MW00761423

American Jewish Year Book

Volume 119

Series Editors

Arnold Dashefsky, University of Connecticut, Storrs, CT, USA
Ira M. Sheskin, University of Miami, Coral Gables, FL, USA

Produced under the Academic Auspices of:
The Center for Judaic Studies and Contemporary Jewish Life,
University of Connecticut
and
The Jewish Demography Project at The Sue and Leonard Miller
Center for Contemporary Judaic Studies, University of Miami

More information about this series at http://www.springer.com/series/11193

Arnold Dashefsky • Ira M. Sheskin

Editors

American Jewish Year Book 2019

The Annual Record of the North American Jewish Communities Since 1899

 Springer

Editors
Arnold Dashefsky
Department of Sociology
Center for Judaic Studies
and Contemporary Jewish Life
University of Connecticut
Storrs, CT, USA

Ira M. Sheskin
Department of Geography
University of Miami
Coral Gables, FL, USA

ISSN 0065-8987   ISSN 2213-9583   (electronic)
American Jewish Year Book
ISBN 978-3-030-40370-6   ISBN 978-3-030-40371-3   (eBook)
https://doi.org/10.1007/978-3-030-40371-3

This Springer imprint is published by the registered company Springer Nature Switzerland AG
The registered company address is: Gewerbestrasse 11, 6330 Cham, Switzerland

This Volume is Dedicated to the Memory of Sidney Goldstein, z"l[1]
Dean of demographers of American Jewry,
regarded by all as a gentleman and a scholar,
and above all else,
a mensch to all who knew him.

---

[1] See addendum in Chap. 15, Sect. 3 for the obituary of Sidney Goldstein.

The Publication of This Volume Was Made Possible by the Generous Support of

The College of Liberal Arts and Sciences at the University of Connecticut (**Interim Dean Davita Silfen Glasberg** and **Dean Juli Wade**)

Center for Judaic Studies and Contemporary Jewish Life at the University of Connecticut (**Sebastian Wogenstein, Interim Director** and **Avinoam Patt, Director**)

The Sue and Leonard Miller Center for Contemporary Judaic Studies (**Haim Shaked, Director**) and its Jewish Demography Project (**Ira M. Sheskin, Director**); and The George Feldenkreis Program in Judaic Studies (**Haim Shaked, Director**)

College of Arts and Sciences at the University of Miami (**Dean Leonidas Bachas** and **Senior Associate Dean Kenneth Voss**)

The Fain Family Endowed Chair at the University of Miami (**William Scott Green, Senior Vice President and Dean of Undergraduate Education**)

Mandell "Bill" Berman (z"l) and the Mandell and Madeleine Berman Foundation **We acknowledge the cooperation of:**

Berman Jewish DataBank, a project of The Jewish Federations of North America (**Mandell Berman (z"l), Founding Chair; Laurence Kotler-Berkowitz, Director**).

The Association for the Social Scientific Study of Jewry (**Leonard Saxe, President**)

We acknowledge the contributions of the men and women who edited the *American Jewish Year Book* **from 1899 to 2008**

Cyrus Adler, Maurice Basseches, Herman Bernstein, Morris Fine, Herbert Friedenwald, H. G. Friedman, Lawrence Grossman, Milton Himmelfarb, Joseph Jacobs, Martha Jelenko, Julius B. Maller, Samson D. Oppenheim, Harry Schneiderman, Ruth R. Seldin, David Singer, Jacob Sloan, Maurice Spector, Henrietta Szold

Academic Advisory Committee

Sidney (z"l) and Alice Goldstein, Honorary Chairs

Carmel U. Chiswick, Research Professor of Economics at George Washington University and Professor Emerita of Economics at the University of Illinois at Chicago

Lynn Davidman, Robert M. Beren Distinguished Professor of Modern Jewish Studies and Professor of Sociology at University of Kansas

Sylvia Barack Fishman, Ph.D., Editor, HBI (Hadassah Brandeis Institute) Series on Gender and Jewish Women; Emerita Professor of Contemporary Jewish Life and Culture at Brandeis University. Recipient of the 2014 Marshall Sklare Award

Calvin Goldscheider, Professor Emeritus of Sociology, Ungerleider Professor Emeritus of Judaic Studies, and Faculty Associate of the Population Studies and Training Center at Brown University. Recipient of the 2001 Marshall Sklare Award

Alice Goldstein, Research Associate Emerita, Population Studies and Training Center, Brown University

Sidney Goldstein (z"l), G. H. Crooker University Professor Emeritus of Sociology, Brown University. Recipient of the 1992 Marshall Sklare Award

Harriet Hartman, Professor of Sociology and Anthropology at Rowan University and Editor-in-Chief of *Contemporary Jewry*. Past President of the Association for the Social Scientific Study of Jewry (ASSJ). Recipient of the 2019 Marshall Sklare Award

Samuel Heilman, Distinguished Professor of Sociology, Harold Proshansky Chair in Jewish Studies at the Graduate Center, and Distinguished Professor of Sociology at Queens College of the City University of New York. Recipient of the 2003 Marshall Sklare Award. Former Editor of *Contemporary Jewry*

Debra R. Kaufman, Professor Emerita of Sociology and Matthews Distinguished University Professor at Northeastern University

Shaul Kelner, Associate Professor of Sociology and Jewish Studies, Vanderbilt University

Barry A. Kosmin, Research Professor of Public Policy & Law and Director of the Institute for the Study of Secularism in Society and Culture at Trinity College, Hartford, Connecticut. Former Director of the North American Jewish DataBank

Laurence Kotler-Berkowitz, Senior Director of Research and Analysis and Director of the Berman Jewish DataBank at The Jewish Federations of North America

Deborah Dash Moore, Professor of History and former Director of the Frankel Center for Judaic Studies at the University of Michigan. Recipient of the 2006 Marshall Sklare Award

Pamela S. Nadell, Professor and Patrick Clendenen Chair in Women's & Gender History, American University; Chair, Critical Race, Gender, and Culture Studies Collaborative; Past President, Association for Jewish Studies; *America's Jewish Women: A History from Colonial Times to Today* (W.W. Norton, 2019)

Bruce A. Phillips, Professor of Sociology and Jewish Communal Service at Hebrew Union College-Jewish Institute of Religion in Los Angeles. Recipient of the 2016 Marshall Sklare Award

Riv-Ellen Prell, Professor Emerita of American Studies and past Director of the Center for Jewish Studies at the University of Minnesota. Past Chair of the Academic Council of the American Jewish Historical Society. Recipient of the 2011 Marshall Sklare Award

Jonathan D. Sarna, University Professor and Joseph H. & Belle R. Braun Professor of American Jewish History at Brandeis University and Chief Historian of the National Museum of American Jewish History. Recipient of the 2002 Marshall Sklare Award. Past President of the Association for Jewish Studies (AJS)

Leonard Saxe, Klutznick Professor of Contemporary Jewish Studies, Director of the Cohen Center for Modern Jewish Studies, and Director of the Steinhardt Social Research Institute at Brandeis University. Recipient of the 2012 Marshall Sklare Award. President of the Association for the Social Scientific Study of Jewry (ASSJ)

Morton Weinfeld, Professor of Sociology and Chair in Canadian Ethnic Studies at McGill University. Recipient of the 2013 Marshall Sklare Award

Preface

Readers of the *Year Book* may find more than an occasional reference in the recent past to Charles Dickens' famous quote about the "best of times," and the "worst of times" (see, for example, Kosmin 2015 and Chap. 4 in this volume) to describe the current situation facing Jews both in the USA and Israel.

Consider that American Jews witnessed, during 2018–2019, mass shootings in Pittsburgh, PA (Tree of Life—Or L'Simcha on October 27, 2018), and in Poway, CA, near San Diego (Chabad of Poway on April 27, 2019). Furthermore, the Anti-Defamation League (ADL) reported that "anti-Semitic incidents remained at near-historic levels in 2018 with 1879 incidents reported…The 2018 total is 48% higher than the number of incidents in 2016 and 99% higher than in 2015" (ADL 2019).

Likewise, in Canada, it was reported that Jews were the "most targeted minority group in Canada for the 3rd consecutive year" (Lazarus 2019). Statistics Canada reported that "the number of incidents dropped to 345 from 360 in 2017." There was a reported decline in hate crimes against Muslims, which fell 50% (to 173), and blacks, which declined by 15% (to 283).

If these reports herald among the "worst of times," what suggests the "best of times"? Consider that in the USA, the Pew Research Center conducted a survey between February 14 and 19, 2019, among US adults to assess how warmly the overall public views various religious groups in the USA (including atheists) on a "feeling thermometer," which has a range of 0 ("coldest and most negative") to 100 ("warmest and most positive"). Of all US religious groups, Jews received the warmest score with a mean thermometer rating of 63, followed by Catholics and Mainline Protestants, each with a score of 60 (Pew Research Center 2019, p. 60).

In contrast, nearly a century ago, Bogardus (1928) asked about 2000 Americans to rate 40 different ethnic groups on a "social distance scale," from "7: would exclude from my country" to "1: to close kinship by marriage." The most favored groups were British, Americans, and Canadians, followed by northern Europeans, and then southern and eastern Europeans. Jews were in the middle; and at the bottom of the social distance scale, were people of color. The dramatic difference between 2019 and 1928 in the position of Jews helps us to understand why intermarriage for Jews has increased (see Phillips 2018).

The above brief discussion is emblematic of our efforts to produce a volume that provides a contemporary portrait of North American Jewish life, which offers an enduring legacy for future generations. Indeed, the *Year Book* has been working at this endeavor across three different centuries: nineteenth, twentieth, and twenty-first. Perhaps, this duality, reflecting the "best of times" and the "worst of times" is best captured by a recent lecture at the University of Connecticut: "Do Americans Love or Hate the Jews? Intermarriage and Antisemitism in the 21st Century" (Phillips 2019).

Clearly, the earliest editors could not have conceived of the level of interest that the latest technology affords to readers of the *Year Book*. As of March 2019, we can report the following:

- **Google** found about over 310,000 references to the *Year Book*
- **Google Scholar** found 6700 references to the *Year Book* in the scientific literature.
- **Google News** found 95 references to the *Year Book*.
- **Wikipedia** has 420 references to the *Year Book*.
- **Springer's website** reported that about 30,000 chapters were downloaded from the 2012–2017 volumes.

In addition, we can also report as follows:

- The "Jewish Population of the United States" and the "World Jewish Population" chapters from the *Year Book* have been downloaded tens of thousands of times from www.jewishdatabank.org and www.bjpa.org.
- Demographic data contained in the *Year Book* are included in the *US Statistical Abstract*, the *World Almanac and Book of Facts*, Wikipedia, the Jewish Virtual Library, and many other places.
- Older issues of the *Year Book* are available at www.ajcarchives.org.

Part I of this volume contains two lead articles: Chap. 1, "Jews in the United States and Israel: A Comparative Look upon Israel's 70th Anniversary," by Uzi Rebhun, Nadia Beider, and Chaim I. Waxman; and Chap. 2, "The Presidential Voting of American Jews," by Herbert F. Weisberg.

The next two chapters in Part I continue our coverage, as in previous years, of domestic and international events. This year, we welcome a new contributor to these pages, J. J. Goldberg, as author of Chap. 3, "American Jews and the Domestic Arena: Focus on the 2018 Midterm Elections." In addition, Mitchell Bard returns to author Chap. 4, "American Jews and the International Arena (August 2018–July 2019): The USA, Israel, and the Middle East."

The first edition of the *Year Book* in 1899 contained three pages entitled "Jewish Statistics" (Adler 1899). This volume contains four chapters. Chapters 5–8 report on the Jewish population of the USA, Canada (two chapters), and the world, by Ira M. Sheskin and Arnold Dashefsky; Charles Shahar; Robert Brym, Keith Neuman, and Rhonda Lenton; and Sergio DellaPergola, respectively.

As returning readers will note, more than half the volume consists of an ever-expanding set of lists. In 2017, we began to subdivide these lists so as to make some of them more concise. For this year, we have organized seven chapters, including:

Chapter 9, Local Jewish Organizations; Chapter 10, Jewish Museums and Holocaust Museums, Memorials, and Monuments; Chapter 11, Jewish Overnight Camps; Chapter 12, National Jewish Organizations; Chapter 13, Jewish Press; Chapter 14, Academic Resources; and Chapter 15, Transitions.

Thus, more than half of the volume consists of directories and lists, which testifies to the dense infrastructure of American Jewish life. The first edition of the *Year Book* (Adler 1899) contained about 300 pages and nearly 90% of the pages consisted of such directories and lists.

Each year the lists in Part II are checked to make certain that all contact information is current. In addition, this year, we added many new Jewish organizations and Jewish publications to these lists that were either new or ones of which we were unaware in the past. Readers should note, however, that even our best efforts to keep the lists current fall short of perfection. We have found that Jewish organizations that disband often leave their website on the internet for several years. Each year, we discover several organizations that should have been deleted several years prior.

While much of the information in Part II is available on the internet (indeed we obtain most of it from the internet), we believe that collating this information in one volume helps present a full picture of the state of North American Jewry today. Part of this picture is demographics; part is the extensive infrastructure of the Jewish community (the organizations and the publications); and part is the enormous contributions made by the less than two percent of the population that is Jewish to the culture and society of the USA and Canada.

In addition, while, for example, a list of Jewish Federations will probably always appear on the internet, a list current as of 2019 will not be there forever. An historian in the year 2119, wishing to examine the history of American Jewry, will have a wealth of data preserved in one volume. Indeed, preserving that history is part of the *raison d'etre* of the *Year Book*.

We hope that the initiatives we have undertaken over the past eight years (2012–2019) will both uphold the traditional quality of the *Year Book* and effectively reflect ever-evolving trends and concerns. We also hope that the *Year Book,* whose existence spans three different centuries, will continue indefinitely.

References

Adler, C. (ed.). 1899. *The American Jewish year book*. Philadelphia, PA: The Jewish Publication Society of America.

Anti-Defamation League. 2019. Audit of anti-Semitic incidents: Year in review 2018. Resource document. www.adl.org/audit2018. Accessed 1 September 2019.

Bogardus, E. S. 1928. *Immigration and race attitudes*. Lexington, MA: D.C. Heath & Company.

Kosmin, B. A. 2015. It's the best of times: It's the worst of times. In *American Jewish year book 2014*, ed. A. Dashefsky and I. M. Sheskin, 61–65. Cham: Springer.

Lazarus, D. 2019. Jews most targeted minority group in Canada for 3rd consecutive year. *Jewish Telegraphic Agency*, July 29.

Pew Research Center. 2019. What Americans know about religion. www.pewresearch.org. Accessed 1 August 2019.

Phillips, B. A. 2018. Intermarriage in the twenty-first century: New perspectives. In *American Jewish year book 2017*, ed. A. Dashefsky and I. M. Sheskin, 31–119. Cham: Springer.

Phillips, B. A. 2019. Do Americans love or hate the Jews? Intermarriage and antisemitism in the 21st Century. Invited talk at the University of Connecticut, Storrs, CT, October 17.

Storrs, CT   Arnold Dashefsky
Coral Gables, FL   Ira M. Sheskin

Acknowledgments

Throughout the past eight years of our editorship, we have viewed our work as a collaborative effort, aided by many individuals, including the authors and reviewers of articles, the staffs at the University of Connecticut and the University of Miami, and the members of the Academic Advisory Committee. We would like to take this opportunity to thank them all for their assistance in preparing the 2019 edition of the *American Jewish Year Book*.

For Part I, we would like to thank the contributing authors of our lead articles: Uzi Rebhun, Nadia Beider, and Chaim I. Waxman for Chap. 1 on "Jews in the United States and Israel: A Comparative Look upon Israel's 70th Anniversary," and Herbert F. Weisberg for Chap. 2 on "The Presidential Voting of American Jews."

In addition, we would like to thank the authors of the articles that have become standard features of the *Year Book* in recent years: J. J. Goldberg for Chap. 3 on "American Jews and the Domestic Arena: Focus on the 2018 Midterm Elections"; Mitchell Bard for Chap. 4 on "American Jews and the International Arena (August 2018–July 2019): The USA, Israel, and the Middle East"; Charles Shahar for Chap. 6 on "Canadian Jewish Population, 2019"; Robert Brym, Keith Neuman, and Rhonda Lenton for Chap. 7 on "2018 Survey of Jews in Canada: Executive Summary," which is a summary of their previously published study of Canadian Jewry; and Sergio DellaPergola for Chap. 8 on "World Jewish Population, 2019." All of these articles form the corpus of each volume. Finally, we would like to express our appreciation to the several reviewers that we consulted in preparation of this volume: Robert Brym, Joshua Comenetz, Lawrence Grossman, Shaul Kelner, Mark Silk, Daniel Staetsky, and Ken Wald.

As we noted in the Preface, Part II on Jewish Lists typically represents more than one-half of the content of recent volumes. We endeavor to review and update annually each of these sections. To do that, we depend on several individuals to whom we owe a great debt of gratitude: Ben Harris and the staff of the JTA (www.jta.org), as well as Sarah Markowitz, Roberta Pakowitz, and Karen Tina Sheskin in Florida, who spent untold hours verifying the many entries. In addition, we would like to thank Amy Lawton, Matthew Parent, and Maria Reger for their excellent editorial assistance, and Pamela Weathers, who serves formally as business manager and program assistant, assisted by Kezia Mann and Charis Nyarko, all at the University of Connecticut Center for Judaic Studies and Contemporary Jewish Life. We owe all of them heartfelt thanks.

We also want to acknowledge the generous support of the College of Liberal Arts and Sciences, headed by former Interim Dean Davita Silfen Glasberg and current Dean Juli Wade, as well as the Center for Judaic Studies and Contemporary Jewish Life, headed by Interim Director Sebastian Wogenstein, and Director Avinoam Patt, all at the University of Connecticut, in facilitating the editorial work involved in producing this volume. Finally, we express our appreciation to Bill Berman, z"l, the founding philanthropist of the Berman Jewish DataBank and the Berman Jewish Policy Archive and to the Mandell and Madeleine Berman Foundation for their generous financial support of the *Year Book*.

At the University of Miami, Chris Hanson and the University of Miami Department of Geography and Regional Studies Geographic Information Systems Laboratory assisted with the production of the maps. We wish to acknowledge the generous support we have received from Deans Leonidas Bachas and Kenneth Voss of the University of Miami College of Arts and Sciences, William Scott Green, Senior Vice Provost and Dean of Undergraduate Education at the University of Miami, and from Haim Shaked, Director of the Sue and Leonard Miller Center for Contemporary Judaic Studies at UM.

Finally, we wish to express our appreciation to our editors at Springer for their support and encouragement. Christopher Coughlin, Anita van der Linden-Rachmat, Marie Josephine Chandramohan, Deepthi Vasudevan, and Joseph Quatela, and their associates at Springer have shared our enthusiasm for the publication of the Year Book. We look forward to our ongoing and mutually beneficial partnership.

Storrs, CT   Arnold Dashefsky
Coral Gables, FL   Ira M. Sheskin

Contents

Part I Review Articles

1 **Jews in the United States and Israel: A Comparative Look upon Israel's 70th Anniversary** 3
Uzi Rebhun, Nadia Beider, and Chaim I. Waxman

2 **The Presidential Voting of American Jews** 39
Herbert F. Weisberg

3 **American Jews and the Domestic Arena: Focus on the 2018 Midterm Elections** 91
J. J. Goldberg

4 **American Jews and the International Arena (August 2018–July 2019): The US, Israel, and the Middle East** 97
Mitchell Bard

5 **United States Jewish Population, 2019** 135
Ira M. Sheskin and Arnold Dashefsky

6 **Canadian Jewish Population, 2019** 233
Charles Shahar

7 **2018 Survey of Jews in Canada: Executive Summary** 247
Robert Brym, Keith Neuman, and Rhonda Lenton

8 **World Jewish Population, 2019** 263
Sergio DellaPergola

Part II Jewish Lists

9 **Local Jewish Organizations** 357
Ira M. Sheskin, Arnold Dashefsky, and Sarah Markowitz

10 Jewish Museums and Holocaust Museums, Memorials, and Monuments 419
Ira M. Sheskin, Arnold Dashefsky, and Sarah Markowitz

11 Jewish Overnight Camps 453
Ira M. Sheskin, Arnold Dashefsky, and Sarah Markowitz

12 National Jewish Organizations 467
Ira M. Sheskin, Arnold Dashefsky, and Sarah Markowitz

13 Jewish Press 641
Ira M. Sheskin, Arnold Dashefsky, and Sarah Markowitz

14 Academic Resources 665
Arnold Dashefsky, Ira M. Sheskin, Amy Lawton, Sarah Markowitz, and Maria Reger

15 Transitions: Major Events, Honorees, and Obituaries 745
Ira M. Sheskin, Arnold Dashefsky, Ben Harris, Roberta Pakowitz, and Matthew Parent

Contributors

Mitchell Bard American-Israeli Cooperative Enterprise, Jewish Virtual Library, Chevy Chase, MD, USA

Nadia Beider The Avraham Harman Institute of Contemporary Jewry, The Hebrew University of Jerusalem, Jerusalem, Israel

Robert Brym Department of Sociology and Centre for Jewish Studies, University of Toronto, Toronto, ON, Canada

Arnold Dashefsky Department of Sociology and Center for Judaic Studies and Contemporary Jewish Life, University of Connecticut, Storrs, CT, USA

Sergio DellaPergola The Avraham Harman Institute of Contemporary Jewry, The Hebrew University of Jerusalem, Jerusalem, Israel

J. J. Goldberg Independent Researcher, New York, NY, USA

Ben Harris JTA, New York, NY, USA

Amy Lawton Department of Sociology and Center for Judaic Studies and Contemporary Jewish Life, University of Connecticut, Storrs, CT, USA

Rhonda Lenton York University, Toronto, ON, Canada

Sarah Markowitz Independent Researcher, Forest Hills, NY, USA

Keith Neuman The Environics Institute, Toronto, ON, Canada

Roberta Pakowitz Independent Researcher, Cooper City, FL, USA

Matthew Parent Center for Judaic Studies and Contemporary Jewish Life, University of Connecticut, Storrs, CT, USA

Uzi Rebhun The Avraham Harman Institute of Contemporary Jewry, The Hebrew University of Jerusalem, Jerusalem, Israel

Maria Reger Center for Judaic Studies and Contemporary Jewish Life, University of Connecticut, Storrs, CT, USA

Charles Shahar The Jewish Community Foundation of Montreal, Montreal, QC, Canada

Ira M. Sheskin Department of Geography and Jewish Demography Project, Sue and Leonard Miller Center for Contemporary Judaic Studies, University of Miami, Coral Gables, FL, USA

Chaim I. Waxman Behavioral Sciences Department, Hadassah Academic College, Jerusalem, Israel

Departments of Sociology and Jewish Studies, Rutgers University, New Brunswick, NJ, USA

Herbert F. Weisberg Department of Political Science, The Ohio State University, Columbus, OH, USA

Part I
Review Articles

Chapter 1
Jews in the United States and Israel: A Comparative Look upon Israel's 70th Anniversary

Uzi Rebhun, Nadia Beider, and Chaim I. Waxman

Jews in the US and Israel exist under two different paradigms of demographic and cultural existence. In the US, Jews are a very small group residing among a non-Jewish majority; In Israel, Jews constitute the overwhelming majority in a state whose *raison d'etre* is to fulfill the rights of Jews to self-determination. The two communities differ on at least five different levels.

First, the separation between "church" and state in the US means that American Jews operate as an independent community that has to raise its own human and financial resources at both local and national levels to establish communal infrastructures and to administer its religious, cultural, educational, and social activities. In Israel, these services are largely provided by the government. These differences are likely to affect the ability to plan and implement policy geared at ensuring group cohesiveness and continuity (Elazar 1989; Liebman and Cohen 1990; Rebhun and Levy 2006).

Second, the local contexts of the US and Israel suggest that Jews in each country are exposed to different general conditions at the macro level. The US has a great influence on the world, including on Israel (sometimes called "Americanization"). Both countries are strong democracies with developed economies, and are members of the Organization for Economic Cooperation and Development (OECD). Nevertheless, each has its own history, political system, geopolitical challenges,

The authors gratefully acknowledge support for this research from the Nachum Ben-Eli Honig Fund.

U. Rebhun (✉) · N. Beider
The Avraham Harman Institute of Contemporary Jewry, The Hebrew University of Jerusalem, Jerusalem, Israel
e-mail: uzi.rebhun@mail.huji.ac.il

C. I. Waxman
Behavioral Sciences Department, Hadassah Academic College, Jerusalem, Israel

Rutgers University (Emeritus), New Brunswick, NJ, USA

© Springer Nature Switzerland AG 2020
A. Dashefsky, I. M. Sheskin (eds.), *American Jewish Year Book 2019*, American Jewish Year Book 119, https://doi.org/10.1007/978-3-030-40371-3_1

natural resources, and economic characteristics. Each has its own ethos and values associated with the country's dominant religion and population composition (Abramson and Troen 2000; Sarna 2004; Shapira 2012, 5).

Third, each Jewish community has a unique history and ethnic structure. The overwhelming majority of American Jews are descendants of Ashkenazi immigrants who arrived from Eastern Europe in the late nineteen and early twentieth centuries. Others are Holocaust survivors or Jews from the Former Soviet Union (FSU) who immigrated in the second half of the twentieth century. Hence, from an ethnic point of view, US Jews are a relatively homogenous population. By contrast, much immigration to Israel derived from Europe, Asia, and North Africa and arrived at very different stages of modernization. Many are Sephardic or Mizrahi Jews. Each group had its specific customs and traditions, with ethnicity being a significant component of their Jewish identity.

Fourth, while US Jews identify with one of the major denominations (Orthodox, Conservative, Reform, or declare that they are "Just Jewish" or cultural Jews), self-definition in Israel distinguishes people differently (as ultra-Orthodox, religious, traditional, or secular). While in the US, special meaning is given to synagogue and other organizational memberships, no such meaning exists in Israel (Goldscheider 2015; Lazerwitz et al. 1998; Levy et al. 2000).

Fifth, factors at both the country level and that of communal belonging help to shape individual patterns for dimensions such as demography, family structure, socio-economic stratification, political orientation, and religio-ethnic connectivity. Moreover, the general system and the communal environment are not static; rather, they are fluid and develop in varied and sometimes contradictory directions resulting in much confusion and uncertainty. Hence, one cannot assume determinism of behaviors, attitudes, and personal feelings (Rebhun 2011).

Despite these major differences, Jews in the US and in Israel largely share a common religious identity, a sense of common peoplehood, an ancient history and language, attachment to the homeland (be it tangible or spiritual), religious rituals, etc. Strong bonds and a sense of mutual dependency exist between these two communities that are reflected in political and economic support and cultural cooperation. Many American and Israeli Jews are connected to one another through familial or social relations. A steady flow of Jews occurs between the two countries with high rates of short-term visits. More recently, advanced technology enables easy and quick consumption of knowledge, which strengthens the connection, albeit virtually, with the other (Rebhun and Lev Ari 2013; Rebhun and Levy 2006; Sheskin 2012; Sasson et al. 2010; Saxe and Chazan 2008; Dashefsky et al. 1992; Waxman 1989).

The 70th anniversary of the State of Israel in 2018 is an appropriate opportunity to assess the demographic and socio-economic developments of the Jewish populations of the US and Israel, trends over time in Jewish identity, and how the two communities have shaped their mutual relations. As much as the data allow, this chapter covers the entire period from 1948 to 2018. To this end, we make use of different sources, both primary and secondary, from various years; as well as generational and age cohort comparisons. The discussion pays attention to the implications of the empirical evidence for communal and worldwide Jewish policy[1].

1.1   Socio-Demography

1.1.1   *Population Size Dynamics*

The documentation of demographic information on US Jews and Israel applies different criteria for defining who is counted as part of the Jewish population. In the US, where the Census Bureau does not ask questions facilitating the identification of Jews, surveys rely on respondents' self-definition as to whether each person regards him/herself as Jewish, be it in terms of religion, ethnicity, culture, nationality, or something else. In Israel, the Israel Central Bureau of Statistics (CBS, the official statistical agency), includes in the Jewish category people who are confirmed as such in the files of the Ministry of Interior, that is persons who are halakhic Jews. It is very likely that respondents to surveys in Israel conducted by private pollsters also meet the religious criteria of group identity.

The core US Jewish population in 1948 was estimated at 5.00 million (Fig. 1.1). By 1958, it increased to 5.45 million and to 5.70 million in 1978. Since then, minor fluctuations (not shown in the graph) occurred with the 1990 National Jewish Population Survey (NJPS 1990) finding 5.50 million Jews and NJPS 2000–2001,

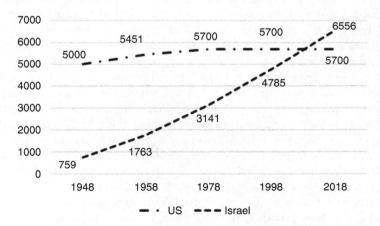

Fig. 1.1 US and Israeli Jewish population size (in thousands). (Sources: For the US: for 1948: Seligman and Swados (1948/1949); for 1958: calculated from Goldstein (1969); for 1978 (reflecting the size in 1980): Schmelz and DellaPergola (1982); for 1998: DellaPergola (1999) (reflecting the size in 1997); for 2018, DellaPergola (2018). For Israel: CBS, *Statistical Abstract 2017* and Statistical Monthly, June 2018)

[1] Throughout this article, and for the sake of simplicity, we refer to the data from both the US and Israel Pew surveys as being collected in 2013 although the later survey is from 2014.

5.30 million. In relative terms, these statistics suggest that from 1948 to 1958, the US Jewish population increased by 9% and by another 5% between 1958 and 1978. Since 1978, the growth rate has been nil (DellaPergola 2018). (See discussion below for additional US estimates.)

The dynamic of the Israeli Jewish population was very different. The first registration of the country's inhabitants in November 1948 recorded about 716,000 Jews. By 1958, this increased to 1.76 million, then to 3.14 million in 1978, 4.79 million in 1998, and 6.6 million in 2018. In the first decade (1948–1958), the pace of growth was 132% and although it remained high, it gradually diminished: to 78% between 1958 and 1978, 52% between 1978 and 1998, and 37% between 1998 and 2018.

The demographic trajectories of American and Israeli Jews gradually narrowed the difference in the size of these populations. By about 2010, the number of Jews in the two communities had converged. Since 2010, Israel's Jewish community became the single largest Jewish community in the world (DellaPergola 2016).

Note that the 2013 Pew Research Center survey (Pew Research Center 2013) found about one million people who self-identified as "part Jewish." Sheskin and Dashefsky (Chapter 5 in this volume) and the Steinhardt Social Research Institute (SSRI) at Brandeis University (www.brandeis.edu/ssri/) who used different methodologies than Pew, also include Jews and "part Jews" in their counts and report 6.7 million or more Jews. Concurrently, at the beginning of 2018, there were in Israel approximately 350,000 people of "no religion," who are immigrants or their descendants who were eligible to immigrate to Israel according to the Law of Return but are not recognized as Jews by the religious establishment (CBS). Strong arguments can be made to include/exclude the above mentioned two groups from the enumeration of Jews in their respective countries (DellaPergola 2014; Saxe et al. 2014). This chapter suggests that the addition of one million people over 13 years (from NJPS 2000 to 2001 to the Pew results in 2013) is not associated with changes in demographic patterns of fertility, life expectancy, or migration. It probably reflects identificational alterations, especially among the children of mixed parentage who do not feel minoritized in present-day America; on the contrary, they view Jews as a privileged sub-group.[2] As such, they feel confident enough to express the Jewish identity that their parents might have chosen to hide. In any case, rather than delving into this dispute, we decided not to consider either group in our statistics to maintain, as much as possible, consistent definitions of the "Jewish population" with earlier data. Were the "part Jewish" and the "no religion" added, the Jewish population in the two countries would be almost identical.

The above dynamics in the size of the Jewish population can be attributed to substantial variation in fertility rates which have been at or below replacement level (2.1 children per women) among American Jews and significantly above replacement level in Israel (DellaPergola 1980; DellaPergola et al. 2000b; CBS, Statistical Abstract n.d. various years); and a much larger net gain from Jewish migration to

---

[2] The first author wishes to thank Sylvia Barak-Fishman for her thoughtful insights in a discussion held at the Jewish People Policy Institute, January 14, 2019.

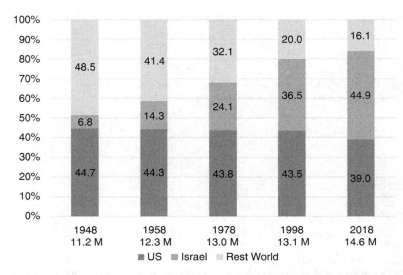

Fig. 1.2 Distribution of world Jewish population. (Sources: Adapted from DellaPergola (1992), DellaPergola (2018); *American Jewish Year Book, 1949*)

Israel than to the US (DellaPergola 2011). (See detailed discussion below.) Likewise, over time, American Jewry has lost hundreds of thousands of core members who adopted another religion or simply discarded a religious preference altogether (Rebhun 2016). Accordingly (Fig. 1.2), the percentage of world Jewry who live in the US somewhat diminished, from 45% in 1948 to 39% in 2018. At the same time, the percentage of world Jewry who live in Israel increased from 7% in 1948 to 24% in 1978, 37% in 1998, and 45% in 2018. The percentage of world Jewry who live in Israel in 2018 is similar to the percentage of world Jews who lived in the US 70 years ago. At no point in modern times has an absolute majority of world Jewry lived in either the US or Israel (DellaPergola 1992, DellaPergola 2018).

American Jews are a small minority within a majority Christian society. Since 1948, the American Jewish population remained stable while the general population increased by 117% from about 150 million in 1948 to about 325 million in 2018. Hence, the percentage of Jews in the American population decreased from 3.4% in 1948 to 2.6% in 1978 and to only about 1.7% today (Table 1.1). This reflects a diminution of more than half in the percentage Jewish in the US over the 70 years. In Israel, upon statehood, Jews accounted for 87% of the population. This percentage decreased to 84% in 1978 and to 75% in 2018. The decreases in percentage Jewish would be moderated slightly if the "part Jewish" in the US and persons of "no religion" in Israel were included. These percentages would rise to 2% in the US and to 79% in Israel.

Table 1.1 Jews as a percentage of the total population, 1948–2018 (percentages)

	1948	1978	2018
US	3.4	2.6	1.7
Israel	86.6	84.0	74.5

Sources: For the US: adapted from www.census.gov; and data from Fig. 1.1; For Israel: CBS, *Statistical Abstract*, various years; and Monthly Statistics, June 2018

Table 1.2 Nativity status of Jews (percentages)

	Total	Native-born	Foreign-born
US 1957	100.0	75.0	25.0
Israel 1957	100.0	32.9	67.1
US 1970	100.0	76.6	23.4
Israel 1970	100.0	46.2	53.8
US 2013	100.0	86.1	13.9
Israel 2016	100.0	76.3	25.6

Sources: For the US in 1957: rough estimate suggested by Goldstein and Goldscheider (1985) and also in accordance with community surveys completed between the late 1930s and mid-1950s (Chenkin 1957). For the US in 1970: *American Jewish Year Book* 1973, For the US in 2013: authors from Pew Research Center (2013). For Israel: CBS, *Statistical Abstract*, various years

1.1.2 Demographic Characteristics

Significant differences are found between the US and Israeli Jewish communities in nativity, fertility, age, and levels of secular education.

Nativity. Both American Jewry and Israel are immigrant absorbing communities. Without disputing the importance of Jewish migration to both communities over the past 140 years, migration to the US was highest between 1880 and 1914 while significant numbers of Jewish immigrants to Israel arrived shortly after statehood and in the 1990s (DellaPergola 2000). These differences in the timing of the largest immigration waves determine the nativity status of the population.

In 1957, an estimated 75% of American Jews were native born (Table 1.2). They include descendants of Jewish immigrants from Central Europe who arrived in the early nineteenth century and the second and third generations of East European Jews from the 1880–1914 mass immigration. In contrast, only 33% of Israeli Jews in 1957 were native born. The overwhelming majority of the foreign born had arrived in Israel after 1948. The percentage of native born in the US remained about the same (77%) by 1970. By 2013 in the US, many Jewish immigrants were lost to mortality and new waves of immigration were generally small; so, the percentage of native born increased to 86%. The percentage of native born among Israeli Jews also increased to 46% by 1970 and 76% by 2013 despite significant immigration in the late 1950s and early 1960s from North Africa and Eastern Europe and the large influx of FSU Jews in the late 1980s and early 1990s. Thus, the number of new immigrants to Israel did not match the significant rate of natural increase.

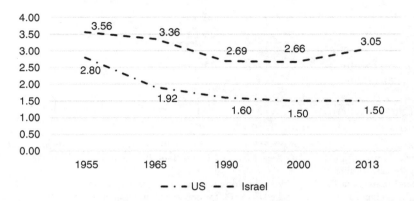

Fig. 1.3 Total fertility rates among Jews. (Sources: For the US: DellaPergola (1980); Kosmin et al. (1991); DellaPergola et al. (2000b); Pew Research Center (2013). For Israel: CBS, *Statistical Abstract*, various years)

The 76% for Israel in 2013 is similar to the share of native born among American Jews in 1957. More generally, the large differences in nativity status between US and Israeli Jews in 1957 (42% points) and 1970 (31% points) decreased substantially to only 10% points in 2013. From an identificational point of view, the meaning of this development is that more people in both the US and Israel each share memories and experiences associated with respective native homelands.

Fertility. The relative stability since 1957 in the nativity status of American Jews was not only affected by a low rate of international migration but was also associated with a fertility rate below the replacement level (2.1 children per women). Indeed, in the mid-1950s, the average number of children per Jewish woman (*Total Fertility Rate* or *TFR*) was 2.8, reflecting the post-WWII "baby boom" (Fig. 1.3). This number decreased to 1.9 in the mid-1960s and from 1990 onward it leveled off at about 1.5. These statistics refer to children born to a Jewish woman who are identified by their parents as Jews ("actual Jewish fertility").

Fertility of Jewish women in Israel has always been higher than in the US (Fig. 1.3). Shortly after statehood, the TFR was 3.5. The rate gradually diminished largely due to the transition to modern demographic patterns among immigrants of Asian and North African background. The large influx of FSU Jews in the 1990s, characterized by small families, further reduced the TFR to 2.66. Since then, the TFR has been increasing – a trend that can be attributed to the increase in fertility among FSU immigrants to levels resembling those of secular Israelis (around two children) (Tolts 2015) and to an increase in the share of religious Jews, especially of ultra-Orthodox Jews (Levy et al. 1993; Pew Research Center 2015), who have on average seven children per woman (Hleihal 2017).

In 1955, the differential in TFR between US and Israeli Jews was 0.76; by 1965, American Jewish fertility decreased at a much faster pace than in Israel and the differences between the two communities increased to 1.4 children. By 1990 and 2000, the differential decreased to about one child; but by 2013, the differential increased to a peak gap of about 1.5. Part of the differential is the result of Israeli Jewry's having a

Table 1.3 Age composition of Jews (percentage)

	Total	20–24	25–44	45–64	65 and over	Index of dissimilarity
US 1957	100.0	6.6	39.5	39.6	14.3	13.1
Israel 1957	100.0	12.9	46.3	32.9	7.9	
US 1970	100.0	12.9	33.1	37.5	16.5	9.1
Israel 1970	100.0	16.7	38.4	32.4	12.5	
US 2013	100.0	8.0	29.5	39.1	23.4	12.9
Israel 2013	100.0	10.5	40.4	30.5	18.6	

Sources: For the US 1957: Adapted from Goldstein (1969). *For Israel: CBS, Statistical Abstract,* various years; For the US 1970: *American Jewish Year Book 1973.* For the US 2013: authors from Pew Research Center (2013)
Note: The Index of Dissimilarity ranges from 0 when the percentage distribution among the age groups is identical in Israel and the US to 100 for maximum variation between the two countries

larger percentage of ultra-Orthodox and modern Orthodox than does American Jewry, but even among those Israelis who are not religious, the fertility rate is higher than that of American Jews. It should also be noted that there is some differential in fertility between ultra-Orthodox women in Israel and in the US of approximately two children in favor of the former. No less important is that US Jewish fertility is below the replacement level (2.1) while that in Israel is significantly above, ensuring population growth.

Age. Thus, it comes as no surprise that the age composition of American Jews is older than that of Israeli Jews (Table 1.3). Already in 1957, the Current Population Survey (CPS) completed by the US Census Bureau found that only 6.6% of the adult Jewish population (age 20 and above) were age 20–24, half the percentage for Israel. Almost twice as many American Jews were age 65 and over than Jews in Israel (14.3% vs. 7.9%). Among American Jews, the two intermediate age groups (25–44 and 45–64) were of very similar size, whereas in Israel the younger of these two cohorts was substantially larger.

By 1970, the percentage for the 20–24 age group among American Jews had increased to 13%, reflecting the maturation of immediate post WWII baby-boom generation (persons born 1946–1950). This increase came at the expense of some diminution in the percentage for the intermediate age cohorts, especially the 25–44 age group, although it did not stop the increase in the percentage for the elderly population. In Israel, the 1957–1970 period shows an increase in the percentage at both ends of the age pyramid. Hence there is now more similarity between the American and Israeli populations, from an index of dissimilarity of 13.2 in 1957 to 9.1 in 1970.[3]

By 2013, the percentage of American Jews in the two youngest age groups decreased in favor of an increase in the percentage for the age 45–64 and age 65 and over cohorts. Although in Israel the two end cohorts behaved similarly to the US,

---

[3] The index of dissimilarity is the percentage of American Jews who would have to be in a different age group so that the American age distribution looks exactly like the Israeli age distribution.

the percentage of Jews age 25–44 increased while the percentage age 45–64 decreased. This resulted in a return to a much higher index of dissimilarity (12.9).

Educational Attainment. Educational attainment is an important indicator of achievement, social status, and prestige both for individuals and the community as a whole. Education is also a good proxy for economic attainment and, thus, quality of life. In the case of a minority group, such as American Jews, this is likely to influence the ability of institutions and organizations to raise money for parochial activities.

Aspiration to acquire higher education is associated with several individual characteristics such as family background, ethnicity, and religiosity. In this regard, American Jews are at an advantage over their peers in Israel. More US Jews are the second or third generation within their families to attend college compared to many Israelis who were raised in families of Holocaust survivors or of immigrants from Muslim countries who frequently did not have educational opportunities. Also, most US Jews were raised in major urban or suburban areas with good educational systems. Many Israelis, on the other hand, especially persons of Sephardic background, received a rather inferior education in Israeli development towns and other peripheral areas of the country. In addition, Ultra-Orthodox Jews are approximately 6–7% of US Jewry whereas Haredim are about 10% of the Israeli Jewish population (Pew Research Center 2013, 2015). Furthermore, US Ultra-Orthodox find it harder to isolate themselves within the religious world and are required by law to provide their children with secular education, while many of their peers in Israel provide mostly religious training and enjoy substantial governmental support.[4] Moreover, US states require school attendance from age 5, 6, or 7 until age 16, 17, or 18.[5]

Indeed, some significant variations are seen in the educational profile of Jews in the US and Israel classified here according to three categories: 1–8 years of education, 9–12 years, and 13 years and more (Fig. 1.4). Around 1960, 30% of American Jews had some post-secondary education (13 or more years), as opposed to 11% in Israel. By 2013, both populations showed impressive increases in post-secondary education to 81% and 45%, respectively. Another important development is the almost total disappearance, both in the US and Israel, of persons with only 1–8 years of schooling. Still, 55% of Jews in Israel in 2013 lack education beyond high school, compared to 19% in the US. It should be noted that data from the 2013 and 2015 Pew surveys, not shown here, suggest that in both countries a similar percentage (71–72%) of those with post-secondary education have, in fact, an academic degree.

---

[4] Note that, in New York, where most ultra-Orthodox in the US reside, recent controversy has arisen as the state tries to enforce the requirement about secular education in ultra-Orthodox schools https://www.haaretz.com/us-news/.premium-ultra-orthodox-in-new-york-threaten-war-after-state-demands-more-secular-education-i-1.6744784.

[5] https://nces.ed.gov/programs/statereform/tab5_1.asp.

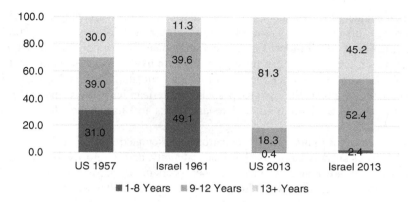

Fig. 1.4 Educational attainment of Jews. (Sources: For the US: Goldstein (1969); authors from Pew Research Center (2013); For Israel: Bachi (1974); authors from Pew Research Center (2015))

Overall, while in 1957 American Jews were more evenly dispersed among the three educational categories, by 2013 the majority experienced at least some type of education beyond high school. In Israel, Jews are fairly equally divided between the two categories of high school education (9–12 years) and post-secondary studies (13 or more years). The index of dissimilarity between American Jews and Israeli Jews, increased from 18.7 in 1957 to 41.1 in 2013. Yet, given the educational achievement of American Jews, any further significant advancement is not likely. By contrast, Jews in Israel still have much room to advance and, with the expansion of opportunities for higher education in Israel, as reflected in the numbers of new colleges opened in the past two decades and the increasing tendency of the Ultra-Orthodox to acquire secular education, the gap between the two populations is likely to narrow over time.

1.2   Jewish Connectivity

Jewish connectivity is multifaceted. It is comprised of both behaviors and attitudes. Each of these modes includes both religious and ethnic/cultural expressions. Some expressions occur in the private sphere and others in public space. But perhaps what makes it difficult to compare Jewish connectivity in the US and Israel is that there are some characteristics which are unique to each of the two societies. One community is not merely less or more Jewish than the other but is rather Jewish in a different way (Rebhun and Levy 2006). Aspects of Jewish connectivity may be important to one community but "Judaically irrelevant to the other" (Liebman and Cohen 1990, 2).

Significant demographic and social differences also exist between American and Israeli Jews which are likely to affect the level and nature of Jewish connectivity. Accordingly, and with due caution, we present here the levels of major connectivity patterns which are shared by Jews in the US and Israel at four different periods in which there were national studies at more or less the same time: 1970, 1990, 2000, and 2013. For the most recent year (2013), we compare Jewish connectivity in the US and Israel by three of the socio-demographic characteristics discussed above: nativity status, age, and education.

1.2.1   Ritual Practice over Time and Space

We focus on five rituals (see Dashefsky et al. 2003 for a similar approach). Some are daily or weekly rituals (lighting Sabbath candles, having separate dishes for meat and dairy, and synagogue attendance) and others are yearly rituals (fasting on Yom Kippur and attending a Passover Seder). For each point in time, a score average is calculated (the sum of percentages for all five rituals divided by five). The score average of the ritual practice index (of ritual observance) among American Jews has remained fairly stable over the past four decades (Table 1.4). If anything, the score average in 2013 was higher than the score average in 1970 and much higher than in 1990. The exception to stability was between 1970 and 1990 which was character-ized by a decrease in four of the five indicators, whereas fasting on Yom Kippur increased somewhat. By 2013, all five indicators were increasing, although only gradually. The rituals which gained the most significant momentum are lighting Sabbath candles, having separate dishes, and synagogue attendance. These may be associated with the increasing share of Orthodox among American Jews. However, it should be noted that in the Pew survey, the questions were phrased differently and that may be influencing these results. For example, rather than asking about main-taining separate dishes, Pew asked about keeping a kosher home. Also, in Pew, there was no High Holidays category for synagogue attendance.

Levels of Jewish identification are substantially higher among Jews in Israel because its culture derives from Judaism and Jewish culture (Rosner and Fuchs 2018), and because Israeli Jewish society has a much higher percentage of religious as well as Sephardi/Mizrahi Jews, who are much more traditional than is American Jewry (Table 1.4). The ritual practice index of Israeli Jews is higher by approximately 20% points over the index score of American Jews. The differentials are especially salient for Sabbath candles and keeping kosher. Interestingly, more Jews in the US attend religious services on the High Holidays or more frequently than Jews in Israel. Detailed data, not presented here, suggest that, among the attendees, more Israelis than American Jews attend services on a daily or weekly basis. The interpretation is that many American Jews, even if not strongly committed, nevertheless feel a need to express their Jewishness on major holidays in a formal, public religious gathering. Similar to the US, the level of Jewish identification in Israel was also fairly stable over time. The slight decrease between 1990 and 2000 should be attributed to a large and mainly secular influx of FSU immigrants: Since then, most of the measurements remained unchanged or increased slightly, including the overall score average.

Table 1.4 Changes in ritual practice (percentages)

	1970	1990	2000	2013
US				
Sabbath candles	29.8	16.3	23.2	22.8
Separate dishes	15.8	13.0	17.2	21.8
Fast on Yom Kippur	46.8	52.8	55.8	57.0
Attend Passover Seder	77.9	63.8	74.4	69.6
Synagogue attendance	67.4	60.7	57.9	77.9
Score Average of Ritual Practice Index	**47.5**	**41.3**	**45.7**	**49.8**
Israel				
Sabbath candles	–	66.3	58.2	57.0
Separate dishes	47.0	47.9	43.7	64.4
Fast on Yom Kippur	–	71.4	67.2	74.1
Attend Passover Seder	–	89.5	93.0	93.4
Synagogue attendance	74.2	66.3	61.0	67.6
Score Average of Ritual Practice Index	–	**67.7**	**64.6**	**71.3**

Sources: For the US: for 1970 (except synagogue attendance: Rebhun (2001). For synagogue attendance for the US 1970: Massarik and Chenkin (1973); For the US and Israel 1990: Rebhun and Levy (2006). For the US and Israel 2013: Authors from Pew Research Center (2013) and Pew Research Center (2015)

Notes: For Sabbath candles the percentage shown is for usually/all the time. For separate dishes for meat and dairy in 2013 the percentage is for "keep kosher at home." For synagogue attendance: the percentage is for High Holidays or once-twice a year or more

1.2.2 Ritual Practice and Demographic Characteristics

Nativity. Although only slightly more than 10% of US Jews are foreign born, the foreign born strengthen the overall levels of ritual practice. For all five indicators, the percentage of foreign born who observe each specific ritual is higher than the percentage among the native-born Jewish population, particularly for Sabbath candles and separate dishes (Table 1.5). The overall score average on the ritual practice index among the foreign born and the native born are 55.9 and 48.9, respectively or a ratio of 1.14. This difference is likely due to the characteristics of two major Jewish immigrant groups (Israelis and Iranians) in the US over the past several decades namely, both of which have relatively strong Jewish identification. Israelis and Iranians compensate for the much weaker ritual practice among Jewish FSU immigrants. (For a discussion of adaptations of these Jewish immigrants to the US, see Gold 2016.)

The opposite is true for Jews in Israel. Native-born Israelis exhibit stronger identification than foreign-born Israelis. This is reflected in all five ritual indicators. The differential is exceptionally large for separate dishes. The overall gap between the two groups is significant: 73.6 for the native born and 64.9 for the foreign born, a ratio of 1.13, which is almost equal to the 1.14 ratio in the US, but in favor of the native born. The weaker observance of foreign-born Jews in Israel as compared with the native born is likely affected by the significant number of FSU immigrants in Israel.

Table 1.5 Ritual practice by nativity status, 2013

	Total	Native-born	Foreign-born
US			
Friday candles	22.8	21.0	34.0
Separate dishes	21.8	20.6	30.0
Fast on Yom Kippur	57.0	56.3	61.3
Attend Passover Seder	69.6	68.8	74.4
Synagogue attendance	77.9	77.6	79.7
Score Average	**49.8**	**48.9**	**55.9**
Israel			
Friday candles	57.1	57.9	50.6
Separate dishes	64.3	69.0	52.9
Fast on Yom Kippur	74.1	75.8	70.1
Attend Passover Seder	93.4	95.6	88.2
Synagogue attendance	67.6	69.6	62.9
Score Average	**71.3**	**73.6**	**64.9**

Sources: Authors from Pew Research Center (2013) and Pew Research Center (2015). See Notes in Table 1.4

Both among the native born and the foreign born, ritual practice in the US is weaker than in Israel. However, because of the different trajectories in the two countries, the ritual practice index differential between the US and Israel is especially high among the native born (24.7 = 73.6 − 48.9) while among the foreign born the differential in the ritual practice index is much lower (9 = 64.9 − 55.9).

Age. Young American Jews score higher on ritual practice than do older American Jews. The score average on the ritual practice index decreases in the next two age groups and then slightly strengthens among the eldest population. The two younger age groups are more likely to light Sabbath candles and keep separate dishes than the middle and older age groups. This is probably the result of the growing percentage of Orthodox youth in American Jewry. As for the rate of synagogue attendance among Jews age 18–29 being the highest, this is also because this age group is the most likely to have young children; and parental synagogue attendance may be part of their Jewish socialization or even required once per month while children are enrolled in supplemental Jewish education. Differences by age for fasting on Yom Kippur and attendance at a Passover Seder are very small. Although the differences between the age groups are not large, they do confirm the idea that the level of ritual observance in the US is stable, with no significant signs of erosion or strengthening.

In Israel, the level of ritual observance as shown by the score average is even more uniform across the age groups. The differential between the group with the lowest score on the ritual practice index (45–64, 70.3) and that with the highest score (65 and over, 72.0) is less than 2% points. Hence, the relationship between religious practices and age is similar for American and Israeli Jews. This is also true for each of the five practices (Table 1.6).

Table 1.6 Ritual practice by age, 2013 (percentages)

	18–29	30–44	45–64	65 and over
US				
Sabbath candles	23.8	27.0	20.2	21.6
Separate dishes	26.6	29.0	18.4	14.9
Fast on Yom Kippur	56.1	56.8	58.0	54.6
Attend Passover Seder	72.8	65.3	66.7	75.4
Synagogue attendance	82.1	75.1	76.9	78.0
Score Average	**52.3**	**50.6**	**48.0**	**48.9**
Israel				
Sabbath candles	57.0	57.7	55.9	58.0
Separate dishes	65.0	65.6	62.0	65.6
Fast on Yom Kippur	77.4	72.5	71.6	76.6
Attend Passover Seder	92.8	94.3	93.8	92.1
Synagogue attendance	65.6	68.7	68.2	67.5
Score Average	**71.6**	**71.8**	**70.3**	**72.0**

Sources: Authors from Pew Research Center (2013) and Pew Research Center (2015). See Notes in Table 1.4

Education. Another characteristic associated with ritual practices is level of secular education. This relationship is inverse: The higher the level of education, the lower is the observance of rituals. This is true for both American and Israeli Jews. Still, the relationship is weaker in the US and only distinguishes between persons without a high school degree, high school graduates, and persons with at least some post-secondary education. No difference is found between those having some college, those having a bachelor's degree, and those having a master's degree or more. The differential between the educational group with the highest level of ritual practice and the lowest level of ritual practice is ten score points.

In Israel, the significant differences are between persons without a high school degree and persons who have a high school degree or higher. A significant difference is also seen between persons with a high school degree or some college, persons with a bachelor's degree, and persons with a master's degree or higher. The differential between the educational groups with the highest and lowest levels of identification is about 25 score average points on the ritual practice index (79.9 - 55.4) compared with the ten points for US Jews. Accordingly, the scores for ritual practice of American Jews and Israeli Jews who have a master's degree or higher are very similar (score average of 48.8 and of 55.4, a differential of less than seven score points).

Some of the results for individual ritual practices are also interesting. Among American Jews, while lighting Sabbath candles, separating dishes, and fasting on Yom Kippur decrease with increasing education, the tendency to attend a Passover Seder increases among people with some college, a bachelor's degree, and a master's degree. For synagogue attendance, the relationship is of a U-shape with the highest level for persons with no high school degree and with a master's degree or higher. In Israel, with very few and only slight fluctuations, the decrease in ritual observances over the educational groups is much smoother (Table 1.7).

Table 1.7 Ritual practice by level of secular education, 2013 (percentages)

	High school in-complete or less	High school graduate	Some college/ vocational degree	BA (including Kollel)	MA or Higher
US					
Sabbath candles	35.5	31.9	22.7	20.3	19.5
Separate dishes	54.7	39.3	22.0	16.9	15.2
Fast on Yom Kippur	66.3	60.4	59.2	56.6	55.5
Attend Passover Seder	59.3	59.6	69.0	71.3	74.2
Synagogue attendance	79.0	80.3	74.6	77.4	79.7
Score	**59.0**	**54.3**	**49.5**	**48.5**	**48.8**
Israel					
Sabbath candles	69.9	59.7	64.9	43.2	39.2
Separate dishes	79.8	70.3	66.2	53.0	39.4
Fast on Yom Kippur	82.6	78.3	78.5	66.6	55.1
Attend Passover Seder	94.7	95.4	94.7	92.2	86.4
Synagogue attendance	73.0	68.0	74.3	61.3	56.7
Score	**79.9**	**74.3**	**75.7**	**63.3**	**55.4**

Sources: Authors from Pew Research Center (2013) and Pew Research Center (2015). See Notes in Table 1.4

1.3   Political Preferences

American Jews typically exhibit liberal political and world views which results in most Jews being Democrats or independents who lean toward the Democratic Party. (See Chap. 2 in this volume for a review of American Jewish political orientations.) Jews were also actively involved in the leadership of socialist movements during the first half of the twentieth century (Dollinger 2000; Forman 2001; Levy 1995; Lipset and Raab 1995). This liberalism is at least partly attributable to their diasporic experience and situation as a minority group which is generally best advanced under liberal regimes (Cohen 1958; Kaplan 2009; Walzer 1986); Jewish religious values (Fuchs 1956; Legge 1995); their high socio-economic status (Lenski 1961; Lipset 1960); historical political socialization in Europe which persists also under the new conditions of America (Lerner et al. 1989); and social and political interests such as

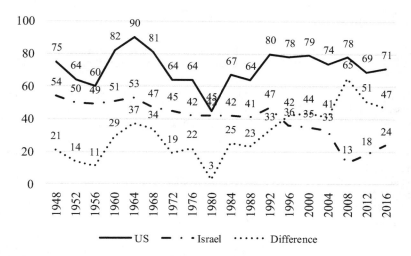

Fig. 1.5 Voting patterns of Jews in the US presidential elections (Democratic candidate) and in Knesset elections in Israel (Labor and Left-Wing parties) (percentages). (Sources: For the US: percentage of Jews voting for the Democratic candidate (Smith and Martinez (2016); Forman (2001); For Israel: percentage of Knesset seats for the Labor Party (including Mapai, Mapam, Ahdut HaAvoda) and Jewish Left parties (Meretz, Shinui). (Knesset of Israel n.d.) (Note: Years refer to US presidential elections. Dates of Knesset elections are sometimes a year earlier or later. The graph skips two Knesset elections (1961, held soon after the 1959 election) and 2006, held between the elections of 2003 and 2009. The results in 1961 and 2006 did not differ much from the 1959 and 2003 elections))

political freedom, economic considerations associated with the occupational structure, and the survival of Israel (Medding 1977).

The political ideology of American Jews is significantly reflected in votes in the US presidential elections. Except for 1980 (after President Jimmy Carter's first term), between 60% and 90% of Jews voted for the Democratic candidate in presidential elections since 1948 (Fig. 1.5). It appears that over the past few elections some decrease in Jewish support of the Democratic Party has occurred. This can be attributed to tensions between African Americans and European Americans, Jews included, over issues such as quotas, affirmative action, and meritocracy (Lipset 1972; Rosenberg and Howe 1976); the crisis in secular liberal thought, and the turn toward extreme leftism which began after World War II (Lipset 1971) but has further strengthened over the past few decades, including anti-Jewish and anti-Israeli sentiments (Chanes 2006; Greenwald 2019); the ascent of the New Right and religious right and its pro-Israel bias; and an increase in the share of Orthodox and Ultra-Orthodox among the Jewish population (Rebhun 2016). Despite these tendencies, some of which are related to transient developments in the overall social and economic configuration of the US, a solid majority of American Jews remain loyal to the Democratic Party.

US Jews have always exhibited stronger liberal inclinations than Jews in Israel, although for many years, the differences were rather small. Between 1948 and 1988, the percentage of American Jews who voted for the Democratic Party was about

20–30% higher than the percentage of Knesset members from the Labor party and left-wing Jewish parties. But since the 1990s, and especially over the past decade, Israelis have largely withdrawn from a socially and economically liberal outlook and from faith in a solution to the Israeli-Arab conflict, resulting in a significant decrease in the representation of leftist parties in the Knesset. This decrease was much more significant than the weakening in the liberal orientation of American Jews. Accordingly, the gap between the two communities in their support for the Democratic Party and leftist parties has widened to about 50%.

1.4   Relationship Between American Jewry and Israel

The relationship between American and Israeli Jews has developed and changed over the 70 years since the founding of Israel. Generally, positive mutual ties between the two communities have prevailed; but some clashes have occurred, particularly between the leaders of the two communities. Long term demographic, economic, social, religious, and political trends have been the catalysts for many of the vicissitudes in the relationship, with specific events often serving as reasons for change.

1.4.1   Historical Background

The establishment of Israel in 1948 was met with ambivalence by many American Jews. Zionism, defined as the idea that a Jewish state should exist in Palestine, had become increasingly popular during the first half of the twentieth century, although a portion of the American Jewish community was opposed to the idea. The concern was that the existence of a Jewish State would prompt allegations of dual loyalty. The situation was exacerbated by Israeli expectations, voiced with customary bluntness by David Ben-Gurion, Israel's first prime minister, that Jews worldwide would settle in Israel. This tension subsided somewhat after the 1950 Ben-Gurion/Blaustein agreement, which established the principle of Israeli non-interference in American Jewish internal affairs and left decisions regarding aliyah to individual American Jews (Liebman 1974, 1977). More crucially, Truman's speedy recognition of Israel enabled American Jews to support both Israel and US government policy. Although the majority of American Jews supported Israel in its first two decades, Israel was somewhat of a peripheral, distant concern (Auerbach 1996).

The events surrounding the 1967 Six-Day War were pivotal in making Israel central to American Jews' personal and communal life. American Jews experienced a strong emotional reaction to both the threat facing Israel and its military victory (Sklare 1993). The following years were marked by stronger support for, and attachment to, Israel, so much so that Elazar (1976) labeled this attitude "incipient 'Israelotry'." An increase also occurred in the number of Americans migrating to Israel, although as a percentage of the American Jewish population the numbers were very small. However, the political shift in Israel from a left to right wing government, military conflicts with both Lebanon and the Palestinians, and political conflicts over the legal status of non-Orthodox Judaism in Israel were associated with increased American Jewish criticism of Israel, a pattern which began in the late 1970s and gained momentum in the 1980s (Sasson 2014; Kelner 2016; Waxman 2016).

A social scientific debate concerning the relationship between American and Israeli Jews emerged during the 1990s, due in part to the availability of survey data. The discourse has become somewhat asymmetrical. The analysis of the possibility of a lessening of the commitment of American Jews toward Israel, termed the "distancing hypothesis" (Cohen 1996, 2002; Cohen and Kelman 2007; Sasson et al. 2010; Sasson 2014) has been the focus of significant social scientific research.[6] The disagreement surrounding the attachment to Israel has focused on whether it has been decreasing and perhaps more crucially, whether attachment is projected to decrease further. However, scant attention is given to the implications of this decrease, if indeed there is such a decrease, for the relationship between the two communities. Rather, attitudes toward Israel are considered to be an indicator of American Jews' ethnic identity, and as such any decrease suggests an alteration in Jewish identity overall (Tabory 2010; Waxman 2010). An alternative approach to the relationship between Israeli and American Jews has tended to focus on the diaspora, rather than America, or perhaps has subsumed all diaspora Jews to American Jewry. Emphasis has been on the homeland–Diaspora dynamic, via analysis of institutional structures, flows of philanthropic dollars, and influence over policy, with the research focused on elite pronouncements, rather than the attitudes of the Jewish population at large (Safran 2005; Sheffer 2002).

1.4.2 Increasing Familiarity by Each Group of the Other

When analyzing the relationship between the Jewish populations of America and Israel, a good starting point may be the degree to which members of each group are familiar with the other. Almost half of American Jews have visited Israel, with a slight minority having visited only once. This percentage has increased from 15% in NJPS 1971 to 22% in NJPS 1990, 41% in NJPS 2000–2001, and 47% in 2013 (Pew Research Center 2013), presumably partially due to the increasing ease of international travel.

Similarly, around two-fifths of Israelis have visited the US, with that number fairly evenly split between persons who have visited once and more than once (Pew Research Center 2015). Aside from visiting, significant numbers settle, with estimates of 300,000 Israelis residing in the US today (Jewish People Policy Institute 2017),[7] while an estimated 1.5% of Israeli Jews are immigrants from America

---

[6] See, in particular, *Contemporary Jewry* 2–3, October 2010.

[7] See Gold (2016) for a range of estimates.

(Rebhun and Waxman 2000). Consequently, large numbers residing in each country have strong ties to family and friends in the other. Indeed, NJPS 2000–2001 found that 45% of American Jews had family or friends residing in Israel, a huge increase from the 25% in NJPS 1990. A serious barrier between the two communities may be language, as 2013 data (Pew Research Center 2013) show that 52% of American Jews know the Hebrew alphabet and only 12% can hold a conversation in Hebrew. The 12% includes Israelis residing in the US.

1.4.3   Jewish Peoplehood

Strong Sense of Belonging to the Jewish People. American and Israeli Jews have a range of ties, but the question is, how strong are these ties? Feeling a "strong sense of belonging" to the Jewish people is a commonly held sentiment among both American and Israeli Jews, although it is slightly less prevalent among American Jews, with 81% of American Jews and 88% of Israeli Jews professing a strong sense of belonging. The somewhat higher levels for Israelis are perhaps due to the collective nature of Israeli religious life and the overlap between national and ethnic identities in Israel. Survey data for the past 50 years consistently demonstrate that the overwhelming majority (88–96%) of Israeli Jews feel a strong sense of belonging to the Jewish people (Levy and Guttman 1976; Levy et al. 1993, 2000; Arian and Keissar-Sugarmen 2012; Pew Research Center 2015).

The evidence is that Israeli Jews have an affinity with American Jews. Sixty-eight percent of Israelis affirm that they have a lot or some things in common with American Jews, including 26% who feel they have "a lot" in common. In fact, while only 13% of American Jews view Israeli Jews as siblings and almost one-third do not relate to them as family members at all, Israeli Jews tend to view their American coreligionists as family members, either as siblings (31%), or relatives (47%) (AJC 2019). Consistently for the past 30 years, about 75% of Israeli Jews feel that American and Israeli Jews share a common destiny. However, Israeli Jews do feel a degree of distance from American Jews, with 57% agreeing that the Jewish people in Israel are a different people from Diaspora Jews in a 1991 survey (Levy et al. 1993), with the percentage holding this view rising to 69% in 1999 (Levy et al. 2000).

Have a Special Responsibility to Take Care of Jews in Need Around the World. A sense of responsibility toward worldwide Jewry is a sentiment shared by 67% of American Jews and 56% of Israeli Jews. The higher percentage among American Jews may be a function of historical patterns of American Jewish philanthropy wherein American Jews have personally contributed time and money to campaigns directed toward the wellbeing of Jews across the world, whereas in Israel the government, rather than the people, has been at the forefront of such efforts.

Age and Peoplehood. For the most part, no clear relationship exists between age and a sense of peoplehood. For American Jews, a sense of belonging to the Jewish people is positively correlated with age, although the relationship is not totally linear (Fig. 1.6). This is interesting as much of the extant research concurs that

American Jewish ethnic attachment increases with age. Indeed, throughout the distancing hypothesis debate the relationship between age and distancing was one undisputed fact,[8] although its interpretation was highly contested. These data indicate that the youngest age group feels a slightly stronger sense of belonging than would have been expected if attachment and age showed a monotonic inverse linear relationship. This is emphatically not a result of a growing Orthodox community as the share of Orthodox Jews among persons under age 30 in this sample is less than their share of persons age 30–39. In fact, what renders the increase in a sense of Jewish peoplehood among persons under age 30 all the more remarkable is the high percentage of persons who are "Jews, No religion" in this age group. It is possible that the great communal efforts directed at fostering a sense of Jewish peoplehood among the young, notably via Taglit-Birthright trips may be bearing fruit. (Saxe and Chazan 2008; Kelner 2010) The trajectory is significant, but at this stage the effect is slight, so it would be wise to reserve judgment until such time as further research corroborates this finding.

Figure 1.6 shows that the relationship between a sense of belonging and age does not exist for Israeli Jews. No relationship is found either for American Jews or Israeli Jews for the statement about a "special responsibility" to take care of Jews in need around the world.

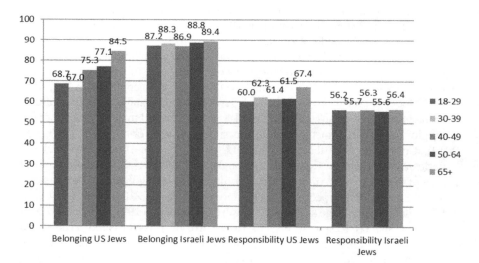

Fig. 1.6 Sense of Jewish peoplehood by age. (Sources: Authors from Pew Research Center (2013) and Pew Research Center (2015))

---

[8] Sheskin (2012) has shown that the relationship at the national level is not true in some local Jewish communities.

Table 1.8 Sense of Jewish peoplehood by religious identity (percentages)

	"Belonging"		"Responsibility"	
	American Jews	Israeli Jews	American Jews	Israeli Jews
Orthodox/*Haredi*	99.7	94.4	91.7	75.9
Conservative/*Dati*	93.3	96.0	82.2	73.7
Reform/*Masorati*	80.7	93.3	66.2	61.2
Just Jewish/*Hiloni*	65.0	81.6	47.1	44.2
Total	**81.3**	**88.1**	**67.4**	**56.0**

Sources: Authors from Pew Research Center (2013) and Pew Research Center (2015)

Belonging and Responsibility by Denominational Subgroups. Significant differences in feelings of peoplehood are found for denominational or religious subgroups (Table 1.8). In America, these categories are Just Jewish, Reform, Conservative, and Orthodox. In Israel, the categories most commonly used are *Hiloni* (Secular), *Masorati* (Traditional), *Dati* (Religious), and *Haredi* (Ultra-Orthodox). For the purpose of clarity, the two sets of subgroups are aligned in the table, but no suggestion is being made that they are exact parallels. But, the patterns they exhibit are definitely similar. For both American and Israeli Jews, for both "belonging" and "responsibility," a marked decrease is found from the most traditional religious affiliation to the least. This fits the pattern established earlier for ritual practice. The only slight deviation from this rule is for Israeli Haredi Jews on the question of belonging. This likely reflects their relative social isolation within Israeli society; but even there, the relationship is very limited.

1.4.4   Israel Attachment

The degree to which American Jews "feel close" to Israel is subject to analysis along two separate planes. It has been viewed as either an indicator of the relationship between Israel and the Diaspora, or as an indicator of Jewish commitment and identity.

This duality of meaning is evidenced by the placement of the question regarding closeness to Israel on the American Jewish Committee (AJC) surveys, which have been completed annually for many years. The question has been included in the Israel section, the "Jewish Identity" section, and the "Background Factors" section (AJC 1995–2011). Interpretations of the closeness of American Jews to Israel are ambiguous and often contradictory. Thus, possible decreases in closeness to Israel may be related to Israeli actions, either foreign or domestic, or to structural shifts in the American Jewish population. The corollary of this is that the implicit blame, or responsibility for ameliorating what is perceived to be a negative situation may be placed either at the door of the Israeli government or the American Jewish community, or both, depending on one's interpretation.

However, it is equally possible to advance an explanation which suggests that, over time, sentiments of closeness or distance between the two communities sharing a religion or ethnicity may fluctuate, without this having profound effects on anything other than that relationship. The counterfactual of Israeli Jews distancing from American Jews demonstrates this point. It would likely be interpreted as a change in the nature of Jewish peoplehood, or the development of an independent Israeli identity, rather than prompting soul searching regarding the future viability of the Jewish project in Israel.

Rates and volumes of charitable donations to Israel were some of the indicators used to measure the relationship between American and Israeli Jews. In the early years of Israel's existence, these donations were of crucial importance to Israel. The current relationship between the US and Israeli Jewish communities is much different; and although there may have been decreases in annual Jewish Federation campaign donations, this is not the indicator it once was both because many other channels for philanthropy to Israel have been created (Sasson 2014) and because Israel's economic need is today much reduced (Cohen 1996; DellaPergola et al. 2000a).

The question most often used to measure American Jews' relationship to Israel is "How emotionally attached are you to Israel?" In 2013, 69% indicated that they were very or somewhat attached to Israel, including 30% who were very attached (Pew Research Center 2013). Surveys conducted by the American Jewish Committee from 1993 to 2011 yield similar results (AJC 1995–2011), which are consistent with an earlier estimate by Liebman and Cohen (1990). According to recent Pew Research Center (2013) data, the Orthodox (61% very attached) are the most attached and the Just Jewish (16% very attached) the least, echoing previous findings.

For Israel attachment, the pattern is not linear for those under 40, but from age 40, attachment does seem to increase with age. The youngest cohort, respondents age 18–29 are significantly more attached to Israel, with 31% declaring themselves "very attached" compared to respondents age 30–39, of whom only 22% feel so close to Israel. Perhaps the heightened sense of connection to Israel among the youngest cohort can be attributed to what has been termed "the Birthright effect" (Sasson 2014, p. 143). (Table 1.9).

Persons who have never visited Israel (16% very attached) exhibit the lowest levels of attachment, with persons who have visited more than once being most attached (68%). It is, however, impossible to know whether visiting Israel causes people to feel more emotionally attached to the country, or whether people who are more attached to Israel are more likely to travel there. The exception to this predicament is Taglit-Birthright trips, which have been shown to increase attachment to Israel (Saxe and Chazan 2008).

Finally, persons who were raised by two Jewish parents are more likely to be more strongly attached than persons raised by one Jewish parent (36% vs. 24%).

Table 1.9 Attachment to Israel among American Jews by age, denomination, visited Israel, and Parents' religion, 2013 (percentages)

	Very attached	Somewhat attached	Very and somewhat attached
Age			
18–29	31.4	37.4	68.8
30–39	22.2	44.3	66.5
40–49	34.9	30.6	65.5
50–64	35.4	41.2	76.6
65 and over	39.3	41.8	81.1
Denomination			
Orthodox	61.4	29.4	90.8
Conservative	48.1	40.8	88.9
Reform	25.5	46.5	72.0
Just Jewish	22.2	34.4	56.6
Visited Israel			
Never	16.3	43.4	59.7
Once	35.8	48.6	84.4
More than once	67.9	24.9	92.8
Parents' Religion			
One Jewish	23.6	38.5	62.1
Both Jewish	36.3	39.5	75.8

Sources: Authors from Pew Research Center (2013)

1.4.5   Israeli Attitudes Toward the Diaspora

For Israelis, although there is a clear sense that Israeli Jews feel a common bond with American Jews, Israeli Jews place a greater emphasis on Jewish life in Israel. The shifting balance of power between Israel and the Diaspora can be charted via the level of support for each of the following two statements:

1. The Jewish people cannot continue to exist without the existence of the State of Israel;
2. The State of Israel cannot exist without a strong connection with Jews in the Diaspora.

In 1976, three quarters of Israeli Jews thought Israel could not survive without Diaspora Jewry and 68% felt that Diaspora Jews were dependent on Israel for their survival. A significant shift toward greater confidence in Israel's prospects occurred by 1991, when the position was reversed, with 77% agreeing that Jews outside Israel were dependent upon Israel for their survival, but only 68% felt that way about Israel's reliance on the Diaspora (Levy et al. 1993). The American Jewish Committee (2019) data demonstrate that the vast majority of Israelis (91%) view the existence of a Jewish state as necessary for the long-term survival of the Jewish people, but only 74% have the same opinion about the necessity for a thriving Jewish Diaspora. Furthermore, for Israeli Jews, residing in Israel is an important

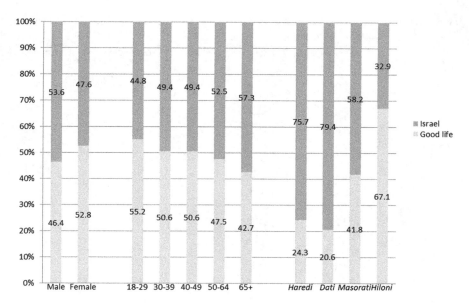

Fig. 1.7 Importance of residing in Israel by gender, age, and religious identity, Israeli Jews. (Source: Authors from Pew Research Center (2015))

aspect of their Jewish identity: One-third averred that residing in Israel is an essential part of what being Jewish means to them, and a further 54% consider it important but not essential. In comparison, 46% or American Jews assert that caring about Israel is an essential part of what being Jewish means to them, with a further 43% categorizing caring for Israel as important but not essential (Pew 2015).

The Pew Research Center (2015) data show near unanimity among Israeli Jews (98%) that it is the birthright of every Jew worldwide to make aliyah, with 87% strongly agreeing with that statement. Although Israeli Jews feel that Israel is central to Jewish life and that all Jews should have the right to live in Israel, on the question of whether this is a responsibility, they are more evenly split. Even when the question is framed fairly narrowly, asking whether:

1. "Jews in Israel should feel free to pursue the good life anywhere in the world, even if it means leaving Israel;" and
2. "Jews in Israel should remain in Israel, even if it means giving up the good life elsewhere."

Accordingly, 46% agreed with the first statement and 47% with the second. A small gender gap exists on this issue (Fig. 1.7), with men (54%) placing greater emphasis on residing in Israel and women (52%) favoring pursuit of the good life over residing in Israel. Older Israelis are more committed to residing in Israel even at the risk of missing out on material comfort than younger Israeli. Secular Jews (*Hiloni*) are the only religious subgroup whose members prioritize pursuit of the good life over residing in Israel, with the *Dati* group (the Religious) being the most committed to residing in Israel despite materialistic constraints.

This fairly high level of acceptance of leaving Israel for material gain is a significant departure from traditional Zionist principles. The correlation of youth with support for this attitude seems to be indicative of a broader societal shift. In terms of ideology, traditional Zionist dogma has given way to a more flexible approach. Where once Jews who chose either not to immigrate to Israel, or to emigrate from it were viewed negatively and referred to derogatively in the national discourse, now, perhaps an indication of the relatively secure position in which Israel finds itself, the tone used is much less strident. Concurrently, there has been a shift from a strong collectivist approach, to a more liberal, individualistic ethos especially over the past 40 years (Rebhun and Lev Ari 2013; Rebhun and Waxman 2000).

1.4.6   The Middle East Conflict

The greatest divergence between American and Israeli Jews is in the political realm. American Jews are more positive about the prospects for peace between Israel and the Palestinians. Three-fifths of American Jews, compared to just over two-fifths of Israeli Jews, believe that a way can be found for Israel and an independent Palestinian state to coexist peacefully (Fig. 1.8). American Jews are much more skeptical about the sincerity of the Israeli government's efforts at peacemaking, perhaps a consequence of their greater optimism about the possibility of peace in the Middle East. Around two-fifths of American Jews believe that the Israeli government is making a sincere effort to bring about peace, compared with a clear majority of Israeli Jews.

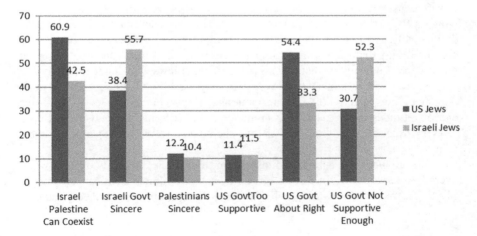

Fig. 1.8 Political views. (Sources: Authors from Pew Research Center (2013) and Pew Research Center (2015))

Although Jews in both countries tend to view the Israeli government as sincerer in its efforts than the Palestinians, American Jews are a little more likely than Israeli Jews to feel that the Palestinian leadership is also making a sincere effort to bring about peace. This is consonant with the aforementioned skepticism on the part of American Jews regarding the sincerity of the Israeli government in its peacemaking efforts.

The inverse of this can be noted with regard to assessments of the American government's role. During the second term of President Barack Obama's administration, when the Pew surveys of Jews in America and Israel asked:

"Now, thinking about the relationship between the US and Israel.... Is the US too supportive of Israel, not supportive enough, or is US support of Israel about right?"

A majority of American Jews felt that America was providing about the appropriate level of support, while Israeli Jews felt America was not sufficiently supportive.[9] Interestingly, similar percentages, but slightly more Israeli Jews, felt that the US government was being overly supportive of Israel. While Jews in America tend to feel an attachment to Israel, it is natural for them to view the actions of their own government more favorably than Israeli Jews do, and the same is naturally true of Israeli Jews' perceptions of the intentions of their government. It is often the case that Diaspora communities represent a certain faction within the political debate in their countries, and therefore their political views may differ from the average citizen. This is true to a small extent regarding issues of peacemaking between Israel and the Palestinians and the role of the American government in providing support for Israel.

The political differences between American and Israeli Jews may be due to the specific environment in which each community operates, or it is possible that the perceptions of American and Israeli Jews differ on political issues because American Jews are, on average, more liberal or left leaning than Israeli Jews (see Sect. 1.3 above). When examined by political ideology, on a five-point scale from very liberal to very conservative for Americans and on a six-point scale from left wing to right wing for Israelis, the political differences between American and Israeli Jews narrow dramatically. For Jews in both countries, positions on the political spectrum tend to correlate with their stance regarding the Arab-Israel conflict and the American government's position on that issue. Thus, American Jews who define themselves as very liberal tend to concur with very left-wing Israelis, while very conservative American Jews tend to hold similar opinions to right-wing Israeli Jews. The difference in attitudes seems to be more a function of the differing political orientation of Jews in America and Israel, rather than their residing in two separate locations (Fig. 1.8).

There are, however, a number of exceptions to this rule, primarily in cases where overall, American and Israeli Jews agree. For example, almost identical percentages, 11.9% of American Jews and 10.4% of Israeli Jews, think that the Palestinians are

---

[9] As noted earlier, the surveys were completed while Barack Obama was President. American Jews overwhelmingly were supportive of Obama, mostly for reasons unrelated to Israel, while Israeli Jews were overwhelmingly anti-Obama.

making sincere efforts toward peace. However, when examined by political leanings, left wing Israelis are more than twice as likely as liberal Americans to consider Palestinian efforts sincere. Similarly, 9.3% of American Jews and 11.5% of Israeli Jews say that the American government is too supportive of Israel. Nevertheless, when examined by political ideology, it can be seen that such a view is held fairly evenly across the political spectrum among American Jews, but in Israel is largely confined to those who identify as left-wing. Conversely, even when examined by political stance, American Jews are more likely to think that their government is giving Israel the appropriate measure of support than Israeli Jews.

On most issues relating to the Middle East conflict, where American and Israeli Jews disagree, American Jews' attitudes are more dovish and Israeli Jews more hawkish. The differences simply express the fact that American Jews tend to be concentrated at the liberal end of the spectrum; whereas in their political approach, Israeli Jews tend to be more right wing. In fact, American conservatives and Israeli rightists would tend to agree with each other as would moderates from each country and liberals/leftists, with each pairing holding strikingly similar views (Fig. 1.9).

Although Israeli Jews overwhelmingly reject taking into account the views of the American Jewish leadership regarding the Israeli-Palestinian conflict (Cohen 2018), overall, Israeli Jews tend to view the influence of American Jews on "the way things are going in Israel" positively. A clear majority (59%) of Israelis feel that Jews in the US have a good influence on Israel; 6% feel they have a bad influence; and just under a third feel that their impact is neutral (Pew Research Center 2015). It seems respondents had in mind political influence on the American government, influence on religious matters such as the status of the Reform and Conservative movements in Israel, or financial influence via philanthropy, more than influence on Israeli policy toward the peace process, which only 31% consider appropriate (AJC 2019).

1.4.7 The Status of Jewish Denominations

Denominations have been a feature of American Jewish life for over a century. In Israel, however, denominations play far less of a role in religious life. The Reform and Conservative movements exist in Israel, but they have only attracted a very small minority of Israelis. Estimates range from 2% (AJC 2018) to 13%, although the movements themselves report only 12,000 adult members (Feferman 2018), which is considerably less than one-tenth of one percent of the adult Jewish Israeli population which, in 2018, was reported by Israel's CBS to be 4,435,800. While there is no official Orthodox movement in Israel, Orthodoxy is considered the default form of Judaism and is the form of Judaism authorized by the State to fulfill religious functions. This divergence is the cause of a high degree of friction in the relationship between American and Israeli Jews. Indeed, a recent survey carried out on behalf of the UJA Federation aimed "to help American Jewish leadership better understand the perspectives of Israeli Jews that are important to both Jewries," with

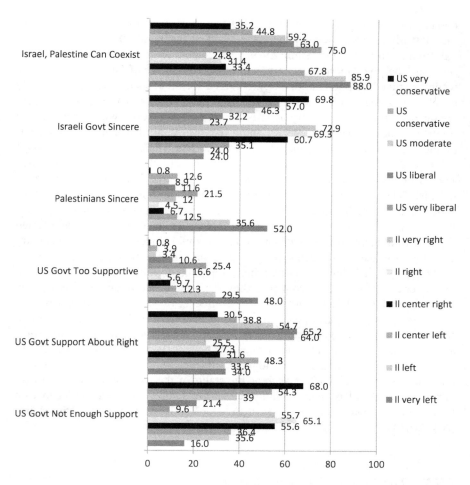

Fig. 1.9 Views on the Israeli-Palestinian conflict by political leanings (percentages). (Sources: Authors from Pew Research Center (2013) and Pew Research Center (2015))

the question of religious pluralism one of the three main areas of inquiry (Cohen 2018).

In the 1990s, one-third of Israeli Jews felt that Conservative, Reform and other non-Orthodox denominations should be granted a status equal to that of the Orthodox; and another third felt they should definitely be given such a status (Levy et al. 2000). However, it seems that this support is primarily at a theoretical level, rather than a practical one, as Israeli Jews tend not to want to attend a non-Orthodox synagogue. For example, if a Conservative or Reform synagogue were in their neighborhood, a majority say they would never attend it, even though 80% of Israeli Jews attend synagogue at least on some occasions (Levy et al. 1993). More recent data (Pew Research Center 2015) suggest that a majority of Israeli Jews (56%) do

Table 1.10 Validity of non-Orthodox conversion among Israeli Jews (percentages)

	All Israeli Jews	Haredi	Dati	Masorti	Hiloni
Valid	38.0	5.1	9.0	28.4	58.0
Invalid	55.5	92.8	88.3	63.2	34.7
Don't know	6.5	2.1	2.7	8.4	7.3

Source: Authors from Pew Research Center (2015)

not consider persons Jewish if they were converted to Judaism by a non-Orthodox rabbi, while 38% would consider them to be Jewish. Rejection of such conversion is strongest among *Haredim*, but majorities of *Dati* and *Masorti* Jews agree as well (Table 1.10). Essentially, the majority of Israeli Jews do not recognize the primary American Jewish denominations (Reform and Conservative) as legitimate sources of Jewish authority, although a significant minority does. The vast majority of Israeli Jews support the current system, whereby State religious services are provided by the Orthodox stream only (Cohen 2018). Similarly, 55% of Israeli Jews reject American Jewish influence on government policy regarding religious pluralism, with 15% in favor of the government taking their views into account to a great extent and 25% to some extent.

1.5 Summary and Projections

The creation of the State of Israel 70 years ago was a tectonic turning point in modern Jewish history. It was followed by dramatic changes in world Jewry's patterns of geographic distribution, demography, and religio-ethnic identification. It also fundamentally changed the nature of the relationship between the Jewish communities inside and outside the Land of Israel. The new political status of Israel as a pivotal player in Jewish affairs is dynamic. This requires occasional assessment of the characteristics of various Diaspora Jewish communities, especially the large and central ones such as that of the US, in comparison to Israel. Indeed, Israel's 70th anniversary is not more special than any other decennial jubilee; but, as we advance in time, scholars have a richer and better empirical infrastructure for exploring these two communities. Accordingly, and as much as data allow, this chapter has traced the socio-demographic, Jewish identification, and political characteristics of Jews in the US and Israel between 1948 and 2018, as well as the relationship between these two largest Jewish communities. The empirical observations have several implications and directions for policy.

Demography. From a demographic perspective, the effect of international migration on the size of the Jewish population in both the US and Israel has recently become very small. In the US, to the extent that the number of Jews increases, this is mainly due to changes in people's self-identification. In Israel, the Jewish population is steadily on the rise mainly due to positive "natural movement" (births minus deaths). Any policy aimed at increasing the size of the

Jewish population in each of the two communities will have to direct its efforts at different trajectories.

Over time, Israel has become a Jewish concentration similar in size or slightly larger than that of the US. If numbers matter, this has implications for the distribution of world Jewish resources. Concurrently, today Israel can largely rely on its own economic strength. The support of American Jews (and of the Jewish Diaspora more generally) is becoming less crucial for its development. In addition, the challenges of vitality facing American Jewry may, at some point, lead American Jews to devote more of their resources to their own material and spiritual support.

We anticipate that the differences in educational attainments between American and Israeli Jews will narrow in the future. Paradoxically, however, this process is somewhat hindered by the migration of Israelis to the US among whom the percentage with academic degrees is twice as high as that of the total Jewish population in Israel (Jewish People Policy Institute 2017). Many of the Israelis in the US work in the high-tech industry and research institutions, and Israel needs to find ways to attract them back and more generally to moderate this brain drain.

Jewish Connectivity. As far as Jewish connectivity is concerned, significant differences exist between American and Israeli Jews, with Israeli Jews demonstrating higher levels of connection across most of the indicators of Jewish identity. An interesting pattern has developed wherein the trajectories among the native born in both countries are similar, while the trajectories among the foreign born are very different. In the US, the foreign born show higher Jewish connectivity than the native born, whereas in Israel, due to the very large immigration of FSU Jews, the native born are more Jewishly connected than the foreign born. Accordingly, any attempts to strengthen Jewish identification should prioritize the population by nativity status differently in the US than in Israel.

Among both American and Israeli Jews, there appears to be a "religiously-shrinking middle" (Cohen 2018)[10] and a growing polarization between the religious and non-religious. Among American Jews, the non-Orthodox are increasingly non-traditional; but their growth rate is limited by low fertility, while the Orthodox are increasing, among other reasons, because of their significantly higher birth rate. Since the Orthodox have higher rates of communal identification, it may be predicted that they will gain in involvement and influence in the American Jewish communal structure.

Among Israeli Jews, on the one hand, there has been a steady decrease in the percentage defining themselves as Traditional and an increase, on the other hand, in the percentage of those defining themselves as *Haredi* and Non-Observant. Whether this will lead to a real rift and polarization, accompanied by increasing strife along religious-secular lines, remains to be seen.

In broad terms, American Jewry increasingly identifies being Jewish with liberal, universalistic norms and values, and Israel increasingly identifies being Jewish with more particularistic norms and values. How this will affect the trajectories of Jewish

---

[10] See also Cohen and Liebman (2019) and the response by Dashefsky and Sheskin et al. (2019).

connectivity of both American and Israeli Jewry in the future also remains to be seen.

American Jewry-Israel Mutual Relationships. Meanwhile, and notwithstanding the strong sense of affinity between American and Israeli Jews, they disagree on a number of issues. Although there has been much concern that American Jewish attachment to Israel will decrease over time, the Pew Research Center (2013) survey does not provide evidence that young American Jews are increasingly alienated from Israel. There is, however, potential for future clashes between the two centers of world Jewry. Both American and Israeli Jews are confident in their positions, but disagree somewhat over issues such as the Israeli/Palestinian conflict and the status of Reform and Conservative denominations in Israel. Given that Israeli Jews welcome the support of American Jews but are opposed to taking their views into account, one can assume that conflicts over contentious issues will arise in the future as they have in recent years. The story of American Jewish-Israeli relations may best be characterized as one of stable and strong connection, punctuated by periodic flare ups over points of contention.

Over the course of the 70 years of Israel's existence, the relationship between American and Israeli Jews has undergone considerable change. Although there has been much concern in recent decades over American Jewish support for Israel, it should be noted that the overwhelming support for Israel in the post-Six-Day War era may represent something of an anomaly. In the 1940s, support for Israel was not considered central to American Jewish identity; and American Jewish support for Israel tended to be ambivalent, or at least tempered, by certain concerns. Ironically, any current decrease in American Jewish support for Israel, although perceived as problematic by community leaders, is of much less concern to Israeli Jews, given their sense of decreased reliance on the Diaspora. Indeed, the entire debate over the degree to which American Jews feel less attached to Israel seems to be a debate about other issues entirely, namely Jewish continuity in America and a frustration with the direction taken by the Israeli government, both in terms of religious and foreign affairs. These issues neatly encapsulate the three central issues framing the discourse regarding the relationship between American and Israeli Jews: The first is internal American, in which the relationship with Israel is simply an indicator of Jewish commitment; the second is religious, between two quite different Jewish communities; and the third is geopolitical, i.e., American Jewish opinion on Israeli foreign policy. On the Israeli side, there has been a decrease in reliance on and an increase in appreciation for the Diaspora, typified by the American Jewish community.

The Jewish communities of the United States and Israel are each characterized by dynamics along with stability in major social, cultural and political attributes. The direction, pace and levels of each such attribute and its specific components may vary from one community to another and at times can overlap. This is largely a result of the unique political and social structure of each country, its Jewish communal organization, and the individual characteristics of the members that comprise them who at the same time are people who share a modern lifestyle and exposure to similar information and knowledge in an era of globalization and advanced technology. In addition, the fluidity of identities and personal behaviors makes it difficult to point to clear and unequivocal trajectories along which these two communities evolve. Perhaps, the concept of diversity can help best to describe the period discussed here and especially the course of the more recent decades. Each of the Jewish communities in the US and in Israel is heterogeneous with many sub-groups and each exhibits peculiar strategies of demographic and cultural survival. Such diversity seems to balance different internal trends within each community. At the same time, it also allows each sub-group to find its peers overseas and to differ and be critical toward different sub-groups in the other country. Intra- and inter-community diversities do not imply weakness, but they require consensus on a number of anchors of group belonging and solidarity.

References

Abramson, G., and I. Troen, eds. 2000. The Americanization of Israel. *Israel Studies* 5 (1): 65–91.

American Jewish Committee. 1995–2011. *Annual surveys of American Jewish public opinion.* http://www.jewishdatabank.org/Studies/details.cfm?StudyID=765.

———. 2018. *Survey of American and Israeli Jewish opinion.* https://www.ajc.org/survey2018.

———. 2019. AJC 2019 *Survey of Israeli Jewish opinion.* https://www.ajc.org/news/survey2019/Israel.

Arian, A., and A. Keissar-Sugarmen. 2012. *Beliefs, observance and values of Israeli Jews.* Jerusalem: The Guttman Center for Surveys of the Israel Democracy Institute.

Auerbach, J.S. 1996. Are we one? Menachem Begin and the long shadow of 1977. In *Envisioning Israel: The changing ideals and images of North American Jews*, ed. A. Gal. Jerusalem: Magnes Press.

Bachi, R. 1974. *The population of Israel.* Jerusalem: The Institute of Contemporary Jewry, The Hebrew University of Jerusalem and Demographic Center, Prime Minister's Office.

Chanes, J.A. 2006. Anti-Semitism. In *American Jewish year book, 2006*, ed. D. Singer and L. Grossman, vol. 106, 64–91. New York: American Jewish Committee.

Chenkin, A. 1957. Jewish population in the United States, 1956. In *American Jewish year book 1957*, ed. M. Fine and J. Sloan, vol. 58, 65–82. New York: American Jewish Committee and Philadelphia: Jewish Publication Society of America.

Cohen, S.M. 1996. Did American Jews really grow more distant from Israel 1983–1992? A reconsideration. In *Envisioning Israel: the changing ideals and images of North American Jews*, ed. A. Gal. Jerusalem: Magnes Press.

———. 2002. Relationship of American Jews with Israel: what we know and what we need to know. *Contemporary Jewry* 23 (1): 132–155.

Cohen, S. M. 2018. *Together and apart: Israeli Jews' views on their relationship to American Jews and religious pluralism.* Unpublished findings from UJA-Federation of Greater New York's Survey of Israeli Jews 2017.

Cohen, S.M., and A.Y. Kelman. 2007. *Beyond distancing: Young adult American Jews and their alienation from Israel.* New York: Andrea and Charles Bronfman Philanthropies.

Cohen, S.M., and C.S. Liebman. 2019. The quality of American Jewish life. In *American Jewish year book, 2018*, ed. A. Dashefsky and I.M. Sheskin, vol. 118, 3–49. Dordrecht: Springer.

Cohen, W. 1958. The politics of American Jews. In *The Jews: Social patterns of an American group*, ed. M. Sklare, 614–626. New York: Free Press.

Dashefsky, A., J. DeAmicis, B. Lazerwitz, and E. Tabory. 1992. *Americans abroad: A comparative study of emigrants from the United States.* New York: Plenum Press.

Dashefsky, A., B. Lazerwitz, and E. Tabory. 2003. A journey of the "straight way" or the "round-about path:" Jewish identity in the United States and Israel. In *Handbook of the sociology of religion*, ed. M. Dillon, 240–260. Cambridge, UK and New York: Cambridge University Press.

DellaPergola, S. 1980. Patterns of American Jewish fertility. *Demography* 17 (3): 261–273.

———. 1992. Major trends of world Jewry: the last hundred years. In *Genetic diversity among Jews: diseases and markers at the DNA level*, ed. B. Bonne-Tamir and A. Adam pp. 3–30. New York and Oxford: Oxford University Press.

———. 1999. World Jewish population, 1997. In *American Jewish year book, 1999*, ed. D. Singer and R.R. Seldin, vol. 99, 543–580. New York: American Jewish Committee.

———. 2000. The global context of migration to Israel. In *Still moving: Recent Jewish migration in comparative perspective*, ed. D. Elazar and M. Weinfeld, 13–59. New Brunswick, NJ and London: Transaction Publishers.

———. 2011. *Jewish demographic policies: population trends and options in Israel and in the diaspora*. Jerusalem: The Jewish People Policy Institute.

———. 2014. End of Jewish/non-Jewish dichotomy? Evidence from the 2013 Pew Survey. In *American Jewish year book, 2014*, ed. A. Dashefsky and I. Sheskin, vol. 114, 32–39. Dordrecht: Springer.

———. 2016. World Jewish Population, 2016. In *American Jewish year book, 2016*, ed. A. Dashefsky and I. Sheskin, vol. 116, 253–332. Dordrecht: Springer.

———. 2018. World Jewish Population, 2018. In *American Jewish year book, 2018*, ed. A. Dashefsky and I. Sheskin, vol. 118. Dordrecht: Springer (forthcoming).

DellaPergola, S., U. Rebhun, and P.R. Raicher. 2000a. The Six-Day War and Israel-Diaspora relations: an analysis of quantitative Indicators. In *The Six-Day War and World Jewry*, ed. E. Lederhendler, 11–50. Bethesda, MD: University of Maryland Press.

DellaPergola, S., U. Rebhun, and M. Tolts. 2000b. Prospecting the Jewish future: population projections, 2000–2080. In *American Jewish year book, 2000*, ed. D. Singer and L. Grossman, vol. 100, 103–146. New York: American Jewish Committee.

Dollinger, M. 2000. *Quest for inclusion: Jews and liberalism in modern America*. Princeton, NJ: Princeton University Press.

Elazar, D.J. 1976. *Community and polity: the organizational dynamics of American Jewry*. Philadelphia: Jewish Publication Society of America.

———. 1989. *People and polity: the organizational dynamics of world Jewry*. Detroit: Wayne University Press.

Feferman, D. 2018. *Rising streams: Reform and Conservative Judaism in Israel*. Jerusalem: Jewish People Policy Institute.

Forman, I.N. 2001. The historical voting behavior of American Jews. In *Jews in American politics*, ed. L.S. Maisel, I.N. Forman, D. Altschiller, and C.W. Bassett, 141–160. Lanham: Rowman & Littlefield.

Fuchs, L. 1956. *The political behavior of American Jews*. Glencoe, IL: Free Press.

Gold, S. 2016. Patterns of adaptation among contemporary Jewish immigrants to the US. In *American Jewish year book, 2015*, ed. A. Dashefsky and I.M. Sheskin, vol. 115, 3–43. Dordrecht: Springer.

Goldscheider, C. 2015. *Israeli society in the 21st century: immigration, inequality, and religious conflict*. Waltham, MA: Brandeis University Press.

Goldstein, S. 1969. Socioeconomic differentials among religious groups in the United States. *American Journal of Sociology* 74 (5): 612–631.

Goldstein, S., and C. Goldscheider. 1985. *Jewish-Americans: Three generations in a Jewish Community*. Lanham, MD: Rowman & Littlefield.

Greenwald, A. 2019. The Democrats' growing Anti-Semitism problem, Commentary, February.

Hleihal, A. 2017. Fertility among Jewish Women in Israel, by Level of Religiosity, 1979–2014. (Working Paper Series, No. 101) Israel Central Bureau of Statistics, Senior Department of Geography and Census. April.

Israel Central Bureau of Statistics (CBS). (n.d., Various years). *Statistical abstract*. Jerusalem.

Jewish People Policy Institute (JPPI). 2017. *Annual Assessment: The Situation and Dynamics of the Jewish people*. Jerusalem.

Kaplan, D.E. 2009. *Contemporary American Judaism: transformation and renewal*. New York: Columbia University Press.

Kelner, S. 2010. *Tours that bind: Diaspora, pilgrimage, and Israeli Birthright tourism*. New York: New York University Press.

Kelner, S. 2016. Veneration and critique: Israel, the sociology of American Judaism and the problematics of sovereignty. *Jewish Studies Quarterly* 23(3): 194–221.

Knesset of Israel (n.d.). *Knesset of Israel*. https://main.knesset.gov.il/About/History/Pages/Lobby.aspx.

Kosmin, B., S. Goldstein, J. Waksberg, N. Lerer, A. Keysar, and J. Scheckner. 1991. *Highlights of the CJF 1990 National Jewish Population Survey*. New York: Council of Jewish Federations.

Lazerwitz, B., A. Winter, A. Dashefsky, and E. Tabory. 1998. *Jewish choices: American Jewish denominationalism*. Albany: SUNY Press.

Legge, J. 1995. Explaining Jewish liberalism in the United States: an exploration of socioeconomic, religious, and communal living variables. *Social Science Quarterly* 76 (1): 124–141.

Lerner, R., A.K. Nagai, and S. Rothman. 1989. Marginality and liberalism among Jewish elite. *Public Opinion Quarterly* 53 (3): 330–352.

Levy, G.B. 1995. *Toward a theory of disproportionate American Jewish liberalism*. New York: Oxford University Press.

Levy, S., and L. Guttman. 1976. Zionism and the Jewishness of Israelis. *Forum on the Jewish People, Zionism and Israel* 24: 39–50.

Levy, S., H. Levinsohn, and E. Katz. 1993. *Beliefs, observances and social interaction among Israeli Jews*. Jerusalem: The Louis Guttman Israel Institute of Applied Social Research.

———. 2000. *A portrait of Israeli Jews: beliefs, observance and values of Israeli Jews*. Jerusalem: The Louis Guttman Israel Institute of Applied Social Research.

Liebman, C.S. 1974. Diaspora Influence on Israel: The Ben-Gurion: Blaustein 'Exchange' and Its Aftermath. *Jewish Social Studies* 36 (3/4): 271–280.

———. 1977. *Pressure without sanctions: The influence of world Jewry on Israeli policy*. Rutherford: Fairleigh Dickinson University Press.

Liebman, C.S., and S.M. Cohen. 1990. *Two worlds of Judaism: The Israeli and American experiences*. New Haven, CT: Yale University Press.

Lipset, S.M. 1960. *Political man: the social basis of politics*. Garden City, NY: Doubleday.

———. 1971. The socialism of fools: the left, the Jews, and Israel. In *The new left and the Jews*, ed. M.S. Chertoff, 103–131. New York: Pitman Publishing Corporation.

———. 1972. *Group life in America: a task force report*. New York: American Jewish Committee.

Lipset, S.M., and E. Raab. 1995. *Jews and the new American scene*. Cambridge, MA and London: Harvard University Press.

Massarik, F., and A. Chenkin. 1973. United States National Jewish Population Survey: A First Report. In *American Jewish year book, 1973*, ed. M. Fine and M. Himmelfarb, vol. 73, 264–315. New York: American Jewish Committee and Philadelphia: Jewish Publication Society of America.

Medding, P.Y. 1977. Towards a general theory of Jewish political interests and behavior. *Jewish Journal of Sociology* 19 (2): 115–144.

Pew Research Center. 2013. *A portrait of Jewish Americans*. http://www.pewforum.org/2013/10/01/jewish-american-beliefs-attitudes-culture-survey/.

———. 2015. *Israel's religiously divided society*. http://www.pewforum.org/2016/03/08/israels-religiously-divided-society/.

Rebhun, U. 2011. Jews and the ethnic scene: A Multidimensional Theory. In *Ethnicity and beyond: Theories and dilemmas of Jewish group demarcation. Studies in contemporary Jewry*, ed. E. Lederhendler, vol. XXV, 91–101.

———. 2016. *Jews and the American religious landscape*. New York: Columbia University Press.

Rebhun, U., and L. Lev Ari. 2013. *American Israelis: Migration, transnationalism, and diasporic identity*. Leiden, Netherlands and Boston: Brill.

Rebhun, U., and S. Levy. 2006. Unity and diversity: Jewish identification in America and Israel 1990–2000. *Sociology of Religion: A Quarterly Review* 67 (4): 391–414.

Rebhun, U., and C.I. Waxman. 2000. The Americanization of Israel: A demographic, cultural and political evaluation. *Israel Studies* 5 (1): 65–91.

Rosenberg, B., Howe., I. 1976. Are the Jews turning Toward the right? In *The new conservatives: a critique from the left*, ed. I. Howe and L. A. Coser, 64-89. New York: New American Library.

Rosner, S., and C. Fuchs. 2018. *Israel Judaism: A cultural Revolution (in Hebrew)*. Hevel Modiin and Jerusalem: Dvir and Jewish People Policy Institute.

Safran, W. 2005. The Jewish Diaspora in a comparative and theoretical perspective. *Israel Studies* 10 (1): 36–60.

Sarna, J. 2004. *American Judaism: a history*. New Haven, CT and London: Yale University Press.

Sasson, T., C. Kadushin, and L. Saxe. 2010. Trends in American Jewish attachment to Israel: an assessment of the distancing hypothesis. *Contemporary Jewry* 30 (2-3): 297–319.

Sasson, T. 2014. *The new American Zionism*. New York: New York University Press.

Saxe, L., and B. Chazan. 2008. *Ten days of Birthright Israel: a journey in young adult identity*. Waltham, MA: Brandeis University Press.

Saxe, L., J. Krasner Aronson, and T. Sasson. 2014. Pew's portrait of American Jewry: A reassessment of the assimilation narrative. In *American Jewish year book, 2014*, ed. A. Dashefsky and I. Sheskin, vol. 114, 71–81. Dordrecht: Springer.

Schmelz, U.O., and S. DellaPergola. 1982. World Jewish population. In *American Jewish year book, 1982*, ed. M. Himmelfarb and D. Singer, vol. 82, 82–96. New York: American Jewish Committee and Philadelphia: Jewish Publication Society of America.

Seligman, B.B., and H. Swados. 1948/1949. Jewish population studies in the United States. In *American Jewish year book, 1948–1949*, ed. H. Schneiderman and M. Fine, vol. 50, 651–782. Philadelphia: Jewish Publication Society of America.

Shapira, A. 2012. *Israel: A history*. Waltham, MA: Brandeis University Press.

Sheffer, G. 2002. A nation and its Diaspora: A re-examination of Israeli-Jewish Diaspora relations. *Diaspora: A Journal of Transnational Studies* 11 (3): 331–338.

Sheskin, I.M. 2012. Attachment of American Jews to Israel: Perspectives from local Jewish community studies. *Contemporary Jewry* 32 (1): 27–65.

Sklare, M. 1993. *Observing America's Jews*. Hanover, MA: Brandeis University Press.

Smith, G. A. and J. Martinez. 2016 (9/11). *How the faithful voted: A preliminary 2016 analysis*. Pew Research Center. http://www.pewresearch.org/fact-tank/2016/11/09/how-the-faithful-voted-a-preliminary-2016-analysis/.

Tabory, E. 2010. Attachment to Israeli and Jewish identity: An assessment of an assessment. *Contemporary Jewry* 30 (2–3): 191–197.

Tolts, M. 2015. Demographic transformations among ex-Soviet migrants in Israel. In *Research in Jewish demography and identity*, ed. E. Lederhendler and U. Rebhun, 151–156. Boston: Academic Studies Press.

Walzer, M. 1986. Is Liberalism (still) good for the Jews? *Moment* (March): 13–19.

Waxman, C.I. 1989. *American aliya: Portrait of an innovative migration movement*. Detroit: Wayne State University Press.

———. 2010. Beyond distancing: Jewish identity, identification, and American's young Jews. *Contemporary Jewry* 30 (2–3): 227–232.

Waxman, D. 2016. *Trouble in the Tribe: The American Jewish Conflict over Israel*. Princeton, NJ: Princeton University Press.

Chapter 2
The Presidential Voting of American Jews

Herbert F. Weisberg

Most American Jews have been voting Democratic since the late-1920s. In every election since 1948, there has been speculation as to whether Jews' affinity to the Democratic Party is about to end; but it has displayed remarkable persistence. Yet, more careful examination reveals that there has been variation in Jews' voting patterns. Partisanship is not static or immutable. Attention to Jewish voting received renewed attention in early 2019 when the Republicans launched a new organization intended to create a Jewish "exodus" from the Democratic Party.

This chapter summarizes the recent surge of research on Jews' politics and supplies great detail on their voting history and voting patterns. Section 2.1 provides a review of the literature. Section 2.2 considers the various factors that have been advanced to explain Jews' voting. Section 2.3 offers a brief analysis of their voting turnout and their political participation more generally. Section 2.4 presents a lengthy history of their presidential voting, including analysis of voting trends. Section 2.5 focuses on three factors that affect Jews' voting: ideology, partisanship, and Israel. Section 2.6 turns to the contemporary period, including their voting in the 2016 election, the impact of the Trump administration, and the 2018 election. Section 2.7 provides a brief conclusion.

2.1 Literature

Attention has been paid to the Jewish vote at least as far back as the Lincoln elections (Sarna and Shapell 2015, pp. 178–182). However, there was little literature on the topic until the advent of public opinion polling in the 1930s and the subsequent development of social science surveys.

H. F. Weisberg (✉)
Department of Political Science, The Ohio State University, Columbus, OH, USA
e-mail: weisberg.1@osu.edu

© Springer Nature Switzerland AG 2020
A. Dashefsky, I. M. Sheskin (eds.), *American Jewish Year Book 2019*, American
Jewish Year Book 119, https://doi.org/10.1007/978-3-030-40371-3_2

2.1.1 Early Literature

The Jewish vote was noticed in the 1936 *Washington Post* (11 Oct., p. B1) on the first Gallup pre-election poll, entitled "Roosevelt Is Strongest With Catholics, Jews." A decade later, a journal article analyzing several religious groups (Allinsmith and Allinsmith 1948) found the Jewish vote was anomalous since they were a relatively prosperous group but voted on the liberal side. The Jewish vote was mentioned in books by early pollster Sam Lubell (1951). The first major national study of American voting behavior (Campbell et al. 1960, p. 302) showed that their voting was distinctively Democratic in the 1950s.

By the mid-1950s, Jewish voting attracted the attention of three dissertation students. Lawrence Fuchs' 1955 dissertation, *The Political Behavior of American Jews*, explained Jewish liberalism in terms of their Judaic values. By contrast, Werner Cohn's 1956 dissertation, *Sources of Jewish Liberalism*, focused on the European origins of Jews' liberalism. Maurice Guysenir's 1957 dissertation, *Jewish Voting Behavior in Chicago's 50th Ward*, concentrated on the class basis of their voting. Cohn's work appeared as a chapter in an edited volume (Cohn 1958) and Guysenir's (1958) in a journal article, while Fuchs (1956) published his as a book.

Fuchs' study was the first full-length book on Jewish voting. It treats Jews as an ethno-religious group, justifying "ethno-religious politics [as] basically a product of ethno-religious pluralism in American life" (p. 19). Four chapters examine Jewish American political history, starting from Jews being Jeffersonian Democrats, then transitioning in the Civil War period in which Northern Jews abandoned the Democratic Party, followed by a lengthy treatment of "the Republican years" with a transition in the 1920s, leading up to "the Democratic return" since the 1930s. Then, Fuchs turned to the 1952 election, analyzing a survey he conducted in a Boston ward. The next four chapters discuss Jews relationship to the Democratic Party, their Socialist tradition, split-ticket voting, and minor party voting. The final chapter focuses on "sources of Jewish internationalism and liberalism," with an emphasis on the role of Jewish values (discussed further below). Fuchs placed his study in the nascent field of voting studies, but the reviews of the book were generally lukewarm because its evidence base was not as systematic as the early sociological analysis of voting.

On the twentieth anniversary of the publication of his pioneering book, Fuchs revisited the topic in an introductory essay for a special bicentennial issue of *American Jewish Historical Quarterly*. Fuchs (1976, p. 182) duly noted that Liebman (1973) had pointed out that the most religious Jews were not the most liberal and had consequently concluded that Fuchs' focus on Judaic values was "tenuous." While Fuchs admitted that American politics had entered a new era, he maintained that Torah-based values still had "something to do with the persistence of Jewish liberalism." Fuchs insisted (p. 189), "What they [Jews] are not going to lose is an overwhelming commitment to the basic structure of constitutional liberalism and to social justice—not as long as they remain Americans and Jews."

John Kennedy's successful 1960 campaign to become the nation's first president who was Catholic increased the focus on the nexus between religion and politics. That brought attention to the Jewish vote in 1960 (Brenner 1964), including what may be the first discussion in the *American Jewish Year Book* of the direction of the Jewish vote (Dawidowicz 1961).

2.1.2   The 1970s–1990s

The first accessible compilation of the Jewish vote in presidential elections was in a book by *Washington Post* correspondent Stephen Isaacs (1974, pp. 151–153). *Jews and American Politics* is an anecdotal work based on interviews that he conducted with Jewish political personalities. He recounted several stories involving Jewish politicians, presidential campaign aides, bureaucrats, and fellow reporters.

Three additional books related to Jewish voting were published during this period. They described the history of Jews' politics, but each also had political objectives. Nathaniel Weyl's (1968) *The Jew in American Politics* argued that Jewish support for liberals was misplaced. William Heitzmann's (1975) *American Jewish Voting Behavior* concluded that Jews would return to the Republican Party. El Azhary (1980) performed a state-by-state analysis of several elections to claim that the importance of Jews' votes was exaggerated; he based his estimates of Jews' votes in each state on Jews' national vote, although too few were interviewed (just 30–53 nationally, depending on the year) for his estimates to be reliable at the state level.

Additionally, Alan Fisher, Arthur Hertzberg, Milton Himmelfarb, and Seymour Martin Lipset, among others, published popular journal articles on the Jewish vote in the 1970s and 1980s. As to be discussed in Sect. 2.2, the factors contributing to Jews' liberalism were considered at a theoretical level by Peter Medding (1977) and Geoffrey Levey (1996), while Steven M. Cohen and Charles Liebman (1997) provided important empirical analysis of that liberalism. Cohen (1983) presented particularly insightful survey-based analysis of modernity effects on their politics. The American Jewish Committee (AJC) began its Annual Survey of American Jewish Opinion in the 1980s, which led to several useful reports (see www.JewishDataBank.org).

2.1.3   The Early 2000s

The 2000s began with the publication of Sandy Maisel and Ira Forman's (2001) *Jews in American Politics*, an edited collection of broad-ranging essays that cover a wide set of topics on contemporary Jewish politics. Most notably for current purposes, Ira Forman (2001) contributed a historical review of American Jewish voting behavior, and Anna Greenberg and Kenneth Wald (2001) wrote a survey-based analysis of Jewish liberalism. Rafael Medoff's (2002) *Jewish Americans and Political Participation* included a historical chapter on the Jewish vote along with examination of Jewish participation in politics more generally.

Ira Sheskin (2013, 2016) has used modern probability-based surveys to examine Jews' politics in several American cities, contributing important analyses of the geography and demography of the Jewish vote.

The most recent studies of Jews' politics are the book-length analyses of Jewish liberalism by Wald (2019) and of Jewish voting by Weisberg (2019), both of which will be described in more detail throughout this chapter.

2.1.4 Problems in Studying Jews' Voting

Studying Jews' presidential voting has been challenging because Jews are such a small proportion of the total population. As to be discussed below, the first studies of Jewish voting were based primarily on predominantly Jewish voting precincts in a few major cities. Thus, the standard estimates of the Jewish vote through 1932, as published in Isaacs (1974) and repeated in Forman (2001), have been traced by Weisberg (2012) back to historian David Burner's (1968) data for predominantly Jewish "sanitary districts" in Manhattan. However, there also would have been non-Jews living in those precincts, and the voting of Jews in those precincts might have been different from that of Jews living in religiously heterogeneous areas across the rest of the nation.

National political surveys have been conducted since the mid-1930s, but they contain too few Jews to permit reliable generalizations. To compensate for that fact, the standard estimates of the Jewish vote for the 1936–1968 elections, as published in Isaacs and Forman, apparently were based on combining several poll results (e.g., Levy and Kramer 1972, p. 103). That strategy has also been used for measuring the distinctiveness of Jews' politics, which requires comparing Jews to comparable non-Jews. While the average numbers of Jews per survey in the 1948–2016 American National Election Studies (ANES) surveys and the 1972–2016 General Social Survey (GSS) are only in the low to middle 40s, their surveys over the years can be combined to analyze Jews' political distinctiveness on repeated questions.[1] Using that approach, Smith (2005), Djupe (2007), Abrams and Cohen (2016), and Weisberg (2019) have shown that the relative liberalism of non-Orthodox Jews is continuing, though it is restrained.

National media exit polls that have been conducted since 1972 are now used to estimate the Jewish vote. Their accuracy depends on whether the precincts they happen to sample include ones where Orthodox Jews live within walking distance of their synagogues as well as a proper representation of Jews living in more

---

[1] Both conducted 31 surveys over these time periods, with the ANES interviewing 1388 Jews (an average of 45 each year) and the GSS 1246 (an average of 40 each year).

religiously heterogeneous areas. The "standard" estimates of Jewish voting since then are based on the main media exit poll. Weisberg (2012) revised estimates of the Jewish vote historically by including a wider variety of national exit polls, while the Solomon Report (Mellman et al. 2012) provided more complete estimates of Jews' voting that incorporated state exit polls and gave considerable detail on the demographics of the Jewish vote.

Advocacy organizations have sponsored occasional national surveys as well as recent Election-Day "exit" polls of Jews. Those surveys are generally either phone or internet based, but their samples of Orthodox and young Jews may not be representative because those groups are difficult to contact and interview without persistent multi-day attempts. Eric Uslaner and Mark Lichbach (2009) and Uslaner (2015) have made good use of advocacy group polls to examine the impact of attitudes regarding Israel on Jews' voting.

The most important development, though, has been the advent of large-scale national surveys of Jews, starting with the National Jewish Population Surveys, which included party identification and political ideology in both the 1990 and 2000–2001 surveys (see esp. Kotler-Berkowitz 2005). Most notably, the 2013 Pew Research Center Survey of US Jews conducted lengthy phone interviews with 3475 Jews chosen through random-digit-dialing (RDD) after stratifying counties based on their Jewish population size. The methodology of these surveys has improved considerably over recent years, with the best surveys using probability-based sampling. Even the most complex sampling of Jews has been challenged because of low response rates (Klausner 2013), though studies find that probabilistic surveys are quite accurate regardless (MacInnis et al. 2018).

Another important problem in surveying Jews is whom to include as Jewish. Most surveys (especially exit polls) only interview "Jews by religion" (JBR), those who answer they are Jewish when asked if they are Protestant, Catholic, or Jewish. That misses the 22% of "Jews of no religion" (JNR), those who say they have no religion (otherwise called "nones"), but, when asked, would say there are other reasons that they consider themselves Jewish. In particular, when asked if their parents were Jewish and/or if they were raised Jewish, most of the JNR respond affirmatively. Surveys show they are more Democratic than Jews by religion, partly because the JBR include Orthodox Jews, who are mostly Republican. JNR are about 10 percentage points more Democratic and nearly 25 points more liberal than JBR (Weisberg 2019, p. 113). The party split for JBR in the Pew survey was 68% Democratic, 7% Independent, and 25% Republican, versus 78%, 10%, and 12% for JNR.[2] The difference was even larger on ideology: JBR split 43% liberal, 35% moderate, and 22% conservative, versus 67%, 22%, and 11% for JNR (Weisberg 2019, fn 6, p. 245). As a result, Jews should be considered to be more Democratic and more liberal than media surveys and exit polls typically show.

---

[2] The 2013 Pew survey results in this chapter are based on reanalysis looking only at US citizens. As in the Pew Report (Pew Research Center 2013), the JNR are included along with the JBR in this chapter.

The 2013 Pew Research Center Survey of US Jews and the 2012 Public Religion Research Institute's (PRRI) Jewish Values Survey also asked about political issues and measured presidential approval, which is a plausible substitute for a vote question, since it was asked in close proximity to a presidential election. Laurence Kotler-Berkowitz (2017) gives an important analysis of politics in the Pew data, and Weisberg (2019) contributes a parallel analysis of the Pew and PRRI data.

2.2 Factors Affecting American Jews' Politics

Countless explanations have been offered over the years for Jews' predominantly liberal politics and Democratic voting, often focusing on the apparent paradox of a relatively affluent social group being politically liberal.

2.2.1 Early Explanations

Social psychological explanations of their liberalism that were offered in the mid-twentieth century emphasized how Jews fit into society at that time. For example, as a minority group that was trying to assimilate, Kurt Lewin (1941) described Jews as "marginal men," estranged from their traditional roots while being alienated from the general society. Liebman (1973) saw political emancipation as allowing Jews to rid themselves of Jewish traditions, leading to estrangement from their roots while still being alienated from society. He considered their liberalism to be a consequence of their "faith that the application of human intellect can create a constantly progressing universal cosmopolitan society" (p. 150). Edward Shapiro (2000, p. 167) emphasized Jews' alienation from power and from authority as leading to their interest in both anarchism and liberalism.

Another explanation was a status inconsistency argument. Seymour Martin Lipset (1963, p. 256) saw Jews' leftist voting as due to their "inferior status position (social discrimination)." As Gerhard Lenski (1967) detailed, Jews had higher "achieved status" in terms of education, occupation, and income than the status ascribed to them because of how non-Jews perceived their religion. His theory claimed that Jews react to that inconsistency by opposing the social order that is responsible for the injustice; so, they support the party that advocates social change.

However, Levey (1996) countered that the ties of marginality and of status inconsistency to Jews' liberal politics are unclear, particularly because most Jews retained some of their Jewish identity. At most, he argued, such inconsistency would lead to radical responses, rather than liberal politics. In any case, even if marginality, alienation, estrangement, status inconsistency, and/or status inferiority were useful ways of thinking about Jews' position in society in the 1940–1970s, they have less relevance in the early 2000s when there is greater acceptance of American Jews.

A related explanation is that Jews became liberal in the US because of social discrimination. Benjamin Ginsberg (1993, p. 140) pointed out that the expanded public sector gave them employment opportunities as well as outlawing discrimination that affected them. He stated (p. 143) "Jews are, as a group, more dependent upon the domestic state than are other whites and, hence, are more likely to support domestic state spending," though he argued this makes them likely to support the Democratic party but not necessarily likely to adopt liberalism as an ideology.

Additionally, some historical explanations of Jewish liberalism have been proposed. For example, Werner Cohn's (1958) explanation went back to the aftermath of the political emancipation of Jews during the French Revolution, when Christian forces on the political right wanted to revoke equality for Jews. Similarly, antisemitism has usually been associated with the political right, so Jews were pushed toward the left. The immigrant experience is also often cited, with Jews favoring socialism because of the harsh working and living conditions many faced when they arrived in the US. More recently, Henry Feingold (1992, 2014) emphasized Jews being urban, urbane, and cosmopolitan as explanations of their politics.

In his work on Jewish political behavior, Fuchs (1955, 1956) focused on a different set of explanations: Jewish insecurity (due to their history as a repressed minority) and a Jewish value system (love of learning, charity, and non-asceticism), combined with Jews' high level of group solidarity. Those explanations, however, have not been treated well over the years. Fuchs did not make clear why their minority status would make Jews vote Democratic. Furthermore, if Judaic factors were responsible for American Jews voting liberal and Democratic, then the most religiously observant Jews should be the most liberal and Democratic. Instead, by the latter part of the twentieth century, Orthodox Jews were generally more conservative and Republican than non-Orthodox Jews. Critics argued that it was illogical to accept Judaic explanations that fit better for the most secular Jews than for the most observant.

Two additional explanations of Jews' liberalism reflect the changed status of Jews in America. Cohen and Liebman (1997) emphasized religious modernism as a factor pushing Jews in the liberal direction. Among other explanations, Greenberg and Wald (2001) pointed to self-interest in the sense that Jews have advanced politically and economically because of the liberal US system.

2.2.2 Recent Explanations

The most recent full-blown explanatory systems are those of political scientists Wald (2019) and Weisberg (2019). Wald describes American Jews' worldview as classical liberalism, which focuses on individual rights but not economic egalitarianism. He applies three general theories of political behavior: contextual analysis, political opportunity structure, and threat perception. The aspect of context that Wald emphasizes is the Americanness of American Jews, particularly their being granted full citizenship rights and their being part of a secular state. The political opportunity structure in the US gave Jews full legal protection. Wald particularly emphasizes the ban on religious tests for office in Article VI of the Constitution. Jews saw the Democrats and liberals as protectors of the separation of church and state under which Jews were prospering. Even if Jews faced some discrimination and antisemitism in the US, the levels were far below those experienced in Europe.

Threat perception theory (Medding 1977) argues that Jews react to the greatest perceived threat to their interests. Thus, some Jews moved away from liberal politics and Democratic voting in the 1970s and 1980s out of reaction to threats they perceived from the black power movement and from attacks on Israeli policies from the left. However, some Jews moved back to the Democratic Party in the 1990s when they perceived a larger threat from the Christian Right. Wald's book, *The Foundations of American Jewish Liberalism,* masterfully expands on these three macro-level explanations with detailed historical examination of different periods of American Jewish history.

Weisberg's (2019) book, *The Politics of American Jews*, instead focuses on the micro-level in applying three social-psychological factors to understand Jews' politics: their self-interest, their values, and their social identity, with Jews' minority consciousness affecting all three. Self-interest has usually been interpreted as pocketbook economics, as when Himmelfarb amusingly pointed to the paradox that Jews earn like Episcopalians while they vote like Puerto Ricans. Weisberg interprets economic self-interest more broadly, in terms of appreciating the economic system in which Jews have prospered. Additionally, Jews' self-interest includes protecting fellow Jews (including Jews abroad and especially in Israel), being accepted, and having religious liberty.

As to values, Weisberg applies the theory of universal values that Shalom Schwartz (1994) based on his studies of motivational values in several nations. One dimension of values is self-transcendence (emphasizing universalism and benevolence) versus self-enhancement (seeking power, achievement, and hedonism). The other dimension is conservation (valuing tradition, conformity, and security) versus openness to change (desiring stimulation and self-direction). Schwartz found people tend to emphasize values that are near one another on the values circle (Fig. 2.1). Another values theory is Inglehart's (1977) focus on materialist versus post-materialist values, based on experiences in people's pre-adult years: economic deprivation leads to materialist values while affluence leads to focus on support for freedom of speech and having a say in government decisions. Weisberg also sees a role for Fuchs' Judaic values, but he recognizes that the Orthodox may emphasize different Judaic values (such as the value of concern for the people of Israel) than the social justice values (*tikkun olam*) that motivate many Conservative and Reform Jews. He argues that self-interest was important in immigrant Jews becoming Democrats during the Great Depression, and that their values kept them in the Democratic fold when the Republican Party was captured by the Christian Right.

Social psychologists today emphasize social identity in understanding group behavior, with people being biased in favor of their in-groups as opposed to their out-groups. Religion is a potent social identity, and it increases in importance when Jews have high levels of interaction with other Jews. Out-groups have historically

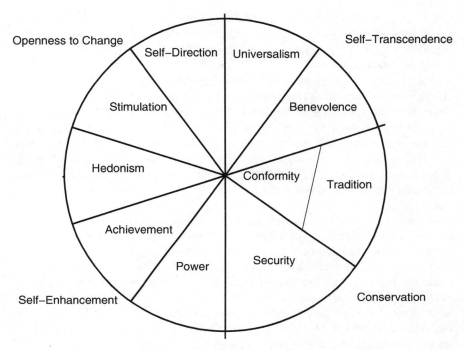

Fig. 2.1 Schwartz universal values circle. (Source: Based on Schwartz and Huismans 1995)

threatened Jews, which also increases Jews' social identity as Jews. Furthermore, social identity can become politicized when a group sees its partisan ties as part of the group's social identity. Thus, after the Jewish vote became predominantly Democratic in the New Deal period, many of the next generation of Jews were raised learning that "we Jews are Democrats," which became part of their social identity *as Jews* (see also Wald 2019, Chap. 9). Of course, many other Jews were raised in Republican families and learned that "we Jews are Republicans;" but they have been a minority in the American Jewish community. Being Democratic has become the "dominant politicized social identity" of American Jews.

Weisberg's argument is in several parts. Jews' minority consciousness has directly affected their self-interest and their values, with that being intensified when they are subject to prejudice and discrimination. Their self-interest led most initially to be Democrats; their values kept them Democrats; their politicized social identity makes their Democratic identification resistant to change. As Dawidowicz and Goldstein (1974, p. 300) describe being Democratic, it has become a "family group tradition—a habit and custom difficult to shed." Jews are a people of tradition, and Weisberg terms their politics "the Politics of Tradition."

Neither Wald's nor Weisberg's explanations are as simple as early explanations of Jews' politics as just reflecting their "marginality" or their "alienation." Instead, both are intended to be broad explanatory systems that can be applied universally, can account for exceptions, and can deal with changes. For example, changes in threat perception can lead to partisan change under the Wald system, while conflict between a group's self-interest and its values can cause partisan change in Weisberg's system.

Additionally, the factors that affect American Jews' ideology and political party choice can vary over time. The reasons that most Jews were liberal in the 1930s are likely different from the reasons that most were liberal in the 1960s and why most are liberal in the early 2000s. Wald would say this reflects changes in the political context, in the political opportunity structure, and in perceived threats, while Weisberg would point to changes in Jews' self-interest and in their values between different eras. For example, the needs and issues that enthused many Jews to vote for Socialist Party candidates in the early 1900s were very different from their liberal positions on moral issues such as abortion and gay rights that motivate many Jews today to back the Democratic Party. Thus, explanations of Jews' politics can be time-specific. That the explanations that Fuchs offered in the 1950s do not hold today does not mean that they were incorrect when originally advanced. The difficulty, however, is that reliable evidence as to Jews' politics in earlier periods is not available. For example, the lack of large-scale surveys prevents testing whether Fuchs' focus on Judaic values as an explanation of Jewish liberalism held for the most observant Jews in the 1950s, which was before the Haredim (fervently Orthodox) became a large part of American Orthodoxy. Still, there are not sufficient tests of Wald's explanations or Weisberg's. In particular, surveys of American Jews' Shalom Schwartz values would be useful, as would be direct measures of their subjective self-interest.

2.3   Voting Turnout

Jews are known for their very high level of voter registration, voting turnout, and for their high level of political participation more generally. A high turnout is useful for magnifying the effect of their votes, since Jews constitute only about 2% of the US population.

Surveys often report that more than 90% of Jews have voted. However, this is likely an exaggeration, since voters are more likely to cooperate with a survey interviewer than non-voters. After all, surveys often find more than 70% of their respondents claiming to have voted, whereas the highest proportion of eligible voters turning out to vote in national elections was in the 50% range from 1972 through 2000 and barely above 60% since then (US Election Project 2019).

Furthermore, studies show that the proportion of Jews who vote is not much higher than the voting proportion for non-Jews with similar socio-demographic characteristics and similar socio-economic status. The cumulative American National Election Studies (ANES) and the General Social Survey (GSS) data permit such comparisons with non-Jews. While those surveys show about a 20% point difference between the turnout rates of Jews and non-Jews in 1992–2012, that difference falls to only about four points when compared to non-Jews with similar characteristics and income (Weisberg 2019, Chap. 6). Jews' apparent turnout advantage is largely due to their being an older group with high levels of education and income.

Looking at political participation more generally, Wald (2016) finds that Jews were not politically hyperactive when compared to a matched sample of non-Jews in Roper Organization polls in the late 1980s and early 1990s. Similarly, Weisberg's (2019, Chap. 6) analysis of ANES data found only slight differences in political participation and campaign donations between Jews and comparable non-Jews. Wald (2019, Chap. 10) states that Jews contribute to campaigns disproportionately, as they do to charities. He emphasized the Democratic skew of Jews' campaign donations, albeit the largest Jewish megadonors in the 2010s elections, Sheldon and Miriam Adelson, gave to the Republican side.

Overall, whether in voting, campaign participation, or political contributions, the high activity level of Jews is basically what should be expected given their demographics and socio-economic status. Politicians would benefit from Jews' high level of political involvement, just as candidates would benefit from the involvement of similarly situated non-Jews.

2.4   The History of Jews' Presidential Voting

2.4.1   The First Century of US Elections: Becoming Politicized

There is little solid evidence as to how Jews voted in early presidential elections, though there is information about their likely self-interest.

2.4.1.1   From 1788 to 1824

The party competition in the 1796–1816 elections was between John Adams's Federalist Party and Thomas Jefferson's Democratic-Republican Party. Jews' self-interest was split between economic interests and desire to have full civil rights. Those who were creditors and those involved in manufacturing goods that competed with European goods had economic reasons to support the Federalists as the party of a strong central government (Forman 2001, p. 145). However, the Federalists were anti-immigrant, as illustrated by their enacting the Alien and Sedition Act of 1798, whereas the Jeffersonians strongly supported religious freedom.

There were some incidents in this period in which Jews and Jewish interests were poorly treated. In part, this was because few early presidents knew many Jews (there were only about 3000–5000 Jews in the US during this period—see Fig. 5.1 in this volume), so their images of Jews were often based on the Old Testament Hebrews. For example, John Adams characterized those who held loans as "as avaricious as any Jews in Jews' Quarter," and Thomas Jefferson called Judaism a "depraved religion." Few Jews received presidential appointments. Early presidents gave Uriah Phillips Levy several high Navy appointments, but he was court-marshaled six times. Mordecai Manuel Noah was recalled as consul to Tunis, when it became known that he was Jewish. Given these incidents, the primary non-economic political motivation of Jews during this period was likely a desire to obtain greater acceptance.

Marcus (1989, p. 527) claims that "a substantial number" of Jews were Federalists, though mentioning (p. 579) that Federalists attacked their opposition as the party of Jews. By contrast, Fuchs (1956, Chap. 2) entitles his chapter on this period "Jeffersonians All;" and Forman (2001, p. 145) emphasizes that a dozen Jewish officeholders during that period were Jeffersonians. Lipset and Raab (1995, p. 153) describe Jews being Democratic-Republicans as "an early example of Jews' political behavior running counter to their economic interests. But it was less a matter of Jews voting against their own self-interest than of their defining self-interest beyond the pocketbook. The qualities inherent in a free and achievement-oriented America were most important for the well-being of Jews."

While there were restrictions on Jews' civil liberties in several of the original 13 American colonies, the states all allowed Jews to vote by the time the US Constitution came into effect (Chyet 1958; Marcus 1989, p. 512). Still, Jews had limited impact in the early elections because many states did not use popular vote to choose their presidential electors. For example, Virginia was the only state with a popular vote for electors in 1800 that had a Jewish community; and Jefferson would have easily carried his home state even without Jews' votes.

2.4.1.2   From 1828 to 1856

The party competition in the 1828–1856 elections was between the Democratic and Whig parties. Presidents generally had greater familiarity with Jews than earlier presidents. Several had Jewish friends, and presidents also had more contact with the Jewish community. For example, Zachary Taylor (Whig) met with Rabbi Isaac Mayer Wise in the White House; and Franklin Pierce (Dem.) signed an act of Congress that enabled the incorporation of the District of Columbia's first synagogue.

Presidents also began to appoint Jews to public office on a more regular basis. Andrew Jackson (Dem.) appointed Mordecai Noah as Overseer to the Port of New York, John Tyler (Whig) nominated Warder Cresson as US consul to Palestine, and Franklin Pierce (Dem.) appointed August Belmont as American Ambassador to The Hague. Most notably, Millard Fillmore (Whig) offered Louisiana Senator Judah Benjamin an appointment to the US Supreme Court, though he turned down the offer because he preferred to remain in the Senate.

As in earlier years, Jews' self-interest would have been divided between economic interests and immigration concerns. The Whig Party supported a strong federal government with a national bank, which was attractive to Jews engaged in finance. That could explain Jewish support for the Whigs among the Sephardim in

New York City (Sarna 1981, pp. 100–101). The dominant view, however, is that most Jews, especially in New York, were Democrats (e.g., Fuchs 1956, pp. 33–35), partly out of opposition to the anti-immigrant element in the Whig Party. Jewish support for the Democratic Party is said to have increased when President Martin Van Buren (Dem.) ordered the American consul in Damascus to protect its Jews when many were attacked in 1840 (the "Damascus Affair").

The Jewish vote was still small, with perhaps 5000 Jews in the US at the beginning of this period and about 200,000 by the end (Fig. 5.1 in this volume). The increase in Jewish immigration after the 1848 European revolutions would have had minimal impact in pre-Civil War elections since there is a 5-year waiting period to obtain American citizenship and vote.

The antebellum era ended with two high-profile foreign policy decisions that underlined the limited acceptance of Jewish interests. President James Buchanan (Dem.) instructed the American ambassador to work to get the Swiss cantons to remove restrictions on Jews, but he rejected requests from Jewish leaders to renegotiate the commercial treaty with Switzerland that allowed expulsion of American Jews (Adams 2014, pp. 19–20). Additionally, Buchanan refused Jews' requests to protest to the Vatican over their taking a 6-year old Jewish boy, Edgardo Mortara, from his parents in 1858 on the claim that a maid had baptized him, possibly because challenging the Pope would have upset the larger number of Catholic voters (Adams 2014, p. 22).

2.4.1.3 From 1860 to 1880

With slavery as the dominant issue, the anti-slavery Republican Party became the Democratic Party's main competition. Some German Jews would have been attracted to the Republican Party's abolitionist position (Mazur 1990, p. 80). However, abolitionists were not popular among Jews because many were evangelical Protestants, who tried to convert Jews and because several used anti-Jewish rhetoric (Sarna 2004, p. 113). Some writers claim that Jews would have been drawn to the Democratic Party because it favored equal rights for white men regardless of their religion (Forman 2001; p. 146).

Forman (2001, p. 147) asserts that "at the eve of the Civil War most Jews remained in the Democratic constituency." Yet Fuchs (1956, p. 35) argues that "by 1860, Democrats were the exception among Jews in the North," and Weyl (1968, p. 56) states that most Jews lived in the north by 1860 and "a decided majority of them sympathized with the Republican Party." By the time of the Civil War, it is likely that Jews were split like the nation as a whole, with most northerners supporting the Republicans and most southerners the Democrats.

The Republican presidents from 1860 through 1884 gave Jews more recognition than previous presidents. Abraham Lincoln's several associations with Jews have been documented by Sarna and Shapell (2015). Most important, Lincoln cancelled General Ulysses S. Grant's General Orders No. 11 that expelled Jews "as a class" from the Department of Tennessee. When Grant ran for president, he wrote a letter explaining and disavowing the Order (Sarna 2012, pp. 75–76). As president, he appointed more Jews to office than any president before him, from which Sarna (2012, p. 148) concluded that Grant learned from his mistakes and "significantly empowered" Jews during his presidency.

Republican Presidents Rutherford B. Hayes, James Garfield, and Chester Arthur all spoke against Russia in its treatment of Jews. The German Jews who immigrated to the US in the mid-1800s were assimilating during this period, with many becoming prosperous business people. They wanted to be accepted as Americans, to have their religious liberty respected, and to have their coreligionists abroad protected. They could reasonably see these Republican presidents as supportive of those interests, which led the best-known Jews in the north to be Republicans.

The standard view is that most northern Jews were Republican (Fuchs 1956, p. 44), especially German Jews (Forman 2001, pp. 148–149), while most southern Jews were Democrats. That would not have been very distinctive, since the north voted Republican and the south Democratic. Diner (1992) describes Republicans as having a slight edge among Jews, which accords with the middle-class status that many central European Jewish immigrants had achieved. There was, however, considerable local variation. Chicago Jews from Bohemia (Czechoslovakia) were Democrats, as were Jews in Los Angeles, and Jews in New York City followed the Tammany Hall machine until the 1870s (Diner 1992). Jews were dispersed across the country, which minimized their electoral impact since their numbers in any single state would have been too small to affect most elections. In any case, they were still a small percentage of the population: only about 280,000 Jews resided in the country in 1880 (Fig. 5.1 in this volume).

2.4.2   The 1884–1932 Elections: Adjusting to Massive Immigration

The immigration between 1881 and 1924 of more than two million Jews from Eastern Europe (especially Russia and Romania) had the potential of considerably changing the politics of American Jews. By 1924, more than 3.6 million Jews lived in the US (Fig. 5.1 in this volume). Progressive economic reforms to improve working conditions would have been in the self-interest of these new immigrants, but neither major party initially nominated progressive presidential candidates on a consistent basis. Indeed, in some elections both major parties nominated establishment candidates who would not have appealed to these new immigrants. These immigrants sometimes joined the German Jews in supporting a progressive Republican candidate, while voting Democratic in other elections. The immigrants also contributed considerable energy to Socialist politics.

2.4.2.1   From 1884 to 1892

The Republican Party was still the party of the Union in the 1880s, while the Democratic Party regained strength in the South after Reconstruction ended. German Jews would have predominated in the Jewish electorate through the early 1890s because few Russian Jews were in the US long enough to attain citizenship.

Grover Cleveland was the Democratic presidential candidate in the 1884–1892 elections, winning the popular vote all three times but losing the Electoral College to Republican Benjamin Harrison in 1888. Rischin (1962, p. 272) published voting data for an assembly district in New York City's Lower East Side, an area in which new immigrants would have predominated. That district had narrow Republican presidential leads in 1884 and 1888. The 1892 election featured a rematch between Cleveland and Harrison, both of whom in their presidencies had criticized Russia's treatment of Jews and had appointed Jews to important positions. The election focused on economic issues including tariffs (which Cleveland wanted to lower) and the gold standard (which he wanted to maintain). Both Rischin's data and Allswang's (1971, p. 42) for Chicago show Cleveland winning about 60% of the 1892 vote of predominantly Jewish districts, though that might have been countered by the vote of German Jews in other districts.

2.4.2.2   From 1896 to 1912

Political historians consider the 1896 election to be a realigning election, establishing an era of Republican dominance. Populist leader William Jennings Bryan became the Democratic presidential nominee that year, promising to end the gold standard. Monetizing silver was popular in the western states, but not in the eastern states which became solidly Republican.

By this time, the immigration of Jews from Eastern Europe was large enough to impact the character of American Jewry, though many were not yet citizens. Prominent Jewish leaders were arguing against having a "Jewish vote." They contended it would look bad if such a small minority voted as a bloc, and they claimed that could rebound against Jewish interests.

This argument, though, had partisan implications. The leaders advocating neutrality were German Jews (N. Cohen 1984), many of whom supported the Republican Party. They were motivated, in part, by fear that bloc voting would result in Democratic voting by non-Jews (Dalin 1992, p. 58). It is telling also that Louis Marshall, one of the most influential leaders who encouraged Jewish political neutrality (Dalin 1992), himself started a Yiddish newspaper to support the Republican Party (Dawidowicz 1963, p. 188). That suggests that the opposition by German Jews to a "Jewish vote" was partly an attempt to dissuade eastern European Jews from voting Democratic *en masse* since their large numbers would have overwhelmed the Republican votes of German Jews.

Additionally, many Jews voted for Socialist presidential candidates during this period. Manor (2009) gave a provocative interpretation of this Socialist vote, stating that "most if not all votes given to the SP [Socialist Party] in fact benefited the Republicans" in that they took away votes that otherwise would have gone to the Democrats. A cynical reading is that establishment German Jews who supported the Republican Party were acceptant of Socialist voting by other Jews if that kept the Democrats from winning power.

With most new immigrants living in New York City and a few other large cities, it is possible to study the vote in predominantly Jewish voting districts. However, Russian Jewish immigrants who were tightly packed in tenement housing in those districts were more progressive in their politics than assimilated German Jews who were dispersed across those cities. Thus, these estimates probably underrepresent the Republican voting by German Jews.

The vote in predominantly Jewish precincts oscillates over this period, as illustrated by Rischin's and Allswang's data in Table 2.1. Estimates based on averaging the vote in multiple studies in New York, Chicago, and Boston[3] (see right section of Table 2.1) show Jews supporting Republican presidential candidates William McKinley in 1896 and Theodore Roosevelt in 1904, favoring Democrat William Jennings Bryan in 1900 and 1908, and then giving large votes to both Democrat Woodrow Wilson and Progressive Theodore Roosevelt in 1912. Notably, those 1896–1908 candidates won barely over 50% of the vote, with the Socialist candidates taking about 10%. Rischin (1962, p. 224) attributed the alternation of the presidential vote in New York's Eighth Assembly District to immigration-related issues as well as a reaction to American policy toward Russia's treatment of Jews.

By contrast, the received wisdom is that Jews voted Republican during these years, with a possible exception of 1900 (Howe 1976, p. 362) and the four-way split in 1912 (Fuchs 1956, p. 58). Fuchs (pp. 50–51) advanced three reasons for their Republican voting, each of which can be challenged. First, he claimed that the immigrants followed the "older and wiser Jewish heads already here" who were mainly Republican; but the Socialist support of many immigrants violates that claim. Second, Fuchs credited their gratitude for being given refuge in the States extended to the administrations in power at the time, though it is sometimes asserted that Jews appreciated the help that Democrats gave new immigrants in New York City. Fuchs' third point was that the Jews disliked the Irish who controlled the eastern Democratic Party; Jews were local Republican Party leaders in Boston (Gamm 1989) and New Haven (Dahl 1961); however, that was not necessarily the case in other cities.

A more likely explanation is that established German Jews and the new Russian Jewish immigrants voted differently from one another because they differed in their self-interest. The Russians favored whichever party nominated the more progressive candidate. While Bryan's "Cross of Gold" metaphor in 1896 was regarded as anti-semitic, he was considered more progressive than the 1900 and 1908 Republican nominees, when he opposed "trusts" (monopolies, in today's terms). Republican

---

[3] Because of the large proportion of American Jews who lived in New York City, this averaging gives extra weight for New York by counting its vote equally with the average of multiple studies for the other cities.

Table 2.1 Estimates of the presidential vote of Jews, 1896–1912

Year	New York estimate[a]			Chicago estimate[b]			Composite estimate[c]			
	Democrat (%)	Republican (%)	Other (%)	Dem. (%)	Rep. (%)	Other (%)	Dem. (%)	Rep. (%)	Other (%)	Basis
1896	37 Bryan	50 **McKinley**	13 Palmer	41			37	54	9	2 cities
1900	49 Bryan	43 **McKinley**	8 Debs	54			56	38	6	3 cities
1904	39 Parker	45 **TRoosevelt**	16 Debs	36			39	48	13	3 cities
1908	51 Bryan	34 **Taft**	15 Debs	52			51	38	11	3 cities
1912	37 **Wilson**	12 Taft	39 TRoosevelt	34	29	19	35	21	32	3 cities
			12 Debs			18			12	

Note: Winners are bolded. Other column lists candidate with more than 1% of the vote who was most popular with Jews
[a]Source: Rischin (1962, p. 272) for NY 8th Assembly District
[b]Source: Allswang (1971, pp. 42 and 218–220)
[c]The composite averages multiple data sources for each city

Roosevelt was the more progressive candidate in 1904, and both Roosevelt and Wilson were considered progressive candidates in 1912. That variation corresponds to the oscillation of the vote in predominantly Jewish districts, even if the winning margins were small. By contrast, the self-interest of the establishment German Jews led them to give a strong Republican vote throughout, which might have made the combined Jewish presidential vote Republican through 1908 as Fuchs claimed.

2.4.2.3   From 1916 to 1932

Table 2.2 shows Jewish voting estimates for the 1916–1932 elections, again based on predominantly Jewish voting districts in major cities. The 1916 election was the first for which there is a standard estimate of the Jewish vote. While, as mentioned earlier, it is based on Burner's (1968) estimates for predominantly Jewish districts in Manhattan, it ignores his Chicago data, as well as other data for Chicago and other cities. The composite column on the right updates Weisberg's (2012) multi-city averages. Importantly, as more Russian Jews immigrated to the country, they outnumbered the German Jews, though many delayed becoming citizens.[4] By 1930, 4.2 million Jews lived in the US (Fig. 5.1).

Before Wilson ran for reelection in 1916, he vetoed an immigration bill that would have made Jewish immigration more difficult by imposing a literacy requirement, and he appointed Louis Brandeis as the first Jewish justice on the Supreme Court. With these two actions, he easily secured the Jewish vote. However, the early 1920s elections offered Jews little ideological choice. Neither major-party candidate in 1920 was a progressive. Republican Warren Harding, when he was a newspaper editor during antisemite Herman Ahlwardt's trip to America, had attacked Ahlwardt in his newspaper as a "Jew-baiter" while praising Jews as being among America's "most patriotic and devoted" citizens. Democrat James Cox may have been the more progressive of the major party candidates, but the data for each city show that the Jewish vote went in Harding's direction, with a higher vote for Eugene Debs, the Socialist candidate, than for Cox.[5]

By contrast with Harding's clear win of the Jewish vote in 1920, there is complete disagreement as to how Jews voted in the 1924 election. Neither Republican Calvin Coolidge nor Democrat John W. Davis was progressive. Fuchs (1956, p. 64 and p. 141) describes Jews as apathetic toward the campaign, but they should instead be considered to be dissatisfied with all the candidates. There were three major issues that were of considerable interest to the Jewish population: the recently imposed immigration quotas, the increased power of the Ku Klux Klan, and

---

[4] Less than a fifth of foreign-born adult males in a largely Jewish New York district in 1910 were naturalized and so could vote (Goren 1961), and similarly only a fifth of Kessner's (1981, p. 232) random sample of 1500 New York City Jewish families in 1925 were on the voting rolls.

[5] Marks and Burbank's (1990) multivariate regression analysis confirms a significant Socialist vote in 1920 and 1912 among the Russian-born, who would have been largely Jewish.

Table 2.2 Estimates of the presidential vote of Jews, 1916–1932

Year	Standard estimate (based on New York)[a]			Chicago estimate[b]			Composite estimate[c]			
	Democrat (%)	Republican (%)	Other (%)	Dem. (%)	Rep. (%)	Other (%)	Dem. (%)	Rep. (%)	Other (%)	Basis
1916	55 Wilson	45 Hughes	0 Benson	57	43		53	36	11	3 cities
1920	19 Cox	43 Harding	38 Debs	28	61	11	19	53	28	3 cities
1924	51 Davis	27 Coolidge	22 LaFollette	37	43	20	34	44	22	4 cities
1928	72 Smith	28 Hoover	0 Thomas	78	22		64	34	2	4 cities
1932	82 FDRoosevelt	18 Hoover	0 Thomas	85	15		68	24	8	4 cities

Note: Winners are bolded. Other column lists candidate with more than 1% of the vote who was most popular with Jews
[a]Source: Forman (2001), based on Burner (1968)
[b]Source: Burner (1968, pp. 239–242)
[c]Source: Updated from Weisberg (2012)

prohibition, which Jews opposed. The major party platforms were almost identical and did not address those three issues.

Coolidge would have been unpopular with Jews, since he had signed the controversial Johnson-Reed Act that was designed to curb Jewish immigration by imposing limits on the basis of national origins in the 1890 census. Yet, the Russian Jewish immigrants would have little reason to favor Davis, who had defeated popular New York governor Al Smith for the party's nomination. Fuchs (1956, p. 141) stresses that Davis' Wall Street background would have been considered a negative, given the Socialist tradition among Jews. Senator Robert LaFollette, the Progressive candidate could have attracted Jewish votes after he was endorsed by the Socialist Party, but he had voted for the Johnson-Reed Act.

Burner's Manhattan data, which are the basis for the standard statistics on Jewish voting, show a Democratic vote by Jews. However, Fuchs (1956, p. 64) asserts that Coolidge obtained more votes than Davis in most Jewish wards in New York.[6] Indeed, Burner's (1968) Chicago data show that more Jews voted Republican than Democratic in 1924, as does other data for Chicago, Boston, and Philadelphia.

Thus, the usual claim that Jews started voting Democratic in 1924 is open to dispute. Neither major party attracted Jews to move *en masse* in its direction. Jews' dissatisfaction with the major party candidates is also evident in the increasing Socialist and Progressive vote in 1920 and 1924. Gamm's (1989, p. 60) analysis of the Jewish vote in Boston shows that different groups of Jews were responding differently in these early 1920s elections. Republicans won more of the Jewish vote than Democrats in middle and working class districts, but the Socialist vote (24%) was higher than the Democratic vote in working class (likely Russian Jewish) districts in 1920. By 1924, the LaFollette vote (43%) was essentially tied with the Republican vote in working class districts, and at 27% it was nearly double the 15% Democratic vote in lower-middle districts. Furthermore, voting turnout was low: just over 40% in upper-middle (likely German Jewish) districts, and only about 25% in working class precincts. This low turnout and growing Socialist vote emphasize how Jews were not entrenched in either major party.

Thus, the data, while only approximations, suggest that Jews were very divided in their voting through 1924. The Jewish vote apparently swung back and forth between the parties, likely due to differences between establishment Jews who were voting Republican and newer immigrants whose voting enthusiasm depended on the candidates.

The Jewish vote shifted decidedly to the Democratic side starting in 1928 with increasing proportions in the following elections, as the Democrats increasingly addressed issues that were important to the new immigrants. Republican 1928 nominee Herbert Hoover had several prominent German Jewish supporters (Wentling and Medoff 2012), but most New York Jews were already supportive of their governor Al Smith, who was the Democratic nominee. The attack on Smith as the candidate of "Rum and Romanism" would have bolstered his support among Jews,

---

[6]Another reason to doubt the Manhattan-based standard figures is that they overstate the Socialist voting of Jews in 1920 while missing their Socialist voting in 1916, 1928, and 1932.

reminding them of his anti-Prohibition stance (with which most agreed) and that he was the candidate of big-city immigrants. The Republican vote nationally rose by 4% points in 1928, but the Jewish vote swung distinctively in the Democratic direction. With the exception of Philadelphia data, Jewish voting estimates based on predominantly Jewish precincts show Smith easily carried the Jewish vote.

The shift of Jews away from the Republicans in the 1928 election accelerated in 1932 after the Great Depression started under Hoover. Intriguingly, Norpoth's (2019) analysis of a Houser Poll finds that ending prohibition, rather than economics, was the major issue that differentiated 1928 Hoover voters who stayed with Hoover in 1932 from those who switched to Franklin Roosevelt. Prohibition repeal would have resonated with Jewish voters. The Jewish vote went solidly for Roosevelt, though the Philadelphia vote appears to have been close. With the country in a serious depression, the Socialist vote by Jews also increased.

The composite estimates in Table 2.2 show the Republicans won more of the Jewish vote in 1920–1932 than the standard figures show, but they agree that Jews were voting predominantly Democratic by 1928. With the Democrats calling for the end of Prohibition and then with Roosevelt's vigorous moves to stem the Depression, the self-interest of the Russian Jews was soon to put them firmly on the Democratic side.

2.4.3   The 1936–1968 Elections: Mobilized Democrats

The Great Depression caused a major shift in the focus of national politics, with the federal government for the first time being considered accountable for the state of the economy.

2.4.3.1   From 1936 to 1948

Jewish voting estimates for this period are based on national face-to-face polling that began by the 1936 election, though religion was not a standard question in the early polls and few polls were taken around presidential elections. The "standard figures" columns in Table 2.3 give Isaacs' (1974, p. 281, n. 1) estimates, which he indicated are "those commonly accepted by Jewish organizations," and presumably are based on Gallup (AIPO) Polls. Gallup averages from other sources are also shown in the table. The right-most columns give Weisberg's (2012) values, averaging surveys taken within a few months of the election.[7] Note that the pre-1950s Gallup Polls used quota sampling, in which interviewers could select whom to interview so long as their respondents included the right proportion of men, women, older people, etc.; that sampling technique was largely abandoned as it was one

---

[7]Weisberg's 1936–1944 estimates use weights derived by Berinsky and Schickler (2011) to correct for Gallup's quota sampling.

Table 2.3 Estimates of the presidential vote of Jews, 1936–1968

	Standard estimate[a]			Gallup average[b]			Composite estimate[c]			
Year	Democrat (%)	Republican (%)	Other (%)	Dem. (%)	Rep. (%)	Other (%)	Dem. (%)	Rep. (%)	Other (%)	Basis
1936	**FDRoosevelt** 85	Landon 15		85	15		87	13		2 polls
1940	**FDRoosevelt** 90	Willkie 10		84	16		91	9		2 polls
1944	**FDRoosevelt** 90	Dewey 10		91	9		91	9		5 polls
1948	**Truman** 75	Dewey 10	15 H.Wallace	54	28	18	54	24	22	3 polls
1952	Stevenson 64	**Eisenhower** 36		72	28		75	23	2	6 polls
1956	Stevenson 60	**Eisenhower** 40		71	29		71	29		7 polls
1960	**Kennedy** 82	Nixon 18		85	15		86	14		4 polls
1964	**Johnson** 90	Goldwater 10					94	6		4 polls
1968	Humphrey 81	**Nixon** 17	2 Geo.Wallace	88	10	2	88	10	2	4 polls

Note: Winners are bolded. Other column lists candidate with more than 1 % of the vote who was most popular with Jews
[a]Source: Isaacs (1974)
[b]Source: Ladd and Hadley (1975) for 1936–1960, Ladd and Lipset (1973, p. 72) for 1968
[c]Source: Updated from Weisberg (2012)

reason why the polls erroneously predicted that Thomas Dewey would win the 1948 election.

Polls show that Jews were voting strongly Democratic when Roosevelt ran for reelection in the 1936–1944 elections, though this conclusion is based on limited data since few polls asking about voting were conducted near those elections. Gamm's (1989, p. 60) analysis of Jewish voting districts in Boston provides important perspective on how the Jewish vote had changed. He found upper-middle class (German) Jewish districts still voting slightly on the Republican side in 1928, but not in 1932 or 1936; the lower-middle class districts were narrowly Democratic in 1928 and more solidly Democratic thereafter. Working class (Russian) districts voted strongly Democratic in each of these years, with more than 90% of the vote in working class districts in 1936 being Democratic.

Gamm's other important finding involves Jews' election turnout. Lower-middle class turnout increased from the low 40% range in 1928 and 1932 to just over 50% in 1936 and 60% in 1940, and working class precincts turnout went from 30% in 1928 and 1932 to 44% in 1936 and then 53% in 1940. Thus, not only was Jews' Democratic vote increasing, but their impact was accelerating due to higher turnout levels. The realignment of the Jewish vote was fueled by mobilization of previous nonvoters into the electorate as the Depression, Prohibition repeal, and Roosevelt's alignment with anti-German forces in the prelude to World War II gave immigrants important reasons to naturalize and to vote.

This mobilization was an important part of Jews' realignment into the Democratic Party. Analyses of urban voting by Andersen (1979) and by Petrocik (1981) demonstrate how the New Deal Realignment can largely be accounted for by mobilization of previous non-voters, rather than conversion of long-time Republican supporters into Democratic voters. While neither researcher focused on Jews, their insights apply equally for Jews. German Jewish merchants who had been voting Republican likely kept doing so because of concern that New Deal reforms would threaten their economic status. Meanwhile, many Russian Jews who had not been voting consistently for either party, if indeed they had voted at all, became loyal Democrats when they benefited from the New Deal.

When Harry Truman ran against Republican Thomas Dewey in 1948, former vice-president Henry Wallace ran as a Progressive Party candidate. Wallace claimed that Truman's support for Israel was insufficient, even though Truman had given immediate recognition to Israel's proclamation of statehood. In particular, Wallace criticized Truman for preventing US citizens of military age from going to Israel and for imposing an arms embargo that mainly hurt Israel since the Palestinians could get arms elsewhere (Medoff 2012).

Wallace's candidacy pulled nearly a quarter of Jewish votes away from the Democrats in 1948, though that could have been due to his leftist stands as much as to his stance on Israel. Surveys also show a higher Republican vote by Jews, which fits with pollster Sam Lubell's (1951, pp. 207–213) interviews indicating realignment in their vote after the decade when Jews had an "emotional attachment" to Franklin Roosevelt due to his opposition to Nazi Germany. Still, the estimates suggest that a slight majority of American Jews voted for Truman.

2.4.3.2   From 1952 to 1968

As Jews moved to the suburbs and had more contact with non-Jews in the 1950s, the Jewish vote was widely expected to become more like the national vote. Both 1952 candidates had the potential to attract Jewish votes. Dwight Eisenhower's role as commander of the Allied Forces in Europe that defeated the Nazis and liberated the concentration camps would have appealed to Jews, but many were drawn to Adlai Stevenson's liberal intellectual image. Fuchs' Boston survey (1955, pp. 93–94, 98) confirmed that Eisenhower did best among Jews living in suburban areas and who had the most contact with non-Jewish primary groups. However, revised figures for 1952 show that just a quarter of Jews nationally voted for Eisenhower.[8] The only change from 1948 was a greater Democratic vote due to Wallace's Progressives returning to the Democratic fold.[9] The 1956 election was a repeat Eisenhower-Stevenson contest. Republican voting by Jews increased slightly, but surveys show that most still considered themselves Democrats.

In contrast to 1950s elections, both 1960 candidates raised concerns among Jews. There was resentment against Richard Nixon for his 1950 Senate campaign in which he accused his opponent, Helen Gahagan Douglas, of communist sympathies and questioned her Jewish husband's loyalty. At the same time, there was lingering antipathy against John Kennedy's father, Joseph Kennedy, who was considered anti-semitic and pro-Nazi Germany when he was American ambassador to Great Britain in 1938–1940. Jewish support for Kennedy was also expected to be lukewarm due to his Catholicism, though his strong statement in favor of separation of church and state eased those concerns. National surveys found a solid increase in Democratic vote among Jews in 1960.

The Democratic vote by Jews returned to the 90% level of the Roosevelt 1940s elections when Lyndon Johnson defeated Barry Goldwater in 1964. However, the Jewish vote was seen as potentially up for grabs in the turbulent 1968 campaign. Democrat Hubert Humphrey had helped overcome Minneapolis' rampant antisemitism when he was that city's mayor, but many young Jews blamed Lyndon Johnson's Democrats for the Vietnam War. Jews' relations with blacks had become more distant after the urban riots of the 1960s (Himmelfarb 1969), causing some Jews to prefer the Republican Party's stronger stand on law and order. Still, Jewish relations with Nixon had always been frosty. Bringing in a full set of polls shows that Nixon's showing among Jews was weak in 1968, with Humphrey receiving the great bulk of their vote.

The 1936–1968 period was when the Jewish vote became distinctively Democratic. Jews remained loyal Democrats through the 1950s and 1960s as other groups abandoned the New Deal coalition. Jews' Republican vote increased in the 1948–1956 elections, but it fell in the 1960s. The composite survey estimates in Table 2.3 show a lower Republican vote by Jews for the 1952–1968 elections than

---

[8] Medoff's examination of precinct-based analysis for the 1950s also estimates the Eisenhower vote at only about 25% (Wentling and Medoff 2012, p. 163 and n. 410).

[9] The margins of error for the Jewish vote after pollsters switched to probability-based sampling are probably in the range of 5%–7%.

usually claimed. Expectations in the 1950s that the Jewish vote might realign proved to be illusory. Instead, being Democratic was becoming part of the Jewish social identity of most Jews.

2.4.4   The 1972–2016 Elections: Stability Amidst Disruption

The American political party system experienced several changes starting in the early 1970s. The power of party bosses drastically diminished, the party system "dealigned" with an increase in the number of political Independents, and "candidate-centered" politics replaced "party-centered politics." By the end of the century, the political parties became increasingly polarized ideologically, with the Republican Party becoming more conservative and the Democrats more consistently liberal.

Meanwhile, the generations of Jews who came of voting age during the 1960s and 1970s were less concerned with their economic status and security than earlier generations had been. Growing up under post-war economic prosperity, these new generations adopted post-materialist values and were more concerned about their individual rights. Those values kept most of them in the Democratic Party, albeit for different reasons than the economic reasons that brought their parents and grandparents into that party. Meanwhile, "neoconservative" Jews left the Democratic Party in the 1970s because they rejected the politics of the New Left, opposed affirmative action and the welfare state, and were adamantly anti-Communist as well as strong supporters of Israel. However, other Jews found they could not join the Republican Party when it adopted the Christian Right's conservative positions on morality issues like abortion and homosexuality.

2.4.4.1   From 1972 to 1988

Starting in 1972, several media organizations began conducting exit polls on Election Day. When asking people their religion, exit polls likely miss people of Jewish heritage who consider themselves culturally or ethnically Jewish but who do not practice the Jewish religion. The standard voting figures for these elections in Table 2.4 are based on the exit polls published by the *New York Times*. The Solomon Report (Mellman et al. 2012) also included state exit polls along with national ones, while Weisberg (2012) averaged several national exit polls.

The 1972–1988 period became one of somewhat diminished Democratic voting by Jews. That began with Richard Nixon's reelection against liberal Senator George McGovern. Most Jews still voted Democratic, but they more were more supportive of Nixon in 1972 than in 1960 or 1968. Fisher's (1976) analysis of survey data through 1972 found that there was no diminution of Jews' liberalism, nor did he find any lessening of Jewish support civil rights even though there were disputes between the Jewish and black communities in New York City. However, Himmelfarb (1970,

Table 2.4 Estimates of the presidential vote of Jews, 1972–2016

Year	Standard estimate[a] Democrat (%)	Republican (%)	Other (%)	Solomon report[b] Dem. (%)	Rep. (%)	Other (%)	Composite estimate[c] Dem. (%)	Rep. (%)	Other (%)	Basis
1972	64 McGovern	34 **Nixon**		66	32		66	33		1 exit
1976	64 **Carter**	34 Ford		64	33		68	31		1 exit
1980	45 Carter	39 **Reagan**	15 Anderson	44	37	19	44	36	19	2 exits
1984	67 Mondale	31 **Reagan**		68	31		66	32	1	4 exits
1988	64 Dukakis	35 **GHWBush**		67	32		69	30	1	5 exits
1992	80 **WmClinton**	11 GHWBush	9 Perot	77	15	8	74	16	10	2 exits
1996	78 **WmClinton**	16 Dole	3 Perot	79	15	6	78	16	6	2 exits
2000	79 Gore	19 **GWBush**	1 Nader	79	17	4	78	21	1	2 exits
2004	74 Kerry	25 **GWBush**		77	21		76	24		2 exits
2008	78 **Obama**	21 McCain	Nader	74	23		78	21	1	1 exit
2012	69 **Obama**	30 Romney	2 Johnson				68	32		1 exit/1 poll
2016	71 HClinton	24 **Trump**	5 Johnson				70	25	5	1 exit/1 poll

Note: Electoral College winners are bolded. Other column lists candidate with more than 1% of the vote who was most popular with Jews

[a]Source: Forman (2001) through 2000; later are from the *New York Times*

[b]Source: Mellman et al. (2012)

[c]Source: Updated from Weisberg (2012)

1973) spotted an unusual class divide forming, with upper class Jews voting more Democratic than working class Jews.

Gerald Ford, as president after Nixon's resignation, allowed planned fighter jet sales to Israel to go ahead only after securing an agreement for withdrawing of Israeli troops from the Suez Canal. The Democratic vote nationally increased by more than 10% points from 1972 to 1976 when Jimmy Carter defeated Ford, but the Jewish vote was essentially unchanged.

Carter appointed more Jews to his cabinet than any previous president. He successfully negotiated a peace treaty between Israel and Egypt, but the American Jewish community viewed him as hostile to Israel when he did not allow the US ambassador to veto a UN Security Council resolution that deplored Israel's West Bank settlements (Lazarowitz 2010). Carter's reelection campaign was weakened by economic hyperinflation and by the Iranian hostage crisis.

More Jews voted for Carter in the 1980 election than for Ronald Reagan, but the Democratic vote percentage among Jews fell below 50%. Independent candidate John Anderson won nearly a fifth of the Jewish vote, reflecting considerable dissatisfaction with Carter's presidency as well as unease with Reagan's conservative politics. Reagan's portion of the Jewish vote in 1980 was the highest Republican vote in decades, giving Republicans thoughts of moving the Jewish vote to their side. Instead, that became the high point for the Republican vote among Jews. Several voting divisions were apparent among Jews in 1980. Himmelfarb (1981) found that higher-income Jews were voting more Republican. He also reported Jewish women were more likely to vote for Carter than Jewish men, an early indication of what became known as the gender gap.

Himmelfarb cited the Borough Park area of Brooklyn as an Orthodox area that voted for Reagan in 1980. In the first half of the twentieth century, the Orthodox were largely eastern European Jews who practiced traditional Judaism. There is no reason to believe their voting had differed from that of other Jews. However, the growth of several Hasidic sects that moved to the US in the 1940s changed the composition of American Orthodoxy. Over the next few elections, the traditional values of Orthodox Jews led many to shift to the Republican side as the Democratic Party adopted liberal positions on morality issues.

Reagan's policies as president were more pro-Israel than Carter's, though AIPAC vigorously fought against his plans to sell AWACS surveillance planes to Saudi Arabia. Jews were also uncomfortable with how close Reagan was to the Christian Right. While 1984 Democratic candidate Walter Mondale had a strong pro-Israel voting record in the Senate, the Jewish rift with the Democratic Party widened when Jesse Jackson made derogatory references to Jews as "Hymies" and New York City as "Hymietown" when he was running for the party's nomination.

Jews reverted to their traditional support of Democratic presidential candidates in 1984 with Reagan's vote share falling a few percentage points. The National Jewish Coalition for Reagan-Bush commissioned its own exit poll in seven Jewish precincts, and it found Reagan winning 41% of the Jewish vote. However, Reagan's pollsters sharply criticized that poll because it was not a probability sample (Weisberg 2012), explaining that the politics of Jews who live in areas of Jewish concentration may differ from that of other Jews. The higher Republican vote that poll obtained suggests that it achieved a good sample of ultra-Orthodox areas that were turning Republican without sufficiently sampling Jews living in less Orthodox areas.

In 1988, the Jewish vote moved a few more percentage points back in the Democratic direction, as did the overall national vote. Two important demographic groups were changing their party loyalties during this period in ways that affected Jews. Blacks had become solidly Democratic, but their demands made some Jews reconsider their loyalty to the Democratic Party. Meanwhile, evangelical Protestants became estranged from the Democratic Party on moral issues; and most moved to the Republican Party, which made many Jews uncomfortable with that party. Polls in 1988 showed that the proportion of Jews who would not vote Democratic if African American activist Rev. Jesse Jackson were on that party's ticket was more than equaled by the proportion who would not vote Republican if fundamentalist Rev. Pat Robertson were on that party's ticket (Cohen 1989, pp. 9–12; Wald and Sigelman 1997, p. 153).

Most Jews still voted Democratic during the 1972–1988 period, but the Republican vote by Jews in those presidential elections was higher than in any election since the Depression. That could have been a turning point toward political realignment of Jews, but instead was a prelude to returning to higher Democratic voting.

2.4.4.2   From 1992 to 2016

Jews increased their Democratic presidential voting again starting in 1992. President George H.W. Bush sent Patriot anti-missile batteries to Israel when Iraq fired Scud missiles at them during the multi-national military attack on Iraq after it seized Kuwait. However, Bush refused to authorize requested loan guarantees for Israel unless it stopped expanding its West Bank settlements, and he made a public statement against AIPAC's lobbying on the issue. Secretary of State James Baker's foreign policy was perceived as tough on Israel, though he denied the many claims that he used an obscenity in stating it was unnecessary to pay attention to Jews because they had not voted for Bush.

Bush ran for reelection in 1992 against Bill Clinton, with billionaire H. Ross Perot mounting a strong independent candidacy. The Republican Convention that year became known for Pat Buchanan's "culture war speech," in which he denounced Bill and Hillary Clinton for promoting radical feminism, abortion on demand, homosexual rights, and discrimination against religious schools. The Democratic vote nationally fell, but the Jewish vote for the Democrats increased to 74%. Only 16% of Jews voted for Bush, with 10% voting for Perot. As Lipset and Raab (1995, p. 166) maintained, "Jewish support for the GOP was undermined by severely critical anti-Israeli remarks made by President Bush and Secretary of State Baker and by the visible presence of the religious right at the Republican convention."

Clinton appointed three Jews to his first-term cabinet and nominated two for the Supreme Court. He won reelection in 1996 with 78% of the Jewish vote, their highest Democratic vote since the 1960s, with the Republican vote by Jews staying at just 16%.

George W. Bush ran against Vice President Al Gore in 2000. Gore's choice of Senator Joe Lieberman as his vice-presidential running mate led to a strong Democratic vote by Jews, with Orthodox Jews reportedly joining in (see Table 2.4 and the more detailed presentation of post-2000 exit polls in Table 2.5). Gore won

Table 2.5   National polls of the Jewish vote, 2000–2018

Year	Election polls[a]		Number of Jews	Solomon Report (including state polls)	Average of Nov.-Dec. national polls by non-advocacy groups
2000	Voter News Service exit poll	79–19–1Nader	306	79–17	78D–21R–1Nader
	Los Angeles Times exit poll	77–22–1Nader			
	American Jewish Committee (Sept.)	75–11–3Nader	1010		
2004	National Election Pool exit poll	74–25	267	77–21	76R–24R
	Los Angeles Times exit poll	78–22			
	National Jewish Democratic Council (July)	75–22–3Other	817		
	American Jewish Committee (Aug.)	69–24	1000		
2008	National Election Pool exit poll	78–21	102	74–23	78D–21R
	American Jewish Committee (Sept.)	57–30	914		
2012	National Election Pool exit poll	69–30			68D–32R
	Cooperative Congressional Election Study	66–33	868		
	J Street	70–30	800		
	Workmen's Circle	68–32	2067		
	Republican Jewish Coalition	68–32[b]	1000		
	Workmen's Circle (May)	59–21	1000		
	American Jewish Committee (Sept.)	65–24	1040		
2016	Edison Research exit poll	71–24–5Other			70D–25R–5Other
	Cooperative Congressional Election Study	68–28–4Other	1179		
	J Street	70–25–5Other	731		
	American Jewish Committee (Oct.)	61–19–9Other	1002		

(continued)

Table 2.5 (continued)

Year	Election polls[a]		Number of Jews	Solomon Report (including state polls)	Average of Nov.-Dec. national polls by non-advocacy groups
2018	Edison Research exit poll (CNN)	79–17			74D–22R
	Cooperative Congressional Election Study	71–22	1068		
	AP: VoteCast	71–28			
	J Street	76–19	983		
	Mellman Group (JEI) pre-election (Oct.)	74–26	800		

Note: Values show the percentage Democrat (D), the percentage Republican (R), and, if stated, the percentage for "other" candidates

[a]Some exit polls are reported slightly differently by different sources, perhaps due to recalculation after early publication using incomplete polls

[b]The major-party split among actual voters in the RJC poll was 65–34

the popular vote, but Bush became president when he won the Electoral College vote. The Jewish vote may have been decisive, albeit unintentionally. Florida's Palm Beach County used a confusing "butterfly ballot" in that election. Statistical analysis found that the vote for third-party candidate Pat Buchanan was higher in Palm Beach County precincts with a high Gore vote than in those with a high Bush vote, which was the opposite pattern of other counties, supporting the claim that many Buchanan votes in Palm Beach were unintended (Brady et al. 2001). There is a sizable elderly Jewish population in that county (see Appendix in Chap. 5), and it would appear that many accidentally voted for Buchanan, who has made several remarks that are considered antisemitic. The Florida vote was so close that there was a recount; hence, those unintended votes may have given Bush the presidency (Hasen 2012), though the same would hold for other groups whose members were confused by the poor ballot design.

Bush's policies were strongly pro-Israel, though he spoke in June 2002 in favor of an independent Palestinian state. Surveys show that the Jewish vote remained solidly Democratic in 2004, though a few percentage points lower than in 2000.

The Jewish vote stayed strongly Democratic at 78% in 2008 when Barack Obama defeated John McCain. While there might have been questions about Jews' willingness to support an African-American candidate, the Republican administration's responsibility for and handling of the nation's fiscal crisis dominated over such considerations.

Thus, in the 1992–2008 period, Democratic presidential candidates averaged just over three-quarters of the Jewish vote. Whereas the Republicans had captured about 30% from 1972 through 1988, they pulled in only 16–24% from 1992 to 2008. This drop in the Republican vote among Jews coincided with the increased identification of the Republican Party with the Christian Right, as highlighted by Buchanan's 1992 culture war speech. That is consistent with the finding that Jews who are negative toward the Christian Right are significantly less Republican in partisanship than other Jews, even with other variables controlled (Uslaner and Lichbach 2009; Weisberg 2019, pp. 88–89).

In his first term, Obama took a strong stand against expansion of Israeli settlements in the West Bank, though he also pushed Congress to approve American funding an Iron Dome defense system for Israel that could shoot down incoming missiles. Obama signed enhanced restrictions against Iran for its nuclear program into law in 2010, but he resisted Israeli Prime Minister Bibi Netanyahu's call to set a "clear red line" on that nuclear program with military action to be taken if Iran crossed that line.

In campaigning against Obama's reelection in 2012, Mitt Romney attacked Obama for the slow economic recovery and also for being insufficiently supportive of Israel. Obama won reelection, though with a lower vote percentage than at the height of the 2008 fiscal crisis (Weisberg 2015). The Democratic presidential vote among Jews fell to 68%. Uslaner (2015) and Weisberg (2014) describe the context of the fight for the 2012 Jewish vote in further detail.

The 2016 election and its aftermath will be discussed later in this chapter. Hillary Clinton received about the same vote among Jews in 2016 as Obama won in 2012; Donald Trump's vote dropped a few percentage points from Romney's, with about a 5% vote for third-party candidates. The Democratic vote among Jews was back down in 2012 and 2016 to its level in the 1970s and 1980s, while the 2016 Republican vote fell back to its 1992–2008 level.

2.4.5 Trends Over Time

More American Jews voted for Democratic than Republican presidential candidates from 1928 through 2016, but there has been more variation in the Jewish vote than is usually recognized. Figure 2.2 charts the Democratic vote for president by Jews in these elections along with the overall vote result. The Jewish vote during this period was more Democratic than the national presidential vote, with a gap usually between 15% and 35% points depending on the year.

Jews' voting shifted in the Democratic direction in the 1928 and 1932 elections, but it did not become solidly Democratic until 1936. After staying in the 90% range in 1940 and 1944, Jews' support for the Democrats waned slightly from 1948 through 1956. Then, the Jewish vote became distinctively Democratic in the 1960s. The Republican voting of Jews increased in the 1970s and 1980s. It looked in 1980 like Jews were tempted to realign politically, but instead their vote became more Democratic again in the 1990s and early 2000s.

The Republican presidential vote by Jews tracks the national Republican vote over the years fairly closely, with a 0.70 correlation, whereas a 1.0 correlation would mean they move totally together. (The two trend lines in Fig. 2.2 are correlated at just 0.55, because of the large deviations involving third-party voting by Democratic Jews in 1948 and 1980.)

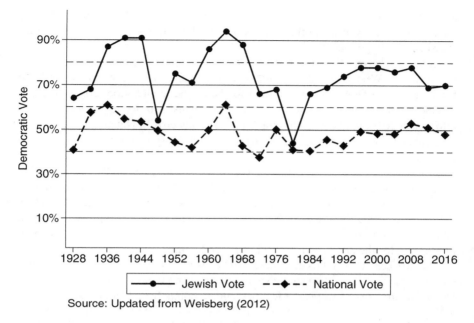

Source: Updated from Weisberg (2012)

Fig. 2.2 Democratic vote by Jews and nationally, 1928–2016

2.5 Factors Affecting Jews' Voting

This section examines three important factors relating to Jews' voting: ideology, party identification, and relations with Israel.

2.5.1 Ideology

Surveys confirm the liberal self-identification of most Jews. The 2013 Pew Research Center Survey of US Jews found that 49% of Jews said they were politically liberal versus 19% politically conservative. That is in sharp contrast to the 21% liberal and 38% conservative for the public at large in Pew's 2013 polls.

However, surveys consistently find that Jewish liberalism is less complete than it is usually portrayed. Cohen and Liebman's (1997) analysis of General Social Survey (GSS) data found that Jews' liberalism was substantially reduced when comparing them with non-Jews who had similar socio-demographic characteristics. Tom Smith's (2005, p. 56) analysis of GSS data likewise concluded that seeing liberalism "as the defining difference [between Jews and non-Jews] is wrong."

Researchers have instead found that Jews' liberalism is "selective" (Liebman and Cohen 1999, p. 200). Thus, Abrams and Cohen (2016, p. 122) described Jews being more liberal on social issues than on regulation of business, and even less so as regards economic regulation. Weisberg (2019) showed Jews' attitudes to be distinctively liberal on school prayer, morality issues, and science issues, but not on economic matters, welfare, affirmative action, or immigration. More specifically, Jews are not much more liberal than comparable non-Jews with similar ideological positions on such issues as whether the government should reduce income inequality and whether the government should help solve more problems. No differences exist on affirmative action for women, while differences are small on affirmative action for blacks. By contrast, there are double-digit percentage differences between comparable Jews and non-Jews on gay issues, marijuana legalization, and abortion as well as on accepting the theory of evolution.

The implication of these studies is that many Jews are not particularly liberal on economic issues even though they are liberal on moral issues. Based on that finding, Weisberg (2019, Chap. 11) applied a four-category classification of Jews' political ideology that differentiates between attitudes on economic and social issues:

1. **Progressives**, who are liberal on both social and economic issues, favoring governmental regulation of the economy but opposing laws limiting individual rights on such matters as abortion and gay marriage,
2. **Libertarians**, who oppose government regulations in both economic and moral realms,
3. **Communitarians**, who favor government regulation in both economic and moral arenas, and
4. **Traditionalists**, who are conservative on both moral and economic issues, favoring government enforcement of moral norms but favoring laissez-faire economics with minimal government economic regulations.

Table 2.6 presents analysis of the General Social Survey (GSS) data from 1972 through 2016. The economic question is whether the government should do more or less to reduce income differences with those choosing the middle option being classified as "ambiguous." The morality issue question is whether the person approves

Table 2.6 Comparison of the ideological profile of Jews and non-Jews, GSS 1972–2016

	Jews		Non-Jews	
	% in this category	% of partisans who are Democrats[a]	% in this category	% of partisans who are Democrats[a]
Progressive	34	87	27	71
Libertarian	32	62	20	37
Communitarian	6	72[b]	20	67
Traditionalist	5	50[b]	13	37
Ambiguous[c]	22	57	20	46
Total	100		100	
Sample size	316			

Source: Analysis of 1972–2016 General Social Survey
[a]Democrats include leaners to the Democratic Party
[b]Based on 20 or fewer people
[c]This category consists of those who were neutral on the economic question

of suicide if a person has an incurable disease. Since most Jews are liberal on morality issues, most are Progressives or Libertarians rather than Traditionalists or Communitarians.

As to be expected, Table 2.6 finds that Progressives who are partisans are predominantly Democrats. However, Libertarians are divided politically, with Jewish Libertarians favoring Democrats over Republicans by a 5-to-3 ratio and non-Jewish Libertarians splitting 5-to-3 in the Republican direction.

2.5.2 Partisanship

Most political scientists regard people's party identification as an important long-term factor affecting their votes. Yet, party identification is not identical to voting since partisans sometimes defect to the other party's nominee, as when many Democrats voted against George McGovern in 1972. The polarization of American politics has decreased such defections, though many Republicans cast Democratic votes in the 2008 election held during the fiscal crisis, and there were defections in both directions in the 2016 Clinton-Trump contest.

When asked their party identification, many Americans say they are Independents rather than Democrats or Republicans. However, when asked a follow-up question as to whether they are closer to the Democratic or Republican party, most Independents answer that they lean to one party or the other. Studies show that these leaners vote for that party's presidential candidate at least as much as people who consider themselves weak Democrats or weak Republicans. As a result, it is common to combine these leaners with partisans into a measure of "leaned partisanship."

2.5.2.1 Jews' Party Identification

Since the measurement of party identification began in the 1950s, surveys have consistently found that Jews predominantly identify as Democratic. The 2013 Pew Jewish study found that 70% of Jews who were US citizens were Democrats (or Democratic-leaning Independents) while only 22% were Republicans (or Republican-leaning Independents). These figures fluctuate in surveys, due as much to sampling issues as to real changes. For example, 68% of registered Jewish voters in Pew's 2017 polling (Pew Research Center 2018) identified as Democrats versus 22% Republicans, which is within sampling error of the 2013 Pew results.

Furthermore, studies consistently find that Jews are significantly more Democratic than non-Jews with similar socio-demographic characteristics (Campbell et al. 1960; Manza and Brooks 1997; Stanley and Niemi 2006; Wald 2015; Weisberg

2019). Indeed, Wald's (2019, Chap. 2) calculations show they are more Democratic than the non-Jew who is their closest match on demographics and economic status.

While this discussion has focused on national trends, it is important to recognize that there is also subnational variation. The Jewish communities in different cities differ from one another in their socio-economic, age, and denominational compositions, which leads to differences in their partisanship and voting. As shown in tables in Chap. 5, the percentage of Jews registered to vote is upwards of 90% in many cities, with New York being an important exception. The percentage of Republican identification is below 20% in most of the surveyed cities; Houston at 31% and St. Petersburg at 25% are exceptions, with those two being the only cities in which large proportions of non-Orthodox are Republican. Sheskin (2013, 2016) has summarized community surveys that illustrate these differences; see also the most recent studies under the "US Local" tab at www.JewishDataBank.org.

2.5.2.2   Changes over Time

Table 2.7 shows the party identification of Jews since 2000 according to a wide variety of polls of Jews. The first three columns display the answers to the basic question of whether people consider themselves Democrats, Republicans, or Independents. The two columns on the right show "leaned partisanship," which combines Independents who lean toward a party with that party's partisans. The results of these different polls are remarkably similar, especially since these polls did not use identical party identification question wording, differed in who they classified as Jews, and were administered through different survey modes. Jews were predominantly Democratic across this period, with about two-thirds of Jews being Democratic or leaning in that direction versus only about one-quarter of Jews being on the Republican side.[10] Additionally, there is remarkably little trend in these data. When new poll results are published, it is tempting to interpret each slight change from previous polls, but this analysis emphasizes their considerable constancy.

Pew's leaned partisan data shows that the Democratic lead among Jews increased near the end of Clinton's presidency (1993–2000) and stayed high through the George W. Bush presidency (2001–2008) but fell during the Obama presidency (2009–2016). The Democratic lead over the Republicans among Jews dropped from an average of 48% during the Bush years to 40% over the Obama years (see Table 2.8). Leaned partisanship has also varied over the years among the public as a whole, with the Democrats having opened up a small lead over the Republicans since 1994. As a result, the Democratic lead among Jews, while still substantial, was actually a few points less distinctive by 2016 than in 1994.

---

[10] Averaging Pew Research Center poll results on yearly leaned partisanship totals from 1994 through 2017 obtains virtually the same result.

Table 2.7 Polls of Jews' party identification, in percentages

Year	Poll	Method[a]	Party identification Dem.	Indep/Other	Rep.	Leaned party ID Dem.	Rep.
2000	AJC	M	59	32	9		
2000–2001	NJPS	P	59	27	14		
2001	AJIS	P	42	39	19		
2002	AJC	M	48	34	18		
2003	AJC	M	51	33	16		
2004	AJC	M	54	30	16		
2004	NJDC		60	26	14	74	19
2005	AJC	M	54	30	16		
2006	AJC	M	54	31	15		
2007	AJC	M	58	27	15		
2007	NSAJ	P	62	24	14		
2007	RLS	P				66	24
2008	AJC		56	27	17		
2009	AJC		53	31	16		
2010	AJC		50	35	15		
2011	AJC		45	39	16		
2012	AJC-spring	IP	52	29	19		
2012	AJC-fall		55	29	16		
2012	PRRI	IP	49	38	13		
2012	J Street	I-1	56	26	18	67	26
2012	RJC	P-1	56	25	19		
2012	WC		59	21	20		
2013	AJC	IP	52	33	15		
2013	Pew	P	55	32	13	70	22
2014	J Street	I-1	59	26	15	68	21
2015	Iran-Cohen		55	33	12		
2015	Iran-J Street		53	29	18	64	25
2015	AJC	IP	49	32	19		
2016	AJC	P	51	31	18		
2016	J Street	I-1	59	22	19	68	25
2016	PRRI	P	47	33	20		
2016	CCES	I	54	26	20	63	26
2016	CCAP		53	27	20	62	28
2017	AJC		57	28	15		
2018	AJC	P	51	33	16		
2018	J Street		58	27	15	71	21
2018	JEI					68	25
2018	AJC	P	51	33	16		
2018	CCES	I	53	26	21	62	28
2019	JEI					65	25

(continued)

Table 2.7 (continued)

Year	Poll	Method[a]	Party identification			Leaned party ID	
			Dem.	Indep/Other	Rep.	Dem.	Rep.
2019	AJC		49	32	18		

AJC American Jewish Committee, *AJIS* American Jewish Identity Study, *CCAP* Cooperative Campaign Analysis Project, *CCES* Cooperative Congressional Election Survey, *JEI* Jewish Electoral Institute, *NJDC* National Jewish Democratic Coalition, *NJPS* National Jewish Population Survey, *NSAJ* National Survey of American Jews, *PRRI* Public Religion Research Institute, *RJC* Republican Jewish Coalition, *RLS* Religious Landscape Study (Pew Research Center), *WC* Workmen's Circle, *P* phone, *I* internet, *M* mail, *IP* internet panel, *1* one–day poll

2.5.2.3 Partisanship and Ideology

Table 2.9 provides useful evidence as to the nature of the relationship between Jews' party identification and their political ideology. The left-hand side of the table shows that very few Jewish Democrats are politically conservative and equally few Jewish Republicans are liberals. Thus, in the current period of partisan polarization, Jews who are partisans have not been adopting the ideological positions associated with the opposite party.

In contrast, the right-hand side of the table demonstrates that nearly 40% of Jewish political conservatives are not Republicans. A much lower proportion of Jewish political conservatives are Republicans than the proportion of Jewish liberals who are Democrats, a result that holds for a wide variety of surveys (Weisberg 2011). Thus, ideology does not lead to partisanship for Jews today as much as partisanship seems to rule out having the ideology associated with the opposite party. This suggests that partisanship leads to ideology for Jews today. However, this does not rule out the possibility that the ideology predominated over partisanship in earlier periods; so, the leftward views of many Jews in the early 1930s Depression days may have led them to the Democratic Party.

2.5.2.4 Exceptions

There are some important exceptions to the Democratic predominance among Jews. Jews from the Former Soviet Union (FSU) and other ex-Communist nations have been less liberal and Democratic (Wald 2019; Weisberg 2019). Similarly, three-fifths of the respondents in FSU households in the large 2018 Detroit Jewish Population Study (Sheskin 2018) who identified with a major party were Republicans, compared to just 22% of other Jews. Similarly, American Jews from Israel in the 2013 Pew survey were also less liberal and Democratic (Weisberg 2019, Chap. 3). Another exception involves income: while upper-income Jews are famously less Republican than upper-income non-Jews, survey analysis finds Jews with higher incomes are somewhat more Republican than Jews with lower incomes (Weisberg 2019, pp. 185, 187, 220, 224).

Table 2.8 Polling averages for partisanship by presidential administration, Pew data

| Presidency | Years | Jews | | | Total public | | |
		Democratic (%)	Republican (%)	Difference[a] (%)	Democratic (%)	Republican (%)	Difference (%)
Wm. Clinton	1994–2000	69	25	45	47	44	3
G.W. Bush	2001–2008	70	23	48	48	42	6
Obama	2009–2016	67	27	40	48	43	5

Source: Calculated from Pew Research Center (2018)
[a]Differences may not add up because of rounding

Table 2.9 Jews' partisanship and self-declared ideology compared, 2013 Pew Survey

	Democrat (%)	Independent (%)	Republican (%)		Liberal (%)	Moderate (%)	Conservative (%)
Liberal	66	23	7	Democrat	93	60	30
Moderate	26	52	36	Independent	4	14	9
Conservative	9	25	57	Republican	2	27	61
Total	101	100	100	Total	99	101	100

Source: Analysis of 2013 Pew Research Center Survey of US Jews

The largest exception to Democratic dominance among Jews involves the Orthodox. Survey evidence on this is mixed, likely because the separation of the Haredi from secular society leads them to eschew participation in surveys. The 2013 Pew survey, which phoned designated respondents back repeatedly so they would be interviewed, found that most Orthodox are Republican: both the ultra-Orthodox (58% Republican to 35% Democratic) and the Modern Orthodox (56–38%). The Republican preference of the Orthodox is also evident in the 2018 Detroit study, with 77% of Orthodox partisans being Republican versus a fifth of the non-Orthodox. Precinct analysis (e.g., Fingerhut 2008; Rocklin 2017) confirms that ultra-Orthodox areas strongly vote Republican. (Election Day phone and internet polls often find the Orthodox voting Democratic, probably because of low response rates among very observant Jews.) Overall, the religious difference between the Orthodox and the non-Orthodox yields larger political divisions among Jews than socio-demographic differences such as age, gender, or income (Kotler-Berkowitz 2017).

2.5.2.5 Predictors of Partisanship

Some studies have used regression analysis to disentangle the separate effects of possible predictors of Jews' party identification. Kotler-Berkowitz (2017) finds that denomination is a strong predictor, with the Orthodox and Conservative being less Democratic than the Reform. Those born in the Former Soviet Union are less Democratic, while higher income Jews are more Democratic. As to age, Kotler-Berkowitz shows that Jews under age 30 and age 65 or over are significantly more Democratic than those age 50–64. Men are significantly more Republican, the inter-married and never married significantly more Democratic. Jews in the South are significantly more Republican as compared to those in the Northeast.

Analyzing both a 2004 survey conducted for the National Jewish Democratic Coalition (see also Uslaner and Lichbach 2009) and the 2012 PRRI survey, Weisberg (2019, Chap. 5) found that ideology is a significant predictor of Jews' party identification. Attitudes toward the Christian Right and evangelicals are also significant predictors: The more negative Jews feel toward those groups, the more Democratic they are. Higher income Jews are more Republican. In the 2004 survey, those who were favorable toward civil unions for gays were more Democratic, though in 2012 attitudes toward gay marriage did not have a significant effect when attitudes toward the Christian Right were controlled. This result leaves ambiguous whether morality issues have a significant effect on Jews' partisanship beyond attitudes toward the Christian Right. As Wald (2019, Chap. 9) emphasizes, Jews' views on the Christian Right are related to views on church-state separation. Unfortunately, surveys have not asked questions that distinguish whether attitudes toward church-state separation, rather than attitudes toward the Christian Right, might underlie Jews' partisanship.

Denomination is not significant in Weisberg's (2019, Table 12.4) analysis of party identification in the 2012 PRRI and 2013 Pew surveys when issue questions are included. The significant predictors in both surveys are instead economic questions, moral issues, and attitudes on the Middle East, along with gender. Denomination still has indirect effects on Jews' partisanship since the Orthodox have distinctive attitudes on moral issues.

There is a gender gap in partisanship in the Jewish community. The gender gap in voting in the American general public began in 1980, with women less likely to vote for Ronald Reagan than men. By the mid-1900s, many non-Orthodox Jewish women were pushing for recognizing a greater role for women in Jewish religious services, including having bat mitzvah ceremonies and reading from the Torah. This activism extended into politics as well, with Jewish women playing an important role in the push for an Equal Rights Amendment (ERA) and with prominent Jewish feminists advocating gender equality more generally. Jewish women are significantly more Democratic in their partisanship than Jewish men, even with attitudes on issues controlled (Weisberg 2019, p. 189).

2.5.2.6 Party Realignment

There is discussion every few decades of whether American Jews might realign to the Republican Party; but, in the end, they have reverted back to strong Democratic voting. Voting behavior studies find that party identification, once established, is fairly resistant to change. Young people are typically less attached to a party, with many starting off as Independents; but strength of partisanship tends to increase with age as one votes for the same party repeatedly. Yet, groups sometimes change their partisanship in response to changes by the parties on issues basic to the group's self-interest.

The Republican Party has tried to use support for Israel as a wedge issue to convince Jews to vote Republican. Support for Israel has traditionally been bipartisan, but there has been a recent increase in sympathy for the Palestinians among the Democratic left while the Republican Party has become unconditionally supportive of Israel's stands. Democrats are still committed to Israel's security, but weakening of that commitment could cause some Jewish Democrats to switch parties. Similarly, support for the Boycott, Divestment, and Sanctions (BDS) movement by prominent Democratic politicians would likely cause some Jews to switch to the Republican side. Still, the current large number of Jewish Democrats in Congress (all 9 Jewish Senators and 27 of 29 Jewish Representatives in 2019) helps signal Jewish voters to stay on the Democratic side.

In looking for possible change in the Jewish vote, it is important to recognize which types of Jews are and are not Republicans. First, while the 2013 Pew Jewish survey found that most Orthodox Jews are Republican, it also shows that most Republican Jews are not Orthodox. To the contrary, Republican Jews are split fairly evenly across Jewish denominations. Second, while Jews who take consistent hardline positions on Middle East issues are more Republican than Jews who take consistent positions in the opposite direction, the hardliners are not a majority of Jewish

Republicans. Further, the hardliners are split quite evenly between being Republicans and Democrats (Weisberg 2019, Chap. 12).

Traditionalist Jews who want minimal government economic regulations but favor government restrictions on morality issues are predominantly Republican; they constitute, however, less than 10% of American Jews. And they are considerably outnumbered by Progressive Jews who want minimal government restrictions on moral issues but favor more government intervention in economic matters; predictably, they are predominantly Democratic.

Another large group are Libertarian Jews who want minimal government regulation on both economic and morality matters; they give the Democrats only a slight advantage. They could support either party, depending on the candidates and/or the issues. Libertarians who are hardline on Middle East issues are mainly Republican, and Libertarians who take the opposite positions on Middle East issues are mainly Democrats; however, many Jewish Libertarians are not consistently on either side regarding Middle East issues, and they are not firmly in either partisan camp. They are likely to drift to the Democratic side when a Republican candidate campaigns on Christian Right moral issues and/or is associated with right-wing antisemitism. However, they could move toward the Republican side when a Democratic candidate campaigns on economic justice issues and/or is seen as acceptant of left-wing antisemitism. These Libertarians are not fully committed to either party, so they could change their party depending on how American politics evolves in the future.

While Israel and antisemitism are relevant issues for many Jews, most of non-Orthodox are more concerned with issues that directly affect themselves or their children. Depending on their life circumstances, those issues are typically jobs, climate change, childcare, the safety of their children in a gun culture, health insurance provisions regarding preexisting conditions, and/or keeping their Medicare benefits, all issues on which the Democrats have an advantage.

Israel is probably a more salient issue for the older generation than for young Jews, but older Jews already considered that issue in choosing their party identification. Many in that generation are uncomfortable when some progressive politicians use antisemitic tropes, but many were also upset with President Trump's rhetoric after the Charlottesville, Virginia "Unite the Right" march. Typically, older people have developed stronger party identification as they have voted for the same party for several decades, making it less likely for them to change parties, though they still could change if left-wing antisemitism threatens their security.

2.5.3 Israel as a Voting Issue

Analyses of voting by the general public rarely considers foreign policy matters, but it is important to examine the role of Israel in Jews' voting decisions. The topic is controversial, partly because it raises questions of whether American Jews would be considered disloyal if they voted on the basis of what is best for Israel.

Also, there is disagreement as to whether changes in Jews' voting for incumbent presidents seeking reelection have been due to their handling of relations with Israel. For example, decreases in Democratic voting by Jews in 1948, 1980, and 2012 from their votes in the preceding presidential elections have sometimes been interpreted as due to Jews dissatisfaction with the incumbent president's support for Israel. However, some observers contend that views on Israel are already incorporated into Jews' partisanship, so that views on relations with Israel do not have an added effect. Furthermore, in each election mentioned above, the drop in Democratic support among Jews simply mirrors vote change among the population at large. The vote for Roosevelt's reelection in 1944 was partly a vote against changing leaders in wartime, so a decrease in Democratic voting was natural after the war ended. Carter's vote fell in 1980 among the general public because of the high inflation rate and the Iranian hostage crisis. The Obama vote in 2008 was partly because people were blaming the incumbent Republican Party for the fiscal crisis; so, it was natural for it to drop in 2012, when people were less upset with the previous Republican administration.

Articles by Wald and collaborators (Wald and Martinez 2001; Wald and Williams 2006) have been important in showing how attitudes on Israel affect American Jews' political behavior. However, survey findings always depend on how a question is asked. For example, most Jews answer affirmatively when surveys ask whether Israel is important in their voting decision; but few choose Israel as one of the most important factors in their voting decisions when they are offered a list of a dozen different issues.

Rather than rely on people's explanations of their voting, statistical analysis can be used to examine the correlates of voting with other variables controlled. Attitudes on Israel or on Israeli policies were significantly related to Jews' presidential voting and presidential approval in 2004, 2012, and 2016, even when party identification was statistically controlled (Uslaner and Lichbach 2009; Cohen and Abrams 2012; Uslaner 2015; Weisberg 2019, Table 12.1).

The most important article on this topic is Uslaner and Lichbach (2009). It found that attitudes on Israel and attitudes toward evangelicals were both strong factors affecting Jews' voting intentions in 2004. In that election, George W. Bush emphasized his strong support for Israel. Meanwhile, conservative forces, with strong backing from evangelical groups and from the Republican Party, sponsored ballot issues in several states that would prohibit gay marriage. Uslaner and Lichbach termed the battle for Jewish votes that year a "two-front war," with attitudes on Israel and attitudes toward evangelicals being countervailing factors. The Israel issue worked in the Republican direction. However, more Jewish voters were concerned about the political power of evangelicals, which pushed the Jewish vote toward the Democrats.[11] Weisberg's (2019, Chap. 12) survey analysis similarly finds

---

[11] Evangelical support for same-gender marriage could be seen an instance of their wanting to have their religious views enacted into law, regardless of the traditional separation between church and state. However, questions on moral issues, on church-state separation, and on attitudes toward the

attitudes on Israeli policies and morality issues are countervailing forces in affecting Jews' party identification, ideology, and approval of the incumbent president.

2.6   The 2016 and 2018 Elections

While Jews have largely voted Democratic since the late 1920s, the split in 2015 in the American Jewish community over the Iran nuclear accords provided a potential opportunity for Republican gains in the 2016 election.

2.6.1   The 2016 Campaign

Hillary Clinton was well-known with Jewish voters from her role as First Lady in Bill Clinton's presidency, followed by her election as US senator from New York, and then her service as Obama's secretary of state. Bill Clinton's popularity with Jewish voters was an asset for her candidacy. As secretary of state, she was strongly supportive of Israel, though the Iran nuclear accords were a potential liability even if negotiations were concluded by her successor.

Donald Trump sought votes in 2016 among Jews and among evangelical Christians by promising to recognize Jerusalem as Israel's capital and to withdraw from the Iran nuclear accords (the Joint Comprehensive Plan of Action). In February 2016, Trump said he would be neutral in the Israeli-Palestinian dispute, but by March he declared himself "very pro-Israel."

Israeli Prime Minister Benjamin Netanyahu avoided favoring either candidate. Sheldon and Miriam Adelson contributed considerable financial backing for the Trump campaign, but his backing from other leading Jewish Republicans was tepid (Sales 2016).

Trump pointed to his Jewish son-in-law, daughter, and grandson in claiming he would be a good president for Jews; but he was criticized throughout the campaign for connections and flirtations with antisemitism. Steve Bannon, a prominent campaign aide, was former editor of the alt-right Breitbart News service that was known for antisemitic comments. During the campaign, Trump tweeted a graphic of Hillary Clinton, with a background of dollar signs and a statement calling her corrupt, that was on a star that resembled the Star of David. His final campaign ad attacked global special interests for bleeding the country dry financially, with video clips of three prominent Jews. In July 2016, his son-in-law Jared Kushner wrote an article defending Trump against charges of antisemitism; and Kushner repeated that defense in a post-election November 2016 interview after Bannon was appointed as the chief presidential strategist.

Christian right have not been asked in the same surveys of Jews, making it difficult to assess their relative importance in affecting Jews' political positions.

2.6.2   The Jewish Vote in 2016

The American Jewish Committee's (AJC) pre-election poll found a substantial Clinton lead over Trump. Assuming the usual drop-off to about 5% in early intentions to vote for minor party candidates, the poll results among those planning to vote were equivalent to Clinton winning 72% of the Jewish vote versus 23% for Trump. As displayed in Table 2.5, exit polls found Jews voting about 70% for Clinton and 25% for Trump, with about 5% for minor party candidates.[12] Thus, the Democratic vote by Jews in 2016 was in line with that in the 2012 election, but with a decline in the Republican vote because of the increased minor party vote.

J Street released cross-tabulations for Jewish voting in 2016 that can be compared with its 2012 polling (Table 2.10). Nearly all Jewish Democrats voted for Clinton versus only three-quarters of Republican Jews voting for Trump, though little of that Republican drop-off went to Clinton.

The highest Clinton vote was among Reform (76%) and Conservative (71%) Jews. The Orthodox were shown as splitting 56% Clinton and 39% Trump, though this probably understates their Trump vote because ultra-Orthodox Jews are likely to avoid participating in 1-day polls; by contrast, the 2012 and 2016 Cooperative Congressional Election Study (CCES) surveys show the Orthodox voting more

Table 2.10 Jewish vote: 2012, 2016, and 2018 J Street election-day polls, in percentages

	2012		2016			2018 Congress	
	Obama	Romney	Clinton	Trump	Other	Dem	Rep
Overall	70	30	70	25	5	76	19
Democratic	93	7	94	5	2	97	1
Republican	13	87	15	76	9	18	77
Reform	78	21	76	21	3	79	16
Conservative	63	37	71	25	4	77	20
Orthodox	59	41	56	39	4	62	30
Other	70	29	67	26	7	77	17
Liberal	89	10	87	7	6	93	4
Moderate	70	30	60	35	5	71	22
conservative	37	62	44	53	3	24	67
Men	66	34	63	31	7	73	20
Women	73	26	77	20	3	79	17
Age 18–39	68	31	73	20	6	75	21
Age 40–64	71	29	65	30	6	72	21
Age 65 and over	69	30	73	25	2	83	13
Not college graduate	70	29	62	31	6	69	24
College graduate	70	29	72	24	4	79	16
Post graduate	69	31	76	19	5	81	16

[12] Edison Research was the main media exit poll. The Comparative Congressional Election Study is a large academic survey, while J Street is the progressive group that lobbies for a two-state solution for the Israeli-Palestinians dispute.

Republican (Weisberg 2019, Chap. 14). Whereas only 3–4% of those who affiliate with one of the major branches of Judaism voted for a third-party, 7% of "other" Jews did so.

There were three notable demographic changes among Jews' voting between 2012 and 2016. First, the gender gap doubled in size with a 14% point greater Democratic vote among Jewish women than men in 2016, up from 7 points in 2012. The gender gap nationally also increased considerably in 2016, moving up to 12% points due to the controversial nature of Trump's candidacy as well as having a woman on the ballot. Second, an educational divide opened up: Clinton did best among Jews with a post-graduate degree (76%) and college graduates (72%), whereas Trump did best among Jews without a college degree (31%). There were no educational differences among Jews in their 2012 presidential voting, but the 2016 difference fits with Trump's general appeal to those without college education. Third, there were age differences: Clinton's vote was highest (73%) among Jews under age 40 and those age 65 and over, whereas Trump did best (30%) among persons age 40–64. (National exit polls likewise found Trump's best showing was winning 63% of the vote of whites age 45–64.)

2.6.3   Jews and the Early Trump Administration

The first 2 years of the Trump administration included several actions that were favorable to Jews and to Israel, while antisemitic incidents increased sharply.

Trump was the first Republican president to appoint Jews to his initial cabinet, continuing Dr. David Shulkin as Veterans Affairs secretary and naming Steven Mnuchin to the treasury post. Several other Jews were given prominent positions in the administration, including Trump's son-in-law Jared Kushner.

Antisemitic incidents spiked after the 2016 election, including over 150 bomb threats phoned to Jewish Community Centers and other Jewish organizations around the nation in early 2017. Those bomb threats unsettled Jewish communities around the nation. After not having spoken out against those threats during the previous months, Trump vigorously denounced them in his February 28, 2017 speech to Congress.

The August 12, 2017 Charlottesville, Virginia "Unite the Right" march, which included Ku Klux Klan (KKK) members and neo-Nazis, turned violent. Trump's initial statement condemned "the egregious display of hatred, bigotry, and violence on many sides;" and he said there were "some very fine people on both sides." Both the Republican Jewish Coalition and AIPAC publicly asked for greater moral clarity and rejected attempts to suggest moral equivalence between the white supremacists and the counter-protestors. A few days later, Trump read a statement condemning the "hatred, bigotry, and violence," including that by "the KKK, neo-Nazis, white supremacists, and other hate groups;" but he subsequently emphasized that "there are two sides to a story" and repeated that "there is blame on both sides."

According to American Jewish Committee's (AJC) annual polling of Jews, the proportion who viewed antisemitism as a "very serious problem" in the US increased from 19% in autumn 2016 to 41% 1 year later, with 84% in 2017 viewing it as at least a "serious problem." Weisberg (2019, Table 14.2) found that perceptions of the severity of antisemitism were significant and behind only party identification and ideology in explanatory power for approval of Trump's presidency in the 2017 survey. Furthermore, antisemitism's perceived severity was tied with ideology for second place behind party identification in a multivariate analysis of presidential vote recall in the 2017 AJC survey, after not being significant in a comparable analysis of presidential vote intention in the 2016 AJC poll (Weisberg 2019, Table 14.2). These results suggest that the level of polarization of American politics has become so high that Jews' perceptions of antisemitism have become politicized.

In May 2018, Trump ordered the American embassy moved from Tel Aviv to Jerusalem, and he pulled the US out of the multination Iran nuclear accord. Interviewing for the April–May 2018 AJC survey ended as the embassy was moved. Approval of Trump's handling US-Israel relations was at 34% in that sample, while 57% disapproved. Also, 55% felt that the status of US Jews was less secure than a year earlier, 18% more secure, and 24% about the same.

2.6.4   The 2018 Election and Its Aftermath

As the 2018 congressional election approached, polls showed considerable Jewish opposition to President Trump. The Gallup Poll found only 26% of Jews in 2018 approving of the manner in which Trump was handling his job as president versus 71% disapproving. An early October 2018 online poll of Jews conducted for the Jewish Electorate Institute (JEI) found that approval of his handling of relations with Israel was at 51% among Jews, in contrast to the AJC 34% reading earlier in the year. Of those who stated their voting plans for the 2018 election, 74% indicated they would vote Democratic versus 26% Republican.

The Shabbat morning killing of 11 people at the Tree of Life Synagogue in the Squirrel Hill area of Pittsburgh occurred on October 27, 2018, just 10 days before the congressional election. President Trump called the act "pure evil" and again condemned antisemitism, while musing about whether the outcome would have been different if the congregation had armed guards.

Election Day polls show a strong Democratic vote by Jews in the 2018 election. Each of the polls in Table 2.5 found at least a 70% Democratic vote. The average poll result was a 74% Democratic vote and 22% Republican. The most striking result in these polls involved a question in J Street's poll asking Jews "How much do you think Donald Trump's comments and policies are responsible for the recent shootings that took place at the synagogue in Pittsburgh?" 39% answered "very responsible," 33% "somewhat responsible," 12% "not really responsible," and only 16% "not at all responsible."

Table 2.10 above includes the congressional vote results from the 2018 J Street poll. Democratic Jews were more unified than in the two previous elections, whereas there was some defection on the Republican side. Politically liberal Jews voted more Democratic and politically conservative Jews voted more Republican than in recent presidential elections. The largest shifts in the Democratic direction were among men and among persons age 65 and over. The Democratic vote increased across all education categories.

The 2018 election further increased the number of Jews in Congress. With Jacky Rosen's election from Nevada, there are once again nine Jewish Senators and all are Democrats. The "blue wave" House election brought in several new Jewish Democrats. The 116th Congress (2019–2020) contains 29 Jewish Representatives, all but two (Lee Zeldin from New York and David Kutsoff from Tennessee) being Democrats.

The aftermath of the 2018 election saw an increase in concern with antisemitism from the left. In particular, Rep. Ilhan Omar, a newly elected Democratic representative from Minnesota (of Somali origin), who favors the Palestinian side in the Israeli-Palestinian conflict, made a series of tweets and comments that suggested that Jewish financiers were buying off US politicians, raised questions about "allegiance to a foreign country," and expressed concern about a powerful lobby, referring obviously to the American Israel Public Affairs Committee (AIPAC). These comments, questioning the loyalty of American Jews and raising traditional antisemitic tropes, lit a firestorm of reactions. While she offered apologies, the House of Representatives passed a resolution condemning all types of hatred, including both antisemitism and anti-Muslim. Furthermore, there has been increased concern with antisemitism on American campuses against Jewish students who take public pro-Israel positions. Additionally, some Democratic progressives support the Boycott, Divestment, Sanctions (BDS) movement against the Israeli presence in the West Bank, a movement which is seen by critics as an attempt to delegitimize Israel.

An early May 2019 internet survey by the Jewish Electorate Institute provided the first measure of the relative concern about antisemitism from the political left versus the right. Jews were asked which of four matters were most concerning to them: 38% chose President Trump encouraging ultra-right extremists committing violent acts, 28% chose Republicans tolerating antisemitism and alliances with white nationalists within their ranks, and 7% chose Republicans encouraging Islamophobia that leads to more violence. By contrast, only 27% chose Democrats tolerating antisemitism in their own ranks. The 27% figure is very close to the proportion of Republicans in the sample, which emphasizes how politicized the topic has become.

As part of a new campaign to promote a Jewish exodus from the Democratic Party, the Trump 2020 reelection effort is attempting to label the Democratic Party as "anti-Jewish." Comparing the 2018 CCES survey with the 2016 CCES shows a very small increase in Republican identification among Jews in the Orthodox and Conservative movements. The same pattern occurs in comparing the 2019 AJC survey with its 2018 and 2017 surveys. These changes could just reflect sampling error, but they hint at shifts associated with President Trump's Middle East moves. Still, with politics so polarized, it is likely to be more difficult to shift the Democratic leanings of the much larger number of Jews who are neither Orthodox nor Conservative.

The spring 2019 American Jewish Committee Survey of American Jewish Opinion found 71% viewed Trump's job performance unfavorably, only 36% approved of his handling relations with Israel, and the party split was 49% Democratic versus 18% Republican. As to how secure Jews were in the US, 65% considered Jews to be less secure than a year earlier, versus 15% considering them more secure. How secure they saw Jews was significantly related to their party identification and their approval of Trump's presidency, whereas how hostile they considered the climate on college campuses toward pro-Israel students was not significant in multivariate analysis.

2.7 Conclusions

Jews realigned their voting behavior in the late 1920s and 1930s to support for the Democratic Party. At several times since then, analysts considered Jews' voting to be at a crossroads. While there have been some shifts in the Republican direction, their voting has always reverted back to strong Democratic support.

There was once again talk of Jewish realignment in the 2010s. Not only was there Republican voting among the 10% of Jews who are Orthodox, but there was enough Republican presidential voting among the non-Orthodox to reduce the Jewish Democratic vote down to the 70% level. The controversy over the Iran nuclear accords could have sparked further movement in the Republican direction in 2016. Instead, Donald Trump's election has, at least temporarily, slowed down such movement. His withdrawal from the Iran nuclear accords and his recognition of Jerusalem as Israel's capital may have brought some Jews to the Republican side, though polls showed that many Jewish Americans supported the accords and many opposed immediately moving the embassy. In any case, Trump's initial responses to the increased antisemitic threats, the Charlottesville march, and the Pittsburgh shooting instead led to increases in Jewish support for the Democrats in the 2018 election. Surveys suggest that Jews' disapproval of the Trump administration was causing a hardening of opposition to the Republican Party, though the specter of antisemitism from the left may counterbalance that.

References

Abrams, S.J., and S.M. Cohen. 2016. The persisting liberalism of (most) American Jews: The Pew survey of 2013 in historical context. In *Minority voting in the US*, ed. K.L. Kreider and T.J. Baldino, vol. 2, 95–123. Santa Barbara, CA: Praeger.

Adams, P. 2014. *Politics, faith, and the making of American Judaism*. Ann Arbor: University of Michigan Press.

Allinsmith, W., and B. Allinsmith. 1948. Religious affiliation and politico-economic attitude: A study of eight major US religious groups. *Public Opinion Quarterly* 12 (3): 377–389.

Allswang, J.M. 1971. *A house for all peoples: Ethnic politics in Chicago, 1890–1936.* Lexington: University Press of Kentucky.

Andersen, K. 1979. *The creation of a Democratic majority, 1928–1936.* Chicago: University of Chicago Press.

Berinsky, A. J., and E. Schickler. 2011. The American mass public in the 1930s and 1940s [Computer file]. Individual surveys conducted by the Gallup Organization [producers], 1936–1945: Roper Center for Public Opinion Research, University of Connecticut [distributor].

Brady, H.E., M.C. Herron, W.R. Mebane Jr., J.S. Sekhon, K.W. Shotts, and J. Wand. 2001. Law and data: The butterfly ballot episode. *PS: Political Science and Politics* 34 (1): 59–69.

Brenner, S. 1964. Patterns of Jewish-Catholic Democratic voting and the 1960 presidential vote. *Jewish Social Studies* 26 (3): 169–178.

Burner, D. 1968. *The politics of provincialism: The Democratic party in transition, 1918–1932.* New York: Knopf.

Campbell, A., P.E. Converse, W.E. Miller, and D.E. Stokes. 1960. *The American voter.* New York: Wiley.

Chyet, S.F. 1958. The political rights of Jews in the US, 1776–1840. *American Jewish Archives* 10 (1): 14–75.

Cohen, N.W. 1984. *Encounter with emancipation: The German Jews in the US, 1830–1914.* Philadelphia: Jewish Publication Society of America.

Cohen, S.M. 1983. *American modernity and Jewish identity.* New York: Tavistock.

———. 1989. *The dimensions of American liberalism.* New York: American Jewish Committee.

Cohen, S. M., and S. Abrams. 2012. *Workmen's Circle/Arbeter Ring 2012 American Jews' political values survey.* http://www.bjpa.org/Publications/downloadFile.cfm?FileID=13871. Accessed 20 Aug 2015.

Cohen, S.M., and C.S. Liebman. 1997. American Jewish liberalism: Unraveling the strands. *Public Opinion Quarterly* 61 (3): 405–430.

Cohn, W. 1958. The politics of American Jews. In *The Jews: Social patterns of an American group,* ed. M. Sklare, 614–626. Glencoe, IL: Free Press.

Dahl, R.A. 1961. *Who governs?* New Haven: Yale University Press.

Dalin, D.G. 1992. Louis Marshall, the Jewish vote, and the Republican party. *Jewish Political Studies Review* 4 (1): 55–84.

Dawidowicz, L.S. 1961. Religion in the 1960 Presidential campaign. *American Jewish Year Book* 62: 111–128.

———. 1963. Louis Marshall's Yiddish newspaper, The Jewish World. *Jewish Social Studies* 25 (2): 102–132.

Dawidowicz, L.S., and L.J. Goldstein. 1974. The American Jewish liberal tradition. In *The Jewish Community in America,* ed. M. Sklare, 285–300. New York: Behrman House.

Diner, H.R. 1992. *A time for gathering: The second migration, 1820–1880.* Baltimore: Johns Hopkins.

Djupe, P.A. 2007. The evolution of Jewish pluralism: The public opinion and political preferences of American Jews. In *From Pews to Polling Places,* ed. J.M. Wilson, 185–212. Washington, DC: Georgetown University Press.

El Azhary, M.S. 1980. *Political cohesion of American Jews in American politics: A reappraisal of their role in presidential elections.* Washington, DC: University Press of America.

Feingold, H.L. 1992. *A time for searching: Entering the mainstream, 1920–1945.* Baltimore: Johns Hopkins University Press.

———. 2014. *American Jewish political culture and the liberal persuasion.* Syracuse, NY: Syracuse University Press.

Fingerhut, E. 2008. *Some stats on the Orthodox Jewish vote. JTA, 25 Nov.* http://www.jta.org/2008/11/26/news-opinion/the-telegraph/some-stats-on-the-orthodox-jewish-vote. Accessed 25 Apr 2016.

Fisher, A. 1976. Continuity and erosion of Jewish liberalism. *American Jewish Historical Quarterly* 66 (2): 322–348.

Forman, I.N. 2001. The politics of minority consciousness: The historical voting behavior of American Jews. In *Jews in American politics*, ed. L.S. Maisel and I.N. Forman, 141–160. Lanham, MD: Rowman and Littlefield.

Fuchs, L.H. 1955. American Jews and the presidential vote. *American Political Science Review* 49 (2): 385–401.

———. 1956. *The political behavior of American Jews*. Glencoe, IL: Free Press.

———. 1976. Introduction. *American Jewish Historical Quarterly* 66 (2): 181–189.

Gamm, G.H. 1989. *The making of the New Deal Democrats: Voting behavior and realignment in Boston, 1920–1940*. Chicago: University of Chicago Press.

Ginsberg, B. 1993. *The fatal embrace: Jews and the state*. Chicago: University of Chicago Press.

Goren, A. 1961. A portrait of ethnic politics: The socialists and the 1908 and 1910 congressional elections on the East Side. *Publication of the American Jewish Historical Society* 50 (March): 202–238.

Greenberg, A., and K.D. Wald. 2001. Still liberal after all these years? In *Jews in American Politics*, ed. L.S. Maisel and I.N. Forman, 161–193. Lanham, MD: Rowman and Littlefield.

Guysenir, M.G. 1958. The Jewish vote in Chicago. *Jewish Social Studies* 20 (4): 195–214.

Hasen, R.L. 2012. *The Voting Wars: From Florida 2000 to the Next Election Meltdown*. New Haven: Yale University Press.

Heitzmann, W.R. 1975. *American Jewish voting behavior: A history and analysis*. San Francisco: R and E Research Associates.

Himmelfarb, M. 1969. Is American Jewry in crisis? *Commentary* 47 (3): 33–42.

———. 1970. Jewish class conflict? *Commentary* 49 (1): 37–42.

———. 1973. The Jewish vote (again). *Commentary* 55 (6): 81–85.

———. 1981. Are Jews becoming Republican. *Commentary* 72 (2): 27–31.

Howe, I. 1976. *World of our fathers*. New York: Harcourt Brace-Jovanovich.

Inglehart, R. 1977. *The silent revolution: Changing values and political styles among western publics*. Princeton: Princeton University Press.

Isaacs, S.D. 1974. *Jews and American politics*. Garden City, NY: Doubleday.

Kessner, T. 1981. Jobs, ghettoes, and the urban economy, 1880–1935. *American Jewish History* 71: 228–236.

Klausner, S. Z. 2013. *Pew Study of American Jewry: A few grains of salt. Jewish Free-Culture Society*. http://jewishfreeculture.org/news/pew-study-of-american-jewry-a-few-grains-of-salt-by-dr-samuel-klausner-2/. Accessed 5 Oct 2015.

Kotler-Berkowitz, L.A. 2005. Ethnicity and political behavior among American Jews: Findings from the National Jewish Population Survey 2000–01. *Contemporary Jewry* 25 (1): 132–157.

———. 2017. The structure of political divisions among American Jews. *Contemporary Jewry* 37 (1): 5–27.

Ladd, E.C., Jr., and C.D. Hadley. 1975. *Transformations of the American party system*. New York: Norton.

Ladd, E.C., Jr., and S.M. Lipset. 1973. *Academics, politics, and the 1971 election*. Washington, DC: American Enterprise Institute.

Lazarowitz, A. 2010. Ethnic influence and American foreign policy: American Jewish leaders and President Jimmy Carter. *Shofar* 29 (1): 112–136.

Lenski, G.E. 1967. Status inconsistency and the vote: A four nation test. *American Sociological Review* 32 (2): 298–301.

Levey, G.B. 1996. The liberalism of American Jews: Has it been explained? *British Journal of Political Science* 26 (3): 369–401.

Levy, M.R., and M.S. Kramer. 1972. *The ethnic factor: How America's minorities decide elections*. New York: Simon & Schuster.

Lewin, K. 1941. *Self-hatred among Jews*. Contemporary Jewish Record, June.

Liebman, C.S. 1973. *The ambivalent American Jew*. Philadelphia: Jewish Publication Society of America.

Liebman, C.S., and S.M. Cohen. 1999. Jewish liberalism revisited. In *Jews in America*, ed. R.R. Farber and C.I. Waxman, 197–200. Hanover, NH: Brandeis University Press.

Lipset, S.M. 1963. *Political man*. Garden City, NY: Anchor Books.

Lipset, S.M., and E. Raab. 1995. *Jews and the new American scene*. Cambridge, MA: Harvard University Press.

Lubell, S. 1951. *The future of American politics*. New York: Harper and Brothers.

MacInnis, B., J.A. Krosnick, A.S. Ho, and M. Cho. 2018. The accuracy of measurements with probability and nonprobability survey samples. *Public Opinion Quarterly* 82 (4): 707–744.

Maisel, S.L., and I.N. Forman, eds. 2001. *Jews in American politics*. Lanham, MD: Rowman and Littlefield.

Manor, E. 2009. *Forward: Immigrants, Socialists, and Jewish politics in New York: 1890–1917*. Brighton: Sussex Academic Press.

Manza, J., and C. Brooks. 1997. The religious factor in US presidential elections. *American Journal of Sociology* 103 (1): 38–81.

Marcus, J.R. 1989. *US Jewry, 1776–1985*. Vol. 1. Detroit: Wayne State University Press.

Marks, G., and M. Burbank. 1990. Immigrant support for the American Socialist party, 1912 and 1920. *Social Science History* 14 (2): 175–202.

Mazur, E.H. 1990. *Minyans for a prairie city: The politics of Chicago Jewry, 1850–1940*. New York: Garland.

Medding, P.Y. 1977. Towards a general theory of Jewish political interests and behaviour. *Jewish Journal of Sociology* 19 (2): 115–144.

Medoff, R. 2002. *Jewish Americans and political participation: A reference handbook*. Santa Barbara, CA: ABC-CLIO.

———. 2012. *Many Jewish voters turned against Truman in '48*. http://wymaninstitute.org/articles/2012-9-jewish-voters-against-truman.php. Accessed 17 Sept 2015.

Mellman, M.S., A. Strauss, and K.D. Wald. 2012. *Jewish American voting behavior, 1972–2008*. Washington, DC: Solomon Project.

Norpoth, H. 2019. The American voter in 1932: Evidence from a confidential survey. *PS: Political Science and Politics* 52 (1): 14–19.

Petrocik, J.R. 1981. *Party coalitions: Realignments and the decline of the New Deal party system*. Chicago: University of Chicago Press.

Pew Research Center. 2013. *A portrait of Jewish Americans: Findings from the Pew Research Center Survey of US Jews. 1 Oct*. http://www.pewresearch.org/wp-content/uploads/sites/7/2013/10/jewish-american-full-report-for-web.pdf. Accessed 15 Nov 2018.

———. 2018. *Party identification trends, 1992–2017. 20 Mar*. http://www.people-press.org/2018/03/20/party-identification-trends-1992-2017/. Accessed 17 July 2018.

Rischin, M. 1962. *The promised city*. Cambridge, MA: Harvard University Press.

Rocklin, M. 2017. *Are American Jews shifting their political affiliation? Mosaic, 18 Jan*. https://mosaicmagazine.com/observation/2017/01/are-american-jews-shifting-their-political-affiliation/. Accessed 6 Mar 2017.

Sales, B. 2016. *Few Republican Jewish Coalition leaders open wallets for Donald Trump. JTA, 1 Nov*. http://www.jta.org/2016/11/01/news-opinion/politics/few-republican-jewish-coalition-leaders-open-wallets-for-donald-trump. Accessed 21 Nov 2016.

Sarna, J.D. 1981. *Jacksonian Jew*. New York: Holmes and Meier.

———. 2004. *American Judaism: A history*. New Haven, CT: Yale University Press.

———. 2012. *When General Grant expelled the Jews*. New York: Schocken Books.

Sarna, J.D., and B. Shapell. 2015. *Lincoln and the Jews*. New York: Thomas Dunne Books.

Schwartz, S.H. 1994. Are there universal aspects in the structure and contents of human values? *Journal of Social Issues* 50 (4): 19–45.

Schwartz, S.H., and S. Huismans. 1995. Value priorities and religiosity in four western religions. *Social Psychology Quarterly* 58 (2): 88–107.

Shapiro, E. S. 2000. Waiting for righty? An interpretation of the political behavior of American Jews. *Michael*, 155–179.

Sheskin, I.M. 2013. Geography, demography, and the Jewish vote. In *American Politics and the Jewish Community*, ed. D. Schnur, 37–76. West Lafayette, IN: Purdue University Press.

———. 2016. An introduction to the Jewish voter. In *Minority voting in the US*, ed. K.L. Kreider and T.J. Baldino, vol. 2, 61–94. Santa Barbara, CA: Praeger.

———. 2018. The 2018 Detroit Jewish Population Study. Detroit: Jewish Federation of Metropolitan Detroit.

Smith, T.W. 2005. *Jewish distinctiveness in America: A statistical portrait*. New York: American Jewish Committee.

Stanley, H.W., and R.G. Niemi. 2006. Partisanship, party coalition, and group support, 1952–2004. *Presidential Studies Quarterly* 36 (2): 172–188.

US Election Project. 2019. http://www.electproject.org/national-1789-present. Accessed 8 Apr 2019.

Uslaner, E.M. 2015. What's the matter with Palm Beach county? *Politics and Religion* 8 (4): 699–717.

Uslaner, E.M., and M. Lichbach. 2009. Identity versus identity: Israel and Evangelicals and the two-front war for Jewish votes. *Politics and Religion* 2 (3): 395–419.

Wald, K.D. 2015. The choosing people: Interpreting the puzzling politics of American Jewry. *Politics and Religion* 8 (1): 4–35.

———. 2016. Politically hyperactive? The civic participation of American Jews. *Politics, Groups, and Identities* 4 (4): 545–560.

———. 2019. *The foundations of American Jewish liberalism*. Cambridge: Cambridge University Press.

Wald, K.D., and M.D. Martinez. 2001. Jewish religiosity and political attitudes in the US and Israel. *Political Behavior* 23 (4): 377–397.

Wald, K.D., and L. Sigelman. 1997. Romancing the Jews: The Christian Right in search of strange bedfellows. In *Sojourners in the wilderness*, ed. C.E. Smidt and J.M. Penning, 139–168. Lanham, MD: Rowman and Littlefield.

Wald, K.D., and B.D. Williams. 2006. American Jews and Israel: The sources of politicized ethnic identity. *Nationalism and Ethnic Politics* 12: 205–237.

Weisberg, H. F. 2011. The distinctiveness of the Jewish-American voter. Paper presented at the Symposium on Jewish Political Behavior, Frankel Institute for Advanced Judaic Studies, University of Michigan, Ann Arbor, 10–11 Nov.

Weisberg, H.F. 2012. Reconsidering Jewish presidential voting statistics. *Contemporary Jewry* 32 (3): 215–236.

———. 2014. Tradition! Tradition? Jewish voting in the 2012 election. *PS: Political Science and Politics* 47 (3): 629–635.

———. 2015. The decline in the white vote for Barack Obama in 2012: Racial attitudes or the economy? *Electoral Studies* 40: 449–459.

———. 2019. *The politics of American Jews*. Ann Arbor, MI: University of Michigan Press.

Wentling, S.S., and R. Medoff. 2012. *Herbert Hoover and the Jews*. Washington, DC: Wyman Institute.

Weyl, N. 1968. *The Jew in American politics*. New Rochelle, NY: Arlington House.

Chapter 3
American Jews and the Domestic Arena: Focus on the 2018 Midterm Elections

J. J. Goldberg

While midterm elections—those not coinciding with a presidential contest—are rarely of great long-term significance, those held on November 6, 2018 were an exception. They constituted what is called a "wave election," in which a large shift in voting patterns significantly weakens the incumbent party and strengthens the opposition. In this case, the American electorate repudiated a sitting president by decisively shifting control of the US House of Representatives from the Republicans to the Democrats. Republicans maintained control of the US Senate. In the 115th Congress, before the 2018 elections, Republicans held a 235 to 196 advantage over the Democrats in the House, with four seats vacant. However, in the new 116th Congress, the balance of power was almost exactly reversed: 235 Democrats, 198 Republicans, and 1 independent, with 1 vacancy remaining. Also, Democrats enjoyed a net gain of eight state governorships and seven state legislative chambers.

3.1 The Midterms and the Jewish Vote

Since most politically active Jews are Democrats, the 2018 outcome had dramatic implications for the Jewish community. For one thing, Democratic advances in the House increased the number of Jews in that body from 22 to 28, a 27% increase. This was the most significant shift in Jewish congressional representation in either direction since 1994, when eight Jewish representatives lost their seats—seven Democrats and one Republican—during that year's Republican sweep.

Of the 22 Jewish incumbents in 2018, three did not seek reelection: Sander Levin of Michigan, who retired at age 87 after 36 years in the House; Jacky Rosen of Nevada, who ran successfully for the US Senate; and Jared Polis of Colorado, who

J. J. Goldberg (✉)
Independent Researcher, New York, NY, USA

© Springer Nature Switzerland AG 2020
A. Dashefsky, I. M. Sheskin (eds.), *American Jewish Year Book 2019*, American Jewish Year Book 119, https://doi.org/10.1007/978-3-030-40371-3_3

was elected governor. Thus, while the number of Jewish freshmen entering the House in January 2019 was eight, the net gain was five.

Jewish House Members in the 116th Congress (January 3, 2019) (* indicates freshman):

Suzanne Bonamici (D-OR)
David Cicilline (D-RI)
Steve Cohen (D-TN)
Susan Davis (D-CA)
Ted Deutch (D-FL)
Eliot Engel (D-NY)
Lois Frankel (D-FL)
Josh Gottheimer (D-NJ)
David Kustoff (R-TN)
*Andy Levin (D-MI)
*Mike Levin (D-CA)
Alan Lowenthal (D-CA)
Nita Lowey (D-NY)
*Elaine Luria (D-VA)
Jerrold Nadler (D-NY)
*Dean Phillips (D-MN)
Jamie Raskin (D-MD)
*Max Rose (D-NY)
Jan Schakowsky (D-IL)
Adam Schiff (D-CA)
Brad Schneider (D-IL)
*Kim Schrier (D-WA)
Brad Sherman (D-CA)
*Elissa Slotkin (D-VA)
Debbie Wasserman-Schultz (D-FL)
*Susan Wild (D-PA)
John Yarmuth (D-KY)
Lee Zeldin (R-NY)

Jewish Senate Members in the 116th Congress (January 3, 2019) (* indicates freshman):

Michael Bennet (D-CO)
Richard Blumenthal (D-CT)
Ben Cardin (D-MD)
Dianne Feinstein (D-CA)
Jacky Rosen (D-NV)*
Bernie Sanders (D-VT)
Brian Schatz (D-HI)
Charles Schumer (D-NY)
Ron Wyden (D-OR)

Some ambiguity exists about the Jewish identity of Suzanne Bonamici and Mike Levin, the former a non-Jew married to a Jew (but attending synagogue with her family) and the latter the offspring of an intermarriage, raised in both his mother's Catholic faith and his father's Jewish faith and describing himself as "culturally Jewish" (http://sdjewishjournal.com/sdjj/january-2019/no-gambler-an-interview-with-congressman-mike-levin/). A similar issue surrounds Michael Bennet (D-CO), whose mother is Jewish and whose father is Christian, who said he was "proud" of both heritages, but is not known to describe himself as Jewish; in May 2019, Bennet announced his candidacy for president.

The Democrats' House victory made the ranking members of the chamber's 24 committees in the old Congress—the leaders of the minority Democrats—into committee chairs in the new Congress. That meant that six of the committees, one-fourth of the total, would now be chaired by Jewish members. Two of them, now among Congress's most visible figures, would lead the congressional investigations of the Trump-Russia affair: Representative Jerrold Nadler (D-NY) chairing the Judiciary Committee and Adam Schiff (D-CA) chairing the Intelligence Committee. As a result, Adam Schiff played a major role in the impeachment investigations faced by Trump in 2019.

Two other new Jewish chairs would head committees that oversaw US-Israel relations: Eliot Engel at Foreign Affairs and Nita Lowey at Appropriations—which, among other things, handles aid to Israel. The two remaining Jewish committee chairs were Budget Chairman John Yarmuth (D-KY) and Ethics Chairman Ted Deutch (D-FL).

New Yorkers Engel and Lowey, representing the southern and northern halves of Westchester County respectively, were among seven pairs of Jewish representatives and one trio—17 members in all, three-fifths of the Jewish total—serving districts that adjoined one another. The others were Jerry Nadler and newcomer Max Rose along the Brooklyn waterfront; Bradley Schneider and Jan Schakowsky in Chicago and its northern suburbs; Adam Schiff and Brad Sherman in Los Angeles' San Fernando Valley; Steve Cohen and David Kustoff in Memphis and its western suburbs; Josh Gottheimer of New Jersey and Susan Wild of Pennsylvania, whose districts meet along a 35-mile stretch of the Delaware River; newcomers Andy Levin and Elissa Slotkin, whose suburban Detroit districts met at a single traffic intersection; and the veteran trio of Debbie Wasserman-Schultz, Ted Deutch, and Lois Frankel lined up from south to north in South Florida. Ironically, the district represented by Kustoff, the only Republican on this list, was next door to that of Cohen, the most combatively liberal Jewish member.

The significance of this phenomenon of clustered Jewish representatives is not clear, but given the high proportion of such cases it seems to deserve further study. At the outset it should be noted that more than half of all Jewish House members appear to represent districts with significant Jewish populations, including at least 12 of the 17 in clustered districts. The relationship between Jewish House members and Jewish voters deserves in-depth examination.

On the Senate side, Jacky Rosen (D-NV), a Democrat and a former synagogue president, ousted Republican incumbent Dean Heller, becoming the ninth Jewish senator, all Democrats. Also of note in the 2018 midterms, two Jews, both Democrats, were elected state governors. Jared Polis became the first Jewish governor of Colorado and the first openly gay governor of any state. And in Illinois, billionaire J.B. Pritzker, a major donor to the Democratic Party and to Jewish causes whose family founded and controls the Hyatt Hotel chain, became that state's third Jewish governor.

Maintaining their familiar voting profile, Jews in 2018 were considerably more likely to support Democrats than Republicans. While final vote tallies (https://cook-political.com/analysis/house/house-charts/2018-house-popular-vote-tracker) showed Americans overall preferring Democrats to Republicans by 53% to 45%, exit polls showed Jewish voters favored Democrats by 79% to 17% (https://www.pewresearch.org/fact-tank/2018/11/07/how-religious-groups-voted-in-the-mid-term-elections/) or: (https://www.cnn.com/election/2018/exit-polls).

But there was another way to look at these numbers. The election was held just ten days after the mass murder of Jews in a Pittsburgh synagogue, allegedly by a right-wing white nationalist, widely blamed on President Trump's divisive rhetoric, and just a year after Trump described a Klan/neo-Nazi/white nationalist rally in Charlottesville, Virginia, as including "some very fine people." In that context, the 17% of Jews voting Republican in 2018 presumably represent a "rock-bottom, never-Democratic" hard core of Republican Jews willing to dismiss Trump's seeming flirtation with the far right. While admittedly a small share of the Jewish vote, it exceeded the approximately 10% that Republican presidential candidates had achieved among Jews in 1940, 1944, 1948, 1964, and 1992 (https://www.jewishvirtuallibrary.org/jewish-voting-record-in-u-s-presidential-elections).

And there were signs that demographic shifts in the American Jewish community could bring future gains to the Republican column. First, there were about a half-million Russian-born Jews and their children in the country whose historical memory of state socialism made most of them politically conservative.

Second, and even more significant, might be the future growth of the Orthodox population, who tend to be more socially conservative and hawkish than other Jews. Politically, Orthodox Jews tend to self-identify as Republican or leaning Republican far more than the non-Orthodox. According to a study by the Pew Research Center, while only 18% of non-Orthodox Jews identified with or leaned Republican, 57% of the Orthodox did.

In the 1990 National Jewish Population Survey, 7% of US Jewish adults were Orthodox. In the 2013 Pew Survey (*A Portrait of Jewish Americans*), 10% of Jewish adults were Orthodox. While this increase is not statistically significant (particularly given the different methodologies of the two surveys), the change is in the expected direction. And Orthodox Jews are much younger than was the case 25 years ago and are much less likely to be Orthodox in Name Only (OINO), meaning that they do not just call themselves Orthodox, but also behave in a truly Orthodox manner. This future increase in Orthodox will largely be due to a considerably higher birthrate—an average of 4.1 children per family as compared to 1.7 children for non-Orthodox families. So, in Detroit, for example, while 9% of Jewish households are Orthodox, such is the case for 15% of Jewish adults, and 37% of Jewish children.

3.2   The Israel Factor

For both the Russians and the Orthodox—and other Jews as well—the steadily widening gulf between the parties over support for Israel has increased the attractiveness of the Republicans. A much-publicized survey by the Pew Research Center in January 2018 asked whether respondents sympathized more with Israel or the Palestinians in their conflict. It found that 79% of self-identified Republicans chose Israel while 6% favored the Palestinians. Among Democrats, 27% sided with Israel and 25% with the Palestinians. (The remainder in both cases either chose both or neither.) A similar survey by the Gallup organization two months later found Republicans siding with Israel at a rate of 87% and Democrats at 49%.

An analysis by the Jewish Virtual Library (www.jewishvirtuallibrary.org) of Gallup polls from 1975 to 2019 indicates that preference for Israel among persons over age 45 averaged 64% among Republicans and 45% among Democrats; preference for Palestinians averaged 10% among Republicans and 18% among Democrats. In polls by both Gallup and Pew, up until about 2001, the two parties' sympathies with Israel and the Palestinians rose and fell in close tandem, separated by a gap of about 8–10 points, well below the 44-year average gap of nearly 20 points. After 2001, though, the parties began to diverge dramatically, with Republicans' sympathy for Israel rising and Democrats' plummeting until the two parties show, in 2019, a 40-point (Gallup) or 50-point (Pew) gap.

A further study by Pew in January 2018 subdivided the two parties into their moderate and more extreme wings, the latter being conservative Republicans and liberal Democrats. In this new four-way breakdown, three of the four subgroups sympathized more with Israel, albeit by varying margins; only the fourth group, liberal Democrats, sided more with Palestinians. Among Conservative Republicans, 81% preferred Israel versus 5% preferring Palestinians; moderate Republicans preferred Israel by 70% to 8%; 35% of moderate Democrats chose Israel and 17% the Palestinians; and liberal Democrats preferred the Palestinians by 35% to 19%.

Notably, the gap between the two parties widened significantly between 2016 and 2018. For conservative Republicans, the percentage supporting Israel remained about the same (79% and 81%). For moderates, the percentage increased from 65% to 70%. Among Democrats, in contrast, a sharp decrease is seen in pro-Israel feeling. Among moderate Democrats, pro-Israel sympathies decreased from 53% to 35%. Among liberal Democrats, pro-Israel sentiment decreased from 33% to 19%; and pro-Palestinian feeling increased from 22% to 35%. The release of these polls showing declining levels of grass-roots Democratic sympathy for Israel put party leaders on the defensive in facing Jewish voters, donors, and wavering centrists in swing states. (The significant decrease in support among Democrats in just two years is somewhat suspect—eds.)

These findings also reinforced the widespread assumption that Israel's standing among Democrats and liberals suffered from Israel's close identification with Donald Trump. Trump fared particularly well among Israelis— and their strongest American supporters—simply by contrast with Barack Obama, who was widely disliked by Israelis and hawkish American Jews. Asked in a Ma'agar Mohot poll in February 2016 which US president over the past 30 years was "the worst for Israel," 63% of Israelis chose Obama. Not only had Israeli Prime Minister Netanyahu enthusiastically embraced Trump following the November 2016 US election, but Israel's right and center were reportedly cheering for Trump even before his election, when it emerged that his top Middle East advisors would be three Orthodox Jews with hawkish views on the conflict: his bankruptcy lawyer David Friedman; his company's executive vice-president and chief legal counsel Jason Greenblatt; and Trump son-in-law Jared Kushner. Friedman was a particularly active supporter of the Israeli right, serving as president of American Friends of Bet El Yeshiva Center, effectively the chief fundraiser for a key bastion of the settler movement, from 2011 until he was named US ambassador to Israel in February 2017. Kushner and his family were donors to Friedman's Bet El charity and similar causes, and Netanyahu had been an occasional visitor in their home.

Greenblatt, named presidential special representative for international negotiations in January 2017, was named to head the president's Middle East peace team, which also included Kushner and Friedman. In a rare interview with PBS NewsHour in July 2019, Greenblatt said that he "can't think of single instances" in which Israel had made mistakes, that he regarded Israel as the victim in the conflict, and that he preferred to refer to Israeli settlements in the West Bank as "communities" rather than settlements.

Netanyahu himself told Trump directly that "Israel has never had a better friend than you," during the March 2019 signing ceremony where Trump formally recognized Israel's 1981 *de facto* annexation of the Golan Heights, captured from Syria in 1967. A 37-nation survey conducted by Pew in June 2017, six months into Trump's presidency, found that Israel was one of just two countries where a majority expressed confidence in Trump: Israelis' approval of Trump stood at 69%, topped only by the Philippines at 78%.

Yet, some observers questioned whether Trump's embrace of Israel and its prime minister or the Democrats' growing grass-roots disenchantment with the Jewish state were necessarily decisive in explaining American Jewish political behavior. Surveys of Jewish opinion had shown for decades that Israel does not figure highly in American Jews' voting choices. When asked to name the most important issue when deciding for whom to vote, only 6–8% chose US-Israel relations, far behind the strong double-digit figures for such concerns as healthcare, economy/jobs, and national security. And yet, a 2015 American Jewish Committee survey that for the first time asked respondents to name their first, second, and third most important voting issues indicated that Israel was considered one of the top three by 22%, suggesting that American support for Israel may be playing a more significant role in Jewish voters' decision-making than previously known.

Chapter 4
American Jews and the International Arena (August 2018–July 2019): The US, Israel, and the Middle East

Mitchell Bard

Any time Israel can avoid a major armed conflict, it is a good year; nevertheless, 2018–2019 had a Dickensian quality as it was the best of times for the alliance between the governments of the US and Israel, but the worst (or at least very bad) times for relations between Israelis and American Jews. Paradoxically, the former was partially responsible for the latter.

Times are always complicated when it comes to American and Israeli Jews and their governments, but this year had a series of challenges, many of which were atypical. The political upheaval in Israel was unusual even for that tumultuous system. Prime Minister Benjamin Netanyahu was under siege from multiple allegations of criminal activity, his government unexpectedly fell due to disagreements over drafting yeshiva students, a variety of legislative initiatives were introduced that critics labeled undemocratic, and the inability of Netanyahu to form a new _ government triggered a new election.

The political turmoil occurred while Palestinians continued protesting in Gaza, Iran and Hezbollah were attempting to establish beachheads in Syria from which to attack Israel, Israeli relations were improving with Egypt and the Gulf States and troubling new discoveries were made about Iran's effort to build a nuclear bomb. Netanyahu was helped by his friendship with President Trump, who announced US recognition of Israeli sovereignty over the Golan Heights and ratcheted up pressure on both Iran and the Palestinians.

Netanyahu's closeness to Trump, meanwhile, exacerbated existing tensions with American Jews, most of whom loathe Trump. Liberal American Jews, already upset about what they view as the lack of religious pluralism in Israel, were angered further when Netanyahu reneged on an agreement to provide egalitarian prayer space at the Western Wall, his government's adoption of the Nation State Law many

M. Bard (✉)
American-Israeli Cooperative Enterprise, Jewish Virtual Library, Chevy Chase, MD, USA
e-mail: weisberg.1@osu.edu

© Springer Nature Switzerland AG 2020
A. Dashefsky, I. M. Sheskin (eds.), *American Jewish Year Book 2019*, American Jewish Year Book 119, https://doi.org/10.1007/978-3-030-40371-3_4

viewed as discriminatory, and his pre-election campaign pledge to annex Jewish settlements in the West Bank.

Adding to the toxic mix was the start of the US presidential campaign in which more than 20 Democrats were vying for the nomination to face Trump in 2020. Given the overwhelming number of Jews in the party, it is no great leap of imagination to expect the Democratic nominee to get most of the Jewish vote (see Chap. 2 in this volume). The positions of many of the candidates are troubling for some Jewish voters, however, as some want to reverse some of the policies Trump adopted that they favored, such as withdrawing from the Iran deal. For the most part, the candidates' views appear similar to those of traditional Democrats who have been reliably pro-Israel, but not uncritical. The cozy relationship between Jews and Democrats was also shaken in 2019 by the outspokenness of two freshman members of Congress who support the Boycott, Divestment, and Sanctions (BDS) movement and made several antisemitic remarks.

4.1 New House Members Generate Controversy

While Congress has always had critics of Israel, none have received more attention than newcomers Reps. Ilan Omar (D-MN) and Rashida Tlaib (D-MI), both supporters of the BDS movement, whose antisemitic comments roiled the Democratic Party and prompted discussion about whether the party was turning on Israel. The two women had been in office only a few weeks before they ignited controversy.

Omar came to Congress having made antisemitic statements in the past, notably this 2012 tweet: "Israel has hypnotized the world, may Allah awaken the people and help them see the evil doings of Israel."[1]

After taking office, she retweeted a post describing how she and Rep. Tlaib were facing punishment from House Minority Leader Kevin McCarthy (R-CA) for criticizing Israel. "It's all about the Benjamins, baby," Omar wrote in response, adding that the American-Israel Public Affairs Committee (AIPAC) could be paying politicians to take pro-Israel positions.[2]

She later further impugned the motives of Israel's supporters and intimated Jews were guilty of dual loyalty when she said, "I want to talk about the political influence in this country that says it is okay to push for allegiance to a foreign country."[3] This remark was condemned in a joint statement by Speaker Nancy Pelosi, Majority Leader Steny Hoyer, Majority Whip James E. Clyburn, Assistant Speaker Ben Ray Luján, Caucus Chairman Hakeem Jeffries and Caucus Vice Chair Katherine Clark:

---

[1] Mike Brest, "Rep. Omar Defends Tweet Claiming, 'Israel Has Hypnotized The World,' Says It's Not About Religion," *Daily Caller*, (January 16, 2019).

[2] Victoria Albert, Rep. Ilhan Omar Criticized for 'Anti-Semitic' Tweet, *Daily Beast*, (February 11, 2019).

[3] Zack Beauchamp, "The Ilhan Omar anti-Semitism controversy, explained, Vox," (March 6, 2019).

> We are and will always be strong supporters of Israel in Congress because we understand that our support is based on shared values and strategic interests. Legitimate criticism of Israel's policies is protected by the values of free speech and democratic debate that the United States and Israel share. But Congresswoman Omar's use of anti-Semitic tropes and prejudicial accusations about Israel's supporters is deeply offensive. We condemn these remarks and we call upon Congresswoman Omar to immediately apologize for these hurtful comments.[4]

Several individual Democrats also reproached Omar, including Rep. Eliot Engel (D-NY) who said, "Anti-Semitism in any form is unacceptable, and it's shocking to hear a member of Congress invoke the anti-Semitic trope of 'Jewish money'" and Rep. Nita Lowey (D-NY) who commented, "There is no defense for invoking anti-Semitic tropes."[5]

Omar's response to her colleagues was another tweet: "I should not be expected to have allegiance/pledge support to a foreign country in order to serve my country in Congress or serve on committee."

Former Chicago Mayor Rahm Emanuel wrote in *The Atlantic*: "No one is questioning the right of members of Congress and others to criticize Israeli policies. But Omar is crossing a line that should not be crossed in political discourse. Her remarks are not anti-Israel; they are anti-Semitic."[6]

Speaker Pelosi yielded to her progressive colleagues, such as Ayanna Pressley (D-MA), who insisted that there must be "equity in our outrage," that all forms of hate needed to be denounced, and that "there is no hierarchy of hurt."[7] The House subsequently adopted a watered-down resolution that did not condemn Omar and, rather than simply express its opposition to antisemitism, condemned nearly every form of bigotry.

Trump and other Republicans criticized the Democrats' timidity. Trump tweeted, "It is shameful that House Democrats won't take a stronger stand against Antisemitism in their conference. Antisemitism has fueled atrocities throughout history and it's inconceivable they will not act to condemn it!"[8]

Republicans, and some Jews, argued that the failure to act more forcefully against Omar, for example, removing her from the influential House Foreign Affairs Committee, was normalizing antisemitism at the highest level of American politics and would seep into other parts of society as it already has on college campuses.[9]

---

[4] "Democratic Leadership Statement on Anti-Semitic Comments of Congresswoman Ilhan Omar," Nancy Pelosi, Speaker of the House, (February 11, 2019), https://www.speaker.gov/newsroom/21119/. Accessed July 25, 2019.

[5] Lindsey McPherson, "House Democratic leaders, chairmen criticize Omar for 'anti-Semitic trope,'" *Roll Call*, (February 11, 2019).

[6] Rahm Emanuel, "I've Faced the Charge of Dual Loyalty," *The Atlantic,* (March 7, 2019).

[7] "Rep. Pressley Issues Statement in Support of Rep. Omar," Press Release, US Congresswoman Ayanna Pressley, (March 6, 2019).

[8] Natalie Andrews and Kristina Peterson, "House Democrats Split Over Measure Tied to Ilhan Omar's Comments," *Wall Street Journal*, (March 6, 2019).

[9] See, for example, Mort Klein, "Morton Klein: Democratic Party Fails to Condemn Antisemitic Democrats," *Breitbart*, (March 21, 2019) and Victoria Albert, "Trump: Ilhan Omar Should Resign from House or Foreign Affairs Committee Over Controversial Israel Tweets," *Daily Beast*, (February 12, 2019).

Democrats responded by talking about the broader problems of racism and violence in America and attributing some of the blame to the president.

Omar continued to enrage friends and foes alike. In January 2019, for example, Omar compared Israel to Iran and said, "We still uphold it as a democracy in the Middle East. I almost chuckle because I know that if we see that any other society we would criticize it, call it out." She also said she was upset that the US did not have "an equal approach" when dealing with Israel and the Palestinians and was aggravated by America's pro-Israel bias. She also made demonstrably false statements, such as "Israel institute[s] laws that recognize it as a Jewish state and does not recognize the other religions that are living in it."[10]

Meanwhile, Tlaib also proved to be a lightning rod for critics of the Democrats. On her first day in office, Tlaib displayed a map with a note posted over Israel that read "Palestine."[11] She also expressed the popular antisemitic canard that Jews have dual loyalty and care more about Israel than the US. "They forgot what country they represent," Tlaib tweeted in reference to supporters of anti-boycott legislation. "This is the US where boycotting is a right & part of our historical fight for freedom & equality."[12] Later, she claimed the comments were not directed at Jewish members.

Tlaib also provoked Jewish ire with this comment in May:

> There's always kind of a calming feeling when I think of the tragedy of the Holocaust, that it was my ancestors—Palestinians—who lost their land and some lost their lives, their livelihood, their human dignity, their existence, in many ways, has been wiped out … in the name of trying to create a safe haven for Jews, post-Holocaust, post-tragedy and the horrific persecution of Jews across the world at that time. And I love the fact that it was my ancestors that provided that in many ways.[13]

While much of the uproar over her comment focused on whether she was minimizing the Holocaust by saying she had a "calming feeling" when she thought about it, her falsification of history was undeniable.

In the same interview where she mentioned the Holocaust, Tlaib expressed her support for a one-state solution. This, of course, means Israel must disappear and be replaced by a state based on "equality" where no one is oppressed and everyone "can feel free and safe."

Omar later retweeted a *New York Times* op-ed that suggested Jesus was a Palestinian, which Rabbi Abraham Cooper, associate and director of the Global Social Action Agenda at the Simon Wiesenthal Center, called "grotesque."[14] The

---

[10] Lukas Mikelionis, "Rep. Ilhan Omar slammed for saying she 'chuckles' when Israel is called a democracy, compares it to Iran," *Fox News*, (January 31, 2019).

[11] Aaron Bandler, "Rep. Tlaib's D.C. Office Map Has 'Palestine' Sticky Note Over Israel," *Jewish Journal*, (January 3, 2019).

[12] @Rashida   Tlaib,   Twitter,   January   6,   2019,   https://twitter.com/rashidatlaib/status/1082095303325609984?lang=en Accessed July 29, 2019.

[13] Allison Kaplan Sommer, "Tlaib Says She Is Humbled Her Ancestors Provided 'Safe Haven' for Jews After Holocaust," *Haaretz*, (May 11, 2019).

[14] Aaron Bandler, "Wiesenthal Center: 'Grotesque' for Omar, NYT to Say Jesus Was Palestinian," *Jewish Journal*, (April 22, 2019).

Times subsequently issued a correction: "Because of an editing error, an article last Saturday referred incorrectly to Jesus's background. While he lived in an area that later came to be known as Palestine, Jesus was a Jew who was born in Bethlehem."[15]

Defenders of Omar and Tlaib adopted a new strategy—accusing their critics of inciting violence and putting the congresswomen's lives in danger. One of the first examples followed the uproar over antisemitic remarks by Rep. Omar. Senator Kirsten Gillibrand (D-NY) admitted that Omar may have used antisemitic tropes but said her detractors "should not be using Islamophobic language and imagery that incites violence."

A few weeks later, after Omar's comment that "some people did something" on 9/11 set off another firestorm, she accused her critics of engaging in "dangerous incitement." Senator Elizabeth Warren (D-MA) defended her and accused Trump of "inciting violence against a sitting congresswoman" when he denounced her.

When Rabbi Shmuley Boteach took out a full-page ad in *New York Times* pointing out the speciousness of Tlaib's comment that Palestinians lost their land, dignity, and lives "in the name of trying to create a safe haven for Jews, post the Holocaust," one of the most vitriolic critics of Israel, James Zogby, supported Tlaib's position and tweeted, "It's not an ad, it's incitement."[16]

4.1.1 Bipartisanship Continues

While the new members of the House provoked controversy, they had no impact on legislation proposed to strengthen the US-Israel relationship. Support for Israel remains bipartisan, with both parties believing in strategic cooperation, maintaining Israel's qualitative military edge and generally backing its position regarding its Arab neighbors. In 2018, for example, Congress approved the terms of the 2016 Memorandum of Understanding which promised Israel a record $38 billion in military aid over 10 years.

While Omar and Tlaib became the first House members to openly support BDS, 398 members voted for a resolution opposing the global boycott movement against Israel in July 2019. No one spoke in opposition to the resolution during the floor debate. Though far weaker than legislation adopted in the Senate, which would make it illegal under federal statute to boycott Israel and grant federal protection to state and local governments that refuse to invest in or contract with companies which boycott Israel, the vote put the House on record as condemning the boycott.[17]

---

[15] Eric V Copage, "As a Black Child in Los Angeles, I Couldn't Understand Why Jesus Had Blue Eyes," *New York Times*, (April 19, 2019).

[16] Shaked Karabelnicoff, "Boteach's NYT Ad Skewered On Twitter For Attacking Rashida Tlaib," *Jerusalem Post*, (June 5, 2019).

[17] "House Passes Resolution Opposing Boycott Against Israel," Jewish Virtual Library, https://www.jewishvirtuallibrary.org/house-passes-resolution-opposing-boycott-against-israel. Accessed July 28, 2019.

The House also passed the US-Israel Cooperation Enhancement and Regional Security Act, which authorized increasing military aid to Israel to $38 billion over 10 years and added another $55 million for other cooperative programs. It also expands existing cooperation in several areas, including cyber security, industrial research, space, desalination, post-traumatic stress and food security.[18]

The Palestinian International Terrorism Support Prevention Act was also adopted with bipartisan support. This legislation imposes sanctions on those who support Palestinian terrorist groups such as Hamas and Palestinian Islamic Jihad. The bill also calls on the administration to cut off and sanction international networks of support for terrorist groups like Hamas and Islamic Jihad.[19]

Senate action and the president's signature were still needed for these bills to become law; nevertheless, they sent a strong signal that the US Congress, and specifically the Democratic-controlled House, have not wavered in support of Israel.

One other piece of legislation provoked controversy from both Israelis and Palestinians. The Anti-Terrorism Clarification Act was passed unanimously in the House and Senate in 2018. This law was designed to allow American victims of terrorism to sue countries receiving US foreign aid in American courts over alleged complicity in "acts of war."[20] The legislation was prompted by the decision of a circuit court to throw out a judgement against the PLO due to a lack of jurisdiction. The Palestinians subsequently said they would not accept any US aid and Israelis worried this would threaten security cooperation with the Palestinian Authority. Congress subsequently was considering amending the law to allow security and humanitarian assistance for the Palestinians.

4.2   Iran

For the Israeli government, the threat from Iran is the top priority. The Netanyahu government was elated when Trump pulled the US out of the nuclear deal negotiated by his predecessor (the JCPOA) and has cheered on the administration's imposition of sanctions aimed at exerting "maximum pressure" to bring Iran back to the negotiating table.

Over the past year, a variety of new sanctions were imposed on Iranian officials, government entities, and individuals, in addition to companies and individuals outside Iran doing business with the Islamic Republic or aiding its military efforts. The administration targeted the iron, steel, aluminum, copper and petroleum industries. Despite warnings it would provoke violence against American assets, the

---

[18] "US-Israel Cooperation Enhancement and Regional Security Act (H.R. 1837)," AIPAC Bill Summary, (March 2019).

[19] Omri Nahmias, "House Passes Bill That Calls To Sanction Palestinian Terror Groups," *Jerusalem Post*, (July 25, 2019).

[20] Yolande Knell, "US stops all aid to Palestinians in West Bank and Gaza, *BBC News*, (February 1, 2019).

administration also designated the Islamic Revolutionary Guards Corps as a Foreign Terrorist Organization.

Proponents of the deal had argued the US could not successfully impose unilateral sanctions; however, they were proven wrong as governments and businesses were given the choice of trading with Iran or doing business with the US. Not surprisingly, Iran was the loser.

To give an example of some of the impact of the sanctions:

- Volkswagen AG agreed to end almost all its business in Iran. Other German companies, Adidas AG, and Daimler AG, have also said they will scale back or abandon their activities in Iran.[21]
- Despite Berlin's pledge to keep the Iranian nuclear deal alive, German banks began refusing to process payments from Iran. Only 40–50 of Germany's 900 cooperative banks and scores of Austrian banks are still processing payments linked to Iranian deals.[22]
- South Korea's Hyundai Engineering & Construction company scrapped a $521 million deal to build a petrochemical complex in Iran.[23]
- Germany's largest telecom company, Deutsche Telekom, reportedly cut off phone and internet service to Iran's Bank Melli, which is accused of funneling money to terrorist groups.[24]
- The Chinese Bank of Kunlun Co. told its clients in April 2019 it was ceasing transfers with Iran. Huawei, the world's second-largest smartphone maker, laid off most of its Iranian staff and Lenovo, the world's largest computer manufacturer, "banned its Dubai-based distributors from selling to Iran after a warning from the US Treasury Department."[25]
- On March 25, 2019, France announced that it would halt flights to and from French airports by Iran's Mahan Air. The move followed Germany's January ban on flights by the Iranian airline.[26]

The Trump administration announced April 22, 2019, it would not renew waivers that allowed Italy, Greece, Taiwan, South Korea, Japan, China, Turkey, and India to buy Iranian oil without facing US sanctions. "This decision is intended to bring

---

[21] Nick Wadhams, "US Says VW to Leave Iran in Symbolic Win for Trump, *Bloomberg*, (September 19, 2018).

[22] Mathias Brüggmann, Elisabeth Atzler and Frank Wiebe, "German banks pull plug on trade with Iran," *Handelsblatt*, (October 2, 2018).

[23] "South Korea's Hyundai E&C cancels $521 million petrochemicals deal, cites Iran financing failure," Reuters, (October 29, 2018).

[24] Benjamin Weinthal, "Germany's largest telecom company stops service for Iranian 'terror bank,'" *Jerusalem Post*, (November 26, 2018).

[25] Benoit Faucon and Sune Engel Rasmussen, "Asian Companies Pull Back from Iran Amid US Pressure," *Wall Street Journal*, (April 24, 2019).

[26] Farzin Nadimi, "How Sanctions Are Affecting Iran's Airline Industry," Washington Institute, (April 17, 2019).

Iran's oil exports to zero, denying the regime its principal source of revenue," according to a statement issued by the White House.[27]

Despite fears by critics that oil prices would spike because of America's effort to block Iranian exports, the price declined below the level they were at prior to signing the nuclear accord. During the first 2 years of oil sanctions under President Barack Obama, prices spiked to more than $100 per barrel. By contrast, following the imposition of sanctions by President Trump, the price declined. Brent crude prices fell more than 20% from their 4-year peak of $86.74. After ending the waivers, the administration reassured the markets, "The US, Saudi Arabia and the United Arab Emirates, three of the world's great energy producers, along with our friends and allies, are committed to ensuring that global oil markets remain adequately supplied."[28] The prediction appeared to be accurate as the price of oil in July was around $55, and this was despite rising tensions in the Persian Gulf.

Still, the Europeans, hungry for business opportunities, and petrified of the possibility that Iran might pull out of the deal, have tried to create a mechanism to circumvent American sanctions and placate the Iranians. That mechanism, the Instrument for Supporting Trade Exchange (Instex) was designed to evade US sanctions by allowing goods to be bartered between Iranian companies and foreign ones without direct financial transactions or using the dollar. The US vigorously opposed its creation and reiterated the administration's position that "entities that continue to engage in sanctionable activity involving Iran risk severe consequences that could include losing access to the US financial system and the ability to do business with the United States or US companies."[29] The Iranians were not mollified either, as Iran's supreme leader Ayatollah Ali Khamenei dismissed the trade mechanism as a "bitter joke."[30]

The Europeans continued to defend the nuclear deal despite the failure of Iran to moderate its behavior. The EU agreed to impose its own sanctions at the beginning of January 2019 after proof was discovered of Iran's role in plots to assassinate dissidents on European soil.[31]

As the US ratcheted up pressure on Iran, the regime became increasingly belligerent and began to play a game of brinksmanship. According to Dennis Ross, the Iranians decided they could not simply wait for Trump to be defeated because of the impact sanctions were having on their economy. Their currency had already lost 60% of its value, inflation was soaring, and consumer goods were becoming scarcer

[27] Nick Wadhams, Glen Carey, and Margaret Talev, "Trump to Escalate Iran Feud by Ending Waivers; Oil Prices Climb," *Bloomberg*, (April 21, 2019).

[28] Nick Wadhams, Glen Carey, and Margaret Talev, "Trump to Escalate Iran Feud by Ending Waivers; Oil Prices Climb," *Bloomberg*, (April 21, 2019).

[29] Steven Erlanger, "3 European Nations Create Firm to Trade With Iran, but Will Anyone Use It?" *New York Times*, (January 31, 2019).

[30] "Iran leader dismisses Europe trade mechanism as 'bitter joke,'" *Daily Mail*, (March 21, 2019).

[31] Taylor Heyman, "EU agrees on sanctions against Iranian intelligence services," *The National*, (January 8, 2019); Raf Sanchez, "Iran hired criminals to assassinate dissidents in the Netherlands, Dutch government claims," *The Telegraph*, (January 9, 2019).

and provoking civil unrest. The situation was expected to get worse because the administration withdrew waivers granted to eight countries to buy Iranian oil, which was expected to reduce exports from approximately one million barrels a day to as little as 300,000 a day.[32]

Months before the announcement on the waivers, Iranian President Hassan Rouhani admitted, "Today the country is facing the biggest pressure and economic sanctions in the past 40 years."[33]

In an effort to impose costs on the US and its allies, and blackmail the Europeans to work harder to meet their demands to circumvent American sanctions, Iran sabotaged oil tankers, its Houthi allies in Yemen attacked Saudi targets, Iranian-backed Shia militias in Iraq fired missiles at bases where US forces are located and, on June 20, 2019, shot down an American drone.

After the downing of the drone, the administration prepared a retaliatory air strike that Trump called off 10 min before it was scheduled after a general told him that 150 people would probably die in the attack.[34]

As tensions mounted, talk of the possibility of war increased. As it did, the anti-semitic trope of blaming the Jews for pushing America into a conflict with Iran once again rose to the fore. Former Obama adviser Ben Rhodes claimed Netanyahu was pushing the US to confront Iran as did Democratic presidential candidate Tulsi Gabbard.[35] Another supporter of the nuclear agreement, the Brookings Institution's Bruce Riedel, wrote a piece headlined, "Don't let Israel and Saudi Arabia drag the US into another war."[36] The antisemitic Mondoweiss website ran a headline that claimed, "Israel wants the Trump administration to attack Iran, but US mainstream media ignores Netanyahu's instigating."[37] Mondoweiss apparently missed this NBC headline: "From Bolton To Bibi To Riyadh, Trump Faces Calls For Confronting Iran."[38] And, in the grand tradition of antisemitic conspiracy theories, Philip Giraldi, Executive Director of the Council for the National Interest, wrote:

> The United States is moving dangerously forward in what appears to be a deliberate attempt to provoke a war with Iran, apparently based on threat intelligence provided by Israel. The claims made by National Security Advisor John Bolton and by Secretary of State Mike Pompeo that there is solid evidence of Iran's intention to attack US forces in the Persian

[32] Dennis Ross, "Will Iran 'break out' for a nuclear weapon, and what can Trump do?" *The Hill*, (July 14, 2019).

[33] Thomas Erdbrink, "Iran Faces Worst Economic Challenge in 40 Years, President Says," *New York Times*, (January 30, 2019).

[34] Michael D. Shear, Helene Cooper and Eric Schmitt, "Trump Says He Was 'Cocked and Loaded' to Strike Iran, but Pulled Back," *New York Times*, (June 21, 2019).

[35] Seth J. Frantzman, "US Far Left And Far Right Blame Netanyahu For Trump's Iran Policy," *Jerusalem Post*, (May 19, 2019).

[36] Bruce Riedel, "Don't let Israel and Saudi Arabia drag the US into another war," *Daily Beast*, (May 14, 2019).

[37] James North, "Israel wants the Trump administration to attack Iran, but US mainstream media ignores Netanyahu's instigating," Mondoweiss, (May 6, 2019).

[38] "From Bolton To Bibi To Riyadh, Trump Faces Calls For Confronting Iran," *NBCnews*, (May 15, 2019).

Gulf region is almost certainly a fabrication, possibly deliberately contrived by Bolton and company in collaboration with Prime Minister Benjamin Netanyahu.[39]

Netanyahu did not call on the US to attack Iran; rather he continued to lobby for tougher measures to bring Iran back to the negotiating table to strengthen the nuclear deal by closing the loopholes and including the areas Obama omitted, such as Iran's production of ballistic missiles and sponsorship of terror. Israelis also had reason to be concerned if the US attacked Iran because of the possibility Hamas and Hezbollah might respond by launching missiles at Israel. Trump, however, appeared averse to a military confrontation, in part because he had campaigned on the promise to avoid foreign entanglements and to withdraw troops from the Middle East.

In addition to Iran's hostile acts, the regime ended all doubt about compliance with the nuclear deal by publicly announcing it planned to exceed the limit on the amount of enriched uranium it would stockpile and then declaring it would ignore the restrictions on uranium enrichment and increase the purity level from 3.67% to 5% with threats to go to 20%—the level it was at prior to the agreement—if the Europeans did not satisfy their demands to counter American sanctions.

Despite the violation of the accord, the EU announced it would not "snapback" sanctions as Obama had promised would occur in the event of Iranian transgressions. In an apparent bid to play for time to avoid further inflaming the situation, European Union foreign policy chief Federica Mogherini asserted that none of the signatories to the deal considered the breaches to be significant enough to act. "Technically all the steps that have been taken, and that we regret have been taken, are reversible," she said following a meeting of EU foreign ministers. "We invite Iran to reverse the steps and go back to full compliance."[40]

Before Trump's decision to withdraw from the agreement, Iran was already cheating (e.g., by refusing to allow inspections of its military sites—the places most likely to have nuclear research going on) and taking advantage of various loopholes (e.g., work on naval propulsion reactors). German intelligence services also revealed ongoing Iranian efforts to obtain materials for weapons of mass destruction. In addition, Israel disclosed Iran's secret trove of documents, proving that Iran lied about its past work on developing nuclear weapons and creating the suspicion that the materials were hidden so that the project could resume when the JCPOA expired, if not before.

In a speech to the UN in September 2018, Netanyahu said Israel had discovered a warehouse used to store nuclear equipment and material and that Iran had removed 15 kg of undeclared enriched uranium from the facility in August 2018. In July 2019, sources indicated the IAEA found evidence of radioactive materials in the

---

[39] Philip Giraldi, "Pandering to Israel Means War With Iran," Strategic Culture Foundation, (May 9, 2019).
[40] "Iran nuclear deal breaches not yet significant, EU says," BBC, (July 15, 2019).

warehouse, which would be a serious breach of the nuclear agreement, but the agency was not making the information public.[41]

For critics of the agreement, this was more proof of its flaws and the wisdom of Trump's decision to withdraw from the deal. Proponents, however, seemed unbothered by the disclosures. Former Secretary of State John Kerry, the architect of the deal, had reportedly advised the Iranians earlier to wait for Trump to leave office.[42] Given that several of the Democratic candidates announced they would rejoin the agreement, Iran has reason to hope for a return to the Obama policies. The Netanyahu government would see this as a disaster unless the agreement was modified.

4.3   No More Pretension of Evenhandedness

One of the marked changes in US-Israel relations from Obama to Trump has been the tone. While Obama and his top advisors were routinely critical of Israeli actions, particularly regarding settlements. Trump and his advisers have not publicly criticized Israel's behavior and have mostly applauded it.

The shift has been dramatic at the United Nations where Obama ended his term by abstaining on Security Council Resolution 2334 condemning Israeli settlements. Trump's ambassador to the UN, Nikki Haley, by contrast, was a vigorous and outspoken champion of Israel before resigning her post at the end of 2018. She is credited with devising a diplomatic strategy of "pairing initiatives hostile to Israel with US-led counter-initiatives that demand UN members hold the other side accountable for its part in the conflict," according to Michael Wilner. "Resolutions calling on the UN to condemn Hamas and Hezbollah, Haley charged, put members in an uncomfortable dilemma—forcing them either to change course or reveal their biases."[43]

Haley's performance at the UN has made her quite popular in the Jewish community, where she is now a sought-after speaker and viewed by some as a potential future presidential nominee they could support.[44] Haley's interim successor Jonathan Cohen has adopted a lower profile, but the administration has not retreated from its vigorous support for Israel. In February 2019, for example, the US blocked a UN resolution denouncing Israel for expelling international monitors from Hebron.[45] In July, the US blocked an attempt by Kuwait, Indonesia, and South Africa to get the

---

[41] Barak Ravid, "UN finds evidence of radioactive material in Iranian warehouse, Israeli officials say," Israel's *Channel 13 News*, (July 11, 2019).

[42] See, for example, editorial "Colluding with Iran," *Washington Times*, (September 17, 2018).

[43] Michael Wilner, "Top 10 Headlines of 2018: American Politics," *Jerusalem Post*, (December 30, 2018).

[44] "Jewish Groups Can't Get Enough Of Nikki Haley, 'Nikki For President!'" *Jerusalem Post*, (April 10, 2019).

[45] "US Blocks UN Resolution Denouncing Israeli Expulsion of Hebron Monitoring Group," Reuters, (February 7, 2019).

Security Council to condemn Israel's demolition of Palestinian homes built illegally on the outskirts of Jerusalem.[46]

Following his decision to recognize Jerusalem as Israel's capital and move the US embassy there from Tel Aviv, the president announced via tweet on March 21, 2019, that the US would recognize Israeli sovereignty over the Golan Heights upending another longstanding US position. "After 52 years it is time for the United States to fully recognize Israel's Sovereignty over the Golan Heights, which is of critical strategic and security importance to the State of Israel and Regional Stability," Trump tweeted.[47]

The Golan decision was welcomed by Netanyahu and most supporters of Israel but, like the Jerusalem decision, sent the foreign policy establishment into apoplexy. The US had resisted taking this step since Israel captured the area in 1973 because of the expectation that a Syrian-Israeli peace agreement would involve a compromise on the Golan Heights. "You don't change 52 years of US policy in a tweet, 4 days before you're about to see the Israeli prime minister at the White House and 21 days before he's running for reelection," said former State Department official Aaron David Miller. He added that past administrations never considered such a move. "The issue was not recognizing Israeli sovereignty of Golan but trying to facilitate any number of Israeli prime ministers' efforts to broker an agreement between Israel and Syria," Miller said.[48]

Trump, however, recognized the practical reality that while Israel once considered withdrawing from part of the Golan Heights in exchange for peace with Syria, the civil war in Syria had at least for the foreseeable future erased that possibility. The threats of an unstable Syria, Iranian efforts to establish a base there and the presence of Hezbollah and Islamist forces near the border made it clear that any compromise on the Golan would constitute an unreasonable risk to Israel's security (something opponents of prior negotiations had long maintained).

As Miller noted, the decision was also controversial because the announcement came just 3 weeks before Israel's April election. Although Trump denied it, the announcement was viewed as an effort to help Netanyahu.[49]

Much like his "maximum pressure" campaign against Iran, President Trump has used a stick rather than carrots in his approach to the Palestinians, continuing to punish the Palestinians for their unwillingness to change their policies or enter negotiations. The passage of the Taylor Force Act in March 2018 required the administration to cut aid to the Palestinian Authority if it continued to pay convicted terrorists and their families (the Knesset passed a similar law to deduct terrorists'

---

[46] "US Blocks UN Rebuke of Israeli Demolition of Palestinian Home in East Jerusalem," Reuters, (July 25, 2019).

[47] Jeremy Diamond and Jennifer Hansler, "Trump says it's time for US to recognize 'Israel's Sovereignty over the Golan Heights,'" CNN, (March 22, 2019).

[48] Adam Taylor, "No president has recognized Israel's control of the Golan Heights. Trump changed that with a tweet," *Washington Post*, (March 22, 2019).

[49] Loveday Morris, "Trump's statement on Golan Heights sparks accusations of election meddling in Israel," *Washington Post*, (March 22, 2019).

salaries from Palestinian taxes collected by Israel)[50] and the Palestinians responded by increasing the payments.[51]

The administration subsequently cut $200 million in aid to the Palestinian Authority[52] and later announced it would no longer contribute to the UN Relief and Works Agency (UNRWA).[53] The administration also announced it was ordering the closure of the mission of the Palestinian Liberation Organization because "the PLO has not taken steps to advance the start of direct and meaningful negotiations with Israel," condemned the US peace plan, and was seeking an investigation of Israel by the International Criminal Court.[54]

In a conference call with Jewish leaders soon after the aid cuts, the President said, "I stopped massive amounts of money that we were paying to the Palestinians and the Palestinian leaders. We were—the United States was paying them tremendous amounts of money. And I'd say, you'll get money, but we're not paying you until we make a deal. If we don't make a deal, we're not paying."[55]

In February 2019, the administration announced the US would cut all aid to the Palestinians. That decision was made after the Anti-Terrorism Clarification Act came into effect. The US had been providing $60 million for Palestinian security forces. Israel supported the funding because cooperation between Israeli and Palestinian security agencies was viewed as one of the few positive relationships and one that helped both sides keep order and prevent the establishment of Hamas terror cells in the West Bank. The Palestinian Authority said it would not accept any American aid, however, because of a fear of lawsuits.[56]

Netanyahu also upset many officials on both sides of the aisle when he appealed to right-wing voters during his election campaign by declaring his intention to annex the settlements if reelected. Asked if he would annex only the settlement blocs, which most Israelis—and Palestinian negotiators—have agreed would be part of Israel in any two-state solution, Netanyahu said "yes" and added, "I'm going to apply sovereignty, but I don't distinguish between settlement blocs and the isolated settlement points, because from my perspective every such point of settlement is Israeli," he said. "We have a responsibility as the Israeli government. I won't

[50] "Knesset passes law to deduct terrorists' salaries from tax funds," *Israel Hayom*, (July 3, 2018).

[51] Abbas Keeps on Defying US, Says PA Will Fund "Pay to Slay" Program Until Last Penny," *The Tower*, (July 25, 2018).

[52] David Brunnstrom, "Trump cuts more than $200 million in US aid to Palestinians," Reuters, (August 24, 2019).

[53] Karen DeYoung, Ruth Eglash and Hazem Balousha, "US ends aid to United Nations agency supporting Palestinian refugees," *Washington Post*, (August 31, 2018).

[54] "US officially announces closure of PLO mission in Washington," *Times of Israel*, (September 10, 2018).

[55] "Trump: Iran lost its mojo since I quit nuke deal; I did a great thing for Israel," *Times of Israel*, (September 6, 2018).

[56] Stephen Farrell and Maayan Lubell, "Trump administration cuts all aid to Palestinians in the occupied West Bank and Gaza," Reuters, (February 1, 2019).

uproot anyone and I won't place them under Palestinian sovereignty. I'll look out for everyone."[57]

This prompted members of Congress to introduce resolutions opposing annexation of the West Bank and calling for a two-state solution to the Israeli-Palestinian conflict.[58] Even some of Israel's staunchest supporters spoke out. For example, a statement by Reps. Eliot Engel (D-NY), Nita Lowey (D-NY), Ted Deutch, (D-FL) and Brad Schneider (D-IL) said: "As strong, life-long supporters of Israel, a US-Israel relationship rooted in our shared values, and the two-state solution, we are greatly concerned by the possibility of Israel taking unilateral steps to annex the West Bank."[59]

South Carolina Republican Lindsey Graham, another staunch friend of Israel, cosponsored a resolution with Chris Van Hollen (D-MD) calling for a two-state solution. "I can't envision a one-state solution," Graham said. "It won't work. I mean, you'd have to disenfranchise the Palestinians, (and) that won't work. If you let them vote, as one state, they'll overwhelm the Israelis. That won't work. So if you want to have a democratic, secure Jewish state, I think you have to have two states...".[60]

The administration reaction was more muted in part because officials did not want to comment just days before the Israeli election. Hence Secretary of State Mike Pompeo refused to answer questions on the subject.[61]

When asked what the US would do if Israel unilaterally annexed the West Bank, US ambassador to Israel David Friedman said, "We really don't have a view until we understand how much, on what terms, why does it make sense, why is it good for Israel, why is it good for the region, why does it not create more problems than it solves." Friedman added, "These are all things that we'd want to understand, and I don't want to prejudge."[62] Friedman also said, however, "Under certain circumstances, I think Israel has the right to retain some, but unlikely all, of the West Bank," which supporters of settlements and their opponents interpreted as an endorsement of Netanyahu's position when, in fact, the substance of the remark was

---

[57] David M. Halbfinger, "Netanyahu Vows to Start Annexing West Bank, in Bid to Rally the Right," *New York Times*, (April 6, 2019).

[58] Barak Ravid, "Senate draft resolution challenges Netanyahu on West Bank annexation," Axios, (June 6, 2019).

[59] Ron Kampeas, "Some of Israel's best American friends worried by Netanyahu's annexation talk," JTA, (April 13, 2019).

[60] Eric H. Yoffie, "Trump Ally Lindsey Graham: America's Most Unlikely Campaigner Against Israeli Annexation," *Haaretz*, (June 19, 2019).

[61] Amir Tibon, "Trump Admin Refuses to Discuss Netanyahu's Remarks on Annexing West Bank," *Haaretz*, (April 8, 2019).

[62] Ron Kampeas, "David Friedman gave Netanyahu half a nod for West Bank annexation. What happens next?" JTA, (June 11, 2019).

consistent with longstanding US policy as well as UN Security Council Resolution 242.[63]

4.4   The "Ultimate Deal"

The Palestinians dismissed the Trump administration early on and decided it would have nothing to do with it. This was a case of cutting off their nose to spite their face as it gained them no sympathy. In fact, the world, especially their fellow Arabs, were showing increasing signs of weariness with the Palestinian issue. No one was rushing to their defense or to replace American funding.

The administration's three top officials working on the much-anticipated peace plan—Jared Kushner, David Friedman, and Jason Greenblatt—are seen by the Palestinians (and others) as unabashed supporters of Israel. Friedman, America's ambassador to Israel, had been a supporter of the settlements before entering the government and his statements and behavior, such as using a sledgehammer at the unveiling of a new archaeological site in Jerusalem's City of David, which lies underneath the Palestinian neighborhood of Silwan, reinforced the view among Palestinians that he is not an honest broker.[64]

The unveiling of the peace initiative was repeatedly delayed as Kushner claimed to be refining it. The plan to release it after Israel's April election had to be shelved when Netanyahu failed to form a government and new elections had to be scheduled for September. The administration does not want to present the plan until a new government is in place, which would probably be at least several weeks after the election, which would mean delaying it until near the end of 2019. At that point, the administration may be reluctant to forward a plan that will surely be contentious just prior to the 2020 US election.

Meanwhile, the administration did release what it figured would be the less-controversial economic component of its plan at a conference in Bahrain in July 2019. Kushner explained the rationale: "One who is more hopeful and sees an opportunity for his or her family will put energy into pursuing opportunity, instead of blaming others for their current misfortune." He said, "That is why agreeing on an economic pathway forward is a necessary precondition to what has previously been an unsolvable political situation."[65]

Preparations for the conference got off to an inauspicious start, however, when the Palestinians announced they were boycotting the meeting, arguing that the US was essentially trying to "buy off Palestinian political aspirations by financial

[63] Ron Kampeas, "Friedman Gave Netanyahu Half A Nod For West Bank Annexation," JTA, (June 13, 2019).

[64] Raphael Ahren, "US envoy Friedman defends sledgehammering open controversial archaeological site," *Times of Israel*, (July 1, 2019).

[65] Herb Keinon, "Kushner In Bahrain: Economic Prosperity Is Pathway To Mideast Peace," *Jerusalem Post*, (June 26, 2019).

means."[66] Without Palestinian participation, it became politically impossible to invite the Israelis (though some business people attended) so the conference was held without the parties involved.

The Arab states ignored the Palestinians' call to boycott the conference, though some did send lower-level officials. Palestinian businesspeople were also warned not to attend by the Palestinian Authority. The 15 who did were arrested, threatened and harassed when they returned.[67]

Despite being impoverished and almost completely dependent on foreign aid, the Palestinians thumbed their noses at the offer of investments worth billions of dollars in part because they would be "administered by a multilateral development bank" rather than the corruption-laced Palestinian Authority to ensure that "all the Palestinians—not just the wealthy and connected—share in the benefits of peace."

The 38-page "Peace to Prosperity" plan calls on Arab states to supply $50 billion in development aid to the Palestinians.[68] Two of the goals are to double the GDP of the Palestinians and create one million jobs over the next 10 years. The funding includes money to create economic opportunities for women and grants for a variety of projects, from building hospitals to promoting tourism to upgrading the Gaza power plant. It also seeks to encourage regional integration and cooperation.

While the Palestinians rejected the initiative out of hand, the Israelis had one major objection, the $5 billion proposal for a highway and railway between the West Bank and Gaza Strip. They fear this indicates the administration sees the two areas as a single territorial unit, possibly a Palestinian state (though the administration has never said this was part of their vision) and would pose a security threat. This is similar, however, to the proposal Prime Minister Ehud Barak agreed to in 2000 and other two-state plans have included a link of some kind between Gaza and the West Bank.

Greenblatt tried to reassure the Israelis during the conference when he said, "We are not suggesting any corridor whatsoever that doesn't completely make Israel comfortable that it will not be a danger to Israel."[69]

None of the Arab states jumped at the opportunity to put up the money, especially given that the US did not offer any monetary contribution. Nevertheless, Ahmed Charai argued that "Kushner's great insight is that economic development should come first and shape the discussion for a political solution. His second insight is that a single 'grand bargain' is not realistic; that an evolutionary and gradual approach that builds trust along with economic milestones is more likely to

---

[66] David Makovsky, "Jared Kushner's all-or-nothing mistake in the Middle East," *Washington Post*, (July 1, 2019).

[67] Khaled Abu Toameh, "Hebron Businessman Who Attended Bahrain: I'm Afraid For My Life," *Jerusalem Post*, (July 1, 2019).

[68] "Peace to Prosperity," The White House, Undated, released in July 2019.

[69] Barak Ravid, "Netanyahu wary of West Bank-Gaza corridor in Trump peace plan," Axios, (July 16, 2019).

succeed."[70] Others argued, however, that it was pointless to focus on economics without fulfilling Palestinians' political demands.[71]

4.5   Syria

Throughout the Syrian civil war, Israel has been actively engaged in proactive measures to prevent Iran from establishing bases in Syria, to prevent Hezbollah and other hostile forces from being ensconced near Israel's northern border, and to prevent the transfer of weapons to Lebanon for Hezbollah. The US has tacitly supported Israel's bombing campaign targeting Iranian bases, arms depots, and convoys smuggling weapons.

Trump shocked and alarmed Israel, however, when he announced in December 2018 he was planning to withdraw all US forces from Syria because, he said, ISIS had been defeated. Israelis feared this would clear the way for Iran to strengthen its position in the country and allow its proxies to pose a greater threat to Israel. Trump was convinced to reverse the decision after pressure from a bipartisan group of lawmakers.[72] He subsequently announced he was sending 1500 additional troops to the region—not to Syria—to reinforce security for existing American and allied forces, and to deter attacks from Iran.[73]

The US was also working with Israel to remove all Iranian forces from Syria. In June 2019, an unprecedented trilateral conference of Israeli, Russian, and American national security advisers met in Jerusalem to discuss countering Iran. Russia held the key because of its dominant role in protecting the Assad regime in Syria and its good relations with both Israel and Iran.

Though Russian adviser Nikolai Patrushev said Israeli airstrikes in Syria were "undesirable," Russia has not interfered and reportedly has an unwritten agreement that it will not do so if none of its interests are threatened. Still, he rejected the American and Israeli view that Iran represents "the main threat to regional security." He made no promises about encouraging or forcing Iranian forces to leave Syria. He said that he was aware of Israel's security concerns and was discussing the issue with the Iranians but emphasized that Iran "was and remains our ally and partner."[74]

---

[70] Ahmed Charai, "Kushner's Middle East Plan Wins Its First Round," *The National Interest*, (June 29, 2019).

[71] Loveday Morris, "Kushner presents vision of a Middle East at peace but no details how to get there," *Washington Post*, (June 25, 2019).

[72] Anne Gearan and Karoun Demirjian, "Trump vowed to leave Syria in a tweet. Now, with a Sharpie, he agreed to stay," Washington Post, (March 5, 2019).

[73] Lucas Tomlinson and Alex Pappas, "Trump approves Pentagon plan to send more US troops to Middle East," Fox News, (May 24, 2019).

[74] Judah Ari Gross, "In trilateral Jerusalem summit, Russia sides with Iran, against Israel and US," *Times of Israel*, (June 25, 2019).

4.6 One Source of Tension

Under Trump, unlike past administrations, the US has found little to complain about Israel's policies. One exception is a deal Israel signed with China. In 2015, Shanghai International Ports Group won a tender to operate the newly constructed container terminal at Haifa for 25 years. As Dale Aluf, observed, "all seemed kosher" until US-China relations grew tense in 2018 and the "Americans started to ask questions about the Haifa terminals and the potential implications it has for both theirs, and Israel's national security." Since Haifa port is used by the US Sixth Fleet, the US expressed concern about the possibility of Chinese espionage.[75]

In recent years, Israel has increasingly turned to Asia for new markets and China has become Israel's second leading trade partner. This is not the first time, however, that Israel's efforts to develop closer relations has run afoul of American security interests. In 2000, Israel agreed to sell China Phalcon radar planes, a deal worth about $250 million, but objections by members of Congress and the Clinton administration prompted Israel to cancel the deal.[76]

According to Assaf Orion, Israel finds itself trying to balance "between tapping China's considerable potential for the advancement of its economy against management of the entailed risks: both direct, to Israel's own security, and indirect, to its strategic relations with the US, a central pillar of Israel's national security."[77] This is likely to be an ongoing issue for years to come as America and China compete for influence.

4.7 Public Opinion

New polls released in 2018–2019 regarding American public opinion toward Israel provoked a mixture of hysteria and misinformation typified by these headlines in *Haaretz* and the *Times of Israel*, respectively: "New Poll Shows Support for Israel Plummeting Among US Liberals, Millennials and Women"[78] and "New poll: Americans' support for Israel falls to lowest point in a decade."[79]

[75] Dale Aluf, "Israel's China challenge," *Times of Israel*, (July 12, 2019).

[76] Jane Perlezjuly, "Israel Drops Plan To Sell Air Radar To China Military," *New York Times*, (July 13, 2000).

[77] Assaf Orion, "Tectonics, Techno-economics, and National Security: The Strategic Clash between the United States and China, and Implications for Israel," INSS Insight No. 1192, (July 15, 2019).

[78] Chemi Shalev, "New Poll Shows Support for Israel Plummeting Among US Liberals, Millennials and Women," *Haaretz*, (October 26, 2018).

[79] Eric Cortellessa, "New poll: Americans' support for Israel falls to lowest point in a decade," *Times of Israel*, (March 6, 2019).

Overall support for Israel fell from its all-time high of 64 to 59%—its lowest point since 2009—but remained well above the historical average of 48% since the Six-Day War. Support since 2000, has also been higher than previous decades.[80]

In addition, 69% of Americans said that they had a favorable opinion of Israel, ranking it eighth behind Canada, the UK, Japan, Germany, France, India, and South Korea. By contrast, just 21% of Americans had a favorable opinion of the Palestinian Authority, placing it near the bottom of the rankings with Afghanistan, Iraq, Iran, Syria, and North Korea.

Most concern has focused on an alleged decline in Democratic support for Israel. Yes, 76% of Republicans compared to 43% of Democrats were more sympathetic toward Israel than the Palestinians; however, since 1993, Democratic support for Israel has averaged only 46%. In the mid-70s, the figure was even lower. Democratic support for the Palestinians, however, has increased to an average of 20% since 1993 (30% this year), and that is more than double the percentage of Republicans.

Support for Israel among liberal Democrats has remained consistent for a decade. When asked their attitude toward Israel, for example, 58% of liberal Democrats and 66% of moderate/conservative Democrats had a favorable view, and only 9% viewed Israel very unfavorably.

The real story is the growth of Republican support for Israel. Back in the mid-1970s, Republicans were more supportive than Democrats, but their numbers were in the 40s and the partisan gap was virtually zero. Since 1993, however, Republicans have averaged 67% with a partisan gap of 22% points (it was 33% points this year).

There has also been a lot of discussion about declining support for Israel among younger Americans. That notion is bolstered by the data on sympathy for Israel and the Palestinians across age groups: 18–34 (47–29%), 35–54 (57–21%), and 55+ (70–15%).

This should not be surprising, however, if put into historical context. Older Americans are typically more sympathetic to Israel. The disparity across age groups may appear alarming; however, if past trends persist, today's young people will become more supportive of Israel over time. Of course, Jews being Jews, that "if" is magnified when we read exaggerated accounts of the atmosphere toward Israel and Jews on college campuses.

Gallup analyst Lydia Saad concluded:

> Americans' overall views toward Israel and the Palestinian Authority have changed little in the past year, with roughly seven in 10 viewing Israel very or mostly favorably and two in 10 viewing the Palestinian Authority in the same terms…. While liberal Democrats are no less favorable toward Israel today than they have been over the past two decades, they have grown more favorable toward the Palestinians.

---

[80] "American Public Opinion Polls," Jewish Virtual Library, https://www.jewishvirtuallibrary.org/american-public-opinion-polls. Accessed July 29, 2019.

4.8 Israeli-American Jewish Ties Fray

Relations between Israeli and American Jews remained a major topic of conversation. The Reform and Conservative movements stayed angry over how their Israeli branches were treated and the non-recognition of their rabbis, weddings, and conversions. Liberal Jews more broadly were upset by Netanyahu's decision to renege on an agreement to open an egalitarian prayer space at the Western Wall, his close relationship with President Trump, and his seeming disinterest in peace with the Palestinians.

The differences have grown to the point where the *New York Times* headlined a story, "American Jews and Israeli Jews Are Headed for a Messy Breakup." The paper quoted from a letter to the Israeli government from Rabbi Steven Wernick, chief executive of the United Synagogue of Conservative Judaism, the umbrella organization of the Conservative movement in North America, which said: "I do not believe we can talk about a 'gap' between Israel and the Diaspora. It is now a 'canyon.'"[81]

The disdain on the part of some Israelis for non-Orthodox Jews particularly rankles American Jews. Following the massacre at the Tree of Life Synagogue in Pittsburgh in October 2018, Israel's Ashkenazi chief rabbi would not describe the site as a synagogue, calling the Conservative shul "a place with a profound Jewish flavor."[82]

Conservative rabbis were outraged a few months earlier when a Conservative rabbi in Israel, Dov Haiyun, was arrested for conducting a non-sanctioned wedding in Haifa. He was released, but the incident raised the possibility other rabbis could be prosecuted for performing marriages without government authority, which means the sanction of the Orthodox Chief Rabbinate.[83]

More American Jewish anger followed comments in July 2019 by Israeli Education Minister Rafi Peretz, a rabbi from the ultranationalist Jewish Home Party, who said that intermarriage among American Jews is "like a second Holocaust." In a comment not directed specifically at American Jews, which still angered many, he later said, conversion therapy could change the sexual orientation of gay men and lesbians.[84]

---

[81] Jonathan Weisman, "American Jews and Israeli Jews Are Headed for a Messy Breakup," *New York Times*, (January 4, 2019).

[82] Judy Maltz, "9 low points in Israel-Jewish Diaspora relations in 2018," *Haaretz*, (December 20, 2018).

[83] Ben Sales, "Why Israel nabbed a rabbi for performing a wedding, and why people are incensed," *Times of Israel*, (July 21, 2018).

[84] Ruth Eglash, "Israel's education minister sparks outrage after advocating gay conversion therapy," *Washington Post*, (July 14, 2019).

Though Israeli officials are well-aware of the conflicts with American Jews, much of the Israeli public is oblivious. For example, less than 30% of Israelis are familiar with the Western Wall compromise.[85]

Since relatively few Israelis identify with Reform or Conservative Judaism, they are not particularly moved by protests from the leaders of the movements in America. They also have little patience for American Jews—unless they have similar opinions—who pontificate about matters of peace and security from the comfort of their homes 6000 miles away where they pay no Israeli taxes, face no threat from terrorists, and do not have to send their children to the military.

For many years, Israeli officials adhered to the unwritten rule to refrain from criticizing their government while abroad. That convention broke down in the 1980s when, first, Labor Party officials and, later, Likudniks began to come to the US when they were in the opposition and encourage American Jews to speak out against the governing party. This emboldened American Jewry, which had typically observed the convention of avoiding public criticism of the Israeli government. This remains the policy of most establishment organizations but is ignored by others.

American Jewry was generally supportive of Israel's actions in Gaza, Lebanon, and Syria, but liberals, especially, were unhappy with the lack of engagement with the Palestinians. Netanyahu's campaign promise to annex the settlements was welcomed by right-wing Jews, but widely condemned by others. While this was expected from left-wing organizations such as J Street, it was more unusual to hear criticism from "establishment" organizations, eight of which wrote to President Trump warning that annexation would "create intense divisions" in the US and "greater conflict between Israelis and Palestinians."[86]

Prior to the April 2019 election, Netanyahu pressured the right-wing Bayit Yehudi party to unite with the even more extreme Otzma Yehudit party, which is composed of followers of Meir Kahane who support annexation of the disputed territories and call for removing "the enemies of Israel from our country," a reference to Israeli Arabs.

Establishment American Jewish organizations are typically reticent to publicly criticize any Israeli prime minister, or comment on Israeli elections, but Netanyahu's action crossed an invisible line. The Anti-Defamation League ADL, for example, said, "There should be no room for racism & no accommodation for intolerance in Israel or any democracy. ADL previously has spoken out on hate-filled rhetoric of leaders of the Otzma Yehudit Party. It is troubling that they are being legitimized by this union."[87] The American Jewish Committee (AJC) said, "The views of Otzma Yehudit are reprehensible. They do not reflect the core values that are the very foundation of the State of Israel."[88] AIPAC said it agreed with AJC and that it "has a

---

[85] Maayan Jaffe-Hoffman, "Israelis Are 'Ignorant' Of World Jewry And Its Concerns—New Survey," *Jerusalem Post*, (July 22, 2019).

[86] Ron Kampeas, "Some of Israel's best American friends worried by Netanyahu's annexation talk," JTA, (April 13, 2019).

[87] Jonathan Greenblatt, @JGreenblattADL, (February 25, 2019).

[88] "AJC Statement on Otzma Yehudit Party," AJC, (February 21, 2019).

longstanding policy not to meet with members of this racist and reprehensible party" while Malcolm Hoenlein, Executive Vice Chairman of the Conference of Presidents of Major American Jewish Organizations, called the development "very disturbing."[89]

As Batya Ungar-Sargon observed, "Partnering with avowed racists, it turns out, was a step too far, even for American Jewish organizations devoted to hawkish Israel policy. It's not just American Jews, either. After years of an increasing divide, American Jews were joined by our Israeli counterparts, many of whom spoke up vociferously against Netanyahu."[90]

While the close relationship between Trump and Netanyahu was cheered by more conservative members of the pro-Israel community and Israelis, it upset liberal American Jews who are rabidly anti-Trump. For many, the president's positive steps to strengthen the US-Israel relationship were offset by his other policies, his behavior, his demeaning of the office, and the allegations about collusion with the Russians and obstruction of justice.

One variable affecting the relationship is the growing confidence of Israelis as their society has evolved from perhaps a Third World country to a First World country. It is not just the oft-mentioned "Start-up Nation" that has produced this change. "Not that long ago," Anshel Pfeffer observed, there was a clear material difference between life in Israel and the west. Most Israelis didn't own a car or fly on vacations abroad. There was one black-and-white channel on television and the variety of cheeses in most stories was limited to white and yellow. The transformation of the Israeli economy in the last quarter of a century, not only changed all that, but removed one of the chief distinctions between Israeli and western Diaspora life."[91]

Furthermore, while American Jews were talking about the increase in antisemitism in the US, BDS and two horrific shootings at synagogues that shook the community, Israelis were having a very good year. According to Pfeffer:

> For Israelis, 2018 was a bumper year with a blooming economy, now growing for a straight decade, attaining for the first time ever an AA credit rating and with its all-time lowest unemployment figures. On the security front, despite a few scares, no major war or intifada broke out. Gaza nearly boiled over but was pacified with Qatari money. There were a few murders in the West Bank but the corrupt Palestinian Authority kept a lid on any major unrest. And across the northern border, Iran and Hezbollah were kept in check. Nothing was solved, but then no one expected that to happen.

Some of the divisions among Jews can be seen in poll data collected by the AJC. In their 2019 surveys of American and Israeli Jews AJC found that both (68% of Israelis and 71% of Americans) were confident relations between the two would be the same or stronger in 5 years; however, they don't have the same sense that Jews are one family. More than one-fourth (28%) of American Jews do not consider Israelis to be part of their family (23% of Israelis felt the same toward Americans).

[89] Batya Ungar-Sargon, "Netanyahu Just Saved Liberal Zionism," *Forward*, (February 25, 2019).

[90] Batya Ungar-Sargon, "Netanyahu Just Saved Liberal Zionism," *Forward*, (February 25, 2019).

[91] Anshel Pfeffer, "This Year, Israelis Lived It Up While Diaspora Jews Were on a Downer," *Haaretz*, (December 28, 2018).

Roughly one-third of Israelis considered American Jews siblings (31%) or extended family (36%). Only 13% of Americans felt that Israelis were siblings; 43% see them more as extended family.[92]

Surprisingly more Israelis (74%) than Americans (65%) say a thriving diaspora is vital for the future of the Jewish people. Nearly all Israelis (91%) believe in the importance of a thriving Israel compared to 72% of Americans.

Less surprising is the large difference in Israelis' approval of Trump's handling of US-Israeli relations. A whopping 79% of Israelis approve somewhat or strongly while 59% of American Jews disapproved. American Jews were even more disapproving (71%) of Trump's overall job performance.

On specific policies, 69% of Israelis approved of the US pulling out of the Iran deal. The AJC did not ask American Jews their opinion in 2019, but 68% disapproved of Trump's handling of the Iran issue in 2017.[93]

More than two-thirds (71%) of American Jews feel caring about Israel is an important part of being a Jew. So perhaps it is not surprising that 57% believe it is appropriate to try to influence Israeli policy on issues such as security and peace negotiations with the Palestinians. Israelis, feel differently, however, with 63% saying it is inappropriate. This represents one of the most serious divisions between the two. It would be interesting to see the results of a question as to whether American Jews should have a say in issues related to pluralism and religion, such as the Nation-State Law, conversion, and funding for the Reform and Conservative movements in Israel.

From Israelis' perspective, it is probably a good thing that American Jews do not have a say on matters of peace and security. Israelis' souring on the two-state solution is reflected by the 51% who oppose it even with a demilitarized Palestinian state (a popular formula that would likely be impossible to enforce). Nearly two-thirds (64%) of Americans, however, continue to favor this solution.

This difference of opinion is also reflected in attitudes toward the settlements. One-fourth of American Jews favor dismantling all the settlements compared to only 6% of Israelis; 66% of Americans would dismantle some or all the settlements compared to 43% of Israelis. The gap is similar between the 50% of Israelis and 28% of Americans who oppose removing any settlements.

Israeli and American Jews cannot even agree on US recognition of the Golan (asked before Trump did so) with Israelis favoring the move by a margin of 88%–50%. This result helps explain why it is unlikely Trump will gain Jewish votes in 2020 as many do not support what others view as his pro-Israel policies.

Many Jews, especially liberal Democrats, are also turned off by the close relationship between Trump and Netanyahu as they have a strong dislike for both, which intensified as the prime minister seemed to share the president's affinity for authoritarian leaders (such as Russia's Vladimir Putin for Trump and Hungary's Viktor

---

[92] "AJC 2019 Survey of Israeli Jewish Opinion," and "AJC 2019 Survey of American Jewish Opinion," American Jewish Committee, (June 2, 2019).

[93] AJC 2017 Survey of American Jewish Opinion," AJC, (August 10-28, 2017).

Oban for Netanyahu) and adopt Trump's approach to his critics. Facing the possibility of multiple indictments, for example, Netanyahu has dismissed the accusations as inventions by his enemies and repeatedly attacked the media for "fake news."[94]

As Yossi Klein Halevi explained:

> Israeli Jews believe deeply that President Trump recognizes their existential threats. In scuttling the Obama-era Iran nuclear deal, which many Israelis saw as imperiling their security, in moving the American Embassy from Tel Aviv to Jerusalem, in basically doing whatever the government of Benjamin Netanyahu asks, they see a president of the United States acting to save their lives.

> American Jews, in contrast, see President Trump as their existential threat, a leader who they believe has stoked nationalist bigotry, stirred anti-Semitism and, time and time again, failed to renounce the violent hatred swirling around his political movement.[95]

The Reut Institute warned in 2017 that the growing gap between Israel and World Jewry "has widened to the point of endangering the role of Israel as the nation-state of the Jewish people" and that this "presents a major threat to Israel's national security." Reut noted that Israel "relies heavily on the [American] Jewish community's commitment to and support of Israel." The group's report argued that the issue regarding the Western Wall "is not just a struggle for progressive Judaism in Israel but a matter of national security." The conclusion was that "Israel must formulate a strategic framework towards World Jewry."[96]

Many people worry about the future because the schism between Israelis and Americans is not just between Orthodox and non-Orthodox or Liberals and Conservatives, it is also generational. If you think about American Jews who are in college today, born around 2000 or later, they were toddlers during the second intifada and teens during the last Israeli "wars" fought in Gaza. They have never known a time when Israel has faced an existential threat so is it any wonder they might believe Israel should just make whatever concessions are necessary to end the conflict with the Palestinians.[97] Jonathan Weissman put it this way:

> Older American Jews, more viscerally aware of the Holocaust and connected to the living history of the Jewish state, are generally willing to look past Israeli government actions that challenge their values. Or they embrace those actions. Younger American Jews do not typically remember Israel as the David against regional Goliaths. They see a bully, armed and indifferent, 45 years past the Yom Kippur War, the last conflict that threatened Israel's existence.[98]

---

[94] Ruth Eglash, "Under investigation and up for reelection, Netanyahu's kinship with Trump has never been clearer," *Washington Post*, (March 19, 2019).

[95] Jonathan Weisman, "American Jews and Israeli Jews Are Headed for a Messy Breakup," *New York Times*, (January 4, 2019).

[96] "Mapping the Relationship between Israeli State Agencies & World Jewry," Reut Group, (October 2017).

[97] Mitchell Bard, "Young Jews Need Their Spinach," *New York Jewish Week*, (May 30, 2003).

[98] Jonathan Weisman, "American Jews and Israeli Jews Are Headed for a Messy Breakup," *New York Times*, (January 4, 2019).

To close the growing chasm, the Jewish Federation of North America (JFNA) held its annual General Assembly (GA) in Tel Aviv with the theme, "We need to Talk." More than 2500 people from Israel and the Diaspora attended, but Judy Maltz noted there was one notable no-show—Israel's Minister of Diaspora Affairs, Naftali Bennett.[99]

4.9 The New York Times

Many Jews take it as an article of faith that the media is biased. As the "paper of record," the *New York Times*, naturally gets the most attention and has long been criticized for one-sided and misleading coverage related to Israel. Media watchdogs can produce a laundry list of examples of articles and editorials that have appeared in the paper over the decades to illustrate the problem. The op-ed page has long been far more open to opinions, especially written by Jews, that are critical of Israel.

In April 2019, the *Times* reached a new low when the paper's international edition published a cartoon of Donald Trump wearing a yarmulke, being walked by a dog with the face of Prime Minister Benjamin Netanyahu and a Star of David collar. "The offensive image published in the *New York Times* international edition was anti-Semitic propaganda of the most vile sort," said Jonathan A. Greenblatt, ADL's CEO and National Director. "This type of content normalizes anti-Semitism by reinforcing tropes of Jewish control and does so at a time when anti-Semitism is surging. And to come on the same day a man attacked a synagogue because he believed such myths—this was not simply a management misstep but a moral failing of major proportions. The *New York Times* owes the Jewish community more than an apology. We need accountability and action."[100]

The international backlash prompted the *Times* to apologize in an editorial note: "A political cartoon in the international print edition of *The New York Times* … included anti-Semitic tropes…. The image was offensive, and it was an error of judgement to publish it."[101] A statement on April 28, 2019, said, "Such imagery is always dangerous, and at a time when anti-Semitism is on the rise worldwide, it's all the more unacceptable."[102] After making excuses and blaming "a single editor without adequate oversight," the paper published another offensive cartoon a few

---

[99] Judy Maltz, "9 low points in Israel-Jewish Diaspora relations in 2018," *Haaretz*, (December 20, 2018).

[100] "ADL Reacts to Offensive *New York Times* Cartoon," ADL, (April 28, 2019).

[101] Marcy Oster, "*New York Times* acknowledges publishing cartoon with 'anti-Semitic tropes,'" JTA, (April 28, 2019).

[102] Zachary Halaschak, "NYT apologizes for anti-Semitic cartoon a day after acknowledging 'error in judgment,'" *Washington Examiner*, (April 28, 2019).

days later featuring Netanyahu with blacked-out eyes, holding a stone tablet emblazoned with a Star of David while appearing to take a selfie with a smartphone.[103]

The paper subsequently announced it would no longer print political cartoons in the international edition.

The problems at the *Times* extend beyond cartoons. The paper added a new op-ed columnist, Michele Goldberg, who immediately made an impression by writing a column arguing that anti-Zionism is not anti-Semitism[104] and followed that up with another defending Omar Barghouti and the BDS movement after the Trump administration refused to grant Barghouti a visa. "The B.D.S. movement doesn't engage in or promote violence. Its leaders try to separate anti-Zionism and anti-Semitism," she claimed. Goldberg further misstated the goals of the movement as "agnostic on a final dispensation of the Israeli-Palestinian conflict." Finally, in protesting Barghouti's ban from the US, she asserted: "Barghouti threatens America's defenders not because he's hateful, but because he isn't."[105]

The truth was that Barghouti was not barred for his views. Reasons for denying visas are not disclosed. Still, his views are well-known and quite different from Goldberg's description:

• "[Palestinians have a right to] resistance by any means, including armed resistance. [Jews] aren't indigenous just because you say you are.... [Jews] are not a people...."[106]

• "Good riddance! The two-state solution for the Palestinian-Israeli conflict is finally dead. But someone has to issue an official death certificate before the rotting corpse is given a proper burial and we can all move on and explore the more just, moral and therefore enduring alternative for peaceful coexistence between Jews and Arabs in Mandate Palestine: the one-state solution."[107]

• "You cannot reconcile the right of return for refugees with a two-state solution.... a return for refugees would end Israel's existence as a Jewish state."[108]

The *Times* doubled down on Goldberg's defense of the BDS movement by printing a letter from Barghouti in which he quoted Jewish philosopher Joseph Levine, saying, "The very idea of a Jewish state [in Palestine] is undemocratic, a violation of the self-determination rights of its non-Jewish citizens, and therefore morally problematic." Barghouti added the reference to Palestine. He omitted however, that

---

[103] "'The New York Times' to scrap daily political cartoons over anti-Semitism controversy," Jewish News Syndicate, (June 11, 2019).

[104] Michelle Goldberg, "Anti-Zionism Isn't the Same as Anti-Semitism," *New York Times*, (December 7, 2018).

[105] Michelle Goldberg, "Anti-Zionists Deserve Free Speech," *New York Times*, (April 15, 2019).

[106] Roberta P. Seid, "Omar Barghouti at UCLA: A speaker who brings hate," *Jewish Journal*, (January 16, 2014).

[107] Omar Barghouti, "The Essential Obstacle to a Just Peace in Palestine," *Counterpunch*, (December 13-14, 2003).

[108] Ali Mustafa, "Boycotts work": An interview with Omar Barghouti," Electronic Intifada, (May 31, 2009).

Levin's article, also published by the *Times*, argued that Israel has no right to exist and that saying so is not antisemitic.

The *New York Times Magazine* published a lengthier defense of BDS, essentially a hit piece on Israel and the pro-Israel community written by Nathan Thrall. Later it was disclosed, though not by the *Times*, that the author works for an organization whose major donor is Qatar, the principal funder of Hamas.[109]

To its credit, the *Times* did hire two strong supporters of Israel—Bari Weiss and Bret Stephens—but they hardly offset the plethora of news stories and columns by regular critics of Israeli government policies such as Thomas Friedman, Nicholas Kristof, and Roger Cohen.

Addressing the cartoon controversy Stephens explained why the paper has a credibility problem:

> The reason is the almost torrential criticism of Israel and the mainstreaming of anti-Zionism, including by this paper, which has become so common that people have been desensitized to its inherent bigotry. So long as anti-Semitic arguments or images are framed, however speciously, as commentary about Israel, there will be a tendency to view them as a form of political opinion, not ethnic prejudice. ... the publication of the cartoon isn't just an "error of judgment," either. The paper owes the Israeli prime minister an apology. It owes itself some serious reflection as to how it came to publish that cartoon—and how its publication came, to many longtime readers, as a shock but not a surprise.

In his analysis of the paper's coverage of Zionism and Israel from 1896–2016, Jerold Auerbach explained why readers would not be surprised given the inversion of the paper's motto:

> All the news "fit to print" became news that fit the *New York Times'* discomfort with the idea, and since 1948 the reality, of a thriving Jewish democratic state in the historic homeland of the Jewish people.[110]

4.10   Relentless Campus Battles

The campus has been a battleground for decades, only the names and tactics have changed. Today, the Jewish community is investing a great deal of time, money and energy into fighting the antisemitic BDS campaign.

Most of the focus remains on college campuses where the drumbeat of publicity of incidents has created the widespread perception that the campuses are on fire with anti-Israel activity. There are indeed serious issues related to BDS; however, some context is necessary. While several thousand faculty, for example, support boycotting Israel, the total number of faculty in the US at 4-year institutions totals

[109] Nathan Thrall, "How the Battle Over Israel and Anti-Semitism Is Fracturing American Politics," *New York Times Magazine*, (March 28, 2019).

[110] Jerold S. Auerbach, *Print to Fit: The New York Times, Zionism and Israel, 1896-2016*, (Boston: Academic Studies Press, 2019), p. xx.

approximately 625,000.[111] Similarly, from 2005 to 2019, only 68 universities, less than 2% of the 4298 degree-granting postsecondary institutions,[112] have had BDS-related student council votes.[113]

In 2012–2013, student governments proposed 10 BDS resolutions; the following year, the number jumped to 19; and in 2014–2015, there were 27. That trend set off alarm bells; however, 2014–2015 turned out to be the peak. During the 2018–2019 academic year, the number dwindled again to 10, and eight of the resolutions were rejected. In addition, the University of Oregon ruled the previous year's resolution was unconstitutional.

No university has endorsed BDS, and dozens of presidents, deans, and chancellors have repudiated the antisemitic campaign.[114] Due to the lack of success of the divestment campaigns, Israel's detractors have often adopted more confrontational approaches such as trying to shout down speakers.

One activist saw developments differently. Jonathan Elkhoury, an Arab-Christian member of Reservists on Duty (RoD), an organization that sends IDF veterans to campuses to counter BDS, said that in the past "we were often pushed, spat on, verbally and even physically assaulted when visiting campuses." He said this still happened occasionally, "but for the most part what we saw was a more calm and cohesive language among all SJP groups across the US, whether in their demonstrations or with regards to their lectures."[115]

New York University, which has one of the largest Jewish student populations in the country, became the scene of several anti-Israel activities. The university awarded Students for Justice in Palestine (SJP)—a promoter of antisemitism that is responsible for creating a climate of intolerance toward Jews—the university's highest honor for a student organization. Shortly thereafter, the Department of Social and Cultural Analysis (SCA) voted to boycott NYU's own satellite campus in Tel Aviv. This was followed by a commencement speech by a graduate of that department, Steven Thrasher, who said he was "so proud" of NYU's chapters of Students for Justice in Palestine, Jewish Voice for Peace, the Graduate Student Organizing Committee labor union, and SCA for supporting BDS "against the apartheid state government in Israel." Thrasher was hired to teach courses on social justice at Northwestern. The president of NYU and the president and provost of Northwestern condemned Thrasher's remarks, but there was no punishment.

[111] National Center for Education Statistics, https://nces.ed.gov/ipeds/TrendGenerator/app/answer/5/12. Accessed July 17, 2019.

[112] Josh Moody, "A Guide to the Changing Number of US Universities," *US News and World Report*, (February 15, 2019).

[113] "Campus Divestment Resolutions in the USA," Jewish Virtual Library, https://www.jewishvirtuallibrary.org/campus-divestment-resolutions. Accessed July 17, 2019.

[114] "University Statements Rejecting Divestment and the Academic Boycott of Israel," Jewish Virtual Library, https://www.jewishvirtuallibrary.org/university-statements-rejecting-bds. Accessed July 29, 2019.

[115] Lidar Gravé-Lazi, "Campus activists call-in 'reserves' to counter new anti-Israel tactics," JNS, (June 5, 2019).

There was a different outcome after another issue came to light, namely the possibility that professors are refusing to write letters of recommendation for students who want to study in Israel. We know of at least one case because University of Michigan professor John Cheney-Lippold admitted that is what he did because he supports the boycott of Israel.

Journalist Mitch Albom criticized Cheney Lippold for weaponizing a letter of recommendation. He noted that no one is required to write a letter of recommendation, but the decision is supposed to be based on merit not politics. "Forget the puzzlement of discouraging study in perhaps the only nation in the Middle East that has laws protecting free speech," Albom wrote. "What about the academic notion that if you want to understand something, you should go and examine it?"

Albom also noted the professor's hypocrisy. Cheney Lippold said that he would be happy to write the student a recommendation to study somewhere else. "What place, I wonder would meet his approval?" Albom asked. "China? Russia?" Albom added that "if being accused of a human rights violation by the United Nations is his criterion, he couldn't write a recommendation to study in America."[116]

Usually faculty malpractice goes unpunished because they are shielded by a misapplication of "academic freedom." In this case, however, the university disciplined the professor, denying him a merit raise and his planned sabbatical.[117] That was the good news, the bad news is that more than 1000 professors have signed a petition supporting Cheney-Lippold, with many saying they would do the same thing.[118]

4.11   Fighting the Boycotters

The BDS movement has had even less success beyond the campus. In fact, it produced a backlash. To date, 27 US states have adopted measures aimed at combating the boycott. In January 2019, the Senate's first legislative action was to pass a bill that included the Anti-Boycott Act. The House, however, refused to take up the Senate bill due to objections from members who said it violated the First Amendment. House Speaker Nancy Pelosi (D-CA) also feared a vote would expose fissures between the insurgent progressive wing of the party, which includes two avid proponents of the boycott—Reps. Ilan Omar (D-MN) and Rashida Tlaib (D-MI)—and Jews and other pro-Israel Democrats. Instead, as noted above, the House adopted a non-binding resolution in July 2019 that condemned the boycott movement and expressed support for a two-state solution. Lead sponsor Brad Schneider (D-IL) said, "I am deeply proud that more than three-quarters of my House colleagues,

[116] Mitch Albom, "Michigan professor let politics dictate student's education," *Detroit Free Press*, (September 23, 2018).

[117] Kim Kozlowski, "UM disciplines prof over Israel letter controversy," *Detroit News*, (October 9, 2018).

[118] "Stand with John Cheney-Lippold," Change.org, https://www.change.org/p/stand-with-john-cheney-lippold. Accessed July 22, 2019.

with overwhelming majorities of both parties, have co-sponsored my resolution making clear that Congress supports a strong US-Israel relationship, is committed to achieving a negotiated two-state solution, and forcefully condemns the Global BDS Movement."[119]

Not surprisingly Omar and Tlaib were two of the Democrats who voted against the resolution. Omar went further and introduced her own bill supporting the boycott, though not explicitly mentioning Israel. "In twisting the knife," Rep. Lee Zeldin responded, "the text of Omar's pro-BDS resolution goes so far as attempting to draw a moral equivalency with boycotting Nazi Germany."[120] This comparison between boycotts of Israel, Nazi Germany and the Soviet Union drew fire from pro-Israel groups as well. "Millions of Holocaust survivors and their descendants, as well refugees from Soviet oppression living in Israel, will find such comparisons unfathomable," said Democratic Majority for Israel president and CEO Mark Mellman. "I find them odious. In an effort led by parties of the left, the German Parliament officially labeled BDS as 'anti-Semitism'—and they were right."[121]

Meanwhile, one new tactic adopted by the boycotters, led by Jewish Voice for Peace (JVP), is to protest training programs and other information exchanges between American police departments and other first responders and their counterparts in Israel. Referring to the campaign as "Deadly Exchange," JVP argues that these programs "solidify partnerships between the US and Israeli governments to exchange methods of state violence and control, including mass surveillance, racial profiling, and suppression of protest and dissent." According to JVP, "When US law enforcement trade tactics with the Israeli police and military, Israel deepens its military occupation and the US heightens its violence of policing."[122]

In April 2018, Durham, North Carolina became the first and, so far, only US city to ban its police department from participating in international exchanges with the Israeli military or police. The BDS proponents hope to replicate this success elsewhere.[123] They targeted Georgia, for example, where law enforcement professionals from that state and others such as North Carolina and Tennessee have traveled to Israel to study the counterterrorism techniques and emergency management methods of their Israeli colleagues since 1993 as part of the Georgia International Law Enforcement Exchange (GILEE) program. The Georgia Association of Chiefs of Police endorsed the GILEE program and denounced the "Deadly Exchange"

---

[119] Ron Kampeas, "Congress tackles the anti-Israel boycott, but bipartisanship is fleeting," *JTA*, (July 19, 2019).

[120] Rep. Lee Zeldin, "Ilhan Omar is wrong—anti-Israel and anti-Semitic BDS movement must be condemned," *Fox News*, (July 23, 2019).

[121] Jackson Richman," Pro-Israel groups slam Omar comparing BDS to boycotts of Nazi Germany, Soviet Union," *JNS*, (July 18, 2019).

[122] Jewish Voice for Peace website, https://jewishvoiceforpeace.org/. Accessed July 22, 2019.

[123] Miriam Elman, "Georgia police groups slam Jewish Voice for Peace's antisemitic "Deadly Exchange" campaign," Legal Insurrection, (January 1, 2019), https://legalinsurrection.com/2019/01/georgia-police-groups-slam-jewish-voice-for-peaces-antisemitic-deadly-exchange-campaign/. Accessed July 26, 2019.

campaign, saying that any claims that the professional programs were training Americans to oppress minorities lacked "any foundation in the facts or history of such exchanges" and the claim that "such training leads to deadly encounters in the US is utterly fallacious and slanderous." The Chiefs' statement added that "participants receive a better understanding of how to network with their citizenry and enhance the service delivery to these underserved communities."[124] A similar statement was issued by the Georgia Sheriffs' Association.[125]

In 2019, defenders of antisemites adopted a new strategy. No longer content to cry "free speech" and accuse their enemies of McCarthyism, they now accuse critics of inciting violence and putting lives in danger. After Omar came under withering criticism from many of her colleagues, Republicans, and the Jewish community, others came to her defense using the new tactic to try to silence them.

4.12   Intersectionality

"Intersectionality" has become a popular buzzword, particularly on college campuses. The word refers to the idea that race, class, gender, and other individual characteristics "intersect" with one another and overlap, and that all injustices are interconnected. Women and minorities (theoretically including Jews, but in certain instances excluding them) are seen as victims of white oppression.

Jewish Voice for Peace summarizes how intersectionality is applied to Israel by linking the Palestinians' plight to "the struggles of students of color, student survivors of sexual assault, and all others who on campus fight against oppression, whether imperialism, racism, patriarchy, police violence, or other systemic inequities."[126]

RoD's Elkhoury noted, for example, how many campuses replaced "Apartheid Week" with "Oppression Week," in an effort to "frame the narrative that Israel equals white supremacy." He said "it was clear that this was a well-thought-out strategy directed to coincide with the debate currently going on in the US regarding oppressed minorities."[127]

Ziva Dahl noted that "in the 'jabberwocky' of multicultural victimhood, Western, white, wealthy, cis-male,[128] and Israel (the collective Jew) are inherently evil, while

---

[124] "Statement of GACP Support of International Law Enforcement Exchange Training Programs," Georgia Association of Chiefs of Police, (December 14, 2018).

[125] "Georgia International Law Enforcement Exchange (GILEE)," Georgia Sheriffs' Association, (December 19, 2018).

[126] Ziva Dahl, "'Intersectionality' and the Bizarre World of Hating Israel," *Observer*, (March 15, 2016).

[127] Lidar Gravé-Lazi, "Campus activists call-in 'reserves' to counter new anti-Israel tactics," JNS, (June 5, 2019).

[128] A "cis" person is a person who was assigned a gender and sex at birth with which they feel comfortable.

third-world people of color, women, LGBTQ and Palestinians are automatically good…. Today, to the sanctimonious social justice warrior, Jews are part of the oppressor class."[129]

The persecuted feel solidarity with other victimized groups, but often ignore the inconsistencies of their positions. Thus, for example, some LBGQT and women's organizations support the Palestinian cause and simply ignore the treatment of gays and women by Palestinians.

"With the advent of 'intersectionality,'" Dahl adds, "Jewish students must pass an Israel litmus test to prove their commitment to social justice. Jewish students are being marginalized on campuses, many feeling the need to hide their pro-Israel and Jewish identities to 'get along' in this hostile environment."[130]

The pressure extends beyond the classroom, for example, to Black Lives Matter and the Women's movement. The platform of the former compares Israel to racist South Africa and accuses it of engaging in genocide against the Palestinians.[131]

Similarly, the leaders of the Women's March have sparked controversy with their comments about Jews and Israel. Two of them, Tamika Mallory and Linda Sarsour, were criticized for their ties to Louis Farrakhan and asked to step down for allowing antisemitism to seep into the movement.[132] Sarsour was also criticized for, among other things, accusing Jews of dual loyalty, condemning the creation of a Congressional Black-Jewish caucus, and co-signing an article that accused Jews of waging "profound war on black people and people of color."[133] She said, "on an issue like Palestine, you gotta choose the side of the oppressed … if you're on the side of the oppressor, or you're defending the oppressor, and you're actually trying to humanize the oppressor, then that's a problem."[134]

In 2017, organizers of Chicago's Dyke March asked three participants carrying LGBT pride flags with a Star of David over the traditional rainbow to leave. Dyke March organizers said they acted because the flags "made people feel unsafe" and the march was "anti-Zionist."[135] This treatment of Jews has continued. The 2019 DC

---

[129] Ziva Dahl, "'Intersectionality' and the Bizarre World of Hating Israel," *Observer*, (March 15, 2016).

[130] Ziva Dahl, "'Intersectionality' and the Bizarre World of Hating Israel," *Observer*, (March 15, 2016).

[131] "INVEST-DIVEST," The Movement for Black Lives, https://policy.m4bl.org/invest-divest/. Accessed July 23, 2019.

[132] Just prior to going to press, it was announced that co-chairs of the Women's March, Linda Sarsour, Tamika Mallory, and Bob Bland, left the board, as reported by *The Washington Post* and JTA ("Sarsour, Other Leaders Accused of Anti-Semitism Leave Women's March," JTA, September 16, 2019).

[133] "Women's March founder calls on leaders to resign for 'allowing anti-Semitism,'" JTA, (November 20, 2018); Ben Sales, "Linda Sarsour apologizes to Jewish members of Women's March over anti-Semitism," *Times of Israel*, (November 21, 2018); Ariel Sobel, "OMG, Just Shut Up: An Open Letter to Linda Sarsour," *Jewish Journal*, (July 10, 2019).

[134] Alex Joffe and Asaf Romirowsky, "Americans' Two Conceptions of Israel," Begin-Sadat Center for Strategic Studies," (February 19, 2019).

[135] James Kirchick, "Dykes Vs. Kikes," *Tablet*, (June 26, 2017).

Dyke March organizers, self-proclaimed anti-Zionists from the radical Jewish organization IfNotNow, said they were banning "Israeli flags, as well as flags that resemble Israeli flags, such as a pride flag with a Star of David in the middle."[136]

Protestors from the Zionist progressive organization Zioness showed up to the march with Jewish Pride flags—a rainbow-striped flag with a Star of David in the middle. They were initially blocked at the entrance to the march by Jewish marshals from IfNotNow but would not back down and were ultimately allowed to march.[137]

4.13 The Attack on Birthright

One of the most successful programs for educating young Jews has been Birthright Israel, which brings young adults to Israel for 10 days. Primarily targeted at Jews who have never been to Israel, the program seeks to introduce them to the history, culture, and geography of the country in the hope it will give them a better appreciation of life in Israel, help them feel closer to the Jewish homeland, and inspire them to return.

Except for some specialized trips specifically geared to political activists, the itineraries are mostly apolitical. This has upset some Jews on the left and extreme left, who complain the trips ignore the Israeli-Palestinian issue and fail to present the Palestinian narrative.

In the summer of 2018, a handful of activists from IfNotNow, a newly formed group of young Jews who are critical of Israeli policies, went on Birthright trips with the intention of staging a protest by leaving the trip. They also harassed students at Kennedy Airport on their way to Israel, distributing flyers full of misinformation about Israel.[138] The walkouts and protests attracted press attention—Jews criticizing Israel is a classic man bites dog story that journalists find compelling—even landing the group on the front page of the *New York Times*.[139] Just a few days before the article appeared, the group sent a private email to its members saying it was suspending the protests because of internal divisions over how they were handled and how the organization would proceed in the future. One of the authors of the email said the group was in a "reevaluation phase."[140]

The student arm of another organization highly critical of the Israeli government and Birthright, J Street, offered its own tour of Israel for the first time in the summer of 2019. "We need to stop the erasure of Palestinians on organized trips to Israel," J

[136] Aiden Pink, "DC Dyke March Bans Jewish Pride Flag," *Forward*, (June 6, 2019).

[137] Samantha Cooper, "Pride and prejudice at LGBTQ weekend," *Washington Jewish Week*, (June 12, 2019).

[138] Mitchell Bard, "When Will IfNotNow Get Its Facts Right?" *Algemeiner*, (July 12, 2018).

[139] Farah Stockman, "Birthright Trips, a Rite of Passage for Many Jews, Are Now a Target of Protests," *New York Times*, (June 11, 2019).

[140] Aiden Pink, "IfNotNow Made An Impact With Its Birthright Protests. Now It's Stopping Them," *Forward*, (June 13, 2019).

Street says on its website advertising their "Let Our People Know Trip." The agenda is clear by the fifth day when the theme is "The Israeli-Palestinian Conflict and the Occupation 101."[141]

Participants on the first trip got the message J Street hoped to convey. Six participants wrote in the *Forward*, "we feel more connected to Israel, Palestine, and the people who live there than we ever did before." They said they were reminded of "collectively trying to eliminate the oppression of people" and "inspired to take action." They had nothing to say about doing anything for Israelis but vowed to "catalyze a just end to the Occupation."[142] Another student who went on the trip was more explicit about the impact it had on him, "I went to Israel with J Street a Zionist. But I was no longer a Zionist when I returned."[143]

4.14   The 2020 Election

When AIPAC held its annual Policy Conference in March 2019, 15 Democrats had announced plans to run for president. A controversy arose when the left-wing advocacy group MoveOn called on the candidates to boycott the conference.[144] Vice President Mike Pence subsequently told attendees that eight Democratic candidates heeded the call and that "anyone who aspires to the highest office in the land should not be afraid to stand with the strongest supporters of Israel."[145] This was one of many instances during the year where a Republican tried to suggest the Democratic Party no longer supports Israel, implying Jews should switch their allegiance.

The media was filled with headlines about the candidates skipping the conference, that this was "another sign of their turn to extremism,"[146] and Trump accused Democrats of being "anti-Israel" and "anti-Jewish."[147]

The truth was more nuanced. AIPAC typically does not invite candidates to speak in non-election years, so no one declined the opportunity to address the group. Of

---

[141] J Street website, https://jstreet.org/let-our-people-know/let-our-people-know-trip/#.XTt5-uhKhaR. Accessed July 26, 2019.

[142] AJ Nadel, Channah Powell, Elam Klein, Ethan Wellerstein, Gabriella Kamran, and Simone Pass Tucker, "We Went To See The Occupation. We Came Back More Connected To Israel," *Forward*, (July 24, 2019).

[143] Jesse Steshenko, "J Street's Birthright Replacement Trip To Israel Killed My Zionism," *Forward*, (July 17, 2019).

[144] Iram Ali, "MoveOn: 2020 Presidential Candidates Should Not Attend AIPAC Conference," MoveOn, (July 23, 2019).

[145] Glenn Kessler, "Did eight Democratic candidates 'boycott' the AIPAC conference?" *Washington Post*, (March 27, 2019).

[146] Editorial Board, "Dems' AIPAC boycott is another sign of their turn to extremism," *New York Post*, (March 22, 2019).

[147] John Verhovek, "Trump slams 2020 Democrats for skipping AIPAC: 'They're totally anti-Israel,'" *ABCnews*, (March 21, 2019).

the candidates, seven were serving in Congress and four met with AIPAC delegations on the day of the conference dedicated to lobbying.

Sen. Bernie Sanders was the only candidate who said he was not attending because, his spokesman said, he was "concerned about the platform AIPAC is providing for leaders who have expressed bigotry and oppose a two-state solution."

Sen. Elizabeth Warren (D-MA) and Rep. Tulsi Gabbard (D-HI) did not attend or meet with constituents in person, but Warren sent her foreign policy advisor to meet with the Massachusetts delegation. This is not unusual as members sometimes are unavailable and set up meetings with their staff. Pete Buttigieg said he was not invited to the conference and Beto O'Rourke and John Delaney said they had scheduling conflicts. O'Rourke said his decision was not a slap at AIPAC, he just thought campaigning was a better way to spend his time.

Three candidates—Kamala Harris, Kirsten Gillibrand, and Amy Klobuchar—did not attend the conference but met with their constituents on Capitol Hill. Cory Booker met an AIPAC delegation at the convention center but did not attend the meeting.

Israel's detractors still declared victory. James Zogby tweeted, for example, "A few years ago, only @BernieSanders had the courage to skip #AIPAC. Now more Democrats are saying No! Thank you @MoveOn. & thank you Bernie for leading the way. It's so important to say No to occupation & Netanyahu's anti-Arab bigotry".[148]

The first debates for the more than two dozen Democratic candidates were held in the summer of 2019 and the campaign will be all-consuming as the election approaches. For Jewish voters, the choice is likely to be Trump or Obama 2.0.

Most Jews do not vote solely on a candidate's position on Israel. In fact, one poll indicated Israel ranks at the bottom of a list of 16 policy priorities of Jewish voters.[149] This assumes, however, that none of the candidates are viewed as hostile to Israel. Obama, for example, unquestionably lost some Jewish votes in 2012 because of his positions related to Israel and the perception of Jimmy Carter as anti-Israel, and his general failure in his first term on many issues, contributed to his share of the Jewish vote dropping from 71% in 1976 to 45% in 1980.[150]

Based solely on his policy toward Israel—his tone, military assistance, political backing, recognition of Jerusalem and the Golan Heights, tough line on the Palestinians—Trump can make a strong pitch for Jewish support. On the other hand, several of these policies caused consternation for liberal Jews because they are seen as harming the prospects for peace.

Apart from Joe Biden and Bernie Sanders, the Democratic candidates do not have significant records on Israel. Biden has long been viewed as a friend of Israel,

---

[148] "Several Democratic Presidential Candidates to Boycott AIPAC," *The Palestine Chronicle*, (March 22, 2019).

[149] "Domestic Issues Dominate The Priorities Of The Jewish Electorate," Jewish Electorate Institute, (May 22, 2019).

[150] "US Presidential Elections: Jewish Voting Record," Jewish Virtual Library, https://www.jewishvirtuallibrary.org/jewish-voting-record-in-u-s-presidential-elections. Accessed July 29, 2019.

though some voters may associate him with less friendly Obama policies during his time as Vice President, while Sanders is a fierce critic of Israeli government policies despite his time spent on a kibbutz in the 1960s. In general, if a Democrat is elected, they are likely to return to the approach of Obama and other Democratic presidents, more critical of Israel and solicitous of the Palestinians. Though there are differences among the candidates, if one were elected, they will probably pursue policies along these lines (some candidates said early on they would do one or more):

- Rejoin the nuclear deal.
- Keep the US embassy in Jerusalem but freeze the process of constructing a new building and reopen the consulate as the diplomatic liaison with the Palestinian Authority.
- Reiterate support for a two-state solution in which Jerusalem will be the shared capital.
- Restore aid to the Palestinian Authority and UNRWA and reopen the Palestine Liberation Organization office in Washington.[151]

With the possible exception of Sanders who, in addition to being extremely critical of Israeli government policies, is too far to the left even for most liberal Jews, whomever the Democrats nominate will likely do better than the average of 75% of the Jewish vote. Trump managed to nearly equal the Republican average of 25% of the Jewish vote in 2016 (he got 24%), but general dissatisfaction with his behavior and domestic policies are likely to lose him votes in 2020 despite his pro-Israel record, although Gallup found that 26% of Jews still approve of Trump's conduct as president.[152]

Republicans, including the president, attempted to paint Democrats as moving to the extreme left and tolerating antisemitism within their party because of the timid response to Tlaib and Omar. Republicans subsequently began to talk of a "Jexodus:" Jews leaving the Democratic Party for the Republicans. Despite years of trying to entice Jews to switch parties, however, there is no evidence they are having any success. Gallup's poll found that only 16% of Jews identified as Republican, which is consistent with the 18% figure in the 2019 American Jewish Committee survey.[153]

The best chance for Republicans to pick up Jewish votes is if the Democrats nominate one of the candidates from the far left for the presidency. Even then, unless it is someone considered hostile to Israel, it is unlikely that Trump will significantly increase his share of the Jewish vote. Absent proof of wrongdoing beyond what was presented in the Mueller Report, Jews who do base their votes on policy toward Israel, particularly Orthodox Republicans who supported Trump in 2016, are likely to stick with him.

---

[151] Alayna Treene and Barak Ravid, "Top 2020 Dems wouldn't reverse Trump's Jerusalem embassy decision," Axios, (July 14, 2019).

[152] RJ Reinhart, "One in Six US Jews Identify as Republican," Gallup, (March 14, 2019).

[153] AJC 2019 Survey of American Jewish Opinion, American Jewish Committee, (June 2, 2019).

Still, Trump spent part of the summer of 2019 trying to paint Omar, Tlaib, and two other congresswomen, Alexandria Ocasio-Cortez of New York and Ayanna Pressley of Massachusetts, who refer to themselves as the "squad," as the face of the party. When he said they should "go back and help fix the totally broken and crime-infested places from which they came" and made repeated comments along similar lines, his remarks were widely condemned, including by many Jews, as racist.

Trump subsequently provoked anger in the Jewish community when he began to cite criticism of Israel and antisemitic remarks as justification for his attacks on the squad. In one tweet, for example, he said, "I don't believe the four Congresswomen are capable of loving our Country. They should apologize to America (and Israel) for the horrible (hateful) things they have said." In another he said the women should "apologize to our Country, the people of Israel and even to the Office of the President, for the foul language they have used, and the terrible things they have said."[154]

Nathan Guttman asserted Trump was "using Israel as a shield for racist attacks and justifying the targeting of non-white members of Congress by pointing to harsh words they've used to criticize Israel" as part of a campaign strategy. "This leaves Israel and its supporters in the US with two bad options," Guttman said, "Either ignore Trump's use of Israel in a racist context and face the accusation of being acquiescent to bigotry, or take a forceful stance against Trump's comment and be exposed to claims of not standing up to attacks, at times vicious, launched against Israel by progressive politicians."[155]

Many Jews have been hesitant to criticize Trump because of his pro-Israel positions. Given the importance the president places on loyalty, some fear he could turn on Israel if Jews turn on him, especially after hearing him praise evangelical Christians while complaining that Jews were not showing enough appreciation for his support for Israel.[156]

The racist remarks crossed a line, however, for even some of his staunchest Jewish supporters—Orthodox Jews—as evidenced by a statement by the Orthodox Rabbinical Council of America that condemned "the most recent outburst of racist rhetoric in the highest levels of government." Although it did not mention Trump, the object of their dissatisfaction was clear. The statement went on to say: "Whether statements that question the loyalty of American Jews when the safety and security of Israel is at stake or rallies that call upon descendants of immigrants to return to countries they never knew, we see these pronouncements as dangerous to the core values of our faith and the foundations of American society."[157]

---

[154] Marcy Oster, "Trump involves Israel again in criticizing 4 Democratic congresswomen," JTA, (July 21, 2019).

[155] Nathan Guttman, "The Political Battle Over BDS and Free Speech," *Moment*, (July 23, 2019).

[156] Anshel Pfeffer, "Donald Trump Thinks the Jews Aren't Grateful Enough," *Haaretz*, (September 22, 2018).

[157] Ron Kampeas, "Rabbinical Council of America condemns racism at 'highest levels of government,'" JTA, (July 19, 2019).

Democrats and many Jewish organizations rallied around the congresswomen. For many Jews, the chants at a Trump rally to "Send her [Omar] back" were reminiscent of the reaction to Jews throughout history, the Nazi rally at Nuremberg and the neo-Nazi march in Charlottesville where white supremacists chanted, "Jews will not replace us."

Even while they attracted sympathy, however, Tlaib and Omar did the party no favor by opposing the bipartisan bill criticizing the BDS movement and then introducing their own bill to support boycotting Israel. It was clear that the Democratic Party's effort to marginalize the squad—Pelosi said, "They're four people, and that's how many votes they got"[158]—was being undermined by both the congresswomen and the President.

Still, the Republican dream of a realignment of the Jewish vote remains just that. Responding to Trump's tweet that "Jewish people are leaving the Democratic Party," Frank Newport, a Gallup senior scientist, said that "the stability of Jewish support for the Democratic Party over the past decade suggests that such a shift in allegiance is unlikely."[159]

---

[158] Julie Hirschfeld Davis, "Tensions Between Pelosi and Progressive Democrats of 'the Squad' Burst Into Flame," *New York Times*, (July 9, 2019).

[159] Frank Newport, "Americans' Views of Israel Remain Tied to Religious Beliefs," Gallup, (March 19, 2019).

Chapter 5
United States Jewish Population, 2019

Ira M. Sheskin and Arnold Dashefsky

The 2019 *American Jewish Year Book* (*AJYB*) cumulative estimate for the US Jewish population is 6.97 million and is based, as in previous years, on the aggregation of more than 900 local estimates. More than three-quarters of the 6.97 million is based on scientific sample surveys of US Jewish communities. The above number compares to the estimate of 5.92 million in 1980.[1] For an explanation of the difference between our estimate and the estimate provided by Sergio DellaPergola in Chap. 8 of this volume, see Sect. 5.3 below.

One difficulty facing researchers seeking to provide an accurate assessment of the nature of the American Jewish population is estimating the number and percent of Jews of Color.[2,3] Kelman et al. (2019) highlighted this issue in a recent report

---

[1] "The best guidance to this complicated field [Jewish demography] is to be found in the annual volumes of the *American Jewish Year Book*, which publishes analytical articles, summaries of surveys of Jewish population, and estimates of Jewish population by state and community" (Glazer 1989/1972/1957, p. 189).

[2] The term "Jews of Color" refers to individual Jews who may possess African, Asian, Hispanic or Latinx, or Native American heritage and derive their Jewish identity by having been raised as Jews or by conversion. Ironically, in the early part of the twentieth century, American Jews were regarded as less than "white" (Brodkin 1998) because their "Yiddishkeit" made them different.

[3] We would like to thank Laurence Kotler-Berkowitz, Senior Director, Research and Analysis and Director, Berman Jewish DataBank at The Jewish Federations of North America and Bruce A. Phillips, Professor of Sociology and Jewish Communal Service at Hebrew Union College for reviewing this section on Jews of Color. We also thank Joshua Comenetz, Population Mapping Consultant, for his review of the entire chapter.

I. M. Sheskin (✉)
Department of Geography and Jewish Demography Project, Sue and Leonard Miller Center for Contemporary Judaic Studies, University of Miami, Coral Gables, FL, USA
e-mail: isheskin@miami.edu

A. Dashefsky
Department of Sociology and Center for Judaic Studies and Contemporary Jewish Life, University of Connecticut, Storrs, CT, USA

© Springer Nature Switzerland AG 2020
A. Dashefsky, I. M. Sheskin (eds.), *American Jewish Year Book 2019*, American Jewish Year Book 119, https://doi.org/10.1007/978-3-030-40371-3_5

focusing on Jews of Color. The authors undertook a meta-analysis of various Jewish national and local Jewish community studies to determine the size of the population of Jews of Color. They summarized their "educated guess" as follows: "We can approximate that Jews of Color represent at least 12%–15% of American Jews" (2019, p. 2). They also reported that "more younger people identify as nonwhite than older people do." Consequently, they stated that "with cohort replacement, this means that the future of American Jewry is diverse" (2019, p. 2).

The "at least 12%–15%" estimate by Kelman et al. (2019) is substantially higher than the Pew estimate of 6% (Pew Research Center 2013, p. 46).[4] The 6% Pew figure is just about equal to the 7% found in the 1990 National Survey of Religious Identification (NSRI) (Kosmin and Lachman 1991, p. 7) and the 5% from the 2000–2001 National Jewish Population Survey (Kotler-Berkowitz et al. 2003), which indicate that the percentage nationally (with the possibility of undercounts as in the US Census) does not appear to have increased between 1990 and 2013.[5,6] This is particularly surprising given that the percentage of all Americans who are non-Hispanic white has decreased from 75.6% in 1990 to 63.7% in 2000 and 60.6% in 2017.

Note that the 6% in the Pew 2013 study is comprised of 2% black (non-Hispanic), 3% Hispanic, and 2% other/mixed races. (This adds to 7% due to rounding.) These data are consistent with Pew surveys of religion among both blacks and Hispanics (www.pewforum.org).

But, as intermarriage (Phillips 2018) continues among American Jews at high levels, the share of Jews of Color in the Jewish population may increase. Such an increase may also occur as Jews adopt children who may be "of Color" and as non-Jewish persons of color decide to identify as Jewish.[7]

---

[4] The 12%–15% mostly relies on the estimate made by the American Jewish Population Project (Kelman et al. 2019).

[5] The NSRI was part of the 1990 National Jewish Population Survey. Note that the data from all three national surveys are for the respondent only so as to make the results comparable among the three studies. Also, all three studies used a random digit dialing procedure and did not employ mailing lists. (Mailing lists might tend to underestimate Jews of Color.) Note as well that only asking population group questions of respondents does not significantly underestimate a population group. In the Miami (2015a) local Jewish community study (which asked Hispanic and Sephardic status of all adults in the household, but not race), 13% of Jewish respondents were Hispanic, compared to 15% of all Jewish adults. For Sephardic Jews, the percentages were 16% and 17%, respectively.

[6] Not only did the percentage of Jews who are Jews of Color not change significantly since 1990, neither has the *number*. In part, because of the influx of Jews from the former Soviet Union and the increase of young ultra-Orthodox, who are both quite unlikely to be Jews of Color, the number of US Jews has increased from 5,981,000 in 1990 to the current 6,968,000 in 2019. Thus, in both years (because the estimate of the percentage of Jews of Color decreased from 7% to 6% from 1990 to 2013 and the number of Jews increased by about one million), the number of Jews of Color has been relatively stable at about 420,000. Note that, in all years, we are assuming that the percentage of Jews of Color among children age 0–17 is about the same as among Jewish adults.

[7] The possibility of conversion of Persons of Color to Judaism in large numbers seems unlikely, as the US becomes increasingly secular (Pew Research Center 2013) and because Judaism is not a

The *Jews of Color* report brings attention to two of the larger local Jewish community studies to support the "at least 12%–15%" finding. The 2017 San Francisco Bay Area Jewish community study (Cohen et al. 2017) shows that 13% *of Jews* in the 10-county Bay Area are Jews of Color.

The 2011 New York Jewish population study (Cohen et al. 2011) shows that 12% *of Jewish households* are multiracial. This does NOT mean that 12% of Jews are Jews of Color. Also, in *some* multiracial households, it could be that it is a non-Jew who is the person of color.

It should also be noted that many Jews who might identify as Hispanic are, in fact, Ashkenazi and are much less likely to be "of Color." For example, in Miami, about 60% of Hispanic Jews consider themselves Ashkenazi (Sheskin 2015a). In many cases, these are Jews whose parents or grandparents fled the Holocaust to places like Cuba and Argentina and then settled in the US. A similar argument can be made against assuming that all Sephardic and Mizrahi Jews are Jews of Color (Levin 2019). It is for this reason that Be'chol Lashon uses the term "diverse Jews" and not "Jews of Color."

While some researchers may disagree with the estimate of Jews of Color that Kelman et al. (2019) produced, Kelman and his colleagues are correct in asserting that this sub-population is relatively "invisible" to many members of the Jewish community as well as to researchers. Part of the reason for this "invisibility" may be due to Jews of Color being less likely to participate in the formal Jewish community.[8]

The recommendations of Kelman et al. (2019, p. 16) are worth considering for future studies of American Jewry:

1. Utilize more sensitive sampling frames to discern Jews of Color.
2. Employ consistency in wording across multiple surveys (a long-standing recommendation of the Berman Jewish DataBank and *American Jewish Year Book*).
3. Devise questions that address "self-identified race, perceived race, and known ancestry geographic origins."
4. Adopt consistent weighting schemes for future national and local Jewish community surveys.
5. Utilize federal guidelines in regard to race and ethnicity to create consistency with Decennial Census data and the American Community Survey.

Our conclusions are that the percentage of Jews of Color is probably closer to 6% nationally than to "at least 12%–15%" and that this percentage has not increased *significantly* since 1990 but is likely to do so in the future. The many methodological issues in trying to estimate this population are covered well in Kelman et al. (2019). Regardless of the true percentage, we think readers would likely agree that, whether the true percentage is around 6%, 9%, or 12–15%, the Jewish community needs to make certain that all Jews are made to feel welcome.

---

proselytizing faith. On the other hand, as the diversity of the country increases, the number of Jews of Color could increase.

[8] See The Jewish Community Study of New York: 2011, Special Study of Nonwhite, Hispanic, and Multiracial Jewish Households at www.jewishdatabank.org.

Advocates for Jews of Color also make a case for equitable representation in Jewish organizations, communal policy making, and in the distribution of resources. Some signs of recognition of this diversity and the need to be inclusive are evident in the American Jewish community. This subject is also highlighted by the existence of at least four national Jewish organizations devoted to advancing Jewish diversity: the Jewish Multiracial Network (https://www.jewishmultiracialnetwork.org), the Jews of Color Field Building Initiative (Geller and Hemlock 2019) (https://jewsof-colorfieldbuilding.org), Jews in ALL Hues (www.jewsinallhues.org), and Be'chol Lashon (www.globaljews.org) (see Chap. 12). The Religious Action Center of Reform Judaism has also examined the subject (www.rac.org) and, among others, *The New York Jewish Week, The Times of Israel* (Ain 2019), and *Moment Magazine* (Pogrebin 2019) have featured recent articles on it.

The Miami Jewish community study (Sheskin 2015a) showed significant diversity: 33% of adults in Jewish households are foreign born and 3% of adults in Jewish households are from the former Soviet Union. Fifteen percent of Jewish adults are Hispanic, 9% are Israelis, and 17% are Sephardic Jews. (These groups are not mutually exclusive.) Recognizing the ethnic and racial diversity of the Miami Jewish population, the Federation has hired an inclusion specialist. In addition, the Federation's Board of Directors recently approved a Diversity and Inclusion Statement[9] to make an affirmative expression of its commitment to an inclusive and diverse community, one in which all are welcome. Even among Hispanic Jews, significant diversity exists: 24% of Hispanic Jewish adults come from Cuba, 18% from Argentina, 16% from Venezuela, 14% from Colombia, 6% from Peru, and 40% from other places.

In sum, despite our disagreement over estimates of Jews of Color, we are indebted to Kelman et al. (2019) for their research and for highlighting the significance of this diverse population for scholars and practitioners. **Indeed, the 6% which Jews of Color represent within American Jewry is three times greater than the 2% that American Jews constitute of the total US population.**

Given this introduction, this chapter, as in previous years, examines the size, geographic distribution, and selected characteristics of the US Jewish population. Section 5.1 addresses the procedures employed to estimate the Jewish population of more than 900 local Jewish communities and parts thereof. Section 5.2 presents the major changes in local Jewish population estimates since last year's *Year Book*. Section 5.3 examines population estimates for the country as a whole, the 4 US Census Regions, each state, the 9 US Census Divisions, the 21 largest US Metropolitan Statistical Areas (MSAs), the 21 largest Combined Statistical Areas (CSAs), and the 52 Jewish Federation Service Areas (JFSAs) with 20,000 or more Jews. Section 5.4 examines changes in the size and geographic distribution of the Jewish population at national, state, and regional scales from 1980 to 2019.

---

[9] The Statement reads: "The Greater Miami Jewish Federation strives to create a caring, inclusive and united community rooted in Jewish values and traditions. We embrace and value differences, such as ethnicity and national origin, religious denomination and spiritual practice, race, age, gender, gender identity, sexual orientation, socio-economic levels and mental and physical ability."

Section 5.5 presents a description of local Jewish community studies and a vignette on a recently completed community study: Detroit (MI). Section 5.6 presents five tables that compare local Jewish communities on political affiliation and voting registration and relate to Chap. 2 in this volume. Section 5.7 presents an atlas of US Jewish communities, including a national map of Jews by county and 14 regional and state maps of Jewish communities.

5.1   Population Estimation Methodology

The authors have endeavored to compile accurate estimates of the size of the Jewish population in each local Jewish community, working within the constraints involved in estimating the size of a rare population.[10] This effort is ongoing, as every year new local Jewish community studies are completed and population estimates are updated. The current Jewish population estimates are shown in the Appendix for about 900 Jewish communities and geographic subareas of those communities. A by-product of this effort is that the aggregation of these local estimates yields an estimate of the total US Jewish population, an estimate that actually may be a bit too high, as explained briefly in Sect. 5.3 below and in more detail by Sheskin and Dashefsky (2006). The national estimate presented below, however, is in general agreement with the 2013 estimates of the Pew Research Center (2013) and the Steinhardt Social Research Institute at Brandeis University (see Sect. 5.3 below).

These estimates are derived from four sources: (1) Scientific Estimates; (2) US Census Bureau Estimates; (3) Informant Estimates; and (4) Internet Estimates.

5.1.1   Source One: Scientific Estimates

Scientific Estimates are most often based on the results of surveys using random digit dial (RDD) telephone procedures (Sheskin 2001, p. 6) or Address Based Sampling (ABS) procedures (Link et al. 2008). In other cases, Scientific Estimates are based on Distinctive Jewish Name (DJN) studies.[11]

---

[10] For a description of some earlier efforts at estimating Jewish population in the US, see Kosmin, Ritterband, and Scheckner (1988), Marcus (1990), and Rabin (2017). See also Dashefsky and Sheskin (2012).

[11] See Sheskin (1998), Abrahamson (1986), Kaganoff (1996), Kosmin and Waterman (1989), and Lazerwitz (1986). The fact that about 8%–12% of US Jews, despite rising intermarriage rates, continue to have one of 36 Distinctive Jewish Names (Berman, Caplan, Cohen, Epstein, Feldman, Freedman, Friedman, Goldberg, Goldman, Goldstein, Goodman, Greenberg, Gross, Grossman, Jacobs, Jaffe, Kahn, Kaplan, Katz, Kohn, Levin, Levine, Levinson, Levy, Lieberman, Rosen, Rosenberg, Rosenthal, Rubin, Schwartz, Shapiro, Siegel, Silverman, Stern, Weinstein, and Weiss) facilitates making reasonable estimates of the Jewish population. See also Mateos (2014) on the uses of ethnic names in general.

DJN studies are sometimes used to estimate the Jewish population of an area by itself, or of areas contiguous to other areas in which an RDD telephone survey was completed,[12] or to update a population estimate from an earlier RDD study. In a few cases, a Scientific Estimate is based on a scientific study using a different methodology (neither RDD nor DJN).[13]

5.1.2 Source Two: US Census Bureau Estimates

Three New York Jewish communities inhabited by Hasidic sects are well above 90% Jewish:

1. Kiryas Joel in Orange County (Satmar Hasidim);
2. Kaser Village in Rockland County (Viznitz Hasidim); and
3. New Square in Rockland County (Skverer Hasidim).

Thus, US Census data were used to determine the Jewish population in those communities.

Although Monsey, another community in Rockland County with a Hasidic population, is not 90% or more Jewish, US Census Data on race and language spoken at home were used to derive a conservative estimate of the Jewish population in this community.

In addition, Hasidic Jews constitute such a large portion of the population of Lakewood, NJ, that growth in that population can be estimated from the American Community Survey (completed annually by the US Census Bureau).

Note that the decennial census has never asked religion. Two Census Bureau surveys did ask religion: An 1890 Census Bureau survey interviewed 10,000 Jewish households (Billings 1890) and the March 1957 Current Population Survey (CPS) asked religion (Bureau of the Census, no date, ca 1958).[14] Our thanks go to Joshua Comenetz, a geographer at the US Census, for his assistance with these estimates.

5.1.3 Source Three: Informant Estimates

Informants at the more than 140 Jewish Federations and the more than 300 Jewish Federations of North America (JFNA) "network communities" were contacted via email. Responses were emailed to the authors. These informants generally have

---

[12] For an example, see footnote 4 in Sheskin and Dashefsky (2008).

[13] Note that while we have classified DJN and "different methodology" methods as Scientific, the level of accuracy of such methods is well below that of the RDD or ABS methodology. Most studies using a "different methodology" have made concerted efforts to enumerate the known Jewish population via merging membership lists and surveying known Jewish households. An estimate of the unaffiliated Jewish population is then added to the affiliated population.

[14] For methods for estimating the ultra-Orthodox population from US Census data, see Comenetz (2006).

access to information about the number of households on the local Jewish Federation's mailing list and/or the number who are members of local synagogues and Jewish organizations. For communities that did not reply and for which other information was not available, estimates were retained from previous years.

5.1.4 Source Four: Internet Estimates

For some communities, we were able to update Jewish population estimates from Internet sources, such as newspaper, Jewish Federation, and synagogue websites. For example, the Goldring/Woldenberg Institute of Southern Jewish Life (www.isjl. org/history/archive/index.html) has been publishing vignettes on existing and defunct Jewish communities in 13 Southern States (Alabama, Arkansas, Florida, Georgia, Kentucky, Louisiana, Mississippi, North Carolina, Oklahoma, South Carolina, Tennessee, Virginia, and Texas). These provide useful information for updating the estimates for Jewish communities in these states.

We also consulted the websites of the Reform (www.urj.org) and Conservative (www.uscj.org) movements. Both have listings of affiliated synagogues. If a city is listed on one of these websites as having a synagogue that had not previously been listed in the *Year Book*, an entry is added to the *Year Book* as appropriate.

5.1.5 Other Considerations in Population Estimation

The estimates for more than 85% of the total number of Jews reported in the Appendix are based on Scientific Estimates or US Census Bureau estimates. Thus, less than 15% of the total estimated number of US Jews is based on the less-reliable Informant or Internet Estimates. An analysis by Sheskin and Dashefsky (2007, pp. 136–138) strongly suggests a greater reliability of Informant Estimates than was previously assumed. It should also be noted that only 12 estimates, accounting for 0.16% of the total estimated number of US Jews, are derived from Informant Estimates that are more than 20 years old.

All estimates are of Jews living in households (and in institutions, where data are available) and do not include non-Jews living in households with Jews. The estimates include Jews who are affiliated with the Jewish community, as well as Jews who are not. Different studies and different informants use different definitions of "who is a Jew." The problem of defining who is, and who is not, a Jew is discussed in numerous books and articles. Unlike most religious groups, "being Jewish" can be both a religious and an ethnic identity. The 2000–2001 National Jewish Population Survey (NJPS 2000–2001) (Kotler-Berkowitz et al. 2003) suggests that about one-fifth of US Jews are "Jews of no religion." This is consistent with the Pew Research Center result (Pew Research Center 2013, p. 7). Kosmin and Keysar (2013, p. 16) suggest that 30–40% of US Jews identify as "secular." One does not cease to be a Jew even if one is an atheist or an agnostic or does not participate in synagogue services or rituals. The exception to this rule, according to most Jewish identity authorities, is when a person born Jewish formally converts or practices another monotheistic religion or professes any form of Messianic Judaism.

During biblical times, Jewish identity was determined by patrilineal descent. During the rabbinic period, this was changed to matrilineal descent. In the contemporary period, Orthodox and Conservative rabbis officially recognize only matrilineal descent, while Reform (as of 1983) and Reconstructionist rabbis recognize, under certain circumstances, both matrilineal and patrilineal descent. Furthermore, Orthodox rabbis only recognize as Jewish those Jews-by-Choice who were converted by Orthodox rabbis.

In general, social scientists conducting survey research with US Jews do not wish to choose from the competing definitions of who is a Jew and have adopted the convention that all survey respondents who "consider themselves to be Jewish" (with the exceptions noted above) are counted as such. But, clearly the estimate of the size of the Jewish population of an area can differ depending on whom one counts as Jewish—and also, to some extent, on who is doing the counting.

Note that, for the most part, we have chosen to accept the definition of "who is a Jew" that was applied in each community by the researcher conducting a scientific demographic study in the community, even in cases where we disagree with that definition. In particular, this impacts the 2011 New York study (Cohen et al. 2011), which included in its total number of Jews about 100,000 persons who responded that they considered themselves Jewish in some way, although they identified their religion as Christian. Note that the world Jewish population chapter by Sergio DellaPergola (Chap. 8 in this volume) does not include these 100,000 persons in the total for the New York metropolitan area. This issue also arises, although to a lesser extent, in some California Jewish communities.

Population estimation is not an exact science. If the estimate of Jews in a community reported herein differs from the estimate reported last year, readers should not assume that the change occurred during the past year. Rather, the updated estimate in almost all cases reflects changes that have been occurring over a longer period of time that only recently have been documented.

5.2   Changes and Confirmations of Population Estimates

This year, 314 estimates in the Appendix were either changed or confirmed. A complete accounting of the changes made between the estimates in the 2018 and 2019 *Year Books* can be found in the Excel version of the Appendix which will be available at www.jewishdatabank.org in fall of 2020. New scientific studies were completed in Palm Beach County, FL. The more significant changes include:

Alabama. Based on a new informant estimate, the Jewish population of Birmingham increased from 5500 to 6300.

California. In the *San Francisco Bay Area,* the Jewish Federation of the East Bay (Oakland) merged with the Jewish Community Federation & Endowment Fund of

San Francisco, the Peninsula, Marin and Sonoma Counties. Thus, while the number of Jews in these areas did not change, the presentation of these numbers is different in this volume compared to 2018. The total for San Francisco is now 310,600 and it is now the third largest Federation service area in the US.

Connecticut. Based on a new informant estimate, the Jewish population of Greenwich increased from 7000 to 7500.

Florida. Based on new scientific studies, the estimate of the Jewish population of South Palm Beach County was changed from 131,300 to 136,100. The estimate for West Palm Beach was changed from 124,250 from 127,200. The estimate for Martin County was changed from 3100 to 8200.

Based on a new informant estimate, the Jewish population of Fort Walton Beach increased from 200 to 400.

Georgia. Based on a new informant estimate, the Jewish population of Augusta increased from 1400 to 1600.

Louisiana. Based on a new informant estimate, the Jewish population of New Orleans increased from 11,000 to 12,000.

North Carolina. Based on a new informant estimate, the Jewish population of Durham-Chapel Hill increased from 6000 to 7500. Based on a new informant estimate, the Jewish population of Raleigh-Cary increased from 6000 to 15,000. This significant increase was reviewed and approved by Ira Sheskin and by Laurence Kotler Berkowitz of the Jewish Federations of North America.

New York. Based on a new informant estimate, the Jewish population of Buffalo was decreased from 12,050 to 11,000.

Pennsylvania. Based on a new informant estimate, the Jewish population of Hazleton-Tamaqua decreased from 300 to 100.

Tennessee. Based on a new informant estimate, the Jewish population of Nashville increased from 8000 to 9000.

Texas. Based on a new informant estimate, the Jewish population of Austin increased from 20,000 to 30,000.

Vermont. Based on new informant estimates, the Jewish population of Stowe increased from 150 to 1000. The estimate for Burlington increased from 3300 to 3500.

Washington. Based on a new informant estimate, the Jewish population of Seattle increased from 63,400 to 64,650.

5.3   National, Regional, State, and Urban Area Totals

This Section examines population estimates for (1) the US as a whole, (2) the four US Census Regions, (3) the nine US Census Divisions, (4) each state, (5) the 21 largest Metropolitan Statistical Areas (MSAs), (6) the 21 largest Combined Statistical Areas (CSAs), and (7) the 52 largest Jewish Federation Service Areas (JFSAs).

5.3.1 National Jewish Population Estimates

More than a century ago, in the second volume of the *American Jewish Year Book*, the editor observed the following in regard to the US Jewish population:

> As the census of the United States has, in accordance with the spirit of American institutions, taken no heed of the religious convictions of American citizens, whether native-born or naturalized, all statements concerning the number of Jews living in this country are based on estimates, though several of the estimates have been most conscientiously made (Adler 1900, p. 623).

Figure 5.1 shows changes in the US Jewish population based on a variety of historic estimates from 1780 to the current year. Not shown on the graph is that the Jewish population of the US as of 1654 was 23, a number derived from court records when a boat load of Jewish refugees arrived in New Amsterdam (renamed New York in 1664). They came to the Dutch colony from Recife, Brazil, when it was ceded by the Dutch to the Portuguese.

The 1960 entry of 5,531,500 Jews is derived from the only time (1957) in the twentieth century that the US Census Bureau queried religion on a sample survey. All estimates for the time line from 1970 to the present are based on sample surveys, or, as in the current estimate reported in this chapter, an aggregate of local Jewish community estimates.

Figure 5.1 shows that the growth of the US Jewish population was fueled by four periods of Jewish migration (Sachar 1992; Dimont 1978).

Sephardic Migration (1654–1810) The Spanish Inquisition, which started in 1492, gave Jews the choice of conversion to Christianity or expulsion from Spain. Many migrated to parts of the Ottoman Empire, as the Ottoman Sultan welcomed Jews

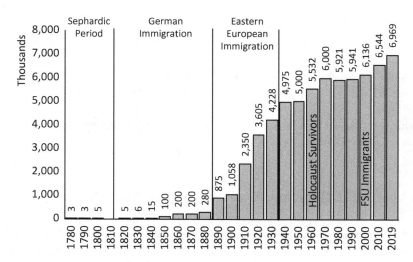

Fig. 5.1 Growth of the US Jewish population (Source: American Jewish Historical Society until 1980; American Jewish Year Book, 1990 to current date)

expelled from Spain. Others found their way to North America. These Jews were mostly shopkeepers and merchants. Not having been allowed to own land in most European countries, Jews did not develop farming skills. Thus, during colonial times, while 80% of Americans in general were farmers, the vast majority of Jews were urbanites. The earliest Jewish congregations were to be found in New Amsterdam (NY), Newport (RI), Savannah (GA), Philadelphia (PA), and Charleston (SC). During this period, the Jewish population increased to about 5000.

German Migration (1810–1880) While Napoleon's message of liberty, equality, and fraternity had improved conditions for Jews in Europe and had freed them from the confines of the ghetto in many areas (resulting in the Haskala, or Enlightenment movement, in Jewish history), with the end of the Napoleonic era, restrictions and difficulties were again faced by Jews in many areas, particularly in Germany (Hertzberg 1989). This led to a new wave of migration to the US. Many of these German immigrants were involved in retail trade, particularly in the garment industry. Some, who began peddling goods from push carts, gradually developed retail outlets, which evolved into major department stores, including Abraham and Strauss, Gimbel's, Bloomingdale's, Macy's, and others. When the Gold Rush of 1849 began, Jewish merchants left the East and became storekeepers in the West.

By 1880, two hundred new synagogues were established, which provided immigrant Jews with a place to pray as well as a familiar milieu and a center for networking and socialization. B'nai B'rith began as a (non-religious) group designed to maintain some aspects of Jewishness and to provide self-help. The German Jews also brought with them a new innovation in Jewish worship, Reform Judaism, which emerged in Hamburg at the end of the second decade of the nineteenth century. Economically, many German Jews prospered and, as they moved into the better neighborhoods and the non-Jews moved out, created "gilded" ghettos. Other German Jews remained poor. This German migration changed the American Jewish community from one in which most Jews were American born, to one in which most were foreign born. During this period, the Jewish population rose to about 280,000.

Eastern European Migration (1880–1930) The third period of Jewish migration began with the fall of czar Alexander II in Russia in 1881. Following this change in leadership, pogroms (anti-Jewish riots) occurred in Russia in 1881 and in Kishinev in 1903 and 1905 (Pasachoff and Littman 1995, pp. 218–221 and 236–239). Jews began to arrive in significant numbers in New York, Baltimore, Philadelphia, Boston, all prominent ports of entry, as well as Chicago (Sanders 1988, p. 167).

This migration was to change the culture of American Jewry from one dominated by German Jews, who by 1880 were, because of very high levels of assimilation, well on their way to becoming another Protestant denomination, to one dominated by more religious Eastern European Jewish migrants. More than 90% of Jewish migrants during this period were from Russia. In total, 3,715,000 Jews entered the US between 1880 and 1929. During this period, 8% of migrants to the US were Jewish (Barnavi 1992: pp.194–195). Fifteen percent of all European Jewry moved to the US during this period.

The Jewish immigrants came to the US to stay. The rate of reverse migration was only 5% for the Jewish population, compared to 35% for the general immigrant population (Sherman 1965, p. 61). This difference is probably related to the fact that while "economic opportunity" was a "pull" factor to the US for all immigrant groups, the "push" factor (antisemitism) for Jews to leave Europe was clearly more significant than for most, if not all, other ethnic groups.

At first, the German Jews wanted to spread the new Jewish immigrants throughout the country. The concept was that if the Jewish population became too geographically clustered, a reaction would occur among non-Jews, resulting in antisemitism. This led to the Galveston plan in the early 1900s, which attempted to divert some of the immigrants headed for northeastern cities, particularly New York, to Galveston, Texas (Sanders 1988, pp. 235–240). This plan failed, as Jews wanted to move to the large northeastern cities that already had large Jewish populations, where they could find *landsmannschaftan* or *landsleite*, cultural societies with membership from their former country, or even their former city (Shamir and Shavit 1986). This large-scale migration increased the US Jewish population to about five million by 1940.

Modern Migration (1930 to the present) The First (1921) and Second (1924) Johnson Acts (Sanders 1988, pp. 386–387) were passed by Congress, practically halting Jewish (and other Eastern and Southern European) immigration (Friesel 1990, p. 132). Unfortunately, this closing of the door to immigration occurred at the worst time for European Jews, as the next two decades saw the rise of Hitler and the Holocaust. Those Jews who came to the US during World War II clearly came as refugees, not merely as immigrants. Between 1933 and 1937, fewer than 40,000 Jews were permitted to enter the US. In total, about 110,000 Jews were permitted entry from 1938 to 1941. Wyman's (1984) *The Abandonment of the Jews* provides significant detail on this period.

After the birth of Israel in 1948, most of the world's Jewish migrants, especially displaced survivors of the Holocaust, migrated to Israel. However, Jewish migrants continued to enter the US, including 160,000 Holocaust survivors (Shapiro 1992, p. 126). Since the mid-1960s, more than 600,000 Jews have immigrated to the US from the former Soviet Union (Gold 2015).

During the past few decades, significant numbers of Israelis have moved to the US, resulting in between 120,000 and 350,000 American Israelis (Sheskin 2010; Gold 2015). Most live in New York, Los Angeles, and South Florida.

Smaller numbers of Jews have come to the US from a variety of other locations. Jewish migrants also came from the Arab world starting in 1948. Over ten thousand Hungarian Jews arrived just after the 1956 Hungarian revolution. A few thousand Cuban Jewish migrants came to Miami in the late 1950s and early 1960s. Starting in the 1970s and continuing to the present day, Jews from a number of Middle American and South American countries have moved to Miami (Sheskin 2015a). After the fall of the Shah of Iran in 1979, Jews came from Iran (particularly to Los Angeles).

5.3.2   Recent US Jewish Population Estimates

As stated above, estimating the number of US Jews is dependent upon one's definition of who is Jewish. Nevertheless, it is interesting that three different methodologies have recently produced estimates of the number of US Jews; and all three are in general agreement:

1. **AJYB 2019**: Based on a simple summation of local Jewish community estimates in the Appendix, the estimated size of the US Jewish community in 2019 is 6.968 million Jews, a significant increase of about 43,000 from the 2018 estimate of 6.925 million. This estimate is based on the aggregation of local estimates of more than 900 US Jewish communities and parts thereof. The bulk of the estimate is based on studies conducted over the past decade.

   For reasons discussed in Sheskin and Dashefsky (2006), it is unlikely that the number of US Jews really is as high as 6.968 million. Some percentage of part-year households (households who spend part of the year in one community and part in another), college students (who may be counted in both their home and school communities), and households who moved from one community to another between local Jewish community studies are likely to be double-counted in the Appendix. Thus, allowing for some double counting (see below), the *American Jewish Year Book* estimate is about 6.8–6.9 million.

2. **SSRI 2019**: The Steinhardt Social Research Institute (SSRI) Brandeis Meta-Analysis estimate of 7.49 million (Tighe et al. 2019) is based on an "averaging" of the percentage of Jews found in tens of national studies conducted over the past decade that happened to ask a question about religion (https://ajpp.brandeis.edu). Note that DellaPergola (2013) takes serious issue, among other matters, with: a) the fact that the SSRI estimates are based on adults only; b) SSRI's methodology for estimating the number of children; and c) SSRI's method for extrapolating the number of Jews "not by religion" from surveys that only estimate adult Jews by religion. See Chap. 8 in this volume for further elucidation of this issue.

3. **Pew 2013**: The Pew Research Center estimate (www.pewresearch.com) is 6.7 million. This includes 5.7 million persons who are Jewish and one million who are partly Jewish. This estimate is based on a national RDD study conducted in 2013 (Pew Research Center 2013). However, with the advent of a high percentage of households who rely solely on cell phones, the lower response rates on cell phones, and the increasing tendency of households with landlines to only answer calls from known phone numbers, conducting RDD surveys has become increasingly challenging and response rates on this and other surveys reflect this.

Thus, we have three recent estimates of the number of US Jews, all using different methodologies, each with their own significant shortcomings. Yet, all three methods yield relatively comparable estimates.

A different estimate of the US Jewish population (5.7 million) is employed in Chap. 8 of this volume on World Jewish Population. In that chapter, Sergio

DellaPergola relies on the Pew Research Center estimate, but, to be comparable with definitions accepted and used in other countries, and to keep to a consistent concept of "core Jewish" population worldwide, he does not include the one million persons who identify as "part Jewish" (who are included in the *American Jewish Year Book*, Pew, and SSRI totals). Thus, given our inclusion of about one million "part Jewish" persons (plus the 200,000 persons by which our 2019 estimate is higher than the Pew 2013 estimate) we would estimate 15.9 million Jews in the world. Therefore, according to our calculations, 43% (6.9 million) of Jews live in the US and 42% (6.7 million) in Israel.

5.3.3   Regional Jewish Population Estimates

Table 5.1 shows that, on a regional basis, the Jewish population is distributed very differently from the US population as a whole. Map 5.1 shows the definitions of the Census Regions and Census Divisions.

While only 17% of all Americans live in the Northeast, 44% of Jews live there. While 21% of all Americans live in the Midwest, only 11% of Jews do. While 38% of all Americans live in the South, only 22% of Jews do. Approximately equal percentages of all Americans and Jews live in the West (23–24%).

Table 5.1 Jewish population by census region and census division, 2019

Census region/division	Jewish population		Total population	
	Number	Percentage distribution	Number	Percentage distribution
Northeast	**3,074,620**	**44.1**	**56,111,079**	**17.2**
Middle Atlantic	2,614,635	37.5	41,257,789	12.6
New England	459,985	6.6	14,853,290	4.5
Midwest	**734,330**	**10.5**	**68,308,744**	**20.9**
East North Central	591,755	8.5	46,931,883	14.3
West North Central	142,575	2.0	21,376,861	6.5
South	**1,541,155**	**22.1**	**124,753,948**	**38.1**
East South Central	45,850	0.7	19,112,813	5.8
South Atlantic	1,297,275	18.6	65,322,408	20.0
West South Central	198,030	2.8	40,318,727	12.3
West	**1,618,495**	**23.2**	**77,993,663**	**23.8**
Mountain	308,570	4.4	24,552,385	7.5
Pacific	1,309,925	18.8	53,441,278	16.3
Total	**6,968,600**	**100.0**	**327,167,434**	**100.0**

Notes: (1) The total number of US Jews is probably about 6.8–6.9 million due to some double-counting between states (Sheskin and Dashefsky 2006); (2) While this table presents our best estimates of Jews for 2019, the more than 900 estimates that have been aggregated to derive this table are most frequently from previous years but remain the best estimates for the current date. For the dates of all 900 estimates, see the Appendix; (3) the total population data are from www.census.gov (July 1, 2018 estimates)

Map 5.1   US Census regions and divisions

5.3.4   State Jewish Population Estimates

The first data column of Table 5.2 shows the number of Jews in each state. Eight states have a Jewish population of 200,000 or more: New York (1,771,000); California (1,183,000); Florida (644,000); New Jersey (545,000); Illinois (298,000); Pennsylvania (298,000); Massachusetts (293,000); and Maryland (237,000). Seven states have between 100,000 and 200,000 Jews: Texas (176,000); Virginia (151,000); Ohio (148,000); Georgia (129,000); Connecticut (118,000); Arizona (107,000); and Colorado (103,000).

The third column of Table 5.2 shows the percentage of the population in each state that is Jewish. Overall, about 2.1% of Americans are Jewish, but the percentage is about 4% or higher in New York (9.1%), the District of Columbia (8.2%), New Jersey (6.1%), Massachusetts (4.2%), and Maryland (3.9%).

The final column of Table 5.2 shows the percentage of the total US Jewish population that each state represents. The four states with the largest shares of the Jewish population—New York (25%), California (17%), Florida (9%), and New Jersey (8%)—account for 60% of the 6.968 million US Jews reported in Table 5.2. These four states account for only 27% of the total US population. The Jewish population, then, is very geographically concentrated, particularly compared to the total population. In fact, using a measure known as the index of dissimilarity or the segregation index (Burt, Barber, and Rigby 2009, pp. 127–129), 38% of Jews would have to change their state of residence for Jews to be geographically distributed among the states in the same proportions as the total population. The same measure for 1980

Table 5.2 Jewish population by state, 2019

State	Number of Jews	Total population	Percentage Jewish	% of total US Jewish population
Alabama	10,325	4,887,871	0.2	0.1
Alaska	5750	737,438	0.8	0.1
Arizona	106,725	7,171,646	1.5	1.5
Arkansas	2225	3,013,825	0.1	0.0
California	1,182,990	39,557,045	3.0	17.0
Colorado	102,600	5,695,564	1.8	1.5
Connecticut	118,350	3,572,665	3.3	1.7
Delaware	15,100	967,171	1.6	0.2
District of Columbia	57,300	702,455	8.2	0.8
Florida[a]	643,895	21,299,325	3.0	9.2
Georgia	128,720	10,519,475	1.2	1.8
Hawaii	7100	1,420,491	0.5	0.1
Idaho	2125	1,754,208	0.1	0.0
Illinois	297,735	12,741,080	2.3	4.3
Indiana	25,245	6,691,878	0.4	0.4
Iowa	5275	3,156,145	0.2	0.1
Kansas	17,425	2,911,505	0.6	0.3
Kentucky	11,200	4,468,402	0.3	0.2
Louisiana	14,900	4,659,978	0.3	0.2
Maine	12,550	1,338,404	0.9	0.2
Maryland	236,600	6,042,718	3.9	3.4
Massachusetts	293,080	6,902,149	4.2	4.2
Michigan	87,905	9,995,915	0.9	1.3
Minnesota	45,600	5,611,179	0.8	0.7
Mississippi	1525	2,986,530	0.1	0.0
Missouri	64,275	6,126,452	1.0	0.9
Montana	1395	1,062,305	0.1	0.0
Nebraska	9350	1,929,268	0.5	0.1
Nevada	76,300	3,034,392	2.5	1.1
New Hampshire	10,120	1,356,458	0.7	0.1
New Jersey	545,450	8,908,520	6.1	7.8
New Mexico	12,625	2,095,428	0.6	0.2
New York	1,771,320	19,542,209	9.1	25.4
North Carolina	45,935	10,383,620	0.4	0.7
North Dakota	400	760,077	0.1	0.0
Ohio	147,815	11,689,442	1.3	2.1
Oklahoma	4425	3,943,079	0.1	0.1
Oregon	40,650	4,190,713	1.0	0.6
Pennsylvania	297,865	12,807,060	2.3	4.3
Rhode Island	18,750	1,057,315	1.8	0.3

(continued)

Table 5.2 (continued)

State	Number of Jews	Total population	Percentage Jewish	% of total US Jewish population
South Carolina	16,820	5,084,127	0.3	0.2
South Dakota	250	882,235	0.0	0.0
Tennessee	22,800	6,770,010	0.3	0.3
Texas	176,480	28,701,845	0.6	2.5
Utah	5650	3,161,105	0.2	0.1
Vermont	7135	626,299	1.1	0.1
Virginia	150,595	8,517,685	1.8	2.2
Washington	73,435	7,535,591	1.0	1.1
West Virginia	2310	1,805,832	0.1	0.0
Wisconsin	33,055	5,813,568	0.6	0.5
Wyoming	1150	577,737	0.2	0.0
Total	6,968,600	327,167,434	2.1	100.0

See the Notes on Table 5.1
[a]Excludes 65,000 Jews who live in Florida for 3–7 months of the year and are counted in their primary state of residence

was 44%, indicating that Jews are less geographically concentrated in 2019 than they were in 1980, when the four states with the largest Jewish populations—New York (36%), California (13%), Florida (8%), and New Jersey (8%)—accounted for 64% of the 5.921 million US Jews.

5.3.5   Urban Area Jewish Population Estimates

Estimates of the Jewish population are provided for three different definitions of urban areas: Metropolitan Statistical Areas (MSAs) (Table 5.3), Combined Statistical Areas (CSAs) (Table 5.4), and Jewish Federation Service Areas (JFSAs) (Table 5.5).

Metropolitan Statistical Areas (MSAs) are geographic entities delineated by the US Office of Management and Budget (OMB) for use by Federal statistical agencies in collecting, tabulating, and publishing Federal statistics. Each MSA has a core urban area with a population of at least 50,000. Each MSA consists of one or more counties and includes the counties containing the core urban area, as well as any adjacent counties that have a high degree of social and economic integration (as measured by commuting to work) with the urban core.

Combined Statistical Areas (CSAs), also defined by OMB, consist of two or more adjacent MSAs or micropolitan areas (essentially MSAs where the major city is between 10,000 and 50,000 population), that have substantial employment interchange. Thus, CSAs are always geographically larger than MSAs.

Table 5.3 Jewish population in the top 21 metropolitan statistical areas (MSAs), 2019

MSA rank	MSA name	Population Total	Jewish	% Jewish
1	New York-Newark-Jersey City, NY-NJ-PA	19,979,477	2,107,800	10.6
2	Los Angeles-Long Beach-Anaheim, CA	13,291,486	617,480	4.6
3	Chicago-Naperville-Elgin, IL-IN-WI	9,498,716	294,280	3.1
4	Dallas-Fort Worth-Arlington, TX	7,539,211	75,005	1.0
5	Houston-The Woodlands-Sugar Land, TX	6,997,384	51,640	0.7
6	Washington-Arlington-Alexandria, DC-VA-MD-WV	6,249,950	297,290	4.8
7	Miami-Ft. Lauderdale-Pompano Beach, FL	6,198,782	535,500	8.6
8	Philadelphia-Camden-Wilmington, PA-NJ-DE-MD	6,096,372	283,450	4.6
9	Atlanta-Sandy Springs-Alpharetta, GA	5,949,951	119,800	2.0
10	Boston-Cambridge-Newton, MA-NH	4,875,390	257,460	5.3
11	Phoenix-Mesa-Chandler, AZ	4,857,962	82,900	1.7
12	San Francisco-Oakland-Berkeley, CA	4,729,484	244,000	5.2
13	Riverside-San Bernardino-Ontario, CA	4,622,361	23,625	0.5
14	Detroit-Warren-Livonia, MI	4,326,442	71,750	1.7
15	Seattle-Tacoma-Bellevue, WA	3,939,363	62,350	1.6
16	Minneapolis-St. Paul-Bloomington, MN-WI	3,629,190	44,500	1.2
17	San Diego-Chula Vista-Carlsbad, CA	3,343,364	100,000	3.0
18	Tampa-St. Petersburg-Clearwater, FL	3,142,663	51,350	1.6
19	Denver Aurora-Lakewood, CO	2,932,415	95,000	3.2
20	St. Louis, MO-IL	2,805,465	61,300	2.2
21	Baltimore-Columbia-Towson, MD	2,802,789	115,800	1.9
Total Population in Top 21 MSAs		127,808,217	5,527,280	4.3
Total US Population		327,167,434	6,968,600	2.1
Percentage of Population in Top 21 MSAs		39.1%	79.3%	

Notes: (1) See www.census.gov/geographies/reference-files/time-series/demo/metro-micro/delin-eation-files.html for a list of the counties included in each MSA; (2) Total population data are for July 1, 2018; (3) Jewish population of 5,527,280 excludes 65,000 part-year residents who are included in MSAs 7, 13, and 18. See also the Notes on Table 5.1. (3) CSA 7 above includes Palm Beach County

Table 5.4 Jewish population in the top 21 combined statistical areas (CSAs), 2019

CSA rank	CSA name	Population Total	Jewish	% Jewish
1	New York-Newark, NY-NJ-CT-PA	22,679,948	2225,700	9.8
2	Los Angeles-Long Beach, CA	18,764,814	685,575	3.7
3	Chicago-Naperville, Elgin IL-IN-WI	9,866,910	294,685	3.0
4	Washington-Baltimore-Arlington, DC-MD-VA-WV-PA	9,778,360	414,220	4.2
5	San Jose-San Francisco-Oakland, CA	9,666,055	362,500	3.8
6	Boston-Worcester-Providence, MA-RI-NH-CT	8,285,407	297,863	3.6
7	Dallas-Fort Worth, TX-OK	7,957,493	75,065	0.9
8	Philadelphia-Reading-Camden, PA-NJ-DE-MD	7,204,035	300,090	4.2
9	Houston-The Woodlands, TX	7,197,883	51,767	0.7
10	Miami-Fort Lauderdale-Port-St. Lucie, FL	6,913,262	550,760	8.0
11	Atlanta-Athens-Clarke County-Sandy Springs, GA	6,775,511	120,675	1.8
12	Detroit-Warren-Ann Arbor, MI	5,353,002	81,250	1.5
13	Phoenix-Mesa, AZ	4,911,851	82,900	1.7
14	Seattle-Tacoma, WA	4,853,364	67,710	1.4
15	Orlando-Deltona-Daytona Beach, FL	4,096,575	39,100	1.0
16	Minneapolis-St. Paul, MN-WI	4,014,593	44,500	1.1
17	Cleveland-Akron-Canton, OH	3,599,264	85,828	2.4
18	Denver-Aurora, CO	3,572,798	95,495	2.7
19	Portland-Vancouver, Salem, OR-WA	3,239,335	37,900	1.2
20	St. Louis-St. Charles-Farmington, MO-IL	2,909,777	61,300	2.1
21	Charlotte-Concord, NC-SC	2,753,810	12,665	0.5
Total Population in Top 21 CSAs		154,394,046	5,931,148	3.8
Total US Population		327,167,434	6,968,600	2.1
Percentage of Population in Top 21 CSAs		47.2%	85.1%	

Notes: (1) See www.census.gov/geographies/reference-files/time-series/demo/metro-micro/delineation-files.html for a list of the counties included in each CSA; (2) Total population data are for 2018; (3) Jewish population of 5,931,148 excludes 56,400 part-year residents who are included in CSA 10 and 15 See also the Notes on Table 5.1

Table 5.5 Jewish population of Jewish federation service areas with 20,000 or more Jews, 2019

	Community	Number of Jews
1	New York	1,538,000
2	Los Angeles	519,200
3	San Francisco	310,600
4	Washington	295,500
5	Chicago	291,800
6	Boston	248,000
7	Philadelphia	214,700
8	Broward County	149,000
9	South Palm Beach	136,100
10	West Palm Beach	127,200
11	Miami	123,200
12	Atlanta	119,800
13	Middlesex-Monmouth (NJ)	122,000
14	Northern NJ	119,400
15	MetroWest NJ	115,000
16	Rockland County (NY)	102,600
17	San Diego	100,000
18	Denver	95,000
19	Baltimore	93,400
20	Ocean County (NJ)	83,000
21	Phoenix	82,900
22	Cleveland	80,800
23	Orange County (CA)	80,000
24	Las Vegas	72,300
25	Detroit	71,750
26	Dallas	70,000
27	Seattle	64,650
28	St. Louis	61,100
29	Southern NJ	56,700
30	Houston	51,000
31	Pittsburgh	49,200
32	San Jose	39,400
33	Portland (OR)	36,400
34	Orange County (NY)	37,300
35	Hartford	32,800
36	Orlando	31,100
37	Austin	30,000
38	San Gabriel (CA)	30,000
39	Minneapolis	29,300
40	St. Petersburg	28,000
41	Cincinnati	27,000
42	Milwaukee	25,800

(continued)

Table 5.5 (continued)

	Community	Number of Jews
43	Columbus	25,500
44	Upper Fairfield County (CT)	24,450
45	Long Beach (CA)	23,750
46	New Haven	23,000
47	Tampa	23,000
48	Tucson	22,400
49	Sacramento	21,000
50	Albany (NY)	20,500
51	Palm Springs (CA)	20,000
52	Somerset (NJ)	20,000

Jewish Federation Service Areas (JFSAs) are areas served by local Jewish Federations[15] and are the result of historical forces and the geographic distribution of the Jewish population. History has produced service areas that vary significantly in size and population. UJA-Federation of New York serves an 8-county area with 1,538,000 Jews, while three Jewish Federations serve parts of Fairfield County (CT), which has about 50,000 Jews.

The JFSAs rarely align themselves geographically with MSAs or CSAs. Thus, the JFSA estimates in Table 5.5 are often quite different from the estimates for MSAs and CSAs found in Tables 5.3 and 5.4. The JFSAs are generally smaller than the geographic areas of the MSAs and much smaller than CSAs. The Appendix definitions generally reflect JFSAs. For example, the Appendix and Table 5.5 show the Jewish population of the Baltimore JFSA to be 93,400, while Table 5.3 shows a Jewish population of 115,800, because the Baltimore-Columbia-Towson, MD MSA covers a larger geographic area than the Baltimore JFSA. Table 5.4 shows that the Jewish population of the Washington-Baltimore-Arlington CSA is 414,220.

Table 5.3 provides data for the 21 largest **MSAs** in 2019. Thirty-nine percent of all Americans live in the 21 largest MSAs, as do 79% of US Jews, and while Jews

---

[15] Among US Jewish communities, more than 140 are served by organizations known as Jewish Federations. The Jewish Federations of North America is the central coordinating body for the local Jewish Federations. A Jewish Federation is a central fundraising and coordinating body for the area it serves. It provides funds for various Jewish social service agencies, volunteer programs, educational institutions and programs, and related organizations, with allocations being made to the various beneficiary agencies by a planning or allocation committee. A local Jewish Federation's broad purposes are to provide "human services (generally, but not exclusively, to the local Jewish community) and to fund programs designed to build commitment to the Jewish people locally, in Israel, and throughout the world." In recent years, funding programs to assure Jewish continuity have become a major focus of Jewish Federation efforts. Most planning in the US Jewish community is done either nationally (by The Jewish Federations of North America and other national organizations) or locally by Jewish Federations. Data for local Jewish Federation service areas is essential to the US Jewish community and to planning both locally and nationally (Sheskin 2009, 2013).

are only 2.1% of all Americans, they constitute 4.3% of the population of the top 21 MSAs.

The New York-Newark-Jersey City, NY-NJ-PA MSA and Miami-Fort Lauderdale-Pompano Beach, FL MSAs are 10.6% and 8.6% Jewish, respectively, while the Los Angeles-Long Beach-Anaheim, CA, Washington-Arlington-Alexandria, DC-VA-MD-WV, Philadelphia-Camden-Wilmington, PA-NJ-DE-MD, Boston-Cambridge-Newton, MA-NH, and San Francisco-Oakland-Berkeley, CA MSAs are all 4.6–5.3% Jewish.

Table 5.4 provides data for the 21 largest **CSAs** in 2019. Forty-seven percent of all Americans live in the 21 largest CSAs, as do 85% of US Jews, and while Jews are only 2.1% of all Americans, they constitute 3.8% of the population of the top 21 CSAs.

The New York-Newark, NY-NJ-CT-PA CSA is 9.8% Jewish, while the Miami-Fort Lauderdale-Port St. Lucie, FL CSA is 8.0% Jewish. The Boston-Worcester-Providence, MA-RI-NH-CT, Washington-Baltimore-Arlington, DC-MD-VA-WV-PA, Los Angeles-Long Beach, CA, Philadelphia-Reading-Camden, PA-NJ-DE-MD, and San Jose-San Francisco-Oakland, CA CSAs are all 3.6–4.2% Jewish.

Table 5.5 provides data for the **JFSAs** with 20,000 or more Jews in 2019. The Jewish Federation service areas with 200,000 or more Jews are New York (1,538,000), Los Angeles (519,200), San Francisco (310,600), Washington (295,500), Chicago (291,800), Boston (248,000), and Philadelphia (214,600). Note that the Florida community numbers in this table include part-year residents.

5.4   Changes in the Size of the Jewish Population, 1980–2019

This section examines changes in the geographic distribution of the Jewish population from 1980 to 2019. In examining the maps, note that the dot symbols are randomly placed within each state (Maps 5.2, 5.3, and 5.4). For additional information about the geographic distribution of American Jews over time, see the previous editions of the *American Jewish Year Book* and de Lange (1984), Gilbert (1985), Friesel (1990), Marcus (1990), Barnavi (1992), Gilbert (1995), Sheskin (1997), Ahituv (2003), and Rebhun (2011). For perspectives on Jewish population change in the future, see Goldscheider (2004) and DellaPergola (2011).

5.4.1   National Level Changes

Overall, the data reveal an increase of just over one million (18%) Jews from 1980–2019 from 5.921 million in 1980 to 6.968 million in 2019. Most of the increase is clearly due to migration, including the influx of over 600,000 Jews from the Former Soviet Union (Gold 2015), the existence of as many as 350,000 Israelis

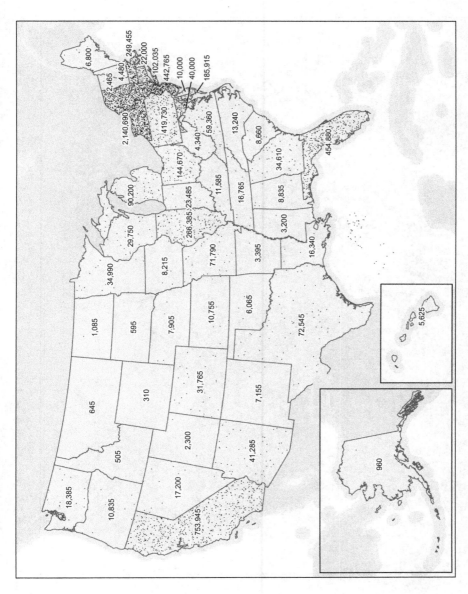

Map 5.2   Jewish population, 1980 (Each dot represents 1,500 Jews)

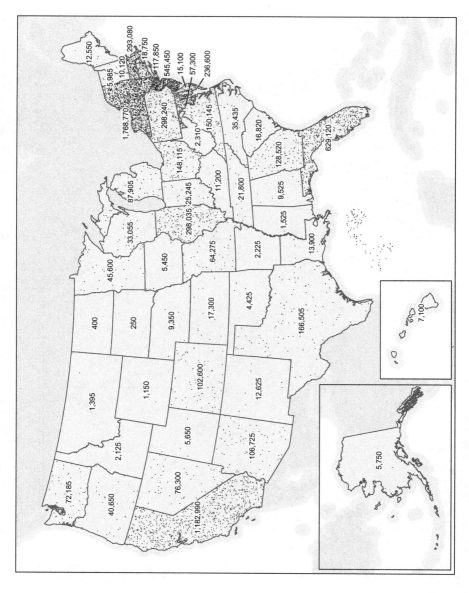

Map 5.3 Jewish population, 2019 (Each dot represents 1,500 Jews)

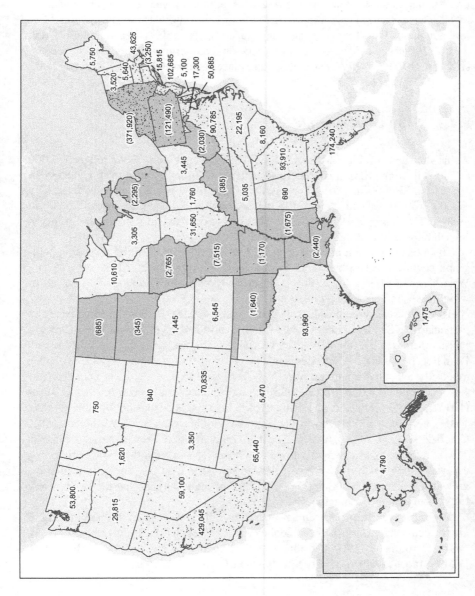

Map 5.4 Changes in Jewish population, 1980-2019 (Each dot represents 1,500 Jews)

(Sheskin 2010 and Gold 2015) in the US, and migration from Central and South America (Gold 2015) from places like Argentina, Colombia, Venezuela, and Peru. But this increase in the estimate is not entirely *actual* growth in the Jewish population. Rather, at least some of this increase is due to improved estimates produced by local Jewish community studies. In addition, the internet was not available to researchers in 1980. Today we list many places in Appendix A that were not listed in the 1980 *Year Book,* having found evidence on the internet as to their existence and size. (The 1980 *Year Book* listed about 650 places compared to the current over 900.)

5.4.2   State Level Changes

At the state level (Table 5.6), the number of Jews in New York decreased by 369,000 (17%), reflecting primarily the decrease in the New York City area, from 1,998,000 in 1980 to 1,538,000 in 2019. The number of Jews in Pennsylvania decreased by 122,000 (29%), reflecting primarily the decrease in Philadelphia, from 295,000 in 1980 to 214,700 in 2019. The only other notable decrease in states with significant Jewish population is Missouri (7500, 11%).

The most significant *percentage* decreases not referenced in the preceding paragraph occurred in North Dakota (63%), South Dakota (58%), Mississippi (52%), West Virginia (47%), Iowa (36%), Arkansas (35%), and Oklahoma (27%), all of which have small Jewish populations.

The number of Jews in California increased by 429,000 (57%), reflecting increases particularly in San Francisco, Orange County, and San Diego. The number of Jews in Florida increased by 189,000 (42%), reflecting increases particularly in Broward and Palm Beach Counties.[16] Other significant increases include New Jersey (103,000, 23%), especially reflecting migration from New York City to the suburbs in northern New Jersey; Georgia (94,000, 272%), reflecting most notably the growth in Atlanta; Texas (104,000, 143%), reflecting largely the growth in Dallas and Houston; Virginia (91,000, 154%), reflecting the growth in the northern Virginia suburbs of Washington, DC; Colorado (71,000, 223%), reflecting primarily the growth in Denver; Arizona (65,000, 159%), reflecting particularly the growth in Phoenix; Nevada (59,000, 344%), reflecting especially the growth in Las Vegas; Washington State (55,000, 299%), reflecting the growth in Seattle, and Maryland (51,000, 27%), reflecting the growth in the Montgomery County suburbs of Washington, DC.

The most significant *percentage* increases not referenced in the previous paragraph occurred in Alaska (499%), Idaho (321%), Oregon (275%), Wyoming (271%), North Carolina (247%), Vermont (190%), Utah (146%), and New Hampshire (126%), most of which have relatively small Jewish populations.

---

[16] The number of Jews in Florida in 2019 excludes Jews in part-year households ("snowbirds"). The historical record does not indicate the portion of the population that was part year in 1980.

Table 5.6 Changes in Jewish population by state, 1980–2019

State	1980	2019	Increase/(decrease)	Percentage change
Alabama	8835	10,325	1490	16.9
Alaska	960	5750	4790	499.0
Arizona	41,285	106,725	65,440	158.5
Arkansas	3395	2225	(1170)	−34.5
California	753,945	1,182,990	429,045	56.9
Colorado	31,765	102,600	70,835	223.0
Connecticut	102,035	118,350	16,315	16.0
Delaware	10,000	15,100	5100	51.0
District of Columbia	40,000	57,300	17,300	43.3
Florida	454,880	643,895	189,015	41.6
Georgia	34,610	128,720	94,110	271.9
Hawaii	5625	7100	1475	26.2
Idaho	505	2125	1620	320.8
Illinois	266,385	297,735	31,350	11.8
Indiana	23,485	25,245	1760	7.5
Iowa	8215	5275	(2940)	−35.8
Kansas	10,755	17,425	6670	62.0
Kentucky	11,585	11,200	(385)	−3.3
Louisiana	16,340	14,900	(1440)	−8.8
Maine	6800	12,550	5750	84.6
Maryland	185,915	236,600	50,685	27.3
Massachusetts	249,455	293,080	43,625	17.5
Michigan	90,200	87,905	(2295)	−2.5
Minnesota	34,990	45,600	10,610	30.3
Mississippi	3200	1525	(1675)	−52.3
Missouri	71,790	64,275	(7515)	−10.5
Montana	645	1395	750	116.3
Nebraska	7905	9350	1445	18.3
Nevada	17,200	76,300	59,100	343.6
New Hampshire	4480	10,120	5640	125.9
New Jersey	442,765	545,450	102,685	23.2
New Mexico	7155	12,625	5470	76.5
New York	2,140,690	1,771,320	(369,370)	−17.3
North Carolina	13,240	45,935	32,695	246.9
North Dakota	1085	400	(685)	−63.1
Ohio	144,670	147,815	3145	2.2
Oklahoma	6065	4425	(1640)	−27.0
Oregon	10,835	40,650	29,815	275.2
Pennsylvania	419,730	297,865	(121,865)	−29.0
Rhode Island	22,000	18,750	(3250)	−14.8
South Carolina	8660	16,820	8160	94.2
South Dakota	595	250	(345)	−58.0

(continued)

Table 5.6 (continued)

State	1980	2019	Increase/(decrease)	Percentage change
Tennessee	16,765	22,800	6035	36.0
Texas	72,545	176,480	103,935	143.3
Utah	2300	5650	3350	145.7
Vermont	2465	7135	4670	189.5
Virginia	59,360	150,595	91,235	153.7
Washington	18,385	73,435	55,050	299.4
West Virginia	4340	2310	(2030)	−46.8
Wisconsin	29,750	33,055	3305	11.1
Wyoming	310	1150	840	271.0
Total	5,920,895	6,968,600	1,047,705	17.7

See Notes 1 and 2 on Table 5.1

5.4.3 Regional Level Changes

Table 5.7 shows that the changes in the geographic distribution of Jews by Census Region and Census Division from 1980–2019, to some extent, reflect the changing geographic distribution of Americans in general. The percentage of Jews in the Northeast decreased from 57% in 1980 to 44% in 2019. The 12% of Jews in the Midwest decreased to 11% in 2019. The percentage of Jews in the South increased from 16% to 22%, and the percentage of Jews in the West increased from 15% to 23%. In sum, the Jewish population shifted from the Northeast to the West and the South.

The final column of Table 5.7 shows that the number of Jews in the Northeast decreased by 9% (316,000) from 1980 to 2019 and the number of Jews in the Midwest increased by 6% (45,000). The number of Jews in the South increased by 62% (591,000). The number of Jews in the West increased by 82% (728,000).

5.5 Local Jewish Community Studies

Most local Jewish community studies produce information about the size and geographic distribution of the Jewish population, migration patterns, basic demographics (e.g., age, marital status, secular education, employment status, income), religiosity, intermarriage, membership in the organized Jewish community, Jewish education, familiarity with and perception of Jewish agencies, social service needs, visits and emotional attachment to Israel, experience with and perception of antisemitism, usage of Jewish and general media, philanthropy, and other areas of interest.

In 2018, one local scientific Jewish community study with probability sampling was completed in Detroit.

Table 5.7 Changes in Jewish population by census region and census division, 1980–2019

Census region/ division	1980		2019		
	Number of Jews	Percentage distribution	Number of Jews	Percentage distribution	Percentage change
Northeast	**3,390,420**	**57.3**	**3,074,620**	**44.1**	**9.3**
Middle Atlantic	3,003,185	50.7	2,614,635	37.5	12.9
New England	387,235	6.5	459,985	6.6	18.8
Midwest	**689,825**	**11.7**	**734,330**	**10.5**	**6.5**
East North Central	554,490	9.4	591,755	8.5	6.7
West North Central	135,335	2.3	142,575	2.0	5.4
South	**949,735**	**16.0**	**1,541,155**	**22.1**	**62.3**
East South Central	40,385	0.7	45,850	0.7	13.5
South Atlantic	811,005	13.7	1,297,275	18.6	60.0
West South Central	98,345	1.7	198,030	2.8	101.4
West	**890,915**	**15.0**	**1,618,495**	**23.2**	**81.7**
Mountain	101,165	1.7	308,570	4.4	205.0
Pacific	789,750	13.3	1,309,925	18.8	65.9
Total	**5,920,895**	**100.0**	**6,968,600**	**100.0**	**17.7**

See Notes 1 and 2 on Table 5.1

5.5.1   Detroit, MI (2018)

This 2018 study covers the service area of the Jewish Federation of Metropolitan Detroit in Michigan. The study area includes Oakland, Wayne, and Macomb County. The consultant was Ira M. Sheskin of the University of Miami. The field work was completed by SSRS (Dr. David Dutwin) of Glen Mills, PA (Sheskin 2018). One thousand two hundred telephone interviews were completed, using a combination of RDD sampling, Distinctive Jewish Name sampling, Jewish Federation list sampling, and lists of cell phone numbers with non-local area codes but with Detroit billing addresses. Previous scientific community studies of the Detroit Jewish population were conducted in 1989 and 2005.

Population Size and Geography. This study finds that 83,800 persons live in 31,500 Jewish households in Detroit, of whom 70,800 persons (85%) are Jewish. Detroit is the 26th largest US Jewish community. Including Jews living in institutions, the total Jewish population of Detroit is 71,750.

From 2005 to 2018, the number of Jewish households increased by 1500 (5%); the number of persons in Jewish households increased by 5800 (7%); but the number of Jews in Jewish households decreased by 700 (1%). Of course, the decrease in Jews in Jewish households is within the margin of error but stands in contrast to the increase in households and persons. This is almost certainly due to the doubling of the percentage of married couples who are intermarried between 2005 and 2018.

The percentage of Detroit households who are Jewish remained about the same (1.9% in 2005 and 2.1% in 2018).

In 2018, 72% of Jewish households live in the Core Area and 28%, in the Non-Core Area. 22% of Jewish households live in West Bloomfield, 15% in Oak Park-Huntington Woods, 14% in Bloomfield-Birmingham-Franklin, 11% in Wayne County, and 9% in Farmington.

From 2005 to 2018, the number of persons in Jewish households in the Core Area increased by about 1700 persons (3%) from 2005 to 2018. The number of persons in Jewish households in the Non-Core Area increased by 4100 persons (24%). The number of persons in Jewish households increased in Bloomfield-Birmingham-Franklin (7050, 103%), West Oakland County (3550, 114%), Macomb County (2550, 300%), East Oakland County (2000, 95%), and Wayne County (1450, 18%). Significant decreases were seen in Farmington (5900, 45%) and West Bloomfield (3400, 18%). The number of Jewish households in the City of Detroit, consistent with the significant decrease in households in Detroit in general (based on data from the American Community Survey), decreased from 1900 households in 2005 to 800 households in 2018.

The 62% of adults in Jewish households who were born in Detroit increased from 57% in 2005. The 62% is the highest of about 40 comparison Jewish communities. Ten percent of adults in Jewish households are foreign-born. Five percent of Jewish households contain an LGBT adult.

The 4% of new Jewish households (in residence for 0–4 years in Detroit) is the third lowest of about 45 comparison Jewish communities and compares to 3% in 2005. The 87% of households in residence for 20 or more years is the highest of about 45 comparison Jewish communities and compares to 88% in 2005. Thus, Detroit is a Jewish community with local roots.

Forty-nine percent of adult children from Jewish households in which the respondent is age 50 or over *who have established their own homes* live in Detroit, which is the fifth highest of about 30 comparison Jewish communities.

Demography. Eighteen percent of persons in Jewish households in Detroit are age 0–17; 23% are age 18–34; 15% are age 35–49; 23% are age 50–64; and 21% are age 65 and over. The 23% age 18–34 is the fourth highest of about 45 comparison Jewish communities. The 18% under age 17 decreased from 25% in 2005. The 23% age 18–34 increased from 12% in 2005. The 15% age 35–49 compares to 17% in 2005. The 23% age 50–64 compares to 22% in 2005. The 21% age 65 and over decreased from 24% in 2005. The median age of persons in Jewish households declined from 47.1 years in 2005 to 45.7 years in 2018.

The 2.66 average household size compares to 2.60 in 2005.

Among about 35 comparison Jewish communities, the 19% of Jewish households with only children age 18 and over at home is the third highest. Among about 45 comparison Jewish communities, the 23% of married households with no children at home is the fourth lowest. Among 40 comparison Jewish communities, the 6% of married households with no children at home age 50–64 is the second lowest.

The 57% of adults in Jewish households who are currently married is the fifth lowest of about 45 comparison Jewish communities. The 57% decreased from 66% in 2005. The 26% who are single, never married is the second highest of 40 comparison Jewish communities. The 26% increased from 17% in 2005. The 5% who are currently widowed is the fifth lowest of 40 comparison Jewish communities. The 5% decreased from 12% in 2005.

In 1989, 61% of adults under age 35 were currently married. This decreased to 24% in 2005 and to 17% in 2018, indicating a tendency for the current generation to marry later in life. This has important implications for synagogues since most households do not join a synagogue until they marry.

The 76% of adults age 25 and over in Jewish households with a 4-year college degree or higher is above average among about 40 comparison Jewish communities and has increased significantly from 63% in 2005. The 76% is well above the 34% for all American adults (both Jewish and non-Jewish) age 25 and over.

Forty-four percent of adults in Jewish households are employed full time; 15% are employed part time; 2% were unemployed at the time of the survey; 19% are retired; 5% are homemakers; 12% are students; and 3% are disabled. The 33% of persons age 65 and over in Jewish households who are employed full time or part time has increased from 29% in 2005.

The median Jewish household income of $107,000 (in 2017 dollars) is about average and the $135,000 median household income (in 2017 dollars) of households with children is about average among about 45 comparison Jewish communities. The $107,000 overall median household income (in 2017 dollars) compares to $110,000 (in 2017 dollars) in 2005.

Eight percent of Jewish households earn an annual income under $25,000. The 2.0% of households with incomes below the Federal poverty levels is about average among about 30 comparison Jewish communities.

On a subjective measure of financial status, 18% of respondents in Jewish households report that they are "well off"; 26% "have some extra money"; 29% "have enough money"; 24% are "just managing to make ends meet"; and 4% "cannot make ends meet."

Jewish Connections. Nine percent of Jewish respondents in Detroit identify as Orthodox; 20%, Conservative; 2%, Reconstructionist; 35%, Reform; 4%, Humanist; and 31%, Just Jewish. The 9% Orthodox is the seventh highest, the 20% Conservative is below average, the 35% Reform and the 35% Just Jewish/Humanist are about average among about 45 comparison Jewish communities.

From 2005 to 2018, the percentage Orthodox changed slightly from 11% to 9%. The percentage Conservative decreased by 9% points; the percentage Reform remained about the same; and the percentage Just Jewish increased by 13% points.

Sixty-two percent of Jewish respondents feel that being Jewish is very important in their lives; 31%, somewhat important; 6%, not too important; and 1%, not at all important. The 62% is about average among about 20 comparison Jewish communities and compares to 73% in 1989.

Ninety-nine percent of Jewish respondents are proud to be Jewish. Ninety-one percent of Jewish respondents agree with the statement "I have a strong sense of belonging to the Jewish people," and 81% agree with the statement "I have a special responsibility to take care of Jews in need around the world."

Having a mezuzah on the front door is observed by 69% of households. Participating in a Passover Seder is always/usually observed by 74% of households and lighting Chanukah candles, by 71%. Lighting Sabbath candles is always/usually observed by 22% of households. Of the 41% of Jewish households who never light Sabbath candles, 5% always/usually do something else to observe the Sabbath. Keeping a kosher home is observed by 19% of households and keeping kosher in and out of the home, by 13% of respondents. While 8% of respondents refrain from using electricity on the Sabbath, 18% of households always/usually have a Christmas tree in the home (and 25% always/usually/sometimes have one).

Among the comparison Jewish communities, Detroit exhibits average levels of religious practice, except for keeping kosher in the home and outside the home and the use of electricity on the Sabbath, which are among the highest of the comparison communities.

The percentage who have a mezuzah on the front door decreased from 77% in 2005 to 69% in 2018. The 74% who always/usually participate in a Passover Seder decreased from 82% in 2005 to 74% in 2018. The 71% who always/usually light Chanukah candles decreased from 77% in 2005 to 71% in 2018. The 22% who always/usually light Sabbath candles decreased from 29% in 2005 to 22% in 2018. The 19% who keep a kosher home changed from 22% in 2005. The 13% who keep kosher in and out of the home changed from 14% in 2005. The 8% who refrain from electrical use on the Sabbath changed from 10% in 2005. Thus, in general home religious practice has decreased from 2005 to 2018.

The percentage who always/usually/sometimes have a Christmas tree in the home increased from 15% in 2005 to 25% in 2018.

The 23% of Jewish respondents who attend synagogue services once per month or more and the 31% who never attend services are both about average among about 40 and 35 comparison Jewish communities, respectively.

The 30% of married couples in Jewish households who are intermarried is well below average among about 45 comparison Jewish communities and compares to 16% in 2005. Thirty-nine percent of children age 0–17 in intermarried households are not being raised Jewish and 17% are being raised part Jewish.

Memberships. The 39% synagogue membership of Jewish households in Detroit is about average among about 45 comparison Jewish communities and has decreased from 50% in 2005 and 52% in 1989. The lower synagogue membership rate in 2018 is likely due to the aging of the population and an increasing age at first marriage.

The 52% of Jewish households with children and the 19% of intermarried households who are synagogue members are both about average among about 45 comparison Jewish communities.

In the past year, 71% of Jewish households participated in or attended religious services or programs at, or sponsored by, a local synagogue; and 13% participated in or attended religious services or programs at, or sponsored by, Chabad.

The 8% of Jewish households who are members of the Jewish Community Center (JCC) located in Detroit compares to 15% in 2005. The 8% is below average among about 45 comparison JCCs. The 51% who participated in a JCC program in the past year is the third highest of about 45 comparison JCCs and compares to 45% in 2005 and 76% in 1989. Thus, while membership is low, participation is high.

The 19% of households who are members of or regular participants in a Jewish organization (other than a synagogue or JCC) is the sixth lowest of about 40 comparison Jewish communities and has decreased from 36% in 2005.

The 45% of Jewish households who are *associated with the Jewish community* (someone in the household is a member of a synagogue, JCC, or Jewish organization) is the seventh lowest of about 40 comparison Jewish communities and compares to 64% in 2005.

Adult Jewish Education. Of respondents in Jewish households in Detroit who were born or raised Jewish, the 81% who had some formal Jewish education as children is about average among about 35 comparison Jewish communities, as is the 13% who attended a Jewish day school as children among 35 comparison Jewish communities. The 13% compares to 15% in 2005.

The 51% of respondents who were born or raised Jewish who attended or worked at a Jewish overnight camp as children is the highest of about 30 comparison Jewish communities. The 51% increased from 42% in 2005. The 47% who participated in a Jewish youth group as teenagers is the fourth highest of about 25 comparison Jewish communities. The 24% of college attendees who participated in Hillel/Chabad (other than on the High Holidays) while in college is about average among about 25 comparison Jewish communities.

In the past year, 31% of Jewish respondents attended an adult Jewish education program or class; 37% engaged in "any other type" of Jewish study or learning (on their own, online, with a friend, or with a teacher); and 57% visited a Jewish museum or attended a Jewish cultural event, such as a lecture by an author, a film, a play, or a musical performance.

Children's Jewish Education. The 63% of Detroit's Jewish children age 0–5 in a preschool/child care program who attend a Jewish preschool/child care program (*Jewish market share*) is about average among about 35 comparison Jewish communities. Sixty-three percent of households with Jewish children have received children's books in the mail from the PJ Library.

Of children age 5–12 in private school, 86% attend a Jewish day school (*Jewish market share*), which is the sixth highest of about 40 comparison Jewish communities.

Eighty-one percent of Jewish children age 5–12 and 49% of Jewish children age 13–17 currently attend formal Jewish education. The 82% of Jewish children age 13–17 who received some formal Jewish education at some time in their childhood is about average among about 40 comparison Jewish communities.

Israel. The 63% of Jewish households in Detroit in which a member visited Israel is the second highest of about 25 comparison Jewish communities and has increased from 58% in 2005. The 33% of households with Jewish children age 6–17 who have sent a Jewish child on a trip to Israel is the fourth highest of about 35 comparison

Jewish communities. Forty-six percent of households with Jewish children age 6–17 (whose Jewish children have not visited Israel) did not send a Jewish child on a trip to Israel because of cost.

The 50% of Jewish respondents who are extremely or very emotionally attached to Israel is about average among about 30 comparison Jewish communities and has decreased from 56% in 2005.

Thus, the connection of Detroit's Jewish population to Israel is quite strong.

Seventy percent of Jewish respondents had conversations with other Jews in Detroit about the political situation in Israel. Forty percent of Jewish respondents who have had such conversations frequently/sometimes hesitate to express their views about the political situation in Israel because those views might cause tension with other Jews in Detroit.

Anti-Semitism. The 16% of respondents in Jewish households in Detroit who personally experienced anti-Semitism in the local community in the past year is about average among about 30 comparison Jewish communities. The 16% compares to 15% in 2005. The 13% of households with Jewish children age 6–17 in which a Jewish child age 6–17 experienced anti-Semitism in the local community in the past year is about average among about 25 comparison Jewish communities and has decreased from 18% in 2005.

The 45% of respondents in Jewish households who perceive a great deal or moderate amount of anti-Semitism in the local community is the fourth highest of about 25 comparison Jewish communities and compares to 61% in 2005.

Thus, both the experience with (among children) and perception of anti-Semitism have decreased since 2005.

Holocaust Survivors. Just 1% (300 households) of *households* contain a survivor, 5% (1670 households) contain a child of a survivor, and 12% (3650 households) contain a grandchild of a survivor. Overall, 14% (4500 households) of households contain a survivor, and/or the child of a survivor, and/or the grandchild of a survivor. Only 0.5% (300 adults) of *Jewish adults* consider themselves to be survivors, 3% (1800 adults) consider themselves to be children of survivors, and 7% (4000 adults) consider themselves to be grandchildren of survivors. Data from Jewish Family Service suggests the estimates of the number of survivors may be low.

Media. Thirty percent of Jewish respondents in Detroit always read the *Detroit Jewish News*; 4%, usually; 40%, sometimes; and 27%, never. The 34% who always/ usually read the *Detroit Jewish News* is about average among about 25 comparison Jewish newspapers and compares to 57% in 2005.

The 28% of Jewish respondents in Detroit who visited the local Jewish Federation website in the past year is the second highest of about 20 comparison Jewish communities.

Philanthropy. The 42% of Jewish households in Detroit who donated to the local Jewish Federation in the past year is above average among about 45 comparison Jewish communities and has decreased significantly from 55% in 2005.

The 58% of Jewish households who donated to other Jewish charities (Jewish charities other than Jewish Federations) in the past year is above average among about 40 comparison Jewish communities and has decreased from 68% in 2005. The 67% who donated to *any* Jewish charity in the past year is above average among about 40 comparison Jewish communities and has decreased from 78% in 2005. The 79% who donated to non-Jewish charities in the past year is about average among about 40 comparison Jewish communities and has decreased from 85% in 2005.

Twenty-seven percent of respondents age 50 and over do not have wills; 58% have wills that contain no provisions for charities; 9% have wills that contain provisions for Jewish Charities (including 2% who have a provision for the Jewish Federation of Metropolitan Detroit); and 6% have wills that contain provisions for Non-Jewish Charities only.

The 32% who volunteered for Jewish organizations in the past year is the fifth highest of about 25 comparison Jewish communities and has decreased from 42% in 2005. The 41% who volunteered for non-Jewish organizations in the past year is about average among about 25 comparison Jewish communities and compares to 37% in 2005.

Helping Jews locally who are in financial need and providing services for the Jewish Elderly are the two major motivations that respondents in Jewish households consider to be the most important in their decision to donate to Jewish causes.

Politics. Fifteen percent of respondents think of themselves as Republican; 51%, Democrat, and 34%, Independent. Ninety-seven percent of respondents are registered to vote and 94% of registered voters voted in the last presidential election.

5.6   Comparisons Among Jewish Communities

Since 2000, about 45 US Jewish communities have completed one or more *scientific* Jewish community studies. Each year, this chapter presents tables comparing the results of these studies. This year, five tables are presented: (1) political party; (2) percentage of respondents who are Republican by age; (3) percentage of respondents who are Republican by Jewish identification; (4) registered to vote; and (5) registered to vote for respondents under age 35. These tables were selected because they complement the discussion in Chap. 2 of this volume.

The comparisons among Jewish communities should be treated with caution, because the studies span a 15-year period, use different sampling methods, use different questionnaires (Bradburn et al. 2004), and differ in other ways (Sheskin and Dashefsky 2007, pp. 136–138; Sheskin 2005). Note that many more comparison tables may be found in Sheskin (2001) and Sheskin (2015b).

Table 5.8 Political party community comparisons

Base: respondents

Community	Year	Republican (%)	Democrat	Independent	Something else
Washington	2003	11	69	17	4
Minneapolis	2004	9	66	19	6
St. Paul	2004	13	63	18	6
Bergen	2001	11	63	19	6
Seattle	2000	8	63	25	4
San Francisco	2004	9	61	12	18
St. Petersburg	2017	25	56	19	0
Broward	2016	17	56	26	1
Indianapolis	2017	16	55	29	0
Miami	2014	18	53	21	9
Detroit	2018	15	51	34	0
Omaha	2017	17	51	33	0
Houston	2016	31	41	24	5

These tables contain relatively few references to the 45 local Jewish community studies completed since 2000. Many communities, because most studies are sponsored by the local Jewish Federation, which is a non-partisan organization, have felt a reluctance to ask a political question until recently. More communities are now recognizing that understanding political preference is important in understanding local Jewish communities.

5.6.1 Political Party

Table 5.8 shows that the percentage of respondents who identify as Republican varies from 8 to 9% in Seattle, San Francisco, and Minneapolis to 31% in Houston, although most communities have percentages between 11% and 18%. St. Petersburg is another "outlier" at 25%. Houston's high value could be due to its location in a Republican state, but the Houston metropolitan area generally votes Democratic. And, while Nebraska is also a Republican state, only 17% of Jews are Republican in Omaha.

5.6.2 Political Party by Age

Table 5.9 shows political party by age. The thesis that younger Jews are more likely to be Republican receives only minimal support. The high value Republican for respondents under age 35 for Detroit and Bergen is more related to the large young

Table 5.9 Percentage Republican by age community comparisons

Base: Jewish respondents

Community	Year	Under 35 (%)	35–49 (%)	50–64 (%)	65–74 (%)	75+ (%)
Houston	2016	36	25	35	28	31
Omaha	2017	4	21	11	29	23
Miami	2014	21	21	19	15	15
Broward	2016	20	19	22	14	10
St. Paul	2004	14	15	7	7	5
Detroit	2018	21	14	16	13	15
Bergen	2001	22	14	10	6	4
Minneapolis	2004	17	13	6	5	3
Washington	2003	9	13	10	13	6
Seattle	2000	0	13	28	2	2
Indianapolis	2017	13	10	30	14	12
St. Petersburg	2017	NA	10	30	29	23
San Francisco	2004	12	8	8	7	13

Orthodox population in those two communities, and, as will be seen in the next table, the Orthodox do tend to vote more Republican than other Jewish groups. Some tendency does exist, with the exception of Houston, Omaha, and St. Peterburg, for a low percentage of Republicans among the two older age groups (65–74 and 75 and over). A few communities do show a higher percentage of Republicans among younger respondents (Bergen, Broward, Miami, St. Paul, Minneapolis), but most of the differences are relatively minor.

5.6.3   Political Party by Jewish Identification

Table 5.10 shows political party by Jewish identification. Note that respondents typically are asked whether they consider themselves to be Orthodox, Conservative, Reconstructionist, Reform, or Just Jewish. Such Jewish identification is a self-identification and is not necessarily based on (nor consistent with) synagogue membership, ideology, or religious practice. In fact, discrepancies between Jewish identification and practice are sometimes evident. For example, respondents may identify as Orthodox or Conservative but report that they do not keep kosher. Respondents may identify as Reform but report that they never attend synagogue services. Also, respondents may identify as Conservative and belong to a Reform synagogue, or to no synagogue at all. Thus, what is being examined here is really a philosophical position and not always a behavioral description.

The thesis that Orthodox Jews are more likely to be Republican than other groups is supported by the table. Only in Bergen and Indianapolis are Orthodox Jews *not*

Table 5.10 Percentage Republican by Jewish identification

Base: Jewish respondents

Community	Year	Orthodox (%)	Conservative (%)	Reform (%)	Just Jewish (%)
Houston	2016	52	37	26	31
Omaha	2017	36	15	12	20
Miami	2014	43	16	15	16
Broward	2016	40	17	15	18
St. Paul	2004	45	8	7	14
Detroit	2018	40	16	12	14
Bergen	2001	12	8	14	13
Minneapolis	2004	54	7	7	11
Washington	2003	28	9	12	9
Seattle	2000	9	0	1	20
Indianapolis	2017	14	16	14	19
St. Petersburg	2017	NA	34	12	30
Twin Cities	2004	45	8	7	13

Note: Due to a small sample size, a combined number for Minneapolis/St. Paul is presented for Orthodox

more likely to be Republican. For example, in Detroit, 40% of the Orthodox are Republican, compared to 16% of Conservative Jews, 12% of Reform Jews, and 14% of the Just Jewish. Yet, note that in only two communities (Houston and Minneapolis) are a majority of Orthodox Jews Republican; and in those cases, the percentages are just over half (52 and 54%).

5.6.4   Registered to Vote

Table 5.11 shows that very large percentages of Jewish respondents who are citizens are registered to vote, ranging from 88% in New York to 98% in Omaha. This compares to 59% for all Americans nationwide from the US Census Bureau's 2014 Current Population Survey (CPS). Given the upcoming presidential election in 2020, note that it appears likely that whatever the percentage that adult Jews are of all American adults in a metropolitan area, their share of the vote will likely average about 30% higher than their share of the population, thereby increasing their voting power.

5.6.5   Registered to Vote for Respondents Under Age 35

Table 5.12 shows that very large percentages of Jewish respondents under age 35 who are citizens are registered to vote, ranging from 72% in New York to 100% in Omaha. This compares to 45% for all Americans nationwide under age 35 in 2014

Table 5.11 Registered to vote community comparisons

Base: Jewish respondents		
Community	Year	%
Omaha	2017	98
Detroit	2018	97
Broward	2016	96
Columbus	2013	96
S Palm Beach	2005	96
W Palm Beach	2005	96
Washington	2003	96
Indianapolis	2017	95
St. Petersburg	2017	95
Miami	2014	95
Houston	2016	94
Bergen	2001	92
New York	2011	88
US (Current Population Survey)	2014	59

Table 5.12 Registered to vote under age 35 community comparisons

Base: Jewish respondents under age 35		
Community	Year	%
Omaha	2017	100
W Palm Beach	2005	94
Washington	2003	94
Indianapolis	2017	93
Miami	2014	93
Detroit	2018	92
St. Petersburg	2017	92
Broward	2016	87
Houston	2016	86
Columbus	2013	85
S Palm Beach	2005	83
Bergen	2001	82
New York	2011	72
US (Current Population Survey)	2014	45

from the US Census Bureau's 2014 Current Population Survey (CPS). Note that in almost all cases, the percentage under age 35 is lower than the overall percentage shown in Table 5.11.

Only Detroit asked if registered respondents actually voted in the last presidential election (2016). About 94% under age 35 claimed to have voted.

5.7 Atlas of US Jewish Communities

This Section presents regional and state maps showing the approximate sizes of each Jewish community. State maps are presented for the states with the largest Jewish populations. In a few cases, states with smaller Jewish populations are presented on the maps because of proximity. For example, Delaware is presented on the Maryland map. The Appendix should be used in conjunction with the maps, as it provides more exact population estimates and more detailed descriptions of the geographic areas included within each community. Note that in some places, county names are utilized, and in other cases, town or city names appear. In general, we have tried to use the names that reflect the manner in which the local Jewish community identifies itself. In some cases, because of spacing issues on the maps, we have deviated from this rule.

The rankings of the population sizes and the population sizes of the communities within the US are from Table 5.5, which is based on the Jewish populations of Jewish Federation service areas.

Map 5.5 shows the percentage of Jews by county (Comenetz 2011). As expected, the percentages are highest in the Northeast, California, and Florida. Note that in some cases, particularly in the West, where counties are generally larger, it may seem that the Jewish population is spread over larger areas of a state than is actually the case. For example, San Bernardino County (CA), the largest county in area in the US, covers 20,105 square miles and is larger than nine US states. Almost all Jews in this county live in the southwestern section of the county, but on the map a very large area is shaded.

Large areas of the country have virtually no Jewish population. Rural, agrarian areas, in particular, are often devoid of any Jewish population. In Europe, from which most US Jews can trace their ancestry, Jews often did not become farmers, because (1) during many eras and in many geographic locations, Jews were not allowed to own land; and (2) as a people who often felt that they could be expelled at any time, Jews did not tend to invest in real estate, which clearly could not be taken with them if they were expelled. Thus, when Jews came to the US, they tended to settle in urban areas. This is still the trend.

While these maps present our best estimates for 2019, note that the date on most estimates are most frequently from previous years. They remain, however, the best estimates available for the current year. For the dates of all estimates, see the Appendix.

5.7.1 New England (Maps 5.6 and 5.7)

Connecticut (Map 5.6). The estimates for Hartford (32,800 Jews), New Haven (23,000), and Upper Fairfield County[17] (24,450) are based on 2000, 2010, and 2000 RDD studies, respectively. Hartford is the largest Jewish community in Connecticut,

---

[17] Only the Westport, Weston, Wilton, Norwalk areas of Upper Fairfield County were included in the survey in 2000.

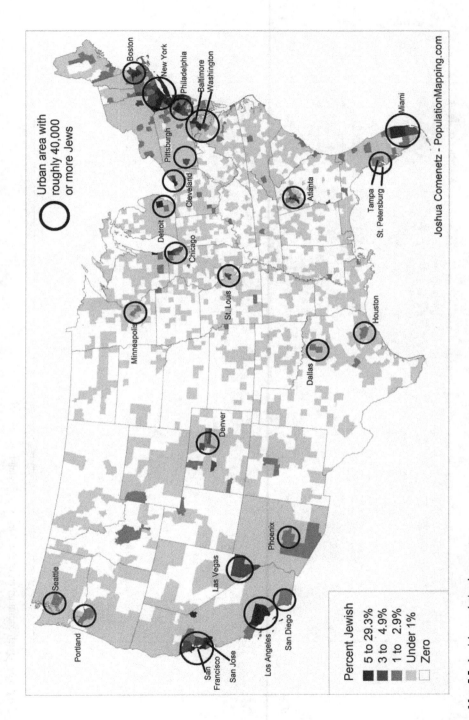

Map 5.5 Jewish population by county

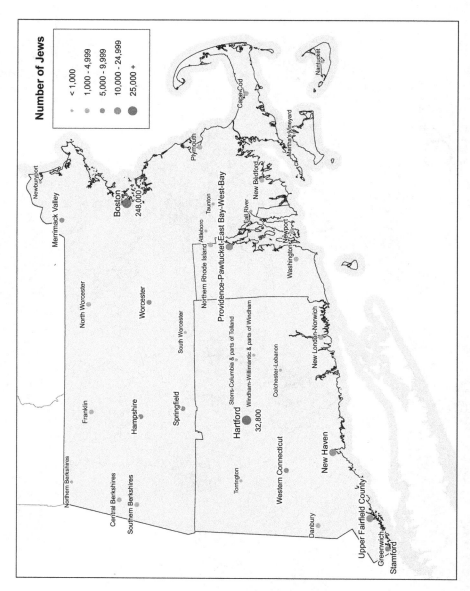

Map 5.6 Jewish communities of Southern New England

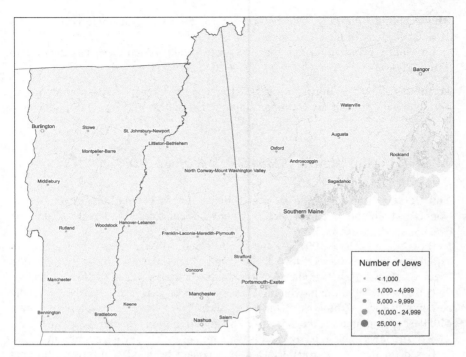

Map 5.7 Jewish communities of Northern New England

accounts for 28% of the Jews in Connecticut, and is the 35th largest US Jewish community. New Haven is the 46th largest US Jewish community.

The estimate for Western Connecticut (8000) is based on a 2010 DJN study.

All other estimates are Informant/Internet Estimates.

Maine (Map 5.7). Based on a 2007 RDD study, 8350 Jews live in Southern Maine (Portland). The estimates for Oxford County (South Paris) (750 Jews), Androscoggin County (Lewiston-Auburn) (600), and Sagadahoc (Bath) (400) are DJN estimates. All other estimates are Informant/Internet Estimates.

Massachusetts (Map 5.6). Based on a 2015 RDD study, 248,000 Jews live in Boston. Boston is the largest Jewish community in Massachusetts, accounts for 85% of the Jews in Massachusetts, and is the 6th largest US Jewish community.

The estimate for Worcester (9000 Jews) is based on a 2014 Informant update of a 1986 RDD study. An estimate of 7050 Jews (including part-year residents) for the Berkshires (2008) is based on a scientific study using a different methodology (neither RDD nor DJN). Attleboro, based on a 2002 DJN estimate, has 800 Jews. All other estimates are Informant/Internet Estimates.

New Hampshire (Map 5.7). Manchester (4000 Jews) is the largest Jewish community in New Hampshire. Most of the estimates are Informant/Internet Estimates.

Rhode Island (Map 5.6). The estimate of 18,750 Jews in the state is based on a 2002 RDD study of the entire state.

For more information on the Jews of Rhode Island, see Goodman and Smith (2004).

Vermont (Map 5.7). Burlington (3500 Jews) is the largest Jewish community in Vermont. All estimates are Informant/Internet Estimates.

5.7.2   Middle Atlantic *(Maps 5.8, 5.9, and 5.10)*

New Jersey (Map 5.8). The most significant Jewish populations are in Bergen County, Monmouth County, Ocean County, Southern New Jersey, Middlesex County, and Essex County.

Based, in part, on a 1997 RDD study in Monmouth and a 2008 RDD study in Middlesex, the now merged Jewish community, called the Jewish Federation in the Heart of New Jersey (Middlesex-Monmouth), contains 122,000 Jews, including 70,000 Jews in Monmouth (which includes 6000 part-year residents who live in the community for 3–7 months of the year) and 52,000 Jews in Middlesex County. Middlesex-Monmouth is the largest Jewish community in New Jersey, accounts for 21% of the Jews in New Jersey, and is the 13th largest US Jewish community

Based, in part, on a 2001 RDD study updated by a 2016 Informant/Internet Estimate, 119,400 Jews live in the service area of the Jewish Federation of Northern New Jersey, including 100,000 in Bergen County, 8000 in northern Passaic County, and 11,400 in Hudson County. Northern New Jersey is the 2nd largest Jewish community in New Jersey, accounts for 22% of the Jews in New Jersey, and is the 14th largest US Jewish community

Based, in part, on a 1998 RDD study, updated with a 2012 DJN study, 115,000 Jews live in the service area of the Jewish Federation of Greater MetroWest NJ, including 48,200 in Essex County, 30,300 in Morris County, 24,400 in Union County, 7400 in northern Somerset County, and 4700 in Sussex County. Greater MetroWest is the third largest Jewish community in New Jersey, accounts for 21% of the Jews in New Jersey, and is the 15th largest US Jewish community.

The estimate for Ocean County (83,000 Jews) is based on an Informant/Internet Estimate that is derived, in part, from a count of a mailing list said to be a complete listing of the ultra-Orthodox community in the Lakewood area. Ocean County is the 20th largest US Jewish community.

Other communities with RDD studies in New Jersey include Southern New Jersey (2013) (56,700), and Atlantic and Cape May Counties (2004) (20,400, including 8200 part-year residents). The 1991 Southern New Jersey (Cherry Hill) study was updated with a 2013 scientific study using a different methodology (neither RDD nor DJN). Southern New Jersey is the 29th largest US Jewish community.

A 2012 DJN study estimates 20,000 Jews for the service area of the Jewish Federation of Somerset, Hunterdon & Warren Counties, including 11,600 Jews in

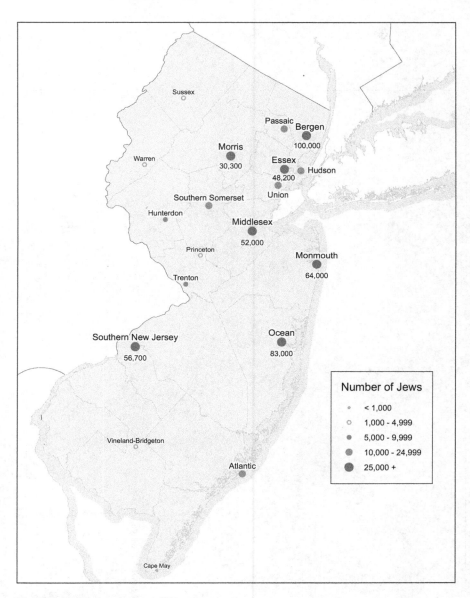

Map 5.8 Jewish communities of New Jersey

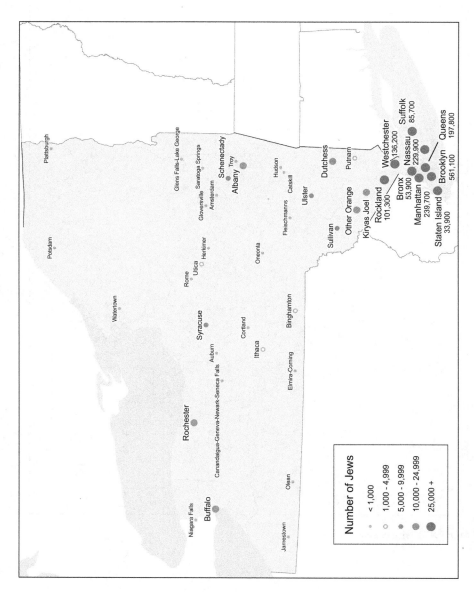

Map 5.9 Jewish communities of New York

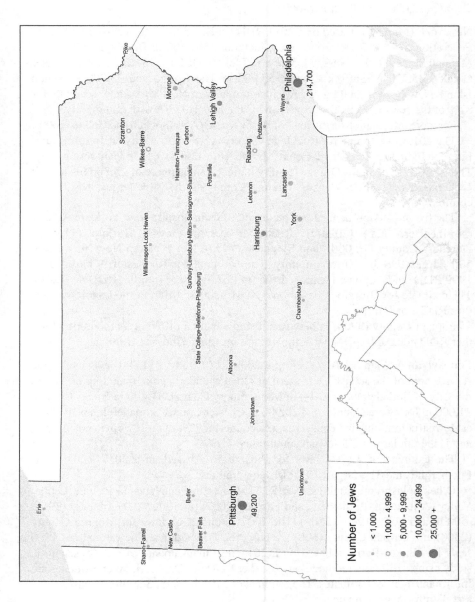

Map 5.10 Jewish communities of Pennsylvania

southern Somerset County, 6000 in Hunterdon County, and 2400 in Warren County. Somerset, Hunterdon & Warren Counties is the 52nd largest US Jewish community.

All other estimates are Informant/Internet Estimates, including southern Passaic County (12,000) and Trenton (6000).

New York (Map 5.9). Based on a 2011 RDD study, 1,538,000 Jews live in the UJA-Federation of New York service area, including 561,100 in Brooklyn, 239,700 in Manhattan, 229,900 in Nassau County, 197,800 in Queens, 136,200 in Westchester County, 85,700 in Suffolk County, 53,900 in The Bronx, and 33,900 in Staten Island. New York is the largest Jewish community in New York State, accounts for 87% of the Jews in New York State, and is the largest US Jewish community.

For more information on the Jews of Brooklyn, see Abramovitch and Galvin (2002).

The 101,300 estimate for Rockland County is based primarily on an Informant/Internet Estimate. Rockland County is the 16th largest US Jewish community. The 37,000 estimate for Orange County includes an estimate of 25,300 for Kiryas Joel, based on the US Census. Orange County is the 34th largest US Jewish community.

The five most significant Jewish communities in upstate New York are Albany (Northeastern NY) (20,500), Rochester (19,900 Jews), Buffalo (11,000), Dutchess County (10,000), and Syracuse (7000). Northeastern New York is the 50th largest US Jewish community. The estimate for Rochester is based on a 1999 RDD study, updated using a different methodology (neither RDD nor DJN). The estimate for Buffalo is based on a study using a different methodology (neither RDD nor DJN).

Putnam County (3900) is based on a study using a different methodology (neither RDD nor DJN). All other estimates are Informant/Internet Estimates.

Pennsylvania (Map 5.10). Based on a 2009 RDD study, 214,700 Jews live in the service area of the Jewish Federation of Greater Philadelphia, including 66,900 in the City of Philadelphia, 64,500 in Montgomery County, 41,400 in Bucks County, 21,000 in Delaware County, and 20,900 in Chester County. Philadelphia is the largest Jewish community in Pennsylvania, accounts for 72% of the Jews in Pennsylvania, and is the 6th largest US Jewish community.

The estimate of 49,200 Jews for Pittsburgh is based on a 2017 RDD study. Pittsburgh is the 31st largest US Jewish community.

Other Jewish communities with RDD studies in Pennsylvania include Lehigh Valley (Allentown, Bethlehem, and Easton) (2007) (8050 Jews), Harrisburg (2016) (5000), and York (1999) (1800). The 2007 estimates of Jews for Monroe County (2300) and Carbon County (600) are based on DJN studies. The estimate of 1800 Jews for Wilkes-Barre is based on a 2014 Informant update of a 2005 scientific study using a different methodology (neither RDD nor DJN). All other estimates are Informant/Internet Estimates. The estimate of 3100 Jews for Scranton is based upon a 2008 informant estimate.

5.7.3 Midwest *(Maps 5.11, 5.12, 5.13, and 5.14)*

Illinois (Map 5.11). Based on a 2011 RDD study, Chicago (291,800 Jews) is the largest Jewish community in Illinois, accounts for 98% of the Jews in Illinois, and is the 5th largest US Jewish community.

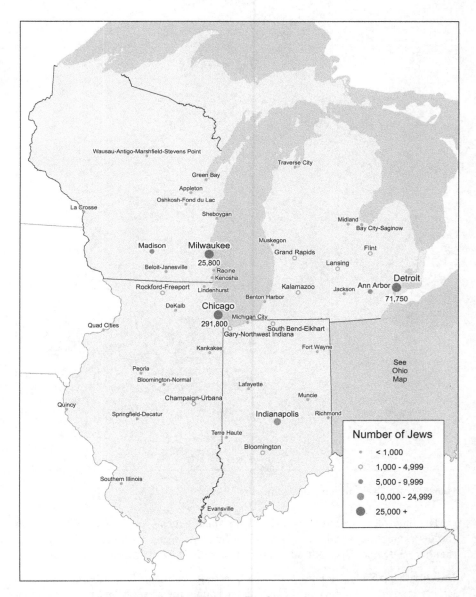

Map 5.11 Jewish communities of the Midwest—Part 1

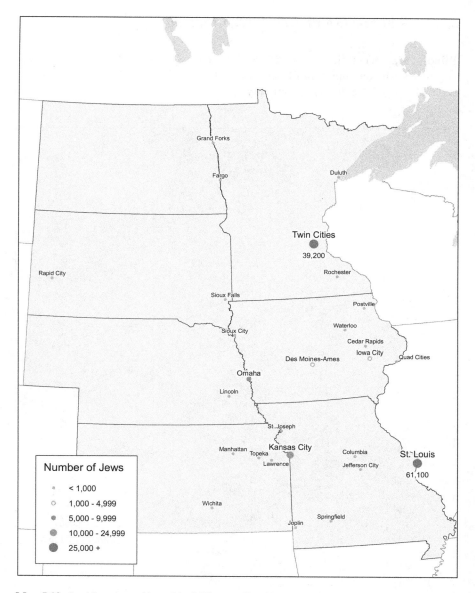

Map 5.12 Jewish communities of the Midwest—Part 2

The only other scientific estimate is for Quad Cities (750, of which 300 live in Illinois), which is based on a 1990 scientific study using a different methodology (neither RDD nor DJN). All other estimates are Informant/Internet Estimates.

Indiana (Map 5.11). Based on a 2017 RDD study, Indianapolis (17,900 Jews) is the largest Jewish community in Indiana and accounts for 71% of the Jews in Indiana. All estimates are Informant/Internet Estimates.

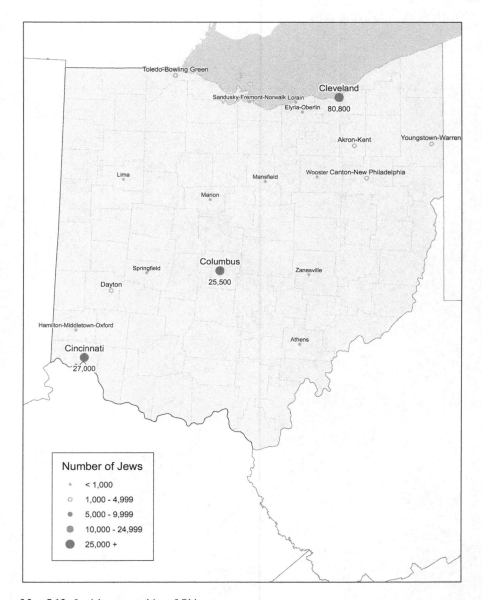

Map 5.13 Jewish communities of Ohio

Iowa (Map 5.12). Des Moines-Ames (2800 Jews) is the largest Jewish community in Iowa, based on a *1956* scientific study using a different methodology (neither RDD nor DJN), updated by an Informant Estimate between 1997 and 2001. Des Moines-Ames accounts for 45% of the Jews in Iowa. The only other scientific estimate is for Quad Cities (450, of which 275 live in Iowa), which is based on a 1990

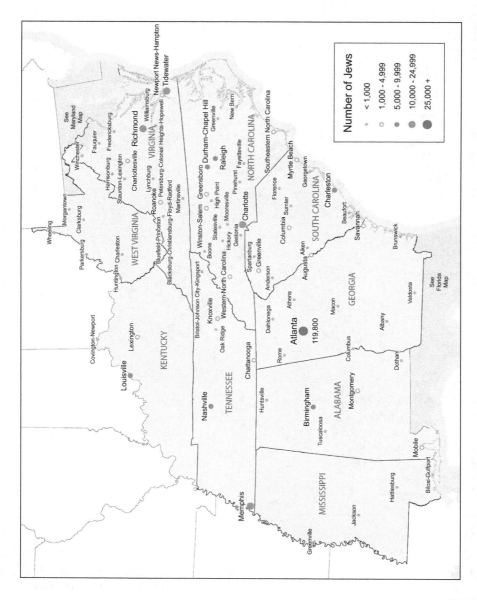

Map 5.14 Jewish communities of the South

scientific study using a different methodology (neither RDD nor DJN) and updated with an Informant Estimate. All other estimates are Informant/Internet Estimates.

Kansas (Map 5.12). The Kansas portion of the Kansas City Jewish community contains 16,000 Jews, based on a 1985 scientific study using a different methodology (neither RDD nor DJN), updated in 2015. Kansas City is the largest Jewish community in Kansas, accounting for 92% of the Jews in Kansas. Adding in the 2000 Jews who live in the Missouri portion of Kansas City, yields a combined population of 18,000. All other estimates are Informant/Internet Estimates.

Michigan (Map 5.11). Detroit (71,750 Jews), the largest Jewish community in Michigan, accounts for 82% of the Jews in Michigan, and is the 25th largest US Jewish community. The estimate is based on a 2018 RDD study.

The estimate for Ann Arbor (8000) is based on a 2010 DJN study, updated by a 2014 Informant Estimate. Flint (1300) is based on a *1956* scientific study using a different methodology (neither RDD nor DJN), updated by a 2009 Informant Estimate. All other estimates are Informant/Internet Estimates.

Minnesota (Map 5.12). The combined Twin Cities Jewish community of Minneapolis and St. Paul, with 39,200 Jews based on a 2004 RDD study (partially updated with a 2010 DJN study), is the largest Jewish community in Minnesota and accounts for 86% of the Jews in Minnesota. Minneapolis, with 29,300 Jews, is the 39th largest US Jewish community. In addition, St. Paul has 9900 Jews the estimate of 5300 Jews for the counties surrounding the Twin Cities is based on a 2004 DJN study. All other estimates are Informant/Internet Estimates.

Missouri (Map 5.12). St. Louis (61,100 Jews), based on a 2014 RDD study, is the largest Jewish community in Missouri, accounts for 95% of the Jews in Missouri, and is the 28th largest US Jewish community.

The Missouri portion of the Kansas City Jewish community contains 2000 Jews, based on a 1985 scientific study using a different methodology (neither RDD nor DJN), updated in 2015. All other estimates are Informant/Internet Estimates.

Nebraska (Map 5.12). Omaha (8800 Jews), based on a 2017 RDD estimate, is the largest Jewish community in Nebraska and accounts for 94% of the Jews in Nebraska. The estimate for Lincoln is an Informant/Internet Estimate.

North Dakota (Map 5.12). The estimates for both Fargo (150 Jews) and Grand Forks (150) are based on Informant/Internet Estimates.

Ohio (Map 5.13). Cleveland, with 80,800 Jews, based on a 2011 RDD study, is the largest Jewish community in Ohio, accounts for 55% of the Jews in Ohio, and is the 22nd largest US Jewish community.

The next two largest Jewish communities in Ohio are Cincinnati, with 27,000 Jews, and Columbus, with 25,500. These estimates are based on RDD studies in 2008 and 2013, respectively. Cincinnati is the 41st largest US Jewish community and Columbus is the 43rd largest. Cleveland, Cincinnati, and Columbus combined account for 90% of the Jews in Ohio.

The estimates for Dayton (4000 Jews), Akron-Kent (3000), Toledo-Bowling Green (2300), Youngstown-Warren (1300), and Canton-New Philadelphia (1000) are based on older scientific studies using a different methodology (neither RDD nor DJN), and most were updated recently by Informant/Internet Estimates. All other estimates are Informant/Internet Estimates.

South Dakota (Map 5.12). The estimates for both Sioux Falls (100 Jews) and Rapid City (100) are based on Informant/Internet Estimates.

Wisconsin (Map 5.11). Milwaukee (25,800 Jews), based on a 2011 RDD study, is the largest Jewish community in Wisconsin, accounts for 78% of the Jews in Wisconsin, and is the 42nd largest US Jewish community. All other estimates are Informant/Internet Estimates.

5.7.4 South *(Maps 5.12 and 5.14, 5.15, 5.16, and 5.17)*

Alabama (Map 5.14). Birmingham (6300 Jews) is the largest Jewish community in Alabama and accounts for 61% of the Jews in Alabama. All estimates are Informant/Internet Estimates.

Arkansas (Map 5.17). Little Rock (1500 Jews) is the largest Jewish community in Arkansas and accounts for 67% of the Jews in Arkansas. All estimates are Informant/Internet Estimates.

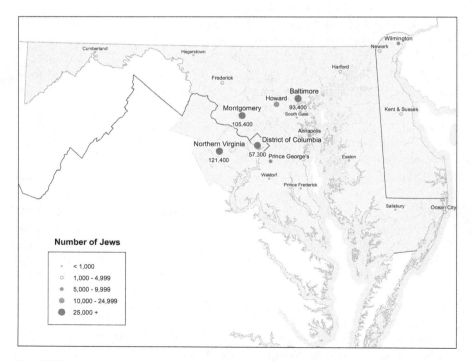

Map 5.15 Jewish communities of Maryland, Delaware, DC, and Northern Virginia

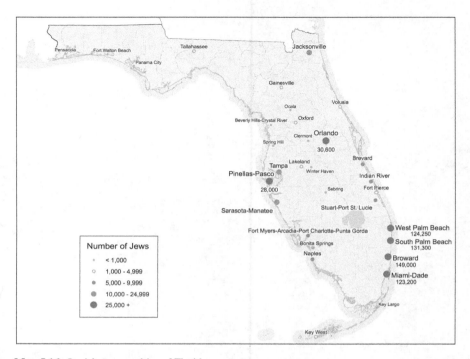

Map 5.16 Jewish communities of Florida

Delaware (Map 5.15). The estimates of Jewish population in Delaware are all based on a 1995 RDD study, updated with a 2006 DJN study. Wilmington (7600 Jews) is the largest Jewish community in Delaware and accounts for 50% of the Jews in Delaware. The other Jewish communities are Newark (4300) and Kent and Sussex Counties (Dover) (3200).

District of Columbia/Greater Washington (Map 5.15). Based on a 2017 RDD study, 295,500 Jews live in the service area of the Jewish Federation of Greater Washington, including 105,400 in Montgomery County (MD), 121,400 in Northern Virginia, 57,300 in the District of Columbia, and 11,400 in Prince George's County (MD). Greater Washington is the 4th largest US Jewish community.

Florida (Map 5.16). Based on RDD studies, 535,000 Jews, including 54,500 part-year residents, live in the three South Florida counties (Broward County, Miami-Dade County, and Palm Beach County[18]): Broward County (2016) 149,000 Jews, including 5300 part-year residents; South Palm Beach (2018) 136,100, including 22,500 part-year residents; West Palm Beach (2018) 127,200, including 22,500 part-year residents; and Miami (2014) 123,200, including 4200 part-year residents.

---

[18] Palm Beach County consists of two Jewish communities: The South Palm Beach community includes Greater Boca Raton and Greater Delray Beach. The West Palm Beach community includes all other areas of Palm Beach County from Boynton Beach north to the Martin County line.

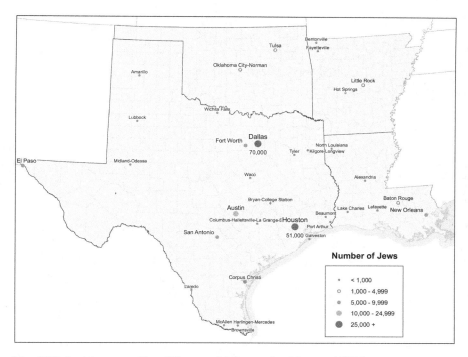

Map 5.17 Jewish communities of Texas, and Arkansas, Louisiana, and Oklahoma

Broward County (149,000) is the 8th largest US Jewish community, Miami (123,200) is the 11th largest, South Palm Beach (136,100) is the 9th largest, and West Palm Beach (127,200) is the 10th largest. Excluding part-year residents, these four communities account for 75% of the Jews in Florida.

Other important Jewish communities in Florida include the service area of the Jewish Federation of Pinellas (St. Petersburg) & Pasco Counties (28,000, including 1500 part-year residents), Orlando (31,100, including 500 part-year residents), Tampa (23,000), Sarasota (15,500, including 3300 part-year residents), and Jacksonville (13,000, including 100 part-year residents). St. Petersburg-Pasco (28,000) is the 40th largest US Jewish community, Orlando (31,100) is the 36th largest, and Tampa (23,000) is the 47th largest.

The estimates for Sarasota, Jacksonville, and St. Petersburg are based on RDD studies (2001, 2002, and 2017 respectively). The RDD study for Orlando (1993) is considerably older, but was updated with a 2010 DJN study. The estimate for Tampa is based on a 2010 DJN study.

The estimates for Naples (7530, including 3200 part-year residents) is based on a scientific study (neither RDD nor DJN) and the estimate for Tallahassee (2800) is based on a 2010 DJN study. The estimate of 11,800 Jews (including 900 part-year residents) for Stuart-Port St. Lucie is based on a 2018 RDD study for Stuart and a 2004 RDD study for St. Lucie. All other estimates are Informant/Internet Estimates, including Fort Myers-Arcadia-Port Charlotte-Punta Gorda (7500).

For more information on the Jews of South Florida, see Greenbaum (2005).

Georgia (Map 5.14). Atlanta (119,800 Jews), based on a 2006 RDD study, is the largest Jewish community in Georgia, accounts for 93% of the Jews in Georgia, and is the 12th largest US Jewish community. The only other significant Jewish community in Georgia is Savannah (4300), whose estimate, like all the other communities in Georgia, is based on an Informant/Internet Estimate.

Kentucky (Map 5.14). Based on a 2006 scientific study using a different methodology (neither RDD nor DJN), Louisville (8300 Jews) accounts for 74% of the Jews in Kentucky. Lexington (2500), which is based on an Informant/Internet Estimate, is the only other significant Jewish community. All other estimates (except Covington-Newport, which is based on an RDD study) are Informant/Internet Estimates.

Louisiana (Map 5.17). New Orleans (12,000 Jews), based on a 1984 RDD study, updated in 2009 (post-Katrina) with a scientific study using a different methodology (neither RDD nor DJN) and in 2019 with an Informant/Internet estimate, accounts for 79% of the Jews in Louisiana. All other estimates are Informant/Internet Estimates.

Maryland (Map 5.15). Based on a 2014 RDD study, the largest Jewish community in Maryland is Montgomery County (105,400 Jews), which is part of the service area of the Jewish Federation of Greater Washington. (See District of Columbia above.) Montgomery County accounts for 45% of the Jews in Maryland.

Based on a 2010 RDD study, Baltimore (93,400) is the second largest Jewish community in Maryland, accounts for 39% of the Jews in Maryland, and is the 19th largest US Jewish community.

The estimate of 17,200 Jews for Howard County (Columbia) is based on a 2010 RDD study. Three communities, the Maryland portion of the service area of the Jewish Federation of Greater Washington (Montgomery and Prince George's Counties), Baltimore, and Howard County, account for 96% of the Jews in Maryland.

Based on a 2010 DJN estimate, 3500 Jews live in Annapolis. All other estimates are Informant/Internet Estimates

Mississippi (Map 5.14). The estimates for all four small Jewish communities in Mississippi are Informant/Internet Estimates.

North Carolina (Map 5.14). Charlotte (12,000 Jews), based on a 1997 RDD study, is the largest Jewish community in North Carolina. Durham-Chapel Hill (7500), Raleigh-Cary (15,000), Western North Carolina (4200), and Greensboro (3000) are other significant communities. With the exception of Western North Carolina, which is based on a scientific study using another methodology (neither RDD nor DJN), the other estimates are Informant/Internet Estimates. Winston-Salem (1200) is based on a 2011 DJN estimate. All other estimates are Informant/Internet Estimates.

Oklahoma (Map 5.17). Based on a 2010 DJN study, the largest Jewish community in Oklahoma is Oklahoma City-Norman (2300 Jews). The estimate for Tulsa (2000) is an Informant/Internet Estimate.

South Carolina (Map 5.14). Charleston (9000 Jews), based on an Informant Estimate, is the largest Jewish community in South Carolina and accounts for 54%

of the Jews in South Carolina. The estimate for Greenville (2000) is based on a DJN study. All other estimates are Informant/Internet Estimates.

Tennessee (Map 5.14). The estimates for Memphis (10,000 Jews) and Nashville (9000), the two largest Jewish communities in Tennessee, are based on scientific studies using another methodology (neither RDD nor DJN). Memphis and Nashville combined account for 83% of the Jews in Tennessee. The estimates for Knoxville (2000), Chattanooga (1400), and Oak Ridge (150) are based on DJN studies. Bristol-Johnson City-Kingsport (125) is an Informant/Internet Estimate.

Texas (Map 5.17). Dallas (70,000 Jews) is the largest Jewish community in Texas, accounts for 42% of the Jews in Texas, and is the 26th largest US Jewish community. The estimate for Dallas is based on a 1988 RDD study, updated by a 2013 scientific study using a different methodology (neither DJN nor RDD).

Houston (51,000) is the second largest Jewish community in Texas, accounts for 31% of the Jews in Texas, and is the 30th largest US Jewish community. The estimate for Houston is based on a 2016 RDD study. Dallas and Houston combined account for 73% of the Jews in Texas.

The only other RDD study completed in Texas was in 2007 in San Antonio (9200). Based on a 2007 DJN study, an additional 1000 Jews live in counties surrounding San Antonio.

All other estimates are Informant/Internet Estimates, including Austin (30,000), El Paso (5000), and Fort Worth (5000).

For more information on the Jews of Texas, see Weiner and Roseman (2007).

Virginia (Maps 5.14 and 5.15). Based on a 2017 RDD study, Northern Virginia (121,400 Jews) is the largest Jewish community in Virginia and is part of the service area of the Jewish Federation of Greater Washington. (See District of Columbia above.) Northern Virginia accounts for 81% of the Jews in Virginia.

Other significant Jewish communities in Virginia are Tidewater (mainly Norfolk and Virginia Beach) (10,950), based on a 2001 RDD study, and Richmond (10,000), based on a 1994 RDD study, updated with a 2011 DJN study. All other estimates are Informant/Internet Estimates.

West Virginia (Map 5.14). Charleston (975 Jews) is the largest Jewish community in West Virginia and accounts for 42% of the Jews in West Virginia. All estimates are Informant/Internet Estimates.

5.7.5   West *(Maps 5.18 and 5.19)*

Alaska (Map 5.18). Anchorage (5000 Jews) is the largest Jewish community in Alaska and accounts for 87% of the Jews in Alaska. All estimates are Informant/Internet Estimates.

Arizona (Map 5.18). Based on a 2002 RDD study, Phoenix (82,900 Jews) is the largest Jewish community in Arizona, accounts for 78% of the Jews in Arizona, and is the 21st largest US Jewish community.

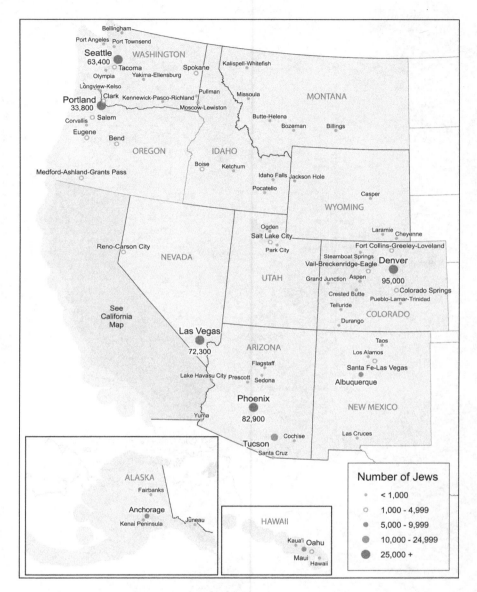

Map 5.18   Jewish community of the West

A 2002 RDD study of Tucson estimated 22,400 Jews (including 1000 part-year residents), making it the second largest Jewish community in Arizona and accounts for 20% of the Jews in Arizona. Tucson (21,400, excluding the part-year residents) is the 48th largest US Jewish community. Phoenix and Tucson combined account for 98% of the Jews in Arizona.

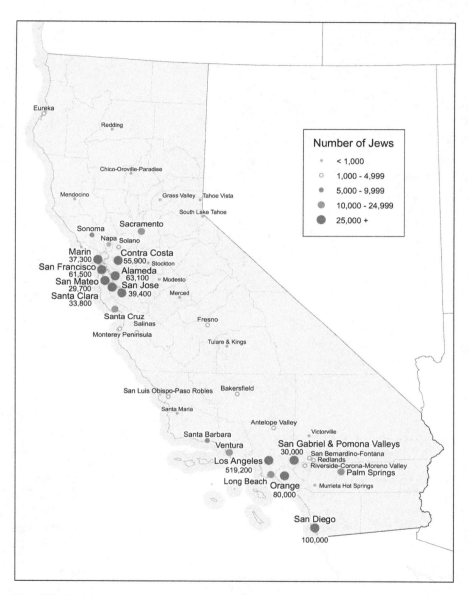

Map 5.19 Jewish communities of California

The estimates for Cochise County (450) and Santa Cruz County (100) are based on 2002 DJN studies. All other estimates are Informant/Internet Estimates.

California (Map 5.19). Based on a 1997 RDD study, 519,200 Jews live in the service area of the Jewish Federation of Greater Los Angeles, which is the largest Jewish community in California, accounts for 44% of the Jews in California, and is the 2nd largest US Jewish community.

Based on a 2017 study, 310,600 Jews live in the service area of the Jewish Community Federation & Foundation of San Francisco, the Peninsula, Marin and Sonoma Counties, including 61,500 in San Francisco County, 37,300 in Marin County, 33,800 in parts of Santa Clara County, 29,700 in San Mateo County, 15,100 in Santa Cruz County, and 8200 in Sonoma County. This Federation recently absorbed (from the now defunct Jewish Federation of the East Bay) Alameda County (63,100), Contra Costa County (55,900), Napa County (2100), and Solano County (3900). San Francisco area is the 2nd largest Jewish community in California, accounts for 26% of the Jews in California, and is the 3rd largest US Jewish community.

Based on a 2003 RDD study, updated by a 2014 Informant/Internet Estimate, 100,000 Jews live in San Diego, which is the 3rd largest Jewish community in California and the 17th largest US Jewish community. Based on a 2017 RDD study, 39,400 Jews live in San Jose, which is the 32nd largest US Jewish community.

Based on a 1993 scientific study using a different methodology (neither RDD nor DJN), 21,000 Jews live in Sacramento, which is the 49th largest US Jewish community.

Based on Informant/Internet Estimates, 80,000 Jews live in Orange County (excluding parts included in Long Beach); 30,000, in San Gabriel and Pomona Valleys; 23,750, in Long Beach; 15,000, in Ventura County (excluding the Simi-Conejo area included in Los Angeles); and 8500, in Santa Barbara. Orange County is the 23rd largest US Jewish community, San Gabriel and Pomona Valleys is the 38th largest, and Long Beach is the 45th.

Based on a 1998 RDD study updated by an Informant/Internet Estimate in 2015, 20,000 Jews (including 9000 part-year residents) live in Palm Springs.

DJN studies were completed in 2011 in the Monterey Peninsula (4500), and Fresno (3500). All other estimates are Informant/Internet Estimates.

For more information on the Jews of California, see Kahn and Dollinger (2003).

Colorado (Map 5.18). Denver (95,000 Jews), based on a 2007 RDD study, updated by a 2016 Informant/Internet Estimate, is the largest Jewish community in Colorado, accounts for 93% of the Jews in Colorado, and is the 18th largest US Jewish community.

The estimates for Colorado Springs (2500) and Vail-Breckenridge-Eagle (1500) are based on DJN studies completed in 2010 and 2011, respectively. All other estimates are Informant/Internet Estimates.

Hawaii (Map 5.18). Oahu (Honolulu) (5200 Jews), based on a 2010 DJN study, is the largest Jewish community in Hawaii and accounts for 73% of the Jews in Hawaii. All other estimates are Informant/Internet Estimates.

Idaho (Map 5.18). Boise (1500 Jews) is the largest Jewish community in Idaho and accounts for 71% of the Jews in Idaho. Estimates for all four small Jewish communities in Idaho are based on Informant/Internet Estimates.

Montana (Map 5.18). Estimates for all five small Jewish communities are based on Informant/Internet Estimates.

Nevada (Map 5.18). Las Vegas (72,300 Jews), based on a 2005 RDD study, updated by a 2009 Informant Estimate, is the largest Jewish community in Nevada, accounts for 95% of the Jews in Nevada, and is the 24th largest US Jewish community. Based on a 2011 DJN study, 4000 Jews live in Reno-Carson City.

New Mexico (Map 5.18). Albuquerque (7500 Jews), based on a 2011 DJN study, is the largest Jewish community in New Mexico and accounts for 59% of the Jews in New Mexico. All other estimates are Informant/Internet Estimates, including Santa Fe-Las Vegas (4000).

Oregon (Map 5.18). The service area of the Jewish Federation of Greater Portland (36,400 Jews), based on a 2011 scientific study using a different methodology (neither RDD nor DJN), includes 33,800 Jews in Portland and 2600 in Vancouver (WA) and is the 33rd largest US Jewish community. Portland is the largest Jewish community in Oregon, accounts for 83% of the Jews in Oregon, and is the 33rd largest US Jewish community.

The estimate for Bend (1000) is based on a 2010 DJN study. All other estimates are Informant/Internet Estimates.

Utah (Map 5.18). Salt Lake City (4800 Jews), based on a 2010 DJN study, is the largest Jewish community in Utah and accounts for 85% of the Jews in Utah. All other estimates are Informant/Internet Estimates.

Washington (Map 5.18). Seattle (64,650 Jews), based on a 2014 RDD study and updated with an Informant Estimates in 2019, is the largest Jewish community in Washington, accounts for 88% of the Jews in Washington, and is the 27th largest US Jewish community.

The estimate for Clark County (2600) is based on a 2011 scientific study using a different methodology (neither RDD nor DJN). All other estimates are Informant/Internet Estimates.

Wyoming (Map 5.18). Estimates for all four small Jewish communities are Informant/Internet Estimates.

5.8 Conclusion

While it might be more appropriate to provide a range of estimates for the US Jewish population, running from a low of 5,700,000 by DellaPergola (see Chap. 8) to 7,100,000 by Tighe et al. (2019), the current number reported in this chapter of 6,800,000–6,900,000 provides a reasonable estimate, one which is supported by the 2013 Pew figure of 6,700,000. The difference between the low figure of 5,700,000, on the one hand, and the AJYB estimate and the Pew estimate on the other hand, results from not counting the "partly Jewish" in the low figure. As one professional observer put it, "It's not like we have a set of estimates claiming 15 million and another claiming 3 million. That they are all between 6.7 and 7.5 million, using different methods, is quite astounding."

In conclusion, the problem of assessing the composition of and changes in a rare population, like US Jews, is complicated by a shifting sense of personal identity, i.e., of how one defines oneself (see Dashefsky et al. 2003). Consequently, in addition to the standard demographic variables of fertility, mortality, and net migration, there are also accessions and secessions from the Jewish population based on identity shifts. Thus, the move to recognize patrilineal descent by some Jewish denominations and the growth of intermarried households have provided further challenges to offering an accurate estimate of the US Jewish population. Nevertheless, our effort is to provide, in one source, the best possible estimates for the national, state, regional, urban, and local areas of the US Jewish population, as a reference for today and a legacy for posterity.

Acknowledgments The authors thank the following individuals and organizations:

1. The Jewish Federations of North America (JFNA) and former staff members at its predecessor organizations (United Jewish Communities and Council of Jewish Federations), including Jim Schwartz, Jeffrey Scheckner, and Barry Kosmin, who authored the *AJYB* US Jewish population chapters from 1986 to 2003. Some population estimates in this report are still based on their efforts;
2. Laurence Kotler-Berkowitz, Senior Director of Research and Analysis and Director of the Berman Jewish DataBank at The Jewish Federations of North America;
3. Amy Lawton and Maria Reger, Editorial Assistants, Pamela Weathers, Program Assistant, and Kezia Mann, Student Administrative Assistant, all at the Center for Judaic Studies and Contemporary Jewish Life at the University of Connecticut, for their excellent assistance;
4. Chris Hanson and the University of Miami Department of Geography's Geographic Information Systems Laboratory for assistance with the maps; and
5. Joshua Comenetz for the new estimates for Jewish population in Hasidic communities.

Appendix

This Appendix presents detailed data on the US Jewish population in four columns:

Date Column. This column provides the date of the latest Scientific Estimate or Informant/Internet Estimate for each geographic area. This chapter's former authors provided only a range of years (pre-1997 or 1997–2001) for the last informant contact. For estimates after 2001, exact dates are shown. For communities for which the date is more recent than the date of the latest scientific study shown in boldface type in the Geographic Area column, the study estimate has been confirmed or updated by an Informant/Internet Estimate subsequent to the scientific study.

Geographic Area Column. This column provides estimates for more than 900 Jewish communities (of 100 Jews or more) and geographic subareas thereof. The number of estimates for each state ranges from three in Delaware, North Dakota, Oklahoma, and South Dakota to more than 75 in California (91), New York (87), and Florida (77). Many estimates are for Jewish Federation service areas. Where possible, these service areas are disaggregated into smaller geographic subareas. For example, separate estimates are provided for such places as West Bloomfield, Michigan (part of the service area of the Jewish Federation of Metropolitan Detroit) and Boynton Beach (Florida) (part of the service area of the Jewish Federation of Palm Beach County). This column also indicates the source of each estimate:

Communities with estimated Jewish population of 100 or more, 2019

Date	Geographic Area	# of Jews	Part-Year
	Alabama		
2017	Auburn	100	
2019	Birmingham (Jefferson County)	6300	
2014	Dothan	200	
2016	Huntsville	750	
2014	Mobile (Baldwin & Mobile Counties)	1350	
2014	Montgomery	1100	
2008	Tuscaloosa	200	
	Other Places	325	
	Total Alabama	**10,325**	
	Alaska		
2008	Anchorage (Anchorage Borough)	5000	
2013	Fairbanks (Fairbanks North Star Borough)	275	
2012	Juneau	300	
2016	Kenai Peninsula	100	
1997–2001	Other Places	75	
	Total Alaska	**5750**	
	Arizona		
2002	**Cochise County (2002)**[a]	450	
2017	Flagstaff (Coconino County)	1000	500
1997–2001	Lake Havasu City	200	
2019	**Northwest Valley (Glendale-Peoria-Sun City) (2002)**	10,900	
2019	**Phoenix (2002)**	23,600	
2019	**Northeast Valley (Scottsdale) (2002)**	34,500	
2019	**Tri Cities Valley (Ahwatukee-Chandler-Gilbert-Mesa-Tempe) (2002)**	13,900	

Communities with estimated Jewish population of 100 or more, 2019			
Date	Geographic Area	# of Jews	Part-Year
2019	*Greater Phoenix Total (2002)*	82,900	
2008	Prescott	300	
2002	**Santa Cruz County (2002)**[a]	100	
2008	Sedona	300	50
2019	**West-Northwest (2002)**	3450	
2019	**Northeast (2002)**	7850	
2019	**Central (2002)**	7150	
2019	**Southeast (2002)**	2500	
2019	**Green Valley (2002)**	450	
2019	*Jewish Federation of Southern Arizona-Tucson (Pima County) Total (2002)*	21,400	1000
2016	Other Places	75	
	Total Arizona	106,725	1550
	Arkansas		
2016	Bentonville	175	
2008	Fayetteville	175	
2001	Hot Springs	150	
2010	Little Rock	1500	
2007	Other Places	225	
	Total Arkansas	2225	
	California		
1997–2001	Antelope Valley (Lancaster-Palmdale in LA County)	3000	
1997–2001	Bakersfield (Kern County)	1600	
1997–2001	Chico-Oroville-Paradise (Butte County)	750	
1997–2001	Eureka (Humboldt County)	1000	
2011	**Fresno (Fresno County) (2011)**[a]	3500	
2016	Grass Valley (Nevada County)	300	
2018	Long Beach (Cerritos-Hawaiian Gardens-Lakewood-Signal Hill in Los Angeles County & Buena Park-Cypress-La Palma-Los Alamitos-Rossmoor-Seal Beach in Orange County)	23,750	
2009	**Airport Marina (1997)**	22,140	
2009	**Beach Cities (1997)**	17,270	
2009	**Beverly Hills (1997)**	20,500	
2009	**Burbank-Glendale (1997)**	19,840	
2009	**Central (1997)**	11,600	
2009	**Central City (1997)**	4710	
2009	**Central Valley (1997)**	27,740	
2009	**Cheviot-Beverlywood (1997)**	29,310	
2009	**Culver City (1997)**	9110	
2009	**Eastern Belt (1997)**	3900	
2009	**Encino-Tarzana (1997)**	50,290	
2009	**Fairfax (1997)**	54,850	

Communities with estimated Jewish population of 100 or more, 2019

Date	Geographic Area	# of Jews	Part-Year
2009	**High Desert (1997)**	10,920	
2009	**Hollywood (1997)**	10,390	
2009	**Malibu-Palisades (1997)**	27,190	
2009	**North Valley (1997)**	36,760	
2009	**Palos Verdes Peninsula (1997)**	6780	
2009	**San Pedro (1997)**	5310	
2009	**Santa Monica-Venice (1997)**	23,140	
2009	**Simi-Conejo (1997)**	38,470	
2009	**Southeast Valley (1997)**	28,150	
2009	**West Valley (1997)**	40,160	
2009	**Westwood (1997)**	20,670	
2009	***Los Angeles (Los Angeles County, excluding parts included in Long Beach, & southern Ventura County) Total (1997)***	519,200	
2010	Mendocino County (Redwood Valley-Ukiah)	600	
1997–2001	Merced County	190	
1997–2001	Modesto (Stanislaus County)	500	
2011	**Monterey Peninsula (2011)**[a]	4500	
1997–2001	Murrieta Hot Springs	550	
2016	Orange County (excluding parts included in Long Beach)	80,000	
2015	**Palm Springs (1998)**	2500	900
2015	**Cathedral City-Rancho Mirage (1998)**	3300	5900
2015	**Palm Desert-Sun City (1998)**	3700	1900
2015	**East Valley (Bermuda-Dunes-Indian Wells-Indio-La Quinta) (1998)**	1200	250
2015	**North Valley (Desert Hot Springs-North Palm Springs-Thousand Palms) (1998)**	300	50
2015	***Palm Springs (Coachella Valley) Total (1998)***	11,000	9000
2010	Redlands	1000	
2016	Redding (Shasta County)	150	
2016	Riverside-Corona-Moreno Valley	2000	
1997–2001	**Sacramento (El Dorado, Placer, Sacramento, & Yolo Counties) (1993) (except Lake Tahoe area)**[d]	21,000	
2015	Salinas	300	
2010	San Bernardino-Fontana	1000	
2016	**North County Coastal (2003)**	27,000	
2016	**North County Inland (2003)**	20,300	
2016	**Greater East San Diego (2003)**	21,200	
2016	**La Jolla-Mid-Coastal (2003)**	16,200	
2016	**Central San Diego (2003)**	13,700	
2016	**South County (2003)**	1600	
2016	***San Diego (San Diego County) Total (2003)***	100,000	
2018	**Alameda County (2018)**	63,100	
2018	**Contra Costa County (2018)**	55,900	
2018	**Marin County (2018)**	37,300	

Communities with estimated Jewish population of 100 or more, 2019

Date	Geographic Area	# of Jews	Part-Year
2018	**Napa County (2018)**	2100	
2018	**San Francisco County (2018)**	61,500	
2018	**San Mateo County Total (2018)**	29,700	
2018	**Santa Clara County (part) (2018)**	33,800	
2018	**Santa Cruz County (2018)**	15,100	
2018	**Solano County (Vallejo) (2018)**	3900	
2018	**Sonoma County (Petaluma-Santa Rosa) (2018)**	8200	
2018	***Jewish Community Federation & Endowment Fund of San Francisco, the Peninsula, Marin & Sonoma Counties (2018)***	310,600	
2019	***Jewish Federation of Silicon Valley Total (Parts of Santa Clara County) (San Jose)***	39,400	
2018	***San Francisco Bay Area Total***	350,000	
2018	**Santa Clara County (2018) Total**	73,200	
1997–2001	San Gabriel & Pomona Valleys (Alta Loma-Chino-Claremont-Cucamonga-La Verne-Montclair-Ontario-Pomona-San Dimas-Upland)	30,000	
2016	San Luis Obispo-Atascadero (San Luis Obispo County)	1000	
2019	Santa Barbara (Santa Barbara County)	8500	
1997–2001	Santa Maria	500	
2016	South Lake Tahoe (El Dorado County)	100	
2016	Stockton	900	
2016	Tahoe Vista	200	
2016	Tulare & Kings Counties (Visalia)	350	
1997–2001	Ventura County (excluding Simi-Conejo of Los Angeles)	15,000	
2016	Victorville	100	
1997–2001	Other Places	450	
	Total California	1,182,990	9000
	Colorado		
2014	Aspen	750	
2010	**Colorado Springs (2010)[a]**	2500	
2008	Crested Butte	175	
2016	Durango	200	
2018	**Denver (2007)**	32,500	
2018	**South Metro (2007)**	22,400	
2018	**Boulder (2007)**	14,600	
2018	**North & West Metro (2007)**	12,900	
2018	**Aurora (2007)**	7500	
2018	**North & East Metro (2007)**	5100	
2018	***Greater Denver (Adams, Arapahoe, Boulder, Broomfield, Denver, Douglas, & Jefferson Counties) Total (2007)***	95,000	
2013	Fort Collins-Greeley-Loveland	1500	
2016	Grand Junction (Mesa County)	300	
2015	Pueblo	150	

Communities with estimated Jewish population of 100 or more, 2019			
Date	Geographic Area	# of Jews	Part-Year
2016	Steamboat Springs	300	
Pre-1997	Telluride	125	
2011	**Vail-Breckenridge-Eagle (Eagle & Summit Counties) (2011)**[a]	1500	
1997–2001	Other Places	100	
	Total Colorado	102,600	
	Connecticut		
Pre-1997	Colchester-Lebanon	300	
2014	Danbury (Bethel-Brookfield-New Fairfield-New Milford-Newtown-Redding-Ridgefield-Sherman)	5000	
2019	Greenwich	7500	
2009	**Core Area (Bloomfield-Hartford-West Hartford) (2000)**	15,800	
2009	**Farmington Valley(Avon-Burlington-Canton-EastGranby-Farmington-Granby-New Hartford-Simsbury) (2000)**	6400	
2009	**East of the River (East Hartford-East Windsor-Enfield-Glastonbury-Manchester-South Windsor in Hartford County & Andover-Bolton-Coventry-Ellington-Hebron-Somers-Tolland-Vernon in Tolland County) (2000)**	4800	
2009	**South of Hartford (Berlin-Bristol-New Britain-Newington-Plainville-Rocky Hill-Southington-Wethersfield in Hartford County, Plymouth in Litchfield County, Cromwell-Durham-Haddam-Middlefield-Middletown in Middlesex County, & Meriden in New Haven County) (2000)**	5000	
2009	**Suffield-Windsor-Windsor Locks (2000)**	800	
2009	***Jewish Federation of Greater Hartford Total (2000)***	32,800	
2016	**The East (Centerbrook-Chester-Clinton-Deep River-Ivoryton-Killingworth-Old Saybrook-WestbrookinMiddlesexCounty&Branford-EastHaven-Essex-Guilford-Madison- North Branford-Northford in New Haven County) (2010)**	4900	
2016	**The West (Ansonia-Derby-Milford-Seymour-West Haven in New Haven County & Shelton in Fairfield County) (2010)**	3200	
2016	**The Central Area (Bethany-New Haven-Orange-Woodbridge) (2010)**	8800	
2016	**Hamden (2010)**	3200	
2016	**The North (Cheshire-North Haven-Wallingford) (2010)**	2900	
2016	***Jewish Federation of Greater New Haven Total (2010)***	23,000	
1997–2001	New London-Norwich (central & southern New London County)	3800	
2010	**Southbury (Beacon Falls-Middlebury-Naugatuck-Oxford-Prospect-Waterbury-Wolcott in New Haven County & Washington-Watertown in Litchfield County) (2010)**[a]	4500	

Communities with estimated Jewish population of 100 or more, 2019

Date	Geographic Area	# of Jews	Part-Year
2010	**Southern Litchfield County (Bethlehem-Litchfield-Morris-Roxbury-Thomaston-Woodbury) (2010)[a]**	3500	
2010	*Jewish Federation of Western Connecticut Total (2010)[a]*	8000	
2009	Stamford (Darien-New Canaan)	12,000	
2006	Storrs-Columbia & parts of Tolland County	500	
1997–2001	Torrington	600	
2000	**Westport (2000)**	5000	
2000	**Weston (2000)**	1850	
2000	**Wilton (2000)**	1550	
2000	**Norwalk (2000)**	3050	
2014	Bridgeport (Easton-Fairfield-Monroe-Stratford-Trumbull)	13,000	
2000	*Federation for Jewish Philanthropy in Upper Fairfield County Total (2000)*	24,450	
2006	Windham-Willimantic & parts of Windham County	400	
	Total Connecticut	118,350	
	Delaware		
2018	**Kent & Sussex Counties (Dover) (1995, 2006)[b]**	3200	
2018	**Newark (1995, 2006)[b]**	4300	
2018	**Wilmington (1995, 2006)[b]**	7600	
	Total Delaware (1995, 2006)[b]	15,100	
	Washington, DC		
2017	**Total District of Columbia (2003)**	57,300	
2017	**Lower Montgomery County (Maryland) (2017)**	87,000	
2017	**Upper Montgomery County (Maryland) (2017)**	18,400	
2017	**Prince George's County (Maryland) (2017)**	11,400	
2017	**North-Central Northern Virginia (2017)**	24,500	
2017	**Central Northern Virginia (2017)**	23,100	
2017	**East Northern Virginia (2017)**	54,400	
2017	**West-Northern Virginia (2017)**	19,400	
2017	*Jewish Federation of Greater Washington Total (2017)*	295,500	
	Florida		
2016	Beverly Hills-Crystal River (Citrus County)	350	
2016	Brevard County (Melbourne)	4000	
2016	Clermont (Lake County)	200	
2019	Fort Myers-Arcadia-Port Charlotte-Punta Gorda (Charlotte, De Soto, & Northern Lee Counties)	7000	
2017	Bonita Springs-Southern Lee County[d]	500	500
2017	Jewish Federation of Lee & Charlotte Counties (Total)	7500	500
1997–2001	Fort Pierce (northern St. Lucie County)	1060	
2019	Fort Walton Beach	400	
2017	Gainesville	2500	
2017	**Jacksonville Core Area (2002, 2015)[e]**	8800	

Communities with estimated Jewish population of 100 or more, 2019

Date	Geographic Area	# of Jews	Part-Year
2017	**The Beaches (Atlantic Beach-Jacksonville Beach-Neptune Beach-Ponte Vedra Beach) (2002, 2015)**[e]	1900	
2017	**Other Places in Clay, Duval, Nassau, & St. Johns Counties (including St. Augustine) (2002, 2015)**[e]	2200	
2017	*Jacksonville Total (2002, 2015)*[e]	12,900	100
2016	Key Largo	100	
2014	Key West	1000	
	Total Monroe County	1100	
Pre-1997	Lakeland (Polk County)	1000	
2019	Marco Island[d]	400	600
2019	Other Collier County (Naples)[d]	3930	2600
2019	Jewish Federation of Collier County (Naples) (2017)[d]	4330	3200
1997–2001	Ocala (Marion County)	500	
2016	Oxford (Sumter County)	2000	
2017	**North Orlando (Seminole County & southern Volusia County) (1993, 2010)**[b]	11,900	300
2017	**Central Orlando (Maitland-parts of Orlando-Winter Park) (1993, 2010)**[b]	10,600	100
2017	**South Orlando (parts of Orlando & northern Osceola County) (1993, 2010)** [b]	8100	100
2017	*Orlando Total (1993, 2010)*[b]	30,600	500
2016	Panama City (Bay County)	100	
2015	Pensacola (Escambia & Santa Rosa Counties)	800	
2017	**North Pinellas (Clearwater) (2017)**	8800	800
2017	**Central Pinellas (Largo) (2017)**	2300	500
2017	**South Pinellas (St. Petersburg) (2017)**	10,950	200
2017	*Pinellas County (St. Petersburg) Subtotal (2017)*	22,050	1500
2017	**Pasco County (New Port Richey) (2017)**	4450	
2012	Hernando County (Spring Hill)	350	
2017	**Jewish Federation of Florida's Gulf Coast Total (2017)**	26,850	1500
2015	**Sarasota (2001)**	8600	1500
2015	**Longboat Key (2001)**	1000	1500
2015	**Bradenton (Manatee County) (2001)**	1750	200
2015	**Venice (2001)**	850	100
2015	*Sarasota-Manatee Total (2001)*	12,200	3300
2018	**East Boca (2018)**	24,400	3700
2018	**Central Boca (2018)**	32,200	9900
2018	**West Boca (2018)**	18,600	400
2018	*Boca Raton Subtotal (2018)*	75,200	14,000
2018	**Delray Beach (2005)**	38,400	8500
2018	*South Palm Beach Subtotal (2018)*	113,600	22,500
2018	**Boynton Beach (2018)**	30,400	5500
2018	**Lake Worth (2018)**	25,600	2500

Communities with estimated Jewish population of 100 or more, 2019

Date	Geographic Area	# of Jews	Part-Year
2018	**Town of Palm Beach (2018)**	1700	1400
2018	**West Palm Beach (2018)**	11,000	1300
2018	**Wellington-Royal Palm Beach (2018)**	9600	1100
2018	**North Palm Beach-Palm Beach Gardens-Jupiter (2018)**	26,400	10,700
2018	*West Palm Beach Subtotal (2018)*	104,700	22,500
2018	*Palm Beach County Total (2018)*	218,300	45,000
2018	**North Dade Core East (Aventura-Golden Beach-parts of North Miami Beach) (2014)**	36,000	2200
2018	**North Dade Core West (parts of North Miami Beach-Ojus) (2014)**	18,500	200
2018	**Other North Dade (parts of City of Miami) (north of Flagler Street) (2014)**	9500	100
2018	*North Dade Subtotal (2014)*	64,000	2500
2018	**West Kendall (2014)**	17,500	200
2018	**East Kendall (parts of Coral Gables-Pinecrest-South Miami) (2014)**	6800	100
2018	**Northeast South Dade (Key Biscayne-parts of City of Miami) (2014)**	11,900	400
2018	*South Dade Subtotal (2014)*	36,200	700
2018	**North Beach (Bal Harbour-Bay Harbor Islands-Indian Creek Village-Surfside) (2014)**	4300	400
2018	**Middle Beach (parts of City of Miami Beach) (2014)**	9800	500
2018	**South Beach (parts of City of Miami Beach) (2014)**	4800	100
2018	*The Beaches Subtotal (2014)*	18,900	1000
2018	*Miami-Dade County Total (2014)*	119,000	4200
2019	**East (Fort Lauderdale) (2016)**	9400	400
2019	**North Central (Century Village-Coconut Creek-Margate-Palm Aire-Wynmoor) (2016)**	8000	1800
2019	**Northwest (Coral Springs-Parkland) (2016)**	27,200	1200
2019	**Southeast (Hallandale-Hollywood) (2016)**	24,000	1000
2019	**Southwest (Cooper City-Davie-Pembroke Pines-Weston) (2016)**	39,400	300
2019	**West Central (Lauderdale Lakes-North Lauderdale-Plantation-Sunrise-Tamarac) (2016)**	35,700	600
2019	*Broward County Total (2016)*	143,700	5300
	Southeast Florida (Broward, Miami-Dade, & Palm Beach Counties) Total	481,000	54,500
2016	Sebring (Highlands County)	150	
2019	**Stuart (Martin County) (2018)**	8000	200
2004	**Southern St. Lucie County (Port St. Lucie) (1999, 2004)[b]**	2900	
2019	*Stuart-Port St. Lucie (Martin-St. Lucie) Total (1999, 2004, 2018)[b]*	10,900	900
2015	**Tallahassee (2010)[a]**	2800	
2017	**Tampa (Hillsborough County) (2010)[a]**	23,000	

Communities with estimated Jewish population of 100 or more, 2019

Date	Geographic Area	# of Jews	Part-Year
2016	Vero Beach (Indian River County)	1000	
2017	Volusia (Daytona Beach) (excluding southern parts included in North Orlando) & Flagler Counties *Jewish Federation of Volusia and Flagler Counties*	4500	
Pre-1997	Winter Haven	300	
2019	Other Places	25	
	Total Florida	643,895	68,200
	Georgia		
2009	Albany	200	
2012	Athens	750	
2012	**Intown (2006)**	28,900	
2012	**North Metro Atlanta (2006)**	28,300	
2012	**East Cobb Expanded (2006)**	18,400	
2012	**Sandy Springs-Dunwoody (2006)**	15,700	
2012	**Gwinnett-East Perimeter (2006)**	14,000	
2012	**North & West Perimeter (2006)**	9000	
2012	**South (2006)**	5500	
2012	*Atlanta Total (2006)*	119,800	
2019	Augusta (Burke, Columbia, & Richmond Counties)	1600	
2009	Brunswick	120	
2015	Columbus	600	
2009	Dahlonega	150	
2015	Macon	750	
2010	Rome	100	
2016	Savannah (Chatham County)	4300	
2009	Valdosta	100	
2009	Other Places	250	
	Total Georgia	128,720	
	Hawaii		
2012	Hawaii (Hilo)	100	
2011	Kauai	300	
2008	Maui	1500	1000
2010	**Oahu (Honolulu) (2010)[a]**	5200	
	Total Hawaii	7100	1000
	Idaho		
2015	Boise (Ada, Caldwell, Weiser, Nampa, & Boise Counties)	1500	
2014	Ketchum-Sun Valley-Hailey-Bellevue	350	
2014	Moscow (Palouse)	100	
2009	Pocatello	150	
	Other Places	25	
	Total Idaho	2125	
	Illinois		
2015	Bloomington-Normal	500	

Communities with estimated Jewish population of 100 or more, 2019

Date	Geographic Area	# of Jews	Part-Year
2015	Champaign-Urbana (Champaign County)	1400	
2019	Decatur	100	
2019	**City North (The Loop to Rogers Park, including North Lakefront) (2010)**	70,150	
2019	**Rest of Chicago (parts of City of Chicago not included in City North) (2010)**	19,100	
2019	**Near North Suburbs (Suburbs contiguous to City of Chicago from Evanston to Park Ridge) (2010)**	64,600	
2019	**North/Far North (Wilmette to Wisconsin, west to include Northbrook, Glenview, Deerfield, etc.) (2010)**	56,300	
2019	**Northwest Suburbs (includes northwest Cook County, parts of Lake County, & McHenry County) (2010)**	51,950	
2019	**Western Suburbs (DuPage & Kane Counties & Oak Park-River Forest in Cook County) (2010)**	23,300	
2019	**Southern Suburbs (south & southwest Cook County beyond the City to Indiana & Will County) (2010)**	6400	
2019	*Chicago (Cook, DuPage, Kane, Lake, McHenry, & Will Counties) Total (2010)*	291,800	
1997–2001	DeKalb	180	
2016	Lindenhurst (Lake County)	100	
2019	Peoria	800	
2019	**Quad Cities-Illinois portion (Moline-Rock Island) (1990)[d]**	175	
2019	**Quad Cities-Iowa portion (Davenport & surrounding Scott County) (1990)[d]**	275	
2005	*Quad Cities Total (1990)[d]*	450	
2015	Quincy	100	
2019	Rockford-Freeport (Boone, Stephenson, & Winnebago Counties)	650	
2015	Southern Illinois (Alton-Belleville-Benton-Carbondale-Centralia-Collinsville-East St. Louis-Herrin-Marion)	500	
2019	Springfield-Decatur (Morgan, & Sangamon Counties)	830	
	Other Places	325	
2015	*Jewish Federation of Southern Illinois, Southeast Missouri and Western Kentucky (Alton-Belleville-Benton-Carbondale-Centralia-Collinsville-East St. Louis-Herrin-Marion in Southern Illinois, Cape Girardeau-Farmington-Sikeston in Southeast Missouri, & Paducah in Western Kentucky) Total*	650	
	Total Illinois	297,735	
	Indiana		
2017	Bloomington	1000	
2017	Evansville	500	
1997–2001	Fort Wayne	900	
2012	Gary-Northwest Indiana (Lake & Porter Counties)	2000	
2017	**North of Core (2017)**	9200	
2017	**Core Area (2017)**	6100	

Communities with estimated Jewish population of 100 or more, 2019

Date	Geographic Area	# of Jews	Part-Year
2017	**South of Core (2017)**	2600	
2017	**Jewish Federation of Greater Indianapolis Total (2017)**	17,900	
2014	Lafayette	400	
2015	Michigan City (La Porte County)	300	
1997–2001	Muncie	120	
2017	Richmond	100	
2019	South Bend-Mishawaka-Elkhart (Elkhart & St. Joseph Counties)	1650	
2019	Benton Harbor (Michigan)	150	
2019	*Jewish Federation of St. Joseph Valley Total*	1800	
2017	Terre Haute (Vigo County)	100	
	Other Places	275	
	Total Indiana	25,245	
	Iowa		
2017	Cedar Rapids	400	
1997–2001	**Des Moines-Ames (1956)[d]**	2800	
2014	Fairfield	200	
2017	Iowa City/Coralville (Johnson County)	750	
2017	Postville	150	
2019	**Quad Cities-Illinois portion (Moline-Rock Island) (1990)[d]**	175	
2019	**Quad Cities-Iowa portion (Davenport & surrounding Scott County) (1990)[d]**	275	
2005	*Quad Cities Total (1990)[d]*	450	
2014	Sioux City (Plymouth & Woodbury Counties)	300	
2014	Waterloo (Black Hawk County)	100	
	Other Places	300	
	Total Iowa	5275	
	Kansas		
2016	**Kansas City-Kansas portion (Johnson & Wyandotte Counties) (1985)[d]**	16,000	
2016	**Kansas City-Missouri portion (1985)[d]**	2000	
2016	*Kansas City Total (1985)[d]*	18,000	
2017	Lawrence	300	
2014	Manhattan	175	
2014	Topeka (Shawnee County)	300	
2019	Wichita	625	
2019	Other Places	25	
2019	Mid-Kansas Jewish Federation (Total)	650	
	Total Kansas	17,425	
	Kentucky		
2008	**Covington-Newport (2008)**	300	
2018	Lexington (Bourbon, Clark, Fayette, Jessamine, Madison, Pulaski, Scott, & Woodford Counties)		
	Jewish Federation of the Bluegrass	2500	

Communities with estimated Jewish population of 100 or more, 2019

Date	Geographic Area	# of Jews	Part-Year
2015	**Louisville (Jefferson County) (2006)**[d]	8300	
2013	Other Places	100	
2015	*Jewish Federation of Southern Illinois, Southeast Missouri and Western Kentucky (Alton-Belleville-Benton-Carbondale-Centralia-Collinsville-East St. Louis-Herrin-Marion in Southern Illinois, Cape Girardeau-Farmington-Sikeston in Southeast Missouri, & Paducah in Western Kentucky) Total*	650	
	Total Kentucky	11,200	
	Louisiana		
2017	Alexandria (Allen, Grant, Rapides, Vernon, & Winn Parishes)	300	
2016	Baton Rouge (Ascension, East Baton Rouge, Iberville, Livingston, Pointe Coupee, St. Landry, &West Baton Rouge Parishes)	1500	
2008	Lafayette	200	
2008	Lake Charles	200	
2019	**New Orleans (Jefferson & Orleans Parishes) (1984, 2009)**[e]	12,000	
2007	Monroe-Ruston	150	
2007	Shreveport-Bossier	450	
2007	*North Louisiana (Bossier & Caddo Parishes) Total*	600	
2007	Other Places	100	
	Total Louisiana	14,900	
	Maine		
2007	**Androscoggin County (Lewiston-Auburn) (2007)**[a]	600	
2017	Augusta	300	
2017	Bangor	1500	
2007	**Oxford County (South Paris) (2007)**[a]	750	
2017	Rockland	300	
2007	**Sagadahoc County (Bath) (2007)**[a]	400	
2018	**Portland (2007)**	4425	
2018	**Other Cumberland County (2007)**	2350	
2018	**York County (2007)**	1575	
2018	*Southern Maine Total (2007)*	8350	
2014	Waterville	225	
	Other Places	125	
	Total Maine	12,550	
	Maryland		
2010	**Annapolis (2010)**[a]	3500	
2018	**Pikesville (2010)**	31,100	
2018	**Park Heights-Cheswolde (2010)**	13,000	
2018	**Owings Mills (2010)**	12,100	
2018	**Reisterstown (2010)**	7000	
2018	**Mount Washington (2010)**	6600	

Communities with estimated Jewish population of 100 or more, 2019

Date	Geographic Area	# of Jews	Part-Year
2018	**Towson-Lutherville-Timonium-Interstate 83 (2010)**	5600	
2018	**Downtown (2010)**	4500	
2018	**Guilford-Roland Park (2010)**	4100	
2018	**Randallstown-Liberty Road (2010)**	2900	
2018	**Other Baltimore County (2010)**	3700	
2018	**Carroll County (2010)**	2800	
2018	***Baltimore Total (2010)***	93,400	
2017	Cumberland	275	
2017	Easton (Talbot County)	500	
2017	Frederick (Frederick County)	1200	
2017	Hagerstown (Washington County)	325	
2017	Harford County	1600	
2010	**Howard County (Columbia) (2010)**	17,200	
2016	**Lower Montgomery County (2003)**	87,000	
2016	**Upper Montgomery County (2003)**	18,400	
2016	**Prince George's County (2003)**	11,400	
2016	***Jewish Federation of Greater Washington Total in Maryland (2003)***	116,800	
2017	Ocean City	1000	
2012	Prince Frederick (Calvert County)	100	
2017	Salisbury	400	
2017	Waldorf	200	
2012	South Gate	100	
	Total Maryland	236,600	
	Massachusetts		
2016	**Attleboro (2002)[a]**	800	
2016	**State of Rhode Island (2002)**	18,750	
2016	***Jewish Alliance of Greater Rhode Island Total***	19,550	
2019	**Northern Berkshires (North Adams) (2008)[d]**	600	80
2019	**Central Berkshires (Pittsfield) (2008)[d]**	1600	415
2019	**Southern Berkshires (Lenox) (2008)[d]**	2100	2255
2019	***Berkshires Total (2008)[d]***	4300	2750
2019	**Brighton-Brookline-Newton & Contiguous Areas (2015)**	70,700	
2019	**Cambridge-Somerville-Central Boston (2015)**	66,800	
2019	**Greater Framingham (2015)**	21,100	
2019	**Northwestern Suburbs (2015)**	11,200	
2019	**Greater Sharon (2015)**	10,400	
2019	**North Shore (2015)**	30,000	
2019	**Southwestern Suburbs (2015)**	5300	
2019	**Northern Suburbs (2015)**	14,400	
2019	**South Area (2015)**	18,100	
2019	***Boston Total***	248,000	
1997–2001	Cape Cod (Barnstable County)	3250	

Communities with estimated Jewish population of 100 or more, 2019

Date	Geographic Area	# of Jews	Part-Year
2017	Fall River	600	
2013	Martha's Vineyard (Dukes County)	375	200
2005	Andover-Boxford-Dracut-Lawrence-Methuen-North Andover-Tewksbury	3000	
2005	Haverhill	900	
2005	Lowell	2100	
2005	*Merrimack Valley Jewish Federation Total*	6000	
2014	Nantucket	100	400
2019	New Bedford (Dartmouth-Fairhaven-Mattapoisett)	3000	
1997–2001	Newburyport	280	
2014	Plymouth	1200	
2012	**Springfield (Hampden County) (1967)[d]**	6600	
2012	Franklin County (Greenfield)	1100	
2012	Hampshire County (Amherst-Northampton)	6500	
2012	*Jewish Federation of Western Massachusetts Total*	14,200	
2014	Taunton	400	
2018	**Worcester (central Worcester County) (1986)**	9000	
2018	South Worcester County (Southbridge-Webster)	500	
2018	North Worcester County (Fitchburg-Gardner-Leominster)	1000	
2018	*Jewish Federation of Central Massachusetts (Worcester County) Total*	10,500	
	Other Places	75	
	Total Massachusetts	293,080	3,350
	Michigan		
2017	**Ann Arbor (Washtenaw County) (2010)[a]**	8000	
2012	Bay City-Saginaw	250	
2016	South Bend-Mishawaka-Elkhart (Elkhart & St. Joseph Counties) (Indiana)	1650	
2016	Benton Harbor-St. Joseph	150	
2016	***Jewish Federation of St. Joseph Valley Total***	1800	
2019	**West Bloomfield (2017)**	15,200	
2019	**Bloomfield Hills-Birmingham-Franklin (2017)**	12,400	
2019	**Farmington (2017)**	6300	
2019	**Oak Park-Huntington Woods (2017)**	12,800	
2019	**Southfield (2017)**	5600	
2019	**East Oakland County (2017)**	3600	
2019	**North Oakland County (2017)**	3700	
2019	**West Oakland County (2017)**	4450	
2019	**Wayne County (2017)**	5000	
2019	**Macomb County (2017)**	2700	
2019	***Detroit (Macomb, Oakland, & Wayne Counties) Total (2017)***	71,750	
2009	**Flint (1956)[d]**	1300	
2018	Grand Rapids (Kent County)	2000	

Communities with estimated Jewish population of 100 or more, 2019

Date	Geographic Area	# of Jews	Part-Year
2017	Jackson	200	
2012	Kalamazoo (Kalamazoo County)	1500	
2016	Lansing	1800	
2015	Lenawee & Monroe Counties	200	
2007	Midland	120	
2007	Muskegon (Muskegon County)	210	
2017	Traverse City	150	
2007	Other Places	275	
2015	*Jewish Federation of Greater Toledo (Fulton, Lucas, & Wood Counties in Ohio & Lenawee & Monroe Counties in Michigan) Total*	2300	
	Total Michigan	87,905	
	Minnesota		
2015	Duluth (Carlton & St. Louis Counties)	600	
2017	Rochester	400	
2015	**City of Minneapolis (2004)**	5200	
2015	**Inner Ring (2004)**	16,100	
2015	**Outer Ring (2004)**	8000	
2015	**Minneapolis (Hennepin County) Subtotal (2004)**	29,300	
2019	**City of St. Paul (2004, 2010)[b]**	4000	
2019	**Southern Suburbs (2004, 2010)[b]**	5300	
2019	**Northern Suburbs (2004, 2010)[b]**	600	
2019	**St. Paul (Dakota & Ramsey Counties) Subtotal (2004, 2010)[b]**	9900	
	Twin Cities Total	39,200	
2004	**Twin Cities Surrounding Counties (Anoka, Carver, Goodhue, Rice, Scott, Sherburne, Washington, & Wright Counties) (2004)[a]**	5300	
	Other Places	100	
	Total Minnesota	45,600	
	Mississippi		
2015	Biloxi-Gulfport	200	
2008	Greenville	120	
2008	Hattiesburg (Forrest & Lamar Counties)	130	
2008	Jackson (Hinds, Madison, & Rankin Counties)	650	
	Other Places	425	
	Total Mississippi	1525	
	Missouri		
2014	Columbia	400	
2009	Jefferson City	100	
2017	Joplin	100	
2016	**Kansas City-Kansas portion (Johnson & Wyandotte Counties) (1985)[d]**	16,000	

Communities with estimated Jewish population of 100 or more, 2019

Date	Geographic Area	# of Jews	Part-Year
2016	**Kansas City-Missouri portion (1985)**[d]	2000	
2016	***Kansas City Total (1985)***[d]	18,000	
2009	St. Joseph (Buchanan County)	200	
2019	**Creve Coeur Area (2014)**	13,550	
2019	**Chesterfield (2014)**	12,150	
2019	**University City/Clayton (2014)**	9100	
2019	**Olivette/Ladue (2014)**	6200	
2019	**St. Charles County (2014)**	5900	
2019	**St. Louis City (2014)**	5150	
2019	**Des Peres/Kirkwood/Webster (2014)**	2750	
2019	**Other North County (2014)**	4400	
2019	**Other South County (2014)**	1900	
2019	***St. Louis Total (2014)***	61,100	
2009	Springfield	300	
	Other Places	75	
2015	*Jewish Federation of Southern Illinois, Southeast Missouri and Western Kentucky (Alton-Belleville-Benton-Carbondale-Centralia-Collinsville-East St. Louis-Herrin-Marion in Southern Illinois, Cape Girardeau-Farmington-Sikeston in Southeast Missouri, & Paducah in Western Kentucky) Total*	650	
	Total Missouri	64,275	
	Montana		
2017	Billings (Yellowstone County)	250	
2009	Bozeman	500	
2017	Helena	120	
2015	Kalispell-Whitefish (Flathead County)	250	
2017	Missoula	200	
1997–2001	Other Places	75	
	Total Montana	1395	
	Nebraska		
2014	Lincoln	400	
2019	**East Omaha (2017)**	1900	
2019	**West Omaha (2017)**	5700	
2019	**Other Areas (2017)**	1200	
2019	**Omaha Total (2017)**	8800	
2012	Other Places	150	
	Total Nebraska	9350	
	Nevada		
2019	**Northwest (2005)**	24,500	
2019	**Southwest (2005)**	16,000	
2019	**Central (2005)**	6000	
2019	**Southeast (2005)**	18,000	
2019	**Northeast (2005)**	7800	
2019	***Las Vegas Total (2005)***	72,300	

Communities with estimated Jewish population of 100 or more, 2019

Date	Geographic Area	# of Jews	Part-Year
2011	**Reno-Carson City (Carson City & Washoe Counties) (2011)**[a]	4000	
	Total Nevada	76,300	
	New Hampshire		
1997–2001	Concord	500	
1997–2001	Franklin-Laconia-Meredith-Plymouth	270	
Pre-1997	Hanover-Lebanon	600	
2001	Keene	300	
1997–2001	Littleton-Bethlehem	200	70
1997–2001	**Manchester (1983)**[d]	4000	
1997–2001	Nashua	2000	
2008	North Conway-Mount Washington Valley	100	
2014	Portsmouth-Exeter (Rockingham County)	1250	
1997–2001	Salem	150	70
2014	**Strafford (Dover-Rochester) (2007)**[a]	700	
1997–2001	Other Places	50	
	Total New Hampshire	10,120	140
	New Jersey		
2004	**The Island (Atlantic City) (2004)**	5450	6700
2004	**The Mainland (2004)**	6250	600
2004	*Atlantic County Subtotal (2004)*	11,700	7300
2004	**Cape May County-Wildwood (2004)**	500	900
2004	*Jewish Federation of Atlantic & Cape May Counties Total (2004)*	12,200	8200
2018	**Pascack-Northern Valley (2001)**	11,900	
2018	**North Palisades (2001)**	18,600	
2018	**Central Bergen (2001)**	22,200	
2018	**West Bergen (2001)**	14,300	
2018	**South Bergen (2001)**	10,000	
2018	Other Bergen	23,000	
2018	*Bergen County Subtotal*	100,000	
2018	**Northern Hudson County (2001)**	2000	
2018	Bayonne	1600	
2018	Hoboken	1800	
2018	Jersey City	6000	
2018	*Hudson County Subtotal*	11,400	
2018	Northern Passaic County	8000	
2018	*Jewish Federation of Northern New Jersey (Bergen, Hudson, & northern Passaic Counties) Total*	119,400	
2019	**Camden County (1991, 2013)**[e]	34,600	
2019	**Burlington County (1991, 2013)**[e]	15,900	
2019	**Northern Gloucester County (1991, 2013)**[e]	6200	

Date	Geographic Area	# of Jews	Part-Year
	Communities with estimated Jewish population of 100 or more, 2019		
2019	*Jewish Federation of Southern New Jersey Total (1991, 2013)*[e]	56,700	
2019	**South Essex (Newark) (1998, 2012)**[b]	12,200	
2019	**Livingston (1998, 2012)**[b]	10,500	
2019	**North Essex (1998, 2012)**[b]	13,000	
2019	**West Orange-Orange (1998, 2012)**[b]	9000	
2019	**East Essex (1998, 2012)**[b]	3500	
2019	*Essex County Subtotal (1998, 2012)*[b]	48,200	
2019	**West Morris (1998, 2012)**[b]	13,700	
2019	**North Morris (1998, 2012)**[b]	13,400	
2019	**South Morris (1998, 2012)**[b]	3200	
2019	*Morris County Subtotal (1998, 2012)*[b]	30,300	
2019	**Northern Somerset County (2012)**[a]	7400	
2019	**Sussex County (1998, 2012)**[b]	4700	
2019	**Union County (2012)**[a]	24,400	
2019	*Jewish Federation of Greater MetroWest NJ (Essex, Morris, northern Somerset, Sussex, & Union Counties) Total (2012)*	115,000	
2008	**North Middlesex (Edison-Piscataway-Woodbridge) (2008)**	3600	
2008	**Highland Park-South Edison (2008)**	5700	
2008	**Central Middlesex (East Brunswick-New Brunswick) (2008)**	24,800	
2008	**South Middlesex (Monroe Township) (2008)**	17,900	
	Middlesex County Subtotal (2008)	52,000	
2006	**Western Monmouth (Freehold-Howell-Manalapan-Marlboro) (1997)**	37,800	
2006	**Eastern Monmouth (Asbury Park-Deal-Long Branch) (1997)**	17,300	
2006	**Northern Monmouth (Hazlet-Highlands-Middletown-Union Beach) (1997)**	8900	
	Monmouth County Subtotal (2008)	64,000	6000
2006	*Jewish Federation in the Heart of New Jersey Total*	116,000	6000
2018	Lakewood	74,500	
2018	Other Ocean County	8500	
2018	*Ocean County Total*	83,000	
2009	Southern Passaic County (Clifton-Passaic)	12,000	
1997–2001	Princeton	3000	
2019	**Hunterdon County (2012)**[a]	6000	
2019	**Southern Somerset County (2012)**[a]	11,600	
2019	**Warren County (2012)**[a]	2400	
2019	*Jewish Federation of Somerset, Hunterdon & Warren Counties Total (2012)*[a]	20,000	
1997–2001	**Trenton (most of Mercer County) (1975)**[d]	6000	

Communities with estimated Jewish population of 100 or more, 2019

Date	Geographic Area	# of Jews	Part-Year
2015	Vineland area (including southern Gloucester & eastern Salem Counties) (Jewish Federation of Cumberland, Gloucester and Salem Counties)	2000	
1997–2001	Other Places	150	
	Total New Jersey	**545,450**	**14,200**
	New Mexico		
2011	**Albuquerque (Bernalillo County) (2011)[a]**	7500	
2016	El Paso (Texas)	5000	
2016	Las Cruces	500	
2016	*Jewish Federation of Greater El Paso (Total)*	5500	
2009	Los Alamos	250	
2011	Santa Fe-Las Vegas	4000	
Pre-1997	Taos	300	
1997–2001	Other Places	75	
	Total New Mexico	**12,625**	
	New York		
2019	Albany (Albany County)	12,000	
2019	Amsterdam	100	
2019	Catskill	200	
2019	Glens Falls-Lake George (southern Essex, northern Saratoga, Warren, & Washington Counties)	800	
2019	Gloversville (Fulton County)	300	
2019	Hudson (Columbia County)	500	
2019	Saratoga Springs	600	
2019	Schenectady	5200	
2019	Troy	800	
2019	Jewish Federation of Northeastern New York (Total)	20,500	
1997–2001	Auburn (Cayuga County)	115	
1997–2001	Binghamton (Broome County)	2400	
2019	**Buffalo (Erie County) (2013)**	10,700	
2019	**Other Western New York (parts of Cattaraugus, Chautauqua, Genesee, Niagara, & Wyoming Counties) (2013)[d]**	300	
2019	*Jewish Federation of Greater Buffalo Total (2013)*	11,000	
1997–2001	Canandaigua-Geneva-Newark-Seneca Falls	300	
1997–2001	Cortland (Cortland County)	150	
2019	Dutchess County (Amenia-Beacon-Fishkill-Freedom Plains-Hyde Park-Poughkeepsie-Red Hook-Rhinebeck)	10,000	
2009	Elmira-Corning (Chemung, Schuyler, southeastern Steuben, & Tioga Counties)	700	
1997–2001	Fleischmanns	100	
1997–2001	Herkimer (Herkimer County)	130	
1997–2001	Ithaca (Tompkins County)	2000	
1997–2001	Jamestown	100	

Communities with estimated Jewish population of 100 or more, 2019			
Date	Geographic Area	# of Jews	Part-Year
2019	**Northeast Bronx (2011)**	18,300	
2019	**Riverdale-Kingsbridge (2011)**	20,100	
2019	**Other Bronx (2011)**	15,500	
2019	***Bronx Subtotal (2011)***	53,900	
2019	**Bensonhurst-Gravesend-Bay Ridge (2011)**	47,000	
2019	**Borough Park (2011)**	131,100	
2019	**Brownstone Brooklyn (2011)**	19,700	
2019	**Canarsie-Mill Basin (2011)**	24,500	
2019	**Coney Island-Brighton Beach-Sheepshead Bay (2011)**	56,200	
2019	**Crown Heights (2011)**	23,800	
2019	**Flatbush-Midwood-Kensington (2011)**	108,500	
2019	**Kings Bay-Madison (2011)**	29,400	
2019	**Williamsburg (2011)**	74,500	
2019	**Other Brooklyn (2011)**	46,400	
2019	***Brooklyn Subtotal (2011)***	561,100	
2019	**Lower Manhattan East (2011)**	39,500	
2019	**Lower Manhattan West (2011)**	33,200	
2019	**Upper East Side (2011)**	57,400	
2019	**Upper West Side (2011)**	70,500	
2019	**Washington Heights-Inwood (2011)**	21,400	
2019	**Other Manhattan (2011)**	17,700	
2019	***Manhattan Subtotal (2011)***	239,700	
2019	**Flushing-Bay Terrace-Little Neck Area (2011)**	26,800	
2019	**Forest Hills-Rego Park-Kew Gardens Area (2011)**	60,900	
2019	**Kew Gardens Hills-Jamaica-Fresh Meadows Area (2011)**	41,600	
2019	**Long Island City-Astoria-Elmhurst Area (2011)**	12,100	
2019	**The Rockaways (2011)**	22,500	
2019	**Other Queens (2011)**	33,900	
2019	***Queens Subtotal (2011)***	197,800	
2019	**Mid-Staten Island (2011)**	18,800	
2019	**Southern Staten Island (2011)**	8800	
2019	**Other Staten Island (2011)**	6300	
2019	***Staten Island Subtotal (2011)***	33,900	
2019	***New York City Subtotal (2011)***	1,086,400	
2019	**Five Towns (2011)**	25,000	
2019	**Great Neck (2011)**	28,700	
2019	**Merrick-Bellmore-East Meadow-Massapequa Area (2011)**	38,500	
2019	**Oceanside-Long Beach-West Hempstead-Valley Stream Area (2011)**	45,900	
2019	**Plainview-Syosset-Jericho Area (2011)**	35,800	
2019	**Roslyn-Port Washington-Glen Cove-Old Westbury-Oyster Bay Area (2011)**	34,800	

Communities with estimated Jewish population of 100 or more, 2019

Date	Geographic Area	# of Jews	Part-Year
2019	**Other Nassau (2011)**	21,200	
2019	*Nassau County Subtotal (2011)*	229,900	
2019	**Commack-East Northport-Huntington Area (2011)**	19,300	
2019	**Dix Hills-Huntington Station-Melville (2011)**	16,500	
2019	**Smithtown-Port Jefferson-Stony Brook Area (2011)**	16,500	
2019	**Other Suffolk (2011)**	33,400	
2019	*Suffolk County Subtotal (2011)*	85,700	
2019	**South-Central Westchester (2011)**	46,200	
2019	**Sound Shore Communities (2011)**	18,900	
2019	**River Towns (2011)**	30,800	
2019	**North-Central & Northwestern Westchester (2011)**	25,300	
2019	**Other Westchester (2011)**	15,000	
2019	*Westchester County Subtotal (2011)*	136,200	
2019	*New York Metro Area (New York City & Nassau, Suffolk, & Westchester Counties) Total (2011)*	1,538,000	
1997–2001	Niagara Falls	150	
2009	Olean	100	
1997–2001	Oneonta (Delaware & Otsego Counties)	300	
2019	**Kiryas Joel (2018)[c]**	25,300	
2019	Other Orange County (Middletown-Monroe-Newburgh-Port Jervis)	12,000	
2019	*Orange County Total*	37,300	
1997–2001	Plattsburgh	250	
1997–2001	Potsdam	200	
2016	**Putnam County (2010)[d]**	3900	
2019	**Brighton (1999, 2010)[e]**	10,100	
2019	**Pittsford (1999, 2010)[e]**	3800	
2019	**Other Places in Monroe County & Victor in Ontario County (1999, 2010)[e]**	6000	
2019	*Rochester Total (1999, 2010)[e]*	19,900	
2019	**Kaser Village (2018)[c]**	5400	
2019	**Monsey (2018)[c]**	22,000	
2019	**New Square (2018)[c]**	8600	
2019	Other Rockland County	66,600	
	Rockland County Total	102,600	
1997–2001	Rome	100	
Pre-1997	Sullivan County (Liberty-Monticello)	7425	
2018	Syracuse (western Madison, Onondaga, & most of Oswego Counties)	7000	
2014	Ulster County (Kingston-New Paltz-Woodstock & eastern Ulster County)	5000	
2019	Utica (southeastern Oneida County) (Jewish Community Federation of the Mohawk Valley)	1100	
1997–2001	Watertown	100	

Date	Geographic Area	# of Jews	Part-Year
	Communities with estimated Jewish population of 100 or more, 2019		
1997–2001	Other Places	400	
	Total New York	1,771,320	
	North Carolina		
2011	**Buncombe County (Asheville) (2011)[d]**	2530	415
2011	**Hendersonville County (Henderson) (2011)[d]**	510	100
2011	**Transylvania County (Brevard) (2011)[d]**	80	130
2011	**Macon County (2011)[d]**	60	30
2011	**Other Western North Carolina (2011)[d]**	220	160
2011	***WNC Jewish Federation (Western North Carolina) Total (2011)[d]***	3400	835
2009	Boone	60	225
2016	**Charlotte (Mecklenburg County) (1997)**	12,000	
2019	Orange County	3900	
2019	Durham County	3075	
2019	Other (Chatham & parts of Wake County)	525	
2019	Jewish Federation of Durham-Chapel Hill[d]	7500	
2012	Fayetteville (Cumberland County)	300	
2009	Gastonia (Cleveland, Gaston, & Lincoln Counties)	250	
2019	Greensboro	3000	
2015	Greenville	300	
2011	Hickory	250	
2009	High Point	150	
2009	Mooresville (Iredell County)	150	
2009	New Bern	150	
2009	Pinehurst	250	
2019	Raleigh-Cary (Wake County)	15,000	
2014	Southeastern North Carolina (Elizabethtown-Whiteville-Wilmington)	1600	
2011	Statesville (Iredell County)	150	
2015	**Winston-Salem (2011)[a]**	1200	
2010	Other Places	225	
	Total North Carolina	45,935	1060
	North Dakota		
2008	Fargo	150	
2011	Grand Forks	150	
1997–2001	Other Places	100	
	Total North Dakota	400	
	Ohio		
2016	**Akron-Kent (parts of Portage & Summit Counties) (1999)[d]**	3000	
Pre-1997	Athens	100	
2006	**Canton-New Philadelphia (Stark & Tuscarawas Counties) (1955)[d]**	1000	
2019	**Downtown Cincinnati (2008)**	700	

Communities with estimated Jewish population of 100 or more, 2019

Date	Geographic Area	# of Jews	Part-Year
2019	**Hyde Park-Mount Lookout-Oakley (2008)**	3100	
2019	**Amberley Village-Golf Manor-Roselawn (2008)**	5100	
2019	**Blue Ash-Kenwood-Montgomery (2008)**	9000	
2019	**Loveland-Mason-Middletown (2008)**	5500	
2019	**Wyoming-Finneytown-Reading (2008)**	2000	
2019	**Other Places in Cincinnati (2008)**	1300	
2019	**Covington-Newport (Kentucky) (2008)**	300	
2019	*Jewish Federation of Cincinnati Total (2008)*	27,000	
2019	**The Heights (2011)**	22,200	
2019	**East Side Suburbs (2011)**	5,300	
2019	**Beachwood (2011)**	10,700	
2019	**Solon & Southeast Suburbs (2011)**	15,300	
2019	**Northern Heights (2011)**	10,400	
2019	**West Side/Central Area (2011)**	11,900	
2019	**Northeast (2011)**	5000	
2019	*Cleveland (Cuyahoga & parts of Geauga, Lake, Portage, & Summit Counties) Total (2011)*	80,800	
2019	**Perimeter North (2013)**	4700	
2019	**Bexley area (2013)**	5400	
2019	**East (2013)**	6400	
2019	**Downtown/University (2013)**	9000	
2019	*Columbus Total (2013)*	25,500	
2019	**Dayton (Greene & Montgomery Counties) (1986)**[d]	4000	
1997–2001	Elyria-Oberlin	155	
1997–2001	Hamilton-Middletown-Oxford	900	
1997–2001	Lima (Allen County)	180	
Pre-1997	Lorain	600	
1997–2001	Mansfield	150	
1997–2001	Marion	125	
1997–2001	Sandusky-Fremont-Norwalk (Huron & Sandusky Counties)	105	
1997–2001	Springfield	200	
2019	**Toledo-Bowling Green (Fulton, Lucas, & Wood Counties) (1994)**[d]	2300	
1997–2001	Wooster	175	
2019	**Youngstown-Warren (Mahoning & Trumbull Counties) (2002)**[d]	1300	
1997–2001	Zanesville (Muskingum County)	100	
1997–2001	Other Places	425	
2015	*Youngstown Area Jewish Federation (including Mahoning & Trumbull Counties in Ohio & Mercer County in Pennsylvania) Total*	1700	
2015	*Jewish Federation of Greater Toledo (Fulton, Lucas, & Wood Counties in Ohio & Lenawee & Monroe Counties in Michigan) Total*	2300	

Communities with estimated Jewish population of 100 or more, 2019

Date	Geographic Area	# of Jews	Part-Year
	Total Ohio	147,815	
	Oklahoma		
2019	**Oklahoma City-Norman (Cleveland & Oklahoma Counties) (2010)[a]**	2300	
2019	Tulsa	2000	
2012	Other Places	125	
	Total Oklahoma	4425	
	Oregon		
2010	**Bend (2010)[a]**	1000	
1997–2001	Corvallis	500	
1997–2001	Eugene	3250	
1997–2001	Medford-Ashland-Grants Pass (Jackson & Josephine Counties)	1000	
2019	**Portland (Clackamas, Multnomah, & Washington Counties) (2011)[d]**	33,800	
2019	**Clark County (Vancouver, WA) (2011)[d]**	2600	
2019	***Greater Portland Total (2011)[d]***	36,400	
1997–2001	Salem (Marion & Polk Counties)	1000	
1997–2001	Other Places	100	
	Total Oregon	40,650	
	Pennsylvania		
2014	Altoona (Blair County)	450	
1997–2001	Beaver Falls (northern Beaver County)	180	
1997–2001	Butler (Butler County)	250	
2007	**Carbon County (2007)[a]**	600	
1997–2001	Chambersburg	150	
2018	Erie (Erie County)	500	
2016	**East Shore (1994)**	3000	
2016	**West Shore (1994)**	2000	
1994	***Harrisburg Total (1994)***	5000	
2019	Hazelton-Tamaqua	100	
2014	Johnstown (Cambria & Somerset Counties)	150	
2014	Lancaster	3000	
2014	Lebanon (Lebanon County)	165	
2018	**Allentown (2007)**	5950	
2018	**Bethlehem (2007)**	1050	
2018	**Easton (2007)**	1050	
2018	***Lehigh Valley Total (2007)***	8050	
2015	Mercer County (Sharon-Farrell)	300	
2007	**Monroe County (2007)[a]**	2300	
2016	**Bucks County (2009)**	41,400	
2016	**Chester County (Oxford-Kennett Square-Phoenixville-West Chester) (2009)**	20,900	

Communities with estimated Jewish population of 100 or more, 2019

Date	Geographic Area	# of Jews	Part-Year
2016	**Delaware County (Chester-Coatesville) (2009)**	21,000	
2016	**Montgomery County (Norristown) (2009)**	64,500	
2016	**Philadelphia (2009)**	66,900	
2016	***Greater Philadelphia Total (2009)***	214,700	
2008	Pike County	300	
2019	**Squirrel Hill (2017)**	14,800	
2019	**Rest of Pittsburgh (2017)**	12,800	
2019	**South Hills (Mt. Lebanon-Upper St. Clair) (2017)**	8800	
2019	**North Hills (Hampton, Fox Chapel, O'Hara) (2017)**	5400	
2019	**Other Places in Greater Pittsburgh (2017)**	7400	
2019	***Greater Pittsburgh (Allegheny, Beaver, Butler, Washington, & Westmoreland Counties) Total (2017)***	49,200	
1997–2001	Pottstown	650	
1997–2001	Pottsville	120	
1997–2001	Reading (Berks County)	2200	
2008	Scranton (Lackawanna County) (Northeastern Pennsylvania)	3100	
2009	State College-Bellefonte-Philipsburg	900	
1997–2001	Sunbury-Lewisburg-Milton-Selinsgrove-Shamokin	200	
1997–2001	Uniontown	150	
2008	Wayne County (Honesdale)	500	
2019	**Wilkes-Barre (Luzerne County, excluding Hazelton-Tamaqua) (2005)[d]**	1800	
2014	Williamsport-Lock Haven (Clinton & Lycoming Counties)	150	
2009	**York (1999)**	1800	
1997–2001	Other Places	900	
2015	*Youngstown Area Jewish Federation (including Mahoning & Trumbull Counties in Ohio & Mercer County in Pennsylvania) Total*	1700	
	Total Pennsylvania	297,865	
	Rhode Island		
2019	**Attleboro, MA (2002)[a]**	800	
2019	**Providence-Pawtucket (2002)**	7500	
2019	**West Bay (2002)**	6350	
2019	**East Bay (2002)**	1100	
2019	**South County (Washington County) (2002)**	1800	
2019	**Northern Rhode Island (2002)**	1000	
2019	**Newport County (2002)**	1000	
2019	**Total Rhode Island (2002)**	18,750	
2019	**Jewish Alliance of Greater Rhode Island Total**	19,550	
	South Carolina		
2009	Aiken	100	
2009	Anderson	100	
2009	Beaufort	100	

Date	Geographic Area	# of Jews	Part-Year
	Communities with estimated Jewish population of 100 or more, 2019		
2018	Charleston (Charleston, Dorchester, and Berkley Counties)	9000	
2015	Columbia (Lexington & Richland Counties)	3000	
2009	Florence	220	
2009	Georgetown	100	
2010	**Greenville (2010)**[a]	2000	
2012	Myrtle Beach (Horry County)	1500	
1997–2001	Spartanburg (Spartanburg County)	500	
2009	Sumter (Clarendon & Sumter Counties)	100	
2009	Other Places	100	
	Total South Carolina	16,820	
	South Dakota		
2009	Rapid City	100	
2014	Sioux Falls	100	
1997–2001	Other Places	50	
	Total South Dakota	250	
	Tennessee		
2013	Bristol-Johnson City-Kingsport	125	
2019	**Chattanooga (2011)**[a]	1400	
2016	**Knoxville (2010)**[a]	2000	
2018	**Memphis (2006)**[d]	10,000	
2019	**Davidson County (2016)**	6450	
2019	**Williamson County (2016)**	1700	
2019	**Other Central Tennessee (2016)**	850	
2019	**Nashville (2016) Total**	9000	
2010	**Oak Ridge (2010)**[a]	150	
2009	Other Places	125	
	Total Tennessee	22,800	
	Texas		
2012	Amarillo (Carson, Childress, Deaf Smith, Gray, Hall, Hutchinson, Moore, Potter, & Randall Counties)	200	
2019	Austin (Travis, Williamson, Hays, Bastrop, & Caldwell Counties)	30,000	
2014	Beaumont	300	
2011	Brownsville	200	
2011	Bryan-College Station	400	
2011	Columbus-Hallettsville-La Grange-Schulenburg (Colorado, Fayette, & Lavaca Counties)	100	
2015	Corpus Christi (Nueces County)	1000	
2019	**North Dallas (1988, 2013)**[e]	12,500	
2019	**Plano-Frisco-Richardson-Allen-McKinney (1988, 2013)**[e]	14,700	
2019	**Central Dallas-Downtown-Uptown (1988, 2013)**[e]	23,500	
2019	**East Dallas (1988, 2013)**[e]	1300	
2019	**Denton-Flowermound-Lewisville (1988, 2013)**[e]	900	
2019	**South Dallas-Duncanville-Cedar Hill (1988, 2013)**[e]	200	

Communities with estimated Jewish population of 100 or more, 2019

Date	Geographic Area	# of Jews	Part-Year
2019	**Addison-Carrolton-Farmers Branch (1988, 2013)[e]**	2700	
2019	**Other Places in Dallas (1988, 2013)[e]**	14,200	
2019	*Dallas (southern Collin, Dallas, & southeastern Denton Counties) Total (1988, 2013)[e]*	70,000	
2016	El Paso	5000	
2016	Las Cruces (New Mexico)	500	
2016	*Jewish Federation of Greater El Paso (Total)*	5500	
2016	Fort Worth (Tarrant County)	5000	
2011	Galveston	600	
2011	Harlingen-Mercedes	150	
2019	**Core Area (2016)**	19,800	
2019	**Memorial (2016)**	5100	
2019	**Central City (2016)**	6000	
2019	**Suburban Southwest (2016)**	5800	
2019	**West (2016)**	3600	
2019	**North (2016)**	7300	
2019	**Southwest (2016)**	3000	
2019	**East (2016)**	400	
2019	*Houston (Harris County & parts of Brazoria, Fort Bend, Galveston & Montgomery Counties) Total (2016)*	51,000	
2011	Kilgore-Longview	100	
2017	Laredo	150	
2012	Lubbock (Lubbock County)	230	
2011	McAllen (Hidalgo & Starr Counties)	300	
2012	Midland-Odessa	200	
2011	Port Arthur	100	
2007	**Inside Loop 410 (2007)**	2000	
2007	**Between the Loops (2007)**	5600	
2007	**Outside Loop 1604 (2007)**	1600	
2007	*San Antonio Total (2007)*	9200	
2007	**San Antonio Surrounding Counties (Atascosa, Bandera, Comal, Guadalupe, Kendall, Medina, & Wilson Counties) (2007)[a]**	1000	
2014	Tyler	250	
2014	Waco (Bell, Coryell, Falls, Hamilton, Hill, & McLennan Counties)	400	
2012	Wichita Falls	150	
2011	Other Places	450	
	Total Texas	176,480	
	Utah		
1997–2001	Ogden	150	
2009	Park City	600	400
2010	**Salt Lake City (Salt Lake County) (2010)[a]**	4800	
1997–2001	Other Places	100	

Communities with estimated Jewish population of 100 or more, 2019

Date	Geographic Area	# of Jews	Part-Year
	Total Utah	5650	400
	Vermont		
1997–2001	Bennington	500	
2008	Brattleboro	350	
2019	Burlington	3500	
1997–2001	Manchester	325	
2008	Middlebury	200	
2008	Montpelier-Barre	550	
2008	Rutland	300	
1997–2001	St. Johnsbury-Newport (Caledonia & Orleans Counties)	140	
2019	Stowe	1000	
Pre-1997	Woodstock	270	
	Total Vermont	7135	
	Virginia		
2013	Blacksburg-Christiansburg-Floyd-Radford	250	
2015	Charlottesville	2000	
2012	Fauquier County (Warrenton)	100	
2013	Fredericksburg (parts of King George, Orange, Spotsylvania, & Stafford Counties)	500	
2013	Harrisonburg	300	
2013	Lynchburg	350	
2019	Newport News-Hampton	2250	
2019	Williamsburg	750	
2019	*United Jewish Community of the Virginia Peninsula Total*	3000	
2008	**Norfolk (2001)**	3550	
2008	**Virginia Beach (2001)**	6000	
2008	**Chesapeake-Portsmouth-Suffolk (2001)**	1400	
2008	***United Jewish Federation of Tidewater Total (2001)***	10,950	
2017	**North-Central Northern Virginia (2017)**	24,500	
2017	**Central Northern Virginia (2017)**	23,100	
2017	**East Northern Virginia (2017)**	54,400	
2017	**West-Northern Virginia (2017)**	19,400	
2016	***Jewish Federation of Greater Washington Total in Northern Virginia (2017)***	121,400	
2013	Petersburg-Colonial Heights-Hopewell	300	
2011	**Central (1994, 2011)**[b]	1300	
2011	**West End (1994, 2011)**[b]	1200	
2011	**Far West End (1994, 2011)**[b]	4100	
2011	**Northeast (1994, 2011)**[b]	1200	
2011	**Southside (1994, 2011)**[b]	2200	
2011	***Richmond (City of Richmond & Chesterfield, Goochland, Hanover, Henrico, & Powhatan Counties) Total (1994, 2011)***[b]	10,000	

Communities with estimated Jewish population of 100 or more, 2019

Date	Geographic Area	# of Jews	Part-Year
2013	Roanoke	1000	
2013	Staunton-Lexington	100	
2013	Winchester (Clarke, Frederick, & Warren Counties)	270	
2013	Other Places	75	
	Total Virginia	150,595	
	Washington		
1997–2001	Bellingham	525	
2011	**Clark County (Vancouver) (2011)[d]**	2600	
1997–2001	Kennewick-Pasco-Richland	300	
2011	Longview-Kelso	100	
1997–2001	Olympia (Thurston County)	560	
Pre-1997	Port Angeles	100	
2009	Port Townsend	200	
2014	Pullman (Whitman County, Palouse)	100	
2019	**South Seattle (Southeast Seattle-Southwest Seattle-Downtown) (2014)**	16,500	
2019	**North Seattle (Northeast & Northwest Seattle) (2014)**	16,400	
2019	**Bellevue (2014)**	6300	
2019	**Mercer Island (2014)**	6400	
2019	**Redmond (2014)**	3000	
2019	**Rest of King County (2014)**	9400	
2019	**Island, Kitsap, Pierce, & Snohomish Counties (2014)**	6650	
2019	*Seattle Total (2014)*	64,650	
1997–2001	Spokane	1500	
2009	Tacoma (Pierce County)	2500	
1997–2001	Yakima-Ellensburg (Kittitas & Yakima Counties)	150	
1997–2001	Other Places	150	
	Total Washington	73,435	
	West Virginia		
2011	Bluefield-Princeton	100	
2007	Charleston (Kanawha County)	975	
1997–2001	Clarksburg	110	
1997–2001	Huntington	250	
1997–2001	Morgantown	200	
Pre-1997	Parkersburg	110	
1997–2001	Wheeling	290	
1997–2001	Other Places	275	
	Total West Virginia	2310	
	Wisconsin		
2015	Appleton & other Fox Cities (Outagamie, Calumet, & northern Winnebago Counties)	200	
1997–2001	Beloit-Janesville	120	
1997–2001	Green Bay	500	
1997–2001	Kenosha (Kenosha County)	300	

Communities with estimated Jewish population of 100 or more, 2019			
Date	Geographic Area	# of Jews	Part-Year
1997–2001	La Crosse	100	
2017	Madison (Dane County)	5000	
2019	**City of Milwaukee (2011)**	4900	
2019	**North Shore (2011)**	13,400	
2019	**Waukesha (2011)**	3200	
2019	**Milwaukee County Ring (2011)**	4300	
2019	***Milwaukee (Milwaukee, southern Ozaukee, & eastern Waukesha Counties) Total (2011)***	25,800	
1997–2001	Oshkosh-Fond du Lac	170	
1997–2001	Racine (Racine County)	200	
1997–2001	Sheboygan	140	
2015	Wausau-Antigo-Marshfield-Stevens Point	300	
1997–2001	Other Places	225	
	Total Wisconsin	33,055	
	Wyoming		
1997–2001	Casper	150	
2012	Cheyenne	500	
2008	Jackson Hole	300	
2008	Laramie	200	
	Total Wyoming	1150	

1. Scientific Estimates. Estimates in boldface type are based on scientific studies, which, unless otherwise indicated, are Random Digit Dial (RDD) studies. The boldface date in the Geographic Area column indicates the year in which the field work was conducted. Superscripts are used to indicate the type of Scientific Estimate when it is not RDD:

   (a) indicates a Distinctive Jewish Name (DJN) study
   (b) indicates a DJN study used to update a previous RDD study (first date is for the RDD study, second date is for the DJN-based update)
   (c) indicates the use of US Census data
   (d) indicates a scientific study using a different methodology (neither RDD nor DJN)
   (e) indicates a scientific study using a different methodology (neither RDD nor DJN) that is used to update a previous RDD study (first date is for the RDD study, second date is for the other scientific study)

2. Informant/Internet Estimates. Estimates for communities not shown in boldface type are generally based on Informant/Internet Estimates

# of Jews. This column shows estimates of the number of Jews for each area or subarea, exclusive of part-year Jews.

Part-Year. For communities for which the information is available, this column presents estimates of the number of Jews in part-year households. Part-year households are defined as households who live in a community for 3–7 months of the year. Note that part-year households are probably important components of other communities but we have no documentation of such.

Jews in part-year households form an essential component of some Jewish communities, as many join synagogues and donate to Jewish Federations in the communities in which they live part time. This is particularly true in Florida, and, to a lesser extent, in other states with many retirees. Presenting the information in this way allows the reader to gain a better perspective on the size of Jewish communities with significant part-year populations, without double-counting the part-year Jewish population in the totals. Note that Jews in part-year households are reported as such in the community that is most likely their "second home."

Excel Spreadsheet. The Excel spreadsheet used to create this Appendix and the other tables in this chapter is available at www.jewishdatabank.org. This spreadsheet also includes information on about 250 *Other Places* with Jewish populations of less than 100, which are aggregated and shown as the last entry for many of the states in this Appendix. The spreadsheet also contains Excel versions of the other tables in this chapter as well as a table showing some of the major changes since last year's *Year Book* and a table showing the calculations for the indices of dissimilarity referenced above.

References

Abrahamson, M. 1986. The unreliability of DJN techniques. *Contemporary Jewry* 7 (1): 93–98.

Abramovitch, I., and S. Galvin, eds. 2002. *Jews of Brooklyn*. Hanover, NH: Brandeis University Press.

Adler, C. 1900. *American Jewish year book 1900–1901*. Vol. 2. Philadelphia: The Jewish Publication Society of America.

Ahituv, S. 2003. *Historical atlas of the Jewish people*. New York: Continuum.

Ain, S. 2019, June 5 Jews of color: "We don't feel comfortable in the synagogue." *The Times of Israel*.

Barnavi, E. 1992. *A historical atlas of the Jewish people: From the time of the patriarchs to the present*. New York: Alfred A. Knopf.

Billings, J.S. 1890. *Vital Statistics of the Jews on the United States. Census Bulletin No. 19*. Washington: Census Office.

Bradburn, N.M., S. Sudman, and B. Wansink. 2004. *Asking questions: The definitive guide to questionnaire design—for market research, political polls, and social and health*. New York: Josses-Bass.

Brodkin, K. 1998. *How Jews became whitefolks: What that says about race in America*. New Brunswick, NY: Rutgers University Press.

Bureau of the Census. No Date, CA 1958. "Tabulations of Data on the Social and Economic Characteristics of Major Religious Groups," 1957. Washington DC (mimeo).

Burt, J.E., G.M. Barber, and D.L. Rigby. 2009. *Elementary statistics for geographers*. 3rd ed. New York: Guilford Press.

Cohen, S.M., J.B. Ukeles, and A. Grosse. 2017. *A portrait of Bay Area Jewish life and communities*. San Francisco: The Jewish Community Federation of San Francisco, the Peninsular, Marin and Sonoma Counties.

Cohen, S.M., J.B. Ukeles, R. Miller, P. Beck, S. Shmulyian, and D. Dutwin. 2011. *Jewish Community Study of New York 2011*. New York: UJA-Federation of New York.

Comenetz, J. 2006. Census-Based estimation of the Hasidic Jewish population. *Contemporary Jewry* 26: 35–74.

———. 2011. Jewish maps of the United States by counties. www.jewishdatabank.org/Studies/details.cfm?StudyID=602.

Dashefsky, A., B. Lazerwitz, and E. Tabory. 2003. A journey of the "straight way" or the "roundabout path": Jewish identity in the United States and Israel. In *Handbook of the sociology of religion*, ed. M. Dillon, 240–260. Cambridge/New York: Cambridge University Press.

Dashefsky, A. and I. Sheskin. 2012. *Estimating a rare population: The case of American Jews*. Paper presented at the Southern Demographic Association, Williamsburg, VA.

De Lange, N. 1984. *Atlas of the Jewish world*. New York: Facts on File.

DellaPergola, S. 2011. *Jewish demographic policies: Population trends and options in Israel and in the diaspora*. Jerusalem: The Jewish People Policy Institute.

———. 2013. How many Jews in the United States? The demographic perspective. *Contemporary Jewry* 33: 15–42.

Dimont, M.I. 1978. *The Jews in America, The roots, history, and destiny of American Jews*. New York: Simon and Schuster.

Friesel, E. 1990. *Atlas of modern Jewish history*. New York: Oxford University Press.

Gilbert, M. 1985. *The Illustrated Atlas of Jewish Civilization*. New York: MacMillan.

———. 1995. *The Routledge atlas of Jewish history*. 8th ed. London: Routledge.

Geller, L. and L. Hemlock 2019. Jews of color belonging: We all have work to do. at www.ejewishphilanthropy.com.

Glazer, N. 1989/1972/1957. American Judaism: Second edition revised with a new introduction. Chicago: The University of Chicago Press.

Gold, S. 2015. Patterns of adaptation among contemporary Jewish immigrants to the US. In *American Jewish year book 2015*, ed. A. Dashefsky and I.M. Sheskin, vol. 115, 3–44. Cham, SUI: Springer.

Goldscheider, C. 2004. *Studying the Jewish future*. Seattle: University of Washington Press.

Goodman, G.M., and Ellen Smith. 2004. *The Jews of Rhode Island*. Hanover, NH: Brandeis University Press.

Greenbaum, A., ed. 2005. *Jews of South Florida*. Hanover, NH: Brandeis University Press.

Hertzberg, A. 1989. *The Jews in America: Four centuries of an uneasy encounter*. New York: Simon and Schuster.

Kaganoff, B.C. 1996. *A dictionary of Jewish names and their history*. Northvale, NJ: Jason Aronson.

Kahn, A.F., and M. Dollinger, eds. 2003. *California Jews*. Hanover, NH: Brandeis University Press.

Kelman, A.Y., A.H. Tapper, I. Fonseca, and A. Saperstein. 2019. *Counting the inconsistencies: An analysis of American Jewish population studies with a focus on Jews of Color*. San Francisco: University of San Francisco, Stanford University, and Jews of Color Field Building Initiative.

Kosmin, B., and S. Waterman. 1989. The Use and Misuse of Distinctive Jewish Names in Research on Jewish Populations. In *Papers in Jewish demography 1985*, ed. U.O. Schmelz and S. DellaPergola, 1–9. Jerusalem: Hebrew University Press.

Kosmin, B.A., and A. Keysar. 2013. American Jewish secularism: Jewish life beyond the synagogue. In *American Jewish year book 2012*, ed. A. Dashefsky and I.M. Sheskin, vol. 109–112, 3–54. Cham, SUI: Springer.

Kosmin, B.A., and S.P. Lachman. 1991. *Research report, The National Survey of Religious identification, 1989–1990*. New York: The Graduate School and University Center of the City University of New York.

Kosmin, B.A., P. Ritterband, and J. Scheckner. 1988. Counting Jewish populations: Methods and problems. In *American Jewish year book*, vol. 88, 204–241. New York: American Jewish Committee and the Jewish Publication Society.

Kotler-Berkowitz, L., S.M. Cohen, J. Ament, V. Klaff, F. Mott, and D. Peckerman-Neuman. 2003. *The National Jewish Population Survey 2000–01: Strength, challenge and diversity in the American Jewish population.* New York: United Jewish Communities.

Lazerwitz, B. 1986. Some comments on the use of Distinctive Jewish Names in surveys. *Contemporary Jewry* 7 (1): 83–91.

Levin, S. September 16, 2019. Jewish Diversity and Sephardic and Mizrahi Jews. *ejewishphilanthropy.*

Link, Michael W., Michael P. Battaglia, Martin R. Frankel, Larry Osborn, and Ali H. Mokdad. 2008. A comparison of Address-Based Sampling (ABS) versus Random-Digit Dialing (RDD) for General Population Surveys. *Public Opinion Quarterly, Spring* 72: 6–27.

Marcus, J.R. 1990. *To count a people.* Lanham, MD: United Press of America.

Mateos, P. 2014. *Names, ethnicity, and populations.* Dordrecht: Springer.

Pasachoff, N., and R.J. Littman. 1995. *Jewish history in 100 nutshells.* Northvale, NJ: Jason Aronson.

Pew Research Center. 2013. *A portrait of Jewish Americans: Findings from a Pew Research Center survey of U.S. Jews.* Washington, DC: Pew Research Center.

Phillips, B.A. 2018. Intermarriage in the twenty-first century: New perspectives. In *American Jewish Year Book 2017*, ed. A. Dashefsky and I.M. Sheskin, vol. 117, 31–119. Cham: Springer.

Pogrebin, L. C. March 14, 2019 Jews of Color are us. *Moment Magazine.*

Rabin, S. 2017. "Let us endeavor to count them up": The nineteenth-century origins of American Jewish demography. *American Jewish History* 101 (4): 419–440.

Rebhun, A. 2011. *The Wandering Jew in America.* Boston: Academic Studies Press.

Sachar, H.M. 1992. *A history of the Jews in America.* New York: Alfred A. Knopf.

Sanders, R. 1988. *Shores of refuge, A hundred years of Jewish immigration.* New York: Henry Holt.

Shamir, I., and S. Shavit. 1986. *Encyclopedia of Jewish History.* New York: Facts on File Publications.

Shapiro, E.S. 1992. *A time for healing: American Jewry since World War II.* Baltimore: John Hopkins University Press.

Sherman, C.B. 1965. *The Jew within American society.* Detroit: Wayne State University Press.

Sheskin, I.M. 1997. The changing spatial distribution of American Jews. In *Land and community: Geography in Jewish studies*, ed. Harold Brodsky, 185–221. Bethesda, MD: University Press of Maryland.

———. 1998. A methodology for examining the changing size and spatial distribution of a Jewish population: A Miami case study. *Shofar, Special Issue: Studies in Jewish Geography* 17 (1): 97–116.

———. 2001. *How Jewish communities differ: Variations in the findings of local Jewish demographic studies.* New York: City University of New York, North American Jewish Data Bank at www.jewishdatabank.org.

———. 2005. Comparisons between local Jewish community studies and the 2000-01 National Jewish Population Survey. *Contemporary Jewry* 25: 185–192.

———. 2009. Local Jewish community studies as planning tools for the American Jewish community. *Jewish Political Studies Review* 21 (1–2): 107–135.

Sheskin, I. M. 2010. "Jewish Israelis in the United States," International Geographic Union Regional Conference, Tel Aviv (2010) (available from author on request).

Sheskin, I.M. 2013. Uses of local Jewish community study data for addressing national concerns. *Contemporary Jewry* 33 (1–2): 83–101.

———. 2015a. *The 2014 Greater Miami Jewish Federation Population Study: A Portrait of Jewish Miami.* Miami: The Greater Miami Jewish Federation.

———. 2015b. *Comparisons of Jewish communities: A compendium of tables and bar charts.* Storrs, CT: Berman Institute, North American. Jewish DataBank and The Jewish Federations of North America at www.jewishdatabank.org.

————. 2018. *The 2018 Detroit Jewish population study: A profile of Jewish Detroit*. Detroit: The Jewish Federation of Metropolitan Detroit.

Sheskin, I.M., and A. Dashefsky. 2006. Jewish population in the United States, 2006. In *American Jewish year book 2006*, ed. D. Singer and L. Grossman, vol. 106, 133–193. New York: American Jewish Committee. www.jewishdatabank.org.

————. 2007. Jewish population in the United States, 2007. In *American Jewish year book 2007*, ed. D. Singer and L. Grossman, vol. 107, 133–205. New York: American Jewish Committee. www.jewishdatabank.org.

————. 2008. Jewish population in the United States, 2008. In *American Jewish year book 2008*, ed. D. Singer and L. Grossman, vol. 108, 151–222. New York: American Jewish Committee. www.jewishdatabank.org.

Tighe, E., R. Magidin de Kramer, D. Parmer, D. Nussbaum, D Kallista, X. Seabrum, and L. Saxe. 2019. *American Jewish population project, summary and highlights 2014*. Waltham, MA: Brandeis University, Steinhardt Social Research Institute at http://www.brandeis.edu/ssri.

Weiner, H.A., and K.D. Roseman, eds. 2007. *Lone stars of David: The Jews of Texas*. Hanover. NH: Brandeis University Press.

Wyman, D. 1984. *The abandonment of the Jews: America and the Holocaust, 1941–1945*. New York: Pantheon Books.

Chapter 6
Canadian Jewish Population, 2019

Charles Shahar

The Canadian Jewish population has seen only modest growth in the past 20 years, following a more significant increase between 1981 and 1991. The latter decade coincided with the beginning of significant immigration by Jews from the Former Soviet Union. Jews reside in every region of Canada including the Northern Territories, although they are concentrated heavily in the major urban centers. The metropolitan area of Toronto is home to 188,710 Jews and includes about half (48.2%) of Canada's Jewish population. The Montreal community numbers 90,780 Jews. The median age of Canadian Jews is slightly older than the national average but much older than ethnic groups with large numbers of more recent immigrants.

There are 36,040 Sephardim living in Canada with the majority residing in Montreal (22,225). The Sephardic population in Montreal has been on the ascendancy since a large influx arrived in the late 1960s. However, this growth has slowed recently, with a gain of only 1000 individuals between 2001 and 2011.

Winnipeg has the fifth largest Jewish community in Canada, comprising 3.5% (13,960) of the country's Jewish population. It was recently surpassed by Ottawa in terms of the size of its Jewish population. The community has faced a number of challenges in the past few decades, including a steadily declining Jewish population since its peak in 1961 of 19,376 Jews. Despite these challenges, the Winnipeg community has a long history of Jewish commitment and affiliation.

Chapter 7, following, presents a revised executive summary of the more recent *2018 Survey of Jews in Canada*. It differs from the current chapter in that it is a sample survey of Jews in Montreal, Toronto, Winnipeg, and Vancouver, where 82% of Canadian Jews reside. The current chapter relies on the 2011 National Household Survey, a government poll of a 20% random sample of Canadian households with a response rate of nearly 74%. Chapter 7 presents details on Jewish beliefs, behavior, and belonging.

C. Shahar (✉)
The Jewish Community Foundation of Montreal, Montreal, QC, Canada
e-mail: Charles.Shahar@jcfmontreal.org

© Springer Nature Switzerland AG 2020
A. Dashefsky, I. M. Sheskin (eds.), *American Jewish Year Book 2019*, American Jewish Year Book 119, https://doi.org/10.1007/978-3-030-40371-3_6

For many decades, the census of the Canadian population has provided an important opportunity to obtain a demographic "snapshot" of the Canadian Jewish community. A major census is distributed at the start of every decade and contains a wealth of information related to the social, cultural, and economic characteristics of Canadian Jews. The two questions used to identify Jews, namely religion and ethnicity, are located on the census "long-form."

A census is also distributed in the middle of every decade, but it does not contain a religion question and, therefore, is much less useful for identifying Jews. However, the most recent mid-decade census (2016) has alarmed those who rely on census data for gaining important information about Jewish populations in Canada.

"Jewish" was not included as a sample response choice among the 28 ethnic categories listed as examples in the 2016 Census. Examples were based mostly on the most frequent single ethnic origins reported in the 2011 National Household Survey. Unfortunately, the number of ethnic Jews fell below the threshold in 2011.

The omission of the "Jewish" ethnicity sample choice, and the fact that the actual choices represented only national or aboriginal groups, rather than cultural groups, resulted in a severe response bias among Jews. The numbers of Canadians who indicated a Jewish ethnicity diminished by 54% between 2011 and 2016, from 309,650 to only 143,660 individuals.

This has implications for the next major census in 2021. Although those who will say they are Jewish by religion will be identified as being Jewish in 2021, there is concern that those who say they have "no religion," but who may identify as Jews on a cultural (ethnic) level, may not do so if they do not have a prompt upon which to base their response.

The number of Jews who say they have no religion has been rising steadily. If the ethnicity variable is thus compromised, it may be difficult to maintain a definition of Jewishness that is as inclusive as possible for the 2021 Census, thus limiting the ability of community leaders and planners to make informed decisions that will ultimately impact their constituents in profound ways. As of July 2018, discussions are underway with Statistics Canada to see what options might be available to address this issue.

The current report is based on the 2011 National Household Survey (NHS). Citing privacy issues, the Federal government decided to make the census long form voluntary in 2011, and a survey methodology was employed.[1] The 2011 NHS was distributed to one-third of Canadian households, compared to the 20% who receive the long-form in the case of the 2001 or 2016 censuses. Whereas the response rate for the census was nearly universal, it was 73.9% for the NHS. Moreover, because the sample was voluntary, it was difficult to know whether certain populations were less inclined to respond, such as economically disadvantaged individuals, the less educated, and recent immigrants.[2]

---

[1] Statistics Canada reverted to using a census methodology with a change in national governments in 2015.

[2] In the case of Jewish communities, it is possible that the ultra-Orthodox were also under-represented in the final count.

Statistics Canada applied rigorous statistical treatments to deal with possible gaps in the data and assured users that it would only release information if it had confidence in its reliability. An examination of the final data sets related to Jewish communities, along with such key variables as poverty and intermarriage, seemed to indicate that the data did "make sense" in light of statistical trends extrapolated from previous censuses.

Respondents were identified as Jews according to the "Jewish Standard Definition," formulated by Jim Torczyner of McGill University in 1971, which used a combination of religious and ethnic identification. However, because the ethnicity variable has been slowly eroding in terms of its usefulness in identifying Jews, the Jewish Standard Definition was revised in 2011 and expanded to include a further set of variables, such as having an Israeli ethnicity and having knowledge of Hebrew or Yiddish.[3] All in all, this "Revised Jewish Standard Definition" did not result in a substantial increase to the final count of Canadian Jews as it only added about 6300 persons.

Despite the limitations of the 2011 NHS, this instrument nonetheless represents an important opportunity for academic researchers as well as community leaders and planners to understand the demographic situation of the Canadian Jewish population better. We are fortunate to have a national survey that includes questions related to ethnicity and religion (as the American census does not).[4] Also, the NHS has a much larger scope than the Canadian Jewish community can undertake on its own.[5]

6.1   Basic Demographics

According to the NHS, the Jewish population of Canada numbered 391,665 persons in 2011.[6] This represented an increase from 2001, when there were 374,060 Jews. Between 2001 and 2011, the Canadian Jewish population thus increased by 17,605 persons, or 4.7% (Table 6.1 and Figure 6.1).

The gain between 2001 and 2011 was slightly larger than that between 1991 and 2001. In the latter decade, the community increased by 14,950 persons, or 4.2%. In

---

[3] For a more comprehensive description of the erosion of the utility of and the problems associated with using both the ethnicity and religion variables in identifying Canadian Jews, see Weinfeld and Schnoor (2015).

[4] Specifically, the US Census asks only one ethnicity-related question identifying respondents of Hispanic or Latino descent. The American Community Survey, an annual demographic study of the US population, does ask questions on "ancestry" and language spoken at home.

[5] The NHS did not ask specific questions such as denominational affiliation, levels of religious observance, attitudes toward Israel, etc. For these data, the Jewish community needs to develop its own survey tools.

[6] All 2011 NHS data cited in this chapter were derived from Statistics Canada, special order tabulations for Jewish Federations of Canada—UIA, CO-1421. Most of the descriptions related to the data were adapted from Shahar (2014a, b; 2015).

Table 6.1 Jewish population of Canada: a historical summary

	Jewish population	Change from previous census	% Change from previous census
2011	391,665	17,605	4.7%
2001	374,060	14,950	4.2%
1991	359,110	45,245	14.4%
1981	313,865	27,315	9.5%
1971	286,550	32,182	12.7%
1961	254,368	49,532	24.2%
1951	204,836	36,251	21.5%
1941	168,585	12,819	8.2%
1931	155,766	30,321	24.2%
1921	125,445	50,685	67.8%
1911	74,760	58,267	353.3%
1901	16,493	–	–

Note: 1991 to 2011 are based on the Revised Standard Jewish Definition described in the methodological discussion above. The rest of the figures are based on the Jewish Standard Definition (1971 and 1981) or were derived from either the religion or ethnicity variables individually (1901 to 1961). For information on the Jewish population of Canada from 1851 to 1941, see Rosenberg (1946)

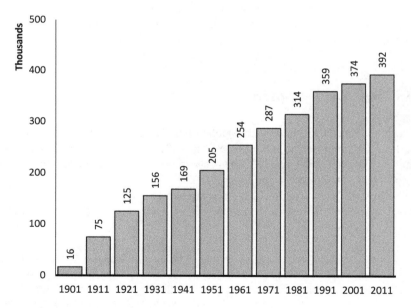

Fig. 6.1 Growth of the Canadian Jewish population. (Sources: Statistics Canada)

short, at least for the past 20 years, the growth rate of the Canadian Jewish population has not been remarkable, but compares well with growth rates in European countries and also with the United States.

A more pronounced increase for the Canadian Jewish community was evident between 1981 and 1991 when it increased by 45,245 persons, or 14.4%. This is likely related to the beginning of significant immigration to Canada by Jews from the former Soviet Union (FSU), and to a lesser extent from South Africa. In fact, this gain of 45,245 persons was the largest increase experienced by the national Jewish population since the large influx of immigrants in the 1950s.

All in all, the number of Canadian Jews has been rising steadily since the turn of the past century. In the 1930s, restricted Jewish immigration to Canada slowed some of the growth experienced in previous decades. Significant levels of immigration then resumed immediately after World War II.

Jews constituted 1.2% of the total Canadian population of 32.9 million in 2011, compared to 2.1% for the US (see Chap. 5). The total Canadian population has been increasing at a faster pace than the Jewish population. For instance, between 1991 and 2011, the Jewish population grew by 9.1%, compared to 21.7% for Canada's total population.

According to the 2011 NHS, the Jewish community, including single and multiple origin responses, ranked seventeenth among ethnic groups in Canada. The ten largest ethnic affiliations were British (6.5 million), Canadian (6.0 million), French (3.7 million), German (2.4 million), Aboriginal (1.8 million), Chinese (1.5 million), Italian (1.4 million), East Indian (1.1 million), Ukrainian (1 million), and Polish (644,700). It is noteworthy that the Jewish population ranked twelfth among ethnic groups in 2001, five rankings above its current status.

In 2011, the Jewish community ranked seventh with respect to religious identity. The five largest religious groups in Canada were Catholics (12.8 million), Protestants (8.7 million), Muslims (1.0 million), Christian Orthodox (550,690), and Hindus (497,965).

Almost one-quarter (23.9%) of the total Canadian population, or about 7.9 million persons, indicated that they had no religious identity. This category included persons who defined themselves as agnostics, atheists, or humanists or who did not identify with any religion at all. It is not clear to what extent highly secular Jews said they had no religious identity. It is thus possible that these individuals were under-represented in the final count of Jews (unless they indicated a Jewish ethnicity).

Finally, the Canadian Jewish community was the fourth largest Jewish community in the world in 2012 (using the year closest to the Canadian census, but see Chap. 8 for current figures). Israel had the largest Jewish population followed by the US, France (480,000), and Canada (391,665). The Jewish populations of the United Kingdom and the Russian Federation numbered 291,000 and 194,000, respectively.

The Canadian Jewish community constituted 2.8% of the total 13,746,100 Jews in the world in 2012 and 5.0% of the 7,845,000 Jews living in the Diaspora in 2012. The Jewish population of Canada comprised 6.8% of the Jews residing in North America.

6.2   Provincial and Metropolitan Population Distributions

Table 6.2 and Map 6.1 show the distribution of Jewish populations across provinces and territories. More than half (57.9%, or 226,610 persons) of Jews in Canada reside in Ontario.

Table 6.2 Jewish population distribution: provinces and territories

Province/territory	Jewish population	% of Canadian Jewish population
Nova Scotia	2910	0.8%
New Brunswick	860	0.2%
Newfoundland/Labrador	220	0.1%
Prince Edward Island	185	0.0%
(Total Atlantic Canada)	**(4175)**	**(1.1%)**
Quebec	93,625	23.9%
Ontario	226,610	57.9%
Manitoba	14,345	3.7%
Saskatchewan	1905	0.5%
Alberta	15,795	4.0%
British Columbia	35,005	8.9%
Yukon	145	0.0%
Northwest Territories	40	0.0%
Nunavut	20	0.0%
Total Canada	**391,665**	**100.0%**

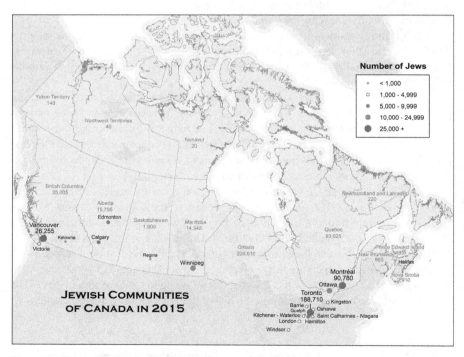

Map 6.1 Geographic distribution of the Jewish population of Canada

Table 6.3 Twenty largest Canadian Jewish communities

Metropolitan area/province	Jewish population	% of Canadian Jewish population
Toronto, ON	188,710	48.2%
Montreal, QC	90,780	23.2%
Vancouver, BC	26,255	6.7%
Ottawa, ON	14,010	3.6%
Winnipeg, MB	13,690	3.5%
Calgary, AB	8335	2.1%
Edmonton, AB	5550	1.4%
Hamilton, ON	5110	1.3%
Victoria, BC	2740	0.7%
London, ON	2675	0.7%
Halifax, NS	2120	0.5%
Kitchener/Waterloo, ON	2015	0.5%
Oshawa, ON	1670	0.4%
Windsor, ON	1515	0.4%
Barrie, ON	1445	0.4%
St. Catharines-Niagara, ON	1375	0.4%
Kingston, ON	1185	0.3%
Guelph, ON	925	0.2%
Regina, SK	900	0.2%
Kelowna, BC	900	0.2%
Total		94.9%

Quebec has 93,625 Jewish residents and about a quarter (23.9%) of the total Jewish population of Canada. British Columbia has 35,005 Jews, or 8.9% of the total Jewish population of Canada.

All other provinces have less than 5% of the national Jewish population. Alberta has 15,795 Jewish residents, or 4% of the country's Jewish population. Manitoba has 14,345 Jews, or 3.7% of the total. The Atlantic Provinces have 4175 Jews, or 1.1% of the country's total Jewish population. Saskatchewan has 1905 Jews, or 0.5% of the country's total.

There are 145 Jews in the Yukon, 40 in the Northwest Territories, and 20 in Nunavut. Although these last numbers are small, it is nonetheless instructive that Jews populate every region of the country, including the northern territories.

Table 6.3 and Map 6.1 present the 20 largest Jewish communities in Canada, which account for 95% of Canada's Jewish population. The Toronto metropolitan area is home to 188,710 Jews and includes about half (48.2%) of Canada's Jewish population. The Montreal community numbers 90,780 Jews and constitutes about a quarter (23.2%) of the Jewish population of Canada. Vancouver has a Jewish population of 26,255, representing 6.7% of the national Jewish population.

The rest of the Jewish communities in Canada each number less than 15,000 persons. For instance, Ottawa has 14,010 Jews, Winnipeg has 13,690, Calgary has 8335, Edmonton has 5550, and Hamilton has 5110.

6.3   Focus on the Age of the Jewish Population

The Canadian Jewish population has a somewhat larger proportion of children (age 0–14) than the total population (18.2% and 17.0% respectively). The Jewish population has a similar percentage in the age 15–24 cohort compared with the total Canadian population (13.4% and 13.2% respectively).

In the economically productive age 25–44 cohort, the discrepancy between the two distributions is more marked. Less than a quarter (23.5%) of Jews fall into this age cohort, compared to 26.7% of Canada's total population. The Jewish community also has a somewhat smaller proportion in the age 45–64 cohort than the overall Canadian population (28.0% and 29.3% respectively).

Finally, a comparison of the two age distributions shows that the Jewish community has a significantly larger proportion of persons age 65 and over (16.9%) than the total Canadian population (13.9%).

The median age of the national Jewish population is 40.5 years, slightly higher than that of Canada's overall population (40.1 years) but a bit lower than the median age of 42 for US Jews, based on the 2000–2001 National Jewish Population Survey. Ethnic groups with the oldest median ages include the British (48.7 years), Americans (45.9 years), French (44.8 years), Germans (40.7 years), Jews (40.5 years), Greeks (40.4 years), and Poles (40.3 years). These ethnic groups generally involve older, more established communities whose peak periods of immigration to Canada have long passed. Since there has not been a large influx of recent immigrants among these groups, their median ages remain at fairly high levels.

The youngest median ages were reported by the Pakistani (26.0 years), African (27.9 years), Aboriginal (28.4 years), Arab (29.3 years), Latin American (30.1 years), Caribbean (31.2 years), and Korean (33.7 years) communities. Most of the latter populations have a large number of more recent immigrants, many of whom settled in Canada in the past two decades. This infusion of people, often involving younger families, has revitalized these communities and has kept their median ages lower than the rest of the population.

6.4   Focus on Sephardim[7]

The term "Sephardim" initially referred to Jews living in Spain, who were expelled during the "Inquisition" in the 1490s. The term now refers to descendants of those Jews, who ultimately settled in areas such as North Africa, Holland, England, Turkey and the Balkans, and who originally spoke Judeo-Spanish languages. It also

---

[7] Previous foci have appeared in the *American Jewish Year Book 2018* (Shahar 2019) on "Seniors", in the *American Jewish Year Book 2017* (Shahar 2018) on "Poverty", in the *American Jewish Year Book 2016* (Shahar 2017) on "Holocaust Survivors", and the *American Jewish Year Book 2015* (Shahar 2016) on "Intermarriage."

refers to Jews who were connected to the Judeo-Spanish culture before the Inquisition, and lived in Arab countries and Iran, where they spoke a variety of Judeo-Arabic and Judeo-Persian languages.

The Sephardic community of Canada comprises 36,040 individuals. In fact, Canada has the seventh largest Sephardic community in the world, following those of Israel, France, United States, Argentina, Brazil and Spain. The rich cultural heritage of Sephardim has contributed to the intricate fabric of the Jewish community in Canada, particularly in Montreal.

The Sephardic community in Montreal has a long history. In the late eighteenth century, Sephardim were among the first Jews to settle in the province of Quebec. The oldest surviving synagogue in Montreal, the Spanish and Portuguese Congregation, is of Sephardic origin. It was founded in 1768, and was the first such congregation in Canada.

The most significant period of Sephardic immigration began following the 1967 Six Day War between Israel and its Arab neighbors. A large influx of Sephardim, mostly from Morocco, settled in Montreal between 1967 and 1987. More recent Sephardic immigrants have come mainly from Israel and Western Europe.

Since many speak French as their mother tongue, and this is the dominant language of the province of Quebec, Sephardim have generally adjusted well to life in Montreal. Jews of Sephardic origin occupy key positions of leadership and influence in the Jewish community, have developed thriving businesses, and enjoy political representation in the general community.

There are 22,225 Sephardim residing in the Montreal metropolitan area. Sephardim comprise 24.5% of the 90,780 members of the Montreal Jewish community. There are also 715 individuals of mixed (Sephardic and Ashkenazi) extraction living in Montreal.

The Sephardic community has been on the ascendancy since their arrival in greater numbers to Montreal in the late 1960s. However, their increases slowed somewhat between 2001 and 2011, when there was a gain of only 1000 individuals. On the other hand, the Ashkenazi population declined by 3380 individuals in that decade, and contributed to an overall decline of 3% in the Jewish population of Montreal. An influx of Jewish immigrants from France in recent years may change the composition of Montreal Jewry somewhat if it continues.

The largest Sephardic age cohort is middle-aged adults between 45 and 64 years of age (5570 individuals). Many of those between 45 and 64 years represent the children of Sephardim who immigrated to Montreal in the late 1960s and throughout the 1970s. There is also a significant representation of Sephardim in the 25–44-year age group (5315 individuals).

About one in five Sephardim (20.4%) are seniors, or 4540 individuals. As large numbers of middle-aged Sephardim enter their senior years, the proportion of elderly will likely increase significantly.

There are 9735 Canadian-born Sephardim living in Montreal, comprising 43.8% of the Sephardic community. The rest of the Sephardic population (56.2%) are immigrants. More than a quarter (28.3%) of Sephardim were born in Morocco, followed by France (7.6%) and Israel (6.4%).

The percentage of adult Sephardim that have a university degree has increased significantly from 35.7% in 2001 to 45.7% in 2011.

There are 4080 Sephardim living below the poverty line in the Montreal metropolitan area, or 18.4% of the total Sephardic population.[8] The poverty level among Sephardim is lower than that of the rest of the Jewish community (20.5%).

Those who are particularly vulnerable to poverty include Sephardic seniors living alone (47.7%); Sephardic adults between 15 and 64 years living alone (47.3%); and Sephardim living in female single parent families (32.7%).

6.5   Focus on a Community: Winnipeg[9]

Winnipeg has the fifth largest Jewish community in Canada, comprising 3.5% of the country's Jewish population. It was recently surpassed by Ottawa in terms of the size of its Jewish population.

The community has faced a number of challenges in the last few decades, including a steadily declining Jewish population since its peak in 1961 of 19,376 Jews. Other challenges include a burgeoning elderly cohort; and the fact that the community is more spread out than ever before, straining the reach of its service delivery.

Despite these challenges, the Winnipeg community has a long history of Jewish commitment and affiliation. The variety and availability of Jewish services in Winnipeg are those usually found in considerably larger communities. Several community initiatives, particularly related to immigration, have been launched in the last two decades. The result is an increasingly diverse population as evident in the cultural makeup and orientations of community institutions.

In 2011, the Jewish population of Winnipeg was 13,690. Jews comprised 1.9% of Winnipeg's total population of 714,640.

The Jewish population figure for 2011 represented a loss from 2001, when there were 14,820 Jews in this metropolitan area. Between 2001 and 2011 the Jewish population declined by 1130 people, or 7.6%.

The population loss between 2001 and 2011 was somewhat greater than between 1991 and 2001. In the latter decade, the community declined by 415 people or 2.7%. The current decline is also a little more significant than the one experienced between 1981 and 1991, when the community decreased by 935 people or 5.8%.

All in all, the demographic trends suggest that the Jewish population is continuing to decrease. This is perhaps surprising given the level of Jewish immigration to

---

[8] The "poverty line" in this report refers to the low-income cutoff (LICO), which is defined by Statistics Canada as "an income threshold at which families are expected to spend 20 percentage points more than the average family on food, shelter and clothing."

[9] The corresponding chapter in the previous *American Jewish Year Book 2018* (Shahar 2019) focused on Ottawa, on Greater Vancouver in the *American Jewish Year Book 2017* (Shahar 2018), on Toronto in the *American Jewish Year Book 2016* (Shahar 2017) and on Montreal in the *American Jewish Year Book 2015* (Shahar 2016).

Winnipeg in the last decade, particularly from individuals originating in the former Soviet Union, Israel and Argentina. Sources from the organized community suggest that the great majority of these newcomers have remained in Winnipeg and have planted their roots there.

Regarding the age distribution of the Winnipeg Jewish community, after showing a very dramatic loss between 1991 and 2001, the 25–44-year age group continued to decrease in the last decade, from 3210 to 2915 individuals.

The 45–64-year cohort remained at about the same level between 2001 and 2011, after demonstrating dramatic gains in the previous decade. This cohort represents the Baby Boomer generation.

The number of seniors 65+ years continued to decline in the last decade, from 3180 to 2580 individuals. On the other hand, the local Jewish community has a much larger proportion of elderly (18.8%) than Winnipeg's total population (13.1%). In fact, Winnipeg has the second highest percentage of seniors of any major Jewish community in Canada, behind only Montreal (20.4%).

The median age of the Winnipeg Jewish community actually decreased between 2001 and 2011, from 44.4 to 43.1 years, but it is still significantly older than that of the Canadian Jewish population (40.5 years).

There are 2000 Jews living below the poverty line in the Winnipeg metropolitan area. The poor comprise 14.6% of a total population of 13,690 Jews residing in the local community.

The level of poverty among children 0–14 years in the Winnipeg Jewish population is 20.2%, almost double the rate found in 2001. There are 470 children in the local Jewish community who live in economically disadvantaged circumstances.

Almost one of seven elderly Jews (65+ years) is poor, but senior women are significantly more likely to be disadvantaged than men (20.8% and 4.7% respectively).

In terms of the intermarriage rate, 25.4% of Jewish spouses / partners are married to, or partnered with, non-Jews in the Winnipeg metropolitan area.

The intermarriage rate among Winnipeg's Jewish population (25.4%) is slightly lower than that of the Canadian Jewish population (26.3%). Although the intermarriage rates of Jewish communities across Canada generally increase as one moves westward, the Winnipeg community is an exception, likely because it has a long history of Jewish commitment and affiliation.

In cases where both spouses are less than 30 years of age, the level of intermarriage is a striking 75.6%; although the small number of Jewish couples in this age group suggests that this figure should be interpreted with caution, as sampling error may account for this finding. It is 19.4% when both spouses are at least 40 years old.

Regarding the youngest children of intermarried couples, about a quarter (26.7%) are identified by their parents as Jews; about half (55.3%) are assigned no religious affiliation; and the rest (17.9%) are identified as having other religions. Whether it is the husband or the wife who is of the Jewish faith has a significant bearing on the religious orientation of their children, with the latter being much more inclined to be identified as Jewish if the mother is identified as such.

6.6 Summary

The Canadian Jewish population has seen only modest growth in the past twenty years, following a more significant increase between 1981 and 1991. The latter decade coincided with the beginning of significant immigration by Jews from the FSU. Jews reside in every region of Canada, including the Northern Territories, although they are concentrated heavily in the major urban centers. The metropolitan area of Toronto is home to 188,710 Jews and includes about half (48.2%) of Canada's Jewish population. The Montreal community numbers 90,780 Jews. The median age (40.5 years) of Canadian Jews is slightly older than the national average but much older than ethnic groups with large numbers of more recent immigrants.

There are 36,040 Sephardim living in Canada with the majority residing in Montreal (22,225). The Sephardic population in Montreal has been on the ascendancy since a large influx arrived in the late 1960s. However, this growth has slowed recently, with a gain of only 1000 individuals between 2001 and 2011. The percentage of Sephardic seniors is expected to increase significantly as the Baby Boomers turn elderly. More than half (56.2%) of Sephardim residing in Montreal are immigrants and more than a quarter (28.3%) were born in Morocco.

Winnipeg has the fifth largest Jewish community in Canada, comprising 3.5% (13,960) of the country's Jewish population. It was recently surpassed by Ottawa in terms of the size of its Jewish population. The community has faced a number of challenges in the last few decades, including a steadily declining Jewish population since its peak in 1961 of 19,376 Jews. Other challenges include a burgeoning elderly cohort; and the fact that the community is more spread out than ever before, straining the reach of its service delivery. Despite these challenges, the Winnipeg community has a long history of Jewish commitment and affiliation.

References

Rosenberg, L. 1946. The Jewish population of Canada: A statistical summary from 1851 to 1941. In *American Jewish year book*, ed. H. Schneiderman and J. Maller, vol. 48, 19–50. New York: American Jewish Committee. Dordrecht: Springer.

Shahar, C. 2014a. 2011 National Household Survey analysis: The Jewish population of Canada. In *Part 1: Basic demographics and Part 2: Jewish populations in geographic areas*. Toronto: Jewish Federations of Canada—UIA. See www.jewishdatabank.org.

———. 2014b. 2011 National Household Survey analysis: The Jewish community of Winnipeg. In *Part 1: Basic demographics and Part 2: Jewish populations in geographic areas*. Toronto: Jewish Federations of Canada—UIA. See www.jewishdatabank.org.

———. 2015. 2011 National Household Survey analysis: The Jewish community of Montreal. In *The Sephardic community*. Toronto: Federations of Canada—UIA. See www.jewishdatabank.org.

———. 2016. Jewish population of Canada, 2015. In *American Jewish year book 2015*, ed. A. Dashefsky and I.M. Sheskin, vol. 115, 261–271. Dordrecht: Springer.

———. 2017. Canadian Jewish population, 2016. In *American Jewish year book 2016*, ed. A. Dashefsky and I.M. Sheskin, vol. 116, 241–251. Dordrecht: Springer.

————. 2018. Canadian Jewish population, 2017. In *American Jewish year book 2017*, ed. A. Dashefsky and I.M. Sheskin, vol. 117, 285–295. Dordrecht: Springer.

————. 2019. Canadian Jewish population, 2018. In *American Jewish year book 2018*, ed. A. Dashefsky and I.M. Sheskin, vol. 118, 349–360. Dordrecht: Springer.

Weinfeld, M., and R.F. Schnoor. 2015. The demography of Canadian Jewry, the "census" of 2011: Challenges and results. In *American Jewish year book 2014*, ed. A. Dashefsky and I.M. Sheskin, vol. 114, 285–300. Dordrecht: Springer.

Chapter 7
2018 Survey of Jews in Canada: Executive Summary

Robert Brym, Keith Neuman, and Rhonda Lenton

The first Jew to settle in what is now Canada was an employee of the Hudson's Bay Company. He arrived in 1732. Today, Canadian Jews number about 392,000 and form the world's third or fourth largest Jewish community.

As late as the first half of the twentieth century, Canadian Jews experienced a high level of discrimination in accommodation, employment, property ownership, and everyday interaction. Despite these impediments, they proved to be highly resilient. They achieved rapid upward mobility and made many important contributions to Canadian medicine, jurisprudence, science, education, government, the economy, and the arts.

Upward mobility and increasing acceptance on the part of the Canadian mainstream have had what many community members regard as a downside: These social processes heightened the prospect of cultural assimilation, loss of traditional languages, and intermarriage. Many in the community are also deeply concerned about the recurrence of a stubborn malady; since the early 2000s, anti-Israel sentiment has sometimes engendered antisemitism, and over the past few years, the rise of "white nationalism" (dimly mirroring the same trend in the US) has resulted in increased anti-Jewish harassment and violence. Although the latter circumstance did not motivate this survey, it is part of the context in which the 2018 Survey of Canadian Jews was conducted.

What is known about the identities, values, opinions, and experiences of Jews in Canada today? The basic demographics of the Jewish population are captured every

R. Brym (✉)
Department of Sociology and Centre for Jewish Studies, University of Toronto,
Toronto, ON, Canada
e-mail: rbrym@chass.utoronto.ca

K. Neuman
The Environics Institute, Toronto, ON, Canada

R. Lenton
York University, Toronto, ON, Canada

© Springer Nature Switzerland AG 2020
A. Dashefsky, I. M. Sheskin (eds.), *American Jewish Year Book 2019*, American Jewish Year Book 119, https://doi.org/10.1007/978-3-030-40371-3_7

5 years through national censuses conducted by Statistics Canada, which document the number who identify as Jewish ethnically and/or religiously, where they live, and their basic characteristics (e.g., age, gender, and education).[1] However, this research does not provide a full understanding about the Jewish experience in Canada, and such knowledge is becoming increasingly important given the dynamic changes taking place in society generally, and in the Jewish world in particular (e.g., assimilation, intermarriage, and antisemitism). It is remarkable that the Canadian Jewish community is one of the least studied in the world—in sharp contrast to that of the US and the UK.

7.1   Overview

This research provides the first empirically-based portrait of the identity, practices, and experiences of Jews in Canada, based on a survey conducted in four cities containing 82% of the country's Jewish population (Toronto, Montreal, Vancouver, and Winnipeg). For simplicity throughout this chapter, the expression "Canadian Jews who live in one of the four cities containing 82% of the country's Jewish population" is shortened to "Canadian Jews." Four overarching themes emerge from the survey, which we consider next.

7.1.1   Changing Basis of Identification

Identifying oneself as a Jew is not what it used to be. Two or three centuries ago, being Jewish meant practicing a distinct religion. Today, only one in three Canadians who identifies as Jewish considers religion very important in his or her life, and just six in ten say they believe in God or a universal spirit (compared to seven in ten of all Canadians). For most Canadian Jews today, the basis of Jewish identity is less about religion than about culture, ethnicity, or a combination of culture, ethnicity, and religion.

Consider that one of the most important expressions of Jewish identity involves families getting together over a meal to mark a Jewish holiday. What does this practice mean? For a growing number of Canadian Jews, the practice seems to be chiefly a means of achieving conviviality in the family and, beyond that, solidarity

---

[1] The previous Chap. 6 presents data on the Canadian Jewish population from the 2011 National Household Survey (NHS). Canada's Conservative government cancelled the 2011 census, replacing it with the voluntary NHS, in which 73.9% of Canada's population participated. The main non-participants were low-income and Indigenous Canadians. We declined to use data from the 2016 census because a problematic change in the wording of the ethnicity question resulted in a 54% drop in the count of Canadian Jews from 2011 to 2016 (Brym 2017). This chapter is slightly modified from Brym et al. (2019).

with the larger community. The purely religious significance of the practice is less important than it was in the past.

7.1.2 Community Resilience

It would be wrong to conclude that change in the basis of Jewish identification signifies that widespread assimilation is taking place among community members. To be sure, the rate of intermarriage is growing. A small minority of Jews display a Christmas tree (or, among relatively recent immigrants from the former Soviet Union, a New Year's tree) in their homes. The quickly growing Vancouver Jewish community stands out in its degree of religious, ethnic, and cultural assimilation. However, the Canadian Jewish community as a whole remains surprisingly cohesive across generations. A range of indicators tells us that. Whether we examine the weekly ritual of lighting candles at the onset of the Sabbath, belonging to Jewish organizations, donating to Jewish causes, or regularly attending synagogue services, we find little difference between young adults and elderly Jews.

Universally, discrimination increases group cohesiveness, and Canadian Jews are no exception in this regard.[2] Perceptions of the level of antisemitism in Canada contribute to community cohesion. The survey examined Canadian Jews' views on discrimination against various racial, religious, ethnic, and sexual minorities. The results suggest that, by and large, Canadian Jews assess the extent and threat of antisemitism realistically.

7.1.3 Canadian Jewish Exceptionalism

The cohesiveness of the Canadian Jewish community contrasts with that of the Jewish community in the US. We know this from previous research—but the magnitude of the difference revealed by this survey is so large that it nonetheless strikes one as remarkable. Intermarriage is far more common in the US than in Canada, the ability to read or speak Hebrew is much less widespread, visiting Israel is a lot less common, and so on.

Since World War II, the story of the Jewish diaspora has been dominated by historical events and social processes occurring in the US and the former Soviet Union. In both cases, community cohesiveness is on the decline. Lost in the

---

[2] Discrimination is a form of social conflict, and as sociologist Georg Simmel (1955: 98–99) pointed out in 1908, "Conflict may not only heighten the concentration of an existing unit, radically eliminating all elements which might blur the distinctiveness of its boundaries against the enemy; it may also bring persons and groups together which have otherwise nothing to do with each other."

dominant narrative is the story of Canadian exceptionalism (Brym et al. 2020). The Jewish communities in Montreal and Winnipeg are shrinking in size, but those in Ottawa, Toronto, Calgary, and Vancouver are growing, as is the Canadian Jewish population as a whole (albeit slowly). The overall result is that Canada's Jews are on the verge of becoming the second largest Jewish community in the diaspora, next in size only to the much larger American Jewish community. (Research conducted by the Pew Research Center [2015] finds that the Jewish population of Canada already exceeds that of France, although Chap. 8 in this volume shows France as number two in the diaspora (at 45,000) and Canada as number three at 392,000.) In short, evidence of Canadian Jewish population growth and resilience suggests the need for a modification of the dominant diaspora narrative.

7.1.4 Heterogeneity

Cohesiveness does not imply homogeneity. Far from it. This report documents that Canadian Jews vary widely in denominational affiliation, subethnic identification, strength of ties to the community, Jewish upbringing, and much else. Geographical differences exist too: a strong east/west pattern emerges, with the large Montreal and Toronto communities being the most cohesive, the Vancouver community in many respects looking more like a part of the US than of Canada, and Winnipeg sitting between these extremes, although closer to the eastern model.

Heterogeneity extends to support for different Canadian political parties and differences of opinion concerning key issues in the Jewish world, notably attitudes toward Israel's West Bank settlement policy. Among those with an opinion on the subject, nearly three times more Canadian Jews believe that West Bank settlements hurt Israel's security than believe the settlements help Israel's security. Some people think of the Canadian Jewish community as a monolith. This research should disabuse them of that impression.

7.2 Highlights

Following are the main highlights from the study.

7.2.1 Canadian Jewish Population

Canada's approximately 392,000 Jews comprise about 1% of the country's population. They are highly urbanized, with more than 87% living in just six census metropolitan areas: nearly one-half in Toronto, nearly one-quarter in Montreal, and nearly one-sixth in Vancouver, Winnipeg, Ottawa, and Calgary combined. The country's Jewish population is growing slowly, but trends vary by city. Vancouver is the country's fastest growing Jewish community, followed by Ottawa, Toronto, and Calgary. In contrast, the Jewish populations of Montreal and Winnipeg have been declining.

The age and sex distribution of Canadian Jews is much like that of the entire Canadian population, but is somewhat more likely to include immigrants. More than eight in ten Canadian Jews define themselves as of Ashkenazi ancestry (from Western Europe and Eastern Europe), and one in ten as of Sephardi or Mizrahi ancestry (from Southern Europe, North Africa, and the Middle East). The educational attainment of the Canadian Jewish population is extraordinarily high; eight in ten Jewish adults between the ages of 25 and 64 have completed at least a bachelor's degree, compared to fewer than three in ten in the population at large.

7.2.2   Jewish Identity

Jews in Canada identify as Jewish in a variety of ways. About one-half consider themselves to be Jewish mainly as a matter of religion, by culture, or by ancestry/descent, while the other half emphasize two or more of these aspects.

Identification by all three of these aspects is most common among Jews who are Orthodox or Conservative, and those who are actively involved in their local Jewish community. By comparison, identification as Jewish mainly through culture or ancestry/descent is most prevalent among those who affiliate as Reform, or are not attached to any denomination or movement.

Two-thirds of Canadian Jews say that being Jewish is very important in their lives, with most of the rest indicating that it is at least somewhat important. By comparison, only three in ten place this level of importance on religion, although a majority say they believe in God or a universal spirit.

What do Canadian Jews consider to be essential aspects of being Jewish? At the top of the list are leading a moral and ethical life, remembering the Holocaust, and celebrating Jewish holidays; a majority identify each of these as "essential" to what being Jewish means to them. In a second tier, at least four in ten identify as essential such attributes as working for justice and equality in society, caring about Israel, being intellectually curious, being part of a community, and having a good sense of humor. By comparison, no more than one in five places such importance on observing Jewish law, attending synagogue, and participating in Jewish cultural activities.

What Canadian Jews consider as being essential to being Jewish varies by age cohort. In particular, members of the youngest cohort are much less likely than those in the oldest cohort to consider a sense of humor to be an essential element of Jewishness. This difference may be due partly to the depletion among young adults of Jewish humor's richest reservoir—the Yiddish language, which was the mother tongue of nearly all Canadian Jews in 1931, but is spoken by just a few percent of Canadian Jews today. A second noteworthy difference is that younger Jews are considerably less likely than older Jews to consider caring for Israel an essential aspect of Jewishness, a trend that has been noted in the US for some time.

Comparisons with American Jews. How Canadian and American Jews identify as Jewish is broadly similar. American Jews are somewhat more likely to pin their identity to religion, culture or ancestry/descent rather than a combination of these aspects. They are less apt to say that being Jewish and being religious is very important to them personally, although they are more likely than Canadian Jews to express belief in God or a universal spirit. And what they consider essential aspects of being Jewish is comparable to what is articulated by Canadian Jews, but with less emphasis on being part of a community.[3]

7.2.3 Jewish Life and Practice

Most Jews in Canada consider themselves to be part of an established Jewish denomination or movement. About six in ten affiliate with one of the three mainstream denominations, the largest being Conservative, followed by Orthodox or Modern Orthodox, and Reform. One in ten report being part of one of the smaller Jewish movements, including Reconstructionism, Humanistic Judaism or Jewish Renewal, Hasidism, or something else. Three in ten are not affiliated with any particular type of Judaism, including some who say they are "just Jewish."

Six in ten report they or someone in their household belong to a synagogue, temple or prayer group, and this represents the majority across all denominations/ movements and even applies to three in ten Jews who do not identify with a particular denomination. Membership does not, however, translate into regular attendance: only one in six attend services at least once or twice a month outside of special occasions such as weddings, funerals and bar/bat mitzvahs. Apart from synagogues and temples, close to half of Canadian Jews say they belong to one or more other types of Jewish organizations, such as a Jewish community center. Three in ten do not belong to any type of Jewish organization.

Even more prevalent than organization membership is providing financial support to Jewish organizations and causes. Eight in ten Jews in Canada report having made such a donation in the previous year (2017). This proportion is highest among those who belong to a denomination or movement, but such contributions have also been made by a majority of Canadian Jews who are unaffiliated and those with an annual household income under $75,000.

Apart from formal memberships and affiliation, being Jewish in Canada is about social connections. More than half report that either all or most of their current friends are Jewish, with very few indicating that hardly any or none of them are

---

[3] The data for American Jews is from a study conducted by the Pew Research Center (2013). Some of the observed difference between Canadian and American Jews may be due to the fact that the Canadian survey included only cities with a Jewish population of about 13,000 or more, while the Pew survey included Jews in communities of all sizes as well as in rural areas.

Jewish. Having a high proportion of Jewish friends is most closely linked to denominational affiliation, being most prevalent among Orthodox/Modern Orthodox Jews, and least so among Reform Jews and those who affiliate with smaller denominations and movements.

Remarkably little difference exists between age cohorts in their degree of religious involvement (e.g., attending religious services, lighting Sabbath candles) and in their degree of community participation (e.g., belonging to Jewish organizations, donating to Jewish causes, having close Jewish friends). This finding suggests that, all else being equal, the Canadian Jewish community is unlikely to become much less cohesive as younger generations age. On the other hand, inter-city differences in religious involvement and community participation are large, with community cohesiveness at a very high level in Montreal and Toronto, but declining as one moves west (notably in Vancouver, which approaches American levels of community cohesiveness).

Comparisons with American Jews. American Jews are as likely as Canadian Jews to have a Jewish affiliation, but are much less involved in their local community. Six in ten identify with one of the three mainstream denominations (predominantly Reform, and least apt to be Orthodox or Modern Orthodox), and like Canadian Jews about one-third have no affiliation. But American Jews are half as likely as Canadian Jews to belong to a synagogue, and even less likely to belong to other types of Jewish organizations. Only one-half have made a financial donation to Jewish organizations and causes (compared with 80% of Canadian Jews), and comparatively few have a preponderance of Jewish friends.

7.2.4   *Jewish Upbringing*

A significant feature of the Jewish population in Canada is the continuity of identification and practice across generations. Nine in ten Canadian Jews report that both of their parents are Jewish, and a comparable proportion say they were raised in the Jewish religion. Being raised in the Jewish religion is most widespread among Orthodox/Modern Orthodox Jews, but it is also the experience of most Jews who are currently unaffiliated. Among the small percentage who were not raised in the Jewish religion, about half say they were raised in a secular Jewish tradition.

A key component of continuity is the prevalence of Jewish education, with most Jews in Canada having participated in one or more types of Jewish education when growing up. Jewish education is most likely to include attendance at an overnight summer camp, Hebrew school or Sunday school, but close to one-half have attended a Jewish day school or yeshiva and have done so for an average of 9 years.

Also important to Jewish upbringing is the coming-of-age tradition of becoming bar or bat mitzvah, typically at age 12 for girls and age 13 for boys. Nine in ten Canadian Jewish men and four in ten Canadian Jewish women have done so, in most cases as a youth but for a small proportion as an adult. The gender difference is due largely to the fact that bat mitzvahs did not become common practice until the

1970s. Consequently, the prevalence of this experience is largely a function of generation, as it is reported by eight in ten Canadian Jews age 18–29, compared with little more than one-third among those age 75 and older. Notably, becoming bar or bat mitzvah is common even among Jews who are not currently synagogue members or affiliated with any denomination or movement.

Most Canadian Jews claim some knowledge of the Hebrew language, with three-quarters saying they know the alphabet, six in ten indicating they can read at least some Hebrew words in a newspaper or prayer book, and four in ten claiming to be able to carry on a conversation in the language. Such knowledge is most widely indicated by Jews who are Orthodox/Modern Orthodox, people under age 30, and first-generation Canadians.

The positive effect of Jewish schooling on community cohesion is evident. Comparing those who did not attend a Jewish day school or yeshiva with those who attended such schools for 9 or more years shows that the latter are much more likely to believe that being part of a Jewish community, celebrating holidays with family, and caring about Israel are essential parts of being Jewish. Those who attended a Jewish day school or yeshiva for 9 or more years are also significantly less likely to have intermarried.

Comparisons with American Jews. One of the major distinctions between the two Jewish communities is the extent of Jewish education in the formative years. American Jews are as likely as Canadian Jews to say they were brought up in the Jewish religion. But they are half as likely to have attended a Jewish day school or yeshiva, and less apt to have attended a Jewish overnight summer camp, Sunday school or Hebrew school. Consequently, many fewer American Jews know the Hebrew alphabet or can carry on a conversation in Hebrew. At the same time, one-half of American Jews have become bar or bat mitzvah, not far behind the Canadian proportion of six in ten.

7.2.5   Intermarriage and Child Upbringing

Assimilation is a widespread concern in the Canadian Jewish community, and a key indicator is intermarriage (Brym and Lenton 2020). Just over three-quarters of Jews who are married or in a common-law relationship have a spouse who is Jewish by religion. Having a Jewish spouse is almost universal among those who are Orthodox/Modern Orthodox or Conservative, and somewhat less so among those who affiliate with Reform or another denomination or movement. Just over half of those who are unaffiliated have a Jewish spouse. Intermarriage is highest among Jews in the youngest age cohort (nearly one-third among people between the ages of 18 and 29), declining to one in five among those age 75 and over. In general, intermarriage is less common in cities with large Jewish marriage pools, but Vancouver is exceptional. With a Jewish population nearly twice as large as Winnipeg's, it has a higher intermarriage rate.

Most Canadian Jewish parents report raising their children in the Jewish religion. This practice is almost universal among Orthodox/Modern Orthodox and Conservative Jews, but is also reported by about half of those who are unaffiliated, those who do not belong to Jewish organizations, and those who themselves were not raised in a Jewishly religious home. Moreover, most Jewish parents with children under age 18 believe their children will grow up to have a connection to Jewish life that is as strong, if not stronger, than their own.

Comparisons with American Jews. In Canada, intermarriage rates are increasing for all ethnic and religious groups; but they are increasing faster for Jews than for Christians. Still, intermarriage is far more common among American Jews than among Canadian Jews, at a rate of 50% (compared with 23% among Canadian Jews). Largely because of intermarriage, American Jewish parents are less likely to report raising their children in the Jewish religion. This difference is most striking among Jews who are not affiliated with any denomination or movement, with American Jews less than one-third as likely as their Canadian counterparts to be raising their children in the Jewish religion.

7.2.6   Discrimination and Antisemitism

Antisemitism has a long history in Canada and continues to be experienced among Jews today. Close to four in ten Canadian Jews report having experienced discrimination in the past 5 years due to their religion, ethnicity/culture, sex and/or language. This is comparable to the experience of Muslims in Canada, and well above that of the population at large.

Specifically, about one in ten Canadian Jews say he or she has been called offensive names or snubbed in a social setting in the past year because of being Jewish. Even more common is attracting criticism from others for taking a position for or against the policies and actions of Israel; many have refrained from expressing opinions about this topic to avoid such a reaction. Close to four in ten say they have downplayed being Jewish in one or more types of situations, such as at work or while travelling outside the country. Across the board, experiences of discrimination are closely linked to age, with Jews age 18–29 most likely to report such incidents.

While Jews in Canada are mindful of the burden of antisemitism, they do not see themselves as the most significant target of persecution in the country. They are more likely to believe that Indigenous Peoples, Muslims and Blacks in Canada are frequent targets of discrimination, and are more likely to hold this view than Canadians as a whole.

Respondents' perceptions of discrimination against Jews are quite realistic if one considers official statistics on hate crime as one indicator of the actual level of anti-Jewish sentiment in Canada. In seven of the 12 years between 2006 and 2017, Jews ranked second in the number of hate crimes committed against Canadian minority groups. Jews ranked third in four of the 12 years and first in one of the 12 years. On average, about 0.6 (mainly non-violent) hate crimes per 100,000 Canadians are committed against Jews each year (Brym 2019).

The same percentage of Montreal and Toronto Jews think they are often the object of discrimination, which is somewhat surprising given the historically higher level of antisemitism in Quebec than in Ontario as measured by surveys. Younger Jews are less likely than older Jews to report believing that Jews experience frequent discrimination; but they are more likely to report experiencing discrimination themselves, possibly because younger Jews are more exposed to non-Jews in their daily lives, while older Jews grew up when discrimination was more common, and their perceptions may be influenced by memory of an earlier era.

Comparisons with American Jews. Most of the questions in this section were not included in the Pew Survey of American Jews, so direct comparisons cannot be made. American Jews are as likely as Canadian Jews to report having been called offensive names or been snubbed in social settings over the previous year. American Jews also share with their Canadian counterparts the view that other groups in society (e.g., Muslims, Blacks) are more likely than Jews to be the target of discrimination; and they are more likely to express this opinion than is the general public in the United States.

7.2.7   Connection to Israel

Canadian Jews have a strong connection to Israel. A large majority express an emotional attachment to Israel and have spent time in the country. Eight in ten have visited Israel at least once and have done so an average of five times to date. One in six report having lived in Israel for 6 months or more. Travel to Israel is most prevalent among Jews who are Orthodox/Modern Orthodox, but it is common across the population, especially among Jews under 45 years of age and those with a post-graduate degree.

While Jews may share a connection to Israel, they do not agree when it comes to Israeli politics. Canadian Jews are divided in their views about the Israeli government's commitment to a peace settlement with the Palestinians and the building of settlements on the West Bank in terms of their legality and impact on the security of Israel. Critical opinions of Israel are most evident among younger Jews, and those who are Reform or unaffiliated.

Opinions are also divided when it comes to how Jews view Canada's relations with Israel. A plurality endorses Canada's current level of support for Israel, but a significant minority believe it is not supportive enough. Opinions are closely linked to federal political party affiliation, with a majority of Liberal Party supporters judging the country's support of Israel to be about right, and a majority of Conservative Party supporters maintaining Canada provides too little support.

Substantial minorities of Jews who support the left-leaning New Democratic Party and Green Party believe Canada is too supportive of Israel.[4]

Comparisons with American Jews. American Jews have a much weaker connection to Israel than do Canadian Jews. They are only half as likely to feel a strong attachment to Israel and half as likely to have ever visited Israel. At the same time, Canadian and American Jews are similarly divided in their opinions about the political situation in Israel, in terms of the government's commitment to peace, Israeli settlements in the West Bank, and their own country's support for Israel. The one notable difference is that American Jews are more apt to hold an opinion (whether positive or negative), while Canadian Jews have a greater tendency to say they are unsure or decline to offer an opinion.

7.2.8   Connection to Local Jewish Community

A large majority Canadian Jews feel somewhat, if not strongly, connected to Jewish life in their city. Such connection is largely a function of denominational affiliation and active involvement; strong connection is most prevalent among Orthodox/ Modern Orthodox Jews, those with mostly Jewish friends, those who belong to multiple Jewish organizations, Israeli Jews, and those who live in Montreal. A strong connection is least evident among Jews from the former Soviet Union, those who identify mainly by ancestry/descent, and residents of Vancouver.

Reasons for not wanting to become more connected to Jewish life tend to fall into one of three broad themes. Some Jews do not want to become more connected because they are simply not interested in doing so. Others indicate obstacles that make it difficult, such as lack of time, other priorities, access to the necessary connections or resources, and personal limitations (e.g., health issues). A third theme concerns not feeling Jewish enough, which in some cases is about not identifying or feeling comfortable with the local community.

Many Jews express interest in becoming more connected to the local Jewish community, but they also tend to be the same people who are already feeling strongly connected. The types of activities and programs most likely to be of interest are, in order, those that are educational (lectures, courses, book clubs), cultural (the performing arts, movies, concerts), and social (activities that connect people). Some would like to see programs and activities tailored for specific groups, notably families and young children.

---

[4] The Liberal and Conservative parties are the main political parties in Canada. The Liberal party was in power at the time of the survey, with 39.5% of seats in parliament. Except for the Conservative party (with 31.9% of seats), all parties in parliament are to the left of the Democratic party in the US. The New Democratic Party (with 19.7% of seats) is similar to the left wing of the US Democratic party. At the time of the survey, the Green Party had 3.5% of seats and the Bloc Québécois, 4.7%.

Based on the survey results, the Canadian Jewish community includes roughly 37,000 Sephardim, 25,000 Jews born in the former Soviet Union (FSU), and 17,000 Jews born in Israel. Comparing members of these subgroups to the Canadian Jewish population as a whole, it is only among Jews born in the FSU that one finds a substantially larger proportion that feel less than very connected to their local Jewish community. However, Jews born in the FSU, as well as Sephardim and Jews born in Israel, seem to be significantly more eager to increase their connection to Jewish life in their city than are members of the Canadian Jewish population at large. Members of the three subgroups rank-order the kinds of programs and activities they would like to engage in much like the entire Jewish community does: Educational programs and activities lead the list, followed by cultural and social programs and activities. Religious programs and activities, and those intended for specific groups, such as children and families, rank lowest.

7.3 About the 2018 Survey of Jews in Canada

In 2013, the Pew Research Center published the results of a comprehensive survey of American Jews that examined the identities, values, opinions, and experiences of US Jews. To address the gap in knowledge about these issues among Canadian Jews, the Environics Institute for Survey Research (Executive Director, Keith Neuman), in partnership with Professor Robert Brym (SD Clark Professor of Sociology at the University of Toronto) and Professor Rhonda Lenton (President and Vice-Chancellor, York University) conducted a landmark national survey of Jews in Canada in 2018.

The survey focuses on what it means to be Jewish in Canada today—specifically, patterns of Jewish practice, upbringing, and intermarriage; perceptions of antisemitism; attitudes toward Israel; and personal and organizational connections that, taken together, constitute the community. This research is modelled closely on the 2013 Pew Survey of American Jews to provide the basis for cross-national comparison and to set a high research standard.

The principal investigators assembled the necessary institutional resources, funding, and research expertise required to launch a study of this scope. This included securing financial support from the UJA Federation of Greater Toronto, Federation CJA (Montreal), the Jewish Community Foundation of Montreal, the Jewish Foundation of Manitoba, and the Anne Tanenbaum Centre for Jewish Studies, University of Toronto. The support provided by these organizations made it possible to expand the scope of the research to more effectively cover the Jewish population in particular cities and for particular groups.

The principal investigators also assembled an informal advisory group of community members to provide input for the development of survey themes and questions. This group included Professor Anna Shternshis (Director of the Anne Tanenbaum Centre for Jewish Studies, University of Toronto), Esther Enkin (journalist, and former Ombudsperson of the Canadian Broadcasting Corporation), and Michael Miloff (a consultant in strategic planning to both Jewish and non-Jewish organizations). Through the participation of Federation CJA (Montreal) and the Jewish Foundation of Manitoba, city-specific questions were included in the survey that addressed issues of particular interest to these organizations.

7.3.1   Survey Methodology

Because Canadian Jews constitute only about 1% of the Canadian population, the use of standard survey research methods was not a feasible option given the high costs of using probability sampling to identify and recruit participants.[5] The principal investigators developed a research strategy to make the research sample as comprehensive and representative as possible within the available budget. This strategy entailed two main parts. First, the survey focused on the census metropolitan areas encompassing four cities (Montreal, Toronto, Vancouver, and Winnipeg) that include approximately 82% of the Canadian Jewish population.

Second, a multi-stage sampling plan was developed to complete interviews with Jews in each of the four cities using a combination of sample sources and survey modalities. The primary sampling frame was drawn from a dictionary of several thousand common Jewish surnames that was used to select households with listed landline telephone numbers in census tracts with a minimum of 5% Jewish households. This source was supplemented by requesting referrals from respondents who completed the survey, social media promotion, and on-site recruitment at the Jewish Community Centre in Winnipeg. People were eligible to participate in the survey if they were age 18 or older and self-identified as Jewish or partially Jewish.

The survey was conducted with 2335 individuals by telephone (85% of respondents) or online (15%) between February 10 and September 30, 2018. Quotas were established in each city for age cohort and gender based on the 2011 National Household Survey to ensure adequate representation by these characteristics.[6] In addition to completing the survey with a representative sample in each city, additional surveys were conducted with Jews age 18–44 in Montreal and those who immigrated from the former Soviet Union, in both cases at the request of study sponsors.

The distribution of completed surveys by city is presented in Table 7.1 below. The final city data were weighted by the age and gender distribution of Jews in each city as reported in the 2011 National Household Survey. The final national data were weighted by the size of the Jewish population in each city and the percentage of Jews in each age cohort who were married or living common-law with someone who is not Jewish, again according to the National Household Survey. Because the

---

[5] The 2013 Pew Survey of American Jews used a comprehensive probability sampling strategy, which was made possible by a research budget estimated to be in the millions of dollars.

[6] This extended time period was required because some quotas were considerably more difficult to fill than others (e.g., younger respondents are more difficult to identify and recruit than older ones).

Table 7.1 Survey sample by city

Census metropolitan area	Final sample	% of Canadian Jewish population
Toronto	1135	48%
Montreal	638	23%
Winnipeg	361	4%
Vancouver	201	7%
Total	**2335**	**82%**

survey is not fully based on probability sampling, sampling error cannot be calculated.[7] A more complete description of the survey methodology is presented in the Appendix of the final report.[8]

7.3.2   About the Final Report

The final report from which this summary is excerpted presents the results of the research and covers the following themes: what it means to be Jewish; types of Jewish practice; strength and type of connections to other Jews and to Jewish organizations; patterns of Jewish upbringing; intermarriage; views on Israel; perceptions of, and experiences with, discrimination and anti-Semitism; and connection to the local community. Throughout the report, the results highlight relevant similarities and differences across the Jewish population, by city, age cohort, denominational affiliation, and other characteristics. The Canadian results are compared with those of American Jews based on the 2013 Pew Survey of American Jews where available, and in several cases also compared to results from surveys of the Canadian population at large. Each chapter ends with a commentary with further analysis and interpretation of the results.

Detailed tables presenting results for all survey questions by Jewish population segments are available separately on the Environics Institute website at www.environicsinstitute.org. All results are presented as percentages unless otherwise noted.

References

Brym, R. 2017. More than half of Canada's Jews are missing. *Globe and Mail*. November 7. https://www.theglobeandmail.com/opinion/more-than-half-of-canadas-jews-are-missing/article36813257/ .

Brym, R. 2019. Antisemitic and anti-Israel actions and attitudes in Canada and internationally: a research agenda. *Patterns of Prejudice, 53*(4):407–420.

---

[7] However, as a rough benchmark, we note that 19 of 20 simple random samples of 2335 respondents would result in a maximum margin of error of plus or minus 2.0 percentage points.

[8] See footnote 1.

Brym, R., K. Neuman, and R. Lenton. 2019. *2018 Survey of Jews in Canada*. Toronto: The Environics Institute. https://www.environicsinstitute.org/projects/project-details/survey-of-jews-in-canada.

Brym, R., and Lenton, R. 2020. Jewish religious intermarriage in Canada. *Canadian Jewish Studies* 30 (in press).

Brym, R., Slavina, A., and Lenton, R. 2020. Qualifying the leading theory of diaspora Jewry: an examination of Jews from the former Soviet Union in Canada and the United States. *Contemporary Jewry* 40 (in press).

Pew Research Center. 2013. *A Portrait of Jewish Americans: Findings from a Pew Research Center Survey of U.S. Jews*. Washington, DC: Pew Research Center.

———. 2015. The future of world religions: population growth projections, 2010–2050: Jews. https://www.pewforum.org/2015/04/02/jews/

Simmel, G. 1955. *Conflict and the web of group affiliations*. Trans. K. Wolff and R. Bendix. New York: Free Press.

Chapter 8
World Jewish Population, 2019

Sergio DellaPergola

At the beginning of 2019, the world's Jewish population was estimated at 14,707,400—an increase of 100,900 (0.69%) over the 2018 revised estimate of 14,606,500 (DellaPergola 2019a). The world's total population increased by 1.11% in 2018 (Population Reference Bureau 2018). The rate of increase of world Jewry hence amounted to 62% of that of the total population.

8.1 Assessing Jewish Population[1]

Figure 8.1 illustrates changes in the number of Jews worldwide, in Israel, and in the aggregate in the rest of the world (the *Diaspora*)—as well as changes in the world's total population between 1945 and 2019. The world's *core* Jewish population was estimated at 11 million in 1945. The *core* Jewish population concept addresses a human collective whose identification is mutually exclusive with respect to other subpopulations, while acknowledging that the number of persons who carry multiple cultural and religious identities tends to increase in contemporary societies (Josselson and Harway 2012). While 13 years were needed to add one million Jews from 11 to 12 million after the tragic human losses of World War II and the *Shoah* (Holocaust) (DellaPergola et al. 2000b), 40 more years were needed to add another million from 12 to 13 million. From the 1970s onwards, world Jewry stagnated at nearly *zero population growth* for nearly 20 years but some demographic recovery

---

[1] This chapter is dedicated to the memory of Professor Sidney Goldstein of Brown University, for many years the dean of Jewish demographic research, who passed in 2019. See the obituary later in this volume.

S. DellaPergola (✉)
The Avraham Harman Institute of Contemporary Jewry, The Hebrew University of Jerusalem, Jerusalem, Israel
e-mail: sergioa@huji.ac.il

© Springer Nature Switzerland AG 2020
A. Dashefsky, I. M. Sheskin (eds.), *American Jewish Year Book 2019*, American Jewish Year Book 119, https://doi.org/10.1007/978-3-030-40371-3_8

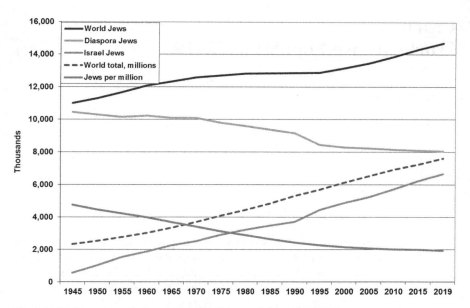

Fig. 8.1 World total population and core Jewish population, 1945–2019

occurred since 2000, mostly reflecting population increase in Israel. It took about 14 years to add another million from 13 to 14 million. In historical perspective and based on the same definitions, world Jewish population has not recovered its size on the eve of World War II—16.5 million—and it may take decades more to do so, if ever.

World Jewish population size reflects a combination of two very different demographic trends in Israel and in the Diaspora. Israel's Jewish population increased linearly from an initial one-half million in 1945 and 630,000 in 1948 to over 6.6 million in 2019. The Jewish population of the Diaspora, from an initial 10.5 million in 1945, was quite stable in number until the early 1970s, when it started decreasing, reaching less than 8.1 million in 2019. The world's total population increased more than threefold from 2.315 billion in 1945 to 7.621 billion by mid-2018. Thus, the relative share of Jews among the world's total population steadily diminished from 4.75 per 1000 in 1945 to 1.93 per 1000 currently—or one per 518 inhabitants in the world.

Two countries, Israel and the US, accounted for over 84% of the 2019 total; 23 countries, each with 10,000 Jews or more, accounted for another 15%, and another 73 countries, each with Jewish populations below 10,000, accounted for the remaining 0.9%. Figure 8.2 shows the size of the 20 largest *core* Jewish populations in 2019.

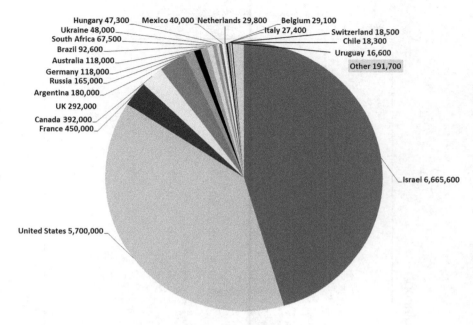

Hungary 47,300__ Mexico 40,000_Netherlands 29,800   _Belgium 29,100
Ukraine 48,000__   __Italy 27,400   __ Switzerland 18,500
South Africa 67,500__   __ Chile 18,300
Brazil 92,600__   Uruguay 16,600
Australia 118,000__
Germany 118,000__   Other 191,700
Russia 165,000__
Argentina 180,000__
UK 292,000
Canada 392,000__
France 450,000__

Israel 6,665,600

United States 5,700,000__

Fig. 8.2 Twenty largest core Jewish populations, 2019

Map 8.1 shows the geographical distribution of the 20 larger Jewish communities worldwide.

Israel's Jewish population (*not* including 426,700 persons not recorded as Jews in the Ministry of Interior's Population Register but who are members of families initially admitted under the *Law of Return*) reached 6,665,600 in 2019 (45.3% of world Jewry by the *core* definition)—out of Israel's total legal population of 8,970,900. This represented a Jewish population increase of 111,100 (1.70%) in 2018. In the same year, the total Jewish population of the Diaspora was estimated to have decreased by 10,200 from 8,052,000 to 8,041,800 (−0.13%). Following the 2013 Pew Research Center (2013) *A Portrait of Jewish Americans*, the US *core* Jewish population was assessed at 5,700,000 and we estimate it to have remained stable, constituting 38.8% of world Jewry in 2019. Core Jews in the US were estimated to have increased slightly since the year 2000, following several years of moderate decline after probably reaching a peak around 1980 (DellaPergola 2013a). Jews in the rest of the world were assessed at 2,341,800 in 2019 (15.9% of world Jewry). Since all of the decline of 10,200 among Diaspora Jews occurred in countries other than the US, that amounted to an annual loss of −0.43% in the aggregate for those countries. For the total world population, growth was 1.4% in less developed countries and zero in the more developed countries where most Jews live.

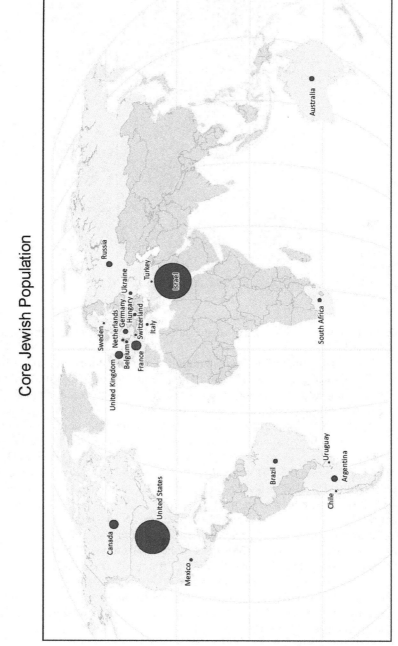

Map 8.1 Countries where 99% of world Jewish population live, 2019

After critically reviewing all available evidence on Jewish demographic trends, it is plausible to claim that Israel hosts the largest *core* Jewish community world-wide. Some dissenting opinions (Saxe and Tighe 2013, Saxe 2019, Sheskin and Dashefsky in this volume) are mostly based on different definitions of the target population. Since Israel's independence in 1948, demography has produced a tran-sition of singular importance for Jewish history and experience—the return of the Jews to a geographical distribution significantly rooted in Israel, their ancestral homeland. This has occurred through daily, slow, and diverse changes reflecting births and deaths, geographical mobility, and the choice of millions of persons to express or to deny a Jewish collective identification not subordinated to nor on par with other explicit religious or ethnic identifications. At the same time, Jewish majority status in Israel faces a significant demographic challenge vis-á-vis the more rapidly growing Palestinian Arab population within the boundaries of the State of Israel as well as in the West Bank and Gaza.

Israel's current Jewish population growth—although slower than during the 1990s—reflects a continuing substantial natural increase generated by a combina-tion of relatively high fertility and a relatively young age composition. These two drivers of demographic growth do not simultaneously exist among any other Jewish population worldwide, including the US. Other than a few cases of growth due to international migration (for example Canada and Australia and, until recently, the US and Germany), and possibly some growth due to local natural increase (plausi-bly in the UK and Mexico, and minimally in Australia) the total number of Jews in Diaspora countries tends to diminish at varying rates.

The fundamental equation of demography is that a population size at a given time reflects an uninterrupted chain of events that change the size of that population from an earlier to a later date. Of the three possible determinants of population change, two are shared by all populations: (a) the balance of vital events (births and deaths) where low Jewish birth rates and an increasingly elderly population gener-ate higher death rates and an overall deficit; and (b) the variable balance of interna-tional migration (immigration and emigration). The third determinant consists of identification changes or *passages* (accessions and secessions)—in this case to and from a Jewish identity—and applies only to subpopulations defined by some cul-tural, symbolic, or other specific characteristic, as is the case for Jews. Identification changes do not affect people's physical presence but rather their willingness or abil-ity to identify with a particular religious, ethnic, or otherwise culturally-defined group.

All this holds true regarding the *core* Jewish population, which does *not* include non-Jewish members of Jewish households, Jews who also hold another religious identification, persons of Jewish ancestry who profess another monotheistic reli-gion, other non-Jews of Jewish ancestry, other non-Jews with family connections to Jews, and other non-Jews who may be interested in Jewish matters. (See further discussion below.) The detailed mechanisms and supporting evidence of Jewish population change have been discussed extensively in previous issues of the *American Jewish Year Book (AJYB)* and will not be repeated here (see DellaPergola 2015a).

Jewish population size and composition reflect the day-by-day interplay of various factors that operate from both outside and inside the Jewish community. The continuing realignment of world Jewish geography toward the major centers of economic development and political power provides a robust yardstick for further explanation and prediction of Jewish demography (DellaPergola et al. 2005; DellaPergola 2017a).

The 2019 Jewish population data were updated from 2018 and previous years in accordance with known or estimated vital events, migrations, and Jewish identification shifts. The world Jewish population estimate results from the sum of national estimates. While individual country estimates can be obtained from nationwide sources as well as from the sum of local sources, in the case of the world's total, in the lack of a global population census, there is no alternative to the summation of local figures. In each of the country update procedures, when data on intervening changes were available, empirically ascertained or reasonably assumed, effects of change were applied accordingly and consistently added to or subtracted from previous estimates. If the evidence was that intervening changes balanced one another in a particular country, Jewish population size was not changed. This procedure has proven highly effective over the years of our monitoring of world Jewish population. Most often, when improved Jewish population estimates reflecting a new census or socio-demographic survey became available, our annually updated estimates proved to be on target. Where needed, previous estimates were adjusted based upon newer, better evidence.

The research findings reported here tend to confirm the estimates reported in previous years and, perhaps more importantly, a coherent and conceptually robust interpretation of the trends prevailing in world Jewish demography (Bachi 1976; Schmelz 1981, 1984; DellaPergola 1995, 1999, 2001, 2011a). While allowing for improvements and corrections, the 2019 population estimates highlight the increasing complexity of socio-demographic and identification factors underlying Jewish population patterns. This complexity is magnified at a time of pervasive internal and international migration and increasing transnationalism, sometimes involving bi-local residences and leading to double counting of people on the move or who permanently share their time between different places. In this study, special attention is paid to avoiding double counts of internationally and nationally mobile and bi-local persons. Even more intriguing can be the position of persons who hold more than one religious, ethnic, or cultural identity and may periodically shift from one to the other. Available data sources only imperfectly allow documenting these complexities; hence, Jewish population estimates are far from perfect. Some errors can be corrected at a later stage, but analysts should resign themselves to the paradox of the *permanently provisional* nature of Jewish population estimates.

8.1.1   *Definitions*

Jewish population definitions obviously critically impact the numbers. A major problem with Jewish population estimates produced by individual scholars or Jewish organizations is the lack of uniformity in definitional criteria—when the issue of defining the Jewish population as well as data quality, is addressed at all. This problem is magnified when one tries to address the Jewish population globally, trying to provide a coherent and uniform definitional framework for Jews who live in very different institutional, cultural, and socioeconomic environments. For analytical purposes, it would not be acceptable to use one definitional standard for one country, and another for another country, although in the daily conduct of Jewish community affairs such differences do prevail across countries.

In such an open, fluid, and somewhat undetermined environment, the very feasibility of undertaking a valid and meaningful study of the Jewish collective—let alone by the use of quantitative tools—generates debates between different intellectual stances facing Jewish population studies (DellaPergola 2014d). In particular, the study of a Jewish population (or of any other subpopulation) requires addressing three main problems:

1. *Defining* the target group on the basis of conceptual or normative criteria aimed at providing the best possible description of that group—which in the case of Jewry is no minor task in itself;
2. *Identifying* the group thus defined based on tools that operationally allow for distinguishing and selecting the target group from the rest of the population—primarily by systematic canvassing of populations and personally ascertaining personal identifications. Identification is also often performed through membership lists, distinctive Jewish names, areas of residence, or other random or non-random procedures; and
3. *Covering* the target group through appropriate field work—through face-to-face interviews, by telephone, by mail, by Internet, or otherwise. Most often in the actual experience of social research, and contrary to ideal procedures, the definitional task is performed at the stage of identification, and the identification task is performed at the stage of actual fieldwork.

It thus clearly appears that the quantitative study of Jewish populations relies mostly on *operational*, not *prescriptive*, definitional criteria. The main conceptual aspects, besides being rooted in social theory, heavily depend on practical and logistical feasibility—not the least, available research budgets. The ultimate empirical step—obtaining relevant data from relevant persons—crucially reflects the readiness of people to cooperate in the data collection effort. In recent years, as response rates and cooperation rates have significantly decreased in social surveys (Keeter et al. 2017), the amount, content, and validity of information gathered have been affected detrimentally. While response rates for Jewish surveys tend to be much better than general surveys, the quality of the data is certainly impacted.

No method exists to counter these decreases in response rates and cooperation rates. Therefore, research findings reflect, with varying degrees of sophistication, only that which is possible to uncover, namely the degree of involvement with or indifference to feeling Jewish by respondents. Something that cannot be uncovered directly can sometimes be estimated through various imperfect indirect techniques. However, there exist unsurmountable limits to what research methodologies can deliver. For example, large representative samples and small qualitative studies are not interchangeable regarding the answers they can provide to specific research questions. Beyond that, we enter the virtual world of beliefs, hopes and fears, myths, and corporate interests. No methodology exists to demonstrate the actual nature of some of these claims—at least not within the limits of a non-fiction and non-advocacy work such as this.

Keeping these limits in mind, four major definitional concepts will be considered here to provide serious comparative foundations to the study of Jewish demography worldwide (Fig. 8.3): (a) the **core Jewish population (CJP)**—the group who consider Judaism their mutually exclusive identification framework, including both those who do see or do not see religion as a major avenue for identification (Jewish only, religion: Circle 1 in Fig. 8.3; Jewish only, no religion: Circle 2 in the figure); (b) the **population with Jewish parent(s) (PJP)**—including those who say they are partly Jewish because their identity is split between two or more different and relevant identification frameworks (Circle 3), and those who say they are not Jewish but have Jewish background in the form of at least one Jewish parent (Circle 4). Taken together Circles 3 and 4 may also be referred to as the "Jewish Connected" population; (c) the **enlarged Jewish population (EJP)**—including others who say they have Jewish background but not a Jewish parent (Circle 5), and all non-Jewish household members who live in households with Jews (Circle 6); and (d) the **Law of Return population (LRP)** (Circle 7). More detail on these definitions is presented in the Appendix.

This typology is relevant because not only it does mark-off alternative population definition approaches but it also delineates different analytic approaches grounded on alternative social theories as well as different possible Jewish institutional strategies in designating the respective catchment constituencies. It is important to realize that the categories in Fig. 8.3 are not static but continuous passages occur across the different circles, from center to periphery and vice-versa, and from the whole configuration outside, and vice-versa. Further definitional extensions (not shown in Fig. 8.3) may address those additional non-Jewish persons who feel some degree of **affinity with Judaism**, sometimes because their more distant ancestors were Jewish or because of other personal cultural or social connections with Jews. Moreover, some studies may have reached people whose **ancestors *ever* were Jewish** regardless of the respondents' present identification. Several socio-demographic surveys indeed ask about the religio-ethnic identification of parents. Some population surveys, however, *do* ask about more distant ancestry. Historians may wish to engage in the study of the number of Jews who ever lived or of how many persons today are descendants of those Jews—for example, *Conversos* who lived in the Iberian Peninsula during the Middle Ages, or the descendants of Jews who lived

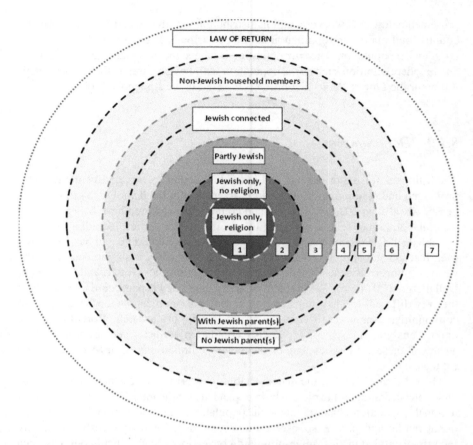

Fig. 8.3 Configuring and defining contemporary Jewish populations, 2019. 1 to 2 = Core Jewish population (CJP); 1 to 4 = Population with Jewish parent(s) (PJP); 1 to 6 = Enlarged Jewish population (EJP); 1 to 7 = Law of Return population (LRP); Areas represented are not proportional to actual populations

during the Roman Empire, or the Lost Tribes (Parfitt 2002; Parfitt and Fisher 2016; Israel Ministry of Diaspora Affairs 2018; Gross et al. 2019). The early Jewish backgrounds of some population groups have been uncovered in recent studies of population genetics (Hammer et al. 2000; Behar et al. 2004, 2010; Carmi et al. 2014; Tian et al. 2015). These long-term issues and analyses are beyond the purpose of the present study.

The adoption of increasingly extended definitional criteria by individual researchers and by Jewish organizations tends to stretch Jewish population definitions with an expansive effect on population estimates beyond usual practices in the past and beyond the limits of the typical *core* definition. These decisions may reflect local needs and sensitivities, but tend to limit the actual comparability of the same Jewish population over time and of different Jewish populations at one given time. As noted, a more coherently comparative approach is followed here. The estimates presented below of Jewish population distribution worldwide and in each continent, country, and major metropolitan area, are consistently anchored to the concept of *core* Jewish population. The *core* definition is indeed the necessary starting point for any broader definition such as the population with Jewish parents, the *enlarged* definition, or the *Law of Return* definition (see detail in the Appendix Table).

8.1.2 Data Sources

The estimates for major regions and individual countries reported below reflect a prolonged and continuing effort to study scientifically the demography of contemporary world Jewry. Data collection and comparative research have benefited from the collaboration of scholars and institutions in many countries, including access to unpublished databases regarding current estimates. It should be emphasized, however, that the elaboration of worldwide estimates for the Jewish populations of the various countries is beset with difficulties and uncertainties (Ritterband et al. 1988; DellaPergola 2014c, d). The problem of data consistency is particularly acute, given the very different legal systems and organizational provisions under which Jewish communities operate in different countries. In spite of our keen efforts to create a unified analytic framework for Jewish population studies, data users should be aware of these difficulties and of the inherent limitations of Jewish population estimates.

Over the past decades, the data available for a critical assessment of the worldwide Jewish demographic picture have expanded significantly. These data consist of national population censuses, national population registers, national and international public and private sponsored surveys, and national or Jewish community records of vital statistics, migration, and conversions. Some of this ongoing data compilation is part of coordinated efforts aimed at strengthening Jewish population research by the Division of Jewish Demography and Statistics at the Institute of Contemporary Jewry of The Hebrew University of Jerusalem. This new evidence generally confirmed our previous estimates, but sometimes suggested upward or downward revisions.

Jewish population projections undertaken by the author, in light of the latest data, also helped in the current assessment. It is quite evident that the cross-matching of more than one type of source about the same Jewish population, although not frequently feasible, can provide either mutual reinforcement of, or important critical insights into, the available data. Other existing estimates of total world Jewish population and of its geographical distribution (Pew Forum on Religion and Public Life 2012; Johnson and Zurlo 2014) provide findings quite close to ours. Unlike our review of hundreds of local and international sources, the Pew comparisons often rely on percentages of Jews from larger general studies. As Jews are usually an extremely small fraction of the total, the resulting Jewish population estimates may be affected by large sampling errors. A full list of the types and quality of documentation upon which Jewish population estimates are based is reported in the **Appendix** below.

8.2   World Jewish Population Size and Distribution by Major Areas

As noted, in our current estimates, we corrected previously published Jewish population data in light of new information. In recent years, the most significant correction was an addition of about 300,000 Jews in the US following the 2013 Pew study. This revision generated retrospective revisions of the whole annual series of data for the US, for the total Diaspora, and for World Jewry since 2000. Table 8.1 provides

Table 8.1 World core Jewish population estimates: original and revised, 1945–2019

Year	World Jewish population			World population		Jews per 1000 total population
	Original estimate[a]	Revised estimate[b]	Annual % change[c]	Total (millions)[d]	Annual % change	
1945, May 1	11,000,000	11,000,000		2315		4.75
1950, Jan. 1	11,303,400	11,297,000	0.59	2526	1.76	4.47
1960, Jan. 1	12,792,800	12,079,000	0.67	3026	1.82	3.99
1970, Jan. 1	13,950,900	12,585,000	0.41	3691	2.01	3.41
1980, Jan. 1	14,527,100	12,819,000	0.18	4449	1.81	2.88
1990, Jan. 1	12,810,300	12,868,000	0.04	5321	1.74	2.42
2000, Jan. 1	13,191,500	13,150,000	0.22	6127	1.42	2.15
2005, Jan. 1	13,034,100	13,460,000	0.47	6514	1.23	2.07
2010, Jan. 1	13,428,300	13,854,000	0.58	6916	1.20	2.00
2015, Jan. 1	14,310,500	14,311,600	0.65	7236	0.91	1.98
2016, Jan. 1	14,410,700	14,407,600	0.67	7336	1.38	1.96
2017, Jan. 1	14,511,100	14,507,600	0.69	7436	1.14	1.95
2018, Jan. 1	14,606,000	14,606,500	0.68	7536	1.13	1.94
2019, Jan. 1	14,707,400		0.69	7621	1.11	1.93

[a]As published in the *American Jewish Year Book*, various years. Some estimates reported here as of Jan. 1 were originally published as of Dec. 31 of the previous year
[b]Based on updated or corrected information. Original estimates for 1990 and after, and all revised estimates: The A. Harman Institute of Contemporary Jewry, The Hebrew University of Jerusalem
[c]Based on revised estimates, except latest year
[d]Mid-year estimates. Source: United Nations Population Division (2018), Population Reference Bureau (2018)

a synopsis of world Jewish population estimates for 1945 through 2019, as first published each year in the *American Jewish Year Book* and retroactively corrected as now, also adjusting all revisions that had been suggested in previous years. These revised estimates depart, sometimes significantly, from the estimates published by other authors until 1980 and since 1981, by ourselves. Thanks to the development over the years of an improved database, these new revisions are not necessarily the same revised estimates that appeared annually in the *AJYB* in the past based on the information that was available on each date. It is possible that further retroactive revisions may become necessary reflecting ongoing and future research.

The time series in Table 8.1 clearly portrays the decreasing rate of Jewish population growth globally between the 1960s and the 1990s. Based on a post-Shoah world Jewish population estimate of 11,000,000, a growth of 1,079,000 occurred between 1945 and 1960, followed by increases of 506,000 in the 1960s, 234,000 in the 1970s, 49,000 in the 1980s, and 282,000 in the 1990s. Since 2000, the slow rhythm of Jewish population growth has somewhat recovered, with an increase of 704,000 through 2010, reflecting the robust demographic trends in Israel and Israel's increasing share of the world total. Between 2010 and 2019, world Jewry increased by 853,400, but Israel's Jewish population increased by 962,000 while the total Diaspora Jewish population decreased by 108,000. Table 8.1 also demonstrates the slower world Jewish population growth rate compared to global population growth, and the declining Jewish share of the world population. In 2019, the share of Jews among the world population (1.93 per 1000) was 40.6% of the 1945 estimate (4.75 per 1000).

Table 8.2 offers an overall picture of the Jewish population by major geographical regions at the beginning of 2019 as compared to 2018. The originally published estimates from the 2018 *American Jewish Year Book* were slightly revised reflecting retroactive corrections due to improved information. These corrections resulted in a net increase of 500 persons in the 2018 world Jewry estimate, reflecting a subtraction of 3600 from the previous estimate for Israel, and a net increase of 4100 in the Jewish Diaspora total.

Looking first at global trends, the number of Jews in Israel increased from the revised 6,554,500 in 2018 to 6,665,600 at the beginning of 2018, an increase of 111,100, or 1.70%. In contrast, the estimated Jewish population in the Diaspora *decreased* from the revised 8,052,000 to 8,041,800—a decrease of 10,200, or −0.13%. These changes reflect continuing Jewish emigration from the former Soviet Union (FSU), and to a lesser extent from France, from the small remnants of Jewish communities in Moslem countries, and from other countries, and the internal decrease due to an excess of deaths over births typical of the aggregate of Diaspora Jewry. In the absence of final accountancy for 2018 we know that in 2017, of a total increase of 108,400 core Jews in Israel, 96,700 reflected the balance of births and deaths, and 11,700 reflected the estimated Israel-Diaspora net migration balance (immigration minus emigration) and to a minor extent net conversion to Judaism (Israel Central Bureau of Statistics n.d.-a annual; Fisher 2015, 2019; Nissim 2018). Israel's net migration balance includes tourists who changed their status to immigrants, returning Israelis, and Israeli citizens born abroad who entered Israel for the

Table 8.2 Estimated core Jewish population, by continents and major geographic regions, 2018 and 2019[a]

Region	2018 Revised[b]		2019		Percentage change 2018–2019	Jews per 1000 total population in 2019
	Estimate	Percent[c]	Estimate	Percent[c]		
World total	**14,606,500**	**100.0**	**14,707,400**	**100.0**	**0.69**	**1.93**
Diaspora	8,052,000	55.1	8,041,800	54.7	−0.13	1.06
US	5,700,000	39.0	5,700,000	38.8	0.00	17.38
Other	2,352,000	16.1	2,341,800	15.9	−0.43	0.32
Israel[d]	6,554,500	44.9	6,665,600	45.3	1.70	743.02
America, total	**6,469,800**	**44.3**	**6,469,900**	**44.0**	**0.00**	**6.38**
North[e]	6,090,600	41.7	6,092,100	41.4	0.02	16.68
Central, Caribbean	57,000	0.4	57,000	0.4	0.00	0.26
South	322,200	2.2	320,800	2.2	−0.43	0.75
Europe, total	**1,349,200**	**9.2**	**1,340,200**	**9.1**	**−0.67**	**1.62**
European Union[f]	1,079,500	7.4	1,078,900	7.3	−0.06	2.11
Other West	20,600	0.1	20,500	0.1	−0.49	1.42
Balkans[g]	17,100	0.1	16,900	0.1	−1.17	0.17
FSU[g]	232,000	1.6	223,900	1.5	−3.49	1.11
Asia, total	**6,589,400**	**45.1**	**6,699,700**	**45.6**	**1.67**	**1.50**
Israel	6,554,500	44.9	6,665,600	45.3	1.70	743.02
FSU	16,000	0.1	15,300	0.1	−4.38	0.17
Other	18,900	0.1	18,800	0.1	−0.53	0.00
Africa, total	**72,600**	**0.5**	**72,000**	**0.5**	**−0.83**	**0.06**
Northern[h]	3400	0.0	3300	0.0	−2.94	0.01
Sub-Saharan[i]	69,200	0.5	68,700	0.5	−0.72	0.07
Oceania[j]	**125,500**	**0.9**	**125,600**	**0.9**	**0.08**	**3.06**

[a]Jewish population: January 1. Total population: mid-year estimates, 2018. Source: United Nations (2018), Population Reference Bureau (2019)

[b]Compare with the original in DellaPergola (2019). The corrections reflecting newly available data are for Israel (−3600), Russia (−2000)

South Africa (−1000), UK (+1000), Australia (+4.500), Austria (+1000), Ukraine (+500), Gibraltar (+100)

[c]Minor discrepancies due to rounding

[d]Includes Jewish residents in East Jerusalem, the West Bank, and the Golan Heights

[e]US and Canada

[f]Including the Baltic countries (Estonia, Latvia, and Lithuania), and the UK

[g]FSU excluding the Baltic countries. Asian regions of Russian Federation and Turkey included in Europe

[h]Including Ethiopia

[i]Including South Africa and Zimbabwe

[j]Including Australia and New Zealand

first time. Therefore, internal demographic change produced 89.2% of the total Jewish population growth in Israel. According to these estimates almost all of the Diaspora's estimated decrease is explained by a negative migration balance. This quite certainly underestimates the actually negative vital balance in most countries, resulting in higher than real population estimates for the aggregate of Diaspora Jewry. Adjustments could be needed in the future.

Recently, for sure, more frequent instances of conversion, accession, or "return" to Judaism can be observed in connection with the absorption in Israel of immigrants from the FSU, Ethiopia, some Latin American countries like Peru, and India. To some extent this same phenomenon of return or first-time accession to Judaism occurs throughout Diaspora communities as well. The addition of such previously non-belonging or unidentified persons tends to contribute both to slowing the decrease in the relevant Diaspora Jewish populations and to a minimal fraction of the increase in the Jewish population in Israel (DellaPergola 2017c).

In descending order by continents, over 45% of world Jewry lived in **Asia**, overwhelmingly in Israel (Table 8.2 and Appendix Table). Asia is defined herein to include the Asian republics of the FSU, but not the Asiatic areas of the Russian Federation and Turkey. The Jewish presence in Asia is mostly affected by trends in Israel which accounts for more than 99% of the continental total. The former republics of the FSU in Asia and the aggregate of the other countries in Asia account each for less than one-half of one percent of the total. Clearly, the fast economic development in Southeast Asian countries like Japan, South Korea, Singapore, and especially China, is attracting Jewish professionals, businesspeople, and technicians. The numbers are still small but growing.

Over 44% of the world's Jews resided in **the Americas**, with 41.4% in North America. The Jewish population in the Americas, estimated at 6,469,900 in 2019, is predominantly concentrated in the US (5,700,000, or 88% of the total Americas), followed by Canada (392,000, 6%), South America (320,800, 5%), and Central America and the Caribbean (57,000, 1%). Since the 1960s, the Jewish population has been generally decreasing in Central and South America, reflecting emigration motivated by recurring economic and security concerns (Schmelz and DellaPergola 1985; DellaPergola 1987, 2008a, 2011b). Panama and Mexico were the exceptions and absorbed Jewish migrants from other countries in the continent. In the Miami Jewish community (Miami-Dade County), the number of members of households containing a Jewish adult from Latin American countries increased from roughly 18,000 in 2004 to 24,500 in 2014 (Sheskin 2015b). In neighboring Broward County (Fort Lauderdale), the same measure increased from 5300 in 1997 to 26,500 in 2016 (Sheskin 2017). Between 2001 and 2018, the total number of immigrants from Latin America to Israel surpassed 25,000 (Israel Central Bureau of Statistics), including many persons highly educated and highly involved in Jewish life (Bokser-Liwerant et al. 2015). Outside the mainstream of the established Jewish community, increased interest in Judaism has appeared among real or putative descendants of *Conversos* whose ancestors left Judaism and converted to Christianity under the pressure of the Inquisition in Spain and Portugal in the fifteenth century. Some of these *Converso* communities have been trying to create permanent frameworks to express their Jewish identity, in part locally, in part through formal conversion to Judaism and migration to Israel. In the long run, such a phenomenon might lead to some expansion of the Jewish population, especially in smaller communities in the peripheral areas of Brazil, Peru, Colombia, and other countries (Israel Ministry of Diaspora Affairs 2018). Persons with such backgrounds are also migrating to Israel (Torres 2017).

Europe, including the Asian territories of the Russian Federation and Turkey, accounted for over 9% of world Jewry. The Jewish population in Europe, estimated at 1,340,200 in 2019, is increasingly concentrated in the western part of the continent and within the European Union (EU). The EU, comprising 28 countries prior to the June 2016 secession vote of the UK (still not fully implemented in late 2019), had an estimated total of 1,078,900 Jews in 2019 (80.5% of the continent's total). The momentous political transformations since the fall of the Berlin Wall and the end of the Soviet Union brought about significant changes in the territorial deployment of Jewish communities in Europe. Revitalization of Jewish community life in the western countries had occurred over the past tens of years through immigration mainly from North Africa and the Middle East but also from the FSU. But more recently, economic recession and rising perceptions of antisemitism across the continent have brought about growing Jewish dissatisfaction and emigration (DellaPergola 2017b; Staetsky 2017; Staetsky et al. 2013; European Union Fundamental Rights Agency-FRA 2013, 2018). Total emigration from the EU to Israel reached a peak of 8406 in 2015 but diminished to 5570 in 2016, 4268 in 2017, and 3628 in 2018. In spite of the unifying project and process, Europe is much more politically fragmented than the US, making it more difficult to create a homogeneous Jewish population database. Nevertheless, several studies have attempted to create such analytic frames of reference (Graham 2004; Kovács and Barna 2010; DellaPergola 1993, 2010b; Staetsky et al. 2013; Staetsky and DellaPergola 2019a). The EU's initially expanding format symbolized an important historical landmark and a promising framework for the development of Jewish life. However, in recent years the EU concept and ideal finds itself under major stress, and the 2016 UK Brexit referendum is only one of its symptoms. Disagreements about migration policies facing large Muslim population increases in different European locations, reflect the unsolved dilemma of defining Europe's own cultural identity and geopolitical boundaries. The four former Soviet republics in Europe (Russia, Belarus, Ukraine, Moldova, excluding the three Baltic republics) have a Jewish population of 223,900 (16.7% of the continental total). The FSU is the area where, in absolute numbers, Jewish population has diminished the most since 1991 (Tolts 2008, 2014, 2015; Konstantinov 2007). Jewish population decrease continued, reflecting emigration, an overwhelming excess of Jewish deaths over Jewish births, high intermarriage rates, and low rates of Jewish identification among the children of intermarriages. The ongoing process of demographic decrease is being alleviated to some extent by the revival of Jewish educational, cultural, and religious activities supported by American and Israeli Jewish organizations (Gitelman 2003). Nevertheless, total migration to Israel from the FSU steadily continued with

14,687 in 2015, 14,471 in 2016, 16,122 in 2017, and 18,887 in 2018 out of a total of 28,118 new immigrants (67%).

Our 2019 assessment of the total *core* Jewish population for the 15 FSU republics in Europe and Asia was 248,100, of whom 232,800 live in Europe (including 8900 in the three Baltic republics already accounted for in the EU) and 15,300 in Asia. Almost as many non-Jewish household members created an *enlarged* Jewish population nearly twice as large as the *core* (Tolts 2006, 2007, 2013, 2015). All other European countries not part of the EU or the FSU, including Turkey, combined comprised 37,400 core Jews (3% of the European total).

Little more than 1% of the world's Jews live in Africa and Oceania combined. The Jewish population in **Africa** is mostly concentrated in South Africa (about 94% of the continental total). Immigration continued to produce some increase in Jewish population in **Oceania** where Australia accounts for 94% of the total.

Overall, between 2018 and 2019 Jewish population size increased primarily in Israel and to a modest extent in North America and Oceania, and decreased to varying degrees in South America, the European Union, other Western Europe, the Balkans, the FSU (both in Europe and Asia), the rest of Asia, and Africa.

8.2.1 Implications of Alternative Jewish Population Definitions

In Table 8.3 we evaluate the Jewish population's regional distribution according to several alternative definitions, as outlined in Fig. 8.3. Updated and revised *core* Jewish population estimates (CJP in the table) are presented, along with the total of those who *have Jewish parents* regardless of their current identity (PJP); the *enlarged Jewish population* inclusive of non-Jewish household members (EJP); and the population eligible for the *Law of Return* (LRP). Detailed country estimates are reported in the Appendix Table. The main purpose of these alternative population boundary definitions is to promote and facilitate comparability across countries. In light of the preceding discussion of definitions, it is clear that Jewish investigators and/or community leaders in different countries sometimes follow local definitional criteria that may differ from the criteria acceptable and used in other countries. This may help explain why Jewish population size in the US or Canada is evaluated quite differently in the present chapter and in other chapters (Sheskin and Dashefsky; Shahar) in this volume. In other words, criteria that may be understood or even preferred in one country may not be meaningful or acceptable in another country. But in a global study like this, maximum comparability can be ensured only if the same criteria are followed consistently for all countries. The prime choice unavoidably must fall on a minimum common denominator. However, by showing the implications of different definitions for Jewish population evaluation, we offer readers an additional tool to better appreciate ongoing population trends in their countries.

Starting from the core Jewish population estimate of 14,707,400 (CJP) in 2019, if we add persons who state they are partly Jewish and non-Jews who have Jewish parents, a broader global aggregate population estimate of 17,917,750 (PJP) is obtained. By adding non-Jewish members of Jewish households, an *enlarged*

Table 8.3 Jewish population by major regions, core definition and expanded definitions (rough estimates), 1/1/2019

Region	Core Jewish population[a] CJP	Population with Jewish parents[b] JPP	Enlarged Jewish population[c] EJP	Law of return population[d] LRP	Difference LRP–CJP Number	Percent distribution	Percent expansion LRP over CJP
World total	**14,707,400**	**17,917,750**	**20,876,400**	**23,674,400**	**8,967,000**	**100.0**	**61**
North America	6,092,100	8,450,200	10,550,300	12,700,400	6,608,300	73.7	108
Latin America	377,800	505,100	605,900	717,900	340,100	3.8	90
European Union[e]	1,078,900	1,336,500	1,633,500	1,910,600	831,700	9.3	77
FSU in Europe[e]	223,900	430,800	632,500	843,000	619,100	6.9	277
Rest of Europe	37,400	46,700	53,400	60,200	22,800	0.3	61
Israel[f]	6,665,600	6,878,950	7,092,300	7,092,300	426,700	4.8	6
FSU in Asia	15,300	25,700	37,100	50,500	35,200	0.4	230
Rest of Asia	18,800	23,400	27,700	31,500	12,700	0.1	68
Africa	72,000	81,700	88,900	97,100	25,100	0.3	35
Oceania	125,600	138,700	154,800	170,900	45,300	0.5	36

[a]Includes all persons who, when asked, identify themselves as Jews, or, if the respondent is a different person in the same household, are identified by him/her as Jews, and do not have another religion. Also includes persons with a Jewish parent who claim no current religious or ethnic identity

[b]Sum of (**a**) core Jewish population; (**b**) persons reported as partly Jewish; and (**c**) all others not currently Jewish with a Jewish parent

[c]Sum of (**a**) core Jewish population; (**b**) persons reported as partly Jewish; (**c**) all others not currently Jewish with a Jewish parent; and (**d**) all other non-Jewish household members (spouses, children, etc.)

[d]Sum of Jews, children of Jews, grandchildren of Jews, and all respective spouses, regardless of Jewish identification

[e]The Former Soviet Union Baltic republics (Estonia, Latvia, and Lithuania) are included in the European Union

[f]Includes Jewish residents of East Jerusalem, the West Bank, and the Golan Heights

estimate obtains of 20,876,400 (EJP). Finally, under the comprehensive three-generation and spouse provisions of Israel's *Law of Return*, the total Jewish and non-Jewish aliyah-eligible population can be roughly estimated at 23,674,400 (LRP). The US holds a significantly larger *Jewish parents population* (PJP) living in households with Jews or other persons with immediate Jewish background than Israel—roughly eight million compared to 6,878,950, respectively.

The results, though tentative, provide interesting indications about the total size and geographical distribution of the populations more or less closely attached to the core Jewish population. The global total of those who have a Jewish parent (PJP) (17,917,750), regardless of their own identification, stands 3,210,350 higher than the 14,707,400 core Jewish population. The total number of household members with at least one core Jew in the household (EJP) is estimated at an additional increment of 2,756,650. Finally, the total eligible for the Law of Return (LRP) is roughly estimated at 23,674,400, an additional increment of 2,798,000. All in all, the difference between the Law of Return population (LRP) and the core Jewish population (CJP) is 8,967,000. Of these roughly estimated nearly nine million partly Jewish, somewhat Jewish-connected, or otherwise included non-Jews, 73.7% live in North America, 9.3% in the EU, 7.3% in the FSU Republics in Europe and Asia, 4.8% in Israel, 3.8% in Latin America, and 1.1% in other countries.

The relative impact of the various population definitions linking the *core* Jewish population (CJP) and the Law of Return population (LRP) is quite different in the three main geographical divisions considered in Fig. 8.4. Since the impact of intermarriage is much lower in Israel than elsewhere, the extensions beyond the core in Israel are quite limited and primarily reflect immigration of intermarried households and, more recently, births in Israel from these households. In other communities outside the US and Israel, the graphic portrays the significant expansion of population aggregates around the CJP. One finally notes that with the emigration—mainly to Israel—of core Jews, the number of other people connected in some way to Judaism does not necessarily diminish across world Jewish communities. Indeed, their propensity to change country of residence may be lower than among core Jews, but they remain nonetheless as a more or less submerged component of the global Jewish population configuration. On the other hand, with the passing of time, as more core Jews pass because of aging,

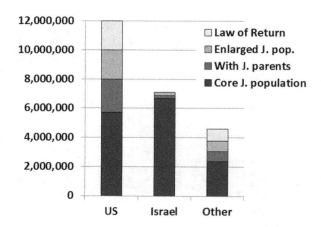

Fig. 8.4 Core and extended Jewish populations in the United States, Israel, and other countries, thousands, 2019

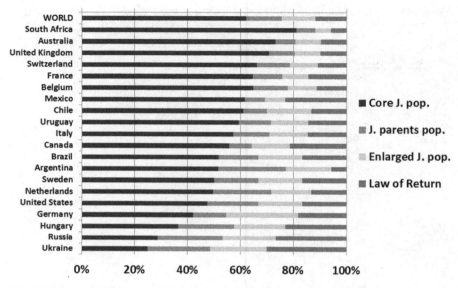

Fig. 8.5 World and 20 largest Diaspora Core, Jewish Parentage, Enlarged, and Law of Return Jewish populations, percentage distributions, 2019. (Source: Appendix Table)

and more of those directly related non-Jews pass too for the same reason, the more distant circles may eventually lose their linkage to the core collective.

Greater detail is provided in Fig. 8.5 on the respective weight of the different population components within the broader Law of Return population in each of the 20 largest Jewish populations worldwide. Countries where the core Jewish population constitutes a larger share relative to the Law of Return definition include South Africa, Australia, the UK, Switzerland, France, Belgium, Mexico, and Chile. Countries where the core constitutes the lowest share of the Law of Return definition include Ukraine, Russia, Hungary, Germany, the US, and the Netherlands.

8.3   Patterns of Jewish Population Distribution in Major Countries

8.3.1   Development and the Jewish Presence

Reflecting global Jewish population stagnation accompanied by an increasing concentration in a few countries, 84.1% of world Jews currently live in two countries, Israel and the US, and 96.4% are concentrated in the ten countries with the most Jews. Thus, the aggregate of just a few major Jewish population centers virtually determines the assessment of world Jewry's total size and trends.

In 2019, over 99% of world Jewry lived in the largest 25 Jewish communities, each evaluated at 10,000 or more. Excluding Israel, 98.4% of Diaspora Jewry lived in the 24 largest communities of the Diaspora, including 71% in the US (Table 8.4).

Table 8.4 25 Countries with core Jewish populations of 10,000 and more, 1/1/2019

Jewish population rank	Country	Core Jewish population	% of total Jewish population			
			In the world		In the diaspora	
			%	Cumulative%	%	Cumulative%
1	Israel[a]	6,665,600	45.3	45.3	[b]	[b]
2	United States	5,700,000	38.8	84.1	70.9	70.9
3	France	450,000	3.1	87.1	5.6	76.5
4	Canada	392,000	2.7	89.8	4.9	81.3
5	United Kingdom	292,000	2.0	91.8	3.6	85.0
6	Argentina	180,000	1.2	93.0	2.2	87.2
7	Russia	165,000	1.1	94.1	2.1	89.3
8	Germany	118,000	0.8	94.9	1.5	90.7
9	Australia	118,000	0.8	95.7	1.5	92.2
10	Brazil	92,600	0.6	96.4	1.2	93.4
11	South Africa	67,500	0.5	96.8	0.8	94.2
12	Ukraine	48,000	0.3	97.2	0.6	94.8
13	Hungary	47,300	0.3	97.5	0.6	95.4
14	Mexico	40,000	0.3	97.7	0.5	95.9
15	Netherlands	29,800	0.2	97.9	0.4	96.2
16	Belgium	29,100	0.2	98.1	0.4	96.6
17	Italy	27,400	0.2	98.3	0.3	97.0
18	Switzerland	18,500	0.1	98.5	0.2	97.2
19	Chile	18,300	0.1	98.6	0.2	97.4
20	Uruguay	16,600	0.1	98.7	0.2	97.6
21	Sweden	15,000	0.1	98.8	0.2	97.8
22	Turkey	14,800	0.1	98.9	0.2	98.0
23	Spain	11,700	0.1	99.0	0.1	98.1
24	Austria	10,000	0.1	99.0	0.1	98.3
25	Panama	10,000	0.1	99.1	0.1	98.4

[a]Includes Jewish residents of East Jerusalem, the West Bank, and the Golan Heights
[b]Not applicable

Besides the two major Jewish populations (Israel and the US), each comprising over five million persons, another seven countries each had more than 100,000 Jews. Of these, three were in Western Europe (France, the UK, and Germany); one in Eastern Europe (Russia); one in North America (Canada); one in South America (Argentina); and one in Oceania (Australia). The dominance of Western countries in global Jewish population distribution is a relatively recent phenomenon and reflects the West's relatively more hospitable socioeconomic and political circumstances *vis-á-vis* the Jewish presence.

The growth, or at least the slower decrease, of Jewish population in the more developed Western countries is accompanied by the persistence of a higher share of Jews among the total population. Indeed, the share of Jews in a country's total population tends to be directly related to the country's level of development (Table 8.5).

Table 8.5 25 largest core Jewish populations per 1000 country's total population and Human Development Indices

Jewish population rank	Country	2019 Core Jewish population	2019 Total population	Jews per 1000 total population	2017 HDI rank[a]
1	**Israel**[b]	**6,665,600**	**8,970,900**	**743.0**	**22**
2	**United States**	**5,700,000**	**328,000,000**	**17.4**	**13**
3	France	450,000	65,140,000	6.9	24
4	Canada	392,000	37,200,000	10.5	12
5	United Kingdom	292,000	66,600,000	4.4	14
6	Argentina	180,000	44,500,000	4.0	47
7	Russia	165,000	147,300,000	1.1	49
8	Germany	118,000	82,800,000	1.4	5
9	Australia	118,000	24,100,000	4.9	3
	Other 100,000 and over	**1,715,000**	**467,640,000**	**3.7**	**22**
10	Brazil	92,600	209,400,000	0.4	79
11	South Africa	67,500	57,700,000	1.2	113
12	Ukraine	48,000	42,300,000	1.1	88
13	Hungary	47,300	9,800,000	4.8	45
14	Mexico	40,000	130,800,000	0.3	74
15	Netherlands	29,800	17,200,000	1.7	10
16	Belgium	29,100	11,400,000	2.6	17
17	Italy	27,400	60,600,000	0.5	28
18	Switzerland	18,500	8,500,000	2.2	2
19	Chile	18,300	18,600,000	1.0	44
20	Uruguay	16,600	3,500,000	4.7	55
21	Sweden	15,000	10,200,000	1.5	7
22	Turkey	14,800	81,300,000	0.2	64
23	Spain	11,700	46,700,000	0.3	26
24	Austria	10,000	8,800,000	1.1	20
25	Panama	10,000	4,200,000	2.4	66
	Other 10,000 & over	**496,600**	**721,000,000**	**0.7**	**46**
	Rest of the world[c]	**130,200**	**6,094,886,100**	**0.0**	**> 100**

[a]*HDI* The Human Development Index, a synthetic measure of health, education and income (measured as US dollar purchase power parity) among the country's total population. See: United Nations Development Programme (2018)

[b]Total Jewish population of Israel includes the Jewish residents of East Jerusalem, the West Bank, and the Golan Heights. Total population includes all residents of Israel, including East Jerusalem and the Golan Heights, but only the Jewish residents and non-Jewish members of Jewish households of the West Bank

[c]Average HDI rank for group of countries

Regarding *core* Jewish populations in 2019, the share of Jews out of the total population was 743.0 per 1000 in Israel (including Jews in East Jerusalem, the West Bank, and the Golan Heights, but excluding Palestinians in the West Bank and Gaza). Israel's population high rate of Jewishness obviously reflects its special positioning in Jewish identity perceptions, but Israel also has become a developed country, and, as such, attractive to prospective migrants. In the US, the *core* Jewish population represented 17.4 per 1000 of total population; Jews comprised 3.7 per 1000 total population on average in the other seven countries with over 100,000 Jews; 0.6 per 1000 on average in the other 16 countries with 10,000 or more Jews; and virtually nil in the remaining countries which comprise the overwhelming majority (80%) of world population.

To further illustrate the increasing convergence between the Jewish presence and the level of socioeconomic development of a country, Table 8.5 reports the latest available Human Development Index (HDI) for each country (United Nations Development Programme 2018). The HDI—a composite measure of a society's level of education, health, and income—provides a general sense of the context in which Jewish communities operate, although it does not necessarily reflect the actual characteristics of the members of those Jewish communities. The latest available HDI country ranks reported in the table are for 2017. Of the 25 countries listed, five are included among the top ten HDIs among 189 countries ranked (Switzerland, Australia, Germany, Sweden, and the Netherlands). Another seven countries are ranked 11th to 25th (Canada, the US, the UK, Belgium, Austria, Israel, and France), six more are between 26th and 50th (Italy, Spain, Chile, Hungary, Argentina, and Russia), six are between 51st and 100th (Uruguay, Turkey, Panama, Mexico, Brazil, and Ukraine), and one (South Africa) occupies a lower rank (113th), pointing to lesser development in the host society. Remarkably, all of the 9 largest Jewish populations, amounting together to 95.7% of world Jewry, live in countries whose HDI ranks among the top 50.

Figure 8.6 demonstrates the relationship that prevails between Jewish population size and the respective countries' human development. The horizontal axis shows the average HDI ranks of world countries regrouped by Jewish population size (as in Table 8.5). The vertical axis indicates the total Jewish population of the same groups of countries. A country's level of development stimulates conditions promoting more than proportionally the size of the local Jewish population. The statistical relationship between the Index of Human Development and the total number of Jews by type of countries is extraordinarily powerful, as indicated by an explained variance of over 85% when including Israel, and over 90% when excluding Israel. The loss of explanatory power following Israel's inclusion means that the strong Jewish presence in Israel cannot be exclusively explained by the environmental circumstances of high development, and obviously draws on deeper historical, cultural, and religious determinants. But in the rest of the world (the Diaspora) the relationship between Human Development and Jewish presence certainly works. As a caveat, it is worth repeating that Jewish communities may display social and economic profiles significantly better than the average population of their respective countries. Nonetheless the general societal context does affect the quality of life of

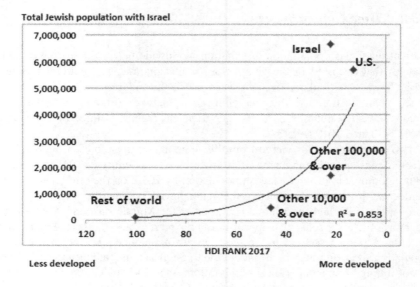

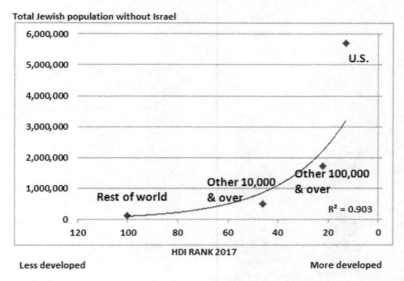

Fig. 8.6 Major groups of countries by Human Development Index (HDI) and total core Jewish population, 2019

each individual, Jews included, everywhere. Changes in the quality of life at the country level foreshadow changes in Jewish population distribution worldwide. Interestingly, the two countries with the largest Jewish populations, the US (ranked 13th in 2017) and Israel (22th) both lost three positions in the HDI ranking versus the previous year. Such fluctuations in development ranking should be monitored carefully as they may critically affect world Jewish population distribution.

8.3.2 Time Comparisons

The current Jewish population distribution worldwide has resulted from dramatic changes that occurred in the geographic, socioeconomic, and cultural profile of world Jewry—particularly over the years since the independence of the state of Israel. As an illustration of the intervening changes, we report the world distribution of core Jewish population by major geographical regions at three points in time: 1948, 1980, and 2019 (Fig. 8.7).

Two opposing trends emerge from this temporal comparison: on the one hand, Israel's Jewish population increased from being a small entity in 1948 to being the central component of world Jewish population by 2019; on the other hand, we see the decline, if not disappearance of the major Jewish population centers in Eastern Europe, the FSU, and the Islamic countries of the Middle East and North Africa. Declines of a lesser scale also appear in Latin America and Southern Africa. North America, and to a lesser extent Western Europe, maintained relatively stable Jewish population sizes, although in the latter case through a significant turnaround of periods of immigration and periods of emigration. As already noted, the tendency over time was much greater consolidation of world Jewry in the two major centers in the US (here with Canada) and Israel, versus a much more dispersed Jewish population worldwide shortly after the end of World War II.

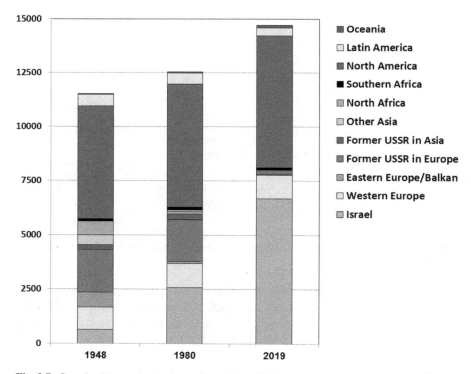

Fig. 8.7 Core Jewish populations by major regions, 1948, 1980, 2019, thousands

A more detailed picture of the changes intervening between 1980 and 2019 is illustrated in Table 8.6. Here we compare the numbers and ranks for the 25 countries with a Jewish population of at least 28,000 Jews in 1980—based on revised estimates and using the list of countries extant upon the breakup of the former Soviet Union, the former Yugoslavia, and the former Czechoslovakia. Striking changes occurred in the population sizes and rankings during the 39 years from 1980 to 2019. Quantitatively, the most remarkable was Israel's Jewish population more than doubling from 3,282,700 to 6,665,600 (103.1%). The greatest percentage growth occurred in Germany (+242.0%). Absolute population increases were recorded in Australia (+68.6%), Canada (+27.3%), and Mexico (+14.3%). The US core Jewish population remained about the same (+0.2%). The other 19 countries witnessed Jewish population reduction, with six countries losing more than 90% of their 1980 population (the five former Soviet republics of Moldova, Uzbekistan, Georgia, Belarus, and Ukraine, and Ethiopia). An entirely different ranking of major

Table 8.6 Largest core Jewish populations as of 1980, and in 2019

Country[a]	1980	Rank	2019	Rank	% Change	Rank diff.
United States	5,690,000	1	5,700,000	2	**0.2**	−1
Israel	3,282,700	2	6,665,600	1	**103.1**	1
Russia	713,400	3	165,000	7	−76.9	−4
Ukraine	634,400	4	48,000	12	−92.4	−8
France	535,000	5	450,000	3	−15.9	2
United Kingdom	390,000	6	292,000	5	−25.1	1
Canada	308,000	7	392,000	4	**27.3**	3
Argentina	242,000	8	180,000	6	−25.6	2
Belarus	135,500	9	9000	25	−93.4	−16
Brazil	110,000	10	92,600	10	−15.8	=
South Africa	108,000	11	67,500	11	−37.5	=
Uzbekistan	100,100	12	3000	37	−97.0	−26
Moldova	80,200	13	1900	44	−97.6	−31
Australia	70,000	14	118,000	9	**68.6**	5
Hungary	65,000	15	47,300	13	−27.2	2
Azerbaijan	44,300	16	7500	29	−83.1	−13
Uruguay	40,000	17	16,600	17	−58.5	=
Mexico	35,000	18	40,000	14	**14.3**	4
Germany	34,500	19	118,000	8	**242.0**	11
Belgium	33,000	20	29,100	15	−11.8	5
Romania	33,000	21	9000	26	−72.7	−5
Italy	32,000	22	27,400	16	−14.4	6
Iran	32,000	23	8300	28	−74.1	−5
Ethiopia	32,000	24	100	78	−99.7	−54
Georgia	28,300	25	1500	51	−94.7	−26

[a]Ranked as of 1980. In bold Jewish population that increased in absolute size. The following countries had Jewish populations among the 25 largest in 2019, but not in 1980: the Netherlands, Switzerland, Turkey, Sweden, Chile, Spain, Austria, and Panama

communities consequently emerged. The top five in 1980 were the US, Israel, Russia, Ukraine, and France; in 2019 they had become Israel, US, France, Canada, and the United Kingdom.

The geographical realignment of the world Jewish population reflects both their past sufferance from political discrimination and persecution, as well as socioeconomic development lags and lack of democracy in the various countries that lost Jewish population. The consequent mass migration from those countries, mostly in Eastern Europe, Asia, and Africa, generated large Jewish population declines. On the other hand, countries that offered a wider range of opportunities and greater freedom witnessed steady Jewish population growth or at least stability.

8.3.3   Dispersion and Concentration

In 2019, 98 countries had at least 100 Jews (Table 8.7). Two countries had Jewish populations of over five million each (Israel and the US), another 7 had more than 100,000 Jews, 2 had 50,000–99,999, 6 had 25,000–49,999, 8 had 10,000–24,999, 9 had 5000–9999, 25 had 1000–4999, and 39 had less than 1000. The 73 communities each with less than 10,000 Jews together accounted for less than 1% of world Jewry.

In only four Diaspora countries did Jews constitute at least 5 per 1000 (0.5%) of the total population. In descending order by the relative share (not size) of their Jewish population, they were Gibraltar (20.0 Jews per 1000 inhabitants), the US (17.4), Canada (10.5), and France (6.9). The case of Israel is very different, with a *core* Jewish population that represents 74.3% of the total legal population, and an *enlarged* Jewish population that represents 79.1% of the total population. In both Israel and the Diaspora, the percentage of Jews out of the total population is decreasing.

By combining the two criteria of Jewish population size and percentage of Jews, we obtain the following taxonomy of the 24 countries with Jewish populations over 10,000 (excluding Israel). Three countries have over 100,000 Jews and at least 5 Jews per 1000 total population: the US, Canada, and France. Five more countries have over 100,000 Jews and at least 1 Jew per 1000 total population: Australia, the UK, the Russian Federation, Argentina, and Germany. Eleven more countries have 10,000 to 99,999 Jews and at least 1 Jew per 1000 total population: Ukraine, South Africa, Hungary, Belgium, the Netherlands, Switzerland, Chile, Uruguay, Sweden, Austria, and Panama. Five countries have 10,000 to 99,999 Jews and less than 1 Jew per 1000 total population: Brazil, Mexico, Italy, Turkey, and Spain.

Over the past decades, the basic typology of size-and-density of Jewish communities throughout the world did not change as much as the underlying changes witnessed by individual countries. Table 8.8 shows the configuration of Jewish populations in 2019 as compared to 1984, the first year for which such tabulation is available (Schmelz and DellaPergola 1986). The 1984 data are reported here unrevised and in the original format of the countries and territories that existed then.

Table 8.7 World core Jewish population distribution, by number and proportion per 1000 total population, 1/1/2019

Number of core Jews in country	Jews per 1000 total population					
	Total	Less than 1.0	1.0–4.9	5.0–9.9	10.0–19.9	20.0+
Number of countries						
Total[a]	98	70	23	1	3	1
100–999	39	35	3	–	1	–
1000–4999	25	24	1	–	–	–
5000–9999	9	6	3	–	–	–
10,000–24,999	8	2	6	–	–	–
25,000–49,999	6	2	4	–	–	–
50,000–99,999	2	1	1	–	–	–
100,000–999,999	7	–	5	1	1	–
1000,000 or more	2	–	–	–	1	1
Jewish population distribution (number of core Jews)						
Total[b]	14,707,400	293,800	1,204,600	450,000	6,092,700	6,665,600
100–999	10,500	8700	1100	–	700	–
1000–4999	54,900	53,000	1900	–	–	–
5000–9999	64,100	45,600	18,500	–	–	–
10,000–24,999	114,900	26,500	88,400		–	–
25,000–49,999	221,600	67,400	154,200	–	–	–
50,000–99,999	160,100	92,600	67,500	–	–	–
100,000–999,999	1,715,000	–	873,000	450,000	392,000	–
1000,000 or more	12,365,600	–	–	–	5,700,000	6,665,600
Jewish population distribution (percent of world core Jewish population)						
Total[b]	100.0	2.0	8.2	3.1	41.4	45.3
100–999	0.1	0.1	0.0	–	0.0	–
1000–4999	0.4	0.4	0.0	–	–	–
5000-9999	0.4	0.3	0.1	–	–	–
10,000–24,999	0.8	0.2	0.6	–	–	–
25,000–49,999	1.5	0.5	1.0	–	–	–
50,000–99,999	1.1	0.6	0.5	–	–	–
100,000–999,999	11.7	–	5.9	3.1	2.7	–
1000,000 or more	84.1	–	–	–	38.8	45.3

[a]Not including countries with fewer than 100 core Jews
[b]Grand total includes countries with fewer than 100 core Jews, for a total of 700 core Jews. Minor discrepancies due to rounding. Israel includes Jewish residents of East Jerusalem, the West Bank, and the Golan Heights

Table 8.8 World core Jewish population distribution, by number of Jews in country, 1984 and 2019

Number of Jews in country	N. of countries		Jewish population		% of world's Jews	
	1984	2019	1984	2019	1984	2019
Total[a]	**74**	**98**	**12,963,300**	**14,707,400**	**100.0**	**100.0**
100–999	23	39	11,000	10,500	0.1	0.1
1000–4999	17	25	41,900	54,900	0.3	0.4
5000–9999	7	9	43,800	55,100	0.3	0.4
10,000–49,999	16	14	362,400	345,500	2.8	2.3
50,000–99,999	2	2	136,500	160,100	1.1	1.1
100,000–999,999	6	7	1,616,000	1,715,000	12.4	11.7
1000,000-4999,999	2	0	5,046,700	0	38.8	0.0
5000,000 or more	1	2	5,705,000	12,365,600	43.9	84.1

[a]Number of countries not including countries with fewer than 100 core Jews. Population and percent figures including countries with fewer than 100 core Jews, for a total of 700
Sources: Schmelz and DellaPergola (1986); Table 8.7 above

The number of countries with at least 100 Jews indeed increased from 74 to 98, following the devolution of the USSR, Yugoslavia, Czechoslovakia, and the addition of several countries with very small Jewish communities that reached the 100-person threshold. The greatest increase was in the number of countries with less than 1000 Jews, from 23 in 1984 to 39 in 2019. At the top of the distribution, two countries in 2019 had more than five million Jews, versus one only in 1984, when two countries had between one and five million Jews: Israel and the USSR. In the meantime, Israel grew and the USSR split into 15 states and lost most of its Jews through emigration.

Countries with between 100,000 and one million Jews comprised 12.5% of total Jewish population in 1984 versus 11.7% in 2019. Of the 15 republics of the FSU, only Russia had more than 100,000 in 2019 when it was joined by two new entries: Germany and Australia. Brazil and South Africa had more than 100,000 Jews in 1984, but fewer in 2019. France, Canada, the UK, and Argentina were included in the 100,000 and over category for both dates, but the gap between Canada and Argentina had more than trebled, from 65,000 to 212,000.

Communities between 10,000 and 100,000 comprised 3.9% of world Jewish population in 18 countries in 1984, versus 3.4% in 16 countries, respectively, in 2019. Among the smaller Jewish communities, those with less than 10,000 Jews comprised at both dates less than 1% of world Jewry, but in 1984 they were distributed across 47 countries and in 2019 across 73 countries. The apparent stability reflected a strong concentration of Jewish population in a few countries at the top of the distribution and a wide dispersion of very small numbers in a large number of countries at the bottom. The transition from a concentration of Jews in one dominant and two secondary centers, to a configuration based on two main centers reflected the quite revolutionary changes undertaken by world Jewry passing from the 20th to the twenty-first century.

8.4   Jewish Population in Major Individual Countries

We turn now to a concise review of the information available and the criteria followed in updating the figures for the largest Jewish populations worldwide. The countries are listed in decreasing order of magnitude of the respective Jewish communities. Given the gradual and slow motion of demographic change, besides a few exceptions, we shall not repeat here the detailed descriptions of sources and patterns that appeared in previous volumes of the *American Jewish Year Book* and refer the reader to those previous volumes.

8.4.1   Israel

Since the end of the first decade of the twenty-first century, Israel is the country with the largest core Jewish population worldwide. It is also the only one displaying a substantial rate of population growth—1.70% in 2018. With a Total Fertility Rate (TFR) of 3.17 children currently born per Jewish woman in 2018, and a relatively young age composition (27% under age 15 and only 13% age 65 and over), the Jewish population in Israel is the one worldwide displaying the highest fertility— largely above generational replacement and currently generating a share of children among the total Jewish population twice that of the elderly. Israel's current Jewish fertility rate is higher than the fertility for the total population of any other developed country and twice or more the current average of *Jewish* children among women in most Diaspora Jewish communities (sometimes called the *effective Jewish fertility rate*). This reflects not only the large family size of the more religious Jewish population component, but also a diffused and persistent desire for children among the moderately traditional and secular, especially among the upwardly mobile (DellaPergola 2009c, d, 2015b). A moderately positive international migration balance also helps to keep Israel's Jewish population increasing. Information on religion is mandatory in official population data regularly collected by the Israel Central Bureau of Statistics (CBS) and in the permanent Population Register maintained by the Ministry of Internal Affairs (Israel Population and Migration Authority). Annual data derive from periodic censuses and detailed accountancy of intervening events (births, deaths, entering the country including immigrants, exiting the country including emigrants, and conversions). In the case of Jews and Judaism, the defining concept is a combination of religion and ethnicity according to rabbinic law (*Halakhah*). At the beginning of 2019, Israel's *core* Jewish population reached 6,665,600, as against a revised total of 6,554,500 in 2017, excluding people who had been missing from the country for 1 year or more. A downward adjustment of −3600 compared to the 2018 estimate reflects late entries and adjustments of demographic events, including conversions and other revisions of personal status. The revised core population combined with the addition of 426,700 "Others"—non-Jewish members of households who immigrated under the

Law of Return or their Israel-born children—formed an *enlarged* Jewish population of 7,092,300 in 2019, of which these "Others" constituted 6.0% (Israel Central Bureau of Statistics). We assume about half of the members of Jewish households who are not recognized as Jewish by the Rabbinate have one Jewish parent. The *Jewish parent* population of Israel is thus estimated at 6,878,950. For the past several years, the main component of Jewish population growth in Israel has been the natural increase resulting from an excess of births over deaths. In 2018, 134,470 Jewish births and 37,744 Jewish deaths produced a net natural increase of 96,726 Jews. This represented 87% of Israel Jews' total growth in 2018. Figure 8.8 demonstrates the changes in birth rates and death rates for Jews and Muslims in Israel between 1980 and 2019. The two birth rate lines in a sense mirror each other, with increases in one population matched by decreases in the other one and vice versa. A major adjustment toward lower natality occurred among Israel's Muslims since the end of the 1990s, accompanied by some increase among Jews. Besides different fertility levels, this largely reflected differences and changes in age compositions and age at marriage of the respective populations (Staetsky 2019). Death rates tended to be low and decreasing among both populations, but they were constantly lower among Muslims due to their much younger age composition. Furthermore, in 2018, the overall birthrate of Jews and Others was 20.1 per 1000 population, versus 23.3 per 1000 for all Arabs including Muslims, Christians, and Druze. These differences significantly affected the respective rates of natural increase with the consequence that in 2018 Muslim population growth continued to be significantly higher than that of Jews, and the share of Arabs among total Israelis continued to increase.

At the time of this writing, the final data on all components of population change for 2018 were not yet released. In 2017, 18,400 Jewish new immigrants and immigrant citizens (Israeli citizens born abroad who entered the country for the first time) arrived in Israel, out of a total of 30,700 immigrants including immigrant citizens (meaning 12,300 were not recorded as Jewish). The net balance of Jewish migrants, minus the balance of Jewish Israelis leaving the country and returning to the country

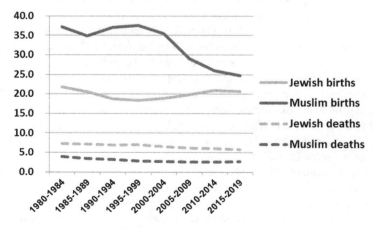

Fig. 8.8 Births and deaths per 1000 population among Jews and Muslims in Israel, 1980–2019

after a prolonged stay abroad was 13,700. Therefore, an estimated 4700 Jews (18,400 − 13,700) plus another 2200 "Others" joined the pool of those who reside abroad permanently or in the long term. These data about Israel's international migration balance point to a steady if moderate level of immigration in comparison to other historical periods, but also to quite low levels of emigration in historical perspective. In 2018, the total number of new immigrants—'olim hadashim, not including immigrant citizens—increased slightly to 28,118 from 26,333 the previous year. The number of converts to Judaism remained only a tiny percentage of the non-Jewish members of Jewish households in Israel, especially among recent immigrants (Fisher 2013, 2015, 2019; Waxman 2013; Nissim 2018). In 2017, the net balance of conversions to and from Judaism was negative: −2000 (Israel Central Bureau of Statistics), probably due to revisions in the personal status of some past converts, following stricter rules pursued by Israel's Central Rabbinate. The conversions balance was 500 for Israeli Muslims, and 600 for Christians. Some increase in religious intermarriage existed in Israel, but the levels of ethnoreligious interaction were overall quite low (DellaPergola 2017d).

Turning now to the territorial aggregate of the State of Israel and of the Palestinian Territory (West Bank and Gaza—WBG), Table 8.9 reports the numbers of Jews, Others (i.e., non-Jewish persons who are members of Jewish households *and* Israeli citizens by the provisions of the Law of Return), Arabs, as well as foreign workers, undocumented tourists, and refugees. Each group's total is shown for different territorial divisions: the State of Israel within the pre-1967 borders, East Jerusalem, the Golan Heights, the West Bank, and Gaza. The percentage of Jews (by the *Law of Return* definition) in each division is also shown. At the beginning of 2019, of a total 6,665,600 *core* Jews, 6,001,700 lived within Israel's pre-1967 borders; 221,800 lived in neighborhoods of East Jerusalem incorporated after 1967; 23,200 on the Golan Heights; and 418,900 lived in the West Bank. Over the years, the pace of Jewish internal migration from Israel's main portion to the West Bank was significantly correlated with levels of unemployment and emigration from Israel (DellaPergola 2019b).

In 2019 *core* Jews represented 74.6% of Israel's total *legal* population of 8,970,900, inclusive of 1,878,600 Arabs and others, but excluding 231,000 foreign workers, undocumented tourists and refugees (Israel Central Bureau of Statistics, Israel Statistical Monthly). In 2018 (the last year with accessible records), the latter group comprised 88,171 legal foreign workers, 18,059 undocumented foreign workers, 74,000 tourists whose visas had expired, 14,778 refuge seekers, and 37,288 illegal entrants (Israel Population and Migration Authority 2019). Israel's *Law of Return* Jewish population of 7,092,300 in 2019 represented 79.1% of the State's total legal population. Israel's Arab population, including East Jerusalem and the Golan Heights, comprised 20.9% of the total legal population. As shown in Table 8.9, the *Law of Return* Jewish population represented 78.7% of total residents within pre-1967 borders (including foreign workers and refugees), 39.6% in East Jerusalem, 47.7% in the Golan Heights, and 14.1% of the West Bank's total population. Since 2005, no Jewish population remains in Gaza.

Table 8.9 Core and enlarged Jewish population, Arab population, foreign workers and refugees in Israel and Palestinian Territory by territorial divisions, 1/1/2019[a]

Area	Core Jewish Population	Others	Core Jewish and others[b]	Arab population and others	Foreign workers and refugees[c]	Total	Percent of Jews and others[d]
	1	2	3	4	5	6	7
Grand total	**6,665,600**	**426,700**	**7,092,300**	**6,361,000**	**231,000**	**13,684,300**	**51.8**
State of Israel[e]	*6,665,600*	*426,700*	*7,092,300*	*1,878,600*	*231,000*	*9,201,900*	*77.1*
Thereof:							
Pre-1967 borders	6,001,700	408,100	6,409,800	1,501,300	231,000	**8,142,100**	78.7
East Jerusalem[f]	221,800	8500	230,300	350,600	–	**580,900**	39.6
Golan Heights	23,200	1200	24,400	26,700	–	**51,100**	47.7
West Bank	418,900	8900	427,800	[g]	–	**427,800**	14.1[h]
Palestinian Territory				*4,482,400*		*4,482,400*	*–*
West Bank	[i]	[i]	[i]	2,595,900	–	**2,595,900**	–
Gaza	0	0	0	1,886,500	–	**1,886,500**	0.0

Source: Israel Central Bureau of Statistics; Israel Population and Migration Authority; PCBS Palestine Central Bureau of Statistics; United Nations Population Fund; and author's estimates
[a]Rounded figures
[b]Enlarged Jewish population
[c]All foreign workers, undocumented residents and refugees were allocated to Israel within pre-1967 borders. Source: Israel Population and Migration Authority (2019)
[d]Column 3 divided by column 6
[e]As defined by Israel's legal system
[f]Estimated from Jerusalem Institute of Israel Studies (2019)
[g]Included under Palestinian Territory
[h]Percent of Jews and others out of total population in the West Bank under Israeli or Palestinian Authority jurisdiction
[i]Included under State of Israel

Regarding the Palestinian population in WBG, in November 2017 the Palestinian Central Bureau of Statistics (PCBS) undertook a new Census which enumerated 4,705,600 persons, of whom 1,875,300 live in Gaza and 2,830,300 in the West Bank—including 281,200 in East Jerusalem. The Census results were about 250,000 lower than the estimated projection of 4,952,168 available from by the Palestinian Central Bureau of Statistics' web site (PCBS 2018). The PCBS Jerusalem's population estimate clearly was an undercount because of their limited access to the city (PCBS 2008, 2009a, b, 2018). This would imply an annual growth rate of 1.84% since 2007 in the West Bank (not including East Jerusalem) and 2.84% in Gaza—as against 2.40% for Muslims in Israel (including East Jerusalem) during the same period (Israel Central Bureau of Statistics). These growth rates were much lower than in the past and pointed to significant differentiation within the Arab/Palestine population. Recall that the total rate of growth of Israeli Jews was 1.70% in 2018 with immigration, and 1.47% without immigration. The Palestinian population's growth rate in WBG was decreasing as well due to net emigration. According to Israel's IDF Civilian Administration in Judea and Samaria (2018), the total of Palestinians recorded in the West Bank population register approached three million, but this figure did not discount sufficiently for Palestinian residents permanently living abroad. Keeping in mind the data in Fig. 8.8, among the Arab population both birth rates and death rates probably continued to be somewhat higher in the Palestinian Territory than in Israel, and significantly higher than among the Jewish population. There was a minor internal migration flow from Gaza to the West Bank, estimated at 2671 persons as of mid-2019 (Hass 2019). In the process, most Christian Palestinians had left Gaza because they felt persecuted there. Our adjusted population estimates for WGB at the beginning of 2019 is 4,482,400, of whom 2,595,900 live in the West Bank and 1,886,500 in Gaza. These figures (always excluding East Jerusalem) are lower than the Palestinian census because they discount for persons, students and others, who actually resided abroad for more than 1 year. Other much lower estimates of WBG population (e.g. Zimmerman et al. 2005a, b; Feitelson 2013) rather than ascertained demographic criteria reflect a political stance and should be dismissed (see also Miller 2015). The Arab population of East Jerusalem, which we have included in Israel's population count, was assessed at 350,600 at the beginning of 2019, and constituted 38.1% of Jerusalem's total population of 920,000 (Israel Central Bureau of Statistics, Choshen et al. 2010, 2012, Jerusalem Institute of Israel Studies 2015, Jerusalem Institute for Policy Research 2016, DellaPergola 2008b). By summing the 1,878,600 Arab population of Israel, including East Jerusalem, and the 4,482,400 estimated Palestinians in WBG, a total of 6,361,000 Arabs/Palestinians obtains for the whole territory between the Mediterranean Sea and the Jordan River, versus a total enlarged Jewish population of 7,092,300. Table 8.10 reports the percentage of Jews according to the *core* and *Law of Return*

Table 8.10 Percent of core and Law of Return Jewish population in Israel and Palestinian Territory, according to different territorial definitions, 1/1/2019

Area	Percentage of Jews[a] by definition	
	Core	Law of return
Grand total of Israel and Palestinian Territory	**48.7**	**51.8**
Minus foreign workers and refugees	49.5	52.7
Minus Gaza	57.6	61.3
Minus Golan Heights	57.8	61.5
Minus West Bank	74.5	79.3
Minus East Jerusalem	77.6	82.5

Source: Table 8.9
[a]Total Jewish population of Israel, including East Jerusalem, the West Bank, and the Golan Heights. In each row, Arabs and others of mentioned area are deducted and the percentages are recalculated accordingly

definitions, out of the total population of the combined territory of Israel and Palestine. Such percent is conditional upon two factors: the definition of who is a Jew, and the territorial boundaries chosen for assessment. Relative to this territorial grand total, we demonstrate the potential effect on the existence and size of a Jewish population majority when gradually and cumulatively subtracting from the initial maximum possible extent the Arab/Palestinian population of designated areas as well as the foreign workers and refugees. The result is gradual growth of the potential Jewish share of total population, along with hypothesized diminishing territorial and total population extents.

A total combined Jewish, Arab, and other population of 13,684,300, including foreign workers, undocumented tourists and refugees, lived in Israel and the Palestinian Territory (WBG) at the beginning of 2019. The *core* Jewish population of 6,665,600 represented 48.7% of this total between the Mediterranean Sea and the Jordan River, of which the State of Israel is part and parcel. Thus, by a rabbinic definition of who is a Jew, the extant Jewish majority not only is constantly decreasing but actually does not exist any longer among the broader aggregate of people currently found over the whole territory between the Sea and the River (DellaPergola 2003a, b, 2007a, 2011a; Soffer and Bistrow 2004; Soffer 2015). If the 426,700 Others (non-Jewish members of Jewish households) are added to the *core* Jewish population, the *Law of Return* Jewish population of 7,092,300 represented 51.8% of the total population in Israel and the Palestinian Territory—a tiny majority. If we subtract from the grand total, the 231,000 foreign workers, undocumented tourists and refugees, the *core* and *enlarged* Jewish populations rise to, respectively, 49.5% and 52.7% of the total population legally resident in Israel and the Palestinian Territory estimated at 13,453,300 in 2019. After subtracting the population of Gaza, the percentages of Jews out of total rise to 57.6% (core) and 61.3% (Law of Return); if subtracting the Druze population of the Golan Heights the Jewish percentages become 57.8% and 61.5%, respectively; if subtracting the Palestinian population of the West Bank, they become 74.5% and 79.3%, respectively; and if also subtracting the Arab population of East Jerusalem the percentages rise to 77.6% and 82.5%. Interestingly, the proponents of much lower Palestinian population estimates argue that the percent Jewish (Law of Return) out of the total population of Israel and West Bank combined is 65% (Ettinger 2019), versus our estimated 61.5%. A spirited and aggressive polemics has been going on for several years about a modest 3.5% difference. The reality is that under current demographic trends, the rate of erosion of the Jewish majority is about 0.1% per year. The same data are graphically presented in Fig. 8.9.

8.4.2 The United States

In the US, in the absence of official census documentation, Jewish population estimates must rely on alternative sources. These are now quite abundant, though of very unequal quality (Goldstein 1981, 1989, 1992; Sheskin 2015a). To assess the current number of Jews in the US one should consider three issues: (1) The need to

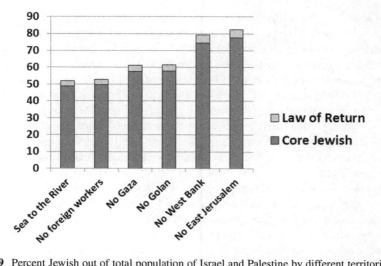

Fig. 8.9 Percent Jewish out of total population of Israel and Palestine by different territorial and Jewish population definitions, 2019

rely on reasoning and empirical evidence grounded in *demographic concepts and research techniques* (discussed above and elsewhere in greater detail, see DellaPergola 2005, 2010a, 2011a, 2013, 2014a, c, d, e); (2) The definitional predicament already discussed above. To perform comparisons over time constant *definition* assumptions are needed. Given ongoing acculturation and assimilation trends in America, but also new meanings attributed to Jewish identity or the rediscovery of submerged identities from the past, group definitions today often may not be the same as past ones; (3) The broader *narratives* within which one seeks to place the findings and their interpretations (Kaufman 2014). Intriguingly, competing narratives and non-comparable empirical and definitional approaches stand behind diverging US Jewish population estimates, with a high-low gap of nearly two million individuals. Opposite interpretations circulate of current and expected trends: rapid growth, stability, or slow decline. Previous to and following the 2013 Pew survey of Jewish Americans, intense debate in and outside the social scientific community entails very different implications at the cognitive level and for Jewish community service planning, matched by a lively media discussion (Heilman 2005, 2013; Pew Research Center 2013; The Jewish Daily Forward 2014). The unescapable underlying condition—hardly acknowledged in professional let alone publicist debate—is the end of a clear dichotomy between Jews and non-Jews in the US (DellaPergola 2015b).

The quest for US Jewish population estimates relies on three major strategies (DellaPergola 2013a). The **first** is to bridge across numerous different national Jewish population estimates available over the years by assessing intervening demographic changes: births and deaths, incoming and outgoing international migration, and identification changes such as accessions to and secessions from identifying as Jewish. In the US, several major data sources allow for a detailed reconstruction of nationwide Jewish population trends since the end of World War II to date. For all purposes, the logic of working nationally to obtain a *national* population estimate is the same logic that explains why, since 1790, a national population census (and not a compilation of local statistics) was held in the US (US Bureau of the Census). The **second** strategy, pursued since the beginnings of US Jewish population studies in the early 1940s (Linfield 1942; Robison 1943), is to construct a national total from a compilation of existing local Jewish population estimates (Sheskin and Dashefsky in this volume). The **third** more recent strategy is to construct a national total through a meta-analysis of a pool of national and local surveys periodically undertaken by public and private bodies, each of which include a small subsample of Jews (Saxe and Tighe 2013). Of the three alternatives, only the first was designed to determine nationwide Jewish population estimates. The second and third methodologies were not, but they do provide valuable grounds for comparative analytic work and in-depth multivariate analysis (Hartman and Sheskin 2012).

Serious attempts to monitor Jewish population size over time at the national level require a reliable baseline figure and updates based on solid empirical research. Each of the existing sources is imperfect, but they do amount to an impressive body of evidence: from historical assessment (Rosenwaike 1980), through the US Census of Religious Bodies (Schwartz et al. 2002), the 1957 Current Population Survey (CPS) (US Census Bureau 1958, 1968; Glick 1960; Goldstein 1969), the 1971 National Jewish Population Study—NJPS 1971 (Massarik 1974; Lazerwitz 1978), the 1990 National Jewish Population Survey—NJPS 1990 (Kosmin et al. 1991), NJPS 2000–2001 (Kotler-Berkowitz et al. 2003) and the American Jewish Identity Survey (AJIS) (Mayer et al. 2001). These various data sets fit well one with another when performing forward-backward Jewish population projections as well as checking with all available data on international migration, age composition, marriage, fertility, survivorship at different ages, and conversions to and from Judaism (Schmelz and DellaPergola 1983, 1988; DellaPergola et al. 1999, 2000a, b; DellaPergola 2005, 2013a; Perlmann 2007). NJPS 2000–2001 yielded an initial estimate of 5200,000 after imputation of persons in homes for the elderly, prisons, military bases, and other institutional settings (Kotler-Berkowitz et al. 2003). Further cohort analysis and projections unveiled under-coverage of over 250,000 individuals born between 1950 and 1970 (Saxe et al. 2006a, 2007; Tighe et al. 2009a, 2011). Evaluation of current migration, fertility, mortality, accessions, and secessions provided revised estimates of 5,367,000 for 2000–2001, and 5,425,000 for 2013—not including the institutionalized (DellaPergola 2013a). A rounded core Jewish population estimate could thus be placed at 5.6–5.7 million around 2010, and this indeed was the estimate suggested by a 2007 Pew survey (Pew Forum on Religion and Public Life 2008; Rebhun 2016). The 2015 Pew study of the US religious landscape confirmed the same orders of magnitude with a slightly higher percent of Jews among the total US adult population (1.9% vs. 1.8%), well within the margins of sampling error (Pew Research Center 2015b). The 2013 Pew *A Portrait of Jewish Americans* (Pew Research Center 2013) found 4.2 million adults and 900,000 children, for a total of 5.1 million Americans with *Jewish religion* (Jews by religion or JBRs) without other religious identities. Another 600,000 persons—500,000 adults and 100,000 children—reported *no religion and Jewish* ("Jews, no religion" or JNRs) without another identity, raising the total to a 5.7 million mutually exclusive Jewish population. This 5.7 million estimate more or less corresponded to a *core* Jewish population concept relying on self-assessment and mutual exclusiveness between religious or ethno-religious populations, and as noted, was fully consistent with the whole body of research on US Jewry since 1957.

As against this quite impressive body of evidence, higher Jewish population estimates were provided by research that instead of one national comprehensive source used compilations of many different smaller databases. Based on their compilation of local estimates, Sheskin and Dashefsky evaluate the US Jewish population at 6,968,000 (see Chap. 5 in this volume). This would be an increase of about 1000,000 over the 1990 *American Jewish Year* Book estimate obtained with the same method. The claimed—though not demonstrated—determinants of this 17% increase include the migration of Jews from the FSU, Israel, Latin America, and other countries.

While local Jewish community studies still are the most important tool for local Jewish community planning, the methodology of summing local studies to obtain a national estimate is problematic, as the authors themselves recognize (Sheskin and Dashefsky 2007, 2010, 2017; Sheskin 2008, 2009). One should acknowledge the diversity of databases and definitions, the lack of synchronization in time, and the very uneven quality of the technical procedures followed, including sometimes embarrassing skill gaps across different polling firms. When it comes to national Jewish population estimates, which as noted local studies were not designed to supply in the first place, local Jewish community summations may risk cumulating significant errors and biases, including double counts of geographically mobile individuals (Rebhun and Goldstein 2006; Groeneman and Smith 2009).

The Brandeis Steinhardt Social Research Institute (SSRI) meta-analysis of a large set of general social surveys is an innovative and ambitious undertaking in the social scientific study of American Jews called the American Jewish Population Project (AJPP) (Saxe et al. 2006b; Tighe et al. 2005, 2009a, b). The Jewish population estimate suggested by SSRI for 2019, based on a synthesis of surveys of the general public conducted between 2012 and 2018, was 7,478,600, plus or minus a margin of error of over 300,000 (SSRI 2019a; Saxe 2019). This figure implies that, since 1990, American Jewry increased by nearly two million persons or about 36%, quite higher than the 32% increase for the US total population and much higher than the 5% increase for non-Hispanic whites. (The Hispanic population increased by 163% from 1990 to 2017. The African-Americans population increased by 38%.) Pew (2013) reports that 93% of American Jews are non-Hispanic whites. Thus, this alleged Jewish population growth of 36% does not seem to be in accordance with extant census data and raises serious questions about the SSRI methodology. Indeed, the AJPP estimated that at least 70,000 Jewish babies were born annually in the US, and that a majority of US Jews did not adhere to any of the major Jewish religious denominations (Tighe et al. 2009a, 2011). These figures can be plausible only if one adopts, rather than a *core* concept of individually-identified Jews, a broadly *enlarged* concept of total population with Jewish background (as already anticipated by Tobin and Groeneman 2003).

Five important caveats should be stressed concerning the SSRI Jewish population estimates (SSRI 2019b):

(a) Jews are over-represented in general sample surveys because of their higher socioeconomic status and educational attainment, and their relatively lower presence among people difficult to cover like the homeless, those without a functioning telephone, or prisoners;
(b) using a sample of US adults—like in the case of most general survey respondents—to obtain estimates for the total population ignores the comparatively lower percentage of children among Jews and thus inflates the Jewish estimate;
(c) in turn the SSRI allocation of children explicitly uses Pew 2013 estimates which include children defined as partly Jewish or of Jewish background;
(d) projecting percentages of Jews among the total population, hence population size, from the percentage of Jewish respondents out of all respondents ignores the multi-religious composition of many Jewish households and thus factors non-Jews into Jewish population estimates; and
(e) the criteria used to estimate the broader aggregate also including Jews of no religion, based on survey data on Jews by religion are problematic.

The latter point (using data on Jews by religion to estimate Jews of no religion) is important in view of attempts to estimate Jewish populations based in surveys which, as they do, include *Jewish* as one option in a question on religious identity (Magidin de Kramer et al. 2018; Hackett 2014). In the SSRI meta-analysis, Jewish population is assessed at the county level through a logistic regression model that predicts the likelihood an adult identifies as Jewish when asked their religion. Factors involved in weighting across the sample of surveys in the model include geographic distribution, sex, age, race/ethnicity, and educational attainment. The model is fit using Bayesian Multilevel estimation with post-stratification (BMP) (SSRI 2019c). In other words, Jewishness of an individual is determined by a blind statistical iteration whose margin of error can be substantial, and not through a direct investigation of the personal religious or otherwise cultural identity of the interviewees. Even if the Jews by religion estimates were accurate, the further attempt to extrapolate the "real" number of Jews from sources that only deal with religion—instead of directly ascertaining the multivariate nature of Jewish identification—are at best speculative. The SSRI estimate of 4.4 million adults *Jews by religion* in 2019 was quite similar to the 4.2 million found by the 2013 Pew survey (Pew Research Center 2013). The SSRI estimate then, while rejecting the reliability of national surveys like Pew, built its own models of the proportion of persons of Jewish origin who declare not to have a religion. The 2013 Pew survey—besides 5.1 million *Jews by religion* (4.2 million adults and 900,000 children)—indeed found 600,000 persons (500,000 adults and 100,000 children) with *no religion and Jewish*, and one million persons (600,000 adults and 400,000 children) with *no religion and partly Jewish* (DellaPergola 2015b). The total of 6.7 million designated in the Pew report as *the net Jewish population* estimate included that million. A further 2.4 million non-Jewish adults with 1.5 million children, for a total of 3.9 million, reported a *Jewish background*. Of these, about one-third had at least one Jewish parent (Pew Research Center 2013), thus raising the total population with at least one Jewish parent (PJP) to about eight million (6.7 + 1.3). The about two-thirds with a Jewish background who did not have a Jewish parent, further expanded the collective to 10.6 million. An additional 1.2 million non-Jewish adults reported some *Jewish affinity*, raising the figure to 11.8 million, not including the children of the latter group. Some of these broader definitions better conform to our *Jewish parents*, *Jewish enlarged*, or *Law of Return* population definitions.

The 2013 Pew study actually confirmed some well-known demographic patterns of US Jews, namely postponed marriage, non-marriage, and small family size (Barack Fishman and Cohen 2017; Hartman 2017). Intermarriage was assessed at 58% of the latest marriage cohorts based on an *extended* Jewish population definition and showing an increase over previous cohorts. Identification with Judaism among children of intermarriages, though on the increase (Sasson et al. 2017), continued to fall below the 50% of all such children and younger adults nationally, which would be the precondition to maintain demographic stability or even determine quantitative gains from intermarriage (Barack Fishman 2004; Dashefsky and Heller 2008; Rebhun 2013; Phillips 2013, 2018). Seven percent of the children raised in in-married households were raised as non-Jews (probably children from previous marriages) versus 67% among intermarried couples.

The current aging composition of US Jewry (also acknowledged by the SSRI study) and other evidence about age-specific birth and death rates based on standard demographic models, plausibly generates annually fewer *Jewish* births nationally (by the *core* definition) than the estimated number of Jewish deaths. The Jewish death rate in the US is one of the least investigated topics in the field of Jewish demographic research and it would be a fair research priority to try to assess it empirically.

Jewish immigration to the US nearly stopped from the FSU but continued at moderate levels from other countries in Western Europe, Latin America, and, to some extent, other countries in the Middle East and South Africa. The evidence for Israelis in the US shows a significant reduction in the influx, largely compensated by returns to Israel (Gold and Phillips 1996, Gold 2002, Cohen 2009, Rebhun and Lev Ari 2010, Rebhun 2014, Israel Central Bureau of Statistics). The number of Israel residents who were allowed lawful permanent resident status in the US was 4324 in 2015, 4652 in 2016, and 4227 in 2017 (US Department of Homeland Security 2017). Accounting for other Jewish migration to the US, and discounting for the about 2500 yearly emigrants to Israel, an annual net migration into the US of 5000 Jews (or slightly more) can be estimated. In other words, net immigration balances the losses due to the likely excess of Jewish deaths over Jewish births (stressing the *core* definition), and the balance of accessions to minus secessions from Judaism. Shifts in lifetime religious preference in American society are comparatively more frequent than in other countries. Different surveys found that Jews, Catholics, and older established Protestant denominations tended to lose membership, while evangelical denominations, Eastern cults, and especially the "religiously undefined" ("none" and not reported) tended to gain (Kosmin and Lachman 1993; Kosmin et al. 2001; Pew Forum on Religion and Public Life 2008; Kosmin and

Keysar 2009; Smith 2009; Pew Research Center 2015a). By the Pew 2013 survey, total secessions from Judaism were double the number of accessions; and by the 2015 Pew survey of the US religious landscape, the net balance of changes of religion resulted in a total lifetime loss of 600,000 persons for the Jewish side (Pew Research Center 2015b). Based on several comparable measures of Jewish identification, the *partly Jewish no-religion* individuals, mainly the children of intermarriages, looked in 2013 more similar to *non-Jews with Jewish background* than to Jews with no religion (*JNRs*), or to Jews by religion for that matter (DellaPergola 2015b).

Following these observations, relying on the 2013 Pew survey and its subsequent updates, stressing that the true predicament of American Jewish demography concerns population definitions, and following the assumption that Jewish identity is mutually exclusive versus other competing religious and ethnic identities, our *core* Jewish population estimate remained stable at 5,700,000 for 2019—the world's second largest. This might be a slight underestimate and national surveys that might be conducted in the near future will clarify he matter. Broader definitional criteria naturally generate higher estimates. Including the partly Jewish with no religion and the pertinent portion of non-Jews with declared Jewish background, about eight million Americans have at least one Jewish parent. The *enlarged* total population including non-Jews in Jewish households approaches ten million. The *Law of Return* population probably approaches 12 million. By each of these expanded criteria, the number of persons included is significantly larger than in Israel.

8.4.3 France

France has the largest Jewish community in Europe. A 2002 national survey suggested 500,000 core Jews, plus an additional 75,000 non-Jewish members of Jewish households (Cohen and Ifergan 2003). Several follow-ups (Cohen 2005, 2007, 2013b) indicated a decreasing Jewish population, primarily due to emigration, mainly to Israel, but also to Canada, the US, and other countries. A survey (Ifop 2015) addressed an enlarged definition of the Jewish population in France but did not provide conclusive information about the size of the Jewish community. Instead, it offered important insights about their past and prospective migration. In retrospect, 39% reported they had relatives living in Israel compared to 31% who had relatives in another country (especially the US, Canada, and the UK). This would correspond to a migrant ratio of 56% to Israel compared to 44% to other countries. Regarding possible future migration, 13% reported they were seriously considering moving to Israel and another 30% had thought about it. The corresponding percentages for migrating to other countries were 13% and 33%, respectively. A previous survey of French Jewish adults age 18 to 40 about their expected country of residence in 5 years found that 33% expected to be living in France, 26% in Israel, 14% in another country, and 27% were not sure (Cohen 2013a). The 2012 European Union Fundamental Rights Agency (FRA) survey on perceptions of antisemitism in

EU countries unveiled that over 40% of French Jews had considered emigrating (European Union Fundamental Rights Agency-FRA 2013). Migration to Israel, after surpassing 2000 annually for several years, actually increased to a historical peak of 6627 in 2015, and lowered again to 2431 in 2018, for a total of over 48,000 between 2001 and 2018. Jewish emigration was also directed toward other western countries and reflected the continuing sense of uneasiness in the face of antisemitism, in part stemming from Islamic fundamentalism and terrorism. Assuming Israel attracted half to two-thirds of the total who departed France, between 72,000 and 96,000 Jews and family members emigrated from France since 2001. Some of these returned to France in the meantime, thus reducing the impact of net migration. Currently more than half of Jews live in the Greater Paris metropolitan region (Cohen and Ifergan 2003; Ifop 2015). Jews of Sephardi ancestry, mostly first, second, or third generation immigrants from North Africa, clearly predominate numerically over those of Central-Eastern European origin who, until World War II, constituted the main component of the Jewish population. Considering these trends, our 2019 core estimate for French Jewry decreased to 450,000—the third largest Jewish population in the world.

8.4.4   Canada

In **Canada,** the quinquennial Census, and more recently National Household Survey (NHS) data on Jewish ethnicity (Statistics Canada 2019)—released in years ending with the digit 1 or 6—can be compared with data on religion—released every decade in years ending with the digit 1 (Statistics Canada 2003a, b; Weinfeld and Schnoor 2015; Shahar 2014, 2016, 2017). Information on religion and ancestry was customarily collected through open-ended questions, where *Jewish* was one of the examples provided as a possible response. The 2016 NHS broke with this tradition and did not provide *Jewish* as an example. Probably as a consequence, the number reporting a Jewish ethnicity collapsed to 143,665 in 2016 from 309,650 in 2011. This makes the new data virtually unusable (see Chap. 7 in this volume). Since 1981, Canadians can declare either a single or a multiple ethnic ancestry (up to four categories, one for each grandparent). Ethnic Jews, as defined by the Canadian Census, can include persons who hold a non-Jewish religion, but these persons are *not* included in the *core* concept used herein. On the other hand, persons without religion who declare a Jewish ethnicity (single or part of a multiple choice) are included in the *core*. The Jewish Federations of Canada-UIA defined this as the *Jewish Standard Definition* (Torczyner et al. 1993; Shahar 2004). The newly suggested *Revised Jewish Standard Definition* also accounts for: (a) persons with no religious affiliation, but who are Israeli by ethnicity; (b) persons with no religious affiliation, but with knowledge of Hebrew or Yiddish as a "non-official" language; (c) persons with no religious affiliation but who were born in Israel; and (d) persons with no religious affiliation who lived in Israel in 2006 (Weinfeld and Schnoor 2015, Shahar 2014, 2016, 2017). This definition provided an estimate of 391,665 in

2011. The latter figure is not strictly comparable with the *core* Jewish population as it includes the fast increasing number of persons for whom Jewish is only one among multiple ethnic identities, some of whom would better be included among the *Jewish parents* Jewish population. In 2011, 329,500 Canadians declared they were Jewish by religion (Weinfeld et al. 2013). Following Jewish ethnicity throughout the past decades provides further clues on Jewish population and identification in Canada. A total of 293,175 ethnic Jews in 1981 increased to a peak of nearly 370,000 in 1991, and has since decreased to 309,650 in 2011. Striking changes actually affected the distribution of Canadians and of Jews among them, by single and multiple ethnicities. The ongoing growth of a new *Canadian* ethnic identity from the merger of pre-existing ethnicities is parallel to the development of a new *American* ethnic identity in the US (Lieberson and Waters 1988). In 1981, 90% or 264,025 of total ethnic Jews declared Jewish as their single ethnicity, but this share decreased to 66% (245,580) in 1991, 53% (186,475) in 2001, 43% (134,045) in 2006, and 37% (115,640) in 2011. Such sharp decrease in Jewish ethnic identification can be explained by an increase in intermarriage which generates growing multiple ancestries among descendants of Jews (Goldman 2009), but also indicates that the relevance of Jewish ethnic (unlike religious) identity is rapidly diminishing, at least as a mutually exclusive category. A systematic evaluation of the Jewish ethnicity variable in the 2016 census (Smith and McLeish 2019) shows the full picture of passages from Jewish and non-Jewish ethnicity declarations, and vice versa, between the 2011 and 2016 censuses. Ethnic origins that replaced *Jewish* mostly included Eastern European countries but also a 4.7% of *Israeli*. The dropping of Jewish ethnicity increased along with increasing generational seniority and acculturation in Canada. It was proportionally more frequent among those listing no religion or religion other than Jewish. On the other hand, among those *adding* Jewish as an ethnicity between 2011 and 2016, the plurality were Christians. While the decrease in responses for *Jewish* as an ethnic origin in 2016 was likely driven by the fact that *Jewish* was no longer among the list of ethnic origin examples, response mobility involving the Jewish ethnic origin is part of a larger pattern that predates the 2016 Census (Smith and McLeish 2019). These trends are confirmed by a 2018 large independent representative survey of Canadian Jews (Brym et al. 2019a). As a general pattern, Canadian Jews displayed significantly higher levels of Jewish identification than Jews in the US (Pew Research Center 2013). Indicators of Jewish religious identification appeared much more resilient than indicators of Jewish ethnicity and community participation (Brym et al. 2019b). Overall, between 2001 and 2011, 21,445 Jews by religion immigrated into Canada, mostly from the FSU, and were reported in Canada in the 2011 NHS. Consequently, the Jewish population by religion which was stable over the same 10 years would have decreased by a similar amount (a potential decrease of 6.5%) were it not for immigration. This, besides minor emigration, reflects a negative balance between Jewish births and Jewish deaths, and passages of people from self-definition as Jews by religion to self-definition of Jews with no religion. Compounding the effects of continuing immigration to Canada, but also some internal attrition because of aging and cultural assimilation, we estimate the Jewish population to have slightly increased in 2018 to 392,000 in 2019—the world's fourth largest Jewish community.

8.4.5   United Kingdom

In the **United Kingdom**, the 2011 Census, including regional totals for Scotland and Northern Ireland, suggested a slight Jewish population increase, from 266,740 in 2001 to 271,259 in 2011 (+1.69%) (United Kingdom Office for National Statistics 2002, 2012; United Kingdom National Records of Scotland NRS 2011; Miller et al. 1996; Kosmin and Waterman 2002; Graham et al. 2007; Graham and Waterman 2005, 2007; Voas 2007; Graham and Vulkan 2007; Graham 2013a, b; Boyd and Staetsky 2013; Graham and Caputo 2015; Staetsky and Boyd 2015). The 2001 national population Census included a voluntary question on religion for the first time since the nineteenth century and apparently somewhat underestimated the Jewish population, especially in areas inhabited by the more religious sectors of UK Jewry (Graham 2011). In 2011, the response rate significantly increased in those areas (Graham et al. 2012). Those who did not report a religion nationally rose from 23% in 2001 to 32% in 2011, but in view of the organized Jewish community's encouragement to participate in the Census, Jewish population was probably less affected by the increase in *no religion* and *not reported*. Mainstream British Jewry is aging, but the higher participation of Haredi Jews in the Census is reflected in a rejuvenating age composition, with an absolute increase of 3% in the percentage under age 15 and a 1% decrease in the percentage age 65 and over. Vital statistics routinely collected by the Board of Deputies of British Jews Community Research Unit on the annual number of Jewish births were quite consistent with the Census returns. A reversal has occurred in recent years from a long negative to a positive balance of Jewish births and deaths (The Board of Deputies of British Jews, Community Research Unit 2005; Vulkan 2012; Casale Mashiah 2018). Intermarriage was on the rise, too, though at moderate levels compared with most other European and Western countries, from 11% of all couples in 1965–1969 to 26% in 2010–2013 (Graham 2016, 2018). Synagogue membership in the UK significantly decreased over time (Casale Mashiah and Boyd 2017). In 2016, 79,597 Jewish households across the UK held synagogue membership, against 92,653 in 1995. While total Jewish households declined from 147,349 in 2001 to 141,503 in 2016, the number of synagogues actually increased from 328 in 1983 to 454 in 2016. The denominational balance also significantly shifted. Between 2010 and 2016, synagogue membership declined by 7.5% for the Central Orthodox, 4.1% for the Reform, 9.1% for the Liberal, and 21.4% for the Sephardi; membership increased by 15.5% for the Masorti, and by 18.4% for the Strictly Orthodox. Jewish education was growing, confirming the growing impact of the Haredi sector on the Jewish birth rate (Staetsky and Boyd 2016). Allowing also for some immigration, we upwardly revised our estimate the UK's core Jewish population at 292,000 in 2019—the fifth largest Jewish community in the world.

8.4.6 Argentina

Argentina has the largest Jewish community in Central and South America. Nearly 6000 Jews emigrated from Argentina to Israel in 2002—the highest number ever in a single year from that country—following the bankruptcy of the country's Central Bank, dire economic conditions, and special incentives offered by Israel. Subsequently, the economic situation stabilized and emigration diminished (Israel Central Bureau of Statistics). By 2014, 4400 persons lived in Jewish households in Miami in which at least one adult was Argentinian (Sheskin 2015b). A 2004 Jewish population survey in the Buenos Aires metropolitan area (AMBA) (Jmelnizky and Erdei 2005) found an *enlarged* Jewish population of 244,000 as part of the over 300,000 who were identified as in some way of Jewish origin or living with a person of Jewish origin. Of the former, 64,000 were Christians and about another 20,000 reported some Jewish ancestry, but did not consider themselves Jewish. Overall, 161,000 people in the AMBA considered self as totally or partly Jewish. Other research suggested significant aging of the *core* Jewish population, reflecting the emigration of younger households in recent years (Rubel 2005) and growing inter-religious couples (Erdei 2014). Argentina's Jewish population was assessed at 180,000 in 2019—the world's sixth largest Jewish community.

8.4.7 Russia

In the **Russian Federation**, Jewish population continued its downward course in the context of a country whose general population had been diminishing for years and only recently started to slowly recover (Tolts 2008, 2014, 2015). After the compulsory item on ethnicity *(natsyonalnost)* on identification documents was canceled, and the Census ethnicity question became optional, the 2010 Russian Census provided a core Jewish population estimated at 157,763, plus another 41,000 undeclared people who likely belonged to the core Jewish population, for a total of 200,600 in 2010 (Tolts 2013). The 2002 Census reported 233,600 Jews, compared to our *core* Jewish population estimate of 252,000 for the beginning of 2003, extrapolated from a February 1994 Russian Federation Microcensus estimate of 409,000 Jews (Goskomstat 1994; Tolts 2004, 2005, 2006, 2007). Comparing the totals and main geographical distributions in 2002 and 2010 (adjusted for under enumeration), the Jewish population diminished by 54,500 (21.4%) reflecting emigration, aging, and a negative balance of births and deaths (Tolts 2018). Over 93,000 (enlarged) Jews migrated to Israel been 2001 and 2018. About half of Russian Jewry was concentrated in Moscow and St. Petersburg, and this basic configuration was not much altered through emigration or vital events. The striking negative balance of Jewish births and deaths, and the recent surge in Jewish emigration generated an extremely elderly age composition and continuing population decrease, only partially compensated by migration from other FSU republics and a moderate amount of returns of previous migrants to Israel (Tolts 2003, 2009, 2015; Cohen 2009). We evaluated Russia's Jewish population at 165,000 in 2019—the world's seventh largest Jewish community.

8.4.8   Germany

In **Germany**, Jewish immigration, mainly from the FSU, brought to the country large numbers of Jewish and non-Jewish household members until 2005. This caused a significant boost in the Jewish population that had previously relied on a few Shoah survivors and several thousand immigrants mostly from Eastern Europe and Israel. Immigration from the FSU diminished to a few hundred annually after the German government, under pressure because of growing unemployment and a struggling welfare system, reduced the benefits to Jewish immigrants (Cohen and Kogan 2005; Dietz et al. 2002; Erlanger 2006). In 2018, 343 new immigrants from the FSU were added to Jewish community membership (besides 251 from other countries: Zentralwohlfhartsstelle der Juden in Deutschland 2019), versus a peak of 8929 in 1999. The total number of *core* Jews registered with the central Jewish community, after increasing consistently since 1989 to a peak of 107,794 at the beginning of 2007, diminished gradually to 96,325 in 2019.

Most of the growth was in the Länders (states) of the former Federal Republic of Germany (FRG) (West Germany). Because of the German national policy to decentralize the geographical absorption of immigrants, no specific area became dominant in Jewish population distribution. The main regional concentrations were in the industrial area of Northern Rein-Westphalia (Düsseldorf, Dortmund, Cologne), Bavaria (Munich), Hesse (Frankfurt), and Berlin. The community-registered Jewish population in Berlin, despite wide reports of a huge increase, diminished from 10,009 at the beginning of 2007 to 9255 in 2019. There is some evidence that Jews who are registered elsewhere might in reality be now living in Berlin (Amt für Statistik Berlin-Brandenburg 2012, 2014; Glöckner 2013; Rebhun et al. 2016). At the end of 2014, the number of officially recorded Israelis in Berlin was 3991 (plus 2774 with dual citizenship) versus 3065 in 2011. This does not account for Israelis and others who may have acquired German citizenship but who do not reside in Germany. Between 2000 and 2015, 33,321 Israelis were granted German citizenship, of which 31,722 kept it and 1599 renounced it (Harpaz 2013; Times of Israel 2017).

German Jews are very aged. In 2018, 227 Jewish births and 1572 Jewish deaths were recorded by the German Jewish community, a loss of 1345 Jews (Zentralwohlfahrtsstelle der Juden in Deutschland 2019). Especially births may suffer of underreporting because of the lack of incentives to register. German Jewry surely enjoys new opportunities for religious, social, and cultural life, but also significantly depends on welfare and elderly services (Schoeps et al. 1999). Allowing for delays in joining the organized community on the part of new immigrants and the choice by some Jews, including temporary migrants, not to affiliate, we estimated Germany's *core* Jewish population at 118,000 in 2019—the world's eighth largest Jewish community.

8.4.9 Australia and New Zealand

Australia's 2016 Census quite surprisingly recorded 91,022 Jews, a decline of 6.5% versus 2011. The explanation is easily found in changes introduced by the Australian Bureau of Statistics in the Census form. The option *No religion* was moved from the bottom to the top in the list of printed options. The result was a dramatic increase by 45.5% in the number of all Australians reporting no religion. Several other religions lost respondents: Anglicans 15.7%, Eastern Orthodox 10.7%, Catholics, 2.7%, and Other Christians 4.7%. Judaism did not appear as a printed option in the questionnaire but only as a write-in option. The suggestion of the *No religion* response option as the first on the list must have affected reporting of Judaism as well. The 2011 Census had reported a Jewish population of 97,336, compared to 88,831 in 2006 and 83,993 in 2001 (Australian Bureau of Statistics 2002, 2007, 2012; Eckstein 2003; Graham 2012, 2014a, b). In view of the general non-response to the 2016 question about religion, but also in view of indications of a lower non-response in more densely Jewish residential areas, adjusted figures suggest totals of 100,800 in 2001 and 112,000 in 2011, a 10-year increase of 11.2% (Graham 2014a).

The Jewish population is highly concentrated in Melbourne and Sydney, which in 2016 together comprised about 85% of the total. Intermarriage in Australia was less frequent than in most other Western large and medium-size communities, but it was on the rise and affecting the effective Jewish birth rate (Graham 2018). The community's rather old age composition reflects a fairly high death rate (Eckstein 2009; Markus et al. 2009, 2011; Forrest and Sheskin 2014). Yet, there possibly existed a small positive difference between an estimated 1200 Jewish births and about 900 Jewish funerals around 2016 (Graham and Narunski 2019). Factors of Jewish population growth were continuing immigration from South Africa, the FSU, and Israel, and moderate though rising intermarriage rates. Based on the new *GEN17 Australian Jewish Community Survey* (Graham and Markus 2018), and a re-evaluation of the 2016 census (Graham and Narunski 2019), we upwardly corrected the previous *core* Jewish population estimate by 4500, raising it to 118,000 in 2019—the world's ninth largest.

In **New Zealand**, likewise Australia, the 2018 census form did not list Judaism (nor other religions) as explicit options as in past censuses and left respondents the choice to write-in their preferred denominations. As a consequence, the percent of those not reporting a religion increased by 38% versus the previous census of 2013. The Jewish population apparently decreased by 23%, to 5274. Of these, 3348 reported Judaism (no further denomination specified), 327 Conservative Judaism, 792 Orthodox Judaism, and 807 Reform Judaism (Statistics New Zealand 2018). In consideration of the evident under-reporting of religion in the 2018 census we kept our estimate of Jews in New Zealand at 7500.

8.4.10   Brazil

In **Brazil**, the 2010 Census reported a national total of 107,329 Jews, of whom 105,432 lived in urban localities and 1987 in rural localities (Instituto Brasilero de Geografia e Estadistica IBGE 2010). The census classified Brazil's population by color, and among Jews, 94,575 were white, 10,429 brown, 1690 black, 492 yellow, and 143 indigenous. By region, 79,910 lived in the Southeast including the major cities, 12,963 in the South, 4266 in the Northeast, 2367 in the North, and 1394 in the Central West (Instituto Brasilero de Geografia e Estadistica 1991, 2000; Decol 1999, 2009). The 2010 census found 51,050 Jews in São Paulo state—36% more than in 2000. While an upward adjustment is reasonable, a 36% increase is not unless the previous census was badly incomplete. There also was a 2.5% increase in Rio de Janeiro (24,451 in 2010) and a decrease of 8.7% in the rest of the Southeastern and Southern states (overall 17,372 in 2010). What cannot be attributed to demography and likely reflects new emerging identifications or misclassifications is a decennial increase of over 8000 people (+125%) in the Northeastern, Northern, and Central-Western states. These growing numbers in the least developed and more peripheral regions of Brazil, but to some extent also in São Paulo, point to inclusion as Jews in the Census population of many thousands of persons who in all probability belong to Evangelical sects and Jehovah's Witnesses, besides possible cases of *Converso* Jewish ancestry. Census data for São Paulo were consistent with systematic documentation efforts undertaken by the local Jewish Federation that found 47,286 Jews (Federação Israelita do Estado de São Paulo FISESP 2002; Milkewitz et al. 2014). Allowing for moderate but growing emigration, our assessment of Brazil's core Jewish population stands at 92,600 in 2019—the world's tenth largest Jewish community.

8.4.11   South Africa

According to the 2001 Census, the white Jewish population of South Africa was 61,675, out of a reported total of 75,555 including nonwhites. Some of these nonwhites may identify with Jewish ancestry, but most probably pertain to messianic Christian denominations. Factoring in an evaluation of the national white non-response rate (14%) and additional factors led to a revised estimate of 72,000 (Saks 2003). After the major wave of departures just before the 1994 internal transferal of power from the apartheid regime to a democratic government, South African Jewry was relatively stable (Dubb 1994; Kosmin et al. 1999; Bruk 2006; Raijman 2015). However, due to the attrition of continuing emigration to Australia, Israel and other countries, and also because of diminishing birth rates versus relatively steady numbers of burials and cremations, the Jewish population surely declined. Jewish school enrollment data were quite stable, but they can mask growing enrollment of non-Jewish pupils. Pending more definitive evidence, we cautiously revised the estimate of South Africa's Jewish population at 67,500 in 2019—the world's eleventh largest Jewish community.

8.4.12 Ukraine

In **Ukraine,** the December 2001 Census yielded an estimate of 104,300 Jews (Ukrainian Ministry of Statistics 2002; Tolts 2002). The 2010 census could not be implemented. Instability, internal cleavage, and war in Ukraine resulted in continuing Jewish emigration and population decline. Over 75,000 (enlarged) Jews migrated to Israel between 2001 and 2018. Between 1989 and 2001, the Jewish population—80% Russian speakers—diminished more sharply in the Western regions where the share of Russians was relatively lower. Patterns of decline of ethnic Russians were similar. The overwhelming concentration of Ukraine's Jews in regions with a predominantly Russian (and often pro-Russian) environment under military dangers had obviously negative consequences for the Jewish community. The 2001 census included 5816 Jews in Crimea, subsequently annexed by Russia and where in 2014 a special census found 3374 Jews (Rosstat 2014). Considering continuing emigration, we assess the 2019 *core* Jewish population at 48,000—the world's twelfth largest Jewish community.

8.4.13 Other Central and South American Countries

In **Mexico**, the third largest Jewish community in Central and South America, the 2010 Census reported a Jewish population of 59,161, plus another 8315 *Neo Israelitas* (New Jews), for a total of 67,476 (Instituto Nacional de Estadística y Geografía 2012). Of these, 62,913—55,138 Jews and 7775 New Jews, respectively, were age 5 and over. The 2000 Census reported 45,260 Jews age 5 and over (Instituto Nacional de Estadística, Geografía e Informatica 2002). Projecting the number of Jews age 5 and over to an estimate inclusive of children age 0–4, the total Jewish population in 2000 would be about 49,000. An in-depth analysis of the 1970 Census (DellaPergola and Schmelz 1978) already had unveiled a significant presence, among those defined as Jews, of persons adherent to other religious denominations, mostly located in distant rural states or peripheral urban areas, with very low levels of educational attainment, exclusive knowledge of local indigenous idioms, and reportedly shoeless (*descalzos*). The further inclusion of a category of *Neo Israelitas* in 2010 leaves open the question of the attribution to Judaism of a population possibly comprising followers of Evangelical sects or Jehovah's Witnesses, as well as descendants of *Conversos*. For the Federal Capital's metropolitan area, Jewish population surveys and other research found general stability of the Jewish population at numbers similar to the Census concerning a conventional definition (Comunidad Judía de México 2015; Bokser Liwerant 2013; Comité Central Israelita de México 2006, 2000; DellaPergola and Lerner 1995). Some international migration operated both ways. Our 2019 Jewish population estimate was kept at 40,000—the world's fourteenth largest Jewish community.

In **Chile**—on the basis of the 2002 Census (Instituto Nacional de Estadistica 2003) and an earlier Jewish population survey (Berger et al. 1995)—the relatively stable core Jewish population was assessed at 18,300 in 2019—the world's nineteenth largest.

Uruguay experienced continuing Jewish emigration (Berenstein and Porzecanski 2001; Porzecanski 2006; Shorer Kaplan 2016). The Jewish population estimate for Uruguay was assessed at 16,600 in 2019—the world's twentieth largest Jewish community.

Panama over the last 20 years received several thousand Jewish immigrants, mostly from other Latin American countries. Its Jewish population in 2019 was estimated at 10,000—the world's twenty-fifth largest Jewish community.

The Jewish community of **Venezuela** now estimated at 7000, continued to shrink rapidly following political chaos and lack of security in the country.

8.4.14   Other European Union Countries

In **Hungary**, Jewish population trends reflect the unavoidably negative balance of Jewish births and deaths in a country whose total population has been diminishing for several years (Stark 1995; Swiss Fund for Needy Victims of the Holocaust/Shoa 2002; Kovács 2013a; Population Reference Bureau 2018). A Jewish survey in 1999 reported a conspicuously larger *enlarged* Jewish population than usually assessed (Kovács 2004). In the 2011 Hungarian Census, only 10,965 reported themselves as Jewish by religion, compared to 13,000 in 2001, clearly an underestimate but indicative of a trend (Hungarian Central Statistical Office 2003, 2013). A new survey in 2017, confirming the substantial gaps in Jewish population size according to different definitions, suggested a minimum-maximum range of 58,936–110,679 Jews for 2015 (Kovács and Barna 2018). Our *core* estimate for 2019, closer to the low of the range, was 47,300—the world's thirteenth largest Jewish community.

In the **Netherlands**, a survey in 2009 found high levels of intermarriage, a growing percentage of elderly, and an increase in the number of Israelis (van Solinge and de Vries 2001; Kooyman and Almagor 1996; van Solinge and van Praag 2010; Tanenbaum and Kooyman 2014). Out of an *enlarged* Jewish population of 52,000, 25% had a Jewish mother and 30% had a Jewish father. Accounting for aging and assuming incoming migration tended to balance emigration, our Jewish population estimate was 29,800 for 2018, the fifteenth largest Jewish community in the world.

In **Belgium**, quite stable numbers reflected the presence of a traditional Orthodox community in Antwerp and the growth of a large European administrative center in Brussels that has attracted Jews from other countries (Cohn 2003; Ben Rafael 2013). Some emigration reflected growing concerns about Islamization, terrorism, and antisemitism. The Jewish population was estimated at 29,100 in 2019, the world's sixteenth largest Jewish community.

In **Italy**, total Jewish community membership—which historically comprised the overwhelming majority of the country's Jewish population—decreased from 26,706 in 1995 to 23,361 in 2018 (Unione delle Comunità Ebraiche Italiane 2002, 2010, 2018; Lattes 2005; Campelli 2013, 2016). Our 2019 estimate of 27,400—the world's seventeenth largest Jewish community—considers some increase of conversions to Judaism and recent emigration.

In **Sweden**, the Jewish population was estimated at 15,000 in 2019—the world's twenty-first largest Jewish community, based on a local survey and on a total estimate of the affiliated community of about 5600 (Dencik 2003, 2013).

In **Spain**, the Jewish population estimate of 11,700 in 2019—the world's twenty-third largest Jewish community—reflected some continuing immigration from Latin America but also continuing emigration. The Spanish government 2015 initiative to offer Spanish citizenship to Jews able to demonstrate ancestry from the medieval expulsion, after a slow beginning, gathered momentum, reaching 132,226 requests (Jones 2019). Most requests came from Latin American countries, 5400 came from the US, and 4900 from Israel. The actual number of naturalizations was expected to be much lower given the quite stringent criteria requested, such as knowledge of Spanish, of the Spanish Constitution, and of Iberian culture. The majority of these requests from Latin American countries probably concerned persons who were not themselves part of the core Jewish population or Law of Return definition but belonged to more distant Jewish identification circles.

A similar law was approved in 2015 in **Portugal** (with an estimated permanent Jewish population provisionally estimated at 600 in 2019) to atone for the expulsions from that part of the Iberian Peninsula (BBC 2015). Brexit fueled an increase in the number of applications for Portuguese citizenship.

In **Austria**, updated Jewish community records and state vital statistics (Statistik Austria 2019; Staetsky and DellaPergola 2019b) suggested an upward revision to a new 2019 10,000 estimate—the world's twenty-fourth largest Jewish community.

In **Poland** the 2011 Census found about 2000 persons who indicated Jewish as their only ethnicity and an additional about 5000 persons who indicated Jewish as their second ethnicity after a mostly Polish first one (Główny Urząd Statystyczny 2012). Jewish community membership was reported at 1222. We provisionally adopted an estimate of 4500 assuming one half of those reporting multiple ethnicities would fall within the *core* Jewish population definition.

In **Ireland**, according to the 2016 census, there were 2557 Jews, a 28.9% increase from 2011 (Ireland Central Statistics Office 2012, 2017).

8.4.15 Other European Countries

In **Switzerland**, in light of Census and emigration data, the estimate was updated to 18,700 in 2018 (Statistik Schweiz 2005, 2012)—the world's eighteenth largest Jewish community.

In **Turkey**, a 2002 survey in Istanbul indicated widespread aging in a community that since has experienced growing emigration and population decline (Filiba 2003; Tuval 2004; Kubovich 2016). Most of the Jews live in Istanbul's European neighborhoods. The 2019 estimate was 14,800 Jews—the world's twenty-second largest Jewish community.

In **Gibraltar** we upwardly adjusted the estimate to 700 in 2019.

8.5 Major Cities and Metropolitan Areas

Changes in the geographic distribution of Jews have affected their distribution not only among countries, but also significantly within countries, and have resulted in a preference for Jews to live in major metropolitan areas. Within metropolitan areas, too, Jews have manifested unique propensities to settle or resettle in specific neighborhoods that were more compatible with their socioeconomic status, and/or more attractive to them because of the vicinity of employment or Jewish community facilities (DellaPergola and Sheskin 2015). Most metropolitan areas include extended inhabited territory and several municipal authorities around the central city. Definitions of urban areas vary by country. It is not easy to create a truly standardized picture of Jews in major cities, as some of the available figures refer to different years and only roughly compare with each other regarding Jewish population definitions and evaluation methods. For example, in the case of a recent Jewish population study of the service area of UJA/Federation of New York (Cohen et al. 2012), we subtracted about 100,000 individuals of the 1,538,000 that were included in the Jewish population count because they were neither born Jewish nor had converted to Judaism. We therefore do not consider them part of the core Jewish population. A similar bias affects the Jewish population estimate for the San Francisco Bay CSA (Phillips 2005). Note that elsewhere in this volume, Sheskin and Dashefsky rely mostly on the estimates resulting from definitions used by the local Jewish federations and often end up with what we define as an enlarged population with Jewish parents (PJP), although not one that includes non-Jews living in households with Jews. The urban areas reported here for the US are Metropolitan Statistical Areas (MSAs), whereas in previous years we reported data for larger Consolidated Statistical Areas (CSAs). Therefore, some of this year's estimates may look lower than in previous years. Similar changes in the definition of Metropolitan areas affected past data for Israel.

The unequivocal outcome of the overwhelmingly urban concentration of Jewish populations globally is shown by the fact that in 2019 more than half (53.4%) of world Jewry lived in only five metropolitan areas (Israel Central Bureau of Statistics; Sheskin and Dashefsky in this volume). These five areas—including the main cities and vast urbanized territories around them—were Tel Aviv, New York-Newark-Jersey City, Jerusalem, Haifa, and Los Angeles-Long Beach-Anaheim (Table 8.11). Two-thirds (66.6%) of world Jewry lived in the five previously mentioned largest areas plus the following six: Miami/Ft. Lauderdale-Pompano Beach, Washington-Arlington-Alexandria, Chicago-Naperville-Elgin, Philadelphia-Camden-Wilmington, Paris, and Boston-Cambridge-Newton. In 2019, the 19 largest metropolitan concentrations of Jewish population, each with 100,000 Jews or more, encompassed 75.8%—over three quarters—of all Jews worldwide.

The Jewish population in the Tel Aviv urban conurbation, extending from Netanya to Ashdod and surpassing 3.5 million Jews by the *core* definition, largely exceeded that in the New York MSA, extending from southern New York State to parts of Connecticut, New Jersey, and Pennsylvania, with 2.1 million Jews. Of the 19 largest metropolitan areas of Jewish residence, eleven were located in the US, four in Israel, and one each in France, the UK, Canada, and Argentina. Nearly all the major areas of settlement of contemporary Jewish populations share distinct features, such as being national or regional capitals, enjoying higher standards of living, with highly developed infrastructures for higher education and hi-tech, and widespread transnational connections. The Tel Aviv area also featured the highest percent of core Jewish among total population (91.1%), followed at a distance by Jerusalem (72.6%), Haifa (66.8%), and Beersheba (57.5%). In the diaspora, the highest percent of Jews in a metropolitan area was in New York (10.6%), followed by Miami-Fort Lauderdale (8.6%), San Francisco (5.2%), Washington (4.8%), and Philadelphia (4.6%).

Unlike our estimates of Jewish populations in individual countries, the data reported here on urban Jewish populations do not fully adjust for possible double counting due to multiple residences. Especially in the US, the differences may be quite significant, in the range of tens of thousands, involving both major and minor metropolitan areas. The respective estimates of part-year residents were excluded from the estimates in Table 8.11. Part-year residency is related to both climate differences and economic and employment factors. Such multiple residences now also increasingly occur internationally. A person from New York or Paris may also own or rent an apartment in Jerusalem or Tel Aviv, and some may even commute weekly (Pupko 2013). The case of Israelis regularly commuting abroad for work has also become more frequent.

8.6   Major Determinants of Demographic Change

The changes in the size and composition of Jewish populations outlined above reflect a chain of interrelated factors each of which in turn depends on a complex array of explanatory determinants. We briefly review here two of these

Table 8.11 Metropolitan areas (CSAs) with core Jewish populations above 100,000, 1/1/2019

Rank	Metropolitan area[a]	Country	Core Jewish population	% Jews out of total population	% Of world Jewish population %	Cumulative %
1	Tel Aviv[b]	Israel	3,569,500	91.1	24.3	24.3
2	New York-Newark-Jersey City	U.S.	2,107,800	10.6	14.3	38.6
3	Jerusalem[c]	Israel	932,900	72.6	6.3	44.9
4	Haifa[d]	Israel	625,600	66.8	4.3	49.2
5	Los Angeles-Long Beach-Anaheim	U.S.	617,500	4.6	4.2	53.4
6	Miami-Ft. Lauderdale-Pompano Beach	U.S.	535,500	8.6	3.6	57.0
7	Washington-Arlington-Alexandria	U.S.	297,300	4.8	2.0	59.1
8	Chicago-Naperville-Elgin	U.S.	294,300	3.1	2.0	61.1
9	Philadelphia-Camden-Wilmington	U.S.	283,500	4.6	1.9	63.0
10	Paris[e]	France	275,000	2.3	1.9	64.9
11	Boston-Cambridge-Newton	U.S.	257,500	3.6	1.8	66.6
12	San Francisco-Oakland-Berkeley	U.S.	244,000	5.2	1.7	68.3
13	Be'er Sheva[f]	Israel	221,300	57.5	1.5	69.8
14	London[g]	U.K.	195,000	1.0	1.3	71.1
15	Toronto[h]	Canada	190,000	3.1	1.3	72.4
16	Buenos Aires[i]	Argentina	159,000	1.2	1.1	73.5
17	Atlanta-Sandy Springs-Alpharetta	U.S.	119,800	2.0	0.8	74.3
18	Baltimore-Columbia-Towson	U.S.	115,800	1.9	0.8	75.1
19	San Diego-Chula Vista-Carlsbad	U.S.	100,000	3.0	0.7	75.8

[a]Most metropolitan areas include extended inhabited territory and several municipal authorities around the central city. Definitions vary by country. The US metropolitan areas are Metropolitan Statistical Areas (MSAs) as defined by the US Office of Management and Budget. See www.census.gov/geographies/reference-files/time-series/demo/metro-micro/delineationfiles.html. A table of the population of the top 20 MSAs can be found in Chap. 5 of this volume. Some of the US estimates are not core Jewish populations and are closer to enlarged Jewish populations. Israel metropolitan areas are defined by the Central Bureau of Statistics
[b]Includes Tel Aviv District, Central District, Ashdod Subdistrict, and sections of Judea and Samaria area. Principal cities: Tel Aviv, Ramat Gan, Bene Beraq, Petach Tikwa, Bat Yam, Holon, Rishon LeZiyon, Rehovot, Netanya, and Ashdod, all with Jewish populations over 100,000
[c]Includes Jerusalem District and parts of the Judea and Samaria District. Includes Bet Shemesh with over 100,000 Jewish population
[d]Includes Haifa District and parts of Northern District
[e]Departments 75, 77, 78, 91, 92, 93, 94, 95
[f]Includes Beersheba Subdistrict and other parts of Southern District
[g]Greater London and contiguous postcode areas
[h]Census Metropolitan Area
[i]Buenos Aires Metropolitan Area A.M.B.A

factors—international migration and age composition—which help understanding the mechanisms behind the demographic polarization that has emerged between Jews in Israel and in the Diaspora.

8.6.1   International Migration

Over the past decades, shifts in Jewish population size in the major regions of the world were primarily determined by large-scale international migration. Unfortunately, international migration of Jews is quite imperfectly documented. Currently, only Israel annually records Jewish immigrants as such by single country of origin (Israel Central Bureau of Statistics). Israeli data, compared over several successive years, may provide, under certain conditions, a sense of the intensity of parallel migration movements of Jews to other countries, although there also are differences in the timing, volume, direction, and characteristics of migrants (DellaPergola 2009a; Amit et al. 2010). Some countries do have records of annual numbers of migrants from Israel, though not distinguishing between Jews and non-Jews (US Department of Homeland Security 2017; Eurostat 2015). Jewish organizations, like HIAS—formerly the Hebrew Immigrant Aid Society (HIAS 2013) in the US or the Zentralwohlfhartsstelle in Germany, record Jewish immigrants on a yearly basis, but the global picture of Jewish migration remains incomplete.

Jewish international migration reached one of its highest peaks ever when the FSU opened its doors to emigration at the end of 1989. Of the estimated over 1.7 million FSU migrants between 1989 and 2018 including non-Jewish household members, over one million migrated to Israel, over 300,000 to the US, and over 225,000 to Germany. Israel's share of the total increased from 18% in 1989 to 83% in the peak years of 1990–1991. It then decreased to 41% in 2002–2004 and increased again in subsequent years—significantly so in 2018. The US significantly lost weight as a destination for FSU migrants since the onset of the twenty-first century, as was the parallel decrease in the attractiveness of Germany since 2005. These remarkable increases and decreases reflect the changing incidence of push factors in the FSU—as a whole and throughout its different regional realities—during times of rapid geopolitical change and shifts in economic opportunities, as well as real or expected disruptions in the societal environment affecting Jewish life. They also reflect the different and significantly variable legal provisions related to migration and socioeconomic options in the main countries of destination.

Beginning with 1948, Israel was the main recipient of Jewish international migration. It gathered 69% of all Jewish migration between 1948 and 1968, and about 60% between 1969 and 2015 (Amit and DellaPergola 2016). Clearly migration, or rather a migration balance producing a net surplus to Israel, reduces the population of the Diaspora and increases the Jewish population of Israel. Table 8.12 shows the number of immigrants to Israel by country of origin in 2017 and 2018. The data reflect the *Law of Return*, not the *core* Jewish population, definition.

Table 8.12 New immigrants to Israel[a], by last country of residence, 2017–2018

Country	2017	2018	Country	2017	2018	Country	2017	2018
Grand Total[b]	**26,333**	**28,118**	Germany	154	170	Kazakhstan	131	203
America—Total[b]	**4225**	**4146**	Greece	9	6	Kyrgyzstan	21	23
North America	**2848**	**2759**	Hungary	52	36	Tadjikistan	7	6
Canada	280	245	Ireland	2	1	Turkmenistan	24	16
United States	2568	2514	Italy	115	74	Uzbekistan	208	200
Central America	**135**	**144**	Luxembourg	1	4	**Other Asia**	**226**	**227**
Bahamas	1	0	Malta	0	7	China	9	19
Costa Rica	16	10	Netherlands	50	62	Hong Kong	7	1
Cuba	5	2	Poland	18	24	India	56	111
Dominican Rep.	3	0	Portugal	4	7	Indonesia	0	1
El Salvador	5	5	Romania	10	22	Iraq	1	1
Guadeloupe	8	1	Slovenia	1	0	Iran	131	76
Guatemala	3	8	Slovakia	1	6	Japan	2	2
Honduras	1	5	Spain	88	63	Korea South	2	0
Jamaica	1	0	Sweden	28	20	Nepal	1	0
Mexico	76	93	United Kingdom	469	514	Philippines	5	2
Panama	16	20	**FSU in Europe**	**15,369**	**18,123**	Singapore	3	3
South America	**1242**	**1243**	Belarus	952	943	Sri Lanka	1	0
Argentina	247	283	Estonia	5	7	Taiwan	1	0
Bolivia	4	5	Latvia	49	48	Thailand	7	7
Brazil	619	586	Lithuania	25	42	Vietnam	0	4
Chile	26	34	Moldova	196	173	**Africa—Total[b]**	**432**	**363**
Colombia	74	84	Russian Fed.	7109	10,474	**Northern Africa**	**143**	**99**
Ecuador	9	13	Ukraine	7027	6428	Ethiopia	43	31
Paraguay	9	8	FSU unspecified	6	8	Morocco	57	52
Peru	57	47	**Other West Eur.**	**87**	**89**	Tunisia	43	16
Uruguay	69	54	Gibraltar	1	2	**Sub-Sahara Afr.**	**289**	**264**
Venezuela	128	129	Monaco	1	5	Congo	3	2
Europe—Total[b]	**20,197**	**22,041**	Norway	1	3	Ghana	0	1
European Union[c]	**4356**	**3628**	Switzerland	84	79	Mozambique	0	1

(continued)

Table 8.12 (continued)

Country	2017	2018	Country	2017	2018	Country	2017	2018
Austria	25	26	**Balkans**	**385**	**201**	Namibia	0	3
Belgium	119	108	Albania	5	0	Ruanda	1	0
Bulgaria	14	6	Serbia	11	12	Nigeria	1	0
Croatia	2	1	Turkey	369	189	Tanzania	1	0
Cyprus	0	5	**Asia—Total[b]**	**1001**	**991**	South Africa	282	256
Czech Republic	13	18	**FSU in Asia**	**775**	**764**	Zimbabwe	1	1
Denmark	12	9	Armenia	48	9	**Oceania—Total**	**140**	**121**
Finland	9	8	Azerbaijan	131	131	Australia	140	117
France	3160	2431	Georgia	205	176	New Zealand	0	4

Source: Israel Central Bureau of Statistics, unpublished data
[a]New immigrants and tourists changing their status to immigrant, not including temporary residents, returning Israelis, and immigrant citizens
[b]Including country unknown
[c]Not including the Baltic countries

In 2018, Jewish international migration slightly increased versus the previous year. In recent years, the volume of Jewish migration was far from the peaks of the past, due to the increasing concentration of Jews in more developed countries and the rapidly decreasing Jewish population in the less developed countries which also were the main areas of Jewish emigration. We already noted the clearly negative relationship that prevails between the quality of life in a country and the propensity of Jews to emigrate. At the same time perceptions and experiences of mounting antisemitism in some countries, particularly in France, stimulated Jewish emigration in more recent years. In the foreseeable future, a continuation of moderate levels of migration can be expected, provided that current geopolitical and socio-economic conditions are not seriously disrupted across the global system, especially in Europe. From this point of view, the UK withdrawal (Brexit) from the European Union might carry significant economic and demographic consequences in the longer term.

In 2018, 28,118 new immigrants arrived in Israel from 87 countries and territories, compared to 26,333 in 2017 (a 6.8% increase and the highest of the past 10 years), 25,010 in 2016, 27,850 in 2015, 24,066 in 2014, and 16,882 in 2013. In 2018, immigration to Israel increased from the European but not the Asian republics of the FSU, Latin America, and Asia, while it diminished from all areas in Europe other than the FSU, North America, Africa, and Oceania. Migration toward other countries did not necessarily follow the same patterns of change over the years. Indeed, Israeli immigration law (the Law of Return) allows for comparatively easier access and immediate citizenship to Jewish migrants and their families, but the integration difficulties experienced in Israel by some immigrants may have created a deterrent. One case in point is immigration from France which, after an all-time peak in 2015 (6627), declined to 4147 in 2016, 3160 in 2017, and 2431 in 2018. Russia was the main country of origin in 2018 (10,474 immigrants vs. 7109 immigrants in 2017), followed by Ukraine (6428 vs. 7027), the US (2514 vs. 2568), and France. No other country had more than 1000 migrants to Israel. Among countries with more than 100 immigrants, minuscule increases occurred from the UK, Argentina, Germany, Venezuela, and India. Declines were recorded from Belarus, Brazil, South Africa, Kazakhstan, Canada, Uzbekistan, Turkey, Georgia, Moldova, Australia, and Belgium. Azerbaijan was stable. Only 31 immigrants arrived from Ethiopia in 2018 compared to 43 in 2017. To these figures, one should add several thousand immigrant citizens (Israeli citizens born abroad and entering the country for the first time) and of returning Israelis, at a time when the Israeli economy was performing relatively better than many Western countries. This made Israel a reasonably attractive option for international migration.

Figure 8.10 demonstrates the annual changes in the number of immigrants to Israel from six of the major countries of origin: Russia, Ukraine, the US, France, the

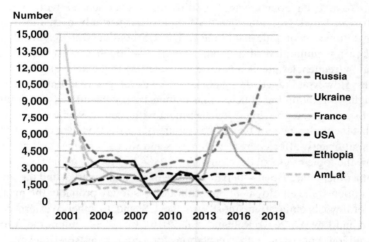

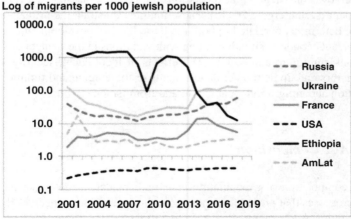

Fig. 8.10 Number of immigrants to Israel from major countries of origin, and rate of immigrants per 1000 Jews 2001–2018

aggregate of Latin American countries, and Ethiopia. Clearly the fluctuations reflected local circumstances in each country and not one common underlying determinant, possibly related to the receiving country Israel. Occasional peaks are related in Ukraine to civil war and the armed conflict with Russia; in Latin America, the collapse of the Central Bank in Argentina in 2002; in France mounting terrorism and antisemitism; and in Ethiopia the variable policies adopted by Israel's government toward bringing more or less of the candidates for immigration who still reside in transition camps in Addis Ababa and elsewhere. The bottom panel of Fig. 8.10 demonstrates the frequency of migration to Israel per 1000 Jewish population in each country of origin and each year (using a logarithmic scale). The highest frequencies initially appeared in Ethiopia, reflecting a systematic repatriation policy which has been discontinued after 2010. The significantly high frequencies in Russia and the Ukraine reflect the security conditions of border areas, but also a quite deeper socioeconomic disease. Increases in France due to security uncertainty seem to have been counteracted by difficulties experienced with immigrants' absorption in Israel. In Latin America the situation partially normalized after the above-mentioned economic bankruptcy. The US continued to feature the lowest propensity for emigration of any other country—though very slowly increasing. Emigration frequencies are clearly ordered according to the level of development of countries. However, France, though being more developed than Latin America featured higher migration frequencies, thus demonstrating the effects of a diminishing sense of security and growing disenchantment with society. While it cannot be disputed that the preference for Israel as a country of destination over competing countries is significantly affected by Jewish norms and values, *aliyah* seems nevertheless to follow the logic of global development.

On the other hand, Israel—in part because of its small market and the limits this imposes upon some employment opportunities—is today probably the main single source of Jewish emigration, mostly to the US and to other Western countries (Rebhun and Lev Ari 2010; Rebhun et al. 2016). Levels of emigration from Israel are overall low, consistent with expectations for a country at Israel's level of human development (DellaPergola 2011c). These findings illustrate the primacy of socioeconomic determinants related to both the basic level of development of a country and its current economic situation, along with variations in the stringency of regulations about immigrant admissions. The effects of ideological, security, and fear-related factors end up as weaker determinants of the volume and timing of Jewish immigration and emigration—namely to and from Israel.

8.6.2 Age Composition

The age composition of a population is a fundamental mediator between demographic processes that precede a certain point in time and the processes that unfold after that point. Age structures are sensitive to the composition of migrants which usually include some over-representation of younger adults and their children.

Exceptions occur when the immigrants include a large share of elderly persons as has been the case for migration from the FSU to Germany, or even to the US and Israel over the past decades. In general, populations in the sending countries tend to become older as a consequence of migration, while populations in the receiving countries tend to become younger. But, as just noted, immigration may also cause aging of the receiving population.

The birth rate, however, is the main determinant of the age composition of a population. Large cohorts reflecting years of high birth rates, as was the case in the US during the baby-boom years (1946–1964), produce a younger population. A persistent high birth rate, as in Israel, produces an expanding population in which each cohort is followed by a slightly larger one, so creating a graphical image of a pyramid. Low birth rates, as typical of most Jewish populations outside of Israel, generate smaller cohorts which sometimes are smaller than those born several years before and in the extreme case may produce a graphic image of an upside down pyramid. In recent years some upward reversal in the Jewish birth rate occurred in the UK, Austria, and possibly Australia. In Fig. 8.11, we demonstrate four different age structures among contemporary Jewish populations, reflecting different stages of demographic transformation. All data refer to the *core* definition.

Israel, here portrayed in 2016 for the sake of comparisons (Israel Central Bureau of Statistics) is the only case where each age group is larger than the one immediately older. The largest age group was 0–14. Israel actually is the only country in the world with a high child dependency ratio (greater than 45%) along with a relatively high old-age dependency ratio (greater than or equal to 15%). It is included by the UN in the double dependency category (United Nations Population Division 2017). At the opposite extreme, Germany in 2018 (Zentralwohlfahrtsstelle der Juden in

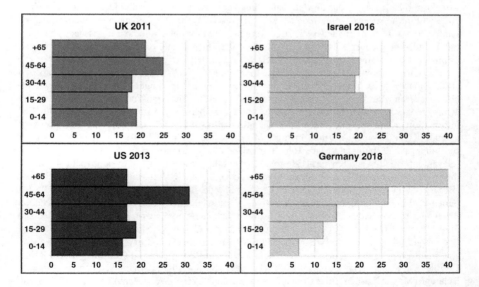

Fig. 8.11 Age structures of selected Jewish populations, 2011–2018, percentages

Deutschland 2018) had an extremely elderly age distribution, where the largest group is 65 and over. The US in 2013 (Pew Research Center 2013), and the UK in 2011 (United Kingdom Office for National Statistics 2012), represent intermediate cases but with some important differences. Both the US and UK Jewish populations underwent significant aging and had relatively low birth rates during the past 50 years. In the US, the effects of the baby boom were visible, with the by far largest age group being those age 45–64 in 2013, born 1949–1968. There were significantly fewer children age 0–14 than young adults age 15–29. In the UK, aging was significant as well, but the effects of the post-World War II baby boom were significantly less and there were again more children than young adults in 2011. Such rejuvenation reflected the growing impact of Haredi Jews among the UK total Jewish population.

As a benchmark for future demographic change, these very different age structures portend very different scenarios. Those countries with large elderly cohorts will unavoidably experience some numerical decline—assuming no major future migrations. Populations that are currently younger will have more of a chance to having children and possibly increasing or keeping their size stable, as well as holding a growing share of world Jewish population.

Acknowledgments Since inception, the *American Jewish Year Book* has documented the Jewish world and has given significant attention to Jewish population issues. Since 1981, responsibility for preparing annual population estimates for world Jewry was taken by the Division of Jewish Demography and Statistics of the A. Harman Institute of Contemporary Jewry at The Hebrew University of Jerusalem. The Division was founded by Roberto Bachi in 1959, was headed by Uziel O. Schmelz until 1986, by the present author until 2010, and by Uzi Rebhun since 2010. Jewish population estimates appeared in the AJYB, then under the aegis of the American Jewish Committee, until 2008. Since 2010, our world Jewish population estimates appeared in the framework of the North American Jewish Data Bank (now the Berman Jewish DataBank), and since 2012 within the renewed *American Jewish Year Book*. World Jewish population estimates as of January 1, 2009 and as of January 1, 2011 were prepared for publication but not issued. The interested reader may consult past AJYB volumes for further details on how the respective annual estimates were obtained (especially Schmelz 1981 and DellaPergola 2015a).

The author expresses warm appreciation to the editors of AJYB during more than 30 years of a close collaboration: Morris Fine, Milton Himmelfarb, David Singer, Ruth Seldin, Lawrence Grossman, and currently Arnold Dashefsky and Ira M. Sheskin. The author also gratefully acknowledges the collaboration of many institutions and persons in various countries who supplied information or otherwise helped in the preparation of this study. Special thanks are due to my colleagues at The Avraham Harman Institute of Contemporary Jewry at The Hebrew University of Jerusalem, Uzi Rebhun and Mark Tolts. I am also indebted to those who over the years provided relevant information and advice at different stages of the present study (in the alphabetical order of the respective cities): Chris Kooyman (Amsterdam), the late Ralph Weill (Basel), Jim Schwartz (Bergen County, NJ), Olaf Glöckner (Berlin), Shmuel Frankel (Bne Berak), Marcos Peckel (Bogota), Simon Cohn, and Claude Kandiyoti (Brussels), András Kovács (Budapest), Ezequiel Erdei, and Yaacov Rubel (Buenos Aires), Tally Frankental (Cape Town), Salomon Benzaquen and Tony Beker de Weinraub (Caracas), Cathleen Falsani, and Tom W. Smith (Chicago), Frank Mott (Columbus, OH), Heike von Bassewitz, and Ellen Rubinstein (Frankfurt a. M.), Frans van Poppel, and Hanna van Solinge (The Hague), Ariela Keysar and Barry Kosmin (Hartford, CT), Maritza Corrales Capestrany (Havana), Lina Filiba (Istanbul), Steven Adler, Benjamin Anderman, Margalit Bejarano, Maya Choshen, Eilat Cohen-Kastro, Susanne Cohen-Weisz, Oren Cytto, Nurit Dovrin, Judith Even, Netanel Fisher, Ahmad Hleihel, Shlomit Levy, Israel Pupko, Uzi Rebhun, Liat Rehavi,

Dalia Sagi, Marina Sheps, Maya Shorer Kaplan, Mark Tolts, Eduardo Torres, Emma Trahtenberg, Chaim I. Waxman, and the late Norma Gurovich (Jerusalem), David Saks (Johannesburg), Roy van Keulen (Leiden), Jonathan Boyd, Richard Goldstein, Marlena Schmool. and Daniel Staetsky (London), Pini Herman, and Bruce Phillips (Los Angeles), Pinhas Punturello (Madrid), John Goldlust, Andrew Markus and Ran Porat (Melbourne), Judit Bokser Liwerant, Susana Lerner, Mauricio Lulka, and Yael Siman (Mexico City), Ira M. Sheskin (Miami), Rafael Porzecanski (Montevideo), Evgueni Andreev and Eugeni Soroko (Moscow), David Bass (Neveh Daniel), the late Vivian Z. Klaff (Newark, DE), Steven M. Cohen, Laurence Kotler-Berkowitz, Lucette Lagnado and Sarah Markowitz (New York), David M. Mizrachi (Panama City), Marcelo Dimentstein, Alberto Senderey, and the late Doris Bensimon-Donat (Paris), Allen Glicksman (Philadelphia), Zbyněk Tarant (Pilsen), Yochanan Moran (Porto), Alice Goldstein, and the late Sidney Goldstein (Providence, RI), Narciso Attía (Quito), Mustafa Khawaja (Ramallah), Orly C. Meron, Carlos Tapiero, and the late Erik H. Cohen (Ramat Gan), Gloria Arbib, and Alberto Levy (Rome), Lars Dencik (Roskilde), David Saltiel (Saloniki), Alberto Milkewitz, Simon Schwartzman, and the late René Decol (São Paulo), Mordechai Abergel (Singapore), Arnold Dashefsky (Storrs, CT), Gary Eckstein, and David Graham (Sydney), Allie A. Dubb (Tel Aviv), Robert Brym, and Gustave Goldman (Toronto), Jeffrey Scheckner (Union, NJ), Thomas Buettner, and Hania Zlotnik (United Nations, NY), Raimund Fastenbauer (Vienna), Sylvia Barack Fishman, Leonard Saxe, Charles Kadushin, Benjamin Phillips, and Elizabeth Tighe (Waltham, MA), Barry R. Chiswick, Carmel U. Chiswick, Alan Cooperman, Conrad Hackett, Neha Sagal, and Greg Smith (Washington, DC), Melita Svob (Zagreb).

   An anonymous reviewer provided useful suggestions to the text and tables. Responsibility for the contents of this article is the author's only.

Appendix

Definitions

In most Diaspora countries, the ***core Jewish population*** (***CJP***—a concept initially suggested by Kosmin et al. 1991) includes all persons who, when asked in a socio-demographic survey, identify themselves as Jews, *or* who are identified as Jews by a respondent in the same household, *and* do not profess another monotheistic religion. Such a definition of a person as a Jew, reflecting *subjective* perceptions, broadly overlaps, but does not necessarily coincide, with *Halakhah* (Jewish law) or other normatively binding definitions. Inclusion does *not* depend on any measure of that person's Jewish commitment or behavior in terms of religiosity, beliefs, knowledge, communal affiliation, or otherwise. The *core* Jewish population includes people who identify as Jews by religion, as well as others who do not identify by religion but see themselves as Jews by ethnicity or other cultural criteria (Jewish only, no religion). Some do not even identify themselves as Jews when first asked, but if they descend from Jewish parents and do not hold another religious identity they should be included. All these people are considered to be part of the *core* Jewish population which also includes all converts to Judaism by any procedure, as well as other people who declare they are Jewish even without formal conversion and do not hold another identity. Persons of Jewish parentage who adopted another monotheistic religion are excluded, as are persons who state being partly Jewish along with another identity, and those of Jewish origin who in censuses or socio-demographic surveys explicitly identify with a non-Jewish religious group without having formally converted. The *core* population concept offers an intentionally comprehensive and pragmatic, mutually exclusive approach compatible with the analytic options offered by many available demographic data sources.

In the Diaspora, such data often derive from population censuses or socio-demographic surveys where interviewees have the option to decide how to answer relevant questions on religious or ethnic identities. In Israel, personal status is subject to Ministry of the Interior rulings, which rely on criteria established by rabbinic authorities and by the Israeli Supreme Court (Corinaldi 2001). In Israel, therefore, the *core* Jewish population does not simply express subjective identification but reflects definite legal rules. This entails matrilineal Jewish origin, or conversion to Judaism, *and* not holding another religion. Documentation to prove a person's Jewish status may include non-Jewish sources.

A major research issue of growing impact is whether *core* Jewish identification can or should be mutually exclusive with other religious and/or ethnic identities. In a much debated study—the 2000–2001 US National Jewish Population Survey-NJPS 2000–2001 (Kotler-Berkowitz et al. 2003)—the solution chosen was to allow for Jews with multiple religious identities to be included in the *core* Jewish population definition under condition that the other identity was not a monotheistic religion. This resulted in a rather multi-layered and not mutually exclusive definition of the US Jewish population. A further category of *Persons of Jewish Background* (PJBs) was introduced by NJPS 2000–2001. Some PJBs were included in the final Jewish population count and others were not, based on a more thorough evaluation of each individual ancestry and childhood. (See further comprehensive discussions of the demography of US Jews in Heilman 2005, 2013.)

The 2013 Pew Research Center's A Portrait of Jewish Americans (Pew Research Center 2013), by introducing the previously not empirically tested concept of *partly Jewish,* helped clarify the demographic picture, but also made the debate about definitions more complicated, and the comparison of results more ambivalent. One intriguing issue concerns the status of the *partly Jewish* as a standard component of the Jewish collective, as some analysts would have it. Following a similar logic, persons with multiple ethnic identities, including a Jewish one, have been included in some total Jewish population counts for Canada. As against this, other researchers would suggest that the *partly Jewish* stand conceptually closer to the other Pew survey categories of *Non-Jews with Jewish background*, or *Non-Jews feeling some Jewish affinity*. Recent research experience indicates that people may shift their identities over time across the different layers of the *core* Jewish definition, and between different *core* and *non-core* statuses. It is not uncommon to see those shifts across the boundary identifying as Jewish and as something else and vice versa in response to the particular context or moment when the question about identity is being tested. At any particular moment, then, there will be a countable Jewish population, which is not necessarily the same as the previous or the following moment.

Emerging from these more recent research developments, the concept of *total population with at least one Jewish parent* (*PJP*) includes the core Jewish population plus anyone currently not identifying as exclusively Jewish but with one or two Jewish parents. In the Pew 2013 survey, the total population with Jewish parents besides the core comprised two sub-groups: (a) persons who report no religion, and declare they are partly Jewish, and (b) persons who report not being Jewish, and declare a Jewish background because they had a Jewish parent (Pew Research Center 2013).

The *enlarged Jewish population* (*EJP*—a concept initially suggested by DellaPergola 1975) further expands by including the sum of: (a) the *core* Jewish population; (b) persons reporting they are *partly Jewish*; (c) all others of Jewish parentage who—by *core* Jewish population criteria—are *not* currently Jewish; (d) all other non-Jews with Jewish background more distant than a Jewish parent; and (e) all respective non-Jewish household members (spouses, children, etc.). Non-Jews with Jewish background, as far as they can be ascertained, include: (a) persons who have adopted another religion, or otherwise opted out, although they may also claim to be Jewish by ethnicity or in some other way—with the caveat just mentioned for recent US and Canadian data; and (b) other persons with Jewish parentage who disclaim being Jewish. It logically follows that most Jews who are identified in the Pew survey as *partly Jewish* or as *PJBs* who are not part of the US *core* Jewish population, as well as many Canadians declaring Jewish as one of *multiple ethnicities,* naturally should be included under the *enlarged* definition. For both conceptual and practical reasons, the *enlarged* definition usually does not include other non-Jewish relatives who lack a Jewish background and live in exclusively non-Jewish households.

The *Law of Return population (LRP)* reflects Israel's distinctive legal framework for the acceptance and absorption of new immigrants. The Law of Return awards Jewish new immigrants immediate citizenship and other civil rights. The Law of Entrance and the Law of Citizenship apply to all other foreign arrivals, some of whom may ask for Israeli citizenship. According to the current, amended version of the *Law of Return* (Gavison 2009), a Jew is any person born to a Jewish mother or converted to Judaism (regardless of denomination—Orthodox, Conservative, Reconstructionist, or Reform) who does not have another religious identity. By ruling of Israel's Supreme Court, conversion from Judaism, as in the case of some ethnic Jews who currently identify with another religion, entails loss of eligibility for *Law of Return* purposes. Thus, all the Falash Mura—a group of Ethiopian non-Jews with Jewish ancestry—must undergo conversion to be eligible for the *Law of Return*. The law itself does not affect a person's Jewish status—which, as noted, is adjudicated by Israel's Ministry of Interior relying on Israel's rabbinic authorities—but only for the specific immigration and citizenship benefits granted under the *Law of Return*. Articles 1 and 4A(a) of this law extend its provisions to *all current Jews, their children, and grandchildren,* as well as to *their respective Jewish or non-Jewish spouses*. As a result of its three-generation and lateral extension, the *Law of Return* applies to a large population—the so-called *aliyah* eligible—whose scope is

significantly wider than the *core* and *enlarged* Jewish populations defined above
(Corinaldi 1998, 2018). It is actually quite difficult to estimate the total size of the
Law of Return population. Rough estimates of these higher figures are tentatively
suggested below.

Some major Jewish organizations in Israel and the US—such as the Jewish
Agency for Israel (JAFI), the American Jewish Joint Distribution Committee (JDC),
and the major Jewish Federations in the US—sponsor data collection and tend to
influence research targets, rendering them increasingly complex and flexible.
Organizations enact their mission toward their respective constituencies based on
perceived interests rather than scientific criteria. The understandable interest of
organizations to function and secure budgetary resources may prompt them to
expand their reach strategies to Jewish populations increasingly closer to the
enlarged and *Law of Return* definitions than to the *core* definition.

Presentation and Quality of Data

Jewish population estimates in this chapter refer to January 1, 2019. Efforts to provide the most recent possible picture entail a short span of time for evaluation of
available information, hence some margin of inaccuracy. For example, a wealth of
the data about Israel's population becomes available annually when the *American
Jewish Year Book* is already in print. Some of Israel's data here are the product of
estimates based on the most recent trends, but may need adjustment when the actual
data are released. Indeed, where appropriate, we revise our previous estimates in
light of newly acquired information. Corrections also were applied retroactively to
the 2018 totals for major geographical regions so as to ensure a better base for comparisons with the 2019 estimates. Corrections of the 2019 estimates, if needed, will
be presented in the future.

**We provide separate estimates for each country with approximately 100 or
more resident core Jews.** Estimates of Jews in smaller communities have been
added to some of the continental totals. For each country, we provide in the Appendix
an estimate of (1) mid-year 2018 total (including both Jews and non-Jews) country
population (Population Reference Bureau 2018); (2) the estimated January 1, 2019
core Jewish population (CJP); (3) the number of Jews per 1000 total population; and
(4) a rating of the accuracy of the Jewish population estimate. The last three columns provide rough estimates of the population with Jewish parents (PJP), the
enlarged Jewish population inclusive of all non-Jewish members in a Jewish household (EJP), and the Law of Return population (LRP). These figures were derived
from available information and assessments on the recent extent and generational
depth of cultural assimilation and intermarriage in the different countries. The quality of such broader estimates of the aggregate of Jews and non-Jews who often share
daily life is much lower than that of the respective core Jewish populations, and the
data should be taken as indicative only.

Wide variation exists in the quality of the Jewish population estimates for different countries. For many Diaspora countries, it might be better to indicate a range for the number of Jews (minimum, maximum) rather than a definite estimate. It would be confusing, however, for the reader to be confronted with a long list of ranges; this would also complicate the regional and world totals. The estimates reported for most of the Diaspora communities should be understood as being the central value of the plausible range for the respective core Jewish populations. The relative magnitude of this range varies inversely with the accuracy of the estimate. One issue of growing significance is related to persons who hold multiple residences in different countries. Based on available evidence, we make efforts to avoid double counting. Wherever possible, we strive to assign people to their country of permanent residence, ignoring the effect of part-year residents. (This is similar to the part-year resident, or "snowbird" issue in estimating the US Jewish population in Sheskin and Dashefsky, in this volume.)

Jewish population data come from a large array of different sources, each with inherent advantages and disadvantages. We report both the main type and the evaluated accuracy of the sources used in this study. In the Appendix Table the main types of sources are indicated as follows:

(C)   National population census. This in theory would be the best source, but undercounts and over counts do occur in several countries which need to be evaluated.

(P)   National population register. Some countries, besides the periodical census, also keep a permanent population register which is constantly updated through detailed accountancy of individual demographic events.

(S)   Survey of the Jewish population, national or inclusive of the main localities, undertaken most often by a Jewish community organization, and sometimes by a public organization.

(J)   Jewish community register kept by a central Jewish community organization.

(E)   Estimate otherwise obtained by a Jewish organization.

Our estimates reflect these sources, but the figures reported below do not necessarily correspond exactly with those indicated in the given sources. When necessary, additional information is brought to bear in deriving our estimates. The three main elements that affect the accuracy of each country's Jewish population estimate are: (a) the nature and quality of the base data, (b) how recent the base data are, and (c) the updating method. A simple code combines these elements to provide a general evaluation of the reliability of data reported in the Appendix Table, as follows:

(A)   Base estimate derived from a national census or reliable Jewish population survey; updated on the basis of full or partial information on Jewish population change in the respective country during the intervening period.

(B)   Base estimate derived from less accurate but recent national Jewish population data; updated on the basis of partial information on Jewish population change during the intervening period.

(C)   Base estimate derived from less recent sources and/or unsatisfactory or partial coverage of a country's Jewish population; updated on the basis of demographic information illustrative of regional demographic trends.

(D)   Base estimate essentially speculative; no reliable updating procedure.

The year in which a country's base estimate or important partial updates were initially obtained is also stated. This is not the current estimate's date but the initial basis for its attainment. An X is appended to the accuracy rating for several countries whose Jewish population estimate for 2018 was not only updated but also revised in light of improved information.

One additional tool for updating Jewish population estimates is provided by several sets of demographic projections developed by the Division of Jewish Demography and Statistics at the Institute of Contemporary Jewry of The Hebrew University of Jerusalem (DellaPergola et al. 2000b; and author's current updating). Such projections, based on available data on Jewish population composition by age and sex, extrapolate the most recently observed or expected Jewish population trends over the first two decades of the twenty-first century. Even where reliable information on the dynamics of Jewish population change is not available, the powerful connection that generally exists between age composition, birth rates, death rates, and migration helps provide plausible scenarios for the developments that occur in the short term. Where better data were lacking, we used findings from these projections to refine the 2019 estimates against previous years. It should be acknowledged that projections are shaped by a comparatively limited set of assumptions and need to be constantly updated in light of actual demographic developments.

Appendix Table　Jewish population by country, core definition and expanded definitions, 1/1/2019

Country	Total population[a]	Core Jewish population[b] CJP	Jews per 1000 total population	Source Type[c]	Source Accuracy rating[d]	Population with Jewish parent[e] PJP	Enlarged Jewish population[f] EJP	Law of Return population[g] LRP
World	**7,620,497,000**	**14,707,400**	**1.93**			**17,917,750**	**20,876,400**	**23,674,400**
America Total	**1,014,023,000**	**6,469,900**	**6.38**			**8,955,300**	**11,156,200**	**13,418,300**
Bermuda	61,000	100	1.64	C	C 2016	200	300	400
Canada	37,200,000	392,000	10.54	C	B 2018	450,000	550,000	700,000
United States	328,000,000	5,700,000	17.38	S	B 2013	8000,000	10,000,000	12,000,000
Total North America[h]	**365,323,000**	**6,092,100**	**16.68**			**8,450,200**	**10,550,300**	**12,700,400**
Bahamas	400,000	300	0.75	C	D 1990	500	700	900
Costa Rica	5,000,000	2500	0.50	J	C 1993	2800	3100	3400
Cuba	11,100,000	500	0.05	S	C 2013	1000	1500	2000
Dominican Republic	10,800,000	100	0.01	E	D 2000	200	300	400
El Salvador	6,500,000	100	0.02	E	C 1993	200	300	400
Guatemala	17,200,000	900	0.05	S	B 1999	1200	1500	1800
Jamaica	2,900,000	200	0.07	J	C 2010	300	400	500
Mexico	130,800,000	40,000	0.31	C,S	B 2010	45,000	50,000	65,000
Netherlands Antilles	324,000	300	0.93	C	C 2016	500	700	900
Panama	4,200,000	10,000	2.38	S	C 2012	11,000	12,000	13,000
Puerto Rico	3,300,000	1500	0.45	J	C 2000	2000	2500	3000
Virgin Islands	105,000	400	3.81	E	D 2016	600	700	800
Other	29,371,000	200	0.01		D 2016	400	600	800
Total Central Amer., Caribbean	**222,000,000**	**57,000**	**0.26**	S		**65,700**	**74,300**	**92,900**
Argentina	44,500,000	180,000	4.04	S	B 2003	260,000	310,000	360,000

Appendix Table (continued)

Country	Total population[a]	Core Jewish population[b] CJP	Jews per 1000 total population	Source Type[c]	Source Accuracy rating[d]	Population with Jewish parent[e] PJP	Enlarged Jewish population[f] EJP	Law of Return population[g] LRP
Bolivia	11,300,000	500	0.04	J	C 2009	700	900	1100
Brazil	209,400,000	92,600	0.44	C	B 2010	120,000	150,000	180,000
Chile	18,600,000	18,300	0.98	C	B 2002	21,000	25,000	30,000
Colombia	49,800,000	2100	0.04	S	C 2010	2800	3500	4500
Ecuador	17,000,000	600	0.04	J	B 2011	800	1000	1200
Paraguay	6,900,000	1000	0.14	C	B 2002	1300	1600	1900
Peru	32,200,000	1900	0.06	S	C 1993	2400	3000	3500
Suriname	600,000	200	0.33	J	D 2000	400	600	800
Uruguay	3,500,000	16,600	4.74	S	B 2013	20,000	24,000	28,000
Venezuela	31,800,000	7000	0.22	S	C 2012	10,000	12,000	14,000
Total South America[h]	**426,700,000**	**320,800**	**0.75**			**439,400**	**531,600**	**625,000**
EUROPE TOTAL	**827,974,000**	**1,340,200**	**1.62**		X	**1,814,000**	**2,319,400**	**2,813,800**
Austria	8,800,000	10,000	1.14	C,J	B 2018	14,000	17,000	20,000
Belgium	11,400,000	29,100	2.55	J	C 2018	35,000	40,000	45,000
Bulgaria	7,000,000	2000	0.29	C,J	C 2011	4000	6000	8000
Croatia	4,100,000	1700	0.41	C,J	C 2001	2400	3100	3800
Cyprus	1,200,000	100	0.08	E	D 2012	200	300	400
Czechia	10,600,000	3900	0.37	C,J	C 2011	5000	6500	8000
Denmark	5,800,000	6400	1.10	S	C 2018	7500	8500	9500
Estonia	1,300,000	1900	1.46	C,P	A 2017	2700	3500	4500
Finland	5,500,000	1300	0.24	P	B 2010	1600	1900	2200
France[i]	65,140,000	450,000	6.91	S	B 2018	550,000	650,000	750,000
Germany	82,800,000	118,000	1.43	J	B 2018	150,000	225,000	275,000

Country	Total population								
Greece	10,600,000	4200	0.40	J	B 2000		5200	6000	7000
Hungary	9,800,000	47,300	4.83	C	C 2018		75,000	100,000	130,000
Ireland	4,900,000	2600	0.53	C	B 2016		3600	5000	6500
Italy	60,600,000	27,400	0.45	S,J	B 2018		34,000	41,000	48,000
Latvia	1,900,000	4600	2.42	C,P	A 2017		8000	12,000	16,000
Lithuania	2,800,000	2400	0.86	C,P	B 2011		4700	7500	10,500
Luxembourg	600,000	600	1.00	J	B 2000		800	1000	1200
Malta	500,000	100	0.20	E	D 2012		200	300	400
Netherlands	17,200,000	29,800	1.73	S	B 2018		43,000	53,000	63,000
Poland	38,400,000	4500	0.12	C,J	C 2018		7000	10,000	13,000
Portugal	10,300,000	600	0.06	C	C 2001		800	1000	1200
Romania	19,500,000	9000	0.46	C,J	B 2002		13,000	17,000	20,000
Slovakia	5,400,000	2600	0.48	C	C 2011		3600	4600	6000
Slovenia	2,100,000	100	0.05	C	C 2003		200	300	400
Spain	46,700,000	11,700	0.25	J	C 2018		15,000	18,000	21,000
Sweden	10,200,000	15,000	1.47	S	C 2018		20,000	25,000	30,000
United Kingdom[j]	66,600,000	292,000	4.38	C,S	B 2018	X	330,000	370,000	410,000
Total European Union 28	**511,740,000**	**1,078,900**	**2.11**				**1,336,500**	**1,633,500**	**1,910,600**
Gibraltar	35,000	700	20.00	C	B 2019	X	800	900	1000
Norway	5,300,000	1300	0.25	P	B 2010		1600	2000	2500
Switzerland	8,500,000	18,500	2.18	C	B 2012		22,000	25,000	28,000
Total other West Europe[b]	**14,434,000**	**20,500**	**1.42**				**24,400**	**27,900**	**31,500**
Bosnia-Herzegovina	3,500,000	500	0.14	C	C 2001		800	1100	1400
North Macedonia	2,100,000	100	0.05	C	C 1996		200	300	400

(continued)

Appendix Table (continued)

Country	Total population[a]	Core Jewish population[b] CJP	Jews per 1000 total population	Source Type[c]	Accuracy rating[d]		Population with Jewish parent[e] PJP	Enlarged Jewish population[f] EJP	Law of Return population[g] LRP
Serbia	7,000,000	1400	0.20	C	C 2001		2100	2800	3500
Turkey[k]	81,300,000	14,800	0.18	S,J	B 2016		19,000	21,000	23,000
Other	5,300,000	100	0.02		D 2016		200	300	400
Total Balkans	**99,200,000**	**16,900**	**0.17**				**22,300**	**25,500**	**28,700**
Belarus	9,500,000	9000	0.95	C	B 2009		17,000	25,000	33,000
Moldova	3,500,000	1900	0.54	C	B 2014		3800	7500	10,000
Russia[k]	147,300,000	165,000	1.12	C	C 2010	X	320,000	460,000	600,000
Ukraine	42,300,000	48,000	1.13	C	C 2001	X	90,000	140,000	200,000
Total FSU Republics	**202,600,000**	**223,900**	**1.11**				**430,800**	**632,500**	**843,000**
[Total FSU in Europe][l]	**208,600,000**	**232,800**	**1.12**				**446,200**	**655,500**	**874,000**
ASIA TOTAL	**4,453,500,000**	**6,699,700**	**1.50**				**6,928,050**	**7,157,100**	**7,174,300**
Israel[m]	8,543,109	6,246,700	731.20	C,P	A 2019	X	6,455,611	6,664,509	6,664,509
West Bank[n]	3,023,700	418,900	138.54	C,P	A 2019	X	423,339	427,791	427,791
Gaza[n]	1,886,500	0	0.00	C,P	A 2019		0	0	0
Total Israel and Palestinian Territory[o]	**13,453,250**	**6,665,600**	**495.46**				**6,878,950**	**7,092,300**	**7,092,300**
[Total State of Israel][p]	**8,970,900**	**6,665,600**	**743.02**				**6,878,950**	**7,092,300**	**7,092,300**
Armenia	3,000,000	100	0.03	C	B 2011		300	500	700
Azerbaijan	9,900,000	7500	0.76	C	B 2009		10,500	15,500	20,500
Georgia	3,900,000	1500	0.38	C	B 2014		3000	5000	7500
Kazakhstan	18,400,000	2600	0.14	C	B 2009		4800	6500	9500
Kyrgyzstan	6,100,000	400	0.07	C	B 2009		700	1000	1500
Turkmenistan	5,900,000	200	0.03	C	D 1995		400	600	800

Country	Total population	Jewish population	Per 1,000					
Uzbekistan	32,900,000	3000	0.09	C	D 1989	6000	8000	10,000
Total former USSR in Asia[b]	**89,200,000**	**15,300**	**0.17**			**25,700**	**37,100**	**50,500**
China[q]	1,401,900,000	3000	0.00	E	D 2015	3200	3400	3600
India	1,371,300,000	4800	0.00	C	C 2011	6000	7500	9000
Indonesia	265,200,000	100	0.00	E	D 2016	200	300	400
Iran	81,600,000	8300	0.10	C	B 2012	10,500	12,000	13,000
Japan	126,500,000	1000	0.01	E	D 2015	1200	1400	1600
Philippines	107,000,000	100	0.00	E	D 2000	200	300	400
Singapore	5,800,000	900	0.16	J	C 2015	1000	1200	1400
South Korea	51,800,000	100	0.00	J	C 2015	200	300	400
Syria[f]	18,300,000	100	0.01	E	D 2015	200	300	400
Taiwan	23,600,000	100	0.00	E	D 2000	200	300	400
Thailand	66,200,000	200	0.00	E	D 2015	300	400	500
Other	831,646,750	100	0.00		D 2016	200	300	400
Total other Asia	**4,350,846,750**	**18,800**	**0.00**			**23,400**	**27,700**	**31,500**
AFRICA TOTAL	**1,284,000,000**	**72,000**	**0.06**			**81,700**	**88,900**	**97,100**
Egypt	97,000,000	100	0.00	J	C 2015	200	300	400
Ethiopia	107,500,000	100	0.00	S	C 2015	500	1000	2500
Morocco	35,200,000	2100	0.06	J	C 2015	2500	2800	3100
Tunisia	11,600,000	1000	0.09	J	C 2015	1200	1400	1600
Total Northern Africa[h]	**342,800,000**	**3300**	**0.01**			**4400**	**5500**	**7600**
Botswana	2,200,000	100	0.05	E	C 1993	200	300	400
Congo D.R.	84,300,000	100	0.00	E	C 1993	200	300	400
Kenya	51,000,000	300	0.01	J	C 1990	500	700	900

(continued)

Appendix Table (continued)

Country	Total population[a]	Core Jewish population[b] CJP	Jews per 1000 total population	Source Type[c]	Accuracy rating[d]		Population with Jewish parent[e] PJP	Enlarged Jewish population[f] EJP	Law of Return population[g] LRP
Madagascar	26,300,000	100	0.00	J	D 2016		200	300	400
Namibia	2,500,000	100	0.04	C	C 1993		200	300	400
Nigeria	195,900,000	100	0.00	E	D 2000		200	300	400
South Africa	57,700,000	67,500	1.17	C,S	B 2018	X	75,000	80,000	85,000
Zimbabwe	14,000,000	200	0.01	C	B 2001		400	600	800
Other	507,300,000	200	0.00		D 2016		400	600	800
Total Sub-Saharan Africa[s]	**941,200,000**	**68,700**	**0.07**				**77,300**	**83,400**	**89,500**
OCEANIA TOTAL	**41,000,000**	**125,600**	**3.06**				**138,700**	**154,800**	**170,900**
Australia	24,100,000	118,000	4.90	C	A 2016	X	130,000	145,000	160,000
New Zealand	4,900,000	7500	1.53	C	B 2006		8500	9500	10,500
Other	12,000,000	100	0.01	C	D 2016		200	300	400

[a]Source, with minor adjustments: Population Reference Bureau (2019) and United Nations Population Division (2018). Mid-year 2018 estimates

[b]Includes all persons who, when asked, identify themselves as Jews, or, if the respondent is a different person in the same household, are identified by him/her as Jews; and do not have another religion. Also includes persons with a Jewish parent who claim no current religious or ethnic identity

[c]Sum of (a) core Jewish population; (b) persons reported as partly Jewish; and (c) all others not currently Jewish with a Jewish parent

[f]Sum of (a) core Jewish population; (b) persons reported as partly Jewish; (c) all others not currently Jewish with a Jewish parent; and (d) all other non-Jewish household members (spouses, children, etc.)

[g]Sum of Jews, children of Jews, grandchildren of Jews, and all respective spouses, regardless of Jewish identification

[c](C) National population census. (P) National population register. (S) Survey of Jewish population. (J) Jewish community register. (E) Estimate.

[d](A) Base estimate derived from national census or reliable Jewish population survey; updated on the basis of full or partial information on Jewish population movements in the respective country during the intervening period. (B) Base estimate derived from less accurate but recent national Jewish population data; updated on the basis of partial information on Jewish population movements during the intervening period. (C) Base estimate derived from less recent sources and/or less reliable or partial coverage of country's Jewish population; updated on the basis of demographic information illustrative of regional demographic

trends. (D) Base estimate essentially speculative; no reliable updating procedure. In categories A, B, and C, the year in which the country's base estimate or important partial updates were obtained is also stated. This is not the current estimate's date but the basis for its attainment. An X is appended to the accuracy rating for several countries, whose Jewish population estimate for 2019 was not only updated but also revised in light of improved information

[h]Including countries and territories not listed because fewer than 100 core Jews live in each of those countries and in all of those countries combined

[i]Including Monaco

[j]Including the Channel Islands and the Isle of Man

[k]Including Asian regions

[l]Including the Baltic countries which are already included above in the EU

[m]Including East Jerusalem and the Golan Heights, not including the West Bank

[n]Author's revised estimates of total Palestinian population on 1/1/2019: West Bank (without East Jerusalem): 2,595,900; Gaza: 1,886,500; Total: 4,482,400. The West Bank also includes 418,900 Jews and 8,900 non-Jewish members of Jewish households, for a total of 427,800 Jews and others. The reported West Bank total of 3,023,700 includes Palestinian, Jewish and other residents

[o]Not including foreign workers and refugees

[p]Israel's total permanent (de jure) population as defined by Israel's legal system, not including foreign workers and refugees

[q]Including Hong Kong and Macao

[r]Jewish population includes Lebanon

[s]Excluding Sudan and Ethiopia included in Northern Africa

References[2]

Adams, S.M., E. Bosch, P.L. Balaresque, S.J. Ballereau, A.C. Lee, E. Arroyo, A.N. López-Parra, M. Aler, M.S. Gisbert Grifo, M. Brion, A. Carracedo, J. Lavinha, B. Martínez-Jarreta, L. Quintana-Murci, A. Picornell, M. Ramon, K. Skorecki, D.M. Behar, F. Calafell, and M.A. Jobling. 2008. The genetic legacy of religious diversity and intolerance: Paternal lineages of Christians, Jews, and Muslims in the Iberian Peninsula. *The American Journal of Human Genetics* 83 (6): 725–736.

Adler, S. 2004. *Emigration among immigrants from Argentina that arrived during the period 1.1.89–31.12.02.* Jerusalem: State of Israel Ministry of Immigrant Absorption, Division of Planning and Research.

Amit, K., A. Borowski, and S. DellaPergola. 2010. Demography: Trends and composition. In *Immigration and nation building: Australia and Israel compared*, ed. A. Markus and M. Semyonov, 15–45. Cheltenham/Northampton: Edward Elgar/Monash University.

Amit, K., and S. DellaPergola. 2016. Demografie und Migration in Israel. In *Ländbericht Israel*, ed. G. Dachs, 125–150. Bonn: Bundeszentrale für politische Bildung.

Amt für Statistik Berlin-Brandenburg. 2012. *Statistisches Jahrbuch Berlin 2012.* Berlin: Amt für Statistik Berlin-Brandenburg.

———. 2014. *Statistisches Jahrbuch Berlin 2014.* Berlin: Amt für Statistik Berlin-Brandenburg.

Australian Bureau of Statistics. 2002. *Population census 2001.* Canberra: Australian Bureau of Statistics.

———. 2007. *Population census 2006.* Canberra: Australian Bureau of Statistics.

———. 2012. *Population census 2011.* Canberra: Australian Bureau of Statistics.

Bachi, R. 1976. *Population trends of world Jewry.* Jerusalem: The Hebrew University, Institute of Contemporary Jewry.

———. 1977. *The population of Israel.* Paris/Jerusalem: CICRED/The Hebrew University and Demographic Center, Prime Minister's Office.

Bass, D. 2011. *Conversions in Israel.* Personal communication.

Barack Fishman, S. 2004. *Double or nothing? Jewish families and mixed marriage.* Hanover/London: Brandeis University Press.

Barack Fishman, S., and S.M. Cohen. 2017. *Family, Engagement, and Jewish Continuity among American Jews*, 6–38. Jerusalem: Jewish People Policy Institute.

BBC. 2015. *Portugal to naturalise descendants of Jews expelled centuries ago.* London: January 29. https://www.bbc.com/news/world-europe-31051223

Behar, D.M., M.F. Hammer, D. Garrigan, R. Villems, B. Bonné-Tamir, M. Richards, D. Gurwitz, D. Rosengarten, M. Kaplan, S. DellaPergola, L. Quintana-Murci, and K. Skorecki. 2004. MtDNA evidence for a genetic bottleneck in the early history of the Ashkenazi Jewish population. *European Journal of Human Genetics* 12: 355–364.

Behar, D.M., B. Yunusbayev, M. Metspalu, E. Metspalu, S. Rosset, J. Parik, S. Rootsi, G. Chaubey, I. Kutuev, G. Yudkovsk, E.K. Khusnutdinova, O. Balanovsky, O. Semino, L. Pereira, D. Comas, D. Gurwitz, B. Bonné-Tamir, T. Parfitt, M.F. Hammer, K. Skorecki, and R. Villems. 2010. The genome-wide structure of the Jewish people. *Nature* 238–242: 1–6, 9 June. http://www.nature.com/dofinder/10.1038/nature09103.

Belstat. 2009. *Population Census of Belarus 2009.* http://belstat.gov.by/homep/ru/perepic/2009/vihod_tables/5.8-0.pdf

Ben Rafael, E. 2013. Belgium. In *Perceptions and experiences of antisemitism among Jews in selected EU member states*, ed. L. Staetsky, J. Boyd, E. Ben-Rafael, E. Cohen, S. DellaPergola, L. Dencik, O. Glöckner, and A. Kovács, 93–94. London: JPR/Institute for Jewish Policy Research; Ipsos MORI.

---

[2] The following is the full list of sources utilized in the preparation of this chapter. Some of the sources may not be listed in the text.

Berenstein, N., and R. Porzecanski. 2001. *Perfil de los egresados de la Red Formal de Educación Judía Uruguaya*. Montevideo: Fundación L.A. Pincus para la educación Judía en la Diáspora, Israel; Consejo de Educación Judía del Uruguay.

Berger, G., M. Tchimino, S. Korinfeld, and V. Zuñiga. 1995. *Estudio Socio-Demográfico de la Comunidad Judía de la Región Metropolitana de Santiago*. Santiago/Buenos Aires: Comité Representativo de las Entidades Judías de Chile-American Joint Distribution Committee, Oficina Buenos Aires-Area Latinoamericana.

Bokser Liwerant, J. 2013. Latin American Jews in the United States: Community and Belonging in Times of Transnationalism. *Contemporary Jewry* 33 (1–2): 121–143.

Bokser-Liwerant, J., S. DellaPergola, L. Senkman, and Y. Goldstein. 2015. *El educador judío latinoamericano en un mundo transnacional. 1. Informe de investigación. 2. Síntesis, conclusiones y recomendaciones del informe de investigación*. Jerusalem: The Hebrew University, Centro Liwerant; Mexico: Universidad Hebraica; Buenos Aires: AMIA.

Boyd, J., and L. Staetsky. 2013. United Kingdom. In *Perceptions and experiences of antisemitism among Jews in selected EU member states*, ed. L. Staetsky, J. Boyd, E. Ben-Rafael, E. Cohen, S. DellaPergola, L. Dencik, O. Glöckner, and A. Kovács, 121–124. London: JPR/Institute for Jewish Policy Research; Ipsos MORI.

Bruk, S. 2006. *The Jews of South Africa 2005—Report on a research study*. Cape Town: South African Jewish Board of Deputies.

Brym, R., K. Neuman, and R. Lenton. 2019a. *2018 Survey of Jews in Canada. Final Report*. Toronto: Environics Institute for Survey Research, University of Toronto, and York University.

Brym, R., A. Slavina, and R. Lenton. 2019b. *Qualifying the Leading Theory of Diaspora Jewry: An Examination of Jews from the Former Soviet Union in Canada and the United States*. Toronto: University of Toronto (publication forthcoming). Paper presented at a symposium in honor of Dr. Mark Tolts, The Hebrew University of Jerusalem, 27 June 2019.

Campelli, E. 2013. *Comunità va cercando, ch'è sí cara …. Sociologia dell'Italia ebraica*. Milano: Franco Angeli.

———. 2016. Le comunità ebraiche italiane: dati, processi, atteggiamenti. In *Sociologia degli ebrei italiani*, ed. G. Pacifici. Milano: Franco Angeli.

Carmi, S., K.Y. Hui, E. Kochav, X. Liu, J. Xue, F. Grady, S. Guha, et al. 2014. Sequencing an Ashkenazi reference panel supports population-targeted personal genomics and illuminates Jewish and European origins. *Nature Communications* 5: 4835.

Casale Mashiah, D. 2018. *Vital Statistics of the UK Jewish population: births and deaths*. London: Jewish Policy Research Institute JPR.

Casale Mashiah, D., and J. Boyd. 2017. *Synagogue membership in the United Kingdom in 2016*. London: Jewish Policy Research Institute JPR.

Choshen, M., E. Bluer, Y. Assaf-Shapira, and I. Doron, eds. 2010. *Statistical yearbook of Jerusalem 2009/2010*. Vol. 24. Jerusalem: Jerusalem Municipality and the Jerusalem Institute for Israel Studies.

Choshen, M., I. Doron, Y. Assaf-Shapira, and E. Bluer, eds. 2012. *Statistical yearbook of Jerusalem 2012*. Vol. 26. Jerusalem: Jerusalem Municipality and the Jerusalem Institute for Israel Studies.

Cohen, E.H. 2005. *Les touristes de France en Israël 2004*. Jerusalem: unpublished paper.

———. 2007. *Heureux comme Juifs en France? Étude sociologique*. Jerusalem: Elkana et Akadem.

———. 2013a. *Les Juifs de France: Un tournant?* Ramat Gan: Bar Ilan University.

———. 2013b. France. In *Perceptions and experiences of antisemitism among Jews in selected EU member states*, ed. L. Staetsky, J. Boyd, E. Ben-Rafael, E. Cohen, S. DellaPergola, L. Dencik, O. Glöckner, and A. Kovács, 95–97. London: JPR/Institute for Jewish Policy Research; Ipsos MORI.

Cohen, E.H., and M. Ifergan. 2003. *Les Juifs de France: Valeurs et identité*. Paris: Fonds Social Juif Unifié.

Cohen, S.M., J.B. Ukeles, and R. Miller. 2012. *Jewish community study of New York, 2011. Comprehensive report*. New York: UJA Federation of New York.

Cohen, Y. 2009. Migration to and from Israel. *Contemporary Jewry* 29 (2): 115–125.

Cohen, Y., and I. Kogan. 2005. Jewish immigration from the Former Soviet Union to Germany and Israel in the 1990s. *Leo Baeck Institute Year Book* 50: 249–265.

Cohen-Weisz, S. 2010. *Like the Phoenix rising from the ashes: Jewish identity and communal reconstruction in Austria and Germany.* Jerusalem: The Hebrew University, Unpublished PhD dissertation.

Cohn, S. 2003. *Résultats élections législatives* (unpublished manuscript). Brussels.

Comité Central Israelita de México. 2000. *Estudio sobre tendencias de la educación judía en México. Censo socio-demográfico de la comunidad judía de México.* México: Comité Central Israelita de México.

———. 2006. *Estudio poblacional de la comunidad judía de México.* México: Comité Central Israelita de México.

Comunidad Judía de Mexico. 2015. *Estudio socio-demográfico 2015.* México: Comunidad Judía de Mexico.

Corinaldi, M. 1998. Jewish identity, Chapter 2. In *Jewish identity: The case of Ethiopian Jewry*, ed. M. Corinaldi. Jerusalem: Magnes Press, Hebrew University.

———. 2001. *The enigma of Jewish identity: The law of return, theory and practice.* Srigim-Lion: Nevo. (in Hebrew).

———. 2018. *Who is a Jew. "Beta Israel": from Ethiopian Exile to Return to Zion.* Tel Aviv: Law Books Publishing House (Hebrew).

Cytto, O. 2007. *Jewish identification in contemporary Spain—A European case study.* Jerusalem: European Forum at The Hebrew University, Helmut Kohl Institute for European Studies in collaboration with Konrad Adenauer Stiftung.

Dashefsky, A., and Z.I. Heller. 2008. *Intermarriage and Jewish journeys in the United States.* Newton Centre: The National Center for Jewish Policy Studies at Hebrew College.

Decol, R. 1999. *Imigraçoes urbanas para o Brasil: o caso dos Judeus.* Campinas: Universidade Estadual, unpublished PhD dissertation.

Decol, R.D. 2009. A demographic profile of Brazilian Jewry. *Contemporary Jewry* 29 (2): 99–113.

DellaPergola, S. 1975. The Italian Jewish population study: Demographic characteristics and trends. In *Studies in Jewish demography: Survey for 1969–1971*, ed. U.O. Schmelz, P. Glikson, and S.J. Gould, 60–97. Jerusalem: The Hebrew University, Institute of Contemporary Jewry, and London: Institute of Jewish Affairs.

———. 1987. Demographic trends of Latin American Jewry. In *The Jewish presence in Latin America*, ed. J. Laikin Elkin and G.W. Merkx, 85–133. Boston: Allen and Unwin.

———. 1992. Recent Trends in Jewish Marriage. In *World Jewish Population: Trends and Policies*, ed. S. DellaPergola and L. Cohen, 56–92. Jerusalem: The Hebrew University, The Institute of Contemporary Jewry.

———. 1993. Jews in the European community: Sociodemographic trends and challenges. In *American Jewish Year Book*, vol. 93, 25–82. New York: American Jewish Committee.

———. 1995. Changing cores and peripheries: Fifty years in socio-demographic perspective. In *Terms of survival: The Jewish world since 1945*, ed. R.S. Wistrich, 13–43. London: Routledge.

———. 1999. *World Jewry beyond 2000: Demographic prospects.* Oxford: Oxford Centre for Hebrew and Jewish Studies.

———. 2001. Some fundamentals of Jewish demographic history. In *Papers in Jewish demography 1997*, ed. S. DellaPergola and J. Even, 11–33. Jerusalem: The Hebrew University.

———. 2002. Demography. In *The Oxford handbook of Jewish studies*, ed. M. Goodman, 797–823. Oxford: Oxford University Press.

———. 2003a. *Jewish demography: Facts, outlook, challenges, Alert paper, 2.* Jerusalem: Jewish People Policy Planning Institute.

———. 2003b. Demographic trends in Israel and Palestine: Prospects and policy implications. In *American Jewish Year Book*, vol. 103, 3–68. New York: American Jewish Committee.

———. 2005. Was it the demography? A reassessment of U.S. Jewish population estimates, 1945–2001. *Contemporary Jewry* 25: 85–131.

————. 2007a. Population trends and scenarios in Israel and Palestine. In *Population resettlement in international conflicts: A comparative study*, ed. A.M. Kacowicz and P. Lutomski, 183–207. Lanham: Rowman & Littlefield.

————. 2007b. Correspondence. *Azure* 27: 3–33.

————. 2008a. Autonomy and dependency: Latin American Jewry in global perspective. In *Identities in an era of globalization and multiculturalism: Latin America in the Jewish world*, ed. J. Bokser Liwerant, E. Ben-Rafael, Y. Gorni, and R. Rein, 47–80. Leiden/Boston: Brill.

————. 2008b. Demography, planning and policy, 2000–2020. In *40 years in Jerusalem*, ed. O. Achimeir and Y. BarSimantov, 39–59. Jerusalem: Jerusalem Institute of Israel Studies. (in Hebrew).

————. 2009a. International migration of Jews. In *Transnationalism: Diasporas and the advent of a new (dis)order*, ed. E. Ben-Rafael and Y. Sternberg, 213–236. Leiden/Boston: Brill.

————. 2009b. Jewish out-marriage: A global perspective. In *Jewish intermarriage around the world*, ed. S. Reinharz and S. DellaPergola, 13–39. London/New Brunswick: Transaction.

————. 2009c. Actual, intended, and appropriate family size among Jews in Israel. *Contemporary Jewry* 29 (2): 127–152.

————. 2009d. *Fertility prospects in Israel: Ever below replacement level? United Nations expert group meeting on Recent and future trends in fertility*. New York: United Nations Secretariat, Department of Economic and Social Affairs, Population Division.

————. 2010a. *World Jewish population, 2010. Current Jewish population reports, Report 2010–2*. Storrs: The North American Jewish Data Bank, the Association for the Social Scientific Study of Jewry, and the Jewish Federations of North America.

————. 2010b. Jews in Europe: Demographic trends, contexts, outlooks. In *A road to nowhere? Jewish experiences in unifying Europe?* ed. J. Schoeps and E. Ben-Rafael, 3–34. Leiden/Boston: Brill.

————. 2011a. *Jewish demographic policies: Population trends and options in Israel and in the diaspora*. Jerusalem: Jewish People Policy Institute.

————. 2011b. Cuántos somos hoy? Investigacón y narrativa sobre población judía en América Latina. In *Pertenencia y Alteridad—Judios en/de America Latina: cuarenta años de cambios*, ed. H. Avni, J. Bokser-Liwerant, S. DellaPergola, M. Bejarano, and L. Senkman, 305–340. Madrid/Frankfurt am Main: Iberoamericana—Vervuert.

————. 2011c. When scholarship disturbs narrative: Ian Lustick on Israel's migration balance. *Israel Studies Review: An Interdisciplinary Journal* 26 (2): 1–20.

————. 2013. World Jewish population, 2012. In *American Jewish Year Book 2012*, ed. A. Dashefsky and I. Sheskin, 213–283. Dordrecht: Springer.

————. 2013a. How many Jews in the US? The demographic perspective. *Contemporary Jewry* 33 (1–2): 15–42.

————. 2014b. World Jewish population, 2013. In *American Jewish Year Book 2013*, ed. A. Dashefsky and I. Sheskin, 279–358. Cham: Springer.

————. 2013c. Italy. In *Perceptions and experiences of antisemitism among Jews in selected EU member states*, ed. L. Staetsky, J. Boyd, E. Ben-Rafael, E. Cohen, S. DellaPergola, L. Dencik, O. Glöckner, and A. Kovács, 103–106. London: JPR/Institute for Jewish Policy Research; Ipsos MORI.

————. 2014a. Jewish peoplehood: Hard, soft and interactive markers. In *Reconsidering Israel-diaspora relations*, ed. E. Ben-Rafael, Y. Gorni, and J. Liwerant, 25–59. Leiden/Boston: Brill.

————. 2014c. Reflections on the multinational geography of Jews after world war II. In *Displacement, migration and integration: A comparative approach to Jewish migrants and refugees in the post-war period*, ed. F. Ouzan and M. Gerstenfeld, 13–33. Leiden/Boston: Brill.

————. 2014d. Jewish demography: Fundamentals of the research field. In *Studies in Contemporary Jewry*, ed. U. Rebhun, vol. 27, 3–36. New York: Oxford University Press.

————. 2014e. Measuring Jewish Populations. In *Yearbook of International Religious Demography 2014*, ed. B.J. Grim, T.M. Johnson, V. Skirbekk, and G.A. Zurlo, 97–110. Leiden/Boston: Brill.

———. 2015a. World Jewish population, 2014. In *American Jewish Year Book 2014*, ed. A. Dashefsky and I. Sheskin, 301–393. Cham: Springer.

———. 2015b. End of Jewish/Non-Jewish Dichotomy? Evidence from the 2013 Pew Survey. In *American Jewish Year Book*, ed. A. Dashefsky and I. Sheskin, vol. 114, 33–39. Cham: Springer.

———. 2016. World Jewish Population 2015. In *American Jewish Year Book 2015*, ed. A. Dashefsky and I. Sheskin, 273–364. Cham: Springer.

———. 2015c. View from a different planet: Fertility attitudes, performances and policies among Jewish Israelis. In *Love, Marriage and Jewish Families Today: Paradoxes of a Social Revolution*, ed. S. Fishman, 123–150. Waltham: Brandeis University Press.

———. 2015d. On Behalf of the Epistemic Community: Contexts and Standards of American Jewishness. *Contemporary Jewry* 35 (2): 129–135.

———. 2017a. World Jewish Population 2016. In *American Jewish Year Book 2016*, ed. A. Dashefsky and I. Sheskin, 241–332. Cham: Springer.

———. 2017b. Jewish Demography in the European Union—Virtuous and Vicious Paths. In *Being Jewish in Central Europe Today*, ed. D. Porat and M. Zoufala. Berlin: De Gruyter (forthcoming).

———. 2017c. Disciplinary, normative and institutional aspects of conversions to Judaism. In *New Ways of Joining the Jewish People*, ed. Tudor Parfitt and Netanel Fisher, 204–223. Cambridge: Cambridge Scholars Publishing.

———. 2017d. Ethnoreligious Intermarriage in Israel: An Exploration of the 2008 Census. *Journal of Israeli History* 36 (2): 149–170. https://doi.org/10.1080/13531042.2018.1532565.

———. 2018. World Jewish Population 2017. In *American Jewish Year Book 2017*, ed. A. Dashefsky and I. Sheskin, 297–377. Cham: Springer.

———. 2019a. World Jewish Population 2018. In *American Jewish Year Book 2018*, ed. A. Dashefsky and I. Sheskin, 361–449. Cham: Springer.

———. 2019b. Reflections on Jewish and Israeli Migrations: The National and the Transnational. In *Paper presented at International Conference People on the Move: Migration and Mobility*. Tel Aviv: Tel Aviv University.

DellaPergola, S., and L. Cohen, eds. 1992. *World Jewish population: Trends and policies*. Jerusalem: The Hebrew University, and Prime Minister Office, The Demographic Center.

DellaPergola, S., and A.A. Dubb. 1988. South African Jewry: A Sociodemographic Profile. In *American Jewish Year Book*, vol. 88, 59–140. Philadelphia/New York: Jewish Publication Society and American Jewish Committee.

DellaPergola, S., and S. Lerner. 1995. La población judía de México: Perfil demográfico, social y cultural. In *México: Asociación de Amigos de la Universidad Hebrea de Jerusalén, and Colegio de Mexico*. Jerusalén: Universidad Hebrea de Jerusalén.

DellaPergola, S., and U.O. Schmelz. 1978. *The Jews of greater Mexico City according to the 1970 population census: First data and critical evaluation*. Jerusalem: Universidad Hebrea, Instituto de Judaísmo Contemporáneo, mimeo.

———. 1989. Demography and Jewish education in the diaspora: Trends in Jewish school-age population and school enrollment. In *Jewish education worldwide: Cross-cultural perspectives*, ed. H.S. Himmelfarb and S. DellaPergola, 43–68. Lanham: University Press of America.

DellaPergola, S., and I.M. Sheskin. 2015. Global Dispersion of Jews: Determinants and Consequences. In The Changing World Religion Map: Sacred Places, Identities, Practices and Politics, ed. S.B. Brunn, Chap. 70, 1311–1343. Cham: Springer.

DellaPergola, S., U. Rebhun, and M. Tolts. 1999. American Jewry: A population projection, 1990–2020. In *Jews in America: A contemporary reader*, ed. R. Rosenberg Farber and C.I. Waxman, 33–50. Hanover/London: Brandeis University Press/University Press of New England.

DellaPergola, S., S. Benzaquen, and T. Beker de Weinraub. 2000a. *Perfil sociodemográfico y cultural de la comunidad judía de Caracas*. Caracas/Jerusalem: The Hebrew University of Jerusalem.

DellaPergola, S., U. Rebhun, and M. Tolts. 2000b. Prospecting the Jewish future: Population pro-jections 2000–2080. In *American Jewish Year Book*, vol. 100, 103–146. New York: American Jewish Committee.
———. 2005. Contemporary Jewish diaspora in global context: Human development correlates of population trends. *Israel Studies* 11 (1): 61–95.
Dencik, L. 2003. *'Jewishness' in postmodernity: The case of Sweden, Paideia report.* Stockholm: The European Institute for Jewish Studies.
———. 2013. Sweden. In *Perceptions and experiences of antisemitism among Jews in selected EU member states*, ed. L. Staetsky, J. Boyd, E. Ben-Rafael, E. Cohen, S. DellaPergola, L. Dencik, O. Glöckner, and A. Kovács, 112–120. London: JPR/Institute for Jewish Policy Research; Ipsos MORI.
Dietz, B., U. Lebok, and P. Polian. 2002. The Jewish emigration from the former Soviet Union to Germany. *International Migration* 40 (2): 29–48.
Dobrin, N. 2006. Marriages of Israelis abroad and the role of former Soviet Union immigrants. *Megamot* 44 (3): 477–506.
Dubb, A.A. 1994. *The Jewish Population of South Africa: The 1991 Sociodemographic Survey.* Cape Town: University of Cape Town, Kaplan Centre.
Eckstein, G. 2003. *Demography of the Sydney Jewish community 2001.* Sydney: unpublished paper.
———. 2009. Intermarriage among Jewish Australians. In *Jewish intermarriage around the world*, ed. S. Reinharz and S. DellaPergola, 139–152. New Brunswick/London: Transaction.
Erdei, E. 2014. *Choosing Each Other: Exogamy in the Jewish Community of Buenos Aires.* Buenos Aires: JDC International Center for Community Development.
Erlanger, S. 2006. *Jewish people policy planning institute annual assessment 2006, deltas creating opportunities and threats, executive report 3.* Jerusalem: JPPPI.
Ettinger, Y. 2019. Israel's Jewish Demography Refutes Pessimism. *The Ettinger Report*, September 29. http://theettingerreport.com/israels-jewish-demography-refutes-pessimism/
European Union Fundamental Rights Agency-FRA. 2013. *Discrimination and hate crime against Jews in EU Member States: Experiences and perceptions of antisemitism.* Vienna: European Union Agency for Fundamental Rights.
———. 2018. *Experiences and perceptions of antisemitism—Second survey on discrimination and hate crime against Jews in the EU.* Luxembourg: Publications Office of the European Union.
Eurostat. 2015. *Immigration by five-year age group, sex and country of previous residence.* http://appsso.eurostatt.ec.europe.eu/nui/print.do. Accessed 6 Jan 2016.
Federação Israelita do Estado de São Paulo FISESP. 2002. *Recadastramento comunitário 2000–01.* São Paulo: FISESP.
Feitelson, Y. 2013. *The demographic processes in the Land of Israel (1800–2013).* Jerusalem: The Institute for Zionist Strategies.
Filiba, L. 2003. *Turkish Jewish community demographic survey 2002–3.* Istanbul: Jewish Community of Turkey Council.
Fisher, N. 2013. A Jewish State? Controversial Conversions and the Dispute Over Israel's Jewish Character. *Contemporary Jewry* 33 (3): 217–240.
———. 2015. *The Challenge of Conversion to Judaism in Israel: Policy Analysis and Recommendations.* Jerusalem: The Israel Democracy Institute (Hebrew).
———. 2019. *"Israeli" Halakha: The Chief Rabbinate's conversion-to-Judaism Policy 1948–2018.* https://academic.oup.com/mj/advance-article-abstract/doi/10.1093/mj/kjy018/5263974
Fishman, S. 2015. American Jewishness Today: Identity and Transmissibility in an Open World. Marshall Sklare Award Lecture. *Contemporary Jewry* 35 (2): 109–128.
Forrest, J., and I.M. Sheskin. 2014. Strands of Diaspora: The Resettlement Experience of Jewish Immigrants to Australia. *Journal of International Migration and Integration* 15 (4): 1–17.
Gavison, R. 2009. *60 years to the law of return: History, ideology, justification.* Jerusalem: Metzilah Center for Zionist, Jewish, Liberal and Humanistic Thought.

Gitelman, Z. 2003. Becoming Jewish in Russia and Ukraine. In *New Jewish identities: Contemporary Europe and beyond*, ed. Z. Gitelman, B. Kosmin, and A. Kovács, 105–137. Budapest/New York: Central European University.

Glick, P.C. 1960. Intermarriage and fertility patterns among persons in major religious groups. *Eugenics Quarterly* 7: 31–38.

Główny Urząd Statystyczny. 2012. *Raport z wyników. Narodowy Spis ludności i mieszkań 2011*. Warsaw: GUS.

Glöckner, O. 2013. Germany. In *Perceptions and experiences of antisemitism among Jews in selected EU member states*, ed. L. Staetsky, J. Boyd, E. Ben-Rafael, E. Cohen, S. DellaPergola, L. Dencik, O. Glöckner, and A. Kovács, 98–100. London: JPR/Institute for Jewish Policy Research; Ipsos MORI.

Gold, S.J. 2002. *The Israeli Diaspora*. London and New York: Routledge.

Gold, S.J., and B.A. Phillips. 1996. Israelis in the United States. In *The American Jewish Year Book*, vol. 96, 51–101. New York: The American Jewish Committee.

Goldman, G. 2009. Intermarriage among Jews in Canada: A demographic perspective. In *Jewish intermarriage around the world*, ed. S. Reinharz and S. DellaPergola, 105–114. New Brunswick/London: Transaction.

Goldstein, S. 1969. Socioeconomic differentials among religious groups in the United States. *The American Journal of Sociology* 74 (6): 612–631.

———. 1981. Jews in the United States: Perspectives from demography. *American Jewish Year Book* 81: 3–59.

———. 1989. American Jewish demography: Inconsistencies that challenge. In *Papers in Jewish demography 1985*, ed. U.O. Schmelz and S. DellaPergola, 23–42. Jerusalem: The Hebrew University.

———. 1992. Profile of American Jewry: Insights from the 1990 National Jewish population survey. *American Jewish Year Book* 92: 77–173.

Goldstein, S., and A. Goldstein. 1997. *Lithuanian Jewry 1993: A demographic and sociocultural profile*. Jerusalem: The Hebrew University, The Institute of Contemporary Jewry.

Goskomstat. 1994. *Mikroperepis' naselenii Rossiiskoi Federatsii 1994*. Moscow: Goskomstat (author's own processing).

Graham, D. 2004. European Jewish identity at the Dawn of the 21st century: A working paper. In *A report for the American Joint Distribution Committee and Hanadiv Charitable Foundation*. Budapest: JPR-Institute for Jewish Policy Research.

Graham, D.J. 2008. *The socio-spatial boundaries of an 'invisible' minority: A quantitative reappraisal of Britain's Jewish population*. Oxford: University of Oxford, St Catherine's College, Un published PhD thesis.

Graham, D. 2011. Enumerating Britain's Jewish population: reassessing the 2001 census in the context of one hundred years of indirect estimates. *The Jewish Journal of Sociology* 53: 7–28.

———. 2012. *Adjusting the Jewish population count in the 2011 Australian census; Methodological summary*. London: JPR-Institute for Jewish Policy Research.

———. 2013a. *2011 census results thinning and thickening: Geographical change in the UK's Jewish population, 2001–2011*. London: Institute for Jewish Policy Research.

———. 2013b. *2011 Census Results (England and Wales): A Tale of Two Jewish Populations*. London: Institute for Jewish Policy Research.

———. 2014a. *The Jewish population of Australia: Key findings from the 2011 census*. Melbourne: JCA and Monash University, Australian Centre for Jewish Civilisation.

———. 2014b. *The Jewish population of New South Wales: Key findings from the 2011 Census*. Melbourne: JCA and Monash University, Australian Centre for Jewish Civilisation.

———. 2016. *Jews in couples. Marriage, intermarriage, cohabitation and divorce in Britain*. London: JPR/Institute for Jewish Policy Research. https://bit.ly/2CHF3GQ.

———. 2018. Britain and Australia, a World Apart, Together: An International Contextualization of Jewish Intermarriage Using Census Data. In *Jewish Population and Identity: Concept and Reality*, ed. S. DellaPergola and U. Rebhun, 3–24. Cham: Springer.

Graham, D., and M.L. Caputo. 2015. *Jewish families and Jewish households: Census insights about how we live*. London: Institute for Jewish Policy Research.

Graham, D., and A. Markus. 2018. *GEN17 Australian Jewish Community Survey: Preliminary Findings*. Melbourne: Australian Centre for Jewish Civilisation, Faculty of Arts, Monash University.

Graham, D., with L. Narunski. 2019. The Jewish population of Australia: Key findings from the 2016 Census. London: Jewish Policy Research Institute JPR.

Graham, D., and D. Vulkan. 2007. *Britain's Jewish community statistics*. London: Board of Deputies of British Jews.

———. 2008. *Britain's Jewish community statistics*. London: Board of Deputies of British Jews.

———. 2010. *Synagogue membership in the United Kingdom in 2010*. London: JPR-Institute for Jewish Policy Research and The Board of Deputies of British Jews.

Graham, D., and S. Waterman. 2005. Underenumeration of the Jewish Population in the UK 2001 Census. *Population, Space and Place* 11: 89–102.

Graham, D.J., and S. Waterman. 2007. Locating Jews by ethnicity: A reply to David Voas 2007. *Population, Space and Place* 13: 409–414.

Graham, D., J. Boyd, and D. Vulkan. 2012. *2011 census results England and Wales: Initial insights about the UK Jewish population*. London: Institute for Jewish Policy Research.

Graham, D., M. Schmool, and S. Waterman. 2007. *Jews in Britain: A snapshot from the 2001 census, JPR report, 1*. London: Institute for Jewish Policy Research.

Grim, B.J., T.M. Johnson, V. Skirbekk, and G.A. Zurlo. 2014. *Yearbook of International Religious Demography*. Leiden/Boston: Brill.

Groeneman, S., and T.W. Smith. 2009. *Moving: The impact of geographical mobility on the Jewish community*. New York: The Jewish Federations of North America.

Gross, A., A. Moryosef, and J. Cohen, eds. 2019. *Iberian New Christians and Their Descendants*. Cambridge: Cambridge Scholars Publishing.

Hackett, C. 2014. Seven things to consider when measuring religious identity. *Religion* 44 (3): 396–413.

Hackett, C., B. Grim, M. Stonawski, V. Skirbekk, N. Kusiakose, and M. Potančoková. 2014. Methodology of the Pew Research *Global Religions Landscape* Study. In *Yearbook of International Religious Demography 2014*, ed. B.J. Grim, T.M. Johnson, V. Skirbekk, and G.A. Zurlo, 167–175. Leiden/Boston: Brill.

Hammer, M., A.J. Redd, E.T. Wood, M.R. Bonner, H. Jarjanazi, T. Karafet, S. Santachiara-Benerecetti, A. Oppenheim, M.A. Jobling, T. Jenkins, H. Ostrer, and B. Bonné-Tamir. 2000. Jewish and Middle Eastern non-Jewish populations share a common pool of Y-chromosome biallelic haplotypes. *Proceedings of the National Academy of Sciences* 97 (12): 6769–6774.

Harpaz, Y. 2013. Rooted Cosmopolitans: Israelis with a European Passport—History, Property, Identity. *International Migration Review* 47 (1): 166–206.

Harpaz, Y., and B. Herzog. 2018. *Report on Citizenship Law: Israel*. S. Domenico di Fiesole: European University Institute.

Hart, R., and E. Kafka. 2006. *Trends in British synagogue membership, 1990–2005/6*. London: The Board of Deputies of British Jews.

Hartman, H. 2017. The Jewish Family. In *American Jewish Year Book 2016*, ed. A. Dashefsky and I. Sheskin, 79–126. Cham: Springer.

Hartman, H., and M. Hartman. 2009. *Gender and American Jews: Patterns in Work, Education & Family in Contemporary Life*. Waltham, MA: Brandeis University Press.

Hartman, H., and I.M. Sheskin. 2012. The Relationship of Jewish Community Contexts and Jewish Identity: A 22-Community Study. *Contemporary Jewry* 32 (3): 237–283.

Hass, A. 2019. The state concedes its attempt to avoid settlement of residents from Gaza to the West Bank. *Haaretz*, September 12 (Hebrew).

Heilman, S., ed. 2005. *Contemporary Jewry* 25.

———., ed. 2013. *Contemporary Jewry* 33(1–2).

HIAS. 2013. *Annual. Statistical report*. New York: The Hebrew Immigrant Aid Society.

Hungarian Central Statistical Office. 2003. *Population Census 2001*. Budapest: KSH.
————. 2013. *Population Census 2011*. Budapest: KSH.
Ifop pour la Fondation Jean Jaurès. 2015. *Enquête auprès des Juifs de France*. Paris: IFOP.
Instituto Brasilero de Geografia e Estatistica IBGE. 1980. *Population census*. Rio de Janeiro: IBGE.
————. 1991. *Population census*. Rio de Janeiro: IBGE.
————. 2000. *Population census*. Rio de Janeiro: IBGE.
————. 2010. *Population census*. Rio de Janeiro: IBGE.
Instituto Nacional de Estadistica. 2003. *Censo 2002: Sintesis de Resultados*. Santiago de Chile: Instituto Nacional de Estadistica.
Instituto Nacional de Estadística, Geografia e Informatica. 2002. *XII Censo General de Población y Vivienda 2000*. Mexico City: Instituto Nacional de Estadística, Geografía e Informatica.
Instituto Nacional de Estadística y Geografía. 2012. *La población con religion Judía en México*. Mexico City: Instituto Nacional de Estadística y Geografía.
Ireland Central Statistics Office. 2012. *Census of Population 2011*. Dublin: Ireland Central Statistics Office.
————. 2017. *Census of Population 2016*. Dublin: Ireland Central Statistics Office.
Israel Central Bureau of Statistics. n.d.-a. *Annual. Statistical abstract of Israel*. Jerusalem: Central Bureau of Statistics. https://www.cbs.gov.il/he/publications/Pages/2018/%D7%94%D7%A9%D7%A0%D7%AA%D7%95%D7%9F-%D7%94%D7%9E%D7%9C%D7%90-2018.aspx.
————. n.d.-b. *Monthly. Israel statistical monthly*. Jerusalem: Central Bureau of Statistics. Accessed http://www.cbs.gov.il.
Israel IDF Civilian Administration in Judea and Samaria. 2018. *Demography in Judea and Samaria*. Jerusalem: Israel Defense Forces.
Israel Ministry of Diaspora Affairs. 2018. *Report of the Consultative Public Commission to Evaluate Israel's Attitudes to World Populations with an Attachment to the Jewish People*. Jerusalem: Ministry of Diaspora Affair. 152 pp.
Israel Population and Migration Authority. 2019. *Data on foreigners in Israel*. Jerusalem: Israel Population and Migration Authority, Division of Policy Planning, 2019 (Hebrew).
Jerusalem Institute of Israel Studies. 2015. *Statistical yearbook of Jerusalem 2015*. Jerusalem: Jerusalem Municipality and Jerusalem Institute for Israel Studies.
Jerusalem Institute for Policy Research. 2016. *Statistical yearbook of Jerusalem 2016*. Jerusalem: Jerusalem Municipality and Jerusalem Institute for Policy Research.
Jmelnizky, A., and E. Erdei. 2005. *Estudio de Población Judía en Ciudad de Buenos Aires y Gran Buenos Aires AMBA*. Buenos Aires: Media, Centro de Estudios para las Comunidades Judías de Latinoamérica, American Joint Distribution Committee.
Johnson, T.M., and G.A. Zurlo. 2014. The World by Religion. In *Yearbook of International Religious Demography 2014*, ed. B.J. Grim, T.M. Johnson, V. Skirbekk, and G.A. Zurlo, 3–82. Leiden/Boston: Brill.
Jones, S. 2019. 132,000 descendants of expelled Jews apply for Spanish citizenship. *The Guardian*. Manchester, October 2. https://www.theguardian.com/world/2019/oct/02/132000-sephardic-jews-apply-for-spanish-citizenship
Josefson, D. 2016. In remote Madagascar, a new community chooses to be Jewish. *JTA*, located June 6, 2016.
Josselson, R., and M. Harway. 2012. *Navigating Multiple Identities: Race, Gender, Culture, Nationality, and Roles*. Oxford: Oxford University Press.
Kadushin, C., B. Phillips, and L. Saxe. 2005. National Jewish population survey 2000–01: A guide for the perplexed. *Contemporary Jewry* 25: 1–32.
Kaufman, D.R., ed. 2014. Demographic Storytelling: The Importance of Being Narrative, *Contemporary Jewry* 34(2).
Keeter, S., N. Hatley, C. Kennedy, and A. Lau. 2017. *What Low Response Rates Mean for Telephone Surveys*. Washington, DC: Pew Research Center.
Kimmerling, B. 1999. Conceptual problems. In *One Land, Two Peoples*, ed. D. Jacoby, 11–22. Jerusalem: The Magnes Press.

Klor, S., and L. Schramm. 2018. *Between Exile and Exodus: Argentinian Jewish Immigration to Israel, 1948–1967.* Detroit: Wayne University Press.

Konstantinov, V. 2007. *Jewish population in the former Soviet Union in the 20th century.* Jerusalem: Lira. (in Russian).

Kooyman, C., and J. Almagor. 1996. *Israelis in Holland: A sociodemographic study of Israelis and former Israelis in Holland.* Amsterdam: Stichting Joods Maatschappelijk Werk.

Korazim, M., and E. Katz. 2003. Patterns of Jewish identity in Moldova: The behavioral dimension. In *New Jewish identities: Contemporary Europe and beyond*, ed. Z. Gitelman, B. Kosmin, and A. Kovács, 159–170. Budapest/New York: Central European University.

Kosmin, B.A., and A. Keysar. 2009. *American religious identification survey ARIS 2008. Summary report.* Hartford: Trinity College.

Kosmin, B.A., and S.P. Lachman. 1993. *One nation under God: Religion in contemporary American society.* New York: Harmony Books.

Kosmin, B., and S. Waterman. 2002. *Commentary on census religion question.* London: JPR-Institute for Jewish Policy Research.

Kosmin, B.A., S. Goldstein, J. Waksberg, N. Lerer, A. Keysar, and J. Scheckner. 1991. *Highlights of the CJF 1990 national Jewish population survey.* New York: Council of Jewish Federations.

Kosmin, B.A., J. Goldberg, M. Shain, and S. Bruk. 1999. *Jews of the New South Africa: Highlights of the 1998 national survey of South African Jews.* London: JPR.

Kosmin, B.A., E. Mayer, and A. Keysar. 2001. *American religious identification survey 2001.* New York: Graduate Center of the City University of New York.

Kotler-Berkowitz, L., S.M. Cohen, J. Ament, V. Klaff, F. Mott, D. Peckerman-Neuman, L. Blass, D. Bursztyn, and D. Marker. 2003. *The National Jewish population survey 2000–01: Strength, challenge, and diversity in the American Jewish population.* New York: United Jewish Communities.

Kovács, A., ed. 2004. *Jews and Jewry in contemporary Hungary: Results of a sociological survey, JPR report No. 1.* London: JPR.

———. 2013a. Hungary. In *Perceptions and experiences of antisemitism among Jews in selected EU member states*, ed. L. Staetsky, J. Boyd, E. Ben-Rafael, E. Cohen, S. DellaPergola, L. Dencik, O. Glöckner, and A. Kovács, 101–102. London: JPR/Institute for Jewish Policy Research; Ipsos MORI.

———. 2013b. Latvia. In *Perceptions and experiences of antisemitism among Jews in selected EU member states*, ed. L. Staetsky, J. Boyd, E. Ben-Rafael, E. Cohen, S. DellaPergola, L. Dencik, O. Glöckner, and A. Kovács, 109–110. London: JPR/Institute for Jewish Policy Research; Ipsos MORI.

———. 2013c. Romania. In *Perceptions and experiences of antisemitism among Jews in selected EU member states*, ed. L. Staetsky, J. Boyd, E. Ben-Rafael, E. Cohen, S. DellaPergola, L. Dencik, O. Glöckner, and A. Kovács, vol. 111. London: JPR/Institute for Jewish Policy Research; Ipsos MORI.

Kovács, A., and I. Barna. 2010. *Identity à la carte: Research on Jewish identities, participation and affiliation in five European countries. Analysis of survey data.* Budapest: The American Joint Distribution Committee.

———. 2018. *Zsidók és zsidóság Magyarországon 2017. Ben egy szociológiai kutatás eredményei.* Budapest: Szombat.

Kubovich, Y. 2016. Turkish Jews Say Raising Anti-Semitism Will Drive Next Generation Away. *Haaretz*, July 3, 2016.

Kulsheresta, P. 2017. The Jews of India. *The Citizen*, July 18, 2017.

Lagnado, L. 2014. *Displacement of Jews from Arab Countries 1948–2012.* New York: unpublished manuscript.

Lattes, Y.A. 2005. *Sull'assimilazione in Italia e i metodi per affrontarla.* Ramat Gan: Bar Ilan University.

Lazerwitz, B. 1978. An estimate of a rare population group—The U.S. Jewish population. *Demography* 15 (3): 389–394.

Lieberson, S., and M.C. Waters. 1988. *From many strands: Ethnic and racial groups in contemporary America, The population of the United States in the 1980s, a census monograph series.* New York: Russell-Sage.

Linfield, H.S. 1942. Statistics of Jews. *American Jewish Year Book* 43: 649–698.

Lustick, I.S. 2011. Israel's migration balance: Demography, politics, and ideology. *Israel Studies Review—An Interdisciplinary Journal* 26 (1): 33–65.

Magidin de Kramer, R., E. Tighe, L. Saxe, and D. Parmer. 2018. Assessing the Validity of Data Synthesis Methods to Estimate Religious Populations. *Journal for the Scientific Study of Religion* 57 (2): 206–220.

Markus, A., N. Jacobs, and T. Aronov. 2009. *Preliminary findings: Melbourne & Sydney, Report series of the Gen08 survey, Report 1.* Melbourne: Monash University, Australian Center for Jewish Civilization.

Markus, A., J. Goldlust, N. Jacobs, T. Baker, T. Munz, A. Goodman, and D. Graham. 2011. *Jewish continuity: Melbourne & Sydney, Report series of the Gen08 survey, Report 2.* Melbourne: Monash University, Australian Center for Jewish Civilization.

Massarik, F. 1974. National Jewish population study: A new United States estimate. In *American Jewish Year Book*, vol. 75, 296–304. New York/Philadelphia: Jewish Publication Society and American Jewish Committee.

Mayer, E., B. Kosmin, and A. Keysar. 2001. *American Jewish identity survey 2001.* New York: The Graduate Center of the City University of New York.

Miles, F.S. 2019. Who Is a Jew (in Africa)? Definitional and Ethical Considerations in the Study of Sub-Saharan Jewry and Judaism. *The Journal of the Middle East and Africa* 10 (1): 1–15.

Milkewitz, A., G. Milevski, and E. Erdei. 2014. *Survey São Paulo Jewish Community March 2014.* São Paulo: Federaçao Israelita do Estado de São Paulo FISESP, American Joint Distribution Committee Escritório Brasil, Knack Investigaçao e Consultoria.

Miller, E. 2015, Jan 5. Right-wing annexation drive fueled by false demographics, experts say. *Times of Israel.* http://www.timesofisrael.com/right-wing-annexation-drive-fueled-by-false-demographics-experts-say/

Miller, S., M. Schmool, and A. Lerman. 1996. *Social and political attitudes of British Jews: Some key findings of the JPR survey.* London: JPR.

Moles, A. 1965. Sur l'aspect théorique du decompte de populations mal definies. In *La vie juive dans l'Europe contemporaine*, 81–87. Brussels: Centre national des hautes études Juives and Institute of Contemporary Jewry of the Hebrew University of Jerusalem.

Morris, P. 2011. *Changing Jewry: A survey of the New Zealand Jewish community.* Auckland: B'nai B'rith.

Nissim, M. 2018. *Conversion in Israel: Report and Recommendations.* Jerusalem: State of Israel (Hebrew).

Parfitt, T. 2002. *The lost tribes of Israel: The history of a myth.* London: Weidenfeld and Nicholson.

Parfitt, T., and N. Fisher, eds. 2016. *Becoming Jewish: New Jews and Emerging Jewish Communities in a Globalized World.* Cambridge: Cambridge Scholars Publishing.

PCBS Palestinian Central Bureau of Statistics. 1998. *Population Housing, and Establishment Census 1997, Statistical Brief (Summary of Census Results).* Ramallah: PCBS.

———. 2008. *Census Semi Final Results in Gaza Strip-Summary (Population and Housing).* Ramallah: PCBS.

———. 2009a. *Census Final Results—Population Report-West Bank.* Ramallah: PCBS.

———. 2009b. *Census Final Results—Population Report-Jerusalem Governorate.* Ramallah: PCBS.

———. 2016. *Estimated Population in the Palestinian Territory Mid-Year by Governorate, 1997–2016.* http://www.pcbs.gov.ps/Portals/_Rainbow/Documents/gover_e.htm

———. 2018. http://www.pcbs.gov.ps/site/881/default.aspx. Accessed 20 Aug 2018.

Perlmann, J. 2007. *Two national surveys of American Jews, 2000–01: A comparison of the NJPS and AJIS, Working paper No. 501.* Annandale-on-Hudson: The Levy Economics Institute of Bard College.

Pew Forum on Religion & Public Life. 2008. *U.S. religious landscape survey: Religious affiliation: Diverse and dynamic*. Washington, DC: Pew Research Center.

———. 2012. *The global religious landscape: A report on the size and distribution of the world's major religious groups as of 2010*. Washington, DC: Pew Research Center.

Pew Research Center. 2013. *A portrait of Jewish Americans: Findings from a Pew research center survey of U.S. Jews*. Washington, DC: Pew Research Center. https://pewrsr.ch/2I8hg4e.

———. 2015a. *The Future of World Religions: Population Growth Projections, 2010–2050*. Washington, DC: Pew Research Center.

———. 2015b. *America's Changing Religious Landscape*. Washington, DC: Pew Research Center.

———. 2016. *Israel's religiously divided society. Deep gulfs among Jews, as well as between Jews and Arabs, over political values and religion's role in public life*. Washington, DC: Pew Research Center.

———. 2017. *The Changing Global Religious Landscape*. Washington, DC: Pew Research Center.

Phillips, B.A. 1997. *Re-examining intermarriage: Trends, textures, strategies*. New York: The Susan and David Wilstein Institute of Jewish Policy Studies, and the American Jewish Committee, The William Petschek National Family Center.

———. 2005. *2004 Jewish community study*. San Francisco: Jewish Community Federation of San Francisco, The Peninsula, Marin and Sonoma Counties.

———. 2013. New demographic perspectives on studying intermarriage in the United States. *Contemporary Jewry* 33 (1–2): 103–120.

———. 2018. Intermarriage in the Twenty-First Century: New Perspectives. In *American Jewish Year Book 2017*, ed. A. Dashefsky and I. Sheskin, 31–119. Cham: Springer.

Population Reference Bureau. 2018. *2017 world population data sheet*. Washington, DC: PRB.

Porzecanski, R. 2006. *El Uruguayo Judío*. Montevideo: Trilce.

Pupko, I. 2013. *Here and there: Transnational immigrants in Israel*. Jerusalem: The Hebrew University, Institute of Contemporary Jewry, unpublished PhD dissertation. (in Hebrew).

Raijman, R. 2015. *South African Jews in Israel. Assimilation in Multigenerational Perspective*. Lincoln-London: University of Nebraska Press.

Rebhun, U. 2013. Jewish Identification in Intermarriage: Does a Spouse's Religion (Catholic vs. Protestant) Matter? *Sociology of Religion: A Quarterly Review* 60 (1): 71–88.

———. 2014. Immigrant Acculturation and Transnationalism: Israelis in the United States and Europe Compared. *Journal for the Scientific Study of Religion* 53 (3): 613–635.

———. 2016. *Jews and the American Religious Landscape*. New York: Columbia University Press.

Rebhun, U., and S. Goldstein. 2006. Changes in the geographical dispersion and mobility of American Jews, 1990–2001. *The Jewish Journal of Sociology* 48 (1): 5–33.

Rebhun, U., and L. Lev Ari. 2010. *American Israelis: Migration, transnationalism, and diasporic identity*. Leiden/Boston: Brill.

Rebhun, U., H. Sünker, D. Kranz, N. Beider, K. Harbi, and M. Shorer-Kaplan. 2016. *Israelis in Contemporary Germany: Social Integration and the Construction of Group Identity*. Jerusalem: The Hebrew University, Wuppertal: Bergische Universität, SWP-German Institute for International and Security Affairs.

Reinharz, S., and S. DellaPergola, eds. 2009. *Jewish intermarriage around the world*. New Brunswick/London: Transaction.

Republic of Moldova, National Bureau of Statistics. 2017. *Anuarul statistic al Republicii Moldova*. Chişinău: National Bureau of Statistics.

Ritterband, P., B.A. Kosmin, and J. Scheckner. 1988. Counting Jewish populations: Methods and problems. In *American Jewish Year Book*, vol. 88, 204–221. New York: American Jewish Committee.

Robison, S. 1943. *Jewish Population Studies*. New York: Conference on Jewish Relations, Jewish Social Studies, 3.

Rosenwaike, I. 1980. A synthetic estimate of American Jewish population movement over the last three decades. In *Papers in Jewish demography 1977*, ed. U.O. Schmelz and S. DellaPergola, 83–102. Jerusalem: The Hebrew University.

Rosstat. 2014. *Special population census of Crimea 2014*. Moscow: Rosstat.

Rubel, Y. 2005. *La Población Judía de la Ciudad de Buenos Aires, Perfil Socio-Demográfico*. Buenos Aires: Agencia Judía para Israel, Iniciativa de Demografía Judía.

Sabah, M. 2012. *Israeli Emigrant Stock*. Jerusalem: Central Bureau of Statistics, Technical Paper Series.

Saks, D. 2003. *Community stable, ageing—Census, South African Jewish report*. Johannesburg: South African Jewish Board of Deputies.

Sasson, T., J. Krasner Aronson, F. Chertok, C. Kadushin, and L. Saxe. 2017. Millennial Children of Intermarriage: Religious Upbringing, Identification, and Behavior Among Children of Jewish and Non-Jewish Parents. *Contemporary Jewry* 37 (1): 99–123.

Saxe, L. 2019. *Director's letter*. Waltham: Brandeis University, Maurice & Marilyn Cohen Center for Modern Jewish Studies. https://www.brandeis.edu/cmjs/constructs/2019/october.html.

Saxe, L., and E. Tighe. 2013. Estimating and understanding the Jewish population in the United States: A program of research. *Contemporary Jewry* 33 (1–2): 43–62.

Saxe, L., B. Phillips, C. Kadushin, G. Wright, and D. Parmer. 2006a. *The 2005 Boston community study: Preliminary findings. A report by the Steinhardt Social Research Institute*. Waltham: Brandeis University for Combined Jewish Philanthropies of Boston.

Saxe, L., E. Tighe, B. Phillips, A. Libhaber, D. Parmer, J. Simon, and G. Wright. 2006b. *Understanding contemporary American Jewry*. Waltham: Brandeis University, Steinhardt Social Research Institute.

Saxe, L., E. Tighe, B. Phillips, C. Kadushin, M. Barnett, D. Grant, D. Livert, A. Libhaber, M. Sud Lokshin, D. Parmer, D. Rindskopf, S. Simon, and G. Wright. 2007. *Reconsidering the size and characteristics of the American Jewish population: New estimates of a larger and more diverse community*. Waltham: Brandeis University, Steinhardt Social Research Institute.

Schick, Marvin. 2005. *A census of Jewish day schools in the United States 2003–2004*. Jerusalem: Avi Chai.

Schmelz, U.O. 1981. Jewish survival: The demographic factors. In *American Jewish Year Book*, vol. 81, 61–117. New York: American Jewish Committee.

———. 1984. *Aging of world Jewry Jerusalem*. Jerusalem: The Hebrew University/ Brookdale Institute.

Schmelz, U.O., and S. DellaPergola. 1983. The demographic consequences of U.S. Jewish population trends. In *American Jewish Year Book*, vol. 83, 141–187. New York: American Jewish Committee.

———. 1985. The demography of Latin American Jewry. In *American Jewish Year Book*, vol. 85, 51–102. New York/Philadelphia: Jewish Publication Society and American Jewish Committee.

———. 1986. World Jewish Population 1984. In *American Jewish Year Book*, vol. 86, 350–364. New York/Philadelphia: Jewish Publication Society and American Jewish Committee.

———. 1988. *Basic trends in American Jewish demography*. New York: American Jewish Committee.

Schnapper, D. 1994. Israélites and Juifs: New Jewish Identities in France. In *Jewish Identities in the New Europe*, ed. J. Webber, 171–178. London: Littman Library of Jewish Civilization.

Schoeps, J.H., W. Jasper, and B. Vogt, eds. 1999. *Ein neues Judentum in Deutschland? Fremd und Eigenbilder der russisch-jüdischen Einwanderer*. Potsdam: Verlag für Berlin-Brandenburg.

Schulman, M. 2003. *National Jewish population survey 2000–01: Study review Memo*, prepared for United Jewish Communities. New York.

Schwartz, J., J. Scheckner, and L. Kotler-Berkowitz. 2002. Census of U.S. synagogues, 2001. *American Jewish Year Book* 102: 112–150.

Shahar, C. 2004. *The Jewish community of Canada*. Toronto: Jewish Federations of Canada-UIA.

———. 2014. *2011 National household survey analysis, the Jewish population of Canada. Part 1, basic demographics; Part 2, Jewish populations in geographic areas*. Toronto: Jewish Federations of Canada-UIA.

———. 2016. Jewish Population of Canada, 2015. In *American Jewish Year Book 2015*, ed. A. Dashefsky and I. Sheskin, 261–271. Cham: Springer.

———. 2017. Canadian Jewish Population, 2016. In *American Jewish Year Book 2016*, ed. A. Dashefsky and I. Sheskin, 241–251. Cham: Springer.

———. 2018. Canadian Jewish Population, 2017. In *American Jewish Year Book 2017*, ed. A. Dashefsky and I. Sheskin, 285–295. Cham: Springer.

Sheskin, I.M. 2008. Four questions about American Jewish demography. *Jewish Political Studies Review* 20 (1–2): 23–42.

———. 2009. *The 2008 Jewish community study of greater Middlesex county, main report*. South River, NJ: Jewish Federation of Greater Middlesex County.

———. 2015a. *Comparisons of Jewish communities: A compendium of tables and bar charts*. Storrs: Mandell Berman Institute, North American Jewish Data Bank and the Jewish Federations of North America.

———. 2015b. *2014 Greater Miami Jewish Federation Population Study: A Portrait of Jewish Miami*. Miami: The Greater Miami Jewish Federation.

———. 2017. *The 2016 Jewish Federation of Broward County population study: a profile of Jewish Broward County*. Davie: The Jewish Federation of Broward County.

Sheskin, I.M., and A. Dashefsky. 2007. *Jewish population of the United States, 2007, American Jewish Year Book*. Vol. 107. New York: The American Jewish Committee, 136–138 and 198–199.

———. 2010. *Jewish population in the United States, 2010, Current Jewish Population Reports, Report 2010–1*. Storrs: The North American Jewish Data Bank, the Association for the Social Scientific Study of Jewry, and the Jewish Federations of North America.

———. 2016. Jewish population in the United States 2015. In *American Jewish Year Book 2015*, ed. A. Dashefsky and I. Sheskin, 163–260. Cham: Springer.

———. 2017. Jewish population in the United States 2016. In *American Jewish Year Book 2016*, ed. A. Dashefsky and I. Sheskin, 153–239. Cham: Springer.

Shorer Kaplan, M. 2016. Ethnic Migration in Comparative Perspective: A Case Study of Migration of Jews from Uruguay to Israel and Other Countries. *Hagira*, 6 (Hebrew).

Smith, T.W. 2009. *Religious switching among American Jews*. New York: The American Jewish Committee.

Smith, T., and S. McLeish. 2019. *Technical report on changes in response related to the census ethnic origin question: Focus on Jewish origins, 2016 Census integrated with 2011 National Household Survey*. Ottawa: Statistics Canada. https://bit.ly/2ZEHbGq.

Soffer, A. 2015. *If I Were Running to Lead Israel in 2015*. Haifa: University of Haifa, Chaikin Chair in Geostrategic Studies. (in Hebrew).

Soffer, A., and Y. Bistrow. 2004. *Israel demography 2004–2020 in the light of disengagement*. Haifa: University of Haifa. (in Hebrew).

SSRI—Steinhardt Social Research Institute. 2019a. *American Jewish Population Project*. Waltham: Brandeis University, SSRI Steinhardt Social Research Institute. https://ajpp.brandeis.edu/map.

———. 2019b. *American Jewish Population Project*. Waltham: Brandeis University, SSRI Steinhardt Social Research Institute. https://ajpp.brandeis.edu/methodology.

———. 2019c. *American Jewish Population Project*. Waltham: Brandeis University, SSRI Steinhardt Social Research Institute. https://ajpp.brandeis.edu/documents/2019/AJPP%20 2019%20Estimation%20Details.pdf.

Staetsky, L.D. 2017. *Are Jews leaving Europe?* London: Jewish Policy Research Institute JPR.

———. 2019. Stalling fertility decline of Israeli Muslims and the demographic transition theory. *Population Studies*.

Staetsky, L.D., and J. Boyd. 2015. *Strictly Orthodox Rising: what the demography of British Jew tells us about the future of the community*. London: Jewish Policy Research Institute JPR.

Staetsky, D., and J. Boyd. 2016. *The rise and rise of Jewish schools in the United Kingdom. Numbers, trends and policy*. London: Jewish Policy Research Institute JPR.

Staetsky, L., J. Boyd, E. Ben-Rafael, E. Cohen, S. DellaPergola, L. Dencik, O. Glöckner, and A. Kovács. 2013. *Perceptions and experiences of antisemitism among Jews in selected EU member states*. London: Jewish Policy Research Institute JPR for Ipsos MORI.

Staetsky, L.D., and S. DellaPergola. 2019a. *Why European Jewish Demography? A fundation paper*, 29 p. London: Jewish Policy Research Institute JPR, European Jewish Demography Unit.
————. 2019b. *Jews in Austria: A Social and Demographic Profile*. London: Jewish Policy Research Institute JPR, European Jewish Demography Unit.
Stark, T. 1995. *A magyar zsidóság statisztikája: Kutatási jelentés*. Budapest: MTA Történettudományi Intézete.
State of Palestine-United Nations Population Fund. 2017. *Palestine 2030. Demographic Change: Opportunities for Development*. State of Palestine: Prime Minister Office, National Population Committee-UNFPA United Nations Population Fund.
Statistics Canada. 2003a. *Selected religions for Canada provinces and territories—20% sample data*. http://www12.statcan.ca/english/census01/products/highlight/Religion/Page.cfm?Lang = E&Geo = PR&View = 1a&Code = 01&Table = 1&StartRec = 1&Sort = 2&B1 = Canada&B2 = 1. Ottawa.
————. 2003b. *Profile of citizenship, immigration, birthplace, generation status, ethnic origin, visible minorities and aboriginal peoples, for Canada, provinces, territories, census divisions and census subdivisions, 2001 census*. http://www12.statcan.gc.ca/english/census01/products/ standard/profiles/Rp-eng.cfm?LANG = E&APATH = 3&DETAIL = 1&DIM = 0&FL= A&FRE E = 0&GC = 0&GID = 0&GK = 0&GRP = 1&PID = 56167&PRID = 0&PTYPE = 55430,53293,55440,55496,71090&S = 0&SHOWALL = 0&SUB = 0&Temporal = 2001&THEME= 57&VID = 0&VNAMEE = &VNAMEF=. Ottawa.
————. 2008. *Ethnic origins 2006 counts for Canada provinces and territories—20% sample data*. http://www12.statcan.gc.ca/census-recensement/2006/dp-pd/hlt/97–562/pages/page.cfm ?Lang=E&Geo=PR&Code=01&Data=Count&Table=2&StartRec=1&Sort=3&Display=All& CSDFilter=5000. Ottawa.
————. 2013a. *2011 National household survey*, Statistics Canada Catalogue no. 99–010-X2011032. Ottawa.
————. 2013b. *2011 National household survey*, Statistics Canada Catalogue no. 99–010-X2011028. Ottawa.
————. 2019. *2011 National Household Survey*. Religion (108), Immigrant Status and Period of Immigration (11), Age Groups (10) and Sex (3) for the Population in Private Households of Canada, Provinces, Territories, Census Metropolitan Areas and Census Agglomerations. https://bit.ly/2EPJqki.
Statistics New Zealand. 2007. *2006 census of population and dwelling*. Auckland: Statistics New Zealand.
————. 2018. *2018 census of population and dwelling*. Auckland: Statistics New Zealand. https:// www.stats.govt.nz/information-releases/2018-census-totals-by-topic-national-highlights.
Statistik Austria. 2003. *Volkszählung 2001: Wohnbevölkerung nach Religion und Staatsangehörigkeit für Bundesländer*. Wien: Statistik Austria.
————. 2019. *Vital statistics. Personal communication to L.D.* Staetsky: JPR.
Statistik Schweiz. 2005. *Wohnbevölkerung nach Religion 2000*. Neuchatel: Bundesamt für Statistik.
————. 2012. *Ständige Wohnbevölkerung ab 15 Jahren nach Religionszugehörigkeit, 2012*. Neuchatel: Bundesamt für Statistik.
Stonawski, M., V. Skirbekk, C. Hackett, M. Potančoková, and B. Grim. 2014. The Size and Demographic Structure of Religions in Europe. In *Yearbook of International Religious Demography 2014*, ed. B.J. Grim, T.M. Johnson, V. Skirbekk, and G.A. Zurlo, 131–142. Leiden/Boston: Brill.
Swiss Fund for Needy Victims of the Holocaust/Shoa. 2002. *Final report*. Bern: Swiss Fund for Needy Victims of the Holocaust/Shoa.
Tal, A. 2016. *The Land is Full. Addressing Overpopulation in Israel*. New Haven-London: Yale University Press.
Tanenbaum, B., and R. Kooyman. 2014. *Jewish feelings, Jewish practice? Children of Jewish intermarriage in the Netherlands*. Paris-Oxford: JDC International Centre for Community Development.

The Board of Deputies of British Jews, Community Research Unit. 2005. *Report on community vital statistics 2004*. London: The Board of Deputies of British Jews, Community Research Unit.

The Jewish Daily Forward. 2014. *Who are we now? Interpreting the Pew study on Jewish identity in America today*. http://www.amazon.com/Interpreting-Study-Jewish-Identity-America-ebook/dp/B00FWVFD2C.

The Jewish People Policy Planning Institute. 2005. *Annual assessment 2004–2005, between thriving and decline*. Jerusalem: The Jewish People Policy Planning Institute.

———. 2007. *The conference on the future of the Jewish people 2007, background policy documents*. Jerusalem: The Jewish People Policy Planning Institute.

———. 2008. *Tomorrow*. Jerusalem: The Jewish People Policy Planning Institute.

Tian, J.Y., H.W. Wang, Y.C. Li, W. Zhang, Y.G. Yao, van Straten, M.B. Richards, and Q.P. Kong. 2015. A genetic contribution from the Far East into Ashkenazi Jews via the ancient Silk Road. *Scientific Reports* 5 (8377): 1–35.

Tighe, E., L. Saxe, D. Brown, J. Dillinger, A. Klein, and A. Hill. 2005. *Research synthesis of national survey estimates of the U.S. Jewish population; project summary, method and analysis plan*. Waltham: Brandeis University, Steinhardt Social Research Institute.

Tighe, E., C. Kadushin, and L. Saxe. 2009a. *Jewish population in the US: 1990 vs. 2000, Working paper*. Waltham: Brandeis University, Steinhardt Social Research Institute.

Tighe, E., D. Livert, M. Barnett, and L. Saxe. 2009b. *Cross-survey analysis to estimate low incidence religious groups*. Waltham: Brandeis University, Steinhardt Social Research Institute.

Tighe, E., L. Saxe, C. Kadushin, R. Magidin De Kramer, B. Nurshadenov, J. Aronson, and L. Cherny. 2011. *Estimating the Jewish population of the United States: 2000–2010*. Waltham: Brandeis University, Steinhardt Social Research Institute.

The Times of Israel. 2017. Over 33,000 Israelis have taken German Citizenship since 2000. 12 February 2007. https://www.timesofisrael.com/over-33000-israelis-have-taken-german-citizenship-since-2000/

Tobin, G., and S. Groeneman. 2003. *Surveying the Jewish population in the United States. Part 1: Population estimate. Part 2: Methodological issues and challenges*. San Francisco: Institute for Jewish & Community Research.

Tolts, M. 2002. *Main demographic trends of the Jews in Russia and the FSU*. Jerusalem: The Hebrew University, The Institute of Contemporary Jewry.

———. 2003. Mass Aliyah and Jewish emigration from Russia: Dynamics and factors. *Eastern European Jewish Affairs* 33: 71–96.

———. 2004. The Post-Soviet Jewish population in Russia and the world. *Jews in Russia and Eastern Europe* 52: 37–63.

———. 2005. *Demographic trends of the Jews in the Former Soviet Union (Final report—Sixth year of study)*. Jerusalem: The Hebrew University, The A. Harman Institute of Contemporary Jewry, Division of Jewish Demography and Statistics.

———. 2006. Contemporary trends in family formation among the Jews in Russia. *Jews in Russia and Eastern Europe* 57: 5–23.

———. 2007. Post-Soviet Jewish demography, 1989–2004. In *Revolution, repression, and revival: The Soviet Jewish experience*, ed. Z. Gitelman and Y. Ro'i, 283–311. Lanham: Rowman & Littlefield.

———. 2008. Population since world war I; migration since world war I. In *The YIVO encyclopedia of Jews in Eastern Europe*, ed. G. Hundert, 1429–1440. New Haven: Yale University Press.

———. 2009. *Some demographic and socio-economic trends of the Jews in Russia and the FSU*. Jerusalem: The Hebrew University, The A. Harman Institute of Contemporary Jewry, Division of Jewish Demography and Statistics.

———. 2013. The Jews in Georgia in the Late Soviet Period: A demographic profile. In *Studies in Caucasian, Georgian, and Bukharan Jewry: Historical, sociological, and cultural aspects*, ed. G. Akhiezer, R. Enoch, and S. Weinstein, 102–116. Ariel: Ariel University, Institute for Research of Jewish Communities of the Caucasus and Central Asia.

————. 2014. Sources for the demographic study of the Jews in the former Soviet Union. *Studies in Contemporary Jewry* 27: 160–177.

————. 2015. Demographic Transformations among Ex-Soviet Migrants in Israel. In *Research in Jewish Demography and Identity*, ed. E. Lederhendler and U. Rebhun, 146–168. Boston: Academic Studies Press.

————. 2016. Demography of the contemporary Russian-Speaking Jewish diaspora. In *The New Jewish Diaspora Russian-Speaking Immigrants in the United States, Israel and Germany*, ed. Z. Gitelman, 23–40. New Brunswick: Rutgers University Press.

————. 2018. Post-Soviet Jewish Demographic Dynamics: An Analysis of Recent Data. In *Jewish Population and Identity: Concept and Reality*, ed. S. DellaPergola and U. Rebhun, 213–229. Cham: Springer.

Torczyner, J.L., S.L. Brotman, K. Viragh, and G.J. Goldmann. 1993. *Demographic Challenges Facing Canadian Jewry; Initial Findings from the 1991 Census*. Montreal: Federation CJA.

Torres, E. 2017. *¿Retorno o entrada primordial en el Judaísmo? La nueva inmigración de América Latina en Israel: 1985–2015*. Jerusalem: The Hebrew University, Ph.D. dissertation submitted to the Faculty of Humanities.

Tuval, S. 2004. *The Jewish community of Istanbul, 1948–1992*. Jerusalem: Ben Zvi Institute. (in Hebrew).

Ukrainian Ministry of Statistics. 2002. *Population census 2001*. Kiev: Ukrainian Ministry of Statistics.

Unione delle Comunità Ebraiche Italiane. 2002. *IV Congresso, Relazione del consiglio*. Roma: Unione delle Comunità Ebraiche Italiane.

————. 2010. *Indagine demografica—Numero degli iscritti delle comunità*. Roma: Unione delle Comunità Ebraiche Italiane.

————. 2018. *Riepilogo Censimento Comunità al 31 dicembre 2017*. Roma: Unione delle Comunità Ebraiche Italiane.

United Kingdom, National Records of Scotland (NRS). 2011. *2011 Scotland's Census*. http://www.scotlandscensus.gov.uk/

United Kingdom Office for National Statistics. 2002. *National report for England and Wales 2001*. London: United Kingdom Office for National Statistics.

————. 2012. *2011 Population Census*. https://www.ons.gov.uk/census/2011census/2011ukcensuses/ukcensusesdata

United Kingdom, Scotland General Register Office. 2002. *2001 Census*. Edinburgh: Scotland General Register Office.

United Nations. 2006. *Demographic Yearbook. Special Census Topics*. New York: United Nations Department of Economic and Social Affairs.

United Nations Development Programme. 2018. *Human Development Indices and Indicators. 2018 Statistical Update*. New York: United Nations Development Programme.

United Nations Population Division. 2017. *World population prospects: The 2017 revision*. New York: United Nations Department of Economic and Social Affairs, Population Division.

US Census Bureau. 1958. *Religion reported by the civilian population in the United States, March 1957, Current population reports, population characteristics, series P-20, No. 79*. Washington, DC: US Census Bureau.

————. 1968. *Tabulations of data on the social and economic characteristics of major religious groups, March 1957*. Washington, DC: US Census Bureau.

————. 2019. *Statistical abstract of the United States*. Washington, DC: US Census Bureau.

US Department of Homeland Security. 2017. *Yearbook of immigration statistics: 2017*. Washington, DC: U.S. Department of Homeland Security, Office of Immigration Statistics. Accessed http://www.dhs.gov/yearbook-immigration-statistics/yearbook/2017.

US Executive Office of the President, Office of Management and Budget. 2013. *Update of statistical area definitions and guidance on their uses, OMB bulletin, 13–01*. Washington, DC: US Executive Office of the President, Office of Management and Budget. https://www.whitehouse.gov/sites/default/files/omb/bulletins/2013/b13-01.pdf.

van Solinge, H., and M. de Vries, eds. 2001. *De Joden in Nederland Anno 2000: Demografisch profiel en binding aan het joodendom*. Amsterdam: Aksant.

van Solinge, H., and C. van Praag. 2010. *De Joden in Nederland anno 2009 continuïteit en veranderin*. Diemen: AMB.

Voas, D. 2007. Estimating the Jewish undercount in the 2001 census: A comment on Graham and Waterman 2005. *Population, Space and Place* 13: 401–407.

Vulkan, D. 2012. *Britain's Jewish Community Statistics 2010*. London: Board of Deputies of British Jews.

Vulkan, D., and D. Graham. 2008. *Population trends among Britain's strictly orthodox*. London: Board of Deputies of British Jews.

Waxman, C.I. 2013. Multiculturalism, conversion, and the future of Israel as a modern state. *Israel Studies Review* 28 (1): 33–53.

Weinfeld, M., and R.F. Schnoor. 2015. The demography of Canadian Jewry, the census of 2011: Challenges and results. In *American Jewish Year Book 2014*, ed. A. Dashefsky and I. Sheskin, 285–299. Cham: Springer.

Weinfeld, M., R.F. Schnoor, and D.S. Koffman. 2013. Overview of Canadian Jewry. In *American Jewish Year Book 2012*, ed. A. Dashefsky and I. Sheskin, 55–90. Dordrecht: Springer.

Zentralwohlfahrtsstelle der Juden in Deutschland. 2018. *Mitgliederstatistik der Jüdischen Gemeinde und Landesverbände in Deutschland für das Yahr 2018*. Frankfurt a.M: ZWJD.

———. 2019. *Mitgliederstatistik der Jüdischen Gemeinde und Landesverbände in Deutschland für das Yahr 2019*. Frankfurt a.M: ZWJD.

———. n.d. *Annual. Mitgliederstatistik; Der Einzelnen Jüdischen Gemeinden und Landesverbände in Deutschland*. Frankfurt a. M: ZWJD.

Zimmerman, B., R. Seid, and M.L. Wise. 2005a. *The million person gap: The Arab population in the West Bank and Gaza, Mideast security and policy studies 65*. Ramat Gan: The Begin-Sadat Center for Strategic Studies.

Zimmerman, B., R. Seid, M.L. Wise, Y. Ettinger, D. Shahaf, E. Sohar, D. Passig, and A. Shvout. 2005b. *Arab population in the West Bank and Gaza: The million and a half person gap*. Washington, DC: American Enterprise Institute.

Part II
Jewish Lists

Chapter 9
Local Jewish Organizations

Ira M. Sheskin, Arnold Dashefsky, and Sarah Markowitz

This chapter provides lists with contact information (name, address, phone number, website) for about 180 Jewish Federations, about 200 Jewish Community Centers, about 185 Jewish Family Services, 15 Jewish Vocational Services, about 50 Jewish Free Loans, and all Israeli embassies and consulates. Note that the 180 Jewish Federations include more than 140 organizations that are associated with the Jewish Federations of North America and some organizations that function as federations for their communities but choose not to be formally associated with JFNA.

For synagogues, college Hillels, and Jewish day schools, websites are provided that contain lists of these organizations, as we simply do not have the resources to update these lists annually. We also do not have the space in this volume to provide extensive lists of these organizations.

The purpose of this chapter is to document the institutional infrastructure of the North American Jewish community and to preserve this information for historical purposes. We expect that historians 100 years from now will look back at the Year Book in researching the history of North American Jewry. In a sense, we are "freezing" the information in time. The information on the internet, of course, changes as frequently as the webmasters update that information, meaning that without this freezing, historians in the future will not have a record of the infrastructure of the community.

I. M. Sheskin (✉)
Department of Geography and Jewish Demography Project, Sue and Leonard Miller Center
for Contemporary Judaic Studies, University of Miami, Coral Gables, FL, USA
e-mail: isheskin@miami.edu

A. Dashefsky
Department of Sociology and Center for Judaic Studies and Contemporary Jewish Life,
University of Connecticut, Storrs, CT, USA

S. Markowitz
Independent Researcher, Forest Hills, NY, USA

© Springer Nature Switzerland AG 2020   357
A. Dashefsky, I. M. Sheskin (eds.), *American Jewish Year Book 2019*, American
Jewish Year Book 119, https://doi.org/10.1007/978-3-030-40371-3_9

Each list is carefully updated each year, but the authors appreciate any corrections noted by our readers. We have found that the lists we can find for Jewish institutions on the internet are far from totally accurate.

9.1 Jewish Federations

9.1.1 Central Coordinating Body for Jewish Federations, United States

The Jewish Federations of North America (formerly **United Jewish Appeal**, **Council of Jewish Federations**, and **United Jewish Communities**). For contact information and a description, see the Jewish Community Coordinating Organizations section of Chap. 12.

9.1.2 Jewish Federations, United States

Alabama
Birmingham
Birmingham Jewish Federation. 3966 Montclair Road, Mountain Brook, AL 35213. (205) 879-0416. (www.bjf.org)

Mobile
Mobile Area Jewish Federation. 705 Regents Way, Mobile, AL 36609. (251) 490-4872. (www.mobilejewishfederation.org)

Montgomery (Central Alabama)
Jewish Federation of Central Alabama. PO Box 20058, Montgomery, AL 36120. (334) 277-5820. (www.jewishmontgomery.org)

Arizona
Phoenix
Jewish Federation of Greater Phoenix. 12701 North Scottsdale Road, Suite 201, Scottsdale, AZ 85254. (480) 634-4900. (www.jewishphoenix.org)

Tucson (Southern Arizona)
Jewish Federation of Southern Arizona. 3718 East River Road, Tucson, AZ 85718. (520) 577-9393. (www.jfsa.org)

Arkansas
Little Rock
Jewish Federation of Arkansas. 18 Corporate Hill Drive, Suite 204, Little Rock, AR 72205. (501) 663-3571. (www.jewisharkansas.org)

California
Fresno (Central California)
Jewish Federation of Central California. 406 West Shields Avenue, Fresno, CA
  93705. (559) 432-2162. (www.jewishfederationcentralcalifornia.org)

Long Beach (West Orange County)
Jewish Federation of Greater Long Beach & West Orange County. 3801 E Willow
  Street, Long Beach, CA 90815. (562) 426-7601. (www.jewishlongbeach.org)

Los Angeles
Jewish Federation of Greater Los Angeles. 6505 Wilshire Boulevard, Los Angeles,
  CA 90048. (323) 761-8000. (www.jewishla.org)

Oakland (East Bay)
Jewish Federation and The Jewish Community Foundation of the East Bay. (Ceased
  to exist as of July 2019)

Orange County
Jewish Federation & Family Services of Orange County. One Federation Way, Suite
  210, Irvine, CA 92603. (949) 435-3484. (www.jewishorangecounty.org)

Palm Springs
Jewish Federation of the Desert. 69710 Highway 111, Rancho Mirage, CA 92270.
  (760) 324-4737. (www.jfedps.org)

Sacramento
Jewish Federation of the Sacramento Region. 2130 21st Street, Sacramento, CA
  95818. (916) 486-0906. (www.jewishsac.org)

San Diego
Jewish Federation of San Diego County. 4950 Murphy Canyon Road, San Diego,
  CA 92123. (858) 571-3444. (www.jewishinsandiego.org)
San Francisco (Alameda, Contra Costa, Marin, Napa, San Francisco, San Mateo,
  Santa Clara, Santa Cruz, Solano, and Sonoma Counties) (As of July 2019, the
  East Bay Federation merged into the San Francisco Federation)
Jewish Community Federation & Endowment Fund of San Francisco, the Peninsula,
  Marin and Sonoma Counties. 121 Steuart Street, San Francisco, CA 94105.
  (415) 777-0411. (www.jewishfed.org)

San Gabriel (Pomona Valleys)
Jewish Federation of the Greater San Gabriel and Pomona Valleys. 114A West Lime
  Avenue, Monrovia, CA 91016. (626) 445-0810. (www.jewishsgpv.org)

San Jose (Silicon Valley)
Jewish Federation of Silicon Valley. 14855 Oka Road, Suite 200, Los Gatos, CA
  95032. (408) 358-3033. (www.jvalley.org)

San Luis Obispo
JCC-Federation of San Luis Obispo. 875 Laureate Lane, San Luis Obispo, CA
  93405. (805) 426-5465. (www.jccslo.com)

Santa Barbara
Jewish Federation of Greater Santa Barbara. 524 Chapala Street, Santa Barbara, CA
   93101. (805) 957-1115. (www.jewishsantabarbara.org)

Ventura
Jewish Federation of Ventura County. 7620 Foothill Road, Ventura, CA 93004.
   (805) 647-7800. (www.jewishventuracounty.org)

Colorado
Aspen
UJA Aspen Valley c/o JEWISHcolorado. 300 South Dahlia Street, Suite 300,
   Denver, CO 80246. (303) 321-3399. (www.jewishcolorado.org/ujaaspenvalley)

Denver-Boulder
JEWISHcolorado. 300 South Dahlia Street, Suite 300, Denver, CO 80246. (303)
   321-3399. (www.jewishcolorado.org)

Connecticut
Bridgeport-Westport (Upper Fairfield County)
Federation for Jewish Philanthropy of Upper Fairfield County. 4200 Park Avenue,
   Suite 300, Bridgeport, CT 06604. (203) 226-8197. (www.jewishphilanthro-
   pyct.org)

Greenwich
UJA-JCC Greenwich. One Holly Hill Lane, Greenwich, CT 06830. (203) 552-1818.
   (www.ujajcc.org)

Hartford
Jewish Federation of Greater Hartford. 333 Bloomfield Avenue, Suite C, West
   Hartford, CT 06117. (860) 232-4483. (www.jewishhartford.org)

New Haven
Jewish Federation of Greater New Haven. 360 Amity Road, Woodbridge, CT 06525.
   (203) 387-2424. (www.jewishnewhaven.org)

New London (Eastern Connecticut)
Jewish Federation of Eastern Connecticut. 28 Channing Street, New London, CT
   06320. (860) 442-8062. (www.jfec.com)

Southbury (Western Connecticut)
Jewish Federation of Western Connecticut. 444 Main Street North, Southbury, CT
   06488. (203) 267-3177. (www.jfed.net)

Stamford-New Canaan-Darien
United Jewish Federation of Greater Stamford, New Canaan and Darien. 1035
   Newfield Avenue, Suite 200, Stamford, CT 06905. (203) 321-1373. (www.
   ujf.org)

Delaware

Wilmington

Jewish Federation of Delaware. 101 Garden of Eden Road, Wilmington, DE 19803.
(302) 427-2100. (www.shalomdelaware.org)

District of Columbia

Washington, DC

Jewish Federation of Greater Washington. 6101 Executive Boulevard, Suite 100,
North Bethesda, MD 20852. (301) 230-7200. (www.shalomdc.org)

Florida

Boca Raton-Delray Beach (South Palm Beach)

Jewish Federation of South Palm Beach County. 9901 Donna Klein Boulevard,
Boca Raton, FL 33428. (561) 852-3100. (www.jewishboca.org)

Daytona Beach (Volusia and Flagler Counties)

Jewish Federation of Volusia & Flagler Counties. 470 Andalusia Avenue, Ormond
Beach, FL 32174. (386) 672-0294. (www.jewishfederationdaytona.org)

Fort Lauderdale (Broward County)

Jewish Federation of Broward County. 5890 South Pine Island Road, Davie, FL
33328. (954) 252-6900. (www.jewishbroward.org)

Fort Myers (Lee and Charlotte Counties)

Jewish Federation of Lee and Charlotte Counties. 9701 Commerce Center Court,
Fort Myers, FL 33908. (239) 481-4449. (www.jewishfederationlcc.org)

Gainesville (North Central Florida)

Jewish Council of North Central Florida. 3835 Northwest 8th Avenue, Gainesville,
FL 32605. (352) 371-3846. (www.jcncf.org)

Jacksonville

Jewish Federation of Jacksonville. 8505 San Jose Boulevard, Jacksonville, FL
32217. (904) 448-5000. (www.jewishjacksonville.org)

Melbourne (Brevard County)

Jewish Federation of Brevard. 210 East Hibiscus Boulevard, Melbourne, FL 32901.
(321) 951-1836. (www.jewishfederationbrevard.com)

Miami

Greater Miami Jewish Federation. 4200 Biscayne Boulevard, Miami, FL 33137.
(305) 576-4000. (www.jewishmiami.org)

Naples (Collier County)

Jewish Federation of Greater Naples. 2500 Vanderbilt Beach Road, Suite 2201,
Naples, FL 34109. (239) 263-4205. (www.jewishnaples.org)

Orlando

Jewish Federation of Greater Orlando. 851 North Maitland Avenue, Maitland, FL
32751. (407) 645-5933. (www.orlandojewishfed.org)

Sarasota and Manatee Counties
Jewish Federation of Sarasota-Manatee. 580 McIntosh Road, Sarasota, FL 34232.
(941) 371-4546. (www.jfedsrq.org)

St. Petersburg (Pinellas, Pasco, and Hernando Counties)
Jewish Federation of Florida's Gulf Coast (formerly Jewish Federation of Pinellas
and Pasco Counties). 13191 Starkey Road, Suite 8, Largo, FL 33773. (727)
530-3223. (www.jewishgulfcoast.org)

Tallahassee
Tallahassee Jewish Federation. PO Box 14825, Tallahassee, FL 32317. (850)
220-0015. (www.jewishtallahassee.org)

Tampa
Tampa Jewish Federation. 13009 Community Campus Drive, Tampa, FL 33625.
(813) 264-9000. (www.jewishtampa.com)

West Palm Beach
Jewish Federation of Palm Beach County. 1 Harvard Circle, Suite 100, West Palm
Beach, FL 33409. (561) 478-0700. (www.jewishpb.org/fed)

Georgia
Atlanta
Jewish Federation of Greater Atlanta. 1440 Spring Street NW, Atlanta, GA 30309.
(404) 873-1661. (www.jewishatlanta.org)

Augusta
Augusta Jewish Federation. 898 Weinberger Way, Evans, GA 30809. (706)
228-3636. (www.jewishaugusta.org)

Columbus
Jewish Federation of Columbus, GA. PO Box 6313, Columbus,
GA 31917. (706) 568-6668. (www.facebook.com/Jewish-Federation-of-
Columbus-GA-396914817040809)

Macon (Middle Georgia)
Jewish Federation of Macon & Middle Georgia. PO Box 5276, Macon, GA 31208.
(www.jewishmacon.org)

Savannah
Savannah Jewish Federation. 5111 Abercorn Street, Savannah, GA 31405. (912)
355-8111. (www.savj.org)

Illinois
Champaign-Urbana
Champaign-Urbana Jewish Federation. 503 East John Street, Champaign, IL 61820.
(217) 367-9872. (www.cujf.org)

Chicago
Jewish United Fund/Jewish Federation of Metropolitan Chicago. 30 South Wells
Street, Chicago, IL 60606. (312) 346-6700. (www.juf.org)

Peoria
Jewish Federation of Peoria. 2000 Pioneer Parkway, Suite 10B, Peoria, IL 61615.
(309) 689-0063. (www.jewishpeoria.org)

Rockford
Jewish Federation of Greater Rockford. 1203 Comanche Drive, Rockford, IL 61107.
(815) 399-5497. (www.jewishrockfordil.org)

Rock Island (Quad Cities)
Jewish Federation of the Quad Cities. 2715 30th Street, Rock Island, IL 61201.
(309) 793-1300. (www.jfqc.org)

Southern Illinois
Jewish Federation of Southern Illinois, Southeast Missouri and Western Kentucky.
3419 West Main Street, Belleville, IL 62226. (618) 235-1614. (www.
simokyfed.com)

Springfield
Jewish Federation of Springfield, Illinois. 1045 Outer Park Drive, Suite 320,
Springfield, IL 62704. (217) 787-7223. (www.shalomspringfield.org)

Indiana
Fort Wayne
Jewish Federation of Fort Wayne. 5200 Old Mill Road, Fort Wayne, IN 46807.
(260) 456-0400. (www.jewishfortwayne.org)

Gary (Northwest Indiana)
Jewish Federation of Northwest Indiana. 585 Progress Avenue, Munster, IN 46321.
(219) 301-0960. (www.federationonline.org)

Indianapolis
Jewish Federation of Greater Indianapolis. 6705 Hoover Road, Indianapolis, IN
46260. (317) 726-5450. (www.jfgi.org)

South Bend (St. Joseph Valley)
Jewish Federation of St. Joseph Valley. 3202 Shalom Way, South Bend, IN 46615.
(574) 233-1164. (www.thejewishfed.org)

West Lafayette
Jewish Federation of Greater Lafayette. PO Box 3802, West Lafayette, IN 47996.
(317) 522-1938. (www.jfgl.org)

Iowa
Davenport (Quad Cities)
Jewish Federation of the Quad Cities. 2715 30th Street, Rock Island, IL 61201.
(309) 793-1300. (www.jfqc.org)

Des Moines
Jewish Federation of Greater Des Moines. 33158 Ute Avenue, Waukee, IA 50263.
(515) 987-0899. (www.jewishdesmoines.org)

Iowa City

Iowa City Jewish Federation. c/o The University of Iowa, Aliber Hillel, 122 East Market Street, Iowa City, IA 52245. (319) 338-0778. (www.iowahillel.org)

Sioux City

Jewish Federation of Sioux City. 815 38th Street, Sioux City, IA 51104. (712) 258-0618. (No website)

Kansas

Kansas City

Jewish Federation of Greater Kansas City. 5801 West 115th Street, Suite 201, Overland Park, KS 66211. (913) 327-8100. (www.jewishkansascity.org)

Wichita (Mid-Kansas)

Mid-Kansas Jewish Federation. 400 North Woodlawn, Suite 8, Wichita, KS 67208. (316) 686-4741. (www.mkjf.org)

Kentucky

Lexington (Central Kentucky)

Jewish Federation of the Bluegrass. 1050 Chinoe Road, Suite 112, Lexington, KY 40502. (859) 268-0672. (www.jewishlexington.org)

Louisville

Jewish Federation of Louisville. 3600 Dutchmans Lane, Louisville, KY 40205. (502) 459-0660. (www.jewishlouisville.org)

Northern Kentucky

Jewish Federation of Cincinnati. 8499 Ridge Road, Cincinnati, OH 45236. (513) 985-1500. (www.jewishcincinnati.org)

Western Kentucky

Jewish Federation of Southern Illinois, Southeast Missouri and Western Kentucky. 3419 West Main Street, Belleville, IL 62226. (618) 235-1614. (www.simokyfed.com)

Louisiana

Baton Rouge

Jewish Federation of Greater Baton Rouge. 4845 Jamestown Avenue, Suite 210, Baton Rouge, LA 70808. (225) 379-7393. (www.jewishbr.org)

New Orleans

Jewish Federation of Greater New Orleans. 3747 West Esplanade Avenue, Metairie, LA 70002. (504) 780-5600. (www.jewishnola.com)

Shreveport (North Louisiana)

North Louisiana Jewish Federation. 245 Southfield Road, Shreveport, LA 71105. (318) 868-1200. (www.jewishnla.org)

Maine

Portland (Southern Maine)

Jewish Community Alliance of Southern Maine. 1342 Congress Street, Portland, ME 04102. (207) 772-1959. (www.mainejewish.org)

Maryland

Baltimore

Associated: Jewish Federation of Baltimore. 101 West Mount Royal Avenue, Baltimore, MD 21201. (410) 727-4828. (www.associated.org)

Bethesda (Montgomery County)

Jewish Federation of Greater Washington. 6101 Executive Boulevard, Suite 100, North Bethesda, MD 20852. (301) 230-7200. (www.shalomdc.org)

Columbia (Howard County)

Jewish Federation of Howard County. 10630 Little Patuxent Parkway, Suite 400, Columbia, MD 21044. (410) 730-4976. (www.jewishhowardcounty.org)

Northeast Maryland

Jewish Federation of Delaware. 101 Garden of Eden Road, Wilmington, DE 19803. (302) 427-2100. (www.shalomdelaware.org)

Massachusetts

Andover (Merrimack Valley)

Merrimack Valley Jewish Federation. PO Box 937, Andover, MA 01810. (978) 688-0466. (www.mvjf.org)

Attleboro

Jewish Alliance of Greater Rhode Island. 401 Elmgrove Avenue, Providence, RI 02906. (401) 421-4111. (www.jewishallianceri.org)

Berkshire County

Jewish Federation of the Berkshires. 196 South Street, Pittsfield, MA 01201. (413) 442-4360. (www.jewishberkshires.org)

Boston

Combined Jewish Philanthropies of Greater Boston. 126 High Street, Boston, MA 02110. (617) 457-8500. (www.cjp.org)

Cape Cod

Jewish Federation of Cape Cod. PO Box 2568, 396 Main Street, Hyannis, MA 02601. (508) 778-5588. (www.facebook.com/Jewish-Federation-of-Cape-Cod-167404356653822)

Fall River

Fall River UJA. 385 High Street, Fall River, MA 02720. (508) 673-7791. (No website)

New Bedford

Jewish Federation of Greater New Bedford. 467 Hawthorn Street, North Dartmouth, MA 02747. (508) 997-7471. (www.jewishnewbedford.org)

Springfield (Western Massachusetts)

Jewish Federation of Western Massachusetts. 1160 Dickinson Street, Springfield, MA 01108. (413) 737-4313. (www.jewishwesternmass.org)

Worcester (Central Massachusetts)

Jewish Federation of Central Massachusetts. 633 Salisbury Street, Worcester, MA 01609. (508) 756-1543. (www.jewishcentralmass.org)

Michigan

Ann Arbor

Jewish Federation of Greater Ann Arbor. 2939 Birch Hollow Drive, Ann Arbor, MI 48108. (734) 677-0100. (www.jewishannarbor.org)

Detroit

Jewish Federation of Metropolitan Detroit. 6735 Telegraph Road, Bloomfield Hills, MI 48301. (888) 902-4673. (www.jewishdetroit.org)

Flint

Flint Jewish Federation. 5080 West Bristol Road, Suite 3, Flint, MI 48507. (810) 767-5922. (www.flintfed.com)

Grand Rapids

Jewish Federation of Grand Rapids. 2727 Michigan NE, Grand Rapids, MI 49506. (616) 942-5553. (www.jewishgrandrapids.org)

Lansing

Greater Lansing Jewish Welfare Federation. 360 Charles Street, East Lansing, MI 48823. (517) 332-1916. (www.jewishlansing.org)

Southeast Michigan

Jewish Federation of Greater Toledo. 6465 Sylvania Avenue, Sylvania, OH 43560. (419) 885-4461. (www.jewishtoledo.org)

Southwest Michigan

Jewish Federation of St. Joseph Valley. 3202 Shalom Way, South Bend, IN 46615. (574) 233-1164. (www.thejewishfed.org)

Minnesota

Minneapolis

Minneapolis Jewish Federation. 111 Cheshire Lane, Suite 50, Minnetonka, MN 55305. (952) 593-2600. (www.jewishminneapolis.org)

St. Paul

Jewish Federation of Greater St. Paul. 790 South Cleveland Avenue, Suite 227, St. Paul, MN 55116. (651) 690-1707. (www.jewishstpaul.org)

Mississippi

Oxford

Jewish Federation of Oxford, Mississippi. (www.jewishfederationoxfordms.org)

Missouri

Kansas City (West Central Missouri)

Jewish Federation of Greater Kansas City. 5801 West 115th Street, Suite 201, Overland Park, KS 66211. (913) 327-8100. (www.jewishkansascity.org

Southeast Missouri
Jewish Federation of Southern Illinois, Southeast Missouri and Western Kentucky. 3419 West Main Street, Belleville, IL 62226. (618) 235-1614. (www. simokyfed.com)

St. Louis
Jewish Federation of St. Louis. 12 Millstone Campus Drive, St. Louis, MO 63146. (314) 432-0020. (www.jewishinstlouis.org)

Nebraska
Lincoln
Jewish Federation of Lincoln. PO Box 67218, Lincoln, NE, 68506. (402) 915-3659. (www.jewishlincoln.org)

Northeast Nebraska
Jewish Federation of Sioux City. 815 38th Street, Sioux City, IA 51104. (712) 258-0618. (No website)

Omaha
Jewish Federation of Omaha. 333 South 132nd Street, Omaha, NE 68154. (402) 334-8200. (www.jewishomaha.org)

Nevada
Las Vegas
Jewish Nevada. 2317 Renaissance Drive, Las Vegas, NV 89119. (702) 732-0556. (www.jewishnevada.org)

New Hampshire
Manchester
Jewish Federation of New Hampshire. 66 Hanover Street, Suite 300, Manchester, NH 03101. (603) 627-7679. (www.jewishnh.org)

New Jersey
Atlantic City (Atlantic and Cape May Counties)
Jewish Federation of Atlantic & Cape May Counties. 501 North Jerome Avenue, Margate, NJ 08402. (609) 822-4404. (www.jewishbytheshore.org)

Bayonne
UJA Federation of Bayonne. 1050 Kennedy Boulevard, Bayonne, NJ 07002. (201) 436-6900. (www.jccbayonne.org/board)

Cherry Hill (Southern New Jersey)
Jewish Federation of Southern New Jersey. 1301 Springdale Road, Suite 200, Cherry Hill, NJ 08003. (856) 751-9500. (www.jewishsouthjersey.org)

Cumberland, Gloucester, and Salem Counties
Jewish Federation of Cumberland, Gloucester and Salem Counties. 1015 East Park Avenue, Suite B, Vineland, NJ 08360. (856) 696-4445. (www.jewishcumberland.org)

Greater MetroWest NJ (Essex, Morris, Sussex, Union, and parts of Somerset Counties)
Jewish Federation of Greater MetroWest NJ. 901 Route 10, Whippany, NJ 07981. (973) 929-3000. (www.jfedgmw.org)

Middlesex and Monmouth Counties
Jewish Federation in the Heart of New Jersey. 230 Old Bridge Turnpike, South River, NJ 08882. (732) 588-1800. (www.jewishheartnj.org)

Northern New Jersey
Jewish Federation of Northern New Jersey. 50 Eisenhower Drive, Paramus, NJ 07652. (201) 820-3900. (www.jfnnj.org)

Ocean County
Jewish Federation of Ocean County. 1235A Route 70, Lakewood, NJ 08701. (732) 363-0530. (www.jewishoceancounty.org)

Princeton (Mercer County)
Jewish Federation of Princeton Mercer Bucks. 4 Princess Road, Suite 211, Lawrenceville, NJ 08648. (609) 219-0555. (www.jewishpmb.org)

Somerset, Hunterdon, and Warren Counties
Jewish Federation of Somerset, Hunterdon & Warren Counties. 775 Talamini Road, Bridgewater, NJ 08807. (908) 758-2006. (www.jfedshaw.org)

New Mexico
Albuquerque
Jewish Federation of New Mexico. 5520 Wyoming Boulevard NE, Albuquerque, NM 87109. (505) 821-3214. (www.jewishnewmexico.org)

New York (Outside New York Metropolitan Area)
Albany-Schenectady-Troy (Northeastern New York)
Jewish Federation of Northeastern New York. 184 Washington Avenue Extension, Albany, NY 12203. (518) 783-7800. (www.jewishfedny.org)

Binghamton (Broome County)
Jewish Federation of Greater Binghamton. 500 Clubhouse Road, Vestal, NY 13850. (607) 724-2332. (www.jfgb.org)

Buffalo
Buffalo Jewish Federation. 2640 North Forest Road, Getzville, NY 14068. (716) 204-2241. (www.jfedbflo.com)

Elmira (Twin Tiers)
Jewish Center and Federation of the Twin Tiers. 1008 West Water Street, Elmira, NY 14905. (607) 734-8122. (www.jewishelmira.org)

Ithaca
Ithaca Area United Jewish Community. PO Box 4214, Ithaca, NY 14852. (www.iaujc.org)

Kingston (Ulster County)
Jewish Federation of Ulster County. 1 Albany Avenue, Suite G-10, Kingston, NY
12401. (845) 338-8131. (www.ucjf.org)

Newburgh (Orange County)
Jewish Federation of Greater Orange County. 292 North Street, 2nd Floor,
Newburgh, NY 12550. (845) 562-7860. (www.jewishorangeny.org)

Poughkeepsie (Dutchess County)
Jewish Federation of Dutchess County. 17 Collegeview Avenue, Poughkeepsie, NY
12603. (845) 471-9811. (www.jewishdutchess.org)

Rochester
Jewish Federation of Greater Rochester. 441 East Avenue, Rochester, NY 14607.
(585) 461-0490. (www.jewishrochester.org)

Rockland County
Jewish Federation of Rockland County. 450 West Nyack Road, West Nyack, NY
10994. (845) 362-4200. (www.jewishrockland.org)

Syracuse (Central New York)
Jewish Federation of Central New York. 5655 Thompson Road, De Witt, NY 13214.
(315) 445-0161. (www.jewishfederationcny.org)

Utica (Mohawk Valley)
Jewish Community Federation of the Mohawk Valley. 2310 Oneida Street, Utica,
NY 13501. (315) 733-2343. (www.jccutica.net)

New York Metropolitan Area
New York City (Bronx, Brooklyn, Manhattan, Queens, Staten Island, and Nassau,
Suffolk, and Westchester Counties)
UJA-Federation of New York. 130 East 59th Street, New York, NY 10022. (212)
980-1000. (www.ujafedny.org)

North Carolina
Asheville (Western North Carolina)
WNC Jewish Federation. PO Box 7126, Asheville, NC 28802. (828) 545-4648.
(www.jewishasheville.org)

Charlotte
Jewish Federation of Greater Charlotte. 5007 Providence Road, Suite 101, Charlotte,
NC 28226. (704) 944-6757. (www.jewishcharlotte.org)

Durham-Chapel Hill
Jewish Federation of Durham-Chapel Hill. 1937 West Cornwallis Road, Durham,
NC 27705. (919) 354-4936. (www.shalomdch.org)

Greensboro
Greensboro Jewish Federation. 5509-C West Friendly Avenue, Greensboro, NC
27410. (336) 852-5433. (www.shalomgreensboro.org)

Raleigh-Cary

Jewish Federation of Raleigh-Cary. 8210 Creedmoor Road, Suite 104, Raleigh, NC 27613. (919) 676-2200. (www.shalomraleigh.org)

Ohio

Akron

Jewish Community Board of Akron. 750 White Pond Drive, Akron, OH 44320. (330) 869-2424. (www.jewishakron.org)

Canton

Canton Jewish Community Federation. 432 30th Street NW, Canton, OH 44709. (330) 445-2404. (www.jewishcanton.org)

Cincinnati

Jewish Federation of Cincinnati. 8499 Ridge Road, Cincinnati, OH 45236. (513) 985-1500. (www.jewishcincinnati.org)

Cleveland

Jewish Federation of Cleveland. 25701 Science Park Drive, Cleveland, OH 44122. (216) 593-2900. (www.jewishcleveland.org)

Columbus

Jewish Federation of Columbus. 1175 College Avenue, Columbus, OH 43209. (614) 237-7686. (www.columbusjewishfederation.org)

Dayton

Jewish Federation of Greater Dayton. 525 Versailles Drive, Centerville, OH 45459. (937) 610-1555. (www.jewishdayton.org)

Toledo

Jewish Federation of Greater Toledo. 6465 Sylvania Avenue, Sylvania, OH 43560. (419) 885-4461. (www.jewishtoledo.org)

Youngstown

Youngstown Area Jewish Federation. 505 Gypsy Lane, Youngstown, OH 44504. (330) 746-3251. (www.jewishyoungstown.org)

Oklahoma

Oklahoma City

Jewish Federation of Greater Oklahoma City. 710 Wilshire Creek Boulevard, Suite 103, Oklahoma City, OK 73116. (405) 848-3132. (www.jfedokc.org)

Tulsa

Jewish Federation of Tulsa. 2021 East 71st Street, Tulsa, OK 74136. (918) 495-1100. (www.jewishtulsa.org)

Oregon

Eugene (Lane County)

Jewish Federation of Lane County. PO Box 5924, Eugene, OR 97405. (541) 484-2541. (www.jewishfedlc.org)

Portland
Jewish Federation of Greater Portland. 6680 Southwest Capitol Highway, Portland,
   OR 97219. (503) 245-6219. (www.jewishportland.org)

Pennsylvania
Allentown-Bethlehem-Easton (Lehigh Valley)
Jewish Federation of the Lehigh Valley. 702 North 22nd Street, Allentown, PA
   18104. (610) 821-5500. (www.jewishlehighvalley.org)

Altoona
Greater Altoona Jewish Federation. 1308 17th Street, Altoona, PA 16601. (814)
   515-1182. (www.greateraltoonajewishfederation.org)

Harrisburg
Jewish Federation of Greater Harrisburg. 3301 North Front Street, Harrisburg, PA
   17110. (717) 236-9555. (www.jewishharrisburg.org)

Lancaster
Jewish Community Alliance of Lancaster. PO Box 5148, Lancaster, PA 17606.
   (717) 569-7352. (www.jcalancaster.org)

North Central Pennsylvania
Jewish Center and Federation of the Twin Tiers. 1008 West Water Street, Elmira,
   NY 14905. (607) 734-8122. (www.jewishelmira.org)

Philadelphia
Jewish Federation of Greater Philadelphia. 2100 Arch Street, Philadelphia, PA
   19103. (215) 832-0500. (www.jewishphilly.org)

Pittsburgh
Jewish Federation of Greater Pittsburgh. 2000 Technology Drive, Pittsburgh, PA
   15219. (412) 681-8000. (www.jfedpgh.org)

Bucks County
Jewish Federation of Princeton Mercer Bucks. 4 Princess Road, Suite 211,
   Lawrenceville, NJ 08648. (609) 219-0555. (www.jewishpmb.org)

Reading
Jewish Federation of Reading/Berks. 1100 Berkshire Boulevard, Suite 125,
   Wyomissing, PA 19610. (610) 921-0624. (www.readingjewishcommunity.org)

Scranton (Northeastern Pennsylvania)
Jewish Federation of Northeastern Pennsylvania. 601 Jefferson Avenue, Scranton,
   PA 18510. (570) 961-2300. (www.jewishnepa.org)

West Central Pennsylvania
Youngstown Area Jewish Federation. 505 Gypsy Lane, Youngstown, OH 44504.
   (330) 746-3251. (www.jewishyoungstown.org)

Wilkes-Barre (Wyoming Valley) (Northeastern Pennsylvania)
Jewish Community Alliance of Northeastern Pennsylvania. 613 S. J. Strauss Lane,
   Kingston, PA 18704. (570) 824-4646. (www.jewishwilkes-barre.org)

Rhode Island
Providence
Jewish Alliance of Greater Rhode Island. 401 Elmgrove Avenue, Providence, RI
    02906. (401) 421-4111. (www.jewishallianceri.org)

South Carolina
Charleston
Charleston Jewish Federation. 176 Croghan Spur Road, Suite 100, Charleston, SC
    29407. (843) 614-6600. (www.jewishcharleston.org)

Columbia
Columbia Jewish Federation. 306 Flora Drive, Columbia, SC 29223. (803)
    787-2023. (www.jewishcolumbia.org)

Greenville
Greenville Jewish Federation. PO Box 5262, Greenville, SC 29606. (864) 606-4453.
    (www.jewishgreenville.org)

North Central South Carolina
Jewish Federation of Greater Charlotte. 5007 Providence Road, Suite 101, Charlotte,
    NC 28226. (704) 944-6757. (www.jewishcharlotte.org)

West Central South Carolina
Augusta Jewish Federation. 898 Weinberger Way, Evans, GA 30809. (706)
    228-3636. (www.jewishaugusta.org)

Tennessee
Chattanooga
Jewish Federation of Greater Chattanooga. 5461 North Terrace Road, Chattanooga,
    TN 37411. (423) 493-0270. (www.jewishchattanooga.com)

Knoxville
Knoxville Jewish Alliance. 6800 Deane Hill Drive SW, Knoxville, TN 37919. (865)
    690-6343. (www.jewishknoxville.org)

Memphis
Memphis Jewish Federation. 6560 Poplar Avenue, Germantown, TN 38138. (901)
    767-7100. (www.jcpmemphis.org/federation)

Nashville (Middle Tennessee)
Jewish Federation of Nashville and Middle Tennessee. 801 Percy Warner Boulevard,
    Suite 102, Nashville, TN 37205. (615) 356-3242. (www.jewishnashville.org)

Texas
Austin
Jewish Federation of Greater Austin. 7300 Hart Lane, Austin, TX 78731. (512)
    735-8010. (www.shalomaustin.org)

Corpus Christi
Combined Jewish Appeal of Corpus Christi. 750 Everhart Road, Corpus Christi, TX
    78411. (361) 855-6239. (www.jcccorpuschristi.org)

Dallas

Jewish Federation of Greater Dallas. 7800 Northaven Road, Dallas, TX 75230. (214) 369-3313. (www.jewishdallas.org)

El Paso

Jewish Federation of Greater El Paso. 7110 North Mesa, El Paso, TX 79912. (915) 842-9554. (www.jewishelpaso.org)

Fort Worth (Tarrant County)

Jewish Federation of Fort Worth & Tarrant County. 4049 Kingsridge Road, Fort Worth, TX 76109. (817) 569-0892. (www.tarrantfederation.org)

Houston

Jewish Federation of Greater Houston. 5603 South Braeswood Boulevard, Houston, TX 77096. (713) 729-7000. (www.houstonjewish.org)

San Antonio

Jewish Federation of San Antonio. 12500 Northwest Military Highway, Suite 200, San Antonio, TX 78231. (210) 302-6960. (www.jfsatx.org)

Waco

Jewish Federation of Waco. 5601 Edmond Avenue, Waco, TX 76710. (254) 776-3740. (www.jfedwaco.org)

Utah

Salt Lake City

United Jewish Federation of Utah. 2 North Medical Drive, Salt Lake City, UT 84113. (801) 581-0102. (www.shalomutah.org)

Virginia

Newport News (Virginia Peninsula)

United Jewish Community of the Virginia Peninsula. 401 City Center Boulevard, Newport News, VA 23606. (757) 930-1422. (www.ujcvp.org)

Norfolk-Virginia Beach (Tidewater)

United Jewish Federation of Tidewater. 5000 Corporate Woods Drive, Suite 200, Virginia Beach, VA 23462. (757) 965-6100. (www.jewishva.org)

Northern Virginia

Jewish Federation of Greater Washington. 6101 Executive Boulevard, Suite 100, North Bethesda, MD 20852. (301) 230-7200. (www.shalomdc.org)

Richmond

Jewish Community Federation of Richmond. 5403 Monument Avenue, Richmond, VA 23226. (804) 285-6500. (www.jewishrichmond.org)

Washington

Seattle

Jewish Federation of Greater Seattle. 2031 Third Avenue, Seattle, WA 98121. (206) 443-5400. (www.jewishinseattle.org)

Southwest Washington
Jewish Federation of Greater Portland. 6680 Southwest Capitol Highway, Portland,
  OR 97219. (503) 245-6219. (www.jewishportland.org)

West Virginia
Charleston
Federated Jewish Charities of Charleston. PO Box 1613, Charleston, WV 25326.
  (304) 345-2320 (www.fjcofcharleston.org)

Wisconsin
Madison
Jewish Federation of Madison. 6434 Enterprise Lane, Madison, WI 53719. (608)
  278-1808. (www.jewishmadison.org)

Milwaukee
Milwaukee Jewish Federation. 1360 North Prospect Avenue, Milwaukee, WI 53202.
  (414) 390-5700. (www.milwaukeejewish.org)

9.1.3 Central Coordinating Body for Jewish Federations, Canada

Jewish Federations of Canada-UIA (formerly **United Israel Appeal of Canada**
and **UIA Federations Canada**). For contact information and a description, see the
National Jewish Organizations, Canada section of Chap. 12.

9.1.4 Jewish Federations, Canada

Alberta
Calgary
Calgary Jewish Federation. 1607 90th Avenue SW, Calgary, AB T2V 4V7. (403)
  444-3152. (www.jewishcalgary.org)

Edmonton
Jewish Federation of Edmonton. 10220 156th Street, Suite 100, Edmonton, AB T5P
  2R1. (780) 487-0585. (www.jewishedmonton.org)

British Columbia
Vancouver
Jewish Federation of Greater Vancouver. 950 West 41st Avenue, Suite 200,
  Vancouver, BC V5Z 2N7. (604) 257-5100. (www.jewishvancouver.com)

Victoria-Vancouver Island
Jewish Federation of Victoria & Vancouver Island. 3636 Shelbourne Street, Victoria,
    BC V8P 4H2. (250) 370-9488. (www.jewishvancouverisland.ca)

Manitoba
Winnipeg
Jewish Federation of Winnipeg. 123 Doncaster Street, Suite C300, Winnipeg, MB
    R3N 2B2. (204) 477-7400. (www.jewishwinnipeg.org)

Nova Scotia
Halifax
Atlantic Jewish Council. 5670 Spring Garden Road, Suite 309, Halifax, NS B3J
    1H6. (902) 422-7491. (www.theajc.ns.ca)

Ontario
Hamilton
Hamilton Jewish Federation. 1605 Main Street West, Hamilton, ON L8S 1E6. (905)
    648-0605, ext 305. (www.jewishhamilton.org)

London
London Jewish Federation. JCC London, 536 Huron Street, London, ON N5Y 4J5.
    (519) 673-3310. (www.jewishlondon.ca)

Ottawa
Jewish Federation of Ottawa. 21 Nadolny Sachs Private, Ottawa, ON K2A 1R9.
    (613) 798-4696, ext. 231. (www.jewishottawa.com)

Toronto
UJA Federation of Greater Toronto. 4600 Bathurst Street, Toronto, ON M2R 3V2.
    (416) 635-2883. (www.jewishtoronto.com)

Windsor
Windsor Jewish Federation. 1641 Ouellette Avenue, Windsor, ON N8X 1K9. (519)
    973-1772. www.jewishwindsor.org)

Quebec
Montreal
Federation CJA. 1 Cummings Square (5151 Côte St. Catherine Road), Montreal,
    QC H3W 1M6. (514) 735-3541. (www.federationcja.org)

Montreal
Federation CJA West Island. 96 Roger-Pilon Street, Dollard-des-Ormeaux, QC
    H9B 2E1. (514) 624-5005. (www.federationcja.org/en/who/fcja_westisland)

9.2 Jewish Community Centers

9.2.1 Central Coordinating Body for Jewish Community Centers

JCC Association of North America (formerly **Council of Young Men's Hebrew & Kindred Associations and Jewish Welfare Board**). For contact information and a description, see the Jewish Community Coordinating Organizations section of Chap. 12.

9.2.2 Jewish Community Centers, United States

Alabama
Birmingham
Levite JCC. 3960 Montclair Road, Birmingham, AL 35213. (205) 879-0411. (www. bhamjcc.org)

Arizona
Phoenix
East Valley JCC. 908 North Alma School Road, Chandler, AZ 85224. (480) 897-0588. (www.evjcc.org)

Phoenix
Valley of the Sun JCC. 12701 North Scottsdale Road, Scottsdale, AZ 85254. (480) 483-7121. (www.vosjcc.org)

Tucson (Southern Arizona)
Tucson JCC. 3800 East River Road, Tucson, AZ 85718. (520) 299-3000. (www. tucsonjcc.org)

California
Long Beach (West Orange County)
Barbara and Ray Alpert JCC. 3801 East Willow Street, Long Beach, CA 90815. (562) 426-7601. (www.alpertjcc.org)

Los Angeles
Silverlake Independent JCC. 1110 Bates Avenue, Los Angeles, CA 90029. (323) 663-2255. (www.sijcc.net)

Los Angeles
Valley JCC. 20350 Ventura Boulevard, Suite 100, Woodland Hills, CA 91364. (818) 360-2211. (www.valleyjcc.org)

Los Angeles
Westside JCC. 5870 West Olympic Boulevard, Los Angeles, CA 90036. (323) 938-2531. (www.westsidejcc.org)

Orange County
Merage JCC of Orange County. One Federation Way, Suite 200, Irvine, CA 92603. (949) 435-3400. (www.jccoc.org)

San Diego
Lawrence Family JCC of San Diego County. 4126 Executive Drive, Jacobs Family Campus, La Jolla, CA 92037. (858) 457-3030. (www.lfjcc.org)

San Francisco (Contra Costa County)
Contra Costa JCC. 1550 Parkside Drive, Suite 130, Walnut Creek, CA 94596. (925) 938-7800. (www.ccjcc.org)

San Francisco
JCC of San Francisco. 3200 California Street, San Francisco, CA 94118. (415) 292-1200. (www.jccsf.org)

San Francisco (Alameda County)
JCC of the East Bay. 1414 Walnut Street, Berkeley, CA 94709. (510) 848-0237. (www.jcceastbay.org)

San Francisco (Sonoma County)
JCC, Sonoma County. 1301 Farmers Lane, Santa Rosa, CA 95405. (707) 528-4222. (www.jccsoco.org)

San Francisco (Marin County)
Osher Marin JCC. 200 North San Pedro Road, San Rafael, CA 94903. (415) 444-8000. (www.marinjcc.org)

San Francisco (Santa Clara County)
Oshman Family JCC. 3921 Fabian Way, Palo Alto, CA 94303. (650) 223-8700. (www.paloaltojcc.org)

San Francisco (Monterrey Peninsula) (San Mateo County)
Peninsula JCC. 800 Foster City Boulevard, Foster City, CA 94404. (650) 212-7522. (www.pjcc.org)

San Jose (Silicon Valley)
Addison-Penzak JCC of Silicon Valley. 14855 Oka Road, Suite 201, Los Gatos, CA 95032. (408) 357-7429. (www.svjcc.org)

San Luis Obispo
JCC-Federation of San Luis Obispo. 875 Laureate Lane, San Luis Obispo, CA 93405. (805) 426-5465. (www.jccslo.com)

Santa Barbara
Bronfman Family JCC/Jewish Federation of Greater Santa Barbara. 524 Chapala Street, Santa Barbara, CA 93101. (805) 957-1115. (www.jewishsantabarbara.org)

Colorado

Boulder

Boulder JCC. 6007 Oreg Avenue, Boulder, CO 80303. (303) 998-1900. (www.boulderjcc.org)

Denver

Staenberg-Loup JCC. 350 South Dahlia Street, Denver, CO 80246. (303) 399-2660. (www.jccdenver.org)

Connecticut

Danbury

JCC in Sherman. 9 Route 39, Sherman, CT 06784. (860) 355-8050. (www.jccinsherman.org)

Greenwich

JCC Greenwich. One Holly Hill Lane, Greenwich, CT 06830. (203) 552-1818. (www.jccgreenwich.org)

Hartford

Mandell JCC of Greater Hartford. 335 Bloomfield Avenue, West Hartford, CT 06117. (860) 236-4571. (www.mandelljcc.org)

New Haven

JCC of Greater New Haven. 360 Amity Road, Woodbridge, CT 06525. (203) 387-2424. (www.jccnh.org)

Stamford-New Canaan-Darien

Stamford JCC. 1035 Newfield Avenue, Stamford, CT 06905. (203) 322-7900. (www.stamfordjcc.org)

Delaware

Wilmington

Bernard and Ruth Siegel JCC. 101 Garden of Eden Road, Wilmington, DE 19803. (302) 478-5660. (www.siegeljcc.org)

District of Columbia

Washington, DC

Edlavitch JCC of Washington, DC. 1529 Sixteenth Street NW, Washington, DC 20036. (202) 518-9400. (www.washingtondcjcc.org)

Florida

Boca Raton-Delray Beach (South Palm Beach)

Adolph and Rose Levis JCC. 9801 Donna Klein Boulevard, Boca Raton, FL 33428. (561) 852-3200. (www.levisjcc.org)

Fort Lauderdale (Broward County)

David Posnack JCC. 5850 South Pine Island Road, Davie, FL 33328. (954) 434-0499. (www.dpjcc.org)

Fort Lauderdale (Broward County)
Samuel M. & Helene Soref JCC. 6501 West Sunrise Boulevard, Plantation, FL 33313. (954) 792-6700. (www.sorefjcc.org)

Jacksonville
David A. Stein Jewish Community Alliance. 8505 San Jose Boulevard, Jacksonville, FL 32217. (904) 730-2100. (www.jcajax.org)

Miami
Dave and Mary Alper JCC. 11155 Southwest 112th Avenue, Miami, FL 33176. (305) 271-9000. (www.alperjcc.org)

Miami
Galbut Family Miami Beach JCC. 4221 Pine Tree Drive, Miami Beach, FL 33140. (305) 534-3206. (www.mbjcc.org)

Miami
Michael-Ann Russell JCC. 18900 Northeast 25th Avenue, North Miami Beach, FL 33180. (305) 932-4200. (www.marjcc.org)

Orlando
Jack & Lee Rosen JCC. 11184 South Apopka-Vineland Road, Orlando, FL 32836. (407) 387-5330. (www.rosenjcc.org)

Orlando
Roth Family JCC of Greater Orlando. 851 North Maitland Avenue, Maitland, FL 32751. (407) 645-5933. (www.orlandojcc.org)

Tampa
Tampa JCCs, Bryan Glazer Family JCC. 522 North Howard Avenue, Tampa, FL 33606. (813) 575-5900. (www.jewishtampa.com)

Tampa
Tampa JCCs, JCC on the Cohn Campus. 13009 Community Campus Drive, Tampa, FL 33625. (813) 264-9000. (www.jewishtampa.com)

West Palm Beach
Mandel JCC of the Palm Beaches, Boynton Beach. 8500 Jog Road, Boynton Beach, FL 33472. (561) 740-9000. (https://bb.jcconline.com)

West Palm Beach
Mandel JCC of the Palm Beaches, Palm Beach Gardens. 5221 Hood Road, Palm Beach Gardens, FL 33418. (561) 712-5200. (https://pbg.jcconline.com)

Georgia
Atlanta
Marcus JCC of Atlanta. 5342 Tilly Mill Road, Dunwoody, GA 30338. (678) 812-4000. (www.atlantajcc.org)

Augusta
Augusta JCC. 898 Weinberger Way, Evans, GA 30809. (706) 228-3636. (www. augustajcc.org)

Savannah
Savannah Jewish Educational Alliance. 5111 Abercorn Street, Savannah, GA 31405.
(912) 355-8111. (www.savannahjea.org)

Illinois
Chicago
JCC Chicago, Bernard Horwich JCC. 3003 West Touhy Avenue, Chicago, IL 60645.
(773) 761-9100. (www.jccchicago.org)

Chicago
JCC Chicago, Bernard Weinger JCC. 300 Revere Drive, Northbrook, IL 60062.
(224) 406-9200. (www.jccchicago.org)

Chicago
JCC Chicago, Florence G. Heller JCC. 524 West Melrose Avenue, Chicago, IL
60657. (773) 871-6780. (www.jccchicago.org)

Chicago
JCC Chicago, Hyde Park JCC. 5200 South Hyde Park Boulevard, Chicago, IL
60615. (773) 753-3080. (www.jccchicago.org)

Chicago
JCC Chicago, Lake County JCC. 23280 North Old McHenry Road, Lake Zurich, IL
60047. (847) 901-0620. (www.jccchicago.org)

Chicago
JCC Chicago, Mayer Kaplan JCC Children's Center. 5050 Church Street, Skokie,
IL 60077. (847) 763-3500. (www.jccchicago.org) (Ceased to exist as of 2018)

Indiana
Indianapolis
Arthur M. Glick JCC. 6701 Hoover Road, Indianapolis, IN 46260. (317) 251-9467.
(www.jccindy.org)

Kansas
Kansas City
JCC of Greater Kansas City. 5801 West 115th Street, Overland Park, KS 66211.
(913) 327-8000. (www.thejkc.org)

Kentucky
Louisville
JCC of Louisville. 3600 Dutchmans Lane, Louisville, KY 40205. (502) 238-2791
or (502) 459-0660. (www.jewishlouisville.org/the-j)

Louisiana
New Orleans
New Orleans JCC, Goldring-Woldenberg JCC-Metairie, Harry and Jeanette
Weinberg Building, 3747 West Esplanade Avenue, Metairie, LA 70002. (504)
887-5158. (www.nojcc.org)

New Orleans
New Orleans JCC, Uptown. 5342 St. Charles Avenue, New Orleans, LA 70115.
(504) 897-0143. (www.nojcc.org)

Maine
Portland (Southern Maine)
Jewish Community Alliance of Southern Maine. 1342 Congress Street, Portland,
ME 04102. (207) 772-1959. (www.mainejewish.org)

Maryland
Baltimore
JCC of Greater Baltimore, Downtown Baltimore JCC. 1118 Light Street, Baltimore,
MD 21230. (410) 559-3618. (www.jcc.org)

Baltimore
JCC of Greater Baltimore, Rosenbloom Owings Mills JCC. 3506 Gwynnbrook
Avenue, Owings Mills, MD 21117. (410) 559-3500. (www.jcc.org)

Baltimore
JCC of Greater Baltimore, Weinberg Park Heights JCC. 5700 Park Heights Avenue,
Baltimore, MD 21215. (410) 500-5900. (www.jcc.org)

Columbia (Howard County)
Jewish Federation of Howard County. 10630 Little Patuxent Parkway, Suite 400,
Columbia, MD 21044. (410) 730-4976. (www.jewishhowardcounty.org)

Rockville (Montgomery County)
Bender JCC of Greater Washington. 6125 Montrose Road, Rockville, MD 20852.
(301) 881-0100. (www.jccgw.org)

Massachusetts
Boston
JCC Greater Boston, Leventhal-Sidman JCC. 333 Nahanton Street, Newton, MA
02459. (617) 558-6522. (www.bostonjcc.org)

Boston
JCC Greater Boston, Metrowest. 327 Union Avenue, Framingham, MA 01702.
(508) 879-3300. (www.bostonjcc.org)

Boston
JCC Greater Boston, North of Boston. (617) 841-8009. (www.bostonjcc.org)

Boston
JCC Greater Boston, South of Boston. (781) 795-0510. (www.bostonjcc.org)

Boston (North Shore)
JCC of the North Shore. 4 Community Road, Marblehead, MA 01945. (781)
631-8330. (www.jccns.org)

Boston (North Shore)
North Suburban JCC. 240 Lynnfield Street, Peabody, MA 01960. (978) 471-5520.
(www.nsjcc.org)

Springfield (Western Massachusetts)
Springfield JCC. 1160 Dickinson Street, Springfield, MA 01108. (413) 739-4715. (www.springfieldjcc.org)

Worcester (Central Massachusetts)
Worcester JCC. 633 Salisbury Street, Worcester, MA 01609. (508) 756-7109. (www.worcesterjcc.org)

Michigan
Ann Arbor
JCC of Greater Ann Arbor. 2935 Birch Hollow Drive, Ann Arbor, MI 48108. (734) 971-0990. (www.jccannarbor.org)

Detroit
JCC of Metropolitan Detroit. 6600 West Maple Road, West Bloomfield, MI 48322. (248) 661-1000. (www.jccdet.org)

Minnesota
Minneapolis
Sabes JCC. 4330 South Cedar Lake Road, Minneapolis, MN 55416. (952) 381-3400. (www.sabesjcc.org)

St. Paul
JCC of the Greater St. Paul Area. 1375 St. Paul Avenue, St. Paul, MN 55116. (651) 698-0751. (www.stpauljcc.org)

Missouri
St. Louis
St. Louis JCC, Marilyn Fox Building, Chesterfield. 16801 Baxter Road, Chesterfield, MO 63005. (314) 442-3428. (www.jccstl.com)

St. Louis
St. Louis JCC, Staenberg Family Complex, Creve Coeur. 2 Millstone Campus Drive, St Louis, MO 63146. (314) 432-5700. (www.jccstl.com)

Nebraska
Omaha
JCC of Omaha. 333 South 132nd Street, Omaha, NE 68154. (402) 334-8200. (www.jccomaha.org)

Nevada
Las Vegas
JCC of Southern Nevada. 8689 West Sahara Avenue, Suite 180, Las Vegas, NV 89117. (702) 794-0090. (www.jccsn.org)

New Jersey
Atlantic and Cape May Counties
Milton & Betty Katz JCC of Atlantic County. 501 North Jerome Avenue, Margate City, NJ 08402. (609) 822-1167. (www.jccatlantic.org)

Bayonne
JCC of Bayonne. 1050 Kennedy Boulevard, Bayonne, NJ 07002. (201) 436-6900.
(www.jccbayonne.org)

Cherry Hill (Southern New Jersey)
Betty & Milton Katz JCC of Cherry Hill. 1301 Springdale Road, Cherry Hill, NJ
08003. (856) 424-4444. (www.katzjcc.org)

Greater MetroWest NJ (Essex County)
JCC MetroWest, Leon & Toby Cooperman JCC. 760 Northfield Avenue, West
Orange, NJ 07052. (973) 530-3400. (www.jccmetrowest.org)

Greater MetroWest NJ (Union County)
JCC of Central New Jersey. 1391 Martine Avenue, Scotch Plains, NJ 07076. (908)
889-8800. (www.jccnj.org)

Greater MetroWest NJ (Union County)
YM-YWHA of Union County, Harry Lebau Jewish Center, 501 Green Lane, Union,
NJ 07083. (908) 289-8112. (www.uniony.org)

Middlesex County
JCC of Middlesex County. 1775 Oak Tree Road, Edison, NJ 08820. (732) 494-3232.
(www.jccmc.org)

Monmouth County
Charles & Brenda Saka DSN Community Center. 244 Norwood Avenue, Oakhurst,
NJ 07755. (732) 686-9595. (www.dsnlive.org)

Monmouth County
JCC Jersey Shore. 100 Grant Avenue, Deal, NJ 07723. (732) 531-9100. (www.
jccjerseyshore.org)

Northern New Jersey
Kaplen JCC on the Palisades. 411 East Clinton Avenue, Tenafly, NJ 07670. (201)
569-7900. (www.jccotp.org)

Princeton (Mercer County)
JCC Princeton Mercer Bucks and JCC Abrams Camps. 148 Cedarville Road, East
Windsor, NJ 08520. (609) 606-7070. (www.jccabramscamps.org)

Somerset, Hunterdon, and Warren Counties
Shimon and Sara Birnbaum JCC. 775 Talamini Road, Bridgewater, NJ 08807. (908)
725-6994. (www.ssbjcc.org)

New Mexico
Albuquerque
Ronald Gardenswartz JCC of Greater Albuquerque. 5520 Wyoming Boulevard NE,
Albuquerque, NM 87109. (505) 332-0565. (www.jccabq.org)

New York (Outside New York Metropolitan Area)

Albany (Northeastern New York)

Sidney Albert Albany JCC. 340 Whitehall Road, Albany, NY 12208. (518) 438-6651. (www.saajcc.org)

Binghamton (Broome County)

Binghamton JCC. 500 Clubhouse Road, Vestal, NY 13850. (607) 724-2417. (www. binghamtonjcc.org)

Buffalo

JCC of Greater Buffalo, Benderson Family Building, Amherst. 2640 North Forest Road, Amherst, NY 14068. (716) 688-4033. (www.jccbuffalo.org)

Buffalo

JCC of Greater Buffalo, Holland Family Building, Buffalo. 787 Delaware Avenue, Buffalo, NY 14209. (716) 886-3145. (www.jccbuffalo.org)

Elmira (Twin Tiers)

Jewish Center and Federation of the Twin Tiers. 1008 West Water Street, Elmira, NY 14905. (607) 734-8122. (www.jewishelmira.org)

Newburgh (Orange County)

Newburgh JCC. 290 North Street, Newburgh, NY 12550. (845) 561-6602. (www. newburghjcc.org)

Rochester

JCC of Greater Rochester. 1200 Edgewood Avenue, Rochester, NY 14618. (585) 461-2000. (www.jccrochester.org)

Rockland County

JCC Rockland. 450 West Nyack Road, West Nyack, NY 10994. (845) 362-4400. (www.jccrockland.org)

Schenectady (Northeastern New York)

Robert & Dorothy Ludwig JCC of Schenectady. 2565 Balltown Road, Schenectady, NY 12309. (518) 377-8803. (www.schenectadyjcc.org)

Syracuse (Central New York)

JCC of Syracuse. 5655 Thompson Road, DeWitt, NY 13214. (315) 445-2360. (www.jccsyr.org)

Utica (Mohawk Valley)

JCC of the Mohawk Valley. 2310 Oneida Street, Utica, NY 13501. (315) 733-2343. (www.jccutica.net)

New York Metropolitan Area

Bronx

Bronx House. 990 Pelham Parkway South, Bronx, NY 10461. (718) 792-1800. (www.bronxhouse.org)

Bronx
Mosholu Montefiore Community Center. 3450 DeKalb Avenue, Bronx, NY 10467.
(718) 882-4000. (www.mmcc.org)

Bronx
The Riverdale Y. 5625 Arlington Avenue, Bronx, NY 10471. (718) 548-8200. (www.
riverdaley.org)

Brooklyn
Boro Park Y. 4912 14th Avenue, Brooklyn, NY 11219. (718) 438-5921. (www.
boroparky.org)

Brooklyn
Edith & Carl Marks JCH of Bensonhurst. 7802 Bay Pkwy, Brooklyn, NY 11214.
(718) 331-6800. (www.jchb.org)

Brooklyn
Kings Bay Y. 3495 Nostrand Avenue, Brooklyn, NY 11229. (718) 648-7703. (www.
kingsbayy.org)

Brooklyn
Morris and Paulette Bailey Sephardic Community Center. 1901 Ocean Parkway,
Brooklyn, NY 11223. (718) 627-4300. (www.scclive.org)

Brooklyn
Shorefront YM-YWHA of Brighton-Manhattan Beach. 3300 Coney Island Avenue,
Brooklyn, NY 11235. (718) 646-1444. (www.shorefronty.org)

Manhattan
14th Street Y. 344 East 14th Street, New York, NY 10003. (212) 780-0800.
(www.14streety.org)

Manhattan
92nd Street Y. 1395 Lexington Avenue, New York, NY 10128. (212) 415-5500.
(www.92y.org)

Manhattan
Educational Alliance. 197 East Broadway, New York, NY 10002. (212) 780-2300.
(www.edalliance.org)

Manhattan
JCC Harlem. 318 West 118th Street, New York, NY 10026. (212) 865-1215. (www.
jccmanhattan.org/communities/jccharlem)

Manhattan
Marlene Meyerson JCC Manhattan. 334 Amsterdam Ave, New York, NY 10023.
(646) 505-4444. (www.jccmanhattan.org)

Manhattan
Moise Safra Center. 30 East 82nd Street, New York, NY 10028. (212) 359-0700.
(www.moisesafracenter.org)

Manhattan

YM & YWHA of Washington Heights & Inwood. 54 Nagle Avenue, New York, NY 10040. (212) 569-6200. (www.ywashhts.org)

Nassau County

Barry and Florence Friedberg JCC, Long Beach. 310 National Boulevard, Long Beach, NY 11561. (516) 431-2929. (www.friedbergjcc.org)

Nassau County

Barry and Florence Friedberg JCC, Merrick/Bellmore. 225 Fox Boulevard, Merrick, NY 11566. (516) 379-938. (www.friedbergjcc.org)

Nassau County

Barry and Florence Friedberg JCC, Oceanside. 15 Neil Court, Oceanside, NY 11572. (516) 766-4341. (www.friedbergjcc.org)

Nassau County

Marion & Aaron Gural JCC. 207 Grove Avenue, Cedarhurst, NY 11516. (516) 569-6733. (www.guraljcc.org)

Nassau County

Mid-Island Y JCC. 45 Manetto Hill Road, Plainview, NY 11803. (516) 822-3535. (www.miyjcc.org)

Nassau County

Sid Jacobson JCC. 300 Forest Drive, East Hills, NY 11548. (516) 484-1545. (www.sjjcc.org)

Queens

Commonpoint Queens Bay Terrace Center. 212-00 23rd Avenue, Bayside, NY 11360. (718) 423-6111. (www.commonpointqueens.org)

Queens

Commonpoint Queens Central Queens. 67-09 108th Street, Forest Hills, NY 11375. (718) 268-5011. (www.commonpointqueens.org)

Queens

Commonpoint Queens Sam Field Center. 58-20 Little Neck Parkway, Little Neck, NY 11362. (718) 225-6750. (www.commonpointqueens.org)

Staten Island

JCC of Staten Island, Aberlin/North JCC. 485 Victory Boulevard, Staten Island, NY 10301. (718) 475-5290. (www.sijcc.org)

Staten Island

JCC of Staten Island, Avis/South Shore JCC. 1297 Arthur Kill Road, Staten Island, NY 10312. (718) 475-5270. (www.sijcc.org)

Staten Island

JCC of Staten Island, Bernikow/Mid-Island JCC. 1466 Manor Road, Staten Island, NY 10314. (718) 475-5200. (www.sijcc.org)

Suffolk County
Suffolk Y JCC. 74 Hauppauge Road, Commack, NY 11725. (631) 462-9800. (www.
suffolkyjcc.org)

Westchester County
Harold & Elaine Shames JCC on the Hudson. 371 South Broadway, Tarrytown, NY
10591. (914) 366-7898. (www.shamesjcc.org)

Westchester County
JCC of Mid-Westchester. 999 Wilmot Road, Scarsdale, NY 10583. (914) 472-3300.
(www.jccmw.org)

North Carolina
Asheville (Western North Carolina)
Asheville JCC. 236 Charlotte Street, Asheville, NC 28801. (828) 253-0701. (www.
jcc-asheville.org)

Charlotte
Sandra and Leon Levine JCC. 5007 Providence Road, Charlotte, NC 28226. (704)
366-5007. (www.charlottejcc.org)

Durham-Chapel Hill
Charlotte and Dick Levin JCC. 1937 West Cornwallis Road, Durham, NC 27705.
(919) 354-4936. (www.levinjcc.org)

Raleigh-Cary
Raleigh-Cary JCC. 12804 Norwood Road, Raleigh, NC 27613. (919) 676-6170.
(www.shalomraleigh.org/jcc)

Ohio
Akron
Jerry Shaw JCC of Akron. 750 White Pond Drive, Akron, OH 44320. (330)
867-7850. (www.shawjcc.org)

Canton
Canton JCC. 432 30th Street NW, Canton, OH 44709. (330) 452-6444. (www.jew-
ishcanton.org)

Cincinnati
Manuel D. and Rhoda Mayerson JCC. 8485 Ridge Road, Cincinnati, OH 45236.
(513) 761-7500. (www.mayersonjcc.org)

Cleveland
Mandel JCC of Cleveland. 26001 South Woodland Road, Beachwood, OH 44122.
(216) 831-0700. (www.mandeljcc.org)

Columbus
JCC of Greater Columbus. 1125 College Avenue, Columbus, OH 43209. (614)
231-2731. (www.columbusjcc.org)

Dayton

JCC of Greater Dayton. 525 Versailles Drive, Centerville, OH 45459. (937)
    610-1555. (www.jewishdayton.org)

Toledo

YMCA and JCC of Greater Toledo. 1500 North Superior Street, 2nd Floor, Toledo,
    OH 43604. (419) 729-8135. (www.ymcatoledo.org)

Youngstown

JCC of Youngstown. 505 Gypsy Lane, Youngstown, OH 44504. (330) 746-3251.
    (www.jccyoungstown.org)

Oklahoma

Tulsa

Charles Schusterman JCC. 2021 East 71st Street, Tulsa, OK 74136. (918) 495-1111.
    (www.csjcc.org)

Oregon

Portland

Mittleman JCC. 6651 Southwest Capitol Highway, Portland, OR 97219. (503)
    244-0111. (www.oregonjcc.org)

Pennsylvania

Allentown-Bethlehem-Easton (Lehigh Valley)

JCC of the Lehigh Valley. 702 North 22nd Street, Allentown, PA 18104. (610)
    435-3571. (www.allentownjcc.org)

Bucks County

JCC Princeton Mercer Bucks and JCC Abrams Camps. 148 Cedarville Road, East
    Windsor, NJ 08520. (609) 606-7070. (www.jccabramscamps.org

Harrisburg

JCC of Greater Harrisburg. 3301 North Front Street, Harrisburg, PA 17110. (717)
    236-9555. (www.jewishharrisburg.org)

Lancaster

Jewish Community Alliance of Lancaster. (Operates without a JCC building.) PO
    Box 5148, Lancaster, PA 17606. (717) 569-7352. (www.jcalancaster.org)

North Central Pennsylvania

Jewish Center and Federation of the Twin Tiers. 1008 West Water Street, Elmira,
    NY 14905. (607) 734-8122. (www.jewishelmira.org)

Philadelphia

Charles & Elizabeth Gershman Y. 401 South Broad Street, Philadelphia, PA 19147.
    (215) 545-4400. (www.gershmany.org)

Philadelphia

Kevy K. and Teddy Kaiserman JCC. 45 Haverford Road, Wynnewood, PA 19096.
    (610) 896-7770. (www.phillyjcc.com)

Philadelphia
Kleinlife. 10100 Jamison Avenue, Philadelphia, PA 19116. (215) 698-7300. (www.
kleinlife.org)

Pittsburgh
JCC of Greater Pittsburgh, South Hills. 345 Kane Boulevard, Pittsburgh, PA 15243.
(412) 278-1975. (www.jccpgh.org)

Pittsburgh
JCC of Greater Pittsburgh, Squirrel Hill. 5738 Forbes Avenue, Pittsburgh, PA 15217.
(412) 521-8010. (www.jccpgh.org)

Reading
Jewish Cultural Center of Reading, PA. 1100 Berkshire Boulevard, Suite 125,
Wyomissing, PA 19610. (610) 921-0624. (www.readingjewishcommunity.org)

Scranton (Northeastern Pennsylvania)
Scranton JCC. 601 Jefferson Avenue, Scranton, PA 18510. (570) 346-6595. (www.
scrantonjcc.org)

Wilkes-Barre (Wyoming Valley) (Northeastern Pennsylvania)
Friedman JCC. 613 S.J. Strauss Lane, Kingston, PA 18704. (570) 824-4646. (www.
jewishwilkes-barre.org)

York
York JCC. 2000 Hollywood Drive, York, PA 17403. (717) 843-0918. (www.yor-
kjcc.org)

Rhode Island
Providence
Dwares JCC. 401 Elmgrove Avenue, Providence, RI 02906. (401) 421-4111. (www.
jccri.org)

South Carolina
Charleston
Charleston JCC Without Walls. 1630-2 Meeting Street, Charleston, SC 29405.
(843) 571-6565. (www.charlestonjcc.org)

Columbia
Katie and Irwin Kahn JCC. 306 Flora Drive, Columbia, SC 29223. (803) 787-2023.
(www.jcccolumbia.org)

Tennessee
Chattanooga
Jewish Cultural Center. 5461 North Terrace Road, Chattanooga, TN 37411. (423)
493-0270. (www.jewishchattanooga.com)

Knoxville
Arnstein JCC/Knoxville Jewish Alliance. 6800 Deane Hill Drive SW, Knoxville,
TN 37919. (865) 690-6343. (www.jewishknoxville.org)

Memphis
Memphis JCC. 6560 Poplar Avenue, Memphis, TN 38138. (901) 761-0810. (www.
jccmemphis.org)

Nashville (Middle Tennessee)
Gordon JCC. 801 Percy Warner Boulevard, Nashville, TN 37205. (615) 356-7170.
(www.nashvillejcc.org)

Texas
Austin
JCC Austin. 7300 Hart Lane, Austin, TX 78731. (512) 735-8000. (www.shalo-
maustin.org)

Corpus Christi
JCC of Corpus Christi. 750 Everhart Road, Corpus Christi, TX 78411. (361)
855-6239. (www.jcccorpuschristi.org)

Dallas
Aaron Family JCC of Dallas. 7900 Northaven Road, Dallas, TX 75230. (214) 506-
-2563. (www.jccdallas.org)

Houston
Evelyn Rubenstein JCC of Houston. 5601 South Braeswood, Houston, TX 77096.
(713) 729-3200. (www.erjcchouston.org)

Houston
Evelyn Rubenstein JCC of Houston, Houston West. 1120 Dairy Ashford, Houston,
TX 77079. (281) 556-5567. (www.erjcchouston.org)

San Antonio
Barshop JCC of San Antonio. 12500 Northwest Military Highway, San Antonio, TX
78231. (210) 302-6820. (www.jccsanantonio.org)

Utah
Salt Lake City
I.J. & Jeanne Wagner JCC. 2 North Medical Drive, Salt Lake City, UT 84113. (801)
581-0098. (www.slcjcc.org)

Virginia
Newport News (Virginia Peninsula)
United JCC of the Virginia Peninsula. 401 City Center Boulevard, Newport News,
VA 23606. (757) 930-1422. (www.ujcvp.org)

Norfolk-Virginia Beach (Tidewater)
Simon Family JCC. 5000 Corporate Woods Drive, Suite 100, Virginia Beach, VA
23462. (757) 321-2338. (www.simonfamilyjcc.org)

Northern Virginia
JCC of Northern Virginia. 8900 Little River Turnpike, Fairfax, VA 22031. (703)
323-0880. (www.jccnv.org)

Richmond
Carole and Marcus Weinstein JCC. 5403 Monument Avenue, Richmond, VA 23226.
   (804) 285-6500. (www.weinsteinjcc.org)

Washington
Seattle
Samuel and Althea Stroum JCC of Greater Seattle, Mercer Island Campus. 3801
   East Mercer Way, Mercer Island, WA 98040. (206) 232-7115. (www.sjcc.org)

Seattle
Samuel and Althea Stroum JCC of Greater Seattle, Seattle Campus. 2618 Northeast
   80th Street, Seattle, WA 98115. (206) 526-8073. (www.sjcc.org)

Wisconsin
Milwaukee
Harry & Rose Samson Family JCC. 6255 North Santa Monica Boulevard, Whitefish
   Bay, WI 53217. (414) 967-8200. (www.jccmilwaukee.org)

9.2.3   Jewish Community Centers, Canada

Alberta
Calgary
Calgary JCC. 1607 90th Avenue SW, Calgary, AB T2V 4V7. (403) 253-8600.
   (www.calgaryjcc.com)

British Columbia
Vancouver
JCC of Greater Vancouver. 950 West 41st Avenue, Vancouver, BC V5Z 2N7. (604)
   257-5111. (www.jccgv.com)

Victoria-Vancouver Island
JCC of Victoria. 3636 Shelbourne Street, Victoria, BC V8P 4H2. (250) 477-7185.
   (www.jccvictoria.ca)

Manitoba
Winnipeg
Rose & Max Rady JCC. 123 Doncaster Street, Winnipeg, MB R3N 2B3. (204)
   477-7510. (www.radyjcc.com)

Ontario
Hamilton
JCC of Hamilton. 1605 Main Street West, Hamilton ON L8S 1E6. (905) 648-0605.
   (www.hamiltonjcc.com)

London
JCC of London. 536 Huron Street, London, ON N5Y 4J5. (519) 673-3310. (www.
   jewishlondon.ca)

Ottawa
Soloway JCC. 21 Nadolny Sachs Private, Ottawa, ON K2A 1R9. (613) 798-9818.
(www.jccottawa.com)

Toronto
Miles Nadal JCC. 750 Spadina Avenue, Toronto, ON M5S 2J2. (416) 924-6211.
(www.mnjcc.org)

Toronto
Prosserman JCC. 4588 Bathurst Street, Toronto, ON M2R 1W6. (416) 638-1881.
(www.prossermanjcc.com)

Toronto
Schwartz/Reisman Centre. 9600 Bathurst Street, Suite 240, Vaughan, ON L6A 3Z8.
(905) 303-1821. (www.srcentre.ca)

Windsor
Windsor JCC. 1641 Ouellette Avenue, Windsor, ON N8X 1K9. (519) 973-1772.
(www.jewishwindsor.org)

Quebec
Montreal
Ben Weider JCC. 5400 Westbury Avenue, Montreal, QC H3W 2W8. (514) 737-6551.
(www.ymywha.com)

9.3 Jewish Human Service Agencies (Jewish Family Services, Jewish Vocational Services, Jewish Free Loans)

9.3.1 Central Coordinating Body for Jewish Human Service Agencies

Network of Jewish Human Service Agencies (formerly **Association of Jewish Family & Children's Agencies**). For contact information and a description, see the Jewish Community Coordinating Organizations section of Chap. 12.
    Note: When multiple locations exist in one community, only the main office is listed.

9.3.2 Jewish Family Service Agencies, United States

Alabama
Birmingham
Collat Jewish Family Services of Birmingham. 3940 Montclair Road, Suite 205,
Birmingham, AL 35213. (205) 879-3438. (www.cjfsbham.org)

Dothan

Blumberg Family Jewish Community Services of Dothan. 2733 Ross Clark Circle, Dothan, AL 36301. (334) 793-6855, ext. 270. (www.bfjcs.org)

Arizona

Phoenix

Jewish Family & Children's Service. 4747 North 7th Street, Suite 100, Phoenix, AZ 85014. (602) 279-7655. (www.jfcsaz.org)

Tucson (Southern Arizona)

Jewish Family & Children's Service of Southern Arizona. 4301 East Fifth Street, Tucson, AZ 85711. (520) 795-0300. (www.jfcstucson.org)

Arkansas

Little Rock

Family Services Fund. Jewish Federation of Arkansas, 18 Corporate Hill Drive, Suite 204, Little Rock, AR 72205. (501) 663-3571. (www.jewisharkansas.org/family-services)

California

Fresno (Central California)

Jewish Family Services. 1340 West Herndon Avenue, Fresno, CA 93711. (559) 432-0529. (www.jewishfederationcentralcalifornia.org/jewish-family-services)

Long Beach (West Orange County)

Jewish Family & Children's Service of Long Beach/West Orange County. 3801 East Willow Street, Long Beach, CA 90815. (562) 427-7916. (www.jfcslong-beach.org)

Los Angeles

Jewish Family Service of Los Angeles. 3580 Wilshire Boulevard, Suite 700, Los Angeles, CA 90010. (323) 761-8800. (www.jfsla.org)

Orange County

Jewish Federation & Family Services of Orange County/JFFS Family Services, Orange County. 1 Federation Way, Suite 220, Irvine, CA 92603. (949) 435-3460. (www.jewishorangecounty.org, www.familyservicesoc.org)

Palm Springs

Jewish Family Service of the Desert. 490 South Farrell, Suite C-208, Palm Springs, CA 92262. (760) 325-4088. (www.jfsdesert.org)

Sacramento

Jewish Family Service. Jewish Federation of the Sacramento Region, 2130 21st Street, Sacramento, CA 95818. (916) 205-0688. (www.jewishsac.org/jfs)

San Diego

Jewish Family Service of San Diego. Turk Family Center, 8804 Balboa Avenue, San Diego, CA 92123. (858) 637-3210. (www.jfssd.org)

San Francisco

Jewish Family & Children's Services of San Francisco, the Peninsula, Marin and Sonoma Counties. Miriam Schultz Grunfeld Professional Building, 2150 Post Street, San Francisco, CA 94115. (415) 449-1200. (www.jfcs.org)

San Francisco (Alameda County)

Jewish Family & Children's Services of the East Bay. 2484 Shattuck Avenue, Suite 210, Berkeley, CA 94704. (510) 704-7475. (www.jfcs-eastbay.org)

San Francisco (Contra Costa County)

Jewish Family & Children's Services of the East Bay. 1855 Olympic Boulevard, Suite 200, Walnut Creek, CA 94596. (925) 927-2000. (www.jfcs-eastbay.org)

San Gabriel/Pomona Valleys

Jewish Counseling and Referral Network. Jewish Federation of the Greater San Gabriel and Pomona Valleys, 114A West Lime Avenue, Monrovia, CA 91016. (626) 445-0810. (www.jewishsgpv.org/our-work/jcrn)

San Jose (Silicon Valley)

Jewish Family Services of Silicon Valley. 14855 Oka Road, Suite 202, Los Gatos, CA 95032. (408) 556-0600. (www.jfssv.org)

San Luis Obispo

Jewish Family Services. JCC-Federation of San Luis Obispo, 875 Laureate Lane, San Luis Obispo, CA 93405. (805) 426-5465. (www.jccslo.com/jewish-family-services.html)

Santa Barbara

Jewish Family Service of Greater Santa Barbara. Jewish Federation of Greater Santa Barbara, 524 Chapala Street, Santa Barbara, CA 93101. (805) 957-1115. (www.jewishsantabarbara.org/jewish-family-service)

Ventura

Ventura County Jewish Family Service. 740 East Main Street, Ventura, CA 93001. (805) 641-6565. (www.jfsvc.org)

Colorado

Boulder

Jewish Family Service. 6007 Oreg Avenue, Boulder, CO 80303. (303) 415-1025. (www.jewishfamilyservice.org/services/boulder-jfs)

Denver

Jewish Family Service of Colorado. 3201 South Tamarac Drive, Denver, CO 80231. (303) 597-5000. (www.jewishfamilyservice.org)

Connecticut

Bridgeport-Westport

Elayne & James Schoke Jewish Family Service of Fairfield County. 4200 Park Avenue, Suite 300, Bridgeport, CT 06604. (203) 921-4161. (www.ctjfs.org)

Fairfield
Jewish Family Service. 325 Reef Road, Fairfield, CT 06824. (203) 366-5438. (www.
jfsct.org)

Greenwich
Jewish Family Services of Greenwich. One Holly Hill Lane, Greenwich, CT 06830.
(203) 622-1881. (www.jfsgreenwich.org)

Hartford
Jewish Children's Service Organization. PO Box 370386, West Hartford, CT 06137.
(www.jcsohartford.org)

Hartford
Jewish Family Services of Greater Hartford. 333 Bloomfield Avenue, Suite A, West
Hartford, CT 06117. (860) 236-1927. (www.jfshartford.org)

New Haven
Jewish Family Service of New Haven. 1440 Whalley Avenue, New Haven, CT
06515. (203) 389-5599. (www.jfsnh.org)

Southbury (Western Connecticut)
Brownstein Jewish Family Service. Jewish Federation of Western Connecticut, 444
Main Street North, Southbury, CT 06488. (203) 267-3177, ext. 310. (www.jfed.
net/jewish-family-service)

Stamford
Elayne & James Schoke Jewish Family Service of Fairfield County. 733 Summer
Street, Suite 602, Stamford, CT 06901. (203) 921-4161. (www.ctjfs.org)

Delaware
Wilmington
Jewish Family Services of Delaware. 99 Passmore Road, Wilmington, DE 19803.
(302) 478-9411. (www.jfsdelaware.org)

District of Columbia
Washington, DC
Jewish Social Service Agency. The Ina Kay Building, 200 Wood Hill Road,
Rockville, MD 20850. (301) 838-4200. (www.jssa.org)

Washington, DC
Jewish Social Service Agency. The Elsie & Marvin Dekelboum Building, 6123
Montrose Road, Rockville, MD 20852. (301) 881-3700. (www.jssa.org)

Washington, DC
Jewish Social Service Agency. 3025 Hamaker Court, Suite 450, Fairfax, VA 22031.
(703) 204-9100. (www.jssa.org)

Florida
Boca Raton-Delray Beach (South Palm Beach)
Ruth & Norman Rales Jewish Family Service. 21300 Ruth & Baron Coleman
Boulevard, Boca Raton, FL 33428. (561) 852-3333. (www.ralesjfs.org)

Fort Lauderdale (Broward County)
Goodman Jewish Family Services of Broward County. 5890 South Pine Island
Road, Suite 201, Davie, FL 33328. (954) 370-2140. (www.jfsbroward.org)

Jacksonville
Jewish Family & Community Services. 8540 Baycenter Road, Jacksonville, FL
32256. (904) 448-1933. (www.jfcsjax.org)

Lee and Charlotte Counties
Jewish Family Services. Jewish Federation of Lee and Charlotte Counties, 9701
Commerce Center Court, Fort Myers, FL 33908. (239) 481-4449. (www.jewish-
federationlcc.org)

Miami
Jewish Community Services of South Florida. 735 Northeast 125th Street, North
Miami, FL 33161. (305) 576-6550. (www.jcsfl.org)

Naples (Collier County)
Jewish Family & Community Services of Southwest Florida. 5025 Castello Drive,
Naples, FL 34103. (239) 325-4444. (www.jfcsswfl.org)

Orlando
Jewish Family Services of Greater Orlando. The George Wolly Center, 2100 Lee
Road, Suite A, Winter Park, FL 32789. (407) 644-7593. (www.jfsorlando.org)

Pinellas and Pasco Counties
Gulf Coast Jewish Family & Community Services. 14041 Icot Boulevard,
Clearwater, FL 33760. (727) 479-1800. (www.gulfcoastjewishfamilyandcom-
munityservices.org)

Sarasota and Manatee Counties
Jewish Family & Children's Service of the Suncoast, Harry & Jeanette Weinberg
Campus. 2688 Fruitville Road, Sarasota, FL 34237. (941) 366-2224. (www.jfcs-
cares.org)

Tampa
Tampa Jewish Family Services. 13009 Community Campus Drive, Tampa, FL
33625. (813) 960-1848. (www.tjfs.org)

Volusia and Flagler Counties
Social Service Council of the Jewish Federation of Volusia & Flagler Counties. 470
Andalusia Avenue, Ormond Beach, FL 32174. (386) 672-0294. (www.jewish-
federationdaytona.org)

West Palm Beach
Fred & Gladys Alpert Jewish Family Service of Palm Beach County. 5841 Corporate
Way, Suite 200, West Palm Beach, FL 33407. (561) 684-1991. (www.alp-
ertjfs.org)

Georgia
Atlanta
Jewish Family & Career Services of Atlanta. 4549 Chamblee Dunwoody Road, Atlanta, GA 30338. (770) 677-9300. (www.jfcsatl.org)

Augusta
Jewish Family Services. Augusta Jewish Federation, 898 Weinberger Way, Evans, GA 30809. (706) 831-3184. (www.jewishaugusta.org/community/jewish-family-services)

Savannah
Jewish Family Services. Savannah Jewish Federation, 5111 Abercorn Street, Savannah, GA 31405. (912) 355-8111. (www.savj.org/jewish-family-services)

Hawaii
Honolulu
Jewish Community Services of Hawaii. PO Box 235805, Honolulu, HI 96823. (808) 258-7121. (www.jcs-hi.org)

Illinois
Chicago
Jewish Child & Family Services of Chicago. 216 West Jackson Boulevard, Suite 800, Chicago, IL 60606. (855) 275-5237 or (312) 357-4800. (www.jcfs.org)

Chicago
Yehi Ohr – Jewish Institute for Psychological Advancement – Addiction (Substance Use Disorder). 3553 West Peterson Avenue, Suite 104, Chicago, Illinois 60659. (773) 234-3870. (www.linkedin.com/company/yehi-ohr%2D%2D-jewish-institute-for-psychological-advancement)

Indiana
Gary (Northwest Indiana)
Jewish Community Services and Programs. Jewish Federation of Northwest Indiana, 585 Progress Avenue, Munster, IN 46321. (219) 301-0960. (www.federationon-line.org/social-services.html)

Indianapolis
Jewish Family Services at the Reuben Center. Albert & Sara Reuben Senior and Community Resource Center, 6905 Hoover Road, Indianapolis, IN 46260. (317) 259-6822. (www.jewishindianapolis.org/jfs)

South Bend (St. Joseph Valley)
Jewish Family Services. Jewish Federation of St. Joseph Valley, 3202 Shalom Way, South Bend, IN 46615. (574) 233-1164. (www.thejewishfed.org/programs/jewish-family-services-jfs)

Iowa

Des Moines

Jewish Family Services. Jewish Federation of Greater Des Moines, 33158 Ute Avenue, Waukee, IA 50263. (515) 987-0899, ext. 210. (www.jewishdesmoines. org/our-pillars/jewish-family-services)

Kansas

Kansas City

Jewish Family Services of Greater Kansas City. 5801 West 115th Street, Suite 103, Overland Park, KS 66211. (913) 327-8250. (www.jfskc.org)

Kentucky

Lexington (Central Kentucky)

Jewish Family Services. Jewish Federation of the Bluegrass, 1050 Chinoe Road, Suite 112, Lexington, KY 40502. (859) 269-8244. (www.jewishlexington.org/ get-involved/jewish-family-services)

Louisville

Jewish Family & Career Services. 2821 Klempner Way, Louisville, KY 40205. (502) 452-6341. (www.jfcslouisville.org)

Louisiana

New Orleans

Jewish Children's Regional Service. Executive Tower, 3500 North Causeway Boulevard, Suite 1120, Metairie, LA 70002. (504) 828-6334. (www.jcrs.org)

New Orleans

Jewish Family Service of Greater New Orleans. 3330 West Esplanade Avenue, Suite 603, Metairie, LA 70002. (504) 831-8475. (www.jfsneworleans.org)

Maine

Portland (Southern Maine)

Michael Klahr Jewish Family Services. Jewish Community Alliance of Southern Maine, 1342 Congress Street, Portland, ME 04102. (207) 772-1959. (www. mainejewish.org)

Maryland

Baltimore

Jewish Community Services. 5750 Park Heights Avenue, Baltimore, MD 21215. (410) 466-9200. (www.jcsbaltimore.org)

Columbia (Howard County)

Social Services & Resources. 10630 Little Patuxent Parkway, Suite 400, Columbia, MD 21044. (410) 730-4976. (www.jewishhowardcounty.org/socialservices)

Rockville (Montgomery County)

Jewish Social Service Agency. The Ina Kay Building, 200 Wood Hill Road, Rockville, MD 20850. (301) 838-4200. (www.jssa.org)

Rockville (Montgomery County)
Jewish Social Service Agency. The Elsie & Marvin Dekelboum Building, 6123 Montrose Road, Rockville, MD 20852. (301) 881-3700. (www.jssa.org)

Silver Spring
Jewish Social Service Agency. 9900 Georgia Avenue, Silver Spring, MD 20902. (301) 587-9666. (www.jssa.org)

Massachusetts
Boston
Jewish Family & Children's Service. 1430 Main Street, Waltham, MA 02451. (781) 647-5327. (www.jfcsboston.org)

Boston
Jewish Family Service of Metrowest. 475 Franklin Street, Suite 101, Framingham, MA 01702. (508) 875-3100. (www.jfsmw.org)

New Bedford
Jewish Family Services. Jewish Federation of Greater New Bedford, 467 Hawthorn Street, North Dartmouth, MA 02747. (508) 997-7471. (www.jewishnewbedford.org/jewish_family_services.html)

Springfield (Western Massachusetts)
Jewish Family Service of Western Massachusetts. 15 Lenox Street, Springfield, MA 01108. (413) 737-2601. (www.jfswm.org)

Worcester (Central Massachusetts)
Jewish Family & Children's Service. PO Box 16770, Worcester, MA 01601. (508) 755-7460. (www.jfcsboston.org)

Michigan
Ann Arbor
Jewish Family Services of Washtenaw County. 2245 South State Street, Suite 200, Ann Arbor, MI 48104. (734) 769-0209. (www.jfsannarbor.org)

Detroit
Jewish Family Service of Metropolitan Detroit. Graham & Sally Orley and Joseph & Suzanne Orley Building, 6555 West Maple Road, West Bloomfield, MI 48322. (248) 592-2313. (www.jfsdetroit.org)

Flint
Jewish Community Services. 619 Wallenberg Street, Flint, MI 48502. (810) 767-5922. (www.jcsflint.org)

Minnesota
Minneapolis
Jewish Family and Children's Service of Minneapolis. 5905 Golden Valley Road, Golden Valley, MN 55422. (952) 546-0616. (www.jfcsmpls.org)

St. Paul
Jewish Family Service of St. Paul. 1633 West 7th Street, St. Paul, MN 55102. (651)
698-0767. (www.jfssp.org)

Missouri
Kansas City
Jewish Family Services of Greater Kansas City, Missouri Office. 425 East 63rd
Street, Kansas City, MO 64110. (816) 333-1172. (www.jfskc.org)

St. Louis
Jewish Family & Children's Service. 10950 Schuetz Road, St. Louis, MO 63146.
(314) 993-1000. (www.jfcs-stl.org)

Nebraska
Omaha
Jewish Family Service. 333 South 132nd Street, Omaha, NE 68154. (402) 330-2024.
(www.jfsomaha.com)

Nevada
Las Vegas
Jewish Family Service Agency. 2309 B Renaissance Drive, Las Vegas, NV 89119.
(702) 732-0304. (www.jfsalv.org)

New Jersey
Atlantic and Cape May Counties
Jewish Family Service of Atlantic & Cape May Counties. 607 North Jerome Avenue,
Margate, NJ 08402. (609) 822-1108. (www.jfsatlantic.org)

Cherry Hill (Southern New Jersey)
Samost Jewish Family & Children's Service of Southern NJ. 1301 Springdale Road,
Suite 150, Cherry Hill, NJ 08003. (856) 424-1333. (www.jfcssnj.org)

Clifton-Passaic
Jewish Family Service and Children's Center of Clifton-Passaic. 110 Main Avenue,
Passaic, NJ 07055. (973) 777-7638. (www.jfsclifton.org)
Greater MetroWest NJ (Essex, Morris, Sussex, Union, and parts of Somerset
Counties)
Jewish Family Service of MetroWest New Jersey. 256 Columbia Turnpike, Suite
105, Florham Park, NJ 07932. (973) 765-9050. (www.jfsmetrowest.org)

Greater MetroWest NJ (Union County)
Jewish Family Service of Central New Jersey. 655 Westfield Avenue, Elizabeth, NJ
07208. (908) 352-8375. (www.jfscentralnj.org)

Middlesex County
Jewish Family Services of Middlesex County. 32 Ford Avenue, 2nd Floor, Milltown,
NJ 08850. (732) 777-1940. (www.jfvs.org)

Monmouth County
Jewish Family and Children's Service of Greater Monmouth County. 705 Summerfield Avenue, Asbury Park, NJ 07712. (732) 774-6886. (www.jfcsmonmouth.org)

Northern New Jersey
Jewish Family Service of Northern New Jersey. 1485 Teaneck Road, Teaneck, NJ 07666. (201) 837-9090. (www.jfcsnnj.org)

Ocean County
Jewish Family & Children's Service. Jewish Federation of Ocean County, 1235A Route 70, Lakewood, NJ 08701. (732) 363-8010. (www.jewishoceancounty.org/jewish-family-and-childrens-service)

Princeton (Mercer County)
Jewish Family & Children's Service of Greater Mercer County. 707 Alexander Road, Suite 102, Princeton, NJ 08540. (609) 987-8100. (www.jfcsonline.org)

Somerset, Hunterdon, and Warren Counties
Jewish Family Services of Somerset, Hunterdon and Warren Counties. 150-A West High Street, Somerville, NJ 08876. (908)725-7799. (www.jewishfamilysvc.org)

New Mexico
Albuquerque
Jewish Care Program. Jewish Federation of New Mexico, 5520 Wyoming Boulevard NE, Albuquerque, NM 87109. (505) 348-4451. (www.jewishnewmexico.org/jewish-care-program)

Santa Fe
Jewish Care Program. Temple Beth Shalom, 205 East Barcelona Road, Santa Fe, NM 87505. (505) 303-3552. (www.jewishnewmexico.org/jewish-care-program)

New York (Outside New York Metropolitan Area)
Albany (Northeastern New York)
Jewish Family Services of Northeastern New York. 877 Madison Avenue, Albany, NY 12208. (518) 482-8856. (www.jfsneny.org)

Binghamton (Broome County)
Jewish Family Service. 500 Club House Road, Vestal, NY 13850. (607) 724-2332. (www.binghamtonjcc.org/community/jewish-agencies)

Buffalo
Jewish Family Service of Buffalo & Erie County. 70 Barker Street, Buffalo, NY 14209. (716) 883-1914. (www.jfsbuffalo.org)

Kingston (Ulster County)
Jewish Family Services of Ulster County. 280 Wall Street, Kingston, NY 12401. (845) 338-2980. (www.jfsulster.org)

Orange County
Jewish Family Service of Orange County. 720 Route 17M, Middletown, NY 10940. (845) 341-1173. (www.jfsorange.org)

Poughkeepsie (Dutchess County)
Jewish Family Services of Dutchess County. Jewish Federation of Dutchess County, 17 Collegeview Avenue, Poughkeepsie, NY 12603. (845) 471-9817. (www.jew-ishdutchess.org/the-jewish-family-service-of-dutchess-county/jfs-counseling-and-referral)

Rochester
Jewish Family Service of Rochester. 441 East Avenue, Rochester, NY 14607. (585) 461-0110. (www.jfsrochester.org)

Rockland County
Rockland Jewish Family Service. 450 West Nyack Road, Suite 2, West Nyack, NY 10994. (845) 354-2121. (www.rjfs.org)

Schenectady (Northeastern New York)
JFS without Walls. Robert & Dorothy Ludwig JCC of Schenectady, 2656 Balltown Road, Schenectady, NY 12309. (518) 482-8856. (www.schenectadyjcc.org/main/jewish-family-services)

Syracuse
Syracuse Jewish Family Service at Menorah Park. Hodes Way, 4101 East Genesee Street, Syracuse, NY 13214. (315) 446-9111, ext. 234. (www.sjfs.org)

New York Metropolitan Area
Bronx
Bronx Jewish Community Council. 2930 Wallace Avenue, Bronx, NY 10467. (718) 652-5500. (www.bjcconline.org)

Bronx
Jewish Community Council of Pelham Parkway. 2157 Holland Avenue, Bronx, NY 10462. (718) 792-4744. (www.jccpelhamparkway.org)

Brooklyn
Bensonhurst Council of Jewish Organizations. 8635 21st Avenue, Suite 1B, Brooklyn, NY 11214. (718) 333-1834. (www.bencojo.org)

Brooklyn
Boro Park Jewish Community Council. 4912 14th Avenue, 3rd Floor, Brooklyn, NY 11219. (718) 972-6600. (www.bpjcc.org)

Brooklyn
Council of Jewish Organizations of Flatbush. 1523 Avenue M, 3rd Floor, Brooklyn, NY 11230. (718) 377-2900. (www.cojoflatbush.org)

Brooklyn
Crown Heights Central Jewish Community Council. 387 Kingston Avenue, Brooklyn, NY 11225. (718) 771-9000. (www.chcentral.org)

Brooklyn
Jewish Child Care Association. 858 East 29th Street, Brooklyn, NY 11210. (917) 808-4800. (www.jccany.org)

Brooklyn
Jewish Community Council of Canarsie, Starrett City (Main) Office. 1170 Pennsylvania Avenue, Suite 1B, Brooklyn, NY 11239. (718) 495-6210. (www. canarsiejcc.org)

Brooklyn
Jewish Community Council of Greater Coney Island. 3001 West 37th Street, Brooklyn, NY 11224. (718) 449-5000. (www.jccgci.org)

Brooklyn
Jewish Community Council of Kings Bay. 3495 Nostrand Avenue, Brooklyn, NY 11229. (718) 648-7703. (www.kingsbayy.org)

Brooklyn
Jewish Community Council of Marine Park. 2076 Flatbush Avenue, Brooklyn, NY 11234. (718) 407-1832. (www.jccmp.org)

Brooklyn
Shorefront Jewish Community Council. 128 Brighton Beach Avenue, 4th Floor, Brooklyn, NY 11235. (718) 743-0575. (www.shorefrontjcc.org)

Brooklyn
United Jewish Organizations of Williamsburg and North Brooklyn. 32 Penn Street, Brooklyn, NY 11249. (718) 643-9700. (www.unitedjewish.org)

Manhattan
Jewish Board of Family and Children's Services. 135 West 50th Street, 6th Floor, New York, NY 10020. (212) 582-9100. (www.jbfcs.org)`

Manhattan
Jewish Community Council of Washington Heights-Inwood. 121 Bennett Avenue, Suite 11A, New York, NY 10033. (212) 568-5450. (www.jccwhi.org)

Manhattan
Jewish Association Serving the Aging. 247 West 37th Street, New York, NY 10018. (212) 273-5200. (www.jasa.org)

Manhattan
Metropolitan Council on Jewish Poverty. 77 Water Street, 7th Floor, New York, NY 10005. (212) 453-9500. (www.metcouncil.org)

Manhattan
United Jewish Council of the East Side. 235 East Broadway, New York, NY 10002. (212) 233-6037. (www.ujces.org)

Queens
Flushing Jewish Community Council. 43-43 Bowne Street, Flushing, NY 11355. (718) 463–0434. (www.flushingjcc.net)

Queens

Jackson Heights-Elmhurst Kehillah. 37-06 77th Street, Jackson Heights, NY 11372. (718) 457-4591. (www.jhekehillah.org)

Queens

Jewish Community Council of the Rockaway Peninsula. 1525 Central Avenue, Far Rockaway, NY 11691. (718) 327-7755. (www.jccrp.org)

Queens

Northeast Queens Jewish Community Council. 58-20 Little Neck Parkway, Little Neck, NY 11362. (718) 343-6779. (www.northeastqueensjewish.org)

Queens

Queens Jewish Community Council. 119-45 Union Turnpike, Forest Hills, NY 11375. (718) 544-9033. (www.qjcc.org)

Staten Island

Council of Jewish Organizations. 984 Post Avenue, Staten Island, NY 10302. (718) 720-4047. (www.cojosi.com)

Westchester County

Westchester Jewish Community Services. 845 North Broadway, White Plains, NY 10603. (914) 761-0600. (www.wjcs.com)

North Carolina

Asheville (Western North Carolina)

Jewish Family Services of Western North Carolina, 2 Doctor's Park, Suite E, Asheville, NC 28801. (828) 253-2900. (www.jfswnc.org)

Charlotte

Jewish Family Services. Shalom Park, 5007 Providence Road, Suite 105, Charlotte, NC 28226. (704) 364-6594. (www.jfscharlotte.org)

Durham-Chapel Hill

Jewish Family Services. Jewish Federation of Durham-Chapel Hill, 1937 West Cornwallis Road, Durham, NC 27705. (919) 354-4936. (www.shalomdch.org/explore-federation/about-us/who-we-are/jewish-family-services)

Greensboro

Jewish Family Services of Greensboro. Greensboro Jewish Federation, 5509-C West Friendly Avenue, Greensboro, NC 27410. (336) 852-4829. (www.jfs-greensboro.org)

Raleigh-Cary

Raleigh-Cary Jewish Family Services. 8210 Creedmoor Road, Suite 104, Raleigh, NC 27613. (919) 676-2200. (www.raleighcaryjfs.org)

Ohio

Akron

Jewish Family Service of Akron. 750 White Pond Drive, Akron, OH 44320. (330) 867-3388. (www.jfsakron.org)

Canton
Jewish Family Services. 432 30th Street NW, Canton, OH 44709. (330) 445-2402.
(www.jewishcanton.org/jfs.html)

Cincinnati
Jewish Family Service of the Cincinnati Area. 8487 Ridge Road, Cincinnati, OH
45236. (513) 469-1188. (www.jfscinti.org)

Cleveland
Bellefaire JCB. Main Campus, One Pollock Circle, 22001 Fairmount Boulevard,
Cleveland, OH 44118. (800) 879-2522 or (216) 932-2800. (www.belle-
fairejcb.org)

Cleveland
Jewish Family Service Association of Cleveland. 24075 Commerce Park Road,
Beachwood, OH 44122. (216) 292-3999. (www.jfsa-cleveland.org)

Columbus
Jewish Family Services. 1070 College Avenue, Columbus, OH 43209. (614)
231-1890. (www.jfscolumbus.org)

Dayton
Jewish Family Services of Greater Dayton. Jewish Federation of Greater Dayton,
525 Versailles Drive, Centerville, OH 45459. (937) 610-1555. (www.jewishday-
ton.org/jewish-family-services)

Toledo
Jewish Family Service of Greater Toledo. Jewish Federation of Greater Toledo,
6465 Sylvania Avenue, Sylvania, OH 43560. (419) 724-0401. (www.jewishto-
ledo.org/jfs)

Youngstown
Jewish Family Services. 517 Gypsy Lane, Youngstown, OH 44504. (330) 746-7929.
(www.jewishyoungstown.org/jewish-family-services/jewish-family-
services-home-page)

Oregon
Eugene (Lane County)
Jewish Family Services. Jewish Federation of Lane County, PO Box 5924, Eugene,
OR   97405.   (541)   484-2541.   (www.jewishfedlc.org/jewish-family-
services)

Portland
Jewish Family & Child Service. 1221 Southwest Yamhill Street, Suite 301, Portland,
OR 97205. (503) 226-7079. (www.jfcs-portland.org)

Pennsylvania
Bucks County
Jewish Family & Children's Service of Greater Mercer County. 707 Alexander Road, Suite 102, Princeton, NJ 08540. (609) 987-8100. (www.jfcsonline.org)

Harrisburg
Jewish Family Service of Greater Harrisburg. 3333 North Front Street, Harrisburg, PA 17110. (717) 233-1681. (www.jfsofhbg.org)

Lancaster
Jewish Family Service of Lancaster. Congregation Shaarai Shomayim, 75 East James Street, Lancaster, PA 17602. (717) 537-1863. (www.jfslancaster.org)

Allentown-Bethlehem-Easton (Lehigh Valley)
Jewish Family Service of the Lehigh Valley. 2004 West Allen Street, Allentown, PA 18104. (610) 821-8722. (www.jfslv.org)

Philadelphia
Jewish Family and Children's Service of Greater Philadelphia. 2100 Arch Street, 5th Floor, Philadelphia, PA 19103. (866) 532-7669. (www.jfcsphilly.org)

Pittsburgh
Jewish Family & Children's Service of Pittsburgh. 5743 Bartlett Street, Pittsburgh, PA 15217. (412) 422-7200. (www.jfcspgh.org)

Reading
Jewish Family Service of the Jewish Federation of Reading. 1100 Berkshire Boulevard, Suite 125, Wyomissing, PA 19610. (610) 921-0624. (www.readingjewishcommunity.org/community/jfs)

Scranton (Northeastern Pennsylvania)
Jewish Family Service of Northeastern Pennsylvania. 615 Jefferson Avenue, Suite 204, Scranton, PA 18510. (570) 344-1186. (www.jfsnepa.org)

York
Jewish Family Services of York. 2000 Hollywood Drive, York, PA 17403. (717) 843-5011. (www.jfsyork.org)

Rhode Island
Providence
Jewish Collaborative Services of Rhode Island. 1165 North Main Street, Providence, RI 02904. (401) 331-1244. (www.jcsri.org)

South Carolina
Charleston
Charleston Jewish Social Services. 1645 Raoul Wallenberg Boulevard, Charleston, SC 29407. (843) 614-6494. (www.charlestonjfs.org)

Columbia
Jewish Family Service. Columbia Jewish Federation, 306 Flora Drive, Columbia, SC 29223. (803) 787-2023, ext. 220. (www.jewishcolumbia.org/our-programs/jewish-family-service)

Tennessee
Chattanooga
Care Network Services. Jewish Federation of Chattanooga, 5461 North Terrace Road, Chattanooga, TN 37411. (423) 493-0270. (www.jewishchattanooga.com/social-services)

Knoxville
Jewish Family Services. Knoxville Jewish Alliance, 6800 Deane Hill Drive, Knoxville, TN 37919. (865) 690-6343, ext. 18. (www.jewishknoxville.org/jfs)

Memphis
Jewish Family Service at the Memphis JCC. 6560 Poplar Avenue, Memphis, TN 38138. (901) 767-8511. (www.jccmemphis.org/jfs/jfs)

Nashville (Middle Tennessee)
Jewish Family Service of Nashville and Middle Tennessee. 801 Percy Warner Boulevard, Suite 103, Nashville, TN 37205. (615) 356-4234. (www.jfsnashville.org)

Texas
Austin
Jewish Family Service. Shalom Austin, 7300 Hart Lane, Austin, TX 78731. (512) 250-1043. (www.shalomaustin.org/jfs)

Dallas
Jewish Family Service of Greater Dallas. 5402 Arapaho Road, Dallas, TX 75248. (972) 437-9950. (www.jfsdallas.org)

Fort Worth (Tarrant County)
Jewish Family Services of Fort Worth & Tarrant County. 4049 Kingsridge Road, Fort Worth, TX 76109. (817) 569-0898. (www.tarrantfederation.org/help-people-in-need)

Houston
Jewish Children's Regional Service, Houston Branch Office. PO Box 218702, Houston, TX 77218. (832) 767-9097. (www.jcrs.org)

Houston
Jewish Family Service. 4131 South Braeswood Boulevard, Houston, TX 77025. (713) 667-9336. (www.jfshouston.org)

San Antonio
Jewish Family Service of San Antonio, Texas. 12500 Northwest Military Highway, Suite 250, San Antonio, TX 78231. (210) 302-6920. (www.jfs-sa.org)

Utah
Salt Lake City
Jewish Family Service. 1111 East Brickyard Road, Suite 218, Salt Lake City, UT
    84106. (801) 746-4334. (www.jfsutah.org)

Virginia
Newport News (Virginia Peninsula)
Jewish Family Service of Tidewater, Peninsula Office. 401 City Center Boulevard,
    Newport News, VA 23606. (757) 223-5635. (www.jfshamptonroads.org)

Norfolk-Virginia Beach (Tidewater)
Jewish Family Service of Tidewater. 5000 Corporate Woods Drive, Suite 400,
    Virginia Beach, VA 23462. (757) 321-2222. (www.jfshamptonroads.org)

Northern Virginia
Jewish Social Service Agency. 3025 Hamaker Court, Suite 450 Fairfax, VA 22031.
    (703) 204-9100. (www.jssa.org)

Richmond
Jewish Family Services. 6718 Patterson Avenue, Richmond, VA 23226. (804)
    282-5644. (www.jfsrichmond.org)

Washington
Seattle
Jewish Family Service of Seattle. 1601 16th Avenue, Seattle, WA 98122. (206)
    461-3240. (www.jfsseattle.org)

Spokane
Spokane Area Jewish Family Services. 1322 East 30th Avenue, Spokane, WA
    99203. (509) 747-7394. (www.sajfs.org)

Wisconsin
Madison
Jewish Social Services of Madison. 6434 Enterprise Lane, Madison, WI 53719.
    (608) 442-4081. (www.jssmadison.org)

Milwaukee
Jewish Family Services. 1300 North Jackson Street, Milwaukee, WI 53202. (414)
    390-5800. (www.jfsmilw.org)

9.3.3 Jewish Family Service Agencies, Canada

Alberta
Calgary
Jewish Family Service Calgary. 5920-1A Street SW, Suite 420, Calgary, AB T2H
    0G3. (403) 287-3510. (www.jfsc.org)

Edmonton
Jewish Family Services Edmonton. 8702 Meadowlark Road, Suite 100, Edmonton
AB T5R 5W5. (780) 454-1194. (www.jfse.org)

British Columbia
Vancouver
Jewish Family Service Agency. 475 East Broadway, Suite 201, Vancouver, BC V5T
1W9. (604) 257-5151. (www.jfsa.ca)

Victoria-Vancouver Island
Jewish Family Services of Vancouver Island. 3636 Shelbourne Street, Victoria, BC
V8P 4H2. (250) 704-2744. (www.jfsvi.ca)

Manitoba
Winnipeg
Jewish Child and Family Service. 123 Doncaster Street, Suite C200, Winnipeg, MB
R3N 2B2. (204) 477-7430. (www.jcfswinnipeg.org)

Ontario
Hamilton
Hamilton Jewish Social Services. 30 King Street East, Dundas, ON L9H 5G4. (905)
627-9922, ext. 21. (www.hamiltonjss.com)

Ottawa
Jewish Family Services of Ottawa. 2255 Carling Avenue, Suite 300, Ottawa, ON
K2B 7Z5. (613) 722-2225. (www.jfsottawa.com)

Toronto
Jewish Family & Child Service of Greater Toronto. 4600 Bathurst Street, 1st Floor,
Toronto, ON M2R 3V3. (416) 638-7800. (www.jfandcs.com)

Quebec
Montreal
Agence Ometz. 1 Cummings Square, 5151 Côte Ste-Catherine Road, Montreal, QC
H3W 1M6. (514) 342-0000. (www.ometz.ca)

9.3.4   Jewish Vocational Services, United States

California
Los Angeles
JVS SoCal. 6505 Wilshire Boulevard, Suite 200, Los Angeles, CA 90048. (323)
761-8888. (www.jvs-socal.org)
San Francisco (Alameda, Contra Costa, Marin, Napa, San Francisco, San Mateo,
Santa Clara, Santa Cruz, Solano, and Sonoma Counties)
Jewish Vocational Service. 225 Bush Street, Suite 400, San Francisco, CA 94104.
(415) 391-3600. (www.jvs.org)

Florida

Tampa

TampaBay-Job-Links. 1211 West Shore Boulevard, Suite 300, Tampa, FL 33607. (813) 344-0200. (www.tbjl.org)

Illinois

Chicago

JVS Chicago. 216 West Jackson Boulevard, Suite 700, Chicago, IL 60606. (855) 463-6587. (www.jcfs.org/jvs)

Kansas

Kansas City

Jewish Vocational Service, Jewish Community Campus (Career Skills and Connection). 5801 West 115th Street, Overland Park, KS 66211. (913) 327-8130. (www.jvskc.org)

Kentucky

Louisville

Jewish Family & Career Services. 2821 Klempner Way, Louisville, KY 40205. (502) 452-6341. (www.jfcslouisville.org)

Massachusetts

Boston

JVS Boston. 75 Federal Street, 3rd Floor, Boston, MA 02110. (617) 399-3131. (www.jvs-boston.org)

Michigan

Detroit

JVS Human Services. 29699 Southfield Road, Southfield, MI 48076. (248) 559-5000. (www.jvsdet.org)

Missouri

Kansas City

Jewish Vocational Service, Main Office. 4600 The Paseo, Kansas City, MO 64110. (816) 471-2808. (www.jvskc.org)

St. Louis

MERS Missouri Goodwill Industries. 1727 Locust Street, St. Louis, MO 63103. (314) 241-3464. (www.mersgoodwill.org)

New Jersey

Greater MetroWest NJ (Essex, Morris, Sussex, Union, and parts of Somerset Counties)

Jewish Vocational Service of MetroWest. 354 Eisenhower Parkway, Plaza 1 Suite 2150, Livingston, NJ 07039. (973) 674-6330. (www.jvsnj.org)

New York Metropolitan Area

Brooklyn

Vocational Support. Jewish Community Council of Greater Coney Island. 3001 West 37th Street, Brooklyn, NY 11224. (718) 449-5000. (www.jccgci.org/our-services)

Ohio
Cincinnati
JVS Career Services. 4540 Cooper Road, Suite 300, Cincinnati, OH 45242. (513)
   936-9675. (www.jvscareers.org)

Pennsylvania
Philadelphia
JEVS Human Services Philadelphia. 1845 Walnut Street, 7th Floor, Philadelphia,
   PA 19103. (215) 854-1800. (www.jevshumanservices.org)

9.3.5   Jewish Vocational Services, Canada

Ontario
Toronto
JVS Toronto. 74 Tycos Drive, Toronto, ON M6B 1V9. (416) 787-1151. (www.jvs-
   toronto.org)

9.3.6   Central Coordinating Body for Jewish Free Loans

International Association of Jewish Free Loans (formerly **International
Association of Hebrew Free Loans** and **Association of Hebrew Free Loans**). For
contact information and a description, see the Jewish Community Coordinating
Organizations section of Chap. 12.

9.3.7   Jewish Free Loans, United States

Arizona
Phoenix
Jewish Free Loan. 3443 North Central Avenue, Suite 707, Phoenix, AZ 85012.
   (602) 230-7983. (www.jewishfreeloan.org)

Tucson (Southern Arizona)
Hebrew Free Loan Association of Tucson. 6890 East Sunrise Drive, Suite 120-310,
   Tucson, AZ 85750. (520) 297-5360. (www.freeloan.org)

California
Los Angeles
Jewish Free Loan Association. 6505 Wilshire Boulevard, Suite 715, Los Angeles,
   CA 90048. (323) 761-8830. (www.jfla.org)

San Diego

JFS Hand Up Loan. Jewish Family Service of San Diego, Turk Family Center, 8804 Balboa Avenue, San Diego, CA 92123. (858) 637-3210. (www.jfssd.org)

San Francisco

Hebrew Free Loan Association. 131 Steuart Street, Suite 520, San Francisco, CA 94105. (415) 546-9902. (www.hflasf.org)

Colorado

Denver-Boulder

Jewish Interest Free Loan of Colorado. Temple Sinai, 3509 South Glencoe, Denver, CO 80237. (303) 759-0841. (www.sinaidenver.org/jifl.html)

Connecticut

New Haven

Hebrew Burial & Free Loan Association of New Haven. PO Box 3783, Woodbridge, CT 06525. (203) 772-8488. (www.hbflanh.org)

District of Columbia

Washington, DC

Hebrew Free Loan Association of Greater Washington. 10421 Motor City Drive, #342044, Bethesda, MD 20817. (301) 859-0346. (www.hebrewfreeloandc.org)

Florida

Jewish Educational Loan Fund. See entry under Georgia.

Miami

Hebrew Free Loan Association of South Florida. 18900 Northeast 25th Avenue, MARJCC, Lipton Building, Suite 216, North Miami Beach, FL 33180. (305) 692-7555. (www.hebrewloan.org)

Georgia

Atlanta

Jewish Educational Loan Fund. 4549 Chamblee Dunwoody Road, Atlanta, GA 30338. (770) 396-3080. (www.jelf.org)

Atlanta

Jewish Interest Free Loans of Atlanta. 5115 New Peachtree Road, Suite 200A, Chamblee, GA 30341. (404) 268-5665. (www.jifla.org)

Maryland

Baltimore

Hebrew Free Loan Association of Baltimore. 5752 Park Heights Avenue, Baltimore, MD 21215. (410) 466-9200, ext. 216. (www.hebrewfreeloan.org)

Bethesda (Montgomery County)

Hebrew Free Loan Association of Greater Washington. 10421 Motor City Drive, #342044. Bethesda, MD 20817. (301) 859-0346. (www.hebrewfreeloandc.org)

Massachusetts
Springfield (Western Massachusetts)
Hebrew Free Loan Association of Greater Springfield. 1160 Dickinson Street, Springfield, MA 01108. (413) 736-6573. (www.hflaspringfield.org)

Michigan
Detroit
Hebrew Free Loan of Detroit. 6735 Telegraph Road, Suite 300, Bloomfield Hills, MI 48301. (248) 723-8184. (www.hfldetroit.org)

Minnesota
Minneapolis-St. Paul
Jewish Free Loan Program (JFLP). Jewish Family and Children's Service of Minneapolis, 5905 Golden Valley Road, Golden Valley, MN 55422. (952) 546-0616. (www.jfcsmpls.org/our-services/financial-assistance)

Missouri
St. Louis
Jewish Loan Association. Jewish Family & Children's Service. 10950 Schuetz Road, St. Louis, MO 63146. (314) 513-1678. (www.jfedstl.org/our-work/what-we-fund/get-funded)

New Jersey
Burlington, Camden, Gloucester, and Mercer Counties (Southern New Jersey)
Hebrew Free Loan Society of Greater Philadelphia. 8231 Old York Road, Elkins Park, PA 19027. (267) 709-9652. (www.hflphilly.org)

Greater MetroWest NJ (Essex, Morris, Sussex, Union, and parts of Somerset Counties)
Hebrew Free Loan of New Jersey. Jewish Federation of Greater MetroWest NJ, 901 Route 10, Whippany, NJ 07981. (973) 765-9050. (www.hebrewfreeloanofnj.org, www.jfedgmw.org/hebrew-free-loan)

Middlesex and Monmouth Counties
Hebrew Free Loan of New Jersey. Jewish Federation in the Heart of New Jersey, 230 Old Bridge Turnpike, South River, NJ 08882. (732) 588-1800. (www.hebrewfreeloanofnj.org, www.jewishheartnj.org/getsupport/individuals-and-families/hebrew-free-loans)

New York (Outside New York Metropolitan Area)
Buffalo
Western New York Hebrew Benevolent Loan Association. 2640 North Forest Road, Suite 200, Getzville, NY 14068. (716) 204-0542. (www.wnyhbla.org)

Syracuse (Central New York)
Hebrew Interest-free Loan Program of Central New York. Jewish Federation of Central New York, 5655 Thompson Road, De Witt, NY 13214. (315) 445- 2040 x118. (www.jewishfederationcny.org/?page_id=10061)

New York Metropolitan Area
New York City (Bronx, Brooklyn, Manhattan, Queens, Staten Island, and Nassau, Suffolk, and Westchester Counties)
Hebrew Free Loan Society. 675 Third Avenue, Suite 1905, New York, NY 10017. (212) 687-0188. (www.hfls.org)

North Carolina
Jewish Educational Loan Fund. See entry under Georgia.

Ohio
Cleveland
HFLA of Northeast Ohio. 23300 Chagrin Boulevard, Suite 204, Beachwood, OH 44122. (216) 378-9042. (www.interestfree.org)

Oregon
Portland
Jewish Free Loan of Greater Portland. Jewish Federation of Greater Portland, 6680 Southwest Capitol Highway, Portland, OR 97219. (503) 892-7417.

Pennsylvania
Philadelphia
Hebrew Free Loan Society of Greater Philadelphia. 8231 Old York Road, Elkins Park, PA 19027. (267) 709-9652. (www.hflphilly.org)

Pittsburgh
Hebrew Free Loan Association of Pittsburgh. 4307 Murray Avenue, Pittsburgh, PA 15217. (412) 422-8868. (www.hflapgh.org)

Rhode Island
Providence
Greater Providence Hebrew Free Loan. 400 Reservoir Avenue, Suite LLA, Providence, RI 02907. (401) 781-1949. (www.jewishrhody.com/stories/new-merged-hebrew-free-loan-association-is-here-to-help,9755)

South Carolina
Jewish Educational Loan Fund. See entry under Georgia.

Texas
Austin
Hebrew Free Loan Association of Austin. 3571 Far West Boulevard, #233, Austin, Texas 78731. (512) 677-4352. (www.hfla.org)

Dallas
Dallas Hebrew Free Loan Association. PO Box 671235, Dallas, TX 75367. (214) 696-8008. (www.dhfla.org)

Fort Worth (Tarrant County)
Tarrant County Hebrew Free Loan Association. 4049 Kingsridge Road, Fort Worth, TX 76109. (817) 569-0898. (www.tchfla.org)

Houston
Hebrew Free Loan Association of Houston. 10101 Fondren Road, Suite 449, Houston, TX 77096. (713) 724-8997. (www.hfla.net)

San Antonio
Hebrew Free Loan Association of San Antonio. PO Box 780264, San Antonio, TX 78278. (210) 736-4352. (www.hfla-sa.org)

Virginia
Excluding Metro DC Area
Jewish Educational Loan Fund. See entry under Georgia.
Northern Virginia
Hebrew Free Loan Association of Greater Washington. 10421 Motor City Drive, #342044, Bethesda, MD 20817. (301) 859-0346. (www.hebrewfreeloandc.org)

Washington
Seattle
Hebrew Free Loan Association of Washington State. PO Box 141, Mercer Island, WA 98040. (206) 397-0005. (www.hflawa.org)

Southwest Washington
Jewish Free Loan of Greater Portland. Jewish Federation of Greater Portland, 6680 Southwest Capitol Highway, Portland, OR 97219. (503) 892-7417.

Wisconsin
Milwaukee
Milwaukee Jewish Free Loan Association. 409 East Silver Spring Drive, Milwaukee, WI 53217. (414) 961-1500. (www.mjfla.org)

9.3.8   Jewish Free Loans, Canada

Alberta
Calgary
Calgary Jewish Family Loan Association. 25 Ceduna Lane SW, Calgary, AB T2W 6H5. (403) 281-6026. (www.cjfla.org)

Edmonton
Jewish Free Loan Association of Edmonton. Jewish Federation of Edmonton, 10220 156th Street, Suite 100, Edmonton, AB T5P 2R1. (780) 487-0585. (www.jew-ishedmonton.org/about-us/board/local-partners-beneficiaries/jewish-free-loan-ass)

British Columbia
Vancouver
Hebrew Free Loan Association of Vancouver. 950 West 41st Avenue, Suite 305A, Vancouver, BC V5Z 2N7. (604) 428-2832. (www.hfla.ca)

Manitoba
Winnipeg
The Asper Helping Hand Initiative. 201 Portage Avenue, Suite 2810, Winnipeg, MB
    R3B 3K6. (204) 989-5537. (www.asperfoundation.com/helping-hand)

Ontario
Ottawa
Ottawa Hebrew Free Loan Association. 2255 Carling Avenue, Suite 301, Ottawa,
    ON K2B 7Z5. (613) 722-2225, ext. 319. (www.ottawahfl.org)

Toronto
Jewish Free Loan Toronto. 4600 Bathurst Street, Suite 340, Toronto, ON M2R 3V3.
    (416) 635-1217. (www.jewishfreeloan.ca)

Quebec
Montreal
Hebrew Free Loan Association of Montreal. 6525 Decarie Boulevard, Suite 202,
    Montreal, QC H3W 3E3. (514) 733-7128. (www.hflamtl.org)

9.4   Directories of Synagogues, College Hillels, and Jewish Day Schools

Orthodox Union (www.ou.org/synagogue-finder)
A list of Orthodox synagogues by state

Chabad Centers (www.chabad.org/centers/default_cdo/jewish/Centers.htm)
A list of Chabad Centers by state, city, or zip code

Young Israel (www.youngisrael.org/find-a-young-israel.html)
A list of Young Israel synagogues by state

United Synagogue of Conservative Judaism (www.uscj.org)
A list of Conservative synagogues by state, city, or zip code

Union for Reform Judaism (www.urj.org/congregations)
A list of Reform synagogues by state, city, or zip code

Jewish Reconstructionist Movement (www.jewishrecon.org/directory)
A list of Reconstructionist synagogues by state

Sephardic Synagogues (http://americansephardifederation.com/syn_us.html)
A list of Sephardic synagogues by state

Society for Humanistic Judaism (www.shj.org/communities/find-a-community)
A list of Humanist communities by state
Alliance for Jewish Renewal (www.aleph.org/locate)
A list of Jewish Renewal synagogues by state

Hillel Foundations on College Campuses (www.hillel.org/home)
A guide to Jewish life on college campuses by state, city, or zip code

Jewish Day Schools (www.lookstein.org/school_db.php?School=&City) and
(www.jewishvirtuallibrary.org/jewish-schools-in-the-united-states)
A list of Jewish day schools by state or city

9.5   Israeli Embassies and Consulates

9.5.1   Israeli Embassy and Consulates, United States

Embassy of Israel
3514 International Drive NW, Washington, DC 20008. (202) 364-5500. (www.
    israelemb.org)
Jurisdiction: DC, MD, VA

Atlanta
Consulate General in Atlanta
1100 Spring Street NW, Suite 440, Atlanta, GA 30309. (404) 487-6500. (www.
    embassies.gov.il/atlanta)
Jurisdiction: GA, KY, MO, NC, SC, TN, WV

Houston
Consulate General in Houston
24 Greenway Plaza, Suite 1500, Houston, TX 77046. (832) 301-3500. (www.
    embassies.gov.il/houston)
Jurisdiction: AR, KS, LA, NM, OK, TX

Los Angeles
Consulate General in Los Angeles
11766 Wilshire Boulevard, Suite 1600, Los Angeles, CA 90025. (323) 852-5500.
    (www.embassies.gov.il/la)
Jurisdiction: AZ, CA (southern), CO, HI, NV, UT, WY

Miami
Consulate General in Miami
100 North Biscayne Boulevard, Suite 1800, Miami, FL 33132. (305) 925-9400.
    (www.embassies.gov.il/miami)
Jurisdiction: AL, FL, MS, Puerto Rico

Midwest
Consulate General to the Midwest
500 West Madison Street, Suite 3100, Chicago, IL 60661. (312) 380-8800. (www.
    embassies.gov.il/chicago)
Jurisdiction: IL, IN, IA, MI, MN, NE, ND, SD, WI

New England
Consulate General to New England
20 Park Plaza, Boston, MA 02116. (617) 535-0200. (www.embassies.gov.il/boston)
Jurisdiction: CT, ME, MA, NH, RI, VT

New York
Consulate General in New York
800 Second Avenue, New York, NY 10017. (212) 499-5000. (www.embassies.gov.
il/new-york)
Jurisdiction: DE, NJ, NY, OH, PA

San Francisco
Consulate General in San Francisco
456 Montgomery Street, Suite 2100, San Francisco, CA 94104. (415) 844-7500.
(embassies.gov.il/san-francisco)
Jurisdiction: AK, CA (northern), ID, MT, OR, WA

9.5.2   Israeli Embassy and Consulates, Canada

Embassy of Israel
50 O'Connor Street, Suite 1005, Ottawa, ON K1P 6L2. (613) 750-7500. (www.
embassies.gov.il/ottawa)
Jurisdiction: Ottawa and Eastern Ontario (up to and including Kingston)

Quebec
1 Westmount Square, Suite 650, Westmount, QC H3Z 2P9. (514) 940-8500. (www.
embassies.gov.il/montreal)
Jurisdiction: NB, NL, NS, PE, QC

Toronto
2 Bloor Street East, Suite 400, Toronto, ON M4W 1A8. (416) 640-8500. (www.
embassies.gov.il/toronto)
Jurisdiction: AB, BC, MB, NT, NU, ON (west of Kingston), SK, YT

Chapter 10
Jewish Museums and Holocaust Museums, Memorials, and Monuments

Ira M. Sheskin, Arnold Dashefsky, and Sarah Markowitz

This chapter provides lists with contact information (name, address, phone number, website) for about 130 Jewish museums and about 150 Holocaust museums.

The purpose of this chapter is to document the institutional infrastructure of the North American Jewish community and to preserve this information for historical purposes. We expect that historians 100 years from now will look back at the *Year Book* in researching the history of North American Jewry. In a sense, we are "freezing" the information in time. The information on the internet, of course, changes as frequently as the webmasters update that information, meaning that without this freezing, historians in the future will not have a record of the infrastructure of the community.

The list is carefully updated each year, but the authors appreciate any corrections noted by our readers. We have found that the lists we can find for Jewish institutions on the internet are far from totally accurate.

10.1 Jewish Museums

Note: For Holocaust Museums, see Sect. 10.2 below.

Note: Section 10.1 does not list the numerous local Jewish historical societies and associations nor Jewish genealogical organizations.

I. M. Sheskin
Department of Geography and Jewish Demography Project, Sue and Leonard Miller Center for Contemporary Judaic Studies, University of Miami, Coral Gables, FL, USA

A. Dashefsky (✉)
Department of Sociology and Center for Judaic Studies and Contemporary Jewish Life, University of Connecticut, Storrs, CT, USA
e-mail: Arnold.dashefsky@uconn.edu

S. Markowitz
Independent Researcher, Forest Hills, NY, USA

© Springer Nature Switzerland AG 2020   419
A. Dashefsky, I. M. Sheskin (eds.), *American Jewish Year Book 2019*, American Jewish Year Book 119, https://doi.org/10.1007/978-3-030-40371-3_10

10.1.1   Central Coordinating Body for Jewish Museums

Council of American Jewish Museums. For contact information and a description, see the Jewish Cultural Organizations section of Chap. 12.

10.1.2   Jewish Museums, United States

Alabama
Huntsville Jewish Heritage Center (Temple B'nai Sholom) *(2017). 103 Lincoln Street SE, Huntsville, AL 35801. (256) 536-4771. Displays highlighting Jewish holidays, Jewish life cycle events, beliefs, culture, and history of Judaism, and sacred Jewish objects, symbols, and traditions; artifacts from historic Jewish events, the Holocaust, and the Declaration of the State of Israel; and the original Sanctuary mantel, artifacts, and the desk used by the Temple's early rabbis; video screening a documentary tracing the history of the Huntsville Jewish community and the contributions of the Jewish community to the cultural, civic, and economic life of Huntsville and North Alabama. (www.templebnaisholom.com/visit)*

Alaska
Alaska Jewish Museum and Cultural Center (2013). 1221 East 35th Avenue, Anchorage, AK 99508. (907) 770-7021. *Collection of original documents, photographs, visual art, books, and cultural artifacts that tells the story of the Jewish experience in Alaska, showcases untold Jewish contributions to Alaska's history, art, and culture, and celebrates Alaska's heroic humanitarian rescues of Jewish refugees during the establishment of the State of Israel. (www.alaskajewishmuseum.com)*

Arizona
Arizona Jewish Historical Society/Cutler-Plotkin Jewish Heritage Center (1981) (2001). 122 East Culver Street, Phoenix, AZ 85004. (602) 241-7870. *Archival collection with over 50,000 primary source documents, photographs, artifacts, oral history and video interviews with Arizona's Jewish residents, and other memorabilia pertaining to the Jewish experience in Arizona and the American Southwest, housed in the restored home of Phoenix's first synagogue. (www.azjhs. org/Exhibits.html)*
  Jewish History Museum/Stone Avenue Temple (2008). 564 South Stone Avenue, Tucson, AZ 85701. (520) 670-9073. *Exhibitions of items and artifacts, depicting the Jewish heritage and history of the Jewish people of Southern Arizona, and preservation of the historic Stone Avenue Temple building—the first synagogue built in the Arizona Territory—in which the museum is housed. (www.jewishhistorymuseum.org)*
  Sylvia Plotkin Judaica Museum (Congregation Beth Israel) (1967). 10460 North 56th Street, Scottsdale, AZ 85253. (480) 951-0323. *Judaic artifacts from*

around the world built on a theme of holiness, as manifested in Torah, Shabbat, holiday observances, and life cycle events, offering insight into the 5000 years of Jewish culture. (www.cbiaz.org/museum)

Arkansas

Museum of Jewish Life-Agudath Achim (Congregation Agudath Achim) (2016). 7901 West Capitol Avenue, Little Rock, AR 72205. (501) 225-1683. *Collection depicting Jewish life cycle events and ritual observance, Jewish culture, and Jewish war heroes, demonstrating how Jews were not only citizens of their own community but great contributors to their city, state, and world around them; interactive displays about the Holocaust. (www.lrsynagogue.org/museum)*

California

Aliyah Bet and Machal Museum (American Jewish University) (2006). American Jewish University, 15600 Mulholland Drive, Bel Air, CA 90077. (888) 853-6763 or (310) 476-9777. *Exhibit documenting the history of the American and Canadian men and women who served on the ships to smuggle Holocaust survivors through the British blockade into Palestine (Aliyah Bet) or as volunteers with the Israeli armed forces (Machal) during Israel's war of independence. (www.israel-vets.com/two_museums.html)*

American Jewish University Permanent Collection. Familian Campus, 15600 Mulholland Drive, Bel Air, CA 90077. (310) 476-9777. *Works of art in various media, embodying the changing dynamics of Jewish lives since nineteenth century to the present. (www.aju.edu/exhibition-spaces/permanent-collection)*

Contemporary Jewish Museum (1984). 736 Mission Street, San Francisco, CA 94103. (415) 655-7800. *Contemporary perspectives on Jewish culture, history, art, and ideas, exploring the diversity of the Jewish experience. (www.thecjm.org)*

Elizabeth S. & Alvin I. Fine Museum (Congregation Emanu-El) (1957) (1981) (1999). 2 Lake Street, San Francisco, CA 94118. (415) 751-2535. *Jewish art and history on various themes, featuring works by internationally renowned Jewish artists as well as recognizing emerging Jewish talent and highlighting the contributions of artists with personal ties to the temple. (www.emanuelsf.org/community/museum)*

Gotthelf Art Gallery (San Diego Center for Jewish Culture at Lawrence Family JCC). 4126 Executive Drive, La Jolla, CA 92037. (858) 457-3030. *Contemporary artists and a wide variety of visual media, exploring the richness and diversity of Jewish culture. (www.sdcjc.org/gag)*

Jewish Heritage Museum (The Reutlinger Community for Jewish Living). 4000 Camino Tassajara, Danville, CA 94506. (925) 648-2800. *Judaica from Europe, the Middle East, and North Africa documenting the history of the Jewish people around the world. (www.rcjl.org/jewish-heritage-museum)*

The Magnes Collection of Jewish Art and Life (University of California, Berkeley) (1962) (2010). 2121 Allston Way, Berkeley, CA 94720. (510) 643-2526. *One of the world's preeminent Jewish collections in a university setting, containing art, objects, texts, music, and historical documents about Jews and Jewish culture in the Global Diaspora and the American West. (www.magnes.berkeley.edu)*

Milken Archive of Jewish Music (1990). 1250 Fourth Street, Santa Monica, CA 90401. (310) 570-4746. *Largest collection of American Jewish music, with about 600 recorded works as well as oral histories with composers, cantors, educators, and performers; photographs and historical documents; video footage from recording sessions, interviews, and live performances; and an extensive collection of program notes and essays. (www.milkenarchive.org)*

Platt and Borstein Galleries (American Jewish University). Familian Campus, 15600 Mulholland Drive, Bel Air, CA 90077. (310) 476-9777. *Exhibitions and educational programs exploring creative practice, cultures, and ideas, with an emphasis on contemporary work, seeking to deepen and enhance the understanding of visual arts as critical facets of society as well as inseparable from Jewish thinking, values, and histories. (www.aju.edu/exhibition-spaces/platt-and-borstein-galleries)*

Skirball Museum (Skirball Cultural Center) (1875) (1972) (1996). 2701 North Sepulveda Boulevard, Los Angeles, CA 90049. (310) 440-4500. *Collection of some 25,000 objects of art and history relating to daily life and practice, customs, and values from biblical to contemporary times, reflecting Jewish life in virtually every era and every part of the world, and documenting experiences and accomplishments of the Jewish people over 4000 years from antiquity to America. (www.skirball.org/exhibitions/collections)*

Colorado

Mizel Museum (1982). 400 South Kearney Street, Denver, CO 80224. (720) 785-7300. *Artifacts, fine art, video, and photography exploring the diversity of Jewish life, culture, and history, addressing today's social justice issues through the lens of Jewish history and values, and connecting universal Jewish values to the larger world. (www.mizelmuseum.org)*

Temple Israel Museum (2012). 201 West 4th Street, Leadville, CO 80461. (303) 709-7050. *Permanent exhibition that documents pioneer Jewish life with a collection of artifacts about Leadville, Colorado, its resident Jews, Temple Israel as a frontier synagogue, and life in a mining town in the 1880s and 1890s, housed in historic restored synagogue building. (www.jewishleadville.org/museum.html)*

Connecticut

Chase Family Gallery (Mandell JCC). 335 Bloomfield Avenue, West Hartford, CT 06117. (860) 236-4571. *Art in all forms — painting, sculpture, photography, glass, and ceramics — ranging from contemporary to classical to avant-garde from local, national, and worldwide artists and craftspeople. (www.mandelljcc.org)*

The Museum of Jewish Civilization (Maurice Greenberg Center for Judaic Studies at University of Hartford) (2003). Mortensen Library, Harry Jack Gray Center, University of Hartford, 200 Bloomfield Avenue, West Hartford, CT 06117. (860) 768-5729. *A teaching museum with exhibits depicting the story of Jewish civilization. (www.hartford.edu/academics/schools-colleges/arts-sciences/academics/departments-and-centers/greenberg-center-for-judaic-studies/museum-of-Jewish-civilization.aspx)*

District of Columbia

Lillian and Albert Small Jewish Museum/Historic 1876 Synagogue (Jewish Historical Society of Greater Washington) (1969). 701 Third Street, NW (corner of G Street), Washington, DC 20001. (202) 789-0900. *(Closed pending completion of new facility in 2021.) History of the Jewish community in the Greater Washington DC area from the mid-1800's to the present and preservation of the oldest surviving synagogue in DC — landmark 1876 Adas Israel Congregation building — in which the museum is housed. (www.jhsgw.org)*

National Museum of American Jewish Military History (1958). 1811 R Street, NW, Washington, DC 20009. (202) 265-6280. *Artifacts depicting the contributions of Jewish Americans who served in the US Armed Forces to the peace and freedom of the US, highlighting their courage, heroism, and sacrifices. (www. nmajmh.org)*

Florida

Aliyah Bet and Machal Museum/Museum of American and Canadian Volunteers in Israel's War of Independence (University of Florida Hillel) (2005). Norman H. Lipoff Hall, Hillel Building, University of Florida, 2020 West University Avenue, Gainesville, FL 32603. (532) 372-2900. *Exhibit documenting the history of the American and Canadian men and women who served on the ships to smuggle Holocaust survivors through the British blockade into Palestine (Aliyah Bet) or as volunteers with the Israeli armed forces (Machal) during Israel's war of independence. (www.israelvets.com/two_museums.html)*

Harold and Vivian Beck Museum of Judaica (Beth David Congregation). 2625 Southwest Third Avenue, Miami, FL 33129. (305) 854-3911. *Sephardic and Ashkenazi artifacts, Jewish memorabilia, and visual arts, depicting Jewish life cycle events, festivals, and Shabbat. (www.bethdavidmiami.org/rentals)*

Jewish Museum of Florida-FIU (Florida International University) (1995). 301 Washington Avenue, Miami Beach, FL 33139. (786) 972-3176. *Florida Jewish experience, telling the story of 250 years of Florida Jewish life, history, arts, culture, and the immigration experience, and exploring the diversity of Jewish life and the influence of Florida Jews on Florida, the nation, and the world; located in two restored historic buildings that were formerly synagogues. (www.jmof.fiu.edu)*

Judaica Museum of Temple Beth Sholom. 1050 South Tuttle Avenue, Sarasota, FL 34237. (941) 955-8121. *Jewish arts, culture, and lifestyle, including Jewish life cycle, holidays, and Holocaust, reflecting the diversity and eclectic culture of Jewish life. (www.templebethsholomfl.org.gpesi.com/Programs/JudaicaMuseum.aspx)*

Georgia

The Breman Museum (also known as **William Breman Jewish Heritage Museum**) (1996). 1440 Spring Street, NW, Atlanta, GA 30309. (678) 222-3700. *Exhibits celebrating the Jewish experience, particularly the lessons and memories of the Holocaust, as well as the history of the Jewish people in the southern US, Jewish life in Georgia, and Atlanta's Jewish history. (www.thebreman.org)*

Lawrence and Nancy Gutstein Museum (Congregation Mickve Israel) (1975) (2015). 20 East Gordon Street, Savannah, GA 31401. (912) 233-1547.

Artifacts depicting the Jewish history of the Jews of Savannah, Georgia, covering a wide range of topics, from politics to slavery to religion and many more. (www. mickveisrael.org/museum-tours)

Illinois

Frank Rosenthal Memorial Collection (Temple Anshe Sholom). 20820 Western Avenue, Olympia Fields, IL 60461. (708) 748-6010. *Extensive private collection of Judaica gathered by Rabbi Frank F. Rosenthal. (No website)*

Museum at Spertus Institute of Jewish Learning and Leadership. 610 South Michigan Avenue, Chicago, IL 60605. (312) 322-1700. *A diverse range of Jewish religious objects from around the world as well as fine art, rare books, and historical artifacts that preserve the material culture of the Jewish people. (https://collection.spertus.edu), (www.spertus.edu/exhibits)*

Rosengard Museum (Congregation Beth Shalom). 3433 Walters Avenue, Northbrook, IL 60062. (847) 498-4100. *Judaic ritual and ceremonial objects, Megillot Esther, items for Jewish life cycle events, and Jewish artwork. (www.bethshalomnb.org/rosengard-museum)*

Indiana

Goldman Memorial Museum (Congregation Achduth Vesholom) (1928) (1931). 5200 Old Mill Road, Fort Wayne, IN 46807. (260) 744-4245. *Museum established at oldest Jewish congregation in Indiana, featuring historic objects associated with the area's Jewish individuals and families and displays on topics such as Jewish holidays, the role of Jewish merchants in the first half of the 20th century, and prominent members of the Jewish community as well as a collection of interviews done in the 1980s and 1990s of survivors of the Holocaust. (www.templecav.org/About/OurStory.aspx)*

Iowa

Iowa Jewish Historical Society Museum (Jewish Federation of Greater Des Moines) (1996) (2002). 33158 Ute Avenue, Waukee, IA 50263 (in the Bucksbaum Arts Wing of The Caspe Terrace Complex). (515) 987-0899. *Collection of historical artifacts documenting the lives of Jewish Iowans from 1833—the year that the first permanent Jewish settler arrived in Iowa—to the present day, focusing on Iowa's Jewish families, religious institutions, political participation, and educational, social, philanthropic, and economic activities, and providing personal perspectives and insight into all aspects of Jewish life in Iowa. (www.jewishdesmoines.org/our-pillars/iowa-jewish-historical-society/visit-museum), (www.jewishdesmoines.org/our-pillars/iowa-jewish-historical-society/our-collection)*

Kansas

The Epsten Gallery (also known as **Kansas City Jewish Museum of Contemporary Art** and **The Museum Without Walls**) (1991). 5500 West 123rd Street (123rd and Nall at Village Shalom), Overland Park, KS 66209. (913) 266-8414. *Jewish culture and experience through traditional and contemporary art, celebrating the common humanity within our diverse society. (www.epstengallery.org)*

Louisiana

Museum of the Southern Jewish Experience (1986) (2000). 818 Howard Avenue, New Orleans, LA 70113. (Opening in New Orleans in 2020; previously located in Natchez, MS.) *History of the Southern Jewish experience. (www.msje.org)*

Maine

Maine Jewish Museum. 267 Congress Street, Portland, ME 04101. (207) 773-2339. *Jewish history, art, and culture of Maine, housed in the restored historic Etz Chaim Synagogue, reflecting the contributions and accomplishments of Maine's original Jewish immigrants and their families; rotating exhibits by contemporary Jewish artists from Maine; objects and architecture depicting religious practices and beliefs; photo exhibit of Holocaust survivors who settled in Maine, accompanied by excerpts of their oral testimonies. (www.mainejewishmuseum.org)*

Maryland

Goldman Art Gallery (Gildenhorn/Speisman Center for the Arts of the Bender JCC of Greater Washington). 6125 Montrose Road, Rockville, MD 20852. (301) 881-0100. *Meaningful exhibits and imagery revolving around the Jewish experience, identity, and culture. (www.benderjccgw.org/arts-culture-jewish-life/goldman-art-gallery)*

The Goldsmith Museum/Hendler Learning Center (Chizuk Amuno Congregation) (2001, Museum) (2004, Learning Center). 8100 Stevenson Road, Baltimore, MD 21208. (410) 486-6400. *Judaica donated and collected over decades by Chizuk Amuno Congregation, depicting the history of Jewish Baltimore and the congregation, and celebrating the various facets of Jewish life, including worship. The Learning Center features a time line of Jewish history from the Biblical period to the present against a backdrop of world civilization, including museum quality artifacts, original documents, and reproductions of paintings, maps, photographs, and prints. (www.chizukamuno.org/learning/museum), (www.chizukamuno.org/learning/hendler)*

The Jewish Museum of Maryland (1960). Herman Bearman Campus, 15 Lloyd Street, Baltimore, MD 21202. (410) 732-6400. *Art, rare objects, historical photographs, clothing, ceremonial objects, oral histories, videos, and hands-on activities depicting the Jewish experience in America, with special attention to Jewish life in Maryland, and the historic Lloyd Street and B'nai Israel Synagogues. (www.jewish-museummd.org)*

Massachusetts

Mayyim Hayyim Art Gallery (Mayyim Hayyim Living Waters Community Mikveh) (2006). 1838 Washington Street, Newton, MA 02466. (617) 244-1836, ext. 211 or ext. 203. *Exhibits in a variety of media by local and regional contemporary artists of all ethnicities and religions that provide original perspectives about immersion in particular and about ritual in general, providing a forum for the exploration of the role of the arts as an expression of Jewish life. (www.mayyimhayyim.org/Gallery)*

The Vilna Shul: Boston's Center for Jewish Culture (1919). 18 Phillips Street, Boston, MA 02114. (617) 523-2324. *Boston's oldest surviving immigrant-era synagogue, exploring the Boston Jewish historical, cultural, and spiritual experience. (www.vilnashul.org)*

Wyner Museum (Temple Israel of Boston) (1984). 477 Longwood Avenue, Boston, MA 02215. (617) 566-3960. *Judaica collection that tells important stories of the congregation and its families. (www.tisrael.org/wyner-museum)*

Yiddish Book Center (1980). 1021 West Street, Amherst, MA 01002. (413) 256-4900. *World's first Yiddish museum, featuring extensive exhibits on Yiddish and Jewish culture, in addition to its extensive library of Yiddish books. (www.yiddish-bookcenter.org)*

Michigan

Goodman Family Judaic & Archival Museum (Temple Israel). 5725 Walnut Lake Road, West Bloomfield, MI 48323. (248) 661-5700. *Artifacts from antiquity to modern times that represent the historical, artistic, and cultural development of the Jewish people, demonstrating how Jewish art is firmly rooted to ritual and bound to spiritual life. (www.temple-israel.org/museum)*

Janice Charach Gallery (JCC of Metropolitan Detroit). 6600 West Maple Road, West Bloomfield, MI 48322. (248) 432-5579. *Exhibitions featuring Jewish and non-Jewish established and emerging artists, and including glass, ceramics, multi-media, painting, fiber arts and photography. (https://gallery.jccdet.org)*

Mississippi

Hebrew Union Congregation Museum (also known as **Goldstein Nelken Solomon Century of History Museum**) (2003). 504 Main Street, Greenville, MS 38701. (662) 332-4153. *Exhibits chronicling the personal history of the Hebrew Union Congregation from 1880 till the present time, and about families, writers, and military veterans. (www.hebrewunion.net)*

Temple B'nai Israel (1905). 213 South Commerce Street, Natchez, MS 39120. (601) 362-6357. *Houses the oldest Jewish congregation in Mississippi and offers a guided tour of the historic building; Of Passover and Pilgrimage, an exhibit documenting the history and everyday life of Natchez's Jewish families; and The Natchez Jewish Experience, an award-winning documentary film. (www.isjl.org/templebnai-israel%2D%2D-natchez.html)*

Nebraska

Henry & Dorothy Riekes Museum (Nebraska Jewish Historical Society) (JCC of Omaha) (1995). 333 South 132nd Street, Omaha, NE 68154. (402) 334-6441. *First permanent Jewish Museum in Nebraska and an historic representation of the Orthodox synagogue known as "The Kapulier Shul" (B'nai Jacob—Adas Yeshuron), and also includes an exhibit dedicated to Shaare Zion (popularly known as "The Riekes Shul") and the Herbert Goldstein Wall of Synagogue History, which has a timeline history of the Temple and Synagogue buildings in Nebraska and Council Bluffs, Iowa, depicting Jewish life and culture since the mid-1800s. (www.nebraska-jhs.com/hen.php)*

New Jersey

Jewish Heritage Museum of Monmouth County (2008). 310 Mounts Corner Drive, Freehold, NJ 07728. (732) 252-6990. *Multi-media exhibit, photographs, artifacts, and collected stories depicting the rich and unique history of the Jewish residents of Monmouth County and their contribution to the community. (www. jhmomc.org)*

The Jewish Museum of New Jersey (Congregation Ahavas Sholom) (2003). 145 Broadway, Newark, NJ 07104. (973) 485-2609. *Exhibits portraying 400 years of the rich cultural heritage of New Jersey's Jewish people, with an emphasis on tolerance and diversity, housed in the last surviving synagogue in Newark. (www. jewishmuseumnj.org)*

The Sam Azeez Museum of Woodbine Heritage/Woodbine Brotherhood Synagogue (2003). 610 Washington Avenue, Woodbine, NJ 08270. (609) 861-5355 or (609) 626-3831. *History and heritage of the Russian Jews who settled in the 1890s in Woodbine, the experimental agricultural industrial colony envisioned by Baron de Hirsch, housed in the historic Woodbine Brotherhood Synagogue. (www. thesam.org)*

New York (Outside New York Metropolitan Area)

Benjamin and Dr. Edgar R. Cofeld Judaic Museum (Temple Beth Zion). 805 Delaware Avenue, Buffalo, NY 14209. (716) 836-6565. *Collection of Judaica artifacts, most of which have been donated or bequeathed by congregants, rotated for viewing according to the holidays. (www.tbz.org/about-tbz/tbz-places-spaces)*

Gomez Mill House (1984). 11 Millhouse Road, Marlboro, NY 12542. (845) 236-3126. *Experiential tours of one of the oldest continuously lived in residences in the US and the oldest surviving Jewish dwelling in North America (1714), focusing on the contributions of former Mill House owners to the multi-cultural history of the Hudson River Valley and the role of American Jews as pioneers. (www.gomez.org)*

Hanukkah House Museum (Temple Concord) (1996). 9 Riverside Drive, Binghamton, NY 13905. (607) 723-7355. *Seasonal teaching museum and exhibition housed in historic Kilmer Mansion (which Temple Concord used as their synagogue until their new synagogue was built adjacent to it), depicting the history of Hanukkah and Jewish life in a creative and engaging way with a new and different exhibit each year in addition to some permanent exhibits. (www.facebook.com/ events/temple-concord/hanukkah-house-museum/380965355316526)*

Historic Beth Joseph Synagogue and Gallery. 59 Lake Street, Tupper Lake, NY 12986. (518) 359-7229 or (518) 359-3328. *A small museum of local Jewish history and religious artifacts from local families that perpetuate the memory of the people and industry in Tupper Lake and the Adirondacks, housed in a landmark restored synagogue (referred to as "The Peddler's Synagogue") built in 1905 by Eastern European Orthodox Jews. (www.tupperlake.com/arts-culture/ beth-joseph-synagogue)*

Torah Animal World. 57 Old Falls Road, Fallsburg, NY 12733. (877) 752-6286. *Taxidermy exhibits of animals of the Mishna. (www.torahanimalworld.com)*

New York Metropolitan Area
Alan & Helene Rosenberg Jewish Discovery Museum (Suffolk Y JCC). 74 Hauppauge Road, Commack, NY 11725. (631) 462-9800. *Hands-on museum where children and their families experience learning about Jewish life, history, values, traditions, and heroes as well as Israel and the Hebrew language through interactive displays. (www.syjcc.org/index.php/jewish-life)*

American Jewish Historical Society (1892). Center for Jewish History, 15 West 16th Street, New York, NY 10011. (212) 294-6160. *Oldest national ethnic historical organization in the nation, documenting the history of the Jewish presence in the US from 1654 to the present and containing a collection of unique treasures that reflect the variety of American Jewish culture as expressed in the synagogue, ritual practice, the home, entertainment, and sports. (www.ajhs.org/museum-holdings)*

American Sephardi Federation (1973). Center for Jewish History, 15 West 16th Street, New York, NY 10011. (212) 548-4486. *Collects and showcases rare artifacts, photographs, historical sites, oral histories, and original art by modern Sephardic artists, and hosts high-profile exhibitions, preserving and promoting the Greater Sephardic history, traditions, and rich mosaic culture as an integral part of the Jewish experience. (www.americansephardi.org)*

Bukharian Jewish Museum (2003). Jewish Institute of Queens/Queens Gymnasia, 60-05 Woodhaven Boulevard, Elmhurst, NY 11373. (718) 897-4124 or (718) 426-9369. *Collection of artifacts that tells the 2500-year history of the Bukharian Jews of Central Asia and paints an interactive picture of the life and culture of the region. (www.bukharianjewishcongress.org/museums/1311-bukharian-jewish-museum), (www.vimeo.com/46589644)*

Center for Jewish History (2000). 15 West 16th Street, New York, NY 10011. (212) 294-8301. *A collaborative home for five partner organizations: American Jewish Historical Society, American Sephardi Federation, Leo Baeck Institute, Yeshiva University Museum, and YIVO Institute for Jewish Research, whose combined archives comprise the world's largest and most comprehensive archive of the modern Jewish experience outside of Israel, and include artworks, textiles, ritual objects, recordings, films, and photographs. (www.cjh.org)*

Derfner Judaica Museum (The Hebrew Home at Riverdale) (1982). Jacob Reingold Pavilion, 5901 Palisade Avenue, Riverdale, NY 10471. (718) 581-1596. *Collection of Jewish ceremonial art donated by Riverdale residents Ralph and Leuba Baum, the majority of which were used primarily by European Jews before the Holocaust, and rotating exhibits featuring contemporary artists, exploring themes drawn from the permanent collection, or highlighting Jewish art and culture. (www.riverspringhealth.org/derfner-judaica-museum)*

Dr. Bernard Heller Museum in New York (Hebrew Union College-Jewish Institute of Religion) (formerly **Hebrew Union College-Jewish Institute of Religion Museum**) (1983) (2018). Brookdale Center, One West 4th Street, New York, NY 10012. (212) 824-2218. *Art by contemporary artists of all faiths exploring Jewish identity, history, culture, spirituality, and experience, and exhibitions that interpret core Jewish values, texts, and beliefs and that foster a deeper* *appreciation for Jewish heritage; also has traveling exhibitions. (www.huc.edu/ research/museums/huc-jir-museum-new-york)*

Elsie K. Rudin Judaica Museum (Temple Beth-El of Great Neck) (1960). 5 Old Mill Road, Great Neck, NY 11023. (516) 487-0900. *Judaica artifacts, including a collection of antique Judaica used in family religious observances, and contemporary Judaica art, including one of the finest collections in the world of 20th century artist Ilya Schor's work. (www.tbegreatneck.org/about-temple-beth-el/our-museum-art-n-architecture/elsie-k-rudin-judaica-museum)*

George Kopp Jewish Military Hall of Heroes (Suffolk Y JCC). 74 Hauppauge Road, Commack, NY 11725. (631) 462-9800. *Contributions to the peace and freedom of the US of Jewish men and women who served in the US Armed Forces. (www. syjcc.org/index.php/jewish-life)*

Gladys & Murray Goldstein Cultural Center (Temple Israel of New Rochelle). 1000 Pinebrook Boulevard, New Rochelle, NY 10804. (914) 235-1800. *Judaic art, archaeological artifacts, contemporary Israeli art, commemorative photographs, and storied objects illustrating the Jewish people's contributions to art and culture. (https://tinr.org/cultural-center)*

Herbert & Eileen Bernard Museum of Judaica (Temple Emanu-El) (1928). One East 65th Street, New York, NY 10065. (212) 744-1400, ext. 259. *Three galleries of Jewish art, religious ornaments, and Temple memorabilia exploring the intersections of Jewish identity, history, and material culture as well as the history of Temple Emanu-El. (www.emanuelnyc.org/museum)*

Jewish Children's Museum (2004). 792 Eastern Parkway, Brooklyn, NY 11213. (718) 467-0600. *Hands-on exhibits for children and their families focusing on Jewish holidays, biblical history, Israel, contemporary Jewish life, Jewish values and traditions, and other aspects of Jewish culture. (www.jcm.museum)*

The Jewish Museum (1904). 1109 Fifth Avenue, New York, NY 10128. (212) 423-3200. *Collection comprises nearly 30,000 objects, ranging from archaeological artifacts to works by today's cutting-edge artists, reflecting global Jewish identity; major exhibitions of an interdisciplinary nature, often employing a combination of art and artifacts interpreted through the lens of social history; monograph shows of significant artists; permanent exhibition tells the story of the Jewish people through diverse works of art, antiquities, and media. (www.thejewishmuseum.org)*

Katherine and Clifford H. Goldsmith Gallery (Leo Baeck Institute). Center for Jewish History, 15 West 16th Street, New York, NY 10011. (212) 744-6400 or (212) 294-8340. *Exhibitions on a variety of themes exploring the history and culture of German-speaking Jewry, illustrated with items from its own art collections. (www.lbi.org/about/visiting-lbi/katherine-and-clifford-h-goldsmith-gallery)*

Kehila Kedosha Janina Synagogue and Museum (1997). 280 Broome Street, New York, NY 10002. (212) 431-1619 or (516) 456-9336. *History and customs of Kehila Kedosha Janina Synagogue, built in 1927 on New York City's Lower East Side by Romaniote Jews from Janina, Greece, and the story of this tiny and obscure Jewish community from their entry into Greece in the first century to their current life in America. (www.kkjsm.org)*

The Laurie M. Tisch Gallery (Marlene Meyerson JCC Manhattan). 334 Amsterdam Avenue, New York, NY 10023. (646) 505-4452. *Changing multi-disciplinary exhibits, ranging from solo artist shows to historical multi-media exhibits and touring shows from museums and galleries around the world, that offer new perspectives on the rich history and values of the Jewish community. (www.jccmanhattan.org/arts-ideas/laurie-m-tisch-gallery/about)*

The Library of the Jewish Theological Seminary (1893). 3080 Broadway, New York, NY 10027. (212) 678-8000. *One of the greatest collections of Judaica in the world — treasures representing Jewish life and creativity from ancient times to the present, including books, manuscripts, archival documents, recordings, and Jewish art, exploring the literary and cultural heritage of the Jewish people, Jewish history, and the shared Jewish experience. (www.jtsa.edu/library)*

The Living Torah Museum (2002). 1601 41st Street, Brooklyn, NY 11218. (877) 752-6286. *Exhibits of ancient artifacts explicitly mentioned in the Torah and from the Biblical Period as well as items mentioned in the Mishna and Talmud; exhibition of the 39 prohibitions of the Sabbath; and a great Torah personalities gallery depicting the life and times of some of the greatest Torah scholars of yesteryear. (www.torahmuseum.com)*

Museum at Eldridge Street (1986). 12 Eldridge Street, New York, NY 10002. (212) 219-0302. *Interactive displays on immigrant history — especially about the culture, history, and traditions of Eastern European Jewish immigrants who settled in New York City's Lower East Side — as well as Jewish practice and historic preservation, housed within the historic Eldridge Street Synagogue built in 1887. (www.eldridgestreet.org)*

National Jewish Sports Hall of Fame and Museum (Suffolk Y JCC) (1975). 74 Hauppauge Road, Commack, NY 11725. (631) 462-9800. *Plaques honoring Jewish individuals who have distinguished themselves in the field of sports, fostering Jewish identity through athletics and commemorating sports heroes who have emerged from a people not commonly associated with sports, and a vast collection of sports memorabilia. (www.syjcc.org/index.php/jewish-life)*

Rabbi Irving and Marly Koslowe Judaica Gallery (Westchester Jewish Center). 175 Rockland Avenue (Palmer and Rockland Avenues), Mamaroneck, NY 10543. (914) 698-2960. *Revolving exhibitions of fine art, folk art, and photography, culled from contemporary artists, historical content, and members' collections, that mirror the Jewish world, in microcosm. (www.wjcenter.org/community/judaicagallery)*

Tenement Museum (1988). 103 Orchard Street, New York, NY 10002 (1992). (877) 975-3786. *America's immigrant history and experience, Jewish and non-Jewish, related through viewing restored apartments of past residents of New York City's Lower East Side from different time periods, including the restored apartment of the German-Jewish Gumpertz family. (www.tenement.org)*

Torah Animal World (2008). 1601 41st Street, Brooklyn, NY 11218. (877) 752-6286. *Taxidermy exhibits of animals and birds of the Torah, animals of the Talmud, animals mentioned in the Tefillah, and exhibits of other animals from Jewish texts. (www.torahanimalworld.com)*

Yeshiva University Museum (1973). Center for Jewish History, 15 West 16th Street, New York, NY 10011. (212) 294-8330. *Collection of more than 10,000 artifacts, exhibitions, installations, and programs, depicting Jewish communities, culture, and art around the world and throughout history; providing interpretations of Jewish life past and present from a multidisciplinary perspective; and presenting the work of emerging and established artists who treat Jewish themes and perspectives. (www.yumuseum.org)*

YIVO Institute for Jewish Research (1925) (1940). Center for Jewish History, 15 West 16th Street, New York, NY 10011. (212) 246-6080. *History of 1000 years of Jewish life throughout Eastern Europe, Germany, and Russia and its continuing influence in America, including largest collection of Yiddish-language materials in the world and home of the largest collection of Holocaust primary documentation in North America. (www.yivo.org)*

North Carolina

Judaic Art Gallery of the North Carolina Museum of Art (1983). 2110 Blue Ridge Road, Raleigh, NC 27607. (919) 839-6262. *One of the finest collections of Jewish ceremonial art in the US, embracing a wide variety of forms and artistic styles from four continents and spanning three centuries, celebrating the spiritual and ceremonial life of the Jewish people. (www.ncartmuseum.org/art/view/judaic)*

The Rosenzweig Gallery (Judea Reform Congregation) (early 1990s). 1933 West Cornwallis Road, Durham, NC 27705. (919) 489-7062. *Rotating exhibits of Judaic art and artifacts, including religious prints and books and traveling exhibits of highly acclaimed Israeli and regional artists. (www.judeareform.org/rosenzweiggallery)*

Ohio

Maltz Museum of Jewish Heritage: The Museum of Diversity & Tolerance (2005). 2929 Richmond Road, Beachwood, OH 44122. (216) 593-0575. *History of the Jewish immigrant experience in Cleveland and the growth and evolution of Cleveland's Jewish community, focusing on tolerance and diversity, with stories of individuals and families—past and present—that come to life through state-of-the-art exhibitions, interactives and films, oral histories, photographs, and artifacts; The Temple-Tifereth Israel Gallery features an internationally-recognized collection of Judaica, and a special exhibition gallery features important exhibitions of national and international acclaim. (www.maltzmuseum.org)*

Skirball Museum (Hebrew Union College-Jewish Institute of Religion) (1913). 3101 Clifton Avenue, Cincinnati, OH 45220. (513) 487-3098. *Permanent exhibit comprised of seven thematic galleries containing Jewish archaeological artifacts and ceremonial and ritual objects that portray the cultural, historical, and religious heritage of the Jewish people, including themes of immigration, American Judaism with emphasis on Cincinnati and HUC-JIR, archaeology, Torah study, Jewish festivals and life cycles, the Holocaust, and modern Israel. (www.huc.edu/research/museums/skirball-museum-cincinnati)*

The Temple Museum of Jewish Art, Religion and Culture (The Temple-Tifereth Israel) (1955). Jack and Lilyan Mandel Building, 26000 Shaker Boulevard,

Beachwood, OH 44122. (216) 831-3233. *One of the first museums of Judaica in North America, containing a collection of artifacts and fine and ritual arts that embodies the Jewish experience from ancient to present times throughout the world. (www.ttti.org/the-temple-museum-of-jewish-art-religion-and-culture)*

Oklahoma
The Sherwin Miller Museum of Jewish Art (1965). 2021 East 71st Street, Tulsa, OK 74136. (918) 492-1818. *Largest collection of Judaica in the American Southwest, including art and artifacts showing the history of the Jewish people from the pre-Canaanite era through the settling of the Jewish community in Tulsa and the Southwest, as well as a Holocaust exhibition containing objects donated by Oklahoma veterans who helped liberate the German concentration camps and artifacts brought to Oklahoma by Jewish refugees from Nazi Germany; special exhibits and events showcase works representing Jewish artists from historic to modern times. (www.jewishmuseumtulsa.org)*

Oregon
Oregon Jewish Museum and Center for Holocaust Education (1989). 724 Northwest Davis Street, Portland, OR 97209. (503) 226-3600. *The Pacific Northwest's only Jewish museum and largest collection of the documented and visual history of Oregon's Jews, examining the history of the Jewish experience in Oregon from 1850 to the present, and a history of the Holocaust that employs the stories of Oregon survivors, and an exhibit on discrimination as a tool used to affect varied groups of people over the history of the region. (www.ojmche.org)*

Pennsylvania
American Jewish Museum (JCC of Greater Pittsburgh) (1998). Squirrel Hill Campus, 5738 Forbes Avenue, Pittsburgh, PA 15217. (412) 697-3231 or (412) 521-8010. *Contemporary Jewish art from throughout the country that facilitates dialogue about art, philosophy, and culture to promote interfaith and intergenerational explorations, and traveling exhibitions from world-class museums. (www.jccpgh.org/jewish-life-arts-events/american-jewish-museum)*

Leon J. and Julia S. Obermayer Collection of Jewish Ritual Art (Congregation Rodeph Shalom) (1985). 615 North Broad Street, Philadelphia, PA 19123. (215) 627-6747. *More than 500 works of Jewish ceremonial art, illustrating life cycles, events, and holidays and demonstrating the unique relationship between the Jews' quest for beauty in articles used in religious rites and art of the countries in which they lived. (www.rodephshalom.org/community/obermayer-collection-jewish-ritual-art)*

National Museum of American Jewish History (1976). 101 South Independence Mall East, Philadelphia, PA 19106. (215) 923-3811. *Repository of the largest collection of Jewish Americana in the world with more than 30,000 artifacts and only museum in the US dedicated exclusively to exploring and interpreting the American Jewish experience in the context of American history, presenting a history of Jewish life in America depicted through original artifacts, telling moments, and state-of-the* *art interactive media and, exploring the religious, social, political, and economic lives of American Jews. (www.nmajh.org)*

The Philadelphia Museum of Jewish Art (Congregation Rodeph Shalom) (1975). 615 North Broad Street, Philadelphia, PA 19123. (215) 627-6747. *Contemporary art that illuminates the Jewish experience in the broadest range of mediums by artists of diverse backgrounds, including a permanent collection of important works by accomplished artists, located within historic Congregation Rodeph Shalom. (www.rodephshalom.org/community/philadelphia-museum-jewish-art)*

Temple Judea Museum (Reform Congregation Keneseth Israel) (1984). 8339 Old York Road, Elkins Park, PA 19027. (215) 887-2027 or (215) 887-8700. *Judaica artifacts from around the world, both historic and contemporary collections, including antique and contemporary Judaica, Israeliana, rare books, historic and art photography, a comprehensive textile collection, ceremonial objects, paintings, prints, works on paper, 3-D crafts and folk objects, and a variety of ephemera, relating to the entire history of the Jewish people and Israel and displayed through original, curated exhibitions. (www.kenesethisrael.org/museum)*

Rhode Island

Rhode Island Jewish Museum (Congregation Sons of Jacob) (2017). 24 Douglas Avenue, Providence, RI 02908. (401) 274-5260. *Preservation of the historic Sons of Jacob Synagogue, celebrating Rhode Island Jewish history and the Smith Hill immigrant experience; murals and intricate paper-cut artwork created by Samuel Shore, the first president of Congregation Sons of Jacob. (www.rhodeislandjewishmuseum.org)*

Touro Synagogue/Touro Synagogue Foundation (1763). 85 Touro Street, Newport, RI 02840. (401) 847-4794, ext. 207 or ext. 201. *History of Touro Synagogue and the Jews of Newport, Rhode Island, including the original of George Washington's Letter to the Hebrew Congregations of Newport, Rhode Island, and various exhibits exploring how Rhode Island contributed to America's notions of religious freedom, the contributions to American economic, social, and political life of individuals who played an important role in the early history of the US, and the Colonial Jewish Burial Ground. (www.tourosynagogue.org)*

South Carolina

Kahal Kadosh Beth Elohim Museum (Kahal Kadosh Beth Elohim). 90 Hasell Street, Charleston, SC 29401. (843) 723-1090. *History of the historic Kahal Kadosh Beth Elohim congregation, the first Reform Jewish congregation in the US and now the fourth oldest Jewish congregation in the continental US, and its members, depicted through documents, photographs, ceremonial objects, and other memorabilia. (www.kkbe.org/museum)*

Temple Sinai Jewish History Center (2018). 11–13 Church Street, Sumter, SC 29150. (803) 773-2122 or (803) 775-0908. *Permanent exhibit about Jewish history in South Carolina and Sumter, including a large section devoted to the Holocaust and Sumter's ties to the Holocaust, housed in historic Reform synagogue. (www.sumtercountymuseum.org/templesinai)*

Tennessee

Belz Museum of Asian & Judaic Art-Judaic Gallery (formerly **Peabody Place Museum**) (2004) (2007). 119 South Main Street, Concourse Level, Memphis, TN 38103. (901) 523-2787. *Modern Judaica and contemporary Israeli art reflecting the artistic journey of some of Israel's most celebrated contemporary artists, including the largest displayed collection of Daniel Kafri's work outside of Israel. (www.belzmuseum.org), (www.belzmuseum.org/galleries/#images-preview1-1)*

Temple Israel Museum (1994). 1376 East Massey Road, Memphis, TN 38120. (901) 761-3130. *Jewish ritual art featuring The Herta and Justin H. Adler Judaica Collection, including the works of artisans from Germany, France, Morocco, Egypt, Poland, Russia, Israel, and America. (www.timemphis.org/about-temple/museum)*

Texas

The Mollie & Louis Kaplan Museum of Judaica (Congregation Beth Yeshurun) (1972). 4525 Beechnut Street, Houston, TX 77096. (713) 666-1881. *Judaica and art depicting the history, religion, culture, and customs of the Jewish people, including many works of Judaica rescued from Europe after World War II. (www.bethyeshurun.org/learn/mollie-louis-kaplan-museum-judaica)*

The National Center for Jewish Art at the Museum of Biblical Art (2014). 7500 Park Lane, Dallas, TX 75225. (214) 368-4622. *Special collection by 20th century and contemporary Jewish and Israeli artists—particularly art from the art colonies in Safed and Ein Hod in Israel—as well as historical and religious artifacts and ceremonial items for study, teaching the basics of Judaism and the Jewish faith through art. (www.biblicalarts.org/ncja)*

Virginia

Beth Ahabah Museum and Archives (Congregation Beth Ahabah) (late 1970s). 1109 West Franklin Street, Richmond, VA 23220. (804) 353-2668. *Richmond's museum of Jewish history, art, and culture, exhibiting materials that relate to Jewish history and culture, with particular emphasis on Richmond, Virginia, and containing four galleries of changing exhibitions that retell the stories of Richmond's long Jewish history. (www.bethahabah.org/bama)*

Jewish Museum & Cultural Center (Chevra T'helim Synagogue) (2008). 607 Effingham Street, Portsmouth, VA 23704. (757) 391-9266. *Artifacts and exhibits that reflect the history of Virginia's Hampton Roads (Tidewater) Jewish community, housed in the restored historic Chevra T'helim Synagogue, a rare surviving example of Eastern European Jewish Orthodoxy. (www.jewishmuseumportsmouth.org)*

Wisconsin

Jewish Museum Milwaukee (Milwaukee Jewish Federation) (2008). Helfaer Community Service Building, 1360 North Prospect Avenue, Milwaukee, WI 53202. (414) 390-5730. *Displays and interactive features, exploring the breadth of Jewish life and culture, both within the state of Wisconsin and beyond, with major sections on Jewish immigration to the US, Jewish belief and community, earning a living,* *intolerance and the Holocaust, Israel, and contributions of Milwaukee's Jews to tikkun olam (repairing the world). (www.jewishmuseummilwaukee.org)*

The Rabbi Ronald and Judy Shapiro Museum of Judaica (Congregation Shalom). 7630 North Santa Monica Boulevard, Milwaukee, WI 53217. (414) 352-9288. *Collection of Jewish art and Judaica. (www.cong-shalom.org/support-us/fund-cards)*

10.1.3   Jewish Museums, Canada

British Columbia
Jewish Museum & Archives of British Columbia (1971). Peretz Centre for Secular Jewish Culture, 6184 Ash Street, Vancouver, BC V5Z 3G9. (604) 257-5199. *Collection of documents, photographs, artifacts, and oral histories, recounting the rich 150-year history of Jews in British Columbia; walking tours and online, traveling exhibits, and temporary exhibits (no permanent exhibits on display). (www.jewishmuseum.ca)*

Manitoba
Marion and Ed Vickar Jewish Museum of Western Canada (Asper Jewish Community Campus) (1998). 123 Doncaster Street, Suite C140, Winnipeg, MB R3N 2B2. (204) 477-7460. *Photographs, Jewish newspapers, cemetery information, oral histories, manuscripts, Yiddish music collections, and films, depicting the Jewish history of settlement in Western Canada and the social history of lives and events in the Jewish community of Western Canada over more than a century. (www.jhcwc.org/about/jewish-museum-of-western-canada)*

New Brunswick
Saint John Jewish Historical Museum (1986). 91 Leinster Street, Saint John, NB E2L 1J2. (506) 633-1833. *Permanent and changing exhibits with displays of documents and artifacts, exploring the Jewish history of Saint John. (www.jewishmuseumsj.com)*

Ontario
Jacob M. Lowy Collection (Library and Archives Canada) (1977). 395 Wellington Street, Room 237A, Ottawa, ON K1A 0N4. (613) 995-7960. *Collection of rare and old Hebraica and Judaica books, monographs, and manuscripts in multiple languages and from several continents, including incunables and the first and early editions of Talmud, codes of law, responsa, legal and biblical commentaries, and mystical texts. (www.bac-lac.gc.ca/eng/lowy-collection/pages/lowy-collection.aspx)*

Koffler Gallery (Koffler Centre of the Arts) (1980). Artscape Youngplace, 180 Shaw Street, Suite 104-105, Toronto, ON M6J 2W5. (647) 925-0643. *Contemporary visual art, mainly by Canadian artists, that reflects diverse cultural, material, and aesthetic perspectives, positioning the contemporary Jewish experience in a context* *of comparative discussions of identity, memory, and place; promoting ideals of social justice, equality, and inclusiveness; and affirming the power of art to provide common ground and activate social change. (www.kofflerarts.org)*

The Morris & Sally Justein Jewish Heritage Museum (Baycrest Health Sciences). 3560 Bathurst Street, 1st Floor (near Bathurst Street entrance), Toronto, ON M6A 2E1. (416) 785-2500, ext. 5622. *Collection of Judaic artifacts, exploring the history and beauty of the Judaic heritage, and a Museum on Wheels program that brings curated artifacts from the permanent collection to clients in the hospital, nursing home, and day programs. (www.baycrest.org/Baycrest/Living-at-Baycrest/Amenities/Museum)*

Reuben & Helene Dennis Museum (Beth Tzedec Congregation) (1965). 1700 Bathurst Street, Toronto, ON M5P 3K3. (416) 781-3514, ext. 232. *Judaica collection containing more than 2500 artifacts, including ceremonial objects, representing Jewish art and history from ancient times to the present. (www.beth-tzedec.org/page/museum)*

Quebec
Aron Museum (Temple Emanu-El-Beth Sholom) (1953). 4100 Sherbrooke Street West, Westmount, QC H3Z 1A5. (514) 937-3575. *Canada's first museum of Jewish ceremonial art objects and one of the most important collections of Judaica in Canada, containing over 300 outstanding examples of ceremonial art from around the world. (www.templemontreal.ca/programming/museum-gallery)*

Edward Bronfman Museum (Congregation Shaar Hashomayim) (1967). 450 Kensington Avenue, Westmount, QC H3Y 3A2. (514) 937-9471. *Permanent exhibit of ceremonial objects that are an integral part of the Jewish life cycle, reflecting the rituals of Jewish life and the Jewish holiday cycle, and archival photos and objects representing the history of Congregation Shaar Hashomayim, and rotating exhibits showcasing artifacts from the various aspects of Jewish life as well as the historical contribution of the congregation to the Montreal Jewish community-at-large. (www.shaarhashomayim.org/museum)*

Museum of Jewish Montreal (2010) (2016). 4040 St. Laurent Boulevard, #R01, Montreal, QC H2W 1Y8. (514) 840-9300. *Exhibits depicting the diverse histories and experiences of Montreal's Jewish community. (www.imjm.ca)*

10.1.4   Online/Virtual Jewish Museums, United States

Aliyah Bet & Machal Virtual Museum: North American Volunteers in Israel's War of Independence. American Veterans of Israel Legacy Corp., 11 East 44th Street, New York, NY 10017. (212) 490-0900. *Relates the history and most of the names of the approximately 1500 American and Canadian men and women, including Jews and Christians, who risked their lives in the service of the Jewish people from 1946 to 1949, serving on the ships to smuggle Holocaust survivors through the*

British blockade into Palestine (Aliyah Bet) or as volunteers with the Israeli armed forces (Machal). (www.israelvets.com)

American Jewish Heroes and Heroines of America Exhibits. *Twelve online exhibits with more than 450 articles, documenting the contributions and sacrifices that American Jews have made to help make the US a leader in the world. (www. seymourbrody.com)*

Diarna: The Geo-Museum of North African and Middle Eastern Jewish Life (2010). c/o Digital Heritage Mapping, 1435 Centre Street, Newton Center, MA 02459. (857) 288-8075. *A digital preservation of the physical remnants of Jewish history (synagogues, schools, and other structures that once comprised Mizrahi Jewish life) and a record of place-based oral histories throughout the North African and Middle Eastern region (Diarna means "Our homes" in Judeo-Arabic). (www. diarna.org)*

Jewish-American Hall of Fame (1969) (2012). c/o American Numismatic Society, 75 Varick Street, 11th Floor, New York, NY 10013. (212) 571-4470. *Virtual tour through 500 years of Jewish-American history, featuring people, places, and events that are recognized by the Jewish-American Hall of Fame and have significantly influenced future generations, illustrated by the commemorative medals issued. (www.amuseum.org/jahf)*

Jewish Baseball Museum (2016). *Showcases the rich relationship between Jews and baseball and the impact each has had on the other, telling the compelling stories of the Jewish players, executives, and others who have had a profound impact on the game; celebrating the game's many influencers, from heroes to journeymen; telling the story of the integration of Jews into the fabric of American life; and featuring artifacts that provide a direct connection to the history of the game. (www.jewishbaseballmuseum.com)*

Jewish Museum of the American West (2013). Western States Jewish History Association, 285 Sierra Woods Drive, Sierra Madre, CA 91024. (562) 405-4176. *Tells the story of the "Third Golden Age of Judaism" when early Jewish pioneers were a major factor in creating the basic foundations of the American Wild West and explains how and why they were so successful, featuring individual "exhibition halls" on each of the states (US) and provinces (Canadian) west of the Mississippi. (www.jmaw.org)*

Jewish Women's Archive (1995). One Harvard Street, Brookline, MA 02445. (617) 232-2258. *World's largest collection of information on Jewish women and most extensive collection of material anywhere on American Jewish women, featuring online exhibits that use digital technology to document Jewish women's stories, explore in-depth their struggles and successes, elevate their voices, and inspire them to be agents of change. (www.jwa.org)*

The Kabbalah Museum. *Makes available for close review and study online the original writings of Rav Ashlag, Rav Brandwein, and the Rav. (www.kabbalahmuseum.org)*

Living Museum (2006). Edmond J. Safra Plaza, 36 Battery Place, New York, NY 10280. (646) 437-4310. *A project of the Museum of Jewish Heritage-A Living Memorial to the Holocaust to help middle school students in Jewish day and supple-*

mentary schools form a personal connection to modern Jewish history by showing how their lives and that of their families fit into the modern Jewish experience, offering exhibitions or organized displays of artifacts made up of images of objects that reflect an aspect of the history of the family that owns, lent, or has donated the artifacts on display which taken together reflect the ups and downs of Jewish experience during the course of modern Jewish history. (www.living-museum.org/site)

Museum of Family History. *Multimedia, interactive website, including a collection of photographs and documents and exhibitions of sight and sound, exploring modern Jewish history and culture; recounting the stories of Jewish families—their struggles and triumphs; and honoring the Jewish people and the Jewish family unit in particular. (www.museumoffamilyhistory.com)*

Museum of the Yiddish Theatre. *Collection of photographs, play programs and theatre reviews, newspaper articles, sheet music, audio recordings and video clips, and other documents of historical significance, chronicling the evolution and progression of the Yiddish theatre in the US. (www.museumoffamilyhistory.com/moyt/atm.htm)*

The Virtual Museum of the Milken Archive of Jewish Music. 1250 Fourth Street, Santa Monica, CA 90401. (310) 570-4746. *Virtual museum presenting the largest collection of American Jewish music, with roughly 600 recorded works as well as oral histories with composers, cantors, educators, and performers; photographs and historical documents; video footage from recording sessions, interviews, and live performances; and an extensive collection of program notes and essays. (www.milkenarchive.org/articles/virtual-exhibits)*

The Washington Jewish Museum (Washington State Jewish Historical Society). 3801 East Mercer Way, Mercer Island, WA 98040. (206) 774-2277. *History of Washington State's Jewish community presented through stories and digital artifacts from the museum's own collection and the collections of members of the state's Jewish community. (www.wsjhs.org/museum)*

10.1.5 Online/Virtual Jewish Museums, Canada

Interactive Museum of Jewish Montreal (2010). 4040 St. Laurent Boulevard, #R01, Montreal, QC H2W 1Y8. (514) 840-9300. *Maps Jewish Montreal from its origins in the 1760s until today, providing written descriptions for the sites on the map and linking them to images from archives from around the world; connects exhibits to personal stories, narrations, songs, poems, and films, allowing the viewer to interact with the community's history; also offers walking tours and pop-up exhibitions. (www.imjm.ca)*

Jewish Canadian Military Museum (Ceased to exist as of 2019)

10.1.6   Traveling Jewish Museums, United States

Barr Foundation Judaica (2018). 1369 Laskin Road, Suite One, Virginia Beach, VA 23451. (757) 627-0291. *Private collection of antique and contemporary Torah pointers (known by the Hebrew word for "hand," yad), created by artists from different ages and cultures and of diverse materials, including wood, precious metals, jewels, ceramics, and paper, available as a traveling exhibit. (www.barrfoundationyads.com)*

Down Home Museum Exhibit (Jewish Heritage Foundation of North Carolina at Duke University) (2011). Center for Jewish Studies, Jewish Heritage Foundation of North Carolina, Duke University, 230 Gray Building, Box 90964, Durham, NC 27708. (919) 660-3504. *Traveling exhibition taking an experiential, values-oriented approach in telling the narrative of Jewish life in North Carolina. (www.jhfnc.org/programs/down-home-museum-exhibit), (https://sites.duke.edu/downhome/explore-the-exhibit)*

10.2   Holocaust Museums, Memorials, and Monuments

Note: Section 10.2 does not list Holocaust Education and Documentation Centers, except when they define themselves as museums. The list also does not include Holocaust organizations that provide resources to teachers as required to teach the Holocaust in the schools.

10.2.1   Central Coordinating Body for Holocaust Museums

Association of Holocaust Organizations. For contact information and a description, see the Jewish Holocaust Organizations section of Chap. 12.

10.2.2   Holocaust Museums, Memorials, and Monuments, United States

Arizona
Center for Holocaust Education and Human Dignity. East Valley JCC, 908 North Alma School Road, Chandler, AZ 85224. (480) 897-0588. (www.evjcc.org/holocaust-education)

Holocaust History Center of Tucson. Jewish History Museum, 564 South Stone Avenue, Tucson, AZ 85701. (520) 670-9073. (www.jewishhistorymuseum.org/holocaust-history-museum)

California

Bronfman Family JCC Holocaust Museum. 524 Chapala Street, Santa Barbara, CA 93101. (805) 957-1115. (www.jewishsantabarbara.org/portraits-of-survival)

Chiune Sugihara Memorial, Hero of the Holocaust. South Central Avenue and East 3rd Street in Little Tokyo (1 block from Japanese American National Museum), Los Angeles, CA 90013. (www.publicartinpublicplaces.info/chiune-sugihara-2002-by-Ramon-G-Velazco)

Desert Holocaust Memorial. Civic Center Park, Fred Waring Drive and San Pablo Avenue, Palm Desert, CA 92255. (760) 324-4737. (www.waymarking.com/waymarks/WMCFHD_Holocaust_Memorial_of_the_Desert_Palm_Desert_CA)

Erna and Arthur Salm Holocaust & Genocide Memorial Grove (Sonoma State University). Center for the Study of the Holocaust & Genocide, 1801 East Cotati Avenue, Rohnert Park, CA 94928. (707) 664-4076 or (707) 664-2112. (http://web.sonoma.edu/holocaustgrove)

Holocaust Memorial at Legion of Honor. Lincoln Park, 34th Avenue and Clement Street, San Francisco, CA 94121. (415) 863-3330 or (415) 750-3600 or (415) 750-3636. (www.roadsideamerica.com/story/14442)

Holocaust Memorial (Beth Jacob Congregation). 3778 Park Boulevard, Oakland, CA 94610. (510) 482-1147. (www.bjsd.org/history)

Holocaust Memorial Garden (Lawrence Family JCC). Jacobs Family Campus, 4126 Executive Drive, La Jolla, CA 92037. (858) 457-3030. (www.sdcjc.org/ajl/holocaust_edu.aspx)

Los Angeles Museum of the Holocaust and Holocaust Monument/Martyrs Memorial. Pan Pacific Park, 100 South The Grove Drive, Los Angeles, CA 90036. (323) 651-3704. (www.lamoth.org), (www.publicartinla.com/sculptures/young_holocaust.html)

The Museum of Tolerance. Simon Wiesenthal Plaza, 9786 West Pico Boulevard, Los Angeles, CA 90035. (310) 772-2505 or (310) 553-8403. (www.museumoftolerance.com)

Nancy & Irving Chase Family Holocaust Memorial Garden (Merage JCC of Orange County). 1 Federation Way, Suite 200, Irvine, CA 92603. (949) 435-3400. (www.jccoc.org/jewishjourneys/nancy-irving-chase-family-holocaust-memorial-garden)

"Never Again" Holocaust Memorial (Jewish Federation of Silicon Valley). Gloria and Ken Levy Family Campus, 14855 Oka Road, Los Gatos, CA 95113. (408) 358-3033. (www.waymarking.com/waymarks/WM7FV5_Never_Again_Holocaust_Memorial_Los_Gatos_CA)

"Wallenberg Lives" Holocaust Memorial to Raoul Wallenberg. Menlo Park Civic Center, Laurel Street, Menlo Park, CA 94025. (www.waymarking.com/waymarks/WM58G0_Wallenberg_Lives_Menlo_Park_California)

Colorado

Babi Yar Park. 10451 East Yale Avenue, Denver, CO 80231. (303) 394-9993. (www.mizelmuseum.org/exhibit/babi-yar-park-a-living-holocaust-memorial)

Holocaust Memorial Social Action Site (University of Denver). Holocaust Awareness Institute, Sturm Hall, 2000 East Asbury Avenue, Suite 157, Denver, CO 80208. (303) 871-3020. (www.du.edu/ahss/cjs/hai/hmsas)

Connecticut

Hartford Remembers the Holocaust Exhibit (University of Hartford). Museum of Jewish Civilization, Mortensen Library, Harry Jack Gray Center, 200 Bloomfield Avenue, West Hartford, CT 06117. (860) 768-5729. (www.hartford.edu/academics/schools-colleges/arts-sciences/academics/departments-and-centers/greenberg-center-for-judaic-studies/museum-of-Jewish-civilization.aspx)

Holocaust Memorial (Mandell JCC of Greater Hartford). 335 Bloomfield Avenue, West Hartford, CT 06117. (860) 236-4571. (www.waymarking.com/waymarks/WMD6WJ_Holocaust_Memorial_West_Hartford_CT)

New Haven Memorial Tribute to the Six Million. Edgewood Park (corner of Whalley and West Park Avenues), New Haven, CT 06515. (203) 946-8028. (www.ctmonuments.net/2010/03/holocaust-memorial-new-haven)

Delaware

Garden of the Righteous Gentiles and Children's Memorial (Bernard and Ruth Siegel JCC). 101 Garden of Eden Road, Wilmington, DE 19803. (302) 478-5660. (www.tclf.org/landscapes/garden-righteous-gentiles)

Holocaust Memorial. Freedom Plaza, Louis L. Redding City County Building, 800 North French Street, Wilmington, DE 19801. (https://collections.ctdigitalarchive.org/islandora/object/50002:1466)

District of Columbia

Art and Remembrance. 5614 Connecticut Avenue NW, #131, Washington, DC 20015. (301) 654-7286. (www.artandremembrance.org)

United States Holocaust Memorial Museum. 100 Raoul Wallenberg Place, SW, Washington, DC 20024. (202) 488-0400. (www.ushmm.org)

Florida

Florida Holocaust Museum. 55 Fifth Street South, St. Petersburg, FL 33701. (727) 820-0100. (www.flholocaustmuseum.org)

Frisch Family Holocaust Memorial Gallery (Jewish Family & Community Services). 8540 Baycenter Road, Jacksonville, FL 32256. (904) 448-1933. (www.jacksonvilleholocaustmemorial.com)

Holocaust Documentation and Education Center. 303 North Federal Highway, Dania Beach, FL 33004. (954) 929-5690. (www.hdec.org)

Holocaust Memorial Miami Beach. 1933-1945 Meridian Avenue, Miami Beach, FL 33139. (305) 538-1663. (www.holocaustmemorialmiamibeach.org)

Holocaust Memorial Resource & Education Center of Florida. 851 North Maitland Avenue, Maitland, FL 32751. (407) 628-0555. (www.holocaustedu.org)

The Holocaust Museum & Education Center of Southwest Florida. 975 Imperial Golf Course Boulevard, Naples, FL 34110. (239) 263-9200. (www.holocaustmuseumswfl.org)

Georgia

Besser Holocaust Memorial Garden (Marcus JCC of Atlanta). Zaban Park, 5342 Tilly Mill Road, Dunwoody, GA 30338. (678) 254-1804 or (678) 812-4161. (www.atlantajcc.org/interior-pages/jewish-life-and-learning-besser-memorial-garden)

The Breman Museum/Weinberg Center for Holocaust Education. 1440 Spring Street NW, Atlanta, GA 30309. (678) 222-3700. (www.thebreman.org)

Museum of History and Holocaust Education (Kennesaw State University). KSU Center, 3333 Busbee Drive, Kennesaw, GA 30144. (470) 578-2083 or (470) 578-6896. (http://historymuseum.kennesaw.edu)

Idaho

Idaho Anne Frank Human Rights Memorial/Wassmuth Center for Human Rights. 777 South 8th Street, Boise, ID 83702. (208) 345-0304. (www.annefrankmemorial.org/memorial-location-boise-idaho)

Illinois

Bernard and Rochelle Zell Holocaust Memorial (Spertus Institute for Jewish Learning and Leadership). 610 South Michigan Avenue, Chicago, IL 60605. (312) 322-1700. (www.tmexhibits.com/portfolio/zell.html)

Holocaust Monument. Village Green, 5213 Oakton Street (between Skokie Village Hall and Skokie Public Library), Skokie, IL 60077. (www.waymarking.com/waymarks/WMC19M_Holocaust_Monument_Skokie_IL), (www.sheerithapleitah.com/sample-page/135-2)

Illinois Holocaust Museum & Education Center. 9603 Woods Drive, Skokie, IL 60077. (847) 967-4800. (www.ilholocaustmuseum.org)

Paul and Gabriella Rosenbaum Garden-Holocaust Survivors' Garden. 140 East Oak Street (intersection of North Michigan Avenue), Chicago, IL 60611. (www.motherearthliving.com/Gardening/Holocaust-Survivors-Garden?slideshow=1)

Peoria Holocaust Memorial. Peoria Riverfront Museum, 123 Washington Street (corner of Washington and Liberty Streets), Peoria, IL 61602. (309) 689-0063. (www.peoriaholocaustmemorial.org)

Indiana

Albert and Sara Reuben Holocaust Memorial Garden (Jewish Federation of Greater Indianapolis). Max and Mae Simon Jewish Community Campus, 6705 Hoover Road, Indianapolis, IN 46260. (317) 715-6976. (www.jewishindianapolis.org/holocaust-education)

CANDLES Holocaust Museum and Education Center. 1532 South Third Street, Terre Haute, IN 47802. (812) 234-7881. (www.candlesholocaustmuseum.org)

Iowa

Iowa Holocaust Memorial. Iowa State Capitol (West Terrace, near the corner of East Grand Avenue and East 7th Street), Des Moines, IA 50319. (515) 987-0899, ext. 212. (www.iowaholocaustmemorial.com)

Kansas

Memorial to the Six Million (JCC of Greater Kansas City). 5801 West 115th Street, Overland Park, KS 66211. (913) 327-8000. (www.kcfountains.com/single-post/2016/11/17/Memorial-to-the-Six-Million)

Louisiana

Alexandria Holocaust Memorial. Corner of Fourth and Elliott Streets, Alexandria, LA 71301. (318) 445-7702. (www.alexandriapinevillela.com/places/alexandria-holocaust-memorial)

New Orleans Holocaust Memorial. Woldenberg Park (at Canal Street, adjacent to the Aquarium of the Americas), New Orleans, LA 70130. (www.holocaustmemorial.us)

Maine

Holocaust and Human Rights Center of Maine (University of Maine at Augusta). Michael Klahr Center, 46 University Drive, Augusta, ME 04330. (207) 621-3530. (www.hhrcmaine.org)

Maryland

Baltimore Holocaust Memorial. Holocaust Memorial Park, (intersection of Lombard and Gay Streets, adjacent to Baltimore City Community College), Baltimore, MD 21202. (410) 542-4850. (www.josephsheppard.com/Holocaust/NewMemorial.htm), (www.josephsheppard.com/Holocaust/AboutMemorial.htm)

Massachusetts

Groton Dunstable Penny Project Memorial (formerly Million Penny Project Memorial) (Groton-Dunstable Regional Middle School). 344-346 Main Street, Groton, MA 01450. (978) 448-6155. (www.facebook.com/pg/The-Groton-Dunstable-Penny-Project-183095678395734/about)

New Bedford Holocaust Memorial. Buttonwood Park, US-6 and Newton Street (Rockdale Avenue and Maple Street), New Bedford, MA 02740. (508) 991-6175. (www.lib.umassd.edu/archives/jewish-tour/holocaust-memorial)

New England Holocaust Memorial. Between Congress and Union Streets, and between North and Hanover Streets (near Faneuil Hall), Boston, MA 02109. (617) 457-8755. (www.nehm.org)

Sugihara Memorial Garden (Temple Emeth). 194 Grove Street, Chestnut Hill, MA 02467. (617) 469-9400. (www.templeemeth.org/AboutUs/SugiharaMemorial/tabid/169/Default.aspx)

Michigan

Holocaust Memorial Center Zekelman Family Campus. 28123 Orchard Lake Road, Farmington Hills, MI 48334. (248) 553-2400. (www.holocaustcenter.org)

Holocaust Memorial (University of Michigan). Central Campus, Raoul Wallenberg Plaza (east side of Rackham Building, Felch Park), Ann Arbor, MI 48109. (734) 615-8765. (www.localwiki.org/ann-arbor/Raoul_Wallenberg_Plaza), (www.arts.umich.edu/museums-cultural-attractions/holocaust-memorial)

Missouri

Holocaust Museum & Learning Center. 12 Millstone Campus Drive, St. Louis, MO 63146 (first floor of Kaplan Feldman Complex, formerly known as the Kopolow Building). (314) 442-3711. (www.hmlc.org)

Nevada

Warsaw Ghetto Remembrance Garden (Temple Beth Sholom). 10700 Havenwood Lane, Las Vegas, NV 89135. (702) 804-1333. (www.bethsholomlv.org/remembrance-garden)

New Hampshire

New Hampshire Holocaust Memorial. Rotary Common Park, 315 Main Street, Nashua, NH 03060. (www.nhpr.org/post/holocaust-memorial-opens-nashua#stream/0)

New Jersey

Esther Raab Holocaust Museum & Goodwin Education Center (Betty & Milton Katz JCC). 1301 Springdale Road, Cherry Hill, NJ 08003. (856) 751-9500, ext. 1249. (www.jcrcsnj.org/goodwin)

Gan Hazikaron, The Avrum and Yocheved Holocaust Memorial Garden (Kaplen JCC on the Palisades). 411 East Clinton Avenue, Tenafly, NJ 07670. (201) 569-7900. (www.tobikahn.com/jcc-new-jersey.html)

Holocaust Memorial. Cooper River Park-Memorial Grove, 203-299 North Park Boulevard, Cherry Hill, NJ 08109. (856) 216-2117. (www.waymarking.com/waymarks/WM4EK6_Holocaust_Memorial_Memorial_Grove_Cherry_Hill_NJ)

Holocaust Remembrance Garden (Brookside Place School). 700 Brookside Place, Cranford, NJ 07016. (908) 709-6244. (www.nj.com/news/local/index.ssf/2009/06/elementary_students_build_gard.html)

Liberation Monument. Liberty State Park, Morris Pesin Drive (South Overlook Field), Jersey City, NJ 07305. (201) 915-3440 or (201) 915-3403. (www.libertystatepark.com/liberation_monument_photos.htm)

New Mexico

Holocaust & Intolerance Museum of New Mexico. 616 Central Avenue SW, Albuquerque, NM 87102. (505) 247-0606. (www.nmholocaustmuseum.org)

Holocaust Memorial. One Civic Plaza NW (3rd Street NW and Tijeras Avenue NW), Albuquerque, NM 87102. (www.waymarking.com/waymarks/WM5JJ6_The_Holocaust_Memorial_Albuquerque_NM)

New York (Outside New York Metropolitan Area)

Goldsworthy Holocaust Memorial Garden of Stones (Cornell University). F. R. Newman Arboretum (at Southeast corner), Cornell Plantations, 1 Plantations Road, Ithaca, NY 14850. (607) 255-2400. (www.iaujc.org/goldsworthy-holocaust-memorial-cornell-plantations)

Holocaust Memorial (Orangetown Jewish Center). 8 Independence Avenue, Orangeburg, NY 10962. (845) 359-5920. (www.theojc.org/shoah-memorial-project.html)

Holocaust Memorial (Temple Beth Tzedek). 1641 North Forest Road, Williamsville,NY14221.(716)838-3232.(www.btzbuffalo.org/history/2009/h-mem-reded/brochure.pdf)

Holocaust Memorial (Temple Israel). 4737 Deerfield Place, Vestal, NY 13850. (607)   723-7461.   (www.facebook.com/pg/TempleIsraelVestal/photos/?tab=album&album_id=112072211417)

Holocaust Museum & Center for Tolerance and Education (formerly Holocaust Museum & Study Center) (Rockland Community College). 145 College Road, Library Media Center, 2nd Floor, Suffern, NY 10901. (845) 574-4099. (www.holocauststudies.org)

Safe Haven Holocaust Refugee Shelter Museum. 2 East 7th Street, Oswego, NY 13126. (315) 342-3003. (www.safehavenmuseum.com)

New York Metropolitan Area

Amud Aish Memorial Museum/Kleinman Holocaust Education Center. 5923 Strickland Avenue, Brooklyn, NY 11234. (718) 759-6200. (www.amudaish.org)

Anne Frank Memorial Garden and Anne Frank Memorial Sculpture. Arboretum Park (Threepence and Wilmington Drives, OFF Bagatelle Road), Melville, NY 11747. (631) 351-3000. (www.huntingtonny.gov/filestorage/13747/99544/25735/47409/Guide_for_Anne_Frank_Memorial_Garden_at_Arboretum_Park.pdf), (www.huntingtonny.gov/Anne-Frank-Memorial-Sculpture)

Center for Social Justice and Human Understanding (formerly Center on the Holocaust, Diversity and Human Understanding) (Suffolk County Community College). Ammerman Campus, Huntington Library 102, 533 College Road, Selden, NY 11784. (631) 451-4117.

Garden of Remembrance. Michaelian Office Building. 148 Martine Avenue, White Plains, NY 10601. (914) 696-0738. (http://parks.westchestergov.com/garden-of-remembrance)

Garden of Remembrance (Brotherhood Synagogue). 28 Gramercy Park South, New York, NY 10003. (212) 674-5750. (www.mapio.net/pic/p-15769549)

Harriet and Kenneth Kupferberg Holocaust Center (formerly Kupferberg Holocaust Resource Center & Archives) (Queensborough Community College). 222-05 56th Avenue, Bayside, NY 11364. (718) 281-5770. (http://khc.qcc.cuny.edu)

Holocaust Memorial & Tolerance Center of Nassau County. Welwyn Preserve, 100 Crescent Beach Road, Glen Cove, NY 11542. (516) 571-8040. (www.hmtcli.org/museum/permanent-exhibit)

Holocaust Memorial Garden (Jericho Jewish Center). 430 North Broadway, Jericho, NY 11753. (516) 938-2540. (www.jerichojc.com/about-us-2/our-history)

Holocaust Memorial Monument. Kennedy Plaza, Park Avenue (between Center Street and National Boulevard), Long Beach, NY 11561. (516) 431-1000. (www.axishistory.com/various/50-museums/museums-memorials/791-holocaust-memorials-long-beach-new-york-usa)

Holocaust Memorial Park. West End Avenue between Emmons Avenue and Shore Boulevard, Brooklyn, NY 11235. (646) 801-0739. (www.thmc.org)

Holocaust Memorial (Park Avenue Synagogue). 50 East 87th Street, New York, NY 10128. (212) 369-2600. (www.waymarking.com/waymarks/ WMA8Y4_Holocaust_Memorial_Park_Avenue_Synagogue_New_York_ City_NY)

The Holocaust Museum & Study Center of the Bronx High School of Science (Stuart S. Elenko Collection). 75 West 205th Street, Bronx, NY 10468. (718) 817-7700. (www.bxscience.edu/apps/news/show_news.jsp?REC_ID= 270392&id=1)

Holocaust Resource Center (Temple Judea of Manhasset). 333 Searingtown Road, Manhasset, NY 11030. (516) 621-8049. (www.temple-judea.com/ holocaust-center)

"Hope" Raoul Wallenberg Memorial. Corner of First Avenue and 47th Street, New York, NY 10017. (212) 737-3275. (www.waymarking.com/waymarks/ WMCWR1_Raoul_Wallenberg_Memorial_New_York_NY)

Memorial to All Victims of the Holocaust (also known as Memorial to Victims of the Injustice of the Holocaust). Appellate Division Courthouse of New York State, 27 Madison Avenue, New York, NY 10010. (212) 340-0400. (www.waymarking.com/way-marks/WMGCPM_Memorial_To_All_Victims_Of_The_Holocaust_New_York_NY)

Monument of the Holocaust (Hebrew Union College-Jewish Institute of Religion). Dr. Bernard Heller Museum (in the Petrie Great Hall), The Brookdale Center, One West 4th Street, New York, NY 10012. (212) 824-2218. (www.samgru-bersjewishartmonuments.blogspot.com/2008/10/exhibitopn-arbit-blatas-in-new-york.html)

Museum of Jewish Heritage-A Living Memorial to the Holocaust. Edmond J. Safra Plaza, 36 Battery Place, New York, NY 10280. (646) 437-4202. (www.mjhnyc.org)

Warsaw Ghetto Memorial. Riverside Park, Warsaw Ghetto Memorial Plaza, South end of the Promenade at 83rd Street, New York, NY 10115. (212) 870-3070. (www.riversideparknyc.org/places/warsaw-ghetto-memorial)

North Carolina

Holocaust Memorial. Marshall Park (next to sidewalk facing South McDowell Street near the intersection with East Martin Luther King Jr. Boulevard), 800 East 3rd Street, Charlotte, NC 28202. (704) 432-4280. (www.docsouth.unc.edu/com-mland/monument/882)

Margaret & Lou Schwartz Butterfly Garden/Children's Holocaust Memorial Sculpture (Jewish Federation of Greater Charlotte). Shalom Park, 5007 Providence Road, Suite 102, Charlotte, NC 28226. (704) 366-5007. (www.shalomcharlotte. com/butterfly-memorial)

Ohio

Holocaust Memorial (JCC of Youngstown). 505 Gypsy Lane, Youngstown, OH 44504. (330) 746-3251. (www.ochge.org/neo-memorials/holocaust-memorial-on-the-grounds-of-the-jewish-community-center-in-youngstown)

Holocaust Memorial Statue: To Life. Ohio Governor's Residence and Heritage Garden, 358 North Parkview Avenue, Columbus, OH 43209. (614) 644-7644. (https://en.wikipedia.org/wiki/Ohio_Governor%27s_Mansion#Exterior)

Memorial to the Six Million Martyrs of the Nazi Holocaust "Last Embrace" (JCC of Youngstown). 505 Gypsy Lane, Youngstown, OH 44504. (330) 746-3251.(www.ochge.org/neo-memorials/memorial-to-the-six-million-martyrs-of-the-nazi-holocaust)

The Nancy & David Wolf Holocaust & Humanity Center Museum (formerly Holocaust and Humanity Center). 1301 Western Avenue (Union Terminal), Suite 2101, Cincinnati, OH 45203. (513) 487-3055. (www.holocaustandhumanity.org)

The Ohio Holocaust & Liberators Memorial. Ohio State House-South Plaza, 1 Capitol Square, Columbus, OH 43215. (614) 752-9777 or (888) 644-6123 or (513) 487-3055. (www.ohioholocaustmemorial.org)

Toledo Holocaust Memorial "For This the Earth Mourns"/Toledo Holocaust Memorial Park (Jewish Federation of Greater Toledo). 6465 Sylvania Avenue, Sylvania, OH 43560. (419) 885-4461. (www.ochge.org/nwo-memorials/toledo-holocaust-memorial)

Oregon
Oregon Holocaust Memorial. Washington Park, Southwest Washington Way and Wright Avenue, Portland, OR 97205. (www.portlandoregon.gov/parks/finder/index.cfm?action=ViewPark&PropertyID=1330)

Oregon Jewish Museum and Center for Holocaust Education (1989). 724 Northwest Davis Street, Portland, OR 97209. (503) 226-3600. The Pacific Northwest's only Jewish museum and largest collection of the documented and visual history of Oregon's Jews, examining the history of the Jewish experience in Oregon from 1850 to the present, and a history of the Holocaust that employs the stories of Oregon survivors, and an exhibit on discrimination as a tool used to affect varied groups of people over the history of the region. (www.ojmche.org)

Pennsylvania
Gary and Nancy Tuckfelt Keeping Tabs: A Holocaust Sculpture (Community Day School). 6424 Forward Avenue, Pittsburgh, PA 15217. (412) 521-1100. (www.com-day.org/give/keepingtabs)

Holocaust Awareness Museum and Education Center (Kleinlife). 10100 Jamison Avenue, Suite 210, Philadelphia, PA 19116. (215) 464-4701. (www.hamec.org)

Holocaust Center of Pittsburgh. 826 Hazelwood Avenue, Pittsburgh, PA 15217. (412) 421-1500. (www.hcofpgh.org)

Holocaust Memorial for the Commonwealth of Pennsylvania. Riverfront Park, Front and Sayford Streets, Harrisburg, PA 17101. (717) 236-9555. (www.jewishharrisburg.org/community-directory/harrisburg-holocaust-monument)

Holocaust Memorial Sculpture "The Six Million" (York JCC). 2000 Hollywood Drive, York, PA 17403. (717) 843-0918. (www.yorkjcc.org/jewish-life/holocaust-memorial)

Holocaust Memorial (Temple Covenant of Peace). 1451 Northampton Street, Easton, PA 18042. (610) 253-2031. (www.tcopeace.org/history.html)

Horwitz-Wasserman Holocaust Memorial Plaza. 16th Street and Ben Franklin Parkway, Philadelphia, PA 19103. (215) 809-2474. (www.philaholocaustmemorial.org)

Monument to the Six Million Jewish Martyrs. (Incorporated into new Horwitz-Wasserman Holocaust Memorial Plaza in 2018)

Puerto Rico

Holocaust Memorial Monument (JCC of Puerto Rico/Shaare Zedeck Synagogue). 903 Ponce de Leon Avenue, San Juan, PR 00907. (787) 724-4157. (www.jccpr.org/holocaust-monument.html)

Rhode Island

Rhode Island Holocaust Memorial. Memorial Park on South Main Street, Providence River Greenway (Providence River Walk), Providence, RI 02903. (401) 453-7860 or (401) 421-4111. (www.jewishallianceri.org/rhode-island-holocaust-memorial), (www.riholocaustmemorial.org/yadvashem)

Sandra Bornstein Holocaust Education Center Memorial Garden. 401 Elmgrove Avenue, Providence, RI 02906. (401) 453-7860. (www.bornsteinholocaustcenter.org/memorial-garden)

South Carolina

Charleston Holocaust Memorial. Marion Square, Calhoun and Meeting Streets, Charleston, SC 29402. (843) 953-3918. (www.waymarking.com/waymarks/WM4HN4_Charleston_Holocaust_Memorial_Charleston_South_Carolina)

Columbia Holocaust Memorial Monument. Memorial Park, Hampton and Gadsden Streets, Columbia, SC 29201. (803) 787-2023. (www.columbiaholocaust-education.org/memorial.php)

Holocaust Memorial (Beth Israel Congregation). 316 Park Avenue, Florence, SC 29501. (843) 669-9724. (www.bethisraelflorence.org/shoah)

Tennessee

Belz Museum of Asian & Judaic Art-Holocaust Memorial Gallery (formerly Peabody Place Museum) (2014). 119 South Main Street, Concourse Level, Memphis, TN 38103. (901) 523-2787. (www.belzmuseum.org/galleries/#images-preview2-1)

The Children's Holocaust Memorial/Paper Clip Project (Whitwell Middle School). 1 Butterfly Lane, Whitwell, TN 37397. (423) 658-5635. (www.whitwellmiddleschool.org/?PageName=bc&n=69259), (www.tennesseeholocaustmemorials.yolasite.com)

Holocaust Memorial. State Capitol grounds, Charlotte Avenue and 6th Avenue North, Nashville, TN 37219. (615) 343-2563. (www.tnholcom.org/about.php)

Holocaust Memorial. West Hills/John Bynon Park, 7624 Sheffield Drive, Knoxville, TN 37909. (865) 300-7406. (www.mongoose-and.tumblr.com/post/152170787410/holocaust-memorial-west-hills-park-knoxville-tn?is_related_post=1)

Nashville Holocaust Memorial (Gordon JCC). 801 Percy Warner Boulevard, Nashville, TN 37205. (615) 356-7170. (www.nashvilleholocaustmemorial.org)

Texas

Dallas Holocaust and Human Rights Museum (formerly Dallas Holocaust Museum/Center for Education and Tolerance). 300 North Houston Street, Suite 100, Dallas, TX 75202. (214) 741-7500. (www.dhhrm.org)

East Texas Holocaust Memorial "Triumph over Tragedy" (Congregation Beth El). 1010 Charleston Drive, Tyler, TX 75703. (903) 581-3764. (www.si.edu/object/ siris_ari_315367)

El Paso Holocaust Museum and Study Center. 715 North Oregon Street, El Paso, TX 79902. (915) 351-0048. (www.elpasoholocaustmuseum.org)

Holocaust Memorial Museum of San Antonio (Jewish Federation of San Antonio). 12500 Northwest Military Highway, San Antonio, TX 78231. (210) 302-6807. (www.hmmsa.org)

Holocaust Museum Houston. Lester and Sue Smith Campus, 5401 Caroline Street, Houston, TX 77004. (713) 942-8000. (www.hmh.org)

Utah

Price Family Holocaust Memorial (IJ & Jeanné Wagner JCC). 2 North Medical Drive, Salt Lake City, UT 84113. (801) 581-0098. (www.slcjcc.org/ price-family-holocaust-memorial)

Vermont

Holocaust Monument and The Lost Shul Mural (Ohavi Zedek Synagogue). 188 North Prospect Street, Burlington, VT 05401. (802) 864-0218. (www.samgruber-sjewishartmonuments.blogspot.com/2013/12/usa-ohavi-zedek-synagogue-in-burl-ington.html);   (www.lostshulmural.org/about-the-mural/ mural-as-a-holocaust-memorial)

Vermont Holocaust Memorial. PO Box 436, Jeffersonville, VT 05464. (www. holocaustmemorial-vt.org)

Virginia

Virginia Holocaust Museum. 2000 East Cary Street, Richmond, VA 23223. (804) 257-5400. (www.vaholocaust.com)

Washington

The Henry and Sandra Friedman Holocaust Center for Humanity. 2045 2nd Avenue, Seattle, WA 98121. (206) 582-3000. (www.holocaustcenterseattle.org)

Holocaust Memorial (Samuel and Althea Stroum JCC of Greater Seattle). Mercer Island Campus, 3801 East Mercer Way, Mercer Island, WA 98040. (206) 232-7115. (www.alamy.com/stock-photo-holocaust-memorial-monument-at-stroum-jewish-community-center-of-greater-56185171.html)

Holocaust Memorial (Temple Beth Shalom). 1322 East 30th Avenue, Spokane, WA   99203.   (509)   747-3304.   (www.simonkogan.com/collection/ HolocaustMemorial.htm)

Replica of Rhodes Holocaust Memorial (Congregation Ezra Bessaroth). 5217 South Brandon Street, Seattle, WA 98118. (206) 722-5500. (www.rhodesjewishmu-seum.org/rhodesli-diaspora-news/seattle),   (www.ezrabessaroth.net/about-us/ history)

West Virginia

Holocaust Memorial (B'nai Sholom Congregation). 949 Tenth Avenue, Huntington, WV 25701. (304) 522-2980. (www.wv-bnaisholom.org/our-memorial.html)

Wisconsin

Holocaust Memorial. Marshall Park, 2101 Allen Boulevard, Middleton, WI 53562. (608) 266-4711. (www.cityofmadison.com/parks/find-a-park/history.cfm?id=1264

Holocaust Memorial (Jewish Museum Milwaukee, Milwaukee Jewish Federation). Helfaer Community Service Building, 1360 North Prospect Avenue, Milwaukee, WI 53202. (414) 390-5730. (www.bluffton.edu/homepages/facstaff/sullivanm/wisconsin/milwaukee/lieberman/holocaust.html)

10.2.3 Holocaust Museums, Memorials, and Monuments, Canada

Alberta

Holocaust Memorial. 10800 97th Avenue (southeast corner of the grounds of the Edmonton Legislature), Edmonton, AB T5K 2B6. (780) 427-7362. (www. susanowenkagan.com/2015/01/27/commissions-select-projects/1-edmonton-holocaust-memorial)

Holocaust Memorial (Calgary Jewish Community Centre). 1607 90th Avenue SW, Calgary, AB T2V 4V7. (403) 253-8600. (www.waymarking.com/waymarks/WMBZCT_Calgary_JCC_Holocaust_Memorial_Calgary Alberta)

British Columbia

Vancouver Holocaust Education Centre. 950 West 41st Avenue, Suite 50, Vancouver, BC V5Z 2N7. (604) 264-0499. (www.vhec.org)

Manitoba

Freeman Family Foundation Holocaust Education Centre of the Jewish Heritage Centre of Western Canada (Asper Jewish Community Campus). 123 Doncaster Street, Suite C140, Winnipeg, MB R3N 2B2. (204) 477-7460. (www.fffholocaust-educationcentre.org)

Holocaust Memorial. Manitoba Legislative Building (southwest grounds), Osborne Street North and Assiniboine Avenue, Winnipeg, MB R3C 1S4. (www. mhs.mb.ca/docs/sites/holocaust.shtml)

New Brunswick

New Brunswick Internment Camp Museum. 420 Pleasant Drive, Unit 1, Minto, NB E4B 2T3. (506) 327-3573. (www.nbinternmentcampmuseum.ca)

Nova Scotia

The Wheel of Conscience. Canadian Museum of Immigration at Pier 21, 1055 Marginal Road, Halifax NS B3H 4P7. (902) 425-7770 or (855) 526-4721. (www. libeskind.com/work/the-wheel-of-conscience)

Ontario

Canadian Society for Yad Vashem Holocaust Memorial Site at Earl Bales Park/ Holocaust Memorial Flame and Wall of Remembrance. 4169 Bathurst Street, NorthYork,ONM3H3P7.(416)785-1333.(www.yadvashem.ca/wall-of-remembrance-at-earl-bales-park-toronto)

Maxwell and Ruth Leroy Holocaust Remembrance Garden (UJA Federation of Greater Toronto). Joseph & Wolf Lebovic Jewish Community Campus, Reena Community Residence (west side of residence, on Ilan Ramon Boulevard), 927 Clark Avenue West, Thornhill, ON L4J 8G6. (905) 889-6484. (www.reena.org/about/reena-community-residence)

National Holocaust Monument. LeBreton Flats, at the corner of Booth Street and the Sir John A. MacDonald Parkway, west of Parliament Hill, across from the Canadian War Museum, Ottawa, ON K1R. (416) 636-5225. (www.holocaustmonument.ca)

Sarah and Chaim Neuberger Holocaust Education Centre (UJA Federation of Greater Toronto). Sherman Campus, 4600 Bathurst Street, 4th Floor, Toronto, ON M2R 3V2. (416) 635-2883, ext. 5627 or (416) 631-5689. (www.holocaustcentre. com/about/visit)

Quebec

Holocaust Memorial. Arthur Zygielbaum Park, Edgemore Avenue and Wavell Road, Cote-Saint-Luc, QC. (514) 485-6800. (www.museumoffamilyhistory.com/hmc-02.htm)

Montreal Holocaust Museum. 5151 Chemin de la Cote-Sainte-Catherine (Cummings House), Montreal, QC H3W 1M6. (514) 345-2605. (www.museeholocauste.ca/en)

10.2.4   Online/Virtual Holocaust Museums, United States

A Cybrary of the Holocaust (Remember.org: A People's History of the Holocaust and Genocide). (www.remember.org)

Museum of Family History. (www.museumoffamilyhistory.com)

University of Minnesota Center for Holocaust and Genocide Studies. 214 Social Sciences Building, 267 19th Avenue S, Minneapolis, MN 55455. (612) 626-2617. (www.cla.umn.edu/chgs/collections-exhibitions)

10.2.5   Online/Virtual Holocaust Museums, Canada

The Madeleine and Monte Levy Virtual Museum of the Holocaust and the Resistance. 1250 Main Street West, Hamilton, ON L8S 4L8. (905) 525-9140 (http:// library.mcmaster.ca/archives/virtualmuseum)

10.2.6   Other Holocaust Resources Websites

For information on other Holocaust resources, see:

www.ahoinfo.org
www.avotaynuonline.com/2016/01/holocaust-memorial-project
www.jewish-american-society-for-historic-preservation.org/americanholocaust-
    mem.html
www.remember-us.org/pdfs/holocaust-centers.pdf

Chapter 11
Jewish Overnight Camps

Ira M. Sheskin, Arnold Dashefsky, and Sarah Markowitz

This chapter provides lists with contact information (name, address, phone number, website) for about 210 Jewish overnight camps.

The purpose of this chapter is to document the institutional infrastructure of the North American Jewish community and to preserve this information for historical purposes. We expect that historians 100 years from now will look back at the Year Book in researching the history of North American Jewry. In a sense, we are "freezing" the information in time. The information on the Internet, of course, changes as frequently as the webmasters update that information, meaning that without this freezing, historians in the future will not have a record of the infrastructure of the community.

The list is carefully updated each year, but the authors appreciate any corrections noted by our readers. We have found that the lists we can find for Jewish institutions on the Internet are far from totally accurate.

I. M. Sheskin (✉)
Department of Geography and Jewish Demography Project, Sue and Leonard Miller Center for Contemporary Judaic Studies, University of Miami, Coral Gables, FL, USA
e-mail: isheskin@miami.edu

A. Dashefsky
Department of Sociology and Center for Judaic Studies and Contemporary Jewish Life, University of Connecticut, Storrs, CT, USA

S. Markowitz
Independent Researcher, Forest Hills, NY, USA

© Springer Nature Switzerland AG 2020
A. Dashefsky, I. M. Sheskin (eds.), *American Jewish Year Book 2019*, American Jewish Year Book 119, https://doi.org/10.1007/978-3-030-40371-3_11

11.1 Central Coordinating Body for Jewish Overnight Camps

Foundation for Jewish Camp (formerly **Foundation for Jewish Camping**). For contact information and a description, see the Jewish Youth Groups and Youth-Related Organizations section of Chap. 12.

Note: In addition to a year-round office telephone number, some overnight camps have a summer telephone number (S).

11.2 Jewish Overnight Camps, United States

Arizona

Camp Daisy and Harry Stein (Congregation Beth Israel). 3400 Camp Pearlstein Road, Prescott, AZ 86303. (928) 778-0091 (S); (480) 951-0323. (www.camp-stein.org)

Camp Nageela West (National Nageela, Community Kollel of Greater Las Vegas). 3511 Verde Valley School Road, Sedona, AZ 86351. (801) 613-1539. (www.nageelawest.org)

California

Camp Alonim (American Jewish University). 1101 Peppertree Lane, Simi Valley, CA 93064. (877) 225-6646. (www.alonim.com)

Camp Be'chol Lashon (Institute for Jewish and Community Research). 1700 Marshall Petaluma Road, Petaluma, CA 94952. (415) 386-2604. (www.bechol-lashon.org)

Camp Bob Waldorf on Max Straus Campus (Jewish Big Brothers Big Sisters of Los Angeles). 1041 Shirlyjean Street, Glendale, CA 91208. (818) 957-4900 (S); (323) 761-8675. (www.campbobwaldorf.org)

Camp Hess Kramer (Wilshire Boulevard Temple). CSU Channel Islands, 1 University Drive, Camarillo, CA 93012. (424) 230-8944 (S); (213) 835-2196. (www.wbtcamps.org)

Camp JCA Shalom (JCC Camp, Shalom Institute). 8955 Gold Creek Road, Sylmar, CA 91342. (818) 889-5500. (www.campjcashalom.com)

Camp Mountain Chai (JCC Camp). 42900 Jenks Lake Road, Angelus Oaks, CA 92305. (858) 499-1330. (www.campmountainchai.com)

Camp Ramah in California (National Ramah Commission). 385 Fairview Road, Ojai, CA 93023. (310) 476-8571. (www.ramah.org)

Camp Ramah in Northern California (National Ramah Commission). Monterey Bay Academy, 783 San Andreas Road, Watsonville, CA 95076. (415) 688-4572. (www.ramahnorcal.org)

Camp Tawonga (JCC Camp). 31201 Mather Road, Groveland, CA 95321. (415) 543-2267. (www.tawonga.org)

Gan Yisroel West (Chabad - Gan Israel). 56887 Shinn Cabin Lane, North Fork, CA 93643. (310) 910-1770. (www.ganyisroelwest.com)

Gindling Hilltop Camp (Wilshire Boulevard Temple). CSU Channel Islands, 1 University Drive, Camarillo, CA 93012. (424) 230-8944 (S); (213) 835-2196. (www.wbtcamps.org)

Habonim Dror Camp Gilboa (Habonim Dror North America). 38200 Bluff Lake Road, Big Bear, CA 92315. (909) 866-1407 (S); (323) 653-6772. (www.camp-gilboa.org)

JCC Maccabi Sports Camp (JCC Camp). 1000 El Camino Real, Atherton, CA 94027. (415) 997-8844. (www.maccabisportscamp.org)

Moshava Alevy (Bnei Akiva). 3500 Seymour Road, Running Springs, CA 92382. (855) 667-4282. (www.moshavamalibu.org)

URJ 6 Points Sports Academy (Union for Reform Judaism). Occidental College, 1600 Campus Road, Los Angeles, CA 90041. (310) 912-7335. (www.6pointsacademy.org)

URJ Camp Newman (Union for Reform Judaism). Cal Maritime, 200 Maritime Academy Drive, Vallejo, CA 94590. (707) 571-7657 (S); (415) 392-7080. (www.campnewman.org)

Yeshivas Kayitz Los Angeles (Yeshiva Ohr Elchonon Chabad). 7215 Waring Avenue, Los Angeles, CA 90046. (323) 927-3763. (www.yoec.edu/?page_id=812)

Colorado

Camp Bais Yaakov of the Rockies. 5100 West 14th Avenue, Denver, CO 80204. (303) 893-1333. (www.bjhs.org/information/camp-bais-yaakov-of-the-rockies)

Camp Meromim. c/o Yeshiva Toras Chaim, Box 40067 1555 Stuart Street, Denver, CO 80204. (877) 637-6646 (S); (720) 881-2755. (www.campmeromim.com)

JCC Ranch Camp (Robert E. Loup JCC). 21441 North Elbert Road, Elbert, CO 80106. (303) 648-3800 (S); (303) 316-6384. (www.ranchcamp.org)

Maurice B. Shwayder Camp (Temple Emanuel). PO Box 3899, Idaho Springs, CO 80452. (303) 567-2722 (S); (303) 388-4013. (www.shwayder.com)

Ramah in the Rockies (National Ramah Commission). 26601 Stoney Pass Road, Sedalia, CO 80135. (303) 261-8214. (www.ramahoutdoors.org)

Connecticut

Camp Chomeish of New England (Chabad). PO Box 248, 11 Johnsonville Road, Moodus, CT 06469. (203) 816-0770. (www.campchomeish.com)

Camp Laurelwood. 463 Summer Hill Road, Madison, CT 06443. (203) 421-3736. (www.camplaurelwood.org)

Ramah Sports Academy. 1073 North Benson Road, Fairfield, CT 06824. (855) 577-7678. (www.ramahsportsacademy.org)

District of Columbia

BBYO on Campus/BBYO Impact Programs (BBYO). (Summer locations at universities change periodically). 800 Eighth Street NW, Washington, DC 20001. (202) 857-6633. (www.bbyo.org/summer)

(https://issuu.com/bbyosummer/docs/bbyo_fy19_summer_brochure_final_for?e=
31700308/65376743)

Florida

Camp Gan Israel Florida (Chabad - Gan Israel). 7495 Park Lane Road, Lake Worth,
FL 33449. (954) 675-6952 (S); (954) 796-7330. (www.cgiflorida.com)

Camp Shalom of Central Florida. 168 Camp Shalom Trail, Orange Springs, FL
32182. (352) 546-2223 (S); (786) 344-3726. (www.campshalom.net)

Georgia

Camp Barney Medintz (Marcus JCC of Atlanta). 4165 Highway 129 North,
Cleveland, GA 30528. (706) 865-2715 (S); (678) 812-3844. (www.campbarney.org)

Camp Ramah Darom (National Ramah Commission). 70 Darom Lane, Clayton,
GA 30525. (706) 782-9300 (S); (404) 531-0801. (www.ramahdarom.org)

URJ Camp Coleman (Union for Reform Judaism). 201 Camp Coleman Drive,
Cleveland, GA 30528. (706) 865-4111 (S); (770) 671-8971. (www.coleman.urj-
camps.org)

Illinois

Camp Ben Frankel (Jewish Federation of Southern Illinois, Southeast Missouri, and
Western Kentucky). SIU Touch of Nature, 1206 Touch of Nature Road, Makanda,
IL 62958. (618) 453-1121 (S); (618) 235-1614. (www.campbenfrankel.org)

Camp Henry Horner (Jewish Council for Youth Services). 26710 West Nippersink
Road, Ingleside, IL 60041. (847) 740-5010 (S); 312-726-8891. (www.jcys.org/
camp-henry-horner)

Camp Nageela Midwest (National Nageela). 26710 West Nipperskink Road,
Ingleside, IL 60041. (773) 604-4400. (www.campnageelamidwest.org)

Camp Red Leaf (Jewish Council for Youth Services). 26710 West Nippersink
Road, Ingleside, IL 60041. (847) 740-5010 (S); (312) 726-8891. (www.jcys.org/
camp-red-leaf)

Yeshivas HaKayitz (Chicago) (Hebrew Theological College). 7135 North
Carpenter Road, Skokie, IL 60077. (847) 982-2500. (www.htc.edu/yeshivas-hakay-
itz-summer-camp.html)

Indiana

Camp Bnos Ma'arava (Agudath Israel). 4215 East Landry Lane, Marshall, IN
47859. (765) 597-2272 (S); (847) 696-6800. (www.aicamps.com)

Camp Livingston (JCC Camp). 4998 Nell Lee Road, Bennington, IN 47011.
(812) 427-2202 (S); (513) 793-5554. (www.camplivingston.com)

Spark for Teens (Agudath Israel). 4215 East Landry Lane, Marshall, IN 47859.
(765) 597-2272 (S); (773) 279-8400. (www.aicamps.com)

URJ Goldman Union Camp Institute (GUCI) (Union for Reform Judaism). 9349
Moore Road, Zionsville, IN 46077. (317) 873-3361. (www.guci.urjcamps.org)

Iowa

Yeshivas Kayitz at Mesivta of Postville (Chabad). 331 West Tilden Street, Postville,
IA 52162. (563) 864-3893. (www.mesivtapostville.org/yk.html)

Maine

Camp Micah. 156 Moose Cove Lodge Road, Bridgton, ME 04009. (207) 647-8999 (S); (617) 244-6540. (www.campmicah.com)

Camp Modin. 51 Modin Way, Belgrade, ME 04917. (207) 465-4444 (S); (212) 570-1600. (www.modin.com)

JCC Camp Kingswood (JCCs of Greater Boston). 104 Wildwood Road, Bridgton, ME 04009. (207) 647-3969 (S); (617) 558-6531. (www.kingswood.org)

Maryland

Camp Airy (The Camp Airy and Camp Louise Foundation, Inc.). 14938 Old Camp Airy Road, Thurmont, MD 21788. (410) 466-9010. (www.airylouise.org)

Camp Louise (The Camp Airy and Camp Louise Foundation, Inc.). 24959 Pen Mar Road, Cascade, MD 21719. (410) 466-9010. (www.airylouise.org)

Habonim Dror Camp Moshava (Habonim Dror North America). 615 Cherry Hill Road, Street, MD 21154. (410) 893-7079 (S); (301) 348-7339. (www.camp-mosh.org)

NCSY Camp Sports (NCSY). c/o Ner Israel Rabbinical College, 400 Mount Wilson Lane, Baltimore, MD 21208. (212) 613-8349 (S); (212) 613-8349. (https://campsports.ncsy.org)

Massachusetts

BIMA at Brandeis University (Brandeis University). 415 South Street MS 065, Waltham, MA 02454. (781) 736-8416. (www.brandeis.edu/highschool/bima)

Camp Avoda. 23 Gibbs Road, Middleboro, MA 02346. (508) 947-3800 (S); (781) 433-0131. (www.campavoda.org)

Camp Bauercrest. 17 Old Country Road, Amesbury, MA 01913. (978) 388-4732. (www.bauercrest.org)

Camp Kinderland (Friends of Camp Kinderland). 1543 Colebrook River Road, Tolland, MA 01034. (413) 258-4463 (S); (718) 643-0771. (www.campkinder-land.org)

Camp Pembroke (The Cohen Camps). 306 Oldham Street, Pembroke, MA 02359. (781) 294-8006 (S); (781) 489-2070. (www.camppembroke.org)

Camp Ramah in New England (National Ramah Commission). 39 Bennett Street, Palmer, MA 01069. (413) 283-9771 (S); (781) 702-5290. (www.campra-mahne.org)

Genesis at Brandeis University (Brandeis University). 415 South Street MS 065, Waltham, MA 02454. (781) 736-8416. (www.brandeis.edu/highschool/genesis)

URJ 6 Points Sci-Tech Academy (Union for Reform Judaism). The Governor's Academy, 1 Elm Street, Byfield, MA 01922. (857) 246-8677. (www.6pointsscitech.org/east)

URJ Crane Lake Camp (Union for Reform Judaism). 46 State Line Road, West Stockbridge, MA 01266. (413) 232-4257 (S); (201) 722-0400. (www.cranelake.urj-camps.org)

URJ Joseph Eisner Camp (Union for Reform Judaism). 53 Brookside Road, Great Barrington, MA 01230. (413) 528-1652 (S); (201) 722-0400. (www.eisner.urjcamps.org)

Michigan

Camp Agudah Midwest (Agudath Israel). 68299 CR 388 Phoenix Road, South Haven, MI 49090. (269) 637-4048 (S); (847) 696-6800. (www.aicamps.com)

Camp Gan Yisroel-Detroit (Chabad - Gan Israel). 1450 Lake Valley Road Northeast, Kalkaska, MI 49646. (231) 258-5781 (S); (248) 599-2703. (www.cgidetroit.com)

Habonim Dror Camp Tavor (Habonim Dror North America). 59884 Arthur L. Jones Road, Three Rivers, MI 49093. (269) 215-1399. (www.camptavor.org)

Tamarack Camps - Camp Maas (JCC Camp, Fresh Air Society). 4361 Perryville Road, Ortonville, MI 48462. (248) 627-2821 (S); (248) 647-1100. (www.tamarackcamps.com)

Minnesota

Camp Teko (Temple Israel). 645 Tonkawa Road, Long Lake, MN 55356. (952) 471-8216 (S); (612) 374-0321. (www.templeisrael.com/camp-teko)

Yeshivas Kayitz Minnesota (Chabad). (Ceased operation)

Mississippi

URJ Henry S. Jacobs Camp (Union for Reform Judaism). 3863 Morrison Road, Utica, MS 39175. (601) 885-6042. (www.jacobs.urjcamps.org)

Missouri

Camp Sabra (St. Louis JCC). 30750 Camp Sabra Road, Rocky Mount, MO 65072. (314) 442-3290 (S); (314) 442-3151. (www.campsabra.com)

New Hampshire

Camp Tel Noar (The Cohen Camps). 167 Main Street, Hampstead, NH 03841. (603) 329-6931 (S); (781) 489-2070. (www.camptelnoar.org)

Camp Tevya (The Cohen Camps). 1 Mason Road, Brookline, NH 03033. (603) 673-4010 (S); (781) 489-2070. (www.camptevya.org)

Camp Yavneh (Hebrew College). 18 Lucas Pond Road, Northwood, NH 03261. (603) 942-5593. (www.campyavneh.org)

Camp Young Judaea (Friends of Young Judaea). 9 Camp Road, Amherst, NH 03031. (603) 673-3710 (S); (781) 237-9410. (www.cyj.org)

New Jersey

Camp Louemma. 43 Louemma Lane, Sussex, NJ 07461. (973) 875-4403 (S); (973) 287-7264. (www.camplouemma.com)

Yeshivas Kayitz Lamasmidim/Yeshiva Summer Program (Chabad). 226 Sussex Avenue, Morristown, NJ 07960. (973) 998-5348 (S); (973) 267-9404. (www.yspmorristown.com)

New York

Berkshire Hills Eisenberg Camp (UJA-Federation of New York). 159 Empire Road, Copake, NY 12516. (518) 329-3303 (S); (914) 693-8952. (www.bhecamp.org)

Camp Achim. 60 Pleasant Acres Road, Catskill, NY 12414. (845) 357-4740. (www.campachim.com)

Camp Agudah/Machane Ephraim (Agudath Israel). 140 Upper Ferndale Road, Liberty, NY 12754. (845) 292-1100 (S); (212) 797-8172. (www.campagudah.net)

Camp Bnos (Agudath Israel). 344 Ferndale Loomis Road, Liberty, NY 12754. (845) 292-2110 (S); (212) 797-8172. (www.campagudah.net/officialinfo.html)

Camp Bnoseinu (Agudath Israel). 316 Ferndale Loomis Road, Liberty, NY 12754. (845) 292-1700 (S); (212) 797-8172. (www.Campagudah.net)

Camp B'Yachad (Edith & Carl Marks JCH of Bensonhurst). (718) 943-6345. (www.jchb.org/camp-b-yachad)

Camp Chayl Miriam (Agudath Israel). 304 Ferndale Loomis Road, Liberty, NY 12754. (845) 292-1700 (S); (212) 797-8172. (www.Campagudah.net)

Camp Emunah/Bnos Yaakov Yehudah (Chabad). 6660 Route 52 Greenfield Park, Greenfield Park, NY 12435. (845) 647-8742 (S); (718) 735-0225. (www.campe-munah.org)

Camp Gan Israel (Chabad - Gan Israel). 487 Parksville Road, Parksville, NY 12768. (718) 774-4805. (www.campganisrael.com)

Camp HASC (Hebrew Academy for Special Children). 361 Parksville Road, Parksville, NY 12768. (845) 292-6821 (S); (718) 686-2600. (www.camphasc.org)

Camp Kaylie. 400 Mount Vernon Road, Wurtsboro, NY 12790. (845) 888-5008 (S); (718) 686-3261. (www.campkaylie.org)

Camp Kinder Ring (Workmen's Circle/Arbeter Ring). 335 Sylvan Lake Road, Hopewell Junction, NY 12533. (845) 221-2771, ext. 107. (www.campkr.com)

Camp L'man Achai (Chabad). 1590 Perch Lake Road, Andes, NY 13731. (845) 676-3996 (S); (718) 436-8255. (www.camplmanachai.com)

Camp Mesorah. 325 North Pond Road, Guilford, NY 13780. (845) 362-7778. (www.campmesorah.com)

Camp Migdal. 96 Camp Utopia Road, Narrowsburg, NY 12764. (718) 313-0264. (www.campmigdal.org)

Camp Mogen Avraham (Shma Camps). 169 Laymon Road, Swan Lake, NY 12783. (516) 992-6131. (www.shmacamps.org)

Camp Monroe. (Ceased operation as of 2018)

Camp Nageela East (Jewish Education Program of Long Island). 5755 State Route 42, Fallsburg, NY 12733. (516) 374-1528. (www.campnageela.org)

Camp Ramah in the Berkshires (National Ramah Commission). PO Box 515, Wingdale, NY 12594. (845) 832-6622. (www.ramahberkshires.org)

Camp Romimu. 150 Roosevelt Road, Monticello, NY 12701. (845) 794-7400 (S); (718) 327-3000. (www.romimu.com)

Camp Seneca Lake (JCC of Greater Rochester). 200 Camp Road, Penn Yan, NY 14527. (315) 536-9981 (S); (585) 461-2000. (www.campsenecalake.com)

Camp Shomria (Hashomer Hatzair). 52 Lake Marie Road, Liberty, NY 12754. (845) 292-6241 (S); (212) 627-2830. (www.campshomria.com)

Camp Simcha/Camp Simcha Special (Chai Lifeline). 430 White Road, Glen Spey, NY 12737. (845) 856-1432 (S); (212) 699-6661. (www.campsimcha.org)

Camp Sternberg (Shma Camps). 97 Camp Utopia Road, Narrowsburg, NY 12764. (516) 992-6131. (www.shmacamps.org)

Camp Tel Yehudah (Young Judaea). PO Box 69, Barryville, NY 12719. (845) 557-8311 (S); (800) 970-2267. (www.campty.com)

Camp Young Judaea Sprout Lake (Young Judaea). 6 Sprout Lake Camp, Route 82, Verbank, NY 12585. (845) 677-3411 (S); (917) 595-1500. (www.cyjsprout-lake.org)

Dr. Beth Samuels High School Program (Drisha Institute for Jewish Education). 1501 Broadway, Suite 505A, New York, NY 10036. (212) 595-0307. (www.drisha. org/highschool)

Eden Village Camp. 392 Dennytown Road, Putnam Valley, NY 10579. (877) 397-3336. (www.edenvillagecamp.org)

Jewish Girls Retreat (Chabad, YALDAH Magazine). 2155 13th Street, Troy, NY 12180. (614) 547-2267. (www.jewishgirlsretreat.net)

Mitzvah Corps (Union for Reform Judaism, NFTY). (212) 452-6517. (www.mitzvahcorps.org)

Silver Lake Camp. 52 Silver Lake Road, Swan Lake, NY 12783. (845) 583-8600 (S); (954) 227-7700. (www.silverlakecamp.com)

Surprise Lake Camp (UJA-Federation of New York). 382 Lake Surprise Road, Cold Spring, NY 10516. (845) 265-3616. (www.surpriselake.org)

The Zone (Boy's Division). 123 Scotch Valley Road, Stamford, NY 12167. (866) 843-9663. (www.thezone.org)

The Zone (Girl's Division). 964 South Gilboa Road, Gilboa, NY 12076. (866) 843-9663. (www.thezone.org)

URJ Kutz Camp (Union for Reform Judaism, NFTY). 46 Bowen Road, Warwick, NY 10990. (845) 987-6300. (www.kutz.urjcamps.org) (Will close after Summer 2019)

Yachad Camp Programs (Yachad: The National Jewish Council for Disabilities). 11 Broadway, 13th Floor, New York, NY 10004. (212) 613-8369. (www.njcd.org/summerprograms)

Yeshivas Kayitz Kingston (Chabad). 201 Powermill Bridge Road, Kingston, NY 12401. (845) 393-1701. (www.ykkingston.com)

North Carolina
Blue Star Camps. 179 Blue Star Way, Hendersonville, NC 28793. (828) 692-3591 (S); (954) 963-4494. (www.bluestarcamps.com)

Camp Judaea (Young Judaea). 48 Camp Judaea Lane, Hendersonville, NC 28792. (828) 685-8841 (S); (404) 634-7883. (www.campjudaea.org)

Camp Living Wonders. c/o Camp Arrowhead, 1415 Cabin Creek Road, Zirconia, NC 28790. (678) 888-2259. (www.camplivingwonders.org)

URJ 6 Points Sports Academy (Union for Reform Judaism). 5603-B W, Friendly Ave. #286 Greensboro, NC 27410. (561) 208-1650. (www.sports.urjcamps.org), (www.6pointsacademy.org)

Ohio
Camp Wise (Mandel JCC of Cleveland). 13164 Taylor Wells Road, Chardon, OH 44024. (216) 593-6250. (www.campwise.org)

Oregon

B'nai B'rith Camp (JCC Camp, B'nai B'rith Men's Camp Association). PO Box 110, Neotsu, OR 97364. (541) 994-2218 (S); (503) 496-7444. (www.bbcamp.org)

Pennsylvania

BBYO International Kallah (BBYO). 661 Rosehill Road, Lake Como, PA 18437. (570) 635-9200 (S); (202) 857-6633. (www.bbyo.org/summer/kallah)

BBYO International Leadership Training Conference (ILTC) (BBYO). 661 Rosehill Road, Lake Como, PA 18437. (570) 635-9200 (S); (202) 857-6633. (www. bbyo.org/summer/iltc)

B'nai B'rith Perlman Camp (B'nai B'rith). 661 Rose Hill Road, Lake Como, PA 18437. (570) 635-9200 (S); (301) 231-5300. (www.perlmancamp.org)

Camp Chayolei Hamelech (Chabad). 445 Masthope Plank Road, Lackawaxen, PA 18435. (570) 576-0405 (S); (718) 221-0770. (www.chayol.com)

Camp Dina for Girls (UJA-Federation of New York). 355 Bangor Mountain Road, Stroudsburg, PA 18360. (570) 992-2267 (S); (718) 437-7117. (www.camp-dina.com)

Camp Dora for Boys (UJA-Federation of New York). 418 Craigs Meadow Road, East Stroudsburg, PA 18301. (570) 223-0417 (S); (718) 437-7117. (www.camp-doragolding.com)

Camp Gan Israel in the Poconos (Chabad - Gan Israel). 127 Log and Twig Road, Dingmans Ferry, PA 18328. (845) 425-0903. (www.cgipoconos.org)

Camp Gan Israel of Greater Philadelphia (Overnight Camp) (Chabad - Gan Israel). (215) 852-0276. (www.ganisraelphilly.com)

Camp Havaya (formerly Camp JRF) (Jewish Reconstructionist Federation). 108 Rabbi Jeff Way, South Sterling, PA 18460. (833) 226-7428 (www.camphavaya.org)

Camp Kesher/Camp Kesher Junior. 570 Sawkill Road, Milford, PA 18337. (212) 415-5573. (www.92y.org/camps/kesher.aspx)

Camp Lavi. 2656 Upper Woods Road, Lakewood, PA 18439. (570) 798-2009 (S); (201) 684-9084. (www.camplavi.com)

Camp Maor/Maor Performing Arts. 31 Barry Watson Way, Lakewood, PA 18439. (267) 317-8243 (S); (212) 613-8349. (www.campmaor.com)

Camp Morasha. 274 High Lake Road, Lakewood, PA 18439. (570) 798-2781. (www.campmorasha.com)

Camp Moshava (Bnei Akiva). 245 Navajo Road, Honesdale, PA 18431. (570) 253-4271. (www.moshava.org)

Camp Nah-Jee-Wah (New Jersey YMHA-YWHA Camps). 570 Sawkill Road, Milford, PA 18337. (570) 296-8596 (S); (973) 575-3333. (www.nahjeewah.org)

Camp Nesher (New Jersey YMHA-YWHA Camps). 90 Woods Road, Lakewood, PA 18439. (570) 798-2373 (S); (973) 575-3333 (www.campnesher.org)

Camp Poyntelle Lewis Village (Samuel Field Y, UJA-Federation of New York). 584 Cribbs Road, Poyntelle, PA 18439. (570) 448-2161 (S); (718) 279-0690. (www. poyntelle.com)

Camp Ramah in the Poconos (National Ramah Commission). 2618 Upper Woods Road, Lakewood, PA 18439. (570) 798-2504 (S); (215) 885-8556. (www.ramahpoconos.org)

Camp Raninu. 62 Raninu Road, Honesdale, PA 18431. (570) 253-0500 (S); (973) 778-5973. (www.campraninu.com)

Camp Ruach Hachaim. (Ceased operation as of 2016)

Camp Shoshanim (New Jersey YMHA-YWHA Camps). 119 Woods Road, Lakewood, PA 18439. (570) 798-2551 (S); (973) 575-3333. (www.campshoshanim.org)

Camp Stone (Bnei Akiva). 2145 Deer Run Road, Sugar Grove, PA 16350. (814) 489-7841 (S); (216) 382-8062. (www.campstone.org)

Camp Zeke. 31 Barry Watson Way, Lakewood, PA 18439. (212) 913-9783. (www.campzeke.org)

Capital Camps (JCC Camp). 12750 Buchanan Trail East, Waynesboro, PA 17268. (717) 794-2177 (S); (301) 468-2267. (www.capitalcamps.org)

Cedar Lake Camp (New Jersey YMHA-YWHA Camps). 570 Sawkill Road, Milford, PA 18337. (570) 296-8596 (S); (973) 575-3333. (www.campcedarlake.org)

Golden Slipper Camp (Golden Slipper Club & Charities). 164 Reeders Run Road, Stroudsburg, PA 18360. (570) 629-1654 (S); (610) 660-0520. (www.goldenslippercamp.org)

Habonim Dror Camp Galil (Habonim Dror North America). 146 Red Hill Road, Ottsville, PA 18942. (610) 847-2213 (S); (215) 832-0676. (www.campgalil.org)

Pinemere Camp (JCC Camp). 865 Bartonsville Woods Road, Stroudsburg, PA 18360. (570) 629-0266 (S); (215) 487-2267. (www.pinemere.com)

Round Lake Camp (New Jersey YMHA-YWHA Camps). 570 Sawkill Road, Milford, PA 18337. (570) 296-8596, ext. 145 (S); (973) 575-3333, ext. 145. (www.roundlakecamp.org)

Teen Camp (New Jersey YMHA-YWHA Camps). 570 Sawkill Road, Milford, PA 18337. (570) 296-8596 (S); (973) 575-3333. (www.teencamp.org)

Tizmoret Shoshana. c/o Capital Retreat Center, 12750 Buchanan Trail East, Waynesboro, PA 17268. (443) 844-5218 or (443) 844-4133. (www.tizmoretshoshana.org)

URJ 6 Points Creative Arts Academy (Union for Reform Judaism). The Westtown School, 975 Road, West Chester, PA 19382. (410) 609-9870. (www.6pointscreativearts.org)

URJ Camp Harlam (Union for Reform Judaism). 575 Smith Road, Kunkletown, PA 18058. (570) 629-1390 (S); (610) 668-0423. (www.harlam.urjcamps.org)

Rhode Island

Camp JORI. 1065 Wordens Pond Road, Wakefield, RI 02879. (401) 783-7000 (S); (401) 421-4111. (www.campjori.com)

Texas

Camp Gan Israel-South Padre Island (Chabad - Gan Israel). 904 Padre Boulevard, South Padre Island, TX 78597. (956) 467-4323. (www.cgispi.com)

Camp Young Judaea Texas (Young Judaea). 121 Camp Young Judaea Drive, Woodcreek, TX 78676. (512) 847-9564 (S); (713) 723-8354. (www.cyjtexas.org)

URJ Greene Family Camp (Union for Reform Judaism). 1192 Smith Lane Bruceville, TX 76630. (254) 859-5411. (www.greene.org)

Washington

Camp Solomon Schechter. (360) 352-1019 (S); (206) 447-1967. (www.camps-chechter.org)

Sephardic Adventure Camp (Congregation Ezra Bessaroth, Sephardic Bikur Holim Congregation). PO Box 28511, WA 98118. (206) 257-2225. (www.sephardicadventurecamp.org)

URJ Camp Kalsman (Union for Reform Judaism). 14724 184th Street NE, Arlington, WA 98223. (360) 435-9302 (S); (425) 284-4484. (www.kalsman.urj-camps.org)

West Virginia

Emma Kaufmann Camp (JCC of Greater Pittsburgh). 297 Emma Kaufmann Camp Road, Morgantown, WV 26508. (304) 599-4435 (S); (412) 697-3550. (www.emmakaufmanncamp.com)

Wisconsin

BBYO Chapter Leadership Training Conference (CLTC) (BBYO). c/o B'nai B'rith Beber Camp, W 1741 County Road J, Mukwonago, WI 53149. (202) 857-6633. (www.bbyo.org/summer/cltc)

B'nai B'rith Beber Camp (B'nai B'rith). W 1741 County Road J, Mukwonago, WI 53149. (262) 363-6800 (S); (847) 677-7130. (www.bebercamp.com)

Camp Moshava Wild Rose (Bnei Akiva). W8256 County Road P, Wild Rose, WI 54984. (920) 622-3379 (S); (847) 674-9733, ext. 7. (www.moshavawildrose.org)

Camp Ramah in Wisconsin (National Ramah Commission). 3390 Ramah Circle, Conover, WI 54519. (715) 479-4400 (S); (312); 606-9316. (www.ramahwisconsin.com)

Camp Young Judaea Midwest (Young Judaea). E989 Stratton Lake Road, Waupaca, WI 54981. (715) 258-2288 (S); (224) 235-4665. (www.cyjmid.org)

Chavayah Overnight Camp for Girls (JCC of Chicago). 443 West Munroe Avenue, Lake Delton, WI 53940. (773) 516-5883 (S); (844) 452-2244 (www.jccchicago.org/programs/camps/overnight-camps/chavayah-orthodox-camp-girls)

Herzl Camp. 7374 Mickey Smith Parkway, Webster, WI 54893. (715) 866-8177 (S); (952) 927-4002. (www.herzlcamp.org)

JCC Camp Chi (JCC of Chicago). 443 West Munroe Avenue, Lake Delton, WI 53940. (847) 763-3551. (www.campchi.com)

Steve and Shari Sadek Family Camp Interlaken JCC (Harry & Rose Samson Family JCC). 7050 Old Highway 70, Eagle River, WI 54521. (715) 479-8030 (S); (414) 967-8240. (www.campinterlaken.org)

URJ Olin-Sang-Ruby Union Institute (OSRUI) (Union for Reform Judaism). 600 Lac La Belle Drive, Oconomowoc, WI 53066. (262) 567-6277 (S); (847) 509-0990. (www.osrui.org)

11.3 Traveling Camps

Achva (Young Israel Summer Tours) (https://achva.youngisrael.org)

Aryeh Adventures. 65 Shrewsbury Drive, Livingston, NJ 07039. (718) 790-0528. (www.aryehadventures.org)

BBYO Passport (BBYO). 5185 MacArthur Boulevard, #640, Washington, DC 20016. (202) 537-8091. (www.bbyopassport.org/Trips/Summer-Experiences)

Camp Tawonga (JCC Camp). Quests: Adventure Travel on the Road. 131 Steuart Street, Suite 460, San Francisco, CA 94105. (415) 543-2267. (www.tawonga.org)

Etgar 36. PO Box 2212, Decatur, GA 30031. (404) 456-6605. (www.etgar.org)

GIVE WEST (NCSY). 11 Broadway, 13th Floor, New York, NY 10004. (212) 613-8349. (https://givewest.ncsy.org)

Tamarack Camps - (JCC Camp, Fresh Air Society). Travel Trips: Embark on the Adventure of a Lifetime. 6735 Telegraph Road, Suite 380, Bloomfield Hills, MI 48301. (248) 647-1100. (www.tamarackcamps:com/campers/travel-trips)

Union of Reform Judaism Travel Camps (www.urjyouth.org)

USY on Wheels. 120 Broadway, Suite 1540, New York, NY 10271. (212) 533-7800. (www.usy.org/escape/usy-on-wheels)

11.4 Jewish Overnight Camps, Canada

Alberta
Camp BB Riback. 201-24508 Township Road 361, Red Deer County, AB T0M 1R0. (587) 988-9771. (www.campbb.com)

British Columbia
Bais Chana Jewish UnCamp (Bais Chana Women International). Vancouver Island, British Columbia. (718) 604-0088. (www.jewishuncamp.org)

Camp Hatikvah (Camp Hatikvah Foundation, Canadian Young Judaea). 15800 Oyama Road, Oyama, BC V4V 2E4. (604) 263-1200. (www.camphatikvah.com)

Habonim Dror Camp Miriam (Habonim Dror North America). 835 Berry Point Road, Gabriola, BC VOR 1X1. (250) 247-9571 (S); (604) 266-2825. (www.camp-miriam.org)

Manitoba
Camp Massad (Jewish Foundation of Manitoba, The Jewish Federation of Winnipeg). c/o Camp Massad, General Delivery, Winnipeg Beach, MB R0C 3G0. (204) 389-5300 (S); (204) 477-7487. (www.campmassad.ca)

Nova Scotia
Camp Kadimah (Atlantic Jewish Council, Canadian Young Judaea). 1681 Barss Corner Road, Barss Corner, NS B0R 1A0. (902) 644-2313 (S); (416) 634-3089. (www.campkadimah.com)

Ontario

B'nai Brith Camp (JCC Camp). Box 559, Kenora, ON P9N 3X5. (807) 548-4178 (S); (204) 477-7512. (www.bbcamp.ca)

Camp Agudah Toronto (Agudath Israel). 3793 Highway 118 West, Port Carling, ON P0B 1J0. (705) 765-6816 (S); (416) 781-7101. (http://campagudahtoronto.com)

Camp Gan Israel Toronto (Chabad – Gan Israel). 1726 Gan Israel Trail, PO Box 535, Haliburton, ON K0M 1S0. (705) 754-9920 (S); (905) 731-7000, ext. 225. (www.ganisraeltoronto.com)

Camp Leah Rivka. 996 Chetwynd Road, Burks Falls, ON P0A 1C0. (705) 382-3770 (S); (905) 763-8727. (www.camplr.com)

Camp Moshava Ennismore (Bnei Akiva). 1485 Murphy Road RR#1, Ennismore, ON K0L 1T0. (705) 292-8143 (S); (416) 630-7578. (www.campmoshava.org)

Camp Northland-B'nai Brith (Jewish Camp Council of Toronto). 4250 Haliburton Lake Road, Haliburton, ON K0M 1S0. (705) 754-2374 (S); (905) 881-0018. (www.campnbb.com)

Camp Ramah in Canada (National Ramah Commission). 1104 Fish Hatchery Road, Utterson, ON P0B 1M0. (416) 789-2193. (www.campramah.com)

Camp Shalom (Toronto Zionist Council, Canadian Young Judaea). 1110 Brydons Bay Road, Gravenhurst, ON P1P 1R1. (705) 687-4442 (S); (416) 781-3571. (www.campshalom.ca)

Camp Shomria (Hashomer Hatzair). 133 Kenyon Rd, RR#3 Otty Lake Road, Perth, ON K7H 3C5. (416) 736-1339. (www.hashomerhatzair.ca)

Camp Solelim (Canadian Young Judaea). 6490 Tilton Lake Road, Sudbury, ON P3G 1L5. (705) 522-1480 (S); (416) 781-5156. (www.campsolelim.ca)

Camp Walden. 38483 Highway 28 (RR#2), Palmer Rapids, ON K0J 2E0. (613) 758-2365 (S); (888) 254-4274. (www.campwalden.ca)

Habonim Dror Camp Gesher (Habonim Dror North America). Camp Gesher General Delivery, Cloyne, ON K0H 1K0. (613) 336-2583 (S); (416) 633-2511. (www.campgesher.com)

J. Academy (Joseph and Wolf Lebovic Jewish Community Campus). 4250 Haliburton Lake Road, Haliburton, ON K0M 1S0. (905) 303-1821, ext. 3026. (www.leboviccampus.ca)

URJ Camp George (Union for Reform Judaism). 45 Good Fellowship Road, Seguin, ON P2A 0B2. (705) 732-6964 (S); (416) 638-2635. (www.george.urj-camps.org)

Quebec

Camp B'nai Brith of Montreal (Federation CJA of Montreal). 5445 Route 329 North, Sainte-Agathe-des-Monts, QC J8C 0M7. (819) 326-4824 (S); (514) 735-3669. (www.cbbmtl.org)

Camp B'nai Brith of Ottawa. 7861 Chemin River, Quyon, QC J0X 2V0. (819) 458-2660 (S); (613) 244-9210. (www.cbbottawa.com)

Camp Gan Yisroel Montreal (Chabad - Gan Israel). 103 Chemin De La Minerve, La Minerve, QC J0T 1H0. (819) 274-2215 (S); (514) 343-9606. (www.cgimontreal.com)

Camp Kinneret-Biluim (Canadian Young Judaea). 184 Rue Harrisson, Mont Tremblant, QC J8E 1M8. (819) 425-3332 (S); (514) 735-3167. (www.ckb.ca)

Camp Massad. 1780 Chemin du Lac Quenouille, Sainte-Agathe-des-Monts, QC J8C 0R4. (819) 326-4686 (S); (514) 488-6610. (www.campmassad.org)

Camp Pardas Chanah. 1984 Route 117, Val David, QC J0T 2N0. (819) 322-2334 (S); (514) 600-1631. (www.camppc.com)

Camp Wingate. 1580 Chemin Lac des Trois Frères, St. Adolphe d'Howard, QC J0T 2B0. (819) 327-1149 (S); (514) 836-8999. (www.campwingate.com)

Camp Yaldei (The Donald Berman Yaldei Developmental Center). (514) 279-3666, ext. 222. (www.yaldei.org)

Harry Bronfman Y Country Camp (YM-YWHA Jewish Community Centres of Montreal). 130 Chemin Lac Blanc, Huberdeau, QC J0T 1G0. (819) 687-3271 (S); (514) 737-6551, ext. 267. (www.ycountrycamp.com)

Chapter 12
National Jewish Organizations

Ira M. Sheskin, Arnold Dashefsky, and Sarah Markowitz

This chapter provides lists with contact information (name, address, phone number, website) for about 950 national Jewish organizations.

The purpose of this chapter is to document the institutional infrastructure of the North American Jewish community and to preserve this information for historical purposes. We expect that historians 100 years from now will look back at the *Year Book* in researching the history of North American Jewry. In a sense, we are "freezing" the information in time. The information on the Internet, of course, changes as frequently as the webmasters update that information, meaning that without this freezing, historians in the future will not have a record of the infrastructure of the community.

The list is carefully updated each year, but the authors appreciate any corrections noted by our readers. We have found that the lists we can find for Jewish institutions on the Internet are far from totally accurate.

Notes:

1. **Academic organizations dedicated to the study of North American Jewry are found in Chap. 14, Sect. 5.**
2. **The inclusion of an organization does not imply that the editors share the viewpoints espoused by that organization.**
3. **FSU means Former Soviet Union.**

I. M. Sheskin (✉)
Department of Geography and Jewish Demography Project, Sue and Leonard Miller Center for Contemporary Judaic Studies, University of Miami, Coral Gables, FL, USA
e-mail: isheskin@miami.edu

A. Dashefsky
Department of Sociology and Center for Judaic Studies and Contemporary Jewish Life, University of Connecticut, Storrs, CT, USA

S. Markowitz
Independent Researcher, Forest Hills, NY, USA

© Springer Nature Switzerland AG 2020
A. Dashefsky, I. M. Sheskin (eds.), *American Jewish Year Book 2019*, American Jewish Year Book 119, https://doi.org/10.1007/978-3-030-40371-3_12

12.1 National Jewish Organizations, United States

United States Jewish organizations are presented in the following categories:

12.1.1 Jewish Denominational Organizations

12.1.2 Jewish Clergy-Related Organizations

12.1.3 Rabbinical/Cantorial Schools

12.1.4 Jewish Community Coordinating Organizations

12.1.5 Jewish Community Professional Organizations

12.1.6 Jewish Children's Education Organizations

12.1.7 Jewish Adult Education Organizations

12.1.8 Jewish Youth Groups and Youth-Related Organizations

12.1.9 Jewish College Campus Organizations

12.1.10 Jewish Outreach Organizations

12.1.11 Jewish Israel-Related Education Organizations

12.1.12 Jewish Israel-Related Humanitarian Organizations

12.1.13 Jewish Israel-Related Political and Advocacy Organizations

12.1.14 Jewish Organizations Supporting Specific Israeli Institutions

12.1.15 Other Jewish Israel-Related Organizations

12.1.16 Jewish Holocaust Organizations

12.1.17 Jewish Community Relations Organizations

12.1.18 Jewish Philanthropy-Promoting Organizations

12.1.19 Jewish Philanthropic Foundations and Organizations

12.1.20 Jewish Philanthropic Pass-Through/Umbrella Organizations

12.1.21 Jewish Overseas Aid Organizations

12.1.22 Sephardic Organizations

12.1.23 Jewish Russian/FSU Organizations

12.1.24 Other Jewish National Origin Organizations

12.1.25 Yiddish Organizations

12.1.26 Jewish LGBTQ Organizations

12.1.27 Jewish Cultural Organizations

12.1.28 Jewish History/Heritage Organizations

12.1.29 Jewish Social Welfare Organizations

12.1.30 Jewish Legal Organizations

12.1.31 Jewish Medical Organizations

12.1.32 Jewish Organizations for People with Disabilities or Special Needs

12.1.33 Jewish End of Life Organizations

12.1.34 Jewish Media Organizations

12.1.35 Jewish Environmental Organizations

12.1.36 Jewish Academic Organizations

12.1.37 Jewish Fraternities/Sororities

12.1.38 Jewish Sports Organizations

12.1.39 Other Jewish Organizations

Note: We have attempted to place each organization in the category that appears most appropriate for it, although many organizations could easily fit in multiple categories.

12.1.1 Jewish Denominational Organizations

Orthodox
Agudas Chasidei Chabad of United States (also known as **Union of Chabad Chassidim**) (formerly **Agudas HaChasidim Anshei Chabad Beartzot Habris** and **Agudas Chassidei Chabad Beartzot Habris veCanada**) (1924). 770 Eastern Parkway, Brooklyn, NY 11213. (718) 774-4000. The umbrella organization for the worldwide Chabad Lubavitch movement. (No website)

Agudath Israel of America (AIA) (1922). 42 Broadway, New York, NY 10004. (212) 797-9000. AIA serves as a leadership and policy umbrella organization for Orthodox Jews in the US, uniting a diverse cross section of leading Orthodox rabbis, activists, philanthropists, and everyday community members. Its goals are strengthening Jewish communities; strengthening religious education and Torah learning for adults; government and legal advocacy; comprehensive community-based social services, and inspiring Jewish youth. (www.agudathisrael.org)

Chief Bukharian Rabbinate of the United States and Canada (2017). The Chief Bukharian Rabbinate of the United States and Canada is an official rabbinical board for the Bukharian Jewish community. It was created to achieve unity among the various synagogues and other institutions within the Bukharian community in the US and Canada, and its primary function is to establish religious policy in a highly fractured community. (No website)

Jewish Orthodox Feminist Alliance (JOFA) (1997). 205 East 42nd Street, 20th Floor, New York, NY 10017. (212) 679-8500. JOFA is dedicated to expanding the spiritual, ritual, intellectual, and political opportunities for women within the framework of halakha. JOFA advocates meaningful participation and equality for women in family life, synagogues, houses of learning, and Jewish communal organizations to the full extent possible within the framework of halakha. (www.jofa.org)

National Council of Young Israel (NCYI) (1912). 50 Eisenhower Drive, Suite 102, Paramus, NJ 07652. (212) 929-1525. NCYI is a coordinating agency for nearly 150 Orthodox congregations in the US and Canada. Through its network of member synagogues in North America and Israel, NCYI maintains a program of spiritual, cultural, social and communal activity aimed at the advancement and perpetuation of traditional, Torah-true Judaism. NCYI is the only Orthodox synagogue movement that requires the minimum halakhic standards of a mechitza, closed parking facilities on Shabbos and Yom Tov, and that the synagogue's officers be Shomer Shabbos. NCYI also serves as a resource to Yisrael Hatzair, the Young Israel movement in Israel, encompassing over 50 synagogues. (www.youngisrael.org)

Orthodox Union (also known as **Union of Orthodox Jewish Congregations of America**) (OU) (1898). 11 Broadway, New York, NY 10004. (212) 563-4000. OU, the largest US organization of Orthodox synagogues, serves as the national central body of Orthodox synagogues. Its departments include OU Kosher, the national OU kashrut supervision and certification service, Job Board, Synagogue Services Department, Advocacy Center (the OU's public policy arm), Israel Center in Jerusalem, Community Engagement Department, Department of Day School and Educational Services, and OU Press. (www.ou.org)

PORAT: People for Orthodox Renaissance and Torah (2016). Inspired by a commitment to a tolerant and inclusive Modern Orthodox community, PORAT brings together lay and religious leaders to advocate for thoughtful halakhic observance and progressive education. PORAT supports organizations dedicated to ensuring open dialogue with Modern Orthodox tradition while advancing Torah values and advocates for a Modern Orthodoxy willing to engage diverse perspectives on issues relating to religious Zionism, gender equality, conversion to Judaism, agunah, the synthesis of secular culture and Jewish tradition, rabbinic authority, spirituality, relations with other denominations and faiths, and the place of gay and lesbian individuals within the Modern Orthodox community. (www.poratonline.org)

Traditional

Union for Traditional Judaism (1984). 82 Nassau Street, #313, New York, NY 10038. (914) 662-9649. The Union for Traditional Judaism seeks to bring the greatest possible number of Jews closer to an open-minded observant Jewish lifestyle. It supports and encourages traditional Jewish practice among individuals, congregations, institutions, scholars and religious leaders across the spectrum of the Jewish community. (www.utj.org)

Conservative

Federation of Jewish Men's Clubs (FJMC) (1929). 475 Riverside Drive, Suite 820, New York, NY 10115. (212) 749-8100. The Federation of Jewish Men's Clubs is the international umbrella organization for a confederation of more than 250 men's auxiliaries serving over 20,000 men throughout North America. FJMC's mission is to involve Jewish men in Jewish life. FJMC is affiliated with the Conservative/Masorti movement and promotes principles of Conservative Judaism. FJMC develops family education and leadership training programs; offers the Art of Jewish Living series and Hearing Men's Voices series; sponsors the Yom HaShoah Yellow Candle Program, World Wide Wrap event, Hebrew literacy adult-education program, and Keruv program (outreach to families with intermarried members). (www.fjmc.org)

Hazak (1999). 820 Second Avenue, 10th Floor, New York, NY 10017. Hazak is The United Synagogue of Conservative Judaism's organization for mature Jews, providing programming for people 55 and older who are members of affiliated Conservative congregations. (www.uscj.org)

Masorti Foundation for Conservative Judaism in Israel (1983). 3080 Broadway, New York, NY 10027. (212) 870-5880. The Masorti Foundation for Conservative Judaism in Israel is the American organization responsible for raising funds to support the work of the Masorti movement and enable the movement to further its activities in Israel. Legal advocacy is one of the central roles of the movement, which represents the religious rights of Masorti and Conservative Judaism before the Israeli establishment, including government ministries, the Supreme Court, and municipalities. (www.masorti.org)

United Synagogue of Conservative Judaism (USCJ) (formerly **United Synagogue of America**) (1913). 120 Broadway, Suite 1540, New York, NY 10271. (212) 533-7800. USCJ is the primary organization of over 600 congregations practicing Conservative Judaism in North America. USCJ promotes the role of the synagogue in Jewish life to motivate Conservative Jews to perform mitzvot encompassing ethical behavior, spirituality, Judaic learning, and ritual observance. USCJ includes the Fuchsberg Jerusalem Center and The Conservative Yeshiva in Jerusalem. (www.uscj.org)

Women's League for Conservative Judaism (1918). 475 Riverside Drive, Suite 820, New York, NY 10115. (212) 870-1260. The Women's League for Conservative Judaism is the parent body of the approximately 500 Conservative/Masorti women's synagogue groups and sisterhoods in the US, Canada, Puerto Rico, Mexico, and Israel. Its mission is to strengthen and unite synagogue women's groups, their members and individual members, support them in mutual efforts to understand and perpetuate Conservative/Masorti Judaism in the home, synagogue and community, and reinforce their bonds with Israel and with Jews worldwide. Women's League contributes to support The Jewish Theological Seminary. (www.wlcj.org)

World Council of Conservative/Masorti Synagogues (**Masorti Olami**) (1957). 3080 Broadway, New York, NY 10027. (212) 280-6039. The World Council of Conservative/Masorti Synagogues builds, renews and strengthens Jewish life throughout the world. It acts to advance the interests and principles of Masorti Judaism, working with all other arms of the Conservative/Masorti movement to be an effective spokesperson for Masorti Judaism. (www.masortiworld.org)

Reconstructionist

Reconstructing Judaism (formerly **Jewish Reconstructionist Communities** and **Jewish Reconstructionist Federation**) (1954) (2012) (2018). 1299 Church Road, Wyncote, PA, 19095. (215) 576-0800. Reconstructing Judaism is the central organization of the Reconstructionist movement whose mission is to cultivate and support Jewish living, learning, and leadership for a changing world. It envisions a more just and compassionate world where creative Jewish living and learning guide people toward lives of holiness, meaning, and purpose. Reconstructing Judaism trains the next generation of rabbis, supports and uplifts congregations and havurot, fosters emerging expressions of Jewish life, and encourages people to be their best selves—always helping to shape what it means to be Jewish today and to imagine the Jewish future. (www.reconstructingjudaism.org)

Reform

Men of Reform Judaism (MRJ) (formerly **North American Federation of Temple Brotherhoods**) (1923). 633 Third Avenue, New York, NY 10017. (212) 650-4100. MRJ was organized to promote the establishment of affiliated brotherhoods, men's clubs and other local organized men's groups in congregations throughout North America affiliated with the Union for Reform. MRJ programs include Reform on Campus, Achim Corps (Men's Health Initiative, Men's Spirituality Program, Jewish Men's Issues), Ben Abba Zeyde Programs, Yom HaShoah Yellow Candle Program, and sponsorship of the Jewish Chautauqua Society, MRJ's interfaith education arm since 1939. (www.menrj.org)

The Society for Classical Reform Judaism (SCRJ) (2008). 15 Newbury Street, Boston, MA 02116. (617) 247-4700. The SCRJ seeks to preserve and creatively renew the deep spiritual values, rich intellectual foundations, and distinctive worship traditions that have historically distinguished the Reform movement. (www. renewreform.org)

Union for Reform Judaism (URJ) (formerly **Union of American Hebrew Congregations**) (1873). 633 Third Avenue, New York, NY 10017. (212) 650-4000. The URJ, founded by Rabbi Isaac Mayer Wise, is the congregational arm of the Reform Movement. It is a network of more than 900 congregations, lay leaders, clergy and professionals in the US, Canada, the Bahamas, Puerto Rico, and the Virgin Islands with a progressive, inclusive approach. As a member of the World Union for Progressive Judaism, the URJ connects Reform Jews in North America with Liberal/Progressive/Reform congregations around the globe. The URJ provides religious, educational, cultural and administrative programs, as well as camping, Birthright, travel and youth group experiences. (www.urj.org)

Women of Reform Judaism (WRJ) (formerly **National Federation of Temple Sisterhoods**) (1913). 633 Third Avenue, New York, NY 10017. (212) 650-4050. WRJ is the women's affiliate of the Union for Reform Judaism. WRJ programs include Lilith Salons, Social Action Rings, Israel Twinning Program, and Fistula and Maternal Health Program. Through the YES Fund (Youth, Education, and Special Projects), WRJ provides financial support to rabbinic and cantorial students at Hebrew Union College-Jewish Institute of Religion, to the youth programs of the Reform movement, and to programs benefitting women and children in Israel, the FSU, and around the world. (www.wrj.org)

World Union for Progressive Judaism (1926). 633 Third Avenue, 7th Floor, New York, NY 10017. (212) 452-6530. The World Union for Progressive Judaism is the international umbrella organization of the Reform, Liberal, Progressive, and Reconstructionist movements, serving more than 1200 congregations, representing an estimated 1.8 million members in about 45 countries. It promotes and coordinates efforts of Liberal congregations throughout the world, starts new congregations, recruits rabbis and rabbinical students for all countries, and organizes international conferences of Liberal Jews. (www.wupj.org)

Jewish Renewal

ALEPH: Alliance for Jewish Renewal (1962) (1993). 7000 Lincoln Drive, #B2, Philadelphia, PA 19119. (215) 247-9700. ALEPH is a core institution in the Jewish Renewal movement. ALEPH supports and grows the worldwide movement for Jewish renewal by organizing and nurturing communities, developing leadership, training lay and rabbinic leaders, creating liturgical and scholarly resources, and working for social and environmental justice. (www.aleph.org)

Secular/Humanist

Congress of Secular Jewish Organizations (CSJO) (1970). 847 Tyson Avenue, Roslyn, PA, 19001. (267) 625-2756. The CSJO focuses on promoting and educating a secular Jewish world view. Its schools, adult and youth groups function outside the framework of organized religion and carry out programs of education directed toward understanding the Jewish people's past and enriching present Jewish lives. The CSJO promotes creative approaches to holiday celebrations that provide an opportunity to reflect upon the cultural and historic heritage of the Jewish people and to relate their significance to present-day life. (www.csjo.org)

International Federation for Secular & Humanistic Judaism (IFSHJ) (Ceased to exist as of 2014)

International Institute for Secular Humanistic Judaism (IISHJ) (1985). 175 Olde Half Day Road, Suite 123, Lincolnshire, IL 60069. (847) 383-6330. The three primary purposes of the IISHJ are to train rabbis, leaders, teachers and spokespersons; to commission and publish educational materials; and to offer public seminars and colloquia. The IISHJ includes distinguished writers, intellectuals and ordained Secular Humanistic rabbis who serve as faculty, as well as faculty members of major universities throughout the world who serve as part-time lecturers and instructors. (www.iishj.org)

Society for Humanistic Judaism (SHJ) (1969). 28611 West Twelve Mile Road, Farmington Hills, Ml 48334. (248) 478-7610. As the central body for the Humanistic Jewish movement in North America, the SHJ assists in organizing new communities, supporting its member communities and providing a voice for Humanistic Jews. The SHJ gathers and creates educational and programmatic materials and sponsors training programs and conferences for its members. (www.shj.org)

Havurah

National Havurah Committee (1979). 125 Maiden Lane, Suite 8B, New York, NY 10038. (860) 245-1674. The National Havurah Committee is a network of diverse individuals and communities dedicated to Jewish living and learning, community building and tikkun olam. It provides the tools to help people create empowered Jewish lives and communities. It maintains a directory of North American havurot and sponsors a week-long summer institute and regional weekend retreats. (www. havurah.org)

Trans-Denominational

Jewish Emergent Network (JEN) (2016). JEN is comprised of the leaders of seven path-breaking Jewish communities from across the US. These include IKAR in Los Angeles, Kavana in Seattle, The Kitchen in San Francisco, Mishkan in Chicago, Sixth & I in Washington, DC, and Lab/Shul and Romemu in New York. These communities do not represent any one denomination but share a devotion to revitalizing the field of Jewish engagement, a commitment to approaches both traditionally rooted and creative, and a demonstrated success in attracting unaffiliated and disengaged Jews to a rich and meaningful Jewish practice. Each community has taken an entrepreneurial approach to this shared vision, operating outside of conventional institutional models. (www.jewishemergentnetwork.org)

National Council of Synagogues (NCS) (formerly **Synagogue Council of America**) (1926) (1999) 1354 East Broad Street, Suite 108, Columbus, OH 43205. NCS is a partnership of the Reform, Conservative, and Reconstructionist movements in Judaism dealing with interreligious affairs on a national level. It collectively represents over 2500 rabbis and 1500 synagogues. Since its creation, the NCS has been a significant voice and increasingly a recognized address in the Jewish community for engagement in interfaith dialogue, collaborative social and public policy initiatives, and the advancement of intergroup relations. (www.nationalcouncilofsynagogues.org)

Synagogue Studies Institute (formerly **Synagogue 2000** and **Synagogue 3000**) (Ceased to exist)

12.1.2   Jewish Clergy-Related Organizations

Orthodox
Cantorial Council of America (CCA) (1960). Philip and Sarah Belz School of Jewish Music, 500 West 185th Street, New York, NY 10033. (212) 960-5400. The CCA, originally formed at Yeshiva University to provide professional and social resources to Orthodox cantors around the country, is today a worldwide organization. Conventions and regional Mid-Winter Conferences provide sessions designed toward enhancing knowledge of synagogue music and prayer for professional cantors and laymen. The CCA sponsors cantor-in-residence and outreach programs around the country to educate communities in the rich Jewish liturgical traditions and to help all worshipers gain more insight and meaning in their prayers. (www.yu.edu/belz/cantorial-council)

Central Rabbinical Congress of the USA and Canada (CRC) (1952). 85 Division Avenue, Brooklyn, NY 11249. (718) 384-6765. The CRC, founded by Rabbi Joel Teitelbaum, is a rabbinical organization that is a consortium of various Orthodox Jewish groups identified with the most conservative wings of Haredi Judaism in America, including the Satmar Hasidic group. The CRC has consistently opposed Zionism. The CRC represents the same conservative wings of the Haredi world that the Edah HaChareidis represents in Jerusalem. The CRC provides kosher food certification and serves as a religious court. (No website)

International Rabbinic Fellowship (IRF) (2008). 347 West 34th Street, New York, NY 10001. The IRF is a Modern Orthodox rabbinic association whose membership come together for serious study of Torah and halakha and to advocate policies and implement actions on behalf of world Jewry and humankind. It is dedicated to providing advice, programming ideas, and general support to its members to address their professional and spiritual well-being. (www.internationalrabbinicfellowship.org)

Rabbinical Alliance of America (**Igud Harabbonim**) (RAA) (1942). 305 Church Avenue, Brooklyn, NY 11218. (718) 532-8720. The RAA is a national rabbinic organization with more than 800 members consisting of congregational leaders, religious teachers, chaplains, heads of Jewish organizations and communal leaders, united in their commitment to traditional Orthodox Judaism. It seeks to promulgate the cause of Torah-true Judaism through an organized rabbinate that is consistently Orthodox and to elevate the position of Orthodox rabbis nationally and defend the welfare of Jews the world over. (www.rabbinicalalliance.org)

Rabbinical Council of America (RCA) (formerly **Rabbinical Council of the Union of Orthodox Jewish Congregations of America**) (1923) (1935). 305 Seventh Avenue, 12th Floor, New York, NY 10001. (212) 807-9000. The RCA advances the cause and the voice of Torah and the rabbinic tradition by promoting the welfare, interests and professionalism of Orthodox rabbis around the world. It promotes Orthodox Judaism in the community, supports institutions for study of Torah, stimulates creation of new traditional agencies, publishes important Torah and intellectual journals, holds annual conventions and conferences, issues occasional position papers and statements on the issues of the day, and provides numerous services for the Orthodox rabbinate. (www.rabbis.org)

Union of Orthodox Rabbis of the United States and Canada (**Agudath Harabbonim**) (UOR) (1902). 235 East Broadway, New York, NY 10002. (212) 964-6337. The UOR, founded on the Lower East Side of New York by European-born Orthodox rabbis, is one of the oldest Orthodox rabbinic organizations in North America. It was established to address issues facing traditional Jews in North America and to counter assimilationist influences. UOR members consist almost exclusively of rabbis with a Haredi (ultra-Orthodox) world view. The UOR seeks to foster and promote Torah-true Judaism in the US and Canada; assists in the establishment and maintenance of yeshivot in the US; maintains a committee on marriage and divorce and aids individuals with marital difficulties; disseminates knowledge of traditional Jewish rites and practices; publishes regulations on synagogue structure; and maintains a rabbinical court for resolving individual and communal conflicts. (No website)

Vaad HaRabbonim of America/American Board of Rabbis. 276 5th Avenue, Suite 704, 7th Floor, New York, NY 10001. (212) 714-3598. The Vaad HaRabbonim of America promotes Jewish unity through advocacy of religious and human rights for the Jewish people throughout the world. It is an Orthodox rabbinical organization dedicated to the dissemination of authentic (halakhic) Judaism. The Vaad offers distance rabbinical courses leading to smicha (certificate of ordination) and advanced ordination. It provides other vital rabbinical services for the Jewish community. (www.vaadharabbonim.com)

Traditional

Morashah. 82 Nassau Street, #313, New York, NY 10038. (914) 662-9649. Morashah is the rabbinic arm of the Union for Traditional Judaism. Members participate in continuing education, annual conferences and summer kallot (conventions). Morashah provides professional placement, a pension program, professional advancement programs and rabbinic resources. (www.utj.org/morashah)

Conservative

Cantors Assembly (CA) (1947). 55 South Miller Road, Suite 201, Fairlawn, OH 44333. (330) 864-8533. The CA is the professional association of cantors affiliated with Conservative Judaism and the official placement agency for cantors in the Conservative movement. Affiliated with the United Synagogue of Conservative Judaism, the CA serves the needs of its members and congregations and helps preserve and enhance the traditions of the Jewish people. The CA provides retirement and pension programs for its members, publishes materials of Jewish liturgy, music and education, and represents cantors to the Jewish and non-Jewish communities at large. (www.cantors.org)

Rabbinical Assembly (RA) (formerly **Alumni Association of the Jewish Theological Seminary**) (1901). 3080 Broadway, New York, NY 10027. (212) 280-6000. The RA is the international association of Conservative/Masorti rabbis. Its nearly 1600 members serve as congregational rabbis, educators, military and hospital chaplains, professors of Judaica, and officers of communal service organizations throughout the world. The RA publishes learned texts, prayer books, and other works of Jewish interest; administers the work of the Committee on Jewish Law and Standards for the Conservative movement; serves the professional and personal needs of its members through publications, conferences and benefit programs; and administers the affairs of the Conservative Movement's Joint Placement Commission. The RA is a strong supporter of Israel and Zionist activities. It is active in interfaith activities and in promoting and supporting projects of tzedakah, gemilut hesed and social justice. (www.rabbinicalassembly.org)

Reconstructionist

Reconstructionist Rabbinical Association (RRA) (1974). 1299 Church Road, Wyncote, PA 19095. (215) 576-5210. The RRA is the professional association of nearly 300 Reconstructionist rabbis. It serves as a collegial community in which professional and personal support and resources are provided to rabbis; represents the rabbinic voice within the Reconstructionist movement, helping to define Reconstructionist positions on Jewish issues for our time; and represents the Reconstructionist rabbinate to the larger Jewish and general communities. The RRA establishes rituals, documents, liturgy and policies around moments of the Jewish life cycle. The annual RRA convention and regional events serve to connect colleagues with each other and provide ongoing education and professional development. (http://therra.org)

Reform

American Conference of Cantors (ACC) (1953). 1375 Remington Road, Suite M, Schaumburg, IL 60173. (847) 781-7800. The ACC, an affiliate of the Union for Reform Judaism, is the professional organization of the Reform movement's more than 500 ordained or certified cantors. Responsible for raising the professional standards of synagogue musicians, the ACC offers continuing education programs and professional development opportunities for its members. It also sponsors an annual convention. It offers placement services to its members and Union for Reform Judaism congregations through the Joint Cantorial Placement Commission. (www.accantors.org)

Central Conference of American Rabbis (CCAR) (1889). 355 Lexington Avenue, New York, NY 10017. (212) 972-3636. The CCAR is the oldest and largest rabbinic organization in North America. The CCAR's unique contribution to a continued vibrant Jewish community and Reform movement lies in its work fostering excellence in Reform rabbis, enhancing unity and connectedness among Reform Jews, applying Jewish values to a contemporary life, and creating a compelling and accessible Judaism for today and the future. It offers rabbis opportunities for Torah study, professional development, spiritual growth and emotional well-being, specialized services such as placement, pension, mentoring and transition training, and chavruta—a nurturing community among rabbis. The CCAR Press provides liturgy and prayer books to the worldwide Reform Jewish community. (www.ccarnet.org)

National Association of Retired Reform Rabbis (NAORR) (1984). c/o Susan and Julian Cook, Co-Executive Vice Presidents, 2777 South Elmira Street, #17, Denver, CO 80231. (303) 753-1309. NAORRR, an affiliate of the Central Conference of American Rabbis (CCAR), provides support and advocacy for, and fosters fellowship among, retired and about to be retired rabbis, their spouses/partners, and surviving spouses/partners. It seeks to present opportunities for discussion of the practical problems and needs of its members; enable its members to continue their efforts to preserve and promote Judaism; provide opportunities for scholarly stimulation and Torah study; and continue strengthening and supporting the CCAR in its endeavors. (www.naorrr.org)

Women's Rabbinic Network (WRN) (1975). 355 Lexington Avenue, New York, NY 10017. (212) 972-3636. The WRN was created by a group of female rabbinic students to provide the support and advocacy needed in the early years of women in the Reform rabbinate. The organization includes the more than 600 women who have been ordained since 1972 at the Hebrew Union College-Jewish Institute of Religion. The WRN has consistently worked to promote the personal and professional growth of female rabbis and rabbinic students within the Reform movement. (www.womensrabbinicnetwork.org)

Jewish Renewal

OHALAH: Association of Rabbis for Jewish Renewal/Association of Cantors for Jewish Renewal (2011). c/o Beth Chaim Congregation, 1800 Holbrook Drive, Danville, CA 94506. (925) 736-7146. OHALAH (an acronym in Hebrew for Agudat Harabbanim l'Hithadshut Hayahadut) is a pan-denominational association of rabbis, cantors and students of these professions and includes more than 200 diverse rabbis who participate in the transformation and renewal of Judaism. The Rabbinic Pastors Association, a branch of OHALAH, includes rabbinic pastors, chaplains and students of these professions. OHALAH provides continuing education, professional support, ethical guidance and supervision, and collegial fellowship for qualifying rabbis, cantors and rabbinic pastors. (www.ohalah.org)

Secular/Humanist

Association of Humanistic Rabbis (AHR) (1967) (2001). 28611 West 12 Mile Road, Farmington, MI 48334. The AHR is a professional rabbinic organization that supports the values of the movement of Secular Humanistic Judaism, a human-centered approach to Jewish life and culture. It meets annually for fellowship, development of ethical positions, study and sharing of ideas to strengthen the movement and enhance collegial support. (www.humanisticrabbis.org)

Nondenominational

Beit Kaplan: The Rabbinic Partnership for Jewish Peoplehood (2016). Beit Kaplan is a new association of rabbis that strives to work collectively to sustain and inspire Jewish communities that champion the religious and cultural life of the Jewish people, upholding a vision of universal rights and dignity for all people. Inspired by the teachings of Rabbi Mordecai Kaplan, Beit Kaplan affirms a serious commitment to traditional Jewish thought and practice while at the same time valuing democratic ideals, academic inquiry, artistic creativity, and scientific discovery. Beit Kaplan is committed to the State of Israel as the historic and contemporary homeland of the Jewish people. Its mission is to offer rabbis a supportive community of peers; promote unity among rabbis regardless of affiliation, welcoming rabbis across denominational lines who support the goals of the partnership; promote dialogue among rabbis on issues of Jewish thought and practice; and support individuals, couples, and families as they deepen their commitments to Jewish learning and Jewish life. (www. rabbinicpartnership.org)

Cantors World (2003). Planetarium Station, 1274 49th Street, New York, NY 11219. (718) 851-3226. Cantors World was founded with the goal of helping to revive interest in traditional chazzanut through quality and creative programs. A key goal of Cantors World is to continue to promote the role of the cantor in bringing inspiration, dignity and beauty to the prayer service. Cantors World programming consists of several annual concerts and unique presentations, such as 'An Evening of Preparation' for the High Holy Days, a cantorial 'Talent Search', and special 'Shabbat Chazzanut' weekends. (www.cantorsworld.com)

Jewish Ministers Cantors Association of America & Canada/Der Chazzonim Farband (JMCA) (1897). 244 Fifth Avenue, Suite G 274, New York, NY 10001. (800) 977-5622. The JMCA was formed to organize an association of traditional cantors in North America and is the oldest cantorial organization in America. Historically, the JMCA supplied Jewish communities throughout the US and Canada with traditional cantors. (www.thejmca.org)

JWB Jewish Chaplains Council (formerly **Chaplains' Committee of the JWB, Committee for Army and Navy Religious Affairs,** and **Commission on Jewish Chaplaincy**) (1917) (1986). 520 Eighth Avenue, New York, NY 10018. (212) 786-5090. The JWB Jewish Chaplains Council, an agency of the JCC Association, provides full support services to Jewish chaplains and administers ecclesiastical approval for chaplain candidates and Jewish lay leaders in the military. It is a government accredited agency providing for the religious, educational and morale needs of Jewish military personnel, their families and patients in Veterans Affairs hospitals. (www.jcca.org/jwb)

Neshama: Association of Jewish Chaplains (NAJC) (formerly **National Association of Jewish Chaplains**) (1990). 3950 Biscayne Boulevard, Miami, FL 33137. (305) 394 8018. The NAJC is the professional organization of Jewish chaplains worldwide for those serving in a variety of settings including hospitals, hospices, nursing homes, homes for the elderly, other geriatric venues, Jewish community chaplaincy, prisons, mental health settings, law enforcement, fire departments, and the military, as well as in pastoral care training and education. It provides collegial support, continuing education and national conferences for professional growth, professional certification, and resources for the Jewish community on issues of pastoral and spiritual care, and serves as a clearinghouse for chaplaincy positions. (www.najc.org)

North American Boards of Rabbis (2000). 943 Cedarhurst Street, Valley Stream, NY 11581. (516) 579-2880. The North American Boards of Rabbis is an umbrella organization for Boards of Rabbis across the US and Canada that aims to bring together rabbis of the major Jewish movements for dialogue. (No website)

Rabbinic Center for Research and Counseling (1970). 306 South Avenue, Fanwood, NJ 07023. (908) 233-0419. The Rabbinic Center for Research and Counseling is the first organization established to promote research on intermarriage and to serve the needs of intermarrying and intermarried couples. It advocates and encourages rabbinic officiation at intermarriage ceremonies. The Rabbinic Center (1) provides a referral service (for a fee) for those who seek help in matters relating to intermarriage by maintaining a national list of rabbis who officiate at intermarriages; (2) conducts and promotes research on intermarriage; (3) offers pre-marital and marital therapy for intermarried couples and their families; (4) presents a variety of programs specifically geared to the needs of intermarried couples; and (5) serves as an outpatient mental health facility for area residents (in New Jersey). (www.rcrconline.org)

Rabbis and Cantors Retirement Board (RCRB) (2012). 115 West 30th Street, Suite 400, New York, NY 10001. (617) 600-8150. The RCRB administers the Rabbis and Cantors Retirement Plan, which provides rabbis and cantors an opportunity to save for retirement in a tax-advantaged manner. The Plan is available to ordained rabbis and cantors of all denominations throughout the US who meet certain eligibility requirements. (www.rabbisretirementplan.org)

T'ruah: The Rabbinic Call for Human Rights (formerly **Rabbis for Human Rights-North America**) (2002). 266 West 37th Street, Suite 803, New York, NY 10018. (212) 845-5201. T'ruah is an organization of rabbis from all streams of Judaism that acts on the Jewish imperative to respect and protect the human rights of all people. Grounded in Torah and the Jewish historical experience and guided by the Universal Declaration of Human Rights, T'ruah advocates for human rights in North America and Israel. (www.truah.org)

Women Cantors' Network (WCN) (1982). PO Box 609, Natick, MA 01760. The goal of the WCN is to promote the practice of Judaism through the dissemination, development and commissioning of Jewish music and rituals for clergy and lay leaders serving in the cantorate. The WCN provides information and education in areas related to the cantorate and Jewish music through annual conferences and online forums; commissions Jewish music for women's voices; and serves as a forum for discussing practical issues for women in the cantorate by sharing professional knowledge and experiences in a supportive atmosphere. (www.womencantors.net)

12.1.3   Rabbinical/Cantorial Schools

Association of Advanced Rabbinical and Talmudic Schools (AARTS) (1974). 11 Broadway, Suite 405, New York, NY 10004. (212) 363-1991. AARTS is a national accreditation association for Rabbinical and Talmudic schools in the US, which sets educational standards in the field throughout the country. Independently run, AARTS is made up of experts in the field of Rabbinical and Talmudic training. Both undergraduate and graduate programs are evaluated by AARTS and must meet set standards in education, finance and graduate requirements to be considered for accreditation. (No website)

Orthodox

Beth Medrash Govoha (Lakewood Yeshiva) (1943). 617 6th Street, Lakewood Township, NJ 08701. (732) 367-1060. The Lakewood Yeshiva is one of the largest yeshivas in the world and confers rabbinic ordination.
www.facebook.com/pages/Beth-Medrash-Govoha/105508412815036

Hebrew Theological College (1922). 7135 North Carpenter Road, Skokie, IL 60077. (847) 982-2500. Hebrew Theological College is a fully accredited institution, committed to the advancement of scholarship in accordance with the principles of Orthodox Judaism, providing academic programs to produce Torah scholars who will provide rabbinic and lay leadership. It includes Beis Midrash (Men's Division), Bellows Kollel, Blitstein Institute for Women, Bressler School of Advanced Hebrew Studies, Fasman Yeshiva High School, Israel Experience Program, Jewish Studies Online, Kanter School of Liberal Arts and Sciences, Yeshivas Hakayitz Summer Camp. (www.htc.edu)

Jewish Educational Leadership Institute/Miami Smicha Program (2002). 3401 Prairie Avenue, Miami Beach, FL 33140. (646) 450-5354. The Miami Smicha Program is a post-secondary institute that trains students to become chaplains and rabbis. It offers rabbinic ordination for young men who are comfortable with the chevruta (partnered) style of learning. The Miami Smicha Program offers both theoretical and practical learning to its students. Every week and during Jewish holidays, the students visit jails and hospitals, offer classes to the community and lead Shabbat services at various locations throughout the state. (www.jelimiami.com)

Kollel Tiferet Menachem. 7215 Waring Avenue, Los Angeles, CA 90046. (323) 906-7709. Kollel Tiferet Menachem is a West Coast rabbinical seminary of the Chabad Lubavitch, located on the campus of Yeshiva Ohr Elchonon (West Coast Rabbinical Seminary). (No website)

Ner Israel Rabbinical College (1933). 400 Mount Wilson Lane, Pikesville, MD 21208. (410) 484-7200. Ner Israel Rabbinical College trains rabbis and educators for Jewish communities in America and worldwide. It offers bachelor's, master's, and doctoral degrees in Talmudic law, as well as teacher's diplomas, and has articulation agreements with Johns Hopkins University, University of Maryland, Baltimore County, Towson University, and the University of Baltimore. (www.facebook.com/pages/Yeshivas-Ner-Yisroel/108924229126747)

Ohr Somayach Monsey (1979). Tanenbaum Educational Center, 244 Route 306, PO Box 334, Monsey, NY 10952. (845) 425-1370. Ohr Somayach Monsey offers the Meshech Chochmah Rabbinic Training Program, which encompasses both the classical material that prepares one for the rabbinate, together with training in areas that are specifically relevant to a role in reaching out to the unaffiliated. The objective of this program is to train rabbinic leaders, community lay leaders and outreach professionals. The two-year course culminates in rabbinic smicha (ordination). (www.os.edu)

Philip and Sarah Belz School of Jewish Music of the Rabbi Isaac Elchanan Theological Seminary (BSJM) (1954). 500 West 185th Street, New York, NY 10033. (646) 592-4420. The BSJM, a division of the Yeshiva University-affiliated Rabbi Isaac Elchanan Theological Seminary, is the foremost center in the US for the preservation of Jewish music and is dedicated to preparing aspiring professional cantors, ba'alei tefillah, music educators and synagogue laymen to serve the Jewish community throughout the world. The program serves to counter the serious shortage of professionally educated cantors, ba'alei tefillah, and music teachers. (www.yu.edu/belz)

Rabbi Isaac Elchanan Theological Seminary (Yeshiva University) (RIETS) (1896). Glueck Center for Jewish Study, Suite 632, 515 West 185 Street, New York, NY 10033. (646) 592-4455. REITS was the first Orthodox rabbinical seminary in the US and is the western hemisphere's leading center for Torah learning and training for the rabbinate. RIETS provides an educational experience in the classic mold of the great yeshivot. Embodying the historic concept of Torah Lishmah–learning for its own sake–and a responsiveness to community needs, RIETS is a preeminent source of rabbinic leadership, having trained some 2700 of the world's most distinguished Orthodox rabbis, scholars and teachers. (www.yu.edu/riets)

Rabbinical College of America (1956). 226 Sussex Avenue, PO Box 1996, Morristown, NJ 07960. (973) 267-9404.The Rabbinical College of America is an internationally known institution of higher education that seeks to develop scholars thoroughly trained in higher Jewish learning. The campus serves as the New Jersey headquarters of the worldwide Lubavitch movement. The College prepares its students for positions as rabbis, teachers and community leaders. The Rabbinical College is concerned with transmitting the ethical, philosophical and spiritual teachings and values of Judaism, and is committed to the unique philosophy of Chabad Lubavitch Chassidism. (www.rca.edu)

Rabbinical Seminary of America (Yeshiva Chofetz Chaim of Queens/ Yeshivas Rabbeinu Yisrael Meir HaKohen) (RSA) (1933). 76-01 147th Street, Flushing, NY 11367. (718) 268-4700. RSA is a major Orthodox yeshiva and rabbinical school that grants ordination. RSA is at the forefront of a Torah renaissance, producing the rabbis, principals, teachers and outreach workers who are revitalizing Jewish life in North America and beyond. Rabbinical students at Yeshiva Chofetz Chaim often spend a decade or more at the Yeshiva, studying a traditional yeshiva curriculum focusing on Talmud, Mussar (ethics), and Halakha. (www.duvys.com/simple/rsa?aff=JDonations)

Talmudic University (1974). 4000 Alton Road, Miami Beach, FL 33140. (305) 534-7050. Talmudic University's Smicha Program trains young scholars to analyze and decide questions of Jewish law. Additionally, the school strives to imbue each rabbi-in-training with the skills necessary to deal with human and community issues. The Program provides a well-rounded curriculum so that graduates are skilled in all areas of Jewish communal life, while emphasizing the specific area in which the rabbinic student is planning to devote himself. (www.talmudicu.edu)

Yeshiva Gedolah of Greater Miami Rabbinical College (1972). 17330 Northwest 7th Avenue, Miami, FL 33169. (305) 653-8770. Yeshiva Gedolah of Greater Miami Rabbinical College is a post-secondary institution that incorporates undergraduate and graduate level programs leading to rabbinical ordination. It is part of the Lubavitch Educational Center. (www.lecfl.com/about-yeshiva-gedolah)

Yeshiva Pirchei Shoshanim (Smicha Program) (1995). 570 4th Street, Lakewood, NJ 08701. (732) 370-3344. Yeshiva Pirchei Shoshanim offers a smicha program to Torah observant Jewish males that provides for a minimum of 15 months of study. (www.shulchanaruch.com)

Yeshivas Bais Torah Menachem (2008). 832 North Cherokee Avenue, Los Angeles, CA 90038. (323) 936-5226 or (323) 495-3010. Yeshivas Bais Toras Menachem balances a well-rounded curriculum of smicha studies, Chassidus, halakha and hashkafa with various occupational and vocational training opportunities. The smicha program is a two-year program, and the material is taught in a less pressured manner. The program's numerous extra-curricular activities provide vital enrichment and support for its spiritual and social aspirations. The students of Yeshivas Bais Toras Menachem are often engaged by many of the local Shluchim who involve them in outreach programs. (www.sites.google.com/site/smichacom)

Yeshivat Chovevei Torah (YCT) (1999). 3700 Henry Hudson Parkway, 2nd Floor, Riverdale, NY 10463. (212) 666-0036. YCT, founded by Rabbi Avi Weiss, is a Modern Orthodox rabbinical school committed to training and placing open Modern Orthodox rabbis who will lead the Jewish community and shape its spiritual and intellectual character in consonance with modern and open Orthodox values and commitments. YCT cultivates a love of Torah, a philosophy of inclusiveness, and a passion for leadership. Tuition is waived for all students and stipends are available to help meet living expenses. (www.yctorah.org)

Traditional

Institute of Traditional Judaism-The Metivta (1990). 82 Nassau Street, #313, New York, NY 10038. (914) 662-9649. The Institute of Traditional Judaism combines intensive Torah study, a profound love of the entire Jewish people, and a deep regard for the world. It is a nondenominational halakhic rabbinical school dedicated to genuine faith combined with intellectual honesty and the love of Israel. Graduates receive yoreh smicha. (www.utj.org)

Sephardic

Saul & Sally Ashkenazi Sephardic Rabbinical College (SRC) (1998). 730 Avenue S, Brooklyn, NY 11223. (718) 376-0930. The main mission of SRC is to train young rabbinic leaders in the tradition of Sephardic Judaism to teach and lead the community with the experience of seven years of learning on the highest levels of halakha and Talmud as well as to train them in pedagogy and other rabbinic functions to lead Sephardic communities and organizations. (No website)

Conservative

H. L. Miller Cantorial School and **College of Jewish Music of The Jewish Theological Seminary** (formerly **Cantors Institute**) (1952). 3080 Broadway,

New York, NY 10027. (212) 678-8000. The H. L. Miller Cantorial School and College of Jewish Music, affiliated with the Conservative movement, are devoted to Jewish musical studies. They train select advanced students as hazzanim (cantors) for congregational service or as teachers of Jewish music, choral directors, composers or research scholars. The H. L. Miller Cantorial School awards the diploma of hazzan, and the College of Jewish Music awards the master's degree in sacred music. Students are enrolled in both schools full-time and are expected to complete the diploma program and the master of sacred music degree simultaneously, preferably within a five-year period, leading to a career of service, through the joys of music, to the Jewish community. (www.jtsa.edu)

The Jewish Theological Seminary (JTS) (formerly **Jewish Theological Seminary Association**) (1886). 3080 Broadway, New York, NY 10027. (212) 678-8000. One of the world's leading centers of Jewish learning, JTS integrates rigorous academic scholarship and teaching with a commitment to strengthening Jewish tradition, Jewish lives and Jewish communities. The Rabbinical School at JTS offers intensive study, led by a world-class faculty of esteemed scholars, for rabbinic ordination of men and women in the Conservative Movement. The program is known for its textual concentration, emphasizing deep engagement with Torah, Midrash, Talmud, codes, liturgy, and literature. It includes The Davidson School (Jewish Education), The Graduate School, Institute for Jewish Learning, List College (undergraduate), Louis Finkelstein Institute for Religious and Social Studies, Melton Research Center for Jewish Education, Milstein Center for Interreligious Dialogue, Project Judaica. (www.jtsa.edu)

Ziegler School of Rabbinic Studies (American Jewish University) (1996). 15600 Mulholland Drive, Bel-Air, CA 90077. (310) 476 9777 or (888) 853-6763. The Ziegler School of Rabbinic Studies made history when it opened the first independent rabbinical school on the West Coast. Located on the campus of American Jewish University, the Ziegler School is a five-year rabbinical school. The rabbinic program is dedicated to training Conservative rabbis who are not only deeply versed in Jewish texts and committed to Jewish traditional practice, but who can transmit the beauty and richness of Judaism to others. (http://ziegler.aju.edu)

Reconstructionist
Reconstructionist Rabbinical College (1968) (2018). 1299 Church Road, Wyncote, PA 19095. (215) 576-0800. The Reconstructionist Rabbinical College is a progressive rabbinical school where people of all backgrounds engage intensively with Jewish texts, thought and practice. Co-educational, with a curriculum grounded in lively seminar-style courses and chevruta (partnered) study, the College offers a unique specialization in social justice organizing and a pioneering Department of Multi-Faith Studies and Initiatives. Its students' extensive field work reflects the wide variety of roles that graduates of the College play in congregations within and beyond the Reconstructionist movement. The College confers the titles of rabbi and cantor and grants degrees of Master and Doctor of Hebrew Letters and Master of Arts in Jewish Studies. (www.rrc.edu)

Reform

Debbie Friedman School of Sacred Music of Hebrew Union College-Jewish Institute of Religion (formerly **School of Sacred Music**) (1948). Brookdale Center, One West Fourth Street, New York, NY 10012. (212) 674-5300. The Debbie Friedman School of Sacred Music offers a five-year program of full-time graduate study leading to the degree of Master of Sacred Music and Investiture as a cantor. Originally conceived as an institution training cantors for the Reform, Conservative and Orthodox movements, the curriculum still reflects nondenominational origins. The School's faculty teaches the full range of cantorial styles, from traditional through contemporary music. (www.huc.edu/alumni/connect/alumni-associations/debbie-friedman-school-sacred-music)

Hebrew Union College-Jewish Institute of Religion (HUC-JIR) (1875). Cincinnati: 3101 Clifton Avenue, Cincinnati, OH 45220. (513) 221-1875; New York: The Brookdale Center, One West 4th Street, New York, NY 10012. (212) 674-5300; Los Angeles: 3077 University Avenue, Los Angeles, CA 90007. (213) 749-3424. HUC-JIR is the nation's oldest institution of higher Jewish education and the academic, spiritual and professional leadership development center of Reform Judaism. HUC-JIR educates men and women for service to American and world Jewry as rabbis, cantors, educators and communal service professionals, and offers graduate and postgraduate degree programs to scholars of all faiths. The Rabbinical School offers a five-year program of full-time graduate study leading to the Master of Arts in Hebrew Letters degree and ordination. Since 1875, over 2500 men and women have been ordained by HUC-JIR to serve the Reform movement. (www.huc.edu)

Jewish Renewal

ALEPH Ordination Programs-Cantorial Path. 7000 Lincoln Drive #B2, Philadelphia, PA 19119. (215) 247-9700. Instructors in the ALEPH Cantorial Program work with each student to craft different programs that take into account their particular knowledge and abilities. The curriculum includes skills in liturgy and the leadership of prayer, pastoral skills, life-cycle officiation, Jewish literacy and personal spiritual/emotional development. The Program also values courses and practica in counseling, counseling education, relationship and family therapy, group work, Clinical Pastoral Education (CPE), and Social Work. (www.aleph.org/cantorial-program)

ALEPH Ordination Programs-Rabbinic Path. 7000 Lincoln Drive #B2, Philadelphia, PA 19119. (215) 247-9700. The ALEPH Rabbinic Program is built upon the pioneering work of Jewish renewal visionary and ALEPH founder, Reb Zalman Schachter-Shalomi. It is a nondenominational, highly decentralized program of learning for men and women which offers structured, yet highly individualized, guidance and mentorship in pursuing the rigorous studies and practica which can culminate in rabbinic ordination. The Program blends a variety of modalities of learning, including its own retreats, seminars and televideo-conference courses, along with other supervised distance learning programs and courses, as well as course work undertaken in universities, colleges, synagogues and seminaries. (www.aleph.org/rabbinic.htm)

Secular/Humanist
Rabbinic Program of International Institute for Secular Humanistic Judaism
(1992). 175 Olde Half Day Road, Suite 123, Lincolnshire, IL 60069. (847) 383-6330.
The International Institute for Secular Humanistic Judaism Rabbinic Program trains
and ordains Secular Humanistic rabbis. The Rabbinic Program consists of four
years of rigorous course work, including completion of a rabbinic thesis, and a one-
year internship with a Secular Humanistic Jewish community. (www.iishj.org/pro-
grams-rabbinic.html)

Trans-Denominational
Academy for Jewish Religion (AJR) (1956). 28 Wells Avenue, Yonkers, NY 10701.
(914) 709-0900. Initially inspired by Rabbi Stephen Wise's vision to educate rabbis
and other spiritual leaders for klal Yisrael (the entire Jewish community), AJR has
grown into a Jewish seminary of major significance, preparing men and women to
serve the Jewish community as congregational spiritual leaders, chaplains, cantors,
educators and administrators in Jewish communal service organizations. AJR
alumni serve in Conservative, Reform, Reconstructionist, Renewal and unaffiliated
congregations and Jewish settings throughout the US, as well as internationally.
(www.ajrsem.org)

   Academy for Jewish Religion, California (Cantorial School) (AJRCA)
(2000). The Academy for Jewish Religion California, 574 Hilgard Avenue, Los
Angeles, CA 90024. (213) 884-4133. AJRCA's Cantorial School trains men and
women to become cantors. As a trans-denominational, pluralistic school that honors
the wisdom of all the denominations, AJRCA provides its students with the opportunity to study the full range of approaches to Jewish learning, values and practices.
Graduates of the five-year program are ordained as "Hazzan and Teacher in Israel,"
and receive a Master's Degree in Jewish Sacred Music. www.ajrca.edu/
cantorial-school

   Academy for Jewish Religion, California (Rabbinical School) (AJRCA)
(2000). The Yitzhak Rabin Hillel Center for Jewish Life at UCLA, 574 Hilgard
Avenue, Los Angeles, CA 90024. (213) 884-4133. AJRCA's Rabbinical School
trains men and women to become spiritual leaders who will serve all Jews and
Jewish movements, who will be steeped in the teachings and traditions of the sacred
texts, and who will bring a sense of spirituality and holiness to the lives of Jews
today. As a trans-denominational, pluralistic school that honors the wisdom of all
the denominations, AJRCA provides its students with the opportunity to study the
full range of approaches to Jewish learning, values and practices. Graduates of the
five-year program are ordained as "Rabbi and Teacher in Israel," and receive a
Master's Degree in Rabbinic Studies. (www.ajrca.edu/rabbinical-school)

Nondenominational
Rabbinical School of Hebrew College (2003). 160 Herrick Road, Newton Centre,
MA 02459. (617) 559-8600. The Rabbinical School of Hebrew College is a pio-
neering and thriving venture in pluralistic rabbinic education whose mission is to

prepare rabbis to serve an increasingly diverse Jewish community with wisdom, sensitivity and skill. Graduates serve as congregational rabbis in affiliated and independent congregations, Hillel rabbis and executive directors, hospital chaplains, educators and organizational innovators in institutions across the country. (www. hebrewcollege.edu/rabbinical)

Rabbinical Seminary International (1955). 13 Fairmont Street, Elmsford, New York, NY 10523. (212) 864-0261. Rabbinical Seminary International offers a unique individualized program for the training of the Modern Rabbi. (www.rabbinicalseminaryint.org)

School of Jewish Music of Hebrew College (2004). 160 Herrick Road, Newton Centre, MA 02459. (617) 559-8643. The School of Jewish Music/Cantor-Educator Program is an intensive full-time program for men and women that combines either a Master of Jewish Education or Master of Arts in Jewish Studies with pluralistic cantorial ordination. The School prepares cantors who can serve a variety of Jewish communities in diverse roles. (www.hebrewcollege.edu)

Online and Off-Campus Schools

American Seminary for Contemporary Judaism (2004). 885 East Seaman Avenue,Baldwin,NY11510.(516)223-0375.(www.jmwc.org/the-american-seminary-for-contemporary-judaism)

Jewish Spiritual Leaders Institute (2010). 54 Riverside Drive, New York, NY 10024. (201) 338-0165. (www.jsli.net/rabbinical-school), (www.jsli.net/cantorial-school)

Online Smicha (2010). 1022 South Fairview Avenue, St. Paul, MN 55116. (718) 221-0500. (www.onlinesmicha.com)

The Rabbinical Academy/Mesifta Adath Wolkowisk-Cantorial Investiture. 28-18 147th Street, Flushing, NY 11354. (718) 461-1273. (www.adasforlife.org/iRabbinicalAcdy.html)

The Rabbinical Academy/Mesifta Adath Wolkowisk-Rabbinic Program. 540 Derby Avenue, Woodmere, NY 11598. (718) 461-1273. (www.adasforlife.org/iRabbinicalAcdy.html)

12.1.4 Jewish Community Coordinating Organizations

Conference of Presidents of Major American Jewish Organizations (1955). 633 Third Avenue, New York, NY 10017. (212) 318-6111. The Conference of Presidents is the central coordinating body for American Jewry, representing more than 50 national Jewish agencies from across the political and religious spectrums. It is American Jewry's recognized address for consensus policy, collective action and maximizing the resources of the American Jewish community on issues of vital international and national concern. It seeks to strengthen and foster the special US-Israel relationship, address critical foreign policy issues that impact the

American Jewish community, and protect and enhance the security and dignity of Jews around the world. (www.conferenceofpresidents.org)

International Association of Jewish Free Loans (IAJFL) (formerly **International Association of Hebrew Free Loans** and **Association of Hebrew Free Loans**) (1982). 3443 North Central Avenue, Suite 707, Phoenix, AZ 85012. (602) 230-7983. The IAJFL is a nonpolitical network of Hebrew/Jewish free loan agencies throughout the world (most in North America) with the common goal of providing interest-free loans to those in need. Member organizations of the IAJFL each offer assistance through a variety of interest-free loan programs, including assistance for emergencies, such as housing, transportation, clothing, food, and shelter; loans for adoption assistance, small business start-ups, home healthcare, technical and vocational training, and families with children with special needs; and undergraduate and graduate student loans. (www.iajfl.org)

JCC Association of North America (JCC Association) (formerly **Council of Young Men's Hebrew & Kindred Associations** and **Jewish Welfare Board**) (1913) (1990). 520 8th Avenue, New York, NY 10018. (212) 532-4949. JCC Association strengthens and leads JCCs, YM-YWHAs, and camps throughout North America. As the convening organization, JCC Association partners with JCCs to bring together the collective power and knowledge of the JCC Movement. It offers services and resources to increase the effectiveness of JCCs as they provide community engagement and educational, cultural, social, recreational, and Jewish identity-building programs to enhance Jewish life throughout North America. JCC Association supports the largest network of Jewish early childhood centers and Jewish summer camps in North America. It provides leadership in the areas of staff recruitment and training, lay leadership development, field research, professional conferences and workshops, consultation, publications, and specialized programming, enabling each constituent JCC to better serve the needs of its members and community. By supporting the Jewish communal professionals who connect with JCC participants each year, JCC Association encourages engaged lives of purpose and meaning. (www.jcca.org)

The Jewish Federations of North America (JFNA) (formerly **United Jewish Appeal**, **Council of Jewish Federations**, and **United Jewish Communities**) (1939) (1999) (2009). 25 Broadway, Suite 1700, New York, NY 10004. (212) 284-6500. JFNA brings together more than 140 Federations and 300 Network communities to maximize its impact as the central address of North American Jewry. Collectively among the top ten charities in the world, JFNA secures and manages $16 billion in endowment assets. Each year, it raises funds through the Annual Campaign and emergency campaigns, and distributes funds from its foundations and endowments. Thought leaders and advocates in the fields of caregiving, aging, philanthropy, disability, foreign policy, homeland security, and health care, JFNA lobbies in Washington, DC to secure public funds that flow to Jewish communities and support thousands of agencies serving people of all backgrounds, including hospitals, nursing homes, community centers, family and children's service agencies, and vocational training programs. JFNA partners with the Government of

Israel and a variety of agencies to secure the Jewish State. (www.jewishfedera-tions.org)

Jewish Social Justice Roundtable (2009). The Jewish Social Justice Roundtable is a network, currently comprised of more than 50 organizations, that strengthens and aligns the Jewish social justice field in order to make justice a core expression of Jewish life and help create an equitable world in which power is shared and all are free from injustice. (www.jewishsocialjustice.org)

Network of Jewish Human Service Agencies (NJHSA) (formerly **Association of Jewish Family & Children's Agencies**) (1972) (2017). 50 Eisenhower Drive, Suite 100, Paramus, NJ 07652. (201) 977-2400. NJHSA is a membership associa-tion of nonprofit organizations in the US, Canada, and Israel. Its members provide a full range of human services for the Jewish community and beyond, including healthcare, career, employment, and mental health services, as well as programs for youth, family and seniors, Holocaust survivors, immigrants and refugees, people with disabilities, and caregivers. It strives to be the leading voice for human service organizations, to be the go-to place for innovation, best practices, collaboration, and advocacy, as well as to strengthen agencies to better serve their communities. (www.networkjhsa.org)

12.1.5 Jewish Community Professional Organizations

American Board of Ritual Circumcision (2004). (718) 435-3576. The American Board of Ritual Circumcision is an authoritative body that was established to create, disseminate and administer proper standards for the practice of brit milah in accor-dance with sound principles, based on the finest current scientific and medical knowledge. (www.certifiedmohels.org)

Association of Directors of Central Agencies (ADCA). ADCA is the profes-sional network of the heads of central agencies for Jewish education (in some com-munities they are known as bureaus of Jewish education, departments of education of the local federation, or several names associated with the idea of partnership for Jewish learning). This network has members in the US, Canada and England. Members meet virtually and in-person to share information, challenges and suc-cesses and for their own professional development. (No website)

Association of Reform Jewish Educators (ARJE) (formerly **National Association of Temple Educators**) (1955). 633 Third Avenue, 7th Floor, New York, NY 10017. (212) 452-6510. ARJE is the professional association of Reform Jewish professionals who engage and educate youth in synagogues, camps, and other Jewish entities. It is the voice of Reform Jewish education across North America and beyond. (www.reformeducaors.org)

Committee on Ethics in Jewish Leadership. The Committee on Ethics in Jewish Leadership promotes the values of accountability, transparency, democracy, and fairness in American Jewish organizations and institutions. (www.jewishleader-shipethics.org)

Early Childhood Educators of Reform Judaism (ECERJ). 21001 North Tatum Boulevard, Suite 1630-909, Phoenix, AZ 85050. (480) 620-4053. ECERJ provides vision, leadership, programmatic support and resources to Reform Jewish early childhood education programs. It also aims to establish an effective partnership within the temple between ECERJ, temple clergy and temple leadership. (www.ecerj.org)

Experiential Jewish Education Network (2015). The Experiential Jewish Education Network strengthens the professional knowledge, skills, connections, and leadership capability of experiential Jewish educators, increasing success, innovation, collaboration, and engagement in the Jewish community. It supports graduates of several experiential Jewish education programs at Hebrew Union College-Jewish Institute of Religion, The Davidson School of the Jewish Theological Seminary, and Yeshiva University as they implement experiential Jewish education across the Jewish spectrum. (www.ejenetwork.org)

Jewish Youth Directors Association (JYDA) (1971). (561) 247-0549. JYDA is dedicated to the development of professionals in the field of Conservative Jewish youth work and to raising the consciousness of the general Jewish community to the importance of this profession. JYDA develops educational programs and materials, provides conventions and workshops that emphasize the importance of Judaic knowledge, and trains Youth directors and advisors in group work skills, Judaic knowledge, child development, and developing creative and diverse programming. (www.jyda.org)

Joint Retirement Board for Conservative Judaism (JRB) (formerly **The Joint Retirement Board of The Rabbinical Assembly of America, The United Synagogue of America, and The Jewish Theological Seminary of America**) (1945). One Penn Plaza, Suite 1515, New York, NY 10119. (888) 572-3733. The JRB provides retirement, insurance, and planning services for professional staff members of the Rabbinical Assembly, Cantors Assembly, North American Association of Synagogue Executives, Jewish Educators Assembly, Jewish Theological Seminary, and United Synagogue of Conservative Judaism. (www.jrbcj.org)

JPro Network (formerly **Jewish Communal Service Association of North America, Conference of Jewish Communal Service, National Conference of Jewish Communal Service, Conference of Jewish Social Welfare, Conference of Jewish Social Service**, and **National Conference of Jewish Charities**) (1899) (2014). 25 Broadway, Suite 1700, New York, NY 10004. (212) 284-6945. JPro Network connects, educates, inspires, and empowers professionals working in the Jewish community sector. It amplifies the ability of Jewish community professionals to contribute to the vitality of their communities, supporting career growth and serving as the central resource for professional development. JPro supports the Jewish voluntary sector in attracting, motivating, and retaining exemplary talent. (www.jpro.org)

Kenissa: Communities of Meaning Network (formerly **The New Paradigm Spiritual Communities Initiative**) (2016). Kenissa: Communities of Meaning Network connects individuals who are leading contemporary efforts to re-define Jewish life. The Kenissa (Hebrew, entrance-way) Network identifies and convenes leaders of new organizations and communities (particularly in the sectors of social justice, spiritual practice, Jewish learning groups, Jewish prayer groups/minyanim, eco-sustainability, and arts/culture), and creates a capacity-building network to help these emerging communities of meaning thrive. (www.kenissa.org)

Leadership Conference of Secular and Humanistic Jews (LCSHJ) (1982). 175 Olde Half Day Road, Suite 123, Lincolnshire, IL 60069. (847) 383-6330. The LCSHJ facilitates communication and cooperation among leaders in Secular and Humanistic Jewish organizations, as well as to certify and establish ethical standards and professional guidelines for leaders in the movement and provide continuing education for the movement leadership. (www.Iishj.org/lcshj)

Leading Edge (formerly **Jewish Leadership Pipelines Alliance**) (2014). 85 Broad Street, New York, NY 10004. Leading Edge is an unprecedented partnership between Jewish foundations and federations to build a robust talent pipeline for Jewish organizations across North America and cultivate the next generation of professional leaders for Jewish nonprofits. The programs that Leading Edge offers include those aimed at easing CEO transitions, maximizing their contributions, and increasing retention rates; engaging the philanthropic community in understanding the importance of talent building; and helping create great workplace cultures that recruit, retain, and support excellent people who are empowered to do their best work. (www.leadingedge.org)

M^2: The Institute for Experiential Jewish Education (M^2) (2016). (866) 462-4353. M^2 is dedicated to advancing experiential Jewish education—a field dedicated to the development of individual and communal Jewish identity and agency. It develops and provides training and research for educators and organizations in North America and Israel that enable them to craft meaningful learning experiences infused with Jewish values and purpose. With a vision toward elevating the reach, impact, and depth of experiential Jewish education by harnessing current research, cross-disciplinary expertise, cutting-edge methods, and Jewish values, texts, and traditions, M^2 will serve the global Jewish community. (www.ieje.org)

National Association for Temple Administration (NATA) (1941). 3060 El Cerrito Plaza, #331, El Cerrito, CA 94530. (800) 966-6282. NATA is the professional organization for those who serve Reform Synagogues as executives, administrators, or managers. (www.natanet.org)

National Conference of Yeshiva Principals (NCYP) (1957). 1090 Coney Island Avenue, 3rd Floor, Brooklyn, NY 11230. (212) 227-1000, ext. 4535 (Men's Division) and ext. 4580 (Women's Division). The NCYP is a professional organization of Orthodox yeshiva and Jewish day school principals who coach one another, share insights and strategies, and help develop the programs and policies for the National Society for Hebrew Day Schools (Torah Umesorah). (www.chinuch.org/ncyp)

National Organization of American Mohalim (NOAM) (1988). c/o HUC-JIR, 3077 University Avenue, Los Angeles, CA 90007. (213) 765-2180. NOAM was founded to serve as the professional organization for mohalim/mohalot certified by the Brit Mila Board of Reform Judaism, with its main focus to provide continuing education opportunities on an assortment of topics ranging from liturgy to outreach. (www.beritmila.org)

North American Association of Synagogue Executives (NAASE) (1948). 120 Broadway, #1540, New York, NY 10271. (631) 732-9461. NAASE is a volunteer professional organization serving the needs of Jewish Executive Directors of the Conservative Movement. NAASE's mission is to bring together synagogue Executive Directors to further the development of their profession. (www.naase.org)

Program and Engagement Professionals of Reform Judaism (PEP-RJ) (formerly **Program Directors of Reform Judaism**) (2001). c/o Geri Gregory, Temple Beth-El, 211 Belknap Place, San Antonio, TX 78212. PEP-RJ is an affiliate of the Union for Reform Judaism that exists to strengthen congregations by supporting the professional development of its members. It is comprised of full- and part-time Program Directors and congregational staff members whose main responsibilities center on program coordination, membership, adult education, and the like. (www.peprj.org)

Reform Pension Board (RPB) (formerly **Rabbinical Pension Board**) (1944). 355 Lexington Avenue, 18th Floor, New York, NY 10017. (212) 681-1818. The RPB offers a variety of programs and services, including a pension plan, rabbi trust plan, life insurance, long-term disability insurance and pension continuance protection, which are specifically designed for the professionals, congregations, and institutions of the Reform Movement. (www.rpb.org)

12.1.6   Jewish Children's Education Organizations

(See also Jewish Youth Groups and Youth-Related Organizations. For Jewish education organizations for special needs children, see Jewish Organizations for People with Disabilities or Special Needs.)

Aleph Beta (2010). (516) 253-5691. Aleph Beta is committed to the relevance of Jewish learning. It believes Torah study should be evidence-based, intellectually stimulating, emotionally gripping, and relevant to your everyday life. Together with its world-renowned educators, Aleph Beta is building an online library making this amazing material accessible to students around the world. Aleph Beta creates video and other educational materials that delve into Jewish text and other sources in Jewish studies. (www.alephbeta.org)

Areyvut (2002). 147 South **Washington Avenue, Bergenfield, NJ 07621.** (201) 244-6702. Areyvut offers Jewish day schools, educators, synagogues, and community centers unique opportunities to empower and enrich youth by creating innovative and meaningful programs that make these core Jewish values a reality. (www.areyvut.org)

Avoda Arts (Ceased to exist as of 2019)

BimBam (formerly **G-dcast**) (Ceased to exist as of 2019)

Center for Initiatives in Jewish Education (CIJE) (2001). 45 Broadway, Suite 3050, New York, NY 10006. (212) 757-1500. CIJE was founded to enhance and enrich the quality of Jewish education throughout the US by seeking to upgrade the technology and programs available to Jewish day schools and yeshivas so that the education these schools provide is world-class. With its unique "hands-on" approach,

CIJE provides extensive teacher training and support, and CIJE liaisons, mentors, and other personnel regularly visit and communicate with beneficiary schools to make sure that the programs and technology provided are fully realized. CIJE supports over 30,000 students in over 100 schools across the US. (www.thecije.org)

The Consortium for Applied Studies in Jewish Education (CASJE) (2011). (510) 848-2502. CASJE is an active network of scholars, practitioners, funders and evaluators working collaboratively to advance the culture and quality of research in Jewish education, thereby producing an evidence base that can be applied to the problems in this field, to improve and advance practice. (www.casje.com)

Hebrew Charter School Center (HCSC) (2009). 555 Eighth Avenue, Suite 1703, New York, NY 10018. (212) 792-6234. HCSC was created to help advance the Hebrew language charter school movement, joining a growing movement to develop public educational opportunities for young people to learn within a dual language environment. (www.hebrewpublic.org)

Hidden Sparks (2005). 452 Fifth Avenue, 24th Floor, New York, NY 10018. (212) 767-7707. Hidden Sparks helps children with learning differences reach their full potential in school and life. Its goal is to increase the capacity of Jewish day schools to address the varied needs of children with learning difficulties by providing teachers with the tools and teaching strategies to better understand and teach children with social, emotional, and learning differences, as well as to nurture a cadre of trained experts. It aims to help schools develop and implement a system for early identification and assessment of struggling learners supported by administrators and educators. (www.hiddensparks.org)

The iCenter (2008). 95 Revere Drive, Suite D, Northbrook, IL 60062. (847) 418-8336. The iCenter works to advance high-quality, meaningful and innovative Israel education by serving as the national hub and catalyst for building, shaping and supporting the field. (www.theicenter.org)

Institute for Curriculum Services (ICS) (2005). 131 Steuart Street, Suite 205, San Francisco, CA 94105. (415) 977-7433. ICS is dedicated to improving the quality of K-12 education on Jews, Judaism, and Israel in the US by developing standards-aligned curricula and training teachers around the country. (www.icsresources.org)

International March of the Living (1988). 2 West 45th Street, Suite 1500, New York, NY 10036. (212) 869-6800. March of the Living International sponsors the annual educational program, March of the Living (MOTL), which brings students from all over the world to Poland to study the history of the Holocaust and to examine the roots of prejudice, intolerance, and hate. The MOTL is joined each year by thousands of Jewish teens, adults, and survivors from around the world. The March itself, a 3-kilometer walk from Auschwitz to Birkenau on Holocaust Remembrance Day, is a silent tribute to all victims of the Holocaust. After spending a week in Poland visiting other sites of Nazi Germany's persecution and former sites of Jewish life and culture, participants also travel to Israel the following week to celebrate Israel's Independence Day. (www.motl.org)

Jewish Early Childhood Education Leadership Institute (JECELI) (2012). 3080 Broadway, Box 55, New York, NY 10027. (215) 470-4664. JECELI engages select new and aspiring early childhood program directors in intensive Jewish learning, reflective practice, leadership development and community building. Participants work on discovering meaning in texts and ritual; understanding leadership and relationships through Jewish perspectives; fostering spiritual development; integrating Israel into the life of the early childhood program; and facilitating the development of identity. JECELI is a collaboration between The Jewish Theological Seminary and Hebrew Union College-Jewish Institute of Religion. (www.jeceli.org)

Jewish Educators Assembly (JEA) (1951). PO Box 413, Broadway & Locust Avenue, Cedarhurst, NY 11516. (516) 569-2537. JEA's mission is to promote excellence among educators committed to Conservative Jewish education by advancing professionalism, encouraging leadership, pursuing lifelong learning and building community. The JEA serves educators in their efforts to strengthen the Conservative movement and inspire greater Jewish learning. (www.jewisheducators.org)

Jewish Interactive (Ji) (2012). 1856 North Nob Hill Road, #219, Plantation, FL 33322. (646) 701-0017/ (703) 517-5182. Ji's mission is to make quality Jewish and Hebrew education available for all children at home, in school and in-between; provide quality materials presented in an engaging way by creating, supporting, curating, and catalyzing development; and align content provided with Jewish educational values. Ji provides accessible, affordable, and engaging Jewish/Hebrew educational technology products; offers high quality Jewish/Hebrew EdTech training to teachers and children; and maintains advocacy for change in Jewish education. (www.jewishinteractive.org)

The Jewish Lens (TJL) (2006). 25 East 83rd Street, Suite 6C, New York, NY 10028. (917) 387-3811. TJL provides experiential Jewish educational programming, engaging youth and young adults in the exploration of Jewish values, identity and tradition while discovering the diversity and unity of Klal Yisrael (Jewish Peoplehood). TJL's innovative methodology couples the emotional impact of photography with more traditional text-based learning, empowering participants to both strengthen their link to Judaism and then express it through their own photographs and commentary. TJL programs culminate in an in-person and/or online exhibition, which serves as a powerful way to share with the community the students' visual and verbal expressions of what being Jewish means to them. (www.jewishlens.org)

Jewish New Teacher Project (of the New Teacher Center) (JNTP) (2003). New Teacher Center, 110 Cooper Street, 5th Floor, Santa Cruz, CA 95060. (831) 600-2200. JNTP assists Jewish day schools across the US and Canada by increasing teacher effectiveness, teacher retention, and student achievement, and bringing the language of teaching standards, collaboration, and professional development into school culture. JNTP is dedicated to improving student learning by accelerating the effectiveness of beginning teachers in Jewish day schools. Its teacher induction model focuses on improving beginning teachers' classroom practice through high quality, intensive mentoring. (www.jntp.org)

Jewish Scholastic Press Association (JSPA) (2013). c/o Shalhevet High School, 5901 West Olympic Boulevard, Suite 108, Los Angeles, CA 90036. JSPA was formed to provide a journalistic organization for students attending Jewish schools. Membership is open to schools and individuals. (www.jewishscholasticpress.org)

Jewish Teen Education & Engagement Network (formerly **North American Association of Community & Congregational Hebrew High Schools** (NAACCHHS) (2006) (2019). NAACCHHS was established to serve as the umbrella organization for the field of community-based supplementary Jewish secondary education. Its mission is to advocate for member schools while creating, supporting, exchanging and disseminating innovative programs, curricula, best practices and resources to enrich Jewish education in community Hebrew high schools across North America. (www.jteenprofessionals.org)

Lookstein Virtual Jewish Academy (2011). (646) 568-9737. Lookstein Virtual Jewish Academy is an online school of Jewish studies for students in grades 6-12, working to bring Jewish education to Jewish students everywhere, regardless of geographic location or ideological orientation, and to supporting Jewish schools by providing affordable, innovative, differentiated instruction to supplement their existing course offerings. It is deeply committed to enhancing the quality of Jewish education around the world. The staff works with hundreds of Jewish day schools to identify and solve problems facing the Jewish educational world today, translating innovative ideas into practical solutions: curriculum, resources, programs, and community action. (www.looksteinvirtual.org)

Merkos-Central Organization for Jewish Education National Accreditation Board (NAB) (2000). (718) 774-4000. 770 Eastern Parkway, Brooklyn, NY 11213. (718) 771-4000. NAB is the only fully recognized national Jewish accrediting agency in the US and grants accreditation to early childhood, elementary and secondary schools. (www.chinuchoffice.org/templates/articlecco_cdo/aid/261058/jewish/Accreditation.htm)

Merkos L'Inyonei Chinuch International Board of License (MLCIBL). 784 Eastern Parkway, Suite 304, Brooklyn, NY 11213. (718) 774-4000, ext. 360. The MLCIBL for principals, teachers and early childhood educators in Jewish schools serves as a coordinating and standard-setting body, responsible for establishing the professional conditions and procedural requirements for licensing in Chabad Lubavitch as well as other yeshivas and Jewish day schools. (www.chinuchoffice.org/templates/articlecco_cdo/aid/2078756/jewish/Merkos-National-Teachers-License.htm)

Moving Traditions (2005). 8380 Old York Road, Suite 4300, Elkins Park, PA 19027. (215) 887-4511. Moving Traditions inspires people to live fuller lives–and to work for a better world for all–by advocating for a more expansive view of gender in Jewish learning and practice. Partnering with institutions across North America, its flagship educational programs are Rosh Hodesh: It's a Girl Thing! and Shevet Achim: The Brotherhood. (www.movingtraditions.org)

National Committee for the Furtherance of Jewish Education (NCFJE) (1940). 824 Eastern Parkway, Brooklyn, NY 11213. (718) 735-0200. The NCFJE is a multi-faceted charity that protects, feeds, and educates thousands throughout the NY metropolitan area and around the nation. One of the first Chabad Lubavitch charities established in the US, initially it provided Jewish public school students with a free Jewish education but soon expanded to implement a broad range of educational and humanitarian services. The NCFJE disseminates the ideals of Torah-true education among the youth of America; provides education and compassionate care for the poor, sick and needy in the US and Israel, immigrant, legal and prisoner services, family and vocational counseling, crisis intervention, and substance abuse and alcohol education and prevention assistance; sponsors camps, after-school and preschool programs; operates Toys for Hospitalized Children; and advocates for the Jewish community. (www.ncfje.org)

National Jewish Early Childhood Network (NJECN) (1977). c/o Helaine Groeger, 11 Wonder View Court, North Potomac, MD 20878. (301) 354-3203. The NJECN, allied with the National Association for the Education of Young Children, is comprised of individuals who are interested in the unique needs of young Jewish children in an early childhood educational setting. The annual NJECN Conference allows early childhood professionals across the country to meet and share ideas. (No website)

NewCAJE (formerly **CAJE, the Coalition for the Advancement of Jewish Education**) (1976) (2010). 908 Nueces Street, #41, Austin, TX 78701 (857) 288-8765. NewCAJE advocates for Jewish education and for Jewish teachers. It is a pluralistic organization which embraces every denominational division of Judaism and brings together all settings of Jewish education, including day schools, complementary schools, camps, JCCs, independent schools, after school programs, online programs and more. NewCAJE holds conferences annually which create a network of support for Jewish educators and a conduit to innovation, deepen the educators' grasp of both Jewish and educational learning, and emphasize the sharing of information, techniques and problem solutions. (www.newcaje.org)

Ozar Hatorah (1945). 625 Broadway, Floor 5, New York, NY 10012. (212) 253-7245. Ozar Hatorah is an international educational network organization for Sephardic Orthodox Jewish education which originally operated in Mandate Palestine but later focused on religious Jewish education in Muslim countries in the Middle East and North Africa, as well as in the Sephardi communities in France. It establishes schools teaching both religious and secular subjects. (www.shemayisrael.com/ozerhatorah)

Prizmah: Center for Jewish Day Schools (2016). 254 West 54th Street, New York, NY 10019. (646) 975-2800. Prizmah was formed through the merger of five national Jewish day school organizations: Day Schools of Reform Judaism (PARDES), The Partnership for Excellence in Jewish Education (PEJE), The Schechter Day School Network (Schechter), RAVSAK (The Jewish Community Day School Network), and The Yeshiva University School Partnership (YUSP). Its mission is to transform the North American Jewish day school landscape with a pioneering approach that provides day schools with tools to foster the educational excellence, financial vitality, and community support that will make day school education the first choice for Jewish families. Prizmah is a powerful resource, thought leader, and advocate for the day school field. Along with research, data analysis, communities of practice, convenings, and publications, Prizmah offers dozens of programs and services with proven track records of success within the Jewish day school network. (www.prizmah.org)

Project Chazon (1996). 1234 East 29th Street, Brooklyn, NY 11210. (347) 546-5233. Project Chazon presents informative and compelling hashkafah (Hebrew, Jewish worldview) seminars that uplift, reinforce and strengthen the Yiddishkeit of yeshiva, Bais Yaakov, and Jewish day school students across North America and England. In addition, Project Chazon's staff individually counsels, supports, and guides hundreds of wavering and at-risk teenagers, helping them to go on to become independent and productive members of the Jewish community; trains teachers to detect the very earliest signs of trouble and sensitizes them to the special needs of troubled students; and offers community parenting lectures. Project Chazon focuses primarily on high school students but includes eighth grade students as well. (www. projectchazon.com)

ShalomLearning (2011). 160 Herrick Road, Newton Centre, MA 02459. (301) 660-3800. Harnessing the power of technology to improve educational outcomes and enhance learning, ShalomLearning offers an alternative approach to traditional Hebrew school programs that combines the best of traditional Jewish religious education with innovative online learning activities to make Hebrew school more engaging and relevant for students, more accessible for families and more effective for synagogues. (www.shalomlearning.org)

SHEVET: Jewish Family Education Exchange (formerly **The Consortium for the Jewish Family** and **Shirley and Arthur Whizin Institute for Jewish Life**) (Ceased to exist)

Shinui: The Network for Innovation in Part-Time Jewish Education (2014) (215) 320-0389. Shinui is a joint effort by a number of central Jewish education agencies across the US whose mission is to spark, nurture, and spread educational innovation in supplementary (part-time) Jewish education. Its website facilitates the sharing of innovative ideas for supplementary Jewish education that includes the entire family, and also provides webinars for educators and parents on how to manage, assess, and sustain change in a supplementary school setting. (www.shinui.org)

Storahtelling (1999). 125 Maiden Lane, Suite 8B, New York, NY 10038. (212) 908-2536. Storahtelling is a pioneer in Jewish education via the arts and new media. Through innovative leadership training programs and theatrical performances, Storahtelling makes ancient stories and traditions accessible for new generations, advancing Judaic literacy and raising social consciousness. (www.amichai.me/ storahtelling)

Torah Umesorah: The National Society for Hebrew Day Schools (1944). 620 Foster Avenue, Brooklyn, NY 11230. (212) 227-1000. Torah Umesorah is an Orthodox organization that fosters and promotes Torah-based Jewish religious education in North America by supporting and developing a loosely affiliated network of independent private Jewish day schools, yeshivas, and kollels in every city with a significant population of Jews. It establishes Jewish day schools in the US and Canada and provides support services, including personnel placement, curriculum development, principal and teacher training, school supervision, conferences and conventions, and resource materials for teachers. It also publishes text books and other learning materials and has also branched out into providing community support and outreach. (www.torah-umesorah.com)

12.1.7   Jewish Adult Education Organizations

(Includes both formal and informal Jewish education organizations. For Jewish education organizations for college students, see Jewish College Campus Organizations. For Jewish education organizations for adults with special needs, see Jewish Organizations for People with Disabilities or Special Needs.)

At The Well (2015). At The Well is a women's wellness organization rooted in Jewish spirituality and women's health. It connects women in peer-led Well Circles who meet monthly for Rosh Chodesh (the new moon). (www.atthewellproject.com)

Brandeis National Committee (BNC) (formerly **Brandeis University National Women's Committee**) (1948). Goldfarb, MS 132, 415 South Street, Waltham, MA 02453. (781) 736-7588 or (888) 862-8692. The BNC provides support for Brandeis University and its libraries through philanthropy, learning and community. It connects Brandeis, a nonsectarian university founded by the American Jewish community, to its members and their communities through programs that reflect the ideals of social justice and academic excellence. (www.brandeis.edu/bnc)

Center for Modern Torah Leadership (1997). 63 South Pleasant Street, Sharon, MA 02067. The Center for Modern Torah Leadership's mission is to model and foster a vision of fully committed halakhic Judaism that embraces the intellectual and moral challenges of modernity. The Center carries out its mission through the Summer Beit Midrash program, educating up-and-coming leaders to write their own halakhic responsum after an intense five-weeks' study session; The Rabbis and Educators Professional Development Institute; the Campus and Community Education Institutes; weekly Divrei Torah circulated online; and its website containing articles and audio lectures. (www.torahleadership.org)

Chai Mitzvah (2008). 106 Timberwood Road, West Hartford, CT 06117. (860) 206-8363. Chai Mitzvah is an unaffiliated, nondenominational, independent organization whose mission is to guide and inspire all Jews in the lifelong pursuit of meaning through a deeper engagement with Judaism. Chai Mitzvah can be found all throughout the US, Canada, and Israel. Participants can engage in Chai Mitzvah through their synagogue, JCC, community organization, with a group of friends, or individually. Chai Mitzvah encourages informal groups to form around special interests (e.g., business ethics, environment) or special times in one's life (e.g., life-cycle events, milestone birthdays, becoming an empty-nester). The curriculum is specially designed for Chai Mitzvah by leading Jewish educators, incorporating both traditional and contemporary sources, and using both Hebrew and English, with a different topic examined in each of the nine monthly group learning sessions. (www.chaimitzvah.org)

Chofetz Chaim Heritage Foundation (1989). 361 Spook Rock Road, Suffern, NY 10901. (845) 352-3505. The Chofetz Chaim Heritage Foundation is an Orthodox Jewish organization dedicated to spreading the teachings of Rabbi Yisrael Meir Kagan, who was known as the Chofetz Chaim (Seeker of Life, in Hebrew), based on his work of Jewish ethics of the same name, dealing with the prohibitions of gossip, slander and defamation (known as lashon hara in Jewish law). The Foundation has launched innovative methods of promoting the Torah's wisdom on human relations and personal development. (www.powerofspeech.org)

Clal-The National Jewish Center for Learning and Leadership (formerly **National Jewish Conference Center** and **National Jewish Resource Center**) (1974). 440 Park Avenue South, 4th Floor, New York, NY 10016. (212) 779-3300. Clal is a leadership training institute, think tank and resource center whose mission is to create an informed, engaged and dynamic Jewish life. It provides leadership training for lay leaders, rabbis, educators and communal professionals and helps people to re-imagine Jewish life. The Clal faculty provides cutting-edge teaching, lectures, courses, seminars and consulting across the US. Clal's Rabbis Without Borders seeks to position rabbis as American religious leaders and spiritual innovators who contribute Jewish wisdom to the American spiritual landscape. (www.clal.org)

Doc Emet Productions (2008). PO Box 10966, Knoxville, TN 37939. (617) 694-4257. Doc Emet Productions is an independently-funded nonprofit organization that produces and disseminates educational resources in a variety of media that contribute to the strengthening of Jewish identity and Jewish peoplehood as well as promoting the values of freedom and democracy. (www.docemetproductions.com)

Drisha Institute for Jewish Education (1979). 1501 Broadway, Suite 505A, New York, NY 10036. (212) 595-0307. The Drisha Institute for Jewish Education was founded as the world's first center dedicated specifically to women's study of classical Jewish texts. Today, Drisha is a leading center for the study of classical Jewish texts for students from across the US and abroad. Drisha offers full-time programs, summer institutes, classes for engaged couples, summer programs for high school girls, a bat mitzvah program, continuing education programs, High Holiday prayer services and community lectures. (www.drisha.org)

The Florence Melton School of Adult Jewish Learning (1980). 520 8th Avenue, 4th Floor, New York, NY 10018. (847) 714-9843. The Melton School forms an international network of community-based schools offering adults the opportunity to acquire Jewish literacy in an open, trans-denominational, intellectually stimulating learning environment. It is the largest pluralistic adult Jewish education network in the world, with more than 45 Melton Schools in as many cities throughout the US, Canada, and elsewhere, that are attended weekly by more than 5000 students. (www.meltonschool.org)

Hadar (also known as **Hadar Institute** and **Mechon Hadar**) (2006). 190 Amsterdam Avenue, New York, NY 10023. (646) 770-1468. Hadar is an educational institution that empowers Jews from all walks of Jewish life to create and sustain vibrant, practicing, egalitarian communities of Torah, Avodah (service), and Hesed (kindness), and offers a creative response to contemporary questions and challenges. It is a leader in the field of Jewish education and community building, engaging diverse populations in serious Jewish learning with curiosity, creativity, and conviction. Hadar offers year-long and summer intensive learning programs; week-long and month-long immersive programs; the only full-time, gender-egalitarian yeshiva in North America; daytime and evening lectures and classes; an online learning platform that connects Jews around the world with each other through weekly one-on-one havruta (partner) learning; and podcasts, essays, online classes, prayer recordings, and other web resources. (www.hadar.org)

Hasefer-The Jewish Literary Foundation (Ceased to exist as of 2019)

Institute for Jewish Ideas and Ideals (2007). 2 West 70th Street, New York, NY 10023. (917) 775-1755. The Institute for Jewish Ideas and Ideals offers a vision of Orthodox Judaism that is intellectually sound, spiritually compelling and emotionally satisfying. Based on an unwavering commitment to the Torah tradition and to the Jewish people, it fosters an appreciation of legitimate diversity within Orthodoxy. (www.jewishideas.org)

Institute for Jewish Spirituality (1999). 121 West 27th Street, Suite 404, New York, NY 10001 (646) 461-6499. The Institute for Jewish Spirituality promotes an immersive, practice-based approach to deepening contemplative Jewish spiritual life for rabbis, cantors, educators, social justice activists, congregants, and community members. (www.jewishspirituality.org)

JewBelong (2016). PO Box 3013, Memorial Station, Upper Montclair, NJ 07043. (973) 464-4975. JewBelong is an online community that seeks to help find the joy, meaning, relevance, and connection that Judaism has to offer for Jewish people, for people who aren't Jewish but are part of a Jewish community, and for anyone who has felt like a Jewish outsider, especially disengaged Jews. It strives to make Judaism and Jewish practice more comfortable and easier to understand and aims to remove embarrassment about a lack of Jewish knowledge as a barrier to Jewish involvement. (www.jewbelong.com)

Jewish Heritage Foundation (JHF). (2001). 23775 Commerce Park Road, Suite #1, Beachwood, OH 44122. (216) 916-9266. JHF is an educational and research institute whose vision is to motivate and inspire people through the power of Torah. Its main project is Keser Torah Worldwide. It initiates innovative methods of promoting the Torah's wisdom, offering a vast array of projects and programs, including its comprehensive website, Torah phone line, and inspirational classes and learning programs. (www.jewishheritagefoundation.org)

KIVUNIM (1998). 300 Central Park West, Suite 12J2, New York, NY 10024. (917) 930-3092 or (917) 658-5884. KIVUNIM's college-age gap year program inspires its students to forge a lifelong relationship with Israel and the Jewish people through their travels across the world, gaining understanding of Jewish life and history together with that of the many cultures, religions, and worldviews among whom the Jewish people grew in its 2000-year Diaspora. KIVUNIM welcomes students from all backgrounds in the belief that mutual understanding can only enhance the possibilities for greater peace and justice. KIVUNIM students receive a full year of college credit transferrable to and accepted by most colleges and universities across North America. (www.kivunim.org)

Limmud North America (2017). 2001 Wilshire Boulevard, Santa Monica, CA 90403. (310) 867-3640. Limmud North America is the North American network of the international Limmud organization headquartered in the United Kingdom, which pioneered and evolved a unique model of cross-communal Jewish learning. (www.limmud.org/network-of-communities/north-america)

Mesorah Heritage Foundation (1994). 4401 Second Avenue, Brooklyn, NY 11232. (718) 921-9000. The Mesorah Heritage Foundation was created to remove the language barrier from the Jewish literary heritage and make the riches of Jewish eternity available to English-speaking Jews. The Foundation sponsors literature that celebrates the rich Jewish heritage; creates works of intensive scholarship and unexcelled beauty; and produces books that will be read, studied, and cherished for generations. It recruits accomplished translators, scholars, writers, and editors who free the great Jewish texts from the captivity of ancient languages and bring them to English-speaking Jews in books that are beautifully produced and literarily graceful. (www.mesorahheritage.org)

Moishe House (2006). Leichtag Commons, 441 Saxony Road, Barn 2, Encinitas, CA 92024. (855) 598-5509. Moishe House is an international organization providing meaningful Jewish experiences to young adults in their twenties. Its innovative model trains, supports and sponsors young Jewish leaders as they create vibrant home-based communities for their peers. From Shabbat dinners to book clubs to sporting events, residents find ways to connect their peers with the community wherever they are. (www.moishehouse.org)

Nishma (1997). 1740 Ocean Avenue, Suite 8-P, Brooklyn, NY 11230. (718) 338-6515. Nishma is an international Torah research, resource, and educational organization, distinguished by its commitment to the presentation of the halakhic spectrum, its fostering of individual inquiry, and its devotion to the critical investigation of contemporary issues. (www.nishma.org)

OneTable (2014). 79 Madison Avenue, 2nd Floor, New York, NY 10016. (646) 887-3891. OneTable is an online and in-person community available in various cities across the US that helps those in their 20s and 30s find, enjoy, and share Shabbat dinners. OneTable makes it easy for hosts to welcome people to a Shabbat dinner at home, for guests to savor a Friday meal, and for all to experience unique events for Shabbat dinner out. (www.onetable.org)

Orot (1990). PO Box 155, Spring Valley, NY 10977. Orot disseminates the teachings of Rabbi Abraham Isaac Hakohen Kook (1865–1935), the first Ashkenazic Chief Rabbi of Israel, considered one of the greatest Jewish thinkers and mystics of all time. (www.orot.com)

Partners in Torah (1991). 228 Aycrigg Avenue, Passaic, NJ 07055. (973) 221-3650 or (800) 788-3942. Partners in Torah provides a cost-free, relationship-based learning opportunity for Jewish adults to discover Judaism—its culture, history and traditions—at their pace and schedule. (www.partnersintorah.org)

Project Genesis (1993). 122 Slade Avenue, Suite 250, Baltimore, MD 21208. (888) 999-8672 or (410) 602-1350. Project Genesis engages Jews worldwide in Jewish educational programming, regardless of their location or previous background, speaking to Jews around the globe in modern language and with advanced technology. (www.projectgenesis.org)

Reclaiming Judaism (2000). 1532 Pelican Point Drive, BA241, Sarasota, FL 34231. (914) 500-5696. Reclaiming Judaism is dedicated to program, ritual, and resource research and development in order to facilitate meaningful engagement with Judaism among all age groups, bringing together seekers, teachers, and innovators from across the full spectrum of Judaism in the pursuit of Jewish educational excellence and healthy and holy approaches to *klal Yisrael*. Its website provides material on inclusive adult Jewish spiritual practice and meaningful bar/bat mitzvah articles and resources; its program division offers workshops, in-service training, lectures, and guidance sessions; and its nonprofit publishing division is dedicated to creating needed new resources for meaningful Jewish living within a context of respectful pluralism. (www.reclaimingjudaism.org)

The Rohr Jewish Learning Institute (JLI) (1998). 822 Eastern Parkway, Brooklyn, NY 11213. (718) 221-6900. JLI, associated with Chabad Lubavitch, is the largest provider of adult Jewish learning. Its mission is to inspire Jewish learning worldwide and to transform Jewish life and the greater community through Torah study with the goal of creating a global network of informed students connected by bonds of shared Jewish experience. Its divisions/projects include Torah Café, Torah Studies, Rosh Chodesh Society, Sinai Scholars, JLI Teens, MYSHIUR, National Jewish Retreat, The Land, and The Spirit. (www.myjli.com)

Shalom Hartman Institute of North America (SHI-NA) (2010). 475 Riverside Drive, Suite 1450, New York, NY 10115. (212) 268-0300. SHI-NA is shaping the future of North American Jewish life through transformative teaching, educating leaders and enriching the public conversation. SHI-NA guides, oversees and implements Shalom Hartman Institute research, educational programming and curricula to North American Jewry. The Shalom Hartman Institute, based in Israel, is a center of transformative thinking and teaching that addresses the major challenges facing the Jewish people and elevates the quality of Jewish life in Israel and around the world. (www.hartman.org.il/NA_index.asp)

Sinai Retreats (1985). 675 State Route 418, Warrensburg, NY 12885. (518) 623-5757 or (301) 807-2434. Sinai Retreats is a two-week summer program that gives Jewish men and women from diverse backgrounds and affiliations an opportunity to explore what it really means to be Jewish in a warm, open environment that makes it easy to ask straight-forward questions. Students and young, single professionals come together in Warrensburg, New York, to study with leading educators, where they engage in a vibrant excursion through contemporary and classical Jewish thought, and they also participate in recreational activities such as canoeing, swimming, sports, hiking, and water sports. (www.sinairetreats.com)

Testing & Training International (TTI) (1996). 5120 19th Avenue, #3D, Brooklyn, NY 11204. (877) 746-4884 or (718) 376-0974. TTI provides quality higher education for Orthodox Jewish students from around the globe, all while steadfastly conforming to the needs and standards of halakha. TTI is the premier provider of alternative college instruction and career advancement in the Orthodox Jewish world. (www.testingandtraining.com)

Walking Stick Foundation (1997). 16155 Sierra Lakes Parkway, Suite 160-407, Fontana, CA 92336. Walking Stick Foundation is an educational organization dedicated to the restoration and preservation of aboriginal Jewish spirituality, flavoring its programs with ancient and early medieval Hebraic shamanism and mystery wisdom. It offers programs that highlight the aboriginal mystery wisdom of Judaism, and, on occasion, programs featuring Native American and other aboriginal traditions shared with participants by teachers indigenous to those paths. (www.walking-stick.org)

Yeshivat Maharat (2009). 3700 Henry Hudson Parkway, Bronx, NY 10463. (718) 796-0590. Yeshivat Maharat, founded by Rabbi Avi Weiss, is the first institution to train Orthodox women as spiritual leaders and halakhic authorities. Through a rigorous curriculum of Talmud, halakhic decision-making, pastoral counseling, leadership development and internship experiences, Yeshivat Maharat's graduates are prepared to assume the responsibility and authority to be legal arbiters for the community. (www.yeshivatmaharat.org)

Zichron Avos-Jewish Interactive Studies (JIS) (1998). 275 North Highland Avenue, Merion Station, PA 19066. JIS was founded to support the use of the internet for Jewish studies. It seeks to provide accessible Jewish education to Jewish adults at all educational and religious backgrounds, using the internet for offering structured online courses that are based on study of classical Jewish texts. (www.jewishstudies.org)

12.1.8 Jewish Youth Groups and Youth-Related Organizations

Betar USA (1929). 2121 South Cedar Road, Cleveland, OH 44101. (216) 297-9466. Betar USA is part of the Betar Movement, a world Zionist youth movement founded by Vladimir Jabotinsky. Betar is involved in Jewish and Zionist activism. It promotes Israeli issues in the American media and takes an active stance against antisemitism. Its goal is the gathering of all Jewish people in Israel. Betar promotes Jewish leadership on university campuses as well as in local communities. (www.betar.org)

B'nai B'rith Youth Organization (BBYO) (1924, became independent in 2002). 800 Eighth Street, NW, Washington, DC 20001. (202) 857-6633. Organized in local chapters, BBYO is a youth-led international organization offering leadership opportunities and Jewish programming for Jewish youth and teenagers in sixth grade and older. BBYO sponsors trips to Israel, camping, community involvement and college campus experiences for teens. The PANIM Institute for Jewish Leadership and Values, a division of BBYO, offers compelling content and experiences to Jewish institutions and teens focused on service, advocacy, and philanthropy. Its flagship program, Panim el Panim, brings about 1000 Jewish teens from across the country to Washington, DC each year to learn about political and social activism in the context of Jewish learning and values, and empowers Jewish teens to a lifetime of activism, leadership and service. (www.bbyo.org)

Bnei Akiva of the United States & Canada (1934). 520 8th Avenue, 15th Floor, New York, NY 10018. (212) 465-9536. Bnei Akiva of the United States & Canada is the premier religious Zionist youth movement. Bnei Akiva provides high quality religious Zionist education and programs for North American Jewish youth along with their families and communities. It offers school-year and summer educational programming from childhood through the college years. Based on the principles of

Torah v'Avodah, Bnei Akiva encourages aliyah, love of the Jewish people and love of Israel. (www.bneiakiva.org)

Club Z (2012). 20 El Camino Real, Redwood City, CA 94062. (650) 575-4224. Club Z envisions a network of leaders who embrace Zionism, are proud of their Jewish heritage, and address issues of bigotry and antisemitism head-on. It is a national organization for Jewish teens, raising modern-day Zionists who are articulate and knowledgeable leaders. Club Z connects teens to their Jewish identity, Israel, Zionism, and a community of like-minded activists at a key point in their lives with a curriculum that engages teens in deep and dynamic conversations, equipping them with the tools to become informed, lifelong leaders. (www.clubz.org)

Foundation for Jewish Camp (FJC) (formerly **Foundation for Jewish Camping**) (1998). 253 West 35th Street, 4th Floor, New York, NY 10001. (646) 278-4500. As the central address for nonprofit Jewish camps in North America, FJC works with camps from all streams of Jewish belief and practice to promote excellence in their management and programs, and with communities, to increase awareness and promote enrollment. It works aggressively to highlight the value and importance of the nonprofit Jewish camp experience to parents, leaders, and communities. (www.jewishcamp.org)

Habonim Dror North America (HDNA) (1935). 1000 Dean Street, #353, Brooklyn, NY 11238. (718) 789-1796. HDNA is a Progressive Labor Zionist Youth movement (its name means the Builders of Freedom, in Hebrew) whose mission is to build a personal bond and commitment between North American Jewish youth and Israel, and to create Jewish leaders who will actualize the principles of social justice, equality, peace, and coexistence in Israel and North America. HDNA fosters identification with cooperative living in Israel, calling for aliyah, and stimulates study of Jewish and Zionist culture, history and contemporary society. HDNA runs seven summer camps across Canada and the US, an Israel summer program, a year-long Israel program and year-round activities in many areas of the country. (www.habonimdror.org)

Hashomer Hatzair United States (1923). 601 West 26th Street, Suite 325-25, New York, NY 10001. (212) 627-2830. Hashomer Hatzair (The Young Guard, in Hebrew) is a Progressive Zionist Youth Movement that specializes in youth-led experiential Jewish education. Based on the values of equity, community and social responsibility, their camps and year-round activities encourage youth to shape their communities and find personal relevance in Judaism, Jewish peoplehood and Israel. Hashomer Hatzair seeks to educate Jewish youth to an understanding of Zionism as the national liberation movement of the Jewish people. It promotes aliyah to kibbutzim. It is affiliated with the Kibbutz Artzi Federation. It espouses socialist-Zionist ideals of peace, justice, democracy, and intergroup harmony. (www.campshomria.com)

HuJews (2007). 28611 West Twelve Mile Road, Farmington Hills, MI 48334. (248) 478-7610. HuJews is the North American youth organization for Humanistic Judaism, a program of the Society for Humanistic Judaism. HuJews, is dedicated to supporting teens and young adults and connecting them to Humanistic Judaism. It provides resources for Humanistic Jewish youth groups, college students, and campus *havurot*. (www.shj.org/youth-programs/hujews)

Jewish Student Connection (JSC) (formerly **Jewish Student Union**) (2002) (2012). 180 South Broadway, Suite 310, White Plains, NY 10605. JSC is dedicated to establishing nondenominational Jewish clubs in public and secular private high schools. JSC provides teens with the opportunity to explore what "Jewish" means to them personally, and aims to help teens foster proud connections with Jewish culture, with the Jewish people, with Israel and with each other. (No website)

Kadima. 120 Broadway, Suite 1540, New York, NY 10271. (212) 533-7800, ext. 1109. Kadima is the international youth organization for Jewish pre-teens (grades 6-8) affiliated with The United Synagogue of Conservative Judaism. (www.usy. org/kadima)

National Jewish Committee on Girl Scouting (NJCGS) (1972). 33 Central Drive, Bronxville, NY 10708. (914) 738-3986. The National Jewish Girl Scout Committee serves to further Jewish education by promoting Jewish award programs, encouraging religious services, promoting cultural exchanges with the Israel Boy and Girl Scouts Federation, and extending membership in the Jewish community by assisting councils in organizing Girl Scout troops and local Jewish Girl Scout committees. (www.njcgs.org)

National Jewish Committee on Scouting (Boy Scouts of America) (1926). 1325 West Walnut Hill Lane, PO Box 152079, Irving, TX 75015. (972) 580-2000. The National Jewish Committee on Scouting promotes Boy Scouting among Jewish youth; helps Jewish institutions and local council Jewish committees provide Scouting opportunities for Jewish youth; and promotes Jewish values in Scouting through the religious emblems program (Maccabee, Aleph, Ner Tamid and Etz Chaim emblems) and the Shofar Award to recognize outstanding service by adults in the promotion of Scouting among Jewish youth. (www.jewishscouting.org)

National Ramah Commission (1950). 3080 Broadway, New York, NY 10027. (212) 678-8881. The National Ramah Commission is the coordinating body of the camping arm of Conservative Judaism, operating under the educational and religious supervision of The Jewish Theological Seminary, and providing oversight and educational planning on behalf of the network of Ramah camps throughout North America and Israel. (www.campramah.org)

NCSY (formerly **National Conference of Synagogue Youth**) (1954). 11 Broadway, New York, NY 10004. (212) 613-8233. NCSY is the Orthodox Union's international youth movement, founded to provide Jewish teens with an opportunity to build a strong connection to their Jewish roots through inspiration and leadership skills. (www.ncsy.org)

NFTY—North American Federation of Temple Youth (NFTY) (1939). 1 West 4th Street, New York, NY 10012. (212) 650-4070. NFTY is North America's Reform Jewish youth movement that fosters leadership at the national, regional, and congregational level. (www.nfty.org)

Tzivos Hashem: Jewish Children International (1980). 792 Eastern Parkway, Brooklyn, NY 11213. (718) 467-6630. Tzivos Hashem (Army of God, in Hebrew) was founded as a youth group of the Chabad movement to serve both the physical and spiritual needs of Jewish children under the age of Bar/Bat Mitzvah from backgrounds spanning the spectrum of levels of Jewish education and commitment to Jewish affiliation, without regard to social and economic status. (www.tzivo-shashem.org)

United Synagogue Youth (USY) (1973). 120 Broadway, Suite 1540, New York, NY 10271. (212) 533-7800. USY is the youth organization for Jewish teens across North America affiliated with The United Synagogue of Conservative Judaism. (www.usy.org)

Young Judaea (1909). 575 8th Avenue, 11th Floor, New York, NY 10018. (917) 595-2100. Young Judaea is the oldest Zionist youth movement in the US. It seeks to build Jewish identity and Zionist commitment in American Jewish youth and young adults from third grade to college and beyond. Young Judaea is a religiously pluralistic, politically nonpartisan, and peer-led youth movement whose programs and activities focus on instilling in its members three core values: Judaism, Jewish identity, and Zionism. Young Judaea's primary goal is to emphasize Jewish and Zionist education, build connections with Israel, and promote aliyah (immigration to Israel). Young Judaea maintains five summer camps in the US and runs summer and year-long programs in Israel. (www.youngjudaea.org)

12.1.9   Jewish College Campus Organizations

Academic Engagement Network (AEN) (2015). Washington, DC. The AEN is a diverse network of college and university faculty and administrators on campuses across the US that addresses issues relating to Israel. It educates students, faculty, administrators, and the public, and facilitates intelligent, constructive, and civilized discourse about Israel on campuses, while protecting and nurturing the exercise of academic freedom and freedom of expression. Network members serve as resources on their campuses, anticipate and address anti-Israel and antisemitic activities as they arise, and maintain ties to those on other campuses confronting similar challenges. (www.academicengagement.org)

Academic Exchange (also known as **Israel America Academic Exchange**) (AE) (2009). 8383 Wilshire Boulevard, Suite 400, Beverly Hills, CA 90211. (310) 247-7483. The goal of AE is to deepen understanding of Israel within the American academic community. It provides educational missions to Israel for American scholars from various academic fields. Programs offer the opportunity to learn about and experience the region through its religious, political, economic, social, and geographical dimensions, and to meet with Israel's leading academicians, political and military leaders, entrepreneurs, and artists as well as with prominent Palestinian spokesmen and scholars. AE is nonpartisan and seeks diversity of political views, disciplines, and national backgrounds in mission and conference participants. (www.academicexchange.com)

Alums for Campus Fairness (ACF) (2015). 165 East 56th Street, 2nd Floor, New York, NY 10022. (917) 512-4585. ACF organizes alumni to fight the antisemitism that is infecting university and college campuses, and promotes open and fair dialogue on campus regarding the Arab-Israeli conflict. It mobilizes alumni to press their alma maters to provide a safe and welcoming environment for students and faculty who feel a connection to Israel. (www.campusfairness.org)

AMCHA Initiative (2011). PO Box 408, Santa Cruz, CA 95061. AMCHA Initiative is dedicated to investigating, documenting, educating about, and combating antisemitism at institutions of higher education in America. It aims to protect Jewish students from both direct and indirect assault and fear while attending colleges and universities. AMCHA Initiative's research arm carries out systematic, in-depth research and analysis of antisemitic activity and has developed a comprehensive method for defining, documenting, and analyzing manifestations of antisemitic behavior on campus, as well as the institutional structures that legitimize it and allow it to flourish. AMCHA Initiative uses the results of its research and analysis to inform university administrators and the public about the antisemitic incidents, the individuals and groups that are perpetrating them, and to pressure university leaders to act. It also mobilizes community activists and has developed a model of response that can be used to impact campuses across the country. (www.amchainitiative.org)

Chabad on Campus International Foundation (2003). 719 Eastern Parkway, First Floor, Brooklyn, NY 11213 (718) 510-8181.The Chabad on Campus International Foundation is the college wing of the Chabad Lubavitch movement, offering social, educational, and spiritual programs at campuses across America and around the globe. (www.chabad.edu)

The David Project (2002). 800 8th Street, NW, Washington D.C. 20001. (617) 428-0012. The David Project positively shapes campus opinion on Israel by educating, training and empowering student leaders on core campuses across the US and Canada to be thoughtful, strategic and persuasive advocates. Its approach–relational advocacy–emphasizes building relationships with diverse communities on campus and teaching and guiding students in leveraging those relationships to raise understanding and support for Israel. (www.davidproject.org)

Hasbara Fellowships (2001). 315 West 36th Street, Suite 5061, New York, NY 10018. (646) 365-0030. Hasbara Fellowships, a program spearheaded by Aish International, is a leading pro-Israel campus activism organization working with over 120 universities across North America. Hasbara Fellowships was the first formal program for students battling overwhelming anti-Israel propaganda on their campuses in the wake of the second Palestinian intifada. (www.hasbarafellowships.org)

Heritage Retreats (formerly **University Heritage Society**) (1999) (2019). 557 Fenlon Boulevard, Clifton, NJ 07014. (800) 927-0476. University Heritage Society seeks to revitalize Jewish identity among college students and young adults through Jewish educational initiatives designed to enable those that do not strongly identify with their heritage to experience how Judaism is indeed relevant in their lives. (www.heritageretreats.com)

Heshe and Harriet Seif Jewish Learning Initiative on Campus (JLIC) (2000). 11 Broadway, New York, NY 10004. (212) 613-8287. JLIC, a program of the Orthodox Union, in partnership with Hillel, helps Orthodox students navigate the college environment and balance their Jewish commitments with their desire to engage the secular world. It was created to help young men and women thrive in a campus environment and helps Jewish students observe key aspects of Jewish life, such as tefillah, kashrut, Shabbat, and chagim. (www.oujlic.org)

Hillel International (formerly **B'nai B'rith Hillel Foundations** and **Hillel: The Foundation for Jewish Campus Life**) (1923). Charles and Lynn Schusterman International Center, Arthur and Rochelle Belfer Building, 800 Eighth Street, NW, Washington, DC 20001. (202) 449-6500. The largest Jewish campus organization in the world, Hillel provides opportunities for Jewish students at more than 500 colleges and universities to explore and celebrate their Jewish identity through its global network of regional centers, campus Foundations and Hillel student organizations. Hillel student leaders, professionals and lay leaders are dedicated to creating a pluralistic, welcoming and inclusive environment for Jewish college students, where they are encouraged to grow intellectually, spiritually and socially. Hillel helps students find a balance in being distinctively Jewish and universally human by encouraging them to pursue tzedek (social justice), tikkun olam (repairing the world) and Jewish learning, and to support Israel and global Jewish peoplehood. (www.hillel.org)

Israel at Heart (2003). 580 Fifth Avenue, 26th Floor, New York, NY 10036. Israel at Heart seeks to promote a better understanding of Israel and its people, to dispel the unfair portrayal of Israel in the media, and to convey to the public at large Israel's significance as the only free democracy in the Middle East. Israel at Heart's efforts have centered on speaking tours for groups of young Israelis who travel in groups of three to speak about their lives and answer questions about Israel, mainly on college and university campuses across North America. (www.israelatheart.org)

Israel on Campus Coalition (2002). Washington, DC. (202) 735-2573. The Israel on Campus Coalition empowers and expands the network of national Israel supporters, engages key leaders at colleges and universities around issues affecting Israel, counters anti-Israel activities on campus and creates positive campus change for Israel. It offers information, resources, training, leadership opportunities, strategic advice, and tactical assistance to the campus community and other supporters of Israel on campus. (www.israelcc.org)

Jewish Awareness America (JAAM) (2001). JAAM is a national awareness program for Jewish students across North America's universities, dedicated to educating Jewish students and graduates about their Jewish heritage and Jewish values. JAAM was founded by a Haredi rabbi with the aim of producing knowledgeable future Jewish leaders who will make personal, family and communal decisions in light of Jewish teaching and tradition. Its flagship program is the Maimonides Jewish Leaders Fellowship, a Jewish leadership training project for university students in the US and Canada. (No website)

Judaism On Our Own Terms (JOOOT) (2018). JOOOT is a network of students and groups that aims to share resources and knowledge across North American campuses and bring together new independent communities in the process. It is a national movement of independent campus Jewish organizations committed to promoting student self-governance and radical inclusivity—both on their individual campuses and in the wider Jewish community. JOOOT represents a diverse set of communities with various ideologies and missions. (www.jooot.org)

Kahal: Your Jewish Home Abroad (formerly Delegation of Jewish American Students) (2013). 1806 Colfax Street, Evanston, IL 60201. (847) 212-8777. Kahal aspires to give the tens of thousands of Jewish students studying abroad each year the resources, tools, and connections they need to meaningfully engage with the Jewish community and deepen their Jewish identity during one of the most important, meaningful, and enduring experiences of their lives. It creates and facilitates transformational Jewish experiences for study abroad students, helping students to take advantage of the opportunities presented by international Jewish communities and increase their connection to the global Jewish people. Working with local Jewish students, families, organizations, and community leaders, Kahal connects Jewish students to exciting opportunities, such as Shabbat dinners, High Holiday and Passover experiences, connections to local Jewish students, volunteer and internship opportunities, access to grant funding, etc. (www.kahalabroad.org)

Maccabee Task Force (formerly **The Campus Maccabees**) (2015). PO Box 19698, Las Vegas, NV 89132. The Maccabee Task Force was created in 2015 to combat the disturbing spread of antisemitism on America's college campuses. It believes the BDS (Boycott, Divestment, Sanctions) movement is at the forefront of this troubling trend and maintains that BDS is an antisemitic movement that crosses the line from legitimate criticism of Israel into the dangerous demonization of Israel and its supporters. The Maccabee Task Force is determined to help students combat this hate by bringing them the strategies and resources they need to tell the truth about Israel. (www.maccabeetaskforce.org)

MEOR (2005). PO Box 279, Pomona, NY 10970. (212) 444-1020 or (800) 284-4110. MEOR focuses on students attending America's leading academic college campuses with large Jewish populations and provides leadership development and innovative, inspiring, and high-impact Jewish learning to students with promising leadership qualities. (www.meor.org)

Olami. 111 John Street, Suite 1720, New York, NY 10038. (212) 791-7354. In response to the alarming rate of assimilation in the Jewish college communities across the globe, Olami was launched as a worldwide campus and young professional effort to reconnect Jews to their heritage, their faith, and their land. Olami is a network of Jewish outreach efforts aiming to forge a deep, meaningful connection to Judaism based on practice and commitment, by providing valuable resources, funds, leadership, and directional guidance to campus outreach organizations throughout North America and all over the world. On campus, Olami identifies unaffiliated Jewish students and offers a wide-range of opportunities for student transformation and identification through text study, experiential engagement, and educational trips to Israel. Its partnering programs fuse both informal and formal Jewish education modules to create an engaging, inspiring, and motivating environment for further Jewish engagement. (www.olami.org)

Open Hillel (2012). 440 Park Avenue South, 4th Floor, New York, NY 10016. Open Hillel promotes pluralism and open discourse on Israel/Palestine in Jewish communities on campus and beyond. It aims to eliminate Hillel International's

Standards of Partnership for Israel Activities, which exclude individuals and groups from the Jewish community on campus on the basis of their views on Israel. It also works to end similar restrictions on discussion and debate in other broad-based/ umbrella Jewish institutions. (www.openhillel.org)

Students Supporting Israel (SSI) (2012). 5775 Wayzata Boulevard, Suite 700, St. Louis Park, MN 55416. (952) 525-2200. SSI is an independent, nonpartisan, grassroots campus movement that was created by students for students, to organize a strong, united, pro-Israel front on college campuses. With chapters across the US and Canada, its mission is to create a clear and confident pro-Israel voice on college campuses, and to support students in grassroots pro-Israel advocacy. It believes that familiarizing students with current events and Israeli culture, and providing access to knowledge of Israel's history and its day to day reality, will promote a better understanding of the State of Israel. (www.ssimovement.org)

URJ Kesher. 633 Third Avenue, 7th Floor, New York, NY 10017. (202) 370-4026. URJ Kesher, under the umbrella of the Union for Reform Judaism, organizes Birthright Israel trips. (www.gokesher.org)

Young Jewish Conservatives (YJC) (2011). 2480 Briarcliff Road STE 6-181, Atlanta, GA 30329. (404) 217-7910. YJC is a national grassroots coalition that unites politically active conservative young Jews and whose mission is to empower them, providing the tools to defend their values and advocate for conservative causes. (www.youngjewishconservatives.org)

12.1.10 Jewish Outreach Organizations

Aish International/Aish HaTorah (1974). 315 West 36th Street, New York, NY 10018. (212) 391-6710. Aish HaTorah (Fire of Torah, in Hebrew) is a Jewish outreach organization started in Jerusalem by Rabbi Noah Weinberg that seeks to revitalize the Jewish people by providing opportunities for Jews of all backgrounds to discover their heritage in an atmosphere of open inquiry and mutual respect. It is regarded as a world leader in creative Jewish educational programs and leadership training. Aish HaTorah operates dozens of branches and programs on six continents. Beyond Jewish education, Aish HaTorah is known as a staunch defender of Israel and has launched various Israel advocacy programs. (www.aish.com)

American Friends of Lubavitch. 2110 Leroy Place, NW, Washington, DC 20008. (202) 332-5600. American Friends of Lubavitch is directly responsible for events and activities of national and international reach for the Chabad Lubavitch movement, while also serving as Chabad's representative office in the nation's capital. Its special programs and activities include the Capitol Jewish Forum, which offers study groups and events in honor of Jewish holidays for Jewish Congressional staff and Members of Congress, and the National Menorah Council, which supports the annual lighting ceremony of the National Chanukah Menorah on the White House Ellipse and offers creative, logistical, and other support to many communities. (www.afldc.org)

Association for Jewish Outreach Programs (AJOP) (formerly **Association for Jewish Outreach Professionals**) (1987). 5906 Park Heights Avenue, Suite 10, Baltimore, MD 21215. (410) 367-2567. AJOP is an Orthodox Jewish network which was established to unite and enhance the Jewish educational work of rabbis, lay people, and volunteers who work in a variety of settings and seek to improve and promote Jewish Orthodox outreach work with ba'alei teshuvah (returnees, in Hebrew [to Orthodox Judaism]), guiding Jews to live according to Orthodox Jewish values. AJOP was the first major Jewish Orthodox organization of its kind that was not affiliated with the Chabad Hasidic movement. (www.ajop.com)

B3/The Jewish Boomer Platform (2011). (201) 657-66141. B3's mission is to develop a wide range of activities designed to engage—or re-engage—baby boomers in Jewish life based on their emerging needs and interests and connect generational groups. B3's platform strategy creates a single portfolio from which it can craft unique leadership and community building programs designed for local communities. (www.b3platform.org)

Bais Chana Women International (1971). 383 Kingston Avenue, Suite 248, Brooklyn, NY 11213. (718) 604-0088 or (800) 473-4801. Bais Chana Women International, inspired by the teachings of the Lubavitcher Rebbe, has been in the forefront of Jewish women's education as a place where women with little or no formal Jewish education could rediscover their heritage. It serves an international clientele of Jewish women from all walks of life, ages 15 and up, with Jewish education, enrichment and support. Jewish Uncamp is a division of Bais Chana that provides summer programs for Jewish high school girls, age 16-19. (www.baischana.org)

Center for Radically Inclusive Judaism (2018). 321 Walnut Street, #443, Newtonville, MA 02460. (617) 307-9981. The Center for Radically Inclusive Judaism will be the central address for professional and lay Jewish communal leaders who seek to advocate for radically inclusive Judaism with respect to interfaith families. Its mission is to advocate for radically inclusive attitudes and policies toward interfaith families—and for programmatic efforts designed to engage interfaith families in Jewish life and community. (www.cfrij.com)

Chabad Lubavitch (1940). 770 Eastern Parkway, Brooklyn, NY 11213. (718) 774-4000. Chabad Lubavitch is a Hasidic movement and one of the world's largest Jewish organizations, providing outreach and educational activities for Jews of all backgrounds—children and adults—through Jewish community centers, synagogues, early childhood programs, schools, camps, and educational programs. (www.lubavitch.com)

Chabad Lubavitch Youth Organization (CLYO) (1955). 770 Eastern Parkway, Brooklyn, NY 11213. (718) 953-1000. CLYO offers a range of services for Jews of all affiliations, including making arrangements with observant rabbis in Israel to recite kaddish for the Jewish deceased (www.sayKaddish.com), arranging inspirational, growth-oriented Shabbat weekends (www.Shabbaton.org), and maintaining the Levi Yitzchok Library. (www.lubavitchyouth.org)

CKL Foundation (also known as **Chesed, Kindness & Learning Foundation**) (CKL) (2010). 19141 North Bay Road, North Miami Beach, FL 33160. (786) 663-9292. CKL is an organization comprised exclusively of volunteers committed to bringing Mashiach by distributing, free of charge, all over the world, Thank You Prayers that connect the Jewish people to Hashem through trust, gratitude, and appreciation. (www.cklfoundation.org)

Footsteps (2003).114 John Street, #930, New York, NY 10272. (212) 253-0890, ext. 7. Footsteps provides educational, vocational, social, and emotional support to people who have left or want to leave the ultra-Orthodox and Orthodox Jewish community, assisting them with this difficult transition. (www.footstepsorg.org)

Gateways (1998). 11 Wallenberg Circle, Monsey, NY 10952. (845) 290-8710. The mission of Gateways is to nurture and sustain Jewish identity, strengthen connection to Israel and empower its participants to make informed decisions about their Jewish future. Gateways offers a wide array of meaningful immersion-based educational and social programs, including family education, learning programs for colligates and young professionals, services focused on the Russian American Jewish community, singles networking and matchmaking, learning opportunities via the internet, life skills and professional development seminars, and Jewish holiday programs. The organization's flagship program is Gateways Classic Retreats, which offers retreats and seminars for the whole family hosted by Gateways on secular public and Jewish holidays. (www.gatewaysonline.org)

Hineni (1973). 232 West End Avenue, New York, NY 10023. (212) 496-1660. Hineni is a Jewish outreach organization that was one of the first ba'al teshuvah (return to Judaism) movements, encouraging Jews to return to their roots. Hineni's goal is to help Jews infuse their lives with more meaning through their Jewish heritage by offering a wide variety of programs, services, classes and seminars to inspire and teach Jews about the Torah and Jewish traditions. The Hineni Heritage Center in Manhattan offers a comprehensive series of educational programs as well as lectures, publications, audio and video cassettes, family counseling, an introduction service for singles and social gatherings. (www.hineni.org)

InterfaithFamily (2001). 90 Oak Street, Fourth Floor, PO Box 428, Newton Upper Falls, MA 02464. (617) 581-6860. InterfaithFamily empowers people in interfaith relationships—individuals, couples, families and their children—to make Jewish choices, and encourages Jewish communities to welcome them. InterfaithFamily believes that maximizing the number of interfaith families who find fulfillment in Jewish life and raise their children as Jews is essential to the future strength and vitality of the Jewish community. It is the leading producer of Jewish resources and content, either online or in print, that reach out directly to interfaith families. (www.interfaithfamily.com)

Jerusalem U/Imagination Productions Company (formerly **Aish Café** and **Jerusalem Online University**) (2007) (2009). 11110 West Oakland Park Boulevard, Suite 288, Sunrise, FL 33351. (888) 515-5292. Jerusalem U, produced by Imagination Productions Company (a nonprofit organization founded by filmmaker Raphael Shore), provides an online portal for Jewish distance learning with a vision to transform Jewish and Israel education for the 21st century, and to inspire, unify, and activate people of all ages as passionate supporters of Israel and the Jewish people. Jerusalem U breaks new ground in outreach by creating original feature films, engaging film classes and courses, and experiential and interactive learning, all distributed via the internet, social media, television, grassroots campaigns, and partnerships with mainstream pro-Israel and outreach organizations. (www.jerusalemu.org)

Jewish Educational Media (JEM) (1980). 784 Eastern Parkway, Suite 403, Brooklyn, NY 11213. (718) 774-6000. Founded to broadcast the public addresses of the Lubavitcher Rebbe live via satellite around the world, JEM has evolved into the multimedia archive responsible for maintaining a lifetime of images and sounds of the Rebbe, the Lubavitch movement, and Jewish outreach. It operates a one-of-its kind motion picture, audio, and photographic archive serving researchers, scholars, and producers whose primary goal is to render its priceless archival materials accessible, making them meaningful to diverse audiences around the world. Its flagship product, The Living Torah DVD Collection, is viewed by nearly 100,000 people around the world every week and is released in multiple languages. (www.JEMedia. org),   (www.facebook.com/Jewish-Educational-Media-JEM-21762304125)

The Jewish Learning Network (Jnet) (2005). 770 Eastern Parkway, Suite 302, Brooklyn, NY 11213. (877) 563-8246. Jnet provides business people, students, and homemakers of every age and background with the opportunity to study Torah, one on one with a volunteer, from the weekly Parsha to Jewish Law, the Talmud, the spirituality and meaning of Chassidus, and Kabbalah. (www.jnet.org)

Jews for Judaism (1983). PO Box 351235, Los Angeles, CA 90035. (310) 556-3344. The mission of Jews for Judaism is to strengthen and preserve Jewish identity through education and counseling that counteracts deceptive proselytizing targeting Jews for conversion. (www.jewsforjudaism.org)

JOY for Our Youth (JOY) (2000). 1805 Swarthmore Avenue, Lakewood, NJ 08701. (866) 448-3569. JOY addresses the educational, material, emotional, and spiritual needs of Jewish children and their families, providing educational services, youth development programs, and community and family outreach. Outreach efforts include one-on-one telephone classes for individuals interested in learning more about Jewish tradition or history; holiday packages shipped nationwide; and family retreats on the Sabbath and Jewish holidays. JOY funds many different programs and services, providing food, clothing, shelter, health and wellness, education, after school programs, special training, mentoring, tutoring, private counseling, summer programs, and guidance to children ages 6 to 18. (www.givejoy.org)

The Kabbalah Centre/Kabbalah Centre International (formerly **The National Research Institute of Kabbalah**) (1965). (888) 898-8358. The Kabbalah Centre provides students with spiritual tools based on kabbalistic principles that they can apply to improve their own lives and by so doing make the world better. Kabbalah is taught as a universal wisdom that predates the Bible or religion, and it can be studied by anyone regardless of their faith or path. (www.kabbalah.com)

Machne Israel (1941). 770 Eastern Parkway, Brooklyn, NY 11213. (718) 774-4000. Machne Israel is the social service organization of the Chabad Lubavitch movement. (www.lubavitch.com/departments.html)

Merkos L'Inyonei Chinuch (Central Organization for Education) (1941). 770 Eastern Parkway, Brooklyn, NY 11213. (718) 774-4000. Merkos L'Inyonei

Chinuch is the coordinating organization of Chabad Lubavitch's worldwide educational programs, which oversees the Kehot Publication Society and Merkos Publications, the Central Chabad Lubavitch Library. (www.lubavitch.com/departments.html)

Momentum (formerly **Jewish Women's Renaissance Project**) (2008) (2019). 6101 Executive Boulevard, Suite 240, Rockville, MD 20852. (240) 747-7080. Momentum's mission is to empower women to change the world through Jewish values that transform themselves, their families, and their communities. Its flagship program, the MOMentum Year-Long Journey empowers women to connect to Jewish values, engage with Israel, take action, and foster unity, without uniformity. (www.momentumunlimited.org)

National Center to Encourage Judaism (NCEJ) (1995). 8204 Fenton Street, Suite 201, Silver Spring, MD 20910. (301) 802-4254. NCEJ is a private foundation encouraging conversion to and retention in Judaism. It helps synagogues and other Jewish institutions reach out to Jews and non-Jews with programs of learning about Judaism, leading to conversion where individuals choose. NCEJ also supports advertising in general secular (non-Jewish) media about pro-conversion programs. (www.ncejudaism.org)

NJOP (formerly **National Jewish Outreach Program**) (1987). 989 Sixth Avenue, 10th Floor, New York, NY 10018. (646) 871-4444. Established to stem the losses of Jews from Jewish life due to assimilation and lack of Jewish knowledge, NJOP has become one of the largest and most successful Jewish outreach organizations in the world, with programs offered in about 40 countries. NJOP reaches out to unaffiliated Jews, offering positive, joyous Jewish experiences and meaningful educational opportunities. NJOP sponsors the acclaimed Shabbat Across America and Canada and Read Hebrew America and Canada campaigns, as well as free "Crash Courses" in Hebrew Reading, Basic Judaism, and Jewish History. (www.njop.org)

N'shei Chabad (Lubavitch Women's Organization). 770 Eastern Parkway, Brooklyn, NY 11213. (718) 774-4000. N'shei Chabad is the Lubavitch Women's organization, whose activities include seminars and learning programs, speaker's bureaus, resource centers, and an annual convention. (No website)

Oorah (1980). 1805 Swarthmore Avenue, Lakewood, NJ 08701. (732) 730-1000 or (800) 216-6724. Oorah is an Orthodox Jewish outreach organization with the goal of awakening Jewish children and their families to their heritage. (www.oorah.org)

Outreach Judaism (1995). 108-18 Queens Boulevard, Suite 806, Forest Hills, NY 11375. (212) 913-9331 or (800) 315-5397. Outreach Judaism is an international organization that responds directly to the issues raised by missionaries and cults, by exploring Judaism in contradistinction to fundamentalist Christianity. Its goal is to generate a lasting connection between Jewish families and Judaism. (www.outreachjudaism.org)

PunkTorah (2010). PO Box 7414, Richmond, VA 23221. (323) 539-4411. PunkTorah is an online community helping people who have fallen through the cracks of Jewish life. Independent and unaffiliated with any movement in Judaism,

PunkTorah has self-published books, developed The G-d Project video series, founded OneShul (the world's first online, lay led synagogue), hosted events, presented at conferences and synagogues, written for other websites and magazines, and managed a successful social network. PunkTorah offers a variety of educational resources for children and adults on its website. (www.punktorah.org)

Reboot (2002). 44 West 28th Street, 8th Floor, New York, NY 10001. Reboot affirms the value of Jewish traditions and creates new ways for people to make them their own. Inspired by Jewish ritual and embracing the arts, humor, food, philosophy, and social justice, Reboot produces creative projects that spark the interest of young Jews and the larger community. It facilitates the process of addressing the questions of Jewish identity, community, and meaning that each generation must grapple with, providing the tools and methodologies to help "reboot" inherited tradition and make it vital, resonant, and meaningful in modern life. Reboot is responsible for producing some of the most influential and innovative Jewish books, films, music, websites, and large-scale public events in recent years. (www.rebooters.net)

Rising Tide Network (2017). 1838 Washington Street, Newton, MA 02466. (617) 244-1836. Rising Tide Network is a national network of mikva'ot working to open the experience of mikveh to the entire Jewish community, making mikveh accessible to Jews of all denominations, ages, genders, sexual orientations, and abilities (open mikveh movement), in order to help create a vibrant, welcoming, inclusive Jewish future. Memberships are available for communities and individuals working within existing mikva'ot, those looking to establish a new mikveh, or those who simply wish to participate in the open mikveh movement. (www.risingtideopenwaters.org)

Shabbat Tent (2000). 9116 ½ West Pico Boulevard, Suite #2, Los Angeles, CA 90035. (562) 355-2939. Shabbat Tent creates Jewish hospitality and programming at national music and camping festivals. Shabbat Tent finds the festival where Jews in their 20s and 30s already hang out and seamlessly weaves an energizing Shabbat experience into the excitement of the event, offering meals to festivalgoers along with a full spectrum of Shabbat activities, from candle lighting to Havdalah, as well as Jewish yoga and meditation classes or deep theological conversations. Shabbat Tent aims to have a tent at every festival, ensuring that wherever Jews go, they can always access Shabbat. (www.shabbattent.org)

Synagogue Connect (2017). Synagogue Connect has created a global network of synagogues that have opened their doors to warmly welcome Jewish young adults age 18-26 for free High Holiday services with absolutely no requirement of membership affiliation. Synagogues of all denominations are participants. Beyond its main mission, it is the hope of Synagogue Connect that this gesture might encourage an ongoing connection between otherwise unaffiliated college students and rabbis. (www.synagogueconnect.org)

Taharas Hamishpacha International (formerly **Mivtza Taharas Hamishpacha**) (1975). 312 Kingston Avenue, Brooklyn, NY 11213. (718) 756-5700. Taharas Hamishpacha International is dedicated to education and training to promote and strengthen the observance of taharas hamishpacha (Jewish family purity), to preserve family sanctity in the Jewish home, and to the building of mikvaot. (www.mikvah.org), (lubavitch.com/department.html?h=657)

Trybal Gatherings (2017). (202) 536-2929. Trybal Gatherings provides Jewish camp experiences for young adults and their friends, set in picturesque landscapes across North America. It reimagines Jewish gatherings in a modern world by offering innovative, all-inclusive 3-day/4-night getaways for young adults in their 20s and 30s to connect, explore, play, and celebrate in a socially Jewish context. Gatherings include meals, lodging, linens, camp activities, and programming. (www.trybalgatherings.com)

The World Values Network (also known as **This World: The Values Network**) (1999). 313 West 71st Street, New York, NY 10023. (212) 634-7777. The mission of The World Values Network, based on the teachings of Rabbi Shmuley Boteach, is to disseminate universal Jewish values in politics, culture, and media, making the Jewish people a light unto the nations. It believes that Judaism, with its unique emphasis on perfecting the world and celebrating life, can help heal America from some of its greatest challenges, including its high rates of divorce, teen alienation, depression, and growing ignorance and materialism. Its goal is to inspire people to apply Jewish values into their everyday lives, ultimately conveying Jewish values in print and on the airwaves to ensure that America benefits from the core values of the Jewish people and also to inspire Jewish youth with the power of its ideas. (www.worldvalues.us/about)

12.1.11   Jewish Israel-Related Education Organizations

(For organizations that offer Israel-related education on college campuses, see Jewish College Campus Organizations.)

Alexander Muss High School in Israel (AMHSI) (1972). 78 Randall Avenue, Rockville Centre, NY 11570. (212) 472-9300 or (800) 327-5980. AMHSI is a non-denominational, 8-week, English language study abroad program in Israel for high school students that offers college credits. While keeping up with classes from their home school and gaining important college preparatory skills, students also learn about Israel through first-hand experience, where the "classroom" is the land itself and the students travel to the places where history was made. (www.amhsi.org)

Birthright Israel Foundation (1999). PO Box 1784, New York, NY 10156. (888) 994-7723. The Birthright Israel Foundation offers the gift of a free, 10-day educational trip to Israel for Jewish adults ages 18 to 26. The trip aims to strengthen participants' Jewish identity; to build an understanding, friendship and lasting bond with the land and people of Israel; and to reinforce the solidarity of the Jewish people worldwide. (www.birthrightisrael.com)

Center for Israel Education (CIE) (2008). 825 Houston Mill Road NE, Atlanta, GA 30329. (404) 395-6851. The CIE's mission is to be a source destination for learners and educators about modern Israel. Its target audiences include pre-collegiate, college, university and adult learners, lay leaders, and clergy who wish to enrich their knowledge of Israel and the Middle East. The CIE produces and presents Israel's complex story via innovative learning platforms, including workshops, podcasts, source compilations, and timely commentary of current issues. It constructs curriculum, assembles documents, offers curriculum for sale, conducts teacher and student workshops, and engages in discussion about all aspects of modern Israel. (www.israeled.org)

Honeymoon Israel (2014). (347) 292-8809. Honeymoon Israel provides immersive trips to Israel for locally based cohorts of couples that have at least one Jewish partner, early in their committed relationship, creating communities of couples who are building families with deep and meaningful connections to Jewish life and the Jewish people. Its goal is to make participants (including Jewish/Jewish, interfaith, and LGBTQ couples) feel welcome in the Jewish community and to inspire them to incorporate Jewish values into their lives in whatever way works for them. (www.honeymoonisrael.org)

iCenter for Israel Education (2011). 95 Revere Drive, Suite D, Northbrook, IL 60062. (847) 418-8336. The iCenter works to advance high-quality, meaningful, and innovative Israel education by serving as the national hub and catalyst for building, shaping, and supporting the field. The iCenter envisions generations of young North American Jews for whom contemporary Israel is an integral and vibrant part of their personal and collective Jewish identity. This vision includes a pre-K through grade 12 Jewish educational system in North America that fully incorporates Israel—people, land, history, language, and culture—into the very fiber of its overall mission. (www.theicenter.org)

Israel 2.0 (2011). 8 Hampton Road, Clifton, NJ 07012. (973) 519-3013. Israel 2.0's mission is to provide young Jewish adults with the opportunity to reconnect with Israel and their Jewish heritage in a deep and meaningful way by sponsoring two-week educational tours to Israel for Jewish college students and young professionals in North America and offering follow-up programming for participants upon their return. It works in coordination with several Jewish organizations across college campuses and cities throughout the US and Canada and targets adults of all Jewish backgrounds, ages 18-28. (www.israel2point0.org)

Israel Institute (2012). 1250 Eye Street, NW, Suite 710, Washington, DC 20005. (202) 216-2219. The Israel Institute is an independent, nonpartisan, and nonadvocacy organization that enhances knowledge about modern Israel through the expansion of accessible, innovative learning opportunities, on and beyond campus. Its many programs and initiatives advance rigorous teaching, research, and discourse about modern Israel in partnership with academic, research, and cultural institutions. The Israel Institute provides funding and structural opportunities for people and existing institutions interested in deepening the study of modern Israel. Its diverse range of programs and initiatives supports the study of modern Israel at universities and other research and cultural institutions around the world. (www.israelinstitute.org)

itrek (formerly **Israel & Co.**) (2012). 1460 Broadway, New York, NY 10036. (212) 528-1500. itrek introduces tomorrow's leaders in business, law, policy, and STEM to Israel, with a uniquely authentic experience that recognizes Israel's richness and complexity, helping them experience Israel firsthand through peer-led, week-long treks that combine education, culture, and fun. It works with student and faculty leaders at the world's top business, law, policy, and STEM programs. (www.itrek.org)

Keren Nesivos Moshe: The Development Fund for Torah Chinuch in Israel (1998). c/o Daniel Goldberg, 1541 47th Street, Brooklyn, NY 11219. (212) 259-0300. Keren Nesivos Moshe was created in the US to establish a Torah school system specifically geared for children from nonreligious homes whose families want their children to benefit from a religious education. Its goal is to build schools for every child in every town and village in Israel where there is a demand for religious schooling. (www.nesivosmoshe.org)

Masa Israel Journey (2004). (866) 864-3279. Masa Israel Journey offers young Jewish adults ages 18 to 30 immersive, life-changing gap year, study abroad, post-college and volunteer experiences in Israel, connecting them to programs that meet their interests, offering scholarships, providing expertise and supporting them throughout the entire process. It is a joint project of the Government of Israel and the Jewish Agency for Israel with support from The Jewish Federations of North America and Keren Hayesod-UIA. (www.masaisrael.org)

Onward Israel (2012). 633 3rd Avenue, 21st Floor, New York, NY 10017. (212) 339-6945. Onward Israel's programs provide participants with an immersive resume-building experience in Israel, featuring opportunities such as internships, academic courses, and fellowships, providing a global, cross-cultural experience in Israel and direct contact with Israeli peers. The ultimate purpose of this initiative is to increase exponentially the number of Birthright and teen program alumni who return to Israel for an identity-building second visit, eventually reaching a stage where half of all first time visitors partake in a longer more immersive second experience. The intended long-term outcome is a long-lasting connection with Israel and a strong commitment to Jewish life and community at the heart of the next generations. (www.onwardisrael.org)

Shorashim (1983). 1415 North Dayton Street, Unit A1, Chicago, IL 60642. (312) 267-0677. Shorashim (Roots, in Hebrew) is devoted to building bridges between Israeli and North American Jews. Shorashim is the Taglit-Birthright Israel program where groups travel with Israelis for ten days, rather than for only part of the trip. Bicultural programs are the foundation of Shorashim as Americans and Israelis travel, live and learn side by side while they explore Israel. Shorashim is committed to a pluralistic Jewish experience, reaching out to American youth from all the major denominations and to Israelis from both the religious and nonreligious sectors. (www.shorashim.org)

12.1.12   Jewish Israel-Related Humanitarian Organizations

The Abraham Fund Initiatives (1989). 1460 Broadway, New York, NY 10036. (877) 440-3440. The Abraham Fund Initiatives is a fundraising and educational organization dedicated to promoting Jewish-Arab coexistence in Israel. The Abraham Fund Initiatives provides grants to numerous organizations and institutions in Israel in such areas as culture, education, health, and social services. In the US, its educational and cultural programs provide information that enhances understanding about the necessary cooperation between Israel's Jewish majority and Arab minority. (www.abrahamfund.org)

ALL4ISRAEL (2003). 53 Dewhurst Street, Staten Island, NY 10314. (877) 812-7162. ALL4ISRAEL's two major functions are providing emergency help to families in Israel and helping seriously injured victims of terror with medical assistance through its Healing Hands program. (www.all4israel.org)

AMIT (formerly **Mizrachi Women of America** and **American Mizrachi Women**) (1925). 817 Broadway, 3rd Floor, New York, NY 10003. (212) 477-4720 or (800) 989-2648. AMIT enables Israel's youth to realize their potential and strengthens Israeli society by educating and nurturing children from diverse backgrounds within a framework of academic excellence, Jewish values, and Zionist ideals. AMIT operates more than 100 schools, youth villages, surrogate family residences, and other programs, constituting Israel's only government-recognized network of religious Jewish education incorporating academic and technological studies. (www.amitchildren.org)

Central Fund of Israel (1979). 980 Avenue of the Americas, 3rd Floor, New York, NY 10018. The Central Fund of Israel funds projects in Israel, including social-humanitarian, medical, education, religious, security, and community programs. It is operated from the Marcus Brothers Textiles offices in the Manhattan garment district. (No website)

Chabad's Children of Chernobyl (CCOC) (1990). 885 Third Avenue, Suite B290, New York, NY 10022. (212) 681-7800. Founded in response to the devastating nuclear disaster in Chernobyl, CCOC evacuates children from the radioactive Chernobyl region to Israel and provides them with medical care, housing, and an education. CCOC also serves those currently living in the contaminated areas by providing medicine, medical equipment, therapeutic aids and other necessary supplies. (www.ccoc.net)

CHMOL (1980). 5225 New Utrecht Avenue, Brooklyn, NY 11219. (718) 871-4111. CHMOL (Chalukas Mazon L'Shabbos, which means Sabbath food for the needy) provides needy Israeli families with food for the Sabbath and daily living, cash grants to cover holiday expenses, emergency crisis aid, and funds for needy couples getting married. (www.chmol.com)

Colel Chabad (1788). 806 Eastern Parkway, Brooklyn, NY 11213. (718) 774-5446. Colel Chabad, one of the oldest Jewish charitable foundations in existence today, was established by the founder of the Chabad Lubavitch movement, Rabbi Schneur Zalman of Liadi. Colel Chabad's mission is to provide direct, meaningful material help—especially food—to the poorest Jews living in Israel and the FSU. It also provides medical and dental care, care for impoverished children, orphans and widows, and help for immigrants in Israel, and supports religious life in the Ukraine. (www.colelchabad.org)

Development Corporation for Israel (DCI) (formerly **State of Israel Bonds**) (1951). 641 Lexington Avenue, 9th Floor, New York, NY 10022. (800) 229-9650. DCI is an international organization offering securities issued by the government of Israel. Since its inception, DCI has secured worldwide sales over $34 billion in investment capital for the development of every aspect of Israel's economic infrastructure, facilitating the rapid development of Israel's economy and building a global partnership with Israel. Proceeds realized through the sale of Israel bonds have helped in agriculture, commerce, industry, and in the absorption of immigrants. Bonds have funded cultivating the desert, building transportation networks, creating new industries, resettling immigrants, and increasing export capability. (www.israelbonds.com)

Dror for the Wounded Foundation (DFW) (2006). 253 West 35th Street, 15th Floor, New York, NY 10001. (646) 710-3767. DFW helps severely wounded veterans of the Israel Defense Forces by providing them with financial assistance for medical and psychological treatments, education and training, small construction projects, advocacy, and general financial aid. This assistance serves as aid above and beyond that provided by Israel's Ministry of Defense. (www.drorfoundation.org)

Emunah of America (1948). 315 West 36th Street, New York, NY 10018. (212) 564-9045. Emunah of America fund raises to support about 250 educational and social welfare institutions in Israel within a religious framework, including day care centers, kindergartens, children's residential homes, vocational schools for the underprivileged, senior citizen centers, a college of arts and technology, a religious girls' arts high school, crisis and family counseling centers, and Holocaust study center. (www.emunah.org)

Ezras Torah (Torah Relief Society) (1915). 1540 Route 202, Suite 2, Pomona, NY 10970. (845) 362-1608. Ezras Torah is a relief organization that specializes in supplying funds to needy Torah families, primarily in Israel. It provides emergency medical assistance, interest free loans, apartment loans, wedding assistance, widow assistance, simchas and special needs grants, assistance to families in need, high holiday assistance, and maternity grants. (www.ezrastorah.org)

Hadassah, The Women's Zionist Organization of America (1912). 40 Wall Street, New York, NY 10005. (800) 664-5646. Hadassah, one of the largest international Jewish organizations, inspires a passion for and commitment to its partnership with the land and people of Israel. It enhances the health of people worldwide through its support of medical care and research at the Hadassah Medical Organization in Jerusalem, which it founded and funds. Hadassah empowers its members and supporters, as well as youth in Israel and America, through opportunities for personal growth, education, advocacy, and Jewish continuity. It provides support for Youth Aliyah and the Jewish National Fund.It sponsors Young Judaea summer and year-course programs, Jewish and women's health education, health awareness programs, advocacy on Israel, Zionism and women's issues, as well as the Hadassah-Brandeis Institute and Hadassah Foundation. (www.hadassah.org)

Healing Across the Divides (2004). 72 Laurel Park, Northampton, MA 01060. (413) 586-5226. Healing Across the Divides supports health initiatives in Israel and the West Bank that promote the health of Israelis and Palestinians while helping to forge inter-agency cooperation that furthers mutual understanding. (www.healing-divides.org)

Helping Israel Fund (2008). 7999 North Federal Highway, Suite 202, Boca Raton, FL 33487. (561) 869-4606. The Helping Israel Fund raises funds for men and women from disadvantaged socioeconomic backgrounds serving to defend Israel. (www.helpingisraelfund.com)

ISEF Foundation (formerly **Project Renewal**) (1977). 520 8th Avenue, 4th Floor, New York, NY 10018. (212) 683-7772. ISEF's mission is to narrow Israel's socioeconomic gap through higher education for gifted students from disadvantaged backgrounds. Its unique methodology combines scholarship grants with required community service, as well as training in leadership and social awareness. ISEF was founded in response to the challenges Israel faced in fighting for survival while absorbing Jews from Asia, North Africa and elsewhere, recognizing the plight of this underprivileged population of new immigrants who was ill-equipped to merge into Israel's economic and social mainstream. Though originally created by and for Sephardic Jews, today all cultural and ethnic groups in Israeli society who share ISEF's values are represented in its student body. (www.isef.org)

Israel America Foundation (IAF) (1995). 108 West 39th Street, Suite 1001, New York, NY 10008. (212) 869-9477 or (800) 401-9952. The IAF raises funds through outright-giving and planned giving methods through charitable trusts, wills and living trusts to support eight specific Israeli nonprofit organizations. It sponsors programs and seminars in the US for predominantly senior citizens that deal with the problems of senior housing, nursing homes, hospices, etc., and legal instruments, such as disability trusts, living wills with health care proxies, last wills and testaments, and living trusts. (www.israelhome.org)

Israel Cancer Research Fund (ICRF) (1975). 52 Vanderbilt Avenue, Suite 1510, New York, NY 10017. (212) 969-9800 or (888) 654-4273. ICRF is the largest single nationwide charitable organization in North America solely devoted to supporting cancer research in Israel. It was founded by a group of American and Canadian researchers, oncologists, and lay people determined to harness Israel's educational and scientific resources in the fight against cancer. Its dual mission is to support cancer research programs in Israel and to support and encourage Israel's scientists to remain and conduct their groundbreaking research in Israel. ICRF provides millions of dollars in grants to outstanding cancer researchers and supports individuals at all of the major research institutions in Israel. ICRF-funded researchers have been making significant progress and have been able to develop improved chemotherapies, advanced techniques in bone marrow transplantation, and an enhanced understanding of tumor suppressor genes. (www.icrfonline.org)

Israel Children's Cancer Foundation (ICCF) (1998). 141 Washington Avenue, Suite 205, Lawrence, NY 11559. (516) 791-1180. The ICCF is a nonpartisan organization that provides clinical support for Israeli children suffering from cancer, offering assistance to every child in Israel, regardless of race, creed or national origin. It funds six of the largest hospitals and medical centers in Israel which care for 97% of all children diagnosed with cancer in Israel. Priority areas include funding for stem cell/bone marrow transplants, equipment upgrades, and the hiring of nurse practitioners and child life specialists. (www.israelcancer.org)

Israel Service Organization (ISO) (2007). 151 Oxford Road, New Rochelle, NY 10804. (917) 620-4771. Modeled after the American USO, ISO seeks to boost morale for the soldiers in the Israel Defense Forces by putting on high production concerts live on army bases. In addition, ISO organizes letter campaigns and care packages, in conjunction with schools worldwide, which enable people of varying backgrounds from all over the world to show their much needed support for the troops in the IDF. In addition, ISO acts to combat the anti-Israel and anti-IDF media bias. It also works to educate the public about the brave and honorable reaction of the Israeli soldiers in the face of real-time ethical and moral challenges they encounter on a daily basis, such as limiting collateral damage. (www.israelservice.org)

Israel Special Kids Fund (1998). 505 Eighth Avenue, New York, NY 10018. (212) 268-2577. Israel Special Kids Fund is dedicated to improving the quality of life for disabled and seriously ill children, as well as their families, in hospitals and rehabilitation centers in Israel. It organizes holiday programs, birthday parties, bar/bat mitzvah celebrations, sleep-away camps, trips, tours, and hospital recreational activities, and fulfills various dreams come true requests. It has set up an extensive big brother/sister and bikur cholim care project for hundreds of children. (www. israelspecialkids.org)

The Jerusalem Foundation (1966). 420 Lexington Avenue, Suite 1645, New York, NY 10170. (212) 697-4188. The Jerusalem Foundation, founded by the legendary Mayor of Jerusalem, Teddy Kollek, is devoted to improving the quality of life for all Jerusalemites, regardless of ethnic, religious or socioeconomic background, while preserving the city's historic heritage and religious sites. It has pioneered and supported more than 4000 projects, including community centers, sports complexes, parks, children's playgrounds, libraries, theaters, museums, arts schools, science labs, day care centers, homes for the elderly, school facilities, and landscaping. (www.jerusalemfoundation.org)

The Jewish Agency for Israel (formerly **The Jewish Agency for Palestine**) (1929). 633 3rd Avenue, New York, NY 10017. (212) 318-6105. The Jewish Agency for Israel played a central role in founding and building the State of Israel and today serves as the main link between Israel and Jewish communities everywhere, working to ensure the future of a connected, committed, global Jewish people with a strong Israel at its center. It also addresses social issues in Israel, facilitates aliyah, and serves as the Jewish people's "first responder," prepared to address emergencies in Israel and to rescue Jews from countries where they are at risk. The Jewish Agency for Israel North America is the organization's main fundraising arm in North America. (www.jewishagency.org)

JOIN Israel (formerly **Jewish Opportunities Institute**) (1990). 232 Madison Avenue, Suite 608, New York, NY 10016. (212) 561-5343. JOIN Israel rescues people in Israel who are hopelessly stuck in intolerable situations—youth delinquency, dysfunctional families, impoverished elderly, inferior education and literacy, legal and financial strangleholds—through strategic partnership with schools for educational issues, government agencies and local charities for welfare needs, other nonprofits, the larger community, and clients themselves to extend their joint capabilities to solve neglected problems and avoid duplication and waste. (www. joinisrael.org)

Just One Life (1989). 587 Fifth Avenue, Suite 702, New York, NY 10017. (212) 683-6040. Just One Life is a social service organization that assists Israeli expectant mothers who are confronted with financial, emotional or medical difficulties that often accompany an untimely or medically at risk pregnancy by providing professional counseling and financial assistance. Run by a professional team of social workers, Just One Life enables and empowers mothers to choose to continue their pregnancies to term. (www.justonelife.org)

KEDMA USA (2000). 574 West End Avenue, #24, New York, NY 10024. KEDMA is a student organization with branches in the US and Israel that works with university, seminary and yeshiva students, assisting disadvantaged communities in Israel while actualizing the concepts of social justice and tikkun olam through innovative programming. (www.kedisrael.weebly.com)

Kol HaNearim (Voice of the Youth) (KH) (2009). KH provides care for orphans and at-risk children in Israel. The vision is to help these special children develop from receivers to givers and see to it that these children have the tools and support to break the cycle of distress, enabling them to start their own families and lead happy, healthy, and successful lives. Each summer KH brings Jewish high-school volunteers to Israel to organize summer camps for orphans and at-risk children. Throughout the year, KH organizes weekend retreats both in Israel and America, marathons, social events, and volunteering opportunities. (www.kolhanearim.org)

M'ever LaYam (2016). (323) 741-1511. M'ever LaYam creates tangible connections between American Jewish youth and Israel by connecting them with lone soldiers from their communities who are currently serving in the Israel Defense Forces. It was developed with lone soldiers as partners in providing support to North American Jewry and to increase Diaspora Jews' emotional attachment to Israel. M'ever LaYam is very different from other lone soldier organizations in that the lone soldiers also become active participants in building ties to their own communities, and connecting lone soldiers with Jewish students and youth organizations from their home towns fosters educational connections and personal relationships that are strengthened through monthly video sharing, face-to-face meet-ups, and the delivery in Israel of personalized care packages, filled with items that the soldiers request, put together by the students. (www.meverlayam.org)

NA'AMAT USA (formerly **Pioneer Women** and **Pioneer Women's Organization of America**) (1925). 21515 Vanowen Street, Suite 102, Canoga Park, CA 91303. (818) 431-2200 or (844) 777-5222. NA'AMAT USA is part of the world movement of NA'AMAT (Hebrew acronym for Movement of Working Women and Volunteers), which strives to enhance the quality of life for women, children and families in Israel, the US and around the world. NA'AMAT USA supports NA'AMAT Israel in its efforts to enhance the status of women, provide social service programs for women, children and families, change the laws that present special obstacles for women in matters of marriage, divorce and widowhood, and advance equal rights and opportunities for women in Israel. It also furthers Jewish education, supports programs that address domestic violence and sexual harassment, and supports Habonim Dror, the Labor Zionist youth movement. (www.naamat.org)

OneFamily (also known as **OneFamily Fund**) (2001). 1029 Teaneck Road, Suite 3B, Teaneck, NJ 07666. (646) 289-8600. OneFamily empowers Israel's thousands of victims of terror attacks to rebuild their lives, rehabilitate, and reintegrate through emotional, legal, and financial assistance programs. It helps orphans, bereaved parents, widows and widowers, bereaved siblings, wounded victims, and those suffering from post-trauma as a result of terrorist attacks. (www.onefamilyto-gether.org)

One Israel Fund (also known as **YESHA Heartland Campaign**) (1993). 445 Central Avenue, Suite 210, Cedarhurst, NY 11516. (516) 239-9202. One Israel Fund is dedicated to supporting the welfare and safety of the men, women, and children of Judea and Samaria, as well as rebuilding the lives of the Jewish people impacted by the Gaza evacuation. Working in concert with communities, government officials and the Israel Defense Forces, One Israel Fund works to fill the gaps in essential medical, social, recreational, and preventive security services. Its goal is to undertake ongoing fundraising campaigns to help ensure the physical, emotional, and moral well-being of the Jewish families living in each and every community in these areas. (www.oneisraelfund.org)

Operation Embrace (2001). 143 Rollins Avenue, #2011, Rockville, MD 20847. Operation Embrace assists injured survivors of terror attacks in Israel regardless of race or religion, providing emotional support through its trauma centers, as well as direct financial assistance for medical, therapeutic, and rehabilitative needs to provide Israeli victims and survivors of terror with a brighter future and help them rebuild their lives. (www.operationembrace.org)

Operation Lifeshield (2007). 1650 South Powerline Road, Suite G, Deerfield Beach, FL 33442. Operation Lifeshield raises needed funds to build and deliver transportable air raid shelters to areas in Israel most at risk from the threat of missile attacks. Lifeshield shelters, constructed in Israel by a leading manufacturer of steel-reinforced concrete products, are deployed quickly and are available to protect schools, kindergartens, synagogues, parks, sidewalks, bus stops, and senior day centers. (www.operationlifeshield.org)

Poale Agudath Israel of America (1948). 1721 49th Street, Brooklyn, NY 11204. (718) 854-2017. Poale Agudath Israel of America aims to educate American Jews to the values of Orthodoxy and Aliyah, and supports kibbutzim, trade schools, yeshivot, moshavim, kollelim, research centers, and children's homes in Israel. (www.facebook.com/pages/Poale-Agudath-Israel-of-America/138571096191297 ?rf=478018239028933)

Polyphony Foundation (2011). 750 East Main Street, Suite 600, Stamford, CT 06902. (203) 979-8566. Polyphony Foundation's mission is to help bridge the divide between Arab and Jewish communities in Israel by creating a common ground where young people come together around classical music. (www.polyph-onyfoundation.org)

Right Now: Advocates for Asylum Seekers in Israel (also known as **Right Now: Advocates for African Asylum Seekers in Israel**) (2012). Right Now is an international coalition of Jews and allies who are advocating for the rights of the African asylum seekers in Israel through awareness-raising, grassroots campaigns, and direct advocacy. It asks Israel to develop an asylum process consistent with the Refugee Convention, one that would respect the dignity of asylum seekers, protect their human rights, and facilitate meaningful and impartial determinations of refugee status by the government of Israel. Coalition members include Eritrean and Sudanese asylum seekers living in Israel, individuals and rabbis in various cities in the US and Israel as well as a number of international organizations. (www.asylum-seekers.org)

Shmira Project (formerly **Elef LaMate**) (2006) (2012). Baltimore, MD. (240) 393-4836. Shmira (Guard duty, in Hebrew) Project is an ongoing, grassroots program that pairs Israel Defense Forces combat soldiers with Jews around the world, regardless of denomination, who do acts of kindness, prayer, or Torah learning to increase the soldier's spiritual merit and protection, following the ancient practice of pairing physical effort with spiritual effort. Shmira Project is being organized in its present format by the mother of a former IDF paratrooper. (www.shmiraproject.com)

Thank Israeli Soldiers (also known as **Fund for Israel's Tomorrow**) (TIS) (2008). 5185 MacArthur Boulevard, NW, Suite 636, Washington, DC 20016. (201) 620-8540. TIS empowers, embraces, and educates the brave men and women who serve Israel in the Israel Defense Forces and gives Jews around the world an easy way to show appreciation to them. (www.thankisraelisoldiers.org)

Tomchei Israel-Charity for Israel (also known as **Adopt a Family**). (2003). 626 East New York Avenue, Brooklyn, NY 11203. (347) 662-2550. Tomchei Israel collects donations to alleviate the constant threat of poverty and illness many Chabad Lubavitch families face in Israel. Its programs include Adopt a Family, which gives donors the opportunity to make a difference for one family at a time, providing them with dependable assistance; Yom Tov fund, which provides needy families with monetary assistance and more during the Jewish holidays; Kallah Fund, which provides for impoverished brides facing a wedding and marriage; and Emergency Fund, which provides money for families facing a harrowing medical crisis. (www.charityforisrael.com)

United Charity Institutions of Jerusalem (Etz Chaim Torah Center) (1903). 1782 45th Street, Brooklyn, NY 11204. (718) 633-8469. United Charity Institutions of Jerusalem raises funds to support schools, kitchens, clinics, dispensaries, and free loan foundations in Israel. (No website)

United Soup Kitchens in Israel (USK) (2003). 700 Broadway, New York, NY 10003. (800) 531-8004. USK is the nationwide network of free dining facilities serving Israel's neediest. It alleviates poverty by eliminating hunger especially among the oldest and youngest. (www.unitedsoupkitchens.org)

Women's International Zionist Organization USA (WIZO USA) (1982). 950 Third Avenue, Suite 2803, New York, NY 10022. (212) 751-6461. WIZO USA is a member of the international WIZO organization, which has members in over 50 countries working together to improve the lives of women, children, and the elderly living in Israel. Next to the Israeli government, it is the largest provider of social welfare services in the country, with projects including child care centers, schools, shelters for battered women, homes for girls in distress, and programs providing services for the elderly. (www.wizousa.org)

YRF Darca (formerly **Youth Renewal Fund**) (1989). 1460 Broadway, New York, NY 10036. (212) 207-3195. YRF Darca is the philanthropic funding partner for the Darca network of schools in Israel. Darca provides Israeli high school students in lower income communities—regardless of ability, religion, birthplace, geographic or socioeconomic status—an excellent education designed to improve social mobility and quality of life for themselves, their communities, and their country. The schools emphasize academic achievement and the values of tolerance, democracy, and active participation in national and community life. (www.yrf-darca.org)

12.1.13   Jewish Israel-Related Political and Advocacy Organizations

Act for Israel (2011). 5042 Wilshire Boulevard, #13938, Los Angeles, CA 90036. (323) 209-5228. Act for Israel is committed to representing Israel's interests through the use of new media; empowering pro-Israel activists to educate others; and strengthening the ties between Israel and the world through shared interests. Act for Israel is the leading digital platform for pro-Israel activism, relying on the latest internet-based technology to win the war on ideas. Its goal is to correct misinformation, end demonization, stop delegitimization, and to give Israel a well-needed voice. (www.actforisrael.org)

Alliance for Israel (2019). Alliance for Israel is a grassroots organization that reflects the diversity of Israel and the Jewish people and of their allies. Its national membership base confronts Israel's detractors face to face to expose the lies and shame of the supporters of the Boycott, Divestment and Sanctions (BDS) campaign as they attempt to deny the Jewish people their indigenous roots and their right to self-determination in Israel. (www.alliance4israel.org)

Alliance for Middle East Peace (ALLMEP) (2006). 1725 I Street, NW, Suite 300, Washington, DC 20006. (202) 618-4600. ALLMEP is a network of organizations that conduct civil society work in conflict transformation, development, coexistence, and cooperative activities. Working on the ground in the Middle East with Israelis, Palestinians, Arabs, and Jews, its members seek to build a secure, just, and sustainable peace where all can enjoy the rights and freedoms necessary so as to reach their human potential and live in peace with one another with dignity. ALLMEP secures and scales up funding to expand trust-building interactions between Palestinians and Israelis; provides capacity-building support and visibility to amplify the voices and impact of its member organizations in the region; and connects individuals and groups to create a critical mass that live and act in support of peace. (www.allmep.org)

Ameinu (formerly **Po'alei Zion** and **Labor Zionist Alliance**) (1995). 25 Broadway, New York, NY 10004. (212) 366-1194. Ameinu is a national, multi-generational community of progressive American Jews who seek opportunities to foster social and economic justice both in Israel and the US. Its political agenda addresses a range of domestic and international issues, including protection of the environment, support for universal healthcare, preservation of civil liberties, and the ending of foreign and domestic sweatshops. Ameinu promotes its agenda through advocacy and educational programming. It supports efforts to end the Middle East conflict with a negotiated peace with the Palestinians and the Arab States. Ameinu sponsors Habonim Dror Labor Zionist youth movement. (www.ameinu.net)

America-Israel Friendship League (AIFL) (1971). 1430 Broadway, Suite 1804, New York, NY 10018. (646) 892-9142. The AIFL's sole purpose is to make friends for the State of Israel through activities intended to improve the general perception of Israel and to help both Americans and Israelis identify and appreciate their shared commitment to democracy. AIFL is a nonsectarian, nonpartisan organization which seeks to broaden the base of support for Israel among Americans of all faiths and backgrounds and promote a strong and enduring friendship between Americans and Israelis. (www.aifl.org)

American Israel Public Affairs Committee (AIPAC) (formerly **American Zionist Committee for Public Affairs**) (1954). 251 H Street, NW, Washington, DC 20001. (202) 639-5200. AIPAC's mission is to strengthen the ties between the US and its ally Israel to the mutual benefit of both nations. It is a 100,000-member grassroots movement of activists committed to ensuring Israel's security and protecting American interests in the Middle East and around the world. AIPAC advocates for US cooperation with Israel on a wide range of issues, from promoting peace between Israel and its neighbors to facilitating US-Israel exchanges of expertise and equipment for homeland security, defense and counterterrorism to collaborating on technology, science and agricultural products. AIPAC is registered as a domestic lobby. It is supported financially by private donations and receives no financial assistance from Israel nor from any national organization or foreign group. AIPAC is not a political action committee and it does not rate, endorse or contribute to candidates. The American Israel Education Foundation makes annual grants to AIPAC. (www.aipac.org)

The American-Israeli Cooperative Enterprise (AICE) (1993). 2810 Blaine Drive, Chevy Chase, MD 20815. (301) 565-3918. AICE is a nonpartisan organization established to strengthen the US-Israel relationship by emphasizing the fundamentals of the alliance. It provides a vehicle for the research, study, discussion, and exchange of views concerning nonmilitary cooperation and shared interests; explores issues of common historical interest to the peoples and governments of the US and Israel; provides educational materials on Jewish history and culture; and promotes scholarship in the field of Israel studies. AICE's major long-term objective is to bring innovative, successful social and education programs developed and proven in Israel to the US to help address its domestic needs and provide tangible benefits to Americans. It also looks at specific opportunities for introducing novel American programs to Israel. The Jewish Virtual Library is a project of AICE. (www. jewishvirtuallibrary.org)

American Jewish International Relations Institute (AJIRI) (2005). PO Box 42732, Washington, DC 20015. (301) 915-0132. AJIRI was established to monitor, track, and combat anti-Israel voting patterns at the United Nations. It works with concerned and committed Members of Congress, on a bipartisan basis, as well as with other motivated groups and individuals, to positively influence the countries who vote against Israel and the US out of habit, inertia, or because they have never been properly engaged on the subject of their voting pattern, urging them to support UN reforms which will shut down destructive anti-Israel activities that are contrary to the principles of the UN Charter. (www.ajiri.us)

American Jewish League for Israel (AJLI) (1957). 450 Fashion Avenue, Suite 808, New York, NY 10123. (212) 371-1583. AJLI seeks to unite all American Jews, regardless of political, ideological or religious beliefs, to work to support Israel. AJLI is independent and not connected to any political party in Israel. Its University Scholarship program awards qualified American students with partial scholarship grants toward a year of study at one of Israel's prestigious universities. (www.americanjewishleague.org)

American Zionist Movement (AZM) (1939). 40 Wall Street, Suite 706, New York, NY 10005. (212) 318-6100. AZM is a coalition of groups and individuals committed to Zionism—the idea that the Jewish people is one people with a shared history, values, and language. AZM is the American affiliate of the World Zionist Organization, the Zionist Federation in the US. Its mission is to strengthen the connection of American Jews with Israel; develop their appreciation of the centrality of Israel to Jewish life worldwide; deepen their understanding of Israeli society and the challenges it faces; encourage travel, long-term visits, and aliyah; and facilitate dialogue, debate, and collective action to further Zionism in the US and abroad. (www.azm.org)

Americans for A Safe Israel (AFSI) (1970). 1751 Second Avenue, New York, NY 10128. (212) 828-2424. AFSI was founded as an American counterpart to the Land of Israel Movement, asserting Israel's historic, religious, and legal rights to the land regained in the 1967 war. AFSI argues that a strong territorially defensible Israel is essential to US and global security interests in the region and that the "two-state solution" would endanger the world, while bringing about the dissolution of Israel. It is dedicated to the premise that the Jewish communities in Judea, Samaria, and the Golan are the best guarantee against strategic vulnerability. (www.afsi.org)

Americans for Peace Now (APN) (formerly **American Friends of Peace Now**) (1981). 1320 19th Street, NW, Suite 400, Washington, DC 20036. (202) 408-9898. APN, the sister organization of Shalom Achshav (Peace Now), Israel's preeminent peace movement, has developed into the most prominent American Jewish Zionist organization working to achieve a comprehensive political settlement to the Arab-Israeli conflict. APN's mission is to educate and persuade the American public and its leadership to support and adopt policies that will lead to comprehensive, durable, Israeli-Palestinian and Israeli-Arab peace, based on a two-state solution. APN also works to ensure Israel's future and the viability of Israel's democracy and Jewish character through education, activism, and advocacy in the US. It engages in grass-roots political activism and outreach to the American Jewish and Arab American communities, opinion leaders, university students, and the public at large. (www. peacenow.org)

Americans United with Israel (2010). PO Box 73071, Marietta, GA 30007. (404) 563-2227. Americans United with Israel, affiliated with the international organization United for Israel, is deeply committed to the success and prosperity of

Israel. Its primary mission is to educate, inspire, and promote building a strong connection with the People, Country and Land of Israel. Americans United with Israel has developed state-of-the-art, efficient channels of communication to distribute critical information and to teach people around the world the truth about Israel. (www.americaunitedwithisrael.org)

America's Voices in Israel (2002) (2010). 633 3rd Avenue, 21st Floor, New York, NY 10017. (212) 339-6998. America's Voices in Israel is a pioneering program created to bolster Israel's image in the US by bringing media and radio personalities to broadcast live from Israel. It engages influential personalities whose first-hand experiences in Israel provide an effective antidote to the distortions and misrepresentations about the Jewish state that are increasingly promulgated by those who seek to delegitimize and demonize Israel. (www.americasvoices.us)

Anthropologists for Dialogue on Israel & Palestine (ADIP) (2015). ADIP promotes the use of anthropology's critical theories and methods in working toward peace and social justice in Israel/Palestine. It encourages and supports dialogue and engagement among Israelis, Palestinians, and others concerned with the region, taking into account a range of anthropologically based values, including abhorrence of violence and a desire to expose inequalities of power along with acknowledging a wide diversity of opinions and possibilities of action. ADIP opposes the academic boycott against Israeli academia and against Israeli and other anthropologists in particular. (No website)

Artists 4 Israel (A4I) (2009). 1060 South Cochran Avenue, Unit 4, Los Angeles, CA 90019. (718) 757-8738. A4I is an artists' rights group that supports Israel and an Israel advocacy organization inspired by artistic freedom. It empowers artists to express their support for the artistic and cultural freedoms of Israel and the nation's right to exist in peace and security. A4I stands guard against propagandists and politicians who strip art of its meaning and of censors who use criticism of Israel as a guise for stifling creativity and expression. A4I's objectives are to provide artists with information to make their own decisions about Israel and the Middle East; counter the misconception that the arts community does not support Israel; utilize the arts to refute propaganda; inform the public about artistic freedoms and Israel through the arts; and beautify the landscape and strengthen the spirit of the people of Israel and the Middle East. (www.artists4israel.org)

ARZA (Association of Reform Zionists of America) (1978). 633 Third Avenue, 7th Floor, New York, NY 10017. (212) 650-4280. ARZA strengthens and enriches the Jewish identity of Reform Jews in the US by ensuring that a connection with Israel is a fundamental part of that identity. It develops support for and strengthens the Reform movement in Israel. ARZA works in partnership with the Union for Reform Judaism and the Israel Movement for Progressive Judaism and their affiliates, and represents US Reform Jews in national and international Zionist organizations. (www.arza.org)

BlueStar (formerly **BlueStar PR**) (2003). 96 Jessie Street, Suite 310, San Francisco, CA 94105. (415) 543-6300. BlueStar's mission is to humanize perceptions about Israel, and its goal is to inform campus and community conversations on Israel. It uses visual media to build support for Israel's case as a Jewish democracy within secure, recognized borders. Free posters and video resources are offered for download from BlueStar's website, and it also designs and prints custom posters and postcards. (www.bluestarpr.com)

The Center for Jewish Nonviolence (CJNV) (2015). The CJNV engages in creative, nonviolent activism in the occupied Palestinian territories and Israel with the aim of bringing an end to the occupation. It draws upon multiple forms of nonviolence, including direct action to confront the violence of the occupation as well as nonviolent solidarity activism to support Palestinians threatened with eviction from their homes and land with an understanding that existence is resistance. The CJNV believes in the shared humanity and full equality of Palestinians and Israelis alike. It does not take an official position on BDS or on the one-states vs. two-state solution. (www.centerforjewishnonviolence.org)

Committee for Israel (2010) (formerly Emergency Committee for Israel). PO Box 51223, Washington, DC 20091. The Emergency Committee for Israel is committed to mounting an active defense of the US-Israel relationship by educating the public about the positions of political candidates on this issue and by keeping the public informed of the latest developments in both countries. (www.facebook.com/Committee-for-Israel-144505782230721)

Creative Community for Peace (CCFP) (2012). (213) 254-3199. CCFP is an entertainment industry organization that represents a cross-section of the creative world dedicated to promoting music and the arts as a bridge to peace, while supporting artistic freedom, and countering the cultural boycott of Israel. It is an apolitical organization that strives to provide balance to the discourse regarding the Israeli-Palestinian conflict and encourage artists to travel to the region to experience it for themselves. (www.creativecommunityforpeace.com)

Democratic Majority for Israel (DMFI) (2019). DMFI brings together a diverse group of leaders who believe the Democratic Party's vision and values represent what's best for the US and who believe in promoting a close relationship between the US and Israel and a progressive policy agenda. It works to maintain and strengthen support for the US-Israel alliance by educating elected officials, candidates, and the public, while advocating for other progressive policies. (www.demmajorityforisrael.org)

Encounter (2005). 25 Broadway, Floor 9, New York, NY 10004. (212) 284-6776. Encounter is a nonpartisan educational organization cultivating informed and constructive Jewish leadership on the Israeli-Palestinian conflict and dedicated to strengthening the capacity of the Jewish people to be constructive agents of change in resolving the conflict. It does not take specific positions, but its vision is one of genuine peace. Encounter equips rabbis, Jewish professionals, leaders, and philanthropists with first-hand knowledge of Palestinian life, seeding a multi-denominational cadre of Jewish leadership charged with a two-pronged mission: to transform the Israeli-Palestinian conflict and to heal internal Jewish communal rifts formed in its wake. Its North America program provides ongoing capacity-building and training. (www.encounterprograms.org)

Endowment for Middle East Truth (EMET) (2005). PO Box 66366, Washington, DC 20035. (202) 601-7422. EMET (Truth, in Hebrew) is a think tank and policy center with a pro-America and pro-Israel stance that prides itself on providing research and analysis which challenges the falsehoods and misrepresentations that abound in US Middle East policy. EMET works to educate policy-makers by providing pertinent information to US Senators and Members of Congress while combating efforts by other interest groups to influence Congress with misrepresentations about Israel and the Middle East. (www.emetonline.org)

Freeman Center for Strategic Studies (1992). PO Box 35661, Houston, TX 77235. The primary purpose of the Freeman Center is to improve Israel's ability to survive in a hostile world. This is accomplished through research into the military and strategic issues related to the Arab-Israeli conflict and Islamic terrorism and the dissemination of that information to the Jewish and non-Jewish community. (www.freeman.org)

Fuel for Truth (FFT) (2001). 90 Church Street, New York, NY 10008. FFT is a bipartisan organization, run exclusively by volunteers, that aims to strengthen Israel's image in the US by providing young social leaders with the basic facts about the Middle East and the skills necessary to advocate for Israel, be it in a social setting, on social media, or otherwise. It selects, educates, and empowers a diverse group of volunteers to help promote and strengthen Israel's image among their peers and social networks. (www.fuelfortruth.org)

Herut North America (2004). 22 Angela Court, Woodcliff Lake, NJ 07677. (212) 444-9511. Herut North America is a Zionist movement committed to social justice, the unity of the Jewish people, and the territorial integrity of the Land of Israel. It is dedicated to strengthening an independent Jewish nation-state in Israel for all Jews who choose to reunite with their brethren in their ancient homeland. (www.herutna.org)

Hiddush-Freedom of Religion for Israel (2009). 182 East 95th Street, Suite 24G, New York, NY 10128. (646) 334-5636. Hiddush is a nondenominational, nonpartisan, Israel-Diaspora partnership dedicated to promoting religious freedom and equality as guaranteed in Israel's Declaration of Independence. Among the organization's stated goals are the legalization of civil as well as religious marriage and divorce, ensuring recognition for Conservative, Reconstructionist and Reform marriages and conversions, full rights for rabbis of all Jewish denominations, providing equal funding for non-Orthodox religious services, civic equality in education, employment, and military service, and fighting discrimination in the name of religious observance against women and other population groups. (www.hiddush.org)

IfNotNow (2014). PO Box 26425, Washington, DC 20001. IfNotNow is a diverse movement of American Jews working to end the American Jewish community's support for the occupation and gain freedom and dignity for all Israelis and Palestinians. It is a nonviolent volunteer movement across generations and organizational affiliations that celebrates Jewish cultural diversity as a source of resilience. IfNotNow does not take a unified stance on BDS (Boycott, Divestment, Sanctions), Zionism, or the question of statehood. (www.ifnotnowmovement.org)

Israel Action Network (IAN) (2010). 25 Broadway, Suite 1700, New York, NY 10004. (212) 284-6500. The IAN is a strategic initiative of The Jewish Federations of North America, in partnership with the Jewish Council for Public Affairs, to counter the assault on Israel's legitimacy. Its work is grounded in building strong relationships with people of faith, human rights advocates, political and civic leaders, and friends and neighbors in the community. (www.israelactionnetwork.org)

Israel Allies Foundation (IAF) (2008). 1001 Connecticut Avenue, NW, Suite 607, Washington, DC 20036. (202) 280-1178. The IAF is dedicated to promoting communication and information sharing between parliamentarians and legislators the world over who share a belief that the State of Israel has the right to exist in peace within secure borders. It accomplishes its goals through the formation of official parliamentary caucuses in support of Israel and the development of coordinated activities and policy priorities for these caucuses. The IAF seeks to strengthen, facilitate, and unify this coalition of parliamentarians who already support Israel by educating them on the issues facing Israel and by providing relevant information, resources, and tools in order to formulate policy positions and legislative actions. (www.israelallies.org)

The Israel Group (TIG) (2015). PO Box 4332, Valley Village, CA 91617. (833) 600-6001. TIG's mission is protecting Israel in the Diaspora. Through diverse initiatives, TIG proactively combats the political warfare campaigns waged against Israel that are proliferating throughout almost all fabrics of society. Its High School Speakers Program enables high school students to gain the understanding, tools, knowledge, and support necessary to enter college, not as victims, but rather as confident supporters of Israel, able to understand the propaganda and misinformation they will most likely face. (www.theisraelgroup.org)

Israel Institute for Strategic Studies (IISS) (2011). IISS is an independent policy center dedicated to the preservation and the propagation of joint values shared by Israel and the US, as embodied in the US Constitution, and the Zionist movement, as reflected in Israel's Declaration of the Independence. It is more than a monitor in that it sets out its own independent policy proposals, and it is more than a think tank in that it is mission-oriented rather than research-oriented. IISS is on the front-lines in the intellectual battle for Israel's legitimacy. (www.strategic-israel.org)

Israel Policy Forum (IPF) (1993). 355 Lexington Avenue, 14th Floor, New York, NY 10017. (212) 315-1741. Founded with the encouragement of Prime Minister Yitzhak Rabin, IPF is a nonpartisan organization that promotes Israel's future as a Jewish and democratic state by advancing a diplomatic resolution to the Arab-Israeli conflict. It promotes active US engagement to achieve a two-state solution to the conflict and peace and security for Israel with the Palestinians and the Arab states. IPF convenes forums and publishes commentary and analysis that promote pragmatic strategies for achieving regional peace and security, and mobilizes policy experts and community leaders to build support for those ideas in the US and Israel. (www.ipforum.org)

The Israel Project (TIP) (Ceased to exist as of 2019)

J Street (2008). PO Box 66073, Washington, DC 20035. (202) 596-5207. J Street is the political home for pro-Israel, pro-peace Americans who want Israel to be secure, democratic, and the national home of the Jewish people. J Street advocates for the future of Israel as the democratic homeland of the Jewish people, with Israel's Jewish and democratic character depending on a two-state solution, which would result in a Palestinian state living alongside Israel in peace and security. Its aim is to promote American leadership to end the Arab-Israeli and Israel-Palestinian conflicts peacefully and diplomatically. JStreetPAC is a political action committee endorsing federal candidates and capable of making direct political campaign donations. J Street Education Fund aims to educate targeted communities about the need for a two-state solution. J Street Local and J Street U (formerly the Union of Progressive Zionists, and JStreet's on-campus movement) are programs of the J Street Education Fund. (www.jstreet.org)

Jewish Institute for National Security Affairs (JINSA) (1976). 1101 14th Street, NW, Suite 1110, Washington, DC 20005. (202) 667-3900. JINSA is a nonpartisan organization that advocates on behalf of a strong US military, a robust national security policy and a strong US security relationship with Israel and other like-minded democracies. It is an educational organization working within the American Jewish community to explain the link between American defense policy and the security of Israel, and within the national security establishment to explain the key role Israel plays in bolstering American interests. (www.jinsa.org)

The Jewish Peace Lobby (JPL) (1989). PO Box 7778, Silver Spring, MD 20910. (240) 481-2382. JPL, made up of over 5000 members and 400 rabbis, is a legally registered lobby promoting changes in US policy regarding the Israeli-Palestinian conflict. It advocates for Israel's right to peace within secure borders; a political settlement based on mutual recognition of the right of self-determination of both peoples; a two-state solution as the most likely means to a stable peace; the sharing of Jerusalem; halting the settlements; and that the US should put on the table a full American plan for ending the conflict. It works closely with Israeli, Palestinian, European, and American policy-makers. (www.peacelobby.org)

Jewish Political Education Foundation (JPEF) (1995). PO Box 4458, Great Neck, NY 11023. (516) 487-2990. The purposes of JPEF include supporting and enhancing the image of Israel as a strong, democratic, benevolent, and humane nation, of the Jewish people as its people, and of Zionism as the national liberation movement of the Jewish people; supporting the right of Israel's citizens to live within secure and defensible borders; bringing an end to antisemitism; supporting the interests of Jewish Americans and promoting awareness of the issues of concern to them; countering misinformation, distortion, and bias in the media regarding Israel and Jewish issues; and soliciting funds to effect these purposes and to support organizations and institutions of like purpose. (www.jewishpoliticalchronicle.org)

Jewish Voice for Peace (JVP) (1996). 1611 Telegraph Avenue, Suite 1020, Oakland, CA 94612. (510) 465-1777. JVP provides a voice for Jews and allies who believe that peace in the Middle East will be achieved through justice and full equality for both Palestinians and Israelis. It seeks an end to the Israeli occupation of the territories; security and self-determination for Israelis and Palestinians; a just solution for Palestinian refugees based on principles established in international law; an end to violence against civilians; and peace and justice for all peoples of the Middle East. (www.jewishvoiceforpeace.org)

Joint Action Committee for Political Affairs (JAC) (1980). PO Box 105, Highland Park, IL 60035. (847) 433-5999. JAC was founded after the 1980 election when many friends of Israel in the Congress were defeated by an emerging force in American politics–Radical Right political groups that opposed Israel and the values of mainstream American Jewry. JAC is comprised of three organizations that engage in the political process from a Jewish perspective. The Joint Action Committee for Political Affairs is a bipartisan political action committee (PAC) committed to the special relationship between the US and Israel and a social agenda that includes reproductive choice and separation of religion and state. The Joint Action Committee is a nonpartisan advocacy group that promotes JAC's agenda. The JAC Education Foundation educates and engages the Jewish community in electoral politics and issues of Jewish concern. (www.jacpac.org)

Just Vision (2003). 1616 P Street, NW, Suite 340, Washington, DC 20036. (202) 232-6820. Just Vision generates awareness and support for Palestinians and Israelis who pursue freedom, dignity, security and peace using nonviolent means. It tells their under-documented stories through its award-winning films and educational tools that undermine stereotypes, inspire commitment and galvanize action. (www.justvision.org)

Justice for Jews from Arab Countries (JJAC) (2002). 21 Dale Drive, West Orange, NJ 07052. (973) 669-9788. JJAC is a coalition of major Jewish communal organizations operating under the auspices of the Conference of Presidents of Major American Jewish Organizations, the American Sephardi Federation in conjunction with the American Jewish Committee, Anti-Defamation League, B'nai B'rith International, the Jewish Public Council for Public Affairs and the World Sephardic Congress. It is a political advocacy organization whose mission is to represent the interests of Jews from Arab countries. (www.justiceforjews.com)

Kumah (1999). 6520 Richmond Street, #2, Chicago, IL 60645. Through innovative social, multimedia and advocacy projects, Kumah, based in the US and Israel, aims to strengthen the national character of Israel, establish its independence, and aid it in reaching its potential to be a home for the Jewish people, a canvas for a cultural rebirth, and positive catalyst for the Middle East region and the world. Kumah aims to educate the public about Israel and dispel myths and stereotypes about the Middle East. It seeks to enhance the Diaspora's connection to Israel through innovative media projects, speaking events, seminars and tours. (www.yishaifleisher.com/kumah)

Liberate Art (2015). 21031 Ventura Boulevard, Suite 1000, Woodland Hills, CA 91364. (424) 653-6112. Liberate Art is a leader in fighting the cultural boycott campaign (BDS) against Israel and connects the international entertainment industry to Israel. The cultural boycott campaign uses artists and celebrities to spread damaging lies about Israel to millions of people across the globe. Liberate Art educates and inspires hundreds of thousands to combat the cultural boycott campaign with commentary in international publications, speaking engagements, celebrity focused events, educational videos, and interviews on radio, podcasts, and television. (www.liberateart.net)

Librarians for Fairness (2003). Librarians for Fairness is dedicated to bringing information about Israel to libraries around the world and to promoting democratic values. It works to ensure that Israel is represented fairly in libraries through books, periodicals, audiovisuals, online resources, and scheduled events. (www.librarians-forfairness.org)

Magshimey Herut North America (MH North America) (2010). Angela Court, Woodcliff Lake, NJ 07677. (212) 444-9511. MH North America, the North American branch of World Magshimey Herut, is a Zionist organization that reaches out to Jewish communities across North America, strengthening the bond between Jews and the Land of Israel. By working with communities, campuses, high schools, etc., MH North America strives to create Zionist leaders to better represent Israel and combat anti-Israel rhetoric raging in North America today. MH North America's Israel Campus Initiative is designed to educate and promote Israel professional internship opportunities for Jewish young adults. World Magshimey (www.worldmh.org.il)

Mercaz USA (1979). 520 Eighth Avenue, 4th Floor, New York, NY 10018. (212) 533-2061. Mercaz USA is the US Zionist membership organization of the Conservative movement, the voice of Conservative Jewry within the World Zionist Organization, the Jewish Agency for Israel, the American Zionist Movement and the Jewish National Fund to support religious pluralism in Israel and strengthen the connection between Israel and the Diaspora. It fosters Zionist education and aliyah and develops young leadership. (www.mercazusa.org)

Middle East Peace Dialogue Network (1999). PO Box 943, Atco, NJ 08004. (856) 768-0938. The Middle East Peace Dialogue Network believes that a two-state solution to the Israeli-Palestinian conflict is essential to Israel's survival as the national home of the Jewish people and as a vibrant democracy, and that supporting dialogue, reconciliation, and tolerance activities and programs which encourage Israeli-Palestinian interaction is essential to long term peace. (www.mepdn.org)

Middle East Peace Network (MEPN) (1990) (2011). (847) 926-7763. MEPN is a US-based, independent, nonpartisan, nongovernmental organization that uses private diplomacy to complement the activities of the Middle Eastern governments in their pursuit of conflict resolution and lasting peace, primarily between Arabs and Israelis, by facilitating dialogue within and across conflict divides. MEPN works with local, national, and international partners to employ alternative avenues of diplomacy, including people-to-people interactions, citizen diplomacy, transnational mechanisms, and back-channels, to forward the peace process in the Middle East. (www.mepnetwork.org)

National Action Committee Political Action Committee (NACPAC) (1981). 3389 Sheridan Street, #424, Hollywood, FL 33021. (954) 894-3048. NACPAC is a pro-Israel political action committee whose members believe that a strong US-Israel alliance is good for America. (www.nacpac.org)

NORPAC (1992). PO Box 1543, Englewood Cliffs, NJ 07632. (201) 788-5133. NORPAC is a nonpartisan Political Action Committee whose primary purpose is to support candidates and sitting members of the US Senate and House of Representatives who demonstrate a genuine commitment to the strength, security, and survival of Israel. In addition to funding candidates' campaigns, support includes educating candidates on important issues, connecting like-minded

Members of Congress on a particular project, and ensuring that a public position taken is appreciated within the community. (www.norpac.net)

One Jerusalem (2001). 136 East 39th Street, New York, NY 10016. One Jerusalem is a grassroots educational foundation committed to preserving a united Jerusalem as the undivided capital of Israel under Israeli sovereignty, which will protect access to the holy sites of all three major religions. (www.onej.org)

OneVoice International (2002). PO Box 1577-OCS, New York, NY 10113. (212) 897-3985. OneVoice International is a global initiative that supports grassroots activists in Israel, Palestine, and internationally who are working to build the human infrastructure needed to create the necessary conditions for a just and negotiated resolution to the Israeli-Palestinian conflict. The OneVoice movement is driven by a vision of an independent and viable Palestine and a secure Israel free from conflict, where Palestinians and Israelis are able to realize their national and individual aspirations, building a future based upon principles of security, justice, dignity, and peace. OneVoice on Campus is a college fellowship program active on a number of campuses across the Midwest, Mid-Atlantic, New England, and Northeast regions, whose aim is to cultivate and train a team of engaged students throughout the country capable of harnessing the energy on campus to advocate for an end to the Israeli occupation and a peaceful resolution to the Israeli-Palestinian conflict in the form of a two-state solution. (www.onevoicemovement.org)

Our Soldiers Speak (OSS) (2010). PO Box 138 Midtown Station, New York, NY 10018. (516) 672-6662. OSS educates current and future generations of policy makers and influencers by way of its unique, three-pronged strategy: Campus, Congress, Israel. OSS Campus is the vehicle through which the IDF and the Israeli National Police dispatch senior officers to select campuses overseas, having reached hundreds of campuses in several continents to date. OSS Campus speaks to the pro, the anti, and the undecided elements of the global student and faculty community alike. OSS Elite convenes policy and strategy briefings for members of the US Congress by senior-ranked members of the IDF and the Israeli National Police as well as for legislators and policy influencers throughout the western world. OSS Israel recognizes that Israel is her own greatest ambassador. The *Israel Through the Law & Policy Lens* tour of the country brings select graduate and doctoral students, committed to careers in public service, from various countries to Israel annually for an academically rich immersion into the law and policy considerations of the country, with unique follow-up opportunities for tour graduates that result in an ongoing appreciation of the State of Israel and her place among the nations. (www.oursoldiersspeak.org)

Partners for Progressive Israel (PPI) (formerly **Meretz USA**) (1991). 601 West 26th Street, Suite 325-30 New York, NY 10001. (212) 242-4500. PPI, affiliated with the World Union of Meretz, is a progressive American Zionist organization dedicated to two essential goals: the achievement of a durable and just peace between Israel and all its neighbors, especially the Palestinian people, based on a negotiated two-state solution; and the realization of human and civil rights, equality and social justice, and environmental sustainability for all of Israel's inhabitants. It develops and implements hands-on programs that enable the American Jewish community, and its friends, to provide real support for policies of peace, democracy, justice and equality in Israeli society. (www.progressiveisrael.org)

Pro-Israel America (2019). 455 Massachusetts Avenue, NW, #225, Washington, DC 20001. Pro-Israel America works to strengthen support for the US-Israel relationship by independently promoting and supporting the election of pro-Israel candidates to federal office, regardless of party; educating voters about pro-Israel candidates and their Congressional races; and creating a simple, accessible, online portal for members to make pro-Israel campaign contributions. (www.proisraelamerica.org)

Religious Zionists of America (RZA) (1909). 305 7th Avenue, Room 1200, New York, NY 10001. (212) 465-9234. The RZA, the American branch of the World Mizrachi-HaPoel HaMizrachi movement, is an ideological and educational organization that aims to instill in the American Jewish community a commitment to religious Zionism. The RZA seeks to reach all segments of the American Jewish population through adult educational programming in regional chapters, pro-Israel advocacy, promoting aliyah, strengthening and developing a creative curriculum on religious Zionism for Jewish day schools, and encouraging the knowledge and use of Hebrew as an important modality of expression. The RZA supports the Bnei Akiva Zionist youth movement and the Yeshivot Hesder movement in Israel. (www.rza.org)

Scholars for Peace in the Middle East (SPME) (2003). PO Box 2241, Bala Cynwyd, PA 19004. SPME is a grassroots community of scholars who have united to promote honest, fact-based and civil discourse, especially in regard to Middle East issues. SPME believes that ethnic, national and religious hatreds, including antisemitism and anti-Israelism, have no place in institutions, disciplines, and communities, and it employs academic means to address these issues. SPME's mission is to inform, motivate and encourage faculty to use their academic skills and disciplines on campus, in classrooms and in academic publications to develop effective responses to the ideological distortions, including antisemitic and anti-Zionist slanders. SPME welcomes scholars from all disciplines, faiths, and nationalities. (www.spme.net)

StandWithUs (also known as **Israel Emergency Alliance**) (2001). PO Box 341069, Los Angeles, CA 90034. (310) 836-6140. StandWithUs is an international, pro-Israel education and advocacy organization dedicated to informing the public about Israel and to combating the extremism and antisemitism that often distorts the issues. Through print materials, speakers, programs, conferences, missions to Israel, campaigns, and internet resources, it ensures that the story of Israel's achievements and ongoing challenges is told on campuses and in communities, the media, libraries, and churches around the world. (www.standwithus.com)

True Torah Jews Against Zionism (formerly **World Federation for the Furtherance of Torah**) (1955) (2001). 183 Wilson Street, PMB 162, Brooklyn, NY 11211. (718) 841-7053. True Torah Jews, founded by a group of Orthodox Jews, is dedicated to informing the world, and the American public and politicians in particular, that not all Jews support the ideology of the Zionist state called Israel and that the ideology of Zionism is in total opposition to the teachings of traditional Judaism. (www.truetorahjews.org)

Unity Coalition for Israel (UCI) (formerly **Voices United for Israel**) (1991). 3965 West 83rd Street, #292, Shawnee Mission, KS 66208. (913) 648-0022. Organized to cultivate American support for a strong and secure Israel, UCI is composed of more than 200 Jewish and Christian organizations, including churches, synagogues, prayer networks, think tanks, and thousands of individuals, representing more than 40 million Americans who are dedicated to a safe and secure Israel. (www.unitycoalitionforisrael.org)

World Zionist Organization-American Section (1971). 633 3rd Avenue, 21st Floor, New York, NY 10017. (212) 339-6000. World Zionist Organization-American Section is registered to foster the ideals of Zionism and Judaism, and the unity of the Jewish people; to encourage the immigration of Jews to Israel and their resettlement and rehabilitation therein; to encourage, foster and promote the knowledge and study of Hebrew language and literature, Jewish culture, history, philosophy and traditions; and to disseminate, publish and otherwise make available works relating to Judaism, Zionism, Israel and kindred subjects. (No website)

Z Street (2009). 742 Righters Mill Road, Narberth, PA 19072. (610) 664-1184. Z Street (Z for Zionist) is a pro-Israel organization that advocates for the right of the Jewish people to a state, and the right of Jews to live freely anywhere, including areas the world insists are reserved for Arab Palestinians; calls for the circulation of facts—not deceptive "Palestinian" narratives—about the Middle East, Israel, and terrorism; condemns those who revile Israel for actions they ignore when taken by Israel's enemies and virtually all states throughout history; and categorically rejects agreements with, or concessions to, terrorists (or their supporters) who are dedicated to Israel's destruction. (www.zstreet.org)

Zionist Organization of America (ZOA) (1897). 633 3rd Avenue, Suite 31-B, New York, NY 10017. (212) 481-1500. ZOA, the oldest pro-Israel organization in the US, is dedicated to educating the public, elected officials, media, and college/high school students about the truth of the ongoing Arab war against Israel, and is also committed to promoting strong US-Israel relations. It works to protect Jewish college and high school students from intimidation, harassment and discrimination, and fights antisemitism in general. It documents and exposes Palestinian Arab violations of the Road Map plan; leads the efforts on behalf of American victims of Palestinian Arab terrorism; has played a key role in Congress regarding victims of terrorism, keeping Jerusalem unified under Israeli sovereignty, fighting Hamas and Fatah, and working on the imposition of sanctions on Arab countries. ZOA's campaigns have repeatedly led to the defeat of hostile critics of Israel who were nominated for important government positions. (www.zoa.org)

12.1.14   Jewish Organizations Supporting Specific Israeli Institutions

(Organizations Supporting Specific Israeli Institutions are generally Jewish-sponsored US nonprofit tax-exempt public charities whose primary purpose is to raise funds in the US on behalf of, or to make grants to, a specific organization

located in Israel. Such organizations are generally structured to allow American donors who wish to support Israeli organizations to receive a charitable income tax deduction for their donation. A list of some of the major such organizations are listed below. There are many other such organizations that are not listed.)

American Associates, Ben-Gurion University of the Negev (1972). 1001 Avenue of the Americas, 19th Floor, New York, NY 10018. (800) 962-2248 or (212) 687-7721. (www.aabgu.org)

American Committee for Shaare Zedek Medical Center in Jerusalem (1949). 55 West 39th Street, 4th Floor, New York, NY 10018. (212) 354-8801. (www.acsz.org)

American Committee for the Weizmann Institute of Science (1944). 633 3rd Avenue, New York, NY 10017. (212) 895-7900. (www.weizmann-usa.org)

American Friends of ALYN Hospital (1934). 122 East 42nd Street, Suite 1519, New York, NY 10168. (212) 869-8085. (www.alynus.org)

American Friends of Ariel (1991). PO Box 880714, Boca Raton, FL 33488. (www.friendsofariel.org)

American Friends of Ariel University (formerly **American Friends of the Ariel University Center of Samaria**) (1994) (2002). 136 East 39th Street, New York, NY 10016. (212) 710-4325. (www.afau.org)

American Friends of Assaf Harofeh Medical Center (1983). 12367 East Cornell Avenue, Denver, CO 80014. (720) 863-8624. (www.assafharofeh.org)

American Friends of Bar-Ilan University (1955). 160 East 56th Street, New York, NY 10022. (212) 906-3900. (www.afbiu.org)

American Friends of Beit Hatfutsot (1976). 633 Third Avenue, 21st Floor, New York, NY 10017. (212) 339-6034. (www.afbh.us)

American Friends of Beit Issie Shapiro (1987). 25 West 45th Street, Suite 1405, New York, NY 10036 (212) 840-1166. (www.afobis.org)

American Friends of Dental Volunteers for Israel (1984). PO Box 127, New York, NY 10185. (201) 336-0230. (www.americanfriendsofdvi.org)

American Friends of ELI: Israel Association for Child Protection (1999). PO Box 12, Merion Station, PA 19066. (551) 486-6915. (www.eli-usa.org)

American Friends of Herzog Hospital (1941). 57 West 57th Street, Suite 412, New York, NY 10019. (212) 683-3702. (www.afherzoghospital.org)

American Friends of Israel Free Loan Association (1992). c/o Jaffe, 2330 Milton Road, University Heights, OH 44118. (www.israelfreeloan.org.il)

American Friends of Leket Israel (2006). PO Box 2090, Teaneck, NJ 07666. (201) 331-0070. (www.leket.org/en/tag/american-friends-of-leket-israel)

American Friends of Likud (1992). 1324 Lexington Avenue, Suite 125, New York, NY 10128. (212) 308-5595. (www.aflikud.org)

American Friends of Magen David Adom (formerly **American Red Mogen Dovid for Palestine** and **American Red Magen David for Israel**) (1940) (1972). 352 Seventh Avenue, Suite 400, New York, NY 10001. (866) 632-2763 or (212) 757-1627. (www.afmda.org)

American Friends of Meir Medical Center (2004). 500 Southeast Mizner Boulevard, #310, Boca Raton, FL 33432. (561) 866-9140. (www.meirmedical-center.com)

American Friends of Museums in Israel (1974). 36 West 44th Street, Suite 1209, New York, NY 10036. (212) 319-0555. (www.museumsinisrael.org)

American Friends of Neve Shalom/Wahat Al-Salam (also known as **Oasis of Peace**) (1988). 229 North Central Avenue, Suite #401, Glendale, CA 91203. (818) 662-8883. (www.oasisofpeace.org)

American Friends of Nishmat (1990). 520 Eighth Avenue, 4th Floor, New York, NY 10018. (646) 378-5895. (www.afnishmat.org)

American Friends of Rabin Medical Center (1995). 636 Broadway, Suite 618, New York, NY 10012. (212) 279-2522. (www.afrmc.org)

American Friends of Rambam (1969). 420 Lexington Avenue, Suite 1701, New York, NY 10170. (212) 292-4499. (www.aforam.org)

American Friends of Reuth (1951). 600 Columbus Avenue, Suite 9L, New York, NY 10024. (212) 751-9255. (www.americanfriendsofreuth.org)

American Friends of Sheba Medical Center at Tel Hashomer (1993). 575 Madison Avenue, 10th Floor, New York, NY 10022. (212) 605-0360. (www.shebamedical.org)

American Friends of Shenkar (formerly **American Committee for The College for Fashion and Textiles in Israel** and **American Committee for Shenkar College in Israel**) (1970). 315 West 36th Street, New York, NY 10018. (212) 947-1597. (www.facebook.com/americanfriendsofshenkar)

American Friends of Soroka Medical Center (1996). PO Box 184-H, Scarsdale, NY 10583. (914) 725-9070. (www.soroka.org)

American Friends of Tel Aviv University (1955). 39 Broadway, Suite 1510, New York, NY 10006. (212) 742-9070. (www.aftau.org)

American Friends of the Ghetto Fighters' House Museum (1980). 181 The Plaza, Teaneck, NJ 07666. (www.gfh.org.il/eng)

American Friends of The Hebrew University (1925). One Battery Park Plaza, 25th Floor, New York, NY 10004. (800) 567-2348 or (212) 607-8500. (www.afhu.org)

American Friends of the Israel Museum (1968). 545 Fifth Avenue, Suite 920, New York, NY 10017. (212) 997-5611. (www.afimnyc.org)

American Friends of the Israel National Museum of Science (formerly **Friends of MadaTech-The Israel Institute of Science & Technology**) (1985). 729 7th Avenue, 9th floor, New York, NY 10019. (212) 947-5654. (www.israelscience.org)

American Friends of the Israel Philharmonic Orchestra (1972). 122 East 42nd Street, Suite 4507, New York, NY 10168. (212) 697-2949. (www.afipo.org)

American Friends of the Open University of Israel (formerly **Open University Foundation**) (1981). 120 East 56th Street, Suite 900, New York, NY 10022. (212) 712-1800. (www.afoui.org)

American Friends of Tzohar (1989). 1417 Coney Island Avenue, Brooklyn, NY 11230. (718) 258-1212. (www.americanfriendsoftzohar.org)

American Friends of Yad Eliezer (formerly **Yad Eliezer Inc.**) (1981) (1999). c/o Tropper, 410 Glenn Road, Jackson, NJ 08527. (www.af-ye.org)

The American Society for the Protection of Nature in Israel (1986). 28 Arrandale Avenue, Great Neck, NY 11024. (800) 411-0966. (www.natureisrael. org/aspni)

American Society for Yad Vashem (1981). 500 Fifth Avenue, 42nd Floor, New York, NY 10110. (212) 220-4304. (www.yadvashemusa.org)

American Society of the University of Haifa (1967). 80 Broad Street, Suite 2102, New York, NY 10004. (212) 344-2784. (www.asuh.org)

American Technion Society (1940). 55 East 59th Street, New York, NY 10022. (212) 407-6300. (www.ats.org)

Arachim America (1994). 1521 51st Street, Brooklyn, NY 11219. (718) 633-1408. (www.arachimusa.org)

Boys Town Jerusalem Foundation of America (1984). 1 Penn Plaza, Suite 6250, New York, NY 10119. (800) 469-2697. (www.boystownjerusalem.org)

Ezer Mizion (1988). 5225 New Utrecht Avenue, 3rd Floor, Brooklyn, NY 11219. (718) 853-8400. (www.ezermizion.org)

Friends of Israel Disabled Veterans–Beit Halochem (1987). 1133 Broadway, Suite 232, New York, NY 10010. (212) 689-3220. (www.fidv.org)

Friends of Israel Scouts–Tzofim (1995). 575 Eighth Avenue, 11th Floor, New York, NY 10018. (212) 390-8130 or (877) 457-2688. (www.israelscouts.org)

Friends of the Israel Defense Forces (1981). 60 East 42nd Street, Suite 1820, New York, NY 10165. (212) 244-3118 or (888) 318-3433. (www.fidf.org)

Friends of United Hatzalah (2000). 208 East 51st Street, Suite 303, New York, NY 10022. (646) 833-7108. (www.israelrescue.org)

Friends of Yad Sarah (1976). 445 Park Avenue, Suite 1702, New York, NY 10022. (212) 223-7758 or (866) 923-7272. (www.friendsofyadsarah.org)

The Gesher Foundation USA (1970). 511 6th Avenue, Suite 444, New York, NY 10011. (646) 934-6149. (www.gesherusa.org)

Givat Haviva Educational Foundation (1965). 601 West 26th Street, Suite 325-25, New York, NY 10001. (212) 989-9272. (www.givathaviva.org)

Israel Air Force Center Foundation (1992). 136 El Camino Drive, Suite 201, Beverly Hills, CA 90212. (310) 274-2314. (www.iafc-foundation.org)

Israel Lacrosse Association (2011). 1501 Broadway, 21st Floor, New York, NY 10036. (800) 894-5820. (www.lacrosse.co.il)

Israel Tennis & Education Centers Foundation (formerly **Israel Tennis Centers Foundation**) (1978). 57 West 38th Street, Suite 605, New York, NY 10018. (212) 784-9200. (www.itecenters.org)

The Jerusalem Foundation (1966). 420 Lexington Avenue, Suite 1645, New York, NY 10170. (212) 697-4188. (www.jerusalemfoundation.org/about-us/ leadership-worldwide/usa.aspx)

Jewish Institute for the Blind (1983). 369 Lexington Avenue, 3rd floor, New York, NY 10017. (212) 532-4155. (www.jewishblind.org)

Medical Development for Israel/Schneider Children's Medical Center of Israel (1982). 1345 Avenue of the Americas, 2nd Floor, New York, NY 10105. (212) 759-3370. (www.mdinyc.org)

P'eylim Lev L'Achim (formerly **Bnai Torah of Eretz Yisroel**) (1953) (1994). 1034 East 12th Street, Brooklyn, NY 11230. (718) 258-7760. (www.duvys.com/simple/levlachim)

Tel Aviv Museum of Art American Friends (formerly **American Friends of Tel Aviv Museum of Art**) (1974) (2014). Spring Place, 6 Saint John's Lane, New York, NY 10013. (310) 806-1551. (www.tamaf.org)

US Friends of the Menachem Begin Heritage Foundation (1993). 4525 Saguaro Trail, Indianapolis, IN 46268. (www.begincenter.org.il)

12.1.15 Other Jewish Israel-Related Organizations

Allergists for Israel (AFI) (1984). AFI seeks to develop camaraderie by the gathering—nationally and internationally—of allergists/immunologists and other supporters of allergy in Israel at National Academy and College allergy meetings; provide financial support for Israeli allergy fellows for scholarly activities; establish a network of North American and Israeli allergists/immunologists that can communicate internationally and meet in the US and Israel every few years; and develop linkages between American and Israeli allergists/immunologists by sponsoring American allergists/immunologists to visit and speak in Israel. AFI provides support for academic research grants and programs in Israel and opportunities for Israeli allergists/immunologists to come to the US and Canada to participate in mini-fellowships and lectureships. (www.allergists4israel.org)

Aluf Stone (2008). New York, NY. Aluf Stone is the veterans' association of volunteers from outside Israel who served in any branch of the Israel Defense Forces ("lone soldiers") in any of Israel's wars since the War of Independence in 1948. Dedicated to Zionist ideals and the covenant of Jewish mutual responsibility, its mission is to sustain fellowship among members and to preserve the proud record of contribution and sacrifice. (www.mronen.wixsite.com/alufstone)

American Healthcare Professionals and Friends for Medicine in Israel (APF) (formerly **American Physicians and Friends for Medicine in Israel**) (1950). 2001 Beacon Street, Suite 210, Boston, MA 02135. (617) 232-5382. APF is dedicated to advancing the state of medical education, medical research, and health care in Israel by assisting in the training of young Israeli physicians and healthcare professionals and in fostering ties between the North American healthcare community and Israel's healthcare community. (www.apfmed.org)

American Israel Numismatic Association (AINA) (1970). PO Box 20255, Fountain Hills, AZ 85269. AINA is a nonsectarian cultural and educational organization dedicated to the study and collection of Israel's coinage, past and present, and all aspects of Judaic numismatics. Its primary purpose is the development of publications, programs, meetings and other activities which will bring news, history, social and related background to the study and collection of Judaic numismatics and the advancement of the hobby. AINA has sponsored major cultural/social/numismatic events such as national and regional conventions, study tours to Israel, publication of books and other activities of benefit to its members. (www.theshekel.org)

American Veterans of Israel (1949). 11 East 44th Street, New York, NY 10017. (212) 490-0900. The American Veterans of Israel is the organization of Aliyah Bet (in Hebrew, "Immigration B," the term used for clandestine immigration of Holocaust survivors) and Machal (in Hebrew, an acronym for "mitnadvei chutz l'Aretz," volunteers from outside the Land) veterans in the US and Canada who served in the Israeli armed forces during Israel's War of Independence. (www.israel-vets.com)

Association of America-Israel Chambers of Commerce. The Association of America-Israel Chambers of Commerce is a private, nongovernmental business network set up to boost the Israeli and US economies by helping their companies develop business relationships with each other and explore new market opportunities. With regional offices throughout the US, it represents thousands of companies and individuals who share an interest in America-Israel business and promotes America-Israel trade. (www.israeltrade.org)

CHAI: Concern for Helping Animals in Israel (1984). PO Box 3341, Alexandria, VA 22302. (703) 658-9650. CHAI's mission is to prevent and relieve animal suffering in Israel and to elevate consciousness about animals through education. CHAI strives to foster empathy, respect and responsibility toward all living beings, and to inspire and empower people—Jewish, Muslim, and Christian—to recognize the interconnectedness of all life and to make compassionate choices for the good of all. (www.chai-online.org)

Inter-Agency Task Force on Israeli Arab Issues (2006). New York, NY. The Inter-Agency Task Force on Israeli Arab Issues is a coalition of North American Jewish organizations, foundations, private philanthropists, and international affiliates that are committed to the welfare of Israel and support the Jewish state's right to a secure and peaceful existence. (www.iataskforce.org)

The Israel Bridge (TIB) (2006). 209 Coconut Key Drive, Palm Beach Gardens, FL 33418. TIB was created to enable Israeli student-athletes to obtain scholarships at American universities. (www.israelbridge.org)

The Israel Forever Foundation (IFF) (2002). 1146 19th Street, NW, 5th Floor, Washington, DC 20036. (202) 463-8022. The IFF is a nonpolitical, innovative programming philanthropy that develops, supports, and promotes virtual experiential learning opportunities to celebrate and strengthen the personal connection to Israel for people around the world. Its programming includes organizing and sponsoring interactive workshops, educational seminars, and online forums which uphold the ideals of the IFF. Projects of The IFF include Virtual Citizens of Israel Global Community, Iranian Jewish Relief Project, The Balfour Initiative, Plant Israel at Home, The Lone Soldier Project, Individually Israel, and Israel Memory Project. (www.israelforever.org)

Israel Sports Exchange (ISE) (1995). 100 Lanidex Plaza, Parsippany, NJ 07054. (973) 694-2596. ISE offers a high level sports training program for teenage varsity level American swimmers and tennis players in Israel. The program combines intensive training, competition, touring, and home hospitality. Each American participant and their family are asked to commit to hosting Israeli athletes who come to the US to train or compete. The program enables Jewish youth athletes to participate at an affordable cost by subsidizing a substantial portion of the costs involved. (www.israeli-sports-exchange.com)

Israel Venture Network (IVN) (2001). 540 Cowper Street, Suite 200, Palo Alto, CA 94301. (650) 325-4200. IVN is a venture philanthropy network of high-tech entrepreneurs, business executives, venture capitalists, corporations and philanthropists from Israel and the US that combines business acumen and financing with high-impact social programs to work toward the betterment of Israel's social landscape. IVN advances social change in three strategic realms: economic development, environment, and education of underserved populations and regions. (www. ivnus.org)

Maccabi USA/Sports for Israel (formerly **US Committee Sports for Israel**) (1948). 1511 Walnut Street, Suite 401, Philadelphia, PA 19102. (215) 561-6900. Maccabi USA is a volunteer organization that endeavors to perpetuate and preserve the American Jewish community through sports by encouraging Jewish pride, strengthening Jewish bonds, and creating a heightened awareness of Israel and Jewish identity. It seeks to enrich the lives of Jewish youth in the US, Israel, and the Diaspora through athletic, cultural, and educational programs. Maccabi USA sponsors the US team to the World Maccabiah Games in Israel and other Maccabi competitions around the world, and supports programs that embody the Maccabi ideals of Jewish continuity, Zionism, and excellence in sport, such as the JCC Maccabi Games and athletic facilities and programs in Israel. (www.maccabiusa.com)

Nefesh B'Nefesh (2002). 50 Eisenhower Drive, Paramus, NJ 07652. (866) 425-4924. Nefesh B'Nefesh provides persons making aliyah (olim) with employment resources, assistance with governmental absorption, community-based guidance and support, and need-based financial aid in order to make each individual's aliyah as successful as possible. Nefesh B'Nefesh provides guidance through all stages of the aliyah process and provides olim with post aliyah guidance and resources to help each individual integrate smoothly and successfully into Israeli society. (www.nbn.org.il)

Nesiya (1987). c/o Broadway Suites, 149 Madison Avenue, Suite 1178, New York, NY 10016. (516) 203-4611. Nesiya's mission is to inspire North American and Israeli young people from diverse backgrounds to enrich Jewish life for themselves and others through a unique model of experiential learning that combines community building, creative study, the arts, outdoor adventure, and community service. (http://nesiya.org)

The Schechter Institutes (1995). Box #3566, PO Box 8500, Philadelphia, PA, 19178. (866) 830-3321. The mission of The Schechter Institutes is to help fashion an Israeli society and a Jewish world secure in its Jewish roots and strong in its democratic values. (www.schechter.edu)

Seeds of Peace (1993). 370 Lexington Avenue, Suite 1201, New York, NY 10017. (212) 573-8040. Seeds of Peace organizes and implements dialogue and leadership development programs for youth and educators in communities in conflict across the globe. Seeds of Peace has become one of the leading coexistence programs striving to bring Israelis and Palestinians together. As its main program, the organization brings youth and educators from areas of conflict to its camp in Maine. (www.seedsofpeace.org)

Skilled Volunteers for Israel (2012). 1755 York Avenue, #19C, New York, NY 10128. (608) 469-0458. Skilled Volunteers for Israel promotes service and volunteerism among Jewish adults by linking the professional expertise of North American Jews with the critical needs of the Israeli nonprofit sector through limited term volunteer engagements. Volunteers support their own travel and living expenses in Israel and contribute their time and expertise to make a positive impact on Israeli society, serving in such capacities as English tutors, accountants, grant writers, and medical triage. (www.skillvolunteerisrael.org)

Society of Israel Philatelists (1948). The Society of Israel Philatelists promotes interest in, and knowledge of, all phases of Israel philately through sponsorship of chapters and research and study groups, maintenance of a philatelic library, support of public and private exhibitions, a speaker's bureau, new issue service, handbooks/monographs, awards, and an annual convention. (www.israelstamps.com)

TAMID Group (formerly **TAMID Israel Investment Group**) (2008). 1100 Wayne Avenue, Suite 850, Silver Spring, MD 20910. (240) 641-6373. TAMID Group's mission is to train the next generation of top business leaders—and instill in them a strong and lasting connection to Israel. A student-led initiative that pioneers the next generation of American commitment to Israel by connecting students at top universities with the Israeli economy, TAMID Group develops the professional skills of undergraduate students through a comprehensive curriculum geared toward the sustained continuous engagement of business-minded students from all disciplines consisting of an educational program, a student-managed investment fund, a consulting practice, and a summer fellowship in Tel Aviv that sends interns to Israeli startups. TAMID Group has no political or religious affiliations. (www.tamidgroup.org)

US-Israel Science & Technology Foundation (USISTF) (1995). 1300 Pennsylvania Avenue, NW, Suite 700, Washington, DC 20004. (202) 204-3102. The objectives of USISTF, founded by a joint initiative of the US Department of Commerce and the Israel Ministry of Economy to administer all the programs of the US-Israel Science and Technology Commission, are to facilitate joint research and development, cooperation, and scientific exchange between the US and Israel that could lead to cooperative commercial activities, enable the development of emerging technology sectors, and assist in the adaptation of military technology for commercial use. Its mission is to promote the advancement of science and technology and to lessen the burdens of their governments in providing economic assistance to their economies. (www.usistf.org)

Volunteers for Israel-USA/Sar-El (1982). 330 West 42nd Street, Suite 1618, New York, NY 10036. (212) 643-4848 or (866) 514-1948. Volunteers for Israel-

USA connects Americans to Israel through volunteer service and promotes solidarity and goodwill among Israelis, American Jews, and other friends of Israel, while providing aid to Israel through volunteer work. It is the American counterpart to Sar-El in Israel. More than 30,000 American adults have performed civilian work on Israeli Defense Forces bases. Volunteers for Israel-USA partners with military and civilian organizations, and newer additions include a summer International Youth Program, an add-on to Birthright tours, and other volunteer options. (www.vfi-usa.org)

12.1.16   Jewish Holocaust Organizations

American Gathering of Jewish Holocaust Survivors and Their Descendants (formerly **American Gathering of Jewish Holocaust Survivors**) (1982). 122 West 30th Street, Suite 304A, New York, NY 10001. (212) 239-4230. The American Gathering of Jewish Holocaust Survivors and Their Descendants is the umbrella organization of survivor groups and landsmanshaften of North America. The American Gathering maintains a registry (also maintained by the United States Holocaust Memorial Museum in Washington, DC) of Jewish Holocaust survivors who came to North America after World War II and continues to acquire names of survivors, facilitates contacts, collects and displays basic information, and assists survivors in seeking lost relatives via its quarterly newspaper. The Holocaust and Jewish Resistance Teachers' Program of the American Gathering brings teachers—Jewish and non-Jewish—to Poland and Washington, DC to partake in Holocaust-related educational experiences with the goal of advancing education in US secondary schools about the Holocaust and Jewish resistance. (www.amgathering.org)

   Anne Frank Center for Mutual Respect (formerly **Anne Frank Center USA**, **Anne Frank Center, The American Friends of Anne Frank Foundation**, and **Anne Frank Foundation in New York City** (1959) (1977). 1325 Avenue of the Americas, 28th Floor, New York, NY 10019: (212) 431-7993. The Anne Frank Center for Mutual Respect, the US national organization in the worldwide network of Anne Frank organizations, addresses civil and human rights across America. Through educational programs and grassroots organizing, the Center calls out prejudice, counters discrimination, and advocates for the kinder and fairer world of which Anne Frank dreamed. As a Jewish voice for social justice, the Center is dedicated to Tikkun Olam, repairing the world, which means advocating on behalf of all communities, Jewish and non-Jewish alike, fighting hatred of refugees and immigrants, antisemitism, sexism, racism, Islamophobia, homophobia, transphobia, bias against the differently abled, and any other hate that runs counter to the American promise of freedom. In addressing the civil and human rights issues of today, the Center applies historic lessons from Anne Frank's life and the Holocaust to its contemporary advocacy techniques, thus making the Holocaust relevant to successive generations of Americans. (www.annefrank.com)

Association of Holocaust Organizations (AHO) (1985). PO Box 230317, Hollis, NY 11423. (516) 582-4571. AHO serves as an international network of organizations and individuals for the advancement of Holocaust education, remembrance and research. Among its functions and services are annual conferences held every June, a seminar at the United States Holocaust Memorial Museum held every January, co-sponsorship of other conferences and seminars, a listserv for members, a website, and the publication of an annual directory. There are also regional branches which meet independently. (www.ahoinfo.org)

Bet Tzedek Holocaust Survivors Justice Network (HSJN) (2008). 3250 Wilshire Boulevard, 13th Floor, Los Angeles, CA 90010. (323) 939-0506. HSJN partners pro bono attorneys with Jewish social service providers to provide free legal assistance to Holocaust survivors seeking reparations from Germany. It operates in a number of cities in the US and Canada. (www.bettzedek.org/2011/11/holocaust-survivors-justice-network), (www.holocaustsurvivorsprobono.org)

The Blue Card (1939). 171 Madison Avenue, Suite 1405, New York, NY 10016. (212) 239-2251. Originally established by the Jewish community in Germany in the early 1930s to help Jews affected by Nazi persecution through loss of jobs and other forms of oppression, The Blue Card was reestablished in the US in 1939 to aid refugees of Nazi persecution resettling in America. After the Holocaust, the mission of the organization was expanded to help survivors of the Shoah from all European countries. The Blue Card helps Holocaust survivors who live at or near the Federal poverty level with such services as dental care, medicine, rent, food, financial support for the Jewish holidays, financial aid, etc. (www.bluecardfund.org)

Center for Medicine after the Holocaust (CMATH) (2010). 3122 Robinhood Street, Houston, TX 77005. (713) 661-6999. The mission of CMATH is to challenge doctors, nurses, and bioscientists to personally confront the medical ethics of the Holocaust and apply that knowledge to contemporary practice and research, being mindful of the Hippocratic Oath with every step. CMATH is concerned that healthcare personnel, like all human beings, have the capacity to believe they are doing good when they are actually doing harm. By studying the past, CMATH hopes to provide knowledge for today that will prevent the repetition of previous errors. (www.medicineaftertheholocaust.org)

Chambon Foundation (formerly **Friends of Le Chambon**) (1982). 8033 Sunset Boulevard, Los Angeles, CA 90046. (323) 650-1774. The Chambon Foundation, a charity named in honor of the Huguenot mountain village of Le Chambon-sur-Lignon, France, where some 5000 Jews—many of them children— were sheltered from the Nazis by some 5000 Christians, seeks to explore and communicate the necessary and challenging lessons of hope intertwined with the Holocaust's unavoidable lessons of despair. Two specialized divisions of the Chambon Foundation are the Chambon Institute and the Varian Fry Institute. (www.chambon.org)

Children of Jewish Holocaust Survivors (CJHS) (2006). 1042 Willow Creek Road, Suite A101-179, Prescott, AZ 86301. CJHS is dedicated to educating the public in the US and abroad about the intellectual and cultural climate that led to the

Holocaust and the ideas and philosophy that bring about a totalitarian dictatorship. (www.cjhsla.org)

Conference on Jewish Material Claims Against Germany (also known as **Claims Conference**) (1951). 1359 Broadway, Room 2000, New York, NY 10018. (646) 536-9100. The Claims Conference seeks a measure of justice for Jewish victims of Nazi persecution by representing Jewish survivors in negotiations for payments directly to individual survivors and grants to social welfare organizations serving survivors from the German government and other entities once controlled by the Nazis. The Claims Conference also administers compensation programs for Nazi victims; negotiates for the return of and restitution for Jewish-owned property; funds social services that assist elderly, needy Nazi victims; and allocates funds to support Holocaust education, documentation, and research. The Successor Organization of the Claims Conference recovers unclaimed Jewish property in the former East Germany and uses the proceeds primarily to provide vital social services to Holocaust victims around the world. (www.claimscon.org)

The David S. Wyman Institute for Holocaust Studies (2003). 1200 G Street, NW, Suite 800, Washington, DC 20005. (202) 434-8994. The David S. Wyman Institute for Holocaust Studies teaches the history and lessons of America's response to the Holocaust through scholarly research, public events, publications, and educational programs. The Wyman Institute focuses on the abandonment of Europe's Jews during the Nazi era, the efforts to promote rescue, and the moral and historical lessons of those experiences. Bringing together a politically, religiously, and culturally diverse group of concerned individuals and scholars, the Wyman Institute strives to bridge the gap between the scholarly community and the general public, by making the historical record accessible to a broader audience through exhibits, speakers, educational curricula, and other forms of media. (http://new.wymaninstitute.org)

Facing History and Ourselves (1976). 16 Hurd Road, Brookline, MA 02445. (617) 232-1595 or (800) 856-9039. Facing History and Ourselves combats racism, antisemitism, and prejudice and nurtures democracy through education programs worldwide. It engages nearly two million students annually through its network of more than 29,000 educators and reaches the public and the broader educational market through community events and extensive online resources. Through a rigorous investigation of the events that led to the Holocaust, as well as other recent examples of genocide and mass violence, students learn to combat prejudice with compassion, indifference with participation, and myth and misinformation with knowledge. (www.facinghistory.org)

The Flame Society (2011). 3700 Northwest 107th Terrace, South Unit, Coral Springs, FL 33065. (954) 653-8473. The Flame Society's mission is to teach the lessons learned from the Holocaust by creating television programs and classroom educational materials and to provide funding for relevant Holocaust-related projects to ensure that mankind will never forget. (www.theflamesociety.org)

Generations of the Shoah International (GSI) (2002). Formed by leaders of seven established Second and Third Generation groups around the US, GSI is a worldwide network of children and grandchildren of Holocaust survivors. GSI is open to all descendants of survivors—second, third, and future generations—as well as any survivor or child survivor, and also includes many Holocaust institutions in its network. In those geographical areas where no established Holocaust-related group exists, GSI provides members with a critical link to their second and third generation brothers and sisters around the world. (www.genshoah.org)

Holocaust Survivors' Foundation-USA (HSF) (2001). c/o Greater Miami Jewish Federation, 4200 Biscayne Boulevard, Miami, FL 33137. (305) 576-4000. HSF is a national alliance established by the elected leaders of local Holocaust survivor associations across the country whose mission is to give meaningful voice and a more active role to survivors in the negotiations and decisions affecting them directly, including restitution, compensation, settlement of claims and humanitarian funds and other benefits for victims of the Holocaust or their rightful heirs. HSF is dedicated to advocating for survivors and raising the level of awareness within the Jewish community about the hardships and poverty that an alarming percentage of aging and infirm survivors face and ensuring that the allocation of Holocaust-related settlement funds addresses the urgent need for quality home care and other critical social services for every survivor living in America. (www.hsf-usa.org)

International Association of Lesbian and Gay Children of Holocaust Survivors (1991). c/o CBST, 261 Broadway – 8C, New York, NY 10007 (212) 233-7867. The International Association of Lesbian and Gay Children of Holocaust Survivors was formed to honor and remember those homosexuals persecuted or killed by the Nazis and to support gay and lesbian children of Holocaust survivors and their families. It allows its members to share their experiences of being lesbian and gay children of Holocaust survivors and serves as a forum to disseminate the information. (www.infotrue.com/gay.html)

The Jan Karski Institute for Tolerance and Dialogue (2004). 2025 O Street, NW, Washington, DC 20036. (571) 451-3219. The mission of the Jan Karski Institute for Tolerance and Dialogue is to keep the legacy of Jan Karski alive by advancing tolerance, dialogue, and understanding through a variety of programs, activities, and awards leading to reconciliation and peace by means of diplomacy. Programs to accomplish these goals include tolerance education for young people, an annual lecture series on acts of conscience, films and videos promoting tolerance and dialogue, and an annual award program. (www.jankarskiinstituteus.org)

The Jewish Foundation for the Righteous (JFR) (formerly **Foundation to Sustain Righteous Christians** and **Jewish Foundation for Christian Rescuers**) (1986). 80 Main Street, Suite 380, West Orange, NJ 07052. (212) 727-9955. The JFR provides financial support to aged and needy non-Jews (Righteous Gentiles), living in about 20 countries, who risked their lives to save Jews during the Holocaust and preserves the memory and legacy of the rescuers through its national Holocaust education program. The goal of the JFR's education program is to educate middle and high school teachers about the history of the Holocaust and to provide them with the resources to integrate this knowledge into their classrooms. (www.jfr.org)

Jewish Partisan Educational Foundation (JPEF) (2000). 2245 Post Street, Suite 204, San Francisco, CA 94115. (415) 563-2244. JPEF's mission is to develop and distribute effective educational materials about the Jewish partisans and their life lessons, bringing the celebration of heroic resistance against tyranny into educational and cultural organizations. JPEF has produced a comprehensive and thought-provoking new curriculum called RESIST, designed to transmit the enduring understandings arising from the stories of the Jewish partisans. RESIST is designed for students in grades 6-12 in formal and informal settings and is being implemented in Jewish and secular schools worldwide. (www.jewishpartisans.org)

The Kindertransport Association (1993). PO Box 1444, New York, NY 10113. The Kindertransport Association unites the child Holocaust refugees who were saved by the Kindertransport rescue movement and their descendants in North America. It shares their stories, honors those who made the Kindertransport possible, and supports charitable work that aids children in need. (www.kindertransport.org)

Memorial Library and Holocaust Educators Network (also known as **Olga Lengyel Institute for Holocaust Studies and Human Rights**) (1962). 58 East 79th Street, #2F, New York, NY 10075. (212) 249-5384. The Memorial Library's mission is to support Holocaust education and to help teachers from across the US promote an agenda for social justice in their classrooms and communities. In addition to its twelve-day Summer Seminar and its shorter Satellite Seminars, the Library offers mini-grants to participating teachers for innovative projects. Founded originally as a repository for World War II memorabilia, the Memorial Library later turned its attention toward teacher education and, with its support, the Holocaust Educators Network was created, which is a nationwide program designed to bring the lessons of the Holocaust into today's world. To enrich its programs and to support other important work in Holocaust education, the Memorial Library has built relationships with colleges and universities as well as Holocaust organizations and museums. (www.toli.us)

The Memory Project Productions (2008). PO Box 20171, New York, NY 10014. (212) 691-1449. The mission of The Memory Project Productions is to explore ways that engaging in art and exploring personal stories can help people remember and honor their own family stories and understand their place in history, appreciate the value of memory and the creative process, and honor the lives of Holocaust victims, survivors, and rescuers. It is an internationally-recognized project addressing universal themes of loss, love, and resilience that includes traveling museum exhibits, educational programs, and documentary films. (www.memoryprojectproductions.com)

National Association of Jewish Child Holocaust Survivors (NAHOS) (1985). PO Box 670125, Station C, Main Street, Flushing, NY 11367. (718) 998-4266 or (718) 380-5576. NAHOS is a social organization of survivors, second generation individuals, and supporters, whose services include reference, social support and guidance, information, support of indigents, education, perpetuation of memories of the martyrs, and campaigning for adequate and undiluted restitution. (www.shoahsurvivors.wordpress.com)

One by One (1995). PO Box 1709, Brookline, MA 02446. One by One offers dialogue groups, usually held in Germany, which are comprised of Holocaust survivors/victims and their descendants and perpetrators, bystanders, resisters, and their descendants, led by professionally trained facilitators from both sides of the war experience. The One by One dialogue group experience provides an opportunity to meet and learn from descendants from the "other side" and provides a context for using the burdensome legacy of the Holocaust in a constructive manner. One by One also offers the services of its Speakers Bureau to universities and civic and religious organizations, whereby members discuss and model the dialogue process. (www. one-by-one.org)

Remember the Women Institute (1997). 11 Riverside Drive, Suite 3RE, New York, NY 10023. (212) 799-0887. The Remember the Women Institute conducts and encourages research and cultural activities that contribute to including women in history with special emphasis on women in the context of the Holocaust and its aftermath, including post-World War II immigration. Other topics include women marginalized within Jewish religion and inter-religious dialogue, as well as the accomplishments and exclusion of women in Jewish and general history, the effects of genocide on women, exploitation of women, and the effects of culture on memorialization. The projects of the Institute include carrying out research on women and the Holocaust, co-publishing books, creating exhibits, organizing panels at conferences, and cooperating with other institutes and organizations for programs, films, and exhibits. (www.rememberwomen.org)

Simon Wiesenthal Center (1977). 1399 South Roxbury Drive, Los Angeles, CA 90035. (310) 553-9036 or (800) 900-9036. The Simon Wiesenthal Center is a global Jewish human rights organization that confronts antisemitism, hate and terrorism, promotes human rights and dignity, stands with Israel, defends the safety of Jews worldwide, and teaches the lessons of the Holocaust for future generations. (www.wiesenthal.com)

The Survivor Mitzvah Project (2008). 2658 Griffith Park Boulevard, Suite #299, Los Angeles, CA 90039. (213) 622-5050 or (800) 905-6160. The Survivor Mitzvah Project is dedicated to providing direct and continuous financial aid to elderly and forgotten Jewish Holocaust survivors scattered throughout Eastern Europe who are sick, impoverished, isolated and receive no direct financial aid from any other agency, helping to ensure that they may live out their last years with some measure of comfort, support and dignity. (www.survivormitzvah.org)

Voices of the Generations (VOG) (1990). VOG is dedicated to preserving the memory and personal stories of Holocaust survivors. Its mission is to provide an easy to grasp, yet powerful and meaningful introduction to the Holocaust. VOG offers its programs to public schools, community centers, and places of worship throughout the US at no cost. (www.vogcharity.org)

World Federation of Jewish Child Survivors of the Holocaust and Descendants (WFJCSHD) (1997). 67 South Bedford Street, Suite 400W, Burlington, MA 01803. With chapters throughout the US and around the world, the WFJCSHD is comprised of Jewish child survivors of the Holocaust who were persecuted during the Nazi era in ghettos, in camps, in hiding, on the run, or forced to leave Nazi occupied Europe. Its objectives are to represent the interests of the child survivor community and to support one another, to keep alive the memory of the six million Jews–including the 1. 5 million children–murdered during the Holocaust, and to pass on their legacy to future generations. The WFJCSHD pursues these objectives by telling stories of their survival, by community interaction, education, and by holding conferences and fighting antisemitism. (www.holocaustchild.org)

The YIZKOR Project (2010). 198 South Holly Street, Denver, CO 80246. (720) 560-0271. The YIZKOR project was established to remember the six million Jews who perished in the Holocaust as individuals and to honor their memory by helping to support the needs of aging Holocaust survivors and the Righteous Gentiles. The YIZKOR project is dedicated to addressing this critical, time sensitive mission through Yizkor-linked charitable acts and contributions, as well as associated education/remembrance activities for schools, families and communities to honor the memory of those who perished. (www.theyizkorproject.org)

Zachor Holocaust Remembrance Foundation (2009). 2251 North Rampart Boulevard, #2520, Las Vegas, NV 89128. (800) 575-9583. The Zachor Holocaust Remembrance Foundation works to insure that the memory and lessons of the Holocaust are never forgotten. The Foundation provides Zachor Pins free of charge to all speakers and providers of Holocaust education programs to be distributed to their students and listeners. (www.zachorfoundation.org)

Zechor Yemos Olam (ZYO). (212) 227-1000, ext. 4557. ZYO's mission is to foster the study of the Holocaust from a religious perspective in yeshivas and Jewish day schools and to raise community awareness about the need and methodology to teach the Holocaust. ZYO conducts teacher training seminars that guide yeshiva and day school faculty in integrating Holocaust studies into their classroom teaching and creates educational resources for Holocaust education within yeshivas and day schools. ZYO has developed an annual fellowship program to offer intensive comprehensive training to a select group of qualified educators. (www.torahumesorah. org/services-teacher)

12.1.17   Jewish Community Relations Organizations

2 For Seder (2019). (412) 697-3510. 2 for Seder, which was started in honor of one of the victims of the 2018 Tree of Life Synagogue shooting in Pittsburgh, promotes the idea that every American and Canadian Jew can and should be involved in pushing back against antisemitism to protect the next generation and their neighbors from hate. (www.2forseder.org)

AJC (formerly **American Jewish Committee**) (1906). 165 East 56th Street, New York, NY 10022. (212) 751-4000. The AJC's mission is to enhance the well-being of the Jewish people and Israel, and to advance human rights and democratic values in the US and around the world. The AJC protects the rights and freedoms of Jews the world over; combats bigotry and antisemitism and promotes democracy and human rights for all. It includes the Belfer Center for American Pluralism, Jacob Blaustein Institute for the Advancement of Human Rights, Heilbrunn Institute for International Interreligious Affairs, Koppelman Institute for American Jewish-

Israeli Relations, Project Interchange, Ramer Institute for German-Jewish Relations, William Petschek Contemporary Jewish Life Department. (www.ajc.org)

American Council for Judaism (ACJ) (1942). PO Box 888484, Atlanta, GA 30356. (904) 280-3131. The ACJ offers a distinctive alternative vision of identity and commitment for the American Jewish community, interpreting Judaism as a universal religious faith rather than an ethnic or nationalist identity. The ACJ affirms that it is Judaism's religious and ethical ideals that are at the core of Jewish identity and commitment. While Israel has significance for the Jewish experience, the ACJ considers that relationship to be a spiritual, emotional, historical, and humanitarian one, not, however, political. The ACJ embraces the prophetic ideals of Classical American Reform Judaism with its progressive religious values, rich intellectual foundations, and distinctive worship traditions. (www.acjna.org)

American Council for World Jewry (2005). 260 Madison Avenue, 2nd Floor, New York, NY 10016. The American Council for World Jewry is an alliance of Jewish groups and individuals from around the world who share a devotion to Jewish life and the defense of Jewish interests, joining together as partners to ensure their common and collective survival. Its central mission is to articulate the concerns of Jewish communities internationally by building bridges to the US Congress and Executive Branch, and to important political figures in other countries. The Council seeks to devise programs of education and public advocacy, to resist the rampant antisemitism that disfigures so many societies, to support Israel, and to promote the goals of humanitarian and civil rights for all. (www.worldjewry.org)

American Jewish Congress (AJCongress) (1918). 745 Fifth Avenue, 30th Floor, New York, NY 10151. (212) 879-4500. Since its inception, the AJCongress has been on the front lines advocating for the civil rights and civil liberties of minorities, in the belief that Jews are more secure in a society that actively protects the rights of all its citizens. It has been engaged in a continuous fight for equal rights for all Americans regardless of race, religion or national ancestry. The AJCongress was instrumental in establishing the World Jewish Congress; acted as a liaison between the US government and the World Jewish Congress on issues relating to rescue attempts made on behalf of European Jews during World War II; was instrumental in relief efforts for Jewish Holocaust survivors; and coordinated a vigorous effort to help create a Jewish state. It was an outspoken voice in the Civil Rights movement; in the struggle against apartheid in South Africa; to end persecution of Soviet Jews; to free the Jews of Syria, Ethiopia, and Iran; to protest the atrocities in the Balkans and the use of civilians as human shields by Hamas; and to call for a stop to acts of genocide in Darfur and South Sudan. Today, the AJCongress works with members of the UN, the Israeli government, the US Congress, and the President to advance Jewish and Israeli rights, and also strives to engage with local up-and-coming politicians from around the world to expand support for Jewish rights on the grassroots level. (www.ajcongress.org)

Americans Against Antisemitism (AAA). AAA was established to bring together a broad cross-section of Americans who are prepared to combat growing antisemitism when and where it's needed most. Through engaging educational content and social media communications, AAA is building its partnership network and volunteer base so that it can continue to mobilize activists on the ground to hotspots of antisemitism throughout the country. AAA is working with a host of major organizations and government officials and agencies as well as grassroots activists toward its crucial goals. (www.americansaa.org)

Americans for Peace and Tolerance (APT) (2008). 15 Main Street, Suite 118, Watertown, MA 02472. (617) 835-3584. APT is dedicated to promoting peaceful coexistence in an ethnically diverse America by educating the American public about radical ideologies that undermine the academic integrity at American high schools and universities. It is composed of concerned citizens, academics, and community activists who believe peaceful coexistence among diverse ethnic populations is only possible by promoting a climate of tolerance and civil society in the American educational system and community. (www.peaceandtolerance.org)

Anti-Defamation League (ADL) (1913). 605 Third Avenue, New York, NY 10158. (212) 885-7700 or (212) 692-3900. The ADL was founded to stop the defamation of the Jewish people and to secure justice and fair treatment to all. Now the nation's premier civil rights/human relations agency, the ADL fights antisemitism and all forms of bigotry in the US and abroad through information, education, legislation and advocacy. It scrutinizes and exposes extremists and hate groups; monitors hate on the internet; provides expertise on domestic and international terrorism; develops and delivers educational programs; fosters interfaith/intergroup relations; safeguards religious liberty throughout society; mobilizes communities to stand up against bigotry; and defends the security of Israel and Jews worldwide. (www.adl.org)

Be'chol Lashon (In Every Tongue) (2000). PO Box 591107, San Francisco, CA 94159. (415) 386-2604. Be'chol Lashon grows and strengthens the Jewish people through ethnic, cultural and racial inclusiveness. It advocates for the diversity that has characterized the Jewish people throughout history, and through contemporary forces including intermarriage, conversion and adoption. Be'chol Lashon strives to strengthen diverse Jewish communities around the world; educate Jews and the general public about Jewish diversity; and increase the Jewish population by encouraging those who would like to be part of the Jewish people. (www.globaljews.org)

Center for Interreligious Understanding (CIU) (1992). 492-C Cedar Lane, PMB 127, Teaneck, NJ 07666. (201) 804-4776. The CIU operates on the premise that religions have great power and through theological dialogue such power can be harnessed for good. CIU works with and influences religious leaders of all beliefs by exploring their common goals as well as their religions' theological foundations. (www.ciunow.org)

Community Security Service (CSS) (2007). 132 East 43rd Street, #552, New York, NY 10017. (917) 720-5583. CSS proactively protects the people, institutions, and events of the American Jewish community. Partnering with Jewish organizations, governmental authorities, and the police, and with a trained membership of thousands of volunteers, CSS safeguards the Jewish community by training volunteers in professional security techniques, providing physical security, and raising public awareness about safety issues. (www.thecss.org)

The Compassionate Listening Project (TCLP) (formerly **Mid-East Citizen Diplomacy**) (1990) (1997). PO Box 17, Indianola, WA 98342. TCLP is dedicated to empowering individuals and communities to transform conflict and strengthen cultures of peace. It teaches powerful skills for peacemaking within families, communities, on the job, and in social change work, locally and globally, offering a powerful conflict resolution model and concrete skill building. The curriculum for TCLP grew out of many years of reconciliation work on the ground in Israel and Palestine. TCLP has built trusting relationships across political, religious and social divides throughout Israel and Palestine and brings Israelis and Palestinians together for Compassionate Listening trainings and events. TCLP's Jewish-German Compassionate Listening Project brings together Jews, Germans and others affected by World War II to explore beliefs and provide an opportunity to advance healing and reconciliation. (www.compassionatelistening.org)

Conference of Jewish Affairs (CJA) (formerly **National Conference on Jewish Affairs**) (2011). (212) 252-6861. CJA represents the views of countless Jewish individuals and patriots across the country who admire America and believe in the core American principles on which the country was founded, especially those rooted in its Judeo-Christian ethos. CJA believes in free markets and capitalism; judging people as individuals as opposed to indistinguishable members of groups; personal self-defense; reverence for the Constitution; property rights; national sovereignty and patriotism; a strong and capable military; and opportunity for all to succeed. It promotes these values in the name of authentic and historic Judaism. CJA has a deep pride in Israel and her extraordinary achievements, and advocates for a secure and strong Israel, one that maintains itself as a Jewish state. CJA speaks out against the alarming and growing antisemitism coming from leftwing and jihadist sources against the Jewish community, Israel, and students on campus, promoting classic American values that are the best antidote against antisemitism and bigotry. (www.conferenceofjewishaffairs.org)

Council of Centers on Jewish-Christian Relations (CCJR) (2002). The CCJR is an association of centers and institutes in the US and Canada devoted to enhancing mutual understanding between Jews and Christians. The CCJR is dedicated to research, publication, educational programming, and interreligious dialogue that respect the religious integrity and self-understanding of the various strands of the Jewish and Christian traditions. The CCJR serves as a network for the sharing of information, research, and resources among academic and educational organizations. (www.ccjr.us)

Foundation for Ethnic Understanding (FFEU) (1989). 1 East 93rd Street, Suite 1C, New York, NY 10128. (917) 492-2538. The FFEU is dedicated to promoting racial harmony and strengthening relations between ethnic communities. It was formed to promote understanding and cooperation between and among ethnic groups and to reduce the existing tensions among diverse racial and ethnic communities. It promotes programs for Muslim-Jewish relations, Black-Jewish relations, and Latino-Jewish relations. (www.ffeu.org)

Foundation to Combat Anti-Semitism (FCAS) (2019). In pursuit of its vision of a world where people of conscience unite to end antisemitism once and for all,

FCAS catalyzes dynamic new solutions to stop the age-old hatred advanced by those who seek the elimination of Judaism and the Jewish people, and the modern movement to destroy the world's only Jewish state. It focuses on positively impacting attitudes of young people around the world, leveraging social media to deliver educational campaigns and spurring action by people of all backgrounds. Working with a network of global partners, the FCAS helps drive effective rapid response to hate as well as proactive campaigns that galvanize popular support for Jews and the Jewish state. By effectively combatting the rise of antisemitism, notably online and through social media, the long term goals of FCAS include creating a replicable model for fighting other forms of prejudice, racism, and hate crimes. (www.foundationtocombatantisemitism.com)

Institute for Black Solidarity with Israel (IBSI) (formerly **Black Americans to Support Israel Committee**) (2013). IBSI is dedicated to strengthening the relationship between Israel and the Jewish people, and people of African descent through education and advocacy. It condemns the "Zionism is racism" ideology; defends Israel's right to live in peace with its Arab neighbors; seeks to help cultivate a mutually beneficial Israel-Africa alliance; exposes the hypocrisy of anti-Israel Arab Islamists (such as Hamas) who condone and benefit from the trafficking and sale of African slaves while feigning solidarity with Black people. IBSI exists to tell the truth about Israel—a multiethnic, liberal democracy that is diverse by choice. (www.ibsi-now.org)

Institute for the Study of Global Antisemitism and Policy (ISGAP) (2004). 165 East 56th Street, 2nd Floor, New York, NY 10022. (212) 230-1840. ISGAP is a nonpartisan organization committed to fighting antisemitism and dedicated to the promotion of justice, understanding, respect, and harmony. It is the first interdisciplinary research center dedicated to the study of antisemitism based in North America. ISGAP is dedicated to scholarly research into the origins, processes, and manifestations of global antisemitism and of other forms of prejudice, including various forms of racism, as they relate to policy in an age of globalization. Its key goals are to promote excellence in research and to develop accessible social-scientific understanding, with attention being given to policy analysis and consultation in local, national, and international contexts. (www.isgap.org)

Interfaith Alliance (1994). 2101 L Street, NW, Suite 800, Washington, DC 20037. (202) 466-0567. Interfaith Alliance celebrates religious freedom by championing individual rights, promoting policies that protect both religion and democracy, and uniting diverse voices to challenge extremism. It dedicated to protecting the integrity of both religion and democracy in America. It was founded to challenge the bigotry and hatred arising from religious and political extremism infiltrating American politics. Interfaith Alliance promotes legislation that protects the boundaries between religion and government, so that politics doesn't infringe on faith and matters of faith don't infringe on freedom; mobilizes individuals on the grass-roots level (through local affiliates) to make a difference in their own communities; offers a forum to challenge bigotry and defend religious freedom on local issues, including candidate education, religion in the public sphere, and interfaith relations; helps religious leaders and politicians navigate the boundary between politics and religion in a way that safeguards the separation of church and state; and facilitates interfaith dialogue to enhance mutual understanding and respect for religious differences. (www.interfaithalliance.org)

International Fellowship of Christians and Jews (IFCJ) (formerly **Holyland Fellowship of Christians and Jews**) (1983). 30 North LaSalle Street, Suite 4300, Chicago, IL 60602. (800) 486-8844. The IFCJ was founded to promote understanding between Jews and Christians and build broad support for Israel and other shared concerns. Over the years, the IFCJ has been a leader in Jewish-Christian relations, building bridges of goodwill that have led to greater understanding and cooperation between members of both faiths. The IFCJ has helped hundreds of thousands of Jews escape poverty and antisemitism and return to their biblical homeland, funded humanitarian assistance that has touched the lives of millions of Jews in Israel and around the world, and provided life-giving aid to Israel's victims of war. (www.ifcj.org)

J'accuse Coalition for Justice (2018). (215) 436-9224. The J'accuse Coalition for Justice is a think tank and watchdog organization dedicated to combating antisemitism and anti-Zionism. It seeks to achieve justice for Jews and Israel in the public sphere by competing openly in the marketplace of ideas, disseminating the truth in regional and national media, and exposing the often double standards used to demonize and delegitimize both the Jewish people and the Jewish State. (www.jaccusecoalition.org)

Jew in the City (JITC) (2007). PO Box 2168, Teaneck, NJ 07666. JITC's mission is to break down stereotypes about religious Jews and offer a humorous, meaningful outlook into Orthodox Judaism. JITC seeks to reshape the way society views Orthodox Jews and Judaism through social media, corporate cultural diversity training seminars, lectures, and consulting services. The JITC team publicizes the message that Orthodox Jews can be funny, approachable, educated, pro-women, and open-minded. It files friend of the court briefs in support of religious liberty cases. (www.jewinthecity.com)

Jewish Coalition for Religious Liberty (JCRL) (2016). One Penn Plaza, Suite 6102, New York, NY 10019. (202) 930-1857. JCRL is a nondenominational organization of Jewish communal and lay leaders seeking to protect the ability of all Americans to freely practice their faith. It also aims to foster cooperation between Jewish and other faith communities in an American public square in which all supporters of freedom are free to flourish. JCRL files friends of the court briefs in support of religious liberty issues. (www.jcrl.org)

Jewish Council for Public Affairs (JCPA) (formerly **National Jewish Community Relations Advisory Council**) (1944). 116 East 27th Street, 10th Floor, New York, NY 10016. (212) 684-6950. The JCPA is the national coordinating body for the field of Jewish community relations, comprising numerous national and local Jewish community-relations agencies. Its goals are to safeguard the rights of Jews in the US and around the world; to ensure the safety and security of Israel; and to protect, preserve and promote a just American society, one that is democratic, pluralistic and furthers harmonious interreligious, inter-ethnic, interracial, and other intergroup relations. The JCPA has the responsibility to enhance the capacity of member agencies to effectively pursue the public affairs agenda. (www.jewishpub-licaffairs.org)

Jewish Democratic Council of America (JDCA) (2017). 1440 G Street, NW, Washington, DC 20005. (202) 975-0859. As the political voice of Jewish Democrats, JDCA advocates for Jewish values and priorities within the Democratic Party and for the Democratic Party within the Jewish community. (www.jewishdems.org)

Jewish Electorate Institute (JEI) (2018). 1440 G Street, NW, Washington, DC 20002. JEI is an independent, nonpartisan organization dedicated to deepening the public's understanding of Jewish American participation in democracy. It also fosters the active participation of the Jewish community in the democratic process and acts as the foremost resource on Jewish voter political preferences, producing the top research, polling, and analysis critical to understanding the Jewish electorate. (www.jewishelectorateinstitute.org)

Jewish Labor Committee (JLC) (1934). 140 West 31st Street, 2nd Floor, New York, NY 10001. (212) 477-0707. The JLC is the voice of the Jewish community in the labor movement and the voice of the labor movement in the Jewish community. It enables the Jewish community and the trade union movement to work together on important issues of shared interest and concern in pursuit of a shared commitment to economic and social justice. The JLC's activities have included working with the US and international labor movement to combat antisemitism, promote intergroup relations, and engender support for the security of Israel and for Jews in and from the FSU; supporting Yiddish-language and cultural institutions; promoting teaching in public schools about the Holocaust and Jewish resistance; and involvement in all aspects of labor-related causes that touch upon the survival and life of the Jewish people. (www.jewishlabor.org)

Jewish Multiracial Network (JMN) (1997). c/o The Shalom Center, 6711 Lincoln Drive, Philadelphia, PA 19119. (347) 620-4467. JMN advances Jewish diversity through empowerment, education and community building and is committed to working toward full inclusion of Jews of Color and multiracial Jewish families in the larger Jewish community. JMN provides families and educators with resources about diverse and inclusive Jewish communities, facilitates dialogue on ways in which members can marry their cultural traditions with Jewish ritual, hosts workshops at its annual retreats designed to empower and encourage its membership to advocate for inclusion and take leadership positions in their local communities, provides educational summits for Jewish professionals, gives guidance to institutions on appropriate ways to design diversity programming and initiatives, and highlights synagogues that are welcoming to Jews of Color and multiracial Jewish families. (www.jewishmultiracialnetwork.org)

Jewish Peace Fellowship (JPF) (1941). PO Box 271, Nyack, NY 10960. (845) 358-4601, ext. 35. The JPF is a nondenominational organization committed to active nonviolence as a means of resolving conflict. The JPF maintains an active program of draft and peace education, opposition to war and belief in the reconciliation of Israel, Jews, and Palestinians. Originally founded to support Jewish conscientious objectors to the military, JPF continues to support Jewish resistance—individual and communal—to the arms race in the US and Israel and throughout the world. It actively opposes capital punishment, conscription, the Israeli occupation, and US armed interventions. (www.jewishpeacefellowship.org)

Jewish Policy Center (JPC) (1985). 50 F Street, NW, Suite 100, Washington, DC 20001. (202) 638-2411. The JPC provides timely perspectives and analysis of foreign and domestic policies by leading scholars, academics and commentators. It passionately supports a strong American defense capability, US-Israel security cooperation, and missile defense. It supports Israel in its quest for legitimacy and security. The JPC advocates for small government, low taxes, free trade, fiscal responsibility and energy security, as well as free speech and intellectual diversity. (www.jewishpolicycenter.org)

Jewish War Veterans of the United States of America (JWV) (1896). 1811 R Street, NW, Washington, DC 20009. (202) 265-6280. JWV seeks to maintain true allegiance to the US; to foster and perpetuate true Americanism; to combat bigotry and prevent defamation of Jews; to support the State of Israel; to encourage the doctrine of universal liberty, equal rights and full justice for all; to cooperate with and support existing educational institutions and establish new ones; to foster the education of ex-servicemen and ex-servicewomen in the ideals and principles of Americanism; to preserve the memories and records of patriotic service performed by Jewish men and women; and to honor their memory and shield from neglect the graves of the heroic dead. (www.jwv.org)

Jewish World Alliance (also known as **Jspace**) (2011). 149 Madison Avenue, Suite 502, New York, NY 10016. (212) 302-8169. Jewish World Alliance/Jspace seeks to create a strong Jewish identity among the millennial generation; strengthen the Jewish community worldwide by bringing together Jews around the globe to share information, content, experiences, and ideas through its online platforms and offline events; provide to the world accurate, informative news content and education about Israel, Judaism, and the Jewish world, and help combat the alarming worldwide growing antisemitism, anti-Israel bias, and boycott Israel movement; and represent and highlight Israel's vast accomplishments, contributions, and benefits to the world via its online and social reach. (www.jewishworldalliance.org)

Jews for the Preservation of Firearms Ownership (JPFO) (1989). 12500 Northeast 10th Place, Bellevue, WA 98005. (800) 486-6963. JPFO is an educational civil-rights organization that opposes so-called "gun control," seeks to expose the misguided notions that lead people to seek out "gun control" and encourages Americans to understand and defend all of the Bill of Rights for all citizens. It is not a lobby. JPFO was initially aimed at educating the Jewish community about the historical evils that Jews have suffered when they have been disarmed. (www.jpfo.org)

Jews in All Hues (JIAH) (2012). (215) 469-1967. JIAH is an education and advocacy organization that supports multiple-heritage Jews, assisting Jewish communities and organizations in the creation of sustainably-diverse communities. JIAH's goal is to build a future for the Jewish community where a person's heritage is never a barrier to acceptance or integration. Heritage-diverse Jews are people whose identity lies outside the construct of what some consider "mainstream" Judaism in the US. These populations include but are not limited to: adoptee Jews,

Jews with one parent of another religion, Jews by choice, multi-racial Jews, Jews of color, LGBTIQQA Jews and those who may not feel they "fit." (www.jewsinall-hues.org)

Jews of Color Field Building Initiative (2018). 2222 Harold Way, Berkeley, CA 94704. (760) 452-8617. The Jews of Color Field Building Initiative is a national effort focused on building and advancing the professional, organizational, and communal field for Jews of Color. It focuses on grant making, research and field building, and community education, and hosts the nation's first ever philanthropic and capacity building fund expressly dedicated to responding to racial injustice through helping further establish, fortify, and building out the field of support for Jews of Color. (www.jewsofcolorfieldbuilding.org)

Louis D. Brandeis Center for Human Rights Under Law (LBD) (2012). 1717 Pennsylvania Avenue, NW, Suite 1025, Washington, DC 20006. (202) 559-9296. LBD is an independent, nonpartisan institution established to advance the civil and human rights of the Jewish people and promote justice for all. It conducts research, education, and advocacy to combat the resurgence of antisemitism primarily on North American college and university campuses. (www.brandeiscenter.com)

Muslim-Jewish Advisory Council (2016). The Muslim-Jewish Advisory Council is an interfaith national group formed by the Islamic Society of North America and the AJC (American Jewish Committee). Its major goals are to highlight the contributions of Muslims and Jews to American society; create a coordinated strategy to address anti-Muslim bigotry and antisemitism; and protect and expand the rights of religious minorities in the US. The group brings together recognized business, political, and religious leaders in the Jewish and Muslim American communities to jointly advocate on issues of common concern. (www.muslimjewi-shadvocacy.org)

National Association of Jewish Legislators (NAJL) (1977). 116 East 27th Street, 10th Floor, New York, NY 10016. (202) 494-7991. The NAJL is a nonpartisan national organization for Jewish state legislators, supporters and anyone else who wants to participate in a network of elected officials working with Jewish agencies and other elected official networks. The NAJL seeks to improve the quality of life for Jews in America and is supportive of Israel. Issues addressed by the NAJL over the years include anti-Zionist resolutions, religious displays in public spaces, hate crimes, homeland security, Holocaust assets taxation, Israel boycott and divestiture proposals, Tay Sachs disease and kosher law enforcement. (www.najl.net)

National Conference of Shomrim Societies (National Shomrim) (1958). PO Box 598, Knickerbocker Station, New York, NY 10002. The National Conference of Shomrim Societies is comprised of Shomrim chapters from the US, and associate members from the US and all over the world, for the purpose of joining together Jews in the public safety fields. Its mission is to promote the interests of the organization and its members to the community. (www.nationalshomrim.org)

National Jewish Coalition for Literacy (NJCL) (1997). 134 Beach Street, Boston, MA 02111. (617) 423-0063. The NJCL, established by Leonard Fein, is the organized Jewish community's vehicle for mobilizing volunteer tutors and reading partners for at-risk children in kindergarten through third grade. Since its launch, some 50 communities have affiliated with the NJCL, and under its auspices roughly 12,000 volunteers spend 1 h a week working one-on-one with public school children (mostly in inner-city schools). (www.njcl.net)

National Jewish Democratic Council (NJDC) (Ceased to exist as of 2016)

NewGround: A Muslim-Jewish Partnership for Change (2006). 1200 West 7th Street, Suite 906L, Los Angeles, CA 90017. (818) 856-0815. NewGround works to create a world in which trust and partnership replace the current atmosphere of mutual suspicion among Muslims and Jews. It equips Muslims and Jews in America with the skills, resources, and relationships needed to improve Muslim-Jewish relations and cooperation on issues of shared concern. Through a young professional's fellowship, public programming, and consulting, NewGround impacts a wide range of Muslims and Jews—from organizational leaders to the unaffiliated and from liberals to conservatives. (www.mjnewground.org)

Religious Action Center of Reform Judaism (RAC) (1953). 2027 Massachusetts Avenue, NW, Washington, DC 20036. (202) 387-2800. The RAC is the hub of Jewish social justice and legislative activity in Washington, DC. The RAC educates and mobilizes the Reform Jewish community on legislative and social concerns, advocating on many different issues, including economic justice, civil rights, religious liberty, and Israel. The RAC's advocacy work is completely nonpartisan and pursues public policies that reflect the Jewish values of social justice that form the core of the Reform movement's mandate. (www.rac.org)

Republican Jewish Coalition (RJC) (formerly **National Jewish Coalition**) (1985). 50 F Street, NW, Suite 100, Washington, DC 20001. (202) 638-6688. The RJC is the voice for Jewish Republicans. The RJC promotes involvement in Republican politics among its members; sensitizes Republican leaders in government and the party to the concerns of the American Jewish community; articulates Republican ideas and policies within the Jewish community; and promotes principles of free enterprise, small government, national security and a strong national defense, and an internationalist foreign policy. The RJC embraces a pro-Israel foreign policy and supports the elimination of oil dependence. (www.rjchq.org)

Scattered Among the Nations (2001). 180 Grand Avenue, Suite 1380, Oakland, California 94612. (510) 847-8079. Scattered Among the Nations is dedicated to educating the Jewish and non-Jewish world about the beauty and diversity of the Jewish people. It assists geographically and politically isolated Jewish or Judaism-practicing communities to continue embracing the Jewish religion and culture, while documenting these communities as they are today before they disappear through immigration or assimilation. (www.scatteredamongthenations.org)

Secure Community Network (SCN) (2004). 25 Broadway, New York, NY 10004. (212) 284-6940. SCN is the national homeland security initiative of The Jewish Federations of North America and the Conference of Presidents of Major American Jewish Organizations created in response to a heightened security concern among national Jewish leadership. It serves as a central address for law enforcement, homeland security and community organizations as it relates to the safety and security of Jewish institutions and communities across the US. Through information sharing, security awareness, training and security consultation, SCN strives to empower individuals and organizations in establishing a culture of security awareness, preparedness and resiliency throughout American communities. SCN's two main functions are rapid information sharing in crisis situations and enhancing security awareness at Jewish organizations and institutions to protect against terrorism and other threats. (www.scnus.org)

The Shalom Center (formerly a division of the **Reconstructionist Rabbinical College** and part of **ALEPH: Alliance for Jewish Renewal**) (1983). 6711 Lincoln Drive, Philadelphia, PA 19119. (215) 844-8494. The Shalom Center seeks to be a prophetic voice in Jewish, multi-religious and American life. It equips activists and spiritual leaders with awareness and skills needed to lead in shaping a transformed and transformative Judaism. The Shalom Center has addressed Jewish perspectives on such issues as overwork in American society, environmental dangers, unrestrained technology, militarism, corporate irresponsibility, climate crisis, concentrations of political and economic power, peacemaking in the Middle East and interreligious tensions among Jews, Christians and Muslims in the US. (www.theshalomcenter.org)

Sino-Judaic Institute (SJI) (1985). 1252 West College Avenue, Jacksonville, IL 62650. A nondenominational, nonpolitical organization, SJI was founded by an international group of scholars and lay persons to promote understanding between the Chinese and Jewish peoples and to encourage and develop their cooperation in matters of mutual historic and cultural interest. SJI initially served as a vehicle for the study and preservation of Jewish history in China, establishing exhibits on the Kaifeng Jews in Kaifeng and publishing various academic materials. It facilitated the establishment of Jewish Studies programs at various Chinese universities and co-sponsored conferences with Chinese scholars. It promotes the translation into Chinese of basic works on Jews and Israel and helps bring Chinese scholars to Israel and the US for advanced study opportunities. (www.sino-judaic.org)

Sisterhood of Salaam Shalom (2013). PO Box 7117, North Brunswick, NJ 08902. With chapters across a number of states in the US, the Sisterhood of Salaam Shalom builds strong relationships between Muslim and Jewish women based on developing trust and respect and ending anti-Muslim and anti-Jewish sentiment. Members participate in dialogue, socialization, social action projects, and activities to expand their knowledge of each other's practices and beliefs, forming strong friendships. (www.sosspeace.org)

Torah Trumps Hate (2016). Torah Trumps Hate is an organization for Torah-affiliated Jews to educate, empower, and mobilize themselves regarding current social justice issues. Its goal is to inspire changes within the Orthodox community and the larger American society, including racial justice, immigrant and refugee rights, poverty, access to health care, an end to mass incarceration, LGBTQ rights, and the protection of the rule of law. Torah Trumps Hate believes that Jews have an obligation to work for a more just society. (www.torahtrumpshate.com)

Uri L'Tzedek: Orthodox Social Justice. 475 Riverside Drive, Suite 1800, New York, NY 10115. (602) 445-3112. Uri L'Tzedek is an Orthodox social justice organization guided by Torah values and dedicated to combating suffering and oppression. Uri L'Tzedek has created different fellowships that train emerging adults with the skills necessary to become community organizers, social entrepreneurs, and change-agents. The Tav HaYosher, Uri L'Tzedek's ethical seal for kosher restaurants, weaves advocacy for worker rights with kashrut in a manner that creates a new paradigm for ethical living, empowers lay leaders to become social justice advocates, and initiates dialogue about the effects of conspicuous consumption, globalization and community in the Jewish public sphere. (www.utzedek.org)

WoMen Fight AntiSemitism (WMFA) (2019). WMFA welcomes Americans of all genders and races to care about and fight for equality and against antisemitism, calling out antisemitism wherever and whenever it is seen and focusing on the most critical concern for Jews—lack of media attention. It keeps track of locations and organizations adopting the International Holocaust Remembrance Alliance Definition of Antisemitism. WMFA stands firmly against the Boycott, Divestment and Sanctions (BDS) of Israel based on its belief that a true and lasting peace will be through cooperative efforts toward that end between the Palestinians and the Israelis, supporting self-determination for both Jews and Palestinians and supporting candidates and representatives who condemn the BDS movement. (www.womenfightantisemitism.org)

World Jewish Congress (WJC) (1936). 501 Madison Avenue, New York, NY 10022. (212) 755-5770. The WJC is the nonpartisan international organization that seeks to intensify bonds of world Jewry with Israel; secure the rights, status and interests of Jews and Jewish communities and defend them; encourage Jewish social, religious and cultural life throughout the world; support Jewish education and the development of Jewish values, and ensure Jewish continuity; assist Jewish communities in strengthening their Jewish identities and in confronting problems; preserve the memory of the Holocaust and advocate on behalf of survivors and their families; combat antisemitism and all religious, racial or ethnic intolerance, oppression or persecution; participate in inter-faith dialogue; and promote gender equality and the involvement of younger Jews in Jewish communal and organizational leadership. (www.worldjewishcongress.org)

Zachor Legal Institute (2015). 5919 US Highway 84, Red Level, AL 36474. (650) 279-9690. Zachor Legal Institute is a legal think tank and advocacy organization that is taking the lead in creating a framework to wage a legal battle against anti-Israel movements in America. Its primary current focus is combatting BDS (Boycott, Divestment and Sanctions) and antisemitic activities in the commercial sector. Since there is a wide overlap between BDS and terrorist organizations in terms of objectives and methods, Zachor scholarship is also used in the anti-terrorism realm. (www.zachorlegal.org)

Zioness (2017). 633 Third Avenue, 21st floor, New York, NY 10017. The Zioness Movement is a coalition of activists and allies who express their Zionist and progressive values through collective action. An inclusive movement that invites all progressive Zionists to participate, they are driven by the belief that the same values of human rights and self-determination at the heart of progressive causes also underlie Zionism, the movement to achieve self-determination—the expression of the Jewish peoples' dreams of liberation and empowerment after millennia of Jewish struggles for civil rights and equality in the face of persecution, exile, and genocide.

Zioness supports Israel's existence as a Jewish and democratic state; fights for justice and against discrimination for women, people of color, LGBTQ+ individuals, and others whose rights are denied or threatened because of their innate characteristics; acts to stop the spread of antisemitism and the demonization of Jews, Zionism, and Zionists on both the right and the left; and seeks to promote understanding of Judaism and Zionism within progressive circles. (www.zioness.org)

12.1.18   Jewish Philanthropy-Promoting Organizations

Center for Entrepreneurial Jewish Philanthropy (CEJP) (2005). 435 Stratton Road, New Rochelle, NY 10804. (914) 654-0008. CEJP was established to advise and support major Jewish philanthropists in all aspects of their Jewish and Israel-based charitable giving. Its mission is to create a new paradigm in Jewish giving, in which philanthropists are treated as partners and not just funders, emphasizing donor empowerment and choice, leverage and partnership, strategic planning, due diligence and accountability. CEJP's services are provided free of charge, enabling 100% of contributions to support the organizations and projects chosen to be funded. (www.cejp.com)

Jewcer Community Funding (Jewcer) (2012). 4647 Kingswell Avenue, Suite 148, Los Angeles, CA 90027. (424) 245-5927. Jewcer was created as a bridge to connect exciting new ideas to the Jewish people in a participatory way, changing the way young people connected to Jewish projects, ideas, and causes. It helps individuals and organizations successfully engage their communities around participatory philanthropy (crowdfunding and active participation in social good). Jewcer's mission is to empower individuals, organizations, and leaders to engage with communities locally, nationally, and globally to raise support for programs, ideas, and causes designed to benefit the Jewish people and/or Israel. It does this through ongoing mentorship, sharing best practices, offering grants and fiscal sponsorship, and promoting causes via social media and email. (www.jewcer.org)

Jewish Aid Worldwide (formerly **Israel Fund**) (2005). 125 Washington Street, Suite 201, Salem, MA 01970. (978) 744-6501. Jewish Aid Worldwide was founded to assist nonprofit organizations with raising funds by facilitating participation in federal and state workplace giving programs, with primary focus on the Combined Federal Campaign. Jewish Aid Worldwide partners with a number of Israel-related charitable organizations. It is a founding member of the Workplace Giving Alliance, a consortium of 13 federations participating in fundraising campaigns in the public sector, representing over 500 charitable organizations working in nearly every sector of the nonprofit world. (www.jewishaidworldwide.org)

Jewish Causes of Choice (JChoice) (2009). 160 Herrick Road, Newton, MA 02459. (857) 404-0219. JChoice's vision is to encourage hundreds of thousands of young Jews to donate on a regular basis to hundreds of needy causes. It operates a social network to help the next generation of charitable donors find, analyze, and donate to causes. (www.jchoice.org)

Jewish Funders Network (JFN) (1990). 150 West 30th Street, Suite 900, New York, NY 10001. (212) 726-0177. JFN is an international organization dedicated to advancing the quality and growth of Jewish philanthropy. Its mission is to help philanthropists maximize the impact of their giving by assisting them in the identification of needs and challenges. The Jewish Teen Funders Network (JTFN), part of JFN since 2006, serves as a central address for Jewish youth philanthropy programs across North America. JTFN's mission is to provide Jewish teens with hands-on opportunities to engage in collective philanthropic giving with their peers, guided by Jewish values. The Social Venture Fund for Jewish-Arab Equality and Shared Society, part of JFN since 2016, is a philanthropic collaborative that brings together individuals, foundations, and federations who support an equal and inclusive shared society in Israel for the benefit of all of its citizens. (www.jfunders.org), (www.jtfn.org)

JLens Investor Network (2012). 560 Mission Street, Suite 1395, San Francisco, CA 94105. JLens Investor Network is an investor network and consulting organization engaging the Jewish community on impact investing through a Jewish lens. JLens mixes education, consulting, and fund management in order to bring Jewish values to investment. JLens currently advises nearly several thousand donors in the Jewish community on how to manage investment capital. Focusing on investment opportunities inspired by the Jewish value of tikkun olam, JLens' consulting activities help organizations develop, implement, and monitor impact investment policies. (www.jlensnetwork.org)

Jumpstart (2008). 2801 Ocean Park Boulevard, #348, Santa Monica, CA 90405. (424) 273-5867. Jumpstart nurtures compelling and innovative early-stage nonprofits, networks their leaders, and connects them to the resources and expertise they need to succeed. Jumpstart provides strategic advice to philanthropists and other advocates committed to growing emerging organizations to scale and sustainability. (www.jewishjumpstart.org)

Slingshot Fund (2007). 25 Broadway, 9th Floor, New York, NY 10004. (646) 838-2148. The Slingshot Fund is a peer-giving network to support Jewish organizations. Slingshot's mission is to strengthen innovation in Jewish life by developing next-generation funders and providing resources to leverage their impact in the Jewish community. (www.slingshotfund.org)

12.1.19   Jewish Philanthropic Foundations and Organizations

Adelson Family Foundation (2007). The Adelson Family Foundation supports charitable organizations located primarily in Israel and the US that generally fall within the following programmatic categories: healthcare; Holocaust and antisemitism awareness; Israel advocacy and defense; Israel programs; Israel studies on campus; Jewish and Zionist identity and education; media and culture; and welfare. (www.adelsonfoundation.org/AFF)

Alan B. Slifka Foundation (1965). 477 Madison Avenue, 9th Floor, New York, NY 10022. (212) 303-9470. The Alan B. Slifka Foundation makes grants that focus on four program areas, two of which are the perpetuation of Jewish values and education in Israel and the Diaspora and the enhancement of coexistence (social cohesion) within the borders of Israel, essentially between Jews and Arabs, but also between secular and religious elements of Israeli society. (www.slifkafoundation.org)

The Areivim Philanthropic Group (2005). 729 Seventh Avenue, 9th Floor, New York, NY 10019. (212) 792-6291. The Areivim Philanthropic Group, a Jewish funding partnership established by Michael Steinhardt and the late William Davidson, is a unique entrepreneurial consortium of major North American philanthropists who are committed to developing and supporting transformational projects with innovative thinking meant to significantly impact the next generation of Jews through formal and experiential Jewish, Hebrew, and Israel education. (www.areivim.org)

The AVI CHAI Foundation, North America (1984). 1015 Park Avenue, New York, NY 10028. (212) 396-8850. AVI CHAI in North America seeks to ensure the continuity of the Jewish people through fostering high levels of Jewish literacy, deepening religious purposefulness and promoting advocacy for Jewish peoplehood and Israel. Its goal in North America is to advance and sustain education in Jewish day schools and summer camps for the purpose of creating the foundation for an energizing nucleus of youth with the values, commitments, motivation, and skills to lead the Jewish people intellectually, spiritually, communally, and politically in the 21st century. (www.avichai.orgica)

Baron de Hirsch Fund (1891). 130 East 59th Street, Suite 1059, New York, NY 10022. (212) 836-1305. The Baron de Hirsch Fund was established by Baron Maurice de Hirsch to assist new immigrants to New York from Russia and Rumania who arrived in 1890-1891. The fund provided the refugees with job training, help with immediate material necessities, instruction in the English language, and covered transportation costs for those wishing to go live with relatives in other parts of the US. Currently, the fund aids Jewish immigrants in the US and Israel by giving grants to agencies active in resettlement, focusing on educational and vocational training and community development. (No website)

Bnai Zion Foundation (1908). 1430 Broadway, Suite 1804, New York, NY 10018. (212) 725-1211. Bnai Zion Foundation supports humanitarian projects in Israel that transform the lives of thousands. Its projects include Bnai Zion Medical Center, Ahava Village for Children and Youth in Kiryat Bialik, The Quittman Center at Israel Elwyn, The David Yellin Academic College of Education, and the Library of Peace and George W. Schaeffer Music Conservatory in Ma'aleh Adumim. (www.bnaizion.org)

Charles and Lynn Schusterman Family Foundation (1987). 110 West 7th Street, Tulsa, OK 74119; (918) 879-0290. The Charles and Lynn Schusterman Family Foundation is committed to strengthening the Jewish people and public education in the US. The Foundation pursues its mission by providing young people with high-quality education, identity development, leadership training and service opportunities that foster their growth as individuals and as leaders. (www.schusterman.org)

The Covenant Foundation (1990). 1270 Avenue of the Americas, Suite 304, New York, NY 10020. (212) 245-3500. The Covenant Foundation's mission is to celebrate, support and advance excellence and innovation in Jewish education. The Foundation recognizes all denominations. By honoring outstanding Jewish educators and supporting creative approaches to programming, the Foundation works to strengthen educational endeavors that perpetuate the identity, continuity and heritage of the Jewish people. (www.covenantfn.org)

Dorot Foundation (1976). 439 Benefit Street, Providence, RI 02903. (401) 351-8866. The Dorot Foundation is concerned with the transmission of Jewish heritage through the generations. It makes grants which demonstrate a commitment to the Jewish past, present and future by supporting activities in the areas of education, cultural institutions, and social change in Israel, among others. (www.dorot.org)

Fohs Foundation (1937). PO Box 1001, Roseburg, OR 97470. (541) 440-1587. Fohs Foundation seeks to improve Jewish-Arab relations within Israel through structural and institutional reform and through policies and practices that build common interests, mutual responsibility and shared benefits. The foundation supports strategies and initiatives that strengthen Israel's future as a just and prosperous home for its Jewish and Arab communities. (No website)

Harold Grinspoon Foundation (1993). 67 Hunt Street, Suite 100, Agawam, MA 01001. (413) 276-0700. The Harold Grinspoon Foundation is committed to charitable giving, primarily in the Jewish world. The Foundation has several flagship programs, including PJ Library, Sifriyat Pijama (Israeli version of PJ Library), JCamp 180 and Voices & Visions™. PJ Library, in partnership with communities throughout North America provides Jewish children's books and music to families raising young Jewish children. Sifriyat Pijama, in cooperation with the Israeli Ministry of Education, gives Hebrew-language children's books each month to preschoolers. JCamp 180 seeks to sustain and strengthen Jewish camps in North America by providing free professional consulting services and grant-matching opportunities. The Voices & Visions™ program elicits the power of art to communicate great Jewish ideas and aims to inspire conversation, instill pride and spark creativity. (www.hgf.org)

The Harry and Jeanette Weinberg Foundation (1959). 7 Park Center Court, Owings Mills, MD 21117. (410) 654-8500. The Harry and Jeanette Weinberg Foundation provides approximately $100 million in annual grants to nonprofits that provide direct services to low-income and vulnerable individuals and families, primarily in the US and Israel, with emphasis placed on serving older adults and the Jewish community. (www.hjweinbergfoundation.org)

Jim Joseph Foundation (also known as **Shimon Ben Joseph Foundation**) (1987, 2005). 343 Sansome Street, Suite 550, San Francisco, CA 94104. (415) 658-8730. The Jim Joseph Foundation is devoted exclusively to supporting education of American Jewish youth and young adults. Foundation awards support the educational training and development of Jewish educators; expand learning opportunities for young Jews; and build the capacity of high performing organizations serving the field of Jewish education. (www.jimjosephfoundation.org)

Lippman Kanfer Family Philanthropies (formerly **Jerome Lippman Family Foundation**) (1966) (2013). 520 South Main Street, Suite 2457, Akron, OH 44311. (330) 255-6200. Comprised of the Lippman Kanfer Family Foundation and Lippman Kanfer Foundation for Living Torah, the Lippman Kanfer Family Philanthropies is committed to building and sustaining a multi-generational family culture of tzedakah (philanthropy); supporting Jewish life in their hometown of Akron and in the family's other local communities; maintaining the pursuit of justice; strengthening the ecosystem for innovation in the Jewish community; and impacting Jewish life broadly in North America in a strategic way. (www.lippmankanfer.org)

Machne Israel Development Fund (1984). 784 Eastern Parkway, Brooklyn, NY 11213. (718) 493-9250. The Machne Israel Development Fund was established by Rabbi Menachem Mendel Schneerson to serve as a major financial resource of the Chabad Lubavitch institutional network. Formed by a core of prominent Jewish philanthropists dedicated to the growth of Jewish life and the greater vision of Jewish continuity, the Fund has disbursed critical sums toward the support of Chabad Lubavitch centers over the years. (www.lubavitch.com/department. html?h=679)

Maimonides Fund. Maimonides Fund is a private grant-making organization dedicated to education and Jewish identity in North America and Israel. (No website)

Mandell and Madeleine Berman Foundation (1995). 29100 Northwestern Highway, Suite 205, Southfield, MI 48034. The Mandell and Madeleine Berman Foundation supports Jewish education, the study of the contemporary American Jewish community, the revitalization of Jewish Detroit, and efforts promoting the arts, education and workforce development in Detroit. (No website)

Memorial Foundation for Jewish Culture (1965). 50 Broadway, 34th Floor, New York, NY 10004. (212) 425-6606. The Memorial Foundation for Jewish Culture's original mandate was the reconstruction of Jewish cultural life around the world after the Shoah, which was fulfilled through the identification and support of a new generation of scholars, intellectuals, academics, writers, artists, rabbis, educators, and other Jewish communal professionals to replace their earlier counterparts in Europe who were lost in the Holocaust. Subsequently, the Foundation re-fashioned the direction of its program to focus on preserving and intensifying Jewish cultural distinctiveness and enhancing Jewish cultural life in Jewish communities by supporting the training of competent and committed communal, cultural, and professional leaders to deal with the new sociological realities and challenges their communities were confronting. (www.mfjc.org)

The Nathan Cummings Foundation (1949). 475 10th Avenue, 14th Floor, New York, NY 10018. (212) 787-7300. The Nathan Cummings Foundation seeks to build a socially and economically just society that values nature and protects the ecological balance for future generations; promotes humane health care; and fosters arts and culture that enriches communities. The Foundation's approach to grant-making embodies in all of its programs concern for the poor, disadvantaged and underserved; respect for diversity; promotion of understanding across cultures; and empowerment of communities in need. (www.nathancummings.org)

Ne'eman Foundation USA (2000). 18 Hazelton Road, Newton, MA 02459. (888) 341-8590. Ne'eman Foundation USA is dedicated to providing a secure financial link between Israel and the US in addition to helping Israeli nonprofit organizations build a new donor base in the US or strengthen an existing one. It provides Americans with a wide selection of tax-deductible projects in Israel to support, including projects and programs throughout Israel that reduce or eliminate poverty; advance education, religion, and quality of life; promote charitable initiatives for community development; and provide health care services and products that prevent and manage serious threats to health. (www.neemanfoundationusa.com)

New Israel Fund (NIF) (1979). 6 East 39th Street, Suite 301, New York, NY 10016. (212) 613-4400. The NIF is a partnership of Israelis, North Americans, and Europeans dedicated to advancing democracy and equality for all Israelis. Its priorities fall into three major issue areas—human and civil rights, social and economic justice, and religious pluralism—and it also focuses on issues of environmental justice. Widely credited with building Israel's progressive civil society from scratch, the NIF has provided over $200 million to more than 800 cutting-edge organizations since its inception. More than just a funder, NIF is at philanthropy's cutting edge thanks in large part to Shatil, the New Israel Fund Initiative for Social Change, which provides NIF grantees and other social change organizations with hands-on assistance, including training, resources, and workshops on various aspects of nonprofit management. NIF/Shatil is a leading advocate for democratic values, builds coalitions, empowers activists, and often takes the initiative in setting the public agenda. (www.nif.org)

Posen Foundation (Ceased to exist in the US as of 2017)

Righteous Persons Foundation (RPF) (1994). (310) 314-8393. The RPF was established by Steven Spielberg in response to his deeply moving experience of directing the film Schindler's List, whereby he donated his portion of the film's profits to help support a flourishing and meaningful Jewish community that reflects the realities of Jewish life in America today. Since inception, RPF has funded a broad range of innovative approaches to strengthening Jewish identity and community in the US and to preserving the memory of the Holocaust. (www.righteouspersons.org)

The Ronald S. Lauder Foundation (1987). 767 Fifth Avenue, Suite 4200, New York, NY 10153. The Ronald S. Lauder Foundation seeks to revitalize Jewish identity through educational and cultural initiatives that reach out to all Jews. The Foundation has been committed to rebuilding Jewish life in Central and Eastern Europe, primarily by providing Jewish education to children through its support of kindergartens, schools, youth centers and camps, institutions of higher education, and e-learning schools. (www.lauderfoundation.com)

Ruderman Family Foundation (1997). 2150 Washington Street, Newton, MA 02462. (617) 559-9919. Guided by its Jewish values, the Ruderman Family Foundation supports effective programs, innovative partnerships, and a dynamic approach to philanthropy in its core areas of interest: advocating for and advancing the inclusion of people with disabilities throughout society; strengthening the sense of commitment and responsibility toward the American Jewish community among Israeli leadership; and modeling the practice of strategic philanthropy worldwide. It is driven by the values of social justice, equality, and tikkun olam. (www.ruderman-foundation.org)

The Samuel Bronfman Foundation (1995). 420 Lexington Avenue, Suite 331, New York, NY 10170. (212) 572-1025. Guided by the vision of Edgar M. Bronfman, The Samuel Bronfman Foundation seeks to inspire a renaissance of Jewish life. The Foundation cultivates long-term relationships with organizations that advance its mission. The Foundation seeks to facilitate Jewish learning; seeks to empower Jewish youth to lead the Jewish people and the world community; supports a culture of pluralism and mutual respect that celebrates diverse expressions of Jewish life; and affirms the unity of the Jewish people throughout the world and in Israel. (www.thesbf.org)

The Steinhardt Foundation for Jewish Life (formerly **Jewish Life Network/Steinhardt Foundation**) (1994). 729 Seventh Avenue, 9th Floor, New York, NY 10019. (212) 279-2288. The Steinhardt Foundation for Jewish Life, founded by former hedge fund manager Michael Steinhardt, funds projects and programs aimed at improving Jewish education and identity. The Foundation has identified two primary pillars on which to build educational and cultural endeavors that recognize the centrality of Hebrew and Israel in the fabric of Jewish Peoplehood: Modern Hebrew language and extended Israel experiences and internships. One of its signature programs is Taglit-Birthright Israel. The Foundation is also at the forefront of the Hebrew language charter school movement and is involved in Israeli Scouts Atid—an English language track of the Israeli Scouts in the US. (www.steinhardtfoundation.org)

Targum Shlishi (1992). 3029 Northeast 188th Street, Suite 1114, Aventura, FL 33180. (305) 692-9991. Targum Shlishi believes in fostering positive, creative change and supporting causes dedicated to improving the quality of Jewish life worldwide. It supports organizations that are dedicated to education, women's issues, Israel, and justice for Nazi war crimes. Targum Shlishi seeks innovative, unpublicized, and behind-the-scenes initiatives that otherwise might not attract funding. (www.targumshlishi.org)

Taube Foundation for Jewish Life & Culture (2001). 1050 Ralston Avenue, Belmont, CA 94002. The mission of the Taube Foundation for Jewish Life & Culture's is to help support the survival of Jewish life and culture in the face of unprecedented global threat to the Jewish people, especially in Israel; strengthen Jewish identity and sustain Jewish heritage in the US in the face of assimilation; celebrate current Jewish achievement in all aspects of human endeavor; and work for the reform of Jewish institutions, which have often become disconnected from the people they serve. (www.taubephilanthropies.org)

Tikvah Fund (1992). 165 East 56th Street, 4th Floor, New York, NY 10022. (212) 796-1672. The Tikvah Fund is a philanthropic foundation and ideas institution committed to supporting the intellectual, religious, and political leaders of the Jewish people and the Jewish State. Tikvah runs and invests in a wide range of initiatives around the world, including educational programs, publications, and fellowships. Tikvah is politically Zionist, economically free-market oriented, culturally traditional, and theologically open-minded. (www.tikvahfund.org)

UpStart (2006) (2017). 1111 Broadway, 3rd Floor, Oakland, CA 94607. (415) 536-5918. The UpStart network, which reflects the merger in 2017 of Bikkurim, Joshua Venture Group, and the US programs of PresenTense Group into UpStart, includes hundreds of organizations bringing fresh approaches to the realms of spirituality, education, community-building, social change, the arts, and Israel engagement. Its mission is to inspire and empower leaders to dream, build, and grow bold initiatives that enhance the vitality of Jewish life, with a vision of Jewish communities as thriving hubs of innovation, creating a more just, vibrant, and inclusive future. (www.upstartlab.org)

The Wexner Foundation (1984). 8000 Walton Parkway, Suite 110, New Albany, OH 43054. (614) 939-6060. The Wexner Foundation's mission is to promote excellence in Jewish professional leadership by providing financial support and leadership educational programs to graduate students and professionals in the field. The Foundation's goal is to help Jewish professionals, volunteers and Israeli public officials strengthen Jewish communities through its Wexner Graduate Fellowship/ Davidson Scholars Program, Wexner Heritage Program, and Wexner Israel Fellowship. (www.wexnerfoundation.org)

12.1.20 Jewish Philanthropic Pass-Through/Umbrella Organizations

America Gives (formerly **American Support for Israel**) (2008). PO Box 3263, Washington, DC 20010. (917) 512-2968. The mission of America Gives is to encourage American support for Israel and its people, and to strengthen the Jewish community in the US by building a bridge between people who want to help Israel—donors—and the people in Israel making a difference every day in the lives and character of the country—the employees and volunteers of Israel's nonprofit organizations and charities. (www.israelgives.org/pages/international)

Amplifier: The Jewish Giving Circle Movement (2014). 120 East 23rd Street, 5th Floor, New York, NY 10010. Amplifier is a global network of giving circles motivated by Jewish values. It is the first concerted effort to network Jewish giving circles, catalyze the creation of new giving circles, educate circle members on best practices in philanthropy, and create a platform to connect NGOs and Jewish giving circles to each other efficiently and effectively. A giving circle is a group of friends, family, or co-workers who come together to give, pooling their charitable donations and deciding together where to allocate their money. (www.amplifiergiving.org)

The Good People Fund (2008). 384 Wyoming Avenue, Millburn, NJ 07041. (973) 761-0580. The Good People Fund, inspired by the Jewish concept of tikkun olam (repairing the world, in Hebrew), responds to significant problems such as poverty, disability, trauma and social isolation, and collects and distributes funds to small, grassroots organizations, both Jewish and non-Jewish, primarily in the US and Israel. It provides financial support, guidance, and mentoring to charitable activities of modest proportions that are undertaken by people acting singly or in small groups. (www.goodpeoplefund.org)

Hands on Tzedakah (HOT) (2002). 2901 Clint Moore Road, #318, Boca Raton, FL 33496. (561) 922-7574. HOT's mission is to reach out to individuals in need by supporting programs that fall below the radar screen of traditional funding. Its major focus is primarily to support "safety-net" or essential, life-sustaining programs, which include projects that combat hunger, poverty, homelessness, and illness, as well as human service type projects that have to do with quality-of-life programs, such as providing health and mental wellness support to victims of terror, the economically disadvantaged, disabled, abused, elderly, ill, etc. (www.handsontzedakah.org)

KAVOD (1993). 8914 Farnam Court, Omaha, NE 68114. (402) 397-1975. KAVOD is an all-volunteer tzedakah collective—a group of individuals who have chosen to pool their tzedakah resources together so that, as a community, they can have a greater impact in their efforts to repair the world. KAVOD creates new programs and funds existing programs that help Jews and non-Jews living in the US, Israel, and around the world to live in dignity and honor. (www.kavod.org)

Natan (2002). 120 East 23rd Street, 5th Floor, New York, NY 10010. (212) 764-9210. Natan is a giving circle in which members pool their charitable contributions and decide together where the pooled funds should go, enabling people to give in a proactive, thoughtful, empowered way—taking a strategic approach to investing in new ideas to tackle the issues that matter most to them, rather than simply responding to fundraising requests. (www.natan.org)

PEF Israel Endowment Funds (PEF) (formerly **Palestine Endowment Funds**) (1922). 630 Third Avenue, 15th Floor, New York, NY 10017. (212) 599-1260. Established by Justice Louis Brandeis, Rabbi Stephen Wise, Robert Szold, and a group of distinguished Americans to enable the direct distribution of funds to selected and approved charitable organizations in Israel, PEF provides a means for individuals, foundations and charitable institutions to recommend grants to approved Israeli charities at no expense to the donor. Areas of support include primary and secondary education; supporting scientific research; promoting greater tolerance and understanding between religious and secular communities and between Arabs and Jews; the special needs of women, children and families in distress; special education and education for the gifted; veterans' programs; drug abuse; promotion of the arts; and relief for the handicapped. Since inception, over $1 billion has been distributed in Israel. (www.pefisrael.org)

To Save a Life (2003). 6162 Golf Villas Drive, Boynton Beach, FL 33437. To Save a Life provides the opportunity to donate directly, efficiently, and personally to help the people of the US and Israel. It works within the world of little miracles, small charities providing various types of humanitarian aid that are below the radar screen but who make real differences in life. (www.tsal.org)

12.1.21 Jewish Overseas Aid Organizations

American Jewish Joint Distribution Committee (JDC) (1914). 220 East 42nd Street, New York, NY 10017. (212) 687-6200. JDC is the world's leading Jewish humanitarian assistance organization, impacting millions of lives in more than 70 countries. JDC's global network of on-the-ground professionals provides critical social-support services and helps build self-sustaining Jewish communities in Latin America, Africa, Asia, the Middle East, Central and Eastern Europe, and throughout the FSU. JDC works to alleviate hunger and hardship, rescue Jews in danger, create lasting connections to Jewish life, and provide immediate relief and long-term development support for victims of natural and man-made disasters. JDC serves the poorest Jews in the world, including isolated elderly, at-risk families and vulnerable children, and Israel's most disadvantaged citizens, including at-risk children and youth, the elderly, immigrants and people with disabilities. (www.jdc.org)

American Jewish World Service (AJWS) (1985). 45 West 36th Street, New York, NY 10018. (212) 792-2900 or (800) 889-7146. Inspired by Judaism's commitment to justice, AJWS works to realize human rights and end poverty in the developing world. It provides nonsectarian, humanitarian assistance, and emergency relief to people in need in Africa, Asia, Latin America, Russia, Ukraine, and the Middle East; works in partnership with local nongovernmental organizations to support and implement self-sustaining grassroots development projects; and serves as a vehicle through which the Jewish community can act as global citizens. (www.ajws.org)

Chevra USA (2001). PO Box 168, Worthington, OH 43085. Chevra (Friendship, in Hebrew) is a humanitarian organization actively involved in many countries. Chevra is the American entity for this international effort. Chevra makes available Russian/Hebrew prayer books, talesim, mezuzot and other religious items to people in the FSU, and operates soup kitchens there. Chevra assists all Jews seeking to immigrate to Israel, helping them with transportation, passports and paperwork. Chevra has established homes in Israel for elderly Holocaust survivors without family to accommodate their immigration to Israel. (www.chevrahumanitarian.org)

Cuba-America Jewish Mission (CAJM) (1999). 6601 Bradley Boulevard, Bethesda, MD 20817. The CAJM is dedicated to assisting with the revitalization and sustenance of Jewish life in Cuba and working to improve the physical and spiritual well-being of the Jews of Cuba and of new Cuban immigrants to Israel. (www.cajm.org)

Friends of Ethiopian Jews (FEJ) (1998). PO Box 960059, Boston, MA 02196. (202) 262-5390. FEJ was founded by members of the American Association for Ethiopian Jews and other veteran activists dedicated to assisting the Ethiopian Jewish community. FEJ supports grassroots Ethiopian-Israeli organizations working to create full integration and successful absorption in Israel for the Ethiopian Jewish community. Programs supported by FEJ address the areas of employment; housing; education; social life; computer training; assistance for at-risk youth and their families; and access to free legal services. (www.friendsofethiopianjews.org)

Gabriel Project Mumbai (GPM) (2012). PO Box 5025, Bergenfield, NJ 07621. (917) 725-3077. GPM is a Jewish volunteer-based initiative caring for vulnerable children living in India by providing hunger relief, literacy support, health and empowerment to children living in the Mumbai slums. This program aims to change the trajectory of the children's lives while offering young Jewish adults a meaningful and life-transforming experience. (www.gabrielprojectmumbai.org)

Global Jewish Assistance and Relief Network (GJARN) (1992). 511 Avenue of the Americas, Suite 18, New York, NY 10011. (212) 868-3636. GJARN was originally created to provide emergency relief to the collapsed Jewish communities of the FSU. While it continues to provide vital services there, the bulk of its programs today are in providing for the material welfare of needy Jews in Israel, primarily "the working poor" and Holocaust survivors, through The Food Card program. GJARN's programs provide immediate relief with food, clothing, and pharmaceuticals; improve primary medical care and health conditions; and promote the development of civil society. GJARN is also active in rebuilding of Jewish life in Central Africa, Asia, and Europe, where it runs numerous nonsectarian program. (www.globaljewish.org)

HIAS (formerly **Hebrew Immigrant Aid Society**) (1881). 1300 Spring Street, Suite 500, Silver Spring, MD 20910. (301) 844-7300. HIAS is the oldest international migration and refugee resettlement agency in the US, dedicated to assisting persecuted and oppressed people worldwide and delivering them to countries of safe haven. In recent years, as the population of Jewish refugees has diminished, it has directed its expertise to assist refugees and immigrants of all backgrounds. Since its founding, HIAS has assisted more than 4,500,000 people worldwide. (www.hias.org)

Innovation: Africa (formerly **Jewish Heart for Africa**) (2008). 520 8th Avenue, 15th Floor, New York, NY 10018. (646) 472-5380. Innovation: Africa brings Israeli innovation to African villages. Its mission is to bring Israeli technology and expertise to communities that need it. Since its inception, Innovation: Africa has provided light, clean water, food and proper medical care to more than 450,000 people in Ethiopia, Tanzania, Malawi, and Uganda. (www.innoafrica.org)

Jewish Coalition for Disaster Relief (JCDR) (2010). c/o American Jewish Joint Distribution Committee, 220 East 42nd Street, New York, NY 10017. JCDR brings together the experience, expertise, and resources of national, primarily North American, Jewish organizations that seek to assist victims of natural or man-made disasters outside of North America on a nonsectarian basis. Coordinated by the American Jewish Joint Distribution Committee, JCDR maximizes the use of financial resources, coordinates the activities of its member agencies, educates the members' constituencies and the general public about current disaster situations and the Jewish response, and demonstrates the long tradition of Jewish humanitarianism. (www.jcdr.org)

Jewish Cuba Connection (2000). 4 Lighthouse Street, #12, Marina Del Rey, CA 90292. (310) 823-4066. Jewish Cuba Connection helps the Jewish communities of Cuba provide their members with medicine, food and clothing, Jewish educational materials, Sabbath meals, etc. Jewish Cuba Connection has contributed to establishing in Cuba a thriving Sunday School, founding a Jewish senior center and the first Cuban Holocaust Memorial and Study Center, and making physical improvements to synagogues. In addition, it has helped Cuban Jews create a support network for those in need—Jews and non-Jews alike. (www.jewishcubaconnection. hfriman.com/our-mission)

Jewish Healthcare International (JHI) (1999). 1440 Spring Street NW, Atlanta, GA 30309. (678) 222-3722. JHI sends teams of volunteer American and Israeli healthcare professionals on medical missions to communities-in-need in Eastern Europe, the FSU, and other countries with a goal toward developing and enhancing the medical infrastructure in those communities. It provides long-term solutions through educational programs for medical professionals, donations of medications and equipment (with training), and establishment of relationships with local medical institutions that facilitate better access to treatment for patients in the Jewish community. JHI also provides a significant Israel/Diaspora experience whereby healthcare professionals from Israel, the US, and the assisted communities develop long-lasting, mutually beneficial professional and personal relationships. (www. jewishhealthcareinternational.org)

Jewish World Watch (JWW) (2004). 5551 Balboa Boulevard, Encino, CA 91316. (818) 501-1836. Founded as the Jewish response to the genocide in Darfur, JWW is a leading organization in the fight against genocide and mass atrocities, engaging individuals and communities to take local actions that produce powerful global results. It is a global coalition that includes schools, churches, individuals, communities and partner organizations. To date JWW has raised millions of dollars for relief and development projects that impact tens of thousands of people in Sudan and Congo. (www.jww.org)

Kulanu (formerly **Amishav USA**) (1994). 165 West End Avenue, 3R, New York, NY 10023. (212) 877-8082. Kulanu (All of Us, in Hebrew) supports isolated and emerging Jewish communities around the world, many of whom have long been disconnected from the worldwide Jewish community and are not yet recognized by all of world Jewry. Kulanu engages with these dispersed groups and individuals through networking and support, raising awareness and support for emerging communities through education, research, and publications about their histories and traditions. Kulanu does not proselytize. Kulanu helps supply educational materials, scholarships, Jewish ritual objects and prayer books, teachers, and rabbis. (www.kulanu.org)

Migdal International Society (2007). 146 Beach 120th Street, Belle Harbor, NY 11694. (718) 474-2232. Migdal International Society's mission is to provide financial and infrastructural support to a network of existing and developing social and cultural Jewish institutions, particularly in vulnerable communities where life for Jews is made difficult. Yiddishkeit and social justice are at the heart of all of its unique existing and developing programs. Migdal International Society currently supports Jewish community programs in Odessa, Ukraine, including a Jewish museum, early childhood development center, the Jewish theater, Jewish magazine, center for Jewish children and families at risk, library and Jewish community center. (No website)

North American Conference on Ethiopian Jewry (NACOEJ) (1982). 255 West 36th Street, Suite 701, New York, NY 10018. (212) 233-5200. NACOEJ is a grassroots organization founded to help Ethiopian Jews survive in Ethiopia, assist them in reaching Israel, aid in their absorption into Israeli society, and preserve their unique and ancient culture. During the 1980's, NACOEJ sent missions to Jewish villages, bringing in doctors, medicine, clothing, school supplies, money and hope. During the 1980's and 1990's, NACOEJ played a key role in the rescue of Ethiopian Jews from Africa to Israel and subsequently provided food, education, employment and religious facilities to Ethiopian Jews waiting to make aliyah. Currently, NACOEJ assists Ethiopian Jews in Israel by providing them with educational and financial support and cultural programming. (www.nacoej.org)

ORT America (1922) (2007). 75 Maiden Lane, 10th Floor, New York, NY 10038. (212) 505-7700 or (800) 519-2678. ORT America, created through a merger of American ORT and Women's American ORT, is the leading fundraising organization for World ORT, whose global educational network, schools, colleges, and international programs propel more than 300,000 students in many countries around the world to develop careers and lead fulfilling, independent lives. ORT's schools and programs reach under-served students by bridging the gap between aptitude and opportunity, and work to expand knowledge, build autonomy, and strengthen Jewish identity. ORT America Next Generation is a national network of young professionals dedicated to improving communities and making the world a better place through the support of ORT educational initiatives. (www.ortamerica.org)

Scholarship Fund for Ethiopian Jews (SFEJ) (1999). 19202 Black Mangrove Court, Palm Beach, FL 33498. (561) 433-1585. SFEJ is dedicated to the development of a pool of talented, well-educated and highly motivated Ethiopian Israelis who will ultimately enable the community to become fully integrated into Israeli society. It seeks to eliminate prejudice by helping to create a core of Israeli professionals who will serve as role-models. SFEJ raises funds for the promotion of post-secondary education among Ethiopian Israelis. In recent years, its efforts have been focused on the rehabilitation of thousands of at-risk youth in the Ethiopian-Israeli community.   (www.facebook.com/pages/Scholarship-Fund-for-Ethiopian-Jews/980684915286472)

Struggle to Save Ethiopian Jewry (SSEJ) (2000). 459 Columbus Avenue, Suite 316, New York, NY 10024. (646) 450-7735. SSEJ assists desperately poor Jews from Ethiopia seeking to make aliyah to Israel. SSEJ provides funds to run a series of programs in Ethiopia, including: food distributions, employment programs, medical assessments, communal activities and educational missions. Additionally, in Israel, SSEJ runs religious and educational programs during Shabbat and holidays in absorption centers. (www.ssej.org)

12.1.22   *Sephardic Organizations*

American Sephardi Federation (ASF) (1973). Center for Jewish History, 15 West 16th Street, New York, NY 10011. (212) 548-4486. The ASF is the central voice of the American Sephardic community. Its mission is to promote and preserve the spiritual, historical, cultural and social traditions of all Sephardic communities as an integral part of Jewish heritage. The ASF seeks to strengthen and unify the community through education, communication, advocacy and leadership development. (www.americansephardi.org)

Foundation for the Advancement of Sephardic Studies and Culture (FASSAC) (1969). 34 West 15th Street, 3rd Floor, New York, NY 10011. The FASSAC is dedicated to preserving and promoting the complex and centuries-old culture of the Sephardic communities of Turkey, Greece, the Balkans, Europe and the US. Its mission is to encourage the appreciation and understanding of the Sephardic heritage, language and experience in an effort to preserve and document it for future generations. (www.sephardicstudies.org)

Sephardic Community Alliance (2010). 1061 Ocean Parkway, Brooklyn, NY 11230. The Sephardic Community Alliance was established to reinforce and preserve the traditional, ancestral Sephardic way of life based on values that include commitment to halakha, growth through education, respect and tolerance, belief in higher secular education, interaction with society, learning and earning, and support for Israel. The Alliance is committed to serve as a platform for lay leaders to work in unison with community rabbis, institutions, and organizations in promoting the perpetuation of these values. (www.scaupdates.org)

Sephardic Educational Center (SEC) (1980). 6505 Wilshire Boulevard, Suite 320, Los Angeles, CA 90048. (323) 272-4574. As the world's largest international Sephardic organization, the SEC strives to be ambassadors and advocates for Sephardim worldwide and seeks to fulfill the educational and cultural needs of the more than one million Sephardim living in the Diaspora, emphasizing Sephardic history, culture and philosophy. The SEC is dedicated to ensuring Jewish identity and continuity by transmitting the rich Sephardic legacy to Diaspora Jews, especially the youth. (www.secjerusalem.org)

Sephardic Heritage Foundation (1980). 1969 East 1st Street, Brooklyn, NY 11223. (347) 268-0892. Sephardic Heritage Foundation is focused on facilitating the religious and cultural observance of the Jewish Syrian-Sephardic community. By distributing publications, Sephardic Heritage Foundation strives to perpetuate the venerated prayer, sacred traditions and valued customs of one of the oldest uninterrupted Jewish communities of the world, the community of Aram Soba (Aleppo, Syria). (www.sephardicheritage.com)

Sephardic Jewish Brotherhood of America (formerly **Salonician Brotherhood of America**) (1916). 67-67 108th Street, Forest Hills, NY 11375. (718) 685-0080. The Sephardic Jewish Brotherhood of America is a benevolent fraternal organization that was created to promote the industrial, social, educational, and religious welfare of its members. Originally founded as a society to help Sephardic immigrants from Salonica become accustomed to life in the US and to have a place of Sephardic worship and community, and as a volunteer mutual aid and burial society, today the Brotherhood serves nearly 1000 families from across the US and continues to support the Sephardic community in the spirit laid out by its founders. In addition to offering death and monument benefits, scholarships, and funds for the needy, the Brotherhood has expanded its programs to support the future generations of its community and reinvent what it means to be Sephardic in the 21st century. (www.sephardicbrotherhood.com)

12.1.23 Jewish Russian/FSU Organizations

Action for Post-Soviet Jewry (formerly **Action**) (1975). 24 Crescent Street, Suite 306, Waltham, MA 02453. (781) 893-2331. Action for Post-Soviet Jewry was created to help Jews living in the Soviet Union immigrate to the US and Israel. Today, it is dedicated to rebuilding the Jewish community and supporting the revival of Jewish culture in Eastern Europe following the devastations of World War II and religious discouragement under communist rule, and to providing general humanitarian aid to those in need. (www.actionpsj.org)

Alliance of Bukharian Americans (ABA) (2016). 99-47 62 Road, Floor 2, Queens, NY 11374. (347) 229-9396. The mission of the ABA is to unify the Bukharian American community while providing the highest level of representation for its constituents with Federal, state, and local government elected officials. Its objectives are to obtain equitable government funding for nonpublic (Jewish) schools, secure grant funding for afterschool programs, obtain funding for Bukharian Jewish community centers and educational institutions, and ensure that the welfare and security of Israel is not compromised. (www.welcometoaba.org)

Am Echad (2000). 1277 Bartonshire Way, Potomac, MD 20854. (301) 309-8755. Am Echad provides financial and moral support to elderly and disabled Jews in the FSU (specifically St. Petersburg) by helping the loneliest, the most desperate, those with no relatives to help them, and those who are not reached by the efforts of the mainstream Jewish organizations. (www.amechad.net)

American Fund for Lithuanian-Latvian Jews (1993). 8835 Berkley Ridge, Atlanta, GA 30350. The American Fund for Lithuanian-Latvian Jews provides humanitarian aid to Jews in Lithuania and Latvia. It provides funds for programs that support the Jewish senior café and senior meals program in Vilnius, Jewish senior meals program in Siauliai, Jewish community in Panevezys, Jewish hospital in Riga, and Jewish Museum in Vilnius. (www.affllj.peggyspage.org)

Chamah (1953). 420 Lexington Avenue, #300, New York, NY 10170. (212) 943-9690. Chamah, which was founded underground in the FSU and operates in the US, Israel, and Russia, conducts a broad range of humanitarian, social, and educational programs in Israel, Russia, and the US. Its activities include soup kitchens, "Meals on Wheels" programs, home care for the elderly, senior citizen centers, community centers, institutions for underprivileged children, day care centers, youth clubs, medical assistance, education for the young, seminars, and Judaic classes for adults. (www.chamah.org)

Congress of Bukharian Jews of the USA and Canada (also known as **Bukharian Jewish Congress**) (1998). 106-16 70th Avenue, Forest Hills, NY 11375. (718) 520-1111. The Bukharian Jewish Congress was formed to assist the integration of Bukharian Jewish immigrants (who originate in Central Asia and regions of the FSU) into American society and Jewish life, while working to preserve Bukharian traditions, culture, and heritage and enhance the Bukharian Jewish identity, as well as to advocate for Israel and issues of antisemitism. The Congress comprises Jewish centers and synagogues, newspapers and magazines, theaters and yeshivas, funeral homes, foundations, music and dance groups, and grass-root organizations. (www.bukharianjewishcongress.org)

Ezra USA (2002). 311 Sea Breeze Avenue, Brooklyn, NY 11224. (718) 368-9200. Ezra USA, an affiliate of Ezra World, is an international, apolitical youth movement that works with Russian-speaking Jewish students and young adults in North America. Its goals are fighting assimilation; strengthening Jewish self-identification; leadership development in the Jewish community; development of Jewish education; support for the State of Israel; and fostering solidarity and unity among all branches of the Jewish people. Ezra USA is a key provider of birthright trips and post-birthright programming for Russian-speaking Jews, and its diverse programs create joyful, rich, and fun Jewish experiences, including Poland-Israel leadership seminars, Jewish-themed international travel to various countries, Shabbat dinners, and charity events promoting tzedakah as a key Jewish value. (www.ny.ezraus.org)

Federation of Jewish Communities of the CIS (FJC) (1998) 445 Park Avenue, 9th Floor, New York, NY 10022. (212) 262-3688. The FJC was established to revive the Jewish communities of the FSU and is recognized as an umbrella organization that represents and administers a variety of established funds and institutions that operate in the region. The FJC provides humanitarian aid and Jewish education, organizes cultural events and religious services, and helps develop Jewish communities and rebuild Jewish institutions. (www.fjc-fsu.org)

Friends of Kishinev Jewry (1995). 635 Empire Boulevard, Brooklyn, NY 11213. (718) 756-0458. Friends of Kishinev Jewry supports the rebuilding and restoration of the Jewish community in Kishinev in the FSU. It provides for the material needs of the community and preserves the culture, heritage, and spiritual needs for its remaining Jews, offering education, humanitarian, and Jewish community and synagogue services. (www.fokj.org)

Genesis Philanthropy Group (GPG) (2007). 499 Seventh Avenue, 15th Floor, New York, NY 10018. GPG's mission is to develop and enhance a sense of Jewish identity among Russian-speaking Jews worldwide, with emphasis on the FSU, North America, and Israel. It supports and launches projects, programming, and institutions that are focused on ensuring that Jewish culture, heritage, and values are preserved in Russian-speaking Jewish communities across the globe. In North America, GPG's work focuses on expanding and creating programs that foster Jewish identity among the Russian Jewish population of the US and Canada. (www.gpg.org)

National Coalition Supporting Eurasian Jewry (NCSEJ) (formerly **National Conference on Soviet Jewry** and **American Jewish Conference on Soviet Jewry**) (1964) (1964) (1971) (2014). 1120 20th Street, NW, Suite 300N, Washington, DC 20036. (202) 898-2500. NCSEJ is the organized American Jewish community's voice for Jews and Jewish concerns in Eastern Europe and Eurasia. Its mission is to empower and ensure the security of Jews in the 15 independent states of the FSU and Eastern Europe; foster cooperation among the US government, US Jewish organizations, and the Jewish communities and governments of the region; represent the organized US Jewish community; collaborate with other organizations for the provision of humanitarian aid, social services, and educational/communal development assistance throughout the region; and facilitate international Jewish organizations' access to Jewish communities. NCSEJ works closely with key officials, Jewish organizations, and activists to monitor antisemitism in the region as well as government respect for religious freedom, cultural rights, and the right to emigrate freely. (www.ncsej.org)

Project Kesher (1989). 729 Seventh Avenue, 9th Floor, New York, NY 10019. (212) 600-0970. Project Kesher transforms lives through Jewish identity building and social activism in the FSU and among the Russian-speaking population in Israel by empowering women to become agents of social change in the region. It focuses on leadership training, advancing the status of women and girls, building a more tolerant society, Jewish identity and renewal, and economic self-sufficiency. From teenage youth groups, to programs on college campuses, to working with young professionals, its programs energize women through a unique combination of Jewish content and social activism. (www.projectkesher.org)

RAJE–Russian American Jewish Experience (2006). 2915 Ocean Parkway, Brooklyn, NY 11235. (347) 702-5427 or (800) 530-4010. RAJE's mission is to create a vibrant Jewish future for FSU Jews in North America by inspiring young Jews to establish Jewish households, be involved in the Jewish community, to fulfill their spiritual needs through the study and practice of Judaism, and to develop a strong connection with the State of Israel. Its goal is to provide FSU millennials with the positive Jewish experiences they need to help them find meaning in their Jewish heritage and to fall in love with the experience of everything Jewish. The RAJE Fellowship provides talented young people with a unique opportunity to explore their Jewish identity and develop their own unique leadership potential, and RAJE Fellowship alumni are provided with support in their integration into the local framework of Jewish communal organizations. (www.rajeusa.com)

Union of Councils for Jews in the Former Soviet Union (UCSJ) (formerly **Union of Councils for Soviet Jews**) (1970). 2200 Pennsylvania Avenue, NW, East Tower, 4th Floor, Washington, DC 20037. (202) 567-7572. UCSJ originally started as the voice of the refuseniks, working for free emigration from the FSU, democracy, and human rights, and against antisemitism, and it continues to do so today. It is currently working with pro-democracy human rights and religious freedom groups in Russia, Belarus, Ukraine, Moldova, and Kazakhstan. (www.ucsj.org)

12.1.24 Other Jewish National Origin Organizations

30 YEARS AFTER (2007). 2029 Century Park East, Suite 900, Los Angeles, CA 90067. The mission of 30 YEARS AFTER is to promote the participation and leadership of Iranian-American Jews in American political, civic, and Jewish life. The organization has become the Iranian-American community's leading and most recognized civic organization by educating, engaging, and empowering Iranian-American Jews in political affairs. (www.30yearsafter.com)

American Friends of the Jewish Museum of Greece (AFJMG) (1982). PO Box 2010, New York, NY 10185. AFJMG was founded in order to promote and provide much-needed financial support to the Jewish Museum of Greece which was founded in 1977 and is today a thriving center of education and a testament to the history of the Jews of Greece. It is the oldest association affiliated with the Jewish Museum of Greece to bring together Sephardic and Romaniot Jews in North America. (No website)

Association of Friends of Greek Jewry (1997). One Hanson Place, Huntington, NY 11743. (516) 456-9336. The Association of Friends of Greek Jewry is one of the only organizations in the US dedicated exclusively to Greek Jewry. Its primary goal is to continue to support the history and heritage of the Jewish communities of Greece through education, restoration, and preservation initiatives both in the US and around the globe. The Association serves as a resource for both Jews and non-Jews alike to learn about the unique Romaniote Jewish tradition and ensure that those who perished in the Holocaust in Greece will never be forgotten. It raises funds for the restoration of Jewish sites in Greece and works to strengthen Greek Jewish roots in the Diaspora. (www.kkjsm.org/partner-organizations)

Association of Jewish Yemenites in the United States (1991). PO Box 300992, Brooklyn, NY 11230. The Association of Jewish Yemenites in the United States seeks to preserve the Jewish Yemenite tradition; transfer the pursuit of Jewish Yemenite culture to future generations; and expose the rest of the community to the beauty and wisdom of the Jewish Yemenite heritage. (www.jewishyemenites.com)

Beta Israel of North America Cultural Foundation (also known as **BINA Cultural Foundation**) (BINA) (2003). 206 Edgecombe Avenue, Suite 102, New York, NY 10030. BINA is dedicated to fostering the continuity of the Ethiopian Jewish cultural heritage; empowering Ethiopian Jews within the American Jewish community; providing assistance to Ethiopian Jews who come to the US; working for greater understanding and inclusiveness among ethnic groups within the Jewish community; and serving as a bridge between the Jewish, Ethiopian, and African-American communities. BINA's Annual Sheba Film Festival, the only film festival of its kind in the US, introduces the general public to films, artistic exhibitions, and panel discussions about the history, culture, and life experiences of Ethiopian Jews. (www.binacf.org)

Centro Primo Levi (CPL) (2000). 15 West 16th Street, New York, NY 10011. (917) 606-8202. CPL was inspired by the humanistic legacy of writer and chemist Primo Levi, who survived Auschwitz and contributed significantly to the post-World War II debate on the role of memory in modern societies. Partnering with universities and research organizations in Italy, Israel, and the US, CPL fosters and supports those interested in Primo Levi's work and the Italian Jewish past as well as those interested in current perspectives and conversations about the Italian Jewish community today. (www.primolevicenter.org)

Chassida Shmella: Ethiopian Jewish Community of North America (2004). 25 Broadway, Suite 1700, New York, NY 10004. (212) 284-6532. Chassida Shmella is the organization of the Ethiopian Jewish Community of North America, whose mission is to preserve the customs and traditions of the Ethiopian Jewish population and to educate Americans, Israelis, and Ethiopian-Israelis about these customs. Its name, which means Stork in Hebrew (Chassida) and Stork in Amharic (Shmella), is derived from the ancient wish of Ethiopian Jews to return to their beloved Jerusalem, just as it is believed the storks did as they migrated from Jerusalem to Ethiopia. Chassida Shmella's goals include helping the Ethiopian Jewish community in North America to fully integrate into the larger Jewish community while preserving its uniqueness; helping Ethiopian Jews maintain their ties to Israel; and advocating for the Ethiopian Jewish community in Israel and North America. (www.chasmell. webs.com)

Historical Society of Jews from Egypt (HSJE) (1996). PO Box 230445, Brooklyn, NY 11223. HSJE undertakes the responsibility of preserving and maintaining the culture and history of Jews from Egypt. Its goals are to preserve Jewish historical sites and monuments in Egypt; to study and document the history of Jews from Egypt, with emphasis on contemporary history; to reunite families through genealogical research; to assist members through social and welfare organizations; and to direct the efforts and support students undertaking similar work, sponsor lectures, publications, films, and discussion groups. HSJE is attempting to convince the Egyptian government to allow the transfer of the Jewish community's records and religious artifacts to the US. (www.hsje.org)

Indian Jewish Congregation of USA (IJC) (2005). 98-41 64th Road, #1G, Rego Park, NY 11374. The IJC was started primarily to provide support to the Beth El Synagogue in Panvel, India, which suffered significant damage in 2005. Today, IJC conducts religious services for the Indian Jewish community; teaches the culture and tradition of the Jews of India to the second and third generation Indian Jews; conducts religious classes for the community; makes the Indian Jewish community's presence known in the larger Jewish community; ensures that the Indian Jewish culture traditions and mode of religious service are continued; and supports Jews in India by providing scholarships, education, healthcare, and support for various synagogues in India. (www.jewsofindia.org)

Iranian American Jewish Federation (IAJF) (1980). 1317 North Crescent Heights Boulevard, West Hollywood, CA 90046. (323) 654-4700. The IAJF was formed as an umbrella organization whose main objective is defending and protecting the interests and welfare of Jews throughout the world—with special emphasis on Iranian Jews—as well as streamlining the philanthropic activities of its member organizations. It works with other organizations in connection with the issues facing Jews from Iran who apply to the US for refugee status, including assistance with the preparation of such applications and assistance to new community members to settle in the US. The IAJF has secured representation of the Iranian-American Jewish community in the larger American Jewish organizations and has also established close contact with many public officials who have been made aware of the issues faced by the Iranian-American Jewish community. (www.iajf.org)

Israeli-American Council (IAC) (formerly **Israeli Leadership Council** and **Israeli Leadership Club**) (2007). 5900 Canoga Avenue, Suite 390, Woodland Hills, CA 91367. (818) 836-6700. The mission of the IAC, the largest Israeli-American organization in the US, is to build an active and giving Israeli-American community throughout the US in order to strengthen the State of Israel and the next generation, and to provide a bridge to the Jewish-American community. The IAC's goals are to connect the next generation to the community, their Jewish identity, the Hebrew language, and the State of Israel; foster active support of initiatives that further Israel's welfare, security, education, and its relations with the US; serve as a professional and financial resource for initiatives that support the development of an active and unified Israeli-American community with strong connections to Israel; and strengthen the relationships between the Israeli-American community and the Israeli community in Israel. The IAC strives to achieve these goals through programs and events for all ages, as well as by empowering and sponsoring a wide array of nonprofit organizations within the Israeli-American community. (www. israeliamerican.org)

JIMENA: Jews Indigenous to the Middle East and North Africa (2001). 450 Fulton Street, Suite 207, San Francisco, CA 94102. (415) 626-5062. JIMENA is dedicated to educating and advocating on behalf of the 850,000 Jewish refugees from the Middle East and North Africa. Founded in the aftermath of the 2001 World Trade Center terror attacks by a group of former Jewish refugees from the region, JIMENA's co-founders sought to empower students and adult audiences with a deeper, personal understanding of the conflicts and cultural nuances in the region. JIMENA has launched numerous campaigns and projects to ensure that the accurate history of Mizrahi and Sephardic Jews is incorporated into mainstream Jewish and Middle Eastern narratives in order to create balance in attitudes, narratives, and discourse about Middle Eastern refugees and the modern Jewish experience. (www. jimena.org)

North American Council for the Legacy of Polish Jews (2006). 733 Park Avenue, New York, NY 10021. (212) 226-2900. The North American Council for the Legacy of Polish Jews supports the mission of the POLIN Museum of the History of Polish Jews by raising crucial funds for its permanent exhibition and educational programs. The Museum, which stands as a celebration of the Jewish existence in Poland, documents 1000 years of the history of Polish Jews, and across from the Museum stands the memorial to the heroes of the Warsaw Ghetto uprising. The Council supports initiatives that preserve and promote the legacy of Polish Jews, including. the Association of the Jewish Historical Institute of Poland and The Emanuel Ringelblum Jewish Historical Institute. (No website)

Society for the History of Czechoslovak Jews (formerly **Society for the History of Jews in the Czechoslovak Republic**) (1961). Ansonia Station, PO Box 230255, New York, NY 10023. The Society for the History of Czechoslovak Jews studies the history of Czechoslovak Jews; collects material and disseminates information through the publication of books and pamphlets; and conducts an annual memorial service for Czech Holocaust victims. In recent years the focus of the Society has been annual Holocaust commemorations as well as smaller initiatives pertaining to Jewish heritage in the Czech and Slovak republics, including a series of lectures on topics related to the history and culture of Jews in the two countries. (www.shcsj.org)

Yemenite Jewish Federation of America (YJFA) (1994). 1115 51st Street, Brooklyn, NY 11219. YJFA is dedicated to advancing the collective interests of the Yemenite Jewish community in America and worldwide through the establishment of a representative body. It was instrumental in liberating about 1500 Yemeni Jews who immigrated to the US and Israel. YJFA aims to provide cultural enrichment and financial support to Jews of Yemenite heritage living in Israel and the US. It runs assistance programs to help local Yemeni families suffering economic hardship with social services and basic needs; awards higher education scholarships, career guidance, and leadership training to Israeli-Yemeni students from low income families; and helps preserve Yemeni culture throughout the world through community-wide lectures, cultural events, and social activities. (No website)

12.1.25   Yiddish Organizations

Congress for Jewish Culture (1948). PO Box 1590, New York, NY 10159. (212) 505-8040. The Congress for Jewish Culture Our is a home and resource for some of the finest writers, poets, translators, composers, and performers working in the field of Yiddish today. It cultivates the language in all of its manifestations: spoken, printed, sung, or acted. It publishes Yiddish and English books; present concerts, plays and Purim-shpiln; runs classes and literary reading circles; fields Yiddish-related questions; guides people in finding materials for reading circles or research, provides synagogues and community centers with Yiddish programming, and can even translate the writing on the back of photographs (www.congressforjewishculture.org)

CYCO: Central Yiddish Culture Organization (1938). 51-02 21st Street, 7th Floor A-2, Long Island City, NY 11101. (718) 392-0002. CYCO, the world's oldest Yiddish bookstore, was founded by leading Yiddish authors and cultural activists as a nonpartisan, nonprofit Yiddish cultural organization. CYCO developed into the leading publisher of Yiddish books, eventually becoming the publishing wing of the Congress for Jewish Culture. Its mission is to disseminate Yiddish literature and culture of the past 100 years into the 21st century. It promotes, publishes, and distributes Yiddish books, music books, CDs, tapes, and albums. (www.cycobooks.org)

Friends of the Vilnius Yiddish Institute (2002). 2425 Colorado Avenue, Santa Monica, CA 90404. The mission of the Friends of the Vilnius Yiddish Institute is to provide financial and intellectual support for the educational, cultural, and research programs and activities of the Vilnius Yiddish Institute in order to help revive the presence of Jewish secular cultures in Eastern Europe, through the teaching of the Yiddish language and the publication of literary and social science works in Yiddish and other languages, and conduct research relevant to Eastern European Jewish and non-Jewish populations. (www.judaicvilnius.com)

League for Yiddish (also known as **Yiddish League**) (1979). 64 Fulton Street, Suite 1101, New York, NY 10038. (212) 889-0380. The League for Yiddish encourages the development and use of Yiddish as a living language and promotes its modernization and standardization. The League for Yiddish is one of the few organizations in today's Yiddish cultural and linguistic world that conducts its activities almost entirely in Yiddish. It runs cultural and educational events; publishes Yiddish textbooks and English-Yiddish dictionaries; and publishes the all-Yiddish magazine, *Afn Shvel.* (www.leagueforyiddish.org)

National Yiddish Theatre Folksbiene (formerly **Folksbiene**, the "People's Stage," in Yiddish) (NYTF) (1915). Edmond J. Safra Plaza, 36 Battery Place, New York, NY 10280. (212) 213-2120. NYTF is the longest continuously producing Yiddish theatre company in the world. Its mission is to celebrate the Jewish experience through the performing arts and to transmit a rich cultural legacy in exciting new ways that bridge social and cultural divides. NYTF presents plays, musicals, concerts, lectures, interactive educational workshops, and community-building activities in English and Yiddish, with English and Russian supertitles accompanying performances, and uses the arts as a vehicle to educate youth and adults in their Jewish heritage. (www.nytf.org)

The Yiddish Book Center (formerly **National Yiddish Book Center**) (1980). 1021 West Street, Amherst, MA 01002. (413) 256-4900. The Yiddish Book Center works to recover, celebrate, and regenerate Yiddish and modern Jewish literature and culture, and to present innovative educational programs that broaden understanding of modern Jewish identity. Responsible for saving a million Yiddish books, its current priority is advancing knowledge of the content and literary and cultural progeny of the books that have been saved. The Yiddish Book Center offers fellowships and courses for high school students, college students, teachers, and adult learners; translates Yiddish literature into English; and records oral histories and contemporary stories. It publishes an English-language magazine, *Pakn Treger,* with news from the Center and features on Yiddish and Jewish literature and culture. (www.yiddishbookcenter.org)

Yugntruf – Youth for Yiddish (1964). PO Box 596, New York, NY 10276. (212) 796-5782. Yugntruf ("Call to Youth," in Yiddish) sponsors an annual week-long all-Yiddish retreat. (www.yugntruf.org)

12.1.26   Jewish LGBTQ Organizations

A Wider Bridge (2010). 25 Broadway, Suite 1700, New York, NY 10004. (866) 288-5774. A Wider Bridge is the North American LGBTQ organization building support for Israel and its LGBTQ community. It is building a movement of pro-Israel LGBTQ people and allies, with strong interest in and commitment to supporting Israel and its LGBTQ community. A Wider Bridge builds personal rather than political relationships with Israel and LGBTQ Israelis, providing leaders, organizations and communities, both in Israel and North America, with opportunities for engagement, advocacy, and philanthropy, thereby advancing equality in and for Israel. (www.awiderbridge.org)

Eshel (formerly **Nehirim**) (2010). c/o Makom Hadash, 125 Maiden Lane, Suite 8B, New York, NY 10038. (724) 374-3501. Eshel's mission is to create community and acceptance for LGBTQ Jews and their families in Orthodox communities. Eshel trains its members and allies to speak out and act as advocates for LGBTQ Orthodox people and their families; creates bridges into Orthodox communities to foster understanding and support; and helps LGBTQ Orthodox people pursue meaningful lives that encompass seemingly disparate identities while also fulfilling Jewish values around family, education, culture, and spirituality. (www.eshelonline.org)

JQ International (formerly **Queer as Jews**) (2002) (2004). 801 Larrabee Street, Suite 10, West Hollywood, CA 90069. (323) 417-2627. JQ International is a LGBTQ Jewish and ally community whose mission is to advance greater inclusion of LGBTQ Jews and straight allies via identity-building programs and services that embody Jewish values. It provides programs and services that foster a healthy fusion of LGBTQ and Jewish Identity; offers LGBTQ Jews, their friends, families, and loved ones the opportunity to reconnect via specialized programming with a strong sense of self; and establishes pride in a LGBTQ Jewish identity by fostering and strengthening leadership, activism, and social action. (www.jqinternational.org)

Keshet (1996) (2002). 284 Armory Street, J, MA 02130. (617) 524-9227. Keshet works for the full equality and inclusion of LGBTQ Jews in Jewish life. Led and supported by LGBTQ Jews and straight allies, it cultivates the spirit and practice of inclusion in all parts of the Jewish community—synagogues, Hebrew schools, day schools, youth groups, summer camps, social service organizations, and other communal agencies. Through training, community organizing, and resource development, Keshet partners with clergy, educators, and volunteers to equip them with the tools and knowledge they need to be effective agents of change. (www.keshetonline.org)

National Union of Jewish LGBT Students (NUJLS) (1997). 4400 Massachusetts Avenue, NW, Washington, DC 20016. NUJLS aims to bring together Jewish LGBTQ and allied students from different communities around the country to create new friendships and celebrate LGBTQ and Jewish identity. Its mission is to empower Jewish LGBTQ+ students to feel proud of and affirmed in all their identities. Its flagship program is an annual gathering of Jewish LGBTQ students from around the US and Canada for a Shabbat weekend conference, featuring speakers, text study, and workshops on topics such as Judaism and queerness, spirituality, activism, relationships, ethics, coming out, politics, and culture. NUJLS provides an opportunity for student leaders from campuses across North America to build community, network, become re-engaged in Jewish life, and practice Jewish forms of spirituality with a queer context. (www.facebook.com/nujls)

The World Congress: Keshet Ga'avah (formerly **World Congress of Gay and Lesbian Jewish Organizations** and **World Congress of Gay, Lesbian, Bisexual, and Transgender Jews**) (1980). 911 First Street, Alexandria, VA 22314. (703) 298-9925. The World Congress: Keshet Ga'avah aims to be a networking resource for lesbian, gay, bisexual, transgender, queer, intersex, asexual, and other Jews of diverse sexual orientations and gender identities (LGBTQIA+ Jews) from around the world to connect, engage, and support on local, national, continental, and global levels. It envisions a world in which LGBTQIA+ Jews worldwide can enjoy free and fulfilling lives and strives to support local groups and to foster a sense of community among diverse individuals and organizations. The Hebrew subtitle Keshet

Ga'avah (Rainbow of Pride) emphasizes the importance of Hebrew and of Israel to The World Congress. (www.glbtjews.org)

12.1.27   Jewish Cultural Organizations

Alliance for Jewish Theatre (AJT) (formerly **Association for Jewish Theatre, Council of Jewish Theatres,** and **Jewish Theatre Association**) (1979). AJT is made up of theatre-artists, theatres, and other people connected to theatre to promote the creation, presentation, and preservation of both traditional and nontraditional theatrical endeavors by, for, and about the Jewish experience. As the leading organization for Jewish theatre worldwide, its mission is to develop, innovate, promote, and preserve theatre with a Jewish sensibility. (www.alljewishtheatre.org)

America-Israel Cultural Foundation (AICF) (1939). 322 8th Avenue, Suite 1702, New York, NY 10001. (212) 557-1600. AICF supports and develops artistic life in Israel by awarding scholarships to Israeli students of the arts in the disciplines of music, art and design, dance, film and television, and theater, and making grants to dozens of partner institutions helping nurture the best in Israeli culture. (www.aicf.org)

American Guild of Judaic Art (AGJA) (1991). 135 Shaker Hollow, Alpharetta, GA 30022. (404) 981-2308. AGJA is an international membership organization whose mission is to promote awareness of fine art and craft objects created in the Jewish spirit and whose goal is to serve the needs of Jewish artists and those who sell and promote Jewish art. Its membership includes artists, artisans, architects, collectors, gallerists, and anyone interested in the role of Judaica and Judaic art as it relates to home, family, and community. AGJA created what is now known as "Jewish Arts Month," an educational event held in March during which there are online and brick-and-mortar member shows, a national event calendar, an essay contest for adults and youth, and local programs given by members in their communities. (www.jewishart.org)

American Society for Jewish Music (ASJM) (formerly **Mailamm (Makhon Eretz Yisraeli L'-Mada'ey ha-Musika), Jewish Music Forum** and **Jewish Liturgical Society of America**) (1932) (1939) (1963) (1974). c/o Center for Jewish History, 15 West 16th Street, New York, NY 10011. (212) 874-3990. ASJM enables the performance, scholarship, and dissemination of Jewish music and sustains these initiatives through concerts, publications, seminars, conferences, and other projects. ASJM provides global access to Jewish music, research, and scholarship. It publishes a journal, *Musica Judaica*. (www.jewishmusic-asjm.org)

Artis (2004).PO Box 979, New York, NY 10013. (212) 285-0960. Artis supports contemporary artists from Israel whose work addresses aesthetic, social, and political questions that inspire reflection and debate. It is dedicated to broadening international awareness and understanding of contemporary visual art from Israel through grant programs, public programs, research trips, and career development programs, and strives to cultivate a global network of resources that advance opportunities for contemporary artists. Artis connects artists, art professionals, and the public. (www.artiscontemporary.org)

Association for Israel's Decorative Arts (AIDA) (2003). c/o Dale & Doug Anderson, 100 Worth Avenue, Apartment 713, Palm Beach, FL 33480. AIDA fosters the development of contemporary decorative artists from Israel by connecting them to an international audience of galleries, institutions, and collectors. Underlying all of AIDA's activities is the goal of promoting a positive face of contemporary Israel not often seen. Its programs include connecting artists with galleries; exhibiting works at international art fairs and significant craft fairs; providing scholarships, residencies, and summer teaching positions at prominent craft schools; supporting participation in conferences like the National Council on Education for the Ceramic Arts and the Glass Art Society conference; and finding venues for museum shows. (www.aidaarts.org)

Asylum Arts (2015). 68 Jay Street, #503, Brooklyn, NY 11201. (718) 249-6410. Asylum Arts supports contemporary Jewish culture on an international scale, bringing greater exposure to artists and cultural initiatives and providing opportunities for new projects and collaborations. A global network of Jewish artists, with hundreds of members in the US, Israel, Europe, and Latin America, Asylum Arts engages audiences with Jewish ideas and community through the vibrant Jewish and Israeli cultural landscape. It empowers artists and cultural organizations to create experiences to broaden the impact of Jewish culture. Its grant program supports Asylum Arts network artists in creative projects that explore Jewish ideas, themes, history, and identity. (www.asylum-arts.org)

ATARA: The Arts & Torah Association for Religious Artists (2007). ATARA's mission is to encourage artistically gifted observant Jews to develop and express their talents. In order to strengthen the expression of art in accordance with Jewish law, the individuals and groups involved in ATARA have created a network for the community of performing artists who adhere to traditional standards. ATARA encourages the utilization of creative talent in the service of religious values to bring meaning and beauty to others; promotes the creative and performing arts as acceptable ways to communicate and the halakhic system as a standard; supports artists in maintaining the quality of both their art and their religious life; and demonstrates sensitivity to both the creative needs of artists as well as a range of religious outlooks among audience members. (www.artsandtorah.org)

Council of American Jewish Museums (CAJM) (1977). 1058 Sterling Place, Brooklyn, NY 11213. (917) 815-5054. CAJM, the leading forum for Jewish museums in North America, is an association of institutions and individuals committed to enriching American and Jewish culture and enhancing the value of Jewish museums to their communities. Its mission is to strengthen Jewish museums as essential resources and vital centers of culture, knowledge, and discourse, offering programs, networking, and learning opportunities to the Jewish-museum field and highlighting issues pertaining to the presentation of Jewish culture. (www.cajm.net)

Idelsohn Society for Musical Preservation (formerly **Reboot Stereophonic**) (2005). 44 West 28th Street, 8th Floor, New York, NY 10001. (413) 582-0137. The Idelsohn Society for Musical Preservation, named for Abraham Zevi Idelsohn, legendary Jewish musicologist and writer of "Hava Nagila," is an all-volunteer organization made up of individuals from the music industry and academia who believe that Jewish history is best told by the music that has been loved and lost and that music creates conversations otherwise impossible in daily life. The Society accomplishes its mission by re-releasing lost classics and compilations; filming the story of Jewish musicians to build a digitally-based archive of the music and the artists who created it in order to preserve their legacy for future generations; curating museum exhibits that showcase the stories behind the music; and creating concert showcases. (www.idelsohnsociety.com)

The In[heir]itance Project (TIP) (2014). 279 West 117th Street, #1V, New York, NY 10026. (347) 645-2789. TIP is a national arts organization that collaborates with communities around the US throughout the creative process, combining their lived experiences and sacred narratives through a unique methodology of collective research, art making, and reflection. (www.inheiritance.org)

Jewish Art Salon (2008). 1324 Lexington Avenue, UPS Box #120, New York, NY 10128. The Jewish Art Salon is the largest, most-recognized Jewish visual art organization in the world. It is a global network of contemporary Jewish art that provides important programs and resources, and develops lasting partnerships with the international art community and the general public. The Jewish Art Salon presents public events in the US and Israel, and produces art projects with international art institutions. Its art exhibits and events explore Jewish themes, related to current issues. (www.jewishartsalon.org)

Jewish Book Council (JBC) (formerly **National Committee for Jewish Book Week**) (1925) (1940) (1943). 520 8th Avenue, 4th Floor, New York, NY 10018. (212) 201-2920. The mission of the JBC is to promote the reading, writing, publishing, and distribution of quality Jewish content books in English; serve as the national resource center for information about the American Jewish literary scene; serve as the coordinating body of Jewish literary activity in North America in both general and Jewish venues; and serve as the North American representative of Jewish literature on the international scene. Among its long-standing programs and activities are National Book Month and the National Jewish Book Awards. (www.jewishbookcouncil.org)

Jewish Creativity International (JCI) (formerly **Center for Jewish Culture and Creativity**) (1990). 2472 Broadway, #331, New York, NY 10025. (310) 652-5163. JCI advances contemporary Jewish culture through the fiscal sponsorship of independent projects in Jewish arts, culture, and media. It has always taken a special interest in the cultural life of Israel as part of its mission of service to creative artists. Fiscal sponsorship is extended to projects that align with its mission of furthering artistic and cultural creativity, as distinct from primarily religious, educational, or social-welfare activities. (www.jewishcreativity.org)

Jewish Film Presenters Network (JFPN) (2006). c/o Marlene Meyerson JCC Manhattan, 334 Amsterdam Avenue, New York, NY 10023. (646) 505-4444. JFPN works to organize and connect Jewish film festivals across North America and the world, in order to create professional standards, exchange knowledge, and ensure growth and sustainability. The goal of JFPN is to provide festivals, small and large, with the professional tools and guidance which will allow them to raise the quality of their programs, expand their reach, and meet industry standards, all while pursuing their mission and serving the community. JFPN holds a bi-annual conference for its over 300 members and has developed J Film Box, an online resource for the makers and distributors of Jewish films that connects makers and presenters (festivals) of Jewish and Israeli films. (www.jfilmnetwork.com)

Jewish Heritage (1981). 150 Franklin Street, #1W, New York, NY 10013. (212) 925-9067. Jewish Heritage is one of the world's oldest and most active organizations dedicated to enriching the literary bookshelf with works of literature related to Jewish history and culture. By partnering with archives to bring unpublished works to a broad readership and supporting contemporary authors, Jewish Heritage has helped bring to light many books of great literary and historical significance. (No website)

Jewish Plays Project (JPP) (2011). (347) 878-5771. The JPP puts bold, progressive Jewish conversations on world stages; it wants to bring great plays to life. The JPP's innovative and competitive development vehicle invests emerging artists in their Jewish identity; engages Jewish communities in the vetting, selecting, and championing of new voices; and secures mainstream production opportunities for the best new plays. The JPP seeks to have theater join the movement underway in Jewish culture in which artists are creating amazing new pathways to Jewish identity. (www.jewishplaysproject.org)

The Jewish Publication Society (JPS) (1888). 2100 Arch Street, Philadelphia, PA 19103. (215) 832-0600 or (800) 234-3151. JPS is the oldest publisher of Jewish books in the US and a nonprofit, nondenominational educational association whose mission is to enhance Jewish literacy and culture. It publishes and disseminates books of Jewish interest for adults and children on Jewish subjects including TANAKH, Bible commentaries, religious studies and practices, life cycle, folklore, classics, art, history, and thought. JPS publishes works representing the highest levels of scholarship, written in a popular manner, and its authors, donors, and readers represent the entire spectrum of the Jewish community. (www.jewishpub.org)

Jewish Storytelling Coalition (1989). The Jewish Storytelling Coalition provides a web presence for Jewish story and is a national network where performing storytellers and audiences may find one another. The Coalition's website offers a national directory of Jewish storytellers and online posts about current storytelling news and events (JSC News, Views, and Shmooze). (www.jewishstorytelling.org)

Kosher Culture Foundation (2008). 7040 West Palmetto Park Road, #4-848, Boca Raton, FL 33433. (561) 392-2188. The Kosher Culture Foundation promotes and supports Jewish continuity, celebrating the rich diversity of Jewish heritage, observance, and ancestry. Its web portal strives to be the most comprehensive Jewish online resource center on the internet with a focus on Jewish education, kashrut, cultural heritage, community service, and brotherhood for all Jews. The Kosher Culture Foundation serves the full spectrum of Jewish organizations and individuals, nurturing an interest in genuine Jewish values, observance and traditions, providing opportunities for personal growth by recognizing the past, celebrating Jewish culture, and promoting services to the Jewish community worldwide. (www.kosher-culture.org)

Music of Remembrance (MOR) (1998). Magnuson Park, Building 30, 6310 Northeast 74th Street, Suite 202E, Seattle, WA 98115. (206) 365-7770. MOR fills a unique cultural role in the US and throughout the world by remembering the Holocaust through music. With concert performances, educational programs, recordings, and commissions of new works by some of today's leading composers, MOR honors those of all backgrounds who found the strength to create even in the face of persecution, and those who had the courage to speak out against cruelty. It tells stories that communicate urgent moral lessons for today with a scope that extends beyond the Holocaust itself to the experience of others who have been excluded or persecuted for their faith, ethnicity, gender, or sexuality. (www.musico-fremembrance.org)

The National Center for Jewish Film (NCJF) (1976). Brandeis University, 415 South Street, Waltham, MA 02454. (781) 736-8600. The NCJF is a unique, independent, nonprofit motion picture archive, distributor, resource center and exhibitor whose mission is the collection, preservation, and exhibition of films with artistic and educational value relevant to the Jewish experience and the dissemination of these materials to the widest possible audience. The NCJF exclusively owns the largest collection of Jewish content film in the world, outside of Israel, including feature films, documentaries, newsreels, home movies, and institutional films dating from 1903 to the present. It is the world's premiere resource for and about Jewish film and has led the revival of Yiddish Cinema. (www.jewishfilm.org)

National Jewish Theater Foundation (NJTF) (2007). 7700 Los Pinos Boulevard, Coral Gables, FL 33143. NJTF presents theatrical works that celebrate the richness of Jewish heritage and culture, and promotes the appreciation and preservation of Jewish musical and dramatic theatrical material and history. As one of the leading, fully professional performing arts organization to focus exclusively on Jewish theater, NJTF is committed to educating the public on Jewish content and themes. Its productions have been presented to diverse audiences across America and throughout the world. (www.njtfoundation.org)

Nextbook Inc. (2003). 37 West 28th Street, 8th Floor, New York, NY 10001. (212) 920-3660. Nextbook Inc. is dedicated to supporting Jewish literature, culture, and ideas. Its main projects are Nextbook Press, a series of books on Jewish themes published by Schocken Books, and *Tablet Magazine*, the daily online magazine of Jewish news, ideas, and culture. (www.nextbookpress.com)

Terezin Music Foundation (TMF) (1991). PO Box 203206, Boston, MA 02123. (857) 222-8262. TMF is dedicated to preserving the musical legacy of composers lost in the Holocaust. It recovers, preserves, and performs the music created by prisoners in the Terezín (Theresienstadt) concentration camp, where the Nazis attempted to hide unspeakable horrors behind a facade of art and culture. TMF sponsors and fosters new commissions by emerging composers to create music that provides a vibrant memorial, tribute, and voice to those who perished in the Holocaust and to all who are silenced by war or genocide. Its commissions are performed internationally in major venues by the world's greatest artists to form an enduring memorial and serve as agents of inspiration, healing, and transformation for future generations of artists and audiences. TMF produces concerts, master classes, commemorative events, and programs in Holocaust education in the US and Europe. (www.terezinmusic.org)

Yiddishkayt (1995). 3780 Wilshire Boulevard, Suite 301, Los Angeles, California 90010. (213) 389-8880. Yiddishkayt is a Yiddish cultural and educational organization which aims to preserve, cultivate, and broadcast the treasures of Yiddish, the diversity of *yiddishkayt's* legacy, and the progressive tradition of Jewish European and immigrant life and explore this cultural and moral heritage in the face of the disappearance and neglect of the historical, lived experience of European Yiddish culture. It seeks to inspire current and future generations with the artists, writers, musicians, performers, filmmakers, philosophers, and social justice activists whose *yiddishkayt*—their particular form of critical and compassionate engagement with humanity—emerged from the Jewish communities of Europe as they developed in constant contact with their non-Jewish neighbors. (www.yiddishkayt.org)

Zamir Choral Foundation (1967). 475 Riverside Drive, Suite 1948, New York, NY 10115. (212) 870-3335. The Zamir Choral Foundation promotes choral music as a vehicle to inspire Jewish life, culture and continuity and to foster Jewish identity across generational and denominational lines. Under the organization's guidance and encouragement, many new choirs have formed in communities across North America and Europe. Major programs include the Zamir Chorale, which was founded as the first Hebrew-singing choir in North America; HaZamir: The International Jewish High School Choir, a network of choral chapters across the US and Israel which provides Jewish teens with a high level choral experience in a Jewish environment; Zamir Noded, which provides a high level musical opportunity for young adults aged 18-30 to sing in a Jewish choir; and the annual North American Jewish Choral Festival. (www.zamirchoralfoundation.org)

12.1.28   Jewish History/Heritage Organizations

1654 Society (2004). 2 West 70th Street, New York, NY 10024. (212) 873-0300. The 1654 Society celebrates the history of America's founding Jewish community—a group of 23 people who arrived in the colony of New Amsterdam from Recife, Brazil in 1654—and brings attention to the history of the Jewish people in America. The 1654 Society has been charged with preserving and publishing unique archives and treasures—primary evidence that document myriad Jewish contributions and firmly establish the place of Jews in the founding of America—which assists every American Jew in understanding and taking pride and ownership in their heritage. (www.1654society.org)

Agudath Israel of America National Orthodox Jewish Archives (1978). 42 Broadway, 14th Floor, New York, NY 10004. (212) 797-9000. The Agudath Israel of America National Orthodox Jewish Archives is a unique repository of historical documents, publications, and photographs relating to the growth of Orthodox Jewry in the US and the history of Agudath Israel on an international scope. Holdings include records, papers, graphic material and publications documenting the history of Agudath Israel of America, Agudath Israel worldwide, and Orthodox Jewish organizations and communities in the US and abroad. The collections reflect major themes of 20th century Jewish history, including immigration, relief and rescue of Jews in Nazi-occupied Europe, Jewish educational activities, children's camps, social welfare programs, and political activity. (www.agudathisrael.org/contact)

American Jewish Historical Society (AJHS) (1892). Center for Jewish History, 15 West 16th Street, New York, NY 10011. (212) 294-6160. AJHS is the oldest ethnic, cultural archive in the US, providing access to documents, books, photographs, art, and artifacts that reflect the history of the Jewish presence in the US from 1654 to the present. Its mission is to foster awareness and appreciation of American Jewish heritage and to serve as a national scholarly resource for research through the collection, preservation, and dissemination of materials relating to American Jewish history. AJHS maintains records of the nation's leading Jewish communal organizations and important collections in the fields of education, philanthropy, science, sports, business, and the arts. (www.ajhs.org)

Center for Jewish History (CJH) (2000).15 West 16th Street, New York, NY 10011. (212) 294-8301. The CJH provides a collaborative home for five partner organizations: American Jewish Historical Society, American Sephardi Federation, Leo Baeck Institute, Yeshiva University Museum, and YIVO Institute for Jewish Research. The partners' archives comprise the world's largest and most comprehensive archive of the modern Jewish experience outside of Israel, illuminating history, culture, and heritage. The collections span a thousand years, with more than five miles of archival documents (in dozens of languages and alphabet systems), more than 500,000 volumes, as well as thousands of artworks, textiles, ritual objects, recordings, films, and photographs. (www.cjh.org)

The Friedberg Genizah Project (FGP) (1999). 3 Dove Lane, Lakewood, NJ 08701. (732) 730-9814. FGP was established to facilitate and rejuvenate Genizah research. It is achieving this goal by locating the Genizah manuscripts and then identifying, cataloging, transcribing, translating, rendering them into digital format (i.e., photographing), and publishing them online, thereby enabling scholars to share information and exchange knowledge and ideas, which is creating important and unprecedented collaboration between academic institutions. FGP has released a fully-operational version of its online research platform, where it is now possible to view over 100,000 digitized images of Genizah manuscripts. FGP is operating in a joint venture with The Friedberg Jewish Manuscript Society in Canada. (http://pr.genizah.org)

Heritage Foundation for Preservation of Jewish Cemeteries (also known as **Avoyseinu**) (HFPJC) (2002). 616 Bedford Avenue, Suite 2B, Brooklyn, NY 11249. (718) 640-1470. The HFPJC is committed to assisting Jews in restoring their ancestral cemeteries in Eastern Europe. It has effected the complete restoration of numerous abandoned Jewish cemeteries throughout Hungary, Poland, Romania, Slovakia, Serbia, and western Ukraine. The HFPJC also serves as a reuniting force and liaison between Jews worldwide in restoring their common ancestral grave sites. (www. hfpjc.com)

International Association of Jewish Genealogical Societies (IAJGS) (1988). PO Box 3624, Cherry Hill, NJ 08034. IAJGS is an independent umbrella organization coordinating the activities and annual conference of numerous national and local Jewish genealogical societies around the world. Its major objectives are to collect, preserve, and disseminate knowledge and information with reference to Jewish genealogy, and to assist and promote the research of Jewish family history. (www.iajgs.org)

Jewish American Society for Historic Preservation (JASHP) (1997). 6162 Golf Villas Drive, Boynton Beach, FL 33437. JASHP is a volunteer organization whose purpose is to identify and recognize sites of American Jewish historical interest. It sponsors and promotes programs of local and national historic interest. In cooperation with local historical societies, communities, and houses of worship, JASHP encourages dialogue and interactive recognition of the commonality of the American   experience.   (www.jewish-american-society-for-historic-preservation.org)

Jewish Architectural Heritage Foundation (JAHF) (2004). 515 Huguenot Avenue, Staten Island, NY 10312. JAHF assumes responsibility for managing the maintenance, restoration, renovation, and construction of select Jewish heritage buildings and monuments around the world. The organization's work is philanthropic in nature and is focused on restoring and erecting Jewish public buildings and holy sites. (No website)

Jewish Community Legacy Project (JCLP) (2016). (678) 429-8895. JCLP aims to help mature Jewish communities in small-town America face challenges brought on by dwindling membership and changing demographics. It aids these communities—ardent in their commitment to Jewish life—as they navigate the present and prepare for the future. (www.jclproject.org/jewish-community-legacy-project-jclp.html)

JewishGen (1987). Edmond J. Safra Plaza, 36 Battery Place, New York, NY 10280. (646) 494-5972. Affiliated with the Museum of Jewish Heritage, and committed to ensuring Jewish continuity for present generations and the generations yet to come, JewishGen's mission is to encourage the preservation of Jewish heritage, allowing anyone with Jewish ancestry to research their roots, connect with relatives, and learn about their family history. JewishGen hosts more than 25 million records and provides a myriad of resources and search tools online designed to assist those researching their Jewish ancestry. (www.jewishgen.org)

The Jewish Heritage Foundation (2011). 101 Plaza Real South, # 413, Boca Raton, FL 33432. (561) 866-0771. The Jewish Heritage Foundation is the only organization that is dedicated to locating, recovering, and restoring Judaica (Torahs and megillahs, synagogue artwork and adornments, Torah scroll adornments and related items, religious books, manuscripts, and texts, etc.) to communal and educational uses. It is comprised of a community of leaders, rabbis, Holocaust restitution experts, museum officials, philanthropists, lawyers, accountants, historians, students, and lay people who are committed to returning the pieces of the Jewish people and its history to where they belong. (www.thejewishheritagefoundation.com)

Leo Baeck Institute (LBI) (1955). Center for Jewish History, 15 West 16th Street, New York, NY 10011. (212) 744-6400 or (212) 294-8340. LBI is devoted to the history of German-speaking Jews, whose history is marked by individual as well as collective accomplishments that played a significant role in shaping art, science, business, and political developments in the modern era, and it is committed to preserving the vibrant cultural heritage of German-speaking Jewry, which was nearly destroyed in the Holocaust. Its 80,000-volume library and extensive archival and art collections represent the most significant repository of primary source material and scholarship on the Jewish communities of Central Europe over the past five centuries. (www.lbi.org)

Rhodes Jewish Historical Foundation (1997). 10850 Wilshire Boulevard, #750, Los Angeles, CA 90024. (310) 475-4779. The Rhodes Jewish Historical Foundation was established to preserve the unique Jewish history of Rhodes and support the Jewish Museum of Rhodes. It accumulated an extraordinary amount of original artifacts from Rhodes from various sources around the world that are displayed in the Museum. (www.rhodesjewishmuseum.org)

The Society for Preservation of Hebrew Books (2002). 1472 President Street, Brooklyn, NY 11213. (718) 363-9404. The Society for Preservation of Hebrew Books was founded to preserve old American Hebrew books written by American rabbis and scholars during the early years of the 20th century that are out of print and/or circulation. Its goal is to bring to life these books and to make all Torah publications free and readily accessible. (www.hebrewbooks.org)

Touro Synagogue Foundation (formerly **The Society of Friends of Touro Synagogue**) (1948). 85 Touro Street, Newport, RI 02840. (401) 847-4794, ext. 207. The Touro Synagogue Foundation is dedicated to maintaining and preserving Touro Synagogue as a national historic site, as well as the colonial Jewish cemetery and Patriots Park, and to promoting and teaching religious diversity, colonial Jewish history and the history of Touro Synagogue. The Foundation was instrumental in building Patriots Park, which honors colonial Jewish leaders, and worked with the US Postal Service to create a stamp featuring Touro Synagogue. The Foundation promotes public awareness of Touro Synagogue's preeminent role in the tradition of American religious liberty and annually hosts The George Washington Letter Celebration, commemorating George Washington's letter of 1790 to the Hebrew Congregation in Newport. (www.tourosynagogue.org)

Vaad Mishmereth STaM (1975). 4907 16th Avenue, Brooklyn, NY 11204. (718) 438-4980. Vaad Mishmereth STaM (STaM stands for Sefer Torahs, Tefillin and Mezuzot) is a consumer-protection agency dedicated to preserving and protecting the halakhic integrity of Torah scrolls, tefillin, phylacteries and mezuzot. It publishes material for laymen and scholars in the field of scribal arts; makes presentations and conducts examination campaigns in schools and synagogues; created an optical software system to detect possible textual errors in STaM; and teaches and certifies scribes worldwide. (No website)

World Jewish Heritage Fund (WJH) (2011). 1 Brussels Street, Worcester, MA 01610. (508) 425-7164. The mission of WJH is to preserve Jewish heritage worldwide and promote tourism to a variety of sites and cultural events around the world that are of great importance to the Jewish heritage continuity. WJH has developed an integrated ecosystem, bringing together heritage, travel, and technology, via an innovative, first-of-its-kind platform, reframing the concept of Jewish heritage and adjusting it to the 21st century. (No website)

YIVO Institute for Jewish Research (1925) (1940). Center for Jewish History, 15 West 16th Street, New York, NY 10011. (212) 246-6080. YIVO is home of the largest collection of Holocaust primary documentation in North America and a world-renowned library and archive of Jewish history and culture. It is the only prewar Jewish cultural institution to have survived the Holocaust and a leader in training generations of Jewish Studies scholars. An educational organization dedicated to fostering knowledge of the history and culture of East European Jewry, YIVO brings treasures from its library and archives to broad audiences via a rich array of programs, including lectures, concerts, and exhibitions; adult education offering online and on-site courses, including the world's oldest intensive Yiddish language program; books and scholarly publications; and fellowships for scholars. (www.yivo.org)

12.1.29   Jewish Social Welfare Organizations

Agunah International (1997). 498 East 18th Street, Brooklyn, NY 11226. (212) 249-4523 or (917) 671-7274. Agunah International is an all-volunteer organization that offers its services free of charge to free women trapped in dead marriages ("agunot") by recalcitrant husbands who refuse to grant a "get" (legal Jewish divorce). Its mission is also to promote a systemic halakhic solution to free agunot ("chained women," in Hebrew) by encouraging the rabbinical courts to assert their halakhic authority to dissolve dead marriages by applying the appropriate halakhic concept; alert the Jewish community as to the severity and magnitude of the agunah problem; educate the Jewish community about halakhic precedents and remedies for freeing agunot; counsel women whose husbands use the "get" as a weapon to extort financial gain or custodial rights, or to exact revenge during the divorce process; and provide financial aid for agunot in need. (www.agunahinternational.com)

The Aleph Institute (1981). 9540 Collins Avenue, Surfside, FL 33154. (305) 864-5553. The Aleph Institute, founded at the direction of the Chabad-Lubavitcher Rebbe, Rabbi Menachem Mendel Schneerson, is dedicated to assisting and caring for the wellbeing of members of specific populations that are isolated from the regular community: US military personnel, prisoners, and people institutionalized or at risk of incarceration due to mental illness or addictions. The Aleph Institute addresses their religious, educational, and spiritual needs, advocates and lobbies for their civil and religious rights, and provides support to their families. It is committed to criminal justice reform and recidivism reduction through preventive-education and faith-based rehabilitation programs, re-entry assistance, alternative sentencing guidance and counsel, and policy research and recommendations. (www.aleph-institute.org)

Amudim (2017). 11 Broadway, Suite 1076, New York, NY 10004. (646) 517-0222. Founded on the pillars of kindness, compassion, and dignity, and dedicated to serving community members in times of crisis, Amudim functions as a confidential resource center that provides meaningful assistance, enduring support, and direct referrals for individuals and families impacted by sexual abuse, neglect, addiction, and other crisis-related matters. It fosters change and growth by raising awareness and implementing educational programs within the community. (www. amudim.org)

Areivim (2000). 23 Lake Avenue, Hillburn, NY 10931. (845) 371-2760. Areivim, provides services within the Orthodox community for troubled teenagers and their families. Its personal and all-encompassing approach nurtures emotional well-being and personal responsibility, guiding young adults into a productive future as healthy individuals, spouses, parents, and neighbors. Through a combination of therapeutic guidance and professional oversight, Areivim gives individuals the ability to take powerful ownership of their life choices. Its services include placements, referral, and advocacy; counseling and mentoring; crisis intervention; publications, lectures, and community classes; a short-term emergency homeless shelter; and a boys' yeshiva. (www.areivim.com)

Association of Jewish Aging Services (AJAS) (formerly **North American Association of Jewish Homes and Housing for the Aging**) (1960). 2519 Connecticut Avenue, NW, Washington, DC 20008. (202) 543-7500. AJAS is an association of nonprofit community-based organizations that promotes and supports elder services in the context of Jewish values through education, professional development, advocacy, and community relationships. Its members administer to the needs of the aging through residential health care, assisted living and group homes, independent and congregate housing, and living-at-home service programs. It functions as the central coordinator for homes and residential facilities for Jewish elderly in North America. The AJAS membership is comprised of Jewish-sponsored nursing homes, housing communities, community-based service organizations, and outreach programs throughout the US and Canada. (www.ajas.org)

Avodah (formerly **Avodah: The Jewish Service Corps**) (1998). c/o Makom Hadash, 125 Maiden Lane, Suite 8B, New York, NY 10038. (212) 545-7759. Avodah strengthens the Jewish community's fight against the causes and effects of poverty in the US by engaging participants in service and community building that inspire them to become lifelong leaders for social change whose work for justice is rooted in and nourished by Jewish values. It trains emerging Jewish leaders to take on the most pressing social and economic issues in America. Avodah recruits young adults ages 21-26 from across the US to spend a year in its Jewish Service Corps working full time at leading antipoverty organizations in select cities that are committed to addressing poverty from a variety of different perspectives, including housing, healthcare, education, and hunger, in jobs ranging from direct service (case management, teaching, staffing medical clinics, etc.) to direct advocacy (legal services) to community organizing (for workers' rights, tenants' rights, local policy, etc.). Corps members live together and learn together in a supportive, pluralistic community at the crossroads of social activism and Jewish life. (www.avodah.net)

Bend the Arc: A Jewish Partnership for Justice (formerly **Jewish Fund for Justice**, **Progressive Jewish Alliance**, **The Shefa Fund**, and **Spark: The Partnership for Jewish Service**) (1984). 330 Seventh Avenue, 19th Floor, New York, NY 10001. (212) 213-2113. Bend the Arc: A Jewish Partnership for Justice brings together progressive Jews from across the country to advocate and organize for a more just and equal society, working to transform America to be inclusive, equitable, and supportive of the dignity of every person across race, class, gender, and faith. It is shaping the Jewish social justice movement by training and supporting a new generation of diverse progressive Jewish leadership needed on the frontlines. (www.jewishpartnership.us)

Bend the Arc: Jewish Action (2012). 330 Seventh Avenue, 19th Floor, New York, NY 10001. (212) 213-2113. Bend the Arc: Jewish Action is uniting progressive Jewish voices across America to fight for justice for all and rising up in solidarity with everyone threatened by the Trump and Republican agenda to fight for the soul of the nation. Its objectives are to stand with communities under attack (immigrants, Muslims, people of color, American democracy) and show up in solidarity to fight terrible legislation and policies; hold elected officials accountable and organize and fundraise to replace them with progressive champions; and win local progressive victories (progressive legislation and policies, like criminal justice reform and economic equity). Bend the Arc: Jewish Action has put out the call to communities across the country to organize in Moral Minyans: groups of 10 or more people acting locally as part of a national network of Jewish resistance. (www.bendthearc.us)

B'Kavod (2018). B'Kavod (with respect, in Hebrew) seeks to help Jewish communal institutions and all who work, learn, or worship at them develop cultures of safety, respect, and fairness. It offers training and policy development as well as reporting and helpline services. B'Kavod's training program covers interactions among all stakeholders: staff, board, volunteers, interns, donors, congregants, and program participants. Its community reporting system collects information—anonymously and confidentially—about harassment and misconduct related to Jewish communal institutions. (https://sites.google.com/kamfam.org/bekavod)

B'nai B'rith International (formerly **Independent Order of B'nai B'rith**) (1843). 1120 20th Street, NW, Suite 300 N, Washington, DC 20036. (202) 857-6600 or (888) 388-4224. B'nai B'rith International is dedicated to improving the quality of life for people around the globe and making the world a safer, more tolerant and better place. B'nai B'rith is a national and global leader in advancing human rights; Israel advocacy; ensuring access to safe and affordable housing for low-income seniors and advocacy on vital issues concerning seniors and their families; diversity education; promoting Jewish unity and continuity; a leader in humanitarian aid and disaster relief, and improving communities and helping communities in crisis. With a presence in countries all around the world, B'nai B'rith is the Global Voice of the Jewish Community. (www.bnaibrith.org)

Challah for Hunger (2004). 1900 Market Street, 8th Floor, Philadelphia, PA 19103. (267) 423-4415. Challah for Hunger brings people together to bake and sell challah in an effort to raise money and practice social justice (tikkun olam) in an inclusive environment. The many chapters, on college campuses throughout the US and beyond engage young people in community, tradition, hands-on baking, volunteer service, activism, philanthropy, and advocacy. Each chapter donates 50% of its profits to the national cause through Mazon: A Jewish Response to Hunger, and chooses the hunger relief organizations around the world to support with the other half of its profits. (www.challahforhunger.org)

Ezras Yisroel (1994). 4415 14th Avenue, Brooklyn, NY 11219. (800) 601-4644. Ezras Yisroel seeks to ease the anguish and despair of Jewish families and individuals in the US and Israel suffering from financial instability and crisis. It serves thousands of people each year through a broad range of compassionate social and financial services, including interest-free loans, assistance with Yom Tov expenses, monthly stipends for needy families, assistance with emergency medical expenses and bikur cholim, bridal assistance, assistance for widows and orphans, assistance for Torah scholars, and other vital programs. (www.ezrasyisroel.org)

The Free Sons of Israel (formerly **Independent Order of Free Sons of Israel**) (1849). 461 Leonard Boulevard, New Hyde Park, NY 11040. (516) 775-4919. The Free Sons of Israel is the oldest national Jewish fraternal benefit order for men and women in the US still in existence. Its mission is to assist members in translating into practice the Jewish spiritual heritage to help all American citizens; advance the principles of human equality worldwide; join experience in human understanding with the advances in social science and communications and the influence of laws to achieve these ends; protect all American citizens from oppression; and render fraternal aid and assistance to its members. (www.freesons.org)

Guard Your Eyes (GYE) (2010). PO Box 32380, Pikesville, MD 21282. (646) 600-8100. GYE addresses the growing problem of the struggle with and addiction to inappropriate materials on the internet and related behaviors in Orthodox Jewish communities. The GYE network helps Jews get back on a path of sanity, healing, and self-control through its website, forums, handbooks, empowerment emails, hotlines, and 12-step phone conferences and groups as well as the use of internet filtering solutions. (www.guardyoureyes.com)

Heroes to Heroes Foundation (2015). 96 Linwood Plaza, #305, Fort Lee, NJ 07024. (201) 851-2409. Heroes to Heroes Foundation provides spiritual healing and peer support for American combat veterans who have attempted suicide or are on a path to self-destruction due to moral injury. The Heroes to Heroes program begins with a 10-day journey to Israel, which offers veterans a place where they can unashamedly experience their faith. Upon their return home, teammates stay connected for a minimum of one year and participate in activities that include a weekend reunion featuring a speaker to reinforce lessons learned in Israel and college campus visits to introduce the next generation to the challenges that veterans face and how the journey to Israel impacted their lives. (www.heroestoheroes.org)

Ichud HaKehillos LeTohar HaMachane (Union of Communities for Purity of the Camp) (2011). Ichud HaKehillos LeTohar HaMachane is an Orthodox

Jewish organization whose purpose is to help Jews avoid online pornography habits and other problems that can result from internet usage. It offers advice to Haredi Jews as to how best to use modern technology in a religiously-responsible manner and encourages the use of content-control software. (No website)

In Shifra's Arms (ISA) (2009). PO Box 7212, Silver Spring, MD 20910. (202) 573-7611. ISA is a nonpartisan social service organization, serving the Jewish community nationally, whose mission is to help pregnant women struggling with unplanned or difficult pregnancies to build a positive future for themselves and their children. It offers counseling and practical resources, including referrals, throughout pregnancy and after birth, free of charge (it does not provide medical or adoption services). ISA helps all women, Jewish and non-Jewish, but primarily reaches out to women in the Jewish community because no other agency within the Jewish community is meeting this need. (www.inshifrasarms.org)

Jewish Children's Adoption Network (JCAN) (1990). PO Box 237, Brooklandville, MD 21022. (720) 260-5864. JCAN is the only Jewish adoption exchange in the Western hemisphere. Its primary goal is to find appropriate adoptive homes for Jewish infants and children, most of whom have special needs. JCAN is contacted on a regular basis by rabbis, social workers, agencies, attorneys, and birth families who know of children in need of a home, and JCAN refers families from its database to the custodial agency or person that contacted them. No fees are charged for JCAN's services, which include helping a birth family parent a child, locating resources for help with personal problems or coping with a child's limitations, helping an adoptive family find resources for adoption or parenting, helping families negotiate adoption subsidies, and helping members in starting a search. (www.jewishchildrensadoption.org)

Jewish Community Watch (JCW) (2011) (2014). 244 Fifth Avenue, 2nd Floor, Suite M-285, New York, NY 10001. (718) 841-7056. JCW is dedicated to the prevention of child sexual abuse within the Orthodox Jewish community and to advocating, supporting, and caring for victims all over the world. Its services include victim support assistance; mass awareness events; staff screening for schools and camps; educating the public by promoting child safety, increasing awareness, and eliminating the stigma and shame of abuse; and actively preventing abuse of children by warning about suspected predators in the community and working to have them arrested. (www.jewishcommunitywatch.org)

Jewish Prisoner Services International (JPSI) (1995). PO Box 85840, Seattle, WA 98145. (206) 617-2367 or (888) 614-3812. Originally an agency of B'nai B'rith International, JPSI currently functions as a volunteer outreach program of Congregation Shaarei Teshuvah. It is a pluralistic Jewish chaplaincy organization that primarily focuses on providing Jewish prisoners with the advocacy and materials that will allow them to fully practice their faith while incarcerated, helping them to successfully transition back into the community, and assisting their families (in conjunction with other Jewish social service agencies). JPSI's mission includes making Jewish educational, religious, cultural, and spiritual resources available to prisoners. (www.jpsi.org)

Jewish Pro-Life Foundation (2006). PO Box 292, Sewickley, PA 15143. (412) 758-3269. The Jewish Pro-Life Foundation promotes life-saving solutions to unplanned pregnancy in the Jewish community; provides education about the development, viability, and sanctity of unborn life as well as traditional Jewish law regarding abortion; provides adoption and pregnancy care referrals; teaches about the harmful effects of abortion, and provides support to Jewish women and men who suffer from post abortion syndrome. It is not affiliated with any Jewish denomination, political organization, or the messianic movement. (www.jewishprolifefoundation.org)

Jewish Women International (JWI) (formerly **B'nai B'rith Women** and **Ruth Lodge No. 1, Daughters of Judah**) (1897). 1129 20th Street, NW, Suite 801, Washington, DC 20036. (202) 857-1300 or (800) 343-2823. JWI is the leading Jewish organization working to empower women and girls by ensuring and protecting their physical safety and economic security, promoting and celebrating intergenerational leadership, and inspiring civic participation and community engagement. Inspired by a legacy of progressive women's leadership and guided by Jewish values, JWI works to ensure that all women and girls thrive in healthy relationships, control their financial futures, and realize the full potential of their personal strength. (www.jwi.org)

Jewish Women Watching (1999). PO Box 637, New York, NY 10025. Jewish Women Watching is an anonymous grassroots feminist group monitoring and responding to sexism in the American Jewish community. It aims to rouse the public to challenge and change sexist and oppressive practices in the Jewish community. The organization uses satire and factual evidence to criticize the narrow-minded priorities of the Jewish establishment. It draws attention to issues that would otherwise not be discussed and to voices that are silenced. (www.jewishwomenwatching.com)

JOIN for Justice (formerly **Jewish Organizing Initiative**) (1998) (2011). 359 Boylston Street, Fourth Floor, Boston, MA 02116. (617) 350-9994. JOIN (Jewish Organizing Institute and Network) for Justice is dedicated to training, supporting, and connecting Jewish organizers and their communities. It strengthens the community organizing practice of Jewish organizers, leaders, and entire organizations so that the Jewish community can effectively play a role in America's social justice struggles. JOIN for Justice also promotes and develops the art and science of organizing among Jews in order to strengthen the Jewish community itself by helping build Jewish communities of relationship, mission, and action. Its goal is to identify, recruit, train, develop, place, and mentor hundreds of top quality Jewish organizers in lay and professional positions inside and outside of the Jewish community, transforming and strengthening individuals and institutions as they work for a more just, inclusive, and compassionate society. It targets young adults, clergy, and Jewish institutional leaders for training opportunities. (www.joinforjustice.org)

Kayama (1985).1143 East 12th Street, Brooklyn, NY 11230. (718) 692-1876 or (800) 932-8589. Kayama provides information and assistance with obtaining a legal Jewish divorce ("get"). It helps facilitate the obtaining of a "get" by dealing with all the parties and making the necessary arrangements, and subsidizes the cost of administering the "get" when necessary. Kayama maintains contacts with "get" administrators around the country and throughout the world, so that the "get" can be arranged regardless of where the parties are located. (www.kayama.org)

KosherTroops (2010). 8 Pleasant Ridge Road, New Hempstead, NY 10977. (845) 354-7763 or (845) 282-0907. KosherTroops was founded to help improve the morale and welfare of members of the US armed forces by showing appreciation for their commitment. Its mission is accomplished by sending care packages to deployed and stateside Jewish American troops that include items to help them celebrate the Jewish holidays and Shabbat so that they will feel connected to the Jewish community while away. KosherTroops sends packages to Jewish soldiers stationed around the world, including kosher meals and staples of kosher products to supplement what they receive from the military, as well as letters and cards. (www.koshertroops.com)

L'Asurim (2010). 139 Rodney Street, Brooklyn, NY 11211. (718) 513-2525. L'Asurim provides support for prisoners, helps prevent crime, and advocates for prison well-being and criminal justice reform. It coordinates visits for family, clergy, and volunteers, including arranging for transportation; raises funds for and sends care packages containing kosher food, reading material, and religious items to prisons year-round and especially for the holidays; runs a robust pen pal program, where members of the public are in regular correspondence with inmates; and holds events, where speakers address law and order issues. (www.lasurim.org)

MAZON: A Jewish Response to Hunger (1985). 10850 Wilshire Boulevard, Suite 400, Los Angeles, CA 90024. (310) 442-0020 or (800) 813-0557. Inspired by Jewish values and ideals, MAZON is a national advocacy organization working to end hunger among people of all faiths and backgrounds in the US and Israel. It is committed to ensuring that vulnerable people have access to the resources they need to be able to put food on the table, and is a leading voice in Washington, DC on anti-hunger issues, especially those that involve populations or problems that have been previously overlooked or ignored. MAZON works with policymakers to protect and strengthen federal nutrition programs like SNAP (food stamps) and school meals; educates communities across the country about the realities of hunger and strategies to end it; and partners with like-minded organizations in the US and Israel to advocate to end hunger. MAZON prioritizes its efforts for active duty military families and veterans, senior citizens, and Native Americans; in rural and remote communities; and in the area of nutrition and health. (www.mazon.org)

National Council of Jewish Women (NCJW) (1893). 2055 L Street, NW, Suite 650, Washington, DC 20036. (202) 296-2588. The NCJW is a progressive Jewish grassroots organization of volunteers and advocates inspired by Jewish values that has always been a leading voice for justice—championing the needs of women, children, and families—while taking a progressive stance on such issues as child welfare, women's rights, and reproductive freedom. NCJW strives for social justice by improving the quality of life for women, children, and families in the US and Israel and by safeguarding individual rights and freedoms. (www.ncjw.org)

NECHAMA—Jewish Response to Disaster (1996) (2015). 12219 Nicollet Avenue, Burnsville, MN 55337. (763) 732-0610. NECHAMA (to comfort, in

Hebrew) provides natural disaster response, rebuild, and preparedness training services nationwide. Rooted in the Jewish values of tikkun olam (Hebrew for repairing the world), performing good acts, and helping the stranger, NECHAMA is the only Jewish organization to offer sustained direct services in the US following the onset of a hurricane, tornado, flood, or other natural disaster, providing disaster survivors with critical comfort and hope. NECHAMA is inclusive, welcoming volunteers of all faiths and providing assistance to disaster survivors regardless of religious affiliation. (www.nechama.org)

Organization for the Resolution of Agunot (ORA) (2002). 551 West 181st Street, Suite 123, New York, NY 10033. (212) 795-0791. ORA seeks to eliminate abuse from the Jewish divorce process by working within the parameters of Jewish law and civil law to advocate for the timely and unconditional issuance of a "get" (legal Jewish divorce) It pursues its mission through agunah case advocacy, early intervention programs, and educational initiative for agunah prevention, and its services are provided free of charge. (www.getora.org)

Rabbis Against Gun Violence (2016). 1316 University Avenue, Berkeley, CA 94702. Rabbis Against Gun Violence is a national grassroots coalition of Jewish American leaders and faith activists from across the denominational spectrum mobilized to curb the current gun violence epidemic plaguing American communities. Rooted in and inspired by Jewish values, teachings, texts, history, and traditions, Rabbis Against Gun Violence uses its rabbinic voice to educate and advocate for positive, achievable solutions that will save lives and make communities safer. Informed by the research and advice of policy and legal experts in the field of gun violence prevention, the coalition supports a wide variety of efforts to save lives and to change the culture around gun violence, providing its members with many points of entry. (www.facebook.com/RabbisAgainstGunViolence)

Reaching Out (to Jewish Prisoners) (1965). 383 Kingston Avenue, Room 190, Brooklyn, NY 11213. (718) 771-0770 or (718) 771-3866. Reaching Out, which calls itself the Chabad House for Jewish Prisoners, helps Jews in confinement in the US and abroad, regardless of religious observance, affiliation, background, or lack of one, and also helps non-Jews to follow the universal Seven Noahide Laws (code of ethics and morality) that are applicable to all of mankind. Reaching Out helps Jewish inmates with religious issues that have not been addressed properly by the prison staff; distributes Jewish prayer books, literature, and other religious items; helps prisoners to observe Jewish holidays and assists them with their daily Jewish practices; advocates for making kosher meals available and for other policy changes to enable Jews to better practice their religion and exercise their religious rights. (www.jewishprisoner.com)

Refuat Hanefesh (2016). PO Box 3332, Silver Spring, MD 20918. Refuat Hanefesh is dedicated to decreasing the stigma surrounding mental illness through conversation and education, while providing a safe place for those affected to seek support and advice. It recognizes that those who suffer from mental illness in the Jewish community face unique challenges and find it particularly difficult to confront the stigma and find confidants or professionals who understand their unique values and way of life. Refuat Hanefesh furthers its mission and reaches into the community by hosting live conversations, running creative competitions, and sending its curricula and speakers into schools, synagogues, and other venues. It does not provide psychiatric or medical advice. (www.refuathanefesh.org)

Relief Resources (2001). 5904 13th Avenue, Brooklyn, NY 11219. (718) 431-9501. Relief Resources provides multiple services to individuals suffering from mental health disorders, geared specifically toward members of the Jewish community. Its mission is to guide individuals to the best mental health resources available, which is accomplished through its referral service. Relief Resources maintains a vast database of qualified mental health providers and helps callers find clinicians who are effective in their field of expertise. (www.reliefhelp.org)

Repair the World (formerly **Jewish Coalition for Service**) (2003) (2009). 1460 Broadway, New York, NY 10036. (646) 695-2700. Repair the World makes meaningful service a defining element of American Jewish life by working to inspire American Jews and their communities to give their time and effort to serve those in need in high-quality service opportunities that will have real impact. It works closely with local nonprofits to create authentic and impactful volunteering and education opportunities, and address urgent social challenges. Volunteers help transform neighborhoods, cities, and lives through meaningful service experiences rooted in Jewish values, learning, and history. (www.werepair.org)

Sacred Spaces (2016). 82 Nassau Street, New York, NY 10038. Sacred Spaces is the only institution in the Jewish community dedicated to developing a systemic approach to end sexual, physical, and emotional abuse occurring in Jewish institutions across the denominational spectrum. Sacred spaces provides Jewish organizations—including synagogues, day schools, summer camps, and other professional workplaces—with the professional services necessary to develop robust policies and training to prevent opportunities for abuse and guides them responsibly when abuse occurs; accredits institutions that have invested the requisite policy and training work; and aids institutions in responding to allegations responsibly by providing them with services that ensure that they are legally compliant, victims are supported, future abuse is prevented, and damage to the institution is minimized. (www. jewishsacredspaces.org)

SafetyRespectEquity Coalition (SRE Coalition) (2018). c/o Third Plateau, 209 Kearny Street, San Francisco, CA 94108. The SRE Coalition works to ensure safe, respectful, and equitable Jewish workplaces and communal spaces by addressing sexual harassment, sexism, and gender discrimination. Called upon by the ethical standards of the Jewish tradition to address these issues within the Jewish community, the Coalition also lends its voices and action to the national movement seeking a culture shift in the country. To that end, the Coalition brings together organizations, funders, individuals, and experts to help create lasting, systemic change. The role of the SRE Coalition is to serve as catalyst and resource, aiming to support, coordinate, and amplify change in individual organizations as well as accelerate a broader cultural shift. (www.safetyrespectequity.org)

Sasson V'Simcha (2000). c/o Scheinberg, 135 Flintlock Drive, Lakewood, New Jersey 08701. (914) 506-5090. Sasson V'Simcha is dedicated to helping Jewish men and women meet, date, marry, and build happy, stable Jewish homes. Its resources are available to all Jewish individuals, families, and communities, and its programs and services have reached thousands of Jewish men and women in the US, Canada, Israel, and the UK. Sasson V'Simcha helps marriage-minded men and women deal with dating challenges so they can go on to build relationships that lead to marriage, and also guides family, friends, and communities in the ways they can actively help daters achieve their goals of successful marriages. (www.jewishdatingandmarriage.com)

Shalom Task Force (1992). 500 Seventh Avenue, 8th floor, New York, NY 10018. (212) 742-1478. Shalom Task Force aims to help women and families struggling with troubled relationships at home; sensitize Jewish communities so that women can feel less ashamed to ask for help; offer professional guidance to rabbis who may be approached for advice by someone in a complex and possibly dangerous situation; and provide preventative education and programing to young adults and community members. (www.shalomtaskforce.org)

Technology Awareness Group (TAG) (2010). 1221 Madison Avenue, Lakewood, NJ 08701. (732) 730-1824. Serving mainly the Orthodox Jewish community, TAG's goal is to increase an awareness into the potential pitfalls and dangers associated with the internet and technology as a whole, and provide free community service for computers, smartphones, laptops, tablets, and many other digital devices to have them filtered using the most reliable and up-to-date resources available in order to prevent access to inappropriate material. Its services, offered globally, include installing and configuring Web filtering and monitoring software. (www.taghelpline.org)

Tivnu: Building Justice (2011). 7971 Southeast 11th Avenue, Portland, OR 97202. (503) 232-1864. Tivnu: Building Justice, a 9-month Jewish gap year program of hands-on social justice engagement, integrates direct service for the fulfillment of basic human needs, Jewish learning and living, and leadership development. Tivnu (build, in Hebrew) participants build community, justice, and purpose. They work directly with local social justice organizations on various essential projects, explore Jewish texts and history, and study contemporary socioeconomic issues in order to provide a solid foundation for Jewish social justice work. (www.tivnu.org)

The Workmen's Circle/Der Arbeter Ring (1900). 247 West 37th Street, 5th Floor, New York, NY 10018. (212) 889-6800. Originally founded by Jewish immigrants from Eastern Europe seeking to promote values of social and economic justice through a Jewish lens, The Workmen's Circle today still remains passionately committed to its core principles: Jewish community, the promotion of an enlightened Jewish culture, and social justice. It is a social justice organization that powers progressive Jewish identity through Jewish cultural engagement, Yiddish language learning, multigenerational education, and social justice activism. Through contemporary cultural traditions, joyful holiday celebrations, timely social justice campaigns, vibrant Yiddishkayt ("Jewishness"), and interactive educational programs, The Workmen's Circle connects Jewish adults, children, and families of all affiliations with their cultural heritage, working to build a better and more beautiful world for all. It supports its signature schools and overnight Camp Kinder Ring. (www.circle.org)

12.1.30   Jewish Legal Organizations

American Association of Jewish Lawyers and Jurists (AAJLJ) (1983). 888 17th Street, NW, Suite 400, Washington, DC 20006. (202) 775-0991. The AAJLJ, affiliated with the International Association of Jewish Lawyers and Jurists, represents the American Jewish legal community, defending Jewish interests and human rights in the US and abroad. It educates and advocates around critical issues such as civil rights, human rights, access to justice, social justice, Israel and the Rule of Law, Holocaust issues, and Jewish Law. Through its members, the AAJLJ provides legal support to safeguard human rights and works to combat those who utilize "lawfare" to delegitimize Israel. (www.aajlj.org)

   Beth Din of America (1960). 305 Seventh Avenue, 12th Floor, New York, NY 10001. (212) 807-9042 or (212) 807-9072. Beth Din of America is one of the nation's pre-eminent rabbinic courts, serving the Jewish community of North America as a forum for arbitrating commercial, communal and matrimonial disputes through the din torah process, obtaining Jewish divorces, confirming Jewish personal status issues, and overseeing, together with the Rabbinical Council of America, the protocols and standards national network of rabbinic courts for conversion. (www.bethdin.org)

   International Beit Din (IBD) (2014). 444 West 259th Street, Suite 3A, Riverdale, NY 10471. (718) 543-1471. The IBD, serving clients across the US, Canada, and Europe, writes gittin (bills of divorce) in cases of uncontested divorce; specializes in addressing challenging cases concerning agunot, agunim, and mesuravot get (referring to Jews stranded in relationships where the spouses refuse to grant a divorce); and provides a forum in which women facing "get" abuse (e.g., a husband's threat to withhold the "get," either for reasons of spite or in order to gain financial advantage in divorce negotiations) may find effective relief. (www.internationalbeitdin.org)

   The Lawfare Project (LP) (2010). 633 Third Avenue, 21st Floor, New York, NY 10017. (212) 339-6995. The LP is a legal think tank and litigation fund that arranges pro bono legal representation for the pro-Israel and counterterrorism communities. (www.thelawfareproject.org)

   National Jewish Commission on Law and Public Affairs (COLPA) (1965). 135 West 50th Street, New York, NY 10020. (212) 641-8992. COLPA is a voluntary association of attorneys whose purpose is to represent the observant Jewish community—individuals, schools, synagogues, and communal organizations—on legal, legislative, and public-affairs matters. COLPA is committed to addressing and resolving conflicts through mediation, negotiation, and, when required, litigation, as well as through legislative initiatives, and has played a significant role in a number of key areas affecting Jewish life, including Sabbath observance, kashrut, family law, land use, public health, education, and public and religious institutions, advocating for the rights and interests of individual observant Jews and the observant Jewish community as a whole. (www.jlaw.com/LawPolicy/colpa.html)

12.1.31   Jewish Medical Organizations

A TIME: A Torah Infertility Medium of Exchange (1994). 1310 48th Street, Suite 406, Brooklyn, NY 11219. (718) 686-8912. A TIME offers advocacy, education, guidance, research, and support through its many programs to Jewish men, women, and couples struggling with reproductive health and infertility. Strongly endorsed by leading rabbis and physicians, it provides a wide array of essential services, including medical referrals, adoption services, support groups, therapy, educational events, etc. (www.atime.org)

   Bonei Olam (1999). 1755 46th Street, Brooklyn, NY 11204. (718) 252-1212. Bonei Olam is a worldwide organization whose mission is to help couples who are experiencing infertility to become parents by providing financial assistance to cover the prohibitive costs of fertility treatments and medical procedures. Bonei Olam is recognized in the worldwide medical arena for its leadership role at the forefront of reproductive medicine, research, and technology. Its programs cover work-up, medication, high-risk pregnancy, pre-implantation, genetic diagnosis, pre- and post-cancer fertility, education, awareness, and adoption assistance. Bonei Olam has built a network of doctors and fertility centers across the world, enabling it to offer medical and financial assistance to all applicants. (www.boneiolam.org)

   Child Life Society (2000). 1347 43rd Street, Brooklyn, NY 11219. (718) 853-7123 or (866) 443-5723. Child Life Society, which was created to help make life with cystic fibrosis (CF) as normal and enjoyable as possible, provides vital assistance and programs to Jewish children and adults with CF, providing desperately needed funds to pay for medical equipment, vitamins and food supplements, home care assistance, therapeutic respite, and emotional support. CF is a degenerative, genetic disease for which there is no present cure that afflicts Jewish families with a far greater frequency than most other ethnic groups. (www.childlifesociety.org)

   Dor Yeshorim (also known as **Committee for Prevention of Jewish Genetic Diseases**) (1983). 309 Rutledge Street, 4B, Brooklyn, NY 11211. (718) 384-6060. Dor Yeshorim successfully eliminates the occurrence of fatal and debilitating genetic diseases in Jewish families worldwide through its premarital genetic screening program, genetic research, the development of reliable testing methods, and education outreach, and is supported and endorsed by leading rabbinical authorities and medical experts. It is a leading voice in the genetics field, researching and advancing its genetic expertise on behalf of Jewish communities across the globe. Dor Yeshorim also assists families affected by rare genetic disorders by providing medical referrals and expert genetic guidance, and is instrumental in helping these families prevent the recurrence of genetic disorders in future generations. (www.doryeshorim.org)

   Familial Dysautonomia Hope Foundation (FD Hope) (2001). 121 South Estes Drive, Suite 205-D, Chapel Hill, NC 27514. (919) 969-1414. FD Hope is working to expand and accelerate scientific research leading to a cure and improved treatment options for Familial Dysautonomia (a Jewish genetic disorder with a carrier rate of 1 in 27 Ashkenazi Jews) while improving the lives of the children and adults who are challenged by the disease. It provides publications, advocacy, and patient networking services. (www.fdhope.org)

Halachic Organ Donor Society (HODS) (2001). PO Box 693, New York, NY 10108. (212) 213-5087. HODS's mission is to save lives by increasing organ donations from Jews to the general public. Its goals are to educate Jews about the different halakhic and medical issues concerning organ donation; offer a unique organ donor card that enables Jews to donate organs according to their halakhic belief; and provide rabbinic consultation and oversight for cases of organ transplantation. (www.hods.org)

Hasidah (2011). PO Box 9531, Berkeley, CA 94709. (415) 323-3226. Hasidah (Stork, in Hebrew) raises awareness of infertility, connects people to support, and reduces financial barriers to treatment in the Jewish community, by providing financial assistance for IVF to people who need assistance in the Jewish community throughout the US. Hasidah, whose root in Hebrew (H-S-D) means loving-kindness, was founded on the belief that one of the greatest gifts of loving-kindness is helping couples struggling with infertility to become parents. (www.hasidah.org)

Jewish Diabetes Association (JDA) (1985). 1122 East 14th Street, Brooklyn, NY 11230. (718) 303-5955 or (917) 963-8143. The JDA is the nation's first and leading Jewish nonprofit, nonsectarian health organization devoted to diabetes education and advocacy. With various projects reaching hundreds of communities both in the US and internationally, its mission is to spread the awareness of the need for and possibility of the prevention and optimal control of diabetes and to help improve the lives of all people affected by diabetes, with a strong focus on the correlation between obesity, diabetes, and other diabetes health-related issues, especially coupled with a Jewish lifestyle. (www.jewishdiabetes.org)

Jewish Fertility Foundation (JFF) 60 Lenox Pointe NE, Atlanta, GA (678) 744-7018. The JFF provides financial assistance, educational awareness, and emotional support to Jewish people who have medical fertility challenges.

Jewish Genetic Disease Consortium (JGDC) (2006). 1515 Route 202, #121, Pomona, NY 10970. (855) 642-6900. The JGDC is an alliance of individuals and nonprofit organizations working together to prevent Jewish genetic diseases through education, awareness, and testing. It encourages timely and appropriate genetic screening for all persons of Jewish heritage, whether Ashkenazi, Mizrahi, or Sephardic, as well as interfaith couples. The JGDC educates physicians, rabbis, and Jews of all backgrounds about Jewish genetic diseases in order to increase genetic screening rates and an understanding of the reproductive options available to reduce the incidence of Jewish genetic diseases. (www.jewishgeneticdiseases.org)

Nefesh: The International Network of Orthodox Mental Health Professionals (1992). 3805 Avenue R, Brooklyn, NY 11234. (201) 384-0084. Nefesh is an interdisciplinary organization of Orthodox Jewish mental health professionals providing leadership and interdisciplinary education in the field of personal, family, and community mental health. It provides an opportunity and vehicle for Orthodox Jewish mental health professionals, clergy, and educators to network and collaborate to enhance the emotional well-being and unity of Klal Yisroel. Its diverse members include Torah-observant psychologists, social workers, psychiatrists, marriage and family therapists, professional counselors, psychiatric nurses, chemical dependency counselors, psychotherapists, guidance and pastoral counselors, and graduate students, and its affiliates include Orthodox rabbis, Jewish educators, attorneys, and allied professionals. (www.nefesh.org)

Orthodox Jewish Nurses Association (OJNA) (2008). The OJNA seeks to provide a forum to discuss professional issues related to Orthodox Jewish nurses, arrange social and educational events, and serve the special needs of its members. It strives to promote professionalism and career advancement, and to be a voice for Orthodox Jewish nurses across the world. Representation on OJNA's active Facebook forum spans the US, Israel, and Canada. (www.jewishnurses.org)

Renewal (2006). 5904 13th Avenue, Brooklyn, NY 11219. (718) 431-9831. Renewal is dedicated to assisting people within the Jewish community who are suffering from various forms of kidney disease and to saving lives through kidney donation. It provides guidance and support to help patients and their families navigate all the medical challenges of coping with chronic kidney disease. Renewal's ultimate goal is to obtain a kidney for those who would like to undergo a transplant, with no one having to wait longer than 6 months to find a donor. Renewal provides referrals, guidance, and continuous support to both donor and recipient. It holds donor drives and educational events and publicizes the need for organ donation within the Jewish community. (www.renewal.org)

Sephardic Health Organization for Referral and Education (SHORE) (2013) 3 Forest Lane, Great Neck, NY 11024. (818) 400-2219. SHORE is comprised of organizations, synagogues, prominent members, physicians, and spiritual leaders from the Sephardic community sharing a common goal of combating Sephardic Jewish genetic diseases. Its mission is to increase awareness and educate the community about Sephardic Jewish genetic diseases; encourage genetic testing for carrier status in order to help eliminate genetic diseases in future generations of the Sephardic/Iranian Jewish community; and provide a source of information for affected individuals and their families. (www.shoreforlife.org)

Sharsheret (2001). 1086 Teaneck Road, Suite 2G, Teaneck, NJ 07666. (866) 474-2774 or (201) 833-2341. Sharsheret (Chain, in Hebrew) supports young women and their families facing breast cancer. Its mission is to offer a community of support to women, of all Jewish backgrounds, diagnosed with breast cancer or at increased genetic risk by fostering culturally-relevant, individualized connections with networks of peers, health professionals, and related resources. Sharsheret's free support and educational programs serve all women and men nationwide. It also provides educational resources and offers specialized support to those facing ovarian cancer or at high risk of developing cancer, and creates programs for women and families to improve their quality of life. (www.sharsheret.org)

Uprooted: A Jewish Response to Infertility (2014). 82 Wendell Avenue, Suite 100, Pittsfield, MA 01201. Through programming, advocacy, and ritual creation, Uprooted educates American Jewish leaders in assisting families with fertility challenges and provides national communal support to those struggling to grow their families. Uprooted aims to create an American Jewish community where those struggling to achieve the goal of growing their family feel supported and welcomed. It develops training sessions and resource materials on how to support fertility journeys within local communities and works directly with support groups, clergy, and community leaders to provide insight and best practices on a wide range of fertility related topics with a Jewish perspective. (www.weareuprooted.org)

Yesh Tikva (2015). 324 South Beverly Drive, Suite 354, Beverly Hills, CA 90212. Yesh Tikva was established to increase awareness of infertility throughout the Jewish community and create a Jewish community of support. Resources include support groups, online support forums, platforms for sharing personal stories, and events. Yesh Tikva also aims to increase the sensitivity of those who have not struggled to have to children and to equip them with the resources to help and support those who may be suffering in silence. (www.yeshtikva.org)

12.1.32   *Jewish Organizations for People with Disabilities or Special Needs*

Chai Lifeline (1987). 151 West 30th Street, New York, NY 10001. (212) 465-1300 or (877) 242-4543. Chai Lifeline addresses the emotional, social, and financial needs of seriously ill children, their families, and their communities, and strives to restore normalcy to family life and better enable families to withstand the crises and challenges of serious pediatric illness. It provides creative, innovative, and effective family-centered programs, activities, and services to bring joy to the lives of young patients and their families; engenders hope and optimism in children, families, and communities; educates and involves communities in caring for ill children and their families; and provides support throughout the child's illness, recovery, and beyond. Chai Lifeline has an extensive network of free programs and services to ensure that every family has access to the programs it needs. (www.chailifeline.org)

Friendship Circle International (also known as **The Friendship Circle**) (1994). 816 Eastern Parkway, Brooklyn, NY 11213. (718) 713-3062. The mission of Friendship Circle International, affiliated with the Chabad Lubavitch movement, is to bring happiness and companionship to children and young adults with special needs, as well as energy, support, and peace of mind to their families, with a focus on developing the values of altruism, compassion, and acceptance in its teen volunteers while heightening community awareness and sensitivity and encouraging a sense of responsibility and involvement. Friendship Circle chapters in local communities around the world create meaningful relationships and friendships between teen volunteers and children with special needs. Programs include home visits to children with special needs, winter and summer camps, holiday programs, Children's Torah Circle, sports activities, sibling support programs, teaching life skills, a sponsored walk-a-thon, and fundraising activities. (www.friendshipcircle.com)

Heart to Heart: The American Jewish Society for Distinguished Children (1990). 616 East New York Avenue, Brooklyn, NY 11203. (718) 778-0111. Heart to

Heart provides services that advocate for Jewish infants with special needs to remain at home with their parents and siblings, and when that option is not possible Heart to Heart provides everything necessary to help make the transition to acceptance into an all new, warm and caring family. Current services include finding suitable long-term and short-term living arrangements for babies abandoned at birth; seminars educating, informing, and encouraging parents, teachers, and the community; camp fund for special needs children; advocating for families with children in the Department of Education; setting up inclusion education programs in yeshivas; and shabbatons for families, siblings, and children with disability issues. (www.hearttoheartamerican.org)

JBI International (JBI) (formerly **The Jewish Braille Institute of America**) (1931). 110 East 30th Street, New York, NY 10016. (212) 889-2525 or (800) 433-1531. JBI is dedicated to meeting the Jewish and general cultural needs of the visually impaired, blind, physically handicapped, and reading disabled—of all ages and backgrounds—worldwide. The JBI Library provides individuals who are visually impaired with books, magazines, and special publications of Jewish and general interest in Braille, large print, and audio format, free of charge, that enable them to maintain their connection to the rich literary and cultural life of the Jewish and broader community. JBI also provides services in Israel, the FSU, Eastern and Central Europe, Latin America, Western Europe, and all English speaking countries. (www.jbilibrary.org)

Jewish Deaf Community Center (JDCC) (formerly **Creative Services Group**) (1992). 507 Bethany Road, Burbank, CA 91504. JDCC promotes individual growth, social awareness, productivity and equality by empowering deaf and hard of hearing persons to be full participants in the Jewish community. It exists exclusively for educational, religious, and charitable purposes, receives inquiries and requests nationwide, and does not charge membership fees. (www.jdcc.org)

Jewish Deaf Congress (JDC) (formerly **National Congress of Jewish Deaf**) (1956). The JDC's mission is to provide religious, cultural, and educational experiences for Jewish persons who are deaf and hard of hearing, primarily in North America, and also serves Jewish deaf and hard of hearing persons all over the world through its biennial conferences. (www.jewishdeafcongress.org)

Jewish Deaf Resource Center (JDRC) (1996). PO Box 318, Hartsdale, NY 10530. (917) 705-8941. JDRC builds bridges between Jews who are deaf and hard of hearing and the individuals and organizations which serve the Jewish community throughout North America. JDRC advocates within the Jewish community for issues of concern to the Jewish deaf community; advocates to increase communication access for Jewish deaf individuals to services, rituals, learning, and other Jewish experiences; advises Jewish organizations on the logistics of creating programs and environments that enable full participation by individuals who are Jewish deaf and hard-of-hearing; and seeks to increase representation of individuals who are deaf and hard of hearing in Jewish communal leadership positions. (www.jdrc.org)

The Jewish Heritage for the Blind (1979). 1655 East 24th Street, Brooklyn, NY 11229. (718) 338-4999 or (800) 995-1888. The Jewish Heritage for the Blind is dedicated to servicing and promoting the independence of individuals who are blind or visually impaired to alleviate the difficulty of fully participating in traditional Jewish life. Services include Bar/Bat mitzvah assistance by providing training, resources, and study sessions in preparation for the Torah reading; assistance in arranging friendship meetings, singles get-togethers, and small gatherings for handicapped persons of the Jewish faith; visiting nursing homes, social centers, and facilities for the disabled; and offering the handicapped free burial plots in Jewish cemeteries throughout the US and abroad. (www.jewishheritage.org)

Matan (2000). 520 Eighth Avenue, 4th Floor, New York, NY 10018. (866) 410-5600. Matan educates Jewish leaders, educators, and communities, empowering them to create learning environments supportive of children with special needs, through training Institutes and consultations across North America. By advocating for the inclusion of diverse learners, Matan enables the Jewish community to realize the gift of every individual and fulfill its obligation to embrace all children regardless of learning challenges in every Jewish educational setting. (www.matankids.org)

National Association of Day Schools Serving Exceptional Children (NADSEC) (Ceased to exist)

P'TACH (Parents for Torah for All Children) (1976). 1689 East 5th Street, Brooklyn, NY 11230. (718) 854-8600. P'TACH's mission is to provide the best possible Jewish and secular education to children who have been disenfranchised because of learning differences. P'TACH has established special classes and resource centers in conjunction with yeshivas and Jewish day schools throughout the US, Canada, and Israel as model programs which it utilizes as laboratories in the forefront of research and discovery on how children learn. P'TACH works to promote public understanding of the diverse learning needs of children and to create opportunities and programs to give every child an equal opportunity to a Jewish education by providing intensive training for regular classroom teachers and empowering them to understand and manage differences in learning. (www.ptach.org)

Rosh Pina (2012). (510) 495-0851. Rosh Pina's Cornerstone Certification process offers a way for organizations and institutions to meet the requirements of their special needs populations by leading them on a year-long journey to create meaningful, enduring change, producing a truly inclusive community. Certification not only serves those with special needs but also positively impacts the organization as a whole, ensuring that individuals and families of all abilities are included as integral parts of the Jewish community. (www.rpcornerstone.org)

Yachad: The National Jewish Council for Disabilities (1983). 11 Broadway, 13th Floor, New York, NY 10004. (212) 613-8229. Yachad, with chapters located throughout the US and Canada, is dedicated to addressing the needs of Jewish individuals with disabilities and ensuring their inclusion in every aspect of Jewish life. Yachad's services include social programming; counseling services for individuals and families; weekend retreats; extensive parent support services; sibling services; vocational training and job placement; professional advocates and case managers; summer camps; special needs yeshivas; Shabbat programs; day habilitation programs; Israel Birthright trips for persons with mobility and/or special learning needs; social skills development; lobbying for pro-disability legislation on the local, state and federal levels; and high school and university leadership programming. Its programs include Our Way for the Deaf and Hard of Hearing. (www.yachad.org)

Yad HaChazakah: The Jewish Disability Empowerment Center (2006). 576 Fifth Avenue, Suite 903 New York, NY 10036. (646) 723-3955. Led by Jews with disabilities and in accordance with Torah standards, Yad HaChazakah-JDEC provides guidance, resource information, advocacy, and support networks for people with obvious or hidden disabilities and their families as it promotes access to Jewish community life. It provides learning sessions and informational workshops; offers discussion groups and networking opportunities; helps Jewish community organizations better accommodate students, patrons, and employees with disabilities; and helps raise awareness about how communities can be more inclusive of people with disabilities. (www.yadempowers.org)

12.1.33   Jewish End of Life Organizations

Jewish Cemetery Association of North America (JCANA) (2009). 2425 East Fourteen Mile Road, Birmingham, MI 48009. JCANA is organized for charitable, educational, and religious purposes to preserve Jewish cemetery continuity by assembling, organizing, and disseminating information relative to the Jewish cemeteries of North America. JCANA sustains community awareness relating to end of life issues and traditional Jewish burial practices; advocates for Federal legislation to protect Jewish cemetery rights and contests legislative acts that would infringe on religious freedom; and offers its members timely advice on all aspects of Jewish cemetery management. (www.jcana.org)

The Jewish Funeral Directors of America (JFDA) (1932). 107 Carpenter Drive, Suite 100, Sterling, VA 20164. (800) 645-7700. JFDA is an International association of funeral homes who predominantly serve members of the Jewish faith. It guides, aids and supports its members in honoring the deceased and comforting the bereaved by preserving, promoting and practicing the customs and traditions of the Jewish funeral. (www.iccfa.com/membership/jfda)

The Kaddish Foundation (1987). 277 Saddle River Road, Airmont, NY 10952. (888) 999-7685. The Kaddish Foundation offers Kaddish recital, yizkor, and yahrzeit observance services to Jews as well as Mishnah study for a full year on behalf of the departed. With offices in the US and Jerusalem, it is a worldwide operation endorsed by many Jewish organizations, rabbis, and synagogues. (www.kaddish-foundation.com)

Kavod-The Independent Jewish Funeral Chapels (formerly **National Independent Jewish Funeral Directors**) (2002). 13625 Bishop's Drive, Brookfield, WI 53005. (262) 814-1554. Kavod is a network of independent family-owned Jewish funeral providers created to support one another in a changing environment. Kavod believes that a solid future for funeral service is based on the collective insight and dedication from caring professionals whose unified voice helps to shape and provide the professional standards that families and communities count on in their time of need. Membership in Kavod is by invitation only. (www.nijfd.org)

Kavod v'Nichum (2000). 8112 Sea Water Path, Columbia, MD 21045. (410) 733-3700. Kavod v'Nichum (Honor and Comfort, in Hebrew) encourages and assists the organization of bereavement committees and Chevra Kadisha groups in synagogues and communities in the US and Canada so that they can perform Jewish funeral, burial, and mourning mitzvot; protect and shield bereaved families from exploitation; and provide information, education, and technical assistance that helps bring these important life cycle events back into the synagogue community. It sponsors an annual international conference whose focus is on Chevra Kadisha, Jewish cemeteries, and all aspects of Jewish death practices and is also a sponsor of the Gamliel Institute, which is dedicated to education related to Jewish death, dying, burial, and mourning. (www.jewish-funerals.org)

Misaskim (2004). 5805 16th Avenue, Brooklyn, NY 11204. (718) 854-4548 or (877) 243-7336. Misaskim's mission is to provide support and assistance to individuals experiencing crisis or tragedy by providing vital community services, including safeguarding the dignity of the deceased; advocating for prevention of autopsies and/or cremation; educating government officials, medical examiners, and coroners regarding mandated respect to the Jewish departed; assisting the bereaved with the many challenges during crisis or loss; burial arrangements for the indigent; assistance to widows and orphans; and providing individuals with physical and moral support during these times. Misaskim also provides disaster/accident recovery services and is effectively the American branch of the Israeli organization ZAKA. (www.misaskim.org)

National Association of Chevra Kadisha (NASCK) (formerly **Association of Chevros Kadisha**) (1996). 85-18 117th Street, Richmond Hill, NY 11418. (718) 847-6280. NASCK was created to form a united and cohesive group of Jewish burial societies in the US and Canada, dedicated to traditional Jewish burial practices. The activities of NASCK include registry of Jewish burial societies; education and outreach to the community-at-large; burial society training, seminars, and conferences; website, newsletter, and educational materials; establishing new Jewish burial societies; halakhic hotline; tracking, developing, and assessing legal issues; creating specific innovative programs geared to reducing the incidence of cremation; burying the indigent; grief and bereavement issues; and creating and advancing programs and initiatives to promote traditional Jewish end-of-life values. (www.nasck.org)

National Institute for Jewish Hospice (NIJH) (1985). 732 University Street, North Woodmere, New York 11581. (800) 446-4448 or (516) 791-9888. NIJH serves as a national Jewish hospice resource center that was established to help alleviate suffering in serious and terminal illness. Its members are comprised of business and professional leaders and a consortium of endowing foundations. NIJH serves as a resource and educational center for hospices, hospitals, family service, medical organizations and all health-care agencies, educating them to the issues and challenges of serving the Jewish terminally ill. It provides hospice training and accreditation of Jewish hospice programs in the US and assists facilities in planning conferences, training staff, and designing appropriate workshops to better serve the Jewish terminally ill. A 24-h toll-free number counsels families, patients, and caregivers, and provides locations of hospices, hospitals, health professionals, and clergy of all faiths. (www.nijh.org)

12.1.34 Jewish Media Organizations

70 Faces Media (1917) (2015) 24 West 30th Street, 4th Floor, New York, NY 10001. (212) 643-1890. Formed through the merger of the Jewish Telegraphic Agency (JTA) and My Jewish Learning, 70 Faces Media is a digital media company that aspires to connect as many people as possible to all sides of the unfolding Jewish story. Its brands, which include Alma, Jewniverse, JTA, JTA Archive, Kveller, My Jewish Learning, and The Nosher, collectively serve as a virtual town square, highlighting and hosting a multitude of voices and conversations that inform people about Jewish news, history, traditions, values, entertainment, and culture; reaching people wherever they are in their lives, level of Jewish knowledge, and sense of Jewish identity; and connecting people and communities in North America, Israel, and around the globe. (www.70facesmedia.org)

American Jewish Press Association (AJPA) (1944). c/o KCA Association Management, 107 South Southgate Drive, Chandler, AZ 85226. (480) 403-4602. The AJPA was founded as a voluntary professional association for the English-language Jewish press in North America. Today, its membership consists of newspapers, magazines, websites, other electronic Jewish media organizations, individual journalists, and affiliated organizations throughout the US and Canada. Its mission is to enhance the status of American Jewish journalism; provide a forum for the exchange of ideas and cooperative activities among the American Jewish press; promote robust, independent, and financially healthy Jewish media; foster the highest ethics, editorial quality, and business standards to help its members navigate their challenges and responsibilities, especially those unique to the Jewish media; and share resources and expertise, provide access to professional development, and advocate for collective interests. The AJPA sponsors the competition for the annual Simon Rockower Jewish Journalism Awards for excellence in Jewish journalism. (www.ajpa.org)

Committee for Accuracy in Middle East Reporting in America (CAMERA) (1982). PO Box 35040, Boston, MA 02135. (617) 789-3672. CAMERA is a media-monitoring, research, and membership organization devoted to promoting accurate and balanced coverage of Israel and the Middle East. It systematically monitors, documents, reviews, and archives Middle East coverage. Staffers directly contact reporters, editors, producers, and publishers concerning distorted or inaccurate coverage, offering factual information to refute errors. CAMERA members are encouraged to write letters for publication in the print media and to communicate with correspondents, anchors, and network officials in the electronic media. CAMERA's combination of rigorous monitoring, research, fact-checking, careful analysis, and grassroots efforts have had a documented impact. A nonpartisan organization, CAMERA takes no position with regard to American or Israeli political issues or with regard to ultimate solutions to the Arab-Israeli conflict. (www.camera.org)

Facts and Logic About the Middle East (FLAME) (1994). PO Box 3460, Berkeley, CA 94703. FLAME's purpose is the research and publication of the facts regarding developments in the Middle East and exposing false propaganda that might harm the interests of the US and its allies in that area of the world. It brings the truth about Israel and the Middle East conflict to the attention of an American public that is mostly uninformed and misinformed about these matters, in part because the media—both print and broadcast—are with few exceptions biased against Israel. FLAME publishes monthly hasbarah (educating and clarifying) messages in major US publications, college newspapers, Jewish publications, and small-town newspapers, across the US and Canada, covering an important segment of the population that might otherwise not have access to mainstream media. (www.factsandlogic.org)

Fuente Latina (FL) (2012). 1125 Northeast 125th Street, Suite 300-3, North Miami, FL 33161. (786) 406-6048. FL breaks down geographic, cultural, and linguistic barriers to facilitate Spanish-speaking global media and influencers to cover the current situation and the reality of Israel and the Middle East. Its mission is to increase the formation and understanding of Israel and the Middle East of Hispanics in the US and Latin America. (www.fuentelatina.org)

Haym Salomon Center (HSC) (2014). 5 Revere Drive, Suite 200, Northbrook, IL 60062. (847) 616-9100. HSC is a news and public policy group that produces content often ignored by traditional media outlets. It consists of a team of reporters and Fellows producing news and opinion content from a pro-Western, pro-democracy viewpoint for publication in the mainstream and news media outlets. Their work, combating antisemitism and Islamic terrorism and defending Western values, has been published everywhere from USA Today and the New York Daily News to Fox News, The Hill, and the Wall Street Journal. (www.salomoncenter.org)

HonestReporting (2000). 165 East 56th Street, 2nd Floor, New York, NY 10022. (646) 654-0316. HonestReporting monitors the news for bias, inaccuracy, or other breach of journalistic standards in coverage of the Arab-Israeli conflict, and effects change through education and action. It facilitates accurate reporting for foreign journalists covering the Middle East, providing support services for journalists based in or visiting Israel, the Palestinian territories, and the region to insure the free flow of information. It provides agenda-free services to reporters, including translation services and access to news makers to enable them to provide a fuller picture of the situation. Formed by a small group of British college students looking to respond to unfair coverage of Israel in the wake of the second Intifada, HonestReporting is not aligned with any government, political party, or movement. (www.honestreporting.com)

ISRAEL21c (2001). 44 Montgomery Street, Suite 3700, San Francisco, CA 94104. Israel21c was established as an independent news and education organization with a mission to increase public and media awareness about the Israel that exists beyond the conflict and beyond typical portrayals in the mainstream media.

ISRAEL21c publishes an English-language online news magazine, recognized as the single most diverse and reliable source of news and information about 21st century Israel, whose content is used by individuals, organizations, associations, news services, bloggers, and businesses around the world. Its website offers a vast resource of originally researched and produced articles, videos, images, and blogs by some of Israel's leading journalists, uncovering the country's rich and diverse culture, innovative spirit, wide-ranging contributions to humanity, and democratic civil society. (www.israel21c.org)

Jewish Education in Media (JEM) (1979). PO Box 180, Riverdale Station, New York, NY 10471. JEM is devoted to producing television, film, and video-cassettes for a popular Jewish audience to inform, entertain, and inspire a greater sense of Jewish identity and Jewish commitment. JEM presents the Jewish Broadcasting Service (JBS), formerly Shalom TV, a nonprofit national Jewish television network. JBS programming includes daily news reports from Israel, live event coverage and analysis, and cultural programming of interest to the North American Jewish community. (www.rethinkpartners.com/shalomtv/?page_id=5)

Jewish Internet Defense Force (JIDF) (2000). JIDF is a private, independent, nonviolent protest organization representing a collective of activists operating since the massacre at the Mercaz HaRav Yeshiva in Jerusalem. JIDF is on the cutting edge of pro-Israel digital online advocacy, presenting news, viewpoints, and information to those who share its concerns for Israel, and about antisemitic and jihadist online content, throughout a large network reaching hundreds of thousands via email, Facebook, YouTube, RSS feeds, Twitter and other digital hubs. Its ACTION ALERTS are well known throughout the Jewish and Israel advocacy world, as they have led to the removal of thousands of antisemitic and jihadist pages online. (www.thejidf.org)

Jewish Student Press Service (JSPS) (1971). 440 Park Avenue South, New York, NY 10016. (212) 675-1168. The JSPS is an independent, student-run organization established to provide quality, student-written articles to a thriving network of Jewish campus publications across the country. Many of today's most accomplished Jewish journalists got their start at the JSPS. Since 1991, the JSPS has published its own magazine, *New Voices*, America's only national magazine written and published by and for Jewish college students, with which JSPS continues its tradition of cultivating the next generation of Jewish journalists, creating a Jewish media that speaks to young Jews and empowering Jewish students to take ownership of their heritage. (www.newvoices.org)

The Middle East Media & Research Institute (MEMRI) (1998). PO Box 27837, Washington, DC 20038. (202) 955-9070. An independent, nonpartisan organization that explores the Middle East and South Asia through their media, MEMRI was founded to inform the debate over US policy in the Middle East. MEMRI provides translations from, and original analysis of, the media and other primary sources in the Arab and Muslim world, covering political, ideological, intellectual, social, cultural, and religious trends. It monitors, translates, and analyzes television broadcasts, print media, mosque sermons, schoolbooks, and other important sources in the region. MEMRI research is translated into English, French, Polish, Japanese, and Hebrew. MEMRI's projects address such issues as antisemitism, emerging developments in jihadist movements, and issues of individual liberty and religious and cultural freedom in South Asia, Islamist terrorism in the Arab world and worldwide, and the 9/11 attacks. (www.memri.org)

12.1.35   Jewish Environmental Organizations

Amir (2010). 5 Kresteller Circle, Madison, WI 53719. Amir's goal is to inspire and empower youth through the medium of farming and gardening, helping to foster a more just and compassionate world. Amir facilitates garden and farm-based education for thousands of youth across North America and seeks to provide garden and farm-based education to youth across the world, both at summer camps and in year-round communal spaces. The Amir Farming Fellowship develops leadership and community-organizing skills among college-age students. (www.amirproject.org)

Aytzim: Ecological Judaism (formerly **Green Zionist Alliance**) (2001). 450 Bay Avenue, Somers Point, NJ 08244. (347) 559-4492. Aytzim (Trees, in Hebrew) offers a place for all people, regardless of political or religious affiliation, who care about humanity's responsibility to preserve the Earth and the special responsibility of the Jewish people to preserve the ecology of Israel. It works to educate and mobilize people around the world for Israel's environment; protect Israel's environment and support its environmental movement; improve environmental practices within the World Zionist Organization and its constituent agencies; and inspire people to work for positive change. Aytzim seeks to bridge the differences between and within religions and people—helping to build a peaceful and sustainable future for Israel and the Middle East. (www.aytzim.org)

Canfei Nesharim (2004). Canfei Nesharim (The Wings of Eagles, in Hebrew) is the only organization that is engaging the Orthodox Jewish community to take an active role in protecting the environment. It is building the foundation of a Torah-based environmental movement by creating educational resources and synagogue programs; training leaders and speakers; and inspiring the Jewish community to commit to environmental action. Connecting traditional Torah texts with contemporary scientific findings, Canfei Nesharim educates and empowers Jewish individuals, organizations, and communities to take an active role in protecting the environment in order to build a more sustainable world. It also connects Jewish environmentalists so that they can learn from one another and engage each other in shared campaigns. (www.canfeinesharim.org)

Coalition on the Environment and Jewish Life (COEJL) (1993). 116 East 27th Street, 10th Floor, New York, NY 10016. (212) 532-7436. COEJL deepens and broadens the Jewish community's commitment to stewardship and protection of the Earth through outreach, activism, and Jewish learning. It partners with the full spectrum of national Jewish organizations to integrate Jewish values of environmental stewardship into Jewish life. Through a network of Jewish leaders, institutions, and individuals, COEJL is mobilizing the Jewish community to conserve energy, increase sustainability, and advocate for policies that increase energy efficiency and security while building core Jewish environmental knowledge and serving as a Jewish voice in the broader interfaith community. COEJL serves as the Jewish partner in the National Religious Partnership for the Environment. (www.coejl.org)

GrowTorah (2015). 282 Elm Avenue, Teaneck, NJ 07666. GrowTorah develops educational Torah garden programs for Jewish schools and communal organizations, and envisions a GrowTorah program in every Jewish day school across North America, which will serve as an interdisciplinary experiential laboratory for students to engage with Torah, science, health, Jewish values and ethics, and more. GrowTorah curates educational garden experiences through which participants explore relevant Jewish values and Torah lessons, and learn the fundamentals of gardening, farming, and planting. (www.growtorah.org)

Hazon (2000). c/o Makom Hadash, 125 Maiden Lane, Suite 8B, New York, NY 10038. (212) 644-2332. Hazon (Vision, in Hebrew) is America's largest Jewish environmental group, creating healthier and more sustainable communities in the Jewish world and beyond. Its programs are multi-generational and give entry points for Jews of all backgrounds who are concerned about the environment and the world. Hazon serves a national and international population; members of every denomination and those who are unaffiliated; and inter-generational from children to seniors, including families and singles, with a particular focus on young adults interested in developing the skills to take on leadership roles in their communities and make a difference in the world. Hazon effects change through transformative experiences, thought-leadership, and capacity-building. Its transformative experiences and programs include bike rides, retreats, adventures, workshops, conferences, festivals, vacations, JOFEE (Jewish, Outdoor, Food & Environmental Education), Siach, Makom Hadash, Shmita Project, Shomrei Adamah, Adamah Fellowship, Elat Chayyim, Green Hevra, Hakhel Intentional Communities, Wilderness Torah, and Teva. The Isabella Freedman Jewish Retreat Center is also part of Hazon. (www.hazon.org)

Israel Longhorn Project (2007). 7777 Bodega Avenue, S-107, Sebastopol, CA 95472. (650) 631-9270. The Israel Longhorn Project is an educational and cattle crossbreeding improvement project whose mission is to help Israel and East Africa by introducing a viable breed of beef cattle—Texas longhorn—that can fit and thrive in their semi-desert environments. Texas Longhorn will decrease calve and cattle losses allowing ranchers to use less cattle and less land to raise enough cattle to support themselves and their community. (www.longhornproject.org)

Jewish Climate Action Network (JCAN) (2015). PO Box 731, Medfield, MA 02052. JCAN works through education, activism, and organizing to add an urgent and visionary Jewish voice to the climate crisis. It builds relationships with environmental and justice leaders in Jewish and other communal organizations; inspires and mobilizes Jewish communities to take leadership and participate in bold climate campaigns; and develops and provides informational resources to allies working on climate change action. (www.jewishclimate.org)

Jewish Farm School (2005). 707 South 50th Street, Philadelphia, PA 19143. (877) 537-6286; Eden Village Camp, which administers the farm's programs: 392

Dennytown Road, Putnam Valley, NY 10579. (877) 397-3336. The Jewish Farm School is dedicated to teaching about contemporary food and environmental issues through innovative training and skill-based Jewish agricultural education. Through its programs, the Jewish Farm School addresses the injustices embedded in today's mainstream food systems and works to create greater access to sustainably grown foods, produced from a consciousness of both ecological and social well-being. (www.jewishfarmschool.org)

Jewish Farmer Network (2017). (828) 484-2342. Jewish Farmer Network works to connect Jewish farmers to each other and to the communities of which they are a part: Jewish, local, secular, regional, international. It builds relationships among farmers and growers, from which personal and professional growth follows; connects Jewish farmers to the organizations, services, and education that feed their communities, farms, and selves; and guides Jews at any stage of their growing journey toward both volunteer and work opportunities on farms. (www.jewishfarmer-network.org)

Jewish Initiative for Animals (JIFA) (2016). 329 West Pierpont Avenue, Suite 200, Salt Lake City, UT 84101. (323) 403-5264. An initiative of Farm Forward, JIFA supports innovative programs to turn the Jewish value of compassion for animals into action while building ethical and sustainable Jewish American communities in the process. It collaborates with Jewish nonprofit organizations to produce educational resources that will spark inquiry into how Jewish values should interact with how we treat animals, and provides expert consultation to assist Jewish institutions in reducing their meat consumption and building more ethical supply chains that provide viable alternatives to factory farmed products. (www.jewishinitiative-foranimals.org)

Jewish National Fund (JNF) (1901). 42 East 69th Street, New York, NY 10021. (212) 879-9300 or (888) 563-0099. JNF is the American fundraising arm of Keren Kayemeth Lelsrael, the official land agency in Israel. JNF performs groundbreaking work to develop the land of Israel through a variety of multifaceted initiatives in the areas of water resource development; forestry and ecology; education, tourism, and recreation; community development; security; and research and development. JNF has evolved into a global environmental leader by planting more than 250 million trees, building over 240 reservoirs and dams, developing over 250,000 acres of land, creating more than 2000 parks, providing the infrastructure for over 1000 communities, bringing life to the Negev Desert, and educating students around the world about Israel and the environment. (www.jnf.org)

Jewish Veg (formerly **Jewish Vegetarians of North America** and **The Jewish Vegetarian Society of America**) (1975). 9 Hawthorne Road, Pittsburgh, PA 15221. (412) 965-9210. Jewish Veg's mission is to encourage and help Jews to embrace plant-based diets as an expression of the Jewish values of compassion for animals, concern for health, and care for the environment. (www.jewishveg.org)

Jews for Animal Rights (JAR) (1985). c/o Micah Publications, Inc., 255 Humphrey Street, Marblehead, MA 01945. (781) 631-7601. JAR was founded with the aim of upholding and spreading the Talmudic prohibition against causing suffering to living creatures, known as tza'ar ba'alei hayyim. It promotes the ideas of

Rabbi Abraham Kook on vegetarianism and campaigns to find alternatives to animal testing. (www.facebook.com/JewsForAnimalRights)

Mosaic Outdoor Clubs of America (MOCA) (formerly **Mosaic Outdoor Mountain Club**) (1988). 2885 Sanford Avenue SW 317827, Grandville, MI 49418. (888) 667-2427. MOCA is a network of Jewish outdoor clubs dedicated to organizing outdoor and environmental activities for Jewish singles, couples, and families of all ages. The all-volunteer-run organization integrates Jewish values with an appreciation of the outdoors and promotes appreciation of the outdoors, nature, outdoor skills, and conservation while helping to build Jewish community and continuity. It brings together members of the Jewish community to celebrate and explore the great outdoors in a social setting, which is achieved by sponsoring activities on a national/international scale, and encouraging and facilitating the formation and continuation of local Mosaic clubs for the purpose of sponsoring local/regional activities. Local clubs are located throughout the US, Canada, and Israel. (www.mosaicoutdoor.org)

Pearlstone Center (formerly **The Jack Pearlstone Institute for Living Judaism**) (1982) (2001). 5425 Mt. Gilead Road, Reisterstown, MD 21136. (443) 273-5201. The Pearlstone Center creates common ground for individuals, groups, and families connecting through retreats, conferences, field trips, volunteering, multicultural programs, fellowships, workshops, and celebrations, connecting people to the land so they can understand and value the connection between man and earth and easily focus on the fundamental elements of life, and teaching through motivating, joyous, and hands-on experiences. The environment that the Pearlstone Center creates, and the programming offered fosters, memorable spiritual experiences and ignites vibrant Jewish life. The Pearlstone Center, which sits on 180 acres of forest, fields, and meadows, and whose campus includes an educational farm, embodies, teaches, and inspires the practice of environmental sustainability. (www.pearlstone-center.org)

ReJews (2013). 9325A Neil Road, Philadelphia, PA 19115. (215) 694-0443. ReJews establishes community-focused environmental action by helping schools, synagogues, community centers, restaurants, offices, and businesses establish recycling initiatives and campaigns in their buildings and neighborhoods, highlighting the importance of focusing on building more sustainable communities. ReJews invites all Jewish organizations to receive free official ReJews branded recycling receptacles, and by reporting on the amount that they have recycled and utilized the receptacles, organizations can become eligible to receive rewards through the ReJews incentive program. (www.rejews.org)

SHAMAYIM: Jewish Animal Advocacy (formerly **Shamayim V'Aretz Institute**) (2012). 12631 Imperial Highway, F-106, Santa Fe Springs, CA 90670. (602) 445-3112. SHAMAYIM is a Jewish animal welfare organization that educates leaders, trains advocates, and leads campaigns for the ethical treatment of animals. (www.shamayimvaretz.org)

TorahTrek Center for Jewish Wilderness Spirituality (2001). The TorahTrek Center for Jewish Wilderness Spirituality contributes to vibrant Jewish communities, living in balance with their neighbors and environs, by exposing Judaism's roots in wilderness, facilitating direct experience of the Divine in nature, demonstrating the effectiveness of Judaism as a spiritual practice, and fostering the spiritual growth of individual Jews and Jewish communities. Through leadership training and curriculum development, TorahTrek envisions a Jewish community that takes full advantage of the natural world in mainstream Jewish education for children, youth, and adults. (www.torahtrek.org)

Yiddish Farm Education Center (2010). 71 Dzierzek Lane, New Hampton, NY 10958. (845) 360-5023. Yiddish Farm fosters and promotes expression in the Yiddish language, building bridges of cross cultural engagement that extend from the context of its working organic farm to the world beyond. Its immersive Yiddish programs empower Jews to reclaim Yiddish as a source of Jewish culture, identity, and learning. Its environmental programming brings high quality outdoor education to native Yiddish speakers. The organic farm provides the context, inspiration, and foundations for a future settled Yiddish-speaking agricultural community. Yiddish Farm produces organic shmura matzo for sale as well as organic vegetables and free range eggs for its residents, students, and guests. (www.yiddishfarm.org)

12.1.36   Jewish Academic Organizations

(See additional Jewish academic organizations in Chap. 14, Sect. 5.)

Association of Orthodox Jewish Scientists (AOJS) (1947). 69-09 172nd Street, Fresh Meadows, NY 11365. (718) 969-3669. AOJS is devoted to the orientation of science within the framework of Orthodox Jewish tradition. It aims to assist those endeavors which will help improve the Torah way of life for Jews throughout the modern world, both intellectually and practically. AOJS provides assistance to individuals and institutions in the solution of practical problems encountered by Orthodox Jews and their children in the study or practice of scientific pursuits; studies the applicability of scientific method and knowledge to the strengthening of Torah ideology; and provides consulting services to Rabbinical authorities concerned with the implications of technological developments for the Jewish religious law. (www.aojs.org)

Jewish Alliance for Women in Science (JAWS) (2009). JAWS seeks to promote the entrance of Jewish women into careers related to math and science. To address the realization that Jewish women face unique challenges and issues that are best addressed by other Jewish women who have faced similar hardships and choices, JAWS fosters discussion and the spread of information among Jewish women interested in science careers, functioning as a support system for women trying to balance their social obligations with the lifestyle that a career in science demands. (www.jawscience.webs.com)

National Association of Professors of Hebrew (NAPH) (1950). c/o Esther Raizen, Executive Vice President, The University of Texas at Austin, 204 West 21st Street, Stop F9400, Calhoun Hall 528, Austin, TX 78712. NAPH's mission is to foster scholarship and academic teaching of Hebrew language, literature, and culture of all periods, from the biblical era to the present, in institutions of higher learning. Membership consists of Hebrew scholars, teachers, and graduate students in universities, colleges, and seminaries all over the world. NAPH convenes an annual International Conference on Hebrew Language, Literature and Culture; organizes a series of sessions at the annual conference of the Society for Biblical Literature; publishes *Hebrew Studies*, an internationally recognized scholarly journal covering all periods of Hebrew language, literature, and culture; publishes *Higher Hebrew Education*, an online journal devoted to the methodology and pedagogy of teaching Hebrew in institutions of higher learning; and sponsors Eta Beta Rho, a national scholastic honors society for students of Hebrew in institutions of higher learning. (www.naphhebrew.org)

Society of Jewish Ethics (2003). 1531 Dickey Drive, Atlanta, GA 30322. (404) 712-8550. The Society of Jewish Ethics is an academic organization dedicated to the promotion of scholarly work in the field of Jewish ethics, including the relation of Jewish ethics to other traditions of ethics and to social, economic, political, and cultural problems. It also aims to encourage and improve the teaching of Jewish ethics in colleges, universities, and theological schools; promote an understanding of Jewish ethics within the Jewish community and society as a whole; and provide a community of discourse and debate for those engaged professionally in Jewish ethics. (www.societyofjewishethics.org)

12.1.37   Jewish Fraternities/Sororities

Alpha Epsilon Phi Sorority (AEPhi) (1909). 11 Lake Avenue Extension, Suite 1A, Danbury, CT 06811. (203) 748-0029. AEPhi was founded at Barnard College in NYC by seven Jewish women who wanted to foster lifelong friendship and sisterhood, academics, social involvement, and community service while providing a home away from home for their members. AEPhi continues to thrive on more than 50 college and university campuses in the US and Canada. Today, AEPhi is a Jewish sorority, but not a religious organization, with membership open to all college women, regardless of religion, who honor, respect, and appreciate its Jewish founding and identity and are comfortable in a culturally Jewish environment. (www.aephi.org)

Alpha Epsilon Pi Fraternity (AEPi) (1913). 8815 Wesleyan Road, Indianapolis, IN 46268. (317) 876-1913. Founded by 11 Jewish men at New York University, AEPi is an international Jewish fraternity active on more than 190 campuses in the US and Canada. While AEPi is nondiscriminatory and open to all who are willing to espouse its purpose and values, the fraternity's mission—developing the future leaders of the Jewish communities—is demonstrated every day through acts of brotherhood, tzedakah, social awareness, and support for Jewish communities and Israel. Its basic purpose is to provide the opportunity for Jewish men to join a Jewish organization whose purpose is not specifically religious, but rather social and cultural in nature. AEPi encourages Jewish students to remain loyal to their heritage and offers many opportunities for them to explore their Jewish heritage both culturally and religiously. (www.aepi.org)

Alpha Omega International Dental Fraternity (AO) (1907). 50 West Edmonston Drive, #206, Rockville, MD 20852. (877) 368-6326 or (301) 738-6400. AO is the oldest international dental organization and oldest international Jewish medical organization. It was founded at the University of Maryland by a group of dental students to fight discrimination in dental schools. Today, it is primarily an educational and philanthropic organization with over 100 alumni and student chapters worldwide. Its mission is to offer dentists, oral health professionals, and students a welcoming fraternal community that honors the organization's Judaic heritage, provides opportunities to attain professional excellence, and promotes access to oral health care for all. AO focuses on philanthropic endeavors that support numerous global oral health and humanitarian projects worldwide. (www.ao.org)

Sigma Alpha Epsilon Pi Sorority (Sigma AEPi) (1998). Sigma AEPi is a Jewish-interest sorority founded at the University of California, Davis by six Jewish women, with active chapters today in several states across the country. Its purpose is to promote unity, support, and Jewish awareness, as well as to provide a Jewish experience for its members and the community as a whole. The sorority is devoted to friendship, motivation, opportunity, leadership, and well-being. Its values are unity, trust, strength, sincere sisterhood, and exemplifying Jewish values. (www.sigmaaepi.com)

Sigma Alpha Mu Fraternity (1909). 8701 Founders Road, Indianapolis, IN 46268. (317) 789-8338. Sigma Alpha Mu was founded by eight Jewish sophomores at the City College of New York as a fraternity of Jewish men. Today, the fraternity is active on more than 50 campuses throughout North America, and it attracts members of all beliefs who respect the ideals and traditions of the fraternity and appreciate its great heritage as a fraternity of Jewish men. Sigma Alpha Mu seeks to foster the development of collegiate men and its alumni by instilling strong fraternal values, offering social and service opportunities, encouraging academic excellence, and teaching leadership skills. It encourages students to take an active role on campus and in community service and philanthropy projects and offers leadership opportunities. (www.sam.org)

Sigma Alpha Rho Fraternity International (formerly **Sigma Alpha Rho of America** and **Soathical Club**) (1917). Sigma Alpha Rho is the oldest, continuously run, independent Jewish high school fraternity, formed primarily for the advancement of Jewish student interests in high school. It is a youth run, youth led fraternity open to all Jewish high school students. Its objectives are to provide leadership opportunities; help Jewish youth develop a positive self-image; encourage friendships among Jewish youth; teach young men social skills; and create lifelong friendships and extensive social networks. (www.sarfraternity.org)

Sigma Delta Tau National Sorority (1917). 714 Adams Street, Carmel, IN 46032. (317) 846-7747. Sigma Delta Tau was founded at Cornell University by seven Jewish women, most of whom had experienced the subtle discrimination that was practiced against religious minorities by many Greek organizations at the time. Today, Sigma Delta Tau is a national sorority with over 60 chapters and is not affiliated with any one religion. It is committed to empowering women through scholarship, service, sisterhood, and leadership. Its mission is to enrich the lifetime experience of women of similar ideals, build lasting friendships, and foster personal growth. Sigma Delta Tau provides intellectual, philanthropic, leadership, and social opportunities for all members within a framework of mutual respect and high ethical standards. (www.sigmadeltatau.com)

Zeta Beta Tau Fraternity (ZBT) (1898). 3905 Vincennes Road, Suite 100, Indianapolis, IN 46268. (317) 334-1898. ZBT was founded as the nation's first Jewish fraternity by a group of Jewish students from several New York City universities and was initially formed as a Zionist youth society, which served as a kind of fraternal body for college students who as Jews were excluded from joining existing fraternities. ZBT's mission is to foster and develop in its membership the tenets of intellectual awareness, social responsibility, integrity, and brotherly love. Mindful of its origins, ZBT preserves and cultivates its relationships within the Jewish community. It is committed to its policy of nonsectarian brotherhood and values the diversity of its membership, recruiting men of good character, regardless of religion, race, or creed who are accepting of its principles. In 1989, ZBT became the first fraternity to abolish pledging from its organization and all two-tier membership statuses, and created a brotherhood program that focuses on equal rights, privileges, and responsibilities for all brothers. (www.zbt.org)

12.1.38   Jewish Sports Organizations

Jewish Coaches Association (JCA) (2006). PO Box 167, Tennent, NJ 07763. (732) 322-5145. JCA's primary purpose is to foster the growth and development of Jewish individuals at all levels of sports, both nationally and internationally. JCA addresses significant issues pertaining to the participation and employment of Jewish individuals in sports, particularly in intercollegiate athletics; provides member coaches with professional and leadership development strategies; creates networking opportunities for Jewish coaches and athletic administrators; promotes the coaching and athletic administration profession to Jews around the world; inspires member coaches to coach with integrity and Jewish values and serve as role models to their teams and communities; and recruits Jews into the coaching and athletic administration profession. (www.jewishcoaches.com)

Jewish Motorcyclists Alliance (JMA) (2005). The JMA is a worldwide association of official, organized, Jewish motorcycle clubs that upon its formation included organized groups in the US, Canada, and Australia, Its major goal is to promote the encouragement and mentoring of its membership in activities which will promote worthy educational and charitable activities that are of benefit to the wider Jewish community and the broader non-Jewish community supportive of the goals and aspirations of the Jewish people, as well as to foster awareness and dissemination of anything related to motorcycling of interest to its members. The JMA seeks to create a global environment whereby members of the Jewish faith who ride motorcycles can congregate in person and/or electronically to share and exchange ideas and opinions about matters of concern to the Jewish community at large as well as issues specifically concerning motorcycles and motorcycle riding. The JMA's signature event is the annual Ride to Remember (R2R), which selects a host site and raises funds for a designated Holocaust-related organization or project. (www.jewishmotorcyclistsalliance.org)

Jewish Sports Heritage Association (2014). 19 Wensley Drive, Great Neck, NY 11021. (516) 406-1414. The Jewish Sports Heritage Association was established to educate the public about the role Jewish men and women have played in sports, an area of Jewish accomplishment often overlooked, and to inspire Jewish athletes and Jewish youth to compete and achieve their dreams. (www.jewishsportsheritage.org)

12.1.39   Other Jewish Organizations

Capital Retreat Center (1987). 12750 Buchanan Trail East, Waynesboro, PA 17268. (717) 794-2177. Capital Retreat Center offers year-round retreat services for synagogues, youth groups, and Jewish organizations seeking the ideal venue for exploring professional, personal, and spiritual growth. Experienced informal educators have planned study materials and experiential programs for guests of all ages, including life cycle events, adult seminars and classes, teen discussions and values clarification programs, youth movement programs on a variety of topics and levels, and holiday and Shabbat programming. (www.capitalretreat.org)

Coalition for Jewish Values (CJV) (2017). 2833 Smith Avenue, Suite 225, Baltimore, MD 21209. (301) 727-2700. The CJV advocates for classical Jewish ideas and standards in matters of American public policy. The six officers who set policy for the CJV are traditional Orthodox rabbis who have served the Jewish and greater American communities for decades as leaders, scholars, and opinion makers and who share positions on moral and ethical issues, national security, immigration, economics, education, public safety, and America's relationship with Israel that many describe as "conservative," but which many rabbis perceive as simply following the great teachers of Jewish history. (www.coalitionforjewishvalues.org)

Darim Online (formerly **Panim Online**) (2000). 1600 Warren Avenue North, Seattle, WA 98109. (434) 260-0177. Darim Online's mission is to advance the Jewish community by helping Jewish organizations align their work for success in the digital age and to use today's available tools and strategies to achieve their goals. It is dedicated to helping Jewish organizations understand the implications of technology and changes in society on their work. Darim Online provides training, coaching, and consulting services, as well as participates in national thought leadership conversations to help advance individuals, organizations, and communities. (www.darimonline.org)

The Dorothy and Myer Kripke Institute (Kripke Institute) (2005). (818) 231-1441. The Kripke Institute, whose guiding vision is a Relational Judaism, is dedicated to bringing joyous and meaningful Jewish living into homes and communal organizations. Its goal is to build relationships between individuals and families with the Jewish experience that empowers the self, strengthens family connection, fosters friendships, enhances Jewish learning and practice, creates community, provides a sense of Jewish peoplehood, fosters ties to the State of Israel, encourages tikkun olam, and leads to a personal relationship with God. Housed in the Kripke Institute are the Center for Relational Judaism, SHEVET: Jewish Family Education Exchange, the Center for Jewish Family Literacy, and the Synagogue 2000/3000 Archive. (www.kripkeinstitute.org)

Fair Trade Judaica (FTJ) 2009). (510) 926-2056. FTJ is building a fair trade movement in the Jewish community, linking Jewish values of human dignity, self-sufficiency, and environmental sustainability with fair trade standards assuring fair and livable wages, no child labor, and healthy and safe working conditions. (www.fairtradejudaica.org)

Jewish Grandparents Network (JGN) 10717 Stevenson Road, Stevenson, MD 21153. (2017). JGN's mission is to celebrate and support grandparents as essential family members who make unique contributions to Jewish children, the Jewish people, and the Jewish future. JGN maintains that financial support and personal time, such as paying for Jewish preschool and taking grandchildren to Tot Shabbat, is the role of today's Jewish grandparent. (www.facebook.com/bubbezayde)

LAVAN (2015). 54 West 40th Street, New York NY 10018. LAVAN educates the next generation of Jewish leadership committed to aligning capital with Jewish values, builds local communities of impact investors, and facilitates meaningful dialogue at the nexus of financial decisions and Jewish values. (www.lavanproject.com)

Magen Tzedek Commission (Ceased to exist)

Resetting the Table (RTT) (2013). RTT is dedicated to building communication and deliberation across political divides in American life, primarily surrounding Israel within the American Jewish community. Drawing from conflict resolution expertise, RTT's approach breaks open communication about charged issues among diverse stakeholders, often entering the room skeptical, dismissive, and estranged. RTT has intensively trained dozens of facilitators and crafted hundreds of forums for thousands of participants, many of them clergy, philanthropists, campus professionals, and other community leaders positioned to impact thousands more. (www.resettingthetable.org)

ROI Community (2005). ROI (Remembrance, Observance, Influence) Community is an international network of young activists and change makers who are enhancing Jewish engagement, strengthening Jewish communities, and fostering positive social change globally. Through its capstone Summit and an innovative suite of ongoing opportunities for professional development, networking, and financial support, ROI Community empowers its members, who are driven by Jewish values, to take an active role in shaping the social landscape of Israel and the future of the Jewish and broader worlds. ROI members are creating new and innovative ways to engage wider audiences in Jewish life globally. (www.schusterman.org/jewish-community-and-israel/signature-initiatives/roi-community)

12.2   National Jewish Organizations, Canada

Note: When an organization has a US counterpart, no description is provided here.

Act to End Violence Against Women (formerly **Jewish Women International of Canada, B'nai B'rith Women of Canada,** and **B'nai B'rith Women of Eastern Canada**) (Ceased to exist as of 2018)

ALEPH Canada: Alliance for Jewish Renewal (Canada) (2004). 3245 Gunpowder Trail, Hornby Island, BC V0R 1Z0. (514) 486-8874. See Jewish Denominational Organizations above. (www.alephcanada.ca)

Arab Jewish Dialogue (AJD) (2006). 360 Main Street, 25th Floor, Winnipeg, MB R3C 4H6. (204) 229-6042. The AJD is dedicated to encouraging positive relations between Arabs and Jews in Canada and works to establish dialogue groups across Canada. The AJD's members, many of whom immigrated to Canada from the Middle East, are committed to two states for two peoples and peace and reconciliation in the Middle East. (www.arabjewishdialogue.com)

ARZA Canada (1977). 3845 Bathurst Street, Suite 301, Toronto, ON M3H 3N2. (416) 630-0375. See Jewish Israel-Related Political and Advocacy Organizations above. (www.arzacanada.org)

Ashkenaz Foundation (1995). 455 Spadina Avenue, Suite 303, Toronto, ON M5S 2G8. (416) 979-9901. The Ashkenaz Foundation is dedicated to fostering an increased awareness of Yiddish and Jewish culture through the arts. Through its biennial festival and an expanding slate of year-round programming, the Ashkenaz Foundation showcases the work of leading contemporary artists from Canada and around the world working in music, film, theatre, dance, literature, craft, and visual arts. (www.ashkenaz.ca)

The Association for the Soldiers of Israel-Canada (ASI-Canada) (1971). 788 Marlee Avenue, Suite 201, Toronto, ON M6B 3K1. (416) 783-3053 or (800) 433-6226. ASI-Canada, the Canadian partner of the Association for the Well-being of Israel's Soldiers, is the only nonprofit organization in Canada that supports the well-being of Israel's soldiers on active duty. By initiating, funding, and supporting social, educational, cultural, and recreational programs and facilities, ASI-Canada strives to boost the morale of the men and women of the Israel Defense Forces. (www.asicanada.org)

The Azrieli Foundation (1989). 1010 St. Catherine Street West, Suite 1200, Montreal, QC H3B 3S3. (514) 282-1155. The Azrieli Foundation supports a wide range of initiatives and programs in the fields of education, architecture and design, Jewish community, Holocaust commemoration and education, scientific and medical research, and arts and music. Its mission is to empower individuals, facilitate innovative outcomes for institutions, and increase knowledge and understanding in the search for practical and novel solutions. It encourages creativity and artistry, and ensures Jewish heritage, memory, and a vibrant Jewish future in Israel and the Diaspora. (www.azrielifoundation.org)

Beit Halochem Canada, Aid to Disabled Veterans of Israel (1984). 1600 Steeles Avenue West, Suite 219, Concord, ON L4K 4M2. (905) 695-0611 or (800) 355-1648. (www.beithalochem.ca)

Birthright Israel Foundation of Canada (2001). c/o JFC-UIA, 4600 Bathurst Street, Suite 315, Toronto, ON M2R 3V3. (416) 636-7655. See Jewish Israel-Related Education Organizations above. (www.jewishcanada.org/bri)

B'nai B'rith Canada (1875). 15 Hove Street, North York, ON M3H 4Y8. (844) 218-2624. See Jewish Social Welfare Organizations above. (www.bnaibrith.ca)

Canada Charity Partners (CCP) (2015). 5785 Smart Avenue, Cote Saint-Luc, QC H4W 2M8. (514) 898-2082. The mission of CCP is to promote health and healing, and to advance education, while addressing and relieving poverty and other social issues in Canada and Israel. It empowers grassroots organizations in Canada and Israel to achieve projects that fulfill its charitable objectives. (No website)

Canada-Israel Cultural Foundation (CICF) (1963). 4700 Bathurst Street, 2nd Floor, Toronto, ON M2R 1W8. (416) 932-2260. See Jewish Cultural Organizations above. (www.cicfweb.ca)

Canada-Israel Education Foundation (CIEF) (Ceased to exist as of 2017)

Canada-Israel Industrial Research & Development Foundation (CIIRDF) (1995). 371A Richmond Road, Suite 3, Ottawa, ON K2A 0E7. (613) 724-1284, ext. 227. CIIRDF, established under a formal mandate from the Governments of Canada and Israel, stimulates and funds collaborative research and development between private sector companies in both countries, with a focus on the commercialization of new technologies and the creation of long term business and research partnerships. (www.ciirdf.ca)

Canadian Antisemitism Education Foundation (CAEF) (2004). c/o The Speakers Action Group, PO Box 42044, John Woodbine PO, Markham, ON L3R 0P9. (905) 413-7230. CAEF is dedicated to promoting tolerance and understanding through cross-cultural education, providing Canadians with knowledge and understanding across ethno-racial and faith communities to see the humanity in all, and to confront discrimination. It is comprised of dedicated volunteers who promote programs of tolerance, interfaith education, combatting antisemitism and racism, and enhancing cross-cultural awareness. CAEF recognizes a new form of antisemitism—the phenomenon that applies a double standard to Israel among the nations of the world, judging everything Israel does through a distorted prism and demonizing Israel with false claims of apartheid—and counters it with truth and facts. CAEF projects include the Speakers Action Group, its flagship program, Canadians for Israel's Legal Rights, and Canadians for Balfour 100. (www.speakersaction.com)

Canadian Associates of Ben-Gurion University of the Negev (1973). 1000 Finch Avenue West, Suite 506, Toronto, ON M3J 2V5. (416) 665-8054. (www.bengurion.ca)

Canadian Association of Jews and Muslims (CAJM) (1996). 589 Silverthorne Crescent, Mississauga, ON, L5R 1W7. (416) 938-2872. CAJM's purpose is to bring members of the Jewish and Muslim communities in Canada closer together; pro-mote positive interaction; and work together to counter problems faced by both communities. (www.cajmcanada.wordpress.com)

Canadian Council for Reform Judaism (CCRJ) (1988). 3845 Bathurst Street, Suite 301, Toronto, ON M3H 3N2. (416) 630-0375. See Jewish Denominational Organizations—Reform above. (www.ccrj.ca)

Canadian Council of Conservative Synagogues (CCCS) (2008). 37 Southbourne Avenue, Toronto, ON M3H 1A4. (416) 635-5340, ext. 304. See Jewish Denominational Organizations—Conservative above. (www.canadianccs. weebly.com)

Canadian Forum of Russian-Speaking Jewry (formerly **Canadian Association of Russian Jews**). (2012) See Jewish Russian/FSU Organizations above. (www. worldbeytenu.org/canada)

Canadian Foundation for Masorti Judaism (also known as **Masorti Canada**) (1989). 55 Yeomans Road, Suite 201, Toronto, ON M3H 3J7. (416) 667-1717 or (866) 357-3384. See Jewish Denominational Organizations—Conservative above. (www.masorti.ca)

Canadian Foundation for Pioneering Israel (CFPI) (1976). c/o Roth, 736 Spadina Avenue, Suite 809, Toronto, ON M5S 2J6. CFPI's mission is to increase knowledge and understanding by supporting educational activities in Canada, Israel, and elsewhere, in areas of Jewish culture, literature, and history; youth leadership, education, and camping; social, environmental, and economic justice; community empowerment, pluralism, and peace; and kibbutz life. (No website)

Canadian Foundation for the Education and Welfare of Jews (CFEWJ) (1989). 2939 Bathurst Street, Toronto, ON, M6B 3B2. (416) 785-5899. The CFEWJ operates in the Former Soviet Union, where the practice of Judaism was forbidden under the Soviet regime for many years. It was established to restore a sense of Jewish identity in these areas. (www.canadianfoundation.org)

Canadian Friends of ALYN Hospital (1978). 122 East 42nd Street, #1519, New York, NY 10168. (212) 869-8085. (https://can.alynus.org)

Canadian Friends of Arachim (Ceased to exist)

Canadian Friends of Bar-Ilan University (1955). 1750 Steeles Avenue West, Suite 214, Concord, ON L4K 2L7. (905) 660-3563 or (888) 248-2720. (www. cfbiu.org)

Canadian Friends of Beit Issie Shapiro (1989). 8171 Yonge Street, Suite 157, Thornhill ON L3T 2C6. (https://en.beitissie.org.il/get-involved/overseas-friends/ canada/welcome-2)

Friends of Bnai Zion Canada. 10660 Yonge Street, PO Box 30528, Richmond Hill, ON. L4C 2H0. (647) 430-7743. (www.b-zion.org.il)

Canadian Friends of Boys Town Jerusalem (1972). 3089 Bathurst Street, Suite 211, Toronto, ON M6A 2A4. (416) 789-7241. (www.btjcanada.com)

Canadian Friends of Dental Volunteers for Israel (1985). 69 Yonge Street, PO Box 17001, Toronto, ON M5E 1K0. (416) 699-3910. (www.canadianfriend-sofdvi.org)

Canadian Friends of Givat Haviva (1993). c/o R. Sokolsky, 320 Tweedsmuir Avenue, Suite 201, Toronto ON M5P 2Y3. (416) 651-7347. (www.givathaviva.ca)

Canadian Friends of Haifa University. 400 Walmer Road, Suite 1921, Toronto, ON M5P 2X7. (416) 972-9400. (www.haifa-univ.ca)

Canadian Friends of Herzog Hospital (1977). 3030 Lawrence Avenue East, Suite 301, Toronto, ON M1P 2T7. (416) 256-4222. (www.herzoghospital.ca)

Canadian Friends of Israel Free Loan Association. c/o Mark Borer, 570 Bay Street, Suite 2202, Toronto, ON M5G oB2. (613) 680-6447. (www.israelfree-loan.org.il)

Canadian Friends of Massuah (1987). 970 Lawrence Avenue, Suite 303, Toronto, ON M6A 3B6. (416) 256-2900. (No website)

Canadian Friends of Meir Medical Center (2006). (www.meirfriends.com)

Canadian Friends of Nishmat (1994). 89 Bevshire Circle, Thornhill, ON L4J 5C6. (416) 628-4634. (www.nishmat.net/support/29)

Canadian Friends of Peace Now (1985). 119-660 Eglinton Avenue East, Suite 517, Toronto, ON M4G 2K2. (416) 322-5559 or (866) 405-5387. See Jewish Israel-Related Political and Advocacy Organizations above. (www.peacenowcanada.org)

Canadian Friends of Rambam Medical Centre (1994). 64 Merton Street, First Floor, Toronto, ON M4S 1A1. (416) 481-5552. (www.cfram.ca)

Canadian Friends of Sheba Medical Center (1973). 180 Steeles Avenue West, Suite 223, Thornhill, ON L4J 2L1. (647) 967-2428. (www.shebacanada.org)

Canadian Friends of Soroka Medical Center (2014). 3 Larratt Lane, Richmond Hill, L4C 9J1. (No website)

Canadian Friends of Tel Aviv University (1972). 6900 Boulevard Décarie, Suite 3480, Montreal, QC H3X 2T8. (514) 344-3417. (www.cftau.ca)

Canadian Friends of the Ghetto Fighters' House Museum (formerly **Canadian Friends of the Ghetto Fighters' House and Children's Memorial Institute: Yad-LaYeled**) (1990). 40 King Street West, Toronto, ON M5H 3Y2. (www.gfh.org.il)

Canadian Friends of The Hebrew University of Jerusalem (1944). 4950 Yonge Street, Suite 1202, Toronto, ON M2N 6K1. (416) 485-8000 or (888) 432-7398. (www.cfhu.org)

Canadian Friends of the Israel Museum (1995). 262 Warren Road, Toronto, ON M4V 2S8. (416) 901-2231. (www.cfimonline.org)

Canadian Friends of the Israel Philharmonic Orchestra (2012). c/o Norton Rose Fulbright, 200 Bay Street, Suite 3800, Royal Bank Plaza, South Tower, Toronto, ON M5J 2Z4. (www.afipo.org/cfipo)

Canadian Friends of the Menachem Begin Heritage Foundation (1994). One Yorkdale Road, Suite 601, Toronto, ON M6A 3A1. (416) 785-6000. (www.begin-center.org.il)

Canadian Friends of the Shalom Hartman Institute (1979). 8888 Boulevard Pie IX, Montreal, QC H1Z 4J5. (www.hartman.org.il)

Canadian Friends of the World Union for Progressive Judaism (1974). 3845 Bathurst Street, Suite 301, Toronto, ON M3H 3N2. (416) 630-0375, ext. 299. See

Jewish   Denominational   Organizations-Reform   above.   (www.wupj.org/how-to-donate-from-around-the-world)

Canadian Friends of Wahat al-Salam—Neve Shalom (1999). (www.wasns.org/cdnfriends)

Canadian Friends of Yad Eliezer. c/o Esther Sora Gestetner, 1943 Clinton Avenue, Montreal, QC H3S 1L2. (www.af-ye.org/contact-us)

Canadian Friends of Yad Sarah (1976). 788 Marlee Avenue, North York, ON M6B 3K1. (416) 781-6416. (www.canadianfriendsofyadsarah.com)

Canadian Hadassah-WIZO (also known as **CHW**) (formerly **Hadassah-WIZO Organization of Canada** (1963). 638A Sheppard Avenue West, Suite 209, Toronto ON M3H 2S1. (416) 477-5964 or (855) 477-5964. See Jewish Israel-Related Humanitarian Organizations above. (www.chw.ca)

Canadian Jewish Holocaust Survivors and Descendants (CJHSD) (1999). Center for Israel and Jewish Affairs, 4600 Bathurst Street, 4th Floor, Toronto, ON M6A 3V2. (416) 638-1991, ext. 5126. The CJHSD, an independent, grassroots organization affiliated with the Centre for Israel and Jewish Affairs, represents Canadian survivors at the Jewish Material Claims Conference and advocates on behalf of its members. CJHSD's primary objectives are to represent and speak on behalf of Canadian Jewish Holocaust survivors with a unified voice in partnership with community funding, planning, and service delivery organizations; secure restitution for Canadian Holocaust survivors; increase public awareness about issues that concern survivors; involve children of survivors on issues of importance to the CJHSD; engage in activities concerning the interest and welfare of Canadian Jewish Holocaust survivors. (www.cija.ca/cjhsd)

Canadian Jewish Law Students' Association (CJLSA) (1987). (416) 736-5820. The CJLSA facilities professional development and enables relationship building between Jewish law students across the country. It holds one national conference each academic year. The CJLSA relies heavily on support, both financial and otherwise, from its student-members, as well as lawyers and law firms across Canada. (No website)

Canadian Jewish Political Affairs Committee (2005). (416) 929-9552 or (866) 929-9552. See Jewish Israel-Related Political and Advocacy Organizations above (www.cjpac.ca)

Canadian Magen David Adom for Israel (1976). 6900 Decarie Boulevard, Suite 3155, Montreal, QC H3X 2T8. (800) 731-2848 or (514) 731-4400. (www.cmdai.org)

Canadian Rabbinic Caucus (CRC). 4600 Bathurst Street, 4th Floor, Toronto, ON M2R 3V2. Comprised of Orthodox, Conservative, and Reform rabbis, the CRC meets to discuss emerging issues and serves as a spokesperson on public policy matters affecting Jewish life and freedom of religion in Canada. (www.cija.ca/impact/learn-more/canadian-rabbinic-caucus)

The Canadian Shaare Zedek Hospital Foundation (formerly **Toronto, Ontario Friends of Shaare Zedek**) (1975). 3089 Bathurst Street, Suite 205, Toronto, ON M6A 2A4. (416) 781-3584 or (800) 387-3595. (www.hospitalwitha-heart.ca)

The Canadian Society for the Protection of Nature in Israel (2011). 25 Imperial Street, Suite 200, Toronto, ON M5P 1B9. (647) 346-0619. (www.natureisrael.org/CSPNI)

Canadian Society for Yad Vashem (1986). 265 Rimrock Road, Suite 218, Toronto, ON M3J 3C6. (416) 785-1333 or (888) 494-7999. (www.yadvashem.ca)

Canadian Young Judaea (formerly **Federation of Young Judaea** and **Young Judaea National League of Canada**) (1917). 788 Marlee Avenue, Toronto, ON M6J 0B8. (416) 781-5156. See Jewish Youth Groups and Youth-Related Organizations above. (www.youngjudaea.ca)

Canadian Zionist Cultural Association (CZCA) (1980). 788 Marlee Avenue, Suite 201, Toronto, ON M6B 3K1. (416) 783-3053. CZCA supports humanitarian and educational programs in Israel. It operates camps for widows, orphans, siblings, and parents of fallen soldiers, and provides scholarships for veterans. (No website)

Canadian Zionist Federation (CZF) (formerly **Federated Zionist Organization of Canada, Zionist Organization of Canada,** and **Federation of Zionist Societies of Canada**) (1899) (1925) (1967) (1972). 4600 Bathurst Street, Suite 315, North York, ON M2R 3V2. (416) 636-7655, ext. 5552. CZF, the Canadian affiliate of the World Zionist Organization, is an umbrella organization of Zionist groups in Canada, whose mission is to strengthen the connection of Canadian Jews with Israel; develop their appreciation of the centrality of Israel to Jewish life worldwide; deepen their understanding of Israeli society and the challenges it faces; encourage travel to Israel; provide educational resources; and facilitate dialogue, debate, and collective action to further Zionism in Canada and abroad. (www.canadianzf.ca)

Canadians Helping Israel Asylum Seekers (CHAI) (2017). CHAI was created by a diverse group from the Jewish community who share the goal of assisting African asylum seekers and refugees from Eritrea and Sudan living in Israel who fled injustice and torture in their homelands and want to resettle in Canada. It aims to utilize Canadian resources to respond to the threats by the Israeli government to deport such asylum seekers and refugees to "safe" third countries, mobilizing Canadians to find alternatives to deportation that offer permanent safety to those who turned to the Jewish homeland for protection. CHAI encourages people to take on sponsorship of refugees from Israel to Canada and to advocate to the Canadian government to do more to help. (www.facebook.com/CanadiansHelpingAsylumSeekersInIsrael), (www.letushelpil.org/canada.html)

The Centre for Israel and Jewish Affairs (CIJA) (formerly **Canadian Council for Israel and Jewish Advocacy**, which included **Canadian Jewish Congress**, **Canada-Israel Committee**, and **Quebec-Israel Committee**) (2004) (2011). 4600 Bathurst Street, 4th Floor, Toronto, ON M2R 3V2. (416) 638-1991. CIJA, the advocacy agent of Jewish Federations of Canada-UIA, is a nonpartisan organization dedicated to improving the quality of Jewish life in Canada by advancing the public policy interests of Canada's organized Jewish community. As the Canadian affiliate of the World Jewish Congress, CIJA connects the power of a strong, national network to regional efforts in every Canadian province and to international efforts worldwide. Its priorities encompass a wide range of issues including human rights, religious freedom, social justice, national security, foreign affairs, and Canada-Israel relations. (www.cija.ca)

Chabad (Canadian) Friends of Cuban Jewry (CFCJ) (1993). 87 Lisa Crescent, Thornhill, ON L4J 2N2. (416) 855-4553 or (905) 660-7946. CFCJ provides humanitarian assistance and Jewish educational programs for the Jewish community in Cuba. (www.chabadcuba.wordpress.com)

Chai Folk Arts Council (1979). 123 Doncaster Street, Suite C147, Winnipeg, MB R3N 2B2. (204) 477-7497. The Chai Folk Arts Council exists to preserve, promote, and develop Jewish and Israeli culture through performance and education in music, song, and dance for the benefit of Canadian youth and community. (www.chai.mb.ca)

Chai Lifeline Canada (2006). 300A Wilson Avenue, Toronto, ON M3H 1S8. (647) 430-5933. See Jewish Organizations for People with Disabilities or Special Needs above. (www.chailifelinecanada.org)

Doctors Against Racism and Anti-Semitism (DARA) (2009). 255 Duncan Mill Road, Suite 211, Toronto, ON M3B 3H9. DARA is a grassroots organization of health care professionals whose activities are directed at upholding human rights in the medical realm specifically and academic environments generally. It seeks to educate health care professionals regarding human rights abuses and addresses examples of racism and/or antisemitism in professional associations and in academia; support global knowledge-sharing by medical and scientific communities by opposing boycotts of academics based on nationality, race, or religion; monitor and respond to articles promoting racial or geopolitical bias in scientific journals, at medical conferences, and on university campuses; oppose the actions of tenured academics who promote their personal, political, or philosophical agendas to a captive student body if these agendas fall outside the subject matter which they are responsible to teach. (www.daradocs.org)

Emunah Canada (1943). Lipa Green Centre, 4600 Bathurst Street, Suite 302E, Toronto, ON M2R 3V3. 416-634-3040. See Jewish Israel-Related Humanitarian Organizations above. (www.emunahcanada.org)

Ezer Mizion Canada (2013). 701 Finch Avenue West, North York, ON M3H 4X4. (647) 799-1475. (www.ezermizion.ca)

The Friedberg Jewish Manuscript Society (FJMS) (formerly **Jewish Manuscript Preservation Society**) (2007). 181 Bay Street, Suite 250, Toronto, ON M5J 2T3. The FJMS, which carries out many of its activities in a joint venture with The Friedberg Genizah Project in Lakewood, NJ, was established to educate the public through the study and research of Genizah fragments, manuscripts, and early printings as well as other books and documents as they relate to Judaism and Jews by using advanced software systems freely accessible to everyone, anywhere, anytime. (https://fjms.genizah.org) (In 2019 in process of merging with the National Library of Israel.)

Friends of Simon Wiesenthal Center for Holocaust Studies (FSWC) (1979). 5075 Yonge Street, Suite 902, Toronto, ON M2N 6C6. (416) 864-9735 or (866) 864-9735. FSWC is a human rights organization that works to improve Canadian society and is committed to countering racism and antisemitism, and to promoting the principles of tolerance, social justice, and Canadian democratic values through advocacy and education. It carries out the work of the Wiesenthal Center in Canada by bringing antisemitism, bigotry, racial hatred, and ethnic intolerance to the attention of the Canadian government, the public, and the media. (www.friendsofsimonwiesenthalcenter.com)

Gesher Canada. 2828 Bathurst Street, Toronto, ON M6B 3A7. (416) 623-7555. Gesher Canada's mission is to monitor and intercede on behalf of causes important to the Canadian Orthodox Jewish community; protect the rights and advance the interests of Orthodox Jews and their growing network of educational and religious institutions; and offer a uniquely Orthodox Jewish perspective on contemporary issues of public concern. It takes advocacy positions before federal, provincial, and local governmental or quasi-governmental bodies and agencies. (www.geshercanada.ca)

Hashomer Hatzair Canada (1923). 192 Spadina Avenue, Suite 319, Toronto, ON M5T 2C2. (416) 736-1339. See Jewish Youth Groups and Youth-Related Organizations above. (www.hashomerhatzair.ca)

HESEG Foundation (HESEG) (2006). 161 Bay Street, PO Box 700, Toronto, ON M5J 2S1. (416) 362-7711. HESEG was established by a Canadian couple as a way to recognize and honor the meaningful contribution of Lone Soldiers to Israel by providing them with an opportunity, through education and career development, to start a life in Israel. It funds full academic scholarships and living expenses for former soldiers who served in the Israel Defense Forces, many of whom were Lone Soldiers from all over the world who left behind families and friends, and were driven by their ideals and a commitment to Israel's security and future. (www.heseg.com/en/index-eng.html)

Heshe and Harriet Seif Jewish Learning Initiative on Campus-Canada (2008). 533 Spring Gate Boulevard, Thornhill, ON L4J 5B7. (416) 843-0245. See Jewish College Campus Organizations above. (www.jliccanada.com)

Hillel Canada (formerly **National Jewish Campus Life**) (2003). 4600 Bathurst Street, Suite 315, Toronto, ON M2R 3V3. (416) 636-7655. See Jewish Youth Groups and Youth-Related Organizations above. (www.jewishcanada.org/jewish-identity/hillel-canada)

Holocaust Education and Genocide Prevention Foundation (HEGP) (formerly **Kleinmann Family Foundation**) (1995). 1438 Rue Fullum, Montreal, QC H2K 3M1. (514) 825-1632. The HEGP was mandated by the Canadian government to educate the public about the dangers of prejudice and discrimination. Its mission is to coordinate ongoing lectures for students of Europe and North America; sponsor field trips and provide academic facilitators for visits to various Holocaust museums in Canada and the US; educate and promote public understanding and knowledge of discrimination; produce, distribute, and use educational videos and survivor testimony in schools, cultural organizations, and academic conferences; and curate and exhibit travelling exhibitions. (www.preventinggenocide.org)

HonestReporting Canada (2003). PO Box 6, Station Q, Toronto, ON M4T 2L7. (416) 915-9157. See Jewish Media Organizations above. (www.honestreporting.ca)

Independent Jewish Voices-Canada (IJV) (2008). PO Box 75372, Leslie Street PO, Toronto, ON M4M 1B0. IJV is a grassroots, national human rights organization, composed of a group of Jews in Canada from diverse backgrounds, occupations, and affiliations, with active chapters in cities and on university campuses across the country, whose mandate is to promote a just resolution to the dispute in Israel and Palestine through the application of international law and respect for the human rights of all parties. It opposes Israel's continued occupation of Palestine and works actively with other organizations, nationally and internationally, to challenge Israeli policies of racial and ethnic segregation, discrimination, and military aggression against Palestinians. IJV supports the right of refugees to return to their homes and properties and has adopted the Palestinian call for Boycott, Divestment and Sanctions (BDS) as a nonviolent way to bring pressure on Israel and compel it to make the changes necessary for a real peace. (www.ijvcanada.org)

International Fellowship of Christians and Jews of Canada (2003). PO Box 670, Station K, Toronto, ON M4P 2H1. (888) 988-4325. See Jewish Community Relations Organizations above. (www.ifcj.ca)

Israel Cancer Research Fund (ICRF) (1975). 1881 Yonge Street, Box 29, Suite 616, Toronto, ON M4S 3C4. (416) 440-7780. See Jewish Medical Organizations above. (www.icrf.ca)

Israel Tennis & Education Centers Foundation (formerly **Canada-Israel Children's Centres** and **Israel Tennis Centers Foundation**) (1980). 19 Lesmill Road, Suite 102, Toronto, ON M3B 2T3. (416) 444-5700, ext. 2505. (www.itecenters.org)

The Jerusalem Foundation of Canada (1970). 250 Consumers Road, Suite 301, Toronto, ON M2J 4V6. (877) 484-1289 or (416) 922-0000. (www.jerusalem-foundation.org/about-us/leadership-worldwide/canada.aspx)

Jewish Federations of Canada-UIA (JFC-UIA) (formerly **United Israel Appeal of Canada** and **UIA Federations Canada**) (1967). 4600 Bathurst Street, Suite 315, Toronto, ON M2R 3V3. (416) 636-7655. JFC-UIA's mission is to support Canadian Jewish federations and communities by increasing its philanthropic capabilities, national and international influence, and connection to Israel and each other. It works in partnership with Jewish Federations and regional communities across Canada to strengthen Jewish life and raise funds for programs and services in Canada, Israel, and overseas. JFC-UIA and its agencies provide direct services to independent regional Jewish communities where there is no formally organized Jewish Federation. (www.jewishcanada.org)

Jewish Immigrant Aid Services of Canada (formerly **Emergency Jewish Immigrant Aid Committee** and **Jewish Immigrant Aid Society of Canada**) (1920) (1922) (1954). 2255 Carling Avenue, Suite 300, Ottawa, ON K2B 7Z5. (613) 722-2225. See Jewish Overseas Aid Organizations above. (www.jewishtoronto.com/directory/jewish-immigrant-aid-service-of-canada)

Jewish National Fund of Canada (1901). 5160 Decarie Boulevard, Suite 740, Montreal, QC H3X 2H9. (866) 775-1563 or (514) 934-0313. See Jewish Environmental Organizations above. (www.jnf.ca)

Jewish Russian Charity Fund (Chamah) (1975). 6280 Westbury Avenue, Montreal, QC H3W-2X3. (514) 731-6259. See Jewish Russian/FSU Organizations above. (www.chamah.org)

The Jewish Theological Society of Canada (1991). 491 Lawrence Avenue West, Suite 400, Toronto, ON M5M 1C7. (416) 789-2193. The Jewish Theological Society of Canada is the fundraising organization for the Jewish Theological Seminary, which trains Conservative rabbis, cantors, teachers, and lay people. (No website)

Jews for Judaism (1983). 3110 Bathurst Street, PO Box 54042, Toronto, ON M6A 3B7. (416) 789-0020 or (866) 307-4362. See Jewish Outreach Organizations above. (www.jewsforjudaism.ca)

JSpaceCanada (2010). 30 Rimmington Drive, Thornhill, ON L4J 6J8. JSpaceCanada is a Jewish, progressive, pro-Israel, pro-peace voice in Canada that supports Israel as a democratic homeland for the Jewish people with full recognition of the equality and civil rights of all its citizens. It strongly supports a two-state solution and a lasting agreement that will bring peace to the region; opposes Israel's Jewish settlements as being an obstacle to peace; and opposes all initiatives that attempt to challenge Israel's right to exist or impose boycotts, divestments, or sanctions on Israel. (www.jspacecanada.ca)

KlezKanada (1996). 1 Carré Cummings Square, No. 504, Montréal, QC H3W 1M6. (514) 734-1473. KlezKanada was founded to teach, nurture, and present to a broad public the best of Jewish traditional arts and Jewish culture. Its goal is to foster Jewish cultural and artistic creativity worldwide as both an ethnic heritage and a constantly evolving contemporary culture and identity. From its start as a small summer festival, KlezKanada has become one of the leading Jewish cultural organizations in the world. (www.klezkanada.org)

Kulanu Canada (also known as **Canadian Friends of Kulanu**) (2014). 509 Castlefield Avenue, Toronto, ON M5N 1L7. (647) 345-6249. See Jewish Overseas Aid Organizations above. (www.kulanucanada.org)

Labor Zionist Alliance of Canada (1909). 7005 Chemin Kildare, Cote Saint-Luc, QC H4W 1C1. (514) 484-1789. See Jewish Israel-Related Political and Advocacy Organizations above. (No website)

Leket Canada (2007) PO Box 63057, University Plaza RPO. Dundas, ON L9H 6Y3. (905) 525-5673. (www.leket.org)

Maccabi Canada (1964). 8150 Keele Street, Unit 1, Concord, ON L4K 2A5. (416) 398-0515. See Jewish Sports Organizations above. (www.maccabi-canada.com)

Machne Israel Development Foundation (2004). 300 La Berge du Canal, Suite 306, Lachine, QC, H8R 1R3. See Jewish Philanthropic Foundations and Organizations above. (No website)

March of Remembrance and Hope Canada (MRH) (2001). MRH Canada, sponsored by Jewish Federations of Canada–UIA, is a dynamic educational leadership program whose purpose is to teach students of different religious and ethnic backgrounds about the dangers of intolerance through the study of the Holocaust and to promote better relations among people of diverse cultures and faith backgrounds. The program, which takes place annually in mid-May, takes college and university students from across Canada on a two-day trip to Germany, followed by a six-day visit to Poland, during which the students visit locations in Germany and Poland related to the Holocaust and other World War II genocides. (www.marchofremembranceandhope.org)

March of the Living Canada (1988). 4600 Bathurst Street, Suite 421, Toronto, ON M2R 3V3. (416) 398-6931, ext. 5392. See Jewish Children's Education Organizations above. (www.marchoftheliving.org)

MAZON Canada (1986). 788 Marlee Avenue, Suite 301, Toronto, ON M6B 3K1. (416) 783-7554 or (866) 629-6622. See Jewish Social Welfare Organizations above. (www.mazoncanada.ca)

Mercaz-Canada. 55 Yeomans Road, Suite 201, Toronto, ON M3H 3J7. (416) 667-1717 or (866) 357-3384. See Jewish Israel-Related Political and Advocacy Organizations above. (www.masorti-mercaz.ca)

Mizrachi Canada (formerly known as **Mizrachi Organization of Canada**) (1941). 4600 Bathurst Street, Suite 316, North York, ON M2R 3V2. (416) 630-9266. Mizrachi Canada is a Torah driven, community-focused educational organization committed to Jewish identity and its destiny. It is the umbrella Religious Zionist Organization for many activities in Canada that connects the community with Israel, together with its branches and affiliates across the country, including the Bnei Akiva youth movement, Camp Moshava Ennismore, and Toronto day camp Moshava Ba'Ir.(www.mizrachi.ca)

Na'amat Canada (formerly **Pioneer Women's Organization Incorporated** and **The Women's Organization for the Pioneer Women of Palestine**) (1925) (1945) (1966) (1987). 5555 Westminster Avenue, Suite 212, Montreal, QC H4W 2J2. (514) 488-0792 or (888) 278-0792. See Jewish Israel-Related Humanitarian Organizations above. (www.naamat.com)

National Council of Jewish Women of Canada (1897). 4700 Bathurst Street, Toronto, ON M2R 1W8. (416) 633-5100 or (866) 625-9274. See Jewish Social Welfare Organizations above. (www.ncjwc.org)

Ne'eman Foundation Canada (formerly **Ne'eman Foundation**) (2011). 75 Lisa Crescent, Thornhill, ON L4J 2N2. (888) 341-8590. See Jewish Philanthropic Foundations and Organizations above. (www.neemanfoundation.com)

New Israel Fund of Canada (1985). 801 Eglinton Avenue West, Suite 401, Toronto, ON M5N 1E3. (416) 781-4322 or (855) 781-4322. See Jewish Philanthropic Foundations and Organizations above. (www.nifcan.org)

Nishma (1990). 1057 Steeles Avenue West, PO Box 81684, Toronto, ON M2R 3X1. (416) 630-0588 or (800) 267-6474. See Jewish Adult Education Organizations above. (www.nishma.org)

OneFamily (also known as **OneFamily Fund Canada**) (2004). 36 Eglinton Avenue West, Suite 601, Toronto, ON M4R 1A1. (416) 489-9687. See Jewish Israel-Related Humanitarian Organizations above. (www.onefamilyfund.ca)

ORT Canada (1942). 272 Codsell Avenue, Toronto, ON M3H 3X2. (416) 787-0339. See Jewish Overseas Aid Organizations above. (www.ort.org/whereweare/canada)

The Polish-Jewish Heritage Foundation of Canada (1988). Montreal Chapter: Station Cote St. Luc, C. 284, Montreal, QC H4V 2Y4; Toronto Chapter: 195 Waterloo Avenue, Toronto, ON M3H 3Z3. (514) 487-9558 or (416) 630-1099. The objectives of The Polish-Jewish Heritage Foundation of Canada are to foster a better understanding of Polish-Jewish history and culture; encourage an honest, open-minded dialogue between Poles and Jews; preserve the unique heritage of Polish Jewry; and foster research. The Foundation presents programs (lectures, films, publications, concerts, exhibitions, commemorative events, and book launches) on Jewish life in Poland, Polish-Jewish relations, and the impact of Polish-Jewish thought and creativity. Its membership is comprised mainly of Christians and Jews of Polish origin. (www.polish-jewish-heritage.org/Eng/index.htm)

Rabbinical College of Canada TTL (also known as **Yeshivas Tomchei Temimim Lubavitch**) (1941). 6405 Westbury Avenue, Montreal, QC H3W 2X5. (514) 735-2201, ext. 105. Rabbinical College of Canada is a Chabad Lubavitch rabbinical institution of higher education that provides rabbinical ordinations for its students in the Chabad Hasidic community. (www.chabad.org/centers/default_cdo/aid/117808/jewish/Rabbinical-College-of-Canada-TTL.htm)

Sar-El Canada (also known as **Canadian Volunteers for Israel**) (1982). 788 Marlee Avenue, Suite 315, Toronto ON M6B 3K1. (416) 781-6089. See Other Jewish Israel-Related Organizations above. (www.sarelcanada.org)

Sasson V'Simcha: Canadian Association for Jewish Family Education & Continuity (2000). 60 Dalemont Avenue, Toronto, ON M6B 3C8. (416) 256-4497. See Jewish Social Welfare Organizations above. (www.sassonvsimcha.ca)

Small Wonders (2002). 3845 Bathurst Street, Suite 103, Toronto, ON M3H 3N2. (416) 742-0090. Small Wonders offers support for Jewish couples in Canada experiencing infertility. It offers emotional support, medical advice, financial assistance, and rabbinical support. (www.smallwonders.ca)

StandWithUs Canada (formerly **Antisemitism Must End Now-AMEN**) (2007) (2013). 355 St. Clair Avenue West, Suite 104, Toronto, ON M5P 1N5. (416) 966-0722. See Jewish Israel-Related Political and Advocacy Organizations above. (www.standwithus.com/canada)

State of Israel Bonds-Canada (1953). 1120 Finch Avenue West, Suite 801, Toronto, ON M3J 3H7. (416) 789-3351 or (866) 543-3351. See Jewish Israel-Related Humanitarian Organizations above. (www.israelbonds.ca)

Technion Canada (formerly **Canadian Technion Society**) (1943). 970 Lawrence Avenue West, Suite 206, Toronto ON M6A 3B6. (416) 789-4545 or (800) 935-8864. (www.technioncanada.org)

Thank Israeli Soldiers-Canadian Chapter (also known as **Fund for Israel's Tomorrow**) (2013). (416) 787-9302. See Jewish Israel-Related Humanitarian Organizations above. (www.facebook.com/ThankIsraeliSoldiersCanada)

Torah in Motion (TiM) (1991). 3910 Bathurst Street, Suite 307, Toronto, ON M3H 5Z3. (416) 633-5770 or (866) 633-5770. Torah in Motion brings Jewish history to life and tackles complex, socially relevant issues. It offers classes, webinars, podcasts, online programs, conferences, and panels that feature a diverse cross-section of renowned speakers addressing complex contemporary issues as well as and educational travel experiences. (www.torahinmotion.org)

Transnistria Survivors' Association (1994). c/o Arnold Buxbaum, 500 Glencairn Avenue, #210, Toronto, ON M6B 1Z1. (416) 787-9734. The Transnistria Survivors' Association is an association representing the 6000–8000 survivors of the Transnistria Holocaust living in Canada at the time the association was formed. It works to provide a voice for and raise awareness of this lesser known group of Holocaust survivors; provides social support services; publishes and disseminates information; educates survivors' children and grandchildren to eliminate all forms of hate and discrimination; and liaises with other groups and organizations in the community which have similar scope and objectives. (http://search.ontariojewisharchives.org/Permalink/accessions24766)

Ukrainian Jewish Encounter (UJE) (2008). 1508 Kenneth Drive, Mississauga, ON L5E 2Y5. (905) 891-0242. UJE is a privately organized, multinational initiative launched as a collaborative project involving Ukrainians of Jewish and Christian heritages and others, in Ukraine, Israel, and the diasporas. Its work engages scholars, civic leaders, artists, governments, and the broader public in an effort to strengthen mutual comprehension and solidarity between Ukrainians and Jews. (www.ukrainianjewishencounter.org)

United Hatzalah Canada (2014). 41 Bertal Road, Toronto, ON M6M 4M7. (647) 533-4497. (www.israelrescue.org)

United Jewish People's Order (UJPO) (1926) (1945). 585 Cranbrooke Avenue, Toronto, ON M6A 2X9. (416) 789-5502. The UJPO is a nonpartisan, independent, socialist-oriented, secular cultural and educational organization that supports racial, economic, and environmental justice and promotes secular Jewish culture and education with a commitment to social justice. It develops and perpetuates a progressive secular approach on social and cultural matters, Jewish heritage, the Yiddish language, and holiday and festival celebrations, and sponsors secular Jewish education, musical and cultural groups, concerts, lectures, and public forums. (www.ujpo.org)

Ve'ahavta (1996). 200 Bridgeland Avenue, Unit D, Toronto, ON M6A 1Z4. (416) 964-7698 or (877) 582-5472. Ve'ahavta (Hebrew, "and you shall love") is a Jewish humanitarian organization dedicated to promoting positive change in the lives of people of all faiths who are marginalized by poverty and hardship. It is committed to engaging community members in a meaningful and hands-on way to support its collective mission of tikkun olam (repairing the world) and delivers programs that break down barriers, restore human dignity, and foster capacity-building. (www.veahavta.org)

Weizmann Canada (formerly **The Canadian Society for the Weizmann Institute of Science**) (1964). 55 Eglinton Avenue East, Suite 603, Toronto, ON M4P 1G8. (416) 733-9220 or (800) 387-3894. (www.weizmann.ca)

Yachad, the Canadian Jewish Council for Disabilities. 15 Gorman Park Road, North York, ON M3H 3K3. (416) 986-1985. (No website)

Yaldeinu: The Marcos Soberano Society for Jewish Education and Camping (2007). 196 Citation Drive, Concord, ON L4K 2V2. (905) 482-3374. Yaldeinu (Our

Children, in Hebrew) is an international organization dedicated to preserving the traditions and ideals of Judaism by providing formal and informal education to Jewish children in various parts of the world. Yaldeinu's activities are divided into Jewish day school education and Jewish camping. With a strong sense of Zionism fueling Yaldeinu's mandate, the organization raises funds for distribution in the form of scholarships and camperships. Scholarships are granted to underprivileged children for day school tuition in conjunction with the most reputable Jewish educational institutions in such parts of the world as the FSU and Central/Latin America. Yaldeinu's camping program sponsors children from communities in developing countries with small Jewish populations who are at risk of assimilation to participate in Canadian, Zionist summer camps. (www.yaldeinu.org)

Zaka Foundation (2008). 99 Burncrest Drive, Toronto, ON M5M 2Z6. (416) 785-9297. (www.zaka.us)

Chapter 13
Jewish Press

Ira M. Sheskin, Arnold Dashefsky, and Sarah Markowitz

13.1   Central Coordinating Body for the Jewish Press

American Jewish Press Association. For contact information and a description, see the Jewish Media Organizations section of Chap. 12.

13.2   National Jewish Periodicals and Broadcast Media

13.2.1   *National Jewish Periodicals and Broadcast Media, United States*

614: The HBI eZine (Ceased publication as of 2016)

The Algemeiner (1972). 208 East 51st Street, #185, New York, NY 10022. (212) 376-4988. Independent media voice covering the Middle East, Israel, and matters of Jewish interest around the world. (www.algemeiner.com)

Alma. Online only. Young women's magazine, whose topics include pop culture, dating, news, politics, feminism, identity, rituals, and holidays — all through a Jewish lens, with particular interest in the experiences of self-identifying Jewish

I. M. Sheskin
Department of Geography and Jewish Demography Project, Sue and Leonard Miller Center
for Contemporary Judaic Studies, University of Miami, Coral Gables, FL, USA

A. Dashefsky (✉)
Department of Sociology and Center for Judaic Studies and Contemporary Jewish Life,
University of Connecticut, Storrs, CT, USA
e-mail: Arnold.dashefsky@uconn.edu

S. Markowitz
Independent Researcher, Forest Hills, NY, USA

© Springer Nature Switzerland AG 2020
A. Dashefsky, I. M. Sheskin (eds.), *American Jewish Year Book 2019*, American
Jewish Year Book 119, https://doi.org/10.1007/978-3-030-40371-3_13

women and non-binary individuals navigating life from college through their 20s and 30s. (Owned by 70 Faces Media.) (www.heyalma.com)

Ami Magazine (2010). 1575 50th Street, Brooklyn, NY 11219. (718) 534-8800. Timely news and opinion, investigative and intriguing features, and professional columns directed at an Orthodox audience. (www.amimagazine.org)

AMIT Magazine (1925). 817 Broadway, New York, NY 10003. (212) 477-4720. Published by AMIT, an American Jewish Zionist volunteer organization dedicated to education in Israel. (www.amitchildren.org)

Avotaynu (1985). 794 Edgewood Avenue, New Haven, CT 06515. (475) 202-6575. Magazine for people researching Jewish genealogy, Jewish family trees, or Jewish roots. (www.avotaynu.com)

Beis Moshiach (1994). 744 Eastern Parkway, Brooklyn, NY 11213. (718) 778-8000. Dedicated to spreading the Lubavitcher Rebbe message that the coming of the Moshiach and our ultimate redemption is imminent. (www.beismoshiach-magazine.org)

Binah (2006). 207 Foster Avenue, Brooklyn, NY 11230. (718) 305-5200. Orthodox Jewish women's magazine. (www.binahmagazine.com)

B'nai B'rith Magazine (1886). 1120 20th Street NW, Suite 300 North, Washington, DC 20036. (202) 857-6600. Published by B'nai B'rith International. Information and analysis on topics of interest and concern to the international Jewish community; insight into issues not yet on the radar screen; and news about current and future B'nai B'rith International endeavors. (www.bnaibrith.org/bnai-brith-maga-zine.html)

B'Yachad (Together) online e-reader. 42 East 69th Street, New York, NY 10021. (888) 563-0099. Online only. Published by Jewish National Fund. Coverage of JNF's latest projects and stories of the people who benefit from their work in developing the land of Israel. (www.jnf.org/menu-3/news-media/byachad-magazine)

Calligraphy (Mishpacha). 5809 16th Avenue, Brooklyn, NY 11204. (718) 686-9339. A biannual collection of fiction curated from today's best Jewish writers. (www.mishpacha.com) (www.mishpacha.com/Browse/Listing/896/Calligraphy)

Chabad.org Magazine (1999). 770 Eastern Parkway, Suite 405, Brooklyn, NY 11213. (718) 774-4000 or (718) 735-2000. Online only. Information about Jewish history, discussion of the weekly Torah portion, essays, stories, lifestyle articles, and more. (www.chabad.org/magazine)

Commentary (1945). 561 7th Avenue, 16th Floor, New York, NY 10018. (212) 891-1400. Articles on public affairs and culture, some fiction and poetry. (www.commentarymagazine.com)

Community Magazine (formerly *Aram Soba* newsletter) (2001). 1616 Ocean Parkway, Brooklyn, NY 11223. (718) 645-4460. Covers issues that matter to the Sephardic community. (www.communitym.com)

Conversations (2008). 2 West 70th Street, New York, NY 10023. (917) 960-1549. Print journal of the Institute for Jewish Ideas and Ideals, which discusses major issues in contemporary Orthodox and general Jewish life. (www.jewishideas.org/conversations)

Country Yossi Family Magazine (Ceased publication as of 2017)

Cross-Currents (1998; reorganized online in 2004). Project Genesis-Torah.org, 122 Slade Avenue, Suite 250, Baltimore, MD 21208. (410) 602-1350. Online only. A journal of thought and reflections, from an array of Orthodox Jewish writers. (www.cross-currents.com)

The Daf HaKashrus (1992). 11 Broadway, New York, NY 10004. (212) 563-4000. Published by the Orthodox Union, containing the latest, in-depth information about the world of kashrut. (www.oukosher.org/blog/articles/daf-ha-kashruth)

ejewishphilanthropy. (2007). Online only. Independent online publisher and a facilitator of resource mobilization serving the professional Jewish community, highlighting the latest happenings in the world of Jewish philanthropy. (www.ejewishphilanthropy.com)

Family First, The Jewish Woman's Weekly (Mishpacha). 5809 16th Avenue, Brooklyn, NY 11204. (718) 686-9339. Explores issues relating to family, health, relationships, and personal development, providing a range of informational articles, profiles of inspiring women, discussions of painful social realities, and featuring Torah columns, stories, and serials. (www.mishpacha.com)

Family Table (Mishpacha). 5809 16th Avenue, Brooklyn, NY 11204. (718) 686-9339. A celebration of the pleasures of cooking and entertainment, highlighting diverse culinary themes with recipes, food and venue photography, and best-friend-in-the-kitchen style. (www.mishpacha.com)

Fleishigs (2018). 530 Arlington Road, Cedarhurst, NY 11516. (917) 703-8145. Kosher food magazine—a handbook for all things meat—featuring articles and recipes by experts in the field. (www.fleishigs.com)

The Forward (formerly *Forverts*, and *The Jewish Daily Forward*). (1897 for Yiddish version, 1990 for English version). 125 Maiden Lane, New York, NY 10038. (212) 889-8200. Online only. Coverage of world and national news, Jewish arts and culture, and opinion. (www.forward.com)

Fresh Ink for Teens (formerly *Fresh Ink*) (1995) (2012). 1501 Broadway, Suite 505, New York, NY 10036. (212) 921-7822. Online only. Magazine written by, and for, Jewish students from high schools around the world, covering various topics including high school life, politics, Israel, sports, culture, Judaism and more through original articles, essays, and creative writing pieces. (www.freshinkforteens.com)

Hadassah Magazine (1914). 40 Wall Street, New York, NY 10005. (212) 451-6289. Published by Hadassah, The Women's Zionist Organization of America. Focuses on Jewish women, health, Israel, and culture, including food, travel, and books. (www.hadassahmagazine.org) www.hadassahmagazine.org

Hamodia: The Daily Newspaper of Torah Jewry (1998). 207 Foster Avenue, Brooklyn, NY 11230. (718) 853-9094. Features local, national, and world news as well as sports, entertainment, business, travel news, and more. (www.hamodia.com)

Hamodia Prime News Magazine (2019). 207 Foster Avenue, Brooklyn, NY 11230. (718) 853-9094. A smorgasbord of hard-hitting opinions and news analyses, political and business features, satire, cartoons and quotes, and interviews in glossy magazine format. (www.hamodia.com/new-hamodia-prime)

Hamodia Weekly. 207 Foster Avenue, Brooklyn, NY 11230. (718) 853-9094, ext. 3. Covers every aspect of Jewish life, with special sections dedicated to Israeli and national news roundup and features, a full-color glossy magazine with a dedicated Shabbos section, and a youth news-zine. (www.hamodia.com/subscribe)

haSepharadi (2018). Online only. Engages scholars, academics, students, and artists of diverse disciplines to discuss ancient texts and grapple with contemporary issues in the pan-Sephardic community. (www.hasepharadi.com)

HaYidion: The PRIZMAH Journal (formerly *The RAVSAK Journal*). 254 West 54th Street, 11th Floor, New York, NY 10019. (646) 975-2800. Published by PRIZMAH: Center for Jewish Day Schools. A journal of Jewish education that explores topics of critical interest to day school leaders, advocates, families, and supporters, focusing on various aspects of Jewish day school life from a wide variety of perspectives, offering both theoretical frameworks and pragmatic approaches. (www.prizmah.org/hayidion)

Hevria Magazine (2014). Online only. Literary magazine for creative and out-of-the-box Jews. (www.hevria.com/magazine)

Humanistic Judaism (1969). 28611 West Twelve Mile Road, Farmington Hills, MI 48334. (248) 478-7610. A voice for Jews who value their Jewish identity and who seek an alternative to conventional Judaism that is independent of supernatural authority.
(www.shj.org/about-shj/humanistic-judaism-journal)

Ignite. 11 Broadway, New York, NY 10004. (212) 613-8233. Magazine of NCSY, the Orthodox Union's international youth movement. (www.ncsy.org/ignite)

inFOCUS Quarterly (2007). 50 F Street NW, Suite 100, Washington, DC 20001. (202) 638-2411. Journal of the Jewish Policy Center. (www.jewishpolicycenter.org/infocus)

Inyan Magazine (Hamodia). 207 Foster Avenue, Brooklyn, NY 11230. (718) 853-9094, ext. 234. Torah, halacha and hashkafah, historic and current feature articles, and humor as well as youth pages. (www.hamodia.com/frominyan)

ISRAEL21c (2001). 44 Montgomery Street, Suite 3700, San Francisco, CA 94104. Online only. Diverse and reliable source of news and information about 21st century Israel, offering topical and timely reports on how Israelis from all walks of life and religion innovate, improve, and add value to the world. (www.israel21c.org)

JBI Voice Magazine (1978). 110 East 30th Street, New York, NY 10016. (212) 889-2525. From Jewish Braille Institute, a monthly compilation of articles from periodicals of Jewish interest in English. (www.jbilibrary.org/interior. php?sub=19&op=2)

JBN (Jewish Breaking News). Online only. All Israeli and Jewish-related breaking news and videos. (www.jewishbreakingnews.com)

JCC Association Circle (Ceased publication as of 2017)

Jewcy (Ceased publication as of 2018)

Jewess Magazine (2017). Online only. Geared toward modern Jewish women of all ages seeking inspiration, entertainment, community, and the latest Jewish news. (www.jewessmag.com)

Jewish Action—The Magazine of the Orthodox Union (1950). 11 Broadway, Suite 1301, New York, NY 10004. (212) 563-4000. Thought-provoking articles about issues that affect Orthodox Jewish life today. (www.ou.org/jewish_action)

Jewish Braille Review (1931). 110 East 30th Street, New York, NY 10016. (212) 889-2525. From JBI International, a monthly compilation of articles from periodicals of Jewish interest in Braille, English). (www.jbilibrary.org)

Jewish Currents (formerly *Jewish Life*) (1946). PO Box 130049, Brooklyn, NY 11213. (845) 626-2427. Progressive magazine that carries on the insurgent tradition of the Jewish left through independent journalism, political commentary, and a "counter cultural" approach to Jewish arts and literature. (www.jewishcurrents.org)

Jewish Insider (2012). Online only. A content curation service covering US politics and business news with a Jewish angle. (www.jewishinsider.com)

theJewishInsights.com (formerly *JEWISH Magazine*) (2006). 1970 52nd Street, Brooklyn, NY 11204. (917) 373-2324. Online only. Jewish music magazine. (www.thejewishinsights.com)

The Jewish Link (2003). (323) 965-1544. Online only. News magazine featuring news, articles, and sections on health, food, Jewish holidays, financial literacy, divrei Torah, music/video, etc. (www.thejewishlink.com)

Jewish Literary Journal (2013). Online only. Creative writing of all genres that deals with Jewish themes and Jewish identity. (www.jewishliteraryjournal.com)

Jewish News. Online only. A nonbiased aggregator of news from all sources large and small, publishing information about, for, and pertaining to Jews and the Jewish community, including news op-eds, spirituality sections, community events, and more. (www.jewishnews.com)

Jewish News Today. Online only. Current events and their impact on the Jewish community. (www.jewishnews2day.com)

The Jewish Post and Opinion (National Edition) (1935). 1389 West 86th Street, #160, Indianapolis, IN 46260. (317) 405-8084. Broad spectrum of Jewish news and opinions. (www.jewishpostopinion.com)

The Jewish Press (1960). 4915 16th Avenue, Brooklyn, NY 11204. (718) 330-1100. Eclectic mix of Jewish news, political, and religious commentary, Jewish classifieds, and special features — including puzzles, games, and illustrated stories — for young readers. (www.jewishpress.com)

Jewish Review of Books. (2010). 3091 Mayfield Road, Suite 412, Cleveland Heights, OH 44118. (216) 397-1073. Leading writers and scholars discuss the newest books and ideas about religion, literature, culture, and politics as well as fiction, poetry, and the arts. (www.jewishreviewofbooks.com)

Jewish Sports Review (1997) 1702 South Robertson Boulevard, PMB #174, Los Angeles, CA 90035. (310) 838-6626. Coverage of Jewish athletes. (www.jewishsportsreview.com)

Jewish Times (2002). Mesora of New York, Inc., PO Box 153, Cedarhurst, NY 11516. (516) 569-8888. Online only. A journal on Jewish thought, with original articles on Judaism, Torah, science, Israel, and politics. (www.mesora.org)

The Jewish Veteran (1896). 1811 R Street NW, Washington, 20009. (202) 265-6280. Published by Jewish War Veterans of the USA. Offers valuable information on topics such as Jewish issues, foreign policy, veterans' affairs, military history, and JWV news. (www.jwv.org/media/the-jewish-veteran)

Jewish World Review (1997). Online only. Informational articles related to Judaism, dozens of syndicated columns written mostly by politically conservative writers, advice columns, and cartoons. (www.jewishworldreview.com)

jGirls Magazine (2017). 447 Broadway, Suite 261, New York, NY 10013. (347) 708-2077. Online only. Magazine written by and for self-identifying Jewish girls ages 13-19. (www.jgirlsmagazine.org)

JNS: Jewish News Syndicate (formerly *Jewish News Service*) (2011). Boston, MA. (617) 562-6397. Online only. National news agency serving Jewish community newspapers and media around the world. (www.jns.org)

The JOFA Journal (1998). 205 East 42nd Street, New York, NY 10017. (212) 679-8500. Published by the Jewish Orthodox Feminist Alliance. Editorials, scholarly articles, and updates on issues that resonate with the Orthodox community, including book reviews. (www.jofa.org/jofa-journal)

Joy of Kosher with Jamie Geller Magazine (2011, merged with *Bitayavon*). Kosher Media Network, 1575 50th Street, Brooklyn, NY 11219. (855) 569-6356. High-end kosher cooking magazine full of exclusive tips, recipes, and articles that appeal to all kosher cooks. (www.joyofkosher.com)

Jr. (Mishpacha). 5809 16th Avenue, Brooklyn, NY 11204. (718) 686-9339. A mix that caters to youngsters of many different reading levels, including stories, history and science features that encourage them to explore their world, confidence-building games and projects, and Torah messages. (www.mishpacha.com)

Jspace News (2011). 286 Madison Avenue, Suite 800, New York, NY 10017. Online only. News on Israel, the Middle East, and Jewish world at large. (www.jspacenews.com)

JTA (Jewish Telegraphic Agency) (1962). 24 West 30th Street, 4th Floor, New York, NY 10001. (212) 643-1890. Online only. International news agency serving Jewish community newspapers and media around the world. (www.jta.org)

JWI Magazine (1998) 1129 20th Street NW, Suite 801, Washington, DC 20036. (800) 343-2823. Published by JWI (Jewish Women International). Jewish women's magazine. (www.jwi.org/magazine)

Lehrhaus (2016). Online only. Targets the Orthodox community and includes long-form, accessibly written, scholarly articles; personal reflections and short commentary; musings related to events on the Jewish calendar; cultural criticism; original poetry; and more. (www.thelehrhaus.com)

Kashrus Magazine (1980). PO Box 204, Brooklyn, NY 11204. (718) 336-8544. Source for kosher information. (www.kashrusmagazine.com)

Kol Hamevaser: The Jewish Thought Magazine of the Yeshiva University Student Body (2007). 500 West 185th Street, New York, NY 10033. (212) 960-5400. Dedicated to sparking discussion of Jewish issues on the Yeshiva University campus and beyond. (www.kolhamevaser.com)

Kolmus: The Journal of Torah and Jewish Thought (Mishpacha). 5809 16th Avenue, Brooklyn, NY 11204. (718) 686-9339. A scholarly journal of Jewish thought that brings together some of the premier thinkers in the Jewish world today and gives voice to contemporary Torah scholarship on a wide range of topics, from the esoteric to the scientific. (www.mishpacha.com)

Kosher Today. (207) 842-5419. Online only. A trade newsletter covering the business of kosher food and beverage. (www.koshertoday.com)

Kulanu Magazine (1993). 165 West End Avenue, 3R, New York, NY 10023. (212) 877-8082. Online only. News and more about Jews of all races around the world. (www.kulanu.org/resources/magazines)

The Layers Project Magazine (2017). Online only. Caters to the cultural, emotional, and spiritual needs of Jewish women and seeks to combat the removal of images of women from Jewish media. (www.thelayersprojectmagazine.com)

L'Chaim Weekly Newsletter (1988). 305 Kingston Avenue, Brooklyn, NY 11213.

Lifestyles Magazine. (1963). 134s 6th Avenue, New York, NY 10013. (212) 888-6868. Chronicles the North American Jewish community, and perpetuates, builds, documents, and encourages the culture of philanthropy. (www.lifestyles-magazine.com)

Lilith. (1976). 119 West 57th Street, Suite 1210, New York, NY 10019. (212) 757-0818. Independent, Jewish, and frankly feminist magazine. (www.lilith.org)

Living with Moshiach (1992). 602 North Orange Drive, Los Angeles, CA 90036. Serving the blind and visually impaired. (www.moshiach.net) (www.torah4blind.org)

Martyrdom and Resistance (formerly *Newsletter for the American Federation of Jewish Fighters, Camp Inmates and Nazi Victims*) (1974). 500 Fifth Avenue, 42nd Floor, New York, NY 10110. (212) 220-4304. Published by the American Society for Yad Vashem. (www.yadvashemusa.org/at-a-glance/#MartydomanandResistance)

Matzav.com (2009). Online only. The online voice of Torah Jewry. (www.matzav.com)

Midstream (1954). 633 Third Avenue, 21st Floor, New York, NY 10017. (212) 339-6020. Published by the Theodor Herzl Foundation. A journal exploring a range of Jewish affairs, with a focus on Israel and Zionism. (www.midstreamthf.com)

Mishpacha, Jewish Family Weekly (1984 in Hebrew, 2004 in English). 5809 16th Avenue, Brooklyn, NY 11204. (718) 686-9339. Aims to facilitate the exchange of ideas and values between the varying streams within the Orthodox Jewish world, including the Hasidic, Yeshivish, Sephardic, and Modern Orthodox communities. (www.mishpacha.com)

Moment (1975). 4115 Wisconsin NW, Suite LL10, Washington, DC 20016. (202) 363-6422. Articles of general interest on Jewish affairs and culture. (www.momentmag.com)

Mosaic (formerly *Jewish Ideas Daily*) (2013). Online only. A web magazine advancing ideas, argument, and reasoned judgment in all areas of Jewish endeavor. (www.mosaicmagazine.com)

The Moshiach Times (1980). 792 Eastern Parkway, Brooklyn, NY 11213. (718) 467-6630. Published by Chabad. Jewish children's magazine with stories, games, jokes, puzzles and comics designed for the Orthodox community. (www.tzivoshashem.org/organizations/#moshiach-times)

Na'amat Woman (formerly *Pioneer Women*) (Ceased publication as of 2018)

Nashim Magazine (2018). Where frum women can express themselves, share their stories, and discuss important issues. (www.nashimmagazine.com)

Natural Jewish Parenting (Ceased publication)

Near East Report (1957). American Israel Public Affairs Committee, 251 H Street NW, Washington, DC 20001. (202) 639-5200. Online only. Published by AIPAC. Informs the public about events relating to the Middle East. (www.aipac.org/resources/aipac-publications)

Neshamas (2017). Online only. Literary magazine that accepts only anonymous submissions, often raw and triggering, recognizing that for reasons varying from communal pressure to internal shame publicly published pieces about subjects like abuse, conversion, identity, and such can be incredibly intimidating. (www.neshamas.com)

New Voices Magazine (1991). 440 Park Avenue South, 4th Floor, New York, NY 10016. (212) 674-1168. Online only. America's only national magazine written and published by and for Jewish college students. (www.newvoices.org)

N'shei Chabad Newsletter (1982). 667 Crown Street, Brooklyn, NY 11213. (718) 774-0797. Published by Chabad. Women's magazine containing biographies, divrei Torah, profiles of baalei teshuvah, humor, parenting and health advice, and Chabad history. (www.nsheichabadnewsletter.com)

Outpost (1970). 1751 Second Avenue, New York, NY 10128. (800) 235-3658. Published by Americans for A Safe Israel. Scholarly publication of informative material regarding Israel, the Middle East, and the Arab world. (www.afsi.org/outpost)

PaknTreger (1980). 1021 West Street, Amherst, MA 01002. (413) 256-4900. English-language magazine published by the Yiddish Book Center. Original work that explores aspects of modern Jewish experience and sensibility. (www.yiddishbookcenter.org/language-literature-culture/pakn-treger)

Paper Brigade (formerly *Jewish Book World Magazine*) (2016). 520 8th Avenue, 4th Floor, New York, NY 10018. (212) 201-2920. Literary magazine published by the Jewish Book Council. (www.jewishbookcouncil.org/programs/jbc-annual-lit-mag-paper-brigade)

Poetica Magazine: Reflections of Jewish Thought. 5215 Colley Avenue, #138, Norfolk, VA 23508. Poetry and short story collections on any theme. (www.poetica-magazine.com)

PROTOCOLS (2018). Online only. Provocative, radical writing and art from the global Jewish diaspora, featuring highly-curated Jewish content with attention to leftist and radical politics. (www.prtcls.com)

Sasson Magazine (2017). Online only. Vibrant, online community of believing Jews who aren't scared to talk about the real challenges – and the real joys – of living a full Jewish life. (www.sassonmag.com)

The Scroll (formerly *Think Jewish*) (2008). 770 Eastern Parkway, Suite 405, Brooklyn, NY 11213. (718) 735-2000, ext. 267. (www.mychabad.org/store/the-Scroll.asp)

Sephardic Horizons (2011). Jewish Institute of Pitigliano, 7804 Renoir Court, Potomac, MD 20854. Online only. New ideas in Sephardic studies and creativity in Sephardic culture. (www.sephardichorizons.org)

Sh'ma Now: A Journal of Jewish Sensibilities (formerly *Sh'ma: A Journal of Jewish Ideas*) (1970) (2016). (Ceased publication as of 2019).

Shmais News Service (1997). 832 Winding Oaks Drive, Suite #1A, Palm Harbor, FL 34683. (718) 774-6247. Online only. A Lubavitcher news service. (www.shmais.com)

Sparkit Magazine (Hamodia) (2019). 207 Foster Avenue, Brooklyn, NY 11230. (718) 853-9094. Articles for the young and young at heart. (www.hamodia.com/subscribe)

Tablet (2009). 37 West 28th Street, 8th Floor, New York, NY 10001. (212) 920-3660. Online only. Published by Nextbook Inc. Jewish news, ideas, and culture. (www.tabletmag.com)

TeenPages (Mishpacha). 5809 16th Avenue, Brooklyn, NY 11204. (718) 686-9339. A collection of features, stories, and serials that brings teenagers' experiences to life, including writing by teenagers themselves, and speaks to the special interests and perspectives of this unique stage of life. (www.mishpacha.com)

Tikkun Magazine (1986). 2342 Shattuck Avenue, Suite 1200, Berkeley, CA 94704. (510) 644-1200. Analyzes American and Israeli culture, politics, religion, and history from a leftist-progressive viewpoint. (www.tikkun.org)

Together (1985). 122 West 30th Street, Room 205, New York, NY 10001. (212) 239-4230. Published by The American Gathering of Jewish Holocaust Survivors and Their Descendants. Reflects the collective voice of survivors and the second and third generations, and includes news, opinions, information on education, commemorations, events, book reviews, announcements, searches, and articles on history and personal remembrance. (www.amgathering.org)

Tradition (1958). 915 East 17th Street, Apartment 314, Brooklyn, NY 11230. (212) 807-9000, ext. 1. Online only. Published by Rabbinical Council of America. Semi-scholarly journal from an Orthodox perspective on halakha, religion, and Jewish affairs. (www.traditiononline.org)

Tzivos Hashem Kids (2007). 792 Eastern Parkway, Brooklyn, NY 11213. (718) 467-6630. Published by Chabad. Magazine for Jewish children under age 13 from backgrounds spanning the spectrum of levels of Jewish education and commitment to Jewish affiliation. (www.kids.tzivoshashem.org)

Valour Magazine (2017). 4403 15th Avenue, Suite #421, Brooklyn, NY 11219. Fashion/lifestyle magazine for the modern modest Jewish woman. (www.valour-magazine.com)

Vos Iz Neias? (What's News?) (2005). 12 Desbrosses Street, New York, NY 10013. (845) 458-1222. Online only. Serves the Orthodox Jewish community with up-to-the-minute news, accurate reporting and research, and hard-hitting commentary, raising issues of importance from the religious Jewish viewpoint. (www.vosizneias.com)

WorldJewishDaily.com (formerly *World Jewish Digest*). Online only. A news aggregation website that collects the best of Israel and Jewish news from around the world. (www.worldjewishdaily.com)

Yated Ne'eman (1987). 1451 Route 88, Suite 9, Brick, NJ 08724. (845) 369-1600. An independent Orthodox Jewish weekly newspaper. (www.yated.com)

The Yeshiva World News (2005). 5809 Foster Avenue, Brooklyn, NY 11203. (718) 305-6020. Online only. An independent news source and a news aggregator, known for providing news of interest to the Orthodox Jewish community, including general news items and Israeli news as well as religious news and news tailored around Jewish life cycle events and the Jewish calendar. (www.theyeshiva-world.com)

Yiddish Nayes. (Ceased publication)

Zman Magazine (2010). 25 Robert Pitt Road, Suite #107, Monsey, NY 10952. (845) 290-6161. Articles by gifted, deep-thinking writers from the Torah-observant world. (www.zmanmagazine.com)

ZOA Report. 633 Third Avenue, Suite 31-B, New York, NY 10017. (212) 481-1500. Published by the Zionist Organization of America. (www.zoa.org/zoa-publications)

13.2.1.1 Publications in Yiddish

Afn Shvel (1941). 64 Fulton Street, Suite 1101, New York, NY 10038. (212) 889-0380. Articles of Yiddish cultural, literary, linguistic, and communal interest. (www.leagueforyiddish.org/afnshvel.html)

Di Tsukunft (The Future) (1892). 1133 Broadway, Suite 1019, New York, NY 10010. (212) 505-8040. A literary journal published by the Congress for Jewish Culture. (www.congressforjewishculture.org/category/tsukunft)

Dee Voch (The Week). 4605 13th Avenue, Brooklyn, NY 11219. In Yiddish. (www.twitter.com/deevoch?lang=en)

Der Yid (The Jew): Voice of American Orthodoxy (1953). 191 Rodney Street, Brooklyn, NY 11211. (718) 797-3900. A New York-based Yiddish language newspaper published by Satmar Hasidim, but read worldwide within the broader Haredi community. (www.deryid.org)

Dos Yiddishe Vort Magazine (The Yiddish Word) (1953). 42 Broadway, 14th Floor, New York, NY 10004. Published by Agudath Israel of America. (212) 797-9000. (No website)

Der Yiddisher Moment (The Yiddish Moment) (2011). A universal, nonpolitical Yiddish-language internet newspaper — the only Yiddish journal entirely in Yiddish on the internet — whose mission is the preservation and furtherance of the Yiddish language and Yiddish culture. (www.yiddishmoment.com)

13.2.1.2 Publications in Russian

Alef Magazine (1981). 473 Empire Boulevard, Brooklyn, NY 11225. (212) 943-9690. Published by Chamah. General and Jewish information for Russian-speaking Jews. (www.alefmagazine.com)

Druzhba (Friendship) (1991). 98-81 Queens Boulevard, Rego Park, NY 11374. (718) 275-3318. Published by Ohr Natan (The Educational Center for New Americans). Largest Jewish publication in Russian in the US. (www.inforeklama.com/partners/magazines/druzhba/price_druzhba.htm)

13.2.1.3 Publications in Ladino

Erensia Sefardi (Sephardic Heritage) (1993). 34 West 15th Street, 3rd Floor, New York, NY 10011. Published by the Foundation for the Advancement of Sephardic Studies and Culture, in English and Ladino. (www.esefarad.com/?tag=erensia-sefardi)

13.2.2 National Jewish Periodicals and Broadcast Media, Canada

Canada Jewish Pipeline (2002). (780) 481-8535. Free e-mail bulletin sent to Jewish subscribers all across Canada containing useful information, articles, a little learning, Jewish holiday traditions, announcements, event photos, advertising, and more. (www.canadajewishpipeline.ca)

Communiqué ISRAnet. PO Box 175, Station H, Montreal, QC H3G 2K7. (514) 486-5544. Online only. Published by the Canadian Institute for Jewish Research. French-language e-mail briefing, covering Israel, Jewish and Arab world issues, the role of France in the Middle East, etc. (www.isranet.org/publications)

Dateline: Middle East (1988). PO Box 175, Station H, Montreal, QC H3G 2K7. (514) 486-5544. The Canadian Institute for Jewish Research's student magazine on Israel and the Middle East, covering issues related to the politics, economics, and cultures of the region. (www.isranet.org/publications)

IsraBlog (2014). PO Box 175, Station H, Montreal, QC H3G 2K7. (514) 486-5544. Published by the Canadian Institute for Jewish Research. Opinion-pieces on Israel, Jewish, and Arab Middle Eastern and international affairs issues written by the Institute's internationally-respected academic Fellows. (www.isranet.org/publications)

Isranet Daily Briefing (2000). PO Box 175, Station H, Montreal, QC H3G 2K7. (514) 486-5544. Published by the Canadian Institute for Jewish Research. Covers issues related to Israel, the Arab-Israel conflict, Middle Eastern politics, the Arab world, the Jewish world, the Holocaust, antisemitism, etc. (www.isranet.org/publications)

JewishFiction.net (2010). Online only. English-language journal devoted exclusively to the publishing of Jewish fiction. (www.jewishfiction.net)

UJPO News (1980). 585 Cranbrooke Avenue, Toronto, ON M6A 2X9. (416) 789-5502. Newsletter of United Jewish People's Order, a secular humanist group. (www.ujpo.org/ujpo-news)

13.2.3   National Television/Internet/Radio Stations, United States

Jewish Broadcasting Service (formerly Shalom TV) (2006). PO Box 180, Riverdale Station, Bronx, NY 10471. (201) 242-9460. Jewish Broadcasting Service is an American Jewish television cable network covering the panorama of Jewish life, with programming that reflects and addresses the diversity and pluralism of the Jewish experience. More than 40 million homes in the US and Canada now have access to the free Jewish television service. (www.shalomtv.com)

The Jewish Channel (2007). The Jewish Channel delivers hundreds of five-star movies, original news, and cultural programming, bringing provocative, engaging, and touching Jewish experiences to its viewers. (www.tjctv.com)

Jewish Rock Radio (2009). The mission of Jewish Rock Radio, an internet radio station, is to strengthen Jewish identity and engagement for youth and young adults through the power of music. (www.jewishrockradio.com)

J Root Radio (2011). 2829 Nostrand Avenue, Brooklyn, NY 11229. (718) 951-0605. J Root Radio is an Orthodox Jewish-themed radio station that broadcasts music, rabbinic lectures, and other Jewish-oriented programming in the US, Israel, and around the world, exposing listeners to the intrinsic beauty and depth of the Jewish faith. (www.jrootradio.com)

Talkline Communications Network (1981). PO Box 20108, Park West Station, New York, NY 10025. (212) 769-1925. Talkline with Zev Brenner is the network's flagship syndicated radio and television program, which airs locally in New York and New Jersey and on the internet 24/7. The radio shows are also carried on cable radio across the country and the television programs air on the Jewish Broadcasting Service nationwide. (www.talklinecommunications.com)

JLTV (Jewish Life Television) (2006). (818) 786-4000. JLTV is a 24/7 TV network delivering Jewish-themed programming, with a spotlight on Israel and Jewish life. It offers news, sports, lifestyle, and entertainment programming, including films, documentaries, music, reviews, interviews, and special events. (www.jltv.tv)

National Jewish Television (1979). National Jewish Television is a Jewish television channel seen as a three-hour block every Sunday on religious and public-access television cable TV channels in the US. (No website)

13.3   Local Jewish Periodicals

13.3.1   Local Jewish Periodicals, United States

Alabama
Southern Jewish Life (formerly *Deep South Jewish Voice*) (1990). 14 Office Park Circle, #104, PO Box 130052, Birmingham, AL 35213. (205) 870-7889. (www.sjlmag.com)

Arizona

Arizona Jewish Life (2013). 6680 SW Capitol Highway, Portland, OR 97219. (602) 538-2955. (www.azjewishlife.com)

Arizona Jewish Post (1946). 3718 East River Road #272, Tucson, AZ 85718. (520) 319-1112. Jewish Federation of Southern Arizona. (www.azjewishpost.com)

Jewish News of Greater Phoenix (1948). 12701 North Scottsdale Road, Suite 206, Scottsdale, AZ 85254. (602) 870-9470. (www.jewishaz.com)

Arkansas

Action. 18 Corporate Hill Drive, Suite 204, Little Rock, AR 72205. (501) 663-3571. Jewish Federation of Arkansas. (www.jewisharkansas.org/action-newsletter)

California

J. the Jewish News of Northern California (formerly *The Jewish Bulletin of Northern California*) (1895). 225 Bush Street, Suite 480, San Francisco, CA 94104. (415) 263-7200. (www.jweekly.com)

Jewish Community Chronicle (1947). 3801 East Willow Street, Long Beach, CA 90815. (562) 426-7601. Jewish Federation of Greater Long Beach & West Orange County. (www.jewishlongbeach.org)

Jewish Community News. 69710 Highway 111, Rancho Mirage, CA 92270. (760) 324-4737. Jewish Federation of Palm Springs and Desert Area. (www.jfedps.org)

Jewish Journal of Greater Los Angeles (1986). 3250 Wilshire Boulevard, Los Angeles, CA 90100. (213) 368-1661. (www.jewishjournal.com)

The Jewish Observer Los Angeles (1999). PO Box 261661, Encino, CA 91426. (818) 996-1220. (www.jewishobserver-la.com)

Jlife: SGPV Jewish Life (2017). One Federation Way, Irvine, CA 92603. (949) 734-5074. Jewish Federation of Greater San Gabriel and Pomona Valleys. (www.jlifesgpv.com)

JValley.news (1976). 14855 Oka Road, Suite 200, Los Gatos, CA 95032. (408) 358-3033. Jewish Federation of Silicon Valley. (www.jvalley.org/news)

L'CHAIM: San Diego Magazine (2014). PO Box 27876, San Diego, CA 92198. (858) 776-0550. (www.lchaimmagazine.com)

Los Angeles Jewish News (Ceased publication)

San Diego Jewish Journal (2001). 5665 Oberlin Drive, Suite 204, San Diego, CA 92121. (858) 638-9818. (www.sdjewishjournal.com)

San Diego Jewish Times (1979). 4731 Palm Avenue, La Mesa, CA 91941. (619) 463-5515. (www.sdjewishtimes.com)

San Diego Jewish World (2009). Harrison Enterprises, PO Box 19363, San Diego, CA 92159. (619) 265-0808. Online only. (www.sdjewishworld.com)

The Voice (2012). 2130 21st Street Sacramento, CA 95818. (916) 486-0906. Online only. The Jewish Federation of the Sacramento Region. (www.jewishsac.org/thevoice/?rq=the%20voice)

We Are in America (2006). PO Box 570283, Tarzana, CA 91357. (877) 332-0233. (www.weinamerica.com)

Colorado

Boulder Jewish News (2009). 4800 Baseline Road, Suite E104-448, Boulder, CO 80303. (720) 934-4372. Online only. (www.boulderjewishnews.org)

Intermountain Jewish News (1913). 1177 Grant Street, Denver, CO 80203. (303) 861-2234. (www.ijn.com)

Connecticut

Connecticut Jewish Ledger. (1929). 36 Woodland Street, Hartford, CT 06105. (860) 231-2424. (www.jewishledger.com)

Greenwich Jewish News. One Holly Hill Lane, Greenwich, CT 06830. (203) 552-1818. UJA-JCC Greenwich. (www.ujajcc.org)

The Jewish Link of Bronx, Westchester & Connecticut (2015). PO Box 1027, Bronx, NY 10471. (718) 564-6710. (www.jewishlinkbwc.com)

The New Jewish Voice (formerly *Jewish Voice*) (1975). 1035 Newfield Avenue, Stamford, CT 06905. (203) 321-1373. United Jewish Federation of Greater Stamford, New Canaan and Darien. (www.ujf.org)

Shalom New Haven. 360 Amity Road, Woodbridge, CT 06525. (203) 387-2424. Jewish Federation of Greater New Haven. (www.jewishnewhaven.org/shalom-new-haven)

Delaware

j-VOICE Monthly. 101 Garden of Eden Road, Wilmington, DE 19803. (302) 427-2100. Jewish Federation of Delaware. (www.shalomdelaware.org)

District of Columbia

Kol HaBirah: Voice of the Capitol (2017). 1111 University Boulevard West, Silver Spring, MD 20902. (240) 478-1924. (www.kolhabirah.com)

Washington Jewish Week (formerly *National Jewish Ledger*) (1930). 11900 Parklawn Drive, Suite 300, Rockville, MD 20852. (301) 230-2222. (www.washingtonjewishweek.com)

Florida

Chai Life (Ceased publication as of 2017)

The Chronicle. 3835 Northwest 8th Avenue, Gainesville, FL 32605. (352) 371-3846. Jewish Council of North Central Florida. (www.jcncf.org/chronicle.html)

The Connection (2005). 210 East Hibiscus Boulevard, Melbourne, FL 32901. (321) 951-1836. Online only. Jewish Federation of Brevard County. (www.jewishfederationbrevard.com)

Federation Star (1991). 2500 Vanderbilt Beach Road, Suite 2201, Naples, FL 34109. (239) 263-4205. Jewish Federation of Collier County. (www.jewishnaples.org/federation-star)

Heritage, Florida Jewish News (1976). 207 O'Brien Road, Suite 101, Fern Park, FL 32730. (407) 834-8787. (www.heritagefl.com)

IsraPost (1997). 2128 Hollywood Boulevard, Hollywood, FL 33020. (954) 964-0135. In Hebrew and English. (www.israpost.com)

Jacksonville Jewish News (1988). 8505 San Jose Boulevard, Jacksonville, FL 32217. (904) 448-5000. Jewish Federation of Jacksonville. (www.jewishjacksonville.org/news)

Jewish Journal – Broward, Palm Beach, Miami Dade (1977). 333 Southwest 12th Avenue, Deerfield Beach, Fl 33442. (954) 572-2050. (www.sun-sentinel.com/florida-jewish-journal)

The Jewish News of Sarasota-Manatee (formerly *The Chronicle*) (1971). 580 McIntosh Road, Sarasota, FL 34232. (941) 371-4546. The Jewish Federation of Sarasota-Manatee. (www.jfedsrq.org)

Jewish Press of Pinellas County (1986). 6416 Central Avenue, St. Petersburg, FL 33707. (727) 535-4400. Jewish Press Group of Tampa Bay in cooperation with The Jewish Federation of Pinellas & Pasco Counties. (www.jewishpresstampabay.com)

Jewish Press of Tampa (1988). 6416 Central Avenue, St. Petersburg, FL 33707. (813) 871-2332. Jewish Press Group of Tampa Bay in cooperation with Tampa Jewish Community Center & Federation. (www.jewishpresstampabay.com)

Jewish Way (JW) (2010). 1920 East. Hallandale Beach Boulevard, Suite 509, Hallandale Beach, FL 33009. (954) 613-9318. (www.jwmagazine.com)

L'Chayim (2003). 9701 Commerce Center Court, Ft. Myers, FL 33908. (239) 481-4449. Jewish Federation of Lee and Charlotte Counties. (www.jewishfederationlcc.org/lchayim)

Southern Jewish Life (formerly *Deep South Jewish Voice*) (1990). 14 Office Park Circle, #104, PO Box 130052, Birmingham, AL 35213. (205) 870-7889. (www.sjlmag.com)

Georgia

The Atlanta Jewish Times (1925). 270 Carpenter Drive NE, Suite 320, Atlanta, GA 30328. (404) 883-2130. (www.atlantajewishtimes.com)

The Jewish Georgian (1990). 9755 Dogwood Road, Suite 101, Roswell, GA 30075. (404) 236-8911. (www.jewishgeorgian.com)

Savannah Jewish News. (1960). 5111 Abercom Street, Savannah, GA 31405. (912) 355-8111. Savannah Jewish Federation. (www.savj.org/savannah-jewish-news)

Illinois

The Chicago Jewish News (1994). 4638 West Church Street, Skokie, IL 60076. (847) 966-0606. (www.chicagojewishnews.com)

JUF News. 30 South Wells Street, Chicago, IL 60606. (312) 346-6700. Jewish United Fund/Jewish Federation of Metropolitan Chicago. (www.juf.org)

Iowa

The Greater Des Moines Jewish Press. 33158 Ute Avenue, Waukee, IA 50263. (515) 987-0899. Jewish Federation of Greater Des Moines. (www.jewishdesmoines.org/our-pillars/jewish-press)

Indiana

Indiana Jewish Post and Opinion (1935). 1389 West 86th Street, #160, Indianapolis, IN 46260. (317) 405-8084. (www.jewishpostopinion.com)

Kansas

The Kansas City Jewish Chronicle (1920). 4210 Shawnee Mission Parkway, Suite 314A, Fairway, KS 66205. (913) 951-8425. (www.kcjc.com)

Kentucky

Community (1975). 3600 Dutchmans Lane, Louisville, KY 40205. (502) 459-0660. Jewish Community Federation of Louisville. (www.jewishlouisville.org)

Shalom (2004). 1050 Chinoe Road, Suite 112, Lexington, KY 40502. (859) 268-0672. The Jewish Federation of the Bluegrass. (www.jewishlexington.org/shalom-online)

Louisiana

Crescent City Jewish News (2011). 3810 Nashville Avenue, New Orleans, LA 70125. (504) 865-1248. Online only. (www.crescentcityjewishnews.com)

The Jewish Light (formerly *Jewish Community Newspaper*) (1996). 1819 Columbia Street, Suite 205, Covington, LA 70433. (504) 455-8822. (www.jewish-communitynews.org)

The Jewish Newsletter (1995). 3747 West Esplanade Avenue, Metairie, LA 70002. (504) 780-5600. Jewish Federation of Greater New Orleans. Distributed as an insert in *Southern Jewish Life*. (www.jewishnola.com)

Southern Jewish Life (formerly *Deep South Jewish Voice*) (1990). 14 Office Park Circle, #104, PO Box 130052, Birmingham, AL 35213. (205) 870-7889. (www.sjlmag.com)

Maryland

Baltimore Jewish Times (1919). 11459 Cronhill Drive, Suite A, Owings Mills, Maryland 21117. (410) 902-2300. (www.jewishtimes.com)

Washington Jewish Week (formerly *National Jewish Ledger*) (1930). 11900 Parklawn Drive, Suite 300, Rockville, MD 20852. (301) 230-2222. (www.washingtonjewishweek.com)

Where What When (1985). 6016 Clover Road, Baltimore, MD 21215. (410) 358-8509. (www.wherewhatwhen.com)

Massachusetts

Berkshire Jewish Voice. 196 South Street, Pittsfield, MA 01201. (413) 442-4360. Jewish Federation of the Berkshires. (www.jewishberkshires.org/community-events/berkshire-jewish-voice)

Jewish Advocate (1902). 15 School Street, Boston, MA 02108. (617) 367-9100. (www.thejewishadvocate.com)

The Jewish Journal MA (1976). 27 Congress Street, Suite 501, Salem, MA 01970. (978) 745-4111. (www.jewishjournal.org)

Jewish Ledger Western Massachusetts Edition. 36 Woodland Street, Hartford, CT 06105. (860) 231-2424. (www.wmassjewishledger.com)

Shalom Magazine-Massachusetts (2009) Farber Marketing, 12 Edward Drive, Stoughton, MA 02072. (781) 975-1009. (www.issuu.com/shalomma)

Michigan

Detroit Jewish News (1942). 29200 Northwestern Highway, Suite 110, Southfield, MI 48034. (248) 354-6060. (www.thejewishnews.com)

Jewish Reporter. 5080 West Bristol Road, Suite 3, Flint, MI 48507. (810) 767-5922. Flint Jewish Federation. (www.flintfed.com/publications)

Red Thread Magazine (Ceased publication as of 2013)

Washtenaw Jewish News (1978). 2935 Birch Hollow Drive, Ann Arbor, MI 48108. (734) 395-4438. (www.washtenawjewishnews.org)

Minnesota

The American Jewish World (formerly *Jewish Weekly*) (1912). 4820 Minnetonka Boulevard, Suite 104, Minneapolis, MN 55416. (952) 259-5234. (www.ajwnews.com)

Mississippi

Southern Jewish Life (formerly *Deep South Jewish Voice*) (1990). 14 Office Park Circle, #104, Birmingham, AL 35213. (205) 870-7889. (www.sjlmag.com)

Missouri

The Kansas City Jewish Chronicle (1920). 4210 Shawnee Mission Parkway, Suite 314A. Fairway, KS 66205. (913) 951-8425. (www.kcjc.com)

St. Louis Jewish Light (1947). 6 Millstone Campus Drive, St. Louis, MO 63146. (314) 743-3660. Jewish Federation of St. Louis. (www.stljewishlight.com)

St. Louis Jewish Parents Magazine (2015). PO Box 31724, St. Louis, MO 63131. (412) 251-6324. (www.stlouisjewishparents.com)

Nebraska

The Jewish Press (1920). 333 South 132nd Street, Omaha, NE 68154. (402) 334-6448. Jewish Federation of Omaha. (www.jewishomaha.org/jewish-press)

Nevada

David Magazine. 1930 Village Center Circle #3-459, Las Vegas, NV 89134. (702) 254-2223. (www.davidlv.com)

Las Vegas Israelite (1965). PO Box 29240, Las Vegas, NV 89126. (702) 876-1255.

(www.lvisraelite.com)

New Hampshire

The New Hampshire Jewish Reporter. 66 Hanover Street, Suite 300, Manchester, NH 03101. (603) 627-7679. Jewish Federation of New Hampshire. (www.jewishnh.org/news/jewishreporter)

New Jersey

The Jewish Community Voice (1941). 1301 Springdale Road, Suite 250, Cherry Hill, NJ 08003. (856) 751-9500, ext. 1217. Jewish Federation of Southern New Jersey. (www.jewishvoicesnj.org)

Jewish Journal (1999). 320 Raritan Avenue, Suite 203, Highland Park, NJ 08904. (732) 987-4783. Jewish Federation of Ocean County. (www.ocjj.net)

The Jewish Link of New Jersey (2013). PO Box 3131, Teaneck, NJ 07666. (201) 371-3212. (www.jewishlinknj.com)

The Jewish Standard (1931). 1086 Teaneck Road, Teaneck, NJ 07666. (201) 837-8818. (http://jewishstandard.timesofisrael.com)

The Jewish Voice and Opinion (1987). (formerly *The Jewish Voice of Northern NJ*). 73 Dana Place, Englewood, NJ 07631. (201) 569-2845. Online only. (www.jewishvoiceandopinion.com)

New Jersey Jewish News (1947). 1719 State Route 10, Whippany, NJ 07054. (973) 887-3900. (https://njjewishnews.timesofisrael.com)

Passaic-Bergen Jewish News (Ceased publication as of 2012)

The Shopper (referred to as *Lakewood Shopper)* (2004). 72B Park Avenue, Lakewood, NJ 08701. (732) 367-6245. Online only. (www.lakewoodshopper.com)

The VOICE of Lakewood (2005). 235 River Avenue, Lakewood, NJ 08701. (732) 901-5746. (www.thevoiceoflakewood.com)

New Mexico

The New Mexico Jewish Link (1971). 5520 Wyoming Boulevard NE, Albuquerque, NM 87109. (505) 821-3214. Jewish Federation of New Mexico. (www.newmexico-jewishelink.com)

New York (Outside New York Metropolitan Area)

The Jewish Journal. 2640 North Forest Road, Getzville, NY 14068. (716) 204-2241. Buffalo Jewish Federation. (www.buffalojewishfederation.org)

Jewish Ledger (1924). 2535 Brighton-Henrietta Townline Road, Rochester, NY 14623. (585) 427-2468. (www.thejewishledger.com)

Jewish Observer of Central New York (1978). 5655 Thompson Road, DeWitt, NY 13214. (315) 445-2040, ext. 116. Jewish Federation of Central New York. (www.jewishfederationcny.org/?page_id=7)

The Jewish World (1965). 1635 Eastern Parkway, Schenectady, NY 12309. (518) 344-7018. (www.jewishworldnews.org)

Monsey Jewish Times (2017). (845) 270-3106. (www.monseytimes.com)

One Stop Jewish Buffalo (2017). 2730 North Forest Road, #132, Getzville, NY 14068. (716) 777-2351. Online only. (www.onestopjewishbuffalo.com)

The Reporter (1971). 500 Clubhouse Road, Vestal, NY 13850. (607) 724-2332. Jewish Federation of Greater Binghamton. (www.thereportergroup.org)

The Rockland Jewish Standard. 1086 Teaneck Road, Teaneck, NJ 07666. (201) 837-8818. (http://jewishstandard.timesofisrael.com)

The Voice of the Dutchess Jewish Community (1990). 17 Collegeview Avenue, Poughkeepsie, NY 12603. (845) 471-9811. The Jewish Federation of Dutchess County. (www.jewishdutchess.org)

New York Metropolitan Area

5 Towns Jewish Times (2000). PO Box 690, Lawrence, NY 11559. (516) 569-0502. Online only. (www.5tjt.com)

Der Blatt (The Page/The Newspaper) (2000). 76 Rutledge Street, Brooklyn, NY 11249. (718) 625-3400. Published by Satmar Hasidim. In Yiddish. (No website).

Bukharian Jewish Link (2017). (917) 945-9592. (www.bukharianjewishlink.com)
The Bukharian Times. 106-16 70th Avenue, Forest Hills, NY 11375. (718) 261-1595 or (718) 261-2315. In Russian. (www.bukhariantimes.org)
CHAZAQ Family Magazine (2008). 141-24 Jewel Avenue, 2nd Floor, Flushing, NY 11367. (718) 285-9132. (www.CHAZAQ.org)
The Country Vues (1983). PO Box 330, Midwood Station, Brooklyn, NY 11230. (718) 377-8016. Published in the summer for the Catskill Mountain area. (www.thevuesonline.com)
Flatbush Jewish Journal. 1314 Avenue J, Brooklyn, NY 11230. (718) 692-1144. (www.flatbushjewishjournal.com)
HasidicNews.com (1999). Online only. (www.hasidicnews.com) (Ceased publication)
The Jewish Herald (1984). 1689 46th Street, Brooklyn, NY 11204. (718) 972-4000. (No website)
The Jewish Home. PO Box 266, Lawrence, NY 11559. (516) 734-0858. (www.fivetownsjewishhome.com)
Jewish Image (1990). PO Box 290-642, Brooklyn, New York 11229. (718) 627-4624. Sephardic. (www.imageusa.com)
The Jewish Link of Bronx, Westchester & Connecticut (2015). PO Box 1027, Bronx, NY 10471. (718) 564-6710. (www.jewishlinkbwc.com)
Jewish Post (1974). 350 5th Avenue, Suite 2418, New York, NY 10118. (212) 563-9219. (www.jewishpost.com)
The Jewish Star (2002). 2 Endo Boulevard, Garden City, NY 11530. (516) 622-7461. (www.thejewishstar.com)
The Jewish Voice (formerly *Jewish Voice*) (2004). 2150 East 4th Street, New York, NY 11223. (800) 998-0885. (www.jewishvoiceny.com)
LeChaim (2010). 107-14 Queens Boulevard, #100, Forest Hills, NY 11375. (718) 306-4382. In Russian. Published by Ohr Avner Ben Imashalom. (www.facebook.com/lechaimnewspaper)
Long Island Jewish World (1977). 115 Middle Neck Road, Great Neck, NY 11021. (516) 594-4000. (www.facebook.com/LIJewishWorld)
New York Jewish Life (2017). 306 Gold Street, Brooklyn, NY 11201. (929) 274-0762. (www.nyjlife.com)
The New York Jewish Week (1876; reorganized 1970). 1501 Broadway, Suite 505, New York, NY 10036. (212) 921-7822. (https://jewishweek.timesofisrael.com)
Queens Jewish Link (2013). 68-68 Main Street, Queens, NY 11367. (718) 880-2622. (www.queensjewishlink.com)
Shalom Magazine. 98-81 Queens Boulevard, Rego Park, NY 11374. (718) 275-3318. Published by Ohr Natan (The Educational Center for New Americans). (www.shalommagazine.org)
Di Tzeitung (*The Newspaper*) (1988). 1281 49th Street, Brooklyn, NY 11219. (718) 851-6607. Hasidic Yiddish-language newspaper sold at city newsstands in New York, especially in Brooklyn's Williamsburg and Borough Park neighborhoods. (www.ditzeitung.com)

The Vues (1977). PO Box 330, Midwood Station, Brooklyn, NY 11230. (718) 377-8016. (www.thevuesonline.com)

Westchester Jewish Life. (1995). 629 Fifth Avenue, Suite 213, Pelham, NY 10803. (914) 738-7869. (www.westchesterjewishlife.com)

North Carolina

Charlotte Jewish News (1978). 5007 Providence Road, Suite 112, Charlotte, NC 28226. (704) 944-6765. Jewish Federation of Greater Charlotte. (www.charlotte-jewishnews.org)

Miriam's Tent, (1987). 8210 Creedmoor Road, Suite 104, Raleigh, NC 27613. (919) 676-2200. The Jewish Federation of Raleigh-Cary. (www.shalomraleigh.org)

Ohio

Akron Jewish News (1929). 750 White Pond Drive, Akron, OH 44320. (330) 869-2424. Jewish Community Board of Akron. (www.jewishakron.org/news/current-news?page=9)

The American Israelite (1854). 11674 Lebanon Road, Cincinnati, OH 45241. (513) 621-3145. (www.americanisraelite.com)

Cleveland Jewish News (1964). 23880 Commerce Park, Suite 1, Beachwood, OH 44122. (216) 454-8300. (www.clevelandjewishnews.com)

Columbus Jewish News (2019). 23880 Commerce Park, Suite 1, Beachwood, OH 44122. (833) 454-8300. www.columbusjewishnews.com

The Dayton Jewish Observer. 525 Versailles Drive, Centerville, OH 45459. (937) 610-1555. Jewish Federation of Greater Dayton. (www.daytonjewishobserver.org)

The Jewish Journal Monthly Magazine (1987). 505 Gypsy Lane, Youngstown, OH 44504. (330) 746-3251. Youngstown Area Jewish Federation. (www.jewishyoungstown.org/federation/jewish-journal-monthly-magazine)

Local Jewish News (Cleveland). Online only. (www.localjewishnews.com)

The Ohio Jewish Chronicle (Ceased publication as of 2018)

Stark Jewish News (1920). 432 30th Street NW, Canton, OH 44709. (330) 445-2860. Canton Jewish Community Federation. (www.jewishcanton.org)

Toledo Jewish News (1951). 6505 Sylvania Avenue, Sylvania, OH 43560. (419) 724-0363. Jewish Federation of Greater Toledo. (www.jewishtoledo.org/about-us/tjnff)

Oklahoma

Tulsa Jewish Review (1930). 2021 East 71st Street, Tulsa, OK 74136. (918) 495-1100. Jewish Federation of Tulsa. (www.jewishtulsa.org/our-work/tulsa-jewish-review)

Oregon

Oregon Jewish Life (2012). 6680 SW Capitol Highway, Portland, OR 97219. (503) 892-7402. Jewish Federation of Greater Portland. (www.ojlife.com)

Pennsylvania

Community Review (1925). 3301 North Front Street, Harrisburg, PA 17110. (717) 236-9555. Jewish Federation of Greater Harrisburg. (www.jewishharrisburg.org/resources/community-review)

Hakol Lehigh Valley. 702 North 22nd Street, Allentown, PA 18104. (610) 821-5500. Jewish Federation of the Lehigh Valley. (www.jewishlehighvalley. org/hakol)

Jewish Exponent (1887). 2100 Arch Street, Philadelphia, PA 19103. (215) 832-0700. Jewish Federation of Greater Philadelphia. (www.jewishexponent.com)

The Philadelphia Jewish Voice (2005). Online only. (www.pjvoice.org)

The Pittsburgh Jewish Chronicle (1962). 5915 Beacon Street, Pittsburgh, PA 15217. (412) 687-1000. (www.thejewishchronicle.net)

The Reporter of Scranton and Northeastern Pennsylvania (2000). 601 Jefferson Avenue, Scranton, PA 18510. (570) 961-2300. Jewish Federation of Northeastern Pennsylvania. (www.jewishnepa.org/news-events/reporter)

Shalom: The Journal of the Reading Jewish Community. 1100 Berkshire Boulevard, Suite 125, Wyomissing, PA 19610. (610) 921-0624. Jewish Federation of Reading/Berks. (www.readingjewishcommunity.org)

Rhode Island

Jewish Rhode Island (formerly *The Jewish Voice and Herald*) (1973) (2018). 401 Elmgrove Avenue, Providence, RI 02906. (401) 421-4111. Jewish Alliance of Greater Rhode Island. (www.jewishrhody.com)

South Carolina

Charleston Jewish Voice (2001). 176 Croghan Spur Road, Suite 100, Charleston, SC 29407. (843) 614-6600. Online only. Charleston Jewish Federation. (www.jewishcharleston.org/community-resources/communications/charleston-jewish-voice)

Columbia Jewish News. 306 Flora Drive, Columbia, SC 29223. (803) 787-2023. Columbia Jewish Federation. (www.jewishcolumbia.org/cjn)

Tennessee

Hebrew Watchman (1925). 4646 Poplar Avenue, Memphis, TN 38117. (901) 763-2215. (No website)

The Jewish Observer (1934). 801 Percy Warner Boulevard, Nashville, TN 37205. (615) 354-1653. Jewish Federation of Nashville and Middle Tennessee. (www.jewishobservernashville.org)

Jewish Scene (formerly *Jewish Living of the South*) (2006). 1703 Tamhaven Court, Cordova, TN, 38016. (901) 827-7244. (www.jewishscenemagazine.com)

Shofar. 5461 North Terrace Road, Chattanooga, TN 37411. (423) 493-0270. Jewish Federation of Greater Chattanooga. (www.jewishchattanooga.com/about/shofar)

Texas

The Jewish Herald-Voice (1908). 3403 Audley Street, Houston, TX 77098. (713) 630-0391. (www.jhvonline.com)

The Jewish Journal of San Antonio (1973). 12500 NW Military Highway, Suite 200, San Antonio, TX 78231. (210) 302-6960. Jewish Federation of San Antonio. (www.jfsatx.org/jewish-journal-of-san-antonio)

The Jewish Outlook. 7300 Hart Lane, Austin, TX 78731. (512) 735-8057. Shalom Austin. (www.thejewishoutlook.com)

The Jewish Voice. 7110 North Mesa, El Paso, TX 79912. (915) 842-9554. Jewish Federation of Greater El Paso. (www.jewishelpaso.org)

Texas Jewish Post - Dallas (1947). 7920 Belt Line Road, Suite 680, Dallas, TX 75254. (972) 458-7283. (www.tjpnews.com)

Texas Jewish Post - Fort Worth (1947). PO Box 12087, Fort Worth, TX 76110. (817) 927-2831. (www.tjpnews.com)

Virginia
Jewish News (1959). 5000 Corporate Woods Drive, Suite 200, Virginia Beach, VA 23462. (757) 965-6100. United Jewish Federation of Tidewater. (www.jewish-newsva.org)

The Reflector. 5403 Monument Avenue, Richmond, VA 23226. (804) 545-8620. Jewish Community Federation of Richmond. (www.jewishrichmond.org/the-reflector)

Washington Jewish Week (formerly *National Jewish Ledger*) (1930). 11900 Parklawn Drive, Suite 300, Rockville, MD 20852. (301) 230-2222. (www.washingtonjewishweek.com)

Washington
Jewish in Seattle (2015). 2031 Third Avenue, Seattle, WA 98121. (206) 443-5400. Jewish Federation of Greater Seattle. (www.jewishinseattle.org/community-voice/jewish-in-seattle-magazine)

Wisconsin
Madison Jewish News. 6434 Enterprise Lane, Madison, WI 53719. (608) 278-1808. Jewish Federation of Madison. (www.jewishmadison.org/madison-jewish-news)

The Wisconsin Jewish Chronicle (1921). 1360 North Prospect Avenue, Milwaukee, WI 53202. (414) 390-5720. Milwaukee Jewish Federation. (www.jewishchronicle.org)

13.3.2 Local Jewish Periodicals, Canada

Alberta
Edmonton Jewish News (1990). 10632 124th Street NW, Suite A, Edmonton, AB T5N 1S3. (780) 421-7966. (www.edmontonjewishnews.com)

Jewish Free Press (1990). 8411 Elbow Drive, SW Calgary, AB T2V 1K8. (403) 252-9423. (www.jewishfreepress.ca)

British Columbia
Jewish Independent (formerly *Jewish Western Bulletin*) (1930). 291 East Second Avenue, Vancouver, BC V5T 1B8. (604) 689-1520. (www.jewishindependent.ca)

Manitoba
The Jewish Post & News (formerly *The Jewish Post*) (1925). 620 Brock Street, Winnipeg, MB R3N 0Z4. (204) 694-3332. (www.jewishpostandnews.ca)

Winnipeg Jewish Review (2009). Online only. (www.winnipegjewishreview.com)

Nova Scotia

Shalom! (1975). 5670 Spring Garden Road, Suite #309, Halifax, NS B3J 2L1. (902) 422-7491, ext. 221. The Atlantic Jewish Council. (www.theajc.ns.ca/category/shalom-magazine)

Ontario

The Canadian Jewish News (1971). 1750 Steeles Avenue West, Suite #218, Concord, ON L4K 2L7. (416) 932-5095. (www.cjnews.com)

Exodus Magazine (formerly *Exodus Newspaper*) (1983) (2002, became *Exodus Magazine* in English). 5987 Bathurst Street, Suite 3, Toronto, ON M2R 1Z3. (416) 222-7105. Published by the Jewish Russian Community Centre of Ontario (Chabad). (www.jrcc.org/templates/articlecco_cdo/aid/259118/jewish/Exodus-Magazine.htm)

Hamilton Jewish News. 1605 Main Street West, Hamilton, ON L8S 1E6. (905) 628-0058. (www.hamiltonjewishnews.com)

Jewish London Magazine. 536 Huron Street, London, ON N5Y 4J5. (519) 673-3310. London Jewish Federation. (www.jewishlondon.ca)

The Jewish Standard Magazine (1929). 1110 Finch Avenue West, Suite 1029, Toronto. ON M3J 3M2. (905) 417-5252. (www.thejewishstandardmag.com)

Kol Echad (Forest Heights Lodge #2667, B'nai B'rith) 150 Harris Way, Thornhill, L3T 5A8. (www.kolechad.ca)

News & Views (formerly *Windsor Jewish Federation*) (1942). 1641 Ouellette Avenue, Windsor, ON N8X 1K9. (519) 973-1772. Windsor Jewish Federation. (www.jewishwindsor.org)

Ottawa Jewish Bulletin (1937). 21 Nadolny Sachs Private, Ottawa, ON K2A 1R9. (613) 798-4696. Jewish Federation of Ottawa. (www.ottawajewishbulletin.com)

Quebec

The Canadian Jewish News (Montreal) (1971). 6900 Decarie Boulevard, Suite 341, Montreal, QC H3X 2TB. (866) 849-0864. (www.cjnews.com)

The Jewish Standard Magazine (1929). 4340 Avenue Walkley, Montreal, QC H4B 2K5. (514) 489-3124. (www.thejewishstandardmag.com)

LVS-La Voix Sepharad. 5151 Côte Ste-Catherine, Suite 216, Montreal, QC H3W 1M6. (514) 733-4998. Published by the Communauté Sépharade Unifiée du Québec (Unified Sephardic Community of Quebec). (www.csuq.org)

Montreal Jewish Magazine. Online only. (www.montrealjewishmagazine.com)

Shtetl: Your Alternative Jewish Magazine (2011). Online only. (www.shtetlmontreal.com)

Chapter 14
Academic Resources

Arnold Dashefsky, Ira M. Sheskin, Amy Lawton, Sarah Markowitz, and Maria Reger

This chapter provides lists with city locations, degrees offered, and websites for about 240 Jewish Studies Programs, about 70 Holocaust and Genocide Studies Programs, about 30 Israel Studies Programs, about 50 Programs in Hebrew and Yiddish Languages, and about 50 Programs in Jewish Education, Jewish Social Work, and Nonprofit Jewish Management. Programs that do not offer degrees are not listed. All programs with majors also offer minors, so "Minor" is not listed.

The chapter also includes (1) bibliographic information on about 80 books on North American Jewry; (2) names, descriptions, and websites for more than 40 academic journals in or about North American Jewish communities; (3) about 80 scholarly articles on the study of North American Jewish communities; (4) names, descriptions, and websites for about 55 websites and organizations for research on North American Jewish communities; and (5) names, descriptions, and websites for about 50 major Judaic research and Holocaust research libraries. In a special section this year, we present the results of a survey of Judaic Studies Programs completed for the Association for Jewish Studies.

The purpose of this chapter is to document the academic and research resources available to scholars and others researching North American Jewish communitie

A. Dashefsky (✉) · A. Lawton
Department of Sociology and Center for Judaic Studies and Contemporary Jewish Life, University of Connecticut, Storrs, CT, USA
e-mail: Arnold.dashefsky@uconn.edu

I. M. Sheskin
Department of Geography and Jewish Demography Project, Sue and Leonard Miller Center for Contemporary Judaic Studies, University of Miami, Coral Gables, FL, USA

S. Markowitz
Independent Researcher, Forest Hills, NY, USA

M. Reger
Center for Judaic Studies and Contemporary Jewish Life, University of Connecticut, Storrs, CT, USA

© Springer Nature Switzerland AG 2020
A. Dashefsky, I. M. Sheskin (eds.), *American Jewish Year Book 2019*, American Jewish Year Book 119, https://doi.org/10.1007/978-3-030-40371-3_14

Each list is carefully updated each year, but the authors appreciate any corrections noted by our readers. We have found that the websites for these programs on the internet are not always current.

14.1 Programs in Jewish Studies, Holocaust and Genocide Studies, Israel Studies, Hebrew and Yiddish Languages, and Programs in Jewish Education, Jewish Social Work, and Nonprofit Jewish Management

14.1.1 Central Coordinating Body for Programs in Jewish Studies, United States

Association for Jewish Studies For contact information and a description, see Sect. 14.5 in this chapter.

14.1.2 Overview of "Jewish Studies in the Academy in 2018" [1]

As Association for Jewish Studies (AJS) approached its 50th anniversary, it invited every US-based institution with a Jewish Studies department (about 250 institutions) to complete a survey based on the 2017/2018 academic year. AJS received responses from 161 institutions (66%). AJS found that Jewish Studies programs and students were concentrated primarily in the Middle Atlantic, South Atlantic, East North Central, and Pacific regions. Maps that reflect the geographical concentration of courses offered, undergraduate enrollment, faculty affiliated, and faculty teaching primarily in Jewish Studies are available in the full report, downloadable at: https://www.associationforjewishstudies.org/docs/default-source/surveys-of-the-profession/final-report_infographic_7-29-2.pdf?sfvrsn=2.

In 2017/2018, more than 35,000 undergraduates enrolled in a Jewish Studies course. About half of the faculty affiliated with Jewish Studies taught a minority of their courses in Jewish Studies. The other half taught most of their courses in Jewish Studies. The most prevalent Jewish Studies courses covered the Holocaust, European history, Israel and the Middle East, Hebrew Language and Literature, and the Bible. The least prevalent Jewish Studies courses covered topics in education, the social sciences, Sephardi and Mizrahi studies, and Yiddish language and literature. In terms of budget, about half of institutions operated on program budgets that were $10,000 or less per year. AJS found that about 30% of Jewish Studies faculty are in non-tenure track/non-tenured positions. Faculty continued to be dominated by

---

[1] This report was created by Dr. Ilana Horwitz, Dr. Arielle Levites, and Dr. Emily Sigalow.

males—for each female faculty member, there were about two male faculty members.

The key findings are summarized here:

- Number of Jewish Studies Courses Offered: **2109**
- Number of Undergrad Enrollments in Jewish Studies Courses: **35,753**
- Number of Faculty Affiliated with Jewish Studies: **1709**
- Number of Faculty Teaching Primarily in Jewish Studies: **812**
- Over two-thirds of responding institutions offered courses in the Holocaust, religion, European history, Israel and the Middle East, Hebrew language and literature, and the Bible.
- About half of responding institutions offered courses in Jewish thought, Jewish culture, and comparative literature.
- Fewer than one-quarter of responding institutions offered courses in Yiddish language and literature, Sephardi and Mizrahi studies, and topical courses in social sciences, art history, and education.
- About half of institutions operated on program budgets that are $10,000 or less per year.
- About 30% of faculty are working outside the tenure system.
- For every female faculty member, there are about two male faculty members.

Based on respondents' self-assessment, undergraduate enrollment was a key area of concern because it reflected the Jewish Studies program's overall vitality. Other indicators of health included the number of majors/minors, the addition/loss of faculty or faculty lines, and community interest in public programs. About 30% of institutions reported that enrollment in Jewish Studies, especially Israel Studies, had increased. About 50% reported that enrollment had stayed constant. Enrollment in Hebrew language and literature appeared to be on the decline. Jewish Studies was highly affected by changes that were often beyond their control, such as changes in General Education or language requirements, demographic shifts in the student body, and decreasing interest in the humanities. To attract students, institutions introduced new course topics, cross-listing courses, adapting courses to meet General Education requirements, offering freshmen seminars to expose students to Jewish studies early on, being more proactive about partnering with Hillel and Chabad, and offering online courses. However, adding new courses may not increase enrollment and instead might cannibalize other Jewish Studies courses. Institutions rarely mentioned trying to improve student learning experiences, suggesting little attention to the quality of courses offered, pedagogy, or assessment of student learning.

14.1.3   Programs in Jewish Studies, United States

Alabama
University of Alabama, Tuscaloosa, AL. Minor. (https://religion.ua.edu/undergraduate-programs/minor-in-judaic-studies)
   University of South Alabama, Mobile, AL. Minor in Jewish and Holocaust Studies. (www.southalabama.edu/colleges/artsandsci/jewishandholocauststudies)

Arizona
Arizona State University, Tempe, AZ. BA, Undergraduate Certificate. (http://jewishstudies.clas.asu.edu/about)
   University of Arizona, Tucson, AZ. BA, Graduate Certificate. (www.judaic.arizona.edu)

Arkansas
University of Arkansas, Fayetteville, AK. Minor. (https://fulbright.uark.edu/programs/jewish-studies)

California
American Jewish University, Los Angeles, CA. MA. (www.aju.edu) (Not accepting new students for BA for 2018/2019 and 2019/2020 academic years)
   California State University, Chico, Chico, CA. Minor in Modern Jewish and Israel Studies. (www.csuchico.edu./mjis)
   California State University, Fresno, Fresno, CA. Minor, Undergraduate Certificate. (www.fresnostate.edu/socialsciences/historydept/degrees/jewish-studies/index.html)
   California State University, Fullerton, Fullerton, CA. Minor. (http://religion.fullerton.edu/academics/jewish_studies.aspx)
   California State University, Long Beach, Long Beach, CA. BA. (www.cla.csulb.edu/programs/jewishstudies)
   California State University, Northridge, Northridge, CA. BA. (www.csun.edu/humanities/jewish-studies)
   Claremont McKenna College, Claremont, CA. Sequence. (www.cmc.edu/religious-studies/jewish-studies)
   Claremont School of Theology, Claremont, CA. Graduate Certificate in Hebrew Bible. (www.cst.edu/certificate-programs/#JS)
   Graduate Theological Union, Berkeley, CA. PhD, MA, Graduate Certificate. (www.gtu.edu/centersandaffiliates/jewishstudies/study-at-cjs)
   Hebrew Union College - Jewish Institute of Religion, Los Angeles, CA. Doctor of Hebrew Letters/Literature (DHL), MA in Hebrew Letters/Literature. (www.huc.edu)
   Loyola Marymount University, Los Angeles, CA. Minor. (www.lmu.edu/academics/degrees)
   San Diego State University, San Diego, CA. BA. (www.jewishstudies.sdsu.edu/major_minor.htm)
   San Francisco State University, San Francisco, CA. BA. (http://jewish.sfsu.edu)

San Jose State University, San Jose, CA. Minor. (www.sjsu.edu/jwss)

Scripps College, Claremont, CA. BA. (www.scrippscollege.edu/departments/jewish-studies)

Sonoma State University, Rohnert Park, CA. Minor. (www.sonoma.edu/jewishstudies)

Stanford University, Stanford, CA. PhD, MA, PhD Concentration in Education and Jewish Studies (EdJS), BA. (https://jewishstudies.stanford.edu), (https://edjs.stanford.edu)

Touro College Los Angeles, Los Angeles, CA. BA. (www.tcla.touro.edu/academics/programs)

University of California, Berkeley, Berkeley, CA. PhD DE (Designated Emphasis), Minor. (http://jewishstudies.berkeley.edu)

University of California, Davis, Davis, CA. Minor. (http://jewishstudies.ucdavis.edu)

University of California, Irvine, Irvine, CA. Minor. (www.humanities.uci.edu/jewishstudies)

University of California, Los Angeles, Los Angeles, CA. PhD, BA, Minor in Hebrew and Jewish Studies. (www.nelc.ucla.edu/jewish)

University of California, San Diego, San Diego, CA. PhD, MA, BA. (http://jewishstudies.ucsd.edu)

University of California, Santa Barbara, Santa Barbara, CA. Minor. (www.jewishstudies.ucsb.edu)

University of California, Santa Cruz, Santa Cruz, CA. BA, (http://jewishstudies.ucsc.edu/index.html)

University of San Francisco, San Francisco, CA. Minor in Jewish Studies and Social Justice. (www.usfca.edu/arts-sciences/undergraduate-programs/jewish-studies-and-social-justice)

University of Southern California, Los Angeles, CA. BA, Minor in Jewish American Studies. (www.dornsife.usc.edu/jewishstudies/majors-minors)

Colorado

University of Colorado-Boulder, Boulder, CO. BA, Graduate Certificate. (www.colorado.edu/jewishstudies)

University of Denver, Denver, CO. Minor. (www.du.edu/ahss/cjs/index.html)

Connecticut

Charter Oak State College, New Britain, CT. Concentration. (www.charteroak.edu/catalog/current/subject_area_concentrations/judaic_studies.php)

Connecticut College, New London, CT. Minor. (www.conncoll.edu/academics/majors-departments-programs/majors-and-minors/jewish-studies)

Fairfield University, Fairfield, CT. Minor. (www.fairfield.edu/undergraduate/academics/schools-and-colleges/college-of-arts-and-sciences/programs/judaic-studies)

Trinity College, Hartford, CT. BA. (www.trincoll.edu/Academics/MajorsAndMinors/Jewish)

University of Connecticut, Storrs, CT. PhD, MA, BA. (www.judaicstudies.uconn.edu)

University of Hartford, West Hartford, CT. BA. (www.hartford.edu/greenberg)

Wesleyan University, Middletown, CT. Undergraduate Certificate in Jewish and Israel Studies. (www.wesleyan.edu/jis)

Yale Divinity School, New Haven, CT. Concentrated MA in Religion with a Concentration in Hebrew Bible. (https://divinity.yale.edu/academics/degree-and-certificate-requirements/concentrated-master-arts-religion-mar)

Yale University, New Haven, CT. PhD, BA. (https://judaicstudies.yale.edu)

Delaware
University of Delaware, Newark, DE. Minor. (www.cgas.udel.edu/programs/jewish-studies)

District of Columbia
American University, Washington, DC. BA. (www.american.edu/cas/js)

George Washington University, Washington, DC. MA in Jewish Cultural Arts, BA, Graduate Certificate in Jewish Cultural Arts. (https://judaic.columbian.gwu.edu)

Georgetown University, Washington, DC. Minor in Jewish Civilization, Undergraduate Certificate in Jewish Civilization. (https://cjc.georgetown.edu)

Yeshiva College of the Nation's Capital, Washington, DC. Bachelor of Talmudic Law.   (www.yeshiva.edu/YESHIVAGEDOLAH/YeshivaCollegeoftheNationsCapital/tabid/101/Default.aspx)

Florida
Chaim Yakov Shlomo College of Jewish Studies, Surfside, FL. MA in Hebrew Letters, BA in Hebrew Letters. (www.cyscollege.org)

Florida Atlantic University, Boca Raton, FL. BA, Undergraduate Certificate. (www.fau.edu/artsandletters/jewishstudies)

Florida International University, Miami, FL. Undergraduate Certificate. (http://jewishstudies.fiu.edu)

Rollins College, Winter Park, FL. Minor. (www.rollins.edu/jewish-studies/index.html)

Talmudic University of Florida, Miami Beach, FL. Bachelor of Talmudic Law. (www.talmudicu.edu) (www.talmudicu.edu/educational-programs)

University of Central Florida, Orlando, FL. Minor, Undergraduate Certificate. (http://judaicstudies.cah.ucf.edu)

University of Florida, Gainesville, FL. BA, Undergraduate Certificate in European Jewish Studies. (www.jst.ufl.edu), (https://catalog.ufl.edu/UGRD/programs)

University of Miami, Miami, FL. BA. (www.as.miami.edu/judaic)

Yeshiva Gedolah of Greater Miami Rabbinical College, Miami Beach, FL. MA, BA. (www.lecfl.com/about-yeshiva-gedolah)

Georgia

Emory University, Atlanta, GA. PhD, PhD in Jewish History, PhD in Jewish Religious Cultures, BA, Graduate Certificate. (www.js.emory.edu)

Georgia State University, Atlanta, GA. Minor. (https://middleeaststudies.gsu.edu/jewish-studies-minor)

University of Georgia, Athens, GA. PhD in Religion with a Concentration in Jewish Studies, MA in Religion with a Concentration in Jewish Studies. (www.religion.uga.edu/graduate-programs-religion)

Illinois

Hebrew Seminary: A Rabbinical School for Deaf & Hearing, Skokie, IL. MA. (www.hebrewseminary.org)

Northwestern University, Evanston, IL. PhD, MA, BA. (www.jewish-studies.northwestern.edu)

Spertus Institute for Jewish Learning and Leadership, Chicago, IL. DSJS (Doctor of Science in Jewish Studies), Doctor of Hebrew Letters, MA. (www.spertus.edu)

Touro College-Hebrew Theological College, Skokie, IL. BA in Talmud. (www.htc.edu)

University of Chicago, Chicago, IL. PhD (in various Jewish Studies fields), MA, BA. (https://ccjs.uchicago.edu)

University of Chicago Divinity School, Chicago, IL. PhD in the History of Judaism, MDiv (Judaism). (https://divinity.uchicago.edu/areas-study-and-committees-faculty)

University of Illinois at Chicago, Chicago, IL. Minor. (www.lcsl.uic.edu/jewish)

University of Illinois at Urbana-Champaign, Urbana, IL. BA, Graduate Certificate. (www.jewishculture.illinois.edu)

Indiana

Earlham College, Richmond, IN. Minor. (www.earlham.edu/jewishstudies)

Indiana University, Bloomington, IN. PhD Minor, MA, Dual MA in Jewish Studies and History, BA, Undergraduate Certificate. (www.indiana.edu/~jsp/index.shtml)

Purdue University, West Lafayette, IN. BA. (www.cla.purdue.edu/jewish-studies)

Kansas

University of Kansas, Lawrence, KS. BA. (www.jewishstudies.ku.edu)

Kentucky

University of Kentucky, Lexington, KY. Minor. (www.as.uky.edu/about-jewish-studies)

University of Louisville, Louisville, KY. Minor. (www.louisville.edu/humanities/jewish-studies)

Louisiana

Louisiana State University, Baton Rouge, LA. Minor. (www.lsu.edu/hss/jewishstudies)

Tulane University, New Orleans, LA. BA. (https://liberalarts.tulane.edu/departments/jewish-studies)

Maine

Colby College, Waterville, ME. Minor. (www.colby.edu/jewishstudies)

Maryland

Bais HaMedrash and Mesivta of Baltimore, Baltimore, MD. Bachelor of Talmudic Law. (www.bhmb.edu/consumer-information)

Binah Institute of Advanced Judaic Studies for Women, Baltimore, MD. BA. (www.mhec.maryland.gov/institutions_training/Pages/collegeinfodetails.aspx?SIC=260537)

Johns Hopkins University, Baltimore, MD. Minor. (www.krieger.jhu.edu/jewishstudies)

Ner Israel Rabbinical College, Pikesville, MD. Bachelor of Talmudic Law. (www.nirc.edu/collegeprograms)

Towson University, Towson, MD. MA, Minor. (www.towson.edu/academics)

University of Maryland, College Park, MD. MA, MA in Jewish Studies/MA in Hebrew Pedagogy (MA in Hebrew Language Instruction), Combined BA/MA, BA, Graduate Certificate. (www.jewishstudies.umd.edu)

University of Maryland, Baltimore County, Baltimore, MD. Minor. (https://judaicstudies.umbc.edu)

Women's Institute of Torah Seminary/Maalot Baltimore, Baltimore, MD. BA. (www.maalotbaltimore.org)

Massachusetts

Boston College, Chestnut Hill, MA. Minor. (www.bc.edu/bc-web/schools/mcas/sites/jewish.html)

Boston University, Boston, MA. PhD in Religion with a Specialization in Jewish Studies, BA. (www.bu.edu/jewishstudies)

Brandeis University, Waltham, MA. PhD in Near Eastern and Judaic Studies, MA in Near Eastern and Judaic Studies, Joint Degree of MA in Near Eastern and Judaic Studies & Women's, Gender, and Sexuality Studies, Joint Degree of MA in Near Eastern and Judaic Studies & Conflict Resolution and Coexistence, Combined BA/MA in Near Eastern and Judaic Studies, BA in Near Eastern and Judaic Studies. (www.brandeis.edu/near-eastern-judaic)

Clark University, Worcester, MA. Concentration. (www2.clarku.edu/departments/jewishstudies)

Gordon College, Wenham, MA. Concentration. (www.gordon.edu/jewishstudies)

Hampshire College, Amherst, MA. BA. (www.hampshire.edu/jewish-studies/jewish-studies-at-hampshire)

Harvard Divinity School, Cambridge, MA. PhD (Jewish Studies Area of Study), MDiv (Judaism), MTS (Jewish Studies Focus), ThM (Jewish Studies Focus). (www.hds.harvard.edu/academics/degree-programs)

Harvard University, Cambridge, MA. PhD in Near Eastern Languages and Civilizations (Jewish History and Culture Field), MA (AM) in Near Eastern Languages and Civilizations (Jewish History and Culture Field), BA in Near Eastern Languages and Civilizations with a Concentration in Jewish Studies. (https://nelc.fas.harvard.edu)

Hebrew College, Newton Centre, MA. MA, Master of Liberal Jewish Studies (MLJS), Combined MA/BA completion (upon transfer from other schools), BA completion (upon transfer from other schools). (www.hebrewcollege.edu)

Mount Holyoke College, South Hadley, MA. Minor. (www.mtholyoke.edu/acad/jewish)

Northeastern University, Boston, MA. BA. (https://cssh.northeastern.edu/jewishstudies)

Smith College, Northampton, MA. BA. (www.smith.edu/academics/courses-of-study)

Tufts University, Medford, MA. BA. (www.ase.tufts.edu/ilcs/programs/judaic.htm)

University of Massachusetts Amherst, Amherst, MA. BA. (www.umass.edu/jne/judaic-studies-program)

Wellesley College, Wellesley, MA. BA. (www.wellesley.edu/jewishstudies)

Wheaton College, Norton, MA. Minor. (www.wheatoncollege.edu/academics/programs/jewish-studies)

Williams College, Williamstown, MA. Concentration. (http://jewish-studies.williams.edu)

Michigan

Eastern Michigan University, Ypsilanti, MI. Minor. (www.emich.edu/jewishstudies)

Kalamazoo College, Kalamazoo, MI. Concentration. (www.kzoo.edu/programs/jewish-studies)

Michigan State University, East Lansing, MI. Minor. (www.jsp.msu.edu/index.php)

Oakland University, Rochester, MI. Minor. (www.oakland.edu/religiousstudies)

University of Michigan, Ann Arbor, MI. PhD, MA, BA, Graduate Certificate. (www.lsa.umich.edu/judaic)

Wayne State University, Detroit, MI. Minor. (www.judaicstudies.wayne.edu)

Minnesota

Carleton College, Northfield, MN. BA. (https://apps.carleton.edu/curricular/judaic-studies)

University of Minnesota, Minneapolis, MN. BA. (www.cla.umn.edu/jewish-studies)

Missouri

Washington University in St. Louis, St. Louis, MO. PhD, MA, BA. (www.jinelc.wustl.edu)

Nebraska
University of Nebraska-Lincoln, Lincoln, NE. Minor. (www.judaic.unl.edu)

New Hampshire
Dartmouth College, Hanover, NH. Minor. (https://jewish.dartmouth.edu)

New Jersey
Drew University, Madison, NJ. Minor. (www.drew.edu/academics/undergraduate-studies/launch/majors-and-minors/jewish-studies)

Montclair State University, Montclair, NJ. Minor in Jewish American Studies. (www.montclair.edu/academics/jewish-american-studies)

Princeton University, Princeton, NJ. Undergraduate Certificate. (https://judaic.princeton.edu/certificate-program)

Rabbinical College of America, Morristown, NJ. BA in Religious Studies. (www.rca.edu/templates/articlecco_cdo/aid/361824)

Ramapo College of New Jersey, Mahwah, NJ. Minor. (www.ramapo.edu/majors-minors/majors/judaic-studies)

Rowan University, Glassboro, NJ. Concentration. (https://academics.rowan.edu/chss/minors/jewishstudies)

Rutgers University, New Brunswick, NJ. BA. (http://jewishstudies.rutgers.edu) (No longer accepting new students for MA as of 2018)

Seton Hall University, South Orange, NJ. MA in Jewish-Christian Studies, Graduate Certificate in Jewish-Christian Studies. (www.shu.edu/academics/ma-jewish-christian-studies.cfm)

Stockton University, Galloway, NJ. Minor. (www.stockton.edu/general-studies/jewish-studies.html)

New York (Outside New York Metropolitan Area)
Bard College, Annandale-on-Hudson, NY. Concentration. (http://jewish.bard.edu)

Colgate University, Hamilton, NY. Minor, (www.colgate.edu/academics/depart-ments-and-programs/jewish-studies)

Cornell University, Ithaca, NY. PhD in Near Eastern Studies with a Specialization in Judaic Studies, Minor. (www.gradschool.cornell.edu/academics/fields-of-study/field/near-eastern-studies), (www.jewishstudies.cornell.edu)

Ithaca College, Ithaca, NY. Minor. (www.ithaca.edu/hs/minors/jewishstudies)

Marist College, Poughkeepsie, NY. Minor. (www.marist.edu/academics/pro-grams/complete-list)

Ohr Somayach Monsey, Monsey, NY. First Talmudic Degree (BA equivalent). (www.os.edu/college_credits.php)

SUNY-Binghamton University, Binghamton, NY. BA. (www.binghamton.edu/judaic-studies)

SUNY-Cortland, Cortland, NY. Minor. (www2.cortland.edu/departments/jewish-studies)

SUNY-New Paltz, New Paltz, NY. Minor. (www.newpaltz.edu/ugc/las/jewish_stud)

SUNY-Plattsburgh, Plattsburgh, NY. Minor. (www.plattsburgh.edu/programs/jewish-studies-minor.html)

SUNY-University at Albany, Albany, NY. Minor. (www.albany.edu/judaic_studies/index.shtml)

SUNY-University at Buffalo, Buffalo, NY. BA. (www.arts-sciences.buffalo.edu/jewish-thought.html)

Syracuse University, Syracuse, NY. BA. (http://thecollege.syr.edu/academics/interdisciplinary/JewishStudies.html)

Union College, Schenectady, NY. Minor. (www.union.edu/academic/majors-minors/jewish-studies)

University of Rochester, Rochester, NY. Minor. (www.sas.rochester.edu/jst)

Vassar College, Poughkeepsie, NY. BA. (https://jewishstudies.vassar.edu)

New York Metropolitan Area

Academy for Jewish Religion, Yonkers, NY. MA. (www.ajrsem.org)

Barnard College, New York, NY. BA/MA, BA (dual major), BA (dual degree program with The Jewish Theological Seminary Albert A. List College of Jewish Studies). (http://jewish.barnard.edu), (https://admissions.barnard.edu/jts), (www.iijs.columbia.edu/masters-bachelors-program)

Columbia University, New York, NY. PhD, MA, BA (dual degree program with The Jewish Theological Seminary Albert A. List College of Jewish Studies), Joint BA/MA, Special Concentration. (www.iijs.columbia.edu)

CUNY-Baruch College, New York, NY. Minor. (www.baruch.cuny.edu/wsas/areas_of_study/interdisciplinary_studies/jewish_studies.htm)

CUNY-Brooklyn College, Brooklyn, NY. MA, BA, Concentration (for majors in early childhood and childhood education teacher programs). (www.brooklyn.cuny.edu/web/academics/schools/socialsciences/undergraduate/judaic.php)

CUNY-City College of New York, New York, NY. BA. (www.ccny.cuny.edu/jewishstudies)

CUNY-The Graduate Center, New York, NY. MA in Liberal Studies (Jewish Studies Track). (www.gc.cuny.edu/Page-Elements/Academics-Research-Centers-Initiatives/Centers-and-Institutes/Center-for-Jewish-Studies/M-A-Track)

CUNY-Hunter College, New York, NY. BA. (www.hunter.cuny.edu/center-for-jewish-studies)

CUNY-Queens College, Flushing, NY. BA. (www.qc.cuny.edu/Academics/Centers/Jewish/Pages/default.aspx)

Fordham University, Bronx, NY. Minor. (www.fordham.edu/JewishStudies)

Hebrew Union College - Jewish Institute of Religion, New York, NY. Doctor of Hebrew Letters/Literature (DHL), MA in Hebrew Letters/Literature, MA. (www.huc.edu)

Hofstra University, Hempstead, NY. BA. (www.hofstra.edu/academics/colleges/hclas/rel)

The Jewish Theological Seminary, New York, NY. PhD, Doctor of Hebrew Literature (DHL), MPhil, MA in Sacred Music, MA, BA/MA, BA (dual degree program with Barnard College or Columbia University). (www.jtsa.edu/academics)

The New School, New York, NY. Minor. (www.newschool.edu/lang/jewish-culture-minor)

New York University, New York, NY. PhD in Hebrew and Judaic Studies, Joint PhD in Hebrew and Judaic Studies/History, MA in Hebrew and Judaic Studies, BA in Hebrew and Judaic Studies. (www.as.nyu.edu/hebrewjudaic.html)

SUNY-Purchase College, Purchase, NY. Minor. (www.purchase.edu/academics/jewish-studies/index.php)

SUNY-Stony Brook University, Stony Brook, NY. Minor. (www.stonybrook.edu/academics/majors-minors-and-programs/#UndergraduatePrograms)

Touro College-Graduate School of Jewish Studies, New York, NY. PhD, MA. (www.gsjs.touro.edu)

Touro College-Lander College for Men, Kew Gardens Hills, NY. Minor. (www.lcm.touro.edu/academics/program-and-majors)

Touro College-Lander College for Women (The Anna Ruth and Mark Hasten School), New York, NY. BA. (www.lcw.touro.edu/academics/programs%2D%2Dmajors)

Touro College-Lander College of Arts & Sciences (Men's and Women's Programs), Brooklyn, NY. BA. (www.las.touro.edu/men/programs%2D%2Dmajors), (www.las.touro.edu/women/programs-and-majors)

Touro College-School for Lifelong Education, Brooklyn, NY. BA. (www.sle.touro.edu)

Yeshiva University, Stern College for Women, New York, NY. MA in Biblical and Talmudic Interpretation (GPATS Program), BA/MA, BA. (www.yu.edu/stern/departments-programs)

Yeshiva University, Yeshiva College (for Men), New York, NY. PhD, MA, BA/MA, BA. (www.yu.edu/pathways/jewish-studies)

North Carolina

Appalachian State University, Boone, NC. Minor in Judaic, Holocaust and Peace Studies. (www.casminors.appstate.edu/judaic-holocaust-and-peace-studies)

Duke University, Durham, NC. PhD, MA, BA, Undergraduate Certificate. (www.jewishstudies.duke.edu)

Elon University, Elon, NC. Minor. (www.elon.edu/u/academics/arts-and-sciences/jewish-studies)

Piedmont International University, Winston-Salem, NC. Graduate Certificate of Old Testament and Hebrew. (www.piedmontu.edu/graduate-certificate-of-old-testament-and-hebrew)

University of North Carolina at Chapel Hill, Chapel Hill, NC. Concentration, Minor, Graduate Certificate. (www.jewishstudies.unc.edu)

Ohio

Case Western Reserve University, Cleveland, OH. Minor. (http://artsci.case.edu/judaic-studies)

Hebrew Union College - Jewish Institute of Religion, Cincinnati, OH. PhD in Judaic and Cognate Studies, PhD in Modern Jewish History & Culture (joint program with University of Cincinnati), Doctor of Hebrew Letters/Literature (DHL), MA in Hebrew Letters/Literature, MA. (www.huc.edu)

Kent State University, Kent, OH. Minor. (www.kent.edu/jewishstudies)

Miami University, Oxford, OH. Minor. (www.miamioh.edu/cas/academics/programs/jst)

Oberlin College, Oberlin, OH. BA. (www.oberlin.edu/arts-and-sciences/departments/jewish-studies)

Ohio State University, Columbus, OH. PhD, MA, BA, Minor in Jewish Oral History. (www.meltoncenter.osu.edu)

Ohio University, Athens, OH. Undergraduate Certificate. (www.ohio.edu/cas/history/undergrad/jewish-studies.cfm)

University of Cincinnati, Cincinnati, OH. PhD in Modern Jewish History & Culture (joint program with Hebrew Union College –Jewish Institute of Religion Pines School of Graduate Studies, Cincinnati), BA, Graduate Certificate. (www.artsci.uc.edu/departments/history.html), (www.artsci.uc.edu/programs-degrees)

Xavier University, Cincinnati, OH. Minor. (www.xavier.edu/jewish-studies)

Youngstown State University, Youngstown, OH. Minor. (www.ysu.edu/academics/college-liberal-arts-social-sciences/judaic-studies-minor)

Oklahoma

University of Oklahoma, Norman, OK. PhD in Judaic History, MA in Judaic History, BA, Minor in Judaic and Israel Studies. (www.ou.edu/cas/judaicstudies), (www.ou.edu/admissions/academics/arts-sciences/judaic-studies)

Oregon

Portland State University, Portland, OR. BA. (www.pdx.edu/judaic)

University of Oregon, Eugene, OR. BA. (http://judaicstudies.uoregon.edu)

Pennsylvania

Bryn Mawr College, Bryn Mawr, PA. BA. (www.brynmawr.edu/hebrew)

Bucknell University, Lewisburg, PA. Minor. (http://coursecatalog.bucknell.edu/collegeofartsandsciencescurricula/areasofstudy/jewishstudies)

Dickinson College, Carlisle, PA. BA. (www.dickinson.edu/homepage/116/judaic_studies)

Drexel University, Philadelphia, PA. Minor. (www.drexel.edu/coas/academics/departments-centers/global-studies-modern-languages/degrees-programs/judaic-studies)

Franklin & Marshall College, Lancaster, PA. Minor. (www.fandm.edu/judaic-studies)

Gettysburg College, Gettysburg, PA. Minor. (www.gettysburg.edu/academics/religion/programs/judaic-studies)

Gratz College, Melrose Park, PA. MA, BA. (www.gratz.edu/academics)

Haverford College, Haverford, PA. Concentration. (www.haverford.edu/academics/majors-minors-and-concentrations)

Lafayette College, Easton, PA. Minor. (https://jewishstudies.lafayette.edu)

Lehigh University, Bethlehem, PA. Minor. (www.cjs.cas2.lehigh.edu)

Muhlenberg College, Allentown, PA. BA. (www.muhlenberg.edu/main/academics/jewishstudies/majorrequirements)

The Pennsylvania State University, University Park, PA. BA. (www.jewishstudies.la.psu.edu)

Reconstructionist Rabbinical College, Wyncote, PA. Doctor of Hebrew Letters (DHL), MA in Hebrew Letters, MA. (www.rrc.edu/admissions/titles-and-degree-programs)

Susquehanna University, Selinsgrove, PA. Minor in Jewish & Israel Studies. (www.susqu.edu/academics/majors-and-minors/jewish-and-israel-studies)

Temple University, Philadelphia, PA. BA, Undergraduate Certificate in Secular Jewish Studies. (www.cla.temple.edu/jewishstudies) (No longer accepting new students for BA as of Spring 2019)

University of Pennsylvania, Philadelphia, PA. PhD (with Specialization in various Jewish Studies fields), MA (with Specialization in various Jewish Studies fields), BA, Graduate Certificate. (http://ccat.sas.upenn.edu/jwst)

University of Pittsburgh, Pittsburgh, PA. BA, Undergraduate Certificate. (www.jewishstudies.pitt.edu)

University of Scranton, Scranton, PA. Concentration. (http://catalog.scranton.edu/preview_program.php?catoid=40&poid=6751)

West Chester University of Pennsylvania, West Chester, PA. Concentration in Jewish American Studies. (www.wcupa.edu/arts-humanities/ethnicStudies/jewish.asp)

Rhode Island

Brown University, Providence, RI. PhD in Religions of the Ancient Mediterranean (with major/minor fields in various Judaic areas of study), Concentration. (www.brown.edu/academics/judaic-studies)

South Carolina

College of Charleston, Charleston, SC. BA. (http://jewish.cofc.edu)

University of South Carolina, Columbia, SC. Minor. (www.sc.edu/study/colleges_schools/artsandsciences/jewish_studies/index.php)

Tennessee

Middle Tennessee State University, Murfreesboro, TN. Minor in Jewish and Holocaust Studies. (www.mtsu.edu/JHStudies)

University of Memphis, Memphis, TN. BA. (www.memphis.edu/jdst)

University of Tennessee, Knoxville, TN. BA (Interdisciplinary Programs Major)-Judaic Studies Concentration. (http://judaic.utk.edu)

Vanderbilt University, Nashville, TN. PhD in Religion (Hebrew Bible and Ancient Israel), MA, BA. (www.vanderbilt.edu/gdr/degrees/phd.php), (https://admissions.vanderbilt.edu/major)

Texas

Rice University, Houston, TX. Minor.
(https://ga.rice.edu/programs-study/departments-programs/humanities/jewish-studies/#text)

Southern Methodist University, Dallas, TX. Minor. (www.smu.edu/Dedman/academics/programs/jewishstudies/minor)

St. Edward's University, Austin, TX. Minor. (www.stedwards.edu/undergraduate/jewish-studies)

University of Houston, Houston, TX. Minor. (www.uh.edu/class/mcl/jewish-studies)

University of North Texas, Denton, TX. Minor in Jewish and Israel Studies, Undergraduate Certificate in Jewish and Israel Studies. (www.jewishstudies.unt.edu)

The University of Texas at Austin, Austin, TX. BA. (www.liberalarts.utexas.edu/scjs)

The University of Texas at El Paso, El Paso, TX. Minor. (http://catalog.utep.edu/undergrad/college-of-liberal-arts/inter-american-jewish-studies-minor)

Vermont
Middlebury College, Middlebury, VT. Minor. (www.middlebury.edu/academics/jewish)

Virginia
College of William & Mary, Williamsburg, VA. Minor. (www.wm.edu/as/charlescenter/academic-programs/interdisciplinary/structured/judaic-studies)

George Mason University, Fairfax, VA. Minor. (www.religious.gmu.edu/programs/la-minor-reli-js)

Liberty University, Lynchburg, VA. Concentration. (www.liberty.edu/index.cfm?PID=31150#ReligiousStudiesJewishStudiesConcentration)

Old Dominion University, Norfolk, VA. Minor. (www.odu.edu/al/institutes/ijiu/academics)

University of Richmond, Richmond, VA. Minor. (www.jewishstudies.richmond.edu)

University of Virginia, Charlottesville, VA. PhD in Religious Studies with a Concentration in the Study of Judaism, MA in Religious Studies with a Concentration in the Study of Judaism, BA. (www.jewishstudies.as.virginia.edu)

Virginia Commonwealth University, Richmond, VA. Minor, Undergraduate Certificate. (www.judaicstudies.vcu.edu)

Virginia Polytechnic Institute and State University, Blacksburg, VA. Minor. (www.liberalarts.vt.edu/academics/majors-and-minors/judaic-minor.htm)

Washington
University of Washington, Seattle, WA. BA. (www.washington.edu/uaa/advising/academic-planning/majors-and-minors/list-of-undergraduate-majors)

Wisconsin
University of Wisconsin-Madison, Madison, WI. PhD in Classical and Ancient Near Eastern Studies (Option in Hebrew Bible), PhD Minor in Hebrew Bible, MA in Classical and Ancient Near Eastern Studies (Option in Hebrew Bible), BA, BS, Undergraduate Certificate. (www.canes.wisc.edu/graduate-studies-requirements), (www.jewishstudies.wisc.edu)

University of Wisconsin-Milwaukee, Milwaukee, WI. BA. (www4.uwm.edu/jewishstudies)

14.1.4   Central Coordinating Body for Programs in Jewish Studies, Canada

Association for Canadian Jewish Studies (formerly **Canadian Jewish Historical Society**). For contact information and a description, see Sect. 14.5 in this chapter.

14.1.5   Programs in Jewish Studies, Canada

Manitoba
University of Manitoba, Winnipeg, MB. Minor. (www.umanitoba.ca/student/admissions/programs/judaic-studies.html)

Ontario
Carleton University, Ottawa, ON. Minor. (www.carleton.ca/jewishstudies/academics/minor-in-jewish-studies)
Kollel Toronto-Institute for Advanced Judaic Studies, Toronto, ON. PhD in Judaics, PhD in Talmudic Law, Master of Judaics, Master of Talmudic Law, Bachelor of Judaics, Bachelor of Talmudic Law. (www.kollel.com/iajs)
Maimonides College, Hamilton, ON. MA, BA. (www.maimonidescollege.ca/admissions.html)
McMaster University, Hamilton, ON. Minor. (www.religiousstudies.mcmaster.ca/programs/minor-in-jewish-studies)
Queen's University, Kingston, ON. Minor. (www.queensu.ca/artsci/programs-and-degrees/humanities/jewish-studies-program)
University of Ottawa, Ottawa, ON. Minor in Jewish Canadian Studies. (www.arts.uottawa.ca/en/programs)
University of Toronto, Toronto, ON. PhD, MA, BA. (www.cjs.utoronto.ca)
University of Waterloo, Waterloo, ON. Minor. (www.uwaterloo.ca/jewish-studies)
University of Western Ontario, London, ON. BA. (www.history.uwo.ca/jewish_studies/index.html)
York University, Toronto, ON. PhD with a Specialization in Jewish Studies, MA with a Specialization in Jewish Studies, BA, Advanced Undergraduate Certificate in Hebrew and Jewish Studies. (www.yorku.ca/cjs)

Quebec
Concordia University, Montreal, QC. MA, BA. (www.concordia.ca/artsci/research/jewish-studies.html)

McGill University, Montreal, QC. PhD, MA, BA. (www.mcgill.ca/jewishstudies)

Saskatchewan
University of Saskatchewan, Saskatoon, SK. Undergraduate Certificate in Jewish & Christian Origins. (www.usask.ca/programs)

14.1.6   Programs in Holocaust and Genocide Studies, United States

This section omits programs designed specifically for educators related to the mandated teaching of the Holocaust in public schools.

Alabama
University of South Alabama, Mobile, AL. Minor in Jewish and Holocaust Studies. (www.southalabama.edu/colleges/artsandsci/jewishandholocauststudies)

California
American Jewish University, Sigi Ziering Institute: Exploring the Ethical & Religious Implications of the Holocaust, Los Angeles, CA. No degree offered. (www.aju.edu/institutes-groups/sigi-ziering-institute)

Chapman University, Barry and Phyllis Rodgers Center for Holocaust Education, Ralph and Sue Stern Chair in Holocaust Education, Orange, CA. Minor in Holocaust History.   (www.chapman.edu/research-and-institutions/holocaust-education/index.aspx)

Claremont McKenna College, Mgrublian Center for Human Rights, Claremont, CA. Human Rights, Holocaust and Genocide Studies Sequence. (www.cmc.edu/human-rights/human-rights-sequence)

Sonoma State University, Center for the Study of the Holocaust and Genocide, Rohnert Park, CA. No degree offered. (http://web.sonoma.edu/holocaust)

University of California, Los Angeles, Alan D. Leve Center for Jewish Studies, 1939 Society Samuel Goetz Chair in Holocaust Studies, Los Angeles, CA. No degree offered. (www.cjs.ucla.edu/holocaust-studies)

University of California, Santa Cruz, Neufeld-Levin Chair of Holocaust Studies, Santa Cruz, CA. No degree offered. (https://news.ucsc.edu/2017/08/holocaust-alma-heckman.html)

University of Southern California, USC Shoah Foundation Center for Advanced Genocide Research, Los Angeles, CA. No degree offered. (http://sfi.usc.edu/cagr)

Colorado
University of Denver, Holocaust Awareness Institute, Denver, CO. No degree offered. (www.du.edu/ahss/cjs/hai/index.html)

District of Columbia

Georgetown University, Braman Endowed Professorship of the Practice of the Forensic Study of the Holocaust, Washington, DC. No degree offered. (www. georgetown.edu/georgetown-receives-gift-for-forensic-research-on-holocaust), (https://cjc.georgetown.edu/people)

Florida

Florida Atlantic University, Dorothy F. Schmidt College of Arts and Letters, The Center for the Study of Values & Violence after Auschwitz, Raddock Eminent Scholar Chair of Holocaust Studies, Boca Raton, FL. No degree offered. (www.fau. edu/artsandletters/pdf/vav-brochure-2014-.pdf)

Florida Gulf Coast University, Center for Judaic, Holocaust, and Genocide Studies, Fort Myers, FL. No degree offered. (www.fgcu.edu/hc)

Florida International University, Steven J. Green School of International and Public Affairs, Global Jewish Studies Program, Holocaust Studies Initiative, Miami, FL. Undergraduate Certificate in Holocaust and Genocide Studies. (http://jewish-studies.fiu.edu/about-us/holocaust-studies-initiative)

University of Florida, Gainesville, FL. Undergraduate Certificate in Holocaust Studies. (https://people.clas.ufl.edu/goda/holocaust-studies-certificate)

Illinois

Elmhurst College, Holocaust Studies, Elmhurst, IL. Minor in Intercultural Studies-Holocaust Focus. (www.elmhurst.edu/academics/departments/intercultural-studies/programs/areas-study/holocaust-studies)

Northwestern University, Holocaust Educational Foundation, Theodore Zev and Alice R. Weiss – Holocaust Education Foundation Chair in Holocaust Studies, Evanston, IL. Undergraduate Certificate of Achievement in Holocaust Studies. (www.hef.northwestern.edu/links/certificate-in-holocaust-studies)

University of Illinois at Urbana-Champaign, The Initiative in Holocaust, Genocide, and Memory Studies, Urbana, IL. Graduate Certificate in Holocaust, Genocide, and Memory Studies. (www.jewishculture.illinois.edu)

Indiana

Purdue University, Institute for Holocaust and Genocide Studies, Fort Wayne, IN. No degree offered. (www.pfw.edu/ihgs)

Kansas

University of Kansas, Lawrence, KS. Undergraduate Certificate in Holocaust and Genocide Studies. (www.jewishstudies.ku.edu/undergraduate-certificate-holocaust-and-genocide-studies)

Maine

University of Maine at Augusta, Augusta, ME. Minor in Holocaust, Genocide & Human Rights Studies. (www.uma.edu/academics/checksheets/hghrsm)

Maryland

University of Maryland, Baltimore County, Baltimore, MD. Minor Concentration in Holocaust Studies. (https://judaicstudies.umbc.edu/minor-program)

Massachusetts
Boston University, Elie Wiesel Center for Jewish Studies, Boston, MA. Minor in Holocaust, Genocide, and Human Rights Studies, Graduate Certificate in Holocaust, Genocide, and Human Rights Studies. (www.bu.edu/jewishstudies/undergraduate/hghrs-minor)

Clark University, Strassler Family Center for Holocaust and Genocide Studies, Worcester, MA. PhD in History-Holocaust History and Genocide Studies Tracks, PhD in (Social) Psychology with an Interdisciplinary Concentration in Holocaust and Genocide Studies, Undergraduate Concentration in Holocaust and Genocide Studies. (www.clarku.edu/centers/holocaust)

Salem State University, Center for Holocaust and Genocide Studies, Salem, MA. Graduate Certificate in Holocaust and Genocide Studies. (www.salemstate.edu/chgs)

University of Massachusetts Amherst, Institute for Holocaust, Genocide, and Memory Studies, Pen Tishkach Chair of Holocaust Studies, Amherst, MA. No degree offered. (www.umass.edu/ihgms)

Michigan
Michigan State University, William and Audrey Farber Family Chair in Holocaust Studies and European Jewish History, East Lansing, MI. No degree offered. (www.history.msu.edu/people/faculty/amy-simon)

Minnesota
University of Minnesota, Center for Holocaust and Genocide Studies, Minneapolis, MN. No degree offered. (www.cla.umn.edu/chgs)

Missouri
University of Missouri-Kansas City, Kansas City, MO. Graduate Certificate in Holocaust Studies. (http://cas2.umkc.edu/holocaust/default.asp)

Nebraska
University of Nebraska-Omaha, Sam and Frances Fried Holocaust and Genocide Academy, Omaha, NE. Minor in Holocaust and Genocide Studies. (www.unomaha.edu/college-of-arts-and-sciences/holocaust-and-genocide-studies/index.php)

Nevada
University of Nevada, Reno, Gender, Race and Identity Program, Reno, NV. Minor in Holocaust, Genocide & Peace Studies. (www.unr.edu/degrees/gender-race-identity/holocaust-genocide-and-peace-studies-minor)

New Hampshire
Keene State College, Cohen Center for Holocaust and Genocide Studies, Cohen Chair for Holocaust and Genocide Studies, Keene, NH. BA in Holocaust and Genocide Studies. (www.keene.edu/academics/programs/hgs), (www.keene.edu/development/ways/designated/detail/496)

New Jersey
The College of New Jersey, Ewing, NJ. Minor in Holocaust and Genocide Studies. (https://hss.tcnj.edu/interdisciplinary-programs/hgs)

Drew University, Madison, NJ. Minor in Holocaust Studies. (www.drew.edu/academics/undergraduate-studies/launch/majors-and-minors/holocaust-studies)

Kean University, Nathan Weiss Graduate College, Holocaust Resource Center, Union, NJ. MA in Holocaust and Genocide Studies. (www.kean.edu/academics/programs/holocaust-and-genocide-studies-ma)

Ramapo College of New Jersey, Gross Center for Holocaust & Genocide Studies, Mahwah, NJ. No degree offered. (www.ramapo.edu/holocaust)

Rider University, The Julius and Dorothy Koppelman Holocaust/Genocide Resource Center, Lawrenceville, NJ. No degree offered. (www.rider.edu/offices-services/holocaust-genocide-resource-center)

Rowan University, Rowan Center for Holocaust & Genocide Studies, Glassboro, NJ. Holocaust and Genocide Education Certificate of Graduate Study. (https://chss.rowan.edu/centers/RCHGS/index.html),   (www.rowanu.com/programs/holocaust-and-genocide-education-certificate-of-graduate-study)

Stockton University, The Sara & Sam Schoffer Holocaust Resource Center, Galloway, NJ. MA in Holocaust & Genocide Studies, Minor in Holocaust & Genocide Studies. (www.stockton.edu/holocaust-resource)

New York (Outside New York Metropolitan Area)
Hobart and William Smith Colleges, Geneva, NY. Minor in Holocaust Studies. (www.hws.edu/studentlife/abbecenter/academics.aspx)

United States Military Academy, Center for Holocaust and Genocide Studies, West Point, NY. No degree offered. (www.westpoint.edu/chgs/SitePages/Home.aspx)

New York Metropolitan Area
CUNY-The Graduate Center, Center for Jewish Studies, Rosenthal Institute for Holocaust Studies, New York, NY. No degree offered. (www.gc.cuny.edu/Page-Elements/Academics-Research-Centers-Initiatives/Centers-and-Institutes/Center-for-Jewish-Studies)

Manhattan College, Holocaust, Genocide, and Interfaith Education Center, Riverdale, NY. No degree offered. (www.ats.hgimanhattan.com.hostbaby.com/index)

Manhattanville College, Purchase, NY. Minor in Holocaust and Genocide Studies.   (https://mville.smartcatalogiq.com/2018-2019/Undergraduate-College-Catalog/Undergraduate-Programs-of-Study-Majors-Minors-and-Requirements/Holocaust-and-Genocide-Studies-Minor)

Yeshiva University, Emil A. and Jenny Fish Center for Holocaust and Genocide Studies at Yeshiva University, New York, NY. No degree offered. (www.yu.edu/fish-center)

North Carolina

Appalachian State University, Center for Judaic, Holocaust and Peace Studies, Boone, NC. Minor in Judaic, Holocaust and Peace Studies. (www.casminors.appstate.edu/judaic-holocaust-and-peace-studies)

University of North Carolina at Charlotte, Center for Holocaust, Genocide & Human Rights Studies, Charlotte, NC. Minor in Holocaust, Genocide, and Human Rights Studies. (https://globalstudies.uncc.edu/center-holocaust-genocide-human-rights-studies)

Ohio

Youngstown State University, Center for Judaic and Holocaust Studies, Youngstown, OH. No degree offered. (www.ysu.edu/directory/dept/center-judaic-and-holocaust-studies)

Pennsylvania

Albright College, Reading, PA. Minor in Holocaust Studies. (www.albright.edu/academic/undergraduate-programs/holocaust-studies)

Gratz College, Melrose Park, PA. PhD in Holocaust and Genocide Studies, MA in Holocaust and Genocide Studies. (www.gratz.edu/academics)

The Pennsylvania State University, Jewish Studies Program, University Park, PA. Undergraduate Certificate in Holocaust and Genocide Studies. (www.jewish-studies.la.psu.edu/undergraduate/holocaust-and-genocide-studies-certificate)

The Pennsylvania State University, Harrisburg, Center for Holocaust and Jewish Studies, Middletown, PA. No degree offered. (www.harrisburg.psu.edu/center-for-holocaust-and-jewish-studies)

Seton Hill University, National Catholic Center for Holocaust Education, Greensburg, PA. Graduate Concentration in Genocide & Holocaust Studies, Minor in Genocide & Holocaust Studies, Graduate Certificate in Genocide & Holocaust Studies. (www.setonhill.edu/academics/certificate-programs/genocide-and-holo-caust-studies-certificate-or-concentration), (www.setonhill.edu/academics/under-graduate-programs/undergraduate-program-minors)

University of Pittsburgh Law School, Pittsburgh, PA. Law Certificate in Holocaust and Crimes Against Humanity Studies Emphasis. (https://catalog.upp.pitt.edu/pre-view_program.php?catoid=136&poid=43375)

West Chester University of Pennsylvania, West Chester, PA. MA in Holocaust and Genocide Studies, Minor in Holocaust Studies, Graduate Certificate in Holocaust and Genocide Studies. (www.wcupa.edu/arts-humanities/holocaust/aca-demicPrograms.asp)

South Carolina

College of Charleston, Sylvia Vlosky Yaschik Jewish Studies Center, Zucker/Goldberg Center for Holocaust Studies, Charleston, SC. No degree offered. (http://jewish.cofc.edu/jewish-studies-center/index.php)

Tennessee

Middle Tennessee State University, Murfreesboro, TN. Minor in Jewish and Holocaust Studies. (www.mtsu.edu/JHStudies)

Texas

Texas A&M University-Commerce, Commerce, TX. Graduate Certificate in Holocaust Studies. (www.tamuc.edu/academics/graduateSchool/programs/graduatecertificates/holocauststudies.aspx)

University of Texas at Dallas, Ackerman Center for Holocaust Studies, Leah and Paul Lewis Chair in Holocaust Studies, Hillel A. Feinberg Chair in Holocaust Studies, Stan and Barbara Rabin Professor of Holocaust Studies, Richardson, TX. Graduate Certificate in Holocaust Studies. (www.utdallas.edu/ackerman)

Vermont

University of Vermont, The Carolyn and Leonard Miller Center for Holocaust Studies, Burlington, VT. Minor in Holocaust Studies. (www.uvm.edu/cas/holocauststudies)

Virginia

Old Dominion University, Institute for Jewish Studies & Interfaith Understanding, Norfolk, VA. Minor in Holocaust & Genocide Studies. (www.odu.edu/al/institutes/ijiu/academics)

Washington

Pacific Lutheran University, Holocaust and Genocide Studies Programs, Kurt Mayer Chair in Holocaust Studies, Tacoma, WA. Minor in Holocaust and Genocide Studies. (www.plu.edu/hgst)

Western Washington University, The Ray Wolpow Institute for the Study of the Holocaust, Genocide, and Crimes Against Humanity, Bellingham, WA. No degree offered. (https://wp.wwu.edu/raywolpowinstitute)

14.1.7 Programs in Holocaust and Genocide Studies, Canada

British Columbia

University of Victoria, Victoria, BC. MA in Germanic and Slavic Languages (Holocaust Studies Stream). (www.uvic.ca/humanities/germanicslavic/graduate/Holocaust/index.php)

Ontario

Carleton University, Centre for Holocaust Education and Scholarship, Ottawa, ON. No degree offered. (www.carleton.ca/ches)

14.1.8   Central Coordinating Body for Programs in Israel Studies

Association for Israel Studies. Department of Israel Studies, University of Haifa, Eshkol Tower, 1407, 199 Abba Khoushy Avenue, Haifa, 3498838, Israel.

The AIS is an international scholarly society devoted to the academic and professional study of Israel whose membership is composed of scholars from all disciplines in the social sciences and many in the humanities. The *Israel Studies Review* is the journal of the Association for Israel Studies, covering the study of all aspects of society, history, politics, and culture of Israel. (http://reg.co.il/ais/ais/home.ehtml)

Note: The following list includes only institutions with programs whose primary focus is on modern Israel, rather than on Jewish or Middle Eastern studies more broadly.

14.1.9   Programs in Israel Studies, United States

California
California State University, Chico, Modern Jewish and Israel Studies, Chico, CA. Minor in Modern Jewish and Israel Studies. (www.csuchico.edu/mjis)

University of California, Berkeley, Berkeley Institute for Jewish Law and Israel Studies, Berkeley CA. No degree offered. (www.law.berkeley.edu/research/berkeley-institute-for-jewish-law-and-israel-studies)

University of California, Los Angeles, Younes and Soraya Nazarian Center for Israel Studies, Los Angeles, CA. Minor. (www.international.ucla.edu/israel/minor)

Colorado
University of Colorado-Boulder, Boulder, CO. Minor in Hebrew & Israel Studies. (www.colorado.edu/jewishstudies/academics/majors-minors-jewish-studies/minor-hebrew-israel-studies)

Connecticut
Wesleyan University, Middletown, CT. Undergraduate Certificate in Jewish and Israel Studies-Israel Studies Track. (www.wesleyan.edu/cjs/jiscertificate.html)

District of Columbia
American University, Center for Israel Studies, Washington, DC. Minor. (www.american.edu/cas/israelstudies)

Florida
University of Florida, Gainesville, FL. BA in Jewish Studies-Israel Studies Track. (www.jst.ufl.edu/major-minor/israel-studies)

Georgia
Emory University, Institute for the Study of Modern Israel, Atlanta, GA. No degree offered. (www.ismi.emory.edu/home/index.html)

Illinois
Northwestern University, Crown Family Center for Jewish and Israel Studies, Evanston, IL. No degree offered. (www.jewish-israel-studies-center.northwestern.edu/israel-studies)

Maryland
University of Maryland, Joseph and Alma Gildenhorn Institute for Israel Studies, College Park, MD. PhD Concentration in Israel Studies, MA Concentration in Israel Studies, Minor. (www.israelstudies.umd.edu)

Massachusetts
Boston University, Elie Wiesel Center for Jewish Studies, Hebrew and Israel Studies, Boston, MA. No degree offered. (www.bu.edu/jewishstudies)

Brandeis University, Schusterman Center for Israel Studies, Waltham, MA. No degree offered. (www.brandeis.edu/israel-center/index.html)

Michigan
Michigan State University, Michael and Elaine Serling Institute for Jewish Studies and Modern Israel, East Lansing, MI. No degree offered. (www.jsp.msu.edu)

Nebraska
University of Nebraska at Omaha, The Natan & Hannah Schwalb Center for Israel and Jewish Studies, Omaha, NE. No degree offered. (www.unomaha.edu/college-of-arts-and-sciences/schwalb-center/index.php)

New Jersey
Rutgers University, New Brunswick, NJ. Minor in Language and Culture of Ancient Israel. (https://jewishstudies.rutgers.edu/academics/undergraduate/minor-jewish-studies)

New York (Outside New York Metropolitan Area)
SUNY-Binghamton University, Center for Israel Studies, Binghamton, NY. Minor. (www.binghamton.edu/israel-studies)

New York Metropolitan Area
Columbia University, Institute for Israel and Jewish Studies, New York, NY. No degree offered. (www.iijs.columbia.edu)

CUNY-Queens College, Queens, NY. BA in Middle Eastern Studies (Islamic Culture, Sephardic and Israeli Culture). (www.qc.cuny.edu/Academics/Centers/Jewish/Pages/default.aspx)

The Jewish Theological Seminary, New York, NY. Doctor of Hebrew Letters (DHL) in Jewish Studies-Israel Studies Track, MA in Jewish Studies-Israel Studies Track. (www.jtsa.edu/kekst-areas-of-study)

New York University, Skirball Department of Hebrew and Judaic Studies, Taub Center for Israel Studies, New York, NY. No degree offered. (http://as.nyu.edu/hebrewjudaic/taub.html)

Yeshiva University, Center for Israel Studies, New York, NY. No degree offered. (www.yu.edu/cis)

North Carolina
Piedmont International University, Winston-Salem, NC. Minor. (www.piedmontu.edu/israel-studies-minor)

Oklahoma
Oral Roberts University, Center for Israel and Middle Eastern Studies, Tulsa, OK. No degree offered. (www.oru.edu/academics/cimes)

University of Oklahoma, Schusterman Center for Judaic and Israel Studies, Norman, OK. Minor in Judaic and Israel Studies. (www.ou.edu/cas/judaicstudies/courses), (www.ou.edu/admissions/academics/arts-sciences/judaic-studies)

Pennsylvania
Gratz College, Harry Stern Family Institute for Israel Studies, Melrose Park, PA.MA.(www.gratz.edu/today/stern-family-institute-israel-studies-gratz-college-presents-educating-more-shared-society)

Susquehanna University, Jewish & Israel Studies Program, Selinsgrove, PA. Minor in Jewish & Israel Studies. (www.susqu.edu/academics/majors-and-minors/jewish-and-israel-studies)

Tennessee
Vanderbilt University, Nashville, TN. PhD in Religion (Hebrew Bible and Ancient Israel). (www.vanderbilt.edu/gdr/degrees/hebrew.php)

Texas
University of North Texas, Jewish and Israel Studies Program, Denton, TX. Minor in Jewish and Israel Studies, Undergraduate Certificate in Jewish and Israel Studies. (www.jewishstudies.unt.edu)

The University of Texas at Austin, Schusterman Center for Jewish Studies, Institute for Israel Studies, Austin TX. No degree offered. (www.liberalarts.utexas.edu/scjs/israel-studies/index.php)

Washington
University of Washington, Seattle, WA. Stroum Center for Jewish Studies, Israel Studies Program. No degree offered. (www.jewishstudies.washington.edu/israel-studies)

Wisconsin
University of Wisconsin-Madison, Madison, WI. BA in Jewish Studies (Track in Modern Hebrew Language, Literature, and Israeli Culture). (www.jewishstudies.wisc.edu)

14.1.10   Programs in Israel Studies, Canada

Ontario
Canada Christian College & School of Graduate Theological Studies, Israel Studies
Department, Toronto, ON. Graduate Certificate. (www.canadachristiancollege.com/
ccc/israel-studies)

Quebec
Concordia University, Azrieli Institute of Israel Studies, Montreal, QC. Minor.
(www.concordia.ca/artsci/research/azrieli-institute.html)

14.1.11   Programs in Hebrew and Yiddish Languages,
United States

California
University of California, Berkeley, Berkeley, CA. Minor in Hebrew. (http://guide.
berkeley.edu/undergraduate/degree-programs/hebrew)
   University of California, Los Angeles, Los Angeles, CA. PhD Near Eastern
Languages and Cultures with a Specialization in Hebrew, MA in Near Eastern
Languages and Cultures with a Specialization in Hebrew, Minor in Hebrew and
Jewish Studies. (www.nelc.ucla.edu/jewish)
   University of California, San Diego, San Diego, CA. Minor in Hebrew Language
and Literature. (http://jewishstudies.ucsd.edu/undergraduate/hebrew_minor.html)

Colorado
University of Colorado-Boulder, Boulder, CO. Minor in Hebrew & Israel Studies.
(www.colorado.edu/jewishstudies/academics/majors-minors-jewish-studies/
minor-hebrew-israel-studies)
   University of Denver, Denver, CO. Minor in Hebrew, Minor in Judaic Studies
with an Emphasis in Hebrew. (www.du.edu/ahss/langlit/programs/hebrew/
minor.html)

District of Columbia
The Catholic University of America, Washington, DC. PhD in Ancient Near Eastern
Studies with a Focus on Languages of the Hebrew Bible and Related Literatures
(Biblical Hebrew and Aramaic), MA in Ancient Near Eastern Studies with a Focus
on Languages of the Hebrew Bible and Related Literatures (Biblical Hebrew and
Aramaic) (https://semitics.cua.edu)
   Georgetown University, Washington, DC. Minor in Hebrew. (https://cjc.george-
town.edu/hebrewlanguage)

Florida
Florida State University, Tallahassee, FL. Minor in Hebrew. (www.modlang.fsu.
edu/programs/hebrew)

University of Florida, Gainesville, FL. BA in Hebrew. (https://catalog.ufl.edu/UGRD/colleges-schools/UGLAS/FHE_BA)

Georgia
Emory University, Atlanta, GA. Minor in Hebrew. (www.mesas.emory.edu/home/undergraduate/minors/hebrew.html)

Indiana
Indiana University, Bloomington, IN. PhD Minor in Yiddish Studies, Minor in Hebrew, Minor in Yiddish. (www.indiana.edu/~jsp/index.shtml)

Maryland
Johns Hopkins University, Baltimore, MD. Concentration in Hebrew and Yiddish (https://grll.jhu.edu)

University of Maryland, College Park, MD. MA in Jewish Studies/MA in Hebrew Pedagogy (MA in Hebrew Language Instruction), MEd in Second Language Teaching/MA in Hebrew Pedagogy (MA in Hebrew Language Instruction), Minor in Hebrew. (www.jewishstudies.umd.edu/morningstar), (www.sllc.umd.edu/hebrew/undergraduate/minor)

Massachusetts
Boston University, Boston, MA. Minor in Hebrew. (www.bu.edu/academics/cas/programs/world-languages-literatures/minor-hebrew)

Brandeis University, Waltham, MA. BA in Near Eastern and Judaic Studies-Hebrew Language Track, Minor in Hebrew Language, Literature and Culture, Minor in Yiddish and East European Jewish Literature and Culture. (www.brandeis.edu/near-eastern-judaic/hebrew/index.html), (www.brandeis.edu/near-eastern-judaic/undergraduate/minors-language.html)

Tufts University, Medford, MA. Minor in Hebrew. (www.ase.tufts.edu/ilcs/programs/judaic.htm)

University of Massachusetts Amherst, Amherst, MA. Minor in Hebrew. (www.umass.edu/jne/judaic-studies-program)

Michigan
University of Michigan, Ann Arbor, MI. BA in Middle East Studies with a Focus on Hebrew, Minor in Yiddish Studies. (www.lsa.umich.edu/middleeast/languages/fields-of-study/hebrew-and-judaic-studies.html), (www.lsa.umich.edu/judaic)

Wayne State University, Detroit, MI. MA in Near Eastern Languages with a Specialization in Hebrew, BA in Near Eastern Languages with a Concentration in Hebrew, BA in Near Eastern Languages with a Joint Concentration in Arabic and Hebrew, Minor in Hebrew. (www.clas.wayne.edu/languages/near-eastern-languages)

Minnesota
University of Minnesota, Minneapolis, MN. Minor in Hebrew. (www.cla.umn.edu/cnes/undergraduate/majors-minors/minors-cnes)

Missouri
Washington University in St. Louis, St. Louis, MO. BA in Hebrew. (www.jinelc. wustl.edu/undergraduate/hebrew)

New Hampshire
Dartmouth College, Hanover, NH. BA in Hebrew. (www.dartmouth.edu/~damell/ department/major.html)

New Jersey
Rutgers University, New Brunswick, NJ. Minor in Modern Hebrew, Minor in Language and Culture of Ancient Israel. (https://jewishstudies.rutgers.edu/academics/undergraduate/minor-jewish-studies)

New York (Outside New York Metropolitan Area)
SUNY-Binghamton University, Binghamton, NY. BA in Hebrew Studies. (www. binghamton.edu/judaic-studies)
    SUNY-University at Albany, Albany, NY. Minor in Hebrew. (www.albany.edu/ judaic_studies/js_degree_requirements.shtml)

New York Metropolitan Area
Columbia University, New York, NY. PhD in Yiddish Studies, MPhil in Yiddish Studies, MA in Yiddish Studies, BA in Yiddish Studies. (https://germanic.columbia. edu/programs/yiddish)
    CUNY-Brooklyn College, Brooklyn, NY. Minor in Hebrew. (www.brooklyn. cuny.edu/web/academics/schools/socialsciences/undergraduate/judaic.php)
    CUNY-Hunter College, New York, NY. BA in Hebrew, Minor in Hebraic Studies. (www.hunter.cuny.edu/classics/hebrew/home)
    CUNY-Queens College, Queens, NY. BA in Hebrew. (www.qc.cuny.edu/academics/degrees/dah/cmal/pages/middleeasternstudies.aspx)
    Hofstra University, Hempstead, NY. BA in Hebrew. (www.hofstra.edu/academics/colleges/hclas/cll/cll-hebrew-major-ba.html)
    New York University, New York, NY. PhD in Hebrew and Judaic Studies, Joint PhD in Hebrew and Judaic Studies/History, MA in Hebrew and Judaic Studies, BA in Hebrew and Judaic Studies. (www.as.nyu.edu/hebrewjudaic.html)
    Yeshiva University, Stern College for Women, New York, NY. Concentration in Hebrew. (www.yu.edu/stern/ug/hebrew/requirements)
    Yeshiva University, Yeshiva College (for Men), New York, NY. BA in Hebrew, Concentration in Hebrew. (www.yu.edu/pathways/jewish-studies)

North Carolina
Duke University, Durham, NC. BA in Modern Hebrew. (www.jewishstudies.duke. edu/academics/hebrew-language)
    Piedmont International University, Winston-Salem, NC. Graduate Certificate of Old   Testament   and   Hebrew.   (www.piedmontu.edu/ graduate-certificate-of-old-testament-and-hebrew)
    University of North Carolina at Chapel Hill, Chapel Hill, NC. Minor in Modern Hebrew. (www.jewishstudies.unc.edu/academics/academics)

Ohio

Case Western Reserve University, Cleveland, OH. BA in Hebrew. (http://mll.case.edu/undergraduate/hebrew)

Ohio State University, Columbus, OH. BA in Hebrew, Minor in Yiddish. (www.meltoncenter.osu.edu)

University of Cincinnati, Cincinnati, OH. Concentration in Hebrew, Undergraduate Certificate in Modern Hebrew. (www.artsci.uc.edu/departments/judaic/undergrad.html)

Oklahoma

Oral Roberts University, Tulsa, OK. Minor in Hebrew. (www.oru.edu/academics/explore-majors/#)

University of Oklahoma, Norman, OK. Minor in Hebrew. (http://hebrew.ou.edu)

Oregon

Multnomah University, Portland, OR. BA in Hebrew. (www.multnomah.edu/academics/college-majors/hebrew-degree)

Portland State University, Portland, OR. Minor in Hebrew. (www.pdx.edu/wll/hebrew-modern)

Pennsylvania

Drexel University, Philadelphia, PA. Undergraduate Certificate in Hebrew. (www.drexel.edu/coas/academics/departments-centers/global-studies-modern-languages/degrees-programs/modern-languages/hebrew)

The Pennsylvania State University, University Park, PA. Minor in Hebrew. (www.jewishstudies.la.psu.edu/undergraduate/hebrew-minor)

Vermont

Middlebury College, Middlebury, VT. Minor in Hebrew. (www.middlebury.edu/academics/hebrew)

Wisconsin

University of Wisconsin-Madison, Madison, WI. BA in Jewish Studies (Track in Modern Hebrew Language, Literature, and Israeli Culture). (www.languages.wisc.edu/languages/hebrew-modern)

University of Wisconsin-Milwaukee, Milwaukee, WI. BA in Jewish Studies-Hebrew Studies Track. (www.uwm.edu/foreign-languages-literature/undergraduate/hebrew-studies)

14.1.12 Programs in Hebrew and Yiddish Languages, Canada

Ontario

York University, Toronto, ON. Advanced Undergraduate Certificate in Hebrew and Jewish Studies. (www.jest.huma.laps.yorku.ca/certificate)

14.1.13 Programs in Jewish Education, Jewish Social Work, and Nonprofit Jewish Management, United States

California
American Jewish University, Graduate Center for Jewish Education, Los Angeles, CA. MA in Education (MAEd), MA in Teaching (MAT), MAEd in Early Childhood Education, MBA in Nonprofit Management/MAEd (joint degree with AJU Graduate School of Nonprofit Management), Graduate Certificate in Experiential Education. (www.aju.edu/graduate-center-jewish-education)

American Jewish University, Graduate School of Nonprofit Management, Los Angeles, CA. MBA in Nonprofit Management-Jewish Communal Leadership Track, MBA in Nonprofit Management/MA in Education (MAEd) (joint degree with AJU Graduate Center for Jewish Education), Graduate Certificate in Social Entrepreneurship, Graduate Certificate in Fundraising. (www.aju.edu/graduate-school-nonprofit-management)

Hebrew Union College - Jewish Institute of Religion, Executive MA Program in Jewish Education, Los Angeles, CA. Executive MA in Jewish Education. (www.huc.edu/academics/become-leader-in-jewish-education/executive-ma-program-in-jewish-education)

Hebrew Union College - Jewish Institute of Religion, Rhea Hirsch School of Education, Los Angeles, CA. MA in Jewish Education (MAJE), MAJE/MA in Hebrew Letters/Literature (joint degree with HUC-JIR Rabbinical School), MA in Jewish Nonprofit Management/MA in Jewish Education (joint degree with HUC-JIR Zelikow School of Jewish Nonprofit Management), Concentration in Experiential Jewish Education, Graduate Certificate in Day School Teaching (DeleT Program). (www.huc.edu/academics/become-leader-in-jewish-education/ma-in-jewish-education-in-los-angeles)

Hebrew Union College - Jewish Institute of Religion, Zelikow School of Jewish Nonprofit Management, Los Angeles, CA. MA in Jewish Nonprofit Management (MAJNM), MAJNM/MA in Jewish Education (joint degree with HUC-JIR Rhea Hirsch School of Education), MAJNM/MA in Hebrew Letters/Literature (joint degree with HUC-JIR Rabbinical School), MS in Organizational Leadership & Innovation, MSW/MAJNM (joint program with University of Southern California Suzanne Dworak-Peck School of Social Work), MPA/MAJNM (joint program with University of Southern California Sol Price School of Public Policy), Masters in Communication Management (MCM)/MAJNM (joint program with University of Southern California Annenberg School for Communication and Journalism), MBA/MAJNM (joint program with University of Southern California Marshall School of Business), Graduate Certificate in Jewish Organizational Leadership/MA in Hebrew Letters/Literature (joint degree with HUC-JIR Rabbinical School), Graduate Certificate in Jewish Organizational Leadership. (http://zsjnm.huc.edu)

University of Southern California, USC Annenberg School for Communication and Journalism, Los Angeles, CA. MCM (Communication Management)/MA in Jewish Nonprofit Management (joint program with Hebrew Union College – Jewish

Institute of Religion Zelikow School of Jewish Nonprofit Management). (https://annenberg.usc.edu/communication/communication-MCM),   (http://catalogue.usc.edu/preview_degree_planner.php?catoid=8&poid=7640&print)

University of Southern California, USC Marshall School of Business, Los Angeles, CA. MBA/MA in Jewish Nonprofit Management (joint program with Hebrew Union College – Jewish Institute of Religion Zelikow School of Jewish Nonprofit Management). (www.marshall.usc.edu/programs/mba-programs/full-time-mba/academics/dual-degrees-certificates)

University of Southern California, USC Sol Price School of Public Policy, Los Angeles, CA. MPA/MA in Jewish Nonprofit Management (joint program with Zelikow School of Jewish Nonprofit Management at Hebrew Union College – Jewish Institute of Religion). (https://priceschool.usc.edu/programs/masters/dual/mpa-majcs)

University of Southern California, USC Suzanne Dworak-Peck School of Social Work, Los Angeles, CA. MSW/MA in Jewish Nonprofit Management (joint program with Hebrew Union College – Jewish Institute of Religion Zelikow School of Jewish Nonprofit Management). (https://dworakpeck.usc.edu/msw-on-campus/dual-degrees/jewish-nonprofit-management)

Connecticut
Yale Divinity School, Joint Master of Social Work Degree Program, New Haven, CT. MDiv/MSW (joint program with Yeshiva University Wurzweiler School of Social Work). (https://divinity.yale.edu/admissions-aid/application-instructions-and-requirements/joint-degree-applications/joint-master-social-work-degree)

District of Columbia
George Washington University, Experiential Education and Jewish Cultural Arts Program, Washington, DC. MA in Experiential Education & Jewish Cultural Arts. (https://judaic.columbian.gwu.edu/ma-experiential-education-and-jewish-cultural-arts)

George Washington University, Mayberg Center for Jewish Education and Leadership, Washington, DC. Master's Degree in Curriculum and Instruction with a Concentration in Jewish Education. (https://gsehd.gwu.edu/mayberg-center-for-jewish-education-and-leadership)

Florida
Talmudic University of Florida, Miami Beach, FL. Master of Religious Education. (www.talmudicu.edu/educational-programs)

Illinois
Hebrew Seminary: A Rabbinical School for Deaf & Hearing, Skokie, IL. Graduate Certificate of Jewish Education. (www.hebrewseminary.org/Educational_program.aspx)

Spertus Institute for Jewish Learning and Leadership, Center for Jewish Leadership, Chicago, IL. Executive MA in Jewish Professional Studies (EMAJPS), MA in Jewish Professional Studies (MAJPS), Graduate Certificate in Jewish

Leadership, Graduate Certificate in Jewish Leadership for Educators. (www.spertus.edu/center)

University of Chicago Divinity School, Chicago, IL. MDiv & Master of Public Policy (MPP) (joint degree with UChicago Irving B. Harris School of Public Policy Studies), MDiv & Juris Doctor (JD) (joint degree with UChicago Law School), MDiv & Master of Social Work (MSW) (joint degree with UChicago School of Social Service Administration). (https://voices.uchicago.edu/divadmit/mdiv)

Indiana

Indiana University, The Robert A. and Sandra S. Borns Jewish Studies Program, Bloomington, IN. MA in Jewish Studies/Graduate Certificate in Nonprofit Management. (www.indiana.edu/~jsp/graduates/certificate.shtml)

Maryland

Binah Institute of Advanced Judaic Studies for Women, Baltimore, MD. BA in Jewish Education. (www.mhec.maryland.gov/institutions_training/Pages/collegeinfodetails.aspx?SIC=260537)

Ner Israel Rabbinical College, Pikesville, MD. MS in Education (joint program with Johns Hopkins School of Education). (www.nirc.edu/collegeprograms)

Towson University, Baltimore Hebrew Institute, Leadership in Jewish Education and Communal Service Graduate Programs, Towson, MD. MA in Leadership in Jewish Education and Communal Service, MSW/MA in Leadership in Jewish Education and Communal Service (joint program with University of Maryland, Baltimore School of Social Work), MA in Leadership in Jewish Education and Communal Service/MA in Jewish Studies, BA/MA in Family Science and Leadership in Jewish Education and Communal Service, Graduate Certificate in Jewish Communal Service, Graduate Certificate in Jewish Education. (www.towson.edu/cla/centers/baltimorehebrewinstitute/programs.html)

University of Maryland, Baltimore, School of Social Work, Baltimore, MD. MSW/MA in Leadership in Jewish Education and Communal Service (joint program with Towson University Baltimore Hebrew Institute). (www.ssw.umaryland.edu/academics/dual-degrees)

Massachusetts

Brandeis University, Hornstein Jewish Professional Leadership Program, Waltham, MA. Dual MA in Jewish Professional Leadership/MBA in Non-Profit Management, Dual MA in Jewish Professional Leadership/MPP (Public Policy), Dual MA in Jewish Professional Leadership/MA in Near Eastern and Judaic Studies, Dual BA in Near Eastern and Judaic Studies/MA in Jewish Professional Leadership. (www.brandeis.edu/hornstein)

Brandeis University, Master of Arts in Teaching Program, Jewish Day Schools/DeleT, Waltham, MA. MA in Teaching (MAT)-Jewish Day Schools. (www.brandeis.edu/programs/education/mat/jds/index.html)

Hebrew College, School of Jewish Music, Newton Centre, MA. Graduate Certificate in Jewish Sacred Music. (www.hebrewcollege.edu/sjm-certificates)

Hebrew College, Shoolman Graduate School of Jewish Education, Newton Centre, MA. PhD in Educational Studies with a Specialization in Jewish Educational Leadership (joint program with Lesley University), Master of Jewish Education (MJEd), Dual MJEd/MA in Jewish Studies, Combined MJEd/BJEd completion (upon transfer from other schools), BJEd completion (upon transfer from other schools), Graduate Certificate in Interfaith Families Jewish Engagement. (www. hebrewcollege.edu/phd-education), (www.hebrewcollege.edu)

Lesley University, Cambridge, MA. PhD in Educational Studies with a Specialization in Jewish Educational Leadership (joint program with Hebrew College Shoolman Graduate School of Jewish Education). (www.lesley.edu/academics/graduate/jewish-educational-leadership)

Michigan

University of Michigan, School of Social Work, Jewish Communal Leadership Program, Ann Arbor, MI. MSW/Graduate Certificate in Jewish Communal Leadership. (www.ssw.umich.edu/offices/jewish-communal-leadership-program)

New York (Outside New York Metropolitan Area)

SUNY- Binghamton University, Judaic Studies & Public Administration Combined Program, Binghamton, NY. JUST-MPA, BA/MPA in Judaic Studies. (www.binghamton.edu/judaic-studies/mpa.html)

New York Metropolitan Area

Columbia University, Mailman School of Public Health, New York, NY. MA/MPH in Jewish Ethics and Public Health (joint program with The Jewish Theological Seminary Gershon Kekst Graduate School). (www.mailman.columbia.edu/become-student/degrees/dual-degrees)

Columbia University, School of Social Work, New York, NY. MA in Jewish Studies/MSW (joint program with The Jewish Theological Seminary Gershon Kekst Graduate School). (www.socialwork.columbia.edu/the-student-experience/degree-options)

Hebrew Union College - Jewish Institute of Religion, Executive MA Program in Jewish Education, New York, NY. Executive MA in Jewish Education. (www.huc.edu/academics/become-leader-in-jewish-education/executive-ma-program-in-jewish-education)

Hebrew Union College - Jewish Institute of Religion, The Interfaith Doctor of Ministry Program for Education in Pastoral Care, New York, NY. Doctor of Ministry in Interfaith Clinical Education for Pastoral Care. (www.huc.edu/academics/develop-skills-in-pastoral-care)

Hebrew Union College - Jewish Institute of Religion, New York School of Education, New York, NY. MA in Religious Education, MA in Jewish Nonprofit Management/MA in Religious Education, Concentration in Experiential Jewish Education.   (www.huc.edu/academics/become-leader-in-jewish-education/ma-in-religious-education-in-new-york)

The Jewish Theological Seminary, Center for Pastoral Education, New York, NY. Graduate Certificate in Pastoral Care and Counseling. (www.jtsa.edu/cpe)

The Jewish Theological Seminary, Gershon Kekst Graduate School, New York, NY. MA in Jewish Studies/MSW (joint program with Columbia University School of Social Work), MA/MPH in Jewish Ethics and Public Health (joint program with Columbia University Mailman School of Public Health), Joint MA in Jewish Studies/MA in Jewish Education (joint degree with JTS The William Davidson Graduate School of Jewish Education). (www.jtsa.edu/the-gershon-kekst-graduate-school)

The Jewish Theological Seminary, The William Davidson Graduate School of Jewish Education, New York, NY. EdD, Executive EdD, MA in Jewish Education, Joint MA in Jewish Studies/MA in Jewish Education (joint degree with JTS Gershon Kekst Graduate School). (www.jtsa.edu/davidson-graduate-school-of-jewish-education)

New York University, Bronfman Center, New York, NY. Graduate Certificate in Spiritual Leadership and Social Impact (joint program with Yeshivat Chovevei Torah). (www.bronfmancenter.org/certificate-in-spiritual-leadership-and-social-impact)

New York University, Wagner Graduate School of Public Service, New York, NY. MPA in Public and Nonprofit Management and Policy/MA in Hebrew and Judaic Studies (joint degree with NYU Graduate School of Arts & Science). (www.wagner.nyu.edu/education/degrees/dual-degree-program/mpa-judaicstudies)

Touro College-Graduate School of Jewish Studies, New York, NY. MA in Jewish Studies with a Concentration in Jewish Education. (www.gsjs.touro.edu/academics/ma-jewish-education)

Touro College-Lander School for Men, Kew Gardens Hill, NY. BA in Psychology/MA in Jewish Studies with a Concentration in Jewish Education. (www.lcm.touro.edu/academics/program-and-majors/majors/chinuch-track.php)

Yeshiva University, Azrieli Graduate School of Jewish Education & Administration, New York, NY. MS in Jewish Education, MS in Jewish Education/MA in Jewish Studies (joint degree with YU Bernard Revel Graduate School of Jewish Studies), BA in Jewish Studies/MS in Jewish Education (joint degree with YU Stern College and Yeshiva University Yeshiva College). (www.yu.edu/azrieli/prospective-students/masters-programs)

Yeshiva University, Stern College for Women, New York, NY. BA in Jewish Education, Concentration in Jewish Education. (www.yu.edu/stern/ug/jewish-education)

Yeshiva University, Wurzweiler School of Social Work, New York, NY. PhD. in Social Welfare, MSW/PhD in Social Welfare, MSW/JD (joint degree with YU Benjamin N. Cardozo School of Law), MSW/MDiv (joint program with Yale Divinity School), MSW, Graduate Certificate in Jewish Communal Service, Graduate Certificate in Jewish Philanthropy. (www.yu.edu/wurzweiler), (www.yu.edu/pathways/social-work)

Yeshivat Chovevei Torah, Riverdale, NY. Graduate Certificate in Spiritual Leadership and Social Impact (joint program with New York University Bronfman Center). (www.yctorah.org/academics/spiritual-entrepreneurship-certificate-program-with-nyu)

Ohio

Hebrew Union College - Jewish Institute of Religion, Executive MA Program in Jewish Education, Cincinnati, OH. Executive MA in Jewish Education. (www.huc. edu/academics/become-leader-in-jewish-education/executive-ma-program-in-jewish-education)

University of Cincinnati, College of Education, Criminal Justice, and Human Services, School of Education, Cincinnati, OH. Graduate Certificate in Jewish Education. (https://cech.uc.edu/education/grad-programs/je-certificate.html)

Pennsylvania

Gratz College, Melrose Park, PA. EdD in Jewish Education, EdD in Leadership with a Concentration in Jewish Education, MA in Education (MAEd), MAEd with a Concentration in Jewish Instructional Education, MS in Nonprofit Management, MS in Nonprofit Management with a Concentration in Jewish Educational Administration, MS in Nonprofit Management/Graduate Certificate in Jewish Nonprofit Management, MA in Jewish Communal Service (MAJCS), MAJCS/MSW (joint program with University of Pennsylvania School of Social Policy & Practice), Graduate Certificate in Jewish Communal Service (CJCS)/MSW (joint program with University of Pennsylvania School of Social Policy & Practice), MA in Interfaith Leadership, MA in Jewish Professional Studies, BA in Jewish Professional Studies, Undergraduate Certificate in Jewish Education. (www.gratz. edu/academics)

Reconstructionist Rabbinical College, Wyncote, PA. MS in Nonprofit Leadership (NPL)/MA in Hebrew Letters (joint program with University of Pennsylvania School of Social Policy & Practice), MA in Jewish Education (joint program with Gratz College), MS in Nonprofit Management (joint program with Gratz College). (www.rrc.edu/admissions/titles-and-degree-programs)

University of Pennsylvania, School of Social Policy & Practice, Philadelphia, PA. MSW/Graduate Certificate in Jewish Communal Service (CJCS) (joint program with Gratz College), MS in Nonprofit Leadership (NPL)/MA in Hebrew Letters (joint program with Reconstructionist Rabbinical College), NPL/MA in Jewish Communal Service (joint program with Gratz College), NPL/Graduate Certificate in Jewish Nonprofit Management (joint program with Gratz College). (www.sp2. upenn.edu/academics/partnerships)

14.1.14 Programs in Jewish Education, Jewish Social Work, and Nonprofit Jewish Management, Canada

Ontario

York University, Israel and Golda Koschitzky Centre for Jewish Studies, Toronto, ON. BEd with a Concentration in Jewish Teacher Education. (http://cjs.yorku.ca/ students/jewish-teacher-education)

Quebec
McGill University, Montreal, QC. BEd Kindergarten Elementary Education (Jewish Studies Option), BEd Secondary (Jewish Studies Option), MA Education and Society Non-Thesis (Jewish Education Option). (www.mcgill.ca/edu-jttp)

14.2 Major Books on the North American Jewish Communities

The following list was derived from WorldCat, a global catalogue of library collections. The list was limited to non-fiction books about Jews and Judaism in the US and Canada, excluding self-published works, reprints, and those cited in previous volumes of the *Year Book*. Additional details about the books can be found at www. worldcat.org. Additional entries for 2018 can be found in Volume 118 of the *Year Book*, while the entries for 2019 cover the period of published books available during the first half of the year.

2018
Association of Jewish Libraries and Chava Punchuck (eds.). 2018. *The Sydney Taylor Book Award: A guide to the winners, honor books and notables. 50th anniversary edition 1968-2018.* New York, NY: Association of Jewish Libraries.

Beerman, Leonard I. and David N. Myers (eds.). 2018. *The eternal dissident: Rabbi Leonard I. Beerman and the radical imperative to think and act.* S. Mark Taper Foundation Imprint in Jewish Studies. Oakland, CA: University of California Press.

Blair, Sara. 2018. *How the other half looks: The Lower East Side and the afterlives of images.* Princeton, NJ: Princeton University Press.

Bunin Benor, Sarah and Benjamin Hary (eds.). 2018. *Languages in Jewish communities, past and present.* Contributions to the Sociology of Language. Vol. 112. Berlin, Germany: De Gruyter Mouton.

Burger, Ariel. 2018. *Witness: Lessons from Elie Wiesel's classroom.* Boston, MA: Houghton Mifflin Harcourt.

Chmerkovskiy, Valentin. 2018. *I'll never change my name: An immigrant's American dream from Ukraine to the USA to Dancing with the Stars.* New York, NY: Dey Street Books.

Cohen, Mark. 2018. *Not bad for Delancey Street: The rise of Billy Rose.* Brandeis Series in American Jewish History, Culture, and Life. Waltham, MA. Brandeis University Press.

Cooperman, Jessica. 2018. *Making Judaism safe for America: World War I and the origins of religious pluralism.* The Goldstein-Goren Series in American Jewish History. New York, NY: New York University Press.

Davids, Stanley M. and Lawrence A. Englander (eds.). 2018. *The fragile dialogue: New voices of liberal Zionism.* New York, NY: Central Conference of American Rabbis.

Diner, Hasia R. (ed.). 2018. *Doing business in America: A Jewish history.* The Jewish Role in American Life, Vol. 16. West Lafayette, IN: Purdue University Press.

Diner, Hasia R. and Simone Cinotto (eds.). 2018. *Global Jewish foodways: A history.* Lincoln, NE: University of Nebraska Press.

Doniger, Wendy. 2018. *The Donigers of Great Neck: A mythologized memoir.* The Mandel Lectures in the Humanities at Brandeis University. Waltham, MA: Brandeis University Press.

Dorff, Elliot N. 2018. *Modern Conservative Judaism: Evolving thought and practice.* Philadelphia, PA: Jewish Publication Society.

Eleff, Zev (ed.). 2018. *A century at the center: Orthodox Judaism & the Jewish Center.* New Milford, CT: Toby Press.

Epstein, Anita, with Noel Epstein. 2018. *Miracle child: The journey of a young Holocaust survivor.* The Holocaust: History and Literature, Ethics and Philosophy. Boston, MA: Academic Studies Press.

Epstein, Nadine. 2019. *Elie Wiesel: An extraordinary life and legacy.* Washington, DC: MomentBooks.

Fermaglich, Kirsten. 2018. *A Rosenberg by any other name: A history of Jewish name changing in America.* The Goldstein-Goren Series in American Jewish History. New York, NY: New York University Press.

Frank, Gillian, Bethany Moreton, and Heather Rachelle White (eds.). 2018. *Devotions and desires: Histories of sexuality and religion in the twentieth-century United States.* Chapel Hill, NC: University of North Carolina Press.

Goda, Norman J. W. (ed.). 2018. *Rethinking Holocaust justice: Essays across disciplines.* New York, NY: Berghahn Books.

Goldman, Samuel. 2018. *God's country: Christian Zionism in America.* Haney Foundation Series. Philadelphia, PA: University of Pennsylvania Press.

Gower, Adam. 2018. *Jacob Schiff and the art of risk: American financing of Japan's war with Russia (1904-1905).* Palgrave Studies in the History of Finance. Cham, Switzerland: Palgrave Macmillan.

Hart, Bradley W. 2018. *Hitler's American friends: The Third Reich's supporters in the United States.* New York, NY: Thomas Dunne Books, an imprint of St. Martin's Press.

Kaplan, Alice. 2018. *French lessons: A memoir.* Chicago, IL: University of Chicago Press.

Kaplan, Amy. 2018. *Our American Israel: The story of an entangled alliance.* Cambridge, MA: Harvard University Press.

Kaplan, Dana Evan (ed.). 2018. *A life of meaning: Embracing Reform Judaism's sacred path.* New York: Central Conference of American Rabbis.

Keinan, Tal. 2018. *God is in the crowd: Twenty-first-century Judaism.* New York, NY: Speigel & Grau.

Krauthammer, Charles and Daniel Krauthammer (eds.). 2018. *The point of it all: A lifetime of great loves and endeavors.* New York, NY: Crown Forum.

Kupperman, Michael. 2018. *All the answers.* New York, NY: Gallery 13, an imprint of Simon & Schuster.

Lefkowitz, Philip. 2018. *History of a Chicago synagogue: Agudas Achim North Shore Congregation founded October 25, 1884.* New York, NY: Page Publishing.

Lesser, Wendy. 2018. *Jerome Robbins: A life in dance.* Jewish Lives. New Haven, CT: Yale University Press.

Levine, Allan. 2018. *Seeking the fabled city: The Canadian Jewish experience.* Toronto: McClelland & Stewart.

Levisohn, Jon A. and Jeffrey S. Kress (eds.). 2018. *Advancing the learning agenda in Jewish education.* Boston, MA: Academic Studies Press.

Margalith, Dana. 2018. *Tradition as mediation: Louis I. Kahn: The Dominican Motherhouse & the Hurva Synagogue.* Routledge Research in Architecture. New York, NY: Routledge.

Mnookin, Robert H. 2018. *The Jewish American paradox: Embracing choice in a changing world.* New York, NY: PublicAffairs.

Morris, Leslie. 2018. *The translated Jew: German Jewish culture outside the margins.* Cultural Expression of World War II. Evanston, IL: Northwestern University Press.

Oster, Sharon B. 2018. *No place in time: The Hebraic myth in late-nineteenth-century American literature.* Detroit, MI: Wayne State University Press.

Pollin-Galay, Hannah. 2018. *Ecologies of witnessing: Language, place, and Holocaust.* New Haven, CT: Yale University Press.

Rochelson, Meri-Jane. 2018. *Eli's story: A twentieth-century Jewish life.* Detroit, MI: Wayne State University Press.

Ross, Steve. 2018. *From broken glass: My story of finding hope in Hitler's death camps to inspire a new generation.* New York, NY: Hachette Books.

Ruderman, Judith. 2018. *Passing fancies in American Jewish literature.* Bloomington, IN: Indiana University Press.

Saperstein, Marc. 2018. *Agony in the pulpit: Jewish preaching in response to Nazi persecution and mass murder 1933-1945.* Cincinnati, OH: Hebrew Union College Press.

Schindler, Judith and Judy Seldin-Cohen. 2018. *Recharging Judaism: How civic engagement is good for synagogues, Jews, and America.* New York, NY: Reform Judaism Publishing, a division of CCAR Press.

Skinazi, Karen E. 2018 *Women of valor: Orthodox Jewish troll fighters, crime writers, and rock stars in contemporary literature and culture.* New Brunswick, NJ: Rutgers University Press.

Sokoloff, Naomi B. and Nancy E. Berg (eds.). 2018. *What we talk about when we talk about Hebrew: (And what it means to Americans).* The Samuel & Althea Stroum Lectures in Jewish Studies. Seattle, WA: University of Washington Press.

Sokolow, Moshe. 2018. *Reading the Rav: Exploring religious themes in the thought of Rabbi Joseph B. Soloveitchik.* New York, NY: Kodesh Press L.L.C.

Steinberg, Morton M. 2018. *Tradition by the lake: A historical outline of North Suburban Synagogue Beth El.* Highland Park, IL: North Suburban Synagogue Beth El.

Sundquist, Eric J. (ed.). 2018. *Writing in witness: A Holocaust reader.* SUNY Series in Contemporary Jewish Literature and Culture. Albany, NY: State University of New York Press.

Trilling, Lionel and Adam Kirsch (eds.). 2018. *Life in culture: Selected letters of Lionel Trilling.* New York, NY: Farrar, Straus and Giroux.

Walkowitz, Daniel J. 2018. *The remembered and forgotten Jewish world: Jewish heritage in Europe and the United States.* New Brunswick, NJ: Rutgers University Press.

Weiman-Kelman, Zohar. 2018. *Queer expectations: A genealogy of Jewish women's poetry.* SUNY Series in Contemporary Jewish Literature and Culture. Albany, NY: State University of New York Press.

Wolfson, Ron, Nicole Armenta Auerbach, and Lydia Bloom Medwin. 2018. *Relational Judaism handbook: How to create a relational engagement campaign to build and deepen relationships in your community.* Encino, CA: Center for Relational Judaism, Dorothy K. and Myer S. Kripke Institute for Jewish Family Literacy.

Zakai, Avihu. 2018. *The pen confronts the sword: Exiled German scholars challenge Nazism.* Albany, NY: State University of New York Press.

2019

Aarons, Victoria and Holli Levitsky (eds.). 2019. *New directions in Jewish American and Holocaust literatures: Reading and teaching.* SUNY Series in Contemporary Jewish Literature and Culture. Albany, NY: State University of New York Press.

Auerbach, Jerold S. 2019. *Print to fit: The New York Times, Zionism and Israel (1896-2016).* Antisemitism in America. Boston, MA: Academic Studies Press.

Bentley, Paul Roberts. 2019. *Strange journey: John R. Friedeberg-Seeley and the quest for mental health.* Boston, MA: Academic Studies Press.

Biederman, Mark with Randi Biederman. 2019. *Schindler's listed: The search for my father and his lost gold.* The Holocaust: History and Literature, Ethics and Philosophy. Boston, MA: Academic Studies Press.

Blumberg, Ilana M. 2019. *Open your hand: Teaching as a Jew, teaching as an American.* New Brunswick, Camden, and Newark, NJ: Rutgers University Press.

Bookman, Terry. 2019. *Beyond survival: How Judaism can thrive in the 21st century.* Lanham, MD: Rowman & Littlefield.

Brickman, S. Perry. 2019. *Extracted: Unmasking rampant antisemitism in America's higher education.* New York, NY: Morgan James Publishing.

Caputo, Nina and Mitchel Bryan Hart (eds.). 2019. *On the word of a Jew: Religion, reliability, and the dynamics of trust.* Bloomington, IN: Indiana University Press.

Cohen, Judah M. 2019. *Jewish religious music in nineteenth-century America: Restoring the synagogue soundtrack.* Bloomington, IN: Indiana University Press.

Friedmann, Jonathan L. 2019. *Cantor William Sharlin: Musical revolutionary of Reform Judaism.* Jefferson, NC: McFarland & Company.

Hoberman, Michael. 2019. *A hundred acres of America: The geography of Jewish American literary history.* New Brunswick, NJ: Rutgers University Press.

Koffman, David S. 2019. *The Jews' Indian: Colonialism, pluralism, and belonging in America.* New Brunswick, NJ: Rutgers University Press.

Limmer, Seth M. and Jonah Dov Pesner (eds.). 2019. *Moral resistance and spiritual authority: Our Jewish obligation to social justice.* New York, NY: Central Conference of American Rabbis.

Lipstadt, Deborah E. 2019. *Antisemitism: Here and now.* New York, NY: Schocken Books.

Majer, Krzysztof, Justyna Fruzińska, Józef Kwaterko, and Norman Ravvin (eds.). 2019. *Kanade, di goldene medine?: Perspectives on Canadian-Jewish literature and culture = perspectives sur la littérature et la culture juives Canadiennes.* Francopolyphonies, Vol. 25. Leiden, Netherlands: Brill.

Maxwell, Nancy Kalikow. 2019. *Typically Jewish.* Lincoln, NE: University of Nebraska Press, and Philadelphia, PA: The Jewish Publication Society.

Milligan, Amy K. 2019. *Jewish bodylore: Feminist and queer ethnographies of folk practices.* Studies in Folklore and Ethnology: Traditions, Practices, and Identities. Lanham, MD: Lexington Books.

Moffic, Evan. 2019. *First the Jews: Combating the world's longest-running hate campaign.* Nashville, TN: Abingdon Press.

Nadell, Pamela Susan. 2019. *America's Jewish women: A history from colonial times to today.* New York, NY: W. W. Norton & Company.

Rosenfarb, Chava and Goldie Morgentaler (eds.). 2019. *Confessions of a Yiddish writer and other essays by Chava Rosenfarb.* Montreal, QC: McGill-Queen's University Press.

Rubin, Ron. 2019. *Strangers and natives: A newspaper narrative of early Jewish America 1734-1869.* Jerusalem: Urim Publications.

Slomowitz, Alan and Alison Feit (eds.). 2019. *Homosexuality, transsexuality, psychoanalysis and traditional Judaism.* Psychoanalysis in a New Key Book Series. 49. New York, NY: Routledge.

Soloveitchik, Joseph Dov, Shalom Carmy, and Joel B. Wolowelsky (eds.). 2019. *Blessings and Thanksgiving: Reflections on the siddur and synagogue.* New York, NY: OU Press, and New Milford, CT: Maggid Books.

Waldoff, Leon. 2019. *A story of Jewish life in Mississippi.* North American Jewish Studies. Boston, MA: Academic Studies Press.

Weisman, Steven R. 2019. *Chosen wars: How Judaism became an American religion.* New York, NY: Simon & Schuster.

Yanklowitz, Shmuly (ed.). 2019. *Kashrut and Jewish food ethics.* Jewish Thought, Jewish History: New Studies. Boston, MA: Academic Studies Press.

Yudkoff, Sunny S. 2019. *Tubercular capital: Illness and the conditions of modern Jewish writing.* Stanford Studies in Jewish History and Culture. Stanford, CA: Stanford University Press.

14.3   Academic Journals about the North American Jewish Communities

AJS Review. Scholarly articles and book reviews in the field of Jewish Studies. Sponsored by the Association for Jewish Studies and published by Cambridge University Press. (www.associationforjewishstudies.org/publications-research/ajs-review)

ALEPH: Historical Studies in Science and Judaism. A joint publication of the Sidney M. Edelstein Center for the History of Science, Technology, and Medicine; the Institute for Jewish Studies at the Hebrew University; and Indiana University Press. (http://muse.jhu.edu/journal/283)

American Jewish Archives Journal. Articles examining the American Jewish experience through primary source documentation. Sponsored by Temple Emanu-El of New York City and the Dolores and Walter Neustadt Fund. Published by The Jacob Rader Marcus Center of the American Jewish Archives. (www.americanjewisharchives.org/publications/journal)

American Jewish History. Scholarly articles on Jewish life in America. Published by Johns Hopkins University Press. (www.press.jhu.edu/journals/american_jewish_history)

Antisemitism Studies. A double blind peer-reviewed academic publication issued twice a year that provides scholarly articles on the millennial phenomenon of antisemitism in both its past and present manifestations. Journal of the Canadian Institute for the Study of Antisemitism (CISA). Published by Indiana University Press. (www.antisemitismstudies.com/index.html)

Canadian Jewish Studies. An interdisciplinary, peer-reviewed journal published annually that is devoted to original scholarship that illuminates aspects of the Canadian Jewish experience. Sponsored by the Institute for Canadian Jewish Studies at Concordia University and affiliated with the Koschitzky Centre for Jewish Studies at York University, the Jewish Studies Program of the University of Toronto, and Vered Jewish Canadian Studies Program at the University of Ottawa. Published by the Association for Canadian Jewish Studies. (https://cjs.journals.yorku.ca/index.php/cjs/index)

Central Conference of American Rabbis: The Reform Jewish Quarterly. Articles examining Judaism and Jewish life in America. Sponsored by the Central Conference of American Rabbis. (www.ccarnet.org/rabbinic-voice/reform-jewish-quarterly)

Contact. A semi-annual journal that explores vital issues affecting the American Jewish community and the philanthropic vision of The Steinhardt Foundation for Jewish Life. Published by The Steinhardt Foundation for Jewish Life. (www.steinhardtfoundation.org/publications)

Conservative Judaism. Articles on Jewish texts and traditions and examines development in today's Jewish communities. Sponsored by the Rabbinical Assembly and the Jewish Theological Seminary. (www.rabbinicalassembly.org/resources-ideas/cj-journal). Ceased publication in 2014.

Contemporary Jewry. Social scientific considerations of world Jewry, its institutions, trends, character, and concerns. Sponsored by The Association for the Social Scientific Study of Jewry. Published by Springer. (www.springer.com/social+sciences/sociology/journal/12397)

G'vanim. A journal dedicated to Jewish diversity. Published by the Academy for Jewish Religion.

Hebrew Higher Education. An online journal for methodology and pedagogy for teaching of Hebrew in institutions of higher learning. Published by the National Association of Professors of Hebrew. (www.naphhebrew.org/publication/hebrew-higher-education)

Hebrew Studies. Hebrew language and literature studies. Sponsored by the Lucius Littauer Foundation and the Department of Hebrew and Semitic Studies at the University of Wisconsin-Madison. Published by the National Association of Professors of Hebrew. (www.naphhebrew.org/publications/hebrew)

History and Memory. Studies in historical consciousness and collective memory. Edited at the Eva and Marc Besen Institute for the Study of Historical Consciousness at Tel Aviv University. Published by Indiana University Press. (http://muse.jhu.edu/journal/71)

Jewish Culture and History. An interdisciplinary approach to Jewish social history and Jewish cultural studies. Published by Taylor and Francis Group. (www.tandfonline.com/loi/rjch20)

Jewish History. Provides scholarly articles on all facets of Jewish history. Sponsored by Springer Science and Business Media. (www.springer.com/history/journal/10835)

Jewish Journal of Sociology. Social scientific studies of Jewry. Sponsored by Maurice Freedman Research Trust Limited. Last issue was 2015. (www.jewishjournalofsociology.org/index.php/jjs)

Jewish Political Studies Review. The first and only journal dedicated to the study of Jewish political institutions and behavior, Jewish political thought, and Jewish public affairs. Published by the Jerusalem Center for Public Affairs.

Jewish Quarterly Review. The oldest English-language journal of Jewish studies, established in 1889. Published by the University of Pennsylvania Press. (http://jqr.pennpress.org/home)

The Jewish Role in American Life. An Annual Review connected to the University of Southern California's Casden Institute for the Study of the Jewish Role in American Life, which has been bringing new insight to bear upon the important role played by Jewish people in American culture, particularly in the West. In recent volumes, the editors have decided to focus each issue on a single topic and to present articles that largely consider aspects of that topic alone. Published by Purdue University Press. (www.thepress.purdue.edu/series/jewish-role-american-life-annual-review)

Jewish Social Studies: History, Culture, and Society. Historical studies in the modern and early modern periods. A project of the Conference on Jewish Social Studies based at the Taube Center for Jewish Studies at Stanford University and sponsored by the Lucius N. Littauer Foundation. Published by Indiana University Press. (https://jewishstudies.stanford.edu/publications/jewish-social-studies)

Jewish Studies Quarterly. Studies in Jewish history, religion, and culture. Edited from Princeton University and published by Mohr-Siebeck in Tübingen, Germany. (www.mohrsiebeck.com/en/journal/jewish-studies-quarterly-jsq)

Journal of Contemporary Antisemitism. One of the few journals exclusively dedicated to the analysis of antisemitism, focusing on the multiple and changing manifestations of antisemitism in the contemporary world. While the specific focus is on 21st century forms of antisemitism, including but not limited to antisemitism in the Islamic world, in Europe, on the left and the right of the political spectra, secular antisemitism, antisemitism in the church, and anti-Zionism, submissions may include relevant empirical studies dealing with the nineteenth or early twentieth century. Published by Academic Studies Press. (http://journals.academicstudies-press.com/index.php/JCA)

Journal of Jewish Communal Service. The journal of record and authority for Jewish communal leaders. Documents the development of new trends and methodologies that enhance the work of Jewish communal employees. Published by the JPro Network. (https://jpro.org/about-the-journal). Ceased publication in 2013.

Journal of Jewish Identities. An interdisciplinary peer-reviewed forum for contesting ideas and debates concerning the formations of, and transformations in, Jewish identities in its various aspects, layers, and manifestations. (https://muse.jhu.edu/journal/463)

Journal of Jewish Studies. An international academic journal publishing scholarly articles on Jewish history, literature, and religion from Biblical to current times. Published by the Oxford Centre for Hebrew and Jewish Studies. (www.jjs-online.net)

The Journal of Jewish Thought and Philosophy. An international forum for the study of Jewish thought, philosophy, and intellectual history from all historic periods. Published by Brill. (https://brill.com/view/journals/jjtp/jjtp-overview.xml)

Journal of Modern Jewish Studies. Interdisciplinary journal publishing academic articles on modern Jewish studies. (www.tandfonline.com/loi/cmjs20)

Journal of Psychology and Judaism. Explores the relationship between modern psychology and Judaism on philosophical and clinical levels. **Published by Springer Science and Business Media. Last issue was 2000.** (www.researchgate.net/journal/0700-9801_Journal_of_Psychology_and_Judaism)

Journal of Textual Reasoning: Rereading Judaism after Modernity. Textual reasoning is a critical and constructive enterprise that endeavors to create new forms of Jewish thought and life that will respond to contemporary needs while being faithful to the fabric of Jewish traditions of text interpretation and philosophy. Sponsored by the Society of Textual Reasoning founded at the Jewish Theological Seminary in New York. Published by the Electronic Text Center at the University of Virginia. (http://jtr.shanti.virginia.edu/volume-1-number-1/introducing-the-journal-of-textual-reasoning-rereading-judaism-after-modernity)

Judaica Librarianship. A scholarly peer-reviewed annual focused on the organization and management of Judaica and Hebraica. Sponsored by the Association of Jewish Libraries. (http://ajlpublishing.org)

Modern Judaism: A Journal of Jewish Ideas and Experience. Scholarly articles on modern Jewish life and experience. Sponsored by Oxford University Press. (https://academic.oup.com/mj)

The NAASE Journal. The professional journal of the North American Association of Synagogue Executives showcasing a range of articles that parallel the diverse interests of synagogue executives, drawn from the expertise of members and from sources in allied professional fields. (www.naase.org/resources/the-naase-journal)

Nashim: A Journal of Jewish Women's Studies & Gender Issues. Provides an international, interdisciplinary, and scholarly forum in Jewish women's and gender studies, the only one of its kind, for the innovative work being done in the many areas of research that comprise this field. Cofounded by the Hadassah-Brandeis Institute at Brandeis University and the Schechter Institute of Jewish Studies in Jerusalem. Published by Indiana University Press. (http://muse.jhu.edu/journal/243)

Prooftexts: A Journal of Jewish Literary History. Articles on the study of Jewish literature. Published by Indiana University Press. (http://muse.jhu.edu/journal/167)

Review of Rabbinic Judaism: Ancient, Medieval, and Modern. First and only scholarly journal to focus solely on the academic study of Rabbinic Judaism in all time periods. Published by Brill. (https://brill.com/view/journals/rrj/rrj-overview.xml)

Shofar: An Interdisciplinary Journal of Jewish Studies. An interdisciplinary journal of Jewish studies. Sponsored by the Midwest and Western Jewish Studies Associations. Published by Purdue University Press. (https://muse.jhu.edu/journal/181)

Southern Jewish History. The annual peer-reviewed journal of the Southern Jewish Historical Society, published in the fall of each year since 1998. (www.jewishsouth.org/about-southern-jewish-history)

Studies in American Jewish Literature. Studies of Jews and Jewishness in American literature. Published by Penn State University Press. (http://muse.jhu.edu/journal/443)

Studies in Christian Jewish Relations. Peer-reviewed scholarship on the history, theology, and contemporary realities of Jewish-Christian relations and reviews of new materials in the field. Sponsored by the Council of Centers on Jewish-Christian Relations. Published by the Center for Christian-Jewish Learning at Boston College. (http://ejournals.bc.edu/ojs/index.php/scjr)

Studies in Judaism, Humanities, and the Social Sciences. Interdisciplinary peer-reviewed academic journal whose mission is to publish original works of interest on Judaism through the "eyes" of the humanities and the social sciences. Published by Academic Studies Press. (www.academicstudiespress.com/journals/sjhss)

Western States Jewish History. A quarterly journal containing interesting articles about persons, places and/or events that can be considered a part of the Jewish history of the American West, including Canada, Mexico, and the Pacific Rim.

Published for over 40 years by Western States Jewish History Association. (www.jmaw.org/indexes)

Women in Judaism: A Multidisciplinary Journal. A multidisciplinary journal examining topics in gender issues in Judaism. Sponsored by Women in Judaism, Inc. (http://wjudaism.library.utoronto.ca/index.php/wjudaism)

14.4   Scholarly Articles on the Study of the North American Jewish Communities: July 2018–June 2019

The following list is based on a practice first undertaken as an appendix to Volume 7 of *Contemporary Jewry* (1986), under the aegis of the Association for the Social Scientific Study of Jewry. Rena Cheskis-Gold and Arnold Dashefsky edited "Recent Research on Contemporary Jewry."

The current list of articles was constructed by searching *SocINDEX* for the following terms: "holocaust*," "Israel*," "Jew*," "Judaism," "Judaic," and "synagog*." Our initial search for July 2018–June 2019 yielded 1252 articles. This search was supplemented by additional articles derived from journals not included in the above sources but previously cited in the *American Jewish Year Book*. A total of 78 articles were deemed relevant and are listed below.

Dates with asterisks indicate articles that were published before July 2018, but which were inadvertently omitted from the previous volume.

July 2018–June 2019
Aronson, Janet Krasner, Leonard Saxe, Charles Kadushin, Matthew Boxer and Matthew A. Brookner. 2018. A new approach to understanding contemporary Jewish engagement. *Contemporary Jewry* 39(1): 91-113.

Arviv, Tamir. 2018. "Stepbrothers from the Middle East": Negotiations of racial identity among Jewish-Israeli immigrants in Toronto. *Social & Cultural Geography* 19(7): 935-954.

Atwood, Sarah. 2018. "This list is not complete": Minnesota's Jewish resistance to the Silver Legion of America, 1936-1940. *Minnesota History* 66(4): 142-155.

Baskind, Samantha. "Propaganda in the best and purest sense of the word": Early representations of the Warsaw Ghetto in American culture. *American Jewish History* 103(2): 125-145.

Bauman, Mark K. and Leah Burnham. 2018. The Atlanta federal penitentiary and area Jews: A social service case study. *Southern Jewish History* 21(1): 1-60.

Becker, Amy B. and Maureen E. Todd. 2018. Watching the evolution of the American family? Amazon's *Transparent*, ecological systems theory, and the changing dynamics of public opinion. *Journal of Homosexuality* 65(9): 1120-1137.

Ben-Choreen, Tal-Or. 2018. Photographic boxes—art installations: A study of the role of photography in the Israel pavilion at Expo '67. *Canadian Jewish Studies* 26(1): 121-134.

Bernstein, Judah M. 2018. A preacher in exile: Shemaryahu Levin and the making of American Zionism, 1914-1919. *American Jewish History* 102(3): 323-350.

Biggs-Craft, Katherine. 2018. The end of the "Golden Years": Jewish life in Saint John in the 1960s. *Canadian Jewish Studies* 26(1): 204-210.

Bressler, Toby. 2019. The lived experience of Orthodox Jewish nursing students. *Jewish Culture and History* 20(2): 153-165.

Carenen, Caitlin. 2017.∗ Zionism and American Jewish relief efforts in Palestine during World War I. *The American Jewish Archives Journal* 69(2): 1-29.

Celinscak, Mark. 2018. The Holocaust and the Canadian War Museum controversy. *Canadian Jewish Studies* 26(1): 11-30.

Cohen, Jeffrey E. 2018. Generalized discrimination perceptions and American Jewish perception of antisemitism. *Contemporary Jewry* 38(3): 405-433.

Cook, Richard M. 2018. Kazin's Trilling: A Cold War portrait. *Society* 55(6): 506-511.

DellaPergola, Sergio, Ariela Keysar, and Shlomit Levy. 2019. Jewish identification differentials in Israel and in the United States: Similarity structure analysis. *Contemporary Jewry* 39(1): 53-90.

Dempsey, Anna M. 2018. Jill Soloway's Transparent: Transgender memory and a tale of two cities. *Gender & History* 30(3): 803-819.

Dilmaghani, Maryam. 2018. A remnant of the past? Jewish homeownership gaps in Montreal and Toronto, from 1971 to 2011. *Contemporary Jewry* 38(3): 315-343.

Drinkwater, Gregg. 2019. Creating an embodied queer Judaism: liturgy, ritual and sexuality at San Francisco's Congregation Sha'ar Zahav, 1977–1987. *Journal of Modern Jewish Studies* 18(2): 177-193.

Eisen, Ethan, and Yehoshua Berman. 2018. Situational factors related to childhood sexual abuse in the Orthodox Jewish community among adult and juvenile offenders. *Journal of Child Sexual Abuse* 27(5): 537-553.

Ellis, Carolyn, and Jerry Rawicki. 2018. Remembering the past /anticipating the future: A professor from the white working class talks with a survivor of the Holocaust about our troubled world. *Qualitative Inquiry* 24(5): 323-337.

Ferziger, Adam S. 2018. Sanctuary for the specialist: Gender and the reconceptualization of the American Orthodox rabbinate. *Jewish Social Studies* 23(3): 1-37.

Finkelstein, Joel, Savvas Zannettou, Barry Bradlyn and Jeremy Blackburn. 2018. A quantitative approach to understanding online antisemitism. *arXiv e-prints arXiv:1809.01644.* https://arxiv.org/pdf/1809.01644.pdf

Friedman, Joshua B. and Moshe Kornfeld. 2018. Identity projects: Philanthropy, neoliberalism, and Jewish cultural production. *American Jewish History* 102(4): 537-561.

Garland, Libby. 2018. State of the field: New directions for American Jewish migration histories. *American Jewish History* 102(3): 423-440.

Gilman, Ernest B. 2019. Mikhl Likht's Yiddish Modernism. *Jewish Studies Quarterly* 26(1): 80-97.

Gil, Noam. 2018. The undesired: On nudniks in Jewish American fiction. *Journal of Modern Jewish Studies* 17(3): 326-341.

Gordan, Rachel. 2018. "The Fabulous Irishman": Lord Mayor Robert Briscoe's "Unusual Religious and National Combination" in Cold War America. *American Jewish History* 102(3):401-421.

Gordon, Mark W. 2018. Rediscovering Jewish infrastructure: Showcasing surviving eighteenth- and nineteenth-century synagogues. *American Jewish History* 102(4): 563-573.

Hassenfeld, Jonah. 2018. Landscapes of collective belonging: Jewish Americans narrate the history of Israel after an organized tour. *Journal of Jewish Education* 84(2): 131-160.

Hassenfeld, Ziva R. and Jon A. Levisohn. 2019. The challenge of professional development in Jewish studies: Why the conventional wisdom may not be enough. *Journal of Jewish Education* 85(1): 53-75.

Horwitz, Ilana M. 2019. Foregrounding the family: An ethnography of how families make decisions about Hebrew school. *Contemporary Jewry* 39(1): 155-172.

Imhoff, Sarah. 2019. Women and gender, past and present: A Jewish Studies story. *Jewish Social Studies* 24(2): 74-81.

Kahn, Ava F. 2017. * Linked by letters: A doctor with the American expeditionary forces and his Chicago family, a Jewish World War I story. *The American Jewish Archives Journal* 69(2): 30-79.

Kaufman, Matthew. 2019. Between consent and descent: Horace M. Kallen and psychophysical inheritance. *American Jewish History* 103(1): 51-73.

Kelley, Heather H., Ashley B. LeBaron, Lance J. Sussman, Jay Fagan, David C. Dollahite, and Loren D. Marks. 2018. Shalom bayit—Peace of the home: Ritual and tradition in American Jewish families. *Marriage & Family Review* 54(7): 706-718.

Kirschen, Bryan. 2019. Lexical variation among south Florida's Judeo-Spanish-speaking Sephardim. *Journal of Jewish Languages* 7(1): 53-84

Kohn, Shira. 2018. Turning German Jews into Jewish Greeks: Philanthropy and acculturation in the Jewish Greek system's student refugee programs, 1936-1940. *American Jewish History* 102(4): 511-536.

Koplowitz-Breier, Anat. 2018. Modernizing Leah: The biblical Leah in contemporary Anglo-American Jewish women's poetry. *Women's Studies* 47(5): 527-540.

Kotlerman, Ber. 2018. 'They don't pay $1000 a week to just anyone': Sholem Aleichem and early Jewish American movie moguls. *Jewish Culture and History* 19(3): 256-274.

Leffler, Phyllis K. 2018. Insiders and outsiders: Charlotteville's Jews, white supremacy, and antisemitism. *Southern Jewish History* 21(1): 61-120.

Lerner, Loren. 2018. The Canadian Jewish connection to the visual narrative of nationhood at the Jewish Palestine pavilion in New York (1939) and the pavilions of Israel and Judaism in Montreal (1967). *Canadian Jewish Studies* 26(1): 135-153.

Lev Ari, Lilach and Nir Cohen. 2018. Acculturation strategies and ethnic identity among second-generation Israeli migrants in the United States. *Contemporary Jewry* 38(3): 345-364.

Levin, Shmuel. 2018. Test of faith: Haredi communities and the right to education. *International Journal of Law, Policy & Family* 32(3): 334-362.

Light, Caroline. 2018.* Precarious pasts and Jewish collective memory: "Trapped in history" in 2017 America. *Journal of Jewish Identities* 11(1): 191-204.

Ljungquist, Kent. 2018. "First connections with stagecraft": S. N. Behrman finds his vocation. *Studies in American Jewish Literature* 37(2): 145-172.

Luce, Caroline E. 2018. Yiddish writers in Los Angeles and the Jewish fantasy past. *American Jewish History* 102(4): 481-509.

Lustig, Jason. 2018. Building a home for the past: Archives and the geography of American Jewish history. *American Jewish History* 102(3): 375-399.

Marchenko, Alla. 2018. In the eyes of Uman pilgrims: A vision of place and its inhabitants. *Contemporary Jewry* 38(2): 227-247.

Marks, Darren C. 2019. 'Sgt Rock is Jewish?' Joe Kubert, Jews and the Holocaust in American comic books: 1938–2006. *Jewish Culture and History* 20(2): 166-187.

Marks, Loren D., Trevan G. Hatch, and David C. Dollahite. 2018. Sacred practices and family processes in a Jewish context: Shabbat as the weekly family ritual par excellence. *Family Process* 57(2): 448-461.

McLean, Heather. 2018. Regulation and resisting queer creativity: Community-engaged arts practice in the neoliberal city. *Urban Studies* 55(16): 3563-3578.

Milligan, Amy K. 2019. The 'Jewish zealots of tobacco land': The circuit riding rabbi project's impact on small town Jews in North Carolina, 1950-1980. *Jewish Culture and History* 20(1): 62-79.

Mindra, Mihai. 2018. Evangelical and progressive inscriptions in Mary Antin's autobiographical discourse. *Studies in American Jewish Literature* 37(2): 173-199.

Neuman, Eran. 2018. The Israel pavilion for the 1967 International and Universal Exposition in Montreal. *Canadian Jewish Studies* 26(1): 104-120.

Pagis, Michal, Wendy Cadge and Orly Tal. 2018. Translating spirituality: Universalism and particularism in the diffusion of spiritual care from the United States to Israel. *Sociological Forum* 33(3): 596-618.

Rabin, Shari. 2018. Judges and Jews: Congregational conflict and the Protestant secular in 19th-century America. *Religion* 48(4): 659-677.

Reimer, Joseph. 2018. Shabbat-at-camp at three Jewish camps: Jewish learning through ritual participation. *Journal of Jewish Education* 84(4): 359-388.

Robins Sharpe, Emily. 2018. "The heart above the ruins": Miriam Waddington's poetry, the Spanish civil war, and Jewish Canadian literature. *Canadian Jewish Studies* 26(1): 56-74.

Roger, Howard and Michael Cole. 2018. Maurice Eisendrath comes to Toronto: The Rabbi's first year at Holy Blossom. *The American Jewish Archives Journal* 70(1&2): 39-67.

Roginsky, Dina and Rina Cohen. 2018. Trading Jerusalem: Jewish-Arab encounters in a Middle Eastern restaurant in Toronto. *Canadian Jewish Studies* 26(1): 75-98.

Rosmarin, David H., Steven Pirutinsky, Moses Appel, Talia Kaplan and David Pelcovitz. 2018. Childhood sexual abuse, mental health, and religion across the Jewish community. *Child Abuse & Neglect* 81(1): 21-28.

Safran, Gabriella. 2018. Authenticity, complaint, and the Russianness of American Jewish literature. *Prooftexts* 36(3): 255-285.

Schwartz, Stephanie Tara. 2018.∗ The challenge of Jewish difference in Québec. *Journal of Jewish Identities* 11(1): 33-54.

Shain, Michelle. 2018.∗ Understanding the demographic challenge: Education, orthodoxy, and the fertility of American Jews. *Contemporary Jewry*. https://doi.org/10.1007/s12397-018-9249-6

Shain, Michelle. 2019. Beyond belief: How membership in congregations affects the fertility of U.S. Mormons and Jews. *Review of Religious Research*: 1-19. https://doi.org/10.1007/s13644-019-00378-x

Shaul Bar Nissim, Hanna and Matthew A. Brookner. 2019. Ethno-religious philanthropy: Lessons from a study of United States Jewish philanthropy. *Contemporary Jewry* 39(1): 31-51.

Sheskin, Ira M. and Harriet J. Hartman. 2019. Religious diversity and religious participation in U.S. Jewish communities. *The Professional Geographer* 71(1): 39-51.

Sheskin, Ira and Harriet Hartman. 2019. A Profile of LGBT Jewish Households, *G'vanim: The Journal of the Academy for Jewish Religion* 10: 68-93.

Sigalow, Emily. 2018. Breaking down the barriers: The encounter between Judaism and Buddhism in the late nineteenth century. *American Jewish History* 102(4): 459-480.

Sigalow, Emily. 2018.∗ Jewish Buddhists, gender, and social scientific perspectives. *Journal of Jewish Identities* 11(1): 17-31.

Train, Kelly Amanda. 2018. Negotiating new territory: Indian Jewish women in the family in Toronto. *Canadian Jewish Studies* 26(1): 31-55.

Troper, Harold. 2018. A tale of two pavilions. Jewish participation in Expo '67. *Canadian Jewish Studies* 26(1): 154-169.

Ury, Scott. 2019. Migration as redemption: The myth and memory of Jewish migration from Eastern Europe to the New World. *Jewish Culture and History* 20(1): 3-22.

Wamsley, Rachel. 2018. "A pure language (or lip)": Representing Hebrew in colonial New England. *Studies in American Jewish Literature* 37(2): 117-144.

Weinfeld, David. 2018. The Maccabaean and the melting pot: Contributionist Zionism and the American diversity discourse, 1903-1915. *The American Jewish Archives Journal* 70(1&2): 1-37.

Weiss, Amy. 2019. Billy Graham receives Ten Commandments: American Jewish interfaith relations in the age of evangelicalism. *American Jewish History* 103(1): 1-24.

Zakai, Sivan. 2019. From the mouths of children: Widening the scope and shifting the focus of understanding the relationships between American Jews and Israel. *Contemporary Jewry* 39(1): 17-29.

14.5 Websites and Organizations for Research on North American Jewish Communities

AJC Archives (formerly **American Jewish Committee Archives**) (2006). 165 East 56th Street, New York, NY 10022. (212) 891-1433. AJC provides the AJC Survey of American Jewish Opinion the results of which are available at www.jewishdatabank.org. The AJC website contains a wealth of historical information on the American Jewish community. Filled with more than a million documents and hundreds of movies and radio shows, the AJC Archives house an extraordinary range of resources on the past century of American Jewish history, including the full text of the *American Jewish Year Book* from 1899-2008. (www.ajcarchives.org)

Alex Dworkin Canadian Jewish Archives (formerly **Canadian Jewish Congress Charities Committee National Archives**) (1934). Concordia University, 1590 Docteur Penfield Avenue, Montreal, QC H3G 1C5. (514) 931-7531, ext. 271. (Archives moved in summer of 2018, please check for new information online.) The Alex Dworkin Canadian Jewish Archives collects and preserves documentation on all aspects of the Jewish presence in Quebec and Canada, including the historical records of most of the national Jewish organizations that have shaped the present community. Most catalogue descriptions of the holdings can be consulted online through the database of the Canadian Jewish Heritage Network. Notable aspects of the Canadian Jewish community reflected in the collections include immigration, integration into Canadian society, community organization, Zionism, human rights issues and discrimination, oppressed Jewry in other countries, education, literature, and genealogy. (www.cjarchives.ca/en)

American Academy for Jewish Research (AAJR) (1920). 202 South Thayer Street, Suite 2111, Ann Arbor, MI 48103. The AAJR is the oldest organization of Judaic scholars in North America. Fellows are nominated and elected by their peers and thus constitute the most distinguished and most senior scholars teaching Judaic studies at American universities. The AAJR sponsors the Baron Book Prize for the best first book in Judaic studies; a biennial retreat for the Fellows; workshops for graduate students and early career faculty in Judaic studies; and academic sessions at the annual meeting of the Association for Jewish Studies. As the senior organization for Jewish scholarship on this continent, it is committed to enhancing Judaic studies throughout North American universities by creating a dynamic fellowship for its members and by providing programs and opportunities for more junior scholars and students entering the field. (www.aajr.org)

American Association for Polish Jewish Studies (AAPJS) (1984). 34 Kirkland Street, Cambridge, MA 02138. The AAPJS, a sister organization of the Institute for Polish Jewish Studies in Oxford, England, was established to preserve the history of Polish Jewry on a worldwide basis; disseminate the results of its research by means of publications, lectures, conferences, seminars, and documentary films; and focus attention of the American and world public on what is most significant and precious in the legacy of Polish Jewry. The AAPJS publishes an annual journal, Polin: Studies in Polish Jewry, which provides a resource for a growing number of scholars who seek authoritative historical and cultural material on Polish Jewry. (www. aapjstudies.org)

American Jewish Historical Society. For contact information and a description, see the Jewish History/Heritage Organizations section of Chap. 12. (www. ajhs.org)

American Sephardi Federation. For contact information and a description, see the Sephardic Organizations section of Chap. 12. (www.americansephardi.org)

American Values Atlas (AVA) (2014). c/o PRRI, 1023 15th Street NW, 9th Floor, Washington, DC 20005. (202) 238-9424. The (AVA) is a powerful tool for understanding the complex demographic, religious, and cultural changes occurring in the US today that was launched by the Public Religion Research Institute in recognition of the need to provide a more complete portrait of substantial diversity of opinion, identities, and values across the US. The AVA's interactive mapping system allows users to explore the differences and similarities between America's diverse religious, political, and demographic communities, and it also includes specific issue modules, covering topics such as immigration, abortion, LGBT issues, and others. The AVA draws upon 50,000 annual telephone interviews among a random sample of Americans to deliver an unprecedented level of detail about the American cultural and religious landscape. With its large sample size, the AVA provides a rare look at the profiles of smaller religious communities, such as Jews, Muslims, Mormons, Hindus, Buddhists, and others, who are often omitted from depictions of the country's religious population. Its scope also allows its users to explore the increasing diversity of specific regions, all 50 states, and 30 major metropolitan areas. (http://ava.prri.org)

Association for Canadian Jewish Studies (ACJS) (formerly **Canadian Jewish Historical Society**) (1976). c/o Department of Religion, Concordia University, 1455 de Maisonneuve West, Montreal, QC H3G 1M8. (514) 848-2424, ext. 2074. The ACJS is a national member-run organization that brings together academics, students, professionals, and others interested in the study of the Jewish experience in Canada across multiple disciplines, including history, literature, sociology, religion, gender studies, architecture, music, translation, and others. Its regular activities include an annual Springtime conference that brings together scholars, archivists, and associated societies and organizations of Canadian Jewish studies together to share their ideas and help shape the future of the discipline; publication of *Canadian Jewish Studies*, the only journal devoted to the study of Canadian Jewry; and publication of a bi-annual *Bulletin* highlighting news and events pertaining to Canadian Jewish studies. (www.acjs-aejc.ca)

Association for Jewish Studies (AJS) (1969). 15 West 16th Street, New York, NY 10011. (917) 606-8249. The AJS was founded by a small group of scholars seeking a forum for exploring methodological and pedagogical issues in the new field of Jewish Studies. Since its founding, the AJS has grown into the largest learned society and professional organization representing Jewish Studies scholars worldwide. As a constituent organization of the American Council of Learned Societies, the AJS represents the field in the larger arena of the academic study of the humanities and social sciences in North America. The organization's primary mission is to advance research and teaching in Jewish Studies at colleges, universities, and other institutions of higher learning. Its members are university faculty, graduate students, independent scholars, and museum and related professionals who represent the breadth of Jewish Studies scholarship, and its institutional members represent leading North American programs and departments in the field. Publications of the AJS include *AJS Review*, its peer-reviewed, scholarly journal published twice annually, and *AJS Perspectives*, its magazine published bi-annually. (www.associationforjewishstudies.org)

Association for the Social Scientific Study of Jewry (ASSJ) (1971). The ASSJ is a cross disciplinary organization of individuals whose research concerns the Jewish people throughout the world. Members are primarily academics, but also policy analysts, communal professionals, and activists, and are engaged in a wide range of scholarly activity, applied research, and the links between them. Members work throughout the world, primarily in North America, Israel, and Europe. All social scientific disciplines are represented, including sociology, social psychology, social anthropology, demography, contemporary history, social work, political science, geography, and Jewish education. The ASSJ promotes networking among researchers, supports the dissemination of research, and assists in the cultivation of younger scholars. The organization's journal, Contemporary Jewry, which is issued several times a year, publishes research that draws on the range of social scientific fields and methodologies, and encourages cutting-edge research and lively debate. (www.assj.org)

Association for the Sociology of Religion (ASR) (formerly American Catholic Sociological Society) (1938). Department of Sociology, Ball State University, 2000 West University Avenue, North Quad 222, Muncie, IN 47306. The ASR is an international scholarly association that seeks to advance theory and research in the sociology of religion. The ASR encourages and communicates research that ranges widely across the multiple themes and approaches in the study of religion, and is a focal point for comparative, historical, and theoretical contributions to the field. In addition, the ASR facilitates the sharing of members' interests with sociologists in other associations and scholars of religion in other disciplines. It publishes the journal titled *Sociology of Religion: A Quarterly Review*. (www.sociologyofreligion.com)

Association for the Study of Religion, Economics, and Culture (ASREC). Institute for the Study of Religion, Economics and Society, 338 North Glassell Street, Orange, CA 92866. (714) 516-4681. The ASREC exists to promote interdisciplinary scholarship on religion through conferences, workshops, newsletters, websites, working papers, teaching, and research. ASREC supports all manner of social scientific methods, but seeks specially to stimulate work based on economic perspectives and the rational choice paradigm. The economic study of religion and culture comprises a variety of sub-fields, which collectively embrace all aspects of the social-scientific study of religion or culture. (www.asrec.org)

Association of Jewish Libraries (AJL) (1966). PO Box 1118, Teaneck, NJ 07666. (201) 371-3255. The AJL is a volunteer-run professional organization that promotes Jewish literacy through enhancement of libraries and library resources and through leadership for the profession and practitioners of Judaica librarianship. The AJL fosters access to information, learning, teaching, and research relating to Jews, Judaism, the Jewish experience, and Israel, and provides a community for peer support and professional development. AJL membership is open to individuals and libraries, library workers, and library supporters. The diverse membership includes libraries in synagogues, JCC's, day schools, yeshivot, universities, Holocaust museums, and even the Library of Congress. (www.jewishlibraries.org)

The Association of Religion Data Archives (ARDA) (formerly **American Religion Data Archive**) (1997). Department of Sociology, The Pennsylvania State University, 211 Oswald Tower, University Park, PA 16802. (814) 865-6258. The ARDA strives to democratize access to the best data on religion. Going online in 1998, the initial archive was targeted at researchers interested in American religion. The targeted audience and the data collection have both greatly expanded since 1998, now including American and international collections and developing features for educators, journalists, religious congregations, and researchers. Data included in the ARDA are submitted by the foremost religion scholars and research centers in the world. (www.thearda.com)

Berman Jewish DataBank (BJDB) (formerly **North American Jewish Data Bank**) (1986). The Jewish Federations of North America, Wall Street Station, PO Box 157, New York, NY 10268. (212) 284-6500. The BJDB, managed by The Jewish Federations of North America, is the central repository of social scientific studies of North American Jewry. It acquires, archives and provides open access to quantitative studies and related materials on North American Jews and Jewish communities; promotes use of its resources by its stakeholders; and encourages transparency in the public release and reporting of research on North American Jewry. The DataBank archives and makes available electronically questionnaires, reports, and data files from the National Jewish Population Surveys (NJPS) of 1971, 1990 and 2000-01. The Data Bank is the sole distributor of the NJPS 2000-01 data set and has archived a large collection of related materials. In addition to the NJPS studies, the DataBank provides access to other national Jewish population reports, Jewish population statistics, and approximately 200 local Jewish community studies from the major Jewish communities in North America. (www.jewishdatabank.org)

Berman Jewish Policy Archive @ Stanford (BJPA) (2008). Stanford Graduate School of Education, 485 Lasuen Mall, Stanford, CA 94305. The BJPA at Stanford University is the central electronic address for Jewish communal policy. It offers a vast collection of policy relevant research and analysis on Jewish life to the public, free of charge, with holdings spanning from 1900 until today. The library contains tens of thousands of policy relevant documents from leading authors, journals, and organizations. The BJPA's comprehensive, searchable collection ensures that existing research will be easily and instantly accessible to everyone who needs it -- communal professionals, lay leaders, academics, clergy, consultants, students, community members, and anyone else with an interest in the Jewish community. The BJPA intends to serve as a catalyst for new research, new analysis, and new policy discussions. A dynamic hub for a diverse network of Jewish organizations, thinkers, and leaders, the BJPA advances the understanding of contemporary Jewish life by providing a platform for highlighting original research and proactively bringing documents on crucial policy topics into the communal spotlight. (www.bjpa.org)

Canadian Institute for Jewish Research (CIJR) (1988). PO Box 175, Station H, Montreal, QC H3G 2K7. (514) 486-5544. The CIJR is an independent Israel and Jewish issues centered think tank, focused on Middle Eastern foreign policy and international relations. It is an internationally-recognized source of informed analysis and data, an academic institute unique in speaking directly to the public, Jewish and non-Jewish. Through up to date analyses of its respected online, email, fax, and print publications and its massive online Israel & Middle East Data Bank, which holds tens of thousands of articles, op eds, and other data, the CIJR addresses topics and key issues that include current and historical Israel and Judaism/Jewish issues; Islam and the Arab world, including Iraq, Syria, Egypt and the Arab rebellions, Hamas, Hezbollah, Al Qaeda and other terrorist organizations, Middle Eastern human rights issues, and Muslim countries' socio economic dynamics and their persecution of Christians; the Arab Israeli conflict, including the status of the West Bank and Jerusalem, Israel civil rights, the Gaza boycott, and Arab and European delegitimization of Israel; antisemitism, the Holocaust, and Holocaust denial; American, Canadian, European, and Arab-world foreign policy issues; and international affairs perspectives. (www.isranet.org)

Canadian Institute for the Study of Antisemitism (CISA) (2010). PO Box 58029 RPO Bishop Grandin, Winnipeg, MB R2M 2R6. CISA promotes scholarship and facilitates public education on the subject of antisemitism in its classic and contemporary forms. It sponsors the leading academic journal on the subject, *Antisemitism Studies*, and hosts and co-sponsors a number of events each year, including public lectures, book signings, film screenings, conferences, courses, and the Annual Shindleman Family Lecture. (www.canisa.org)

Canadian Jewish Heritage Network (CJHN) (2011). The CJHN is a web presence linking and showcasing the resources of the major organizations involved in Canadian Jewish archival preservation. This site brings together the databases and digitized archival material of the Alex Dworkin Canadian Jewish Archives, the Jewish Public Library Archives of Montreal, the Montreal Holocaust Museum, the Ottawa Jewish Archives, the Saint John Jewish Historical Museum, the Congregation Shaar Hashomayim Museum and Archives, and The Spanish and Portuguese Synagogue Archives. The site contains a detailed searchable index containing descriptions of archival holdings, from the fonds level down to the series, file, or item level in some cases, and a wide variety of digitized archival collections or collection series, which permits substantive scholarly research online. (www.cjhn.ca/en)

Canadian Society for Jewish Studies (CSJS) (2004). Dr. Ira Robinson, c/o Department of Religion, Concordia University, 1455 de Maisonneuve Boulevard West, Montreal, QC H3G 1M8. The CSJS was founded in Winnipeg, MB with the goal to promote and facilitate the development of Jewish Studies in Canada. The purpose of the CSJS is to provide a venue for the presentation of Jewish studies education, research, and information, primarily for faculty members, graduate students, and independent scholars from across Canada. The CSJS represents faculty, librarians, and students at institutions throughout Canada. Membership in the Society is open to all with an active scholarly interest in Canadian Jewish studies. (www.csjs.ca)

Center for Jewish History. For contact information and a description, see the Jewish History/Heritage Organizations section of Chap. 12. (www.cjh.org)

Cohen Center for Modern Jewish Studies (CMJS) (1980). MS 014, Brandeis University, 415 South Street, Waltham, MA 02454. (781) 736-2060. The CMJS is a multi-disciplinary research center that incorporates the latest concepts, theories, and techniques of social science in the study of contemporary Jewish life. The senior research staff are trained in community psychology, social psychology, sociology, and social policy. Research areas include Israel, Jewish education, religious life, and socio-demography. Within each research area there are a number of projects that contribute to scholarly and policy-relevant research on the US Jewish community. Core topics concern the development of ethnic and religious identities and their attendant personal, communal, and societal outcomes. Research incorporates cutting edge methodologies and strives to be rigorous and transparent. In this fashion, the Center contributes to a scholarly understanding of American Jewry and Jewish institutions and provides policy relevant analysis. (www.brandeis.edu/cmjs)

Ethnic Geography Specialty Group (EGSG) (1992). The EGSG of the Association of American Geographers (AAG) promotes the common interests of scholars and professionals researching ethnic geography, provides a forum for the exchange of ideas within the AAG, and encourages members in their research and teaching of ethnic experiences from comparative, national/transnational and global perspectives. The EGSG facilitates the sharing of diverse ideas and information among its members and others interested in ethnic geography; stimulates research, pedagogy, and applications in ethnic geography; aids in the advancement of its members and of the field of ethnic geography; represents ethnic geography within geography as a whole and with other related disciplines as well as the general public; and maintains relations with cognate organizations. (www.ethnicgeography.com)

Geography of Religion and Belief Systems (GORABS) (1978). The GORABS Specialty Group of the Association of American Geographers, the official group for geographers interested in religion, secularization, and other such ontologies, was created to further the geographic study of religious phenomena, including but not limited to religious groups, behavior, material culture, and human environment relations from a religious perspective. (www.aaggorabs.wordpress.com) (http://community.aag.org/communities/community-home?CommunityKey=439a7aec-3325-4 49c-97fe-12634667288f)

Goldring/Woldenberg Institute of Southern Jewish Life (ISJL) (formerly **Museum of the Southern Jewish Experience**) (1986) (2000). 4915 I-55 North, Suite 100A, Jackson, MS 39206. (601) 362-6357. The ISJL preserves, documents, and promotes the practice, culture, and legacy of Judaism in the South. The ISJL's History Department works to preserve and interpret the rich legacy of the southern Jewish experience, preserving historical documents and artifacts covering 13 states. It collects information and documents relating to every Southern Jewish community that has ever existed. Its Encyclopedia of Southern Jewish Communities, designed to present a history of every congregation and significant Jewish community in the South, offers detailed histories of over 200 Jewish communities and congregations in the South, which serves as a valuable resource for researchers, scholars, and people interested in their family history. The ISJL's Oral History Program has collected more than 700 audio and video interviews with Jewish Southerners from all over the region. These recordings — firsthand accounts of life stories and community histories — offer present and future users a unique resource for learning about the personalities, experiences, and memories of Jews in the American South. (www.isjl.org)

The Goldstein-Goren Diaspora Research Center. The Goldstein-Goren Diaspora Research Center is dedicated to the research of the history of the Jewish people and its culture in all diasporas and eras. The Center is an integral part of the Lester and Sally Entin Faculty of Humanities in Tel Aviv University. (www3.tau.ac.il/ggcenter/index.php?lang=english)

Hartford Institute for Religion Research (HIRR) (formerly **Center for Social and Religious Research**) (1981). 77 Sherman Street, Hartford, CT 06105. (860) 509-9542. Hartford Seminary's HIRR has a long record of rigorous, policy relevant research, anticipation of emerging issues, and commitment to the creative dissemination of learning. This record has earned the HIRR an international reputation as an important bridge between the scholarly community and the practice of faith. Its work is guided by a disciplined understanding of the interrelationship between the life and resources of American religious institutions and the possibilities and limits placed on those institutions by the social and cultural context in which they work. The HIRR website presents summaries of current religion research by HIRR faculty as well as the research done by other sociologists of religion. (www.hirr.hartsem.edu)

H-Judaic: Jewish Studies Network (JSN) (formerly **Judaica/He'Asif**). JSN, a member of H-Net Humanities & Social Sciences Online, is the premier digital source concerning Judaica and the academic study and discussion of Judaism — ancient, medieval, and modern. It provides dynamic online information in Judaic Studies: links to syllabi and other online sources of syllabi and materials of interest. (https://networks.h-net.org/h-judaic)

Institute for Jewish & Community Research (IJCR) (1994). 3198 Fulton Street, San Francisco, CA 94118. (415) 386-2604. The IJCR is an independent, nonpartisan think tank that provides innovative research and pragmatic policy analysis on a broad range of issues, including racial and religious identity, philanthropy, and antisemitism, and is devoted to creating a safe, secure, and growing Jewish community. The IJCR provides research to the Jewish community and the general society; utilizes its information to design and develop innovative initiatives; and educates the general public and opinion leaders. The IJCR conducts on-going research in three areas: religious prejudice and the security of the Jewish community, philanthropy, and the growth and vitality of the Jewish people. (www.jewishresearch.org)

Jacob Rader Marcus Center of the American Jewish Archives (AJA) (formerly **American Jewish Archives**) (1947). 3101 Clifton Avenue, Cincinnati, OH 45220. (513) 221-1875. The AJA was established to collect, preserve, and make available for research, materials on the history of Jews and Jewish communities in the Western Hemisphere (primarily focusing on America), including data of a political, economic, social, cultural, and religious nature. It promotes the study and preservation of the Western Hemisphere Jewish experience through research, publications, collection of important source materials, and a vigorous public outreach program. The AJA exists to preserve the continuity of Jewish life and learning for future generations, serving scholars, educators, students, and researchers of all backgrounds and beliefs. The AJA publishes the American Jewish Archives Journal, which features articles on relevant themes in American history. (www.americanjewisharchives.org)

JData. JData is a not for profit project that collects and provides census like information about Jewish educational programs in North America. The data are both collected and accessed via the JData website. The website securely houses the data and offers users multiple ways to utilize data through reports and analyses. (www.jdata.org)

JDC Archives. The JDC Archives houses one of the most significant collections in the world for the study of modern Jewish history. Comprising the organizational records of JDC, the overseas rescue, relief, and rehabilitation arm of the American Jewish community, the archives includes over 3 miles of text documents, 100,000 photographs, a research library of more than 6000 books, 1100 audio recordings including oral histories, and a video collection. (http://archives.jdc.org)

Jewish English Lexicon. The Jewish English Lexicon is a collaborative database of distinctive words that are used in the speech or writing of English-speaking Jews. (www.jel.jewish-languages.org)

The Jewish Federations of North America (formerly **United Jewish Appeal**, **Council of Jewish Federations**, and **United Jewish Communities**). For contact information and a description, see the Jewish Community Coordinating Organizations section of Chap. 12. (www.jewishfederations.org)

Jewish Question Survey Bank (JQSB) (2013). Stanford Graduate School of Education, 458 Lasuen Mall, Stanford, CA 94305. A project of the Berman Jewish Policy Archive at Stanford University and the Berman Jewish DataBank, the JSQB is an online database of survey questions used in Jewish social research. As recent years have seen an increasing number of social scientific surveys of the Jewish population, including studies of the Jewish population, program evaluation, public opinion, and more, open access to the questions used in this research will increase both quality and comparability of future studies, allowing and encouraging researchers to make use of each other's work. (https://jewishquestions.bjpa.org/jsqb)

Jewish Virtual Library (formerly **Jewish Student Online Research Center, JSOURCE**). For contact information and a description, see the Online Libraries section of this chapter, Sect. 14.6. (www.jewishvirtuallibrary.org)

JSTOR. JSTOR is a digital archive of academic journals and other scholarly content, including Jewish Studies as one of the subject areas. (www.jstor.org)

JTA (also known as **Jewish Telegraphic Agency**) (formerly **Jewish Correspondence Bureau**) (1917, JTA) (2011, JTA Digital Archive). JTA is a trusted global source of news, analysis, and features on issues of Jewish interest and concern. JTA prides itself on producing compelling, credible, independent, and high-quality journalism, and it has earned a reputation for journalistic integrity, outstanding reporting, and insightful analysis. Its reporting reflects the wide spectrum of religious, political, and cultural identity within the Jewish community, with its digital properties serving as a town square where Jews of all stripes can debate with and learn about each other. JTA's global reporting provides extensive coverage of political, economic, and social developments affecting Jews all over the world. Its reporting also shines a spotlight on the cultural happenings, influential thinkers and leaders, and milestone events defining the Jewish experience today. Over the years, the Jewish community has come to rely on JTA as a credible source of news and analysis available about events and issues of Jewish interest anywhere in the world. The JTA Archive is a powerful reference tool that offers a perspective on current events and modern Jewish history that is not available anywhere else. With free access to nearly a century of reporting about global events affecting world Jewry, the Archive serves as a rich resource for students and scholars of modern Jewish history. (www.jta.org) (www.jta.org/archive)

The Lindex (1973). The Lindex is the first ethnic database of disease. Since 1973, studies dealing with the disease experience of American and Canadian Jews have been collected and reviewed. There is no comparable database for any ethnic group that covers this array of diseases in this detail for a 12-year period. Data sources include journal articles; conference proceedings; community, insurance, government, hospital and vital statistics reports; doctoral dissertations; and monographs. The Lindex consists of the MicroLindex, which is a database that records numerous variables of each study in the Lindex, and the MacroLindex, which involves a review of each disease associated with every one of the publications in text form, consisting of one or more paragraphs. (http://lindex.umdnj.edu)

Midwest Jewish Studies Association (MJSA) (1988). The MJSA is a broad and interdisciplinary nonprofit organization that brings together scholars of Jewish and non-Jewish backgrounds in a synergistic effort to generate energy, talent, ideas, and resources. The MJSA is designed to facilitate scholarship and pedagogy and offer other valuable resources and services for individuals involved in Jewish Studies at the college and university levels. While its focus is predominantly on Jewish Studies within the traditional American Midwest, the MJSA welcomes scholars and scholarship from all aspects of Jewish Studies—history, anthropology, religion, film studies, English, music, etc.—and by scholars from across the globe. A central event of the MJSA is the annual conference, which is held, on a rotating basis, at various Midwest institutions of higher education. Shofar is a quarterly journal of Jewish studies that is the official journal of the Midwest and Western Jewish Studies Associations. (www.midwestjewishstudies.com/home)

National Association of Professors of Hebrew. For contact information and a description, see the Jewish Academic Organizations section of Chap. 12. (www. naphhebrew.org)

Network for Research in Jewish Education (NRJE) (1987). 4613 North University Drive, #348, Coral Springs, FL 33067. (513) 815-6753. The NRJE was established to encourage, support, and stimulate serious research in Jewish education; to create a community of researchers in the field; and to advocate for increased funding and for proper utilization of research in Jewish education. Its mission is to foster communication, encourage collaboration, and support emerging scholarly research. Through its annual conference, its Emerging Scholar Award and NRJE Research Award, and the quarterly Journal of Jewish Education, the NRJE fosters a community dedicated to Jewish educational research. (www.nrje.org)

Pew Forum on Religion & Public Life (2001). 1615 L Street NW, Suite 800, Washington, DC 20036. (202) 419-4300. The Pew Research Center's Forum on Religion & Public Life seeks to promote a deeper understanding of issues at the intersection of religion and public affairs. The Pew Forum conducts surveys, demographic analyses, and other social science research on important aspects of religion and public life in the US and around the world. It examines a wide range of issues concerning religion and American society, from the shifting religious composition of the US to the influence of religion on politics, and also covers a range of policy issues that often have a religious component. The Pew Forum explores the role religion plays in world affairs through a range of research products, from large public opinion surveys on religion and society to in-depth demographic analyses of the current distribution and future growth trajectory of major religious groups. The Pew Forum also produces research that documents the extent of government and social restrictions on religion around the world. (www.pewforum.org)

Public Religion Research Institute (PRRI) (2009). 1023 15th Street NW, 9th Floor, Washington, DC 20005. (202) 238-9424. PRRI is a nonprofit, nonpartisan organization dedicated to conducting independent research at the intersection of religion, culture, and public policy. Its research explores and illuminates America's changing cultural, religious, and political landscape. PRRI's mission is to help journalists, scholars, pundits, thought leaders, clergy, and the general public better understand debates on public policy issues, and the important cultural and religious dynamics shaping American society and politics. PRRI conducts high quality public opinion surveys and qualitative research, and is committed to independent inquiry and academic rigor. (www.prri.org)

RAMBI—The Index of Articles on Jewish Studies. RAMBI is a selective bibliography of articles in the various fields of Jewish studies and in the study of Israel. Material listed in Rambi is compiled from thousands of periodicals and from collections of articles — in Hebrew, Yiddish, and European languages. (http://web.nli.org.il/sites/nli/english/infochannels/catalogs/bibliographic-databases/rambi/pages/rambi.aspx)

Religion and Politics (1903). 1527 New Hampshire Avenue NW, Washington, DC 20036. (202) 483-2512. Religion and Politics is an organized section of the American Political Science Association. The purpose of the section is to encourage the study of the interrelations between religion and politics, including the politics of religious pluralism; law, religion, and governance; faith, practice, and political behavior; and the politics of secularism, in the US as well as in comparative, historical, and global perspective. Politics and Religion is an international journal publishing high quality peer-reviewed research on the multifaceted relationship between religion and politics around the world." (https://connect.apsanet.org/s11/home)

Religious Research Association (RRA) (formerly **Religious Research Fellowship**) (1951). c/o Kevin D. Dougherty, One Bear Place, #97326, Waco, TX 76798. (254) 710-6232. The RRA is an association of academic and religious professionals working at the intersection of research and practical religious activities. It is an interfaith and international association whose members include college, university, and seminary faculty; religious leaders; organizational consultants; lay persons; and other professionals interested in the intersection of religion and society. The RRA encourages and communicates research across multiple themes and approaches in the study of religion, including: new religious movements; dynamics of denominational and congregational growth; individual and organizational variations in beliefs and practices; relation between personal spirituality and institutional religious involvement; conflict within congregations and denominations; religious experience; ethnic religious groups; religion and family life; religion and political behavior; and comparative analyses of religious behavior and institutions. 'The RRA publishes the Review of Religious Research, which seeks to provide a regular channel for the exchange of information on methods, findings and uses of religious research. (www.rraweb.org)

Society for the Anthropology of Religion (SAR) (formerly the **Anthropology of Religion Section**) (1997). 2300 Clarendon Boulevard, Suite 1301, Arlington, VA 22201. (703) 528-1902. SAR is a section of the American Anthropological Association and facilitates the research and teaching of the anthropology of religion. It supports anthropological approaches to the study of religion from all the subdisciplines: cultural anthropology, archaeology, physical anthropology, linguistic anthropology, and others. It also encourages and helps provide avenues for enhanced communication among scholars sharing the interests of anthropology and religion. SAR publishes the journal *Religion and Society*. (http://sar.americananthro.org)

Society for the Psychology of Religion and Spirituality (SPRS). APA Division Services, 750 First Street NE, Washington, DC 20002. (202) 336-6013. SPRS promotes the application of psychological research methods and interpretive frameworks to diverse forms of religion and spirituality; encourages the incorporation of the results of such work into clinical and other applied settings; and fosters constructive dialogue and interchange between psychological study and practice on the one hand and between religious perspectives and institutions on the other. The division is strictly nonsectarian and welcomes the participation of all persons who view religion as a significant factor in human functioning. SPRS publishes *Psychology of Religion and Spirituality*, a journal of peer-reviewed original articles related to the psychological aspects of religion and spirituality. (www.apa.org/about/division/div36.aspx)

Society for the Scientific Study of Religion (SSSR) (formerly **Committee for the Social Scientific Study of Religion** and **Committee for the Scientific Study of Religion**) (1949). c/o Roman R. Williams, Ph.D., Calvin College, Department of Sociology, Grand Rapids, MI 49546. (616) 526-6026. SSSR is an interdisciplinary academic association that stimulates, promotes, and communicates social scientific research about religious institutions and experiences. It fosters interdisciplinary dialogue and collaboration among scholars from sociology, religious studies, psychology, political science, economics, international studies, gender studies, and many other fields. SSSR's flagship publication, the Journal for the Scientific Study of Religion, is the most cited resource in the field. (www.sssreligion.org)

Steinhardt Social Research Institute (SSRI) (2005). MS 014, Brandeis University, 415 South Street, Waltham, MA 02454. (781) 736-3958. The SSRI is dedicated to providing unbiased, high-quality data about contemporary Jewry. It develops reliable and valid quantitative data about the American Jewish community. It conducts socio demographic research; studies the attitudes and behavior of US Jews; and develops a variety of policy focused analyses of issues such as intermarriage and the effectiveness of Jewish education. The SSRI's work is characterized by the application of cutting edge research methods to provide policy relevant data. SSRI research informs discourse about religious-ethnic identity and, in so doing aids efforts to ensure a vibrant future for the Jewish community. (www.brandeis.edu/ssri)

Western Jewish Studies Association (WJSA) (1995). c/o Dr. Lawrence Baron, Department. of History, San Diego State University, 5500 Campanile Drive, San Diego, CA 92182 (619) 594-5338. The WJSA is a nonprofit organization whose main purpose is to organize and host a Jewish Studies Conference every Spring at alternating sites in the western US and Canada to serve as a forum for Jewish Studies scholars in this region to present their research, discuss pedagogical issues, network with colleagues in their disciplines, and share information about the funding and organization of Jewish Studies programs. Shofar is a quarterly journal of Jewish studies that is the official journal of the Midwest and Western Jewish Studies Associations. (www.wjsa.net)

World Union of Jewish Studies (WUJS) (1957). The Hebrew University of Jerusalem, Rabin World Center of Jewish Studies, Mt. Scopus, Jerusalem, 91240, Israel. The WUJS is an international organization that promotes Jewish studies worldwide. It is the most important parent body for research in Jewish Studies. Its members include scholars, students, and intellectuals from all over the world. Since its establishment, the WUJS has acted toward the advancement of Jewish studies through conferences and publications in order to encourage research and the exchange of ideas between scholars from around the world. The WUJS publishes the academic, peer-reviewed journal, Jewish Studies, along with monographs in the various disciplines of Jewish Studies. (www.jewish-studies.org)

YIVO Institute for Jewish Research. For contact information and a description, see the Jewish History/Heritage Organizations section of Chap. 12. (www.yivo.org), (www.yivoarchives.org)

14.6   Major Judaic Research and Holocaust Research Libraries

14.6.1   Central Coordinating Body for Jewish Libraries

Association of Jewish Libraries (formerly **Jewish Library Association**). For contact information and a description, see this chapter, Sect. 14.5.

14.6.2   Judaic Research, United States

Arizona
Hayden Library at Arizona State University. 300 East Orange Mall, Tempe, AZ 85281. (480) 965-3605. Among other collections, the Hayden Library houses the largest collection of Israeli pulp fiction outside of Israel. The Judaica collections support research and teaching pertaining to Jewish Studies on all ASU campuses. The collections offer a variety of reference tools, scholarly journals and books in print and electronic formats as well as microfilms, maps, videos, DVDs, and music CDs. These library materials cover all areas of research in the interdisciplinary field of Jewish Studies, with particular focus on the Modern era, including History, Religious Studies, Political Science, Yiddish belles-lettres, criticism, and nonfiction, Hebrew language, literature and criticism, Zionism and Israel Studies, and Latin American Judaica. A collection covers the history of Jewish communities in Latin America and their relations with other communities in the region as well as their intellectual and literary output in all mentioned languages. Coverage of works published in Yiddish in Argentina is particularly strong. (https://lib.asu.edu/hayden)

California
Bel and Jack M. Ostrow Library at American Jewish University and the Burton Sperber Memorial Jewish Community Library of Los Angeles (1948, incorporating the Jewish Community Library of Los Angeles). 15600 Mulholland Drive, Bel Air, CA 90077. (310) 440-1238. The Ostrow Library is designed to meet the needs of the University's faculty and students as well as scholars conducting research in all fields of Jewish culture and civilization. With approximately 110,000 print volumes, its holdings include: collections in Bible, Business Administration, Education, Hebrew and English Literature, Israel and Zionism, Jewish History and Archaeology, the Middle East, Philosophy, Rabbinics, Social Science, Theology, and Yiddish; the Rare Book Collection, including the Maslan Bible Collection of approximately 4000 Bibles from as early as the sixteenth century and the Kahlman-Friedmann Collection of Italian Judaica housed in the Lowy-Winkler Family Rare Book Room; the Milken Liberal Arts Collection comprised of acquisitions in the arts and humanities; a large collection of Jewish-themed books and videotapes formerly housed at the Jewish Community Library of Los Angeles as well as a growing

collection of DVDs and CDs; the Gindi Microfilm Collection, which contains manuscript collections from the Jewish Theological Seminary and several Jewish and Israeli newspapers from the turn of the twentieth century; and an extensive collection of dissertations published in the US on Jewish subjects. Students, staff, and visitors to the campus have access to databases containing thousands of journals as well as over 40,000 electronic books. (www.aju.edu/ostrow-academic-library)

Charles E. Young Research Library Department of Special Collections (Hebraica and Judaica Collections) at University of California, Los Angeles (1963). 280 Charles E. Young Drive North, Los Angeles, CA 90095. (310) 825-4732. Presently numbering in excess of 170,000 volumes, the UCLA Library Collections consist of materials relating to Jewish history, religion, language, society, and culture from around the world. While the largest number of holdings are in Hebrew and Yiddish, the collection includes materials in all western languages. Especially noteworthy are the Early Italian Hebraica Collection, which is included in the Ahmanson-Murphy Early Italian Printing Collection Hebrew manuscript holdings, including the Rosenberg-Lewin Collection of Hebrew Manuscripts, Cummings Collection of Hebraica and Judaica, and the Feldman Collection of Hebrew Manuscripts; and a collection of Yizkor books numbering over 500 volumes. (www.library.ucla.edu/yrl)

Doe Memorial Library of University of California, Berkeley Judaica Collection. University of California, Berkeley, CA 94720. (510) 642-6657. With more than 500,000 volumes, the UC Berkeley Judaica collection is one of the finest in the country. It includes Jewish religious texts and commentaries; rabbinic, medieval and modern Jewish history; modern Jewish thought; and comparative literature. More than 60,000 titles are in Hebrew or Yiddish. The collection supports the research and instructional activities of faculty and students in a number of interdisciplinary fields as well as the joint Ph.D. program in Judaic Studies with the Graduate Theological Union. The relevant fields include Near Eastern languages and literature; Talmudic studies, including the Babylonian and Palestinian Talmuds and subsequent texts and commentaries; rabbinic, medieval, and modern Jewish history throughout the world; modern Jewish thought; and comparative literature, including works in Hebrew, Yiddish, English, and other languages. (http://jewishstudies.berkeley.edu/affiliates-resources)

Judaica and Hebraica Collections at Stanford University Libraries (1985). Cecil H. Green Library, 557 Escondido Mall, Stanford, CA 94305. (650) 725-1054. /is (650) 723-1493. The Judaica and Hebraica Collections in the Stanford University Libraries support research and instruction in all aspects of Jewish Studies: history; literature; linguistics; cultural studies; contemporary social, political and cultural developments in the US, Israel, and throughout the world. The Judaica and Hebraica collections at Stanford include particularly extensive coverage of the following areas: Hebrew and Yiddish literature; Hebrew language and linguistics; and Jewish cultural, economic, political, social, religious history and material culture. Stanford has an impressive research base covering the full expanse of Jewish culture in Hebrew, Yiddish, Ladino, German, Russian, and many other languages. (http://library.stanford.edu/guides/jewish-studies-resources)   (https://jewishstudies.stanford.edu/resources/judaica-and-hebraica-collections-sul)

Simon Wiesenthal Center Library and Archives (1978). 1399 South Roxbury Drive, Third Floor, Los Angeles, CA 90035. (310) 772-7605. The Simon Wiesenthal Library contains material for all ages and educational levels, in many languages, with primary emphasis on the Holocaust, genocide, antisemitism, and Jewish communities around the world. In addition to books and periodicals, the Library also holds many other formats, including videos (VHS and DVD), audio cassettes and CDs, educational kits, visual materials (posters, slides, etc.), and microfilm. The Archives is a repository for primary source material, including over 50,000 photographs, thousands of documents, diaries, letters, artifacts and memorabilia, artwork, and rare books. (www.wiesenthal.com/site/pp.asp?c=lsKWLbPJLnF&b=4441267)

Connecticut
Yale University Library Judaica Collection (1915). Sterling Memorial Library, 120 High Street, Room 335A, New Haven, CT 06511. (203) 432-7207. The Yale University Library Judaica holdings have grown slowly but steadily since the University's founding in 1701. Following the receipt of two major gifts in 1915, the Yale Library established a separate Judaica collection which is recognized as one of the major collections of Judaica in the country. The focus of the 95,000 volume collection, which includes manuscripts and rare books, is biblical, classical, medieval, and modern periods of Jewish literature and history, and supports the research needs of the faculty and students of the University's Judaic Studies Program and those of the broader academic community. The social, religious, and cultural lives of the Jewish people are reflected in the Library's collections. Religious law, Sephardic studies, rabbinics, Jewish philosophy and modern thought, talmudica, and Hebrew, Yiddish, and Ladino languages and literatures are all represented in the collection. (https://web.library.yale.edu/international/judaica-collection)

District of Columbia
I. Edward Kiev Judaica Collection, Gelman Library at The George Washington University (1996). 2130 H Street, NW, Washington, DC 20052. (202) 994-6558. The Gelman Library has diverse and wide-ranging holdings in the field of Hebrew and Judaic studies, including modern Judaica, rare books, and archival materials. Foremost among these is the I. Edward Kiev Collection, the leading university collection of pre-modern Hebraica and Judaica, and of Hebrew and Jewish bibliographic literature, in the Washington Research Library Consortium. The Kiev Collection holds more than 28,000 volumes, composed largely of English, Hebrew, and German works published between the eighteenth and twentieth centuries. (www.library.gwu.edu/collections/kiev)

Library of Congress Hebraic Section (African and Middle Eastern Division) (1914). 101 Independence Avenue, SE, Thomas Jefferson Building, Room LJ220, Washington, DC 20540. (202) 707-5422. Long recognized as one of the world's leading research centers for the study of Hebraica and Judaica, the Hebraic Section serves as the Library's primary access point for reference and research activities related to the Ancient Near East, pre-Islamic Egypt, Biblical Studies, Jewish Studies, and ancient and modern Israel. The section has custody of materials in a variety of formats in Hebrew and its cognates, including Yiddish, Ladino, Judeo-Arabic, and

Judeo-Persian as well as Amharic, Coptic, and Syriac. (www.loc.gov/rr/amed/hs/hshome.html)

Florida
Isser and Rae Price Library of Judaica at University of Florida (1981). PO Box 117010, Gainesville, FL 32611. (352) 273-2865. With holdings of over 110,000 volumes, and digital collections comprising more than 180,000 pages of content, the Isser and Rae Price Library of Judaica at the University of Florida, is considered the foremost Jewish studies research collection in the southeastern US. In terms of many of its scarce late nineteenth to early twentieth century imprints, it ranks among the top 20 academic libraries in the world. Furthermore, many thousands of its titles in Hebrew and Yiddish are held by less than ten libraries in the US. A Jewish studies collection of notable depth, scope and singularity, its diversified holdings in English, Hebrew, and other languages support scholarship in virtually every aspect of the Jewish experience, with materials relevant to the ancient, medieval, and modern periods. The Library was built on the core collection of Rabbi Leonard C. Mishkin of Chicago which, at the time of its acquisition in 1977, was the largest personal library of Judaica and Hebraica in the US. (http://cms.uflib.ufl.edu/judaica/Index.aspx) (http://cms.uflib.ufl.edu/judaica/libraryhistory.aspx)

Molly S. Fraiberg Judaica Collections of S. E. Wimberly Library at Florida Atlantic University (1989). 777 Glades Road, Boca Raton, FL 33431. (561) 297-3787. The Molly S. Fraiberg Judaica Collections contain over 70,000 items, including books, periodicals, sheet music, audio-visual materials, and artifacts, a large number of which is in Yiddish, Hebrew, and English. The Fraiberg Collections support the Judaic Studies program at the main campus of Florida Atlantic University, but also serve the needs of the local community. This Judaica library is one of the largest in the southeastern US. (www.library.fau.edu/geninfo/online_tour/speccoll.htm)

Illinois
Asher Library at Spertus Institute for Jewish Learning and Leadership (mid 19350s) (1974). 610 South Michigan Avenue, Chicago, IL 60605. (312) 322-1712. One of North America's largest Jewish libraries, Asher Library serves a diverse populace locally, nationally, and internationally, with a special emphasis on developing collections and services for Spertus students and the Jewish community. Its collection includes Jewish-interest fiction and nonfiction books, plus periodicals, films, and music from all over the world. Asher Library is home to the Chicago Jewish Archives, which collects historical material of Chicago individuals, families, synagogues, and organizations. (www.spertus.edu/library)

Ludwig Rosenberger Library of Judaica at University of Chicago Library (1980). Joseph Regenstein Library, 1100 East 57th Street, Chicago, IL 60637. (773) 702-8442. Hebrew books and Judaica in other languages have been an integral part of the University of Chicago Library since its founding in 1892. Built by many bibliographers and subject and language specialists over the years, the collections are shaped by staff and faculty of the University and by the individuals whose private collections have been acquired and integrated into the Library's collections. The largest of these is the Ludwig Rosenberger Library of Judaica, a collection of over 17,000 titles documenting the social, cultural, and political history of the Jewish people. The Rosenberger Collection is available in the Special Collections Research Center on the first floor of the Joseph Regenstein Library. The Judaica and Hebraica collection today includes tens of thousands of physical volumes as well as rich resources in microfilm. (http://guides.lib.uchicago.edu/jewishstudies) (www.lib. uchicago.edu/scrc/rarebooks/ludwig-rosenberger-collection-judaica

Saul Silber Memorial Library at Hebrew Theological College. 7135 North Carpenter Road, Skokie, IL 60077. (847) 982-2500. The Saul Silber Memorial Library is the largest rabbinic library in the Midwest. It is the prime academic library that supports the curricula and research of faculty and students of Hebrew Theological College. The Library has over 70,000 items that include books in Hebrew, English, and other languages, periodicals, pamphlets, museum objects, microforms, computer CD-ROMs, video and audio tapes, music CDs, manuscripts, and art work. The strongest areas of the collections are in Rabbinic literature (classical texts, their commentaries, and Rabbinic Responsa), Bible, Holocaust Studies, and Jewish history. The Library also has a significant collection on the history of Jews in Chicago. (www.htc.edu)

Maryland

Baltimore Hebrew Institute Judaic Collection at Albert S. Cook Library of Towson University (formerly Joseph Meyerhoff Library at Baltimore Hebrew Institute) (1978). 8000 York Road, Towson, MD 21252. (410) 704-2456. The Baltimore Hebrew Institute Judaic Collection is a specialized collection of Jewish studies that includes material on the Bible and archaeology; Jewish history and rabbinics; Jewish philosophy, political science, and sociology; and Jewish education, language and literature, and the arts. The BHI collection is a rich resource for information about Jewish history, culture, and tradition. Its contents reflect the applied knowledge of Judaism within the context of world civilization, and its scope spans the entire breadth of world history. The collection includes rare books, artifacts, World War II-era Jewish Cultural Reconstruction books, Holocaust survivor testimonies, and Yizkor (memorial) books from across Europe. (http://libraries.towson. edu/using-the-libraries/collections) (https://libraries.towson.edu/university-archives/collections/baltimore-hebrew-institute-special-collections)

Massachusetts

Judaica Collection in Widener Library at Harvard University (1962). Judaica Division, Widener Library Room M, Harvard Library, Harvard University, Cambridge, MA 02138. (617) 495-2985 or (617) 495-3335. The Harvard Judaica Collection documents the life and culture of the Jewish people throughout history — in all places, all languages, and all formats—with particular comprehensive coverage of life and culture in the State of Israel. This collection is a unique research resource for Harvard and the global scholarly community, with materials from around the world in over 50 languages. The current collection has over 820,000 titles (not including digital images), with over 22,000 new titles added each year. The Judaica Collection includes books, pamphlets, periodicals, newspapers, maps, posters, broadsides, photographs, microforms, sound and video recordings, electronic databases, and other formats. Special emphasis is placed on materials in Hebrew, particularly from the State of Israel, which makes up the largest component of the collection The Judaica Collection is a significant part of Harvard Library, and makes up roughly 5% of its collection. Hebrew is the eighth most represented language in the Library's collections. The Judaica Digital Images collection is the largest collection of HOLLIS Images, at over 5.5 million images and growing. (https://library.harvard.edu/collections/judaica-collection)

Yiddish Book Center (1980). 1021 West Street, Amherst, MA 01002. (413) 256-4900. World's first Yiddish museum, featuring extensive exhibits on Yiddish and Jewish culture, in addition to its extensive library of Yiddish books. (www.yiddishbookcenter.org)

Judaica Collection of Robert D. Farber University Archives and Special Collections Department at Brandeis University. Goldfarb Library, Library & Technology Services, MS 045, 415 South Street, Waltham, MA 02453. (781) 736-7777 or (781) 736-4688. An integral component of Special Collections, the Judaica Collection comprises more than 200,000 works housed throughout the Library. The collection documents all aspects of Jewish history, religion, and culture, with a particular focus on the Bible, rabbinics, Jewish philosophy and mysticism, Hebrew and Yiddish literature, and the Holocaust. The microfilm, microfiche, and electronic collections include a wide array of English, German, Hebrew, and Yiddish newspapers; reproductions of Hebrew manuscripts; works on Israel, Zionism, and American Jewish history; the personal papers of Abba Hillel Silver and Chaim Weizmann; rabbinical texts; important bibliographic databases; and other relevant research tools and collections. Many rare and unique Judaica materials are located in Special Collections, including incunabula, rare books, and manuscripts; artifacts; collections documenting the Leo Frank case and the Dreyfus Affair; the personal papers of Louis D. Brandeis, E. M. Broner, Helmut Hirsch, Rose Jacobs, and Stephen S. Wise; and many others. (http://lts.brandeis.edu/research/archives-speccoll/intro.html)

Rae and Joseph Gann Library at Hebrew College. 160 Herrick Road, Newton Centre, MA 02459. (617) 559-8750. The Rae and Joseph Gann Library offers the College community and the public extraordinarily rich collections in print, media, and electronic formats, focusing on Judaica, Jewish studies, and Jewish education for adults and children. The Gann Library is one of the finest Judaica libraries in New England. The Library houses some 90,000 volumes of Jewish studies and Judaica, primarily in Hebrew and English, and includes: multilingual literature, including works in Yiddish, German, Russian and Japanese; music, art and film in multimedia formats; Jewish education curricula for primary and secondary school settings; significant holdings in Responsa literature, Hasidism, Kabbalah, the Middle East, Israel and Jewish ethics, among others; archival documents, rare books and manuscripts in print and microform; and books on reserve and course reserve material. (www.hebrewcollege.edu/library)

Michigan
Judaica Collection of Harlan Hatcher Graduate Library at University of Michigan. Harlan Hatcher Graduate Library South, Judaica-Hebraica Unit, 913 South University Avenue, Ann Arbor, MI 48109. (734) 764-0400. The Judaica holdings of the University of Michigan's Hatcher Graduate Library are rich and extensive. The collection originated in the Library's support of research and instruction in ancient Near Eastern and Hebrew bible studies. Over the years, the Judaica and Hebraica components developed into a diverse and independent collection that supports students, teachers, and the Jean and Samuel Frankel Center for Judaic Studies. The Library's Judaica collection has grown into one that can be favorably compared in depth and title count with the larger collections in other major North American universities and research institutions. The collection includes more than 55,000 titles in Hebrew and Yiddish, as well as Ladino, Aramaic, and other Jewish languages, while Western language Judaica holdings number approximately 43,000. The collection is particularly strong in Modern Hebrew literature, Jewish history, the history of Israel, Judaism, and Hebrew bible studies. Annually, the Library adds about 1000 Hebrew and Yiddish titles to the collection and 1500 Jewish studies titles in Western languages. In addition to the Graduate Library's collections of books and periodicals, the Special Collections Library holds a growing number of rare Hebraica books and manuscripts. (https://lsa.umich.edu/judaic/resources/library-collections/harlan-hatcher-graduate-library.html) (http://guides.lib.umich.edu/Judaica)

New York Metropolitan Area
American Jewish Historical Society Library (1892). 15 West 16th Street, New York, NY 10011. (212) 294-6160 or (917) 606-8217. The American Jewish Historical Society library consists of approximately 50,000 volumes, including both books and serials (journals and periodicals), which are non-circulating. Some of the major topics represented in the library collection are American Jewish religious, intellectual, political, and economic life; Jewish participation in the visual and performing arts; the geographic origins of American Jewry; Jewish immigration to the Americas; gender relations and family structure in American Jewish life; antisemitism; regional and local histories; and Zionism. The Library supports the Archival Collections. The Library also has an open-stack reference collection that researchers may use, consisting of encyclopedias, yearbooks, genealogical reference sources, bibliographies, biographical dictionaries, atlases, and many other useful American Jewish reference publications, which are integrated with the collections of the Leo Baeck Institute, American Sephardi Federation, and the YIVO Institute for Jewish Research in the Reading Room of the Center for Jewish History. This combined reference collection consists of approximately 3000 volumes and includes important resources for research on American, Sephardic, Eastern European, and German Jewry. (www.ajhs.org/library)

   Central Chabad Lubavitch Library (formerly **Library of Agudas Chassidei Chabad-Ohel Yosef Yitzchak Lubavitch**) (1992). 770 Eastern Parkway, Brooklyn, NY 11213. (718) 493-1537. The Central Chabad Lubavitch Library is a research library owned by Agudas Chassidei Chabad (Association of Chabad Chasidim) that contains books on Jewish topics dating back to the earliest days of Jewish publishing. It is one of the largest and most prominent Jewish libraries in the world. The Library is home to 250,000 books, mostly in Hebrew and Yiddish, many of which are rare and unique to the Library. More than 100,000 letters, artifacts, and pictures belonging to and written by and for the seven Lubavitcher Rebbes of Chabad and their Hasidim are included in the collection. Also included in the collection is the siddur of the Baal Shem Tov. Handwritten manuscripts on Chabad philosophy are among the most prized elements of the collection. While the bulk of the collection is comprised of works on Chabad Hasidic philosophy, many works are of more general interest. The Library is utilized by Chabad and general Judaic scholars and viewed by thousands of visitors each year. (www.chabadlibrary.org)

Dorot Jewish Division of the New York Public Library (1897). Stephen A. Schwarzman Building, 476 Fifth Avenue, First Floor, Room 111, New York, NY 10018. (212) 930-0601. The Dorot Jewish Division, which is responsible for administering, developing, and promoting one of the world's great collections of Hebraica and Judaica, contains a comprehensive and balanced chronicle of the religious and secular history of the Jewish people in over a quarter of a million books, microforms, manuscripts, newspapers, periodicals, and ephemera from all over the world. Primary source materials are especially rich in the following areas: Jews in the US, especially in New York in the age of immigration; Yiddish theater; Jews in the land of Israel through 1948; Jews in early modern Europe, especially Jewish-Gentile relations; Christian Hebraism; antisemitism; and world Jewish newspapers and periodicals of the nineteenth and twentieth centuries. The Dorot Jewish Division contains the most extensive collection (over 750) in the US of Yizkor (memorial) books, which document the history of Jewish communities destroyed in the Holocaust, most of which have been digitized and are available for viewing online. (www.nypl.org/about/divisions/jewish-division)

Judaica Collection of Gould Law Library at Touro Law Center. Gould Law Library, Touro College Jacob D. Fuchsberg Law Center, 255 Eastview Drive, Central Islip, NY 11722. (631) 761-7160 or (631) 761-7152. The Gould Law Library's Judaica Collection, with materials representing Jewish law, history, and philosophy from biblical times to the present day, supports Touro Law Center courses on Jewish law as well as the Jewish Law Institute and the Institute on Holocaust Law and International Human Rights. Scholars and members of the Jewish are also welcome to use the collection. Included in the collection are editions of important Jewish texts in English and Hebrew, including the Tanakh (Jewish Bible); Mishna; Babylonian and Jerusalem Talmuds; Mishneh Torah of Maimonides; Turim; Shulhan Arukh and halakhah (legal literature); commentaries, novellae, and responsa of acknowledged Rabbinic scholars; and modern works on issues of Jewish law, philosophy, and history. The collection includes extensive materials related to antisemitism, with a special emphasis on the Holocaust. (www.tourolaw.edu/LawLibrary/?pageid=346)

Library of The Jewish Theological Seminary (1893). 3080 Broadway, New York, NY 10027. (212) 678-8844. Serving the students and faculty of JTS and scholars and researchers around the world, the Library of JTS is home to more than 400,000 circulating volumes. Its collection also includes manuscripts, rare printed books, periodicals, scrolls, ketubot (marriage contracts), ephemeral materials, musical scores, sound recordings, moving images, graphic arts, and archives, making it the largest and most extensive collection of Hebraic and Judaic material in the Western Hemisphere and one of the greatest Judaic studies libraries in the world. The Library has an exceptional collection of rare materials, including the world's largest collection (about 11,000) of Hebrew manuscripts, the most complete collection of early Hebrew printed books (incunables), 43,000 fragments from the Cairo Genizah, and extensive archives, including papers representing the history of Jews in the US, and the Conservative Movement in particular, during the twentieth century, and significant Jewish music archives. (www.jtsa.edu/library)

Library of the Leo Baeck Institute (1955). 15 West 16th Street, New York, NY 10011. (212) 744-6400 or (212) 294-8340. The Library of the Leo Baeck Institute is internationally recognized as the most comprehensive repository for books documenting the history and culture of German-speaking Jewry. Over 80,000 volumes and 1600 periodical titles provide important primary and secondary material. Rich in rarities ranging from early sixteenth century writings to Moses Mendelssohn and Heinrich Heine, first editions and dedication copies of works by more recent prominent writers, many of its volumes were salvaged from famous Jewish libraries that were confiscated and dispersed by the Nazis. Most of the collection deals with central European Jewry during the nineteenth and early twentieth centuries. It also includes material dating back as far as the sixteenth century and is as current as the Jewish population in Germany today. The focus of the collection is on the diverse culture of German-speaking Jewry, especially in the arts, sciences, literature, philosophy, and religion. (www.lbi.org/collections/library)

Lillian Goldman Reading Room at the Center for Jewish History (1999). 15 West 16th Street, New York, NY 10011. (212) 294-8301. The Lillian Goldman Reading Room is the gateway for exploring the diverse history of the Jewish people through the collections housed at the Center for Jewish History. The open-stack collection has reference texts and general information, consisting of 3000 titles, as well as all major publications of the Center partners. The Reading Room has developed an extensive electronic resource library that is available through public computer terminals. Archive and Library collections consist of 500,000 volumes in multiple languages (e.g., Hebrew, Yiddish, Russian, German, Polish, French) from many time periods, as well as over 100 million documents, including organizational records and personal papers, photographs, multimedia recordings, posters, art, and artifacts. (www.cjh.org/scholarship/lillian-goldman-reading-room)

Lillie Goldstein Traveling Judaica Collection of the Gould Law Library at Touro Law Center. Gould Law Library, Touro College Jacob D. Fuchsberg Law Center, 255 Eastview Drive, Central Islip, NY 11722. (631) 761-7152. The Lillie Goldstein Judaica Collection, with its unique designation as a traveling library, was developed to further Touro Law Center's goal of presenting Jewish thought and learning, particularly the Jewish legal tradition, within a scholarly framework.

Established to make available to law schools without Judaica collections the resources necessary to offer courses in Jewish law, the collection includes more than 420 titles in over 700 volumes in Hebrew and/or English, which are duplicates of the core halakha (Jewish law) materials found in the Gould Law Library's Judaica Collection, as well as other materials chosen to enrich the study of Jewish law. The Lillie Goldstein Traveling Judaica Collection is offered as an interlibrary loan for a semester or for an academic year. (www.tourolaw.edu/LawLibrary/?pageid=347)

Mendel Gottesman Library of Hebraica/Judaica at Yeshiva University (1969). 2520 Amsterdam Avenue, New York, NY 10033. (642) 592-4190. The Mendel Gottesman Library of Hebraica/Judaica is one of the world's great Judaic library collections and the Jewish Studies research center at Yeshiva University's Wilf Campus. Occupying three levels in the Gottesman Library Building, the Library offers services and collections for advanced scholarship as well as for the student just beginning to explore the field. With over 300,000 physical volumes, and access to more than 50,000 electronic-journals, several hundred databases, and 428,000 electronic book titles shared with other libraries at the Wilf and Beren Campuses, the Library provides students and faculty members with a vast array of information sources. The Library is particularly strong in the areas of Bible, Rabbinic literature, Jewish history, Jewish philosophy, and Hebrew language and literature. Rare books and manuscript collections as well as archival materials complementtheLibrary'sholdings.(https://library.yu.edu/c.php?g=570456&p=3931655)

Rare Book & Manuscript Library of Columbia University: Judaica Collection (1859). Butler Library, 6th Floor East, 535 West 114th Street, MC1127, New York, NY 10027. (212) 854-8046 or (212) 854-5590. Columbia University has been collecting rare Hebraica and Judaica for over 120 years. The Columbia Judaica collection became truly significant, however, through a generous donation in 1892 from Temple Emanuel, the oldest Reform congregation in New York City. Today, there are about 125,000 volumes in the Judaica collection. The Judaica collection currently contains about 1600 manuscripts, 29 incunabula, 350 sixteenth-century books, thousands of books from the seventeenth to eighteenth centuries, and various archival material relating to prominent people in Jewish Studies. Columbia's Hebrew manuscript collection is one of the largest of its kind in North America and is very diverse, covering many different times and places. The Library also includes one of the most important collections for the study of Byzantine Jewry. Topics include philosophy, kabbalah (including some early works and many manuscripts from the Lurianic school), liturgy, Jewish law, Rabbinic texts and related commentaries, poetry, Bible and its exegesis, responsa, letters from individuals and communities, historical documents, ketubot (marriage contracts), documents from the Cairo Genizah, and other general literature. The collections are open for research and reference use by all members of the Columbia University community and the public. (www.library.columbia.edu/locations/rbml/about.html)

YIVO Library (1925) (1940). 15 West 16th Street, New York, NY 10011. (212) 246-6080, ext. 5102. The YIVO Library is the world's only academic library specializing in the history, languages, literature, culture, folklore, and religious traditions of East European Jewry. Its holdings are particularly strong in documentation of Jewish history, culture, and religion in Eastern Europe; the Holocaust period; the experience of immigration to the US; antisemitism; and the continuing influence of Ashkenazic Jewish culture today. The YIVO Library contains nearly 400,000 volumes of books and periodical editions in twelve major languages, along with pamphlets, periodicals, letterheads, and more, including the unique Vilna Collection of 40,000 volumes with 25,000 rabbinical works from as early as the sixteenth century and treasures rescued by the so-called "Paper Brigade," Jews who risked their lives to hide books and documents inside and outside the Vilna ghetto, thus saving them from Nazi pillage. (Manuscripts and other special collections are held by the YIVO Archives.) The YIVO Library is especially strong in Yiddish literature and theater, Yiddish linguistics and lexicography, and historical writings, including many books and serials found in no other research library in the world. Approximately 40,000 volumes are in Yiddish, making the YIVO Library the largest collection of Yiddish-language works in the world. Best described as a "collection of collections," the YIVO Library has been built through the amalgamation of a number of private and institutional libraries over the last century. (www.yivo.org/Library)

Ohio

American Jewish Periodical Center at Hebrew Union College-Jewish Institute of Religion (1957). Klau Library, Cincinnati, 3101 Clifton Avenue, Cincinnati, OH 45220. (513) 487-3276. The Lucille Klau Carothers American Jewish Periodical Center of Hebrew Union College-Jewish Institute of Religion houses a microform collection of American Jewish newspapers, journals, and magazines published in eight languages. The Center also houses the Klau Library's collection of microform materials. (www.huc.edu/research/libraries/collections/ajpc_archive)

Klau Library in Cincinnati at Hebrew Union College-Jewish Institute of Religion (1975). 3101 Clifton Avenue, Cincinnati, OH 45220. (513) 487-3276. The Klau Library in Cincinnati functions both as a campus library and as the main research library within the HUC-JIR Library system. It acquires, preserves, and provides access to materials in printed, manuscript, and other formats, supporting the teaching functions of the Rabbinic and Graduate programs and meeting the research needs of its various users: the faculty, students, and staff of HUC-JIR Cincinnati; the residents of the Cincinnati metropolitan area; and the broader Judaic academic and general community both in the US and abroad. As the main research library in the system, the Cincinnati Library provides both its depth of resources and various library services to the other HUC-JIR libraries. With 436,000 printed books and many thousands of special collection items including manuscripts, computer files, microforms, maps, broadsides, bookplates, tablets, and stamps, the Klau Library in Cincinnati has the largest Judaica collection in the western hemisphere and is second in size only to the Judaica collection at the Jewish National and University Library in Jerusalem. The Klau Library is one of the three conservators in the world of the negatives of the Dead Sea Scrolls. (www.huc.edu/research/libraries/cincinnati-klau-library)

Pennsylvania
Library of the Herbert D. Katz Center for Advanced Judaic Studies at University of Pennsylvania (formerly **Library of Dropsie College for Hebrew and Cognate Learning**) (ca. 1913). 420 Walnut Street, Philadelphia, PA 19106. (215) 746-1290 or (215) 746-5154. The Library at the Katz Center holds approximately 200,000 volumes, including 32 (17 Hebrew and 15 Latin) incunabula and over 8000 rare printed works, mainly in Hebrew, English, German, French, Yiddish, Arabic, Latin, and Ladino. The rare Hebrew editions offer specimens from a variety of Hebrew printing houses around the world; particularly strong are holdings of early modern rare books printed on the Italian peninsula, including nearly 20% of all Venetian Hebrew imprints.

The Judaica collections at the Penn Libraries, as a whole, constitute one of the world's largest and richest resources on the history and culture of Jews. The collections are dispersed, mainly, among five library locations. The combined holdings currently total between 350,000-400,000 volumes in 24 languages and dialects and in a range of formats from manuscripts to electronic resources. Quantitatively, this amounts to one of the largest Judaica collections in the world. Qualitatively, these holdings cover almost every period and area of Jewish life from the Biblical era to contemporary America and support both undergraduate education and advanced research. (www.library.upenn.edu/lkcajs)

Mordecai M. Kaplan Library at Reconstructionist Rabbinical College (1999). 1299 Church Road, Wyncote, PA 19095. (215) 576-0800, ext. 234 or est. 233. The Mordecai M. Kaplan Library, housed in the Goldyne Savad Library Center, serves the needs of students, faculty and community members. Named after the intellectual founder of Reconstructionist Judaism, the Library offers an excellent collection of Judaica and Hebraica, and Reconstructionist movement publications. The Library contains approximately 50,000 books on Judaica, primarily in English, Hebrew, and Yiddish, as well as periodicals and other materials. (www.rrc.edu/resources/goldyne-savad-library-center)

Robert and Molly Freedman Jewish Music Archive at University of Pennsylvania Annenberg Rare Book and Manuscript Library (1996). The Robert and Molly Freedman Jewish Music Archive, largely regarded as the world's premier private collection of Yiddish music, includes thousands of Yiddish folk and art songs, theater music, comedy, and klezmer music in songbooks, reference works and sound recordings. The music in this collection is a key to Jewish life in Europe and America in the twentieth century. In what scholars consider an incomparable resource, a database in English, Hebrew, and Yiddish of tens of thousands of entries exhaustively index the bulk of the collection and is capable of referencing artists, titles, literary and Biblical references, poems, and other categories of particular interest., making it possible to compare various settings and renditions of familiar songs as well as to discover unknown settings of Yiddish literature to music. (http://sceti.library.upenn.edu/freedman)   (www.giving.library.upenn.edu/your-impact/robert-and-molly-freedman-jewish-music-archive)

Tuttleman Library at Gratz College (formerly **Gratz College Library**) (ca. 1916). 7605 Old York Road, Melrose Park, PA 19027. (215) 635-7300. The

Tuttleman Library, a specialized academic library of Hebraica and Judaica, is a major national and international Judaic resource and serves as the Jewish Public Library of Greater Philadelphia. The Library houses approximately 100,000 items, including books, periodicals, sound recordings in various formats, films, and rare books. The Library's circulating collection includes books on every Jewish topic from Bible and Talmud to modern Jewish fiction, Middle Eastern history and politics, and Jewish life throughout the world. The Theodore H. and Leah Cook Reference Collection includes standard reference works in Judaica and Hebraica, The Catholic Encyclopedia, the Encylopaedia of Islam, as well as on topics including the Holocaust, Middle East, art, music, and Jewish life throughout the world. The Wolk Family Periodical Center includes current subscriptions with extensive holdings of back issues in both scholarly and popular periodicals. Library materials are available in a variety of languages, including English, Hebrew, Yiddish, Ladino, Spanish, German and more. (www.gratz.edu/tuttleman-library)

Tennessee

Mary and Harry Zimmerman Judaica Collection of Jean and Alexander Heard (Divinity) Library at Vanderbilt University (1945) (1988). 419 21st Avenue South, Nashville, TN 37203. (615) 322-2865. The Zimmerman Judaica Collection of books and journals covers thousands of years of Jewish research, culture, and history. It contains encyclopedias of Jewish history, journals, microfilm, and books on every facet of Jewish life and learning-in English, Hebrew, German, Yiddish, and other languages-covering some 4000 years of faith, history, commentary and customs. The collection, now numbering well over 20,000 titles, was begun in 1945 with the gift of the professional library of Professor Ismar Elbogen. Today, the collection is impressive in breadth and depth, and includes textually-oriented study (Jewish works on the Hebrew Scriptures, Mishna, Talmud, Gaonic literature, and liturgy); tradition-oriented research (studies dealing with the religious and cultural dimensions of the Jewish tradition); and historical study (works treating the history of the Jewish people from ancient times to the present). The acquisition of the collection of Professor Nahum N. Glatzer in 1991 strengthened the existing collection and broadened its scope, particularly with its focus on nineteenth and twentieth century European Judaism, and included manuscript and correspondence materials relating to Martin Buber, Franz Rosenzweig, and Leopold Zunz. (www.library. vanderbilt.edu/divinity/services/judaica.php)

14.6.3   Judaic Research, Canada

Jewish Public Library (1914). Cummings House Building, 5151 Côte-Sainte-Catherine Road, Montreal, QC H3W 1M6. (514) 345-2627. The Jewish Public Library recognizes its responsibility to provide a full range of library services to meet the cultural, educational, informational, and recreational needs of all segments of the Jewish community of Montreal. The Jewish Public Library is unique among

Montreal's—and the world's—Jewish institutions. A full service lending and research library containing North America's largest circulating Judaica collection, it is an internationally-recognized resource while also meeting the informational, educational and recreational needs of Jewish Montrealers of all ages and backgrounds. The Main Library holds over 150,000 items in five official languages (English, French, Hebrew, Yiddish and Russian); the 30,000-item Norman Berman Children's Library also offers many activities for children up to 14 years of age; and the Archives help preserve and honor Canada's Jewish history for generations to come. The Library also maintains special, non-circulating collections that include rare books; Jewish Canadiana (newspaper and magazine clippings, pamphlets, chapbooks, and unpublished manuscripts reflecting Canadian Jewry's artistic, cultural, and intellectual life); ephemeral collection (contemporary accounts of Jewish life in the Diaspora and Israel, from a variety of European newspapers in Yiddish, Hebrew, Russian, and other languages); Yizkor (memorial) books; photograph, sheet music, and multimedia archive; and periodicals and academic journals. The Library is also a key provider of adult cultural and educational programming for the community. (www.jewishpubliclibrary.org/en)

14.6.4   Judaic Research, Online Libraries

Jewish Virtual Library (formerly **Jewish Student Online Research Center, JSOURCE**) (1997). AICE, 2810 Blaine Drive, Chevy Chase, MD 20815. (301) 565-3918. The Jewish Virtual Library is a comprehensive online source for information about Jewish history, Israel, US-Israel relations, the Holocaust, Antisemitism, and Judaism. It is a cyber-encyclopedia whose goal is to provide the basic information users need to be informed of the facts about Jewish history and current affairs. It currently has more than 25,000 articles and 10,000 images and is accessed by users in more than 230 countries and territories worldwide. Much of the information in the Library cannot be found anywhere else in the world. The Jewish Virtual Library is a "living" library; it is constantly updating, changing, and expanding. The Library currently has 15 wings: Antisemitism, Biography, History, Holocaust, Israel, Israel Education, Judaic Treasures, Maps, Myths & Facts, Politics, Religion, Travel, US & Israel, Vital Statistics, and Women. Each of these has numerous subcategories. The Library includes the Virtual Israel Experience, which is designed for anyone who plans to visit Israel or wants to learn more about the history of the Jewish state. The Library also includes the Virtual Jewish History World/Virtual Jewish History Tours, which allows users to virtually visit Jewish communities across the world to learn about their history and culture as well as about Jewish heritage, the development of Judaism, the changing nature of Jewish communities, and the connection between the Jewish past and present. (www.jewishvirtuallibrary.org)

Sefaria: A Living Library of Jewish Texts (2012). Sefaria is a free living library of Jewish texts and their interconnections, in Hebrew and in translation. Its scope is Torah in the broadest sense, from Tanakh to Talmud to Zohar to modern texts and all the volumes of commentary in between. Sefaria is created, edited, and annotated by an open community. Having digital texts enables the creation of new, interactive interfaces for the web, tablet, and mobile which allow students and scholars around the world to freely learn and explore the interconnections among Torah texts. (www.sefaria.org)

14.6.5   Holocaust Research, United States

Fortunoff Video Archive for Holocaust Testimonies (1982). Sterling Memorial Library, 130 Wall Street, New Haven, CT 06520. (203) 432-1879. The Fortunoff Video Archive for Holocaust Testimonies is a collection of over 4400 videotaped interviews with witnesses and survivors of the Holocaust which are available to researchers, educators, and the general public. These personal testimonies, which are comprised of over 10,000 recorded hours of videotape, are crucial documents for the education of students and community groups in an increasingly media-centered era. Testimonies were produced in cooperation with 37 affiliated projects across North America, South America, Europe, and Israel. The Fortunoff Archive and its affiliates recorded the testimonies of willing individuals with first-hand experience of the Nazi persecutions, including those in hiding, survivors, bystanders, resistants, and liberators. The Archive stands as a living memorial to counteract forgetfulness, ignorance and malicious denial. Part of Yale University's department of Manuscripts and Archives, the archive is located at Sterling Memorial Library and is open to the public by appointment. (https://web.library.yale.edu/testimonies)

Sala and Aron Samueli Holocaust Memorial Library (2005). Chapman University Leatherby Libraries-4th Floor, One University Drive, Orange CA 92866. (714) 532-7756. (714) 997-6815. The Sala and Aron Samueli Holocaust Memorial Library's permanent and rotating exhibits tell of the individual lives affected, and all too often ended, by the Holocaust. The Library's non-circulating collection includes photographs, documents, oral histories, and books, including a first edition in Dutch of the *Diary of Anne Frank*, as well as reference works to support research on the Holocaust in its historical context. (www.chapman.edu/research/institutes-and-centers/holocaust-education/samueli-holocaust-memorial-library.aspx)

Tauber Holocaust Library (2011). 2245 Post Street, San Francisco, CA 94115. (415) 449-3717. The Tauber Holocaust Library is a non-circulating library that offers a rich resource for students, scholars, researchers, and the general public. Part of the Holocaust Center of Jewish Family and Children's Services of San Francisco, the Peninsula, Marin and Sonoma Counties, this university-level library includes over 13,000 volumes, primarily in English but with a sizable number in more than 12 languages, with a special emphasis on the collection of rare, out-of-print Yizkor (memorial) volumes. The collection deals with every aspect of the Holocaust and focuses on: Jewish life in Europe before the Holocaust; Nazi rise to power and propaganda; Nazi racial theory and antisemitism; anti-Jewish policy and persecution in

Germany and occupied countries; flight, emigration, and refugee life; Nazi occupation of conquered Europe; deportation and execution of Jewish communities; ghettos and concentration camps (transit, labor, and extermination); reaction of the world community to events; resistance and partisan activities; liberation; war trials; post-war displaced persons and immigration; Holocaust memorials and memory; second and third generation healing; and Holocaust denial, in addition to other genocides and genocide in general. The Library holdings include the complete transcripts, in English and in German, of the Nuremberg and various other wartime trials, and the subsequent Nuremberg hearings involving the German military commanders on trial for war crimes, as well as the complete proceedings and transcripts in English of the Adolf Eichmann trial held in Israel. The Library also has a collection of rare books from the Holocaust era, including books published by the Nazi party and Julius Streicher's antisemitic press, and immediate post-war publications, documenting the events of the Holocaust for the first time in print. (https://holocaustcenter.jfcs.org/library-archives)

United States Holocaust Memorial Museum Library (1993). 100 Raoul Wallenberg Place SW, Washington, DC 20024. (202) 488-0400. The non-circulating Library is set up primarily to support research on-site or via online tools. The Library and Archives preserve and make available to the public in its reading rooms the historical record of the Holocaust and support the Museum's wide-ranging efforts in the areas of research, exhibition, publication, education, and commemoration. The Library's published materials include books, serials, historical newspapers, feature films and documentaries, CDs, and DVDs. (www.ushmm.org/research/library)

USC Shoah Foundation Institute for Visual History and Education (formerly **Survivors of the Shoah Visual History Foundation**) (1994). Leavey Library, 650 West 35th Street, Suite 114, Los Angeles, CA 90089. (213) 740-6001. Inspired by his experience making Schindler's List, Steven Spielberg established the Survivors of the Shoah Visual History Foundation to gather video testimonies from survivors and other witnesses of the Holocaust. While most of those who gave testimony were Jewish survivors, the Foundation also interviewed homosexual survivors, Jehovah's Witness survivors, liberators and liberation witnesses, political prisoners, rescuers and aid providers, Roma and Sinti (Gypsy) survivors, survivors of Eugenics policies, and war crimes trials participants. The vast majority of the Holocaust testimonies were recorded between 1994 and 1999. In January 2006, the Survivors of the Shoah Visual History Foundation became part of the Dana and David Dornsife College of Letters, Arts and Sciences at the University of Southern California in Los Angeles, where the testimonies in the Visual History Archive will be preserved in perpetuity. The change of name to the USC Shoah Foundation Institute for Visual History and Education reflects the broadened mission of the Institute: to overcome prejudice, intolerance, and bigotry — and the suffering they cause—through the educational use of the Institute's visual history testimonies. The Visual History Archive currently holds nearly 55,000 World War II era video and is the largest archive of its kind in the world. USC Shoah Foundation digitizes, indexes, and integrates into the Visual History Archive Holocaust testimony taken and owned by other museums and institutions to make them more accessible to scholars, students, educators, and the general public. Today the Institute reaches educators, students, researchers, and scholars on every continent and supports efforts to collect testimony from the survivors and witnesses of other genocides. (http://sfi.usc.edu)

Voice/Vision Holocaust Survivor Oral History Archive at Mardigian Library (1981). University of Michigan-Dearborn, Mardigian Library, 4901 Evergreen Road, Dearborn, MI 48128. (313) 583-6300. The Voice/Vision Archive promotes cultural, racial, and religious understanding through unprecedented worldwide access to its collection of Holocaust survivor narratives. The archive preserves the voices and memories of Holocaust survivors for future generations through powerful audio and video-taped oral histories of survivors who experienced the Holocaust. The archive represents an honest presentation—unembroidered, without dramatization, a scholarly yet austerely moving collection of information and insight. It supports Holocaust research by scholars, students, educators, and the general public through round-the-clock access to survivors' testimonies. (http://holocaust.umd. umich.edu)

14.6.6 Holocaust Research, Canada

Holocaust Literature Research Institute (1992). University of Western Ontario, 1151 Richmond Street, London, ON N6A 3K7. (519) 661-3820. The Holocaust Literature Research Institute was established to preserve Holocaust survivor memoirs. With more than 4000 volumes in 26 languages, this collection of Holocaust stories and witness accounts is the third largest in the world and the second largest outside of Israel. The primary role of the Institute is to search for, collect, and analyze Holocaust survivor narratives and witness accounts. Its activities include the compilation of a catalogued and annotated bibliography of survivor testimonials and witness accounts and building an online database; the development of educational programs, and providing resources and research support. The idea of the bibliography is to provide the public and the scholarly community with references and analysis to texts published by survivors. (www.hlri.ca)

Library and Archives Canada (LAC) 395 Wellington Street, Ottawa, ON K1A 0N4. (613) 996-5115. LAC has developed a publicly accessible thematic guide that provides a list of Holocaust-related material in its holdings. The Research Guide to Holocaust-related Holdings at LAC provides an introduction to material from both archival and published sources that relates to a range of events and decisions before, during and after the Second World War. The guide includes both government and personal documents. (www.bac-lac.gc.ca/eng/holocaust/Pages/holocaust.aspx)

14.6.7   Holocaust Research, Online Libraries

Women and the Holocaust: A Cyberspace of Their Own (2001). This is a website published by an amateur historian that provides a range of excellent resources on women and the Holocaust. The Holocaust produced a set of experiences, responses and memories for Jewish women that do not always parallel those of Jewish men, including the extra burdens of sexual victimization, pregnancy, childbirth, rape, abortion, the killing of newborns, and often the separation from children. Jewish women's lives were endangered as Jewish women, as mothers, and as caretakers of children. The Women and the Holocaust site aims to investigate the Final Solution and the Nazi's views on gender, and looks at the experience of women as victims of genocide, and also as the perpetrators and collaborators of the Nazi regime. The site provides primary sources, including survivor testimonies, a collection of personal poetry writings from Holocaust survivors and others, women's personal memories and letters related to their Holocaust experiences, a collection of articles and essays related to women survivors of the Holocaust and the women that came afterwards, articles and essays about women survivors from the perspective of their roles as mothers, tributes to certain individuals whose experiences and actions before, during, or after the Holocaust are distinctive and deserve special recognition, book and film reviews related to women survivors of the Holocaust and the women that came afterwards, a bibliography of important Holocaust works, and web links, as well as a good range of both academic and general articles and essays. These explore subjects like partisans and resistance fighters, forest-dwellers, survivors' stories, and women involved in the Nazi regime. (www.theverylongview.com/WATH)

Chapter 15
Transitions: Major Events, Honorees, and Obituaries

Ira M. Sheskin, Arnold Dashefsky, Ben Harris, Roberta Pakowitz, and Matthew Parent

This chapter provides a listing of major events in the North American Jewish communities from June 2018 to June 2019, a list of persons honored by the Jewish and general communities from 2018 to 2019, and a list of obituaries of North American Jews from July 2018 to May 2019.

JTA (www.jta.org) provided the material for Sect. 15.1.

The list of persons honored (Sect. 15.2) is presented in the following categories.

Jewish Book Awards
Academic Awards
Jewish Organization Awards
Media Awards
Secular Awards Given to North American Jews
Cultural/Sports/Pulitzer Awards Given to North American Jews
Lists of Influential Jews
US Jewish Politicians

I. M. Sheskin (✉)
Department of Geography and Jewish Demography Project, Sue and Leonard Miller Center for Contemporary Judaic Studies, University of Miami, Coral Gables, FL, USA
e-mail: isheskin@miami.edu

A. Dashefsky
Department of Sociology and Center for Judaic Studies and Contemporary Jewish Life, University of Connecticut, Storrs, CT, USA

B. Harris
JTA, New York, NY, USA

R. Pakowitz
Independent Researcher, Cooper City, FL, USA

M. Parent
Center for Judaic Studies and Contemporary Jewish Life, University of Connecticut, Storrs, CT, USA

© Springer Nature Switzerland AG 2020
A. Dashefsky, I. M. Sheskin (eds.), *American Jewish Year Book 2019*, American Jewish Year Book 119, https://doi.org/10.1007/978-3-030-40371-3_15

15.1 Major Events in the North American Jewish Communities

15.1.1 North American Year in Review June 2018–June 2019

15.1.1.1 June 2018

Twenty-six Jewish groups sign a letter calling the US policy of separating children from their migrant parents "unconscionable." The signatories included three major Jewish religious movements—Conservative, Reform, and Reconstructionist—as well as the American Jewish Committee, the Anti-Defamation League, HIAS, Jewish Women's International, the Jewish Council for Public Affairs and Uri L'Tzedek, an Orthodox social justice organization. https://www.jta.org/2018/06/14/news-opinion/26-jewish-groups-sign-letter-condemning-policy-separates-children-migrant-parents

"The Band's Visit," a musical based on an Israeli film about an Egyptian band stranded in a hardscrabble Negev town, dominates the 72nd annual Tony Awards, winning ten awards, including best musical. The play also took home trophies for best actor in a musical, best direction of a musical, and best original score. https://www.jta.org/2018/06/10/top-headlines/israeli-american-actor-wins-tony-bands-visit

An Israeli court convicts a 19-year-old American-Israeli teenager of making hundreds of bomb threats against Jewish community centers and schools around the US. Michael Kadar was convicted on several counts, including extortion, conspiracy to commit a crime, money laundering and assaulting a police officer. Kadar's threats forced widespread evacuations of American Jewish institutions and sparked fear of resurgent antisemitism in the first three months of 2017. https://www.jta.org/2018/06/28/news-opinion/american-israeli-man-convicted-jcc-bomb-threats

The US withdraws from the UN Human Rights Council, citing the body's bias against Israel. Nikki Haley, the US ambassador to the UN, said the council was "not worthy of its name" and that the decision to withdraw had come after a "good faith" effort to reform the body had failed. https://www.jta.org/2018/06/19/news-opinion/united-states/us-expected-leave-un-human-rights-council-israel-bias

15.1.1.2 July 2018

Jonathan Gold (see Sect. 15.3.1), the renowned Los Angeles food writer who in 2007 became the first restaurant critic to win a Pulitzer Prize, dies at 57. Gold was known for reviewing small, ethnic eateries and even food trucks located throughout the city with as much zest as expensive haute cuisine restaurants. https://www.jta.org/2018/07/22/united-states/jonathan-gold-restaurant-critic-showcased-los-angeles-neighborhoods-dies-57

Sociologist Steven M. Cohen is accused by several women of sexual misconduct, including allegations of inappropriate touching, sexual advances, and inappropriate remarks. A leading researcher of American Jewry, Cohen, who did not deny the allegations and apologized for them, subsequently resigned as director of the Berman Jewish Policy Archive and from his tenured professorship at Hebrew Union College—Jewish Institute of Religion. https://www.jta.org/2018/07/19/united-states/several-women-accuse-leading-jewish-sociologist-sexual-misconduct

Facebook founder Mark Zuckerberg says his company will not delete posts that deny the Holocaust. Zuckerberg, who has come under mounting criticism for permitting the dissemination of misinformation online, said that while he personally found Holocaust denial offensive, Facebook's purpose was not to censor people who say something untrue, only to prevent it spreading across the network. https://www.jta.org/2018/07/19/united-states/mark-zuckerberg-clarifies-remarks-not-deleting-holocaust-denial-posts-facebook

Richard Siegel (see Sect. 15.3.1), the co-editor of the seminal do-it-yourself publication "The Jewish Catalog," dies in Los Angeles at 70. The book, first published in 1973, offered instructions on everything from making a Passover Seder to protesting on behalf of Soviet Jewry. It became an instant best-seller, credited with empowering young Jews who felt alienated from synagogue life and popularizing an ethos of pluralism and gender egalitarianism. https://www.jta.org/2018/07/13/obituaries/richard-siegel-educator-co-edited-jewish-catalog-dead-70

Former NY State Assembly Speaker Sheldon Silver is sentenced to seven years in prison on federal corruption charges. Silver was convicted in a scheme in which a doctor agreed to refer patients to Silver's law firm, a deal that netted Silver over $3 million in referral fees and injury claims in exchange for providing the doctor $500,000 in taxpayer funds for research projects. In a separate scheme, Silver received $700,000 in referral fees from a real estate firm seen as illegal kickbacks by prosecutors. https://www.jta.org/2018/07/27/politics/ex-ny-assembly-speaker-sheldon-silver-gets-7-years-corruption

15.1.1.3   August 2018

The Centers for Disease Control says that one person has died and 17 were taken ill by an outbreak of salmonella in Empire Kosher chicken. Eight of those illnesses required hospitalization. The chicken company noted that "no data that connects this tragic event to our products," but that it is cooperating fully with investigators. https://www.jta.org/2018/08/29/united-states/1-dead-17-sick-from-salmonella-in-empire-kosher-chicken

A study by the Pew Research Center finds that nearly half of American Jews do not identify with organized religion. The survey of over 4700 respondents found that 28% of American Jews are "solidly secular" and another 17% believe in a higher power but have negative views of organized religion. https://www.jta.org/2018/08/29/united-states/nearly-half-of-us-jews-dont-identify-with-organized-religion-study-finds

Victims of Barry Freundel, the disgraced Washington Orthodox rabbi imprisoned for spying on women using the ritual bath adjacent to his synagogue, reached a $14.25 million settlement with the synagogue. Plaintiffs had originally sued the synagogue, Kesher Israel, for $100 million. Prosecutors identified more than 150 women who were videotaped by Freundel. https://www.jta.org/2018/08/28/united-states/victims-mikvah-peeping-rabbi-reach-14-25-million-settlement-synagogue

Neil Simon (see Sect. 15.3.1), the playwright responsible for such Broadway hits as "The Odd Couple" and "Lost in Yonkers," dies in New York at 91. The author of more than 30 plays and about as many movie screenplays, Simon was the winner of both a Pulitzer Prize and a Tony Award. He frequently plumbed the anxieties of middle-class American Jews and the family issues that plagued them in his work. https://www.jta.org/2018/08/26/united-states/award-winning-playwright-neil-simon-dies-91

Hebrew College agrees to sell its Newton, MA, campus 16 years after moving into the newly constructed facility designed by Israeli architect Moshe Safdie. The move allows the college, founded in 1921, to resolve all outstanding debt on the building.https://www.jta.org/2018/08/20/united-states/bostons-hebrew-college-sells-campus-shore-future

World Jewish Congress President Ronald Lauder harshly rebukes Israeli Prime Minister Benjamin Netanyahu and questions whether the Jewish state is "losing its way." The criticism, published in an opinion piece in the *New York Times*, was occasioned by a number of developments, including the arrest of a Conservative rabbi for conducting weddings, the exclusion of same-sex couples from a newly passed surrogacy law, and the adoption of a law declaring Israel the nation-state of the Jewish people. Lauder accused Netanyahu of damaging "the sense of equality and belonging of Israel's Druze, Christian, and Muslim citizens." The op-ed follows a March, 2018, op-ed in *The Times* in which Lauder criticized Israel's turn away from the two-state solution and warned that Israel was turning into a semi-theocracy. https://www.jta.org/2018/08/14/culture/ronald-lauder-helped-make-benjamin-netanyahu-prime-minister-now-hes-publicly-opposing

15.1.1.4   September 2018

Leslie Moonves resigns as CEO of the CBS network after six women accuse him of sexual misconduct. The allegations, published in the *New Yorker*, follow six earlier accusations against Moonves published in July 2018. Moonves denied the claims. https://www.jta.org/2018/09/12/united-states/leslie-moonves-resigns-at-cbs-after-6-more-women-accuse-him-of-sexual-misconduct

Rabbi Rachel Cowan (see Sect. 15.3.1), a pioneer in the Jewish healing movement, dies in NY at 77. Cowan was one of the founders of the Jewish Healing Center and served for 14 years as director of the Jewish Life and Values Program at the Nathan Cummings Foundation in NY, where she helped direct grants for programs that addressed the spiritual dimensions of serious illness. https://www.jta.org/2018/09/02/obituaries/rabbi-rachel-cowan-pioneer-jewish-healing-movement-dies-77

Ari Fuld, an American-born Israeli activist, dies after being stabbed outside a shopping mall in the West bank town of Efrat. A father of four, Fuld chased his attacker and shot him before collapsing. Fuld was well known for his social media posts defending Israel and its military. https://www.jta.org/2018/09/16/israel/israeli-man-killed-stabbing-attack-outside-mall-etzion-bloc

Casino mogul Sheldon Adelson and his wife, Miriam, become the biggest spenders in American politics, having donated $55 million to groups helping to maintain Republican control of the House and Senate in the midterm elections, according to a *New York Times* report. The sum represented a substantial increase from the $46.5 million they had donated at the same point in the 2016 election cycle. https://www.jta.org/2018/09/23/politics/adelsons-55-million-federal-gop-races-makes-biggest-spenders-american-politics

A Canadian federal court denies the appeal of a former Nazi who sought to avoid deportation after having been found to have failed to disclose his past when applying for Canadian citizenship in 1960. The court ruled that it was "reasonable" that Helmut Oberlander, 94, be stripped of his citizenship. https://www.jta.org/2018/09/28/global/ex-nazi-soldier-loses-final-appeal-keep-canadian-citizenship

15.1.1.5   October 2018

In the deadliest attack ever on an American Jewish institution, 11 people are killed and another six injured when a gunman opens fire on the Tree of Life synagogue in Pittsburgh during Shabbat morning services. The alleged gunman, Robert Bowers, had made a post to an online social networking website shortly before the attack accusing the Jewish immigrant group HIAS of bringing "invaders" into the US. The attack was widely condemned by top officials in the US and abroad, with President Donald Trump describing it as an act of "pure evil." https://www.jta.org/2018/10/27/united-states/least-4-reported-dead-pittsburgh-synagogue-shooting

An explosive device is found in the mailbox of the NY home of Jewish billionaire and donor to left-wing causes George Soros. The device was detonated by a police bomb squad. https://www.jta.org/2018/10/23/united-states/bomb-found-mail-box-george-soros-new-york-home?_ga=2.190220905.376452078.1560704134-975108829.1547560004

In a reversal of a 1972 ban, the Conservative movement's religious law authorities move to allow its rabbis to attend intermarriages. The Committee on Jewish Law and Standards issued the new ruling at the same time as it upheld the movement's position that its clergy may only officiate at a marriage in cases where both parties are Jewish. https://www.jta.org/2018/10/22/united-states/conservative-rabbis-can-now-attend-intermarriages

The nearly century-old Hebrew College installs its first female president. Rabbi Sharon Cohen Anisfeld is installed as the college's top official after serving as dean of its pluralistic rabbinical school for 12 years. https://www.jta.org/2018/10/16/united-states/hebrew-college-installs-first-female-president

15.1.1.6   November 2018

The online home rental service Airbnb says it will remove listings of rooms and homes for rent in West Bank Jewish settlements. In a statement, the company said it consulted with experts to learn about the historical disputes in the region to make a decision about whether it should be doing business there. Israel's tourism minister, Yariv Levin, called the decision "discriminatory." https://www.jta.org/2018/11/19/israel/airbnb-remove-listings-west-bank-jewish-settlements

In what is believed to be the largest gift ever to higher education in the US, Michael Bloomberg announces a $1.8 billion gift to Johns Hopkins University to eliminate student loans and financial aid packages for incoming students. In an op-ed announcing the gift, the former New York City mayor and alumnus of the Baltimore university said that denying college entry to students on account of their ability to pay undermines equal opportunity, perpetuates intergenerational poverty and "strikes at the heart of the American dream: the idea that every person, from every community, has the chance to rise based on merit." https://www.jta.org/2018/11/19/united-states/michael-bloomberg-donates-1-8-billion-johns-hopkins-u-make-admissions-need-blind

The Reform movement's rabbinical wing appoints Rabbi Hara Person as its first female chief executive. Person succeeds Rabbi Steven Fox as head of the Central Conference of American Rabbis, which represents 2100 Reform rabbis around the world. https://www.jta.org/2018/11/15/united-states/reform-movements-rabbinical-group-appoints-first-female-leader

Data released by federal law enforcement authorities show that hate crimes against Jews in the US rose by more than a third in 2017. The FBI further shows that Jews accounted for 58% of all religion-based hate crimes. Overall, hate crimes increased by 17% in 2017. https://www.jta.org/2018/11/13/united-states/hate-crimes-jews-rise-37-fbi-reports

Stan Lee (see Sect. 15.3.1), the creator of comic book franchises Spider-Man, the Incredible Hulk, and the X-Men, dies in Los Angeles at 95. Born Stanley Martin Lieber in 1922, Lee was a pioneer in a comic book industry dominated at its outset by second-generation Jewish artists and writers. https://www.jta.org/2018/11/12/united-states/stan-lee-creator-iconic-marvel-comics-superheroes-dead-95

More than 75% of American Jews cast their ballots for Democrats in midterm congressional elections, according to polls. The election, which returned Democrats to the majority in the House of Representatives, also brought eight new Jewish members into the House and two Jews to governorships. In Colorado, Jared Polis became the state's first Jewish governor and the first openly gay man elected governor.

https://www.jta.org/2018/11/06/politics/jared-polis-elected-first-jewish-governor-colorado

https://www.jta.org/2018/11/07/politics/75-percent-jews-voted-democrats-midterms

The American-Israeli man convicted of making hundreds of bomb threats to Jewish community centers and Jewish schools in the US in 2017 is sentenced to ten years in prison in Israel. Michael Kadar had admitted making hundreds of threats against American Jewish institutions that forced widespread evacuations and promoted fears of mounting antisemitism. https://www.jta.org/2018/11/22/israel/american-israeli-behind-jcc-bomb-threats-sentenced-10-years-prison

The NY City Health Department warns of an outbreak of measles in Brooklyn's Orthodox Jewish community where vaccination rates are low. The department said a total of 17 cases had been recorded in the heavily Jewish Brooklyn neighborhoods of Williamsburg and Borough Park, three of which—including the initial case—were acquired by children on a visit to Israel. https://www.jta.org/2018/11/02/health/nyc-warns-measles-outbreak-among-orthodox-jews-brooklyn

Palestinian American activist Linda Sarsour, one of the founders of the Women's March, apologizes for causing harm to the movement's Jewish members and for being too slow to fight antisemitism. "We are deeply sorry for the harm we have caused, but we see you, we love you, and we are fighting with you," Sarsour said. The statement came a day after another of the march's co-founders, Teresa Shook, called on the movement's current organizers to step down because they have "allowed antisemitism."

https://www.jta.org/2018/11/19/united-states/womens-march-co-founder-calls-current-organizers-resign-saying-allowed-anti-semitism

https://www.jta.org/2018/11/20/united-states/linda-sarsour-apologizes-jewish-members-womens-march

15.1.1.7 December 2018

The American Civil Liberties Union announces a lawsuit against the state of Texas over a 2017 law prohibiting government contractors from engaging in boycotts of Israel. The ACLU argued that the law infringes on a legitimate form of political protest, while defenders say it does not inhibit free speech but only extends existing civil penalties for complying with boycott requests from foreign countries. https://www.jta.org/2018/12/19/united-states/aclu-sues-texas-over-anti-boycott-law-meant-to-protect-israel

Political commentator Marc Lamont Hill apologizes for calling for "a free Palestine from the river to the sea" during a UN event in solidarity with the Palestinian people. Hill, a professor of media studies at Temple University, was fired as a commentator by CNN for using the slogan, which Palestinian groups have invoked in rejecting any Israeli sovereignty between the Jordan River and the Mediterranean Sea. "I take seriously the voices of so many Jewish brothers and sisters, who have interpreted my remarks as a call to or endorsement of violence," Hill wrote in an op-ed in the *Philadelphia Inquirer*. https://www.jta.org/2018/12/02/united-states/commentator-marc-lamont-hill-op-ed-apologizes-use-phrase-free-palestine-river-sea

The US Congress passes bipartisan legislation named for the late Elie Wiesel that aims to improve the US response to emerging or potential genocides. The Elie Wiesel Genocide and Atrocities Prevention Act passed the House of Representatives by a vote of 406-5. The measure had been previously passed by the Senate, with 24 cosponsors. https://www.jta.org/quick-reads/congress-passes-legislation-named-for-elie-wiesel-that-aims-to-stop-genocides

15.1.1.8 January 2019

Robert Kraft, the New England Patriots owner, is named the winner of the $1 million Genesis Prize, the so-called Jewish Nobel. Kraft, 77, is the sixth person to win the prize, which honors individuals who serve "as an inspiration to the next generation of Jews through their outstanding professional achievement along with their commitment to Jewish values and the Jewish people." https://www.jta.org/2019/01/09/united-states/new-england-patriots-owner-robert-kraft-wins-1-million-genesis-prize

The storied Jewish newspaper *The Forward* announces it will be ceasing its print edition and laying off its editor-in-chief and 20% of its staff. Founded in 1897, the newspaper began as a Yiddish-language publication and launched an English edition in 1990. *The Forward* will continue to publish online in both English and Yiddish. https://www.jta.org/quick-reads/the-forward-is-ending-its-print-edition

Prominent Democrats launch a pro-Israel group to counter the party's drift away from Israel. "Our mission at Democratic Majority for Israel is to strengthen the pro-Israel tradition of the Democratic Party, fight for Democratic values and work within the progressive movement to advance policies that ensure a strong US-Israel relationship," said Mark Mellman, a longtime Democratic Party pollster who has been active in the pro-Israel community. Other party leaders involved in the effort include Jennifer Granholm, the former governor of MI, Henry Cisneros, a Housing secretary under President Bill Clinton, and Ann Lewis, chief of communications under Clinton and a longtime leading supporter of Hillary Clinton. https://www.jta.org/quick-reads/leading-dems-launch-centrist-pro-israel-faction-to-counter-lefts-influence

Rep. Ilhan Omar disavows a 2012 tweet in which she said Israel had "hypnotized" the world, saying the term was "unfortunate and offensive." One of just two freshman lawmakers to endorse the Boycott, Divestment, and Sanctions (BDS) campaign targeting Israel, the Minnesota Democrat's comment came days after she was named to the US House of Representatives Foreign Affairs Committee. "It's now apparent to me that I spent lots of energy putting my 2012 tweet in context and little energy in disavowing the anti-semitic trope I unknowingly used, which is unfortunate and offensive," the first-term lawmaker said. https://www.jta.org/quick-reads/ilhan-omar-says-her-2012-tweet-about-israel-hypnotizing-the-world-was-offensive-and-unfortunate

15.1.1.9 February 2019

Al Vorspan (see Sect. 15.3.1), who helped organize the Religious Action Center of Reform Judaism and served as the longtime director of its Commission on Social Action, dies at 95. A World War II veteran, Vorspan pushed the Reform movement to create the commission in 1953, and later pressed for the creation of the Religious Action Center, which became the movement's voice in Washington. https://www.jta.org/2019/02/17/obituaries/al-vorspan-jewish-social-justice-leader-for-the-reform-movement-dies-at-95

Rep. Ilhan Omar says in a tweet that the American Israel Public Affairs Committee (AIPAC) pays politicians to be pro-Israel, a falsehood that drew quick rebukes from a number of her Democratic colleagues, including House Speaker Nancy Pelosi, Foreign Affairs Committee Chairman Eliot Engel, and Judiciary Committee Chairman Jerry Nadler. Omar subsequently apologized for the tweet and expressed gratitude to "Jewish allies and colleagues who are educating me on the painful history of anti-Semitic tropes." https://www.jta.org/quick-reads/ilhan-omar-apologizes-for-tweets-saying-aipac-buys-politicians-backing-for-israel

Michael Cohen, the former lawyer for President Donald Trump, cites his father's survival of the Holocaust to explain why he turned on his one-time mentor and employer. "My father survived the Holocaust thanks to the compassion and selfless acts of others," Cohen said in a statement prepared for delivery to US House of Representatives Oversight Committee. "He was helped by many who put themselves in harm's way to do what they knew was right." Cohen, Trump's longtime lawyer, pleaded guilty to fraud and violating campaign finance laws and was preparing to serve three years of jail time. https://www.jta.org/quick-reads/noting-fathers-holocaust-survival-michael-cohen-calls-trump-a-racist-and-conman

The US Senate approves a bill that provides legal cover to states that target the movement to boycott Israel despite opposition from several prominent Democrats. The bill, which passed by a 77-23 margin, has been criticized for infringing on free speech and was opposed by Senators Elizabeth Warren, Cory Booker, Kamala Harris, and Bernie Sanders—all of whom were vying for the 2020 Democratic presidential nomination. Every Republican except Sen. Rand Paul of Kentucky supported the bill. https://www.jta.org/quick-reads/senate-passes-bill-including-anti-bds-measures

A Holocaust survivor who escaped the shooting at the Pittsburgh synagogue where 11 worshippers were killed is a special guest at President Donald Trump's State of the Union address. Judah Samet, 81, survived because he was late to services the morning of the shooting and was warned to stay outside the building. Samet sat in the gallery with First Lady Melania Trump for the address along with 12 other guests, including a police officer who was shot several times battling the gunman. https://www.jta.org/quick-reads/tree-of-life-shooting-survivor-and-pittsburgh-police-officer-named-guests-for-state-of-the-union

15.1.1.10   March 2019

Jewish megadonor Michael Steinhardt is accused of a pattern of sexually inappropriate behavior by seven women. In an expose published by *The New York Times* and the journalism nonprofit ProPublica, the women accused Steinhardt, one of the founders of Birthright Israel and a major supporter of a range of Jewish institutions, of making sexual requests of them while they were relying on or seeking his support. Steinhardt denied the accusations, but acknowledged a pattern of comments "that were boorish, disrespectful, and just plain dumb." https://www.jta.org/2019/03/21/united-states/megadonor-michael-steinhardt-is-accused-by-six-women-of-a-pattern-of-sexual-harassment

President Donald Trump signs a proclamation recognizing Israel's sovereignty over the Golan Heights, becoming the first country to recognize Israeli rule over the strategic plateau captured from Syria in the 1967 war. Israel annexed the territory in 1981.https://www.jta.org/quick-reads/trump-signs-proclamation-recognizing-israeli-sovereignty-over-the-golan-heights

A Gallup poll finds that a majority of Americans sympathize with Israel over the Palestinians, but that the percentage is slipping. Some 59% of Americans said they sympathize more with the Israelis, down from 64% in 2018, Gallup's annual World Affairs survey found. The poll also found that 43% of Democrats sympathized more with Israel, while 76% of Republicans did so. https://www.jta.org/quick-reads/more-americans-sympathize-with-israel-than-the-palestinians-but-support-is-slipping

The American Israel Public Affairs Committee (AIPCA) opens its annual policy conference in Washington with a defiant refusal to be silenced in the face of mounting criticism from the left. "When they try to silence us we speak up, and when they tell us to sit down we stand up, we stand up, We. Stand. Up," AIPAC CEO Howard Kohr said in a fiery opening speech. MoveOn, a progressive grassroots organization, had called on Democratic presidential candidates to boycott the conference, though candidates generally do not appear at AIPAC in non-election years. Some 18,000 activistsattendedtheconference.https://www.jta.org/quick-reads/defiant-aipac-opens-conference-emphasizing-diversity

President Donald Trump calls Democrats the "anti-Jewish" party following a vote in the House of Representatives condemning antisemitism. "The Democrats have become an anti-Israel party. They've become an anti-Jewish party, and that's too bad," Trump said. The House resolution condemned antisemitism primarily, along with Islamophobia and other biases, and specified that charges of dual loyalty were especially harmful. The entire Democratic caucus voted for the resolution, and all but 24 Republicans did as well. The resolution was spurred by several comments made by Democrat Representative Ilhan Omar of Minnesota that appeared to traffic inantisemitictropes.https://www.jta.org/quick-reads/donald-trump-calls-democrats-an-anti-jewish-party

15.1.1.11 April 2019

One person is killed and three injured in a shooting at a Chabad synagogue in Poway, California. Lori Gilbert-Kaye, 60, was killed when a gunman opened fire on the synagogue northeast of San Diego on the last day of Passover. The suspect, John Earnest, 19, was charged with murder as well as federal hate crimes and civil rights violations.https://www.jta.org/quick-reads/police-detain-man-in-san-diego-synagogue-shooting-at-least-4-injured

Airbnb reverses its decision to remove West Bank settlement listings from its website. The online rental service changed its policy after two federal court settlements between the company and two groups of American Jewish plaintiffs who accused the company of discrimination. In a statement posted to its website, Airbnb said it would donate the proceeds from West Bank rentals to humanitarian groups. https://www.jta.org/quick-reads/embargoed-airbnb-will-cancel-its-ban-on-west-bank-settlement-listings

The Anti-Defamation League says there were 1879 antisemitic incidents in the US in 2018, a drop from the 1986 reported in 2017 but still the third-highest total since 1979. The vast majority were incidents of harassment or vandalism, but the number of assaults doubled since 2017, to 39 from 17. In Canada, the number of antisemitic incidents tallied by B'nai B'rith Canada rose to a record high for the third consecutive year, surging to 2041 incidents in 2018 from 1752 reported in 2017. https://www.jta.org/quick-reads/there-were-1879-incidents-in-2018-adl-finds; https://www.jta.org/quick-reads/anti-semitic-incidents-in-canada-rise-to-record-number-for-3rd-straight-year

The New York Times prints a cartoon in its international print edition depicting Israeli Prime Minister Benjamin Netanyahu as a guide dog wearing a Star of David collar and leading President Donald Trump, who is wearing a black yarmulke. The cartoon is broadly condemned as antisemitic, and the newspaper said it was "deeply sorry" to have published an image that included "antisemitic tropes." In a subsequent editorial, the paper called it "an appalling political cartoon" that is "evidence of a profound danger—not only of antisemitism but of numbness to its creep." https://www.jta.org/quick-reads/in-second-statement-new-york-times-apologizes-for-publishing-anti-semitic-political-cartoon

Deputy US Attorney General Rod Rosenstein submits his resignation letter to President Donald Trump. Rosenstein had appointed Robert Mueller as special counsel to look into Russian interference in the 2016 elections and was a key player in overseeing the probe that Trump called a "witch hunt." https://www.jta.org/quick-reads/deputy-ag-rod-rosenstein-submits-resignation-letter

New York City Mayor Bill de Blasio declares a public health emergency over a measles outbreak in Brooklyn's haredi Orthodox community, ordering unvaccinated people living in four zip codes in the heavily Orthodox Brooklyn neighborhood of Williamsburg to get vaccinated or pay fines up to $1,000. A week later, the city closed a yeshiva preschool in Williamsburg for defying a Health Department order to provide medical and attendance records regarding measles vaccinations. According to the city, between October 2018 and April 2019, there were 285 reported cases of measles in Brooklyn's Orthodox community, including 246 children.https://www.jta.org/quick-reads/new-york-city-declares-public-health-emergency-over-measles-outbreak-in-brooklyn-haredi-orthodox-community

https://www.jta.org/quick-reads/new-york-city-shuts-down-brooklyn-yeshiva-preschool-over-measles-vaccination-violations

15.1.1.12   May 2019

American Daniel Atwood becomes the first openly gay man ordained as an Orthodox rabbi at a ceremony in Jerusalem. Atwood had previously been denied ordination by the liberal American Orthodox rabbinical school Yeshivat Chovevei Torah three months prior to his graduation. The school declined to specify the reason for its decision, but it came just months after Atwood and his partner were engaged to marry. Atwood's ordination was granted by Rabbi Daniel Landes, a prominent Israeli-American rabbi. https://www.jta.org/2019/05/27/israel/first-openly-gay-orthodox-rabbi-ordained-in-jerusalem

https://www.jta.org/2019/04/02/united-states/liberal-orthodox-yeshiva-says-it-will-not-ordain-gay-student

Herman Wouk (see Sect. 15.3.1), the bestselling Orthodox Jewish author whose literary career spanned nearly seven decades, dies at 103. Wouk helped usher Judaism into the American mainstream through more than two dozen novels and works of nonfiction, including the Pulitzer Prize-winning *The Caine Mutiny* from 1951, which was a fixture on best-seller lists for two years, and the best-selling *Marjorie Morningstar* from 1955. https://www.jta.org/2019/05/17/obituaries/herman-wouk-dies

The Israeli eatery Zahav wins the 2019 James Beard Foundation award for outstanding restaurant. Jewish chefs Michael Solomonov, a native of Israel, and Steve Cook founded the Philadelphia restaurant, whose name means "gold" in Hebrew, in 2008.https://www.jta.org/quick-reads/israeli-restaurant-zahav-named-best-in-the-us-by-james-beard-awards

15.1.1.13   June 2019

Quebec passes a so-called secularism law banning certain public employees from wearing religious symbols, including yarmulkes and hijabs, at work. The law, which applies to teachers, judges, and police officers, among others, was passed by a 73-35 vote following a contentious debate. "The Jewish community of Quebec is profoundly disappointed by the adoption of Bill 21," Brenda Gewurz, chair of the Centre for Israel and Jewish Affairs in Quebec, said in a statement. "This bill is reckless. It undermines religious freedom and equal access to employment." https://www.jta.org/quick-reads/quebec-passes-law-banning-kippahs-turbans-and-hijabs-for-public-workers

Ryan Braun passes Hank Greenberg to claim the record for most home runs by a Jewish baseball player. The Milwaukee Brewers outfielder hit his 332nd career home run in a game against the Pittsburgh Pirates. https://www.jta.org/quick-reads/ryan-braun-breaks-hank-greenbergs-record-for-most-home-runs-by-a-jewish-player

Rep. Alexandria Ocasio-Cortez comes under fierce criticism for comparing migrant detention centers at the US-Mexico border to "concentration camps." Multiple Jewish groups criticized the Democratic lawmaker's Holocaust comparison, including Yad Vashem, the Anti-Defamation League, the US Holocaust Memorial Museum, and the Jewish Community Relations Council of New York. https://www.jta.org/2019/06/24/politics/how-jews-reacted-to-alexandria-ocasio-cortezs-controversial-concentration-camp-comment

Gary Rosenblatt announces that he will be stepping down as editor and publisher of *The New York Jewish Week* after 26 years. Rosenblatt, 72, will continue to write occasionally for *The Jewish Week* and remain involved in several of its educational projects, according to the newspaper. https://www.jta.org/quick-reads/gary-rosenblatt-stepping-down-as-editor-and-publisher-of-the-new-york-jewish-week

Steven Nasatir, the longest-serving CEO of any Jewish federation in North America, says he will step down as head of Chicago's Jewish United Fund after four decades on the job. The federation has distributed nearly $7 billion to charitable causes since Nasatir took the helm of the federation in 1979. https://www.jta.org/2018/06/11/united-states/man-whos-run-chicagos-jewish-community-almost-40-years-stepping

The White House unveils the economic portion of its Mideast peace plan, which calls for $50 billion of investment in building infrastructure and capacity in the West Bank and the Gaza Strip. Authored by a team lead by President Donald Trump's son-in-law Jared Kushner, the plan was released just days ahead of a conference in Bahrain where Kushner sought to drum up support for it. The plan included no political details and made no mention of Palestinian statehood. https://www.jta.org/2019/06/22/united-states/white-house-unveils-economic-portion-of-peace-plan-including-portions-that-will-unsettle-netanyahu

15.1.2   The Top 11 Jewish Stories of 2018 According to JTA

1) The Pittsburgh shooting
2) The US Embassy move to Jerusalem
3) The Parkland shooting
4) Michael Cohen turns on Trump
5) Jewish Democrats ride the blue wave
6) Antisemitism allegations roil the women's march
7) Natalie Portman snubs Netanyahu
8) A Democratic candidate (Julia Salazar) sparks a debate on Jewish identity

9) The demonization of George Soros
10) Jared and Ivanka on the hot seat
11) Jeremy Corbyn's "existential threat" to British Jewry

15.1.3   The Top 10 Apologies of the Jewish Year According to JTA

1) Larry Kudlow, Trump's economic advisor, for inviting a friend who publishes work by white nationalists to a party in his home
2) Benjamin Netanyahu, after US journalist Peter Beinart was detained at Ben Gurion airport
3) Trayon White, Sr., a Washington, DC, city council member who accused the Rothschilds of controlling the weather, the World Bank, and the federal government
4) Jason Spencer, a Georgia State representative who resigned after he was duped into dropping his pants and using a racial slur on Sacha Baron Cohen's new Showtime series
5) Roseanne Barr apologized to Hungarian-American billionaire George Soros for calling the Jewish philanthropist a Nazi collaborator
6) Steven M. Cohen, a sociologist whose findings have shaped Jewish communal policy for decades, apologized after several women accused him of sexual misconduct
7) MSNBC host Joy Reid apologized for blog posts criticizing the late Israeli Prime Minister Ariel Sharon and questioning Israel's right to its sovereignty
8) Samantha Bee, after calling Ivanka Trump a "feckless c***" on her TBS late night show
9) Michelle Bachmann, the former congresswomen from Minnesota who ran for the Republican presidential nomination in 2012, apologized for calling on Jews to convert to Christianity
10) Quai James, of Yonkers, NY, for posting a video on social media ridiculing the hairstyle of a young Hasidic boy

15.1.4   The 8 Must-Read Jewish News Stories of 5779 (2018–2019) According to JTA

https://www.jta.org/2019/09/24/culture/the-8-must-read-jewish-news-stories-of-5779?utm_source=JTA_Maropost&utm_campaign=JTA_DB&utm_medium=email&mpweb=1161-13729-33285

1) 12 Jews killed in synagogues
2) Jewish democrats win big in 2018 elections

3) Hate crimes against Jews are spiking
4) The Women's March remains a lightning rod with continued charges of antisemitism
5) Israelis vote twice and still don't have a prime minister
6) Israel becomes a wedge issue
7) The #MeToo movement hits the Jewish community
8) A measles outbreak hits the Orthodox community

15.2 Persons Honored by the Jewish and General Communities, 2018 to 2019

15.2.1 Jewish Book Awards

American Academy for Jewish Research, 2018
www.aajr.org
−Baron Book Prize
Sunny Yudkoff, *Tubercular Capital: Illness and the Conditions of Modern Jewish Writing*

Association of Jewish Libraries, 2019
www.jewishlibraries.org
−Sydney Taylor Book Award for Younger Readers
Emily Jenkins, *All-of-a-Kind Family Hanukkah*
−Sydney Taylor Book Award Winner for Older Readers
Jonathan Auxier, *Sweep: The Story of a Girl and Her Monster*
−Sydney Taylor Book Award Winner for Teen Readers
Vesper Stamper, *What the Night Sings*
−Sydney Taylor Manuscript Award Winner
Jessica Littmann, *A Corner of the World*
−Sydney Taylor Reference and Bibliography Award
Marcin Wodziński, *Historical Atlas of Hasidism*
−AJL Jewish Fiction Award
Mark Sarvas, *Memento Park*

Canadian Jewish Literary Awards, 2018
www.cjlawards.ca
−Fiction
Natalie Merrill, *The Ghost Keeper*
−Memoir/Biography
Kathy Kacer with **Jordana Lebowitz**, *To Look a Nazi in the Eye: A Teen's Account of a War Criminal Trial*
−Poetry
Rebecca Papacaru, *The Panic Room*
−Yiddish

Seymour Mayne, *In Your Words: Translations from the Yiddish and the Hebrew*
–Scholarship
Daniel Kupfert Heller, *Jabotinsky's Children: Polish Jews and the Rise of Right-Wing Zionism*
–History
Pierre Anctil, Histoire des Juifs du Québec
–Holocaust Literature
Max Wallace, In the Name of Humanity: The Secret Deal to End the Holocaust
–Children and Youth Fiction
Anne Renaud (author) and **Richard Rudnicki** (illustrator), *Fania's Heart*

Hadassah Magazine Harold U. Ribalow Prize, 2018
www.hadassahmagazine.org
Carol Zoref, *Barren Island*
(for Jewish fiction, both novels and short-story collections)

Jewish Quarterly Wingate Literary Prize, 2019
www.thejc.com
Françoise Frenkel, *No Place to Lay One's Head*
(awarded to the best book, fiction or nonfiction, to translate the idea of Jewishness to the general reader)

Jordan Schnitzer Book Award from the Association for Jewish Studies, 2018
www.associationforjewishstudies.org
–Biblical Studies, Rabbinics, and Jewish History and Culture in Antiquity
Mira Balberg, *Blood for Thought: The Reinvention of Sacrifice in Early Rabbinic Literature*
–Jews and the Arts: Music, Performance, and Visual
David Stern, *The Jewish Bible: A Material History*
–Modern Jewish History and Culture: Europe and Israel
Daniel Kupfert Heller, *Jabotinsky's Children: Polish Jews and the Rise of Right-Wing Zionism*
–Social Science, Anthropology, and Folklore
Michal Kravel-Tov, *When the State Winks: The Performance of Jewish Conversion in Israel*

National Jewish Book Awards by The Jewish Book Council, 2018
www.jewishbookcouncil.org
–Jewish Book of the Year, Everett Family Foundation Award
Beate and Serge Klarsfeld, *Hunting the Truth*
–Biography, Autobiography, Memoir, The Krauss Family Award in Memory of Simon & Shulamith (Sofi) Goldberg
Ehud Barak, *My Country, My Life: Fighting for Israel, Searching for Peace*
–Biography Award, In Memory of Sara Berenson Stone
Ariel Burger, *Witness: Lessons from Elie Wiesel's Classroom*
–Carolyn Starman Hessel Mentorship Award

Susan Shapiro
–Women=s Studies, Barbara Dobkin Award
Alice Shalvi, *Never a Native*
—American Jewish Studies, Celebrate 350 Award
Jack Wertheimer, *The New American Judaism: How Jews Practice Their Religion Today*
–Book Club Award, The Miller Family Award in Memory of Helen Dunn Weinstein & June Keit Miller
Ronald H. Balson, *The Girl from Berlin*
–Children=s Literature
Erica S. Perl, *All Three Stooges*
–Contemporary Jewish Life and Practice, Myra H. Kraft Memorial Award
Leon Wiener Dow, *The Going: A Meditation on Jewish Law*
–Debut Fiction, Goldberg Prize
Bram Presser, *The Book of Dirt*
–Education and Jewish Identity, In Memory of Dorothy Kripke
Barry Scott Wimpfheimer, *The Talmud: A Biography*
–Fiction, JJ Greenberg Memorial Award
Michael David Lukas, *The Last Watchman of Old Cairo*
–History, Gerrard and Ella Berman Memorial Award
Ronen Bergman, *Rise and Kill First: The Secret History of Israel's Targeted Assassinations*
–Holocaust, In Memory of Ernest W. Michel
Omer Bartov, *Anatomy of a Genocide: The Life and Death of a Town Called Buczacz*
–Modern Jewish Thought and Experience, Dorot Foundation Award in Memory of Joy Ungerleider Mayerson
Alan L. Mittleman, *Does Judaism Condone Violence? Holiness and Ethics in Jewish Tradition*
–Poetry, Berru Award in Memory of Ruth and Bernie Weinflash
Erika Meitner, *Holy Moly Carry Me*
–Scholarship, Nahum M. Sarna Memorial Award contributions in spectral theory, functional analysis, and nonrelativistic quantum mechanics
Marcin Wodzinski (author), **Waldemar Spallek** (cartography), *Historical Atlas of Hasidism*
–Sephardic Culture, Mimi S. Frank Award in Memory of Becky Levy
Jonathan Decter, *Dominion Built of Praise: Panegyric and Legitimacy Among Jews in the Medieval Mediterranean*
–Writing Based on Archival Material, The JDC-Herbert Katzki Award
Rebecca Erbelding, *Rescue Board: The Untold Story of America's Efforts to Save the Jews of Europe*

Sami Rohr Prize by The Jewish Book Council, 2019
www.jewishbookcouncil.org
Michael David Lukas, *The Last Watchman of Old Cairo*
(for the contribution of contemporary writers in exploring and transmitting Jewish values)

15.2.2   Academic Awards

American Academy of Religion Awards, 2017–2018
www.aarweb.org
–Book Awards
Nancy Levene, Yale University, *Powers of Distinction: On Religion and Modernity*
Noah Salomon, Carleton College, *For Love of the Prophet: An Ethnography of Sudan's Islamic State*

American Computing Machinery A.M. Turing Award, 2018
https://amturing.acm.org
Yoshua Bengio, Université de Montréal

American Computing Machinery Paris Kanellakis Award, 2018
www.acm.org
Pavel Pevzner, University of California, San Diego
(to honor "specific theoretical accomplishments that have had a significant and demonstrable effect on the practice of computing)
American Jewish Historical Society, 2019 (www.ajhs.org)
–Saul Viener Book Prize
Kirsten Fermaglich, *A Rosenberg by Any Other Name: A History of Jewish Name Changing in America*
–Sid and Ruth Lapidus Fellowship, 2019
Dr. Melissa Klapper, *At Home in the World: American Jewish Women Abroad, 1865–1940.*
Laura Michel, *Benevolent Republicans: Philanthropy, Identity, and Foreign Relations in the Early United States*
Connor Kenaston, *Broadcasting the Gospel of Tolerance: Liberal Religion, Media, and Capitalism in Twentieth-Century America*

American Humanist Association, 2019
www.americanhumanist.org
–Lifetime Achievement Award, 2019
Barry Kosmin, founding director of the Institute for the Study of Secularism in Society and Culture (ISSSC), research professor of Public Policy and Law at Trinity College

Association for Canadian Jewish Studies, 2019
www.acjs-aejc.ca/award
–Marcia Koven Best Student Paper Award
Magdalene Klassen, (McGill University): *Going Out into the World: Humanitarianism, Assimilation, and Gender among Jewish Members of the Imperial Order of the Daughters of the Empire, 1900–1939*
–Distinguished Service Award
Norma Baumel Joseph (Concordia University)

Association for the Social Scientific Study of Jewry, 2019
www.assj.org
–Sklare Award
Harriet Hartman, Sociology, Rowan University
(for significant scholarly contributions to the social scientific study of Jewry)

Breakthrough Prize in Fundamental Physics, 2019
www.breakthroughprize.org
Charles L. Kane *(theoretical condensed matter physicist)*

Breakthrough Prize in Life Sciences, 2019
www.breakthroughprize.org
Adrian R. Krainer *(biochemist and molecular geneticist)*

Dannie Heineman Prize for Mathematical Physics, 2018
www.aps.org)
Barry Simon, Caltech (contributions in spectral theory, functional analysis, and nonrelativistic quantum mechanics)

Foreign Membership in the British Royal Society, 2019
www.royalsociety.org
Professor Barry Barish, Linde Professor of Physics, Emeritus, California Institute of Technology and Distinguished Professor of Physics, University of California, Riverside
David Milstein, Weizmann Institute of Science
James Rothman, Sterling Professor of Cell Biology, School of Medicine, Yale University

Frank Nelson Cole Prizes in Algebra and Number Theory, 2018
www.ams.org
Robert Guralnick, University of Southern California

Gairdner Foundation Awards, 2019
https://gairdner.org
Susan Horwitz, Albert Einstein College of Medicine (pioneer in dissecting the mechanisms of action of chemotherapeutic drug)
Ronald Vale, University of California, San Francisco (for molecular motors)
(for medical and life sciences)

Lasker Award in Basic Medical Research, 2018
www.laskerfoundation.org
Michael Grunstein, UCLA (demonstrated that histones dramatically influence gene activity within living cells and laid the groundwork for understanding the pivotal role of particular amino acids in this process)

Leroy P. Steele Prize for Lifetime Achievement, 2019
www.ams.org
Jeff Cheeger, NYU (for differential geometry and its connections with topology and analysis)
(for Lifetime Achievement in Mathematics)

MacArthur Fellows, 2018
www.macfound.org/programs/fellows
Amy Finkelstein, Massachusetts Institute of Technology
Becca Heller, Human Rights Lawyer

MacArthur Fellows, 2019
www.macfound.org/programs/fellows
Elizabeth Anderson, Philosopher
Joshua Tenenbaum, Cognitive Scientist

National Academy of Science Award in Molecular Biology, 2019
www.nasonline.org
David Reich, Harvard Medical School, geneticist
(has pioneered techniques to study ancient DNA to trace ancient human migrations)

National Academy of Science Award in Neurosciences, 2019
www.nasonline.org
Eve Marder, Brandeis University
(for research over more than 40 years that has provided transformative insight into the fundamental processes of animal and human brains)

Peter Debye Award in Physical Chemistry, 2019
www.acs.org
Daniel Neumark, University of California, Berkeley (physical chemistry and molecular structure and dynamics)

Troland Research Award, 2018
www.nasonline.org
Marlene R. Cohen (for her experimental and theoretical work characterizing the population-level neural mechanisms by which spatial attention enhances the cortical representation of a visual object and facilitates transmission of information about that object)
(awarded to researchers under age 40 in recognition of psychological research on the relationship between consciousness and the physical world)

Wolf Prize, 2019
www.wolffund.org.il
Moshe Safdie, architecture (designed the Yad Vashem Holocaust memorial and museum in Jerusalem and Habitat 67)
Jeffrey Friedman, medicine (Rockefeller University, molecular geneticist, discovered the hormone leptin and its role in regulating body weight)
Gregory Lawler, mathematics (University of Chicago, best known for his work on the Schramm-Loewner evolution)
David Zilberman, agriculture (University of California, combined the biophysical characteristics of agro-economic systems to develop economic models and frameworks for econometric decisions that answer fundamental questions in agriculture, economics, and policy that arise in a number of important areas)

Stephen L. Buchwald, chemistry (Massachusetts Institute of Technology, known for the development of the Buchwald-Hartwig amination and the discovery of the dialkylbiaryl phosphine ligands)

15.2.3   Jewish Organizations Awards

ADL A.I. Botnick Torch of Liberty Award, 2018
Warner Thomas and **Steve Gleason**
(for their influential and respected leadership in their demonstrated commitment to the community and to the values of ADL)

ADL-Kovler Nation of Immigrants Award, 2018
The Honorable Gurbir Grewal
(for standing up and challenging bias and discrimination in all forms)

Association of Jewish Aging Services, 2019
www.ajas.org
–Dr. Herbert Shore Award of Honor
Barbara Gold, Director, Senior Services of West Central Montreal Health Network, Donald Berman Maimonides Geriatric Centre (Montreal, Canada)
–Trustee of the Year Award
Ron Elinoff, River Garden Senior Services, Jacksonville, FL
–Professional of the Year Award
Richard Schwalberg, Chief Operating Officer Menorah Park, Beachwood, OH
–Young Executives of the Year Award
Abby Miles, Manager of Business Analytics, Jewish Association on Aging, Pittsburgh
Sean Gregson, Vice President, Home Care and Hospice, Abramson Senior Care, North Wales, PA
–Jewish Programming Award Winners:

1. Carp Tank, Jewish Home of Rockleigh, NJ
2. Creative Volunteerism, Jewish Association on Aging, Pittsburgh, PA
3. Linkages at Kavod, Kavod Senior Life, Denver, CO
4. Project VAST Hebrew Senior Life, Boston, MA
5. Partnering with Elders: Health and Creativity, The Cedars, Portland, ME
6. Traditions Abramson Senior Care, North Wales, PA

Azrieli Foundation, 2018
www.azrielifoundation.org
–Azrieli Prize for Jewish Music
Avner Dorman, Nigunim for Violin and Orchestra

B'nai B'rith International, 2019
www.bnaibrith.org

–Distinguished Achievement Award
Richard Robinson, Chairman & CEO, Scholastic Inc.

The Charles Bronfman Prize, 2018, 2019
www.thecharlesbronfmanprize.org
Amy Bach, Founder, Executive Director, and President of Measures for Justice, an
   organization that measures criminal justice performance by collecting, cleaning,
   and coding county-level criminal justice data (2018).
David Hertz, Co-Founder and President of Gastromotiva who pioneered a model
   for using food to improve the lives of low-income people (2019)
*(honors humanitarian work, informed by Jewish values, that has broad, global
impact that can change lives and inspire future generations from all walks of life)*

Covenant Foundation Award for Excellence in Jewish Education, 2019
www.covenantfn.org
Dr. Gregory Beiles, Head of School, The Toronto Heschel School and Director,
   The Lola Stein Institute, Toronto, CA
Sally Grazi–Shatzkes, Registered Drama Therapist, Licensed Creative Arts
   Therapist, and Theater Director, Yeshivah of Flatbush, Brooklyn, NY
Risa Strauss, Education Director, Beth Shalom Synagogue and Founding Director,
   Camp Gesher, The Katie and Irwin Kahn Jewish Community Center,
   Columbia, SC
(recognizes excellence and impact in Jewish education)

Covenant Foundation Pomegranate Prize, 2018
www.covenantfn.org
Rabbi Adina Allen, Co-Founder and Creative Director of the Jewish Studio Project
   (JSP) in Berkeley, CA
Maiya Chard-Yaron, Executive Director of Texas Hillel in Austin, TX
Ilana Gleicher-Bloom, Founding Vision Director of Mensch Academy at Mishkan
   Chicago in Chicago, IL
Oren Kaunfer, Madrich Ruchani (Spiritual Educator/Director of Jewish Life) at
   JCDS, Boston's Jewish Community Day School in Watertown, MA ·
Hannah Kearney, Director of Havayah, The Teen Community at Temple Beth
   Elohim in Wellesley, MA.
*(honors rising leaders who have been in the field of Jewish education for up to
ten years)*

Genesis Prize Foundation, 2019
www.genesisprize.org
–Inaugural Lifetime Achievement Award
–Genesis Prize Laureate
Robert Kraft, American philanthropist and owner of the New England Patriots

Hebrew Union College-Jewish Institute of Religion
www.huc.edu
–Sherut L'Am Award

Deborah E. Lipstadt, Emory University

International Jewish Sports Hall of Fame, 2019
www.jewishsports.net
Ruth Aarons, Table Tennis
Sasha Cohen, Figure Skating
Ben Hatskin, Ice Hockey
Kevin Youkilis, Baseball

Jewish American Hall of Fame, 2018, 2019
www.amuseum.org
Hedy Lamarr, Movie star, inventor
Isaac Mayer Wise, Founder of Reform Judaism

Jewish Council for Public Affairs, 2018
http://jewishpublicaffairs.org
−Albert D. Chenin Award
Nancy Kaufman, CEO of National Council of Jewish Women
(given to Jewish leaders whose life work best exemplifies the social justice impera-
*   tives of Judaism, Jewish history, and the protection of the Bill of Rights)*
−Tikkun Olam Award
Rabbi Rachel Ain, Rabbi of the Sutton Place Synagogue in Manhattan
(given to leaders who have worked to bring together communities and have embod-
*   ied good works)*

Jewish Foundation for the Righteous, 2018
www.jfr.org
−Robert I. Goldman Award for Excellence in Holocaust Education
Maureen Carter, K-12 Holocaust Studies program planner for the School District
   of Palm Beach County, FL

Jewish Free Loan, 2019
www.jfla.org
−Honor
Mayim Bialik, actress

Jewish Funders Network, 2019
www.jfunders.org
The JJ Greenberg Memorial Award
David Rittberg, Director of the Charles and Lynn Schusterman Family Foundation's
   US Jewish grantmaking portfolio
(honors foundation professionals engaged in grant making, age 40 and under, who
*   have demonstrated extraordinary leadership in Jewish philanthropy)*

Jewish Labor Committee Human Rights Award, 2018
www.jewishlaborcommittee.org
HIAS, the refugee and immigrant aid organization
Henry A. Garrido, Executive Director, AFSCME District Council 37

Service Employees International Union

Jewish National Fund, 2018
www.jnf.org
–Tree of Life Award
Susan and Marc Sacks, Chicago
(humanitarian award given in recognition of outstanding community involvement,
*   dedication to the cause of American-Israeli friendship, and devotion to the peace*
*   and security of human life)*

Jewish Sports Heritage Association, 2019
www.jewishsportsheritage.org
Ernie Grunfeld, Basketball player and executive

Jewish Women's Archive, 2018
www.wja.org
–Natalia Twersky Award for Educators
Julie Rezmovic-Tonti, middle-school Jewish history teacher, Outreach Coordinator
    at Gesher Jewish Day School

Keshet Hacham Lev Award 2018
www.keshetonline.org
Alyx Bernstein, peer leader in the Keshet LGBTQ and Ally Teen community, first
    openly trans girl to serve on the editorial board of the groundbreaking *JGirls*
    Magazine
Bennett Decker, co-facilitates Keshet LGBTQ and Ally Teen Shabbatonim as a
    Keshet College Fellow, youngest person to become a member of the Keshet's
    Board of Directors
Sawyer Goldsmith, peer leader in the Keshet LGBTQ and Ally Teen community,
    first openly trans person to be elected to the international board of USY and
    serves as Religious Education Vice President

Moment Magazine, 2018, 2019
www.momentmag.com
–Robert S. Greenberger Journalism Award
Jane Mayer, investigative reporter and author (2018)
Evan Osnos, *New Yorker*
–Human Rights Award
Justice Ruth Bader Ginsburg, Supreme Court Justice (2018)
—Moment Creativity Awards
Carol Brown Goldberg, artist (2018)
Esther Coopersmith, former US Representative to the UN (2018)
Aviva Kempner, Filmmaker (2019)
–Moment Community Leadership Award
Lloyd Goldman (2019)
–Women and Power Award
Nina Totenberg, NPR (2019)

–Trailblazer Award
Phyllis Greenberger, Women's Health Advocate (2019)

JPRO Network, 2019
www.jpro.org
–The Ben Mandelkorn Distinguished Service Award, 2017
Rabbi B. Elka Abrahamson and **Gerrald (Jerry) Silverman**
(recognizes significant and sustained contributions to Jewish community organizations)
– Bernard Rodkin Professional Development Israel Fellowship, 2019
Caryn Roman, Sharon Bitensky, Rebecca Hindin, Shelly Parver, *and* **Marina Rostein**
–JPRO Young Professional Award, 2019
Kate Belza O'Bannon and **Arya Marvazy**
(recognizes the achievements of outstanding young Jewish community professionals)

Rabbi Shmuley's This World: The Jewish Values Network, 2019
www.shmuley.com
–Champion of Jewish Values Awards
Marion Wiesel, Co-founder, the Elie Wiesel Foundation for Humanity
Mike Pompeo, 70th US Secretary of State
Sir Clive Gillinson, Executive and Artistic Director of Carnegie Hall
Jason Greenblatt, Special Representative for International Negotiations
Larry Kudlow, Director of the US National Economic Council
(recognizes those who strive to positively affect society)

Simon Wiesenthal Center Humanitarian Award, 2019
www.wiesenthal.com
Bob Iger, Chairman/CEO of Disney
(for his enthusiastic support of the Simon Wiesenthal Center and Museum of Tolerance)

United Synagogue of Conservative Judaism, 2018
www.uscj.org
–Shoshana S. Cardin Leadership Award
Dr. Clifford Nerwen, Synagogue Adath Israel of Riverdale NY for *Safeguarding our Children*
(recognizes an emerging Jewish leader who is making a difference in strengthening and transforming Jewish life through Conservative Judaism)

World Jewish Congress, 2018
www.worldjewishcongress.org
–Teddy Kollek Award for the Advancement of Jewish Culture
Robert Kraft, American philanthropist and owner of the New England Patriots
–Theodor Herzl Award for Individuals Who Promote a Strong Israel and a Safer World

The Rothschild Family
–Shalom Prize
His Majesty Felipe VI of Spain, in recognition of the restitution of civic rights for
   Jews descended from Spaniards

Yivo Institute for Jewish Research, Jan Karski & Pola Nirenska Award, 2018
https://yivo.org
Bella Szwarcman-Czarnota, Warsaw, Poland
*(for authors documenting Polish-Jewish relations and Jewish contributions to
   Polish culture)*

Zionist Organization of America, 2018
www.zoa.org
Mark Levin, Radio host, The Mark Levin Show
Ambassador Richard Grenell, US Ambassador to Germany
Dr. Bob Shillman, World Class Entrepreneur and Philanthropist
Kimberly Guilfoyle, Television host, Fox Five News

15.2.4   Media Awards

Religion Newswriters Association, 2018
www.rna.org
Newspaper Awards
–Excellence in Religion Reporting –Online News Outlets
Elizabeth Eisenstadt Evans, Global Sisters Project (third place)
Nonfiction Religion Book Award
–Excellence for Nonfiction Book
Richard Elliot Friedman, *The Exodus* (second place)

Simon Rockower Awards for Excellence in Jewish Journalism, 2019
www.ajpa.org
See the American Jewish Press Association website for the many awards.

15.2.5   Secular Awards Given to North American Jews

American Academy of Arts and Letters, 2019
www.artsandletters.org
Judith Bernstein, Arts and Letter Award, Art
Robert Alter, Arts and Letters Award, Literature
Michael Singer, Arts and Letters Award, Art
Doron Langberg, John Koch Award, Art

Berggruen Prize, 2018, 2019
www.berggruen.org
Martha Nussbaum, American philosopher (2018)
Ruth Bader Ginsberg, Supreme Court Justice (2019)
(Given to a thinker whose ideas "have profoundly shaped human understanding and advancement in a rapidly changing world")

Carnegie Medal of Philanthropy, 2019
www.medalofphilanthropy.org
Morton L. Mandel

Financial Times Person of the Year Award, 2018
www.ft.com
George Soros, investor and philanthropist

Kennedy Center Honors, 2018
www.kennedy-center.org
Philip Glass, composer

Louisa Gross Horwitz Prize, 2018
https://www.cuimc.columbia.edu/research/louisa-gross-horwitz-prize
Ronald Evans, Salk Institute for Biological Studies (for nuclear hormone signaling and metabolism)

Nobel Prizes, 2018
www.nobelprize.org
William Nordhaus, Yale University, Economics (for integrating climate change into long-run macroeconomic analysis)
Arthur Ashkin, Bell laboratories and Lucent Technologies, Physics (for optical tweezers)

Presidential Medal of Freedom, 2018
www.whitehouse.gov
Miriam Adelson, doctor, philanthropist, and humanitarian

15.2.6   Cultural/Sports Awards Given to North American Jews

Billboard Awards, 2019
www.billboard.com
–Top Artist, Top Male Artist, Top Streaming Artist, Top Billboard 200 Artist, Top Radio Songs Artist, Top Billboard 200 Album, Top Hot 100 Artist, Top Hot 100 Song, Top Rap Artist, Top Rap Male Artist, Top Rock Artist
Drake
Girls Like You—Maroon 5 (Adam Levine) featuring Cardi B
–Top Song Sales Artist

Imagine Dragons (Daniel Platzman)
–Top Soundtrack
The Greatest Showman, Benj Pasek and Justin Paul (producers)
–Top Rap Album
Scorpion—Drake
–Top Streaming Song (Video)
In My Feelings—Drake
–Top Collaboration
Girls Like You—Maroon 5 (Adam Levine) featuring Cardi B
–Top Radio Song
Girls Like You—Maroon 5 (Adam Levine) featuring Cardi B
–Top Selling Song
Girls Like You—Maroon 5 (Adam Levine) featuring Cardi B

Critics' Choice Movie Awards, 2019
www.criticschoice.com/movie-awards
–Best Animated Feature
Spider-Man: Into the Spider-Verse, Avi Arad and Amy Beth Paskal (producers)
–Best Sci-Fi/Horror Movie
A Quiet Place, Michael Bay (producer)
–Best Comedy
Crazy Rich Asians, Nina Jacobson (producer)
–Best Action Movie
Mission: Impossible—Fallout, J.J. Abrams (producer)
–Best Score
Justin Hurwitz, First Man
–Best Song
Mark Ronson, Shallow (from A Star is Born)
–Critics' Choice Creative Achievement Award
Chuck Lorre

Critics' Choice Television Awards, 2019
www.criticschoice.com/television-awards
–Best Drama Series
The Americans, Joe Weisberg and Daniel Sackheim (producers)
–Best Comedy Series
The Marvelous Mrs. Maisel, Amy Sherman-Palladino (creator and executive producer)
–Best Animated Series
BoJack Horseman, Raphael Bob-Waksberg (producer)
–Best Supporting Actor in a Comedy Series
Henry Winkler, Barry
–Best Supporting Actress in a Comedy Series
Alex Borstein, The Marvelous Mrs. Maisel
–Best Supporting Actor in a Drama Series
Noah Emmerich, The Americans

–Best Actress in a Movie/Limited Series
Patricia Arquette, Escape at Dannemora

Daytime Emmys-The Academy of Television Arts & Sciences, 2019
www.emmys.com
–Outstanding Talk Show/Entertainment
The Ellen DeGeneres Show, Andy Lassner (executive producer)
–Outstanding Culinary Program
Valerie's Home Cooking, Marc Schwartz and Ronnie Weinstock (executive producers)
–Lifetime Achievement Award
Judge Judy Sheindlin, television personality and author

Emmys-The Academy of Television Arts & Sciences, 2018
www.emmys.com
–Outstanding Comedy Series
The Marvelous Mrs. Maisel, Amy Sherman-Palladino (creator and executive producer)
–Outstanding Drama Series
Game of Thrones, D.B. Weiss and David Benioff (executive producers)
–Outstanding Variety Sketch Series
Saturday Night Live, Lorne Michaels (executive producer)
–Outstanding Supporting Actor in a Comedy Series
Henry Winkler, Barry
–Outstanding Supporting Actress in a Comedy Series
Alex Borstein, The Marvelous Mrs. Maisel
–Outstanding Directing for a Comedy Series
Amy Sherman-Palladino, The Marvelous Mrs. Maisel
–Outstanding Directing for a Variety Special
Glenn Weiss, The Oscars
–Outstanding Writing for a Comedy Series
Amy Sherman-Palladino, The Marvelous Mrs. Maisel
–Outstanding Writing for a Drama Series
Joe Weisberg and Joel Fields, The Americans
–Outstanding Guest Actress in a Comedy Series
Tiffany Haddish, Saturday Night Live
–In Memoriam
Steven Bochco (producer, writer)
Anthony Bourdain (celebrity chef, author)
Charlotte Rae (actress, comedian, singer)
Mitzi Shore (comedy club owner)
Monty Hall (game show host, producer, philanthropist)

Emmys-The Academy of Television Arts & Sciences, 2019
www.emmys.com
–Outstanding Drama Series

Game of Thrones, David Benioff and D.B. Weiss (executive producers)
–Outstanding Limited Series
Chernobyl, Craig Mazin and Carolyn Strauss (executive producers)
–Outstanding Variety Sketch Series
Saturday Night Live, Lorne Michaels (executive producer)
–Outstanding Supporting Actress in a Comedy Series
Alex Borstein, Susie Myerson in The Marvelous Mrs. Maisel
–Outstanding Supporting Actress in a Drama Series
Julia Garner, Ruth Langmore in Ozark
–Outstanding Supporting Actress in a Limited Series or Movie
Patricia Arquette, Dee Dee Blanchard in The Act
–Outstanding Writing in a Limited Series, Movie or Dramatic Special
Craig Mazin, Chernobyl
–Outstanding Writing for a Variety Series
Last Week Tonight with John Oliver, Josh Gondelman (writer)
–Outstanding Original Music and Lyrics
Antidepressants Are So Not a Big Deal, Rachel Bloom and Adam Schlesinger
    (written for Crazy Ex-Girlfriend)
–Outstanding Writing and Outstanding Informational Series
Anthony Bourdain, Anthony Bourdain Parts Unknown (awarded posthumously)
–In Memoriam
Andre Previn (pianist, conductor, and composer)
Sid Sheinberg, (entertainment executive)
Steve Golin (film and television producer)
Cameron Boyce (actor)
Larry Siegel (comedy writer and satirist)
Peggy Lipton (actress, model, and singer)
Bob Einstein (actor, comedy writer, and producer)
Stan Lee (comic book writer, editor, publisher, and producer)
Lou Weiss (talent agent)
Russell Kagan (television executive)

E! People=s Choice Film Awards, 2018
www.eonline.com
–The Movie
Avengers: Infinity War, Kevin Feige (producer)
–The Comedy Movie
The Spy Who Dumped Me, Susanna Fogel (director)
–The Action Movie
Avengers: Infinity War, Kevin Feige (producer)
–The Female Movie Star
Scarlett Johansson—Avengers: Infinity War

E! People=s Choice Television Awards, 2018
www.eonline.com
–The Drama Show

Riverdale, Jon Goldwater and Sarah Schechter (executive producers)
–The Comedy Show
Orange is the New Black, Jenji Kohan (executive producer)
–The Revival Show
Dynasty, Richard Shapiro, Esther Shapiro, Josh Schwartz, and Brad Silberling
    (executive producers)
–The Daytime Talk Show
The Ellen DeGeneres Show, Andy Lassner (executive producer)
–The Nighttime Talk Show
The Tonight Show Starring Jimmy Fallon, Lorne Michaels (executive producer)

Obie Awards, 2019
www.obieawards.com
–Sustained Excellence in Directing
Leigh Silverman
–Lifetime Achievement Award
Jeffrey Horowitz
World Wrestling Entertainment
–Cruiserweight Champion
Drew Gulak

Forbes List 100 Most Powerful Women, 2018
https://businesstrumpet.com/the-worlds-100-most-powerful-women-in-2018

7. **Susan Wojcicki**, CEO of YouTube
11. **Sheryl Sandberg**, COO of Facebook
14. **Safra Catz**, Oracle Corporation
16. **Adena Friedman**, President and CEO
19. **Ruth Bader Ginsberg**, **Elena Kagan**, Supreme Court Justices
21. **Ruth Porat**, CFO of Alphabet
24. **Ivanka Trump**, White House Aide
31. **Shari Redstone**, Vice-Chair and Controlling owner of Viacom and CBS
36. **Bonnie Hammer,** chairman of NBCUniversal Cable
75. **Judy Faulkner**, CEO and founder of Epic Systems
89. **Kirsten Green**, Founder and Managing Partner of Forerunner Ventures
92. **Ann Wojcicki**, Cofounder and CEO of 23andMe

Golden Globe Awards, 2019
www.goldenglobes.com
–Best Television Series-Drama
The Americans, Joe Weisberg (creator and producer)
–Best Television Series-Musical or Comedy
The Kominsky Method, Chuck Lorre (creator and producer)
–Best Performance in a Television Series-Musical or Comedy
Michael Douglas, The Kominsky Method
–Best Original Film Score
Justin Hurwitz, First Man

–Best Original Song
Shallow, Mark Ronson (songwriter)
–Best Animated Feature Film
Spider-Man: Into the Spider-Verse, Avi Arad and Amy Beth Paskal (producers)
–In Memoriam
Steven Bochco (producer, writer)
Milos Forman (director, screenwriter, actor, professor)
Stan Lee (comic book writer, editor, publisher, producer)
Neil Simon (playwright, screenwriter, author)

Grammy Awards, 2019
www.grammy.com
–Best Dance Recording
Electricity-Silk City & Dua Lipa, featuring Mark Ronson
—Best Rock Song
Masseduction, Jack Antonoff and Annie Clark
–Best Alternative Music Album
Colors, Beck
–Best Compilation Soundtrack for Visual Media
The Great Showman, Benj Pasek and Justin Paul (compilation producers)
–Best Song Written for Visual Media
Shallow, Mark Ronson (songwriter)
–Best Rap Song
God's Plan, Drake
–Special Merit Awards—Trustees Awards
Johnny Mandel, composer and arranger
Lou Adler, music executive, songwriter, film director and producer
–In Memoriam
Mac Miller (rapper, songwriter, record producer)
Alan R. Pearlman (engineer, founder of ARP Instruments, Inc.)
Marty Balin (founder and a lead singer of Jefferson Airplane and Jefferson Starship)
Norman Gimbel (lyricist of popular songs, television, and movie themes)

Juno Awards, 2019
www.junoawards.ca
–Group of the Year
Arkells, Max Kerman
–Rock Album of the Year
Arkells, Rally Cry, Max Kerman
–Video of the Year
Ali Eisner, No Depression—Bahamas

Oscars American Academy of Motion Picture Arts and Sciences, 2019
www.oscars.org
–Best Animated Feature Film
Spider-Man: Into the Spider-Verse, Avi Arad and Amy Beth Paskal (producers)

–Best Adapted Screenplay
BlacKkKlansman, David Rabinowitz and Charlie Wachtel (writers)
–Best Original Song
Shallow (from A Star is Born), Mark Ronson (songwriter)
–Academy Honorary Award
Marvin Levy, publicist
–In Memoriam
Neil Simon (playwright, screenwriter, author)
Martin Bregman (film producer, personal manager)
Milos Forman (director, screenwriter, actor, professor)
Stan Lee (comic book writer, editor, publisher, producer)
William Goldman (novelist, screenwriter, playwright)
James Karen (actor)
Gloria Katz (producer, screenwriter)

Pulitzer Prizes, 2019
www.pulitzer.org/prize-winners-by-year/2018
–Public Service
South Florida Sun Sentinel for reporting on the Parkland shooting by: Tonya Alanez, Susannah Bryan, **David Fleshler**, Stephen Hobbs, Lisa J. Huriash, Paula McMahon, Megan O'Matz, Scott Travis, and **Brittany Wallman**
–Breaking News Reporting
Pittsburgh Post-Gazette for reporting on the Tree of Life synagogue massacre by: Kris Mamula, **Andrew Goldstein**, Paula Reed Ward, Liz Navratil, Shelly Bradbury, Rich Lord, Christopher Huffaker, and Liz Navratil.
–Local Reporting
The Advocate, Baton Rouge, LA for a damning portrayal of the state's discriminatory conviction system by John Simerman, **Jeff Adelson**, Gordon Russell, Dan Swenson, Gordon Russell, and Walt Handelsman
–National Reporting
Staff of the *Wall Street Journal* for uncovering President Trump's secret payoffs to two women during his campaign who claimed to have had affairs with him by Joe Palazzolo, Nicole Hong, **Michael Rothfeld**, Rebecca Davis O'Brien, and Rebecca Ballhaus
–Feature Writing
Hannah Dreier of ProPublica
–Editorial Cartooning
Darrin Bell, freelancer

Screen Actors Guild Awards, 2019
www.sagawards.org
–Outstanding Performance by a Female Actor in a Miniseries or Television Movie
Patricia Arquette, Escape at Dannemora
–Outstanding Performance by an Ensemble in a Comedy Series
The Marvelous Mrs. Maisel, Alex Borstein, Caroline Aaron, Kevin Pollak, and Michael Zegen

–In Memoriam
James Karen (actor)
Charlotte Rae (actress, comedian, singer)
Ricky Jay (magician, actor, bibliophile, writer)
Bob Einstein (actor, comedy writer, producer)

Songwriters Hall of Fame, 2019
www.songwritershalloffame.com
–Johnny Mercer Award, 2019
Carole Bayer Sager
–Visionary Leadership Award
Martin Bandier

Tony Awards, 2019
www.tonyawards.com
–Best Musical
Hadestown, Rachel Chavkin, director
–Best Play
The Ferryman, Sam Mendes, director
–Best Performance by a Leading Actress in a Play
Elaine May, The Waverly Gallery
–Best Direction of a Play
Sam Mendes, The Ferryman
–Best Direction of a Musical
Rachel Chavkin, Hadestown
–Best Sound Design of a Musical
Nevin Steinberg, Hadestown
–Special Tony Award
Judith Light, Isabelle Stevenson Tony Award
–In Memoriam
Neil Simon (playwright, screenwriter)
Alan Wasser (Broadway general manager)
Alvin Epstein (actor, director, acting teacher)
Jerry Frankel (Broadway producer)
William Goldman (novelist, playwright, screenwriter)
Robert Kamlot (Broadway general manager)
Terry Allen Kramer (Broadway producer)
Harvey Sabinson (Broadway press agent, executive director of *The Broadway League*)
Mark Medoff (playwright, screenwriter, actor, professor)
Carole Shelley (actress)
Craig Zadan (Broadway producer)
Glen Roven (composer, lyricist, conductor, producer)
Charlotte Rae (actress comedian, singer)

Time 100, 2019
www.time100.com
Adam Bowen and **James Monsees**, founders of *Juul*, electronic cigarette company
Leah Greenberg and **Ezra Levin**, founders of *Indivisible*, political-activism
   organization

15.2.7 The Forward Fifty, 2018 (www.forward.com)

Forward 50–2018

15.2.7.1 Trump's Jews

Ivanka Trump and Jared Kushner—Senior Advisors
Two people who hold that job title are Ivanka Trump and Jared Kushner, though
they are, of course, so much more and, paradoxically, so much less. There was little
progress this year in their respective portfolios—women and children for Trump,
Middle East peace and other sundries for Kushner—but they clearly exercised
power in other ways. News reports said they shaped the president's response to the
Pittsburgh massacre (the scripted response anyway) and Kushner evidently had a
hand in persuading his father-in-law to excuse the Crown Prince of Saudi Arabia for
the murder of journalist Jamal Khashoggi.

Stephen Miller—Senior Advisor
If the first daughter and her family are meant to represent Orthodox Jewish values
in the White House, the third senior adviser, Stephen Miller, represents the opposite.
When, in June, the administration decided to separate families seeking refuge at the
southern border, Miller—architect of the president's inhumane immigration policy—offered a full-throated endorsement. By doing so, not only did he distance
himself from the majority of American Jews who objected to the policy, he also
distanced himself from his family's immigrant history. His own relatives
denounced him.

Stephen Mnuchin—US Treasury Secretary
Mnuchin surprised everyone this year by simply holding on to his job. In an administration with an unusually high turnover of senior officials, Mnuchin has managed
to avoid Trump's wrath by keeping selectively silent and unendingly loyal. If his
moderate Wall Street predilections are clashing with his boss's unorthodox approach
to tax, trade, and fiscal policy, Mnuchin isn't saying.

David Friedman—US Ambassador to Israel
Friedman relocated his office to Jerusalem from Tel Aviv, a move with grand political and strategic implications. At a dedication ceremony in May, notable for who
spoke (evangelical preachers) and who wasn't invited (Democrats), Trump fulfilled
his promise to move the US Embassy to the contested city, solidifying Jewish claims

and negating Palestinian ones. While American Jews were overwhelmingly wary of the unilateral move, Israelis and white evangelical Christians were thrilled.

Michael D. Cohen—President's Ex-Lawyer

Cohen went from the guy who would take a bullet for his boss to the one who snitched on him. In August, in an extraordinary admission in court, Cohen said that Trump had directed him to pay two women during the 2016 campaign to keep them from publicly speaking about affairs they had with the man now in the White House.

In all, Cohen pleaded guilty to eight criminal counts, including tax fraud and campaign violations. He was sentenced to three years in federal prison and ordered to pay a $50,000 fine. Then on Friday December 7, Cohen got into even more trouble when the special prosecutor's office revealed that he reached out to Russia to arrange a meeting with President Vladimir Putin in late 2015—and that Trump knew about it beforehand.

Sheldon Adelson—Billionaire Philanthropist

The billionaire casino magnate, philanthropist and profligate Republican donor solidified his power this year on many fronts. His privileged seat at the dedication of the US Embassy in Jerusalem was merely one illustration of the force with which he has commandeered American foreign policy to align with the Netanyahu government.

Adelson has used his political access to push his financial self-interests, and the Trump administration is more than happy to oblige. While at first he was a reluctant supporter of the renegade presidential candidate, Adelson bet, and bet big—he was the biggest Republican donor in the midterms—and he won, at least personally. "With Trump occupying the White House, Adelson has found the greatest political ally he's ever had," ProPublica reported.

15.2.7.2 The Other 44

Andre Aciman—Author

An American writer who was born and raised in Alexandria, Egypt, he is currently distinguished professor at the Graduate Center of City University of New York, where he teaches the history of literary theory and the works of Marcel Proust. Aciman previously taught creative writing at New York University and French literature at Princeton and Bard College. In 2009, he was Visiting Distinguished Writer at Wesleyan University. He is the author of several novels, including *Call Me by Your Name* (winner, in the Gay Fiction category, of the 2007 Lambda Literary Award) and a 1995 memoir, *Out of Egypt*, which won a Whiting Award.

Arthur Ashkin—Proving It's Never Too Late to Make History

You don't need to understand what optic tweezers are or how they have revolutionized contemporary physics to understand the achievement of Nobel Prize winner Arthur Ashkin. Indeed, even Bell Labs, his former employer, eschews the scientific to describe the tweezers as grabbing "particles, atoms, viruses and other living cells with their laser beam fingers."

The Nobel committee said that his work "revolutionized laser physics" and opened up "multitude of industrial and medical applications." He also made history because his success, at the age of 96, means he is the oldest person ever to collect a Nobel Prize.

Ady Barkan—Giving His Last Breath to Democracy

Ady Barkan was born to immigrant parents (his mother from Romania by way of Tel Aviv, where she met his father) who became academics in the US. Barkan grew up in what he describes as a "secular Jewish household" and holds dual US and Israeli citizenship. He took an early interest in progressive activism like the fight against anti-gay rights legislation. He went to Yale Law School.

Barkan works for the Center for Popular Democracy. Beginning in 2012, he developed the Fed Up campaign to advocate with the Federal Reserve for the impact of monetary policy on low-income people. Barkan also developed the Be a Hero campaign that supports a range of progressive causes and candidates. During the 2018 Supreme Court confirmation hearings of Brett Kavanaugh, in collaboration with the Maine People's Alliance and Mainers for Accountable Leadership, Barkan and the Be a Hero campaign advocated for Republican US Senator Susan Collins of Maine to vote against the nomination.

Marc Benioff—Entrepreneur

Marc Benioff is an American billionaire internet entrepreneur, author and philanthropist with a net worth of $5.7 billion. He is the founder, chairman and co-CEO of Salesforce, an enterprise cloud computing company. The company he started, Salesforce, has annual revenues of more than $10 billion.

Benioff called out other tech billionaires for opposing a tax to fund homeless services in San Francisco, while buying and promising significant resources to revive *Time* magazine, the struggling old newsstand warhorse.

Jamie Bernstein—Author

Jamie Bernstein, 66, is the eldest daughter of Leonard Bernstein. She gave powerful voice to the experience of having such a remarkable, temperamental father in her memoir *Famous Father Girl,* released this past June.

Max Boot—A Change of Heart

Max Boot is one of those rare public intellectuals with firmly held beliefs who is willing to admit that he was wrong. He's done that a lot in the last year, and garnered enormous attention for it. A Jewish refugee from the Soviet Union who was raised in California and once quipped that he was the only conservative student at Berkeley, Boot's writings have upheld centrist Republican values: socially liberal, economically conservative, in favor of a strong military and American intervention overseas, but wary of "political correctness" and identity politics. Trump's nomination and election victory, though, seriously rattled Boot, 49, a columnist for the *Washington Post* and a fellow at the Council on Foreign Relations. Late last year, he realized how wrong he was to overlook the privilege he enjoyed as a white man. This year, he reversed his skepticism of the danger of climate change.

Then he went even further. Not only had he officially renounced the Republican party after Trump's election, but in a widely-shared, damning column published just before the midterms, Boot exhorted his readers to vote for Democrats. "For every office. Regardless of who they are," he urged. Boot's battle cry resonated widely, bolstered by the publication of his timely book, *The Corrosion of Conservatism: Why I Left the Right*.

Bradd Boxman—Rabbi of Kol Tikvah, Parkland, FL

It was Rabbi Bradd Boxman's day off when he got a call saying that a gunman was loose in Parkland, FL, in school hallways barely half a mile from the synagogue.

About 100 of Kol Tikvah's teens go to Stoneman Douglas, so the first thing Boxman and the staff did was try to locate them. He began texting: "Are you ok?" "Where are you?" Boxman held a small service that afternoon in the sanctuary.

"It was probably, in my career, the most horrific period of time," he said. "As you can imagine, the trauma, the pain, the sorrow, psychological torment … we're still dealing with it today." Several of the students leading the March for Our Lives movement belong to Kol Tikvah, Boxman said, and he was there to support them. Two weeks after the shooting, they organized a bus of 47 and traveled overnight to Tallahassee. They joined the march in Florida's capital and used the opportunity to practice civil disobedience, banging on the doors of senators and legislators to tell their story. At one point, they all dropped to the floor, wanting the politicians to have an experience like walking over dead bodies.

Jeffrey Cohen—Tree of Life Synagogue Member

The day after the Pittsburgh massacre, Dr. Jeffrey Cohen went to see the man who had killed his friends. Cohen, 63, is a member of the Tree of Life synagogue, and is president of Allegheny General Hospital, where Robert Bowers, the shooter, was taken for treatment. Two other Jewish doctors and one Jewish nurse had already treated Bowers. Cohen wanted to see the man for himself. Cohen's act of humanity—and his support for the doctors who treated Bowers—made international headlines. He insisted that though Bowers' act was "heinous," he was not the root of the problem. "It's time for leaders to lead," Cohen said. "And the words mean things. And the words are leading to people doing things like this, and I find it appalling."

Julie Cohen—For The Love of RBG

With all of the love out there for Supreme Court justice Ruth Bader Ginsburg, it was only a matter of time before a documentary came along. 2018's "RBG" gave us a long-awaited cinematic look at RBG's career that was met with near-universal acclaim—and even gave publicity to RBG's personal trainer and his workout regimen for the 85-year-old jurist. One of the women behind the film is Julie Cohen, who co-directed and produced it with fellow Columbia School of Journalism professor Betsy West.

In 2007 Cohen started her own production company, Better Than Fiction Productions. Cohen already has three New York regional Emmys, and she and West walked away from 2018's Critics' Choice Documentary Awards with a win for Best Political Documentary for "RBG."

Stosh Cotler—Building A Nationwide Jewish Resistance

The advocacy group Bend the Arc emerged this year as one of the leaders of the so-called "Jewish Resistance" to President Trump's administration. Led for the past four years by CEO Stosh Cotler, 50, Bend the Arc has been one of the most outspoken groups protesting Trump's immigration policies. They held rallies across the country to condemn Trump's plan to end the DACA program for undocumented immigrants, and continued to hold protests against family separations at the border. Some activists were even arrested at the Capitol in January. Bend the Arc also called the confirmation of Supreme Court Justice Brett Kavanaugh a "national disgrace" with Cotler herself decrying Trump's "limitless hatred, anger, and lies."

Ruchie Freier—Judge, Ambulance Group Founder and Community Leader for Hasidic Women

When Ruchie Freier announced her candidacy for civil court judge in Boro Park, she enlisted the most loyal staff she could find: Her six children. Freier, 53, has pushed boundaries in her Hasidic community—not only is she the first Hasidic female judge in the US, but she has also poured her leadership and expertise into building community institutions, namely, B'Derech, a GED program for Haredi youth at-risk, and a much-lauded Ezras Nashim, a female ambulance team, recently profiled by Paula Eiselt in her film "Queen93."

Dasi Fruchter—A New Voice Within the Orthodox Clergy

Rabbanit Hadas "Dasi" Fruchter, an Orthodox Jewish woman, who turns 29 this month, was ordained at Yeshivat Maharat in The Bronx and has made plans to move to Greater Philadelphia to start her own synagogue. She is currently assistant spiritual leader at Beth Sholom Congregation and Talmud Torah in Potomac, Maryland.

Joel Grey—He Put the Yidl into "Fiddler"

Joel Grey, 86, who won an Oscar for his performance in "Cabaret," has an enviable reputation as a performer. His directorial accomplishments, on the other hand, while impressive, have been relatively few and far between.

So he was somewhat surprised when he received a call from Zalmen Mlotek, musical director of the National Yiddish Theatre Folksbiene, inviting him to direct the Folksbiene's forthcoming production of "Fiddler on the Roof." Joel told Zalmen he'd have to think about it. The next day, Joel had decided: "Having long been an admirer of the show, when Zalmen invited me to direct for the first time ever in the US a Yiddish version that originated in Israel, I could only say 'Yes!'"

Tiffany Haddish—Comedian

The 38-year-old comedian, who is an Ethiopian Jew, has been ready for years—popping up in guest appearances on comedy shows like "That's So Raven," "New Girl" and "Chelsea Lately"—it's only this year that her fame has caught up with her talent. Finally, with as explosive a reputation as her talent deserves, the breakout star of 2017's "Girls Trip" has become a one-woman comedy industry in 2018, starring in four feature films, six music videos and her hit TV show, "The Last O.G." She won an Emmy for her watershed appearance as a "Saturday Night Live" host.

Becca Heller—Refugee Assistance

Heller, 36, won the 2015 Charles Bronfman Prize for her work with the International Refugee Assistance Project (IRAP). She was the youngest recipient in the history of the prize. Since then, her work with IRAP has sharpened even further.

In addition to its work with refugees, IRAP has made legal representation available to others affected by anti-immigrant measures. For example, responding to the Trump administration's attempted Muslim ban, IRAP coordinated to make sure that there were lawyers at every port where people were being detained or threatened with deportation.

Basil Herring—Orthodox Rabbi

Basil Herring is a South African-born rabbi and former executive president of the Rabbinical Council of America (RCA) who is designing a new standard synagogue siddur, translation, and commentary. The previous RCA siddur had been published by Art scroll in 1984. The new *Avodat Halev Siddur* includes women-specific prayers with expanded language (prayers for new mothers after childbirth, prayers for a female head of household, a post-meal zimmun written specifically to be sung by three women); its ritual instructions use the pronoun "one" instead of "he" as default, and even discusses the importance of halakhic prenuptial agreements. Women scholars' commentary range from Nechama Leibowitz to Devra Kay to Yaffa Eliach, among others.

Melody Herzfeld—Drama Teacher in Parkland, FL

There was nary a dry eye in the house when students from Marjory Stoneman Douglas High School performed "Seasons of Love" from the musical "Rent" at the 72nd annual Tony Awards this summer. They were honoring their drama teacher Melody Herzfeld, who hid with 65 students for more than 2 h amidst gunfire at the school in Parkland, FL. She was recognized on theater's biggest night with the 2018 Excellence in Theatre Education Award, an honor given to a theater educator "who has demonstrated monumental impact on the lives of students."

Jodi Kantor—Journalist Who Made a Lasting Impact

On October 5, 2017, *The New York Times* published an explosive front-page story by Jodi Kantor and Megan Twohey, headlined, "Harvey Weinstein Paid Off Sexual Harassment Accusers for Decades."

Kantor, who is 43 and whose grandparents were Holocaust survivors, was raised in NJ and attended the Union for Reform Judaism's Eisner summer camp in Great Barrington, MA. She credits the camp with giving her a level of social consciousness she had never experienced. After graduating from Columbia University she studied at Harvard Law School for a year before becoming a journalist at Slate in 1998. She joined *The New York Times* in 2003 and covered the Obamas, the gender gap at Harvard Business School, and scheduling practices at Starbucks.

But of all her reporting, the Weinstein investigation, which won a Pulitzer Prize, will undoubtedly have the most long-lasting effect. "The Weinstein story is easily one of the most important articles ever published in *The New York Times*," said the newspaper's publisher, A.G. Sulzberger. "It made such a powerful case for change that a year later we're still seeing its ongoing impact across countless industries and around the world."

Katle Kanye—Critic of Hasidic Education

No one knows who he is, but in July, Katle Kanye, the erudite Hasidic blogger with the pseudonym meaning "Just a regular Joe," published a searing book-length indictment of Hasidic education. And it might actually influence Hasidic public opinion since it's written in Yiddish, the way Hasidim in America actually speak. Some of the gaps in the education he sees—both secular and religious—are scandalous. Students graduate without knowing basic mathematics, the months of the American year or even with the ability to give a short Torah lesson.

Debra Katz—Lawyer

Katz represented Christine Blasey Ford before the Senate Judiciary Committee, when sharing her allegation of sexual assault against now-Supreme Court Justice Brett Kavanaugh. A founding partner of Katz, Marshall & Banks in Washington, DC—described as a "Whistleblower & Employment Law Firm"—she is also working on the cases of Irwin Reiter, a longtime Weinstein Company executive who reportedly spoke out against Harvey Weinstein sexually harassing a front desk employee, as well as one of the two women who came to Hillel International with complaints about the behavior of Michael Steinhardt, one of its biggest donors.

Karlie Kloss—A Model Jewish Activist

Karlie Kloss converted to Judaism before marrying her partner of six years, Joshua Kushner. She is a supermodel, entrepreneur, activist, and coder. Kloss, a 26-year-old St. Louis native, rocketed to success as a high fashion runway model in 2008, going on to become arguably the most successful and accomplished model of her generation. As a computer science student at New York University's Gallatin School of Independent Studies she started coding, which led to her developing a not-for-profit charity group to teach young girls coding in an empowering environment. Kloss and Kushner are not only blindingly photogenic, with an apparently enviable relationship and more professional success than you could shake an expensive stick at—they also represent the nascent progressive wing of the Kushner family. The couple attended the Women's March and March for Our Lives together, and Kloss has led the pair in anti-gun violence activism.

Rachel Kushner—Author of "The Mars' Room" and 'Girl Citizen'

Kushner's first novel was set in Cuba in the 1950s, her second in NY and Italy in the 1970s. "The Mars Room" is set in the early 2000s, which brings Kushner nearly to the present. "The Mars Room" was a success, ending up on the shortlist for this year's Man Booker Prize. With it, Kushner, 50 and already a respected writer, entered a new sphere of literary fame. (She was dubbed *The Forward*'s 2018 Sexiest Jewish Intellectual Alive.) In doing so as a "girl citizen," she quietly proposed a model of literary prowess somewhat in opposition to that which has recently dominated American letters. For at least the last half century, the literary world has often, not without a certain snobbishness, suggested that for writers, craft and rigor must come before an effort to be just. Kushner is one of a number of ascendant writers challenging that model.

David Lubell—A Welcoming Jewish American
David Lubell, 42, is a helper with a particularly unique vision for bringing together newcomers and natives as neighbors. His work with the city of Pittsburgh and Welcoming America, the organization that he founded, helped put Pittsburgh in a strong position to get past the tragedy at the Tree of Life Synagogue. He received the Charles Bronfman Prize this year in recognition of how he reached into 190 communities around America, touching the lives of tens of millions of people. With the help of local governments, he provided structure for communities to learn about each other's customs, needs and talents. Regardless of color, beliefs or provenance, the communities that worked together grew stronger together.

Elaine Luria—Congresswoman
Seders tend to be noisy, but Elaine Luria's Seder on an aircraft carrier in the Middle East took the kosher-for-Passover cake. "We're going through the Haggadah … having our little makeshift Seder there while we're launching and recovering aircraft that are striking terrorist targets in Afghanistan," Luria told *The Forward* about a month before she won a tight race—51% to 49%—for a VA congressional district that includes several military facilities and the biggest naval base on the East Coast. As a veteran, a woman and a Jew, the 43-year-old Luria boasted a profile that was valued among Democrat strategists. She was raised in AL and ran as a moderate.

Marc Maron—Comedian
Marc Maron, 55, didn't start out as leading man material. Since 2009 his celebrated podcast "WTF with Marc Maron," has famously hosted Oscar-winning actors, iconic musicians and even a sitting president—all from the clutter of his garage. But in the past two years Maron has gained new recognition for his acting chops, courtesy of the Emmy-nominated Netflix series "GLOW."

Maron started his career as a standup comedian in the 1990s, making regular appearances on the Late Show with David Letterman and more appearances on Late Night with Conan O'Brien than any other comedian. But Maron's move to the host's chair was less successful. In 1993 he was pegged for "Short Attention Span Theater" on Comedy Central, taking over hosting duties from fellow Jew Jon Stewart. The show's cancellation in 1994 did a number on Maron's self-esteem and, as he's mentioned often on "WTF" and in his books, amplified his substance abuse during this period.

Elaine May—Actress, Writer, and Director
Elaine May, 86, writer of The Birdcage," a mid-90s comedy about the clash between a gay couple and their conservative soon-to-be in-laws, "Labyrinth," a terrifyingly weird children's movie about a magical David Bowie, and an actress in "The Graduate"?, May, has been a writer and director lighting up the American comedy scene since the 1950s, when she debuted in a comedy duo with Mike Nichols, an act that Dick Cavett described as "one of the comic meteors in the sky." This fall, May

is appearing on Broadway in a soberer setting, starring in Kenneth Lonergan's play "The Waverly Gallery."

Keren McGinity—Academic Historian

"There needs to be a Jewish response to the #MeToo movement." That was the clarion call from Jewish Studies professor Keren McGinity detailing some of the harassment she had personally suffered in the Jewish institutional world. She is a gender historian who specializes in the changing meanings and experiences of Jewish intermarriage, her story was no less forceful for the irony that one of the few times in which converts, intermarried women, and born Jewish women are treated similarly is when they are being sexually harassed.

McGinity's harasser was Steven M. Cohen, a hitherto widely-respected and cited expert on Jewish demography. Several other women accused him of significant improprieties, leading to his apology and resignation. McGinity's larger, communal, point is still in play. She has set an example by serving on the Sexual Misconduct Task Force of the Association for Jewish Studies.

Jeffrey Myers—Choosing Peace Before Politics

Rabbi Jeffrey Myers was introduced to the world in a photograph of him being rushed away from the Tree of Life synagogue, with a tallit over one shoulder, clutching his kippah to his head. He quickly became the face of Jewish Pittsburgh, speaking at length to the media and eventually taking President Trump and his family on a tour of the devastated synagogue.

On the first Shabbat after the shooting, Myers opened up about why he spoke to Trump, in a sermon given before 1000 worshippers, and the congregants of the three communities who lost members in the massacre. His sermon was an eloquent, impassioned call to his community to meet hate with love—no matter who, no matter when or where. Afterwards, he received a standing ovation. He was the only leader who spoke that morning who directly referenced the president.

Craig Newmark—Founder of Craigslist

Craig Newmark assured reporters that he did not make a donation to the CUNY Graduate School of Journalism out of guilt. Newmark, founder of Craigslist—the online service which has claimed a major part of the billion-dollar classified ad business from newspapers—gave the school $20 million in June in support of journalism and a public school system that was committed to helping students who relied on scholarships, like he once did. In his dedication to journalism, he also donated $1 million to ProPublica, $500,000 to Columbia Journalism Review, $1 million to Data & Society (a research institute) and more than $560,000 to the International Center for Journalists.

In an interview with Recode in July, Newmark said there were three people who had a major influence on his life. The first two were Mr. and Mrs. Levin, his Hebrew School teachers at the Jewish Community Center in Morristown, NJ. The next was his high school US History teacher, Mr. Schulsky.

Jared Polis—Gay, Millionaire, Jewish Governor-Elect of Colorado

On November 6, Jared Polis, 43, was elected to become Colorado's first Jewish governor, and the country's first openly gay governor, when he beat his Republican opponent with 52% to Walker Stapleton's 44%. A Democrat, Polis came to the job from Congress, where he was one of the wealthiest members. He sold an internet access provider he created while a student at Princeton for $23 million, and helped sell his family's online greeting-card company for $780 million in 1999.

Natalie Portman—Divisive Conversation Starter

When Natalie Portman, 37, belatedly declined to come to Israel for the Genesis Prize ceremony, she set off a furor. Citing the "mistreatment of those suffering from today's atrocities," she said she could not travel to accept the prize. She set herself up as an embodiment of principles that were at odds with the government of Israeli Prime Minister, Benjamin Netanyahu, as she stated that "Because I care about Israel, I must stand up against violence, corruption, inequality, and abuse of power."

Aly Raisman—Champion of Gymnastics and Justice

During the 2012 summer Olympic Games in London, the Jewish world watched with particular interest and pride when the American Jewish gymnast Alexandra "Aly" Raisman, then 18, became the first American woman in Olympic history to win a gold medal in the floor exercise. The achievement itself was a dayenu moment, but her routine added ethnic sparkle because she chose to perform to the traditional tune "Hava Nagila" in front of—literally—the entire world.

But Raisman was suppressing a lurid secret: For years she had been subjected to repeated sexual abuse at the hands of the USA Gymnastics team doctor, Larry Nassar.

Raisman and the team she led as captain would bag two more Olympic gold medals—for team events at both the 2012 and 2016 Rio Olympic Games—before Raisman would finally share her experience of Nassar with FBI investigators. Then, in November 2017, on the heels of the burgeoning #MeToo movement and the cultural outing of sexual predators across several industries, Raisman decided to join fellow outspoken gymnasts and go public. *Raisman didn't stop at telling her story; she launched a crusade beginning with her 2017 book, Fierce*, and in subsequent interviews and speeches,

Jacky Rosen—From Shul President to Nevada Senator

Jacky Rosen, 61, has climbed the leadership ladder quickly. In 2016 she was her Las Vegas-area synagogue's president, then in 2017 she was elected to Congress, before winning an even bigger national office—being elected senator for Nevada in 2018. She's the first freshman congresswoman to ever win a Senate seat.

Julia Salazar—Contested Identity, Uncontested Election

Julia Salazar sprang to public attention when she surprisingly defeated incumbent Martin Dilan in the Democratic primary for a New York State Senate seat. A young woman with South American roots coming from the left of the party to shock a centrist. She claims that her Jewish roots had contributed to her political worldview. As a student at Columbia University, however, she identified as a pro-life Christian. Her Sephardi identity was also brought into question as her family history seemed to include limited obvious Jewish engagement. Salazar and her defenders eventually pointed out that, on the one hand, her youth and leftish leanings made her a prime target for right wing media and that, on the other, the fluid nature of many Sephardi communities means that Jewish identity does not work as simply or as rigidly as in many North American Ashkenazi communities. Julia Salazar will be the Jewishly identified state senator for the 18th district of NY.

Abby Schachner—Comedian
In November 2017, Schachner was one of five women to speak to *The New York Times* about Louis CK's inappropriate sexual behavior. The choice to come forward about a phone call she had with CK in 2003 in which he acted inappropriately played a role in his subsequent confession to sexual misbehavior, as well as in his partial ostracization from the comedy community.

Schachner's comedy often plays on her own fears and anxieties. She has written over a dozen solo shows including "Jew Must Be Crazy," "Plate," about eating disorders, and "Shadow Kissers," about her fear of intimacy. She's also been known to use events from her life as creative fuel. Her parent's divorce, which allegedly involved her father Sheldon hiring a hit man to kill her mother (the attempt was unsuccessful), was the subject of her solo show "Schachner v. Schachner."

Brian Schreiber—Creating A Community Hub in The Face of Tragedy
The heart of the Pittsburgh neighborhood of Squirrel Hill is its Jewish Community Center, and so it was no surprise that shortly after the massacre at the Tree of Life synagogue four blocks away, the JCC became the hub of community activities.

The Center, led by President and CEO Brian Schreiber, immediately became a response center for the FBI and the American Red Cross, hosting community briefings and readily-available grief counselors and therapy dogs. In the subsequent days, it hosted a funeral, provided food for overwhelmed community members, and hosted Israeli trauma experts.

As president and CEO of the JCC, a role he has held for the past 20 years, Schreiber oversees more than 900 full-time, part-time, and seasonal staff. He has grown endowment funds from $1 million to over $19 million since 1999, according to the JCC Association.

Howard Schultz—Starbuck's Life Beyond Coffee
Before he stepped down as Starbucks' executive chairman, Howard Schultz announced that the coffee chain would open its restrooms to all visitors, regardless of whether they are paying customers. The policy change was Schultz's way of acknowledging the controversy that hit in the company in May, when two black men were arrested after asking to use the bathroom in a Philadelphia Starbucks. Told it was only for paying customers, they sat down without ordering anything. Then the manager called the police.

Schultz, 65, set the tone of a corporate leader genuinely concerned that his company should do the right thing. He addressed the incident immediately, directly and apologetically, and directed the company to close 8000 stores for a day of racial bias training.

Josh Shapiro—Fast-Rising Star in Pennsylvania Politics

This summer, Pennsylvania's Jewish Attorney General unveiled one of the most shocking documents in the history of the international clergy abuse scandal in the Catholic Church. Josh Shapiro announced the release of a 1400-page grand jury report that claimed church leaders in Pennsylvania had covered for more than 300 Catholic priests accused of abusing more than 1000 children. The report was the result of an 18-month investigation led by Shapiro's office. Shapiro, 45, is a fast-rising star in PA politics; once the youngest chief of staff in the US Congress, later a member of the state legislature. Elected to Attorney General in 2016, he's widely thought to have plans to run for higher office.

Amy Sherman-Palladino—Producer of Mrs. Maisel

Amy Sherman-Palladino is the producer of the "Gilmore Girls" and "The Marvelous Mr. Maisel." "Mrs. Maisel" is centrally concerned with being loud and proud about Jewish humor. Its title character is a young housewife in the 1950s who turns to comedy—often raunchily—after her nebbishy husband leaves her for his secretary. Along the way, Midge Maisel, played by Rachel Brosnahan, befriends Lenny Bruce, bribes bookers with brisket and manages to alienate her rabbi in truly unorthodox ways. It is joyful, kvetchy NY Jewishness, seen through a pastel-tinted mist of nostalgia. The show's massive success—both the series and its cast, including Brosnahan, won laurels at the Golden Globe and Emmy awards.

George Soros—Anti-Semites' Favorite Boogeyman

The newly empowered white nationalist movement has a favorite boogeyman—88-year-old Jewish billionaire and Holocaust survivor George Soros. From neo-Nazi websites like The Daily Stormer to Republican campaign ads, from the NRA to presidential tweets, the racist trope of the Jewish conspiracy has made an unwelcome return—this time it's painted with Soros at its center.

The midterm elections saw members of the Republican Party falsely describe Soros as the funder and string-puller of both the Kavanaugh protests and the refugee caravan trudging from Honduras to seek asylum in America.

Zalman Tiechtel—Making Jewish College Life in Kansas Accessible, Rewarding and Tasty!

Zalman Tiechtel, 37, the University of Kansas, have made Jewish life accessible to those who observe the dietary restrictions 365 days a year, even in the college town of Lawrence. After 13 years at KU, the Tiechtels established a kosher meals program in a dining hall in February. They have been working for years to expand kosher options, including operating a concession stand at Allen Fieldhouse, the home of the Jayhawks' five-time national champion men's basketball team. They've also worked to comfort the community amidst tragedy: After three people in Lawrence were killed in a mass shooting, the same day as a Las Vegas gunman killed 58, the Tiechtels set up a system of "good cards"—instructing recipients to do a good deed within 10 min and then pass it on to someone else.

Julia Turshen—Cooking Food with A Side of Activism

Turshen has spent the last two years fighting back against power. She fed an army of righteously enraged political dissenters in her 2017 book "Feed The Resistance" and then created the website "Equity at The Table" as a way of breaking down the gatekeeping boundaries in the food media industry and getting diverse people diverse jobs. Oh, and she's published "Now & Again," a peaceful paean to home cooking and the magic of leftovers. So, whether you believe in dissent, fairness or the peaceful enjoyment of leftovers, you have to talk about her.

Joe Weisberg—TV Writer
Joe Weisberg is the closest thing we have to a Jewish Ian Fleming. Creator of FX's Emmy-winning spy series, "The Americans," one of Weisberg's first jobs out of college was at the Central Intelligence Agency.

Weisberg eventually left the Agency to teach special education in Queens. He turned to TV writing in 2010. After penning scripts for "Falling Skies" and the DirectTV run of "Damages" he pitched a Cold War espionage family drama about KGB agents posing as every day, nuclear family Yanks.

"The Americans" ran on FX for six acclaimed seasons. Its final episode gained Weisberg his first Emmy for outstanding writing following five nominations. His first series as show runner was such a hit, we can't wait to see what he comes up with next. Here's hoping it keeps the fun wigs from "The Americans."

15.2.8   Jewish Women International 10 Women to Watch, 2018

www.jwi.org

1. **Jenny Abramson**, Abramson is the founder and managing partner of Rethink Impact, the "largest impact-oriented venture capital fund in the country with a gender lens. Joining with her is partner Heidi Patel, a veteran of the world of impact investing. Rethink investors come from 32 states and have a balance of men and women.

2. **Mackenzie** Barth, co-founded Spoon at Northwestern University in 2012. Spoon has grown into a global media company with 300 campus-based chapters and over 11,500 contributors in the US and elsewhere. Its stock in trade is empowering young people to create articles, photos, videos and events highlighting their food interests and educating their peers. Along the way, students receive training to develop skills to take with them into the job world.

3. **Wendy Feldman Block**, Senior managing director at Savills Studley, an international commercial real estate firm specializing in tenant representation,

4. **Rabbi Lizzi Heydemann**, Started Mishkan, an alternative to traditional synagogues, in Chicago where an environment is created in which Judaism is invigorated and without which people do not want to live, a place where people find connection, joy, and purpose.

5. **Dr. Logan Levkoff**, an educator dedicated to perpetuating healthy and positive messages about sexuality and relationships. She teaches widely, has written multiple books about both teen and adult sexuality and is an oft-consulted

expert appearing on such TV shows as *Nightline, Good Morning America*, and *The Today Show*.

6. **Marlee Matlin**, at age 21 won an Academy Award for *Children of a Lesser God*. Most recently, she has appeared in the SyFy series *The Magicians*, and was a regular on the ABC thriller *Quantico*. She was a cast member on *The West Wing*, and received award nominations for her work as a courtroom litigator in the series *Reasonable Doubts*. Her appearances on such iconic shows as *The Practice, Law and Order: SVU, Picket Fences* and *Seinfeld* (she played Jerry's love interest) garnered Emmy Award nominations. She also was cast member of the Peabody Award-winning series *Switched at Birth*, which, according to ABC Family, was "the first mainstream television series to have multiple deaf and hard-of-hearing series regulars and scenes shot entirely in American Sign Language (ASL)."

7. **Dr. Jill Saxon**. Throughout Saxon's life, from the time her team was named number one high school soccer team in the US, to her years as a Navy lieutenant and optometrist serving our nation's heroes during Operation Iraqi Freedom, to her current work as senior director, professional strategy at the global headquarters of Bausch + Lomb, in Bridgewater, NJ, she has strived to excel, while fulfilling her goal to help people.

8. **Beth Chartoff Spector**, senior managing director and head of investor relations and business development for GSO Capital, a division of Wall Street investment powerhouse Blackstone.

9. **Laurie Strongin**, The Hope for Henry Foundation, which Strongin and husband Allen Goldberg founded in 2003, is reinventing how hospitals care for seriously ill children. She serves as the foundation's CEO.

10. **Linda Youngentob.** Through her philanthropic and hands-on involvement in multiple educational organizations throughout Montgomery County, MD, she works to impact the lives of first-generation college students, many from immigrant families, by helping them apply for and succeed in college. With their success and growing financial independence, they can in turn assist their families.

15.2.9   The Jerusalem Post's 50 Influential Jews of 2018

www.jpost.org
Note: North American honorees are in boldface type.

1. Avichai Mandelblit
2. Benjamin Netanyahu
3. **Jared Kushner** and **Ivanka Trump**, presidential advisors
4. **David Friedman**, US Ambassador to Israel
5. **Maggie Haberman**, reporter for the *New York Times*

6. **Steve Mnuchin**, US Secretary of the Treasury
7. **Audrey Azulay**, UNESCO leader
8. Ayelet Shaked
9. **Ronald Lauder**, President, World Jewish Congress
10. Gal Gadot
11. Naftali Bennett and Avigdor Liberman
12. Yossi Cohen and Gadi Eisenkot
13. **Ruth Bader-Ginsberg**, **Elena Kagan**, and **Stephen Breyer**, US Supreme Court Justices
14. **Michael Cohen**, lawyer to President Trump
15. Isaac Herzog
16. **Sheldon Adelson**, businessman and philanthropist
17. Claudia Sheinbaum
18. Miri Regev
19. Esther Hayut
20. Reuven Rivlin
21. **Ron Dermer** and Danny Danon, Israeli Ambassador to the US
22. Roman Abramovich
23. **Mark Zuckerberg** and **Sheryl Sandberg**, Facebook
24. Avi Gabbay and Yair Lapid
25. Gilad Erdan, Gideon Sa'ar and Israel Katz
26. Benny Gantz and Gabi Ashkenazi
27. Netta Barzilai
28. Luciana Berger
29. **Natalie Portman**, actress
30. **Russell Robinson**, CEO of JNF – USA
31. Rabbi Berl Lazar and Rabbi Pinchas Goldschmidt
32. **Howard Kohr**, Executive Director of AIPAC
33. **Simone Zimmerman**, political activist
34. Shari Arison
35. **Sylvan Adams**, philanthropist
36. Nitsana Darshan-Leitner
37. Danny Atar
38. **Mayim Bialik**, actress
39. Shiri Maimon
40. Marie van der Zyl
41. Wendy Kahn
42. Dr. Shmuel Rosenman and **Phyllis Greenberg Heideman,** March of the Living
43. **Bini Zomer**, Noble Energy
44. **Rabbi Ammiel Hirsch**, Reform Judaism leader
45. **Bonnie Hammer**, network executive
46. Sivan Rahav Meir
47. Gidi Mark
48. **Haim Saban**, TV and film productions
49. Or Na'aman
50. **Nicole Krauss**, novelist

15.2.10   US Jewish Politicians

Jews in the US Senate in the 116th Congress (January 2019–January 2021)
Michael Bennet (D-OR)
Richard Blumenthal (D-CT)
Ben Cardin (D-MD)
Dianne Feinstein (D-CA)
Jacky Rosen (D-NV) *
Bernie Sanders (D-VT)
Brian Schatz (D-HI)
Charles Schumer (D-NY)
Ron Wyden (D-OR)

Jews in the US House of Representatives in the 116th Congress (January 2019-January 2021)
Suzanne Bonamici (D-OR)
David Cicilline (D-RI)
Steve Cohen (D-TN)
Susan Davis (D-CA)
Ted Deutch (D-FL)
Eliot Engel (D-NY)
Lois Frankel (D-FL)
Josh Gottheimer (D-NJ)
David Kustoff (R-TN)
Andy Levin (D-MI) *
Mike Levin (D-CA) *
Alan Lowenthal (D-CA)
Nita Lowey (D-NY)
Elaine Luria (D-VA) *
Jerrold Nadler (D-NY)
Dean Phillips (D-MN) *
Jamie Raskin (D-MD)
Max Rose (D-NY) *
Jan Schakowsky (D-IL)
Adam Schiff (D-CA)
Brad Schneider (D-IL)
Kim Schrier (D-WA) *
Brad Sherman (D-CA)
Elissa Slotkin (D-MI) *
Debbie Wasserman-Schultz (D-FL)
Susan Wild (D-PA)
John Yarmuth (D-KY)
Lee Zeldin (R-NY)

Jewish Governors
Jared Polis (D-CO) *
J. B. (Jay Robert) Pritzker (D-IL) *

Jewish Mayors of the Top 50 US Cities
Los Angeles, **Eric Garcetti**
Chicago, **Rahm Emanuel**
Austin, **Steve Adler**
Las Vegas, **Carolyn Goodman**
Minneapolis, **Jacob Frey**
San Antonio, **Ron Nirenberg**
Sacramento, **Darrell Steinberg**
Tucson, **Jonathan Rothschild**
Oakland, **Libby Schaaf**

Jewish US Cabinet Officers
Steven Mnuchin, Secretary of the Treasury
David Shulkin, Secretary of Veterans Affairs

Jewish US Supreme Court Justices
Stephen Breyer
Ruth Bader Ginsburg
Elena Kagan
*Indicates newly-elected

15.3 Obituaries, July 2018 to May 2019

This list of obituaries was culled from JTA (www.JTA.org), the Jewish Federations of North America (www.JFNA.org), *The Forward* (www.forward.com), *Tablet* (www.tabletmag.com), *Jewish Journal* (www.jewishjournal.com), *The New York Times* obituary section online, and the *Toronto Star* online.

Obituaries for notable figures are abridgments of those originally posted by the JTA.

15.3.1 Notable Obituaries, July 2018–May 2019[1]

Tree of Life Synagogue Shooting Victims
Oct. 28, 2018 (JTA)—Here are the names of the victims of the Pittsburgh synagogue shooting

---

[1] For full obituary of notable figures see www.JTA.org.

The 11 victims of Saturday's attack on a Pittsburgh synagogue included two brothers, a married couple, and a physician who assisted patients in the early days of the AIDS crisis.

The chief medical examiner of Pittsburgh's Allegheny County released the names Sunday, one day after a gunman opened fire at Tree of Life Congregation, which houses three separate prayer services. In addition to the 11 victims, two congregants and four police officers were injured. The youngest victim was 54 and the oldest was 97.

At a news conference Sunday, federal officials as well as the mayor of Pittsburgh, Bill Peduto, expressed sympathy for the victims' families and solidarity with the Jewish community of Squirrel Hill, the historically Jewish neighborhood where the shooting took place.

"The Jewish community is the backbone," Peduto said of the Squirrel Hill neighborhood. "It is part of the fabric of Pittsburgh and we will be there in all communities to help our friends in the Jewish community. We've been knocked down before, but we've always been able to stand up because we work together. "We know that we as a society are better than this. We know that hate will never win out."

Jeff Finkelstein, president and CEO of Pittsburgh's Jewish federation, at the news conference called it "an awful, awful period for our Jewish community, and especially for the families that have been affected, and it's real once you hear the names. We'll be there for them and be there to help our Jewish community and the Pittsburgh region heal from this," he said.

Peduto also pushed back against a statement by President Donald Trump that an armed guard could have prevented the carnage at the synagogue. The mayor said that instead of arming more people, the focus should be on stopping irrational hatred and removing guns from the hands of those who seek to do harm. "We shouldn't be trying to find ways to minimize the dangers that occur from irrational behavior," he said. "We should be working to eliminate irrational behavior and the empowerment of people who would seek to cause this type of carnage from continuing. The approach we need to be looking at is how we take the guns, which is the common denominator of every mass shooting in America, out of the hands of those who are looking to express hatred through murder."

The victims are: **David Rosenthal** (54), **Cecil Rosenthal** (59), **Bernice Simon** (84), **Sylvan Simon** (86), **Daniel Stein** (71), **Jerry Rabinowitz** (66), **Richard Gottfried** (65), **Joyce Fienberg** (75), **Rose Mallinger** (97), **Melvin Wax** (88), and **Irving Younger** (69).

ALLEN, Rabbi Daniel

Dec. 17, 2018 (JTA)—Rabbi Daniel Allen, philanthropy executive and Zionist activist, dies at 69

Rabbi Daniel Allen, a noted expert on Jewish philanthropy who led the United Israel Appeal and the Reform movement's Zionist association, has died at age 69. Allen, who lived in West Orange, NJ, died on Sunday night surrounded by his family. He had suffered from amyotrophic lateral sclerosis, the neurodegenerative condition known as Lou Gehrig's disease. From 2012 to 2015 he was senior vice president of the Jewish Federations of North America (JFNA) and executive vice chairman emeritus of its United Israel Appeal (UIA), a subsidiary which acts as a conduit for Jewish humanitarian philanthropy in Israel. He held top leadership roles at UIA beginning in 1988, before it merged with other philanthropies to become part of the JFNA. Allen also served as the executive director of ARZA, the Reform movement's Zionist arm, and as the rabbi of the Emory University Hillel. Born in Reno, Nevada, he earned a bachelor's degree in political science in 1971 from the University of Nebraska-Lincoln and a master's of Hebrew letters from Hebrew Union College (HUC) in 1973. He was ordained at HUC in 1976. Allen served as the CEO of the Greater Hartford Jewish Federation for two years until 2003, and as CEO of American Friends of Magen David Adom for nearly six years until 2009. Allen, known by nearly all as "Danny," was a noted pro-Israel activist and one of the leading experts on American Jewish philanthropy and its impact on Israeli society. He was still working on several projects to help Israel and friends at the time of his death. A close friend, Jennifer Laszlo Mizrahi, said he helped her when she launched The Israel Project and later RespectAbility, a disability rights organization. She described Allen, her former Hillel rabbi at Emory, as "a leaders' leader—a Rabbi's Rabbi. When Jewish organizations denied access to my child due to disability issues, Danny was a calming voice.... He was also a constant feminist inside Judaism, Jewish groups, and Israel." He told *Ha'aretz* in 2016 that he had visited Israel six to seven times a year for more than 25 years. He is survived by his wife of 46 years, Mary Lou (Frishberg) Allen; his children Sarah, Rabbi Uri (Sari) and Noah (Rena); four grandchildren; and his mother Annie Allen of Jerusalem. He is also survived by his siblings Dr. Joel Allen (Debbie), Dr. Miriam Kluska (Avram) and Rabbi Morris Allen (Dr. Phyllis Gorin).

ARENS, Moshe
Jan. 7, 2019 (JTA)— Moshe Arens, Israeli defense minister under 3 prime ministers, dies at 93

Moshe Arens, a veteran Israeli politician and defense minister under three prime ministers, has died. Arens, who first hired Benjamin Netanyahu and is credited with helping him get his start in politics, died Monday in his sleep at his home near Tel Aviv. He was 93. Arens was a member of the Knesset for the Likud party from 1973 to 1992 and again from 1999 to 2003. As ambassador to the US beginning in 1982, Arens brought on Netanyahu as part of the diplomatic corps and later appointed him as ambassador to the UN. Arens served as defense minister under prime ministers Menachem Begin, Yitzhak Shamir and Netanyahu, as well as foreign minister. "I loved you as a son loved his father," Netanyahu said in a tribute on Monday. "There was no greater patriot. Moshe Arens' great contribution to our people and our state will be remembered forever." "Misha was one of the most important ministers of defense the State of Israel ever had. He was not a commander or a general, but a devoted man of learning who toiled day and night for the security of Israel and its citizens," Israel's President Reuven Rivlin said in a statement on Monday. The Israel Defense Forces (IDF) in a statement said that Arens "led the shaping of the face of the Israeli defense establishment over the years," noting that Arens "laid down important elements in the IDF's building of strength, its power, and its technological renewal." Prior to entering politics, Arens was deputy director general at Israel Aircraft Industries (IAI), where he oversaw major development projects, including the Kfir fighter jet project. Before that, from 1957 to 1962, he was a professor of aeronautics at The Technion. Arens, a Lithuania native, immigrated to the US with his family in 1939. During World War II he served in the US Army Corps of Engineers as a technical sergeant. Arens moved to Israel shortly after it declared independence in 1948 and joined the Zionist paramilitary organization the Irgun. In 1951, he returned to the US to study engineering at the Massachusetts Institute of Technology (MIT) and aeronautical engineering at the California Institute of Technology (CIT). In his later years, Arens was a columnist for the left-wing Israeli daily newspaper *Ha'aretz*. He also was chairman of the International Board of Governors of Ariel University Center of Samaria. Jewish Agency Chairman Isaac Herzog in a statement called Arens "a true leader with integrity, reason and eloquence who made great contributions to Israel's security and global standing. Despite our differences, there was always mutual respect between us." He is survived by his wife, Muriel, four children and nine grandchildren.

ARNOW, Robert
Dec. 18, 2018 (JTA)— Robert Arnow, NY philanthropist and real estate developer, dies at 94

Real estate developer and philanthropist Robert H. Arnow—who played a key role in securing the long-term survival of the Jewish Telegraphic Agency (JTA)—died December 15 at his home in Scarsdale, NY. He was 94. Arnow became president of the board of directors of JTA in 1967, at a time when the international news agency faced significant financial challenges. He served as president until 1973, but remained a board member for 45 years, until his death. According to Mark Seal, a former chief executive of JTA, Arnow was essential in negotiating the separation of JTA from the Jewish Agency for Israel and into an independent operation with support from local Jewish federations. Decades later, Arnow would reminisce about his hands-on role during that transition, which included personally carrying over some of the typewriters to the agency's new office. Born in Roxbury, Mass. in 1924, Arnow worked in his father Leon's drug store from an early age. Following his naval service during the World War II, he studied to be a pharmacist at the Massachusetts College of Pharmacy, intending to join his father's business. However, after his marriage to Joan Weiler in 1949, Arnow changed course and went into the real estate development business with his father-in-law Jack Weiler, developing projects such as NY's Grace Building and eventually becoming president of the Weiler-Arnow Management Company. His success in business led to an interest in philanthropy, and he became a supporter of numerous Jewish causes. Among his many roles, Arnow served as the vice president of the United Jewish Appeal of Greater New York, vice-president of the American Association for Jewish Education (later the Jewish Education Service of North America) and a member of the board of Lincoln Center. As chairman of the board of Israel's Ben-Gurion University of the Negev for a decade, he championed the establishment of a center to provide support for Bedouin students. According to his family, he was the first to establish an endowed scholarship fund for Bedouin women. Arnow is survived by his four children, 10 grandchildren and 10 great-grandchildren. His wife Joan, who among other things worked with her husband to bring the television show "Sesame Street" to Israel, died in 2010 at age 80.

BADER, Alfred
Jan. 2, 2019 (JTA)— Alfred Bader, Milwaukee philanthropist and art collector, dies at 94

Alfred Bader, a refugee who escaped Nazi-occupied Vienna as a young teen in 1938, and later became a chemist, businessman, philanthropist for Jewish and other causes, and an influential art collector, has died. Bader's charitable giving established a legacy for Jewish education in Milwaukee, including for its day schools. He died December 23 at his Milwaukee home. He was 94. Bader and his family foundation donated millions of dollars to social, medical, and cultural institutions in Milwaukee, along with Queen's University in Ontario, Canada—his alma mater—and institutions in Great Britain and Israel, where his foundation funds research, treatment and care-giving innovations for people with Alzheimer's disease. Bader was born in 1924 in Vienna, the son of a Jewish father and a Catholic mother, from an aristocratic Hungarian family. After his father died when he was 2 weeks old, he was adopted by his father's sister and raised as a Jew. He later converted to Judaism, according to the Milwaukee *Journal Sentinel*. At 14, he escaped via the Kindertransport to England. In 1940, he was among other war refugees deported to Canada. There he was held for nearly two years at a detention center before he was taken in by Martin Wolff, a Jewish railway engineer in Montreal and a historian of Canadian Jewish life. Wolff welcomed Bader as part of his family and encouraged him to complete his education. Bader's aunt died at the Nazi concentration camp at Theresienstadt. Facing discrimination against Jews in higher education, Bader eventually was accepted at Queen's University and earned dual degrees in chemistry and history. In 1950, on a scholarship, Bader completed his doctorate in organic chemistry at Harvard. A year later, while working as a researcher for Pittsburgh Plate Glass company at their plant in Milwaukee, he co-founded Aldrich Chemical company. It filled a void for researchers who needed a consistent source for hard-to-find, high quality chemical compounds. From the niche market, he built that company and several others into some of the world's largest, according to industry publications. The scope of Bader's philanthropy reflects his lifelong array of interests in science, history and art—subjects he mastered against the odds of the upheaval and challenges of his early life, which he and others have said inspired him to do good and leave a mark. "He had an incredible life," his son Daniel, who oversees Bader Philanthropies, told the *Journal Sentinel*. "He built an incredible dynasty with his business accomplishments. He has a legacy in three different areas—in art, chemistry and philanthropy." His lifelong devotion to collecting led him from an early interest in stamps to a keen eye and passion for art, notably 17th- century Dutch masters, including Rembrandt. Over decades, the Baders donated hundreds of artworks, including their enviable private collection of Dutch and Flemish Baroque art to the Agnes Etherington Art Centre at Queen's University, considered a transformative gift to the museum. The Baders also funded the Isabel Bader Centre for the Performing Arts, which opened in 2014, and donated a 15th-century castle in England to Queen's University that serves as the school's international learning center. Bader, who wrote two autobiographies, is survived by his wife, two sons and seven grandchildren.

BALIN, Marty
Oct. 4, 2018 (JTA)— Jefferson Airplane co-founder Marty Balin is dead at 76

Marty Balin, the co-founder of the iconic 1960s psychedelic rock band Jefferson Airplane, died in Tampa, FL, of unspecified causes. The Rock and Roll Hall of Famer was 76. Born Martyn Jerel Buchwald to Jewish parents in Cincinnati in 1942, Balin was one of the founding members of Jefferson Airplane and a member of its successor band, Jefferson Starship, which played such famous hits as "White Rabbit" and "Somebody to Love" and performed at the iconic Woodstock and Altamont festivals. Balin also was the owner of the Matrix club in San Francisco, where he featured performers such as the Grateful Dead and Santana. Along with his induction in the Rock and Roll Hall of Fame, Balin won a Grammy Lifetime Achievement Award. He continued his musical career until the end of his life. While the cause of his death was not reported, Balin underwent open-heart surgery in 2016 and was known to have suffered from vocal cord paralysis for a time afterward. He is survived by his wife and four daughters.

BEREZIN, Evelyn
Dec. 11, 2018 (JTA)— Evelyn Berezin, who brought first word processor to market, dies at 93

Evelyn Berezin, a Bronx-born daughter of Jewish immigrants from Russia who built and marketed the first computerized word processor, died Saturday in Manhattan. She was 93. A founder in 1969 of the Long Island-based Redactron Corp., Berezin created the Data Secretary, a processor-enhanced typewriter that jump-started a market later to be dominated by IBM and brands like Osborne, Wang, Tandy, and Kaypro. She sold the company to the Burroughs Corp. in 1976 and went on to careers in venture capital and consulting, according to her obituary in *The New York Times*. "Why is this woman not famous?" British writer Gwyn Headley wrote in a 2010 blog post. "Without Ms. Berezin there would be no Bill Gates, no Steve Jobs, no internet, no word processors, no spreadsheets; nothing that remotely connects business with the 21st century."

BLAINE, Hal
Mar. 13, 2019 (JTA)— Hal Blaine, Hall of Fame drummer who played with Elvis and Frank Sinatra, dies at 90

In the 1960s and 1970s, music lovers would likely be digging the drumming of Hal Blaine when they listened to a No. 1 hit. Blaine, who died Monday, played on 40 of them in those decades as a member of the Wrecking Crew, a Los Angeles-based collective of session musicians. Some of those hits: The Ronettes' "Be My Baby," Elvis Presley's "Can't Help Falling in Love," Frank Sinatra's "Strangers in the Night," the Beach Boys' "Good Vibrations," Simon and Garfunkel's "The Boxer" and the Byrds' cover of "Mr. Tambourine Man." On hearing of his death, Brian Wilson of the Beach Boys called him "the greatest drummer ever," The Associated Press reported. Blaine died of natural causes at his home in Palm Desert, California, The Associated Press reported The Rock and Roll Hall of Fame, which inducted him in 2000, called Blaine "the most recorded drummer in history." He also was awarded a Grammy Lifetime Achievement Award last year. Blaine first performed mainly at strip clubs before touring with musicians including Patti Page. He was born Harold Simon Belsky in Holyoke, MA, to Jewish immigrant parents from Russia. He called the community "a small Polish capital, loaded with immigrant Poles and Jews from all over Europe," the AP reported, quoting a 1990 autobiography. When he was 7, his family moved to an all-Jewish neighborhood in Hartford, CT, and at 11 Blaine attended Hebrew school and then celebrated his bar mitzvah. He dropped out of high school in San Bernardino, CA, at 16 and served in a military band in Korea. Blaine was married at least six times, according to *The Washington Post*, and is survived by a daughter and seven grandchildren.

BLOCH, Henry
Apr. 23, 2019 (JTA)— Henry Bloch, founder of H and R Block and philanthropist, dies at 96

Henry Bloch, who with his brother founded the international tax service giant H&R Block, has died at 96. Bloch, a philanthropist who contributed to Jewish causes, among others, died Tuesday surrounded by his family, a memorial site said. Bloch returned to Kansas City from World War II at 24 a decorated veteran of the Army Air Corps, having flown 32 missions as a navigator, most over Germany. He started a bookkeeping service. A decade later, in 1955, he and his brother Richard launched a tax preparation service. It quickly grew, and by the 1970s, Henry Bloch was its face, appearing as an avuncular tax adviser in TV ads. He was so good, other companies asked him to appear in their ads. Richard Bloch, who died in 2004, said they used the "Block" spelling for the company to make sure clients pronounced their name correctly. The brothers did not want to hear clients say they got their taxes "blotched." Henry Bloch founded a foundation in 2011 with his wife, Marion Helzberg Bloch, who died in 2013. It lists seven areas of focus, including "organizations that advance social and economic justice issues in the Jewish community." Among its beneficiaries are the Jewish Community Center of Greater Kansas City, the American Jewish Committee, Jewish Family Services and the Jewish Federation of Greater Kansas City. In 1990, according to *The Washington Post*, he became the center of a controversy when it was reported that he was denied membership in the Kansas City Country Club because he was Jewish. Tom Watson, a top pro golfer, quit the club and rejoined only when the club extended membership to Bloch. Being the target of anti-semitism did not dent Bloch's humorous affect. Asked to comment on the affair, he liked to tell reporters, "It's the first time I ever made the sports page." "Our Dad was passionate about his family and his community, and he will long be remembered for his benevolence, humility and fortitude," the family said on its memorial site. Bloch is survived by four children, 12 grandchildren, and 19 great-grandchildren.

BRAHAM, Randolph Louis
Nov. 27, 2018 (JTA)— Holocaust scholar Randolph Louis Braham, a two-time Jewish National Book Award winner, dies at 95

Randolph Louis Braham, a two-time Jewish National Book Award winner for works on the Holocaust in Hungary and a founding member of the US Holocaust Memorial Museum, has died. He was 95. Braham was a Romania native whose parents and siblings perished at Auschwitz. In 1944, after escaping labor service in the Hungarian army in the Ukraine, he was hidden by a Christian farmer named István Novák, who later was honored by Yad Vashem in Jerusalem as a Righteous Among the Nations. In 1947, Braham came to the US, where he would earn a master's degree and doctorate. His two-volume *The Politics of Genocide: The Holocaust in Hungary* won the 1981 Jewish National Book Award. He won again in 2014 for his three-volume *The Geographical Encyclopedia of the Holocaust in Hungary.* Braham edited over 60 books, most of them dealing with the Holocaust in Hungary, and co-authored or wrote chapters for 50 others. He also published a large number of scholarly articles. He died Sunday of heart failure hours before he was scheduled to deliver a lecture at the Rosenthal Institute for Holocaust Studies at the City University of New York. He was born Adolf Ábrahám in Romania, and attended the Jewish elementary school in his parents' hometown of Des, located in Northern Transylvania, and re-annexed by the Hungarian Kingdom in 1940. In the US, Braham received a master's degree from the City College of New York in 1949, and a doctorate in political science from The New School for Social Research in 1952. He was an emeritus professor at CUNY, where he taught Comparative Political Science from 1956 until 1992, when he retired. Braham was honored with several medals from Hungary, but returned them in 2014 after Prime Minister Viktor Orban praised Miklos Horthy, who led the country following the disintegration of the Austro-Hungarian Empire after World War I. Horthy was a Hitler ally who oversaw the murder of more than 500,000 Holocaust victims together with Nazi Germany.

CHANNING, Carol
Jan. 15, 2019 (JTA)—Carol Channing, the original star of 'Hello Dolly!,' dies at 97

Actress Carol Channing, who originated the starring role in "Hello Dolly!" on Broadway and won a Tony Award for her portrayal of the boisterous widow, has died. She was 97. Channing was the daughter of a Jewish mother and a Christian father and identified as "part Jewish." At 16, she learned that her father was multiracial, with an African-American mother and a German father. She wrote in her memoir of her five-year marriage to her first husband, Theodore Naidish, that she learned to speak fluent Yiddish from his grandfather, Sam Cohen, who lived in Brooklyn's Brighton Beach. The Seattle native first became a star playing flapper Lorelei Lee in the 1949 production of "Gentlemen Prefer Blondes," where she sang the iconic "Diamonds Are a Girl's Best Friend." Channing played Dolly Levi in "Hello Dolly!" winning the Tony in 1964. She played the role for the last time in a 1995 revival. Barbra Streisand was Dolly in the 1969 film version and Bette Midler also won a Tony for her portrayal in the 2017 Broadway revival. Channing was recognized with a Lifetime Achievement Tony Award in 1995 and was inducted into the American Theatre Hall of Fame in 1981. She made guest appearances on many television shows including "Sesame Street," where she performed a parody of "Hello Dolly" called "Hello Sammy," a love song to the Jim Henson character Sammy the Snake. She died Tuesday of natural causes just days before her 98th birthday. Channing was married four times and has one son.

COWAN, Rabbi Rachel
Sep. 2, 2018 (JTA)— Rabbi Rachel Cowan, pioneer in the Jewish healing movement, dies at 77

Rabbi Rachel Cowan, a pioneer in the Jewish healing movement, has died. Cowan died on Friday of brain cancer at her home in Manhattan at the age of 77. She was diagnosed two years ago with glioblastoma, an aggressive form of brain cancer, the same cancer that Sen. John McCain died of days before the rabbi. In 1990, Cowan was one of the co-founders of the Jewish Healing Center, a pioneer in the Jewish healing movement that provides spiritual resources and wisdom to help people deal with the suffering that surrounds personal loss and serious illness. She also served for 14 years as director of the Jewish Life and Values Program at the Nathan Cummings Foundation in NY, where she helped direct grants for programs that addressed the spiritual dimensions of serious illness. Cowan's family could trace its lineage back to the Mayflower. She converted to Judaism years after her marriage to writer and reporter Paul Cowan, the author of *An Orphan in History*, a classic memoir of his assimilated upbringing and eventual embrace of his own Jewish identity. The couple had married in 1965, and then spent time registering black voters in Mississippi and later serving in the Peace Corps in Ecuador. In the 1970s, they became involved in the Jewish revival on the Upper West Side of Manhattan, and belonged to the Ansche Chesed synagogue, which was made up of smaller congregations. Cowan completed her rabbinic studies at Hebrew Union College after the death of her husband in 1988, eight years after her official conversion to Judaism. She turned to the spiritual dimension of healing in part as a reaction to the comforts—and inadequacies—of Jewish tradition she experienced during her husband's struggle with leukemia. "Moses' path—and ours—is to move from the narrow place of doubt, fear, anger, and jealousy to an expansive covenanted life in a community of mutual care and responsibility," she wrote in an essay for *The Torah: A Women's Commentary*, a 2008 collection. "In such a community, all people are holy. They—we—can remind each other that what matters is not the ambition of the self, but the work of helping to make the soul, the home, the office, and the world a safer, wiser, more compassionate place for all. Such a perspective helps each of us to come closer to being a humble servant of God." Cowan is survived by a daughter, Lisa Cowan; a son, Matthew; two sisters, Constance Egleson and Margaret White; a brother, Richard; and four grandchildren.

DAVIDSON, David S.
Feb. 25, 2019 (JTA)— David S. Davidson, prominent judge and leader in Reform movement, dies at 91

David S. Davidson, a prominent judge and leader in the Reform Jewish movement, has died. He served as chair of the Reform movement's Commission on Social Action and as a board member of the Union for Reform Judaism (URJ) and the Religious Action Center (RAC) of Reform Judaism. He also was a founding member of the Reform congregation Temple Emanuel in Kensington, MD. Davidson died Feb. 17 from lymphoma. He was 91. The RAC praised his accomplishments in the movement. "So many of the resolutions of the Movement on issues of social justice bear his mark," the organization said in a statement. "He had a unique talent—he had an extraordinary intellect, coupled with a deft touch, a way for using just the right words, and all in service of our shared commitment to creating a better world." Davidson was the former chief judge of the National Labor Relations Board (NLRB) and later became involved in MD Democratic politics, where he served as an adviser to Sen. Chris Van Hollen. He also served as president of Mobile Med, an organization that provides medical services to low-income residents of MDs Montgomery County. Van Hollen lauded the late judge in a statement. "David was a kind and gentle soul who lived a life of purpose and always brought a reservoir of wisdom and moral clarity to his many endeavors," he said. "He put his keen sense of justice into action to strengthen our community and our country." Davidson, a Springfield, MA native, served in the US Navy during World War II. His grandson, journalist Eric Cortellessa, called him "the most incredible mensch. He lived with an insatiable commitment to protecting the vulnerable, providing care and comfort to those in need, and improving the lives of others. His ethos of humility and altruism embodied all that is good about the human spirit."

DAVIS, David Brion
Apr. 16, 2019 (JTA)— David Brion Davis, historian who wrote landmark trilogy on slavery, dies at 92

David Brion Davis, a Pulitzer Prize-winning historian who wrote a comprehensive trilogy of books on the problem of slavery in western culture, has died. Davis, a professor emeritus of American history at Yale University where he taught for more than 30 years, died on Sunday in Guilford, CT at the age of 92. Davis was the founding director of the Gilder Lehrman Center for the Study of Slavery, Resistance, and Abolition at Yale. He wrote or edited 16 books, but is best known for his slavery trilogy. The first, *The Problem of Slavery in Western Culture*, published in 1966, won a Pulitzer Prize and was a National Book Award finalist. The second, *The Problem of Slavery in the Age of Revolution, 1770–1823*, published in 1975, won the National Book Award as well as the Bancroft Prize, one of the most prestigious in the study of American history. The last book, *The Problem of Slavery in the Age of Emancipation*, was published in 2014 and won the National Book Critics Circle Award. He also wrote on how the role of Jews in the slave trade in the Americas was greatly exaggerated in deliberate efforts to encourage antisemitism. The fundamental problem of slavery, Davis wrote in his first book, "lay not in its cruelty or exploitation, but in the underlying conception of man as a conveyable possession with no more autonomy of will and consciousness than a domestic animal." He received the National Humanities Medal from President Barack Obama in 2014. Davis said in a 2014 interview that his parents had rebelled against their Christian upbringing and that he was raised with no religious heritage. He married a Jewish woman in 1971 and more than a decade later when he was in his 60s he began the process of conversion to Judaism. He had a bar mitzvah at the age of 80. "Judaism resonates with my Niebuhrian view of history and human nature. I also was deeply influenced by Rabbi Abraham Joshua Heschel. I believe in God and pray almost daily and could not be more grateful for my total acceptance as a Jew by many friends, including members of our bible-study weekly Shabbos group, who are mostly modern Orthodox," he said of his religious journey. A statement from Yale's MacMillan Center, for international and area studies, said: "He was an intellectual in pursuit of truth and wisdom. In his presence one always learned something. He was a deeply spiritual man who saw the historian's craft as a search for the minds and souls of people in the past. He devoted his life and career to understanding the place of the inhumane but profoundly important and persistent practices of slavery and racism in the world. He was a philosopher at heart, a lyrical writer, and defined why we do history. We stand on his shoulders."

DONEN, Stanley
Feb. 24, 2019 (JTA)— Filmmaker Stanley Donen, director of 'Singin' in the Rain,' dies at 94

Stanley Donen, the filmmaker and choreographer best known for the 1952 musical "Singin' in the Rain," has died. Donen died Thursday from heart failure in NYC. He was 94. As a child in Columbia, SC, Donen faced antisemitic bullying and used the movies as an escape from the tensions of being one of the few Jews in his community, The Associated Press reported. He became an atheist as a youth. The movies turned him on to the world of dancing and acting. He met Gene Kelly when they worked on the original Broadway production of Rodgers and Hart's "Pal Joey," when Donen, then 16, was in the chorus and Kelly was cast in the lead. They met again in Hollywood and began working together, first with Donen as Kelly's assistant, choreographer, and later as co-director. Donen also worked with actors including Cary Grant, Frank Sinatra, and Fred Astaire. Some of his other notable films include "On the Town" (1949), "Royal Wedding" (1951), "Seven Brides for Seven Brothers" (1954), "Funny Face" (1957), "Indiscreet" (1958), and "Charade" (1963). Though his movies are well-known and beloved, the director never received an Academy Award nomination. In 1998 he was given an honorary Oscar for lifetime achievement. Steven Spielberg told the AP that Donen was a "friend and early mentor. His generosity in giving over so many of his weekends in the late 1960's to film students like me to learn about telling stories and placing lenses and directing actors is a time I will never forget." Donen was married five times and is survived by three of his four children.

ECKSTEIN, Rabbi Yechiel
Feb. 6, 2019 (JTA)— Rabbi Yechiel Eckstein, interfaith activist who raised millions in Christian donations for Israel, dies at 67

To the many colleagues and supporters of Rabbi Yechiel Eckstein, who died Wednesday at the age of 67, he was a man of vision whose enormous drive to succeed both facilitated and complicated his relentless efforts on behalf of the Jewish people. As head of the International Fellowship of Christians and Jews (IFCJ), the NY-born rabbi raised hundreds of millions of dollars in donations—mostly from Christians—for projects benefiting needy Jews and Arabs in Israel and beyond. To many thousands of ordinary Jews and Christians whose lives he touched without ever meeting them, Eckstein was something of a guardian angel, heading a powerful machine that offered everyday assistance and was able to intervene quickly in emergencies, in creative ways cutting through the red tape characteristic of some other Jewish aid groups. The impact left by Eckstein, who died of cardiac arrest at his home in Jerusalem, was reflected in the glowing eulogies that mainstream Jewish groups offered within hours of his death. "He was a tireless worker for the Jewish people and for Israel, and he made significant contributions by fostering evangelical support for Israel," wrote Jonathan Greenblatt, national director of the Anti-Defamation League (ADL). Eckstein, who grew up in Canada and moved to Israel in 1999, began his involvement in interfaith dialogue with the ADL in 1974 and started the IFCJ in 1983. Using TV advertising, his tremendous charisma and tireless outreach legwork in the US, he made unprecedented headway in raising funds for Israel and Jews in crisis situations among evangelicals. Eckstein served as a member of the board and executive committee of the American Jewish Joint Distribution Committee and in 2014, together with IFCJ, received its highest honor, the Raoul Wallenberg Award. He also pushed back against Jewish leaders who distrusted evangelical support of Israel. "[T]he majority of evangelicals are passionately pro-Israel because it is part of their theology to love and support the Jewish people," Eckstein wrote in 2002. "I could not accept the conditional love of those who expect a payback on behalf of my people. I could not embark on a relationship that would compromise my personal integrity and ideals or that of the Jewish community I represent. But having been the first—and most often the only—Jew to build bridges with the right-wing Christian community, I have a view and understanding of their pro-Israel fervor that most people 'on the outside' lack." Israel's influential Tzohar rabbinical group called him a "visionary whose leadership enabled tremendous support for the state and people of Israel, and his actions bettered the lives of countless people all over the country." Isaac Herzog, the chairman of the Jewish Agency for Israel, wrote on Twitter that the Jewish people have lost "a leader who worked tirelessly on their behalf." Eckstein was ordained at Yeshiva University in New York, and held master's degrees from Yeshiva University and Columbia University, where he also completed studies for his doctorate. One of his three daughters, Yael, works at the ICFJ as global executive vice president. Despite repeated conflicts over the years with establishment figures and bodies, the scale of Eckstein's work made his organization too big to ignore or sideline, forcing even his most outspoken critics to work with him or get out of his way. Thanks to Eckstein, "today so many Christians from around the world stand in fellowship with Israel," Rabbi Tuly Weisz, an author and publisher of the Israel National News website wrote in an obituary. "We, Jews and Christians together, mourn the tragic loss of a true bridge builder."

GEFFEN, Rela Mintz
Feb. 4, 2019 (JTA)— Rela Mintz Geffen, former Baltimore Hebrew University president, dies at 75

Rela Mintz Geffen, a sociologist who undertook pioneering studies about the expanding roles of women in Jewish life and ritual, and the often unacknowledged complexity of the modern Jewish family, has died. She was 75. Geffen died Sunday in Philadelphia. The cause was multiple organ failure, according to family members. She was the sixth president of Baltimore Hebrew University, from 2000 to 2007, and was a professor emerita of sociology. Geffen taught sociology at Gratz College in Philadelphia for many years, coordinated its program in Jewish communal service and served five years as dean for academic affairs. Her major fields of interest were sociology of religion and the family and gender roles. She often focused on the Conservative movement. At the time of her death, she was working on a qualitative study of Jewish grand parenting. She published more than 40 articles and book chapters, and authored or edited four books including *Celebration and Renewal: Rites of Passage in Judaism* and *Freedom and Responsibility— Exploring the Challenges of Jewish Continuity,* which was the Centennial Volume of Gratz College, co-edited with Marsha Bryan Edelman. Another book, *Conservative Judaism: Dilemmas and Challenges*, was co-authored with the late Daniel Elazar. Raised in NY, Geffen came from a line of distinguished rabbis. Her father, Rabbi Joel Geffen, served for some four decades as director of field activities and communities education at the Jewish Theological Seminary. Her grandfather, Tobias Geffen, was the longtime rabbi of Congregation Shearith Israel in Atlanta, and is credited with certifying a version of Coca-Cola that is kosher for Passover. Geffen received her bachelor's degree in religious education from JTS and her undergraduate and master's degrees from Columbia University. She earned her doctorate in sociology from the University of Florida. She frequently urged leaders and planners in the Jewish community to acknowledge the growing diversity among Jews, and the complexity of blended families, interfaith families, same-sex marriages and couples who were having children later in life. Her 1978 survey, "The Evolving Role of Women in the Ritual of the American Synagogue," conducted with Elazar, showed the extent to which egalitarian principles were taking hold at Reform and Conservative synagogues. In a 1987 study, she showed how Jewish women were successfully "juggling" marriage, career and childrearing but often without support from their Jewish communities. "Jewish women are committed to the Jewish community, but the Jewish community is not committed to them," she told *The New York Times*. "This is an alienation that I think we cannot afford." Geffen served as president of the Association for the Social Scientific Study of Jewry (ASSJ) and co-editor, with Egon Mayer, of its journal *Contemporary Jewry*.

She was also program and membership vice president of the Association for Jewish Studies (AJS), the major organization of professors of Jewish studies in North America.

GLAZER, Nathan
Jan. 20, 2019 (JTA)— Urban sociologist Nathan Glazer, a founder of neo-conservatism, dies at 95

Urban sociologist Nathan Glazer, considered a founder of neo-conservatism, has died. Glazer died on Saturday at his home in Cambridge, MA at the age of 95. A long-time professor at Harvard University, Glazer was the author of *The Lonely Crowd* and, with Daniel Patrick Moynihan, the seminal *Beyond the Melting Pot*, a study of five racial and ethnic groups in NY. Glazer was a writer and editor for *Commentary* and *The New Republic*, beginning in the 1940s. In 1965, he began writing for the new journal founded by his friends Daniel Bell and Irving Kristol, *The Public Interest*. He became co-editor with Kristol in 1973, a position he held until 2003. According to *The New York Times*, he was not comfortable with the label neoconservative, which Bell described as a "socialist in economics, a liberal in politics, and a conservative in culture"—but mostly, a believer in a muscular US role in foreign affairs. On foreign policy Glazer continued to describe himself as "somewhat left." The son of Yiddish-speaking Jewish immigrants from Russia, Glazer attended the City College of New York, where he met Bell, Kristol, and Irving Howe, who frequently gathered to discuss Marxist philosophy, communism and socialism. He worked in the editorial divisions of Random House and Anchor Books in the 1950s, and served during the Kennedy administration in what is now the US Department of Housing and Urban Development. He taught at the University of California at Berkeley for five years beginning in 1963. He began teaching at Harvard in 1969 and was a professor emeritus of sociology and education there at the time of his death.

GOFFIN, Sherwood
Apr. 4, 2019 (JTA)— Cantor Sherwood Goffin, who served Manhattan's Lincoln Square Synagogue for 50 years, dies at 77

Cantor Sherwood Goffin, the cantor of Lincoln Square Synagogue on Manhattan's West Side for 50 years, has died. Goffin, a resident of Manhattan, died on Wednesday at age 77. Known by many as "The Chaz," Goffin was granted Cantor for Life tenure at the synagogue in 1986, and also served there as the principal for its Feldman Hebrew School, where he taught hundreds of students for their b'nai mitzvahs. He was a teacher of Jewish Liturgy and Folk Music since 1987 at Yeshiva University's Belz School of Jewish Music. He also was the Honorary President of the Cantorial Council of America, the only Orthodox organization of cantors in the world, an affiliate of Yeshiva University. Goffin recorded Jewish music albums, including cantorial music, liturgical music, folk music, and an album from 1970 dedicated to Soviet Jewish refuseniks. He performed until 1995 in venues throughout North America, and in South Africa and Israel, including performances at Carnegie Hall and Alice Tully Hall at Lincoln Center. Goffin was raised in New Haven, CT and attended high school at Mesivta Torah Vodaath in Brooklyn. He received a bachelor's degree in psychology from Yeshiva University in 1963 and a Cantorial Degree from the Belz School of Jewish Music in 1966.

GOLD, Jonathan
Jul. 22, 2018 (JTA)— Jonathan Gold, restaurant critic who showcased diverse Los Angeles neighborhoods, dies at 57

Jonathan Gold, a Los Angeles restaurant critic who said his goal in reviewing both taco stands and fancy French restaurants was to make people less afraid of their neighbors and to visit the entire city, has died. Gold, who was the first restaurant critic to win a Pulitzer Prize, died Saturday at St. Vincent's Medical Center in LA, after being diagnosed with pancreatic cancer earlier in the month. He was 57. Gold won the Pulitzer Prize for criticism in 2007 while writing for *L.A. Weekly*. The judges praised his "zestful, wide-ranging restaurant reviews, expressing the delight of an erudite eater." He was a finalist for the prize again in 2011. He also won several James Beard Foundation journalism awards during his career, including the M.F.K. Fisher prize for distinguished writing in 2011 and the Craig Claiborne Distinguished Restaurant Review Award, which he received in May. Gold was known for reviewing small, ethnic restaurants and even food trucks located throughout the city with as much zest as expensive haute cuisine restaurants. He published more than 1000 reviews from the 1980s until his death. Gold's work and his view of his beloved LA are featured in the 2015 documentary "City of Gold," directed by Laura Gabbert. Following his Pulitzer win, he stopped going incognito to restaurants, since his image was widespread and became well-known. Most of Gold's reviews appeared in two newspapers: *L.A. Weekly* and *The Los Angeles Times*, where he had been the chief critic since 2012. He started at *L.A. Weekly* in 1982 as a proofreader while working on a degree in art and music at UCLA, and soon after became its music editor. In 1986, he began a column in which he explored LAs' ethnic neighborhoods, moving the column to the *Los Angeles Times* from 1990 to 1996. He moved to NY in 1999 to become the NYC restaurant critic for *Gourmet* magazine, but returned to LA in 2001. He returned to the *L.A. Weekly* for a decade and then returned to the *Times*. Gold was born and raised in a Reform Jewish family in South LA. His mother, Judith, was a teacher and school librarian who converted to Judaism and his father, Irwin, was a LA probation officer. He played the cello from childhood, and pursued a degree in music history at UCLA. He briefly led a new wave rock band called Overman. He is survived by his wife, *Los Angeles Times* Arts and Entertainment editor Laurie Ochoa, and two children.

GOLDMAN, William
Nov. 16, 2019 (JTA)— William Goldman, who wrote 'Princess Bride' and 'Butch Cassidy and the Sundance Kid,' dies at 87

William Goldman, a novelist and screenwriter who twice won the Oscars for his work on "All the President's Men" and "Butch Cassidy and the Sundance Kid," died at the age of 87. Goldman, who was Jewish, passed away Thursday night in his

Manhattan home, surrounded by family and friends at the age of 87, friends of his family told Deadline. Goldman began his writing career as a novelist and later transitioned to writing scripts. As a novelist, Goldman wrote the critically-acclaimed "Marathon Man" and "The Princess Bride," among others. He later adapted those two novels for film, turning them into box-office hits that are considered classics. His first film script was "Masquerade" in 1965. Some of his other notable film credits include "Misery" (adapted from the Stephen King novel) and "The Stepford Wives (adapted from the Ira Levin novel). Goldman was born in Chicago and raised in the suburb of Highland Park, IL. He was married to Ilene Jones from 1961 until their divorce in 1991. They had two daughters.

KARLIN, Nurit
Apr. 30, 2019 (JTA)— Nurit Karlin, Israeli-born cartoonist who broke into a men's club at The New Yorker, dies at 80

Nurit Karlin, an Israeli-born artist who crashed the nearly all-male world of *New Yorker* magazine cartoonists, died April 30 at a hospital in Tel Aviv. She was 80. No cause of death was given. An appreciation of Karlin in *The New Yorker*, where she was a regular cartoonist for 14 years beginning in 1974, noted that most of her cartoons, which were usually captionless, "are not really jokes but, rather, visual thoughts that force the viewer to pause and grasp an idea." They include an egg awaiting its future in a bird cage, an envelope from "The Sublime" addressed to "The Ridiculous," and a museum gallery full of mice admiring paintings of mazes. In one of her more poignant images, considering that she was born in Jerusalem, two doves fight over an olive branch. *The New Yorker* noted that for much of her tenure she was the only woman drawing cartoons for the magazine (a drought that ended in 1978 with the hiring of Roz Chast, another Jewish cartoonist). Before coming to the US to study animation at the School of Visual Arts in NY, she served in the Israeli army and studied at the Bezalel Academy of Arts and Design in Jerusalem. Fellow cartoonist Liza Donnelly recalled that when she asked Karlin where she got her ideas, she replied, "If I knew where they came from, I would be the first in line! I used to doodle. Then something would be there." Karlin published a collection of her work, *No Comment*, in 1978. She also wrote and illustrated children's books, including *The Tooth Witch* (1985), *The Dream Factory* (1988) and *I See, You Saw* (1997). Karlin, who never married, is survived by her sister, Dina Wardi, and two nieces. After retiring about 13 years ago, she returned to live in Israel, according to *The New York Times*. She was active in Yesh Din, a group that aims to protect the human rights of Palestinians living under Israeli military control.

KRAMER, Clara
Sep. 27, 2018 (JTA)— Clara Kramer, who survived Holocaust hidden in an underground bunker, dies at 91

Clara Schwarz Kramer, whose 2009 memoir "Clara's War" recounted the 20 months she spent hiding in a bunker beneath a house in the Polish town of Zolkiew during the Holocaust, has died. Kramer died on September 11 at age 91. Longtime residents of Elizabeth, NJ, Kramer and her husband Sol, who died in 2011, were active in numerous causes and communal organizations and took leadership roles in the Jewish Educational Center, Elizabeth; the former Jewish Federation of Central New Jersey; State of Israel Bonds; YM-YWHA of Union County, Jewish Family Service of Central NJ; Central NJ Jewish Home for the Aged; and Trinitas Regional Healthcare Foundation. Clara Schwarz was born in Zolkiew, Poland, in 1927. When the Germans invaded her town in 1942, 18 people, including Clara and her family, went into hiding in a crawl space they dug under one of their homes. They were hidden underground for almost two years by Valentin Beck and his family. While in hiding, Clara kept a diary, which is now held at the US Holocaust Memorial Museum in Washington, DC. On March 25, 1943, 3500 Jews from Zolkiew were marched to a clearing and shot. After the war, she met her husband Sol in the displaced persons camps in Austria and they were married in 1949. They made aliyah to Israel, where their children Philip and Eli were born. They came to America in 1957 and settled in Elizabeth in 1965. Drawn to Elizabeth by its community of Holocaust survivors, Sol established a prominent real estate business and they became active members of that community. With a small group of survivors, she co-founded the Holocaust Resource Center at Kean University, which has provided training on Holocaust education to thousands of teachers. In her 80s, Kramer, together with co-author Stephen Glantz, wrote *Clara's War*, a memoir of her wartime experience hiding from the Nazis. The book was published in over a dozen languages. She was also a helpful source for Philippe Sands, a lawyer and author whose 2016 book *East West Street* discussed the fate of Zolkiew's Jews. Predeceased by a sister, Manya, who was killed by the Nazis, and her husband of 62 years, she is survived by two sons, Philip and Eli; a brother, Alex Orli; a sister, Naomi Kornberg; five grandchildren; and four great-grandchildren.

KRUEGER, Alan
Mar. 19, 2019 (JTA)— Alan Krueger, economist who advised Clinton and Obama, dies at 58

Alan Krueger, an economist who advised presidents Bill Clinton and Barack Obama, has died at the age of 58. Krueger was found dead on Saturday at his home in Princeton, NJ. His family said in a statement released by Princeton University, where he taught since 1987, that the cause of death was suicide. Krueger was the chief economist for the US Department of Labor in 1994 and 1995 under Clinton and was an assistant secretary of the Treasury from 2009 to 2010 and the chair of the White House Council of Economic Advisers from 2011 to 2013 under Obama. "Alan was someone who was deeper than numbers on a screen and charts on a page," Obama said in a statement. "He saw economic policy not as a matter of abstract theories, but as a way to make people's lives better." Krueger was pushing the field of economics toward a more scientific approach emphasizing data over theory. His latest book, which is scheduled to be released in June, discusses the economics of the music industry, according to *The New York Times*. Krueger, Harvard economist Lawrence Katz and economist David Card are known for their research in the early 1990s that found that raising the minimum wage did not, as had been believed, reduce employment for low-wage workers. Krueger graduated from

Cornell in 1983, and earned a doctorate in economics from Harvard in 1987. He is survived by his wife, Lisa, and two children.

LANDA, Rabbi Avraham Tzvi
Mar. 10, 2019 (JTA)— Rabbi Avraham Tzvi Landa, last Chabad yeshiva student to survive Holocaust via Shanghai, dies at 100

Rabbi Avraham Tzvi Landa, the last Chabad yeshiva student to survive the Holocaust by escaping to Shanghai has died. Landa died in his sleep on February 15 at age 100. He was granted a visa in 1940 by Japanese consul Chiune Sugihara and spent the remainder of World War II first in Kobe, and then in Shanghai. He was the last of the group of Polish Chabad yeshiva students to escape the Nazis. Landa had written to Rabbi Yosef Yitzchak Schneersohn, the sixth Lubavitcher rebbe, for advice on how to get out of Vilnius, Poland, where he was in the Chabad yeshiva and received a reply that assured him that God would grant him "… long, good and illuminating days and years, within the tent of Torah." Landau's parents and all but one of his siblings were killed in the Holocaust. He received a visa to the US and arrived in NY in 1946. He was a teacher for decades before taking a job at the US Postal Service. After retirement he taught in synagogues and yeshivas in Borough Park in Brooklyn. He is survived by his four children and many grandchildren and great-grandchildren.

LAQUEUR, Walter
Oct. 4, 2018 (JTA)— Walter Laqueur, the Holocaust survivor who reinvented terrorism studies, dies at 97

Laqueur passed away at his home in Washington, DC, on Sunday. He was 97. Born in Wroclaw, Poland, and raised in Breslau, Germany, he was a teenager when his parents sent him to Mandatory Palestine only days before the 1938 Kristallnacht pogrom. His parents would later die in the Holocaust. In Palestine, Laqueur worked on a kibbutz and as a journalist before leaving to enter academia in Europe and the US. He would later become the chairman of the International Research Council of the Center for Strategic and International Studies and director of the Wiener Library in London. Laqueur wrote extensively about fascism, terrorism, and the decline of Europe, and accurately predicted that rather than democratize following the breakup of the Soviet Union, Russia would fall into the form of populist authoritarianism now known as Putinism. As a terrorism researcher, he helped debunk the popular myth that poverty leads to terrorism. Laqueur also wrote extensively about the Arab-Israeli conflict and the Holocaust. Many of his books, including *A History of Zionism* and *A History of Terrorism*, are considered classics. "Europe will not be buried by ashes, like Pompeii or Herculaneum, but Europe is in decline," *The Washington Post* quoted him as telling the German magazine *Der Spiegel*. "It's certainly horrifying to consider its helplessness in the face of the approaching storms. After being the center of world politics for so long, the old continent now runs the risk of becoming a pawn." He is survived by his wife, Susi Genzen Wichmann; daughters Sylvia Laqueur Graham and Shlomit Laqueur; and four grandchildren.

LEDERMAN, Leon
Oct. 4, 2018 (JTA)— Leon Lederman, Nobel-winning physicist who sold his prize to pay for medical expenses, dies at 96

Leon Lederman, a Jewish-American physicist who won a Nobel Prize for his research on subatomic particles—nearly two decades later he sold the prize to pay for medical expenses—has died. Lederman died Wednesday at a nursing home in Rexburg, Idaho, his wife, Ellen Carr Lederman, told The Associated Press. In 1966, President Lyndon B. Johnson awarded him the National Medal of Science, the highest US government honor for scientific work. Lederman won the 1988 Nobel Prize in Physics with two other Jewish-American scientists, Melvin Schwartz and Jack Steinberger, for discovering the presence of a "ghostlike" particle in the building blocks of matter. Lederman is credited with coining the nickname the "God particle" for the Higgs Boson subatomic particle, which is believed to give mass to matter. In 2015, he sold his Nobel Prize for $765,000 to pay for medical expenses due to suffering from dementia. Lederman, a New York native born to Russian Jewish immigrants, served in the US Army for three years during World War II. He then enrolled at Columbia University, where he earned a doctorate and later became a faculty member. "What he really loved was people, trying to educate them and help them understand what they were doing in science," his wife told AP.

LEE, Stan
Nov. 12, 2018 (JTA)— Stan Lee, creator of iconic Marvel comics superheroes is dead at 95

Stan Lee, who as one of the masterminds behind Marvel Comics created such mega-popular comic book franchises as Spider-Man, the Incredible Hulk and the X-Men, died early Monday morning at Cedars-Sinai Medical Center in LA. He was 95. Born Stanley Martin Lieber in 1922, the son of a Romanian-Jewish immigrant father and what he once called a "nice, rather old-fashioned Jewish lady," Lee drew on themes of his childhood to create a series of memorable pulp heroes whose outsider status in some ways became their superpower. Lee was a pioneer of a comic book industry dominated at its outset by hungry, second-generation Jewish artists and writers, and became one of its most iconic figures. He also lived long enough to see it transformed into a multibillion-dollar multimedia industry that has spawned countless blockbusters based on his characters, including Black Panther, the Mighty Thor, Iron Man, the Fantastic Four, the Incredible Hulk, Daredevil, and Ant-Man. Lee was raised in the Washington Heights neighborhood of Manhattan and attended DeWitt Clinton High School in the Bronx. In 1939, he was brought in to what would become Marvel—and named its interim editor at age 19—although it was not until the early 1960s that he and artist Jack Kirby (born Jacob Kurtzberg) teamed up to put their distinctive stamp on the industry then dominated by DC, which published Superman and Batman comics. According to Arie Kaplan, author of *From Krakow to Krypton: Jews and Comic* Books, Lee and Kirby created "a group of superheroes who weren't sunny or optimistic like rival company DC's heroes. One member of the Fantastic Four, Ben Grimm (aka The Thing) felt like a freak because cosmic rays had transformed him into an orange, granite-skinned monster. With Ben Grimm, Lee and Kirby were using a superhero as a metaphor for Jews, African-Americans, and other minorities." In the introduction to the book *Disguised as Clark Kent: Jews, Comics and the Creation of the Superhero* by Danny Fingeroth, Lee wondered if the antisemitism he and other young comic book writers and artists experienced played a role in their art. "[C]ould it be that there was something in our background, in our culture, that brought us together in the comic book field?" he wrote. "When we created stories about idealized superheroes, were we subconsciously trying to identify with characters who were the opposite of the Jewish stereotypes that hate propaganda had tried to instill in people's minds?" In 1972, Lee was named publisher of Marvel, leaving the editing to others as he went about promoting the Marvel brand. He set up an animation studio in LA, and saw the company eventually grow from TV production into a multimedia giant that has dominated the movie box office. In 2009, the Walt Disney Co. bought Marvel Entertainment for $4 billion. Upon hearing of his death, Lee's Jewish fans offered tributes on Twitter. "In honor of the late great Stan Lee, born Stanley Lieber, you should all read *The Amazing Adventures of Kavalier and Klay* by Michael Chabon, a novel about how American Jews invented superheroes, and why," wrote Peter Sagal, the host of the NPR game show "Wait Wait ... Don't Tell Me!" NBC News correspondent Benjy Sarlin described Lee as "a big source of cultural pride as a kid, both as a New Yorker and as a Jew. It meant a lot to me that so many great comic creators had similar biographies to my grandparents and that their world was reflected in the work itself." Survivors include his daughter and a younger brother, Larry Lieber, a writer and artist for Marvel. Another daughter, Jan, died in infancy.

LIPTON, Peggy
May 11, 2019 (JTA)— Peggy Lipton, star of TV's 'The Mod Squad,' dies at 72

Her death from cancer was announced Saturday by Kidada and Rashida Jones, her daughters from her marriage to composer and music producer Quincy Jones. On "The Mod Squad," which ran on ABC from 1968 to 1973, she played Julie Barnes, one of a trio of young "counterculture" types who are enlisted as undercover cops after their own brushes with the law. It was one of the earliest primetime series to deal with the burning social issues of the day, including abortion, racism, the anti-war movement and police brutality. Lipton later starred in the role of Double R Diner owner Norma Jennings on the cult 1990s TV series "Twin Peaks," and appeared in its 2017 revival. As a singer, she had hits with "Stoney End" in 1968 and "Lu" and "Wear Your Love Like Heaven" in 1970. Born in NY in 1946, she was raised in Woodmere, one of the iconic Five Towns of Long Island that drew a large Jewish population after World War II. In her 2005 memoir, "Breathing Out," she wrote that her grandparents on both sides had emigrated from Russia. Her father, Harold Lipton, was a corporate lawyer; her mother, Rita Benson, was an artist. In the memoir, Lipton describes their neighbors as "immigrants or refugees fleeing racism and a hostile world, all combustible nervous energy, humor, and angst." As a result, "Their children were spoiled." Lipton modeled as a teenager and began getting TV roles after her family moved to LA in 1964. In 1974, she married Jones, with whom she had her two daughters, both of whom became actresses. Rashida Jones is best known for her roles in the comedy series "The Office" and "Parks and Recreation." The couple divorced in 1990. As a biracial couple, Lipton and Jones often faced "ugly" reactions, she said. Lipton once recalled that the girls and their stepsister all "loved" attending synagogue and Passover Seders, but "felt conspicuously black and out of place in Jewish Sunday School where there seemed to be only little fair-skinned white girls." As the Hollywood "It" girl of her era, Lipton was linked with various celebrity men, including Paul McCartney, Elvis Presley, The Who drummer Keith Moon and actor Terrence Stamp. After returning to the business after her marriage to Jones ended, she came to be regarded as a generous and helpful mentor to younger actors, especially those who became successful, as she did, at a young age. "I feel for their need to succeed and being in a business where, if you let yourself be open to its forces, it can tear you up and spit you out," she told an interviewer in 2005. "I didn't let that happen."

LYMAN, Princeton
Aug. 27, 2018 (JTA)— Princeton Lyman, Jewish diplomat who helped plan Operation Moses, dies at 82

Princeton Lyman, the Jewish American diplomat who played a critical role in organizing Operation Moses, the stunning 1984 airlift of Ethiopian Jews, has died at 82. Lyman died Friday at his home in the Washington suburb of Silver Spring, MD, the *Washington Post* reported. He died of lung cancer. The *Post* obituary celebrated the role of Lyman in helping to midwife the transition in South Africa from apartheid to democracy in the early 1990s when he was the US ambassador to the country. Lyman had the trust of F. W. DeKlerk, the last apartheid president of the country, and Nelson Mandela, who led the African National Congress. But he also played a critical behind-the-scenes role a decade earlier, when he was deputy assistant secretary of state for Africa, in organizing the airlift from Sudan to Israel of thousands of Ethiopian Jews who had fled their famine-ravished country only to face indifference and starvation in Sudan. In a 2007 account of the rescue, "Blacks, Jews and Other Heroes," Howard Lenhoff said other US officials eagerly seized credit for the operation. "Lyman remained silent," Lenhoff reported. "Always the consummate professional, Princeton Lyman is an unsung hero of the Ethiopian Jews." Lyman was born in 1935 to immigrant Jewish parents from Lithuania. Asked to explain his unusual first name, he explained in 1999 that he had brothers named Yale, Harvard and Stanford. "I guess it was an extraordinary example of immigrant parents determined that their children would go to universities," he said. "Of course, being very practical, we all ended up in the University of California—not the expensive schools we were named after." He added: "My brother Elliott, who was the only son not named for a university, indeed did not go to college." Lyman was married for 50 years to the former Helen Ermann, who died in 2008. He is survived by his second wife, Lois Hobson, and three daughters, Tova Brinn of Israel, and Sheri Laigle and Lori Bruun, both of MD.

LYON, Avi
Apr. 1, 2019 (JTA)— Avi Lyon, former head of Jewish Labor Committee, is dead at 76

Avram "Avi" Lyon, who was executive director of the Jewish Labor Committee (JLC) from 1997 to 2008, died Monday. He was 76. The cause was pancreatic cancer, his wife, Laurie Ebner-Lyon, wrote on his Facebook page. As head of the JLC, Lyon was active in exposing workers' rights abuses at the Agriprocessors kosher meat processing plant in Postville, Iowa, and assisting Jewish and labor organizations working to combat these abuses, according to the JLC. In 2000, he launched a "Labor Seder" program to strengthen connections between organized labor and the organized Jewish community. According to the JLC, Lyon was involved in liberal and progressive Jewish causes since he was a teenager. He was active in the Ihud Habonim (now Habonim Dror) Labor Zionist Youth Movement and in the Jewish student movement of the 1960s and 1970s. He worked with the Jewish Agency for Israel in the wake of the 1967 Six-Day War, helping to find work for volunteers who traveled to Israel. In the early 1970s, he led the North American Jewish Students' Appeal, a student-run organization promoting Jewish identity and raising funds among college-aged youth. He later worked for a range of educational and advocacy institutions before coming to the JLC in 1997. At the JLC, he was committed to building relationships with other religious and ethnic groups, and worried that other Jewish organizations were neglecting coalition building. "It's not enough to give money to power brokers in Washington," he said in an interview with *Jewish Currents* in 2005, soon after the JLC marked its 70th anniversary. "You always have to have a broader base of support built on a community of interests, and the only way to have that is by really working at it and getting involved with other ethnic and coalition groups in a major way. "The labor movement is an important part of the Jewish past and the Jewish present, and is an important ally to the Jewish community," he added. "We have stood by them, and they have stood by us, and we need to continue to do that. There will be a tremendous price to pay if we isolate ourselves." In retirement, he served on the boards of the Forward Association and Ameinu, the successor to the Labor Zionist Alliance. Lyon is survived by his wife and three daughters.

MILLER, Samuel
Mar. 7, 2019 (JTA)— Samuel Miller, philanthropist who championed Catholic-Jewish ties, dies at 97

Samuel Miller, a Cleveland developer and philanthropist who championed relations between Catholics and Jews, has died. Miller, the co-chairman emeritus of Forest City Realty Trust, Inc. in Cleveland, the real estate development company he helped build into a national giant, died Thursday. He was 97. His son, the veteran Middle East peace negotiator Aaron David Miller, once described his father as a "brilliant, driven man" who was "as tough, smart and intimidating as any man I've ever known. Born to Russian immigrant parents, he served in the navy at Guadalcanal, then went to Harvard, married my mother, and entered the family real estate business, where his toughness and smarts made him an indispensable asset in dealing with the unions and zoning boards," his son wrote in the 2008 book, *The Much Too Promised Land.* Sam Miller was close friends with a local bishop, Anthony Pilla, and together they coordinated bridge-building programs between the Jewish and Catholic communities. Miller supported Jewish organizations in Cleveland and served on the local boards of Jewish and other organizations. He also backed causes in Israel as well. In the late 1980s he helped the Cleveland Diocese save 15 inner-city Catholic schools from closing. Miller had several meetings with Pope John Paul II over the years and was honored with a Lifetime Achievement Award from the Catholic Diocese of Cleveland in 2015. "I'm helping the Jews by helping the Catholics," he told the *Cleveland Jewish News* in 2016, when he received the news-paper's Lifetime Achievement Award. In addition to Aaron, he is survived by his second wife, Maria; sons Abraham and Richard; and daughter, Gabrielle.

POSNER, Rabbi David
Oct. 22, 2018 (JTA)— Rabbi David Posner, who served 40 years at flagship NYC Reform temple, dies at 70

Rabbi David Posner, a spiritual leader at the flagship Reform Temple Emanu-El in NYC for four decades, has died. Posner, who retired from active work at NYC's first Reform congregation in 2012 after serving 10 years as its senior rabbi, died Friday from complications of Alzheimer's disease. He was 70. Following his ordi-nation from Hebrew Union College-Jewish Institute of Religion (HUC-JIR) in Cincinnati in the early 1970s—the Brooklyn native told his parents when he was 10 that he wanted to be a rabbi, according to The *New York Times*—he was asked to join the rabbinical staff at Temple Emanu-El and never left the Manhattan congrega-tion. He was named senior rabbi in 2002, a position he held until his retirement, and was senior rabbi emeritus at the time of his passing. In 2008, Posner was awarded the International Humanitarian Award from the World Union for Progressive Judaism. He served as a member of the board of governors of HUC from 2005 to 2015. "The death of Rabbi David Posner leaves a gaping hole in the heart of the Jewish people and our community," Rabbi David Ellenson, HUC's interim presi-dent, said in a statement. "His brilliance, his love of scholarship and the arts, his sensitivity and care for others, his love for the State of Israel, his leadership of Congregation Emanu-El, in the Reform Movement, and at HUC-JIR, and his con-tributions to Klal Yisrael were unsurpassed." Posner developed relationships with political and faith leaders. He was friends with NY Gov. Eliot Spitzer and mayors Ed Koch and Michael Bloomberg, and had close ties to Cardinals O'Connor, Egan, and Dolan, according to the HUC website. He met his wife, Sylvia, when he was 12 and married her when he was 21. She worked for 43 years as the assistant to the president of HUC. An accomplished pianist, Posner earned a doctorate in piano pedagogy from Columbia University in 1988. His doctoral thesis, "Reviving a Lost Art—Piano Music of Russian-Jewish Origin" centered on the modern Jewish art music composed in St. Petersburg, the cultural heart of czarist Russia during the first decade of the 20th century. While attending HUC, he specialized in the study of Semitic languages, and he received the Ralph Lazarus Prize for ranking first in his class.

RAE, Charlotte
Aug. 6, 2018 (JTA)— Charlotte Rae, who starred as Mrs. Garrett on 'The Facts of Life,' dies at 92

Actress Charlotte Rae, who won acclaim playing the housemother Edna Garrett on the sitcom "The Facts of Life," has died. She was 92. Rae, who was nominated for Emmy and Tony awards, died Sunday at her home in Los Angeles. She was diagnosed last year with bone cancer; she had survived pancreatic cancer. Rae first appeared as Mrs. Garrett in a recurring role as a housekeeper on the popular sitcom "Diff'rent Strokes," and then for seven years on its spinoff, "The Facts of Life," beginning in 1979. Her Emmy nomination was for the show. Her career also featured appearances on more than 50 TV shows. Rae worked in theater before her TV career took off, garnering two Tony nominations—in 1966 as best featured actress in a musical in "Pickwick," and in 1969 for best actress in a play for "Morning, Noon and Night." Her last role in a feature film was alongside Meryl Streep in the 2015 movie "Rikki and the Flash." She also appeared in films such as Woody Allen's "Bananas" in 1971, "Hair" in 1979 and the Adam Sandler comedy "You Don't Mess with the Zohan" in 2008. Rae was born Charlotte Rae Lubotsky in Milwaukee, WI, to Russian Jewish immigrants. Her mother, Esther, was a childhood friend of the future Israeli prime minister Golda Meir, who grew up in Milwaukee. Rae reportedly dropped her Jewish-sounding surname on the advice of an unnamed radio personality. She released her autobiography, "The Facts of My Life," in 2015, co-written by her son Larry Strauss. Rae was married for 25 years to composer John Strauss, but divorced in 1976 when he came out as bisexual. Her son Andrew, who was diagnosed with autism, died in his mid-40s of a heart attack in 1999. She is survived by her son, Larry; three grandchildren; and a sister, Miriam Guten.

SHACHNOW, Sidney
Oct. 4, 2018 (JTA)— Sidney Shachnow, Holocaust survivor who went on to command US forces in Berlin, dies at 83

Sidney Shachnow, a child Holocaust survivor from Lithuania who went on to become a two-star general and the commander of US forces in Berlin during the Cold War, has died. Shachnow died Friday in Southern Pines, NC, where he lived. He was 83. He and his family survived the Holocaust in Lithuania, where he was imprisoned for three years in the Kovno concentration camp, by keeping their heads low and showing restraint. According to his autobiography, "Hope and Honor," the same level-headedness guided him through the pains of assimilation as a young refugee living in Salem, MA, and then through a career in the military. His stint, including a turn in the Green Berets in Vietnam and as an officer in an undercover unit infiltrating East Germany, ended with his command of US forces in Berlin when the Wall came down in 1989. Among the medals he earned were the Bronze Star, the Silver Star and the Purple Heart. His description of his childhood in Lithuania is heartbreaking and includes the shattering experience of witnessing a Lithuanian partisan rape his mother while his father hid under the bed. His mother had ordered his father into hiding, knowing that the discovery of adult males could mean a death sentence, but it appears as if Shachnow could never shake off the experience. "I thought my father would go out and help," he wrote. "He didn't. I thought he was a coward. Maybe I was a coward, too." Shachnow was also on the board of advisers of the Jewish Institute for National Security Affairs (JINSA) and appeared at a Jewish War Veterans event. Shachnow "was an American and Jewish hero," said JINSA's CEO, Michael Makovsky. "He was a very impressive man and his accomplishments were even greater," Jewish War Veterans National Commander Barry Schneider said in a statement. "His contributions to our American military and to Jewish military history has majorly impacted the lives of Americans and Jewish Americans in ways that we cannot even know. Our brother Gen. Shachnow will be sorely missed." Shachnow is survived by his wife, Arlene, four daughters and many grandchildren.

SHINE, Herman
Jul. 24, 2018 (JTA)— Herman Shine, one of the last survivors to have escaped Auschwitz, dies at 95

Herman Shine, who is believed to be one of the last survivors to have escaped Auschwitz, has died. Shine, who worked as a roofer at the Nazi death camp before making a daring escape with his good friend Max Drimmer, died on June 23. He was 95. Fewer than 200 prisoners escaped from Auschwitz. Shine, born Mendel Scheingesicht in Berlin, was arrested in that German city in 1939 and then deported with 1700 other Polish Jews to the Sachsenhausen concentration camp. Shine's father was Polish. He claimed to be a roofer to survive the camp and actually learned how to build roofs. In 1942, Shine was transferred to Auschwitz, where he continued to work as a roofer. While working at an Auschwitz satellite forced labor camp in the town of Gleiwitz, he met a Jewish girl who worked in the camp and was able to return to her home at night. The girl, Marianne, would later become his wife. Drimmer came to Shine with an Auschwitz escape plan and, with the help of a Polish partisan, they managed to break out of Auschwitz and hide on his farm for 3 months. Marianne's family would hide the two men during the final weeks of the war. Shine and Drimmer and their wives immigrated to the US, settling in San Francisco. Shine founded the Standard Roofing Company in 1956 and was a successful businessman until his retirement in 1979. Drimmer, who worked as a plumber and a baker, died in 2012. A documentary about the men, "Escape from Auschwitz: Portrait of a Friendship," was released in 2001. It was updated and re-released in 2015 with additional material. Shine and his wife devoted time to Holocaust education and told their stories to groups throughout the Bay Area.

SIEGEL, Richard
Jul. 13, 2018 (JTA)— Richard Siegel, educator who co-edited 'The Jewish Catalog,' is dead at 70

Richard Siegel, an educator who advocated for Jewish culture and arts and co-edited the seminal "Jewish Catalog" series of guides to "do-it-yourself" Judaism, died Thursday in LA. He was 70 and had been battling cancer for two years, according to a friend and colleague, Barry Holtz, a professor of Jewish education at The Jewish Theological Seminary. Siegel was the director emeritus of the Zelikow School of Jewish Nonprofit Management at Hebrew Union College-Jewish Institute of Religion in LA, which trains communal professionals for work in Jewish organizations. For 28 years, he worked at the National Foundation for Jewish Culture (renamed the Foundation for Jewish Culture), and served as its executive director from 1978 to 2006. According to HUC, he created the Jewish Endowment for the Arts and Humanities to provide funding for artists, scholars and cultural institutions, and initiated the Fund for Jewish Documentary Filmmaking, the Fund for New Play Commissions in Jewish Theater and the 6-Points Fellowships in the Arts. In recent years he worked with his wife, Rabbi Laura Geller, on a forthcoming book *titled Good at Getting Older: A Practical Catalog Grounded in Jewish Wisdom*, to be published by Behrman House. His other books included *The Jewish Almanac* (1981) and *The Writer in the Jewish Community: An Israel-North America Dialogue* (1993). Siegel also was one of the founding members of Minyan M'at, a lay-led congregation that meets at Ansche Chesed, an egalitarian, Conservative synagogue on Manhattan's Upper West Side. "Richard Siegel was a transformative force in the Jewish world through his commitment to strengthening professional education, enhancing Jewish culture and advancing contemporary Jewish identity formation," the Zelikow School said in a statement announcing his death. Raised in Pittsburgh, Siegel received a master's degree in contemporary Jewish studies (now the Hornstein Program) at Brandeis University in 1972 and another master's in Jewish history from the Jewish Theological Seminary in 1974. His master's thesis at Brandeis was subsequently developed into *The Jewish Catalog*. He was the Hillel director, its first, at the State University of New York at Stony Brook from 1974 to 1978, where he founded the Long Island Jewish Arts Festival. He is survived by his wife, the senior rabbi emerita of Temple Emanuel of Beverly Hills, and their children, Andy, Ruth, Josh, and Elana.

SIMON, Neil

Aug. 26, 2018 (JTA)— Neil Simon, Broadway's giant of bickering, wise-cracking couples, dies at 91

Playwright Neil Simon, known for such Broadway hits as "The Odd Couple," "Barefoot in the Park" and "Lost in Yonkers," has died. Simon, who earned a Pulitzer Prize and a Tony Award, died overnight Saturday at New York-Presbyterian Hospital in NYC from complications with pneumonia at age 91. Simon began his career in TV, on the writing staff for Sid Caesar for "Your Show of Shows," working with future Jewish comedy legends Mel Brooks, Carl Reiner, and Larry Gelbart. He later wrote for "The Phil Silvers Show." During his career he wrote more than 30 plays and about as many movie screenplays, some original and most adaptions of his plays. "The Goodbye Girl" won an Academy Award for Richard Dreyfuss, playing the role of an incorrigible actor; "The Heartbreak Kid," starring Charles Grodin and Cybill Shepherd and directed by Elaine May, has been described as a worthy successor to Hollywood's classic screwball comedies and as a disparaging, overly stereotypical portrayal of marital discord among suburban Jews. In 1991 he won both the Tony Award and the Pulitzer Prize for "Lost in Yonkers," another autobiographical comedy. Simon was born in NY to Irving Simon, a garment salesman, and Mamie (Levy) Simon, a homemaker. His parents had what he described as a "tempestuous marriage," in which his father left the family at least eight times. Simon said he took refuge in movie theaters to escape his troubles at home. Those troubles also inspired him to become a writer, which he said helped him to become independent of emotional family issues. An interviewer once asked Simon what effect his being Jewish had on his humor. "That's a tough question," Simon replied. "Humor is a way of expressing your protest and being able to laugh, too. What Jews do is laugh at their predicament, and it's what blacks do, too. I do my funniest writing when I'm in a predicament. If a play is out of town and needs work, I'll do my best work. When I'm in an elevator that's stuck, I can keep everyone laughing. The other thing about Jewish humor—I don't know if it was always this way; I don't know if the Jews in Egypt were making jokes about Pharaoh—is that it takes a great deal of intelligence. It takes an adventurous mind." He was married five times: to dancer Joan Baim, who died of cancer (1953–1973), actress Marsha Mason (1973–1983), twice to actress Diane Lander (1987–1988 and 1990–1998), and to actress Elaine Joyce (1999–2018).

SIPERSTEIN, Barbra
Feb 11, 2019 (JTA)— Transgender rights activist Barbra Siperstein dies at 76

Barbra Casbar Siperstein, who fought for transgender rights in the US after her own gender transition in middle age, has died. Siperstein died February 3 in New Brunswick, NJ, at age 76. Her death came two days after a law named for her went into effect that allows NJ residents to amend the gender on their birth certificates without proof of gender reassignment surgery. The legislation was signed into law by Gov. Phil Murphy, a Democrat, after being vetoed twice by his Republican predecessor, Chris Christie. Siperstein, an Army veteran who was born with the name Barry, told her wife, Carol, that she was transgender in the late 1980s. Her wife was supportive and the couple stayed together until Carol's death in 2001. In the intervening years they had used an amalgamation of their initials and names as an alias, Casbar. While she had been transitioning in stages since telling her wife, Siperstein became a public advocate for gender equality and transgender rights. In 2009, after completing sex reassignment surgery, she officially changed her Hebrew name from Eliezer Banish to Baila Chaya at a ceremony at her Conservative synagogue in Freehold, the *New Jersey Jewish News* reported at the time. Siperstein, known as "Babs," was a principal in her family's eponymous paint and wallpaper chain. She was the first transgender member of the executive committee of the Democratic National Committee, and served from 2011 to 2017. During that time, she successfully worked to convince the party to include gender identity as a category for protected rights. Also during that time, she was a superdelegate for Hillary Clinton at the Democratic National Convention. Siperstein "was never shy to push us to open our hearts and minds, and to move our thinking ever forward," Murphy said in a statement after her death.

VORSPAN, Al
Feb. 17, 2019 (JTA)— Al Vorspan, social justice leader for the Reform movement, dies at 95

Al Vorspan, who helped organize the Religious Action Center (RAC) of Reform Judaism and served as the longtime director of its Commission on Social Action, has died. Vorspan, who also was former senior vice president of the Union for Reform Judaism (URJ), died on Sunday at the age of 95, according to the URJ. Rabbi David Saperstein, RAC's director emeritus, in a statement issued after Vorspan's death, called him one of the g'dolei hador, or "great ones," of Jewish social justice work. A true icon, Vorspan shaped much of social justice work of the Reform Jewish Movement, ensuring it lives at the very heart of Reform Judaism," said Saperstein, who is currently a senior adviser to the URJ. "Beginning in 1953, he helped inspire the creation of congregational social action committees across North America, encouraging Reform Jewish synagogues to partner with their local communities in pursuit of tikkun olam, 'repairing the world.'" Saperstein said Vorspan played "a pivotal role" in founding the RAC. "A mentor, friend, and inspiration to all who knew him, Al Vorspan was, to many, the personification of Reform Judaism's social justice efforts," said Saperstein. URJ President Rabbi Rick Jacobs described Vorspan as "one of the towering giants of Jewish social justice." "Al blazed a trail of courage and conscience that so many of us have walked," Jacobs said in a tweet. "Not since the biblical prophets Amos, Hosea, and Micah walked the earth have we been led by such an inspiring justice leader. Our Reform Movement and our world are bereft, for he cannot be replaced." In 1964, Vorspan was jailed with a group of Reform rabbis who at the request of the Rev. Martin Luther King, Jr. joined in the civil rights protests in St. Augustine, FL. "We came as Jews who remember the millions of faceless people who stood quietly, watching the smoke rise from Hitler's crematoria. We came because we know that, second only to silence, the greatest danger to man is loss of faith in man's capacity to act," he later wrote about his reason for joining the protests. Vorspan, who had fought in the US Navy during World War II, was an early and vociferous opponent of the Vietnam War, which led Sen. Thomas J. Dodd, a member of the Senate Subcommittee on Internal Security, to call him "a vociferous minority" at odds with mainstream Jewish opinion. He also criticized Israel's treatment of the Palestinians, writing in a piece in the *New York Times* magazine in 1988 at the beginning of the first Palestinian Intifada that "Israelis now seem the oppressors, Palestinians the victims." In 1953, Vorspan convinced Rabbi Maurice Eisendrath, who was then president of the Union of American Hebrew Congregations (UAHC)—the precursor to today's URJ—to create the Commission on Social Action. It worked with the Union and the Central Conference of American Rabbis to guide and shape social action in Reform communities and in Washington, DC, according to the RAC website. He then pressed the URJ to create the RAC to make the voice of the Reform movement heard in the halls of Congress. The RAC was voted into existence at the 1961 UAHC Biennial in Washington, DC. He authored several books, which today are standards in Jewish religious education, including *Justice and Judaism, Searching the Prophets for Values*; *Tough Choices: Jewish Perspectives on Social Justice*; and *Jewish Dimensions of Social Justice: Tough Moral Choices for our Times* The last two provide Jewish perspectives and moral policy analysis on issues ranging from abortion to capital punishment and from the Mideast peace process to religious freedom in Israel and the US. He and his wife, Shirley, were married for 72 years until her death on Aug. 27, 2018.

WOUK, Herman
May 17, 2019 (JTA)— Herman Wouk, legendary author who brought Judaism into the mainstream, dies at 103

Herman Wouk, the bestselling Orthodox Jewish author whose literary career spanned nearly seven decades and who helped usher Judaism into the American mainstream, died Friday at age 103. Wouk was the author of two dozen novels and works of nonfiction, including the Pulitzer Prize-winning *The Caine Mutiny* from 1951, which was a fixture on best-seller lists for two years, and the best-selling *Marjorie Morningstar* from 1955. Both books were later adapted for the screen. His novels *The Winds of War* and *War and Remembrance* both became successful TV miniseries. By the mid-1950s, Wouk's popular and financial success as an American Jewish novelist was unmatched. Even more unusual for a writer of Wouk's celebrity was his Orthodox observance and treatment of Jewish religious practice in his writing. Wouk embodied the new postwar possibilities for American Jews and his writing was both cause and effect of the normalization of Judaism within the larger American Judeo-Christian tradition. At the time, Wouk's fame seemed like an incredible feat for an Orthodox Jew. Unlike other Jewish novelists, who had focused on Jewish immigrant culture and tended to portray religious Judaism as foreign and exotic, Wouk made Jewish religious observance appear mainstream in his books. Scenes of a Passover Seder and a bar mitzvah service became scenes of middle-class American life in *Marjorie Morningstar*. As other American celebrities would do, Wouk used his fame to draw attention to his little-understood religion. Serialized in the *Los Angeles Times*, *This Is My God* introduced readers to such Jewish particulars as the laws of kashrut and family purity and the holidays of Sukkot and Shavuot. The book showed, through anecdotes from Wouk's glamorous Manhattan life, that it was possible to be both a modern American and Orthodox. At a time when Jews still encountered quotas at universities and discrimination in hiring and housing, Wouk's example provided inspiration. *This Is My God* became a popular bar mitzvah and confirmation gift for young Jews of all movements. Wouk is survived by two sons, Nathaniel and Joseph, and three grandchildren. His oldest son, Abraham, died in a 1951 swimming pool accident.

YOUNG, Israel (Izzy)
Feb. 6, 2019 (JTA)— Izzy Young, who produced Bob Dylan's first major concert, dies at 90

Izzy Young, the folk music promoter and archivist who produced Bob Dylan's first major concert at Carnegie Chapter Hall in 1961, has died. Young died Monday at his home in Stockholm. He was 90. Israel Young was born in 1928 to Polish immigrants on the Lower East Side. His mother inspired him with Yiddish songs and he worked at his father's bakery in Brooklyn. When Izzy opened the Folklore Center in NY's Greenwich Village in 1957, he wanted it to be a combination of all his passions. It was a music store, a bookstore, an archive, a place where artists could sit for hours listening to old recordings, writing, or schmoozing. Young became a mentor to many of the most renowned beat poets and folk musicians of that era.

Dylan immortalized Young in the 1969 song "Talking Folklore Center":

"On MacDougal Street I saw a cubby hole,
I went in to get out of the cold,
Found out after I'd entered
The place was called the Folklore Center—
Owned by Israel Young—
He's always in back—
Of the center."

Young closed the Greenwich Village shop in 1973 and moved to Stockholm, where he started a similar enterprise, the Folklore Centrum. In 2016, Young shipped 20 boxes to the American Folklife Center in Washington, DC. Inside were journals, manuscripts, photographs and recordings of some of America's greatest musicians, including Pete Seeger and Dylan.

15.3.2 Full List of Obituaries, July 1–December 31, 2018

ALLEN, DANIEL: Rabbi and philanthropist executive, d. 12-16-18.

ARNOW, ROBERT: Philanthropist and real estate developer, d. 12-15-18.

BALIN, MARTY: Musician and Rock and Roll Hall of Famer, d. 9-27-18.

BADER, ALFRED: Milwaukee philanthropist who escaped Nazi-occupied Vienna, d. 12-23-18.

BEREZIN, EVELYN: Brought first word processor to market, d. 12-8-18.

BLUM, WILLIAM: Author, historian, and critic of US foreign policy, d. 12-9-18.

BRAHAM, RANDOLPH LOUIS: Holocaust scholar and author, d. 11-25-18.

COWAN, RABBI RACHEL: Prominent member of Jewish healing movement, d. 8-31-18.

EISENBERG, LARRY: Biomedical engineer, sci-fi author, and prolific limerick writer, d. 12-25-18.

ENGEL-WIJNBERG, SELMA: Holocaust survivor of the Sobibor extermination camp, d. 12-4-18.

EPSTEIN, ALVIN: Actor, director, and authority on the works of Samuel Beckett, d. 12-10-18.

FUCHS, MAX: GI Cantor in Historic Battlefield Service, d. 7-3-18.

GLASSMAN, BERNIE: Prominent Zen Buddhist roshi, raised in Brighton Beach, d. 11-4-2018.

GOLD, JONATHAN: Restaurant critic and Pulitzer Prize winner, d. 7-21-18.

GOLDMAN, WILLIAM: Novelist, screenwriter, and Oscar award winner, d. 11-16-18.

HIRSH, ANITA: Jewish activist and philanthropist, helping Jews around the world, d. 11-1-18.

HORENSTEIN, SIDNEY: Geologist and public educator, d. 12-5-18.

JAY, RICKY: Brooklyn-born actor, author, and magician, d. 11-24-18.

KATZ, GLORIA: Holocaust survivor and Oscar-nominated screenwriter, d. 11-25-18.

KISLAK, JAY: Real estate magnate, historian, and philanthropist, d. 10-3-18.

KLABEN KAHN, HELEN: Author of *Hey, I'm Alive*, and wilderness survivor, d. 12-2-18.

KRAMER, CLARA: Holocaust survivor and author of memoir, d. 9-11-18.

LAQUEUR, WALTER: Holocaust survivor and prominent scholar of terrorism, d. 9-30-18.

LEDERMAN, LEON: Nobel Prize winning physicist, d. 10-3-18.

LEE, STAN: Marvel Comics executive and comic book luminary, d. 11-12-18.

LIEBER, LES: Jazz musician and founder of NYC's "Jazz at Noon," d. 7-10-18.

LIKE, IRVING: Lawyer and prominent New York environmental activist, d. 10-3-18.

LYMAN, PRINCETON: Jewish American diplomat known for his role in Operation Moses, d. 8-24-18.

LUX, DAVE: Holocaust survivor and active member of the LA Museum of the Holocaust, d. 10-29-18.

ORBUCH, SONIA: Jewish resistance fighter and later Holocaust educator, d. 9-30-2018.

POSNER, RABBI DAVID: Spiritual leader at Reform Temple Emanu-El for four decades, d. 10-19-18.

RAE, CHARLOTTE: Stage and screen actor, d. 8-5-18.

RICHTER, BURTON: Physicist and Nobel prize winner, d. 7-18-18.

RIESMAN, MAYRA LANGDON: Found of film review website and pioneer of digital media, d. 11-4-18.

SHACHNOW, SIDNEY: Holocaust survivor and Cold War era American general, d. 9-28-18.

SHINE, HERMAN: Holocaust survivor and one of the few people to escape Auschwitz, d. 6-23-18.[2]

SHUBIK, MARTIN: Economist who predicted the rise of electronic computing, d. 8-22-18.

SIEGEL, RICHARD: Educator and co-editor of *The Jewish Catalog*, d. 7-12-18.

SIMON, NEIL: Pulitzer Prize and Tony Award winning playwright, d. 8-25-18.

WEINTRAUB, PETER: Financial adviser and community activist, d. 10-18-18.

WIENER, ALTER: Concentration camp survivor and advocate for Holocaust education, d. 12-11-18.

ZUCKERMANN, WOLFGANG: Harpsichord maker and writer, d. 10-31-18.

15.3.3   Full List of Obituaries, January 1–May 31, 2019

ADLER, WARREN: Author, playwright, and poet, d. 4-15-19.

ARENS, MOSHE: Israeli defense minister who served in the US Army during WWII, d. 1-7-19.

BLAINE, HAL: Hall of fame drummer and inductee in The Rock and Roll Hall of Fame, d. 3-11-19.

BLOCH, HENRY: Founder of H and R Block and noted philanthropist, d. 4-23-19.

BLOOM, VERNA: Actress best known for co-starring movies in the 1970s, d. 1-9-2019.

CASSEL, SEYMOUR: Actor, d. 4-7-19.

CHANNING, CAROL: Tony Award winner and member of American Theatre Hall of Fame, d. 1-15-19.

COHEN, LARRY: Producer, director, and screenwriter known for B-movie horror, d. 3-23-19.

---

[2] Not published widely in media until July, 2018.

DAVIDSON, DAVID S.: Prominent judge and leader in Reform movement, d. 2-17-19.

DAVIS, DAVID BRION: Historian, expert on slavery, and Pulitzer Prize winner, d. 4-14-19.

DONEN, STANLEY: Filmmaker and choreographer, known for "Singing' in the Rain," d. 2-21-19.

ECKSTEIN, RABBI YECHIEL: Rabbi and interfaith activist, d. 2-6-19.

EINSTEIN, BOB: Actor, comedy writer, and producer, d. 1-2-19.

FRIEDMAN, STANTON: Physicist and prominent UFO researcher, d. 5-13-19.

GEFFEN, RELA MINTZ: Sociologist and former president of Baltimore Hebrew University, d. 2-3-19.

GEMINDER, ROBERT: Holocaust survivor and educator, d. 1-27-19.

GLAZER, NATHAN: Urban sociologist and early advocate of neo-conservatism, d. 1-19-19.

GOFFIN, SHERWOOD: Cantor at Manhattan's Lincoln Square Synagogue for 50 years, d. 4-10-19.

GOLIN, STEVE: Film and television producer, d. 4-21-19.

GREEN, RICHARD: American psychiatrist and sexologist, d. 4-6-19.

HAMBURG, DAVID: Stanford psychiatrist and advocate to end violence, d. 4-21-19.

IGLAUER, EDITH: Writer and "Bard of Canada," d. 2-13-19.

KARLIN, NURIT: Israeli-born artist who became a prominent *New Yorker* cartoonist, d. 4-30-19.

KRUEGER, ALAN: Advisor to Presidents Clinton and Obama, and noted economist, d. 3-16-19.

LANDA, RABBI AVRAHAM TZVI: Last Chabad yeshiva student to survive the Holocaust, d. 2-15-19.

LEDERMAN, HAROLD: Boxing judge and well-known analyst, d. 5-11-19.

LEVY, STEVEN: Actor and comedian, known as part of the duo of "Zito and Bean," d. 1-21-19.

LIEBERMAN, JANET: Educational innovator and advocate for LaGuardia College, d. 3-19-19.

LIPTON, PEGGY: Acclaimed actor and mother of Rashida Jones, d. 5-11-19.

LYON, AVI: Noted labor activist and coalition builder, d. 4-1-19.

MEDOFF, MARK: Playwright, screenwriter, actor, professor, and director, d. 4-23-19.

METZNER, RALPH: Psychologist specializing in LSD and consciousness, d. 3-14-19.

MILLER, DICK: Actor appearing in more than 180 films, d. 1-30-19.

MILLER, SAMUEL: Philanthropist, real estate developer, and advocate for Catholic-Jewish ties, d. 3-7-19.

PICKER, DAVID V.: Producer and film industry executive, d. 4-20-19.

PORTUGAL, YISROEL AVROHOM: Rebbe of Skulen, having lived through the Holocaust, d. 4-1-19.

PREVIN, ANDRÉ: Pianist, composer, arranger, conductor, and film industry musician, d. 2-28-19.

ROBBINS, DAN: Artist and inventor of paint-by-numbers, d. 4-1-19.

SANDLER, BERNICE: Activist for gender equality and advocate of Title IX, d. 1-5-19.

SARGENT, ALVIN: American screenwriter and academy award winner, d. 5-9-2019.

SHORE, SAMMY: Actor, comedian, and co-founder of LA's Comedy Store, d. 5-18-19.

SILVERMAN, SYDEL: Anthropologist and advocate for archival preservation, d. 3-25-19.

SILVERS, ANITA: Authority on disability rights and philosophy professor, d. 3-14-19.

SIPERSTEIN, BARBARA: Army veteran and transgender rights activist, d. 2-3-19.

STEINER, JACQUELINE: Folk singer, songwriter, and social activist, d. 1-25-19.

STERNOFF, NANCY: Jewish feminist leader and prominent organizational strategist, d. 1-12-19.

STEWART, GARY: Prominent figure in the LA rock and roll scene, d. 4-12-19.

URMAN, MARK: Film producer and independent film distributor, d. 1-14-19.

VORSPAN, AL: Social justice activist and noted leader in the Reform movement, d. 2-17-19.

WOUK, HERMAN: Author and fixture in ushering Judaism into the American mainstream, d. 5-17-19.

WRONKER, LILI: Hebrew calligrapher and book illustrator, d. 1-10-19.

YOUNG, ISRAEL (IZZY): Folk music promoter and found of the NYs Folklore Center, d. 2-4-19.

Addendum
GOLDSTEIN, Sidney
Aug. 5, 2019—*American Jewish Year Book* mourns the passing of Sidney Goldstein, 92

Sidney Goldstein died on August 5, 2019 in Lexington, KY. He was born on August 4, 1927 to Max Goldstein and Bella Howscha Goldstein in New London, CT. He earned his B.A. and M.A. at the University of Connecticut in 1949 and 1951 respectively, and his Ph.D. at the University of Pennsylvania in 1953. Although his degrees were in Sociology, his specific interest and lifelong work was in demography. After teaching two years in the Wharton School of the University of Pennsylvania, he joined the Sociology faculty of Brown University, specifically to help develop a specialty in population studies. In 1977, Brown named him the George Hazard Crooker University Professor. He held emeritus status since 1992. He was Director for 25 years of Brown's Population Studies and Training Center, which he helped found.

Sid's specific area of interest was the migration of people within countries, especially their movement from rural to urban areas. Beginning with analyses of migration in the US and Denmark, his focus shifted to less developed countries, including Thailand, China, Vietnam, Ethiopia, Guatemala, and South Africa. In each case, he was especially interested in the impact of rural-urban migration on the welfare and life patterns of the migrants and how they differed from those who were residentially stable. An important component of his work in these countries was the development of local expertise, so that the work that he had begun could be carried further by in-country researchers.

A secondary, but important part of Sid's research focused on the American Jewish population. Applying the analytic methods used in his international research, he furthered the study of Jews at the US community level and then at the national level as Chair of the committee that conducted the 1990 National Jewish Population Survey. For his influence, Sid has been considered the "Dean of American Jewish demographers." He has been recognized for this work by the National Foundation for Jewish Culture and the Council of Jewish Federations (now the Jewish Federations of North America), as well as the Institute of Contemporary Jewry at The Hebrew University of Jerusalem.

In addition to his prolific research, Sid was a consummate teacher. He mentored over 100 students at Brown, not only during their tenure at the university, but also into their careers. His students originated in many parts of the world and now hold key positions in government, research institutes, and international organizations. Many have kept in close touch.

During his career, Sid authored several books, well over 100 monographs and articles, and presented papers at meetings worldwide. He was the recipient of both Guggenheim and Fulbright Fellowships, and research grants from the Social Science Foundation, the United Nations, and the National Academy of Sciences. Other recognitions include being named the 2005 Laureate of the International Union for the Scientific Study of Population, president of the Population Association of America, and receipt of the Chulalongkorn University Medal (Thailand).

In 2011, Sid received the Lifetime Achievement Award from the Association for the Social Scientific Study of Jewry (from which he had also received the Marshall Sklare Award in 1992).

Goldstein was an active member of the RI Jewish community. He served as Vice President and board member of the Bureau of Jewish Education, as board member of the Jewish Federation of RI (now the Jewish Alliance of Rhode Island), and as a member of the RI Jewish Historical Society. He was a long time member of Temple Am David, serving as vice president, board member, and chair of its ritual committee. His first involvement with Jewish demography was when he conducted the Population Survey of the Greater Providence Jewish Community in 1963. Sid also completed the 1987 demographic study for the Jewish Federation of Rhode Island.

CPSIA information can be obtained
at www.ICGtesting.com
Printed in the USA
LVHW081240080720
659895LV00017BA/338

9 783030 403706